The Adventures
in Literature Program

═══

ADVENTURES FOR READERS: BOOK ONE
Teacher's Manual
Test Booklet
Reading/Writing Workshop, Grade 7

ADVENTURES FOR READERS: BOOK TWO
Teacher's Manual
Test Booklet
Reading/Writing Workshop, Grade 8

ADVENTURES IN READING
Teacher's Manual
Test Booklet
Reading/Writing Workshop, Grade 9

ADVENTURES IN APPRECIATION
Teacher's Manual
Test Booklet
Reading/Writing Workshop, Grade 10

ADVENTURES IN AMERICAN LITERATURE
Teacher's Manual
Test Booklet
Lessons in Critical Reading and Writing:
Henry James's *Washington Square* and *Daisy Miller*

ADVENTURES IN ENGLISH LITERATURE
Teacher's Manual
Test Booklet
Lessons in Critical Reading and Writing:
Shakespeare's *Hamlet*

JAMES EARLY

Southern Methodist University, Dallas, Texas
GENERAL EDITOR AND CONTRIBUTOR
Commentaries

ROBERT FREIER

Laura F. Osborn High School, Detroit, Michigan
GENERAL TEACHING CONSULTANT AND CONTRIBUTOR
Teacher's Manual

EMILY ELLISON

Illinois Teacher's College, Chicago–North, Chicago, Illinois
CONSULTANT AND CONTRIBUTOR
Composition and Language Program

A. R. GURNEY, JR.

Massachusetts Institute of Technology, Cambridge, Massachusetts
Drama

JEAN SISK

Baltimore County Board of Education, Baltimore, Maryland
Historical Introductions and "Analysis and Composition"

with LOUIS EISENHAUER

Catonsville Community College, Catonsville, Maryland

THOMAS M. FOLDS

Dean of Education
The Metropolitan Museum of Art, New York, New York
Fine Arts Program

ADVENTURES
in American Literature

CLASSIC EDITION

Harcourt Brace Jovanovich, Inc.

NEW YORK CHICAGO SAN FRANCISCO ATLANTA DALLAS

JAMES EARLY is Associate Professor of English at Southern Methodist University in Dallas, Texas. He received a master's degree and a Ph.D. from Harvard University. Mr. Early has taught English and American literature at Yale University and Vassar College, and is the author of *Romanticism and American Architecture*.

ROBERT FREIER is head of the English Department at Laura F. Osborn High School in Detroit, Michigan. He received a master's degree from the University of Michigan, and has taught at Wayne State University, the University of Detroit, and the University of Michigan. Mr. Freier has served as a consultant for national testing programs and for the Commission on English. He is co-author of *Adventures in Modern Literature*.

EMILY ELLISON teaches at Illinois Teachers College, Chicago–North, Chicago, Illinois. She is a graduate of Wellesley College, from which she also received a master's degree. Mrs. Ellison has served as a consultant on applied linguistics.

A. R. GURNEY, JR. is an Associate Professor of English at the Massachusetts Institute of Technology. He is a graduate of the Yale School of Drama and has produced and published several plays.

JEAN SISK is coordinator of English, Baltimore County Public Schools. She is a graduate of Goucher College and received a master's degree from the University of Maryland. She has served as Supervisor of Secondary English for Baltimore County and has taught English Education at Johns Hopkins University. Miss Sisk is general editor of *Major Writers of America, Shorter Edition*.

LOUIS EISENHAUER is an Associate Professor and Head of the Division of Language and Literature at Catonsville Community College, Catonsville, Maryland. He is a graduate of the University of Maryland and has received a master's degree from Cornell University.

THOMAS M. FOLDS is Dean of Education at The Metropolitan Museum of Art in New York. A graduate of Yale College and Yale School of Fine Arts, Mr. Folds has been an instructor of English and Art Director at Phillips Exeter Academy, New Hampshire, and a Professor of Art and Chairman of the Department of Art at Northwestern University.

Front cover photo by Harbrace.
Coin used as colophon courtesy of The American Numismatic Society.

Copyright © 1973, 1968 by Harcourt Brace Jovanovich, Inc.

PRINTED IN THE UNITED STATES OF AMERICA

ISBN 0–15–335142–X

CONTENTS

EARLY MEN OF LETTERS

THE FLOWERING OF NEW ENGLAND

TRAGEDY AND RENEWAL

THE TRIUMPH OF REALISM

AMERICA AND THE MODERN WORLD

The Fine Arts Program

THE BEGINNINGS OF THE AMERICAN TRADITION

The land was ours before we were the land's.
She was our land more than a hundred years
Before we were her people. She was ours
In Massachusetts, in Virginia,
But we were England's, still colonials
Possessing what we still were unpossessed by,
Possessed by what we now no more possessed. . . .

ROBERT FROST, from "The Gift Outright" *

In the seventeenth century, the New World seemed a land of promise, an opportunity not only for individuals but for humanity as a whole to make a fresh beginning. The land itself was vast and unconquered, promising riches but yielding its bounty only at great cost. Of the 102 passengers who arrived on the *Mayflower* in 1620, nearly half were dead by 1621. Yet the American colonies grew. Men and women continued to emigrate from Europe, some hoping to gain wealth, some to gain the freedom to lead their lives in accordance with their consciences. Many heeded the call of men such as John Smith, founder of the Jamestown Colony, who described the riches of the new world—the fertile ground, the plentiful game and fish— and asked Englishmen, "Who can desire more content, that hath small means or but only his merit to advance his fortunes, than to tread and plant that ground he hath purchased by the hazard of his life?"

* "The Gift Outright" from *Complete Poems of Robert Frost*, copyright 1942 by Robert Frost. Reprinted by permission of Holt, Rinehart and Winston, Inc.

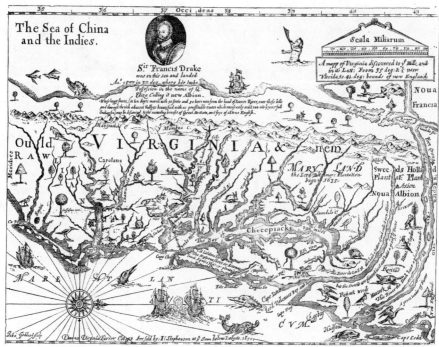

This map, from a book entitled *Virginia,* was published in London in 1651.

THE CONFLICT BETWEEN IDEALS AND REALITIES

Yet men who came to America because of the promise of an easy living found that they would have to struggle hard to survive. Others who sought religious freedom found that they were members of an authoritarian, sternly repressive church. Still others, who dreamed of organizing a perfect society, found that they could not escape the problems that face all societies—keeping order, reconciling conflicting interests, and making men work together for the common good. Thus, even at the very beginning of American history, there was a conflict between ideals and realities. Often Americans have had to strike some kind of balance between their dreams and the hard facts of existence. But, while Americans have sometimes modified their ideals, they have never abandoned them. Therefore, the history of the English colonies in America cannot properly be understood without also understanding the ideals that inspired many colonists: the ideal of religious integrity, and the ideal of political democracy.

TWO COLONIAL TYPES

Different sorts of men came to America for different reasons, and it took many different sorts of men to build the colonies and make them prosper. Yet two distinctive types impressed themselves on our early literature and left a cultural heritage that American writers have continued to draw on ever since. Both types—Puritan and Cavalier—emigrated from England, and both soon began to wrestle with peculiarly American problems and to come to terms with American scenes.

The Puritan. The Puritans came to America to practice Christianity according to their own lights. The word *Puritan* was coined by their opponents and applied to them in scorn. As the name implies, the Puritans wished to purify their religion, to bring Christianity back to the simplicity of the primitive Christian church.

Puritanism is associated with a cheerless, pessimistic outlook, and it is true that the Puritan view of man's nature and his position in the universe is a gloomy one. The Puritans were Calvinists, followers of the Swiss theologian John Calvin. Calvinism emphasizes original sin and man's fall and sees man as an utterly corrupt being who can be regenerated only through God's grace. Because of Christ, man has been given a second chance to be visited by God's grace, but this second chance has been extended only to the "elect," the chosen few whom God has decided to save. All other men are predestined to damnation. (The words *election* and *predestination* are key terms in understanding the Puritan point of view.) No man can know if he is among the elect, but all men are to strive to understand God's will and to spend their lives in an effort to bring themselves closer to Him. Man can bring himself closer to God in two ways: through spiritual growth, by a constant examination of his own soul and conscience; and through understanding the material world around him, since the world

GOOD
N E VV E S
FROM NewEngland:
O R

A true Relation of things very remarkable at the Plantation of *Plimoth* in New-England.

Shewing the wondrous providence and goodnes of God, in their preservation and continuance, *being delivered from many apparant deaths and dangers.*

Together with a Relation of such religious and civill Lawes and Customes, as are in practise amongst the *Indians,* adjoyning to them at this day. As also *what Commodities are there to be raysed for the maintenance of that and other Plantations in the said Country.*

Written by E. W. who hath borne a part in the fore-named troubles, and there lived since their first Arrivall.

LONDON
Printed by I. D. for *William Bladen* and *Iohn Bellamie,* and are to be sold at their shops, at the *Bible* in *Pauls*-Church-yard, and at the three Golden Lyons in Corn-hill, neere the *Royall Exchange.* 1 6 2 4.

TO
ALL WEL-WILLERS
AND FVRTHERES OF
Plantations in *New England:* especially to such as euer haue or desire to assist, the *people of* Plimoth *in their iust proceedings,* Grace, and Peace, bee *multiplyed.*

Ight Honorable and Worshipfull Gentlemen, or whatsoeuer : Since it hath pleased God to stir you vp to be instruments of his glory, in so honorable an enterprise as the inlarging of his Maiesties Dominions. by planting his loyall subiects in so healthfull and hopefull a Countrey as *New-England* is; where the Church of God being seated in sincerity, there is no lesse hope of conuincing the Heathen of their euill wayes, and converting them to the true knowledge and worship of the liuing God, and so consequently the saluation of their soules by the merit of Iesus Christ, then else-where though it be much talked on, & lightly

A 2   or

Title page and interior page of one of the first reports from the New World.

is as much a sign of God's will as the soul. The Puritan saw God in all things and events. Thus William Bradford (page 7) could write that when the Pilgrims had landed safely in America, "they fell upon their knees and blessed the God of heaven who had brought them over the vast and furious ocean."

The Puritan view was not one of unrelieved gloom, however. A totally pessimistic outlook could not have sustained the Puritans through the hardships of the New World. They were a vigorous, hardy people who had dared to dissent from an established church and passionately held to their own beliefs. The most intense of them, men such as Edward Taylor and Jonathan Edwards (pages 19 and 24), could find Puritanism a richly rewarding spiritual and intellectual discipline.

The Puritans left a deep impression on New England, where they settled, and it is the Puritan influence which is responsible for a phrase that is associated with the New England character: "plain living and high thinking." But even more, the Puritans left a heritage for the entire country to draw on, one of aspiration toward higher things, an emphasis on spiritual values, an awareness of the relationship between the outer world of material objects and the inner world of the spirit. If, today in the United States, there is a spirit of self-examination, a zeal to improve the country and uplift the character of its citizens, it is to a large extent inherited from the Puritans.

The Cavalier. The Cavaliers established large plantations in the South and, like the Puritans, were aware of the presence of an omnipotent God. But, unlike the Puritans, the Cavalier planters' deepest interests were likely to be social, economic, and political rather than religious. Their ideals were derived from the English Cavaliers, supporters of the Royalist cause of Charles I and opponents of the Puritans. Like their English counterparts, the American Southern Cavaliers saw life from an aristocratic perspective, their point of view being haughty and somewhat amused.

Yet the Southern Cavalier was, on the whole, faithful not only to his privileges but to his duties. He saw himself as the model of a gentleman, the justification for the existence of a society in which he stood on the highest level. He supported the advancement of the arts and sciences, and he served his colony by helping to run its affairs and by representing it in England. Some Southern planters, like William Byrd (page 13), were highly accomplished men who distinguished themselves in many fields.

America is the richer for its Cavalier and Puritan heritage. If the Puritan upheld an ideal of faithfulness to conscience, the Cavalier promoted a more worldly ideal: that of the man who is an ornament to society not only because of his position but because of his abilities, and who works hard to justify the good fortune of his birth and position. Often the Cavalier, because of the special quality of his point of view, made a contribution to the national literature that no other segment of society could make.

THE BEGINNINGS OF
THE AMERICAN TRADITION

POPULATION
1640 APPROX.: 27,950
1730 APPROX.: 654,950
1800 CENSUS: 5,308,483

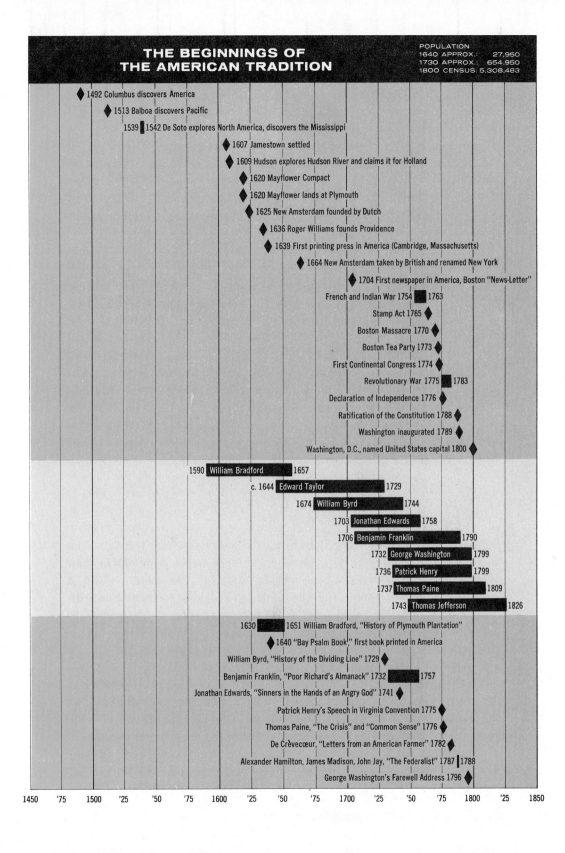

1492 Columbus discovers America

1513 Balboa discovers Pacific

1539 1542 De Soto explores North America, discovers the Mississippi

1607 Jamestown settled

1609 Hudson explores Hudson River and claims it for Holland

1620 Mayflower Compact

1620 Mayflower lands at Plymouth

1625 New Amsterdam founded by Dutch

1636 Roger Williams founds Providence

1639 First printing press in America (Cambridge, Massachusetts)

1664 New Amsterdam taken by British and renamed New York

1704 First newspaper in America, Boston "News-Letter"

French and Indian War 1754 1763

Stamp Act 1765

Boston Massacre 1770

Boston Tea Party 1773

First Continental Congress 1774

Revolutionary War 1775 1783

Declaration of Independence 1776

Ratification of the Constitution 1788

Washington inaugurated 1789

Washington, D.C., named United States capital 1800

1590 William Bradford 1657

c. 1644 Edward Taylor 1729

1674 William Byrd 1744

1703 Jonathan Edwards 1758

1706 Benjamin Franklin 1790

1732 George Washington 1799

1736 Patrick Henry 1799

1737 Thomas Paine 1809

1743 Thomas Jefferson 1826

1630 1651 William Bradford, "History of Plymouth Plantation"

1640 "Bay Psalm Book," first book printed in America

William Byrd, "History of the Dividing Line" 1729

Benjamin Franklin, "Poor Richard's Almanack" 1732 1757

Jonathan Edwards, "Sinners in the Hands of an Angry God" 1741

Patrick Henry's Speech in Virginia Convention 1775

Thomas Paine, "The Crisis" and "Common Sense" 1776

De Crèvecœur, "Letters from an American Farmer" 1782

Alexander Hamilton, James Madison, John Jay, "The Federalist" 1787 1788

George Washington's Farewell Address 1796

1450   '75   1500   '25   '50   '75   1600   '25   '50   '75   1700   '25   '50   '75   1800   '25   1850

By the middle of the eighteenth century, a sense of national identity was beginning to emerge. Americans were becoming conscious of themselves as a people distinct from other peoples. A Frenchman who had settled in New York, Jean de Crèvecoeur, wrote a book called *Letters from an American Farmer* in which he described the growing national spirit: "Here individuals of all nations are melted into a new race of men whose labors and posterity will one day cause great changes in the world." Further, Crèvecoeur wrote: "We have no princes, for whom we toil, starve and bleed: we are the most perfect society now existing in the world. Here man is free as he ought to be. . . ."

The American concern with building a society that existed to protect and enlarge man's freedom, not to limit or destroy it, began as early as 1620 when the Pilgrims drew up the Mayflower Compact. In the second half of the eighteenth century, as the conflict between the colonies and the mother country grew more intense, the concern with the relationship between citizens and their government became correspondingly intense. The pens of some of the most gifted men in America were placed at the service of a cause: freedom and independence. During this turbulent era, literature became the record of the mind rather than of the spirit, of minds which grappled with ideas and translated them into speeches, essays, and great political testaments. The literature of this era—the work of men such as Benjamin Franklin, Patrick Henry, Thomas Paine, Thomas Jefferson, and George Washington—is the literature of dreams in action.

A LITERATURE OF GIFTED AMATEURS

The men who created the literature of colonial America were, by and large, not professional writers. What these men wrote grew out of their busy lives: sermons, histories, journals, speeches, pamphlets, political documents. Yet such gifted writers as Benjamin Franklin, Jonathan Edwards, and Thomas Jefferson could scarcely help creating a notable literature. In the nineteenth century, other writers—Poe, Longfellow, Irving, Hawthorne—would write more specifically literary works: poems, short stories, and novels. These later writers would attempt to support themselves through their writing, and they would be concerned with the practice of literature as a special kind of endeavor, a special career that has its own skills and obligations. Most of the earlier, colonial, writers had no such awareness. Yet their solid achievements formed the beginning of our American literature, the literature of a country-to-be groping for an identity and in need of works of art that would express the national consciousness.

WILLIAM BRADFORD

(1590–1657)

In May, 1621, after Plymouth Colony had been through its first, terrible winter, William Bradford was elected its second governor. Almost half the colony had died during the winter. Only seventeen men, four women, and a few children remained. Except for five years when, at his own request, he served as assistant to the governor instead of as governor, Bradford continued to lead the colony until his death, when Plymouth Colony numbered twenty-five hundred people and was a prosperous enterprise.

William Bradford was born in northern England, the son of a farmer. As a boy of twelve, he became associated with the Congregational Church at Scrooby which had separated from the Church of England. After suffering the ill will of their neighbors, and even imprisonment, for refusing to conform to the practices of the Established Church, the congregation emigrated to the Netherlands in 1608, when Bradford was eighteen. Although well treated by the Dutch, the congregation became uneasy about their isolation in a foreign land where the children might be tempted to leave the small community. They dreamed of founding a colony to advance "the gospel of Christ" in an unsettled part of America. By now, Bradford was prominent in the affairs of the community. Several months after the hazardous sea voyage and the landing at Plymouth, John Carver, the original governor of the colony, died, and Bradford was elected to succeed him. He proved to be an able leader, especially in dealings with the Indians and with the other colonies. One year, during a famine, a neighboring Indian chief sent Bradford a grim challenge in the form of a bundle of arrows wrapped in the skin of a rattlesnake. Although Bradford took up the challenge and replied by returning the snakeskin filled with bullets and gunpowder, the Indians did not carry out their threat to attack the colony. Bradford was also a shrewd trader for Indian furs, and a brave, physically rugged man who once, during a winter storm, rescued the survivors of a shipwreck off Cape Cod.

Although Bradford attended no formal school, he was nevertheless a well-educated man. Undoubtedly he was given lessons by some of the university-trained leaders of the Scrooby congregation. His library included books in French, Dutch, Latin, and Hebrew. Bradford's great history, *Of Plymouth Plantation,* makes no show of learning and deliberately avoids the complicated, highly ornamental style that was popular with other writers of his time. The history's grave and simple eloquence is patterned on the style of writing of the Geneva Bible, the version preferred by the Pilgrims to the more ornate King James version. Bradford's history of the colony is also his own story, revealing his great devotion to the colony and the religious cause it represented. The history also reveals many qualities of the leader who saw Plymouth through its worst years. The meaning of Bradford's life, as he saw it, is summed up in the following verses which he wrote.

"From my years young in days of youth,
   God did make known to me his truth,
   And call'd me from my native place,
   For to enjoy the means of grace.

In wilderness he did me guide,
   And in strange lands for me provide,
   In fears and wants, through weal and woe,
   A Pilgrim passed I to and fro."

Of Their Safe Voyage, and How They Passed the Sea; and of Their Safe Arrival at Cape Cod

FROM *Of Plymouth Plantation*

September 6

THOSE TROUBLES [caused by the unseaworthiness of their ships] being blown over, and now all being compact together in one ship, they put to sea again with a prosperous wind, which continued divers [1] days together, which was some encouragement unto them; yet, according to the usual manner, many were afflicted with seasickness. And I may not omit here a special work of God's providence. There was a proud and very profane young man, one of the seamen, of a lusty, able body, which made him the more haughty; he would always be contemning the poor people in their sickness and cursing them daily with grievous execrations, and did not let [2] to tell them that he hoped to help to cast half of them overboard before they came to their journey's end, and to make merry with what they had; and if he were by any gently reproved, he would curse and swear most bitterly. But it pleased God, before they came half seas over, to smite this young man with a grievous disease, of which he died in a desperate manner, and so was himself the first that was thrown overboard. Thus his curses light on his own head, and it was an astonishment to all his fellows for they noted it to be the just hand of God upon him.

After they had enjoyed fair winds and weather for a season, they were encountered many times with cross winds and met with many fierce storms with which the ship was shroudly [3] shaken, and her upper works made very leaky; and one of the main beams in the midships was bowed and cracked, which put them in some fear that the ship could not be able to perform the voyage. So some of the chief of the company, perceiving the mariners to fear the sufficiency of the ship, as appeared by their mutterings, they entered into serious consultation with the master and other officers of the ship to consider in time of the danger, and rather to return than to cast themselves into a desperate and inevitable peril. And truly there was great distraction and difference of opinion amongst the mariners themselves; fain would they do what could be done for their wages' sake (being now near half the seas over) and on the other hand

---

[1] **divers:** several.
[2] **let:** omit, leave undone.

[3] **shroudly:** an old form of the word *shrewdly*, here used to mean "severely."

they were loath to hazard their lives too desperately. But in examining of all opinions, the master and others affirmed they knew the ship to be strong and firm under water; and for the buckling of the main beam, there was a great iron screw the passengers brought out of Holland, which would raise the beam into its place; the which being done, the carpenter and master affirmed that with a post put under it, set firm in the lower deck and otherways bound, he would make it sufficient. And as for the decks and upper works, they would caulk them as well as they could, and though with the working of the ship they would not long keep staunch, yet there would otherwise be no great danger, if they did not overpress her with sails. So they committed themselves to the will of God and resolved to proceed.

In sundry of these storms the winds were so fierce and the seas so high as they could not bear a knot of sail, but were forced to hull for divers days together. And in one of them, as they thus lay at hull in a mighty storm, a lusty young man called John Howland, coming upon some occasions above the gratings, was, with a roll of the ship, thrown into sea; but it pleased God that he caught hold of the topsail halyards[1] which hung overboard and ran out at length. Yet he held his hold (though he was sundry fathoms under water) till he was hauled up by the same rope to the brim of the water, and then with a boat hook and other means got into the ship again and his life saved. And though he was something ill with it, yet he lived many years after and became a profitable member both in church and commonwealth. In all this voyage there died but one of the passengers, which was William Butten, a youth, servant to Samuel Fuller, when they drew near the coast.

But to omit other things (that I may be brief), after long beating at sea they fell with that land which is called Cape Cod; the which being made and certainly

The *Mayflower*.

known to be it, they were not a little joyful. After some deliberation had amongst themselves and with the master of the ship, they tacked about and resolved to stand for the southward (the wind and weather being fair) to find some place about Hudson's River for their habitation. But after they had sailed that course about half the day, they were amongst dangerous shoals and roaring breakers, and they were so far entangled therewith as they conceived themselves in great danger; and the wind shrinking upon them withal they resolved to bear up again for the Cape and thought themselves happy to get out of those dangers before night overtook them, as by God's good providence they did. And the next day they got into the Cape Harbor where they rid[2] in safety. . . .

Being thus arrived in a good harbor and brought safe to land, they fell upon their knees and blessed the God of heaven who had brought them over the vast and furious ocean, and delivered them from all the perils and miseries thereof, again to set their feet on the firm and stable earth, their proper element. And no marvel if they were thus joyful, seeing wise Seneca[3] was so affected with sailing a few

[1] **halyards:** ropes for hoisting or lowering sails.

[2] **rid:** here, the past tense of "ride."
[3] **Seneca:** a Roman statesman (4? B.C.–A.D. 65).

Reports of the New World

Englishmen who wished to improve their position in life by settling in the American colonies must nevertheless have been anxious about the prospect. They would have to uproot themselves from familiar surroundings, undertake a long and possibly dangerous sea voyage, and finally begin life on a strange continent. That the colonies found sufficient manpower to grow and prosper throughout the seventeenth century was due in no little part to a number of reports about the New World which were written to encourage immigration. The first of these, published in 1588, was by Thomas Hariot, who was chosen by Sir Walter Raleigh to accompany the Roanoke expedition of 1585. In *A Briefe and True Report of the New Found Land of Virginia,* Hariot reported on the abundant natural resources of the Virginia coast. In his conclusion he encouraged colonists by writing, "Why may we not then look for in good hope from the inner parts [of the country] of more and greater plenty, as well of other things, as of those which we have already discovered? . . ."

In the seventeenth century, reports about the New World could tell not only of large expanses of land and abundant resources, but also of colonies successfully founded and of hardships overcome. Among the notable accounts of the American colonies were Francis Higginson's *New England's Plantation* (1630), George Alsop's *Character of the Province of Maryland* (1666), and William Penn's *Some Account of the Province of Pennsylvania* (1681). Perhaps the most interesting reports, however, were written by Captain John Smith, one of the most famous colonizers of America. In all, Smith wrote eight books about the New World. In them he told not only of the riches of the continent but also of his own adventures, including his possibly imaginary rescue from Indians by Pocahontas. (Historians have established that her real name was Matoaka.) Captain Smith's books provide a glimpse of one of the most fascinating figures in the early history of America. In one of these books he wrote what is possibly the most eloquent invitation ever made to colonists:

"Who can desire more content, that hath small means, or but only his merit to advance his fortunes, than to tread and plant that ground he hath purchased by hazard of his life? If he have but the taste of virtue and magnanimity, what to such a mind can be more pleasant than planting and building a foundation for his posterity, got from the rude earth, by God's blessing and his own industry without prejudice to any? . . . What so truly suits with honor and honesty as the discovering things unknown, erecting towns, peopling countries, informing the ignorant, reforming things unjust, teaching virtue; and gain to our native mother-country; a kingdom to attend her; find employment for those that are idle because they know not what to do; so far from wronging any as to cause posterity to remember thee, and remembering thee, ever honor that remembrance with praise?"

An early engraving showing the landing of the Pilgrims at Plymouth.

miles on the coast of his own Italy, as he affirmed, that he had rather remain twenty years on his way by land than pass by sea to any place in a short time, so tedious and dreadful was the same unto him.

But here I cannot but stay and make a pause, and stand half amazed at this poor people's present condition; and so I think will the reader, too, when he well considers the same. Being thus past the vast ocean, and a sea of troubles before in their preparation (as may be remembered by that which went before), they had now no friends to welcome them nor inns to entertain or refresh their weather-beaten bodies; no houses or much less towns to repair to, to seek for succor. It is recorded in Scripture as a mercy to the Apostle and his shipwrecked company [1] that the barbarians, when they met with them (as after will appear) were readier to fill their sides full of arrows than otherwise. And for the season it was winter, and they that know the winters of that country know them to be sharp and violent, and subject to cruel and fierce storms, dangerous to travel to known places, much more to search an unknown coast. Besides, what could they see but a hideous and desolate wilderness, full of wild beasts and wild men—and what multitudes there might be of them they knew not. Neither could

[1] the Apostle . . . company: Acts 28 in the Bible records the kindness shown to St. Paul and his shipwrecked companions by the natives of the island of Milita.

they, as it were, go up to the top of Pisgah [2] to view from this wilderness a more goodly country to feed their hopes; for which way soever they turned their eyes (save upward to the heavens) they could have little solace or content in respect of any outward objects. For summer being done, all things stand upon them with a weather-beaten face, and the whole country, full of woods and thickets, represented a wild and savage hue. If they looked behind them, there was the mighty ocean which they had passed and was now as a main bar and gulf to separate them from all the civil parts of the world. . . .

What could now sustain them but the Spirit of God and His grace? May not and ought not the children of these fathers rightly say: "Our fathers were Englishmen which came over this great ocean, and were ready to perish in this wilderness; but they cried unto the Lord, and He heard their voice and looked on their adversity. Let them therefore praise the Lord, because He is good: and His mercies endure forever."

[2] Pisgah: the mountain in Jordan from which Moses viewed the Promised Land.

FOR STUDY AND DISCUSSION

1. What dangers on sea and on land did the Pilgrims face? How did they survive these dangers?

2. What evidence do you find in the selection of the Pilgrims' belief in providence?

What evidence do you find of Bradford's personal belief in providence?

3. What indications are there of Bradford's wide reading? What other conclusions can you form about Bradford's character from the selection?

4. Study the last two paragraphs of the selection carefully. Why do you think Bradford paused in his narrative? Do you think that this is an especially effective passage? Defend your answer.

PLAIN STYLE AND ORNATE STYLE

At the beginning of his history, Bradford declares his intention of writing "in a plain style with a singular regard unto the simple truth in all things." He here confronts a problem faced by all writers: the relationship between subject matter and style. Bradford chooses to write simply, to set down the plain truth, which a more ornate style might obscure.

Although the English language has changed sufficiently in three hundred years to make Bradford's prose seem a bit strange to modern readers, the simplicity of his style can be illustrated by comparing his writing with a passage written some fifty years before by John Lyly, a writer famous for his ornate style.

"There dwelt in Athens a young gentleman of great patrimony, and of so comely a personage that it was doubted whether he were more bound to Nature for the lineaments of his person or to Fortune for the increase of his possessions. But Nature, impatient of comparisons, and as it were disdaining a companion or copartner in her working, added to this comeliness of body such a sharp capacity of mind that not only she proved Fortune counterfeit, but was half that opinion that she herself was only current [genuine]."

This passage tells only that a young man of Athens was very handsome, very rich, and very intelligent. It is meant to call attention to itself, to make the reader note the exact balance between "to Nature for the lineaments of his person" and "to Fortune for the increase of his possessions" and to admire the elaborate personification (see page 861) of Nature. Lyly's reader may think "How beautifully this is written," but not "What an interesting story is being told."

A reader trying to paraphrase a passage by Bradford will find that it cannot be expressed in a few words, as Lyly's passage was. Bradford rarely attempts to write phrases or sentences that balance each other, nor does he use elaborate figures of speech. Where figures of speech occur, they are expressed vividly and in few words. ("The weather was very cold and it froze so hard as the spray of the sea lighting on their coats; they were as if they had been glazed.") While the sentences are usually longer than those of most modern writers, Bradford's prose has the essential features of a plain style: it is simple, clear, and precise.

LANGUAGE AND VOCABULARY

Though Bradford's style is clear and simple by early seventeenth-century standards, a twentieth-century reader must find modern equivalents for a number of obsolete expressions. For example, "And no marvel if they were thus joyful" should be understood to mean, "And it is not surprising that they rejoiced."

Rewrite the five sentences below as a modern author might write them. On the basis of changes you have made, be prepared to discuss differences between Bradford's English and contemporary English.

1. "Thus his curses light on his own head, and it was an astonishment to all his fellows for they noted that it be the just hand of God upon him."

2. "In sundry of these storms the winds were so fierce and the seas so high as they could not bear a knot of sail . . ."

3. "Being thus arrived in a good harbor . . . they fell upon their knees and blessed the God of heaven . . ."

4. "But here I cannot but stay and make a pause, and stand half amazed at this poor people's present condition . . ."

5. "For summer being done, all things stand upon them with a weather-beaten face, and the whole country, full of woods and thickets, represented a wild and savage hue."

FOR COMPOSITION

Assume that you are unaware of the subsequent history of the Pilgrims. In a brief composition, discuss the colony's chance of survival, based on your reading of the selection from Bradford. Consider what qualities of the Pilgrims, as revealed in the selection, might enable them to survive.

WILLIAM BYRD
(1674–1744)

William Byrd, one of the most influential Virginians of colonial times, was born on a Tidewater plantation but received most of his education in England. There he acquired the manners of a gentleman and was trained in the law. He also studied Greek, Latin, and English literature. He learned to dance and fence well and to speak and write with elegance and wit. He became acquainted with many of the leaders of English literary and intellectual life and was a member of that distinguished organization of scientists, the Royal Society. Most important, he learned the obligations as well as the prerogatives of a landed aristocrat. When he returned to Virginia, much of his time was given to hard work in the administration of his huge plantation and in the service of the colony. He served in the Virginia House of Burgesses and represented Virginia in England on a number of occasions.

Byrd was over thirty when he settled down at Westover, his father's plantation on the James River. There he built the admirably proportioned, steep-roofed brick house that is one of the architectural treasures of Virginia. His life was filled with activity. He gave dances and dinners and arranged fox hunts. He corresponded with friends in England and with the Royal Society. Almost every day he read in Greek, Latin, or Hebrew to keep up his studies in these languages. He made frequent trips to Williamsburg, the colonial capital, for governmental and social reasons. He was proud of his extensive plantation and compared it to a kingdom with flocks and herds and "every sort of trade amongst my own servants, so that I live in a kind of independence of everyone but Providence." Running such a complex, self-sufficient community, however, required much effort. "I must take care to keep all my people to their duty, to set all the springs in motion, and to make everyone draw his equal share to carry the machine forward."

In the spring and fall of 1728, Byrd led a party which surveyed the boundary line between Virginia and North Carolina. The journal he kept during the months he pushed through the rough wilderness formed the basis of his book, *The History of the Dividing Line.* Although the manuscript remained unpublished for many years after Byrd's death, it seems certain that Byrd intended to have it published, with illustrations. It is not the work of a serious New Englander but of a worldly and witty gentleman who was convinced of the loftiness of his position in the New World. Few American writers since William Byrd have been confident enough to write in a humorously condescending style like his.

FROM *The History of the Dividing Line Run in the Year 1728*

March 10

THE SABBATH happened very opportunely to give some ease to our jaded people, who rested religiously from every work but that of cooking the kettle. We observed very few cornfields in our walks and those very small, which seemed the stranger to us because we could see no other tokens of husbandry or improvement. But, upon further inquiry, we were given to understand people [1] only made corn for themselves and not for their stocks, which know very well how to get their own living.

Both cattle and hogs ramble in the neighboring marshes and swamps, where they maintain themselves the whole winter long and are not fetched home till the spring. Thus these indolent wretches, during one half of the year, lose the advantage of the milk of their cattle, and many of the poor creatures perish in the mire, into the bargain, by this ill management.

Some, who pique themselves more upon industry than their neighbors, will now and then in compliment to their cattle cut down a tree whose limbs are laden with moss. The trouble would be too great to climb the tree in order to gather this provender, but the shortest way (which in this country is always counted the best) is to fell it, just like the lazy Indians, who do the same by such trees as bear fruit and so make one harvest for all. By this bad husbandry, milk is scarce in the winter season ... And, in truth, I believe this is ... a very good reason why so many people in this province are marked with a custard complexion.

The only business here is raising of hogs, which is managed with the least trouble and affords the diet they are most fond of. The truth of it is, the inhabitants of North Carolina devour so much swine's flesh that it fills them full of gross humors. For want too of a constant supply of salt, they are commonly obliged to eat it fresh, and that begets the highest taint of scurvy. Thus, whenever a severe cold happens to constitutions thus vitiated, 'tis apt to improve into the yaws,[2] called there very justly the country-distemper. This has all the symptoms of the pox, with this aggravation, that no preparation of mercury will touch it. First it seizes the throat, next the palate, and lastly shows its spite to the poor nose, of which 'tis apt in a small time treacherously to undermine the foundation.

This calamity is so common and familiar here that it ceases to be a scandal, and in the disputes that happen about beauty, the noses have in some companies much ado to carry it. Nay, 'tis said that once, after three good pork years, a motion had like to have been made in the House of Burgesses that a man with a nose should be incapable of holding any place of profit in the province; which extraordinary motion could never have been intended without some hopes of a majority.

April 7

The next day being Sunday, we ordered notice to be sent to all the neighborhood that there would be a sermon at this place and an opportunity of christening their children. But the likelihood of rain got the better of their devotion, and what perhaps might still be a stronger motive, of their curiosity. In the morning we dispatched a runner to the Nottoway [3] town, to let the Indians know we intended them a visit

---

[1] **people:** the North Carolinians.

[2] **the yaws:** a contagious skin disease.

[3] **Nottoway:** an extinct Indian tribe of Virginia.

that evening, and our honest landlord was so kind as to be our pilot thither, being about four miles from his house.

Accordingly in the afternoon we marched in good order to the town, where the female scouts, stationed on an eminence for that purpose, had no sooner spied us but they gave notice of our approach to their fellow citizens by continual whoops and cries, which could not possibly have been more dismal at the sight of their most implacable enemies.

This signal assembled all their great men, who received us in a body and conducted us into the fort. This fort was a square piece of ground enclosed with substantial puncheons, or strong palisades, about ten feet high and leaning a little outwards to make a scalade more difficult. Each side of the square might be about one hundred yards long, with loopholes at proper distances, through which they may fire upon the enemy.

Within this enclosure we found bark cabins sufficient to lodge all their people, in case they should be obliged to retire thither. These cabins are no other but close arbors made of saplings, arched at the top, and covered so well with bark as to be proof against all weather. The fire is made in the middle, according to the Hibernian [1] fashion, the smoke whereof finds no other vent but at the door, and so keeps the whole family warm at the expense both of their eyes and complexion.

The Indians have no standing furniture in their cabins but hurdles to repose their persons upon, which they cover with mats or deerskins. We were conducted to the best apartments in the fort, which just before had been made ready for our reception and adorned with new mats that were sweet and clean.

The young men had painted themselves in a hideous manner, not so much for ornament as terror. In that frightful equipage they entertained us with sundry war

North Carolinian Indians are shown broiling fish over an open fire in this engraving after a watercolor by John White.

dances, wherein they endeavored to look as formidable as possible. The instrument they danced to was an Indian drum, that is, a large gourd with a skin braced taut over the mouth of it. The dancers all sang to this music, keeping exact time with feet, while their heads and arms were screwed into a thousand menacing postures.

Upon this occasion the ladies had arrayed themselves in all their finery. They were wrapped in their red and blue matchcoats,[2] thrown so negligently about them that their mahogany skins appeared in several parts, like the Lacedemonian [3] damsels of old. Their hair was braided with white and blue peak, and hung gracefully in a large roll upon their shoulders.

This peak consists of small cylinders cut out of a conch shell, drilled through, and strung like beads. It serves them both for money and jewels, the blue being of much greater value than the white . . . because they are more scarce. The women wear necklaces and bracelets of these precious materials, when they have a mind to appear lovely. . . . Their shapes are

[1] **Hibernian:** Irish.

[2] **matchcoats:** wool cloths.
[3] **Lacedemonian:** Spartan.

A village of Virginian Indians similar to that described in William Byrd's journal.

vermin that use to be troublesome to other uncleanly people. The little work that is done among the Indians is done by the poor women, while the men are quite idle or at most employed only in the gentlemanly diversions of hunting and fishing.

In this as well as in their wars, they now use nothing but firearms, which they purchase of the English for skins. Bows and arrows are grown into disuse, except only amongst their boys. Nor is it ill policy, but on the contrary very prudent, thus to furnish the Indians with firearms, because it makes them depend entirely upon the English, not only for their trade but even for their subsistence. Besides, they were really able to do more mischief while they made use of arrows, of which they would let silently fly several in a minute with wonderful dexterity, whereas now they hardly ever discharge their firelocks [1] more than once, which they insidiously do from behind a tree and then retire as nimbly as the Dutch horse [2] used to do now and then formerly in Flanders.

We put the Indians to no expense but only of a little corn for our horses, for which in gratitude we cheered their hearts with what rum we had left, which they love better than they do their wives and children.

Though these Indians dwell among the English and see in what plenty a little industry enables them to live, yet they choose to continue in their stupid idleness and to suffer all the inconveniences of dirt, cold, and want, rather than to disturb their heads with care or defile their hands with labor.

The whole number of people belonging to the Nottoway town, if you include women and children, amount to about two hundred. These are the only Indians of any consequence now remaining within the limits of Virginia. The rest are either removed or dwindled to a very inconsiderable number, either by destroying one another or else by the smallpox and other

[1] **firelocks:** muskets.
[2] **horse:** cavalry.

very straight and well proportioned. Their faces are seldom handsome, yet they have an air of innocence and bashfulness that with a little less dirt would not fail to make them desirable. The bear's oil, with which they annoint their persons all over, makes their skins soft and at the same time protects them from every species of diseases. Though nothing has been so fatal to them as their ungovernable passion for rum, with which, I am sorry to say it, they have been but too liberally supplied by the English that live near them.

And here I must lament the bad success Mr. Boyle's [1] charity has hitherto had toward converting any of these poor heathens to Christianity. Many children of our neighboring Indians have been brought up in the College of William and Mary. They have been taught to read and write, and have been carefully instructed in the principles of the Christian religion till they came to be men. Yet after they returned home, instead of civilizing and converting the rest, they have immediately relapsed into infidelity and barbarism themselves.

And some of them too have made the worst use of the knowledge they acquired among the English, by employing it against their benefactors. Besides, as they unhappily forget all the good they learn and remember the ill, they are apt to be more vicious and disorderly than the rest of their countrymen.

I ought not to quit this subject without doing justice to the great prudence of Colonel Spotswood in this affair. That gentleman was lieutenant governor of Virginia when Carolina was engaged in a bloody war with the Indians. At that critical time it was thought expedient to keep a watchful eye upon our tributary savages, who we knew had nothing to keep them to their duty but their fears.

Then it was that he demanded of each nation a competent number of their great men's children to be sent to the college, where they served as so many hostages for the good behavior of the rest and at the same time were themselves principled in the Christian religion. He also placed a schoolmaster among the Saponi Indians, at the salary of fifty pounds per annum, to instruct their children. The person that undertook that charitable work was Mr.

[1] **Mr. Boyle:** the missionary among the Indians.

Indian Literature

Colonists like Byrd regarded the Indians primarily as a people to be conquered or "civilized." Only in the nineteenth century did Americans begin seriously to study Indian culture. The first significant student of Indian culture was Henry Rowe Schoolcraft, who observed the Ojibwa tribes in Michigan. Schoolcraft's work came to the attention of Henry Wadsworth Longfellow (page 205), who used it as the basis for his enormously popular poem, *Hiawatha.* Later anthropological studies have preserved much of the literature of the Indian peoples.

Indian literature is primarily oral, transmitted by word of mouth. Of the stories, myths, and ritual chants recorded by anthropologists, one of the most impressive chants, from the Papage Indians of Arizona, was recorded by Ruth M. Underhill.

The corn comes up;
It comes up green;
Here upon our fields
White tassels unfold.

The corn comes up;
It comes up green;
Here upon our fields
Green leaves blow in the breeze.

Blue evening falls.
Blue evening falls;
Near by, in every direction,
It sets the corn tassels trembling.

In recording Indian myths and poems, American anthropologists not only have preserved much that is beautiful in a dying culture; they have also given the American writer still another resource to draw on as he creates a national literature.

Charles Griffin, a man of good family, who by the innocence of his life and the sweetness of his temper was perfectly well qualified for that pious undertaking. Besides, he had so much the secret of mixing pleasure with instruction that he had not a scholar who did not love him affectionately.

Such talents must needs have been blessed with a proportionable success, had he not been unluckily removed to the college, by which he left the good work he had begun unfinished. In short, all the pains he had undertaken among the infidels had no other effect but to make them something cleanlier than other Indians are.

FOR STUDY AND DISCUSSION

1. Find examples of Byrd's energy, his curiosity, his shrewdness, and his sense of humor. What evidence is there that this selection was written from an aristocratic point of view?

2. Why does Byrd look down on the North Carolinians? What does his attitude toward them tell you about his own view of a well-run farm or community?

3. What does Byrd admire about the Nottoway Indians? What does he deplore about them? In your opinion, does Byrd feel that the Indians should not have been educated at all, or that they should have been educated more thoroughly? Why?

4. Would you say that this selection is written in a plain style or in an ornate style (see page 12)? Explain your answer.

LANGUAGE AND VOCABULARY

The *context* of a word refers to the words that surround it and the total situation in which it is used. As you read, you will often be able to guess the meaning of an unfamiliar word, or the unfamiliar meaning of a familiar word, from the context in which the word is used. For example, the first sentence of the selection contains a word that may not be familiar to all readers.

"The Sabbath happened very opportunely to give some ease to our *jaded* people, who rested religiously from every work but that of cooking the kettle."

From such surrounding words as "ease" and "rested" and from the total situation in which the people find relief by resting, you might guess that "jaded" here means "tired" or "fatigued." In some cases, of course, context will not always be a sufficient clue to meaning. In other cases, the context of a word may be ambiguous, and you may make a wrong guess. Whenever you are not sure about the meaning of an unfamiliar word, look up the word in the dictionary. In many cases, however, the ability to guess the meaning of a word from its context will save you the trouble of looking up the word, thus increasing the ease of your reading and your appreciation of the selection.

Define the italicized words in the following sentences. If you cannot arrive at the meanings of the words from the context of the sentences in which they appear, be sure to refer to the dictionary. Be prepared to explain how you arrived at your definitions.

1. "The truth of it is, the inhabitants of North Carolina devour so much swine's flesh that it fills them full of gross *humors*." (Page 14.)

2. "Accordingly in the afternoon we marched in good order to the town, where the female scouts, stationed on an *eminence* for that purpose, had no sooner spied us but they gave notice of our approach to their fellow citizens . . ." (Page 15.)

3. "This fort was a square piece of ground enclosed with substantial puncheons, or strong palisades, about ten feet high and leaning a little outwards to make a *scalade* more difficult." (Page 15.)

4. "The young men had painted themselves in a hideous manner, not so much for ornament as terror. In that frightful *equipage,* they entertained us with sundry war dances . . ." (Page 15.)

5. "Such talents must needs have been blest with *proportionable* success, had he not been unluckily removed to the college, by which he left the good work he had begun unfinished." (Page 18.)

FOR COMPOSITION

In a brief composition, compare the characters of William Byrd and William Bradford, showing what traits and beliefs the two men had in common as well as the ways in which they were different. Use details from the selections by these men to support your statements.

EDWARD TAYLOR

(1645?–1729)

Edward Taylor, the minister and doctor of a small town for over fifty years, was described by his grandson as "a man of small stature, but firm; of quick passions yet serious and grave; exemplary in piety and for a very sacred observance of the Lord's day." Born in England, he came to Massachusetts as a young man and studied at Harvard University. After being admitted to the ministry, he accepted an invitation to organize a church in Westfield, Massachusetts. Taylor made a hundred-mile trip from the coast to this frontier town, walking through knee-deep snow and over rocks and mountains, finding his way much of the time by following marked trees. During his first years at Westfield, the town was in great danger of assault by Indians, especially during King Philip's War, when Indian raids destroyed many towns nearer Boston. The remaining years of Taylor's ministry were spent in quiet isolation from the world at large. He tended to the spiritual and physical ills of the town. He married twice and had fourteen children. He amassed a sizable library containing books in Hebrew, Greek, and Latin and including handwritten copies of books he had borrowed as a young man, when he could not afford to buy many books. Letters from his old friend and college roommate, Judge Samuel Sewall, enabled Taylor to keep up with affairs in Boston and the more distant world beyond. As a minister, Taylor had a public life; like all poets, he also had an intensely private one. This second, poetic life looked intently at the world of nature and of men and sought to build from these worlds a single, greater world, containing all heaven, earth, and hell.

Edward Taylor would probably be forgotten if his poetry had not been found in the Yale University Library in 1937. Today he is generally regarded as the finest poet writing in America before the nineteenth century. He never meant his poetry to be published, perhaps because of the general Puritan suspicion of all poetry that did not preach a religious lesson. Although Taylor's poetry is religious, it does not preach simple religious lessons. Instead, it seeks to describe the complexity of his own beliefs and feelings, and is modeled on the works of English poets of a somewhat earlier time, particularly on the poems of George Herbert. Herbert used unusual comparisons between religious doctrines and commonplace things to convey the religious significance of all existence. Like Herbert's poetry, Taylor's is sometimes difficult and intellectually challenging because it deals with complex experiences and ideas. His poems do exemplify one Puritan doctrine, however: a belief in the relationship between the things of this world and the things of the next. A similar emphasis upon the tremendous importance of ordinary sights and objects characterizes much American literature from Benjamin Franklin through Ralph Waldo Emerson to the important modern poet, Wallace Stevens.

This gold coin, called an angel, shows the archangel Michael slaying a dragon. The angel, referred to by Edward Taylor in "Meditation Six," was minted in England between the reigns of Elizabeth I and Charles II.

Meditation Six

Canticles 2 : 1. I am . . . the lily of the valleys.

Am I thy gold? Or Purse, Lord, for thy Wealth;
    Whether in mine or mint refined for thee?
I'm counted so, but count me o'er thyself,
    Lest gold-washed face, and brass in Heart I be.
    I Fear my Touchstone° touches when I try   5
    Me and my Counted Gold too overly.

Am I new minted by thy Stamp indeed?
    Mine Eyes are dim; I cannot clearly see.
Be thou my Spectacles that I may read
    Thine Image and Inscription stamped on me.   10
If thy bright Image do upon me stand,
    I am a Golden Angel° in thy hand.

Lord, make my Soul thy Plate°: thine Image bright
    Within the Circle of the same enfoil.°
And on its brims in golden Letters write   15
    Thy Superscription in an Holy style.
    Then I shall be thy Money, thou my Hoard:
    Let me thy Angel be, be thou my Lord.

5. **Touchstone:** a stone used to test the purity of gold and silver. 12. **Golden Angel:** In Taylor's time there was a gold coin called an angel that carried the image of the archangel Michael. 13. **Plate:** gold plate. 14. **enfoil:** enfold.

"Meditation Six" from *The Poetical Works of Edward Taylor,* edited by Thomas H. Johnson, copyright 1939, Rocklands Editions; copyright 1943 by Princeton University Press. Reprinted by permission of Princeton University Press.

The Experience

Oh! that I always breath'd in such an air,
　　As I sucked in, feeding on sweet Content!
Dished up unto my Soul ev'n in that prayer
　　Poured out to God over last Sacrament.°
　　What Beam of Light wrapped up my Sight to find　　5
　　Me nearer God than e'er came in my mind?

Most Strange it was! But yet more Strange that shine
　　Which filled my Soul then to the brim to spy
My nature with thy Nature all Divine
　　Together joined in Him that's Thou and I.　　10
　　Flesh of my Flesh, Bone of my Bone:° there's run°
　　Thy Godhead, and my Manhood in thy Son.

Oh! that that Flame which thou didst on me Cast
　　Might me enflame, and Lighten° everywhere.
Then Heaven to me would be less at last,　　15
　　So much of heaven I should have while here.
　　Oh! Sweet though Short! I'll not forget the same.
　　My nearness, Lord, to thee did me Enflame.

I'll Claim my Right: Give place, ye Angels Bright.
　　Ye further from the Godhead stand than I.　　20
My Nature is your Lord; and doth Unite
　　Better than Yours unto the Deity.
　　God's Throne is first and mine is next; to you
　　Only the place of Waiting-men is due.

Oh! that my Heart thy Golden Harp might be　　25
　　Well tuned by Glorious Grace, that ev'ry string
Screwed to the highest pitch, might unto thee
　　All praises wrapped in sweetest Music bring.
　　I praise thee, Lord, and better praise thee would
　　If what I had, my heart might ever hold.　　30

4. **last Sacrament:** the experience occurred when Taylor last received communion.
11. **Flesh . . . Bone:** an echo of Genesis 2:18. **there's run:** there (in Christ) is where runs.
14. **Lighten:** shine.

FOR STUDY AND DISCUSSION

1. Explain the first line of "Meditation Six." In what way is the poet like gold or a purse? How are these comparisons developed?

2. Explain the pun in line 12 of "Meditation Six." Why is a pun an effective device in a poem of this kind?

3. Describe Taylor's experience (in "The Experience"). What comparisons does he use to convey the quality of the experience? Are they appropriate to the poem? Explain.

4. What in your opinion are the difficulties of describing a religious experience in a poem? How well do you think Taylor succeeds in overcoming these difficulties in "The Experience"?

Huswifery

In this poem, Taylor compares his soul to a spinning wheel. In order to understand the poem, it is necessary to know that on a spinning wheel the distaff holds the raw wool, the flyers control the spinning, the spool winds and twists the yarn, and the reel takes up the finished thread.

Make me, O Lord, thy Spinning Wheel complete.
　Thy Holy Word my Distaff make for me.
Make mine° Affections° thy Swift Flyers neat
　And make my Soul thy holy Spool to be.
　My Conversation make to be thy Reel　　　　　　5
　And reel the yarn thereon spun of thy Wheel.

Make me thy Loom then, knit therein this Twine,
　And make thy Holy Spirit, Lord, wind quills:°
Then weave the Web thyself. The yarn is fine.
　Thine Ordinances° make my Fulling Mills.°　　　10
　Then dye the same in Heavenly Colors Choice,
　All pinked° with Varnished° Flowers of Paradise.

Then clothe therewith mine Understanding, Will,
　Affections, Judgment, Conscience, Memory
My Words and Actions, that their shine may fill　　15
　My ways with glory and thee glorify.
　Then mine apparel shall display before ye
　That I am Clothed in Holy robes for glory.

---

3. **mine:** my. **Affections:** emotions. 8. **quills:** spools on a loom. 10. **Ordinances:** the sacraments. **Fulling Mills:** mills where the cloth was cleaned. 12. **pinked:** decorated. **Varnished:** bright, shining.

"Huswifery" from *The Poetical Works of Edward Taylor,* edited by Thomas H. Johnson, copyright 1939, Rocklands Editions; copyright 1943 by Princeton University Press. Reprinted by permission of Princeton University Press and The New England Quarterly.

COMMENTARY

"Huswifery" (or housewifery) grows out of an intricately developed comparison between a domestic chore and God's bestowal of grace. Such an extended comparison between two startlingly different things (a lowly household task and the means of salvation) is a type of metaphor called a *conceit*. (For a discussion of metaphor, see page 286.) Conceits are associated primarily with the work of seventeenth-century English poets such as John Donne and George Herbert, who introduced many things into their poetry that are not usually considered poetic. For example, Donne compared love with the bite of a flea; Herbert compared the relationship between man and God with that between a tenant and a rich lord. Part of the pleasure in reading such poems lies in recognizing the surprising yet plausible way in which the poet has worked out an involved relationship between things that, on the face of it, have nothing in common. In religious poetry a conceit may serve a deeper purpose than pleasure. It can emphasize the connection between all things, high and low, familiar and strange. Taylor, as a Puritan, believed that since God created everything, He could be served equally well in all human activities—by a housewife as well as by someone exclusively devoted to religious duties. Therefore, it was perfectly natural for him to compare the hope for salvation with the making of homespun clothes.

"Huswifery" is a private conversation between the poet and God, a kind of prayer asking God for the grace to lead a pious, upright life. The comparison introduced in the first line between the poet's soul and a spinning wheel is worked out in detail in the rest of the stanza. The "Holy Word" is like the distaff on which the raw wool is placed before spinning. The poet's emotions are like the flyers that twist and carry the wool. His soul is like the spool that winds the thread on the wheel, while

his conversation, or way of living, is comparable to the reel. The stanza ends with a plea to God to reel in the yarn, which is the stuff of the poet's life.

The second stanza shifts to a comparison with weaving. The poet now asks that he be made like a loom that weaves yarn or twine. The Holy Spirit, or Holy Ghost, is to wind the yarn on the quills, and God, Himself, is to be the weaver. Once the yarn of the poet's life is woven, it is to be purified by God's laws, dyed in "heavenly Colors," and decorated with "Flowers of Paradise." These decorations represent the soul's achieving divine grace, without which salvation is impossible.

Taylor prays that the woven cloth of grace be used to clothe his mental faculties and all his words and actions, so that his way of living will testify to God's glory. In the last two lines of the poem he declares that if God will do what Taylor has asked, the poet will show God that he is clothed in grace and ready for divine salvation.

FOR STUDY AND DISCUSSION

1. Do you think that Taylor's manner of expressing himself is too complicated for sincere religious feeling, or is his manner of expression an honest reflection of complex thoughts and emotions? Defend your answer. Would you call "Huswifery" a deeply felt poem? Why or why not?

2. In the first stanza, the poet is compared both to a spinning wheel and the yarn that is spun on it. In your opinion, is this double comparison an inconsistency that weakens the poem, or does it point to a deeper meaning? Why?

3. The Commentary describes "Huswifery" as a private conversation. How would you characterize the speaker? (That Taylor is a pious man is obvious. What else can you tell about him from the poem?)

FOR COMPOSITION

Write a composition in which you discuss how a poem may relate several apparently unconnected ideas or experiences and create a new experience out of the relationship between them.

JONATHAN
EDWARDS
(1703–1758)

Jonathan Edwards, minister, theologian, philosopher, could write of the "inward, sweet delight in God and divine things" and of "the black clouds of God's wrath now hanging directly over your heads." As a theologian, he strove to reconcile the ecstasy of his own religious experiences with the importance of judgment and damnation in the Puritan point of view. As a minister, he strove to make the Deity a beautiful and terrible presence to his congregation. As a philosopher, he strove to build a coherent system of thought, based on Isaac Newton's physics, John Locke's concept that man's ideas derive from his sensory impressions, and the Puritan doctrine that God chooses those persons whom He will save from damnation. An early American attempt to interrelate all things, Edwards's philosophical system is generally regarded as the most brilliant intellectual construction of the colonial period.

Edwards, the son of a prominent minister, was born in East Windsor, Connecticut. He showed an early interest in science, and at the age of twelve, he wrote a paper on the habits of flying spiders. The same year he entered Yale College. After graduation he served briefly as a minister in New York and then returned to Yale to teach. In 1729, he became minister of the church of Northampton, Massachusetts, succeeding his maternal grandfather, Samuel Stoddard. Stoddard had been the most formidable minister west of Boston, a man of enormous presence and influence who was noted for his religious revivals. Edwards soon surpassed his grandfather's accomplishments. In 1735 he brought about a religious revival which he described in *A Faithful Narrative of the Surprising Work of God in the Conversion of Many Hundred Souls in Northampton, and the Neighboring Towns and Villages*. In 1740 and 1741, aided by the English Methodist, George Whitefield, Edwards led the Great Awakening, a revival that brought most of New England and the neighboring colonies to a high pitch of religious excitement. During the period of the Great Awakening, Edwards was the most powerful man in the Northern colonies. He preached sermons like "Sinners in the Hands of an Angry God," bringing to his congregation a vivid awareness of their wretched state. Although Edwards preached in a simple, restrained manner, using no gestures and gazing at the bell rope at the opposite end of the hall, his sermons had a powerful effect. During the delivery of "Sinners in the Hands of an Angry God," as a local historian noted, "there was heard such a breathing of distress and weeping that the preacher was obliged to speak to the people and desire silence that he might be heard."

When a reaction set in against the emotionalism of the Awakening, Edwards's own congregation turned against him, partly because they considered him too authoritarian. After being dismissed from his pulpit, he spent over six years in poverty and almost complete isolation from New England society. Serving as minister to the Housatonic Indians, he remained at his post during the dangers of the French and Indian War. During this period, he completed his famous philosophical work on the freedom of the will, *A Careful and Strict Enquiry into the Modern Prevailing Notions of That Freedom of Will which Is Supposed to Be Essential to Moral Agency, Virtue and Vice, Reward and Punishment, Praise and Blame.* Toward the end of his ministry to the Housatonics, he wrote his great theological works, *The Nature of True Virtue* and *Dissertation Concerning the End for which God Created the World.* An appointment as president of the College of New Jersey (now Princeton University) put an end to Edwards's isolation, but he died from a smallpox inoculation a little over a month after his arrival in Princeton.

Address to Sarah Pierrepont

According to legend, Edwards, when he was twenty years old, wrote this brief address to his future wife before he had ever seen her.

THEY SAY there is a young lady in [New Haven] who is beloved of that Great Being who made and rules the world, and that there are certain seasons in which this Great Being, in some way or other invisible, comes to her and fills her mind with exceeding sweet delight, and that she hardly cares for anything, except to meditate on Him—that she expects after a while to be received up where He is, to be raised up out of the world and caught up into heaven; being assured that He loves her too well to let her remain at a distance from Him always. There she is to dwell with Him and to be ravished with His love and delight forever. Therefore, if you present all the world before her, with the richest of its treasures, she disregards it and cares not for it and is un-mindful of any pain or affliction. She has a strange sweetness in her mind and singular purity in her affections; is most just and conscientious in all her conduct; and you could not persuade her to do anything wrong or sinful if you would give her all the world, lest she should offend this Great Being. She is of a wonderful sweetness, calmness, and universal benevolence of mind; especially after this Great God has manifested himself to her mind. She will sometimes go about from place to place singing sweetly, and seems to be always full of joy and pleasure; and no one knows for what. She loves to be alone, walking in the fields and groves, and seems to have some One invisible always conversing with her.

FOR STUDY AND DISCUSSION

1. In "Sarah Pierrepont," what qualities in a girl does Edwards seem to admire? Do you think a modern boy would admire these qualities? Explain. In your opinion, is the description of Sarah Pierrepont believable? Why or why not? Do you think there are people like her today?

2. "Sarah Pierrepont" has been called a "short prose poem." What is poetic about the selection?

3. What does this selection reveal of the Puritan viewpoint? (Before answering, you may wish to study pages 2–3.)

FROM *Sinners in the Hands of an Angry God*

WERE IT NOT for the sovereign pleasure of God, the earth would not bear you one moment; for you are a burden to it; the creation groans with you; the creature [1] is made subject to the bondage of your corruption, not willingly; the sun does not willingly shine upon you to give you light to serve sin and Satan; the earth does not willingly yield her increase to satisfy your lusts; nor is it willingly a stage for your wickedness to be acted upon; the air does not willingly serve you for breath to maintain the flame of life in your vitals, while you spend your life in the service of God's enemies. God's creatures are good, and were made for men to serve God with, and do not willingly subserve to any other purpose, and groan when they are abused to purposes so directly contrary to their nature and end. And the world would spew you out, were it not for the sovereign hand of Him who hath subjected it in hope. There are black clouds of God's wrath now hanging directly over your heads, full of the dreadful storm, and big with thunder; and were it not for the restraining hand of God, it would immediately burst forth upon you. The sovereign pleasure of God, for the present, stays [2] His rough wind; otherwise it would come with fury, and your destruction would come like a whirlwind, and you would be like the chaff of the summer threshing floor.

The wrath of God is like great waters that are dammed for the present; they increase more and more, and rise higher and higher, till an outlet is given; and the longer the stream is stopped, the more rapid and mighty is its course, when once it is let loose. It is true that judgment against your evil works has not been executed hitherto; the floods of God's vengeance have been withheld; but your guilt in the meantime is constantly increasing, and you are every day treasuring up more wrath; the waters are constantly rising and waxing more and more mighty; and there is nothing but the mere pleasure of God that holds the waters back that are unwilling to be stopped and press hard to go forward. If God should only withdraw His hand from the floodgate, it would immediately fly open, and the fiery floods of the fierceness and wrath of God would rush forth with inconceivable fury, and would come upon you with omnipotent power; and if your strength were ten thousand times greater than it is, yea, ten thousand times greater than the strength of the stoutest, sturdiest devil in Hell, it would be nothing to withstand or endure it.

The bow of God's wrath is bent, and the arrow made ready on the string, and justice bends the arrow at your heart, and strains the bow, and it is nothing but the mere pleasure of God, and that of an angry God, without any promise or obligation at all, that keeps the arrow one moment from being made drunk with your blood. Thus all you that never passed under a great change of heart, by the mighty power of the Spirit of God upon your souls; all you that were never born again, and made new creatures, and raised from being dead in sin to a state of new, and before altogether unexperienced light and life, are in the hands of an angry God. However you may have reformed your life in many things, and may have had religious affections, and may keep up a form of religion in your families and closets [3] and in the house of God, it is nothing but His mere pleasure that keeps you from being this moment swallowed up in everlasting destruction. However unconvinced you may now be of the truth of what you

---

[1] **the creature:** that which was created by God: the world.

[2] **stays:** restrains.

[3] **closets:** private rooms.

hear, by and by you will be fully convinced of it. Those that are gone [1] from being in the like circumstances with you see that it was so with them, for destruction came suddenly upon most of them when they expected nothing of it, and while they were saying, Peace and safety: now they see that those things on which they depended for peace and safety were nothing but thin air and empty shadows.

The God that holds you over the pit of Hell, much as one holds a spider or some loathsome insect over the fire, abhors you, and is dreadfully provoked: His wrath toward you burns like fire; He looks upon you as worthy of nothing else but to be cast into the fire; He is of purer eyes than to bear to have you in His sight; you are ten thousand times more abominable in His eyes than the most hateful venomous serpent is in ours. You have offended Him infinitely more than ever a stubborn rebel did his prince; and yet it is nothing but His hand that holds you from falling into the fire every moment. It is to be ascribed to nothing else that you did not go to Hell the last night, that you was suffered to wake again in this world after you closed your eyes to sleep. And there is no other reason to be given why you have not dropped into hell since you arose in the morning, but that God's hand has held you up. There is no other reason to be given why you have not gone to Hell, since you have sat here in the house of God, provoking His pure eyes by your sinful wicked manner of attending His solemn worship. Yea, there is nothing else that is to be given as a reason why you do not this very moment drop down into Hell.

O sinner! Consider the fearful danger you are in: it is a great furnace of wrath, a wide and bottomless pit, full of the fire of wrath, that you are held over in the hand of that God whose wrath is provoked and incensed as much against you as against many of the damned in Hell. You hang by a slender thread, with the flames of divine wrath flashing about it, and ready every moment to singe it, and burn it asunder; and you have no interest in any Mediator, and nothing to lay hold of to save yourself, nothing to keep off the flames of wrath, nothing of your own, nothing that you ever have done, nothing that you can do, to induce God to spare you one moment.

How dreadful is the state of those that are daily and hourly in the danger of this great wrath and infinite misery! But this is the dismal case of every soul in this congregation that has not been born again, however moral and strict, sober and religious, they may otherwise be. Oh that you would consider it, whether you be young or old! There is reason to think that there are many in this congregation now hearing this discourse, that will actually be the subjects of this very misery to all eternity. We know not who they are, or in what seats they sit, or what thoughts they now have. It may be they are now at ease and hear all these things without much disturbance, and are now flattering themselves that they are not the persons, promising themselves that they shall escape. If we knew that there was one person, and but one, in the whole congregation that was to be the subject of this misery, what an awful thing would it be to think of! If we knew who it was, what an awful sight would it be to see such a person! How might all the rest of the congregation lift up a lamentable and bitter cry over him! But, alas! instead of one, how many is it likely will remember this discourse in Hell? And it would be a wonder if some that are now present should not be in Hell in a very short time, even before this year is out. And it would be no wonder if some persons, that now sit here in some seats of this meeting house in health, quiet and secure, should be there before tomorrow morning. Those of you that finally continue in a natural condition, that shall keep out of Hell longest, will be there in a little time! your damnation does not slumber; it will come swiftly and, in all probability, very suddenly upon

[1] **are gone:** have died.

many of you. You have reason to wonder that you are not already in Hell. It is doubtless the case of some whom you have seen and known, that never deserved Hell more than you, and that heretofore appeared as likely to have been now alive as you. Their case is past all hope; they are crying in extreme misery and perfect despair; but here you are in the land of the living and in the house of God, and have an opportunity to obtain salvation. What would not those poor damned hopeless souls give for one day's opportunity such as you now enjoy!

And now you have an extraordinary opportunity, a day wherein Christ has thrown the door of mercy wide open, and stands in calling and crying with a loud voice to poor sinners; a day wherein many are flocking to Him and pressing into the kingdom of God. Many are daily coming from the east, west, north, and south; many that were very lately in the same miserable condition that you are in are now in a happy state, with their hearts filled with love to him who has loved them, and washed them from their sins in His own blood, and rejoicing in hope of the glory of God. How awful is it to be left behind at such a day! To see so many others feasting, while you are pining and perishing! To see so many rejoicing and singing for joy of heart, while you have cause to mourn for sorrow of heart, and howl for vexation of spirit! How can you rest one moment in such a condition? Are not your souls as precious as the souls of the people at Suffield,[1] where they are flocking from day to day to Christ?

Are there not many here who have lived long in the world, and are not to this day born again? and so are aliens from the commonwealth of Israel, and have done nothing ever since they have lived but treasure up wrath against the day of wrath? Oh, sirs, your case in an especial manner is extremely dangerous. Your guilt and hardness of heart is extremely great. Do you not see how generally per-

sons of your years are passed over and left, in the present remarkable and wonderful dispensation of God's mercy? You had need to consider yourselves and awake thoroughly out of sleep. You cannot bear the fierceness and wrath of the infinite God. And you, young men and young women, will you neglect this precious season which you now enjoy, when so many others of your age are renouncing all youthful vanities and flocking to Christ? You especially have now an extraordinary opportunity; but if you neglect it, it will soon be with you as with those persons who spent all the precious days of youth in sin, and are now come to such a dreadful pass in blindness and hardness. And you, children, who are unconverted, do not you know that you are going down to Hell, to bear the dreadful wrath of that God who is now angry with you every day and every night? Will you be content to be the children of the devil, when so many other children in the land are converted, and are become the holy and happy children of the King of kings?

And let every one that is yet of Christ, and hanging over the pit of Hell, whether they be old men and women, or middle-aged, or young people, or little children, now hearken to the loud calls of God's word and providence. This acceptable year of the Lord, a day of such great favors to some, will doubtless be a day of as remarkable vengeance to others. Men's hearts harden, and their guilt increases apace at such a day as this, if they neglect their souls; and never was there so great danger of such persons being given up to hardness of heart and blindness of mind. God seems now to be hastily gathering in His elect in all parts of the land; and probably the greater part of adult persons that ever shall be saved, will be brought in now in a little time, and that it will be as it was on the great outpouring of the Spirit upon the Jews in the apostles' days; the election will obtain,[2] and the rest will be blinded.

[2] **election . . . obtain:** Those destined for salvation will be chosen.

[1] **Suffield:** a nearby town.

If this should be the case with you, you will eternally curse this day, and will curse the day that ever you was born to see such a season of the pouring out of God's Spirit, and will wish that you had died and gone to Hell before you had seen it. Now undoubtedly it is as it was in the days of John the Baptist; the ax is in an extraordinary manner laid at the root of the trees, that every tree which brings not forth good fruit may be hewn down and cast into the fire.

Therefore, let everyone that is out of Christ now awake and fly from the wrath to come. The wrath of Almighty God is now undoubtedly hanging over a great part of this congregation: Let everyone fly out of Sodom: [1] "Haste and escape for your lives, look not behind you, escape to the mountain, lest you be consumed." [2]

[1] **Sodom:** a Biblical city destroyed because of the sinfulness of its people.
[2] **Haste . . . consumed:** the angels' warning to Lot, the one upright man in Sodom.

FOR STUDY AND DISCUSSION

1. To which three things does Edwards compare God's wrath? How does he develop each comparison? How does each comparison add to the force of the sermon?

2. In this sermon, Edwards speaks of an angry God. Yet in another of his writings Edwards speaks of God as "majesty and meekness joined together." Are these two conceptions contradictory or not? Explain.

THE FORMS OF DISCOURSE: PERSUASION

One way of classifying writing is according to the forms of discourse: *narration, description, exposition,* and *persuasion.* A writer uses narration to tell about series of events: the selection from Bradford's *Of Plymouth Plantation* is largely narration. Description is used to show how something looks or feels or otherwise appeals to the senses: Byrd's account of the Nottoway Indians is largely description. Exposition presents information, a set of related facts or ideas: the paragraph from Bradford's account which begins, "But here I cannot but stay" (page 11) is largely expository. A piece of writing rarely uses one kind of discourse exclusively. For example, Bradford's narrative uses description to show how rough the sea was, and exposition to present the desperate situation of the Pilgrims.

Persuasive speech or writing seeks to have its audience adopt an opinion, perform an action, or both. Some modern examples of persuasive speaking and writing are political speeches, television commercials, and newspaper editorials. In analyzing persuasive writing, you should consider four aspects of the work: (1) the speaker, (2) the audience, (3) the occasion, (4) the means of persuasion.

1. *The speaker:* A speaker or writer who seeks to persuade usually tries to convince his readers or audience that he is well qualified to offer an opinion. Sometimes he tries to convince his audience that he is much like them and can therefore speak for them. Sometimes he tries to impress the audience by displaying special knowledge. Edwards's congregation knew their minister to be a brilliant and upright man. What is there in the sermon itself that might persuade an audience of Edwards's special qualifications to discuss God's wrath and salvation?

2. *The audience:* A persuasive speech or piece of writing often makes its appeal to a particular audience. For example, a commercial for a toy, meant to appeal to children, is written differently than a commercial for a detergent. Describe Edwards's audience. How does he appeal to it?

3. *The occasion:* Many persuasive works are written for a special occasion, or situation, that may determine the kinds of arguments used. What was the special occasion of Edwards's sermon? How does he make use of this occasion in the sermon?

4. *The means of persuasion:* A great many devices have been developed to change people's minds. A persuasive speaker or writer may argue logically; he may appeal to tradition; he may play on the emotions of his audience. Does Edwards appeal primarily to reason or emotion? Cite specific arguments Edwards uses to sway his audience.

FOR COMPOSITION

Write a composition in which you analyze a modern piece of persuasive writing, perhaps a newspaper or magazine editorial. Consider the four aspects of persuasion: the speaker or writer, the audience, the occasion, the means of persuasion.

BENJAMIN FRANKLIN

(1706–1790)

Benjamin Franklin and Jonathan Edwards were born within three years of each other, yet their careers took vastly different courses. While Edwards was stirring his Northampton congregation to heights of religious enthusiasm, Franklin was busily running a print shop, publishing the Pennsylvania *Gazette* and *Poor Richard's Almanac,* and expounding the virtues of thrift and industry. While Edwards was writing his philosophical work on freedom of the will, Franklin was conducting his experiments with electricity and beginning his career of public service. Edwards, the theologian and philosopher, and Franklin, the ingenious man of affairs, have often been contrasted, yet Franklin seems to leap the bounds of such a contrast. There is too much of him to be accounted for. He was indeed a practical man who grew rich from the results of his inventiveness and hard work, but he was also an idealist who gave a large part of his life to the service of the colonies and new nation. He was a famous scientist who was honored in Europe and a shrewd diplomat who could charm the French by appearing in a backwoodsman's fur cap. Above all, he was an American who set an example for other Americans by constantly testing the resources of his mind and character.

As Franklin relates in his *Autobiography,* he was born in Boston and was apprenticed to his brother James to learn the printer's trade. At the age of seventeen, after a series of quarrels with his brother (described in the selection which follows), Franklin went to New York and then to Philadelphia. Within a few years, he set up his own print shop with a partner. In 1730, he began to publish the Pennsylvania *Gazette,* which later became the *Saturday Evening Post.* 1732 saw the first appearance of *Poor Richard's Almanac,* in which Franklin invented the character of Poor Richard, a printer who lived in the country and supposedly published the almanac. Franklin spiced the pages of his *Almanac* with Poor Richard's sayings, some of which were borrowed and some invented. Where he borrowed he improved, and Franklin's skill as a writer is nowhere more apparent than in his recasting of old proverbs into a more effective form. The old English saying, "A muffled cat was never a good mouser," became in Franklin's hands "The cat in gloves catches no mice." The proverb, "Three may keep counsel, if two be away," became "Three may keep a secret, if two of them are dead." In addition to being a printer, publisher, and writer, Franklin was also a merchant of quills, soap, cheese, rags, lottery tickets, and a salve guaranteed to cure the itch. By 1748, twenty years after he had opened his print shop, he was rich enough to retire from business.

Business concerns alone had never been enough to exhaust Franklin's boundless energy. In 1731, he founded the first circulating library in Philadelphia. In 1736, he began a fifteen-year stint as clerk of the Pennsylvania Assembly. In 1743, he was instrumental in founding the American Philosophical Society. Through the years he became increasingly interested in scientific matters, especially in the phenomenon of electricity. He performed his famous kite experiment in 1752, proving that lightning was electricity. His invention of the lightning rod and his book *Experiments and Observations on Electricity* won him honorary degrees from Harvard, Yale, William and Mary, and Oxford University. The British philosopher David Hume called him America's "first philosopher, and indeed the first great man of letters, for whom we are beholden to her."

Franklin's major involvement in political affairs began in 1757, when he was sent to England to act as agent for the Pennsylvania Assembly. Except for a brief return to Philadelphia, he stayed in England almost until the beginning of the Revolutionary War, eventually representing Georgia, New Jersey, and Massachusetts, as well as Pennsylvania. He moved in cultivated English society, traveled on the Continent, and pled the cause of colonial liberty. In the early 1770's, he wrote a number of essays directed against the English administration that was mismanaging colonial affairs, among them the satires "An Edict by the King of Prussia" and "Rules by Which a Great Empire May Be Reduced to a Small One." In 1775, convinced that his efforts were useless, he returned to America. Together with Jefferson and John Adams, he served on the committee that drafted the Declaration of Independence. Then he was sent to France to win support for the Revolutionary cause. He was vastly popular. Frenchmen expected an American to be a strange, rustic creature, and with great shrewdness Franklin satisfied their expectations by dressing plainly and wearing a fur cap. Those whom his appearance failed to captivate, his wit conquered. In 1778 he effected a military alliance with France, and five years later he helped to negotiate a peace treaty with England. He ended his public life as a delegate to the Constitutional Convention, where his good sense and counsels of moderation were invaluable.

Franklin's life was crammed with activity. He himself exemplified Poor Richard's saying, "Dost thou love life, then do not squander time, for that's the stuff life is made of." But behind all his doings and comings and goings, there was a pattern: first he worked hard to become rich, then for higher purposes. A literary historian has written of him, "Some men cast a shadow over posterity. Franklin throws a light which has affected American life, literature, and science ever since his own day and is still undimmed. He survives as a tremendous national symbol, and yet has never ceased to be a familiar and beloved person."

From the title page of a French translation of *Poor Richard's Almanac* (1777).

FROM HIS *Autobiography*

Franklin began his autobiography while he was vacationing in Twyford, England, in 1771. It is addressed to his son, William Franklin, Governor of New Jersey. The part of the *Autobiography* telling about Franklin's project to achieve moral perfection (page 36) was written thirteen years later in Passy, a suburb of Paris.

DEAR SON: I have ever had pleasure in obtaining any little anecdotes of my ancestors. You may remember the inquiries I made among the remains of my relations when you were with me in England, and the journey I undertook for that purpose. Imagining it may be equally agreeable to you to know the circumstances of my life, many of which you are yet unacquainted with, and expecting the enjoyment of a week's uninterrupted leisure in my present country retirement, I sit down to write them for you. To which I have besides some other inducements. Having emerged from the poverty and obscurity in which I was born and bred to a state of affluence and some degree of reputation in the world, and having gone so far through life with a considerable share of felicity, the conducing means I made use of, which with the blessing of God so well succeeded, my posterity may like to know, as they may find some of them suitable to their own situations and therefore fit to be imitated.

That felicity, when I reflected on it, has induced me sometimes to say that were it offered to my choice, I should have no objection to a repetition of the same life from its beginning, only asking the advantages authors have in a second edition to correct some faults of the first. So I might, besides correcting the faults, change some sinister accidents and events of it for others more favorable. But though this were denied, I should still accept the offer. Since such a repetition is not to be expected, the next thing most like living one's life over again seems to be a recollection of that life, and to make that recollection as durable as possible by putting it down in writing.

Hereby, too, I shall indulge the inclination so natural in old men to be talking of themselves and their own past actions; and I shall indulge it without being tiresome to others who, through respect to age, might conceive themselves obliged to give me a hearing, since this may be read or not as anyone pleases. And lastly (I may as well confess it, since my denial of it will be believed by nobody), perhaps I shall a good deal gratify my own *vanity.* Indeed, I scarce ever heard or saw the introductory words, *"Without vanity I may say,"* etc., but some vain thing immediately followed. Most people dislike vanity in others, whatever share they have of it themselves; but I give it fair quarter wherever I meet with it, being persuaded that it is often productive of good to the possessor, and to others that are within his sphere of action; and therefore, in many cases, it would not be altogether absurd if a man were to thank God for his vanity among the other comforts of life.

And now I speak of thanking God, I desire with all humility to acknowledge that I owe the mentioned happiness of my past life to His kind providence, which led me to the means I used and gave them success. My belief of this induces me to *hope,* though I must not *presume,* that the same goodness will still be exercised toward me in continuing that happiness or enabling me to bear a fatal reverse, which I may experience as others have done; the complexion of my future fortune being known to Him only in whose power it is to bless to us even our afflictions. . . .

My brother had, in 1720 or 1721, begun to print a newspaper. It was the second that appeared in America and was called the *New England Courant.* The only one before it was the *Boston News-Letter.* I remember his being dissuaded by some of his friends from the undertaking, as not likely to succeed, one newspaper being, in their judgment, enough for America. At this time (1771) there are not less than five-and-twenty. He went on, however, with the undertaking, and after having worked in composing the types and printing off the sheets, I was employed to carry the papers through the streets to the customers.

He had some ingenious men among his friends, who amused themselves by writing little pieces for this paper, which gained it credit and made it more in demand, and these gentlemen often visited us. Hearing their conversations and their accounts of the approbation their papers were received with, I was excited to try my hand among them; but, being still a boy, and suspecting that my brother would object to printing anything of mine in his paper if he knew it to be mine, I contrived to disguise my hand and, writing an anonymous paper, I put it in at night under the door of the printing house. It was found in the morning and communicated to his writing friends when they called in as usual. They read it, commented on it in my hearing, and I had the exquisite pleasure of finding it met with their approbation, and that, in their different guesses at the author, none were named but men of some character among us for learning and ingenuity. I suppose now that I was rather lucky in my judges and that perhaps they were not really so very good ones as I then esteemed them.

Encouraged, however, by this, I wrote and conveyed in the same way to the press several more papers which were equally approved; and I kept my secret till my small fund of sense for such performances was pretty well exhausted, and then I discovered [1] it when I began to be considered a little more by my brother's acquaintance and in a manner that did not quite please him, as he thought, probably with reason, that it tended to make me too vain. And, perhaps, this might be one

occasion of the differences that we began to have about this time. Though a brother, he considered himself as my master, and me as his apprentice, and, accordingly, expected the same services from me as he would from another, while I thought he demeaned me too much in some he required of me, who from a brother expected more indulgence. Our disputes were often brought before our father, and I fancy I was either generally in the right or else a better pleader because the judgment was generally in my favor. But my brother was passionate and had often beaten me, which I took extremely amiss; and, thinking my apprenticeship very tedious, I was continually wishing for some opportunity of shortening it, which at length offered in a manner unexpected.*

One of the pieces in our newspaper on some political point which I have now forgotten gave offense to the Assembly. He was taken up, censured, and imprisoned for a month, by the speaker's warrant, I suppose, because he would not discover his author. I too was taken up and examined before the council; but though I did not give them any satisfaction, they contented themselves with admonishing me and dismissed me, considering me, perhaps, as an apprentice who was bound to keep his master's secrets.

During my brother's confinement, which I resented a good deal, notwithstanding our private differences, I had the management of the paper; and I made bold to give our rulers some rubs [2] in it, which my brother took very kindly, while others began to consider me in an unfavorable light, as a young genius that had a turn for libeling and satire. My brother's discharge was accompanied with an order of the House (a very odd one), that *"James Franklin should no longer print the paper called the New England Courant."*

There was a consultation held in our

---

[1] **discovered:** here, revealed.

* I fancy his harsh and tyrannical treatment of me might be a means of impressing me with that aversion to arbitrary power that has stuck to me through my whole life. [Franklin's note.]

[2] **rubs:** here, sarcastic comments.

printing house among his friends, what he should do in this case. Some proposed to evade the order by changing the name of the paper; but my brother, seeing inconveniences in that, it was finally concluded on as a better way to let it be printed for the future under the name of BENJAMIN FRANKLIN; and to avoid the censure of the Assembly, that might fall on him as still printing it by his apprentice, the contrivance was that my old indenture should be returned to me with a full discharge on the back of it to be shown on occasion, but to secure to him the benefit of my service, I was to sign new indentures for the remainder of the term, which were to be kept private. A very flimsy scheme it was; however, it was immediately executed, and the paper went on accordingly under my name for several months.

At length, a fresh difference arising between my brother and me, I took upon me to assert my freedom, presuming that he would not venture to produce the new indentures. It was not fair in me to take this advantage, and this I therefore reckon one of the first errata [1] of my life; but the unfairness of it weighed little with me when under the impressions of resentment for the blows his passion too often urged him to bestow upon me, though he was otherwise not an ill-natured man: perhaps I was too saucy [2] and provoking.

When he found I would leave him, he took care to prevent my getting employment in any other printing house of the town by going round and speaking to every master, who accordingly refused to give me work. I then thought of going to New York as the nearest place where there was a printer; and I was rather inclined to leave Boston when I reflected that I had already made myself a little obnoxious to the governing party, and, from the arbitrary proceedings of the Assembly in my brother's case, it was likely I might, if I stayed, soon bring myself into scrapes. . . . My friend Collins,

therefore, undertook to manage a little for me. He agreed with the captain of a New York sloop for my passage. . . . So I sold some of my books to raise a little money, was taken on board privately, and as we had a fair wind, in three days I found myself in New York, near three hundred miles from home, a boy of but seventeen, without the least recommendation to, or knowledge of, any person in the place, and with very little money in my pocket.

Having a trade and supposing myself a pretty good workman, I offered my service to the printer in the place, old Mr. William Bradford, who had been the first printer in Pennsylvania but removed from thence upon the quarrel of George Keith. He could give me no employment, having little to do and help enough already; but, says he, "My son at Philadelphia has lately lost his principal hand, Aquila Rose, by death; if you go thither, I believe he may employ you." Philadelphia was a hundred miles further; I set out, however, in a boat for Amboy,[3] leaving my chest and things to follow me round by sea.

In crossing the bay, we met with a squall that tore our rotten sails to pieces, prevented our getting into the kill,[4] and drove us upon Long Island. . . .

When we drew near the island, we found it was at a place where there could be no landing, there being a great surf on the stony beach. So we dropped anchor and swung round toward the shore. Some people came down to the water edge and hallowed [5] to us, as we did to them; but the wind was so high, and the surf so loud, that we could not hear so as to understand each other. There were canoes on the shore, and we made signs and hallowed that they should fetch us; but they either did not understand us or thought it impracticable, so they went away, and night coming on, we had no remedy but to wait till the wind should abate; and the mean-

---

[1] **errata** (i·rä′tə): mistakes.
[2] **saucy:** here, impertinent.

[3] **Amboy:** a town on the New Jersey coast.
[4] **kill:** creek or channel.
[5] **hallowed:** called.

time the boatman and I concluded to sleep if we could; and so crowded into the scuttle,[1] and the spray, beating over the head of our boat, leaked through to us. . . . In this manner we lay all night with very little rest; but, the wind abating the next day, we made a shift to reach Amboy before night, having been thirty hours on the water, without victuals or any drink but a bottle of filthy rum, and the water we sailed on being salt.

In the evening I found myself very feverish and went into bed; but, having read somewhere that cold water drunk plentifully was good for a fever, I followed the prescription, sweat plentiful most of the night; my fever left me, and in the morning, crossing the ferry, I proceeded on my journey on foot, having fifty miles to Burlington, where I was told I should find boats that would carry me the rest of the way to Philadelphia.

It rained very hard all the day; I was thoroughly soaked and by noon a good deal tired; so I stopped at a poor inn where I stayed all night, beginning now to wish that I had never left home. I cut so miserable a figure, too, that I found, by the questions asked me, I was suspected to be some runaway servant and in danger of being taken up on that suspicion. However, I proceeded the next day and got in the evening to an inn, within eight or ten miles of Burlington, kept by one Dr. Brown. . . .

At his house I lay that night, and the next morning reached Burlington, but had the mortification to find that the regular boats were gone a little before my coming and no other expected to go before Tuesday, this being Saturday; wherefore I returned to an old woman in the town of whom I had bought gingerbread to eat on the water, and asked her advice. She invited me to lodge at her house till a passage by water should offer; and being tired with my foot traveling, I accepted the invitation. She, understanding I was a printer, would have had me stay at that town and follow my business, being ignorant of the stock necessary to begin with. She was very hospitable, gave me a dinner of ox-cheek with great good will, accepting only of a pot of ale in return; and I thought myself fixed till Tuesday should come. However, walking in the evening by the side of the river, a boat came by, which I found was going toward Philadelphia with several people in her. They took me in, and as there was no wind, we rowed all the way; and about midnight, not having yet seen the city, some of the company were confident we must have passed it and would row no farther; the others knew not where we were; so we put toward the shore, got into a creek, landed near an old fence, with the rails of which we made a fire, the night being cold in October, and there we remained till daylight. Then one of the company knew the place to be Cooper's Creek, a little above Philadelphia, which we saw as soon as we got out of the creek, and arrived there about eight or nine o'clock on the Sunday morning, and landed at the Market-street wharf.

I have been the more particular in this description of my journey and shall be so of my first entry into that city, that you may in your mind compare such unlikely beginnings with the figure I have since made there. I was in my working dress, my best clothes being to come round by sea. I was dirty from my journey; my pockets were stuffed out with shirts and

The city of Philadelphia in the 1720's.

---

[1] **scuttle:** opening or hatchway.

stockings, and I knew no soul nor where to look for lodging. I was fatigued with traveling, rowing, and want of rest; I was very hungry; and my whole stock of cash consisted of a Dutch dollar and about a shilling in copper. The latter I gave the people of the boat for my passage, who at first refused it on account of my rowing; but I insisted on their taking it. A man being sometimes more generous when he has but a little money than when he has plenty, perhaps through fear of being thought to have but little.

Then I walked up the street, gazing about till near the market house I met a boy with bread. I had made many a meal on bread, and, inquiring where he got it, I went immediately to the baker's he directed me to, in Second-street, and asked for biscuit, intending such as we had in Boston; but they, it seems, were not made in Philadelphia. Then I asked for a three-penny loaf and was told they had none such. So not considering or knowing the difference of money, and the greater cheapness nor the names of his bread, I bade him give me three-penny worth of any sort. He gave me, accordingly, three great puffy rolls. I was surprised at the quantity, but took it and, having no room in my pockets, walked off with a roll under each arm and eating the other. Thus I went up Market-street as far as Fourth-street, passing by the door of Mr. Read, my future wife's father; when she, standing at the door, saw me and thought I made, as I certainly did, a most awkward, ridiculous appearance. Then I turned and went down Chestnut-street and part of Walnut-street, eating my roll all the way, and, coming round, found myself again at Market-street wharf near the boat I came in, to which I went for a draught of the river water; and, being filled with one of my rolls, gave the other two to a woman and her child that came down the river in the boat with us and were waiting to go farther.

Thus refreshed, I walked again up the street, which by this time had many clean-dressed people in it who were all walking

the same way. I joined them and thereby was led into the great meeting house of the Quakers near the market. I sat down among them, and, after looking round a while and hearing nothing said, being very drowsy through labor and want of rest the preceding night, I fell fast asleep and continued so till the meeting broke up, when one was kind enough to rouse me. This was, therefore, the first house I was in or slept in in Philadelphia. . . .

It was about this time [1] I conceived the bold and arduous project of arriving at moral perfection. I wished to live without committing any fault at any time; I would conquer all that either natural inclination, custom, or company might lead me into. As I knew, or thought I knew, what was right and wrong, I did not see why I might not always do the one and avoid the other. But I soon found I had undertaken a task of more difficulty than I had imagined. While my care was employed in guarding against one fault, I was often surprised by another; habit took the advantage of inattention; inclination was sometimes too strong for reason. I concluded, at length, that the mere speculative conviction that it was our interest to be completely virtuous was not sufficient to prevent our slipping; and that the contrary habits must be broken and good ones acquired and established before we can have any dependence on a steady, uniform rectitude of conduct. For this purpose I therefore contrived the following method.

In the various enumerations of the moral virtues I had met with in my reading, I found the catalogue more or less numerous, as different writers included more or fewer ideas under the same name. Temperance, for example, was by some confined to eating and drinking, while by others it was extended to mean the moderating of every other pleasure, appetite, inclination, or passion, bodily or mental, even to our avarice and ambition. I proposed to myself, for the sake of clearness,

---

[1] **this time:** about 1729 or 1730, after Franklin had settled in Philadelphia.

to use rather more names, with fewer ideas annexed to each, than a few names with more ideas; and I included under thirteen names of virtues all that at that time occurred to me as necessary or desirable, and annexed to each a short precept, which fully expressed the extent I gave to its meaning.

These names of virtues, with their precepts, were:

1. TEMPERANCE

Eat not to dullness; drink not to elevation.

2. SILENCE

Speak not but what may benefit others or yourself; avoid trifling conversation.

3. ORDER

Let all your things have their places; let each part of your business have its time.

4. RESOLUTION

Resolve to perform what you ought; perform without fail what you resolve.

5. FRUGALITY

Make no expense but to do good to others or yourself; i.e., waste nothing.

6. INDUSTRY

Lose no time; be always employed in something useful; cut off all unnecessary actions.

7. SINCERITY

Use no hurtful deceit; think innocently and justly; and, if you speak, speak accordingly.

8. JUSTICE

Wrong none by doing injuries, or omitting the benefits that are your duty.

9. MODERATION

Avoid extremes; forbear resenting injuries so much as you think they deserve.

10. CLEANLINESS

Tolerate no uncleanliness in body, clothes, or habitation.

11. TRANQUILLITY

Be not disturbed at trifles, or at accidents common or unavoidable.

12. CHASTITY

13. HUMILITY

Imitate Jesus and Socrates.

My intention being to acquire the *habitude* of all these virtues, I judged it would be well not to distract my attention by attempting the whole at once but to fix it on one of them at a time; and, when I should be master of that, then to proceed to another, and so on till I should have gone through the thirteen; and as the previous acquisition of some might facilitate the acquisition of certain others, I arranged them with that view as they stand above. Temperance first, as it tends to procure that coolness and clearness of head, which is so necessary where constant vigilance was to be kept up, and guard maintained against the unremitting attraction of ancient habits and the force of perpetual temptations. This being acquired and established, Silence would be more easy; and my desire being to gain knowledge at the same time that I improved in virtue, and considering that in conversation it was obtained rather by the use of the ears than of the tongue, and therefore wishing to break a habit I was getting into of prattling, punning, and joking, which only made me acceptable to trifling company, I gave Silence the second place. This and the next, Order, I expected would allow me more time for attending to my project and my studies. Resolution, once become habitual, would keep me firm in my endeavors to obtain all the subsequent virtues; Frugality and Industry, freeing me from my remaining debt and producing affluence and independence, would make more easy the practice of Sincerity and Justice, etc., etc. Conceiving then, that, agreeably to the advice of Pythagoras [1] in his Golden

---

[1] **Pythagoras** (pi·thag′ər·əs): a famous Greek philosopher of the sixth century B.C.

Verses, daily examination would be necessary, I contrived the following method for conducting that examination.

I made a little book, in which I allotted a page for each of the virtues. I ruled each page with red ink, so as to have seven columns, one for each day of the week, marking each column with a letter for the day. I crossed these columns with thirteen red lines, marking the beginning of each line with the first letter of one of the virtues, on which line and in its proper column I might mark, by a little black spot, every fault I found upon examination to have been committed respecting that virtue upon that day.

I determined to give a week's strict attention to each of the virtues successively. Thus, in the first week, my great guard was to avoid even the least offense against Temperance, leaving the other virtues to their ordinary chance, only marking every evening the faults of the day. Thus, if in the first week I could keep my first line, marked T, clear of spots, I supposed the habit of that virtue so much strengthened, and its opposite weakened, that I might venture extending my attention to include the next, and for the following week keep both lines clear of spots. Proceeding thus to the last, I could go through a course complete in thirteen weeks, and four courses in a year. And like him who, having a garden to weed, does not attempt to eradicate all the bad herbs at once, which would exceed his reach and his strength, but works on one of the beds at a time and, having accomplished the first, proceeds to a second, so I should have, I hoped, the encouraging pleasure of seeing on my pages the progress I made in virtue, by clearing successively my lines of their spots, till in the end, by a number of courses, I should be happy in viewing a clean book, after a thirteen weeks' daily examination. . . .

The precept of Order requiring that *every part of my business should have its allotted time,* one page in my little book contained the following scheme of employment for the twenty-four hours of a natural day.

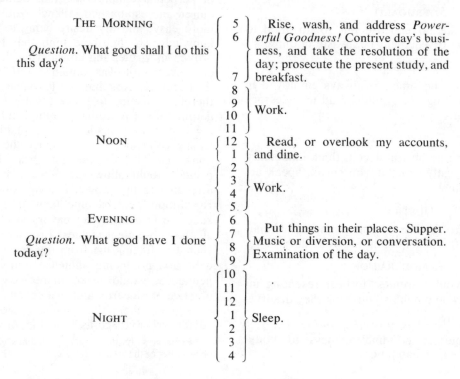

THE MORNING	5	Rise, wash, and address *Powerful Goodness!* Contrive day's business, and take the resolution of the day; prosecute the present study, and breakfast.
Question. What good shall I do this this day?	6	
	7	
	8	Work.
	9	
	10	
	11	
NOON	12	Read, or overlook my accounts, and dine.
	1	
	2	Work.
	3	
	4	
	5	
EVENING	6	Put things in their places. Supper. Music or diversion, or conversation. Examination of the day.
Question. What good have I done today?	7	
	8	
	9	
	10	Sleep.
	11	
	12	
NIGHT	1	
	2	
	3	
	4	

I entered upon the execution of this plan for self-examination and continued it with occasional intermissions for some time. I was surprised to find myself so much fuller of faults than I had imagined; but I had the satisfaction of seeing them diminish. To avoid the trouble of renewing now and then my little book, which, by scraping out the marks on the paper of old faults to make room for new ones in a new course, became full of holes, I transferred my tables and precepts to the ivory leaves of a memorandum book, on which the lines were drawn with red ink that made a durable stain, and on those lines I marked my faults with a black lead pencil, which marks I could easily wipe out with a wet sponge. After a while I went through one course only in a year and afterward only one in several years, till at length I omitted them entirely, being employed in voyages and business abroad, with a multiplicity of affairs that interfered; but I always carried my little book with me.

My scheme of Order gave me the most trouble; and I found that, though it might be practicable where a man's business was such as to leave him the disposition[1] of his time, that of a journeyman printer, for instance, it was not possible to be exactly observed by a master, who must mix with the world and often receive people of business at their own hours. Order, too, with regard to places for things, papers, etc., I found extremely difficult to acquire. I had not been early accustomed to it, and, having an exceeding good memory, I was not so sensible of the inconvenience attending want of method. This article, therefore, cost me so much painful attention, and my faults in it vexed me so much, and I made so little progress in amendment and had such frequent relapses, that I was almost ready to give up the attempt and content myself with a faulty character in that respect, like the man who, in buying an ax of a smith, my neighbor, desired to have the whole of its surface as bright as the edge. The smith consented to grind it bright for him if he would turn the wheel; he turned, while the smith pressed the broad face of the ax hard and heavily on the stone, which made the turning of it very fatiguing. The man came every now and then from the wheel to see how the work went on, and at length would take his ax as it was, without further grinding. "No," said the smith, "turn on, turn on; we shall have it bright by and by; as yet, it is only speckled." "Yes," says the man, *"but I think I like a speckled ax best."*

And I believe this may have been the case with many who, having, for want of some such means as I employed, found the difficulty of obtaining good and breaking bad habits in other points of vice and virtue, have given up the struggle, and concluded that *"a speckled ax was best"*; for something that pretended to be reason was every now and then suggesting to me that such extreme nicety as I exacted for myself might be a kind of foppery[2] in morals, which, if it were known, would make me ridiculous; that a perfect character might be attended with the inconvenience of being envied and hated; and that a benevolent man should allow a few faults in himself, to keep his friends in countenance.

In truth, I found myself incorrigible with respect to Order; and now I am grown old, and my memory bad, I feel very sensibly the want of it. But, on the whole, though I never arrived at the perfection I had been so ambitious of obtaining, but fell far short of it, yet I was, by the endeavor, a better and a happier man than I otherwise should have been if I had not attempted it; as those who aim at perfect writing by imitating the engraved copies, though they never reach the wished-for excellence of those copies, their hand is mended by the endeavor.

It may be well my posterity should be informed that to this little artifice, with the blessing of God, their ancestor owed the constant felicity of his life, down to

---

[1] **disposition:** here, management.

[2] **foppery:** foolishness.

his seventy-ninth year, in which this is written. What reverses may attend the remainder is in the hand of Providence; but, if they arrive, the reflection on past happiness enjoyed ought to help his bearing them with more resignation. To Temperance he ascribes his long-continued health, and what is still left to him of a good constitution; to Industry and Frugality, the early easiness of his circumstances and acquisition of his fortune, with all that knowledge that enabled him to be a useful citizen and obtained for him some degree of reputation among the learned; to Sincerity and Justice, the confidence of his country, and the honorable employs it conferred upon him; and to the joint influence of the whole mass of the virtues, even in the imperfect state he was able to acquire them, all that evenness of temper and that cheerfulness in conversation, which makes his company still sought for and agreeable even to his younger acquaintance. I hope, therefore, that some of my descendants may follow the example and reap the benefit.

It will be remarked that, though my scheme was not wholly without religion, there was in it no mark of any of the distinguishing tenets of any particular sect. I had purposely avoided them; for, being fully persuaded of the utility and excellency of my method, and that it might be serviceable to people in all religions, and

An illustration from *Poor Richard's Almanac,* a best seller of the mid-eighteenth century.

intending some time or other to publish it, I would not have anything in it that should prejudice anyone, of any sect, against it. I purposed writing a little comment on each virtue, in which I would have shown the advantages of possessing it, and the mischiefs attending its opposite vice; and I should have called my book *The Art of Virtue,* because it would have shown the means and manner of obtaining virtue, which would have distinguished it from mere exhortation to be good that does not instruct and indicate the means, but is like the apostle's man of verbal charity who, without showing to the naked and hungry how or where they might get clothes or victuals, only exhorted them to be fed and clothed.—James 2:15–16.

But it so happened that my intention of writing and publishing this comment was never fulfilled. I did, indeed, from time to time put down short hints of the sentiments, reasonings, etc., to be made use of in it, some of which I have still by me; but the necessary close attention to private business in the earlier part of my life, and public business since, have occasioned my postponing it; for, it being connected in my mind with a great and extensive project that required the whole man to execute, and which an unforseen succession of employs prevented my attending to, it has hitherto remained unfinished.

In this piece it was my design to explain and enforce this doctrine: that vicious actions are not hurtful because they are forbidden, but forbidden because they are hurtful, the nature of man alone considered; that it was, therefore, everyone's interest to be virtuous who wished to be happy even in this world; and I should, from this circumstance (there being always in the world a number of rich merchants, nobility, states, and princes, who have need of honest instruments for the management of their affairs, and such being so rare), have endeavored to convince young persons that no qualities were so likely to make a poor man's fortune as those of probity and integrity.

My list of virtues contained at first but

twelve; but a Quaker friend having kindly informed me that I was generally thought proud; that my pride showed itself frequently in conversation; that I was not content with being in the right when discussing any point, but was overbearing and rather insolent, of which he convinced me by mentioning several instances; I determined endeavoring to cure myself, if I could, of this vice or folly among the rest, and I added Humility to my list.

I cannot boast of much success in acquiring the *reality* of this virtue, but I had a good deal with regard to the *appearance* of it. I made it a rule to forbear all direct contradiction to the sentiments of others, and all positive assertion of my own. I even forbade myself, agreeably to the old law of our Junto,[1] the use of every word or expression in the language that imported a fixed opinion, such as *certainly, undoubtedly,* etc., and I adopted, instead of them, *I conceive, I apprehend,* or *I imagine* a thing to be so or so; or *it so appears to me at present.* When another asserted something that I thought an error, I denied myself the pleasure of contradicting him abruptly and of showing immediately some absurdity in his proposition; and in answering I began by observing that in certain cases or circumstances his opinion would be right, but in the present case there *appeared* or *seemed* to me some differences, etc. I soon found the advantage of this change in my manner; the conversations I engaged in went on more pleasantly. The modest way in which I proposed my opinions procured them a readier reception and less contradiction; I had less mortification when I was found to be in the wrong, and I more easily prevailed with others to give up their mistakes and join with me when I happened to be in the right.

And this mode, which I at first put on with some violence to natural inclination, became at length so easy and so habitual

---

[1] **Junto:** the debating society organized by Franklin.

to me that perhaps for these fifty years past no one has ever heard a dogmatical expression escape me. And to this habit (after my character of integrity) I think it principally owing that I had early so much weight with my fellow citizens ˉwhen I proposed new institutions, or alterations in the old, and so much influence in public councils when I became a member; for I was but a bad speaker, never eloquent, subject to much hesitation in my choice of words, hardly correct in language, and yet I generally carried my points.

In reality, there is, perhaps, no one of our natural passions so hard to subdue as *pride*. Disguise it, struggle with it, beat it down, stifle it, mortify it as much as one pleases, it is still alive, and will every now and then peep out and show itself; you will see it, perhaps, often in this history; for, even if I could conceive that I had completely overcome it, I should probably be proud of my humility.

FOR STUDY AND DISCUSSION

1. What reasons does Franklin give for writing his *Autobiography?* Have you read any other autobiographies that you think were written largely for the same reasons? What other reasons might there be for writing an autobiography?

2. Franklin's differences with his brother eventually led Franklin to leave Boston. What arguments could you use to defend Franklin's side of the quarrel? What arguments could you use to defend his brother's side?

3. Why do you think Franklin tells of his journey to Philadelphia in such detail?

4. How may Franklin's project to achieve moral perfection have given him training as a writer and adapter of proverbs? In what ways do you think that Franklin's attempt to achieve humility contributed to his career as a statesman?

5. Find examples of Franklin's talent for pithy phrases and for illustrating his meaning with an appropriate anecdote.

6. As you learned previously, the first part of this *Autobiography* was written in England in 1771 and addressed to Franklin's son, William. The part beginning, "It was about this time I conceived the bold and arduous project

of arriving at moral perfection" (page 36) was written thirteen years later in France. At that time, Franklin, estranged from his son, who had supported the British in the Revolutionary War, was writing for a larger audience. After having studied the *Autobiography,* do you think that Franklin wrote differently for his son than he did for the public, or is there no difference between the two parts of the selection? Support your answer with examples from the selection of differences or similarities.

7. What sort of a man does the selection reveal Franklin to be? Give specific details to support your answer.

8. What can you learn about colonial life from the selection? How did the circumstances of Franklin's life differ from those of the life of Jonathan Edwards and of William Byrd?

LANGUAGE AND VOCABULARY

1. In Franklin's account of his project to achieve moral perfection, he states that he found a number of definitions for *temperance.* Why did he decide to use only one meaning of the word? What other definitions for the word does he give? Look up *temperance* in an unabridged dictionary and find definitions that Franklin does not include. Write a rule of conduct in Franklin's style, using one of the meanings of this word that you found in the dictionary.

2. Look up in the dictionary the following virtues in Franklin's catalogue: *order, resolution, industry, justice, moderation.* On the basis of the definitions you find for these words, be prepared to discuss the various ideas which a word can express and how these ideas may be related to each other. (For example, how is *moderation,* as Franklin uses the word, related to the duties of the moderator of a debate?)

3. Look up the following words and be prepared to give definitions and explanations that show their relation to *temperance: temperament, intemperate, temperature, tempera, distemper.*

FOR COMPOSITION

Compare Benjamin Franklin and Jonathan Edwards as these two men are revealed in their own writings. Consider especially the personalities and the outlooks of the two men.

Rules by Which a Great Empire May Be Reduced to a Small One

This satire first appeared in the *Public Advertiser,* a London newspaper, in 1773.

AN ANCIENT SAGE boasted that, though he could not fiddle, he knew how to make a great city of a little one. The science that I, a modern simpleton, am about to communicate, is the very reverse.

I address myself to all ministers who have the management of extensive dominions, which from their very greatness are become troublesome to govern, because the multiplicity of their affairs leaves no time for fiddling.

I. In the first place, gentlemen, you are to consider that a great empire, like a great cake, is most easily diminished at the edges. Turn your attention, therefore, first to your remotest provinces; that, as you get rid of them, the next may follow in order.

II. That the possibility of this separation may always exist, take special care the provinces are never incorporated with the mother country; that they do not enjoy the same common rights, the same privileges in commerce; and that they are governed by severer laws, all of your enacting, without allowing them any share in the choice of the legislators. By carefully making and preserving such distinctions, you will (to keep to my simile of the cake) act like a wise gingerbread-baker, who, to facilitate a division, cuts his dough half through in those places where, when baked, he would have it broken to pieces.

III. Those remote provinces have perhaps been acquired, purchased, or conquered at the sole expense of the settlers, or their ancestors, without the aid of the mother country. If this should happen to increase her strength, by their growing numbers ready to join in her wars, her commerce, by their growing demand for her manufactures, or her naval power, by greater employment for her ships and seamen, they may probably suppose some merit in this, and that it entitles them to some favor; you are therefore to forget it all or resent it, as if they had done you injury. If they happen to be zealous Whigs, friends of liberty nurtured in revolution principles,[1] remember all that to their prejudice and resolve to punish it; for such principles, after a revolution is thoroughly established, are of no more use; they are even odious and abominable.

IV. However peaceably your colonies have submitted to your government, shown their affection to your interests, and patiently borne their grievances, you are to suppose them always inclined to revolt and treat them accordingly. Quarter troops [2] among them, who by their insolence may provoke the rising of mobs and by their bullets and bayonets suppress them. By this means, like the husband who uses his wife ill from suspicion, you may in time convert your suspicions into realities.

V. Remote provinces must have governors and judges to represent the Royal Person and execute everywhere the delegated parts of his office and authority. You ministers know that much of the strength of government depends on the opinion of the people; and much of that opinion on the choice of rulers placed immediately over them. If you send them wise and good men for governors who study the interest of the colonists and advance their prosperity, they will think their king wise and good, and that he

This watercolor, made by an American artist in 1768, shows British troops drilling on the Boston Common.

wishes the welfare of his subjects. If you send them learned and upright men for judges, they will think him a lover of justice. This may attach your provinces more to his government. You are therefore to be careful whom you recommend for those offices. If you can find prodigals who have ruined their fortunes, broken gamesters, or stockjobbers,[3] these may do well as governors; for they will probably be rapacious and provoke the people by their extortions. Wrangling proctors [4] and pettifogging [5] lawyers, too, are not amiss; for they will be forever disputing and quarreling with their little parliaments. If withal they should be ignorant, wrong-headed, and insolent, so much the better. Attorneys' clerks and Newgate [6]

---

[1] **revolution principles:** a reference to the principles that led the Whigs to depose James II from the throne of England during the "Glorious Revolution" of 1688.

[2] **Quarter troops:** The quartering of troops in Boston led to the Boston Massacre.

[3] **stockjobbers:** speculators in stocks.

[4] **proctors** (prŏk'tərz): court officers.

[5] **pettifogging:** petty or trivial.

[6] **Newgate:** a famous old prison in London.

This engraving, a well-known piece of Revolutionary propaganda, was made by Paul Revere, printer, engraver, inventor, and one of Boston's most famous Sons of Liberty.

solicitors will do for chief justices, especially if they hold their places during your pleasure; and all will contribute to impress those ideas of your government that are proper for a people you would wish to renounce it.

VI. To confirm these impressions and strike them deeper, whenever the injured come to the capital with complaints of maladministration, oppression, or injustice, punish such suitors with long delay, enormous expense, and a final judgment in favor of the oppressor. This will have an admirable effect every way. The trouble of future complaints will be prevented, and governors and judges will be encouraged to further acts of oppression

and injustice; and thence the people may become more disaffected, and at length desperate.

VII. When such governors have crammed their coffers and made themselves so odious to the people that they can no longer remain among them with safety to their person, recall and reward them with pensions. You may make them baronets[1] too, if that respectable order should not think fit to resent it. All will contribute to encourage new governors in the same practice and make the supreme government detestable.

[1] **baronets:** Francis Bernard was made a baronet after having served as royal governor of Massachusetts.

VIII. If, when you are engaged in war, your colonies should vie in liberal aids of men and money against the common enemy upon your simple requisition, and give far beyond their abilities, reflect that a penny taken from them by your power is more honorable to you than a pound presented by their benevolence; despise therefore their voluntary grants and resolve to harass them with novel taxes. They will probably complain to your parliaments that they are taxed by a body in which they have no representative, and that this is contrary to common right. They will petition for redress. Let the parliaments flout their claims, reject their petitions, refuse even to suffer the reading of them, and treat the petitioners with the utmost contempt. Nothing can have a better effect in producing the alienation proposed; for though many can forgive injuries, none ever forgave contempt.

IX. In laying these taxes, never regard the heavy burdens those remote people already undergo in defending their own frontiers, supporting their own provincial governments, making new roads, building bridges, churches, and other public edifices, which in old countries have been done to your hands by your ancestors, but which occasion constant calls and demands on the purses of a new people. Forget the restraints you lay on their trade for your own benefit and the advantage a monopoly of this trade gives your exacting merchants. Think nothing of the wealth those merchants and your manufacturers acquire by the colony commerce; their increased ability thereby to pay taxes at home; their accumulating, in the price of their commodities, most of those taxes and so levying them from their consuming customers; all this and the employment and support of thousands of your poor by the colonists, you are entirely to forget. But remember to make your arbitrary tax more grievous to your provinces by public declarations importing that your power of taxing them has no limits; so that when you take from them without their consent one shilling in the pound, you have a clear

right to the other nineteen. This will probably weaken every idea of security in their property and convince them that under such a government they have nothing they can call their own; which can scarce fail of producing the happiest consequences!

X. Possibly, indeed, some of them might still comfort themselves and say, "Though we have no property, we have yet something left that is valuable; we have constitutional liberty, both of person and of conscience. This king, these lords, and these commons, who it seems are too remote from us to know us and feel for us, cannot take from us our habeas corpus right or our right of trial by a jury of our neighbors; they cannot deprive us of the exercise of our religion." To annihilate this comfort, begin by laws to perplex their commerce with infinite regulations, impossible to be remembered and observed; ordain seizures of their property for every failure; take away the trial of such property by jury and give it to ar-

WILLIAM JACKSON, an *IMPORTER*; at the *BRAZEN HEAD,* North Side of the TOWN-HOUSE, and *Opposite the Town-Pump, in Corn-hill,* BOSTON.

It is desired that the SONS and DAUGHTERS of *LIBERTY,* would not buy any one thing of him, for in so doing they will bring Disgrace upon *themselves,* and their *Posterity,* for *ever* and *ever,* AMEN.

A handbill urging citizens not to buy from a local importer of British goods.

The British tax stamp required on newspapers, advertisements, diplomas, licenses, and many other legal documents.

bitrary judges of your own appointing, and of the lowest characters in the country, whose salaries and emoluments [1] are to arise out of the duties or condemnations, and whose appointments are during pleasure. Then let there be a formal declaration of both houses that opposition to your edicts is treason, and that any person suspected of treason in the provinces may, according to some obsolete law, be seized and sent to the metropolis of the empire for trial; and pass an act that those there charged with certain other offenses shall be sent away in chains from their friends and country to be tried in the same manner for felony. Then erect a new Court of Inquisition among them, accompanied by an armed force with instructions to transport all such suspected persons, to be ruined by the expense if they bring over evidences to prove their innocence or be found guilty and hanged if they cannot afford it. And, lest the people should think you cannot possibly go any farther, pass another solemn declaratory act [2] "that king, lords, commons had, hath, and of right ought to have, full power and authority to make statutes of sufficient force and validity to bind the unrepresented provinces in *all cases whatsoever.*" This will include spiritual with temporal

[1] **emoluments** (i·mol′yə·mənts): fees or profits from office.
[2] **declaratory act:** The Declaratory Act was passed by Parliament in 1766.

and, taken together, must operate wonderfully to your purpose by convincing them that they are at present under a power something like that spoken of in the scriptures, which cannot only kill their bodies, but damn their souls to all eternity by compelling them, if it pleases, to worship the Devil.

XI. To make your taxes more odious and more likely to procure resistance, send from the capital a board of officers to superintend the collection, composed of the most indiscreet, ill-bred, and insolent you can find. Let these have large salaries out of the extorted revenue and live in open, grating luxury upon the sweat and blood of the industrious, whom they are to worry continually with groundless and expensive prosecutions before the above-mentioned arbitrary revenue judges, all at the cost of the party prosecuted, though acquitted, because the king is to pay no costs. Let these men, by your order, be exempted from all the common taxes and burdens of the province, though they and their property are protected by its laws. If any revenue officers are suspected of the least tenderness for the people, discard them. If others are justly complained of, protect and reward them. If any of the under officers behave so as to provoke the people to drub them, promote those to better offices: this will encourage others to procure for themselves such profitable drubbings by multiplying and enlarging such provocations, and all will work toward the end you aim at.

XII. Another way to make your tax odious is to misapply the produce of it. If it was originally appropriated for the defense of the provinces, the better support of government, and the administration of justice, where it may be necessary, then apply none of it to that defense, but bestow it where it is not necessary, in augmented salaries or pensions to every governor who had distinguished himself by his enmity to the people and by calumniating them to their sovereign. This will make them pay it more unwillingly and be more apt to quarrel with those that

The·TIMES are
Dreadful,
Difmal,
Doleful
Dolorous, and
DOLLAR-LESS.

An Emblem of the Effects of the STAMP

Of the fatal Stamp

Thurfday, *October* 31, 1765.

THE

NUMB. 1195.

PENNSYLVANIA JOURNAL;
AND
WEEKLY ADVERTISER.

The Pennsylvania Journal goes out of business because of taxes levied by the Stamp Act.

collect it and those that imposed it, who will quarrel again with them, and all shall contribute to your main purpose of making them weary of your government.

XIII. If the people of any province have been accustomed to support their own governors and judges to satisfaction, you are to apprehend that such governors and judges may be thereby influenced to treat the people kindly and to do them justice. This is another reason for applying part of that revenue in larger salaries to such governors and judges, given, as their commissions are, during your pleasure only; forbidding them to take any salaries from their provinces; that thus the people may no longer hope any kindness from their governors, or (in Crown cases) any justice from their judges. And, as the money thus misapplied in one province is extorted from all, probably all will resent the misapplication.

XIV. If the parliaments of your provinces should dare to claim rights, or complain of your administration, order them to be harassed with repeated dissolutions.[1] If the same men are continually returned by new elections, adjourn their meetings to some country village where they cannot be accommodated, and there keep them during pleasure; for this, you know, is your *prerogative;* and an excellent one it is, as you may manage to promote discontents among the people, diminish their respect, and increase their disaffection.

XV. Convert the brave, honest officers of your navy into tidewaiters [2] and colony officers of the customs. Let those who in time of war fought gallantly in defense of the commerce of their countrymen, in peace be taught to prey upon it. Let them learn to be corrupted by great and real smugglers; but (to show their diligence) scour with armed boats every bay, harbor, river, creek, cove, or nook throughout the coast of your colonies; stop and detain every coaster, every wood-boat, every fisherman; tumble their cargoes and even their ballast inside out and upside down; and, if a penn'orth of pins is found unentered,[3] let the whole be seized and confiscated. Thus shall the trade of your colonists suffer more from their friends in time of peace than it did from their enemies in war. Then let these boats' crews land upon every farm in their way, rob the orchards, steal the pigs and poultry, and

---

[1] **dissolutions:** In 1768, the royal governor threatened to dissolve the Massachusetts House of Representatives.

[2] **tidewaiters:** customs officers who board ships entering port.

[3] **if ... unentered:** if a penny's worth of pins has not been listed in the customs declaration.

insult the inhabitants. If the injured and exasperated farmers, unable to procure other justice, should attack the aggressors, drub them and burn their boats—you are to call this high treason and rebellion; order fleets and armies into their country; and threaten to carry all the offenders three thousand miles to be hanged, drawn, and quartered.[1] O! this will work admirably!

XVI. If you are told of discontents in your colonies, never believe that they are general or that you have given occasion for them; therefore do not think of applying any remedy or of changing any offensive measure. Redress no grievance, lest they should be encouraged to demand the redress of some other grievance. Grant no request that is just and reasonable, lest they should make another that is unreasonable. Take all your informations of the state of the colonies from your governors and officers in enmity with them. Encourage and reward these leasing-makers; [2] secrete their lying accusations, lest they should be confuted, but act upon them as the clearest evidence; and believe nothing you hear from the friends of the people: suppose all their complaints to be invented and promoted by a few factious demagogues,[3] whom if you could catch and hang, all would be quiet. Catch and hang a few of them accordingly, and the blood of the martyrs shall work miracles in favor of your purpose.

XVII. If you see rival nations rejoicing at the prospect of your disunion with your provinces and endeavoring to promote it; if they translate, publish, and applaud all the complaints of your discontented colonists, at the same time privately stimulating you to severer measures, let not that alarm or offend you. Why should it, since you all mean the same thing?

XVIII. If any colony should at their own charge erect a fortress to secure their port against the fleets of a foreign enemy, get your governor to betray that fortress into your hands.[4] Never think of paying what it cost the country, for that would look, at least, like some regard for justice; but turn it into a citadel to awe the inhabitants and curb their commerce. If they should have lodged in such fortress the very arms they bought and used to aid you in your conquests, seize them all; it will provoke like ingratitude added to robbery. One admirable effect of these operations will be to discourage every other colony from erecting such defences, and so your enemies may more easily invade them; to the great disgrace of your government and, of course, the furtherance of your project.

XIX. Send armies into their country under pretense of protecting the inhabitants; but, instead of garrisoning the forts on their frontiers with those troops to prevent incursions, demolish those forts and order the troops into the heart of the country, that the savages may be encouraged to attack the frontiers and that the troops may be protected by the inhabitants. This will seem to proceed from your ill will or your ignorance, and contribute further to produce and strengthen an opinion among them, that you are no longer fit to govern them.

XX. Lastly, invest the general of your army in the provinces with great and unconstitutional powers and free him from the control of even your own civil governors. Let him have troops enow [5] under his command with all the fortresses in his possession; and who knows but (like some provincial generals in the Roman Empire, and encouraged by the universal discontent you have produced) he may take it into his head to set up for himself? If he should, and you have carefully practiced

[1] **If . . . quartered:** The farmers who burned the schooner *Gaspée* on June 10, 1772, were so threatened.

[2] **leasing-makers:** inventors of lies.

[3] **factious demagogues** (fak'shəs dem'ə·gôgz): popular leaders who seek to gain political influence from social unrest and dissention.

[4] **If . . . hands:** In September, 1770, Castle William, built by the colonists in Boston Harbor, was given by Governor Thomas Hutchinson to the British.

[5] **enow:** enough.

these few excellent rules of mine, take my word for it, all the provinces will immediately join him; and you will that day (if you have not done it sooner) get rid of the trouble of governing them, and all the plagues attending their commerce and connection from henceforth and forever.

FOR STUDY AND DISCUSSION

1. Franklin declares, "I address myself to all ministers who have the management of extensive dominions, which from their very greatness are become troublesome to govern, because the multiplicity of their affairs leaves no time for fiddling." Does Franklin really intend to advise ministers how they can have more time for "fiddling"? Explain. Why did Franklin have this selection published in a London rather than in a colonial newspaper?

2. Describe the situation in the colonies that this selection reveals. Cite at least five details in the selection to support your description.

3. In your opinion, does the intensity of Franklin's indignation decrease or increase as the selection proceeds? Do the examples of poor administration grow more serious or less serious? Support your answers by comparing passages from the selection.

4. From studying this essay, what can you conclude about Franklin's real views of the proper management of the colonies?

SATIRE AND IRONY

A writer who attacks an action, a point of view, or a character trait may do so directly by calling it stupid, vicious, or evil. Or he may attack it indirectly by making it seem ridiculous and letting the reader conclude that it is also stupid. A persuasive work that relies on ridicule as its chief weapon and persuades while it amuses is called *satire*. When a satire, such as this selection by Franklin, pretends to advise when it is really issuing a warning, it is using *irony*.

There are several kinds of irony, but all involve a discrepancy between the apparent and the real. A speaker or writer using *verbal irony* will say one thing when he actually means another, as when Mark Antony refers to the conspirators who slew Caesar as "honorable men." *Dramatic irony* depends on a discrepancy between what a character in a literary work says or thinks and the reader's understanding of the situation as it really is. For

example, a character who claims "I'm the smartest person in the whole world!" may reveal himself to be a fool. A third, more complex kind of irony is *irony of situation,* which depends on a discrepancy between purpose and results. A character in Anton Chekhov's story, "A Slander," for example, sets out to stop a rumor about himself but, by telling everyone that the rumor is false, actually spreads it. Underlying all types of irony is a certain kind of attitude toward life. A writer using irony pays his compliments to the subtlety and complexity of all things. Just as a poem may examine a flower, rock, or fence more closely than a reader has ever thought of looking at it, so irony calls for a recognition that nothing may be as simple as it seems. A satire that seems to praise may really be an attack. A character's remark may show how far he is from understanding the truth. An action may have a result quite different from the one intended. To properly appreciate irony, a reader should be aware of the subtle details that establish a writer's attitude toward his subject.

1. Why do you think Franklin chose to write a satire rather than a direct attack on the persons directing England's colonial affairs? In your opinion, would a direct attack have been more or less effective? Why?

2. On which kind of irony—verbal irony, dramatic irony, or irony of situation—does "Rules by Which a Great Empire May Be Reduced to a Small One" depend? Find examples of this kind of irony. Explain how they are ironic.

3. A writer of ironic satire must be sure that his purpose will not be misunderstood. How is Franklin's purpose established by the title and first two paragraphs of the selection?

4. An ironic satire may be more than merely amusing or persuasive. The author may be so fiercely indignant at the injustice he protests that the reader is deeply moved by this indirect form of expression. In your opinion, does Franklin's selection ever rise to this level? If so, where?

FOR COMPOSITION

Write a brief satire attacking a rule or action that you consider unjust. Remember that satire is most effective when it amuses while it persuades. Avoid obvious sarcasm such as "The most brilliant thinker the world has ever known" or "The justice of this move no one would ever question."

PATRICK HENRY
(1736–1799)

Patrick Henry, a backwoods Virginia lawyer, was a tall, awkward-looking man, but listeners soon forgot about his appearance when they heard his words. In 1765, in a speech to the Virginia legislature opposing the Stamp Act, he first demonstrated his gift for memorable phrases: "Caesar had his Brutus; Charles the First had his Cromwell; and George the Third——" Here cries of "Treason! Treason!" interrupted him. He continued, "——and George the Third may profit by their example."

In his youth, Henry showed few of the qualities that were to make him a colonial leader. As a boy, he preferred hunting and fishing to pursuing an education. When he married at the age of eighteen, his parents bought the young couple a farm, but within two years Henry had sold the farm and bought a store with the money. He proved a poor businessman. When, three years later, the store failed, he began to study law and in 1760 passed the bar examination. Henry turned out to be a surprisingly good lawyer and an eloquent pleader, and many clients began to seek his services. In 1763, Patrick Henry became famous as an advocate of colonial rights in the Parson's Cause, a case involving the King of England and the colony of Virginia. Soon after this legal victory Henry was elected to the Virginia legislature.

As a member of the House of Burgesses, he continued to urge the defense of colonial liberty, and in time he came to realize that only by armed resistance could the colonies withstand English oppression. In 1775, the House of Burgesses held a revolutionary convention at which Henry introduced the resolution that "Virginia be immediately put into a posture of defense." There was strong opposition, for the rich planters feared a popular rebellion even more than they feared England. Barely a month before Massachusetts farmers fired on British troops at Lexington and Concord, Henry rose to speak in support of his resolution. The eloquence of his famous speech was overwhelming. For that moment, Henry controlled the destiny of Virginia. Later he became governor of the state and was a delegate to the Constitutional Convention in Philadelphia, where he pressed for the adoption of a Bill of Rights. But never again did the power of his words control a body of men as on March 23, 1775.

Speech in the
Virginia Convention

M R. PRESIDENT: No man thinks more highly than I do of the patriotism, as well as abilities, of the very worthy gentlemen who have just addressed the house. But different men often see the same subject in different lights; and, therefore, I hope it will not be thought disrespectful to those gentlemen, if, entertaining as I do opinions of a character very opposite to theirs, I shall speak forth my sentiments freely and without reserve. This is no time for ceremony. The question before the house is one of awful moment to this country. For my own part, I consider it as nothing less than a question of freedom or slavery. And in proportion to the magnitude of the subject ought to be the freedom of the debate. It is only in this way that we can hope to arrive at truth and fulfill the great responsibility which we hold to God and our country. Should I keep back my opinions at such a time, through fear of giving offense, I should consider myself as guilty of treason toward my country, and of an act of disloyalty toward the Majesty of Heaven, which I revere above all earthly kings.

Mr. President, it is natural to man to indulge in the illusions of hope. We are apt to shut our eyes against a painful truth and listen to the song of that siren till she transforms us into beasts. Is this the part of wise men, engaged in a great and arduous struggle for liberty? Are we disposed to be of the number of those who having eyes see not, and having ears hear not, the things which so nearly concern their temporal salvation? For my part, whatever anguish of spirit it may cost, I am willing to know the whole truth; to know the worst and to provide for it.

I have but one lamp by which my feet are guided, and that is the lamp of experience. I know of no way of judging of the future but by the past. And judging by the past, I wish to know what there has been in the conduct of the British ministry for the last ten years to justify those hopes with which gentlemen have been pleased to solace themselves and the house? Is it that insidious smile with which our petition has been lately received? Trust it not, sir; it will prove a snare to your feet. Suffer not yourselves to be betrayed with a kiss. Ask yourselves how this gracious reception of our petition comports with those warlike preparations which cover our waters and darken our land. Are fleets and armies necessary to a work of love and reconciliation? Have we shown ourselves so unwilling to be reconciled that force must be called in to win back our love? Let us not deceive ourselves, sir. These are the implements of war and subjugation—the last arguments to which kings resort.

I ask gentlemen, sir, what means this martial array, if its purpose be not to force us to submission? Can gentlemen assign any other possible motive for it? Has Great Britain any enemy in this quarter of

The Virginia House of Burgesses

Within a month after Patrick Henry's speech in the House of Burgesses, angry colonists exchanged fire with British troops at the North Bridge in Concord, Massachusetts.

the world, to call for all this accumulation of navies and armies? No, sir, she has none. They are meant for us: they can be meant for no other. They are sent over to bind and rivet upon us those chains which the British ministry have been so long forging.

And what have we to oppose to them? Shall we try argument? Sir, we have been trying that for the last ten years. Have we anything new to offer upon the subject? Nothing. We have held the subject up in every light of which it is capable; but it has been all in vain. Shall we resort to entreaty and humble supplication? What terms shall we find which have not been already exhausted? Let us not, I beseech you, sir, deceive ourselves longer.

Sir, we have done everything that could be done to avert the storm which is now coming on. We have petitioned; we have remonstrated; we have supplicated; we have prostrated ourselves before the throne and have implored its interposition [1] to arrest the tyrannical hands of the ministry and Parliament. Our petitions have been slighted; our remonstrances have produced additional violence and insult; our supplications have been disregarded; and we have been spurned with contempt from the foot of the throne! In vain, after these things, may we indulge the fond [2] hope of peace and reconciliation. There is no longer any room for hope. If we wish to be free, if we mean to preserve inviolate those inestimable privileges for which we have been so long contending, if we mean not basely to abandon the noble struggle in which we have been so long engaged, and which we have pledged ourselves never to abandon until the glorious object of our contest shall be obtained—we must fight! I repeat it, sir, we must fight! An appeal to arms and to the God of Hosts is all that is left us!

They tell us, sir, that we are weak— unable to cope with so formidable an adversary. But when shall we be stronger? Will it be the next week, or the next year? Will it be when we are totally disarmed, and when a British guard shall be stationed in every house? Shall we gather strength by irresolution and inaction? Shall we acquire the means of effectual resistance by lying supinely on our backs and hugging the delusive phantom of hope until our enemies shall have bound us hand and foot? Sir, we are not weak, if we make a proper use of those means which

[1] **interposition:** intervention; entrance into the problem.

[2] **fond:** foolish.

the God of nature hath placed in our power. Three millions of people, armed in the holy cause of liberty, and in such a country as that which we possess, are invincible by any force which our enemy can send against us. Besides, sir, we shall not fight our battles alone. There is a just God who presides over the destinies of nations and who will raise up friends to fight our battles for us. The battle, sir, is not to the strong alone; it is to the vigilant, the active, the brave. Besides, sir, we have no election.[1] If we were base enough to desire it, it is now too late to retire from the contest. There is no retreat but in submission and slavery! Our chains are forged! Their clanging may be heard on the plains of Boston! The war is inevitable—and let it come! I repeat it, sir, let it come!

It is in vain, sir, to extenuate the matter. Gentlemen may cry, Peace, Peace—but there is no peace. The war is actually begun! The next gale that sweeps from the north will bring to our ears the clash of resounding arms! Our brethren are already in the field! Why stand we here idle? What is it that gentlemen wish? What would they have? Is life so dear, or peace so sweet, as to be purchased at the price of chains and slavery? Forbid it, Almighty God! I know not what course others may take; but as for me, give me liberty or give me death!

[1] election: choice.

FOR STUDY AND DISCUSSION

1. The biographical introduction refers to Henry's gift for memorable phrases. What evidence of this gift can you find in the selection?

2. What is the difference between the tone of the first and of the final paragraphs of the speech? Is there a sudden or a gradual change in tone?

3. Henry states, "I know of no way of judging the future but by the past." Do you agree? In your opinion, how reliable is the past as a guide to the future?

THE FORMS OF DISCOURSE: PERSUASION

As we have seen earlier (see page 29), it is helpful in analyzing a persuasive work to consider four aspects: the speaker, the audience, the occasion, and the means of persuasion.

1. *The speaker:* On what basis does Patrick Henry claim the right to be heard? Find sentences in the speech to support your answer. Describe Henry's personality as it is revealed in the speech.

2. *The audience:* In what way might Henry's speech be different if it had been delivered to a mob on the steps of the legislative house or to a group of voters?

3. *The occasion:* How does Henry impress his audience with the urgency of the occasion?

4. *The means of persuasion:* Does this speech appeal more to reason or to the emotions? Or does it appeal equally to both? What specific arguments are offered? What objection to his arguments does Henry refute? Why do you think he brings up this objection instead of trying to make his audience forget it?

UNDERSTANDING ALLUSIONS

When Henry refers to "the song of that siren," he assumes that his listeners will recognize this allusion to Book XII of Homer's *Odyssey*. Such a reference to a well-known source—to the Bible, a play by Shakespeare, or some other literary classic—may often be used by a writer to deepen the meaning and significance of his work. Recognizing such allusions can increase your understanding and enjoyment of literature.

1. Why was the singing of the sirens dangerous?

2. Read Ezekiel 12:2 in the Bible and explain Patrick Henry's remark about "those who having eyes see not, and having ears hear not." How is this allusion related to the last two words of the same sentence, "temporal salvation"?

3. Look up Psalm 119:105. How is this verse related to Henry's statement, "I have but one lamp by which my feet are guided"?

4. Read Luke 22:47–48. What comparison was Henry making when he advised Virginians, "Suffer not yourselves to be betrayed with a kiss"?

5. In what way does the frequent use of Biblical allusions increase the power of Henry's speech?

THOMAS PAINE
(1737–1809)

Just as Patrick Henry's speech brought Virginia into the Revolution, so Thomas Paine's writings helped persuade Americans to become an independent nation and sustained them during the grim years of the war. Paine came late to the struggle. After an unsuccessful life in England as sailor, corset-maker, schoolteacher, and collector of excise taxes, he met Benjamin Franklin, who persuaded him to try his luck in the New World. Paine arrived in Philadelphia in 1774, ten years after James Otis had written *The Rights of the British Colonies Asserted and Proved,* nine years after the enactment of the Stamp Act, four years after the Boston Massacre. Yet almost at once, Paine felt caught up in the events that led to independence. After the Battle of Lexington in 1775, he wrote *Common Sense,* a pamphlet addressed not to the learned man but to the average American who would know in his heart which was the right course to follow. Within a few months, over a hundred thousand copies of the pamphlet were in circulation, its vigorous style and arguments winning thousands of adherents to the cause of independence. George Washington stated that it worked "a powerful change in the minds of many men." After the Continental Congress issued the Declaration of Independence, for which *Common Sense* had prepared the way, Paine joined the army as an aide to General Greene. The first of *The Crisis* papers was written while Paine was with Greene, following the early disheartening events of the war. Published just before Christmas in 1776, it was read to each regiment of the army, including the soldiers who were to cross the Delaware with Washington and attack the British at Trenton. During the next seven years, fifteen more *Crisis* papers appeared, urging Americans to take heart and keep faith with their cause. In 1783, Paine wrote that "the greatest and completest revolution the world ever knew" was "gloriously and happily accomplished."

After the Revolution, Paine became involved in the political affairs of England and France. He was forced to leave England because he defended the French Revolution, and later he was imprisoned in France for advocating that Louis XVI be imprisoned rather than executed. While in prison, Paine himself narrowly escaped execution. In 1802 he returned to America and spent the last years of his stormy life on a farm in New Rochelle, New York.

FROM *The Crisis, Number 1*

THESE ARE the times that try men's souls. The summer soldier and the sunshine patriot will, in this crisis, shrink from the service of their country; but he that stands it *now* deserves the love and thanks of man and woman. Tyranny, like hell, is not easily conquered; yet we have this consolation with us, that the harder the conflict, the more glorious the triumph. What we obtain too cheap, we esteem too lightly: it is dearness only that gives everything its value. Heaven knows how to put a proper price upon its goods, and it would be strange indeed if so celestial an article as *freedom* should not be highly rated. Britain, with an army to enforce her tyranny, had declared that she has a right, not only to *tax,* but "to *bind* us in *all cases whatsoever"*; and if being bound in that manner is not slavery, then there is not such a thing as slavery upon earth. Even the expression is impious, for so unlimited a power can belong only to God.

I have as little superstition in me as any man living, but my secret opinion has ever been, and still is, that God Almighty will not give up a people to military destruction or leave them unsupportedly to perish, who have so earnestly and so repeatedly sought to avoid the calamities of war by every decent method which wisdom could invent. Neither have I so much of the infidel in me as to suppose that He has relinquished the government of the world and given us up to the care of devils; and, as I do not, I cannot see on what grounds the king of Britain can look up to heaven for help against us.

I once felt all that kind of anger which a man ought to feel against the mean principles that are held by the Tories. A noted one, who kept a tavern at Amboy, was standing at his door, with as pretty a child in his hand, about eight or nine years old, as ever I saw, and after speaking his mind as freely as he thought was prudent, finished with this unfatherly expression, "Well! give me peace in my day." Not a man lives on the continent [1] but fully believes that a separation must some time or other finally take place, and a generous parent should have said, "If there must be trouble, let it be in my day, that my child may have peace"; and this single reflection, well applied, is sufficient to awaken every man to duty. Not a place upon earth might be so happy as America. Her situation is remote from all the wrangling world, and she has nothing to do but to trade with them. A man can distinguish himself between temper and principle, and I am as confident as I am that God governs the world, that America will never be happy till she gets clear of foreign dominion. Wars, without ceasing, will break out till that period arrives, and the continent must in the end be conqueror; for though the flame of liberty may sometimes cease to shine, the coal can never expire.

The heart that feels not now, is dead; the blood of his children will curse his cowardice who shrinks back at a time when a little might have saved the whole and made them happy. I love the man that can smile in trouble, that can gather strength from distress and grow brave by reflection. 'Tis the business of little minds to shrink; but he whose heart is firm, and whose conscience approves his conduct, will pursue his principles unto death. My own line of reasoning is to myself as straight and clear as a ray of light. Not all the treasures of the world, so far as I believe, could have induced me to support an offensive war, for I think it murder; but if a thief breaks into my house, burns and destroys my property, and kills or threatens to kill me or those that are in it and to

---

[1] **the continent:** Paine refers here to the North American continent.

Pamphleteers of the American Revolution

Eleven years before the first shots of the Revolutionary War were fired, a preliminary war was being fought by writers. One scholar of the period has written, "The literary controversies of the American Revolution were conducted in little books— books inexpensive to print . . . cheap to buy, easy to read, and, more significant, easy to write . . . intended for instant circulation, designed to change men's minds, addressed to urgent problems, sometimes touching the universal issues that confront men anywhere, any time, in civil society." Of these pamphleteers, Thomas Paine was the most effective, but not the first.

In 1764 a tract by James Otis, a Boston lawyer, appeared. Two years earlier Otis had published a pamphlet on purely local issues. Now, in *The Rights of the British Colonies Asserted and Proved,* Otis discussed an issue of national importance: By what right does a government hold power? Power, Otis held, was "originally and ultimately in the people." Governments existed only to serve the people. "The end of government . . . is above all things to provide for the security, the quiet, and the happy enjoyment of life, liberty, and property." Although in *Rights of the British Colonies* Otis advised the colonists to "use the proper legal measure to obtain redress" for England's injustices, in later pamphlets his tone became more violent, and he warned England, "Revolutions have been. They may be again." It is *The Rights of the British Colonies* which insures Otis's fame as the first American enunciator

of those principles which led to the framing of the Declaration of Independence and the United States Constitution.

In 1767, the English Parliament under the leadership of Charles Townshend passed a series of acts levying import duties on tea, lead, glass, and other articles in common use. To enforce these acts, British officers of law were empowered to enter citizen's houses without search warrants. Such a denial of rights led John Dickinson, a Philadelphia lawyer and legislator, to write *Letters from a Pennsylvania Farmer,* which were published in twenty-one American newspapers and later appeared in book form. Ever afterwards, Dickinson was known as the "Pennsylvania Farmer" for his stirring defense of the rights of Americans and for his searching examination of the principles of political freedom. A free people, he maintained, were not "those over whom government is reasonably and equitably [maintained], but those who live under a government so constitutionally checked and controlled that proper provision is made against its being otherwise exercised."

Other pamphleteers—writers such as Jonathan Mayhew, John Adams, Daniel Dulany—continued to arouse the colonists. Tory writers, including Jonathan Boucher and Joseph Galloway, argued forcefully for conciliation with England. Then, in 1774, a thirty-seven-year-old ex-schoolteacher arrived in Philadelphia. A year later, Thomas Paine's *Common Sense* swept through the colonies and helped found a new nation.

Paine's first *Crisis* paper was read to Washington's troops shortly before their attack on Trenton and Princeton. This contemporary engraving depicts the Battle of Princeton.

"bind me in all cases whatsoever" to his absolute will, am I to suffer it? What signifies it to me whether he who does it is a king or a common man, my countryman or not my countryman; whether it be done by an individual villain or an army of them? If we reason to the root of things, we shall find no difference; neither can any just cause be assigned why we should punish in the one case and pardon in the other.

FOR STUDY AND DISCUSSION

1. What does Paine mean by the "summer soldier and the sunshine patriot"?

2. What answer does Paine have for the timid person who is afraid of England's might? for the one who believes all war is wrong?

3. Give examples of Paine's farsightedness. What did he think of people who ask for "peace in my day"? What evidence is there that he foresees America's future greatness?

4. If you had been an undecided citizen of their day, who would have moved you more strongly to action, Patrick Henry or Thomas Paine? Why?

5. Is Paine's article written primarily in a plain or an ornate style? Find examples of both kinds of styles in this selection.

LANGUAGE AND VOCABULARY

Rewrite the following passage by Paine in what you feel is a good modern style. On the basis of what you have written, be prepared to discuss the changes in expression that have taken place since 1776. Give special consideration to the italicized words and phrases.

"I have as little superstition in me as any man *living,* but my *secret* opinion has ever been, and still is, that God Almighty *will not give up a people to military destruction* or leave them *unsupportedly* to perish, who have so earnestly and so repeatedly sought to avoid the calamities of war by every decent method which *wisdom could invent.* Neither *have I so much of the infidel in* me as to suppose that He has relinquished the government of the world and *given us up to the care* of devils . . ."

FOR COMPOSITION

Write a composition in which you compare Paine's article with Henry's speech as persuasive works. In your composition, consider the following questions: What differences between the two works stem from the fact that one was intended to be heard and the other to be read, as well as heard? Although Paine was not addressing a group of listeners, what evidence is there that, like Henry, he had a specific audience in mind? Which author makes greater use of comparisons? Why? Is Paine's purpose, like Henry's, to persuade his audience to take specific action or to maintain a particular opinion? How does Paine's purpose influence the arguments he uses? Which author, in your opinion, presents a more logical case? Why?

GEORGE
WASHINGTON
(1732–1799)

George Washington was in his own day almost as famous and admired in Europe as in the United States. The English poet Lord Byron called him "the first—the last —the best/ The Cincinnatus of the West," referring to the patriot who led Rome in a time of emergency and then retired to his farm. Throughout Europe, Washington was contrasted with Napoleon, the dictator who had forsaken his republican ideals. Unlike Napoleon, Washington displayed a selfless devotion to ideals. When he gave up the life of a Virginia planter that he preferred, it was not to seek power and glory but to serve the nation which he, more than any other, had helped establish. Years before his election to the Presidency, Americans were calling him the father of his country. After his death, the House of Representatives officially endorsed the sentiment that Washington was "first in war, first in peace, and first in the hearts of his countrymen."

Washington's youth and early manhood were spent as a surveyor, woodsman, and farmer. He gained extensive military experience and a reputation for bravery during the French and Indian War, during which he rose to the rank of colonel. After the War, he devoted most of his time to managing his considerable property, but he also served in Virginia's House of Burgesses, where he opposed British restrictions on colonial liberty. He spent the early months of 1775 organizing military companies in Virginia to fight the British in case armed resistance proved necessary. On June 15, 1775, the Continental Congress appointed him commander-in-chief of the Continental Army. His eventual victory over the British is a remarkable achievement, for he was forced to pit poorly trained and equipped volunteers against an army of professional soldiers. His bravery, his sense of honor, and his willingness to share hardships won the respect and devotion of his men.

In 1789, Washington was inaugurated as the first President of the United States under the new Constitution. As President, he sought to strengthen the federal government and reconcile the opposing parties led by Jefferson and Hamilton. His "Farewell Address," published on September 19, 1796, in *Claypoole's American Daily Advertiser,* a Philadelphia newspaper, conveyed his decision not to seek a third term in office. In the "Address," Washington drew on his wisdom and experience to offer, for the "solemn contemplation" of his fellow citizens, advice to preserve and strengthen the young nation.

FROM *The Farewell Address*

FRIENDS AND FELLOW CITIZENS: The period for a new election of a citizen to administer the executive government of the United States being not far distant, and the time actually arrived when your thoughts must be employed in designating the person who is to be clothed with that important trust, it appears to me proper, especially as it may conduce to a more distinct expression of the public voice, that I should now apprise you of the resolution I have formed to decline being considered among the number of those out of whom a choice is to be made.

I beg you, at the same time, to do me the justice to be assured that this resolution has not been taken without a strict regard to all the considerations appertaining to the relation which binds a dutiful citizen to his country; and that, in withdrawing the tender of service, which silence in my situation might imply, I am influenced by no diminution of zeal for your future interest, no deficiency of grateful respect for your past kindness, but am supported by a full conviction that the step is compatible with both.

The acceptance of, and continuance hitherto in, the office to which your suffrages have twice called me have been a uniform sacrifice of inclination to the opinion of duty and to a deference for what appeared to be your desire. I constantly hoped that it would have been much earlier in my power, consistently with motives which I was not at liberty to disregard, to return to that retirement from which I had been reluctantly drawn. The strength of my inclination to do this, previous to the last election, had even led to the preparation of an address to declare it to you; but mature reflection on the then perplexed and critical posture of our affairs with foreign nations, and the unanimous advice of persons entitled to my confidence, impelled me to abandon the idea.

I rejoice that the state of your concerns, external as well as internal, no longer renders the pursuit of inclination incompatible with the sentiment of duty or propriety, and am persuaded, whatever partiality may be retained for my services, that in the present circumstances of our country you will not disapprove my determination to retire. . . .

In looking forward to the moment which is intended to terminate the career of my public life, my feelings do not permit me to suspend the deep acknowledgment of that debt of gratitude which I owe to my beloved country for the many honors it has conferred upon me; still more for the steadfast confidence with which it has supported me; and for the opportunities I have thence enjoyed of manifesting my inviolable attachment by services faithful and persevering, though in usefulness unequal to my zeal. If benefits have resulted to our country from these services, let it always be remembered to your praise and as an instructive example in our annals that—under circumstances in which the passions, agitated in every direction, were liable to mislead, amidst appearances sometimes dubious, vicissitudes of fortune often discouraging, in situations in which not unfrequently want of success has countenanced the spirit of criticism—the constancy of your support was the essential prop of the efforts and a guaranty of the plans by which they were effected. Profoundly penetrated with this idea, I shall carry it with me to the grave as a strong incitement to unceasing vows that Heaven may continue to you the choicest tokens of its beneficence; that your union and brotherly affection may be perpetual; that the free constitution, which is the work of your hands, may be sacredly maintained; that its administration in every department may be stamped with wisdom and virtue; that, in fine, the happiness of the people of these States under the auspices of liberty may be made complete, by so careful a preservation and so prudent a use of this blessing as will acquire to them the glory of recommending it to the applause, the affection, and adoption of every nation which is yet a stranger to it.

Here, perhaps, I ought to stop. But a solicitude for your welfare, which cannot end but with my life, and the apprehension of danger, natural to that solicitude, urge me on an occasion like the present to offer to your solemn contemplation and to recommend to your frequent review some sentiments which are the result of much reflection, of no inconsiderable observation, and which appear to me all important to the permanency of your felicity as a people. . . .

Interwoven as is the love of liberty with every ligament of your hearts, no recommendation of mine is necessary to fortify or confirm the attachment.

The unity of government, which constitutes you one people, is also now dear to you. It is justly so; for it is a main pillar in the edifice of your real independence, the support of your tranquillity at home, your peace abroad; of your safety; of your prosperity in every shape; of that very liberty which you so highly prize. But as it is easy to foresee that, from different causes and from different quarters, much pains will be taken, many artifices employed, to weaken in your minds the conviction of this truth; as this is the point in your political fortress against which the batteries of internal and external enemies will be most constantly and actively (though often covertly and insidiously) directed, it is of infinite moment [1] that you should properly estimate the immense value of your national Union to your collective and individual happiness, that you should cherish a cordial, habitual, and immovable attachment to it, accustoming yourselves to think and speak of it as of the palladium [2] of your political safety and prosperity, watching for its preservation with jealous anxiety, discountenancing whatever may suggest even a suspicion that it can in any event be abandoned, and indignantly frowning upon the first dawning of every attempt to alienate any portion of our country from the rest or to enfeeble the sacred ties which now link together the various parts.

For this you have every inducement of sympathy and interest. Citizens by birth or choice of a common country, that country has a right to concentrate your affections. The name of *American*, which belongs to you in your national capacity, must always exalt the just pride of patriotism more than any appellation derived from local discriminations. With slight shades of difference, you have the same religion, manners, habits, and political principles. You have in a common cause fought and triumphed together. The independence and liberty you possess are the work of joint counsels and joint efforts, of common dangers, sufferings, and successes. . . .

In contemplating the causes which may disturb our Union, it occurs as a matter of serious concern that any ground should have been furnished for characterizing parties by geographical discriminations, Northern and Southern, Atlantic and Western; whence designing men may endeavor to excite a belief that there is a real difference of local interests and views. One of the expedients of party to acquire influence within particular districts is to misrepresent the opinions and aims of other districts. You cannot shield yourselves too much against the jealousies and heart-burnings which spring from these misrepresentations; they tend to render alien to each other those who ought to be bound together by fraternal affection. . . .

To the efficacy and permanency of your union, a government for the whole is indispensable. No alliances, however strict, between the parts can be an adequate substitute; they must inevitably experience the infractions and interruptions which all alliances in all times have experienced. Sensible of this momentous truth, you

---

[1] **moment:** here, importance.
[2] **palladium:** safeguard.

George Washington's home in Mount Vernon, Virginia, where he retired after deciding against running for a third term as President of the United States of America.

have improved upon your first essay [1] by the adoption of a constitution of government better calculated than your former for an intimate union and for the efficacious management of your common concerns. This government, the offspring of our own choice, uninfluenced and unawed, adopted upon full investigation and mature deliberation, completely free in its principles, in the distribution of its powers, uniting security with energy and containing within itself a provision for its own amendment, has a just claim to your confidence and your support. Respect for its authority, compliance with its laws, acquiescence in its measures, are duties enjoined by the fundamental maxims of true liberty. The basis of our political systems is the right of the people to make and to alter their constitutions of government. But the constitution which at any time exists until changed by explicit and authentic act of the whole people is sacredly obligatory upon all. The very idea of the power and the right of the people to establish government presupposes the duty of every individual to obey the established government.

All obstructions to the execution of the laws, all combinations and associations under whatever plausible character, with the real design to direct, control, counteract, or awe the regular deliberation and action of the constituted authorities, are destructive of this fundamental principle and of fatal tendency. They serve to organize faction, to give it an artificial and extraordinary force; to put in the place of the delegated will of the nation the will of a party, often a small but artful and enterprising minority of the community; and, according to the alternate triumphs of different parties, to make the public administration the mirror of the ill-concerted and incongruous projects of faction rather than the organ of consistent and wholesome plans digested by common councils and modified by mutual interests. . . .

Toward the preservation of your government and the permanency of your present happy state, it is requisite not only that you steadily discountenance [2] irregular oppositions to its acknowledged authority, but also that you resist with care the spirit of innovation upon its principles, however specious the pre-

[1] **essay:** here, attempt.

[2] **discountenance:** disapprove of.

texts. One method of assault may be to effect, in the forms of the constitution, alterations which will impair the energy of the system and thus to undermine what cannot be directly overthrown. In all the changes to which you may be invited, remember that time and habit are at least as necessary to fix the true character of governments as of other human institutions; that experience is the surest standard by which to test the real tendency of the existing constitution of a country; that facility in changes, upon the credit of mere hypothesis and opinion, exposes to perpetual change from the endless variety of hypothesis and opinion; and remember, especially, that for the efficient management of your common interests in a country so extensive as ours, a government of as much vigor as is consistent with the perfect security of liberty is indispensable. Liberty itself will find in such a government, with powers properly distributed and adjusted, its surest guardian. It is, indeed, little else than a name, where the government is too feeble to withstand the enterprises of faction, to confine each member of the society within the limits prescribed by the laws, and to maintain all in the secure and tranquil enjoyment of the rights of person and property. . . .

Let me now take a more comprehensive view and warn you in the most solemn manner against the baneful effects of the spirit of party, generally. . . .

The alternate domination of one faction over another, sharpened by the spirit of revenge natural to party dissension, which in different ages and countries has perpetrated the most horrid enormities, is itself a frightful despotism. But this leads at length to a more formal and permanent despotism. The disorders and miseries which result gradually incline the minds of men to seek security and repose in the absolute power of an individual; and sooner or later the chief of some prevailing faction, more able or more fortunate than his competitors, turns this disposition to the purposes of his own elevation on the ruins of public liberty. . . .

It is important, likewise, that the habits of thinking in a free country should inspire caution, in those entrusted with its administration, to confine themselves within their respective constitutional spheres, avoiding in the exercise of the powers of one department to encroach upon another. The spirit of encroachment tends to consolidate the powers of all the departments in one and thus to create, whatever the form of government, a real despotism. A just estimate of that love of power and proneness to abuse it which predominates in the human heart is sufficient to satisfy us of the truth of this position. The necessity of reciprocal checks in the exercise of political power, by dividing and distributing it into different depositories and constituting each the guardian of the public weal against invasions by the others, has been evinced by experiments ancient and modern, some of them in our country and under our own eyes. To preserve them must be as necessary as to institute them. If, in the opinion of the people, the distribution or modification of the constitutional powers be in any particular wrong, let it be corrected by an amendment in the way which the constitution designates. But let there be no change by usurpation; for, though this in one instance may be the instrument of good, it is the customary weapon by which free governments are destroyed. The precedent must always greatly overbalance in permanent evil any partial or transient benefit which the use can at any time yield. . . .

It is substantially true that virtue, or morality, is a necessary spring of popular government. The rule, indeed, extends with more or less force to every species of free government. Who that is a sincere friend to it can look with indifference upon attempts to shake the foundation of the fabric?

Promote, then, as an object of primary importance, institutions for the general diffusion of knowledge. In proportion as the structure of a government gives force to public opinion, it is essential that public opinion should be enlightened.

As a very important source of strength and security, cherish public credit. One method of preserving it is to use it as sparingly as possible; avoiding occasions of expense by cultivating peace, but remembering also that timely disbursements to prepare for danger frequently prevent much greater disbursements to repel it; avoiding likewise the accumulation of debt, not only by shunning occasions of expense, but by vigorous exertions in time of peace to discharge the debts which unavoidable wars may have occasioned, not ungenerously throwing upon posterity the burden which we ourselves ought to bear. . . .

Observe good faith and justice towards all nations. Cultivate peace and harmony with all. Religion and morality enjoin this conduct; and can it be that good policy does not equally enjoin it? It will be worthy of a free, enlightened, and, at no distant period, a great nation to give to mankind the magnanimous and too novel example of a people always guided by an exalted justice and benevolence. Who can doubt that in the course of time and things, the fruits of such a plan would richly repay any temporary advantages which might be lost by a steady adherence to it? Can it be that Providence has not connected the permanent felicity of a nation with its virtue? The experiment, at least, is recommended by every sentiment which ennobles human nature. Alas! is it rendered impossible by its vices? . . .

The great rule of conduct for us in regard to foreign nations is, in extending our commercial relations, to have with them as little *political* connection as possible. So far as we have already formed engagements, let them be fulfilled with perfect good faith. Here let us stop.

Europe has a set of primary interests which to us have no or a very remote relation. Hence she must be engaged in frequent controversies, the causes of which are essentially foreign to our concerns. Hence, therefore, it must be unwise in us to implicate ourselves, by artificial ties, in the ordinary vicissitudes of her politics or

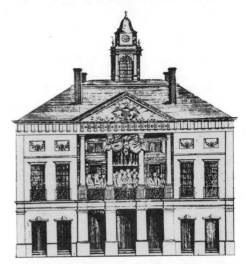

A contemporary engraving showing the inauguration of George Washington at New York's old City Hall, 1789.

the ordinary combinations and collisions of her friendships or enmities. . . .

Taking care always to keep ourselves, by suitable establishments, on a respectably defensive posture, we may safely trust to temporary alliances for extraordinary emergencies.

Harmony, liberal intercourse with all nations, are recommended by policy, humanity, and interest. But even our commercial policy should hold an equal and impartial hand; neither seeking nor granting exclusive favors or preferences; consulting the natural course of things; diffusing and diversifying by gentle means the streams of commerce but forcing nothing; establishing, with powers so disposed, in order to give trade a stable course, to define the rights of our merchants, and to enable the government to support them, conventional rules of intercourse, the best that present circumstances and mutual opinion will permit, but temporary and liable to be from time to time abandoned or varied, as experience and circumstances shall dictate; constantly keeping in view that it is folly in one nation to look for disinterested favors from another, that it must pay with a portion of its independence for whatever it may accept under that character; that, by such acceptance, it may place itself in the condition of having given equivalents for nominal favors, and yet of being reproached with ingratitude for not giving more. There can be no greater error than to expect or calculate upon real favors from nation to nation. It is an illusion, which experience must cure, which a just pride ought to discard.

In offering to you, my countrymen, these counsels of an old and affectionate friend, I dare not hope they will make the strong and lasting impression I could wish, that they will control the usual current of the passions or prevent our nation from running the course which has hitherto marked the destiny of nations. But, if I may even flatter myself that they may be productive of some partial benefit, some occasional good; that they may now and then recur to moderate the fury of party spirit, to warn against the mischiefs of foreign intrigue, to guard against the impostures of pretended patriotism; this hope will be a full recompense for the solicitude for your welfare by which they have been dictated.

How far in the discharge of my official duties I have been guided by the principles which have been delineated, the public records and other evidences of my conduct must witness to you and to the world. To myself, the assurance of my own conscience is that I have at least believed myself to be guided by them. . . .

FOR STUDY AND DISCUSSION

1. The body of the "Farewell Address" falls into two main parts: advice on national affairs and advice on foreign affairs. Make an outline of the points under each.

2. In the matters of public debt and taxes, Washington held beliefs that are still discussed today. What were his views?

3. What distinction did Washington make between *commercial* relations and *political* alliances with foreign powers? What advice did he give?

4. Cite several examples of Washington's advice that the nation has followed and several that it has not followed. What changes since Washington's time have made some of his advice difficult to follow?

5. Point out differences in language, in tone, and in sentence structure between Washington's address and modern Presidential speeches, especially those you may have heard on television or radio. How do you account for the differences?

6. Would you say that the "Farewell Address" is written in a plain or an ornate style? Find sentences from the selection to support your answer.

7. Compare Washington's "Farewell Address" with Patrick Henry's speech and Paine's article. Which do you consider the most effective piece of persuasion? Why?

LANGUAGE AND VOCABULARY

Define the numbered italicized words in the following passage from the "Farewell Address." While you may have to look up some words, you will probably be able to guess the meaning of others from the context. Then write a summary of the passage to show that you understand its total meaning.

"In looking forward to the moment which is intended to (1) *terminate* the career of my public life, my feelings do not permit me to suspend the deep (2) *acknowledgment* of that debt of gratitude which I owe to my beloved country for the many honors it has conferred upon me; still more for the steadfast confidence with which it has supported me; and for the opportunities I have thence enjoyed of (3) *manifesting* my (4) *inviolable* attachment by services faithful and persevering, though in usefulness unequal to my zeal. If benefits have resulted to our country from these services, let it always be remembered to your praise and as an instructive example in our (5) *annals* that—under circumstances in which the passions, (6) *agitated* in every direction, were liable to mislead, amidst appearances sometimes dubious, (7) *vicissitudes* of fortune often discouraging, in situations in which not infrequently want of success has (8) *countenanced* the spirit of criticism—the constancy of your support was the essential prop of the efforts and a guaranty of the plans by which they were effected. Profoundly penetrated with this idea, I shall carry it with me to the grave as a strong incitement to unceasing vows that Heaven may continue to you the choicest tokens of its (9) *beneficence* . . ."

THOMAS JEFFERSON
(1743–1826)

Thomas Jefferson was a lawyer, diplomat, parliamentarian, politician, scientist, architect, inventor, and writer. He served as delegate to Virginia's House of Burgesses, member of the Continental Congress, Governor of Virginia, member of Congress under the Articles of Confederation, minister to France, Secretary of State, Vice-President, and finally as third President of the United States. Yet in his epitaph, he noted the achievements that to him seemed most significant:

HERE WAS BURIED
THOMAS JEFFERSON,
AUTHOR OF THE DECLARATION
OF INDEPENDENCE,
OF THE STATUTE OF VIRGINIA FOR
RELIGIOUS FREEDOM, AND FATHER
OF THE UNIVERSITY OF VIRGINIA

A famous sentence by him may have served almost as well: "I have sworn upon the altar of God eternal hostility against every form of tyranny over the mind of man." He devoted his life to establishing a nation in which free men could develop their intellectual powers, unhampered by restrictions on thought or religion. Although he was sometimes forced into compromises, he returned always to his vision of a society in which the growth of the nation is matched by the growth of the individual. He is America's foremost exponent of the democratic ideal.

The son of a civil engineer and public official, Jefferson attended William and Mary College and then studied law. After practicing for several years, however, he gave up the law. The business of lawyers, he later wrote, "is to question everything, yield nothing, and talk by the hour." Managing his large estate, Jefferson turned to the life of a country gentleman and entered on a political career.

When Jefferson was chosen to draft the Declaration of Independence, he had already published *Summary of the Rights of British America* and was regarded as one of the ablest writers in the Continental Congress. Several men have charged Jefferson with borrowing the ideas in the Declaration from other works, notably from the political writings of John Locke, the English philosopher, and from a pamphlet by James Otis of Massachusetts (see page 56). But, as Jefferson remarked, "I did not consider it as any part of my charge to invent new ideas altogether, and to offer no sentiment which had ever been expressed before." Instead, he aimed to express ideas about man's natural rights that were shared by most Americans and Englishmen. These ideas he stated with an eloquence that has never been matched. When men advocate the doctrine of inalienable rights, they remember Jefferson's famous words, "We hold these truths to be self-evident . . ."

FROM *The Autobiography*

*The Framing of the Declaration
of Independence*

IT APPEARING in the course of these debates that the colonies of New York, New Jersey, Pennsylvania, Delaware, Maryland, and South Carolina were not yet matured for falling from the parent stem, but that they were fast advancing to that state, it was thought most prudent to wait a while for them and to postpone the final decision to July 1, but that this might occasion as little delay as possible a committee was appointed to prepare a declaration of independence. The committee were J. Adams, Dr. Franklin, Roger Sherman, Robert R. Livingston, and myself. Committees were also appointed at the same time to prepare a plan of confederation for the colonies and to state the terms proper to be proposed for foreign alliance. The committee for drawing the declaration of Independence desired me to do it. It was accordingly done, and being approved by them, I reported it to the house [1] on Friday the twenty-eighth of June when it was read and ordered to lie on the table.[2] On Monday, the first of July, the house resolved itself into a committee of the whole and resumed the con-

sideration of the original motion made by the delegates of Virginia, which being again debated through the day, was carried in the affirmative by the votes of New Hampshire, Connecticut, Massachusetts, Rhode Island, New Jersey, Maryland, Virginia, North Carolina, and Georgia. South Carolina and Pennsylvania voted against it. Delaware having but two members present, they were divided. The delegates for New York declared they were for it themselves and were assured their constituents were for it, but that their instructions having been drawn near a twelvemonth before, when reconciliation was still the general object, they were enjoined by them to do nothing which should impede that object. They therefore thought themselves not justifiable in voting on either side and asked leave to withdraw from the question, which was given them. The committee rose and reported their resolution to the house. Mr. Edward Rutledge of South Carolina then requested the determination might be put off to the next day, as he believed his colleagues, though they disapproved of the resolution, would then join in it for the sake of unanimity. The ultimate question whether the house would agree to the resolution of the committee was accordingly postponed to the next day, when it was again moved and South Carolina concurred in voting for it. In the meantime a third member had come post from the Delaware counties and turned the vote of that colony in favor of the resolution. Members of a different sentiment attending that morning from Pennsylvania also, their vote was changed, so that the whole twelve colonies who

[1] **the house:** the Continental Congress.
[2] **to . . . table:** to be placed on the calendar for discussion and voting.

For his painting "The Signers of the Declaration of Independence," the American artist John Trumbull painted most of his portraits from life. In this detail from the painting, Thomas Jefferson places the Declaration on the table. Benjamin Franklin is directly to the right, and John Adams, later second President of the United States, stands at the far left.

were authorized to vote at all gave their voices for it; and within a few days, the convention of New York approved of it and thus supplied the void occasioned by the withdrawing of her delegates from the vote.

Congress proceeded the same day to consider the Declaration of Independence which had been reported and lain on the table the Friday preceding, and on Monday referred to a committee of the whole. The pusillanimous idea that we had friends in England worth keeping terms with still haunted the minds of many. For this reason those passages which conveyed censures on the people of England were struck out, lest they should give them offence. The clause too, reprobating the enslaving the inhabitants of Africa, was struck out in complaisance to South Carolina and Georgia, who had never attempted to restrain the importa-

tion of slaves and who on the contrary still wished to continue it. Our Northern brethren also I believe felt a little tender under those censures; for though their people have very few slaves themselves, yet they had been pretty considerable carriers of them to others. The debates, having taken up the greater parts of the second, third, and fourth days of July, were, in the evening of the last, closed, the declaration was reported by the committee, agreed to by the house, and signed by every member present except Mr. Dickinson. As the sentiments of men are known not only by what they receive, but what they reject also, I will state the form of the declaration as originally reported. The parts struck out by Congress shall be distinguished by a black line drawn under them; and those inserted by them shall be placed in the margin or in a concurrent column.

A DECLARATION BY THE REPRESENTATIVES
OF THE UNITED STATES OF AMERICA,
IN GENERAL CONGRESS ASSEMBLED

When in the course of human events it becomes necessary for one people to dissolve the political bands which have connected them with another, and to assume among the powers of the earth the separate and equal station to which the laws of nature and of nature's God entitle them, a decent respect to the opinions of mankind requires that they should declare the causes which impel them to the separation.

We hold these truths to be self-evident: that all men are created equal; that they are endowed by their creator with inherent and [certain] inalienable rights; that among these are life, liberty, and the pursuit of happiness: that to secure these rights, governments are instituted among men, deriving their just powers from the consent of the governed; that whenever any form of government becomes destructive of these ends, it is the right of the people to alter or abolish it, and to institute a new government, laying its foundation on such principles, and organizing its powers in such form, as to them shall seem most likely to effect their safety and happiness. Prudence indeed will dictate that governments long established should not be changed for light and transient causes; and accordingly all experience hath shown that mankind are more disposed to suffer while evils are sufferable, than to right themselves by abolishing the forms to which they are accustomed. But when a long train of abuses and usurpations begun at a distinguished period and pursuing invariably the same object evinces a design to reduce them under absolute despotism, it is their right, it is their duty to throw off such government, and to provide new guards for their future security. Such has been the patient sufferance of these colonies; and such is now the necessity which constrains them to expunge their former systems of govern- [alter] ment. The history of the present king of Great Britain is a history of unremitting injuries and usurpations, among which ap- [repeated] pears no solitary fact to contradict the uniform tenor of the rest but all have in direct object the establishment of an absolute tyr- [all having] anny over these states. To prove this let facts be submitted to a candid world for the truth of which we pledge a faith yet unsullied by falsehood.

He has refused his assent to laws the most wholesome and necessary for the public good.

He has forbidden his governors to pass laws of immediate and pressing importance, unless suspended in their operation till his assent should be obtained; and when so suspended, he has utterly neglected to attend to them.

He has refused to pass other laws for the accommodation of large districts of people, unless those people would relinquish the right of representation in the legislature, a right inestimable to them, and formidable to tyrants only.

He has called together legislative bodies at places unusual, uncomfortable, and distant from the depository of their public records, for the sole purpose of fatiguing them into compliance with his measures.

He has dissolved representative houses repeatedly <u>and continually</u> for opposing with manly firmness his invasions on the rights of the people.

He has refused for a long time after such dissolutions to cause others to be elected, whereby the legislative powers, incapable of annihilation, have returned to the people at large for their exercise, the state remaining in the meantime exposed to all the dangers of invasion from without and convulsions within.

He has endeavored to prevent the population of these states; for that purpose obstructing the laws for naturalization of foreigners, refusing to pass others to encourage their migrations hither, and raising the conditions of new appropriations of lands.

He has <u>suffered</u> the administration of justice <u>totally to cease in some of these states</u>, refusing his assent to laws for establishing judiciary powers.   obstructed   by

He has made <u>our</u> judges dependent on his will alone, for the tenure of their offices, and the amount and payment of their salaries.

He has erected a multitude of new offices <u>by a self-assumed power</u> and sent hither swarms of officers to harass our people and eat out their substance.

He has kept among us in times of peace standing armies <u>and ships of war</u> without the consent of our legislatures.

He has affected to render the military independent of, and superior to, the civil power.

He has combined with others to subject us to a jurisdiction foreign to our constitutions and unacknowledged by our laws, giving his assent to their acts of pretended legislation for quartering large bodies of armed troops among us; for protecting them by a mock trial from punishment for any murders which they should commit on the inhabitants of these states; for cutting off our trade with all parts of the world; for imposing taxes on us without our consent; for depriving us [   ] of the benefits of trial   in many cases by jury; for transporting us beyond seas to be tried for pretended offences; for abolishing the free system of English laws in a neighboring province, establishing therein an arbitrary government, and enlarging its boundaries, so as to render it at once an example and fit instrument for introducing the same absolute rule into these states; for taking away our charters, abolishing our most valuable laws, and altering fundamentally the forms of our governments; for suspending our own legislatures, and declaring themselves invested with power to legislate for us in all cases whatsoever.

[margin: colonies]

He has abdicated government here withdrawing his governors, and declaring us out of his allegiance and protection.

[margin: by declaring us out of his protection, and waging war against us.]

He has plundered our seas, ravaged our coasts, burnt our towns, and destroyed the lives of our people.

He is at this time transporting large armies of foreign mercenaries to complete the works of death, desolation, and tyranny already begun with circumstances of cruelty and perfidy [ ] unworthy the head of a civilized nation.

[margin: scarcely paralleled in the most barbarous ages, and totally]

He has constrained our fellow citizens taken captive on the high seas to bear arms against their country, to become the executioners of their friends and brethren, or to fall themselves by their hands.

He has [ ] endeavored to bring on the inhabitants of our frontiers the merciless Indian savages, whose known rule of warfare is an undistinguished destruction of all ages, sexes, and conditions of existence.

[margin: excited domestic insurrection among us, and has]

He has incited treasonable insurrections of our fellow citizens, with the allurements of forfeiture and confiscation of our property.

He has waged cruel war against human nature itself, violating its most sacred rights of life and liberty in the persons of a distant people who never offended him, captivating and carrying them into slavery in another hemisphere, or to incur miserable death in their transportation thither. This piratical warfare, the opprobrium of infidel powers, is the warfare of the Christian king of Great Britain. . . . And that this assemblage of horrors might want no fact of distinguished die, he is now exciting those very people to rise in arms among us, and to purchase that liberty of which he has deprived them, by murdering the people on whom he also obtruded them: thus paying off former crimes committed against the liberties of one people, with crimes which he urges them to commit against the lives of another.

In every stage of these oppressions we have petitioned for redress in the most humble terms: our repeated petitions have been answered only by repeated injuries.

A prince whose character is thus marked by every act which may define a tyrant is unfit to be the ruler of a [ ] people who mean to be free. *[free]* Future ages will scarcely believe that the hardiness of one man adventured, within the short compass of twelve years only, to lay a foundation so broad and so undisguised for tyranny over a people fostered and fixed in principles of freedom.

Nor have we been wanting in attentions to our British brethren. We have warned them from time to time of attempts by their legislature to extend a jurisdiction over these our states. We *[an unwarrantable/ us]* have reminded them of the circumstances of our emigration and settlement here, no one of which could warrant so strange a pretension: that these were effected at the expense of our own blood and treasure, unassisted by the wealth or the strength of Great Britain: that in constituting indeed our several forms of government, we had adopted one common king, thereby laying a foundation for perpetual league and amity with them: but that submission to their parliament was no part of our constitution, nor ever in idea, if history may be credited: and, we [ ] appealed *[have]* to their native justice and magnanimity as well as to the ties of *[and we have conjured [1]]* our common kindred to disavow these usurpations which *[them by]* were likely to interrupt our connection and correspondence. They *[would inevitably]* too have been deaf to the voice of justice and of consanguinity,[2] and when occasions have been given them, by the regular course of their laws, of removing from their councils the disturbers of our harmony, they have, by their free election, reestablished them in power. At this very time too they are permitting their chief magistrate to send over not only soldiers of our common blood, but Scotch and foreign mercenaries to invade and destroy us. These facts have given the last stab to agonizing affection, and manly spirit bids us to renounce forever these unfeeling brethren. We must endeavor to forget our former love for them, and hold them as we hold the rest of mankind, enemies in war, in peace friends. We might have been a free and a great people together; but a communication of grandeur and of freedom it seems is below their dignity. Be it so, since they will have it. The road to happiness and to glory is open to us too. We will tread it apart from them, and acquiesce in the necessity which denounces [3] our eternal separation [ ]! *[We must therefore and hold them as we hold the rest of mankind, enemies in war, in peace friends.]*

[1] **conjured:** here, appealed to, begged.

[2] **consanguinity** (kon'sang·gwin'ə·tē): relationship resulting from common ancestry; blood relationship.

[3] **denounces:** here, makes known in a solemn or official manner.

We therefore the representatives of the United States of America in General Congress assembled do in the name and by authority of the good people of these states reject and renounce all allegiance and subjection to the kings of Great Britain and all others who may hereafter claim by, through, or under them: we utterly dissolve all political connection which may heretofore have subsisted between us and the people or parliament of Great Britain: and finally we do assert and declare these colonies to be free and independent states, and that as free and independent states, they have full power to levy war, conclude peace, contract alliances, establish commerce, and to do all other acts and things which independent states may of right do.

And for the support of this declaration we mutually pledge to each other our lives, our fortunes, and our sacred honor.

We therefore the representatives of the United States of America in General Congress assembled, appealing to the Supreme Judge of the world for the rectitude of our intentions, do in the name, and by the authority of the good people of these colonies, solemnly publish and declare that these united colonies are and of right ought to be free and independent states; that they are absolved from all allegiance to the British Crown, and that all political connection between them and the State of Great Britain is, and ought to be, totally dissolved; and that as free and independent states they have full power to levy war, conclude peace, contract alliances, establish commerce and to do all other acts and things which independent states may of right do.

And for the support of this declaration, with a firm reliance on the protection of Divine Providence, we mutually pledge to each other our lives, our fortunes, and our sacred honor.

The Declaration thus signed on the fourth on paper, was engrossed [1] on parchment, and signed again on the second of August.

[1] **engrossed:** here, copied.

FOR STUDY AND DISCUSSION

1. What can you learn from the selection about the process of passing a law or a resolution? What compromises were made? Which delegation voted for the Declaration, although disapproving of it? Which delegation abstained? Why?

2. Note that in the Declaration blame is placed upon the king rather than upon the people of England. Why is this an important distinction?

3. Jefferson states that "the sentiments of men are known not only by what they receive, but what they reject also . . ." What do you learn about the sentiments of the Continental Congress from the parts of the Declaration of Independence which they rejected?

4. Find several examples of changes in phrasing which you think improved the Declaration. Give reasons for your choices. Are there changes in phrasing which you think should not have been made? If so, why?

5. How does the Declaration of Independence justify Jefferson's reputation as an able writer? What memorable phrases can you find in the Declaration?

FOR COMPOSITION

Write a composition in which you make a detailed study of the original and revised versions of the Declaration of Independence. In your composition, consider which changes were made to improve the style of the Declaration and which were made for political reasons. Decide which version of the Declaration you prefer and give specific reasons for your choice.

Letter to
Thomas Jefferson Randolph

Near the end of Jefferson's second term as President, he wrote the following letter to his grandson, who had been sent away to school in Philadelphia. Thomas Jefferson Randolph grew up to become a leading citizen of Virginia, and in 1872 he presided over the Democratic National Convention that nominated Horace Greeley for the presidency.

November 24, 1808
Washington

MY DEAR JEFFERSON: Your situation, thrown at such a distance from us, and alone, cannot but give us all great anxieties for you. As much has been secured for you, by your particular position and the acquaintance to which you have been recommended, as could be done toward shielding you from the dangers which surround you. But thrown on a wide world among entire strangers, without a friend or guardian to advise, so young too and with so little experience of mankind, your dangers are great, and still your safety must rest on yourself. A determination never to do what is wrong, prudence, and good humor, will go far toward securing to you the estimation of the world. When I recollect that at fourteen years of age, the whole care and direction of myself was thrown on myself entirely, without a relation or friend qualified to advise or guide me, and recollect the various sorts of bad company with which I associated from time to time, I am astonished I did not turn off with some of them and become as worthless to society as they were. I had the good fortune to become acquainted very early with some characters of very high standing and to feel the incessant wish that I could ever become what they were. Under temptations and difficulties, I would ask myself what would Dr. Small, Mr. Wythe, Peyton Randolph do in this situation? What course in it will ensure me their approbation? I am certain that this mode of deciding on my conduct tended more to correctness than any reasoning powers I possessed. Knowing the even and dignified line they pursued, I could never doubt for a moment which of two courses would be in character for them. Whereas, seeking the same object through a process of moral reasoning and with the jaundiced eye of youth, I should often have erred. From the circumstances of my position, I was often thrown into the society of horse racers, card players, fox hunters, scientific and professional men, and of dignified men; and many a time have I asked myself, in the enthusiastic moment of the death of a fox, the victory of a favorite horse, the issue of a question eloquently argued at the bar, or in the great council of the nation: well, which of these kinds of reputation should I prefer? That of a horse jockey, a fox hunter, an orator, or the honest advocate of my country's rights? Be assured, my dear Jefferson, that these little returns into ourselves, this self-catechising habit, is not trifling nor useless but leads to the prudent selection and steady pursuit of what is right.

Monticello, Jefferson's home in Virginia, which he designed and built himself.

I have mentioned good humor as one of the preservatives of our peace and tranquillity. It is among the most effectual, and its effect is so well imitated and aided artificially by politeness, that this also becomes an acquisition of first rate value. In truth, politeness is artificial good humor, it covers the natural want [1] of it, and ends by rendering habitual a substitute nearly equivalent to the real virtue. It is the practice of sacrificing to those whom we meet in society all the little conveniences and preferences which will gratify them and deprive us of nothing worth a moment's consideration; it is the giving a pleasing and flattering turn to our expressions, which will conciliate others and make them pleased with us as well as themselves. How cheap a price for the good will of another! When this is in return for a rude thing said by another, it brings him to his senses, it mortifies and corrects him in the most salutary way, and places him at the feet of your good nature in the eyes of the company. But in stating prudential rules for our government in society, I must not omit the important one of never entering into dispute or argument with another. I never saw an instance of one of two disputants convincing the other by argument. I have seen many, on their getting warm, becoming rude and shooting one another. Conviction is the effect of our own dispassionate reasoning, either in solitude, or weighing within ourselves, dispassionately, what we hear from others, standing uncommitted in argument ourselves. It was one of the rules which, above all others, made Doctor Franklin the most amiable of men in society, "never to contradict anybody." If he was urged to announce an opinion, he did it rather by asking questions, as if for information, or by suggesting doubts. When I hear another express an opinion which is not mine, I say to myself, he has a right to his opinion, as I to mine; why should I question it? His error does me no injury, and shall I become a Don

Quixote,[2] to bring all men by force of argument to one opinion? If a fact be misstated, it is probable he is gratified by a belief of it, and I have no right to deprive him of the gratification. If he wants information, he will ask it, and then I will give it in measured terms; but if he still believes his own story and shows a desire to dispute the fact with me, I hear him and say nothing. It is his affair, not mine, if he prefers error. There are two classes of disputants most frequently to be met with among us. The first is of young students just entered the threshold of science, with a first view of its outlines not yet filled up with the details and modifications which a further progress would bring to their knowledge. The other consists of the ill-tempered and rude men in society who have taken up a passion for politics. (Good humor and politeness never introduce into mixed society a question on which they foresee there will be a difference of opinion.) From both of those classes of disputants, my dear Jefferson, keep aloof as you would from the infected subjects of yellow fever or pestilence. Consider yourself, when with them, as among the patients of Bedlam,[3] needing medical more than moral counsel. Be a listener only, keep within yourself, and endeavor to establish with yourself the habit of silence, especially on politics. In the fevered state of our country, no good can ever result from any attempt to set one of these fiery zealots to rights, either in fact or principle. They are determined as to the facts they will believe and the opinions on which they will act. Get by them, therefore, as you would by an angry bull; it is not for a man of sense to dispute the road with such an animal. You will be more exposed than others to have

[1] **want:** here, lack.

[2] **Don Quixote** (don kwik·sət): the hero of a novel by Cervantes (1547–1616). Befuddled by excessive reading of books of chivalry, Don Quixote imagines himself to be a medieval knight who rides forth to right wrongs and combat oppression.

[3] **Bedlam** (bed'ləm): a famous institution for the insane.

Among the furniture Jefferson designed for Monticello is this ingenious chair desk.

these animals shaking their horns at you, because of the relation in which you stand with me. Full of political venom, and willing to see me and to hate me as a chief in the antagonist party, your presence will be to them what the vomit grass is to the sick dog, a nostrum for producing ejaculation. Look upon them exactly with that eye and pity them as objects to whom you can administer only occasional ease. My character is not within their power. It is in the hands of my fellow citizens at large and will be consigned to honor or infamy by the verdict of the republican mass of our country according to what themselves will have seen, not what their enemies and mine shall have said. Never, therefore, consider these puppies in politics as requiring any notice from you, and always show that you are not afraid to leave my character to the umpirage of public opinion. Look steadily to the pursuits which have carried you to Philadelphia, be very select in the society you attach yourself to, avoid taverns, drinkers, smokers, idlers, and dissipated persons generally; for it is with such that broils [1] and contentions arise; and you will find your path more easy and tranquil. The limits of my paper warn me that it is time for me to close with my affectionate adieu,

TH: JEFFERSON

---

[1] **broils:** here, quarrels.

FOR STUDY AND DISCUSSION

1. Explain what Jefferson means by the "self-catechising habit." What effect did it have on his own life? In your opinion, is this habit a difficult or an easy one to acquire? Explain.

2. Why does Jefferson advise his grandson to follow the examples of those whom he admires rather than to guide his conduct "through a process of moral reasoning"? Do you agree with Jefferson's advice? Give reasons for your answer.

3. What do you learn about Jefferson's youth from this letter? What do you learn about the burdens of his high office? What do you learn from the letter about his attitude toward his political enemies?

4. Judging from this letter, would you say that Jefferson was a likable person? Why or why not? What adjectives would you use to describe him?

LANGUAGE AND VOCABULARY

1. Give the meaning of the italicized words, either from their context or by looking them up.
   a. "Under temptations and difficulties, I would ask myself what would Dr. Small, Mr. Wythe, Peyton Randolph do in this situation? What course in it will ensure me their *approbation?*" (Page 73.)
   b. "Whereas, seeking the same object . . . with the *jaundiced* eye of youth, I should often have erred." (Page 73.)
   c. "it [politeness] is the giving a pleasing and flattering turn to our expressions, which will *conciliate* others and make them pleased with us as well as themselves." (Pages 73–74.)
   d. "it brings him to his senses, it mortifies and corrects him in the most *salutary* way, and places him at the feet of your good nature in the eyes of the company." (Page 74.)
   e. "From both of those classes of disputants . . . keep aloof as you would from the infected subjects of yellow fever or *pestilence.*" (Page 74.)

2. On the basis of this letter, discuss Jefferson's resources of vocabulary. Do you think that he had an unusually wide vocabulary which he used naturally, or that he consciously tried to introduce unusual words into his correspondence?

The Beginnings of the American Tradition

Now that you have studied and discussed the selections in the first unit, it is appropriate to look back and see what conclusions you can draw not simply from studying every selection and author as individual entities but by relating them to each other and seeing them all as part of a larger whole. Your first impression of this period in America might be that it was one of literary diversity. The earliest of the authors represented in this unit died in 1657, the last, in 1826. Altogether, the selections in the unit cover a period of about a hundred and fifty years, a much longer period than that covered by any of the other units in this book. In this early period there was no sense of a cohesive cultural and literary life. There was not even much concern with developing such a life. The colonies were struggling to survive and later to win independence. Literature was an almost accidental by-product of the struggle, the product of a number of remarkable individuals.

To relate the selections of this unit to each other, it may be helpful to divide its contents into four historical phases:

    I. COLONIAL BEGINNINGS: Bradford
    II. COLONIAL DEVELOPMENT: Byrd, Taylor, Edwards, Franklin *(Autobiography)*
    III. THE REVOLUTION: Franklin ("Rules by Which a Great Empire May Be Reduced to a Small One"), Henry, Paine
    IV. THE YOUNG NATION: Washington, Jefferson

What do you learn from the selections about each historical phase? For example, what do you learn from the selection from Bradford's history of the hardships experienced in the first phase? What do you learn about Northern colonial life from the selections by Taylor, Edwards, and Franklin? about Southern life from Byrd? What do you learn about the colonist's concern with religion? with politics? What indications of a growing sense of national identity can be found in the writings of Henry, Paine, and Washington? What do you learn about the problems of the new nation from Washington's *Farewell Address?* Why should each of these selections be read for literary as well as historical reasons?

THE CONFLICT BETWEEN IDEALS AND REALITIES

The development of American literature, and of the nation itself, can be seen as a struggle between ideals and realities. The introduction to this unit briefly discusses this struggle. Of the struggle, Marcus Cunliffe, a British scholar, has remarked, "As a society founded with ideal aims, America finds that the ideal is sometimes contradicted by the reality; and that in any case the ideal and the real must always be referred to one another." As you study later American literature, you will see that the conflict between ideals and realities is characteristic of American literature to this day.

1. Study the discussion of the conflict between ideals and realities in the introduction to the unit (pages 1–6). Then consider Professor Cunliffe's statement. What are some of the religious, political, and social ideals expressed by the authors in this unit? Find specific passages to support your answers. What realities—for example, physical hardships, difficulties with England—do you find discussed in the selections? Which writers emphasized the ideals of American life more than the realities? Which seemed more interested in the practical, day-to-day realities? As ideals and realities conflict, each tends to change the other. How did colonial realities change colonial ideals? How did ideals change realities?

2. Religious ideals dominated Puritan New England. Later in our history, political and social ideals became of primary importance. Give examples from the selections that reflect this change.

THE PURITAN AND THE CAVALIER

As is pointed out in the unit introduction, two distinct types emerged in colonial America: the Puritan and the Cavalier. Both types were important in colonial literature; both types made important contributions to the emerging nation. Study the discussion of the Puritan and the Cavalier on pages 2–4. Review the selections by Bradford, Edwards, and Taylor as examples of Puritan writing; review the selection by Byrd as an example of writing by a Cavalier. Then discuss the following questions.

1. Contrast the Puritan and the Cavalier. What ideals were most important to the Puritan? to the Cavalier? What was the attitude of the Puritan toward his fellow man? of the Cavalier? If you were to write compositions called "Portrait of a Puritan" and "Portrait of a Cavalier," what characteristics would you describe? What, in your opinion, would Jonathan Edwards think of William Byrd? What would Byrd think of Edwards?

2. In what ways do the Puritan and the Cavalier traditions influence modern American life? What contemporary writers or public figures might be called the inheritors of the Puritan or the Cavalier tradition?

A VARIETY OF LITERATURE

The great diversity of the selections in this unit has already been mentioned. You may also notice that several types of literature common today, particularly prose fiction, are not included here. In order to come to some conclusions about this period, make a list of authors, selections, and literary forms (for example: Bradford, *Of Plymouth Plantation,* history). Then consider the following questions.

1. Marcus Cunliffe remarks that "the Puritan atmosphere was discouraging to imaginative literature." Do you agree or disagree? Give reasons for

your answer. How do you explain the dearth of poetic, fictional, and dramatic literature during the colonial and revolutionary periods?

2. Of three of the major purposes for writing—to inform, persuade, or entertain—which predominates in the selections you have read? What conclusions about the literature of this period and the society that produced it can you draw from this fact?

PLAIN VERSUS ORNATE STYLE

The Puritans, as you have learned, were the earliest advocates in America of the "plain style," in keeping with a plain way of life (see page 12). Benjamin Franklin wrote a good description of this style: "The words should be the most expressive that the language affords, provided that they are the most generally understood. Nothing should be expressed in two words that can as well be expressed in one; that is, no synonyms should be used, or very rarely, but the whole should be as short as possible, consistent with clearness; the words should be so placed as to be agreeable to the ear in reading; summarily, it should be smooth, clear, and short, for the contrary qualities are displeasing."

1. Select as examples of the plain style four passages from four different writers. To what extent is each passage "smooth, clear, and short"? Do these passages lack any of the qualities Franklin mentions?

2. Select an ornately written passage and rewrite it so that it will conform to Franklin's description of the plain style.

FOR COMPOSITION: THE FORMS OF DISCOURSE

In this unit, you have been studying the forms of discourse (see page 29). Now review the selections in the unit and find at least one sample paragraph of narration, exposition, and description. Then, giving special attention to the following examples of persuasion—"Sinners in the Hands of an Angry God," "Rules by Which a Great Empire May Be Reduced to a Small One," "Speech in the Virginia Convention," and *The Crisis, Number One*— review what you have learned in each case about the speaker (or writer), the audience (or reader), the occasion, and the means of persuasion. How does each author give emphasis to the major points he wishes to make?

ART AND LITERATURE

In addition to literature, the colonies were also developing the art of painting. (Study the plates and accompanying text on pages 79–86.) Early American painters were particularly interested in portrait painting. Explain how one of the portraits on pages 81–83 and 86 conveys the personality of its subject. Show how all the details in the portrait unite to create one dominant impression. Compare this portrait with Edwards's written portrait of Sarah Pierrepont (page 25). What is Edwards trying to convey that a painting cannot?

AMERICAN PAINTING

The Colonial and Federal Periods

Our earliest American painters were primarily artisans skilled in a number of different crafts. As such, they played an important role in colonial life, for as frontier settlements developed into towns, signs had to be painted, saddles made, furniture stained, and so on. By the second quarter of the eighteenth century, painters in prosperous commercial centers like Boston and Charleston were supplementing their incomes by doing portraits of wealthy merchants and landowners. Soon it became possible for a self-taught colonial artist to support himself by devoting his time entirely to the painting of likenesses.

One of these self-taught artists was Ralph Earl of Connecticut, who painted portraits of such stalwart New Englanders as the prominent lawyer and statesman Roger Sherman (PLATE 1). Sherman's figure seems posed a bit stiffly here; yet this awkwardness is effective, for it conveys a feeling of his rugged personality. And the severity of the setting seems to emphasize the density and weight of Sherman's body, so that we almost feel we are in his presence.

Another talented colonial portrait painter was John Singleton Copley of Boston. He, too, was largely self-taught, having learned to draw and compose by copying engravings of famous European paintings. Copley began to paint professionally at eighteen, and within a few years became the leading portraitist in America—a reputation he maintained until he left for England just before the Revolutionary War.

Copley was especially good at portraying older people. One of his finest likenesses was that of Mrs. Sylvanus Bourne (PLATE 2), a seventy-one-year-old widow of a well-known Boston jurist. Copley's brush seems to have captured her expression perfectly just at the instant she put down her book and glanced up at us. And notice how well he has unified his composition by linking the white edges of the woman's bonnet to the larger pattern of grayish-white across her cape, which then gathers into the bow at her waist and finally opens out once more into the billowing folds of her apron.

Few colonialists were more versatile than Charles Willson Peale—painter, inventor, saddler, scientist, soldier, writer, naturalist, and proprietor of a Philadelphia museum. As a painter, Peale maintained that he simply imitated what he saw in front of him. In fact, in one of his large pictures, *The Staircase Group* (PLATE 3), he represented two of his sons so realistically that the picture almost fools the eye. What made the picture especially deceptive was the way Peale exhibited it: he set it in the frame of a doorway and built a wooden step out onto the floor from the bottom of the canvas. President Washington is said to have bowed politely to the painted figures as he walked past the picture on a tour of Peale's museum. Of course, *The Staircase Group* is not merely a "deception," but also a handsome design. See, for instance, how Peale has balanced the winding form of the staircase with a shadow on the back wall, which seems to curve around in the opposite direction.

One of the artists who helped Copley when he returned to London was Benjamin West, a native of Philadelphia who had settled in England in 1763 and who, nine years later, had been appointed "historical painter" to King George III. West was a skillful composer of large groups of figures. In *The Battle of La Hogue* (PLATE 4), a British admiral is shown leading a combined force of English and Dutch sailors and soldiers in a surprise attack on French warships anchored in the harbor of La Hogue. Despite the violence of the battle, some of the figures are posed in rather formal attitudes—somewhat like those of classical Roman statues, which West had admired in Italy many years earlier. Though he lacked the genius of an artist like Copley, West was an important figure in the history of American art because of his influence on the work of many colonial painters who came to study with him in London.

One of West's most talented students was John Trumbull, a graduate of Harvard and a colonel in the Revolutionary Army. From West, Trumbull learned the neoclassical rules of drawing and composition and what were considered the correct attitudes of figures in scenes of violent action. *Death of General Mercer at the Battle of Princeton* (PLATE 5) is a good example. This is one of a series of historical scenes which Trumbull painted to document the Revolution. At least eight of the figures in this picture are portraits of American officers.

Another brilliant pupil from West's studio in London was Gilbert Stuart of Rhode Island. After a successful career as a portrait painter in England and then in Ireland, Stuart came to America in 1793 and was soon showered with commissions. PLATE 6 shows his portrait of Stephen Decatur, a naval hero of the War of 1812. Most of our attention is focused directly on the strong features of this American officer, but notice how Stuart has enlivened the picture by leading our eye from one highlight to another along the gold braid of his uniform.

PLATE 1. RALPH EARL (1751–1801): *Roger Sherman*. About 1777–79. Oil on canvas, $64\frac{5}{8}$ x $49\frac{5}{8}$ inches. (Yale University Art Gallery, New Haven, Connecticut)

PLATE 2. JOHN SINGLETON COPLEY (1738–1815): *Mrs. Sylvanus Bourne*. 1776. Oil on canvas, $50\frac{1}{4}$ x 40 inches. (The Metropolitan Museum of Art, New York, Morris K. Jesup Fund, 1924)

PLATE 3. CHARLES WILLSON PEALE (1741–1827): *The Staircase Group*. 1795. Oil on canvas, 89 x 39½ inches. (Philadelphia Museum of Art, George W. Elkins Collection)

83

PLATE 4. BENJAMIN WEST (1738–1820): *The Battle of La Hogue.* 1778. Oil on canvas, $60\frac{1}{8}$ x $84\frac{3}{8}$ inches. (National Gallery of Art, Washington, D.C., Andrew Mellon Collection)

PLATE 5. JOHN TRUMBULL (1756–1843): *Death of General Mercer at the Battle of Princeton.* About 1787. Oil on canvas, 20 x 30 inches. (Yale University Art Gallery, New Haven, Connecticut)

85

PLATE 6. GILBERT STUART (1755–1828): *Commodore Stephen Decatur*. About 1813. Oil on canvas, 30 x 25 inches. (Smithsonian Institution, Washington, D.C.)

EARLY MEN
OF LETTERS

"The national character is yet in a state of fermentation; it may have its frothiness and sediment, but its ingredients are sound and wholesome; it has already given proofs of powerful and generous qualities, and the whole promises to settle down into something substantially excellent."

WASHINGTON IRVING

For the new nation, the years following the American Revolution were years of tremendous growth and expansion. Between 1791 and 1821, ten new states were admitted to the Union. In 1789, Samuel Slater, an English mechanic with a thorough knowledge of English spinning and weaving machines, emigrated to the United States. With the help of a merchant, he set up his own cotton factory in Rhode Island. The Industrial Revolution had come to the United States. Utilizing the knowledge of machines that Slater had brought with him from England, textile mills sprang up all over New England. In 1803, President Jefferson purchased the Louisiana Territory from France, thus tremendously increasing the territory of the United States. The next year, under Congressional authority, Meriwether Lewis and William Clark began their expedition of the northwestern part of the country. Pioneers, searching for new land to farm, pushed westward over roads and trails, rivers and canals. Involvement in national politics—the struggle between Federalists and Republicans—gave Americans a growing sense of being a part of one country rather than of an alliance of states. The War of 1812 strengthened the American sense of unity and of national identity. But in these early years of the new nation, two elements essential to a strong sense of national identity were missing: a distinctive cultural life and a significant national literature.

From the Lewis and Clark Expedition came first knowledge of the Northwest. This amusing woodcut appeared in the first published account (1811) of the expedition.

THE STRUGGLE FOR CULTURAL INDEPENDENCE

In 1820, Sydney Smith, an English clergyman, writer, and wit, posed the question: "In the four quarters of the globe, who reads an American book?" That same year, Washington Irving's *Sketch Book* appeared and proved enormously popular both in the United States and in England. Three years earlier, William Cullen Bryant's poem "Thanatopsis" had been published in the *North American Review*. In 1823, James Fenimore Cooper's first novel about Natty Bumppo, *The Pioneers,* was published; and four years later, Edgar Allan Poe issued his first collection of poems. All these writers provided an answer to Smith's question, for they produced literary works that were not only read by Americans but admired by educated Europeans. Cooper and Poe, in particular, made important contributions to Western literature and culture. Cooper's idyllic descriptions of life in the American forest and his creation of Natty Bumppo, the frontiersman who combined primitive simplicity with ethical discipline, set an ideal of life for the school-boys of many countries. Poe's cultivation of effects of terror and despair in his tales and poems had a profound effect on the French poet Baudelaire and, through Baudelaire, on modern European poetry.

Yet forty years after the American Revolution, Sydney Smith could pose his question, and it seemed a reasonable question to ask. America had not yet begun to produce its own distinctive literature. Although some able writers had already appeared, notably the poet Philip Freneau and the novelists Charles Brockden Brown and Hugh Henry Brackenridge, the work of these writers did not achieve the popularity that the works of Cooper, Poe, Irving, and Bryant were later to have. Also, America remained under the cultural domination of England long after it had won its political independence. One scholar has estimated that in 1820, seventy percent of the books that Americans read were published in England, while only thirty percent were brought out by American publishers. By 1850, the ratio was reversed. In the third and fourth decades of the nineteenth century, book publishers, literary magazines, and newspapers began to prosper. It became possible for a man with literary ambitions to make a living by his writing, although some writers, like Poe, never did manage to rise above poverty. The story of American literature in the early part of the nineteenth century, then, is the story of American writers trying to work out their own cultural destiny, to create a distinctive literature separate from English literature, and to make this literature a significant part of the national life.

CLASSICISM AND ROMANTICISM

While Americans were trying to create their own literature, they were working within a mode of thought and feeling that dominated most nineteenth-century literature of the Western world. Gradually, near the end of the eighteenth century, there was a shift in the fundamental conception of the artist's role and purpose, which is generally characterized as a shift from *classicism* to *Romanticism*. Both classicism and Romanticism are broad terms that are difficult to define exactly. Many painters, writers, and composers can be seen to have both classical and Romantic qualities. But, by and large, the eighteenth century was a classical period in art, music, and literature, while the first part of the nineteenth century was dominated by Romanticism.

Perhaps the best way to define classicism and Romanticism is in terms of a set of contrasts. One French critic, who was hostile to Romanticism, wrote that it was "a movement to honor whatever classicism rejected. Classicism is the regularity of good sense—perfection in moderation. Romanticism is disorder in the imagination—the rage of incorrectness. A blind wave of literary egotism." However, the German poet Heinrich Heine wrote that "classic art portrays the finite, Romantic art also suggests the infinite." Romanticism has been described as "emotion rather than reason, the heart opposed to the head," as "imagination as contrasted with reason and the sense of fact," and as "a sense of the mystery of the universe and the perception of its beauty." It would be fair to say that classical art most highly esteems the traditional, the normal, and the universal; while Romantic art pursues the original, the strange, and the deeply personal. Classical writers generally try to make their writing conform to what they regard as a universal set of rules; they value clarity, balance, and order. Romantic writers usually try to make their writing a reflection of their inmost feelings, and the qualities they value most highly are originality and emotional sincerity.

When Benjamin Franklin undertook to improve his prose style by imitating Addison, an English writer whom he regarded as a fine stylist, he was being a classicist. On the other hand, William Cullen Bryant was expressing the Romantic point of view when he wrote that "the great spring of poetry is emotion . . . strong feeling is always a sure guide. . . . It may sometimes transgress arbitrary rules or offend against local associations, but it speaks a language which reaches the heart in all countries and all times."

SOME CHARACTERISTICS OF ROMANTICISM

Cooper, Irving, Bryant, and Poe, as part of the Romantic movement, shared certain characteristics with other Romantic writers. Before you read selections by these four writers, you may find it useful to consider the ways in which they exemplify the following characteristics of the Romantic movement:

An appeal to emotion rather than reason. As you have seen, Bryant regarded emotion as the best source for poetry. Poe believed that a writer should carefully construct his story or poem so that it would have one predominant effect (page 138). In the novels of Cooper, the characters who are most highly regarded are usually those who give honest expression to their feelings.

An interest in nature. Perhaps responding to the English poet William Wordsworth's poems celebrating the beauty of the English countryside, Bryant wrote poems such as "The Yellow Violet," "A Forest Hymn," and "To a Waterfowl" (page 112). Some of the finest passages in Cooper's novels describe the beauties of the American wilderness. Both Bryant and Cooper awakened the imagination of later American writers to the possibility of seeing the American wilderness as a wilder, more primitive, more splendid scene than any to be found in Europe. Even Irving, who spent much of his time in Europe and who wrote mostly about European scenes, was alive to the distinctive beauties of his own country. He wrote that an American "never need . . . look beyond his own country for the sublime and beautiful of natural scenery."

An interest in the picturesque and unusual. Romantic writers were seldom interested in the average and the ordinary, but were always pursuing the strange and out-of-the-way. Washington Irving confessed, "I was always fond of visiting new scenes and observing strange characters and manners," and he roamed through Europe searching for picturesque scenes and characters. The search for the unusual is reflected in the tales of Edgar Allan Poe, who did not travel from country to country but explored the dark areas of his own mind.

A spirit of nationalism. Many Romantic writers were concerned with exploring the history and traditions of their own nation and bringing out

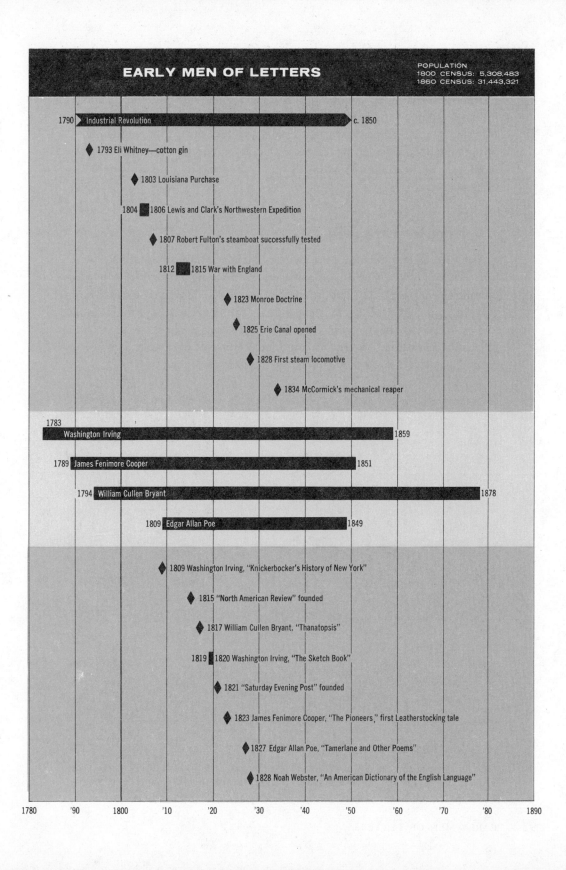

EARLY MEN OF LETTERS

1790 Industrial Revolution c. 1850

1793 Eli Whitney—cotton gin

1803 Louisiana Purchase

1804 1806 Lewis and Clark's Northwestern Expedition

1807 Robert Fulton's steamboat successfully tested

1812 1815 War with England

1823 Monroe Doctrine

1825 Erie Canal opened

1828 First steam locomotive

1834 McCormick's mechanical reaper

1783 Washington Irving 1859

1789 James Fenimore Cooper 1851

1794 William Cullen Bryant 1878

1809 Edgar Allan Poe 1849

1809 Washington Irving, "Knickerbocker's History of New York"

1815 "North American Review" founded

1817 William Cullen Bryant, "Thanatopsis"

1819 1820 Washington Irving, "The Sketch Book"

1821 "Saturday Evening Post" founded

1823 James Fenimore Cooper, "The Pioneers," first Leatherstocking tale

1827 Edgar Allan Poe, "Tamerlane and Other Poems"

1828 Noah Webster, "An American Dictionary of the English Language"

1780   '90   1800   '10   '20   '30   '40   '50   '60   '70   '80   1890

qualities that were special to that nation. In America, as you have seen, Bryant and Cooper described the special beauty of the American landscape. Furthermore, Cooper created the first great American fictional character in Natty Bumppo (page 93). Even Irving, who sometimes tried to be more English than the English, warned English writers not to be contemptuous of the new nation, which would yet produce a great culture. Only Poe was indifferent to the claims of nationalism, arguing that all true art is universal in its significance.

A NATIONAL LITERATURE

Yet Poe, as much as the other writers, helped establish a national literature, not by being a fervid nationalist nor by creating a theory of American literature, but by writing important literary works. The four writers whom you are about to read established a basis for American literature simply and essentially by being good writers, writers whom European readers could respect and in whom Americans could feel a sense of pride and accomplishment. They made a solid beginning for the new nation.

This illustration for "Rip Van Winkle" appeared in *The Sketch Book of Geoffrey Crayon, Gent.* (1848) by Washington Irving, one of the first American men of letters.

JAMES
FENIMORE
COOPER
(1789–1851)

James Fenimore Cooper has given America one of its great heroes, the frontiersman Natty Bumppo who is also known as Deerslayer, Hawkeye, and Leatherstocking. Bumppo, skilled as a woodsman and deadly with a rifle, is a naturally good man, and in his simple innocence he achieves an almost profound nobility. American literature owes him a great deal. He is the grandfather of most cowboy heroes. He is also a distant ancestor of various fictional Americans who arrive from the West to confront sophisticated Easterners or, during a European tour, amaze everyone they meet because they are so fresh and straightforward—in a word, so American! Although Cooper's reputation rests primarily on his creation of Natty Bumppo, he would probably have an honored place in American literature even if he had not written the Leatherstocking Tales. He is our first serious novelist. At a time when Europeans were questioning whether the new nation could develop a significant culture, Cooper, like Irving, showed that an American, writing on American subjects, could be read and admired in England and on the continent.

Expelled from Yale University in 1806 for his pranks, Cooper spent the next two years as a sailor on a merchant vessel; then in 1808, he entered the navy as a midshipman. Later he drew on his experience of the sea to write novels such as *The Pilot* and *The Red Rover*. In 1811, after the death of his father, who was a judge and important landowner in upper New York, Cooper resigned from the navy, married, and settled down to manage his estates and fortune. His first novel, *Precaution,* was written nine years later, as the result of a bet with his wife that he could write a better novel than the one he was reading. It is doubtful that he deserved to win the bet, since *Precaution* is a poor imitation of the kind of English novel that deals with country estates and drawing rooms. It met with little success. Cooper's next novel, *The Spy,* takes place in New York during the Revolutionary War. A far better work than its predecessor, it sold eight thousand copies in four months and established Cooper as a writer of importance. *The Pioneers,* his third novel, is the first of the Leatherstocking Tales. In all Cooper wrote five Leatherstocking Tales—*The Pioneers, The Last of the Mohicans, The Prairie, The Pathfinder, The Deerslayer*—taking Natty Bumppo from his early manhood to his death in a Pawnee village. Although the Leatherstocking Tales have artificial plots and some unconvincing characters, they also have some memorable characters such as Bumppo and his Indian friends, Chingachgook, Uncas, and Hard-Heart, and brilliantly evocative descriptions of the American wilderness. For all their crudities, they are a remarkable achievement, the celebration of a hero who combined the simplicity of the Indian way of life with the moral idealism of his colonial forbears. As a character in *The Prairie* says of Bumppo, "Unlike most of those who lead a border life, he united the better, instead of the worst, qualities of the two people. He was a man endowed with the choicest and perhaps rarest gift of nature; that of distinguishing good from evil."

In 1826, Cooper made a visit to Europe that was to last seven years. When he returned to America, he was keenly aware that the cultivation and refinement he had found in European society were largely absent from his native land. Several years later he published two novels, *Homeward Bound* and *Home as Found,* and a collection of essays, *The American Democrat.* These works contained many sharp comments about the shortcomings of American society, and Cooper was criticized as a false friend of democracy who had "exhausted his powers of invective upon the manners and characters of his countrymen." In his later works he defended the rights of large landowners, who, he believed, would preserve American society from the mob's "vulgar domination." Although many of Cooper's social and political ideas may seem outdated, he posed a problem basic to democracy: reconciling the pursuit of excellence with the principle of majority rule.

Advantages of a Democracy

"Advantages of a Democracy" and "On the Disadvantages of a Democracy" are from *The American Democrat,* a work in which Cooper analyzes the American form of government and comments on its possible dangers. In his introduction Cooper states, "The writer believes himself to be as good a democrat as there is in America. . . . He prefers a democracy to any other system, on account of its comparative advantages, and not on account of its perfection. . . . It will be very apparent to all who read this book that he is not a believer in the scheme of raising men very far above their natural propensities."

THE PRINCIPAL advantage of a democracy is a general elevation in the character of the people. If few are raised to a very great height, few are depressed very low. As a consequence, the average of society is much more respectable than under any other form of government. The vulgar charge that the tendency of democracies is to levelling, meaning to drag all down to the level of the lowest, is singularly untrue, its real tendency being to elevate the depressed to a condition not unworthy of their manhood. In the absence of privileged orders, entails,[1] and distinctions, devised permanently to separate men into social castes, it is true none are great but those who become so by their acts, but, confining the remark to the upper classes of society, it would be much more true to say that democracy refuses to lend itself to unnatural and arbitrary distinctions, than to accuse it of a tendency to level those who have a just claim to be elevated. A denial of a favor is not an invasion of a right.

Democracies are exempt from the military charges, both pecuniary and personal, that become necessary in governments in which the majority are subjects, since no force is required to repress those who, under other systems, are dangerous to the state by their greater physical power.

As the success of democracies is mainly dependent on the intelligence of the peo-

[1] **entails:** restrictions on inheritance that prevent the splitting up of large estates.

ple, the means of preserving the government are precisely those which most conduce to the happiness and social progress of man. Hence we find the state endeavoring to raise its citizens in the scale of being, the certain means of laying the broadest foundation of national prosperity. If the arts are advanced in aristocracies through the taste of patrons, in democracies, though of slower growth, they will prosper as a consequence of general information; or as a superstructure reared on a wider and more solid foundation.

Democracies being, as nearly as possible, founded in natural justice, little violence is done to the sense of right by the institutions, and men have less occasion than usual to resort to fallacies and false principles in cultivating the faculties. As a consequence, common sense is more encouraged, and the community is apt to entertain juster notions of all moral truths than under systems that are necessarily sophisticated. Society is thus a gainer in the greatest element of happiness, or in the right perception of the different relations between men and things.

Democracies being established for the common interests, and the public agents being held in constant check by the people, their general tendency is to serve the whole community and not small portions of it, as is the case in narrow governments. It is as rational to suppose that a hungry man will first help his neighbor to bread,

The United States Capitol Building, Washington, D.C., as it appeared in about 1850.

when master of his own acts, as to suppose that any but those who feel themselves to be truly public servants will first bethink themselves of the public when in situations of public trust. In a government of one, that one and his parasites will be the first and best served; in a government of a few, the few; and in a government of many, the many. Thus the general tendency of democratical institutions is to equalize advantages and to spread their blessings over the entire surface of society.

Democracies, other things being equal, are the cheapest form of government, since little money is lavished in representation, and they who have to pay the taxes have also, directly or indirectly, a voice in imposing them.

Democracies are less liable to popular tumults [1] than any other polities, because the people, having legal means in their power to redress wrongs, have little inducement to employ any other. The man who can right himself by a vote will seldom resort to a musket. Grievances, moreover, are less frequent, the most corrupt representatives of a democratic constituency generally standing in awe of its censure.

As men in bodies usually defer to the right, unless acting under erroneous impressions, or excited by sudden resentments, democracies pay more respect to abstract justice in the management of their foreign concerns than either aristocracies or monarchies, an appeal always lying against abuses, or violations of principle, to a popular sentiment that, in the end, seldom fails to decide in favor of truth.

In democracies, with a due allowance for the workings of personal selfishness, it is usually a motive with those in places of trust to consult the interests of the mass, there being little doubt that in this system the entire community has more regard paid to its wants and wishes than in either of the two others.

[1] **tumults:** here, riots or uprisings.

On the Disadvantages of a Democracy

DEMOCRACIES ARE liable to popular impulses, which, necessarily arising from imperfect information, often work injustice from good motives. Tumults of the people are less apt to occur in democracies than under any other form of government, for, possessing the legal means of redressing themselves, there is less necessity to resort to force, but, public opinion constituting, virtually, the power of the state, measures are more apt to be influenced by sudden mutations [1] of sentiment than under systems where the rulers have better opportunities and more leisure for examination. There is more feeling and less design in the movements of masses than in those of small bodies, except as design emanates from demagogues and political managers.

The efforts of the masses that are struggling to obtain their rights in monarchies and aristocracies, however, are not to be imputed to democracy; in such cases, the people use their natural weapon, force, merely because they are denied any participation in the legal authority.

When democracies are small, these impulses frequently do great injury to the public service, but in large states they are seldom of sufficient extent to produce results before there is time to feel the influence of reason. It is, therefore, one of the errors of politicians to imagine democracies more practicable in small than in large communities, an error that has probably arisen from the fact that, the ignorance of masses having hitherto put men at the mercy of the combinations of the affluent and intelligent, democracies have been permitted to exist only in countries insignificant by their wealth and numbers.

Large democracies, on the other hand, while less exposed to the principal evil of this form of government than smaller, are unable to scrutinize and understand character with the severity and intelligence that are of so much importance in all representative governments, and consequently the people are peculiarly [2] exposed to become the dupes of demagogues and political schemers, most of the crimes of democracies arising from the faults and designs of men of this character, rather than from the propensities of the people, who, having little temptation to do wrong, are seldom guilty of crimes except through ignorance.

Democracies are necessarily controlled by public opinion, and failing of the means of obtaining power more honestly, the fraudulent and ambitious find a motive to mislead and even to corrupt the common sentiment to attain their ends. This is the greatest and most pervading danger of all large democracies, since it is sapping the foundations of society by undermining its virtue. We see the effects of this baneful influence in the openness and audacity with which men avow improper motives and improper acts, trusting to find support in a popular feeling, for while vicious influences are perhaps more admitted in other countries than in America, in none are they so openly avowed.

It may also be urged against democracies that, nothing being more corrupting than the management of human affairs, which are constantly demanding sacrifices of permanent principles to interests that are as constantly fluctuating, their people are exposed to assaults on their morals from this quarter that the masses of other nations escape. It is probable, however, that this evil, while it ought properly to be enumerated as one of the disadvantages of the system, is more than counterbalanced by the main results, even on the score of morals.

[1] **mutations:** here, changes.

[2] **peculiarly:** here, particularly.

In this contemporary drawing a Pennsylvania regiment waits to vote in the election of 1864.

The constant appeals to public opinion in a democracy, though excellent as a corrective of public vices, induce private hypocrisy, causing men to conceal their own convictions when opposed to those of the mass, the latter being seldom wholly right, or wholly wrong. A want of national manliness is a vice to be guarded against, for the man who would dare to resist a monarch shrinks from opposing an entire community. That the latter is quite often wrong, however, is abundantly proved by the fact that its own judgments fluctuate, as it reasons and thinks differently this year or this month even from what it reasoned and thought the last.

The tendency of democracies is, in all things, to mediocrity, since the tastes, knowledge, and principles of the majority form the tribunal of appeal. This circumstance, while it certainly serves to elevate the average qualities of a nation, renders the introduction of a high standard difficult. Thus do we find in literature, the arts, architecture, and in all acquired knowledge, a tendency in America to gravitate towards the common center in this, as in other things; lending a value and estimation to mediocrity that are not elsewhere given. It is fair to expect, however, that a foundation so broad may in time sustain a superstructure of commensurate proportions, and that the influence of masses will in this, as in the other

interests, have a generally beneficial effect. Still it should not be forgotten that, with the exception of those works, of which, as they appeal to human sympathies or the practices of men, an intelligent public is the best judge, the mass of no community is qualified to decide the most correctly on anything which, in its nature, is above its reach.

It is a besetting vice of democracies to substitute public opinion for law. This is the usual form in which masses of men exhibit their tyranny. When the majority of the entire community commits this fault it is a sore grievance, but when local bodies, influenced by local interests, pretend to style themselves the public, they are assuming powers that properly belong to the whole body of the people, and to them only under constitutional limitations. No tyranny of one, nor any tyranny of the few, is worse than this. All attempts in the public, therefore, to do that which the public has no right to do should be frowned upon as the precise form in which tyranny is the most apt to be displayed in a democracy.

Democracies, depending so much on popular opinion, are more liable to be influenced to their injury through the management of foreign and hostile nations than other governments. It is generally known that in Europe secret means are resorted to, to influence sentiment in this way, and we have witnessed in this country open appeals to the people against the acts of their servants, in matters of foreign relations made by foreign, not to say hostile, agents. Perhaps no stronger case can be cited of this weakness on the part of democracies than is shown in this fact, for here we find men sufficiently audacious to build the hope of so far abusing opinion as to persuade a people to act directly against their own dignity and interests.

The misleading of public opinion in one way or another is the parent of the principal disadvantages of a democracy, for in most instances it is first corrupting a community in order that it may be otherwise injured. Were it not for the counteracting influence of reason, which, in the end, seldom, perhaps never, fails to assert its power, this defect would of itself be sufficient to induce all discreet men to decide against this form of government. The greater the danger, the greater the necessity that all well-intentioned and right-minded citizens should be on their guard against its influence.

It would be hazardous, however, to impute all the peculiar faults of American character to the institutions, the country existing under so many unusual influences. If the latter were overlooked, one might be induced to think frankness and sincerity of character were less encouraged by popular institutions than was formerly supposed, close observers affirming that these qualities are less frequent here than in most other countries. When the general ease of society is remembered, there is unquestionably more deception of opinion practiced than one would naturally expect, but this failing is properly to be imputed to causes that have no necessary connection with democratical institutions, though men defer to public opinion, right or wrong, quite as submissively as they defer to princes. Although truths are not smothered altogether in democracies, they are often temporarily abandoned under this malign influence, unless there is a powerful motive to sustain them at the

moment. While we see in our own democracy this manifest disposition to defer to the wrong in matters that are not properly subject to the common sentiment, in deference to the popular will of the hour, there is a singular boldness in the use of personalities, as if men avenged themselves for the restraints of the one case by a licentiousness that is without hazard.

The base feelings of detraction and envy have more room for exhibition and perhaps a stronger incentive in a democracy than in other forms of government, in which the people get accustomed to personal deference by the artificial distinctions of the institutions. This is the reason that men become impatient of all superiority in a democracy and manifest a wish to prefer those who affect a deference to the public rather than those who are worthy.

FOR STUDY AND DISCUSSION

1. To what two kinds of government does Cooper compare a democracy? Find six advantages that Cooper thinks a democracy has over other kinds of government. In your opinion, which of these advantages exist today?

2. What, in Cooper's opinion, is the relationship of public opinion to the defects of a democracy? Do you agree or disagree? Why?

3. Explain Cooper's statement, "The tendency of democracies is, in all things, to mediocrity." Do you think Cooper would make such a statement today? Why or why not?

4. Why, according to Cooper, might a democracy manage its foreign affairs poorly?

5. Do you think that a person reading Cooper's two essays and having no other knowledge of the democratic form of government would conclude that, between a democracy and other forms of government, there is little to choose? Give reasons for your answer.

FOR COMPOSITION

Write a composition in which you discuss what changes Cooper might make in these two essays if he were rewriting them today. Include in your essay specific references to passages in the selections.

WASHINGTON
IRVING
(1783–1859)

In 1820, when James Fenimore Cooper's first, imitative novel appeared, a group of stories and essays called *The Sketch Book of Geoffrey Crayon, Gent.* was being issued in the United States as a series of booklets and, almost immediately afterwards, was published in Great Britain. The English liked it, and it was highly praised in periodicals such as the *Quarterly Review,* where American authors were usually condemned or dismissed. Thus three years before Cooper gained a literary reputation with *The Spy,* Washington Irving was winning an English audience and answering the contemptuous question posed by an English wit: "In the four quarters of the globe, who reads an American book?" Irving won his English readers by appearing to be almost as English as they. Most of the selections in *The Sketch Book* are about aspects of English life. Yet the two selections that are widely read today, "Rip Van Winkle" and "The Legend of Sleepy Hollow," depict American places and types, the quiet villages and rich farms of the Hudson Valley, the stiff New England schoolmaster, and the affable and sometimes lazy Dutch farmers.

As a writer, Irving aimed primarily to amuse and entertain with a quiet essay, an odd tale, or an outrageous piece of humor. He wished to be known not simply as a man of letters but as a gentleman, and much of his work reads like the conversation of a widely read, much traveled man of leisure. Thackeray, the nineteenth-century English novelist, described Irving in his later years as "a delightful example of complete gentlemanhood." Yet Irving was born to a New York businessman's family at a time when business was considered not quite the proper pursuit of a gentleman, and he spent part of his life trying to reconcile his literary ambitions with the need to earn a living.

At the age of nineteen, Irving studied law and also contributed essays to the New York *Morning Chronicle* under the name "Jonathan Oldstyle." After a tour of Europe, he settled down to devote to the practice of law what time he could spare from writing *A History of New York . . . by Diedrich Knickerbocker,* published in 1809. Supposedly written by an eccentric historian, the *History* is an immensely complicated and funny work that pokes fun at history books, the old Dutch families of New York, and President Jefferson. Irving spent the next few years working in the family firm and editing a Philadelphia magazine. In 1815, he went to England to manage a branch of the firm. Three years later, when the firm went bankrupt, he decided to make his living by writing. The books that followed *The Sketch Book*—*Bracebridge Hall, The Alhambra,* and *Tales of a Traveler*—were almost as popular as his first great success. Irving traveled throughout Europe, making important literary and social friendships everywhere and devoting some time to a study of German literature. Highly regarded as a public figure, in 1841 he was appointed minister to Spain. Among his final works were books on the American West and a long biography of George Washington. Before his death, his stories and essays were already being studied in classrooms as models of good writing.

The Devil and Tom Walker

A FEW MILES from Boston in Massachusetts, there is a deep inlet, winding several miles into the interior of the country from Charles Bay and terminating in a thickly wooded swamp or morass. On one side of this inlet is a beautiful dark grove; on the opposite side the land rises abruptly from the water's edge into a high ridge, on which grow a few scattered oaks of great age and immense size. Under one of these gigantic trees, according to old stories, there was a great amount of treasure buried by Kidd the pirate. The inlet allowed a facility to bring the money in a boat secretly and at night to the very foot of the hill; the elevation of the place permitted a good lookout to be kept that no one was at hand; while the remarkable trees formed good landmarks by which the place might easily be found again. The old stories add, moreover, that the Devil presided at the hiding of the money and took it under his guardianship; but this, it is well known, he always does with buried treasure, particularly when it has been ill-gotten. Be that as it may, Kidd never returned to recover his wealth; being shortly after seized at Boston, sent out to England, and there hanged for a pirate.

About the year 1727, just at the time that earthquakes were prevalent in New England and shook many tall sinners down upon their knees, there lived near this place a meager, miserly fellow, of the name of Tom Walker. He had a wife as miserly as himself: they were so miserly that they even conspired to cheat each other. Whatever the woman could lay hands on she hid away; a hen could not cackle but she was on the alert to secure the new-laid egg. Her husband was continually prying about to detect her secret hoards, and many and fierce were the conflicts that took place about what ought to have been common property. They lived in a forlorn-looking house that stood alone and had an air of starvation. A few straggling savin [1] trees, emblems of sterility, grew near it; no smoke ever curled from its chimney; no traveler stopped at its door. A miserable horse, whose ribs were as articulate as the bars of a gridiron, stalked about a field where a thin carpet of moss, scarcely covering the ragged beds of pudding stone, tantalized and balked his hunger; and sometimes he would lean his head over the fence, look piteously at the passer-by, and seem to petition deliverance from this land of famine.

The house and its inmates had altogether a bad name. Tom's wife was a tall termagant, fierce of temper, loud of tongue, and strong of arm. Her voice was often heard in wordy warfare with her husband; and his face sometimes showed signs that their conflicts were not confined to words. No one ventured, however, to interfere

---

[1] savin (sav'in): a North American juniper or red cedar.

between them. The lonely wayfarer shrunk within himself at the horrid clamor and clapperclawing,[1] eyed the den of discord askance, and hurried on his way, rejoicing, if a bachelor, in his celibacy.

One day that Tom Walker had been to a distant part of the neighborhood, he took what he considered a short cut homeward, through the swamp. Like most short cuts, it was an ill-chosen route. The swamp was thickly grown with great gloomy pines and hemlocks, some of them ninety feet high, which made it dark at noonday, and a retreat for all the owls of the neighborhood. It was full of pits and quagmires, partly covered with weeds and mosses, where the green surface often betrayed the traveler into a gulf of black, smothering mud; there were also dark and stagnant pools, the abodes of the tadpole, the bullfrog, and the water snake, where the trunks of pines and hemlocks lay half drowned, half rotting, looking like alligators sleeping in the mire.

Tom had long been picking his way cautiously through this treacherous forest; stepping from tuft to tuft of rushes and roots, which afforded precarious footholds among deep sloughs; or pacing carefully, like a cat, along the prostrate trunks of trees; startled now and then by the sudden screaming of the bittern, or the quacking of a wild duck rising on the wing from some solitary pool. At length he arrived at a firm piece of ground, which ran out like a peninsula into the deep bosom of the swamp. It had been one of the strongholds of the Indians during their wars with the first colonists. Here they had thrown up a kind of fort, which they had looked upon as almost impregnable and had used as a place of refuge for their squaws and children. Nothing remained of the old Indian fort but a few embankments, gradually sinking to the level of the surrounding earth, and already overgrown in part by oaks and other forest trees, the foliage of which formed a contrast to the dark pines and hemlocks of the swamp.

It was late in the dusk of evening when Tom Walker reached the old fort, and he paused there awhile to rest himself. Anyone but he would have felt unwilling to linger in this lonely, melancholy place, for the common people had a bad opinion of it from the stories handed down from the time of the Indian wars, when it was asserted that the savages held incantations here and made sacrifices to the evil spirit.

Tom Walker, however, was not a man to be troubled with any fears of the kind. He reposed himself for some time on the trunk of a fallen hemlock, listening to the boding cry of the tree toad and delving with his walking staff into a mound of black mold at his feet. As he turned up the soil unconsciously, his staff struck against something hard. He raked it out of the vegetable mold and lo! a cloven skull, with an Indian tomahawk buried deep in it, lay before him. The rust on the weapon showed the time that had elapsed since this deathblow had been given. It was a dreary memento of the fierce struggle that had taken place in this last foothold of the Indian warriors.

[1] **clapperclawing** (klap′ər·klô′ing): clawing.

"Humph!" said Tom Walker, as he gave it a kick to shake the dirt from it.

"Let that skull alone!" said a gruff voice. Tom lifted up his eyes and beheld a great black man seated directly opposite him, on the stump of a tree. He was exceedingly surprised, having neither heard nor seen anyone approach; and he was still more perplexed on observing, as well as the gathering gloom would permit, that the stranger was neither Negro nor Indian. It is true he was dressed in a rude half-Indian garb and had a red belt or sash swathed round his body; but his face was neither black nor copper color, but swarthy and dingy, and begrimed with soot, as if he had been accustomed to toil among fires and forges. He had a shock of coarse black hair that stood out from his head in all directions, and bore an ax on his shoulder.

He scowled for a moment at Tom with a pair of great red eyes.

"What are you doing on my grounds?" said the black man, with a hoarse, growling voice.

"Your grounds!" said Tom, with a sneer, "No more your grounds than mine; they belong to Deacon Peabody."

"Deacon Peabody be d——d," said the stranger, "as I flatter myself he will be, if he does not look more to his own sins and less to those of his neighbors. Look yonder, and see how Deacon Peabody is faring."

Tom looked in the direction that the stranger pointed and beheld one of the great trees, fair and flourishing without, but rotten at the core, and saw that it had been nearly hewn through, so that the first high wind was likely to blow it down. On the bark of the tree was scored the name of Deacon Peabody, an eminent man, who had waxed wealthy by driving shrewd bargains with the Indians. He now looked around, and found most of the tall trees marked with the name of some great man of the colony, and all more or less scored by the ax. The one on which he had been seated, and which had evidently just been hewn down, bore the name of Crown-

inshield; and he recollected a mighty rich man of that name, who made a vulgar display of wealth, which it was whispered he had acquired by buccaneering.

"He's just ready for burning!" said the black man, with a growl of triumph. "You see, I am likely to have a good stock of firewood for winter."

"But what right have you," said Tom, "to cut down Deacon Peabody's timber?"

"The right of a prior claim," said the other. "This woodland belonged to me long before one of your white-faced race put foot upon the soil."

"And pray, who are you, if I may be so bold?" said Tom.

"Oh, I go by various names. I am the wild huntsman in some countries; the black miner in others. In this neighborhood I am known by the name of the black woodsman. I am he to whom the red men consecrated this spot, and in honor of whom they now and then roasted a white man, by way of sweet-smelling sacrifice. Since the red men have been exterminated by you white savages, I amuse myself by presiding at the persecutions of Quakers and Anabaptists;[1] I am the great patron and prompter of slave dealers, and the grand master of the Salem witches."

"The upshot of all which is that, if I mistake not," said Tom, sturdily, "you are he commonly called Old Scratch."

"The same, at your service!" replied the black man, with a half-civil nod.

Such was the opening of this interview, according to the old story; though it has almost too familiar an air to be credited. One would think that to meet with such a singular personage, in this wild, lonely place, would have shaken any man's nerves; but Tom was a hard-minded fellow, not easily daunted, and he had lived so long with a termagant wife that he did not even fear the Devil.

[1] **Quakers and Anabaptists:** The Quakers were persecuted in England because of their pacifism and their refusal to take oaths. The Anabaptists, a religious sect that arose in Switzerland in 1523, were subject to persecution because of their opposition to infant baptism.

It is said that after this commencement they had a long and earnest conversation together, as Tom returned homeward. The black man told him of great sums of money buried by Kidd the pirate, under the oak trees on the high ridge, not far from the morass. All these were under his command and protected by his power, so that none could find them but such as propitiated his favor. These he offered to place within Tom Walker's reach, having conceived an especial kindness for him; but they were to be had only on certain conditions. What these conditions were may be easily surmised, though Tom never disclosed them publicly. They must have been very hard, for he required time to think of them, and he was not a man to stick at trifles when money was in view. When they had reached the edge of the swamp, the stranger paused. "What proof have I that all you have been telling me is true?" said Tom. "There's my signature," said the black man, pressing his finger on Tom's forehead. So saying, he turned off among the thickets of the swamp and seemed, as Tom said, to go down, down, down, into the earth, until nothing but his head and shoulders could be seen, and so on, until he totally disappeared.

When Tom reached home, he found the black print of a finger burnt, as it were, into his forehead, which nothing could obliterate. The first news his wife had to tell him was the sudden death of Absalom Crowninshield, the rich buccaneer. It was announced in the papers with the usual flourish that "a great man had fallen in Israel."

Tom recollected the tree which his black friend had just hewn down and which was ready for burning. "Let the freebooter roast," said Tom; "who cares!" He now felt convinced that all he had heard and seen was no illusion.

He was not prone to let his wife into his confidence; but as this was an uneasy secret, he willingly shared it with her. All her avarice was awakened at the mention of hidden gold, and she urged her husband to comply with the black man's terms and

The Profession of Literature

To create a national literature, America had to develop professional men of letters. In the eighteenth century, America's notable writers were principally men like Benjamin Franklin, who regarded writing as merely one of many pursuits. But in the nineteenth century, a different kind of writer appeared: the professional who made the composition of literary works his chief occupation. In order for the professional writer to exist in America, he needed outlets that not only would publish his work but pay him for it. As the country prospered, such outlets ultimately developed.

Book publishers. A number of publishing companies were founded. Those begun by J. and J. Harper, Daniel Appleton, and George Putnam survive to this day.

Annuals. Gift books published once a year, including *The Token, Friendships Offering,* and *The Atlantic Souvenir,* printed stories, poems, and essays.

Magazines and newspapers. Magazines, including *Knickerbocker* and *Graham's,* paid modest fees to authors for their work. Newspapers also paid small sums for fiction and poetry.

Despite the growing number of outlets for their work, life for professional writers was not easy. Edgar Allan Poe was sometimes desperate for lack of funds. Later, Hawthorne and Melville had to turn to nonliterary jobs to survive. As late as 1851, one writer could lament, "Alas! . . . is it not sad that an American author cannot live by magazine writing?"

secure what would make them wealthy for life. However Tom might have felt disposed to sell himself to the Devil, he was determined not to do so to oblige his wife; so he flatly refused, out of the mere spirit of contradiction. Many and bitter were the quarrels they had on the subject; but the more she talked, the more resolute was Tom not to be damned to please her.

At length she determined to drive the bargain on her own account and, if she succeeded, to keep all the gain to herself. Being of the same fearless temper as her husband, she set off for the old Indian fort toward the close of a summer's day. She was many hours absent. When she came back, she was reserved and sullen in her replies. She spoke something of a black man whom she had met about twilight hewing at the root of a tall tree. He was sulky, however, and would not come to terms; she was to go again with a propitiatory offering, but what it was she forbore to say.

The next evening she set off for the swamp, with her apron heavily laden. Tom waited and waited for her, but in vain; midnight came, but she did not make her appearance: morning, noon, night returned, but still she did not come. Tom now grew uneasy for her safety, especially as he found she had carried off in her apron the silver teapot and spoons, and every portable article of value. Another night elapsed, another morning came, but no wife. In a word, she was never heard of more.

What was her real fate nobody knows, in consequence of so many pretending to know. It is one of those facts which have become confounded by a variety of historians. Some asserted that she lost her way among the tangled mazes of the swamp and sank into some pit or slough; others, more uncharitable, hinted that she had eloped with the household booty and made off to some other province; while others surmised that the tempter had decoyed her into a dismal quagmire, on the top of which her hat was found lying.

In confirmation of this, it was said a great black man, with an ax on his shoulder, was seen late that very evening coming out of the swamp, carrying a bundle tied in a checked apron, with an air of surly triumph.

The most current and probable story, however, observes that Tom Walker grew so anxious about the fate of his wife and his property that he set out at length to seek them both at the Indian fort. During a long summer's afternoon he searched about the gloomy place, but no wife was to be seen. He called her name repeatedly, but she was nowhere to be heard. The bittern alone responded to his voice, as he flew screaming by; or the bullfrog croaked dolefully from a neighboring pool. At length, it is said, just in the brown hour of twilight, when the owls began to hoot, and the bats to flit about, his attention was attracted by the clamor of carrion crows hovering about a cypress tree. He looked up and beheld a bundle tied in a checked apron and hanging in the branches of the tree, with a great vulture perched hard by, as if keeping watch upon it. He leaped with joy; for he recognized his wife's apron and supposed it to contain the household valuables.

"Let us get hold of the property," said he consolingly to himself, "and we will endeavor to do without the woman."

As he scrambled up the tree, the vulture spread its wide wings and sailed off, screaming, into the deep shadows of the forest. Tom seized the checked apron, but woeful sight! found nothing but a heart and liver tied up in it!

Such, according to this most authentic old story, was all that was to be found of Tom's wife. She had probably attempted to deal with the black man as she had been accustomed to deal with her husband; but though a female scold is generally considered a match for the Devil, yet in this instance she appears to have had the worst of it. She must have died game, however; for it is said Tom noticed many prints of cloven feet deeply stamped about the tree, and found handfuls of hair that looked as if they had been plucked from the coarse black shock of the woodsman. Tom knew his wife's prowess by experience. He shrugged his shoulders as he looked at the signs of a fierce clapper-clawing. "Egad," said he to himself, "Old Scratch must have had a tough time of it!"

Tom consoled himself for the loss of his property with the loss of his wife, for he was a man of fortitude. He even felt something like gratitude toward the black woodsman, who, he considered, had done him a kindness. He sought, therefore, to cultivate a further acquaintance with him, but for some time without success; the old blacklegs played shy, for, whatever people may think, he is not always to be had for calling for; he knows how to play his cards when pretty sure of his game.

At length, it is said, when delay had whetted Tom's eagerness to the quick and prepared him to agree to anything rather than not gain the promised treasure, he met the black man one evening in his usual woodsman's dress, with his ax on his shoulder, sauntering along the swamp and humming a tune. He affected to receive Tom's advances with great indifference, made brief replies, and went on humming his tune.

By degrees, however, Tom brought him to business, and they began to haggle about the terms on which the former was to have the pirate's treasure. There was one condition which need not be mentioned, being generally understood in all cases where the Devil grants favors; but there were others about which, though of less importance, he was inflexibly obstinate. He insisted that the money found through his means should be employed in his service. He proposed, therefore, that Tom should employ it in the black traffic; that is to say, that he should fit out a slave ship. This, however, Tom resolutely refused; he was bad enough in all conscience; but the Devil himself could not tempt him to turn slave trader.

Finding Tom so squeamish on this point, he did not insist upon it, but proposed, instead, that he should turn usurer; the Devil being extremely anxious for the increase of usurers, looking upon them as his peculiar [1] people.

To this no objections were made, for it was just to Tom's taste.

"You shall open a broker's shop in Boston next month," said the black man.

"I'll do it tomorrow, if you wish," said Tom Walker.

"You shall lend money at two percent a month."

"Egad, I'll charge four!" replied Tom Walker.

"You shall extort bonds, foreclose mortgages, drive the merchants to bankruptcy——"

"I'll drive them to the devil," cried Tom Walker.

"You are the usurer for my money!" said blacklegs with delight. "When will you want rhino?" [2]

"This very night."

"Done!" said the Devil.

"Done!" said Tom Walker.

So they shook hands and struck a bargain.

A few days' time saw Tom Walker seated behind his desk in a counting house in Boston.

His reputation for a ready-moneyed man, who would lend money out for a good consideration, soon spread abroad. Everybody remembers the time of Governor Belcher,[3] when money was particularly scarce. It was a time of paper credit. The country had been deluged with government bills; the famous Land Bank [4] had been established; there had been a rage for speculating; the people had run mad with schemes for new settlements, for building cities in the wilderness; land jobbers went about with maps of grants, and townships,

---

[1] **peculiar:** here, special or particular.

[2] **rhino:** slang for money.

[3] **Belcher:** Jonathan Belcher was governor of Massachusetts from 1730 to 1741.

[4] **Land Bank:** a loan system by which the province advanced money on mortgages on land.

and El Dorados [1] lying nobody knew where, but which everybody was ready to purchase. In a word, the great speculating fever which breaks out every now and then in the country had raged to an alarming degree, and everybody was dreaming of making sudden fortunes from nothing. As usual the fever had subsided; the dream had gone off, and the imaginary fortunes with it; the patients were left in doleful plight, and the whole country resounded with the consequent cry of "hard times."

At this propitious time of public distress did Tom Walker set up as usurer in Boston. His door was soon thronged by customers. The needy and adventurous, the gambling speculator, the dreaming land jobber, the thriftless tradesman, the merchant with cracked credit, in short, everyone driven to raise money by desperate means and desperate sacrifices hurried to Tom Walker.

Thus Tom was the universal friend of the needy and acted like a "friend in need"; that is to say, he always exacted

good pay and good security. In proportion to the distress of the applicant was the highness of his terms. He accumulated bonds and mortgages, gradually squeezed his customers closer and closer, and sent them at length, dry as a sponge, from his door.

In this way he made money hand over hand, became a rich and mighty man, and exalted his cocked hat upon 'Change.[2] He built himself, as usual, a vast house, out of ostentation; but left the greater part of it unfinished and unfurnished, out of parsimony. He even set up a carriage in the fullness of his vainglory, though he nearly starved the horses which drew it; and as the ungreased wheels groaned and screeched on the axletrees, you would have thought you heard the souls of the poor debtors he was squeezing.

As Tom waxed old, however, he grew thoughtful. Having secured the good things of this world, he began to feel anxious about those of the next. He thought with regret on the bargain he had made with his black friend and set his wits to work to cheat him out of the conditions. He became, therefore, all of a sudden, a violent churchgoer. He prayed loudly and strenuously, as if heaven were to be taken by force of lungs. Indeed, one might always tell when he had sinned most during the week, by the clamor of his Sunday devotion. The quiet Christians who had been modestly and steadfastly traveling Zionward were struck with self-reproach at seeing themselves so suddenly outstripped in their career by this new-made convert. Tom was as rigid in religious as in money matters; he was a stern supervisor and censurer of his neighbors, and seemed to think every sin entered up to their account became a credit on his own side of the page. He even talked of the expediency of reviving the persecution of Quakers and Anabaptists. In a word, Tom's zeal became as notorious as his riches.

---

[1] **El Dorados** (dǝ·rä′dōz): literally, "the golden" (Spanish); hence, places of fabulous riches.

[2] **'Change:** Exchange, the place where merchants, brokers, and bankers meet to do business.

Still, in spite of all this strenuous attention to forms, Tom had a lurking dread that the Devil, after all, would have his due. That he might not be taken unawares, therefore, it is said he always carried a small Bible in his coat pocket. He had also a great folio Bible on his counting house desk and would frequently be found reading it when people called on business; on such occasions he would lay his green spectacles in the book, to mark the place, while he turned round to drive some usurious bargain.

Some say that Tom grew a little crack-brained in his old days, and that, fancying his end approaching, he had his horse new shod, saddled and bridled, and buried with his feet uppermost; because he supposed that at the last day the world would be turned upside down; in which case he should find his horse standing ready for mounting, and he was determined at the worst to give his old friend a run for it. This, however, is probably a mere old wives' fable. If he really did take such a precaution, it was totally superfluous; at least so says the authentic old legend, which closes this story in the following manner.

One hot summer afternoon in the dog days, just as a terrible black thunder-gust was coming up, Tom sat in his counting house, in his white linen cap and India silk morning gown. He was on the point of foreclosing a mortgage, by which he would complete the ruin of an unlucky land speculator for whom he had professed the greatest friendship. The poor land jobber begged him to grant a few months' indulgence. Tom had grown testy and irritated, and refused another day.

"My family will be ruined and brought upon the parish," said the land jobber.

"Charity begins at home," replied Tom; "I must take care of myself in these hard times."

"You have made so much money out of me," said the speculator.

Tom lost his patience and his piety. "The devil take me," said he, "if I have made a farthing!"

Just then there were three loud knocks at the street door. He stepped out to see who was there. A black man was holding a black horse, which neighed and stamped with impatience. "Tom, you're come for," said the black fellow, gruffly. Tom shrank back, but too late. He had left his little Bible at the bottom of his coat pocket, and his big Bible on the desk buried under the mortgage he was about to foreclose: never was sinner taken more unawares. The black man whisked him like a child into the saddle, gave the horse the lash, and away he galloped, with Tom on his back, in the midst of the thunderstorm. The clerks stuck their pens behind their ears and stared after him from the windows. Away went Tom Walker, dashing down the streets; his white cap bobbing up and down, his morning gown fluttering in the wind, and his steed striking fire out of the pavement at every bound. When the clerks turned to look for the black man, he had disappeared.

Tom Walker never returned to foreclose the mortgage. A countryman, who lived on the border of the swamp, reported that in the height of the thunder-gust he had heard a great clattering of hoofs and a howling along the road, and running to the window caught sight of a figure, such as I have described, on a horse that galloped like mad across the fields, over the hills, and down into the black hemlock

swamp toward the old Indian fort; and that shortly after, a thunderbolt falling in that direction seemed to set the whole forest in a blaze.

The good people of Boston shook their heads and shrugged their shoulders, but had been so much accustomed to witches and goblins, and tricks of the Devil in all kinds of shapes, from the first settlement of the colony, that they were not so much horror-struck as might have been expected. Trustees were appointed to take charge of Tom's effects. There was nothing, however, to administer upon. On searching his coffers, all his bonds and mortgages were found reduced to cinders. In place of gold and silver, his iron chest was filled with chips and shavings; two skeletons lay in his stable instead of his half-starved horses, and the very next day his great house took fire and was burnt to the ground.

Such was the end of Tom Walker and his ill-gotten wealth. Let all griping money brokers lay this story to heart. The truth of it is not to be doubted. The very hole under the oak trees, whence he dug Kidd's money, is to be seen to this day; and the neighboring swamp and old Indian fort are often haunted in stormy nights by a figure on horseback, in morning gown and white cap, which is doubtless the troubled spirit of the usurer. In fact, the story has resolved itself into a proverb, and is the origin of that popular saying, so prevalent throughout New England, of "The Devil and Tom Walker."

FOR STUDY AND DISCUSSION

1. In his book, *Tales of a Traveler,* Irving claims this tale was "found among the papers of the late Diedrich Knickerbocker," a character Irving invented and used as the imaginary author of *A History of New York,* "Rip Van Winkle," and "The Legend of Sleep Hollow." Irving describes Knickerbocker as an eccentric man interested in strange old tales and historical oddities. What details in "The Devil and Tom Walker" show that a person with these interests is narrating the story?

2. Find statements made by the narrator to indicate that the story is to be believed. Does it matter whether or not you believe it? Can you enjoy the story without believing in it? Explain. Do you think that Irving, as opposed to his imaginary narrator, meant the story to be believed? Find statements in the story that are meant to be taken with a grain of salt.

3. Give examples of Irving's humor by quoting directly from the story. What is funny about the excerpts you have quoted? To answer this question, you will have to make some basic comments about humor.

4. What colors are dominant in the story? Do these have any special significance? Explain your answer.

LANGUAGE AND VOCABULARY

In "The Devil and Tom Walker" there is an unusual word for money: *rhino*. It is interesting to note how many different English words for money there are. How many common English words for money can you think of? How many unusual words for this concept can you find? In the language of the Eskimo there are many different words for snow. What is the significance of the fact that there are few words for the idea of snow in English but many words for the idea of money? For what other ideas do we have a variety of words?

FOR COMPOSITION

1. Washington Irving makes use of a number of old sayings throughout "The Devil and Tom Walker." Sometimes he gives a direct illustration of a saying like "The devil would have his due." At other times a familiar saying is given an ironic twist (page 49). Write a composition in which you examine some of these sayings. Show whether Irving is illustrating these sayings or whether he is giving them an ironic twist. Conclude with a discussion of what these sayings contribute to the story.

2. Use an old saying as the basis of a composition. (Your parents and grandparents are probably a good source of old maxims and proverbs, or you may want to refer to Benjamin Franklin's collection of old sayings in *Poor Richard's Almanac.*) Tell about a situation or a character that illustrates your saying, or write a story in which the saying is given an ironic twist. Your story may be real or invented.

The Author's Account
of Himself

FROM *The Sketch Book
of Geoffrey Crayon, Gent.*

I WAS ALWAYS fond of visiting new scenes and observing strange characters and manners. Even when a mere child I began my travels and made many tours of discovery into foreign parts and unknown regions of my native city, to the frequent alarm of my parents and the emolument of the town crier.[1] As I grew into boyhood, I extended the range of my observations. My holiday afternoons were spent in rambles about the surrounding country. I made myself familiar with all its places famous in history or fable. I knew every spot where a murder or robbery had been committed, or a ghost seen. I visited the neighboring villages and added greatly to my stock of knowledge, by noting their habits and customs and conversing with their sages and great men. I even journeyed one long summer's day to the summit of the most distant hill, whence I stretched my eye over many a mile of terra incognita[2] and was astonished to find how vast a globe I inhabited.

This rambling propensity strengthened with my years. Books of voyages and travels became my passion, and, in devouring their contents, I neglected the regular exercises of the school. How wistfully would I wander about the pier-heads in fine weather and watch the parting ships, bound to distant climes—with what longing eyes would I gaze after their lessening sails and waft myself in imagination to the ends of the earth!

Further reading and thinking, though they brought this vague inclination into more reasonable bounds, only served to make it more decided. I visited various parts of my own country; and had I been merely a lover of fine scenery, I should have felt little desire to seek elsewhere its gratification, for on no country have the charms of nature been more prodigally lavished. Her mighty lakes, like oceans of liquid silver; her mountains, with their bright aerial tints; her valleys, teeming with wild fertility; her tremendous cataracts, thundering in their solitudes; her boundless plains, waving with spontaneous verdure; her broad deep rivers, rolling in solemn silence to the ocean; her trackless forests, where vegetation puts forth all its magnificence; her skies, kindling with the magic of summer clouds and glorious sunshine—no, never need an American look beyond his own country for the sublime and beautiful of natural scenery.

But Europe held forth the charms of storied and poetical association. There were to be seen the masterpieces of art, the refinements of highly cultivated society, the quaint peculiarities of ancient and local custom. My native country was full of youthful promise: Europe was rich in the accumulated treasures of age. Her very ruins told the history of times gone

The ruins of the Colosseum in Rome.

---

[1] **emolument . . . town crier:** The town crier earned fees by crying out the announcement in various districts of the city that a child answering to a certain description was lost.

[2] **terra incognita:** unknown territory.

by, and every moldering stone was a chronicle. I longed to wander over the scenes of renowned achievement—to tread, as it were, in the footsteps of antiquity—to loiter about the ruined castle —to meditate on the falling tower—to escape, in short, from the commonplace realities of the present and lose myself among the shadowy grandeurs of the past.

I had, beside all this, an earnest desire to see the great men of the earth. We have, it is true, our great men in America: not a city but has an ample share of them. I have mingled among them in my time and been almost withered by the shade into which they cast me; for there is nothing so baleful to a small man as the shade of a great one, particularly the great man of a city. But I was anxious to see the great men of Europe; for I had read in the works of various philosophers that all animals degenerated in America, and man among the number. A great man of Europe, thought I, must therefore be as superior to a great man of America, as a peak of the Alps to a highland of the Hudson; and in this idea I was confirmed by observing the comparative importance and swelling magnitude of many English travelers among us, who, I was assured, were very little people in their own country. I will visit this land of wonders, thought I, and see the gigantic race from which I am degenerated.

It has been either my good or evil lot to have my roving passion gratified. I have wandered through different countries and witnessed many of the shifting scenes of life. I cannot say that I have studied them with the eye of a philosopher, but rather with the sauntering gaze with which humble lovers of the picturesque stroll from the window of one print shop to another, caught sometimes by the delineations of beauty, sometimes by the distortions of caricature, and sometimes by the loveliness of landscape. As it is the fashion for modern tourists to travel pencil in hand, and bring home their portfolios filled with sketches, I am disposed to get up a few for the entertainment of my friends.

When, however, I look over the hints and memorandums I have taken down for the purpose, my heart almost fails me at finding how my idle humor has led me aside from the great objects studied by every regular traveler who would make a book. I fear I shall give equal disappointment with an unlucky landscape painter who had traveled on the continent but, following the bent of his vagrant inclination, had sketched in nooks, and corners, and by-places. His sketch book was accordingly crowded with cottages, and landscapes, and obscure ruins; but he had neglected to paint St. Peter's, or the Coliseum;[1] the cascade of Terni,[2] or the bay of Naples; and had not a single glacier or volcano in his whole collection.

[1] **St. Peter's . . . Coliseum:** The Church of St. Peter's and the Coliseum, in Rome, are famous architectural achievements.
[2] **cascade of Terni:** artificial waterfalls in Perugia, Italy.

FOR STUDY AND DISCUSSION

1. In what sense can the author of this essay be called one of the "humble lovers of the picturesque"? Why does he disclaim "the eye of a philosopher"? Why does he compare himself to "an unlucky landscape painter"? This essay is the introduction to *The Sketch Book,* a collection of essays and stories. Would you expect the selections that follow it to be concerned with great men and momentous events? Why or why not?

2. What differences does the author draw between the charms of America and Europe? Do these differences exist now? Did they exist in the first part of the nineteenth century? Explain.

3. Study the fifth paragraph of the selection. Is this paragraph to be taken at its face value or is it ironic? (See page 49.) Defend your answer. Consider especially the sentence, "A great man of Europe, thought I, must therefore be as superior to a great man of America, as a peak of the Alps to a highland of the Hudson; and in this idea I was confirmed by observing the comparative importance and swelling magnitude of many English travelers among us, who, I was assured, were very little people in their own country."

WILLIAM CULLEN BRYANT
(1794–1878)

There were American poets before Bryant who gained a national audience, most notably Philip Freneau, but it is Bryant who is most often called "the father of American poetry." With the exception of Edward Taylor, who was not discovered and read until the twentieth century, Bryant is the first American who produced a body of poetry that can be matched against the achievements of English poets. When Bryant's "Thanatopsis" was submitted to the *North American Review,* one of the editors protested to a fellow editor, "Ah, you have been imposed upon. No one on this side of the Atlantic is capable of writing such verse!" Matthew Arnold, the famous English poet and the most respected literary critic of his time, stated that Bryant's "To a Waterfowl" was the "most perfect brief poem in the language."

Born in Cummington, Massachusetts, Bryant, was the son of a country doctor. As a boy, Bryant roamed the countryside and became "a delighted observer of external nature—the splendors of a winter daybreak . . . the glories of autumnal woods . . . the return of spring, with its flowers." He began "Thanatopsis," his most famous poem, when he was only seventeen. Much of his best poetry was written when he was a young man living in Great Barrington, Massachusetts, and earning a slender living as a lawyer, poet, and book reviewer.

In 1825, at the age of thirty, Bryant left Massachusetts to follow a career of journalism in New York. Within a few years, he was editor and part-owner of the New York *Evening Post,* a partnership that eventually made him wealthy. A shy, retiring man, Bryant developed a formal, austere manner that led James Russell Lowell to write that he was "as quiet, as cool, and as dignified,/ As a smooth silent iceberg" (page 201). Yet he had moments of blazing temper. Once he horsewhipped the editor of a rival paper for publishing some insulting remarks about President Jackson. He threw himself into social causes, championing free speech, free trade, and the abolition of slavery. In 1860, when Abraham Lincoln made his famous Cooper Union speech, it was Bryant who presided at the meeting and introduced the Illinois politician to the New York public. During his busy career as an editor and public figure, Bryant wrote only a few fine poems, but the work of his youth had already established him as one of America's great poets. At the beginning of his New York career, he delivered four "Lectures on Poetry" that contain some of the best literary criticism of the time. Near the end of his life he translated the *Iliad* and the *Odyssey* into English blank verse.

To a Waterfowl

Whither, midst falling dew,
While glow the heavens with the last steps of day,
Far, through their rosy depths, dost thou pursue
   Thy solitary way?

Vainly the fowler's° eye   5
Might mark thy distant flight to do thee wrong,
As, darkly seen against the crimson sky,
   Thy figure floats along.

Seek'st thou the plashy brink
Of weedy lake, or marge of river wide,   10
Or where the rocking billows rise and sink
   On the chafed oceanside?

There is a Power whose care
Teaches thy way along the pathless coast—
The desert and illimitable air—   15
   Lone wandering, but not lost.

All day thy wings have fanned,
At that far height, the cold, thin atmosphere,
Yet stoop not, weary, to the welcome land,
   Though the dark night is near.   20

And soon that toil shall end;
Soon shalt thou find a summer home, and rest,
And scream among thy fellows; reeds shall bend,
   Soon, o'er thy sheltered nest.

Thou'rt gone, the abyss of heaven   25
Hath swallowed up thy form; yet, on my heart
Deeply hath sunk the lesson thou hast given,
   And shall not soon depart.

He who, from zone to zone,
Guides through the boundless sky thy certain flight, 30
In the long way that I must tread alone,
   Will lead my steps aright.

5. **fowler:** hunter.

I Broke the Spell That Held Me Long

I broke the spell that held me long,
The dear, dear witchery of song.
I said, the poet's idle lore
Shall waste my prime of years no more,
For Poetry, though heavenly born,   5
Consorts with poverty and scorn.

I broke the spell—nor deemed its power
Could fetter me another hour.
Ah, thoughtless! how could I forget
Its causes were around me yet?   10
For wheresoe'er I looked, the while,
Was Nature's everlasting smile.

Still came and lingered on my sight
Of flowers and streams the bloom and light,
And glory of the stars and sun;   15
And these and poetry are one.
They, ere the world had held me long,
Recalled me to the love of song.

FOR STUDY AND DISCUSSION

TO A WATERFOWL

1. Point out the stanzas that make up each of the three parts of this poem: the bird as seen by the poet, his meditation about the bird, and his application of these thoughts to his own life.

2. Is the journey described in stanzas 5–7 a symbol for another kind of journey? If so, what kind? When does the journey begin and end? How does the phrase "abyss of heaven" emphasize the symbolic quality of the journey? Why is it significant that the poet sees the bird at sunset? At what point in the poem should you become aware that the poet is writing about more than a specific bird?

3. What images and phrases does the poet use to make the flight of the bird a vivid sight?

4. Read stanza 7 aloud, giving proper attention to the commas and the semicolon. How do the frequent pauses called for indicate the poet's mood? Is the mood destroyed by reading the stanza quickly? Why? Show how pauses in other stanzas also further this mood.

5. The last four lines of this poem have often been memorized because they have meant much to many people. Do you think this philosophy was meaningful only at the time it was written, or is it still meaningful today?

I BROKE THE SPELL

1. Why, according to the poem, did Bryant want to break the spell of poetry? Why was he unsuccessful in his attempt? Does his lack of success reveal anything about poetry or poets?

2. Explain the statement that poetry "Consorts with poverty and scorn." Can you give examples from the lives of poets you have read to support this statement?

3. According to lines 10–12, the poet found the causes of poetry in "Nature's everlasting smile." How does the last stanza state the relationship between nature and poetry?

PERIODIC AND LOOSE SENTENCES

A periodic sentence is one in which the most important part is withheld until the very end. A loose sentence is one in the usual order. The purpose of a periodic sentence is to build suspense by withholding the climax until the end, thus emphasizing the last part of the sentence. In the following periodic sentence by Emerson, what idea is emphasized?

"If you have not slept, or if you have headache, or sciatica, or leprosy, or thunderstroke, I beseech you, by all angels, to hold your peace."

In this sentence, the phrase "hold your peace" is like the last piece of a jigsaw puzzle. The reader must know this phrase to understand the entire sentence, and therefore he waits for the phrase expectantly. If the sentence were altered to begin "I beseech you, by all angels, to hold your peace if you have not slept . . ." the phrase "hold your peace" would lose its emphasis.

Two stanzas of "To a Waterfowl" are periodic sentences. One is the first stanza. What idea is emphasized in this stanza? In which stanza is the other periodic sentence? What idea is emphasized?

Thanatopsis *

To him who in the love of Nature holds
Communion with her visible forms, she speaks
A various language; for his gayer hours
She has a voice of gladness, and a smile
And eloquence of beauty, and she glides   5
Into his darker musings, with a mild
And healing sympathy, that steals away
Their sharpness, ere he is aware. When thoughts
Of the last bitter hour come like a blight
Over thy spirit, and sad images   10
Of the stern agony, and shroud, and pall,
And breathless darkness, and the narrow house,
Make thee to shudder and grow sick at heart—
Go forth, under the open sky, and list
To Nature's teachings, while from all around—   15
Earth and her waters, and the depths of air—
Comes a still voice—Yet a few days, and thee
The all-beholding sun shall see no more
In all his course; nor yet in the cold ground,
Where thy pale form was laid, with many tears,   20
Nor in the embrace of ocean, shall exist
Thy image. Earth, that nourished thee, shall claim
Thy growth, to be resolved to earth again,
And, lost each human trace, surrendering up
Thine individual being, shalt thou go   25
To mix forever with the elements,
To be a brother to the insensible rock
And to the sluggish clod, which the rude swain°
Turns with his share,° and treads upon. The oak
Shall send his roots abroad, and pierce thy mold.   30

Yet not to thine eternal resting place
Shalt thou retire alone, nor couldst thou wish
Couch more magnificent. Thou shalt lie down
With patriarchs of the infant world—with kings,
The powerful of the earth—the wise, the good,   35
Fair forms, and hoary seers of ages past,
All in one mighty sepulcher. The hills
Rock-ribbed and ancient as the sun—the vales

---

* **Thanatopsis** (than'ə·top'sis): a meditation on death. 28. **rude swain:** crude peasant.
29. **share:** plowshare.

Stretching in pensive quietness between;
The venerable woods—rivers that move   40
In majesty, and complaining brooks
That make the meadows green; and, poured round all,
Old Ocean's gray and melancholy waste—
Are but the solemn decorations all
Of the great tomb of man. The golden sun,   45
The planets, all the infinite host of heaven,
Are shining on the sad abodes of death,
Through the still lapse of ages. All that tread
The globe are but a handful to the tribes
That slumber in its bosom. Take the wings   50
Of morning,° pierce the Barcan° wilderness,
Or lose thyself in the continuous woods
Where rolls the Oregon,° and hears no sound,
Save his own dashings—yet the dead are there;
And millions in those solitudes, since first   55
The flight of years began, have laid them down
In their last sleep—the dead reign there alone.
So shalt thou rest, and what if thou withdraw
In silence from the living, and no friend
Take note of thy departure? All that breathe   60
Will share thy destiny. The gay will laugh
When thou art gone, the solemn brood of care
Plod on, and each one as before will chase
His favorite phantom; yet all these shall leave
Their mirth and their employments, and shall come   65
And make their bed with thee. As the long train
Of ages glides away, the sons of men,
The youth in life's green spring, and he who goes
In the full strength of years, matron and maid,
The speechless babe, and the gray-headed man—   70
Shall one by one be gathered to thy side,
By those who in their turn shall follow them.

       So live, that when thy summons comes to join
The innumerable caravan, which moves
To that mysterious realm where each shall take   75
His chamber in the silent halls of death,
Thou go not, like the quarry slave at night,
Scourged to his dungeon, but, sustained and soothed
By an unfaltering trust, approach thy grave,
Like one who wraps the drapery of his couch   80
About him, and lies down to pleasant dreams.

   50–51. **Take . . . morning:** from the Old Testament Psalm 139:9.   51. **Barcan:** pertaining
to Barca, a district in North Africa on the Mediterranean coast.   53. **Oregon:** now known as
the Columbia River, between Oregon and Washington.

1. In what ways, according to the poem, can man commune with nature? Why does the poem begin with this subject?

2. Contrast the two views of death in lines 17–30 and 31–72. What consolation is there in the two facts presented in lines 31–33?

3. How is earth the "great tomb of man"? What are its "decorations"? How can this idea help man accept death as a natural thing? How is this part of the poem (lines 31–45) related to the beginning? (As a help in answering this question, consider the relationship between the words "nature" and "natural.")

4. What contrast is made in the last stanza of the poem? What are the two similes by which the contrast is made? Are these similes appropriate to the meaning and tone of the poem? Suppose the similes concerned a man going to the dentist and a boy eagerly opening his birthday presents? Would these similes be appropriate to the poem?

5. Line 73 of the poem begins "So live . . ." but does not go on to give specific suggestions about how a man should conduct his life. What suggestions might the poet have?

6. All three of Bryant's poems that you have read show a concern with nature. How, according to these poems, can nature affect and enrich man's life?

BLANK VERSE

As you read "Thanatopsis," you probably noticed that while the poem does not use rhyme, it does have a regular rhythm, a pattern of stressed and unstressed syllables. If you were to analyze the rhythm of the first line by counting the number of syllables and placing an accent mark above each stressed syllable

To him who in the love of na ture holds
 1   2   3   4   5   6   7 8   9   10

you would find that this line, as most other lines of the poem, consists of ten syllables, and that the rhythm of the line stems from an alternation of unstressed and stressed syllables. Each group of two syllables, an unstressed followed by a stressed syllable ("To hím"), is a unit of rhythm called an *iamb*. A verse line consisting of five such units is written in *iambic pentameter*. (Notice the use of the prefix "penta-," meaning "five," in such words as "pentameter" and "pentagon.") A poem consisting of verse lines of unrhymed iambic pentameter is written in *blank verse*.

Blank verse is often used in dramatic poems (e.g., Shakespearean plays), narrative poems ("The Death of the Hired Man," page 621), and meditative poems of some length (such as "Thanatopsis"). Of all the regular patterns of rhythm used in poetry, the pattern of blank verse is closest to ordinary speech and is thus the most natural-sounding and flexible pattern; yet, because of a careful, regular use of rhythm, blank verse possesses an emotional power that ordinary speech rarely attains. A poet using blank verse must face an important problem: keeping the rhythm from becoming sing-song and thus monotonous. He usually solves this problem by varying his rhythm. Notice that Bryant introduces variety into the sixth line of "Thanatopsis"

Into his darker musings, with a mild

by reversing the pattern in the first rhythm unit ("Into") and having the stressed syllable come before the unstressed syllable. A number of lines in "Thanatopsis" contain variations in rhythm.

Another way that a poet using blank verse avoids a monotonous rhythm is through a careful use of pauses within lines, called *caesuras*. Notice that in the third line of "Thanatopsis" a caesura occurs after the sixth syllable, whereas in the next line, there is a caesura after the seventh syllable. In a number of lines in "Thanatopsis" there is more than one caesura.

A reader of blank verse should, like the poet, avoid certain dangers. First, the reader should not give all stressed syllables an equal stress, thus imposing a sing-song quality that the poet never intended. Next, the reader should not read the verse exactly as if it were prose, thus ignoring a rhythm which the poet has carefully built up. A good reading of blank verse avoids these two dangers by taking account of the basic rhythm of the poem and of all the devices used to vary that rhythm. (For a further discussion of rhythm in poetry, see page 204.)

1. Find five lines of "Thanatopsis" in which there is a variation of the basic rhythm. Point out the variation. Find two lines where the use of a caesura introduces a variation into the rhythm.

2. Read aloud ten lines or so of "Thanatopsis" to show how blank verse should be properly read. In your reading avoid both a sing-song rhythm and the suppression of rhythm that comes from reading the verse lines as if they were prose.

EDGAR ALLAN POE

(1809–1849)

During a short, unhappy life, Edgar Allan Poe acted a number of literary roles: the nightmare-haunted artist who wrote stories such as "The Fall of the House of Usher," "Ligeia," and "William Wilson"; the pure poet who tried to remove all traces of the prosaic from his poetry and sang of the marvelous angel Israfel, "whose heart strings are a lute"; the coldly analytic craftsman who deliberately built up all the details in a poem or story to achieve an effect that was chosen in advance. Behind these roles, behind the life Poe lived in his writings and imagination, there was an overworked editor and journalist, trying desperately to earn enough money to support himself and his young wife. Hard pressed as he was, Poe left his mark on American and world literature. His poems, with their unreal atmosphere and musical effects, were much admired by the French poet Baudelaire and had a considerable influence on late nineteenth-century French poetry. His definition of the short story, expounded in his review of Hawthorne's *Twice-Told Tales,* led to a recognition of the short story as a distinct form of literature. His three detective stories—"The Murders in the Rue Morgue," "The Mystery of Marie Roget," and "The Purloined Letter"—inspired the creation of Sherlock Holmes and other brilliantly deductive sleuths. But Poe's chief contribution to literature is his exploration of the dark side of human nature, his creation of incidents and symbols that afford disturbing glimpses into a tumultuous world no further away than a twist of the imagination.

Poe was born in Boston, Massachusetts, the son of traveling actors. In 1810, after the desertion of his father, Poe's mother died of consumption in a Richmond, Virginia, rooming house. Poe was taken in by a childless couple, John and Frances Allan, who raised but never formally adopted him. John Allan, a wealthy tobacco merchant, gave Poe a gentleman's education and probably meant to treat him as a son, but Richmond boys of good family never regarded Poe, the son of disreputable actors, as one of them. He grew increasingly moody. Allan disapproved of his ward's literary ambitions and was disappointed by his lack of interest in a business career. When Poe entered the University of Virginia, Allan granted him an allowance that Poe considered inadequate. In less than a year Poe had contracted gambling debts that his guardian refused to pay, and thus he was forced to leave the University. After a bitter quarrel with Allan, Poe left Richmond and worked his way to Boston, where he published his first book, *Tamerlane and Other Poems.* Under the name of Edgar A. Perry, he enlisted in the army and rose to the rank of sergeant-major, but after two years he grew tired of army life. Allan promised to obtain Poe's release from the army on condition that Poe accept an appointment to West Point. Poe agreed and spent an unhappy eight months at the Military Academy. When he learned that Allan had married a young wife, Poe concluded that he had little hope of becoming Allan's heir. Assuming that a poor man could not expect a splendid military career, he deliberately neglected his duties and was dismissed from the Academy.

For a time Poe lived in Baltimore with his father's sister, Mrs. Maria Clemn, and her daughter Virginia. In 1833, after winning a contest with his story "Ms. Found in a Bottle," he was befriended by the Southern novelist John Pendleton Kennedy, who helped him get a job as editor with the *Southern Literary Messenger,* in Richmond. Poe lost the job temporarily because of excessive drinking and an inability to meet deadlines, but he was shortly rehired. As editor of the *Messenger* he raised the circulation enormously and, through his book reviews, gained a reputation for high critical standards and a caustic wit. In 1835, he married his thirteen-year-old cousin, Virginia Clemm. Considering his annual salary of eight hundred dollars too low, he resigned from the *Messenger* in 1837 and left Richmond. For the next few years, Poe worked feverishly at editorial and literary tasks in New York and Philadelphia. Several times he attempted but failed to start a magazine of his own. His *Tales of the Arabesque and Grotesque,* published in 1840 on condition that the publisher take all the profits, attracted little attention. Meanwhile Virginia's health was failing, and in 1842 she suffered her first attack of consumption. Poe went through long spells of depression and drank heavily. In 1845 he finally achieved literary popularity with his poem "The Raven." For the first time he was able to find a publisher who would publish his collection of *Tales* and pay him royalties, but the book sold few copies. As he wrote a friend, "I am as poor as I ever was in my life." In 1846, he managed to gain control of the *Broadway Journal,* but under his direction it failed for lack of funds. The next year, in a bare cottage in New York where Poe often lacked funds to build a fire, Virginia died. Poe went to pieces and spoke of his "terrible agony"; but he wrote an associate, "The truth is, I still have a great deal to do." In the next few years he wrote several more stories and a number of poems, including "The Bells." His most important work of these years is *Eureka,* a long prose poem that examines a series of opposites—attraction and repulsion, spirit and matter, the light and dark sides of man—and shows how they are brought together by the fusing power of God's poetic imagination. Some critics consider *Eureka* the key to Poe's other works.

In the summer of 1849, hoping to begin a new magazine, Poe returned to Richmond. There he encountered his boyhood sweetheart, Elmira Shelton, now a widow, to whom he became engaged. In September, he left Richmond to attend to some work in the North, and a week later, he was found unconscious in Baltimore, in an alley near a tavern. He died shortly thereafter.

To Helen

Helen, thy beauty is to me
  Like those Nicaean barks of yore,
That gently, o'er a perfumed sea,
  The weary, wayworn wanderer bore
To his own native shore.   5

On desperate seas long wont to roam,
  Thy hyacinth° hair, thy classic face,
Thy naiad airs have brought me home
  To the glory that was Greece
And the grandeur that was Rome.   10

Lo! in yon brilliant window niche
  How statuelike I see thee stand,
The agate lamp within thy hand!
  Ah, Psyche, from the regions which
Are Holy Land!   15

7. **hyacinth:** A favorite adjective for hair in the old Greek epics was "hyacinthine," usually meaning beautiful and curling.

FOR STUDY AND DISCUSSION

1. In his review of Hawthorne's *Twice-Told Tales,* Poe writes, "... in almost all classes of composition, the unity of effect or impression is a point of the greatest importance." Does this poem achieve a unity of effect? What do such words and phrases in the first stanza as "gently," "perfumed sea," and "weary, wayworn wanderer," contribute to the effect? To answer this question, you might substitute other words and phrases—"roughly" for "gently," for example—and see how the effect changes.

2. In stanza 2, what noun or pronoun is modified by the phrase, "On desperate seas long wont to roam"?

3. Explain the analogy (see page 859) that is developed in the first and second stanzas. How is the poet like the "weary, wayworn wanderer"? In what ways are Greece and Rome like the wanderer's native shore? Does the phrase "desperate seas" further the analogy or contradict it? What is meant by this phrase?

4. In an earlier version of the poem, lines 1–10 read as follows: "To the beauty of fair Greece/ And the grandeur of old Rome." Which version of these lines is more effective? Give reasons to support your choice.

5. "To Helen" has been praised as an almost perfect poem and attacked as vague and sentimental. Which of these opinions do you think is more nearly correct? Why?

LANGUAGE AND VOCABULARY

Look up the following words and explain how they give a classical feeling to the poem: *Nicaean* (line 2), *naiad* (line 8), *agate* (line 13), *Psyche* (line 14). Does the name "Helen" add to the classical feeling? Explain.

The Bells

I

Hear the sledges with the bells,
    Silver bells!
What a world of merriment their melody foretells!
    How they tinkle, tinkle, tinkle,
      In the icy air of night!   5
    While the stars, that oversprinkle
    All the heavens, seem to twinkle
      With a crystalline delight;
    Keeping time, time, time,
    In a sort of runic° rhyme,   10
To the tintinnabulation that so musically wells
    From the bells, bells, bells, bells,
      Bells, bells, bells—
    From the jingling and the tinkling of the bells.

II

Hear the mellow wedding bells,   15
    Golden bells!
What a world of happiness their harmony foretells!
    Through the balmy air of night
    How they ring out their delight!
      From the molten-golden notes,   20
      And all in tune,
      What a liquid ditty floats
    To the turtledove that listens, while she gloats
      On the moon!
    Oh, from out the sounding cells,   25
What a gush of euphony° voluminously wells!
      How it swells!
      How it dwells
    On the future! how it tells
    Of the rapture that impels   30
    To the swinging and the ringing
      Of the bells, bells, bells,
    Of the bells, bells, bells, bells,
      Bells, bells, bells—
To the rhyming and the chiming of the bells!   35

---

10. **runic** (rōō′nik): pertaining to runes, letters in an ancient alphabet, used in the writing of ancient Teutonic poetry; hence, strange, magical.   26. **euphony** (yōō′fə·nē): pleasant sounds.

Hear the loud alarum bells,
    Brazen bells!
What a tale of terror, now, their turbulency tells!
    In the startled ear of night
    How they scream out their affright!   40
      Too much horrified to speak,
      They can only shriek, shriek,
        Out of tune,
In a clamorous appealing to the mercy of the fire,
In a mad expostulation with the deaf and frantic fire,   45
      Leaping higher, higher, higher,
      With a desperate desire,
    And a resolute endeavor
    Now—now to sit or never,
    By the side of the pale-faced moon.   50
      Oh, the bells, bells, bells!
      What a tale their terror tells
        Of despair!
    How they clang, and clash, and roar!
    What a horror they outpour   55
On the bosom of the palpitating air!
      Yet the ear, it fully knows,
        By the twanging
        And the clanging,
      How the danger ebbs and flows;   60
    Yet the ear distinctly tells,
        In the jangling
        And the wrangling,
    How the danger sinks and swells—
By the sinking or the swelling in the anger of the bells,   65
      Of the bells,
    Of the bells, bells, bells, bells,
      Bells, bells, bells—
In the clamor and the clangor of the bells!

IV

    Hear the tolling of the bells,   70
      Iron bells!
What a world of solemn thought their monody° compels!
    In the silence of the night
    How we shiver with affright
At the melancholy menace of their tone!   75
      For every sound that floats
      From the rust within their throats
        Is a groan.

72. **monody** (mon′ə·dē): a type of music carried by one voice. In ancient Greek times a monody was sung as a dirge or funeral song; hence, the word suggests sorrow and tragedy.

And the people—ah, the people,
They that dwell up in the steeple,   80
    All alone,
And who tolling, tolling, tolling
    In that muffled monotone,
Feel a glory in so rolling
    On the human heart a stone—   85
They are neither man nor woman,
They are neither brute nor human,
    They are ghouls:
And their king it is who tolls;
And he rolls, rolls, rolls,   90
    Rolls
    A paean from the bells;
And his merry bosom swells
    With the paean of the bells,
And he dances, and he yells: 95
Keeping time, time, time,
In a sort of runic rhyme,
    To the paean of the bells,
    Of the bells:
Keeping time, time, time,   100
In a sort of runic rhyme,
    To the throbbing of the bells,
Of the bells, bells, bells—
    To the sobbing of the bells;
Keeping time, time, time,   105
    As he knells, knells, knells,
In a happy runic rhyme,
    To the rolling of the bells,
Of the bells, bells, bells:
    To the tolling of the bells,   110
Of the bells, bells, bells, bells,
    Bells, bells, bells—
To the moaning and the groaning of the bells.

FOR STUDY AND DISCUSSION

1. Contrast the four different kinds of bells. How does Poe use suggestive details to give his descriptions an emotional quality?

2. The sections of this poem grow progressively longer. In fact, the last section is more than three times as long as the first. Account for this difference in length.

DEVICES OF SOUND: ONOMATOPOEIA, ASSONANCE, CONSONANCE, ALLITERATION

"The Bells" is a poem that depends a great deal on sound for its effectiveness. This poem may profitably be studied for the effect that devices of sound have on the poem as a whole.

The most obvious sound device in the poem is *onomatopoeia*, the use of a word whose sound imitates or suggests its meaning. The word *tintinnabulation* in line 11 is a good example.

Another sound device used in the poem is *assonance*, the repetition of vowel sounds in one or two lines or in a part of the line so that these sounds come to dominate the phrase or sentence in which they occur. An example of assonance is "molten-golden notes" (line 20), dominated by the "o" sound.

A third device is *consonance*, the repetition of consonants within a line or group of lines.

Notice, for example, the repetition of *r*'s and *l*'s in line 3.

A fourth device (used more extensively and obviously in "The Raven" than in "The Bells") is *alliteration,* the repetition of initial consonant sounds of words, as in *"runic rhyme"* (line 97).

1. Give examples of onomatopoeia, assonance, consonance, and alliteration in "The Bells." Explain how these heighten the effectiveness of the lines in which they occur.

2. Show how other sound devices—rhyme, rhythm, and repetition—increase the emotional effect of the poem.

3. Compare the last lines of the four sections of the poem (lines 14, 35, 69, and 113). Describe the different effect of these lines and show how each depends on sound devices.

4. Onomatopoeia is a device exemplified by only a relatively small number of English words. Many people feel, however, that some words naturally suggest certain emotional moods. List five words which you consider have light, gay sounds and five others which you feel sound heavy and solemn. On the basis of these words, discuss the extent to which the sound of a word influences its meaning and the extent to which it is possible to separate sound from meaning. For example, it has been said that "cellar door" is one of the most beautiful phrases in English. Do you agree? Why or why not?

FOR COMPOSITION

Write a composition in which you summarize "The Bells," and then explain what qualities of the poem are lost in your summary. (For example, is your summary as emotionally effective as the poem?) Consider whether any summary of a poem can adequately convey the poem's qualities.

The Raven

Once upon a midnight dreary, while I pondered, weak and weary,
Over many a quaint and curious volume of forgotten lore—
While I nodded, nearly napping, suddenly there came a tapping,
As of someone gently rapping, rapping at my chamber door.
" 'Tis some visitor," I muttered, "tapping at my chamber door: 5
    Only this and nothing more."

Ah, distinctly I remember it was in the bleak December,
And each separate dying ember wrought its ghost upon the floor.
Eagerly I wished the morrow—vainly I had sought to borrow
From my books surcease of sorrow—sorrow for the lost Lenore,   10
For the rare and radiant maiden whom the angels name Lenore:
    Nameless here forevermore.

And the silken sad uncertain rustling of each purple curtain
Thrilled me—filled me with fantastic terrors never felt before;
So that now, to still the beating of my heart, I stood repeating,   15
" 'Tis some visitor entreating entrance at my chamber door,
Some late visitor entreating entrance at my chamber door:
    This it is and nothing more."

Presently my soul grew stronger; hesitating then no longer,
"Sir," said I, "or Madam, truly your forgiveness I implore;   20

But the fact is I was napping, and so gently you came rapping,
And so faintly you came tapping, tapping at my chamber door,
That I scarce was sure I heard you"—here I opened wide the door—
    Darkness there and nothing more.

Deep into that darkness peering, long I stood there wondering, fearing,   25
Doubting, dreaming dreams no mortal ever dared to dream before;
But the silence was unbroken, and the stillness gave no token,
And the only word there spoken was the whispered word "Lenore!"
This I whispered, and an echo murmured back the word "Lenore":
    Merely this and nothing more.   30

Back into the chamber turning, all my soul within me burning,
Soon again I heard a tapping somewhat louder than before.
"Surely," said I, "surely that is something at my window lattice;
Let me see, then, what thereat is, and this mystery explore:
Let my heart be still a moment and this mystery explore: 35
    'Tis the wind and nothing more."

Open here I flung the shutter, when, with many a flirt and flutter,
In there stepped a stately Raven of the saintly days of yore.
Not the least obeisance made he; not a minute stopped or stayed he;
But, with mien of lord or lady, perched above my chamber door,   40
Perched upon a bust of Pallas° just above my chamber door:
    Perched, and sat, and nothing more.

Then this ebony bird beguiling my sad fancy into smiling
By the grave and stern decorum of the countenance it wore—
"Though thy crest be shorn and shaven, thou," I said, "art sure no craven,
Ghastly grim and ancient Raven wandering from the nightly shore: 46
Tell me what thy lordly name is on the night's Plutonian° shore!"
    Quoth the Raven, "Nevermore."

Much I marveled this ungainly fowl to hear discourse so plainly,
Though its answer little meaning—little relevancy bore;   50
For we cannot help agreeing that no living human being
Ever yet was blessed with seeing bird above his chamber door,
Bird or beast upon the sculptured bust above his chamber door,
    With such name as "Nevermore."

But the Raven, sitting lonely on the placid bust, spoke only   55
That one word, as if his soul in that one word he did outpour.
Nothing further then he uttered, not a feather then he fluttered,
Till I scarcely more than muttered—"Other friends have flown before;
On the morrow *he* will leave me, as my hopes have flown before."
    Then the bird said, "Nevermore."   60

41. **Pallas** (pal′əs): Pallas Athene, Greek goddess of wisdom, called Minerva by the Romans.
47. **Plutonian** (plo͞o·tō′nē·ən): referring to Pluto, the god who in Greek mythology presided over the regions of the dead.

Startled at the stillness broken by reply so aptly spoken,
"Doubtless," said I, "what it utters is its only stock and store,
Caught from some unhappy master whom unmerciful disaster
Followed fast and followed faster till his songs one burden bore:
Till the dirges of his hope that melancholy burden bore   65
    Of 'Never—nevermore.' "

But the Raven still beguiling all my fancy into smiling,
Straight I wheeled a cushioned seat in front of bird and bust and door;
Then, upon the velvet sinking, I betook myself to linking
Fancy unto fancy, thinking what this ominous bird of yore,   70
What this grim, ungainly, ghastly, gaunt, and ominous bird of yore
    Meant in croaking "Nevermore."

This I sat engaged in guessing, but no syllable expressing
To the fowl whose fiery eyes now burned into my bosom's core;
This and more I sat divining, with my head at ease reclining   75
On the cushion's velvet lining that the lamplight gloated o'er,
But whose velvet violet lining with the lamplight gloating o'er
    She shall press, ah, nevermore!

Then, methought, the air grew denser, perfumed from an unseen censer
Swung by seraphim whose footfalls tinkled on the tufted floor.   80
"Wretch," I cried, "thy God hath lent thee—by these angels he hath sent
    thee
Respite—respite and nepenthe° from thy memories of Lenore!
Quaff, oh quaff this kind nepenthe, and forget this lost Lenore!"
    Quoth the Raven, "Nevermore."

"Prophet!" said I, "thing of evil—prophet still, if bird or devil!   85
Whether tempter sent, or whether tempest tossed thee here ashore,
Desolate yet all undaunted, on this desert land enchanted—
On this home by horror haunted—tell me truly, I implore:
Is there—*is* there balm in Gilead?°—tell me—tell me, I implore!"
    Quoth the Raven, "Nevermore."   90

"Prophet!" said I, "thing of evil—prophet still, if bird or devil!
By that heaven that bends above us, by that God we both adore,
Tell this soul with sorrow laden if, within the distant Aidenn,°
It shall clasp a sainted maiden whom the angels name Lenore:
Clasp a rare and radiant maiden whom the angels name Lenore!"   95
    Quoth the Raven, "Nevermore."

"Be that word our sign of parting, bird or fiend!" I shrieked, upstarting:
"Get thee back into the tempest and the night's Plutonian shore!
Leave no black plume as a token of that lie thy soul hath spoken!

---

    82. **nepenthe** (ni·pen'thē): a drug that destroys pain and brings forgetfulness. 89. **balm in Gilead** (Gil'ē·ad): a healing lotion made in Gilead, a part of ancient Palestine (see Jeremiah 8:22); therefore, relief from affliction. 93. **Aidenn** (ā'den): from the Arabic for Eden.

Leave my loneliness unbroken! quit the bust above my door!   100
Take thy beak from out my heart, and take thy form from off my door!"
    Quoth the Raven, "Nevermore."

And the Raven, never flitting, still is sitting, still is sitting
On the pallid bust of Pallas just above my chamber door;
And his eyes have all the seeming of a demon's that is dreaming,   105
And the lamplight o'er him streaming throws his shadow on the floor:
And my soul from out that shadow that lies floating on the floor
    Shall be lifted—nevermore!

FOR STUDY AND DISCUSSION

1. What details establish an atmosphere and mood at the very beginning of the poem? Describe the room that serves as the poem's setting.

2. How does the bird's reply, "Nevermore," grow in emotional intensity and significance as the poem progresses?

3. Find examples of alliteration in "The Raven." Why do you think Poe makes extensive use of this device?

4. Although the raven has the appearance of an unearthly creature, there is a natural explanation for his appearance. Why then does the narrator call him "prophet still, if bird or devil"? What does the raven symbolize to the narrator? How may the bird have a deeper meaning for the reader? What in the raven's manner makes the poem unusually weird and depressing?

5. It has been said that "The Raven" can be made considerably shorter by omitting the word "nevermore" and that more than a third of "The Bells" can be cut by omitting the word "bells." Should this comment be considered a criticism of Poe, or does it simply call attention to one of his principal methods, the repetition of a key word? Defend your answer.

FOR COMPOSITION

In a famous essay, "The Philosophy of Composition," Poe gives an account of how he wrote "The Raven," first deciding what the effect of the poem was to be, then choosing a subject and poetic devices, and finally working out the form of his stanzas and the details of the narrative. Several biographers of Poe have doubted whether "The Philosophy of Composition" is an entirely accurate presentation of Poe's methods. There is no doubt, however, that the essay reveals something of Poe's attitude toward poetry in general and toward his own poems in particular.

Read "The Philosophy of Composition" and write an imaginary account of the composition of "To Helen" or "The Bells." First present Poe's theory of poetry, then describe the intended effect of the poem that you (as Poe) intend to write, and, finally, tell how you went about achieving that effect.

The Fall of the House of Usher

Son cœur est un luth suspendu;
Sitôt qu'on le touche il résonne.[1]
DE BÉRANGER

DURING THE whole of a dull, dark, and soundless day in the autumn of the year, when the clouds hung oppressively low in the heavens, I had been passing alone, on horseback, through a singularly dreary tract of country, and at length found myself, as the shades of the evening drew on, within view of the melancholy House of Usher. I know not how it was—but, with the first glimpse of the building, a sense of insufferable gloom pervaded my spirit. I say insufferable; for the feeling was unrelieved by any of that half-pleasurable, because poetic, sentiment with which the mind usually receives even the sternest natural images of the desolate or terrible. I looked upon the scene before me—upon the mere house, and the simple landscape features of the domain—upon the bleak walls—upon the vacant eyelike windows —upon a few rank sedges [2]—and upon a few white trunks of decayed trees—with an utter depression of soul which I can compare to no earthly sensation more properly than to the afterdream of the reveler upon opium—the bitter lapse into everyday life—the hideous dropping off of the veil. There was an iciness, a sinking, a sickening of the heart—an unredeemed dreariness of thought which no goading of the imagination could torture into aught of the sublime. What was it—I paused to think—what was it that so unnerved me in the contemplation of the House of Usher? It was a mystery all insoluble;

nor could I grapple with the shadowy fancies that crowded upon me as I pondered. I was forced to fall back upon the unsatisfactory conclusion that while, beyond doubt, there *are* combinations of very simple natural objects which have the power of thus affecting us, still the analysis of this power lies among considerations beyond our depth. It was possible, I reflected, that a mere different arrangement of the particulars of the scene, of the details of the picture, would be sufficient to modify, or perhaps to annihilate its capacity for sorrowful impression; and, acting upon this idea, I reined my horse to the precipitous brink of a black and lurid tarn [3] that lay in unruffled luster by the dwelling, and gazed down— but with a shudder even more thrilling than before—upon the remodeled and inverted images of the gray sedge, and the ghastly tree stems, and the vacant and eyelike windows.

Nevertheless, in this mansion of gloom, I now proposed to myself a sojourn of some weeks. Its proprietor, Roderick Usher, had been one of my boon companions in boyhood; but many years had elapsed since our last meeting. A letter, however, had lately reached me in a distant part of the country—a letter from him—which, in its wildly importunate nature, had admitted of no other than a personal reply. The Ms.[4] gave evidence of nervous agitation. The writer spoke of acute bodily illness—of a mental disorder which oppressed him—and of an earnest desire to see me, as his best and indeed his only personal friend, with a view of attempting, by the cheerfulness of my society, some alleviation of his malady. It was the manner in which all this, and much more, was said—it was the apparent *heart* that went with his request— which allowed me no room for hesitation; and I accordingly obeyed forthwith what I still considered a very singular summons.

---

[1] "His heart is a suspended lute;/ Touch it and the strings resound." From the poem *"Le Refus"* by Pierre Jean de Béranger (1780–1857).

[2] **sedges:** grasslike plants.

[3] **tarn:** a small lake or pool.

[4] **Ms.:** manuscript.

Although, as boys, we had been even intimate associates, yet I really knew little of my friend. His reserve had been always excessive and habitual. I was aware, however, that his very ancient family had been noted, time out of mind, for a peculiar sensibility of temperament, displaying itself, through long ages, in many works of exalted art, and manifested, of late, in repeated deeds of munificent yet unobtrusive charity, as well as in a passionate devotion to the intricacies, perhaps even more than to the orthodox and easily recognizable beauties, of musical science. I had learned, too, the very remarkable fact that the stem of the Usher race, all time-honored as it was, had put forth, at no period, any enduring branch; in other words, that the entire family lay in the direct line of descent, and had always, with very trifling and very temporary variation, so lain. It was this deficiency, I considered, while running over in thought the perfect keeping of the character of the premises with the accredited character of the people, and while speculating upon the possible influence which the one, in the long lapse of centuries, might have exercised upon the other—it was this deficiency, perhaps, of collateral [1] issue, and patrimony with the name, which had, at length, so identified the two as to merge the original title of the estate in the quaint and equivocal appellation of the "House of Usher"—an appellation which seemed to include, in the minds of the peasantry who used it, both the family and the family mansion.

I have said that the sole effect of my somewhat childish experiment—that of looking down within the tarn—had been to deepen the first singular impression. There can be no doubt that the consciousness of the rapid increase of my superstition—for why should I not so term it?—served mainly to accelerate the increase itself. Such, I have long known, is the

[1] **collateral:** related, but not in a direct line of descent.

paradoxical law of all sentiments having terror as a basis. And it might have been for this reason only, that, when I again uplifted my eyes to the house itself, from its image in the pool, there grew in my mind a strange fancy—a fancy so ridiculous, indeed, that I but mention it to show the vivid force of the sensations which oppressed me. I had so worked upon my imagination as really to believe that about the whole mansion and domain there hung an atmosphere peculiar to themselves and their immediate vicinity —an atmosphere which had no affinity with the air of heaven, but which had reeked up from the decayed trees, and the gray wall, and the silent tarn—a pestilent and mystic vapor, dull, sluggish, faintly discernible, and leaden-hued.

Shaking off from my spirit what *must* have been a dream, I scanned more narrowly the real aspect of the building. Its principal feature seemed to be that of an excessive antiquity. The discoloration of ages had been great. Minute fungi overspread the whole exterior, hanging in a fine tangled webwork from the eaves. Yet all this was apart from any extraordinary dilapidation. No portion of the masonry had fallen; and there appeared to be a wild inconsistency between its still perfect adaptation of parts, and the crumbling condition of the individual stones. In this there was much that reminded me of the specious totality of old woodwork which has rotted for long years in some neglected vault, with no disturbance from the breath of the external air. Beyond this indication of extensive decay, however, the fabric gave little token of instability. Perhaps the eye of a scrutinizing observer might have discovered a barely perceptible fissure, which, extending from the roof of the building in front, made its way down the wall in a zigzag direction, until it became lost in the sullen waters of the tarn.

Noticing these things, I rode over a short causeway to the house. A servant in waiting took my horse, and I entered the Gothic archway of the hall. A valet, of stealthy step, thence conducted me, in silence, through many dark and intricate passages in my progress to the studio of his master. Much that I encountered on the way contributed, I know not how, to heighten the vague sentiments of which I have already spoken. While the objects around me—while the carvings of the ceilings, the somber tapestries of the walls, the ebon blackness of the floors, and the phantasmagoric armorial trophies which rattled as I strode were but matters to which, or to such as which, I had been accustomed from my infancy—while I hesitated not to acknowledge how familiar was all this—I still wondered to find how unfamiliar were the fancies which ordinary images were stirring up. On one of the staircases, I met the physician of the family. His countenance, I thought, wore a mingled expression of low cunning and perplexity. He accosted me with trepidation and passed on. The valet now threw open a door and ushered me into the presence of his master.

The room in which I found myself was very large and lofty. The windows were long, narrow, and pointed, and at so vast a distance from the black oaken floor as to be altogether inaccessible from within. Feeble gleams of encrimsoned light made their way through the trellised panes and served to render sufficiently distinct the more prominent objects around; the eye, however, struggled in vain to reach the remoter angles of the chamber, or the recesses of the vaulted and fretted [1] ceiling. Dark draperies hung upon the walls. The general furniture was profuse, comfortless, antique, and tattered. Many books and musical instruments lay scattered about, but failed to give any vitality to the scene. I felt that I breathed an atmosphere of sorrow. An air of stern, deep, and irredeemable gloom hung over and pervaded all.

Upon my entrance, Usher arose from a sofa on which he had been lying at full length, and greeted me with a vivacious warmth which had much in it, I at first thought, of an overdone cordiality—of the constrained effort of the *ennuyé* [2] man of the world. A glance, however, at his countenance convinced me of his perfect sincerity. We sat down; and for some moments, while he spoke not, I gazed upon him with a feeling half of pity, half of awe. Surely, man had never before so terribly altered, in so brief a period, as had Roderick Usher! It was with difficulty that I could bring myself to admit the identity of the wan being before me with the companion of my early boyhood. Yet the character of his face had been at all times remarkable. A cadaverousness of complexion; an eye large, liquid, and luminous beyond comparison; lips somewhat thin and very pallid, but of surpassingly beautiful curve; a nose of a delicate Hebrew model, but with a breadth of nostril unusual in similar formations; a finely molded chin, speaking, in its want of prominence, of a want of moral energy; hair of a more than weblike softness and tenuity; these features, with an inordinate expansion above the regions of the temple, made up altogether a countenance not easily to be forgotten. And now in the mere exaggeration of the prevailing character of these features, and of the expression they were wont to convey, lay so much of change that I doubted to whom I spoke. The now ghastly pallor of the skin, and the now miraculous luster of the eye, above all things startled and even awed me. The silken hair, too, had been suffered to grow all unheeded, and as, in its wild gossamer texture, it floated rather than fell about the face, I could not, even with effort, connect its Arabesque [3] expression with any idea of simple humanity.

In the manner of my friend I was at once struck with an incoherence—an inconsistency; and I soon found this to arise from a series of feeble and futile struggles

[1] **fretted:** carved in patterns.

[2] *ennuyé* (än·nwē·ā′): bored (French).
[3] **Arabesque** (ar′ə·besk′): fantastic.

to overcome an habitual trepidancy—an excessive nervous agitation. For something of this nature I had indeed been prepared, no less by his letter, than by reminiscences of certain boyish traits, and by conclusions deduced from his peculiar physical conformation and temperament. His action was alternately vivacious and sullen. His voice varied rapidly from a tremulous indecision (when the animal spirits seemed utterly in abeyance [1]) to that species of energetic concision—that abrupt, weighty, unhurried, and hollow-sounding enunciation—that leaden, self-balanced, and perfectly modulated guttural utterance, which may be observed in the lost drunkard, or the irreclaimable eater of opium, during the periods of his most intense excitement.

It was thus that he spoke of the object of my visit, of his earnest desire to see me, and of the solace he expected me to afford him. He entered, at some length, into what he conceived to be the nature of his malady. It was, he said, a constitutional and a family evil, and one for which he despaired to find a remedy—a mere nervous affection,[2] he immediately added, which would undoubtedly soon pass off. It displayed itself in a host of unnatural sensations. Some of these, as he detailed them, interested and bewildered me; although, perhaps, the terms and the general manner of their narration had their weight. He suffered much from a morbid acuteness of the senses; the most insipid food was alone endurable; he could wear only garments of certain texture; the odors of all flowers were oppressive; his eyes were tortured by even a faint light; and there were but peculiar sounds, and these from stringed instruments, which did not inspire him with horror.

To an anomalous species of terror I found him a bounden slave. "I shall perish," said he, "I *must* perish in this deplorable folly. Thus, thus, and not otherwise, shall I be lost. I dread the events of the future, not in themselves, but in their results. I shudder at the thought of any, even the most trivial, incident, which may operate upon this intolerable agitation of soul. I have, indeed, no abhorrence of danger, except in its absolute effect—in terror. In this unnerved, in this pitiable, condition, I feel that the period will sooner or later arrive when I must abandon life and reason together, in some struggle with the grim phantasm, FEAR."

I learned, moreover, at intervals, and through broken and equivocal hints, another singular feature of his mental condition. He was enchained by certain superstitious impressions in regard to the dwelling which he tenanted, and whence, for many years, he had never ventured forth —in regard to an influence whose suppositious force was conveyed in terms too shadowy here to be restated—an influence which some peculiarities in the mere form and substance of his family mansion had, by dint of long sufferance, he said, obtained over his spirit—an effect which the physique of the gray walls and turrets, and of the dim tarn into which they all looked down, had, at length, brought about upon the morale of his existence.

He admitted, however, although with hesitation, that much of the peculiar gloom which thus afflicted him could be traced to a more natural and far more palpable origin—to the severe and long-continued illness—indeed to the evidently approaching dissolution—of a tenderly beloved sister, his sole companion for long years, his last and only relative on earth. "Her decease," he said, with a bitterness which I can never forget, "would leave him (him, the hopeless and the frail) the last of the ancient race of the Ushers." While he spoke, the lady Madeline (for so was she called) passed through a remote portion of the apartment, and, without having noticed my presence, disappeared. I regarded her with an utter astonishment not unmingled with dread; and yet I found it impossible to account for such feelings. A

[1] **in abeyance** (ə·bā′əns): suppressed.
[2] **affection:** here, affliction.

sensation of stupor oppressed me as my eyes followed her retreating steps. When a door, at length, closed upon her, my glance sought instinctively and eagerly the countenance of the brother; but he had buried his face in his hands, and I could only perceive that a far more than ordinary wanness had overspread the emaciated fingers through which trickled many passionate tears.

The disease of the lady Madeline had long baffled the skill of her physicians. A settled apathy, a gradual wasting away of the person, and frequent although transient affections of a partially cataleptical [1] character were the unusual diagnosis. Hitherto she had steadily borne up against the pressure of her malady, and had not betaken herself finally to bed; but on the closing in of the evening of my arrival at the house, she succumbed (as her brother told me at night with inexpressible agitation) to the prostrating power of the destroyer; and I learned that the glimpse I had obtained of her person would thus probably be the last I should obtain—that the lady, at least while living, would be seen by me no more.

For several days ensuing, her name was unmentioned by either Usher or myself; and during this period I was busied in earnest endeavors to alleviate the melancholy of my friend. We painted and read together, or I listened, as if in a dream, to the wild improvisations of his speaking guitar. And thus, as a closer and still closer intimacy admitted me more unreservedly into the recesses of his spirit, the more bitterly did I perceive the futility of all attempt at cheering a mind from which darkness, as if an inherent positive quality, poured forth upon all objects of the moral and physical universe in one unceasing radiation of gloom.

I shall ever bear about me a memory of the many solemn hours I thus spent alone with the master of the House of Usher. Yet I should fail in any attempt to convey an idea of the exact character of the studies, or of the occupations, in which he involved me, or led me the way. An excited and highly distempered ideality [2] threw a sulfureous luster over all. His long improvised dirges will ring forever in my ears. Among other things, I hold painfully in mind a certain singular perversion and amplification of the wild air of the last waltz of von Weber. [3] From the paintings over which his elaborate fancy brooded, and which grew, touch by touch, into vaguenesses at which I shuddered the more thrillingly, because I shuddered knowing not why—from these paintings (vivid as their images now are before me) I would in vain endeavor to educe more than a small portion which should lie within the compass of merely written words. By the utter simplicity, by the nakedness of his designs, he arrested and overawed attention. If ever mortal painted an idea, that mortal was Roderick Usher. For me at least, in the circumstances then surrounding me, there arose out of the pure abstractions which the hypochondriac contrived to throw upon his canvas, an intensity of intolerable awe, no shadow of which felt I ever yet in the contemplation of the certainly glowing yet too concrete reveries of Fuseli. [4]

One of the phantasmagoric conceptions of my friend, partaking not so rigidly of the spirit of abstraction, may be shadowed forth, although feebly, in words. A small picture presented the interior of an immensely long and rectangular vault or tunnel, with low walls, smooth, white, and without interruption or device. Certain accessory points of the design served well to convey the idea that this excavation lay at an exceeding depth below the surface of the earth. No outlet was observed in any portion of its vast extent, and no torch or other artificial source of light was discernible; yet a flood of intense

[1] **cataleptical** (kat′ə·lep′tik′l): pertaining to a stroke characterized by a deathlike rigidity.

[2] **distempered ideality:** feverish obsession.

[3] **von Weber** (fon vā′bər): Carl Maria von Weber (1786–1826), a German composer.

[4] **Fuseli:** Johann Heinrich Fuseli (*or* Füssli), a Swiss painter (1742–1825) who lived in England.

rays rolled throughout, and bathed the whole in a ghastly and inappropriate splendor.

I have just spoken of that morbid condition of the auditory nerve which rendered all music intolerable to the sufferer, with the exception of certain effects of stringed instruments. It was, perhaps, the narrow limits to which he thus confined himself upon the guitar which gave birth, in great measure, to the fantastic character of his performances. But the fervid facility of his impromptus could not be so accounted for. They must have been, and were, in the notes, as well as in the words of his wild fantasias (for he not unfrequently accompanied himself with rhymed verbal improvisations), the result of that intense mental collectedness and concentration to which I have previously alluded as observable only in particular moments of the highest artificial excitement. The words of one of these rhapsodies I have easily remembered. I was, perhaps, the more forcibly impressed with it as he gave it, because, in the under or mystic current of its meaning, I fancied that I perceived, and for the first time, a full consciousness on the part of Usher of the tottering of his lofty reason upon her throne. The verses, which were entitled "The Haunted Palace," ran very nearly, if not accurately thus:

I

In the greenest of our valleys,
  By good angels tenanted,
Once a fair and stately palace—
  Radiant palace—reared its head.
In the monarch Thought's dominion—
  It stood there!
Never seraph spread a pinion
  Over fabric half so fair.

II

Banners yellow, glorious, golden,
  On its roof did float and flow
(This—all this—was in the olden
  Time long ago);

And every gentle air that dallied,
  In that sweet day,
Along the ramparts plumed and pallid,
  A wingèd odor went away.

III

Wanderers in that happy valley
  Through two luminous windows saw
Spirits moving musically
  To a lute's well-tunèd law;
Round about a throne, where sitting
  (Porphyrogene!) [1]
In state his glory well befitting,
  The ruler of the realm was seen.

IV

And all with pearl and ruby glowing,
  Was the fair palace door,
Through which came flowing, flowing, flowing
  And sparkling evermore,
A troop of Echoes whose sweet duty
  Was but to sing,
In voices of surpassing beauty,
  The wit and wisdom of their king.

V

But evil things, in robes of sorrow,
  Assailed the monarch's high estate;
(Ah, let us mourn, for never morrow
  Shall dawn upon him, desolate!)
And, round about his home, the glory
  That blushed and bloomed
Is but a dim-remembered story
  Of the old time entombed.

VI

And travelers now within that valley,
  Through the red-litten [2] windows see
Vast forms that move fantastically
  To a discordant melody;
While, like a rapid ghastly river,
  Through the pale door,
A hideous throng rush out forever,
  And laugh—but smile no more.

[1] **Porphyrogene** (pôr′fi·ro·jēn′): pertaining to royalty or "the purple." The word comes from porphyry, a dark-red or purple rock.

[2] **litten:** poetic for lighted.

I well remembered that suggestions arising from this ballad led us into a train of thought wherein there became manifest an opinion of Usher's, which I mention not so much on account of its novelty (for other men have thought thus), as on account of the pertinacity with which he maintained it. This opinion, in its general form, was that of the sentience [1] of all vegetable things. But in his disordered fancy, the idea had assumed a more daring character, and trespassed, under certain conditions, upon the kingdom of inorganization. [2] I lack words to express the full extent, or the earnest *abandon* of his persuasion. The belief, however, was connected (as I have previously hinted) with the gray stones of the home of his forefathers. The conditions of the sentience had been here, he imagined, fulfilled in the method of collocation of these stones—in the order of their arrangement, as well as in that of the many fungi which overspread them, and of the decayed trees which stood around—above all, in the long undisturbed endurance of this arrangement, and in its reduplication in the still waters of the tarn. Its evidence—the evidence of the sentience—was to be seen, he said (and I here started as he spoke), in the gradual yet certain condensation of an atmosphere of their own about the waters and the walls. The result was discoverable, he added, in that silent yet importunate and terrible influence which for centuries had molded the destinies of his family, and which made *him* what I now saw him—what he was. Such opinions need no comment, and I will make none.

Our books—the books which, for years, had formed no small portion of the mental existence of the invalid—were, as might be supposed, in strict keeping with this character of phantasm. We pored together over such works as the *Ververt et Chartreuse* [3] of Gresset; the *Belphegor* of

Machiavelli; the *Heaven and Hell* of Swedenborg; the *Subterranean Voyage of Nicholas Klimm* by Holberg; the *Chiromancy* of Robert Flud, of Jean D'Indaginé, and of De la Chambre; the *Journey into the Blue Distance* of Tieck; and the *City of the Sun* of Campanella. One favorite volume was a small octave edition of the *Directorium Inquisitorium*, by the Dominican Eymeric de Gironne; and there were passages in Pomponius Mela, about the old African Satyrs and Ægipans, over which Usher would sit dreaming for hours. His chief delight, however, was found in the perusal of an exceedingly rare and curious book in quarto Gothic— the manual of a forgotten church—the *Vigiliæ Mortuorum Secundum Chorum Ecclesiæ Maguntinæ.*

I could not help thinking of the wild ritual of this work, and of its probable influence upon the hypochondriac, when, one evening, having informed me abruptly that the lady Madeline was no more, he stated his intention of preserving her corpse for a fortnight (previously to its final interment), in one of the numerous vaults within the main walls of the building. The worldly reason, however, assigned for this singular proceeding, was one which I did not feel at liberty to dispute. The brother had been led to his resolution (so he told me) by consideration of the unusual character of the malady of the deceased, of certain obtrusive and eager inquiries on the part of her medical men, and of the remote and exposed situation of the burial ground of the family. I will not deny that when I called to mind the sinister countenance of the person whom I met upon the staircase, on the day of my arrival at the house, I had no desire to oppose what I regarded as at best but a harmless, and by no means an unnatural precaution. [4]

At the request of Usher, I personally aided him in the arrangements for the

---

[1] **sentience** (sen'shē·əns): consciousness.

[2] **kingdom of inorganization:** the world of inanimate objects.

[3] ***Ververt et Chartreuse,*** etc.: All of the books listed are works of mysticism or magic.

[4] **I will . . . precaution:** Usher wishes to prevent his sister's body from being dissected by doctors. The person with the "sinister countenance" is the family physician.

temporary entombment. The body having been encoffined, we two alone bore it to its rest. The vault in which we placed it (and which had been so long unopened that our torches, half smothered in its oppressive atmosphere, gave us little opportunity for investigation) was small, damp, and entirely without means of admission for light; lying, at great depth, immediately beneath that portion of the building in which was my own sleeping apartment. It had been used, apparently, in remote feudal times, for the worst purposes of a donjon-keep,[1] and, in later days, as a place of deposit for powder, or some other highly combustible substance, as a portion of its floor, and the whole interior of a long archway through which we reached it, were carefully sheathed with copper. The door, of massive iron, had been, also, similarly protected. Its immense weight caused an unusually sharp, grating sound, as it moved upon its hinges.

Having deposited our mournful burden upon trestles within this region of horror, we partially turned aside the yet unscrewed lid of the coffin, and looked upon the face of the tenant. A striking similitude between the brother and sister now first arrested my attention; and Usher, divining, perhaps, my thoughts, murmured out some few words from which I learned that the deceased and himself had been

twins, and that sympathies of a scarcely intelligible nature had always existed between them. Our glances, however, rested not long upon the dead—for we could not regard her unawed. The disease which had thus entombed the lady in the maturity of youth had left, as usual in all maladies of a strictly cataleptical character, the mockery of a faint blush upon the bosom and the face, and that suspiciously lingering smile upon the lip which is so terrible in death. We replaced and screwed down the lid, and, having secured the door of iron, made our way, with toil, into the scarcely less gloomy apartments of the upper portion of the house.

And now, some days of bitter grief having elapsed, an observable change came over the features of the mental disorder of my friend. His ordinary manner had vanished. His ordinary occupations were neglected or forgotten. He roamed from chamber to chamber with hurried, unequal, and objectless step. The pallor of his countenance had assumed, if possible, a more ghastly hue—but the luminousness of his eye had utterly gone out. The once occasional huskiness of his tone was heard no more; and a tremulous quaver, as if of extreme terror, habitually characterized his utterance. There were times, indeed, when I thought his unceasingly agitated mind was laboring with some oppressive secret, to divulge which he struggled for the necessary courage. At times, again, I was obliged to resolve all into the mere inexplicable vagaries[2] of madness, for I beheld him gazing upon vacancy for long hours, in an attitude of the profoundest attention, as if listening to some imaginary sound. It was no wonder that his condition terrified—that it infected me. I felt creeping upon me, by slow yet certain degrees, the wild influences of his own fantastic yet impressive superstitions.

It was, especially, upon retiring to bed late in the night of the seventh or eighth day after the placing of the lady Madeline

---

[1] **donjon-keep:** dungeon.

[2] **vagaries** (və·gâr′ēz): whims.

within the donjon, that I experienced the full power of such feelings. Sleep came not near my couch—while the hours waned and waned away, I struggled to reason off the nervousness which had dominion over me. I endeavored to believe that much, if not all, of what I felt was due to the bewildering influence of the gloomy furniture of the room—of the dark and tattered draperies, which, tortured into motion by the breath of a rising tempest, swayed fitfully to and fro upon the walls, and rustled uneasily about the decorations of the bed. But my efforts were fruitless. An irrepressible tremor gradually pervaded my frame; and, at length, there sat upon my very heart an incubus of utterly causeless alarm. Shaking this off with a gasp and a struggle, I uplifted myself upon the pillows, and peering earnestly within the intense darkness of the chamber, hearkened—I know not why, except that an instinctive spirit prompted me—to certain low and indefinite sounds which came, through the pauses of the storm, at long intervals, I knew not whence. Overpowered by an intense sentiment of horror, unaccountable yet unendurable, I threw on my clothes with haste (for I felt I should sleep no more during the night), and endeavored to arouse myself from the pitiable condition into which I had fallen, by pacing to and fro through the apartment.

I had taken but few turns in this manner, when a light step on an adjoining staircase arrested my attention. I presently recognized it as that of Usher. In an instant afterward he rapped, with a gentle touch, at my door, and entered, bearing a lamp. His countenance was, as usual, cadaverously wan—but, moreover, there was a species of mad hilarity in his eyes—an evidently restrained hysteria in his whole demeanor. His air appalled me—anything was preferable to the solitude which I had so long endured, and I even welcomed his presence as a relief.

"And you have not seen it?" he said abruptly, after having stared about him for some moments in silence— "you have not then seen it?—but, stay! you shall." Thus speaking, and having carefully shaded his lamp, he hurried to one of the casements, and threw it freely open to the storm.

The impetuous fury of the entering gust nearly lifted us from our feet. It was, indeed, a tempestuous yet sternly beautiful night, and one wildly singular in its terror and its beauty. A whirlwind had apparently collected its force in our vicinity; for there were frequent and violent alterations in the direction of the wind; and the exceeding density of the clouds (which hung so low as to press upon the turrets of the house) did not prevent our perceiving the lifelike velocity with which they flew careering from all points against each other, without passing away into the distance. I say that even their exceeding density did not prevent our perceiving this—yet we had no glimpse of the moon or stars, nor was there any flashing forth of the lightning. But the under surfaces of the huge masses of agitated vapor, as well as all terrestrial objects immediately around us, were glowing in the unnatural light of a faintly luminous and distinctly visible gaseous exhalation which hung about and enshrouded the mansion.

"You must not—you shall not behold this!" said I, shuddering, to Usher, as I led him, with a gentle violence, from the window to a seat. "These appearances, which bewilder you, are merely electrical phenomena not uncommon—or it may be that they have their ghastly origin in the rank miasma [1] of the tarn. Let us close this casement; the air is chilling and dangerous to your frame. Here is one of your favorite romances. I will read, and you shall listen: and so we will pass away this terrible night together."

The antique volume which I had taken up was the *Mad Trist* of Sir Launcelot Canning; [2] but I had called it a favorite

[1] **rank miasma** (mī·az′mə): thick, harmful atmosphere.

[2] ***Mad Trist* of Sir Launcelot Canning:** The book and the author were Poe's inventions.

of Usher's more in sad jest than in earnest; for, in truth, there is little in its uncouth and unimaginative prolixity which could have had interest for the lofty and spiritual ideality of my friend. It was, however, the only book immediately at hand; and I indulged a vague hope that the excitement which now agitated the hypochondriac might find relief (for the history of mental disorder is full of similar anomalies) even in the extremeness of the folly which I should read. Could I have judged, indeed, by the wild overstrained air of vivacity with which he hearkened, or apparently hearkened, to the words of the tale, I might well have congratulated myself upon the success of my design.

I had arrived at that well-known portion of the story where Ethelred, the hero of the Trist, having sought in vain for peaceable admission into the dwelling of the hermit, proceeds to make good an entrance by force. Here, it will be remembered, the words of the narrative run thus:

"And Ethelred, who was by nature of a doughty heart, and who was now mighty withal, on account of the powerfulness of the wine which he had drunken, waited no longer to hold parley with the hermit, who, in sooth, was of an obstinate and maliceful turn, but, feeling the rain upon his shoulders, and fearing the rising of the tempest, uplifted his mace outright, and, with blows, made quickly room in the plankings of the door for his gauntleted hand; and now pulling therewith sturdily, he so cracked, and ripped, and tore all asunder, that the noise of the dry and hollow-sounding wood alarumed and reverberated throughout the forest."

At the termination of this sentence, I started and, for a moment, paused; for it appeared to me (although I at once concluded that my excited fancy had deceived me)—it appeared to me that, from some very remote portion of the mansion, there came indistinctly to my ears what might have been, in its exact similarity of character, the echo (but a stifled and dull one certainly) of the very cracking and ripping sound which Sir Launcelot had so particularly described. It was, beyond doubt, the coincidence alone which had arrested my attention; for, amid the rattling of the sashes of the casements, and the ordinary commingled noises of the still increasing storm, the sound in itself had nothing, surely, which should have interested or disturbed me. I continued the story:

"But the good champion Ethelred, now entering within the door, was sore enraged and amazed to perceive no signal of the maliceful hermit; but, in the stead thereof, a dragon of a scaly and prodigious demeanor, and of a fiery tongue, which sate in guard before a palace of gold, with a floor of silver; and upon the wall there hung a shield of shining brass with this legend enwritten—

Who entereth herein, a conqueror hath bin;
Who slayeth the dragon, the shield he shall win.

And Ethelred uplifted his mace, and struck upon the head of the dragon, which fell before him, and gave up his pesty breath, with a shriek so horrid and harsh and withal so piercing, that Ethelred had fain to close his ears with his hands against the dreadful noise of it, the like whereof was never before heard."

Here again I paused abruptly, and now with a feeling of wild amazement, I did actually hear (although from what direction it proceeded I found it impossible to say) a low and apparently distant, but harsh, protracted, and most unusual screaming or grating sound—the exact counterpart of what my fancy had already conjured up for the dragon's unnatural shriek as described by the romancer.

Oppressed, as I certainly was, upon the occurrence of this second and most extraordinary coincidence, by a thousand conflicting sensations, in which wonder and extreme terror were predominant, I still retained sufficient presence of mind to avoid exciting, by any observation, the sensitive nervousness of my companion. I was by no means certain that he had noticed the sounds in question; although, assuredly, a strange alteration had, during the last few minutes, taken place in his demeanor. From a position fronting my own, he had gradually brought round his chair, so as to sit with his face to the door of the chamber; and thus I could but partially perceive his features, although I saw that his lips trembled as if he were murmuring inaudibly. His head had dropped upon his breast—yet I knew that he was not asleep, from the wide and rigid opening of the eye as I caught a glance of it in profile. The motion of his body, too, was at variance with this idea—for he rocked from side to side with a gentle yet constant and uniform sway. Having rapidly taken notice of all this, I resumed the narrative of Sir Launcelot, which thus proceeded:

"And now, the champion, having escaped from the terrible fury of the dragon, bethinking himself of the brazen shield, and of the breaking up of the enchantment which was upon it, removed the carcass from out of the way before him, and approached valorously over the silver pavement of the castle to where the shield was upon the wall; which in sooth tarried not for his full coming, but fell down at his feet upon the silver floor, with a mighty great and terrible ringing sound."

No sooner had these syllables passed my lips, than—as if a shield of brass had indeed, at the moment, fallen heavily upon a floor of silver—I became aware of a distinct, hollow, metallic, and clangorous, yet apparently muffled, reverberation. Completely unnerved, I leaped to my feet; but the measured rocking movement of Usher was undisturbed. I rushed to the chair in which he sat. His eyes were bent fixedly before him, and throughout his whole countenance there reigned a stony

rigidity. But, as I placed my hand upon his shoulder, there came a strong shudder over his whole person; a sickly smile quivered about his lips; and I saw that he spoke in a low, hurried, and gibbering murmur, as if unconscious of my presence. Bending closely over him, I at length drank in the hideous import of his words.

"Not hear it?—yes, I hear it, and *have* heard it. Long—long—long—many minutes, many hours, many days, have I heard it—yet I dared not—oh, pity me, miserable wretch that I am!—I dared not—I *dared* not speak! *We have put her living in the tomb!* Said I not that my senses were acute? I *now* tell you that I heard her first feeble movements in the hollow coffin. I heard them—many, many days ago—yet I dared not—*I dared not speak!* And now—tonight—Ethelred—ha! ha!—the breaking of the hermit's door, and the death-cry of the dragon, and the clangor of the shield—say, rather, the rending of her coffin, and the grating of the iron hinges of her prison, and her struggles within the coppered archway of the vault! Oh! whither shall I fly? Will she not be here anon?[1] Is she not hurrying to upbraid me for my haste? Have I not heard her footstep on the stair? Do I not distinguish that heavy and horrible beating of her heart? Madman!"—here he sprang furiously to his feet, and shrieked out his syllables, as if in the effort he were giving up his soul—"*Madman! I tell you that she now stands without the door!*"

As if in the superhuman energy of his utterance there had been found the potency of a spell, the huge antique panels to which the speaker pointed threw slowly back, upon the instant, their ponderous and ebony jaws. It was the work of the rushing gust—but then without those doors there *did* stand the lofty and enshrouded figure of the lady Madeline of Usher. There was blood upon her white robes, and the evidence of some bitter struggle upon every portion of her emaciated frame. For a moment she remained

[1] **anon** (ə·non'): soon.

trembling and reeling to and fro upon the threshold—then, with a low moaning cry, fell heavily inward upon the person of her brother, and in her violent and now final death agonies, bore him to the floor a corpse, and a victim to the terrors he had anticipated.

From that chamber, and from that mansion, I fled aghast. The storm was still abroad in all its wrath as I found myself crossing the old causeway. Suddenly there shot along the path a wild light, and I turned to see whence a gleam so unusual could have issued; for the vast house and its shadows were alone behind me. The radiance was that of the full, setting, and blood-red moon, which now shone vividly through that once barely discernible fissure, of which I have before spoken as extending from the roof of the building, in a zigzag direction, to the base. While I gazed, this fissure rapidly widened —there came a fierce breath of the whirlwind—the entire orb of the satellite burst at once upon my sight—my brain reeled as I saw the mighty walls rushing asunder —there was a long tumultuous shouting sound like the voice of a thousand waters —and the deep and dank tarn at my feet closed sullenly and silently over the fragments of the *House of Usher*.

COMMENTARY

"The Fall of the House of Usher," which many critics consider Poe's best story, is a fine example of Poe's artistry: his meticulous attention to the function of details in an overall pattern. As you know, Poe believed that the best poems and stories are not written haphazardly or in a frenzy of inspiration but are precisely calculated to achieve a definite effect. As Poe stated, "There should be no word written of which the tendency, direct or indirect, is not to the one preestablished design." The writer should first choose an effect—for example, humor or terror— and then combine "such events as may best aid him in establishing his preconceived effect." In "The Philosophy of Composition" (see page 126), Poe describes his own method of writing a story:

"I say to myself, in the first place— 'Of the innumerable effects, or impressions, of which the heart, the intellect, or . . . the soul is susceptible, what one shall I, on the present occasion, select?' Having chosen a novel . . . and . . . vivid effect, I consider whether it can best be wrought by incident or tone . . . afterward looking . . . for such combinations of event, or tone, as shall best aid me in the construction of the effect."

Before writing "The Fall of the House of Usher," Poe probably selected an effect of irrational terror and decided to achieve his effect by the use of striking incidents and a tone that depends largely on the character and manner of the narrator. He seems to be a normal, sensible fellow, but he has ridden all day through dreary countryside, and, at his first glimpse of the Usher house, he is seized by a strange sensation, "a sickening of the heart." Gradually the narrator is drawn more and more into the strange world of the Ushers, and as he is pulled in, he carries the reader along with him.

The incidents of the story—the supposed death of Usher's sister, Usher's collapse into madness, the destruction of Usher and his mansion—are in themselves calculated to induce an effect of terror. However, the effect of these incidents is vastly enhanced by a systematic use of details to build up an impression of hidden decay and impending doom. The details describing Roderick Usher emphasize his weakness and are omens of his dreadful fate. To the narrator Usher's chin indicates "in its want of prominence . . . a want of moral energy." Usher's sensitivity causes him considerable suffering. He can endure only the blandest of foods. He is oppressed by the odors of all flowers and by even the faintest light. Even his intelligence adds to his suffering. He declares, "I dread the events of the future, not in themselves, but in their results. I shudder at the thought of any, even the most trivial, incident, which may operate upon this intolerable agitation of the soul. I have, indeed, no abhorrence of danger, except in its absolute effect—in terror." Thus, Usher's awareness serves only to increase the terror that finally destroys him.

Between Usher's condition and the state of the antiquated family mansion, there is a significant parallel that Poe's artful use of detail brings out. In his first examination of the mansion, the narrator notices that, although no part of it has fallen, the individual stones are crumbling. While, on superficial examination, the building may seem perfectly sound, it is actually on the verge of destruction. Usher, who has developed a theory that the building is a conscious being exercising a "silent yet importunate and terrible influence" on his family, is in somewhat the same condition as the building—superficially sound, but actually crumbling.

All the details about Usher and his mansion—and the parallel between them—are part of Poe's carefully developed plan to establish a "preconceived effect" of terror. Other details that are part of the plan are taken up in the questions below.

However, a close look at one detail—the tarn—points up one of Poe's most effective devices, the repetition of detail to give heightened significance. The narrator, when he first looks at the tarn, describes it as "black and lurid." When he sees in it a reflection of the mansion, he shudders and imagines "a pestilent and mystic vapor" rising out of the tarn. Later, during the last tumultuous episode of the story, he thinks that the strange luminescence "which hung about and enshrouded the mansion" has its "ghastly origin in the rank miasma of the tarn." Finally, as he flees from the doomed mansion, he sees "the deep and dank tarn at my feet [close] sullenly and silently over the fragments of the *House of Usher.*" Thus the tarn is used to suggest the evil that surrounds and finally destroys the Ushers.

FOR STUDY AND DISCUSSION

1. What is the importance of the fact that "the stem of the Usher race . . . had put forth, at no period, any enduring branch"? What may have been the author's purpose in having the term "The House of Usher" stand for both the family and the family mansion?

2. How is Roderick Usher's malady similar to Lady Madeline's disease? What may have been the author's purpose in revealing that Roderick and Madeline were twins?

3. What is revealed about Roderick through his painting and his music? One of his pictures is described in detail. What is the significance of this picture in the light of what happens later in the story?

4. In Roderick's song, "The Haunted Palace," what does the palace symbolize? Is there any similarity between the picture and the ballad? Explain.

5. Describe the last scene in the story, beginning with the narrator's rising in the middle of the night and encountering Roderick. How is the weather appropriate to this scene? During the scene, the narrator reads from a romance and describes "that well-known portion of the story where Ethelred, the hero of the Trist, having sought in vain for peaceable admission into the dwelling of the hermit, proceeds to make good an entrance by force." What is the significance of this situation, con-

sidering what happens in the Usher mansion? What does the narrator's oral reading of the romance contribute to the mood of the story?

LANGUAGE AND VOCABULARY

1. The author of "The Fall of the House of Usher" builds an atmosphere of gloom from the very first sentence. Following are phrases that Poe uses to help create atmosphere. If you do not already know the meanings of the italicized words, look them up in a dictionary.
   a. "clouds hung *oppressively* low . . ."
   b. "*precipitous* brink of a black and lurid tarn . . ."
   c. "An air of stern, deep, and *irredeemable* gloom . . ."
   d. "the *wan* being before me . . ."
   e. "A *cadaverousness* of complexion . . ."
   f. "One of the *phantasmagoric* conceptions . . ."
   g. "the *luminousness* of his eye . . ."
   h. "an *incubus* of utterly causeless alarm."
   i. "the history of mental disorder is full of similar *anomalies* . . ."

Which of the italicized words can be used *only* when writing about a somewhat dangerous or gloomy situation? Which ones could equally well be used in writing about a quite different situation?

2. Find five or more additional words in this story which add to the atmosphere of gloom. (Examples: *reeked, decayed, ghastly.*) For these words, try to substitute words or phrases which communicate an opposite feeling (e.g., a pleasant feeling).

POE'S EVOCATIVE SENTENCES

The sentences in this story are frequently long and complicated. To understand their basic meaning, you must identify the main clause of a sentence and determine the relationship of this clause to modifying clauses and phrases. At the same time, you should be responsive to the effect that Poe creates in a sentence, partly through a musical rhythm, partly through evocative adjectives and adverbs, and partly through frequent pauses that slow down a sentence and give the reader an opportunity to grasp its full implications. The opening sentence of the story is a typical one:

"During the whole of a dull, dark, and soundless day in the autumn of the year, when the clouds hung oppressively low in the heavens, I had been passing alone, on horseback, through a singularly dreary tract of country, and at length found myself, as the shades of the evening drew on, within view of the melancholy House of Usher."

The main clause of this sentence gives its basic meaning: "I had been passing alone . . . and at length found myself . . . within view of the melancholy House of Usher." To further understand this sentence, you must relate all the modifying clauses and phrases (which give the time of the day, describe the landscape, and so on) to the main clause. To grasp all the implications of the sentence, you must be aware of phrases such as "dull, dark, and soundless day," "oppressively low," and "a singularly dreary tract of country." Finally, you should read this and several other sentences out loud to make yourself aware of their rhythm. Note the pauses: in this sentence there are at least seven.

Choose one of Poe's long sentences to analyze. Determine the main clause in the sentence. Explain the relationship of this clause to modifying clauses and phrases. Note the use of evocative adjectives and adverbs. Read the sentence aloud to determine its rhythm. Be prepared to explain the effect that Poe achieves in the sentence.

FOR COMPOSITION

1. Write a paragraph that creates a single emotional effect. It may be fear, joy, horror, suspicion, pity, or some other emotion that occurs to you. You may wish to describe a scene or narrate a short incident. Construct every sentence and choose every word with care.

Write the effect you intended on the back of your paper, and then exchange papers in class to see if a classmate can guess the effect you have tried to convey.

2. Poe's tales have been admired for their craftsmanship as well as for their imaginative power. They have also been attacked as shallow, tricky works written only to provide cheap thrills. Write a composition in which you answer the following questions: Is Poe more than simply another writer of "horror stories"? If so, what qualities raise him above this level? The English poet and critic Matthew Arnold defined literature as a "criticism of life." Do Poe's tales fit this definition? To what extent can Poe be considered a serious literary artist? Support your general points with specific references to "The Fall of the House of Usher."

Ms. Found in a Bottle*

Qui n'a plus qu'un moment à vivre
N'a plus rien à dissimuler.
                    QUINAULT, *Atys* [1]

O F MY COUNTRY and of my family I have little to say. Ill usage and length of years have driven me from the one, and estranged me from the other. Hereditary wealth afforded me an education of no common order, and a contemplative turn of mind enabled me to methodize the stores which early study very diligently garnered up. Beyond all things the works of the German moralists gave me great delight; not from any ill-advised admiration of their eloquent madness, but from the ease with which my habits of rigid thought enabled me to detect their falsities. I have often been reproached with the aridity of my genius—a deficiency of imagination has been imputed to me as a crime—and the Pyrrhonism [2] of my opinions has at all times rendered me notorious. Indeed a strong relish for physical philosophy has, I fear, tinctured my mind with a very common error of this age—I mean the habit of referring occurrences, even the least susceptible of such reference, to the principles of that science. Upon the whole, no person could be less liable than myself to be led away from the severe precincts of truth by the *ignes fatui* [3] of superstition. I have thought proper to premise thus much lest the incredible tale I have to tell should be considered rather the raving of a crude imagination, than the positive experience of a mind to which the reveries of fancy have been a dead letter and a nullity.

After many years spent in foreign travel, I sailed in the year 18—, from the port of Batavia in the rich and populous island of Java, on a voyage to the Archipelago of the Sunda islands. I went as passenger—having no other inducement than a kind of nervous restlessness which haunted me like a fiend.

Our vessel was a beautiful ship of about four hundred tons, copper-fastened, and built at Bombay of Malabar teak. She was freighted with cotton-wool and oil from the Lachadive islands. We had also on board coir, jaggeree, ghee,[4] cocoanuts, and a few cases of opium. The stowage was clumsily done, and the vessel consequently crank.[5]

We got under way with a mere breath of wind, and for many days stood along the eastern coast of Java, without any other incident to beguile the monotony of our course than the occasional meeting with some of the small grabs [6] of the Archipelago to which we were bound.

One evening, leaning over the taffrail, I observed a very singular, isolated cloud, to the NW. It was remarkable, as well for its color, as from its being the first we had seen since our departure from Batavia. I watched it attentively until sunset, when it spread all at once to the eastward and westward, girding in the horizon with a narrow strip of vapor and looking like a long line of low beach. My notice was soon afterwards attracted by the dusky-red appearance of the moon, and the peculiar character of the sea. The latter was undergoing a rapid change, and the water seemed more than usually transparent. Although I could distinctly see the bottom, yet, heaving the lead, I found the ship in fifteen fathoms. The air now became intolerably hot, and was loaded with spiral

---

* The word *Ms.* is an abbreviation for *manuscript*.

[1] *Qui . . . Atys:* a quotation from *Atys,* a tragedy by Philippe Quinault (1635–1688): "One who has only a moment to live no longer has anything to conceal."

[2] **Pyrrhonism:** a philosophy of skepticism taught by the Greek philosopher Pyrrho (365–275 B.C.)

[3] *ignes fatui:* will-o'-the wisps.

[4] **coir, jaggeree, ghee:** cocoanut fiber, palm sugar, and butter made from the milk of water buffaloes.

[5] **crank:** was unsteady.

[6] **grabs:** two-masted ships.

exhalations similar to those arising from heated iron. As night came on, every breath of wind died away, and a more entire calm it is impossible to conceive. The flame of a candle burned upon the poop without the least perceptible motion, and a long hair, held between the finger and thumb, hung without the possibility of detecting a vibration. However, as the captain said he could perceive no indication of danger, and as we were drifting in bodily to shore, he ordered the sails to be furled and the anchor let go. No watch was set, and the crew, consisting principally of Malays, stretched themselves deliberately upon deck. I went below—not without a full presentiment of evil. Indeed every appearance warranted me in apprehending a simoom.[1] I told the captain my fears—but he paid no attention to what I said, and left me without deigning to give a reply. My uneasiness, however, prevented me from sleeping, and about midnight I went upon deck. As I placed my foot upon the upper step of the companion ladder, I was startled with a loud, humming noise, like that occasioned by the rapid revolution of a mill wheel, and before I could ascertain its meaning, I found the ship quivering to its center. In the next instant, a wilderness of foam hurled us upon our beam-ends, and, rushing over us fore and aft, swept the entire decks from stem to stern.

The extreme fury of the blast proved in a great measure the salvation of the ship. Although completely waterlogged, yet, as all her masts had gone by the board, she rose, after a minute, heavily from the sea, and, staggering awhile beneath the immense pressure of the tempest, finally righted.

By what miracle I escaped destruction, it is impossible to say. Stunned by the shock of the water, I found myself, upon recovery, jammed in between the stern-post and rudder. With great difficulty I gained my feet, and looking dizzily around, was, at first, struck with the idea of our

being among breakers, so terrific beyond the wildest imagination was the whirlpool of mountainous and foaming ocean within which we were engulfed. After a while, I heard the voice of an old Swede, who had shipped with us at the moment of our leaving port. I hallooed to him with all my strength, and presently he came reeling aft. We soon discovered that we were the sole survivors of the accident. All on deck, with the exception of ourselves, had been swept overboard, and the captain and mates must have perished as they slept, for the cabins were deluged with water. Without assistance, we could expect to do little for the security of the ship, and our exertions were at first paralyzed by the momentary expectation of going down. Our cable had, of course, parted like pack-thread at the first breath of the hurricane, or we should have been instantaneously overwhelmed. We scudded with frightful velocity before the sea, and the water made clear breaches over us. The framework of our stern was shattered excessively, and, in almost every respect, we had received considerable injury—but to our extreme joy we found the pumps unchoked, and that we had made no great shifting of our ballast. The main fury of the simoom had already blown over, and we apprehended little danger from the violence of the wind—but we looked forward to its total cessation

[1] **simoom:** a hot, violent wind.

with dismay, well believing that, in our shattered condition, we should inevitably perish in the tremendous swell which would ensue. But this very just apprehension seemed by no means likely to be soon verified. For five entire days and nights—during which our only subsistence was a small quantity of jaggeree, procured with great difficulty from the forecastle—the hulk flew at a rate defying computation, before rapidly succeeding flaws of wind, which, without equalling the first violence of the simoom, were still more terrific than any tempest I had before encountered. Our course for the first four days was, with trifling variations, SE. and by South; and we must have run down the coast of New Holland.[1] On the fifth day the cold became extreme, although the wind had hauled round a point more to the northward. The sun arose with a sickly yellow luster, and clambered a very few degrees above the horizon—emitting no decisive light. There were no clouds whatever apparent, yet the wind was upon the increase, and blew with a fitful and unsteady fury. About noon, as nearly as we could guess, our attention was again arrested by the appearance of the sun. It gave out no light, properly so called, but a dull and sullen glow unaccompanied by any ray. Just before sinking within the turgid sea its central fires suddenly went out, as if hurriedly extinguished by some unaccountable power. It was a dim, silver-like rim, alone, as it rushed down the unfathomable ocean.

We waited in vain for the arrival of the sixth day—that day to me has not arrived —to the Swede, never did arrive. Thenceforward we were enshrouded in pitchy darkness, so that we could not have seen an object at twenty paces from the ship. Eternal night continued to envelop us, all unrelieved by the phosphoric sea-brilliancy to which we had been accustomed in the tropics. We observed too, that, although the tempest continued to rage with unabated violence, there was no longer to

be discovered the usual appearance of surf, or foam, which had hitherto attended us. All around was horror, and thick gloom, and a black sweltering desert of ebony. Superstitious terror crept by degrees into the spirit of the old Swede, and my own soul was wrapped up in silent wonder. We neglected all care of the ship, as worse than useless, and securing ourselves as well as possible to the stump of the mizzenmast, looked out bitterly into the world of ocean. We had no means of calculating time, nor could we form any guess of our situation. We were, however, well aware of having made farther to the southward than any previous navigators, and felt extreme amazement at not meeting with the usual impediments of ice. In the meantime every moment threatened to be our last—every mountainous billow hurried to overwhelm us. The swell surpassed anything I had imagined possible, and that we were not instantly buried is a miracle. My companion spoke of the lightness of our cargo, and reminded me of the excellent qualities of our ship—but I could not help feeling the utter hopelessness of hope itself, and prepared myself gloomily for that death which I thought nothing could defer beyond an hour, as, with every knot of way the ship made, the swelling of the black stupendous seas became more dismally appalling. At times we gasped for breath at an elevation beyond the albatross—at times became dizzy with the velocity of our descent into some watery hell, where the air grew stagnant, and no sound disturbed the slumbers of the kraken.[2]

We were at the bottom of one of these abysses, when a quick scream from my companion broke fearfully upon the night. "See! see!"—cried he, shrieking in my ears—"Almighty God! see! see!" As he spoke, I became aware of a dull, sullen glare of red light which streamed down the sides of the vast chasm where we lay, and threw a fitful brilliancy upon our deck. Casting my eyes upwards, I beheld a spec-

[1] **New Holland:** Australia.

[2] **kraken:** mythical sea monster.

tacle which froze the current of my blood. At a terrific height directly above us, and upon the very verge of the precipitous descent, hovered a gigantic ship of nearly four thousand tons. Although upreared upon the summit of a wave of more than a hundred times her own altitude, her apparent size still exceeded that of any ship of the line[1] or East Indiaman[2] in existence. Her huge hull was of a deep dingy black, unrelieved by any of the customary carvings of a ship. A single row of brass cannon protruded from her open ports and dashed off from their polished surfaces the fires of innumerable battle-lanterns, which swung to and fro about her rigging. But what mainly inspired us with horror and astonishment was that she bore up under a press of sail in the very teeth of that supernatural sea, and of that ungovernable hurricane. When we first discovered her, her stupendous bows were alone to be seen, as she rose up, like a demon of the deep, slowly from the dim and horrible gulf beyond her. For a moment of intense terror she paused upon the giddy pinnacle, as if in contemplation of her own sublimity, then trembled and tottered, and—came down.

At this instant, I know not what sudden self-possession came over my spirit. Staggering as far aft as I could, I awaited fearlessly the ruin that was to overwhelm. Our own vessel was at length ceasing from her struggles, and sinking with her head to the sea. The shock of the descending mass struck her, consequently, in that portion of her frame which was already under water, and the inevitable result was to hurl me with irresistible violence upon the rigging of the stranger.

As I fell, the ship hove in stays[3] and went about, and to the confusion ensuing I attributed my escape from the notice of the crew. With little difficulty I made my way unperceived to the main hatchway, which was partially open, and soon found an opportunity of secreting myself in the hold. Why I did so I can hardly tell. A nameless and indefinite sense of awe, which at first sight of the navigators of the ship had taken hold of my mind, was perhaps the principle of my concealment. I was unwilling to trust myself with a race of people who had offered, to the cursory glance I had taken, so many points of vague novelty, doubt, and apprehension. I therefore thought proper to contrive a hiding place in the hold. This I did by removing a small portion of the shifting boards[4] in such a manner as to afford me a convenient retreat between the huge timbers of the ship.

I had scarcely completed my work, when a footstep in the hold forced me to make use of it. A man passed by my place of concealment with a feeble and unsteady gait. I could not see his face, but had an opportunity of observing his general appearance. There was about it an evidence of great age and infirmity. His knees tottered beneath a load of years, and his entire frame quivered under the burden. He muttered to himself, in a low broken tone, some words of a language which I could not understand, and groped in a corner among a pile of singular-looking instruments and decayed charts of navigation. His manner was a wild mixture of the peevishness of second childhood and the solemn dignity of a god. He at length went on deck, and I saw him no more.

A feeling, for which I have no name, has taken possession of my soul—a sensation which will admit of no analysis, to which the lessons of bygone time are inadequate, and for which I fear futurity itself will offer me no key. To a mind constituted like my own the latter consideration is an evil. I shall never—I know that I shall never—be satisfied with regard to the nature of my conceptions. Yet it is not wonderful that these conceptions are indefinite, since they have their origin in

---

[1] **ship of the line:** the largest class of naval vessels.
[2] **East Indiaman:** commercial ship sailing for the East India Company.
[3] **hove in stays:** shook in the act of turning.

[4] **shifting boards:** boards placed in a hold to prevent the cargo from shifting.

sources so utterly novel. A new sense, a new entity is added to my soul.

It is long since I first trod the deck of this terrible ship, and the rays of my destiny are, I think, gathering to a focus. Incomprehensible men! Wrapped up in meditations of a kind which I cannot divine, they pass me by unnoticed. Concealment is utter folly on my part, for the people *will not* see. It was but just now that I passed directly before the eyes of the mate—it was no long while ago that I ventured into the captain's own private cabin, and took thence the materials with which I write, and have written. I shall from time to time continue this journal. It is true that I may not find an opportunity of transmitting it to the world, but I will not fail to make the endeavor. At the last moment I will enclose the Ms. in a bottle, and cast it within the sea.

An incident has occurred which has given me new room for meditation. Are such things the operations of ungoverned Chance? I had ventured upon deck and thrown myself down, without attracting any notice, among a pile of ratline stuff [1] and old sails in the bottom of the yawl. While musing upon the singularity of my fate, I unwittingly daubed with a tarbrush the edges of a neatly folded studding sail [2] which lay near me on a barrel. The studding sail is now bent upon the ship, and the thoughtless touches of the brush are spread out into the word DISCOVERY.

I have made many observations lately upon the structure of the vessel. Although well armed, she is not, I think, a ship of war. Her rigging, build, and general equipment, all negative a supposition of this kind. What she *is not* I can easily perceive, what she *is* I fear it is impossible to say. I know not how it is, but in scrutinizing her strange model and singular cast of spars, her huge size and overgrown suits of canvas, her severely simple bow and antiquated stern, there will occasionally flash across my mind a sensation of familiar things, and there is always mixed up with such indistinct shadows of recollection an unaccountable memory of old foreign chronicles and ages long ago.

I have been looking at the timbers of the ship. She is built of a material to which I am a stranger. There is a peculiar character about the wood which strikes me as rendering it unfit for the purpose to which it has been applied. I mean its extreme *porousness,* considered independently of the worm-eaten condition which is a consequence of navigation in these seas, and apart from the rottenness attendant upon age. It will appear perhaps an observation somewhat overcurious, but this wood has every characteristic of Spanish oak, *if Spanish oak were distended or swelled by any unnatural means.*

In reading the above sentence a curious apothegm [3] of an old weather-beaten Dutch navigator comes full upon my recollection. "It is as sure," he was wont to say, when any doubt was entertained of his veracity, "as sure as there is a sea where the ship itself will grow in bulk like the living body of the seaman."

About an hour ago, I made bold to thrust myself among a group of the crew. They paid me no manner of attention, and, although I stood in the very midst of them all, seemed utterly unconscious of my presence. Like the one I had at first seen in the hold, they all bore about them the marks of a hoary old age. Their knees trembled with infirmity, their shoulders were bent double with decrepitude, their shriveled skins rattled in the wind, their voices were low, tremulous, and broken, their eyes glistened with the rheum of years, and their gray hairs streamed terribly in the tempest. Around them on every part of the deck lay scattered mathematical instruments of the most quaint and obsolete construction.

[1] **ratline stuff:** ropes used for ladders up the masts.
[2] **studding sail:** a light, auxiliary sail.

[3] **apothegm** (ap′ə·them): a saying or proverb.

I mentioned some time ago the bending of a studding sail. From that period the ship, being thrown dead off the wind, has held her terrific course due south, with every rag of canvas packed upon her from her trucks to her lower studding-sail booms, and rolling every moment her topgallant yardarms [1] into the most appalling hell of water which it can enter into the mind of man to imagine. I have just left the deck, where I find it impossible to maintain a footing, although the crew seem to experience little inconvenience. It appears to me a miracle of miracles that our enormous bulk is not buried up at once and forever. We are surely doomed to hover continually upon the brink of Eternity, without taking a final plunge into the abyss. From billows a thousand times more stupendous than any I have ever seen, we glide away with the facility of the arrowy sea gull; and the colossal waters rear their heads above us like demons of the deep, but like demons confined to simple threats and forbidden to destroy. I am led to attribute these frequent escapes to the only natural cause which can account for such effect. I must suppose the ship to be within the influence of some strong current, or impetuous undertow.

I have seen the captain face to face, and in his own cabin—but, as I expected, he paid me no attention. Although in his appearance there is, to a casual observer, nothing which might bespeak him more or less than man—still a feeling of irrepressible reverence and awe mingled with the sensation of wonder with which I regarded him. In stature he is nearly my own height, that is, about five feet eight inches. He is of a well-knit and compact frame of body, neither robust nor remarkably otherwise. But it is the singularity of the expression which reigns upon the face, it is the intense, the wonderful, the thrilling evidence of old age so utter,

so extreme, which excites within my spirit a sense—a sentiment ineffable. His forehead, although little wrinkled, seems to bear upon it the stamp of a myriad of years. His gray hairs are records of the past, and his grayer eyes are sibyls [2] of the future. The cabin floor was thickly strewn with strange, iron-clasped folios,[3] and moldering instruments of science, and obsolete long-forgotten charts. His head was bowed down upon his hands, and he pored with a fiery unquiet eye over a paper which I took to be a commission, and which, at all events, bore the signature of a monarch. He muttered to himself, as did the first seaman whom I saw in the hold, some low peevish syllables of a foreign tongue, and although the speaker was close at my elbow, yet his voice seemed to reach my ears from the distance of a mile.

The ship and all in it are imbued with the spirit of Eld.[4] The crew glide to and fro like the ghosts of buried centuries, their eyes have an eager and uneasy meaning, and when their figures fall athwart my path in the wild glare of the battle-lanterns, I feel as I have never felt before, although I have been all my life a dealer in antiquities, and have imbibed the shadows of fallen columns at Balbec, and Tadmor, and Persepolis,[5] until my very soul has become a ruin.

When I look around me I feel ashamed of my former apprehensions. If I trembled at the blast which has hitherto attended us, shall I not stand aghast at a warring of wind and ocean, to convey any idea of which the words tornado and simoom are trivial and ineffective! All in the immediate

[1] **topgallant yardarms:** the last yards of sail at the end of a mast called the *topgallant*.

[2] **sibyls:** In ancient Greece, sibyls were women who made prophecies under the inspiration of the gods.
[3] **folios:** large books.
[4] **Eld:** antiquity.
[5] **Balbec, and Tadmor, and Persepolis:** ancient cities. Balbec (usually spelled *Baalbek)* is a village in Lebanon that was once a large, important city. Tadmor is a ruined city northeast of Damascus. Persepolis is the ancient capital of Persia.

vicinity of the ship is the blackness of eternal night, and a chaos of foamless water; but, about a league on either side of us, may be seen, indistinctly and at intervals, stupendous ramparts of ice, towering away into the desolate sky, and looking like the walls of the universe.

As I imagined, the ship proves to be in a current; if that appellation can properly be given to a tide which, howling and shrieking by the white ice, thunders on to the southward with a velocity like the headlong dashing of a cataract.

To conceive the horror of my sensations is, I presume, utterly impossible—yet a curiosity to penetrate the mysteries of these awful regions predominates even over my despair, and will reconcile me to the most hideous aspect of death. It is evident that we are hurrying onwards to some exciting knowledge—some never-to-be-imparted secret, whose attainment is destruction. Perhaps this current leads us to the southern pole itself—it must be confessed that a supposition apparently so wild has every probability in its favor.

The crew pace the deck with unquiet and tremulous step, but there is upon their countenances an expression more of the eagerness of hope than of the apathy of despair.

In the meantime the wind is still in our poop, and as we carry a crowd of canvas, the ship is at times lifted bodily from out the sea—Oh, horror upon horror! the ice opens suddenly to the right, and to the left, and we are whirling dizzily, in im-

mense concentric circles, round and round the borders of a gigantic amphitheater, the summit of whose walls is lost in the darkness and the distance. But little time will be left me to ponder upon my destiny—the circles rapidly grow small—we are plunging madly within the grasp of the whirlpool—and amid a roaring, and bellowing, and shrieking of ocean and of tempest, the ship is quivering, oh God! and—going down.

ANALYSIS AND COMPOSITION

Early Men of Letters

After reading and studying this second unit, you should be aware of a number of differences between the selections in this unit and in the preceding one. One important difference is that these selections were written within a much shorter period of time. Another is that, while the selections in the first unit were largely the work of gifted amateurs, the authors in this unit were all, in one way or another, professional writers. All thought of themselves as literary men, and all of them, to some degree, were commercially successful writers. All approached writing not as the diversion of an idle hour or as a means to a political end, but as a central concern—as something that was important in itself.

OVERVIEW OF THE PERIOD

Review the biographies of the writers in this unit. Remember that these men were all contemporaries, aware of one another's existence, and that Poe made a living at reviewing the works of other writers. Think of these men as all belonging to a literary community. In this light, review the selections you have read. Make a list of the authors, selections, and literary forms represented in this unit, and compare the list with the list you made for the preceding unit. Then discuss the following questions.

1. Which literary forms are new to this period? Which literary forms receive much greater emphasis in this unit than in the preceding one? Which forms that were prominent in the first period are not represented here? How do the selections in this unit reflect the growth of a literary community, a body of professional writers?

2. In the unit introduction it is stated that "The story of American literature in the early part of the nineteenth century . . . is the story of American writers trying to work out their own cultural destiny, to create a distinctive literature separate from English literature, and to make this literature a significant part of the national life" (page 89). Support this statement with specific references to selections in this unit and with details from the lives of Cooper, Irving, Bryant, and Poe.

THE CONFLICT BETWEEN IDEALS AND REALITIES

Although the selections in this unit do not reveal as much of a direct concern with the conflict between ideals and realities as do the earlier selections, this concern is nevertheless reflected in the literature. During this period, the conflict was mainly one between an ideal of democratic life and the reality of political demagogues and mob violence.

1. Which selections most clearly reflect the conflict between ideals and realities in the national life? What do these selections tell you about the conflict? Cite specific details from the selections to support your answer.

2. Which selections can be seen as a turning away from the realities of national life? Does the "unreal" quality of these selections make them any less valuable as literary works? Give reasons to support your answer.

ROMANTICISM AND THE ROMANTIC MOVEMENT

As you have learned, the writers represented in this unit can be considered as part of the Romantic movement that was dominant in the literature, music, and art of the first part of the nineteenth century. Review the discussion of the Romantic movement and the characteristics of Romanticism on pages 89–92. Then consider how the selections you have read exemplify these characteristics.

1. Cite passages that show the tendency of Romantic works to appeal to the emotions rather than to reason. In which selections is reason important? Cite passages that show an interest in the picturesque and unusual. How do Cooper, Bryant, and Irving exemplify the tendency of Romantic writers to build a national literary tradition? Poe, as you have learned, was indifferent to literary nationalism. He wrote, "A 'national' literature! As if any true literature *could be* 'national'—as if the world at large were not the only proper stage for the literary *histrio* [actor]." Do you agree or disagree? Explain.

2. All the writers represented in this unit showed an interest in nature. Cooper, who is represented by two political essays, wrote a number of memorable descriptions of the American wilderness in his novels. The following description of a lake is from *The Deerslayer:*

> "On a level with the point lay a broad sheet of water, so placid and limpid that it resembled a bed of the pure mountain atmosphere, compressed into a setting of the hills and woods. Its length was about three leagues while its breadth was irregular, expanding to half a league, or even more, opposite to the point, and contracting to less than half that distance more to the southward. Of course, its margin was irregular, being indented by bays, and broken by many projecting low points. At its northern, or nearest end, it was bounded by an isolated mountain, lower land falling off east and west, gracefully relieving the sweep of the outline. Still the character of the country was mountainous; high hills or low mountains, rising abruptly from the water, on quite nine-tenths of its circuit. . . .
>
> "But the most striking peculiarities of this scene were its solemn solitude and sweet repose. On all sides, wherever the eye turned, nothing met it but the mirrorlike surface of the lake, the placid view of heaven, and the dense setting of the woods. So rich and fleecy were the outlines of the forest that scarce an opening could be seen, the whole visible earth, from the rounded mountaintop to the water's edge, presenting one varied hue of unbroken verdure. As if vegetation were not satisfied with a triumph

so complete, the trees overhung the lake itself, shooting out toward the light; and there were miles along its eastern shore, where a boat might have pulled beneath the branches of dark Rembrandt-looking hemlocks, quivering aspens, and melancholy pines. In a word, the hand of man had never yet defaced or deformed any part of this native scene, which lay bathed in the sunlight, a glorious picture by the beautiful variety afforded by the presence of so broad an expanse of water."

What Romantic qualities can you find in this description? What sentences from the discussion of Romanticism in the unit introduction may be applied to this passage? What do you learn about nature, as an abstract idea, from the second stanza of Bryant's "I Broke the Spell That Held Me Long" (page 113)? Judging from the passage above from *The Deerslayer,* do you think Cooper would have agreed with Bryant? Explain.

FOR COMPOSITION: THE FORMS OF DISCOURSE

As you have seen from the selections by Irving and Poe and from the passage from Cooper's *The Deerslayer* given above, these writers were masters of descriptive writing. All of them relied on descriptive passages to help set the mood of a scene in a story or novel. As skillful descriptive writers, they were able to organize their descriptions so that all the details united to form a *dominant impression.*

1. Select descriptive passages by Irving and Poe that you consider to be good examples of mood setting. Can the dominant mood or impression of each passage be summarized by a single noun or adjective? If so, suggest some appropriate nouns or adjectives. What is the dominant impression or mood of the descriptive passage from *The Deerslayer?* How do all the details contribute to this impression? How are the details organized in the passages by Irving and Poe?

2. As a preliminary exercise in writing unified descriptions, list the words in the first paragraph of "The Fall of the House of Usher" and the second and third paragraphs of "The Devil and Tom Walker" that contribute most to the unifying moods. Substitute other words that will change the mood of each of these passages.

3. Write a paragraph or two of description. Organize all the details of your description so that they will unite to form a dominant impression and set a mood. On the back of your paper, write a noun or an adjective that will describe this mood. Exchange papers with a classmate and have him guess what mood you were trying to convey.

ART AND LITERATURE

Like its writers, the artists of the young Republic were also a part of the Romantic movement and equally concerned with a Romantic treatment of nature. Make a close study of one of the plates on pages 155 and 156, or on pages 225–30, that seems to you especially Romantic in its treatment of nature. Write a composition in which you show how all the details of the painting combine to suggest a mood.

AMERICAN PAINTING

The Early Nineteenth Century

By the end of the eighteenth century, American painting was developing along a number of widely divergent paths. Gilbert Stuart, John Trumbull, and other prominent American artists continued to work in the aristocratic British manner which they had learned from Benjamin West in London. But at the same time a very different tradition was flourishing in backwoods villages and rural areas. This was the tradition of "primitive" painting. Rooted in medieval folk art, it had been brought over by the early settlers.

Lady with Her Pets (PLATE 1), by a Massachusetts artist named Rufus Hathaway, is one of the most delightful examples of the primitive style. Hathaway knew almost nothing about effects of light and shade or about the rules of perspective. He rendered shapes so distinctly that each detail seems to stand out by itself. Yet the shapes also harmonize with one another. Notice, for example, how the spreading shape of the open fan is repeated by the two feathers sprouting from the top of the woman's bonnet. Primitive paintings such as this one often have qualities seldom found in the work of more formally trained artists—a charming naïveté combined with precise craftmanship and an elegant sense of design.

After the War of 1812 had been successfully concluded, the federal government and many cities and states commissioned artists to paint portraits and historical scenes expressing the nation's growing pride and self-confidence. In 1817, for instance, Thomas Sully painted a picture for the North Carolina State Capitol in which he showed Washington and his troops crossing the Delaware just before their attack on Trenton (PLATE 2). Unlike Trumbull's centrally balanced composition in *Death of General Mercer* (page 80), Sully's picture is heavily weighted on one side. Note how he has grouped all the main figures on the far right. And instead of staging a dramatic battle scene, Sully has evoked a feeling of tension leading *up to* the battle, a mood suggesting impending crisis.

The romantic concern with mood and feeling is even more apparent in the landscapes of Washington Allston, one of the foremost early American artists. Allston painted landscapes not simply to render the outward facts of nature, but also to express something of its power and presence. *Moonlit*

Landscape (PLATE 3) was probably evoked by the artist's memories of places he had seen both in America and Europe. Although this is a very small canvas, it has been painted with a feeling of breadth that we would expect from a picture of much grander scale. But most important is its luminosity of tone, which Allston achieved after careful study of the paintings of Titian and other Venetian masters.

Another important development in American art during the early nineteenth century was that of *genre* painting: pictures which show people in their everyday surroundings. One of the most talented of the early genre masters was William Sidney Mount, who found his subject matter in the community life of backwater areas near his childhood home in Stony Brook, Long Island. In *Eel Spearing at Setauket* (PLATE 4), Mount recorded what must have been a rather commonplace event. Yet through what he chose to emphasize, the artist transformed this ordinary scene into a vivid and compelling pictorial image. The long horizontal shape of the boat, the flat shoreline, and the gradual sloping contours of the landscape all combine to suggest a moment of utter stillness. But this hushed moment is threatened by the diagonal line of the poised spear and by the tension we feel in the alert poses of the two figures.

About this same time, another famous American genre painter, George Caleb Bingham, was working in Missouri on a series of pictures intended as a sort of visual encyclopedia of frontier life. In 1846–47 Bingham painted a number of canvases depicting crews of boatmen aboard rafts on the Upper Mississippi and Missouri Rivers. One of the finest is his *Raftsmen Playing Cards* (PLATE 5), a powerful illusion of three-dimensional space. Each figure seems to occupy a cube of space that has been allotted to him as if he were an actor in a carefully staged tableau. Each figure's gestures have been planned with utmost precision to relate to the gestures of the figures around him. And notice how the group as a whole combines with the converging sides of the raft to form a sort of pyramid, which seems to be partly framed by the soft banks of foliage jutting out into the river. As in many of his other river scenes, Bingham has set the action of the figures against a serene background of infinite space.

The flavor of life in America during this period would be incomplete without at least one picture of the colorful, proud American Indian. PLATE 6 shows a full-length portrait of the most famous of the Indian chiefs along the Mississippi River—*Keokuk, The Watchful Fox.* The artist, a Pennsylvanian named George Catlin, became so fascinated with Indian culture that he spent six years traveling from tribe to tribe throughout the Midwest, documenting what he saw in hundreds of paintings. But Catlin painted only those details he considered significant. What we see here, then, is the result of an artist's selective imagination, rather than merely a literal copy of life.

PLATE 1. RUFUS HATHAWAY (About 1770–1822): *Lady with Her Pets*. 1790. Oil on canvas, 34¼ x 32 inches. (The Metropolitan Museum of Art, New York, Gift of Edgar William and Bernice Chrysler Garbisch, 1963)

PLATE 2. THOMAS SULLY (1783–1872): *Passage of the Delaware.* 1819. Oil on canvas, 146½ x 207 inches. (Courtesy, Museum of Fine Arts, Boston, Gift of the owners of the Boston Museum)

PLATE 3. WASHINGTON ALLSTON (1779–1843): *Moonlit Landscape.* 1819. Oil on canvas, 24 x 25 inches. (Courtesy, Museum of Fine Arts, Boston, Gift of Dr. W. S. Bigelow)

155

PLATE 4. WILLIAM SIDNEY MOUNT (1807–1868): *Eel Spearing at Setauket*. 1845. Oil on canvas, 29 x 36 inches. (New York State Historical Association, Cooperstown, New York)

156

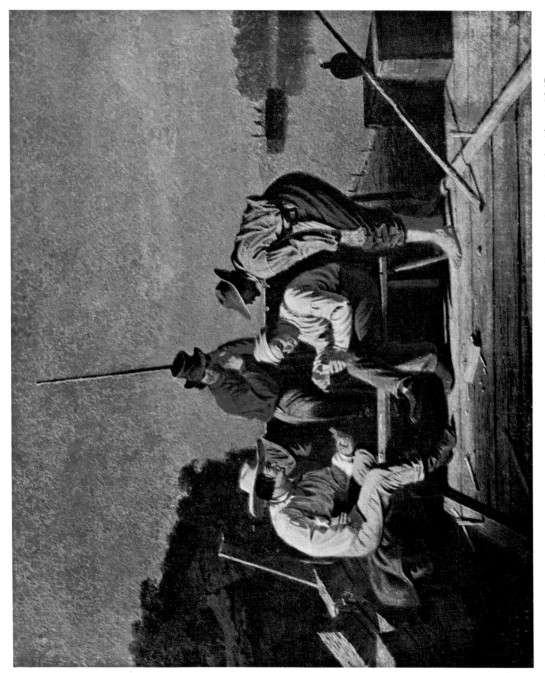

PLATE 5. GEORGE CALEB BINGHAM (1811–1879): *Raftsmen Playing Cards.* About 1847 Oil on canvas, 28 x 36 inches. (Owned by the Right Reverend Paul Moore, Jr.)

157

PLATE 6. GEORGE CATLIN (1796–1872): *Keokuk, The Watchful Fox.* 1834–36. Oil on canvas, 29 x 24 inches. (Smithsonian Institution, Washington, D.C.)

THE FLOWERING OF NEW ENGLAND

"The foregoing generations beheld God and nature face to face; we, through their eyes. Why should not we also enjoy an original relation to the universe? Why should not we have a poetry and philosophy of insight and not of tradition, and a religion by revelation to us, and not the history of theirs? . . . The sun shines today also. There is more wool and flax in the fields. There are new lands, new men, new thoughts. Let us demand our own works and laws and worship."

RALPH WALDO EMERSON

From the beginning of Andrew Jackson's administration to the onset of the War Between the States, the United States was an exciting place in which to live and write. The frontier was pushed to the Rockies, then to the Pacific. The country's transportation system—roads, canals, steamboats, and railroads—grew enormously, making it easier to travel and transport goods from one part of the country to another, and bringing with it a growing sense of nationhood. The West, more and more an important part of the nation, played a decisive part in electing Jackson. On the very day the new President took office, he made it clear that a new era was beginning. After his Inaugural Address, the White House was thrown open to all of Jackson's followers. Crowds of men jammed the rooms, celebrating wildly. Aristocratic Southerners and New Englanders might grumble, but like it or not, the common man's turn in politics had arrived. Jackson himself believed that anyone, no matter what his background or education, was fit to hold a government office: "The duties of all public officers are, or at least admit of being made, so plain and simple that men of intelligence may readily qualify themselves for their performance." Reformers working in various fields advocated broadened suffrage, women's rights, humane treatment of prisoners and of the mentally ill, and abolition of slavery. It seemed that an era of greatness was at hand.

In this era, one characteristic of the Romantic movement became more and more important: a belief in the innate goodness of the individual man. Man, according to many Romantics, was born good. If some men became evil or did evil, it was because society had led them astray. If man acted in accordance with his own instincts and impulses and lived close to nature, he would remain good. Only society tended to corrupt man. With Westerners this belief took the form of a distrust of Eastern society and its complications. With a remarkable individual like Thoreau, this belief took the form of a withdrawal from men and their towns to live in the woods and arrive at universal truths by practicing a simple, contemplative life. With men of great spiritual force like Emerson, this belief took the form of repeated admonitions to individual men to trust themselves, to act in accordance with their own natures, no matter what anyone else might tell them. Americans were optimistic and confident. In this land of free individuals, this time of territorial expansion and industrial growth, who knew what America might not accomplish, was not, indeed, already accomplishing?

But as before (page 2), American ideals were tempered by some harsh realities. While men might hope to build the perfect society, they were very far from achieving it. The industrialization of New England brought with it a brutalization of human life, created ugly mill towns where human beings were packed together in unsightly huts and where even small children were put to hard labor. A Southern poet, William J. Grayson, wrote a bitter description of life in a mill town: "Childhood bestows no childish sports or toys,/ Age neither reverence nor repose enjoys,/ Labor with hunger wages ceaseless strife,/ And want and suffering only end with life."

In the South, there was slavery, a condition of life that New England idealists and reformers were finding harder and harder to accept. While Southerners like Grayson might defend the system of slavery on the grounds that the slave on the plantation was no less fortunate than the Northern laborer and in fact led a happier life, many Americans—among them, Southerners themselves—found the existence of slavery difficult to reconcile with the belief expressed in the Declaration of Independence "that all men are created equal, that they are endowed by their Creator with certain inalienable rights, that among these are life, liberty, and the pursuit of happiness." Gradually, even a thinker like Emerson, who preferred to remain aloof from political questions, found himself drawn to the antislavery cause, and in 1856 he issued a grave warning: "But the hour is coming when the strongest will [toward reconciliation] will not be strong enough. A harder task will the new revolution of the nineteenth century be than was the revolution of the eighteenth century . . . vast property, gigantic interests, family connections, webs of party, cover the land with a network that immensely multiplies the dangers of war."

If this period in American literature ended with grave misgivings, it began with a rush of optimism. America was at last developing its own culture and literature, and in Ralph Waldo Emerson it found a great champion. In 1837 Emerson delivered an address at Harvard which he called "The American Scholar" (page 167) and which is now regarded as one of the most important events in the intellectual life of America. "Our day of dependence, our long apprenticeship to the learning of other lands, draws to a close," Emerson declared, and he proclaimed the beginning of a new age in which America would be the intellectual leader of the world.

New England was alive with the excitement of ideas, vitalized by the sense that *its* cultural and intellectual time had come, as previously the time of Greece and Rome and Florence and England had come. This period in American literature has been called by some scholars the "American Renaissance," to compare it with a great cultural period of the Western world. In his famous book on the period, *The Flowering of New England,* Van Wyck Brooks has described the contribution of the New England writers of this period: "They threw so many ideas into circulation and wrote so sincerely and so well that they came to be accepted as fathers and sages . . . They helped to make their countrypeople conscious of the great world-movements of thought and feeling in which they played parts side by side with the intellectual leaders of the older countries. In their scholarship, their social thought, their moral passion, their artistic feeling, they spoke for the universal republic of letters, giving their own province a form and body in the consciousness of the world."

Although some writers—notably Emily Dickinson and John Whittier— fall outside the following classification, the authors who made New England a significant place in literature can be put into three groups: the transcendentalists, the Brahmins, and the dissenters.

CONCORD: THE TRANSCENDENTALISTS

Although Concord, Massachusetts, was a small town, the writers and thinkers who congregated there had a major influence on the intellectual life of America. Emerson had settled in Concord in 1834. Living nearby were Bronson Alcott, Margaret Fuller, Theodore Parker, Orestes Brownson, and Henry David Thoreau. Gradually these serious people got into the

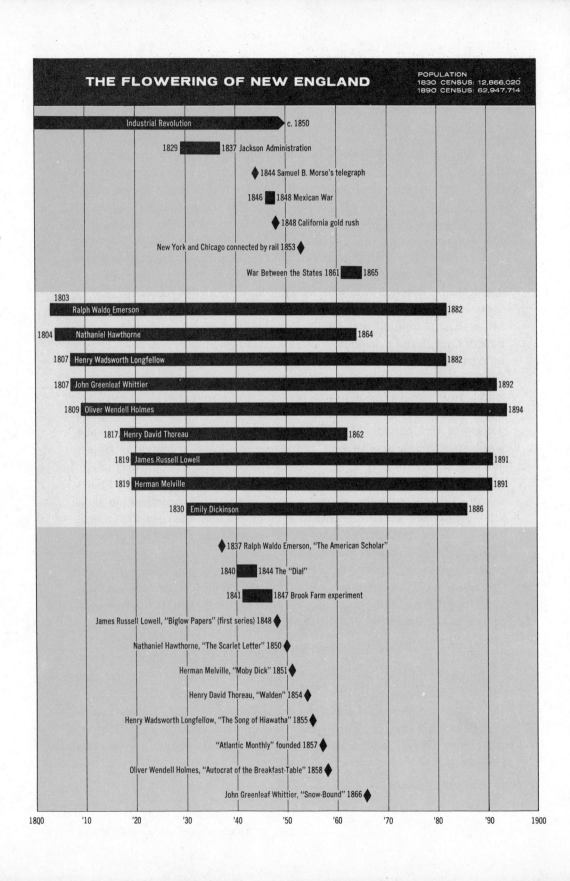

THE FLOWERING OF NEW ENGLAND

POPULATION
1830 CENSUS: 12,866,020
1890 CENSUS: 62,947,714

Industrial Revolution → c. 1850

1829 ■ 1837 Jackson Administration

◆ 1844 Samuel B. Morse's telegraph

1846 ■ 1848 Mexican War

◆ 1848 California gold rush

New York and Chicago connected by rail 1853 ◆

War Between the States 1861 ■ 1865

1803 Ralph Waldo Emerson 1882

1804 Nathaniel Hawthorne 1864

1807 Henry Wadsworth Longfellow 1882

1807 John Greenleaf Whittier 1892

1809 Oliver Wendell Holmes 1894

1817 Henry David Thoreau 1862

1819 James Russell Lowell 1891

1819 Herman Melville 1891

1830 Emily Dickinson 1886

◆ 1837 Ralph Waldo Emerson, "The American Scholar"

1840 ■ 1844 The "Dial"

1841 ■ 1847 Brook Farm experiment

James Russell Lowell, "Biglow Papers" (first series) 1848 ◆

Nathaniel Hawthorne, "The Scarlet Letter" 1850 ◆

Herman Melville, "Moby Dick" 1851 ◆

Henry David Thoreau, "Walden" 1854 ◆

Henry Wadsworth Longfellow, "The Song of Hiawatha" 1855 ◆

"Atlantic Monthly" founded 1857 ◆

Oliver Wendell Holmes, "Autocrat of the Breakfast-Table" 1858 ◆

John Greenleaf Whittier, "Snow-Bound" 1866 ◆

1800   '10   '20   '30   '40   '50   '60   '70   '80   '90   1900

habit of gathering at one another's homes of an afternoon. One of the group humorously described these sessions of conversation as "going to Heaven in a swing." The talk was moral and philosophical and reflected the influence of such English and German writers and philosophers as Wordsworth, Coleridge, Carlyle, Goethe, and Fichte. Although not every member of the group regarded himself as a transcendentalist, eventually the group named itself the Transcendental Club. Out of the Transcendental Club came one of the most influential magazines of the time, *The Dial,* which Emerson and Margaret Fuller edited at different times. Out of the group also came Brook Farm, an experiment in communal living. The philosophy of *transcendentalism,* which members of the club advocated, had a vital effect on many writers of the time, including those who were skeptical or opposed it.

Transcendentalism is difficult to define. Its major importance is not so much as a set of precise doctrines than as a state of mind, a set of attitudes about man, God, and the universe. Put simply, transcendentalism is the view that the basic truths of the universe lie beyond the knowledge we obtain from our senses, a knowledge that a transcendentalist regards as the mere appearance of things. Basic truths, it was felt, can be reached only through instinct and intuition and are a matter of private experience, faith, and conviction. To arrive at the truth, man must go beyond or transcend what his eyes and ears tell him or what he can learn from books. He must listen to his inner soul. Much of the philosophy of transcendentalism is expressed in Emerson's words: "Great men are they who see that spiritual is stronger than any material force, that thoughts rule the world."

Although it was at variance with Puritan doctrines, transcendentalism was in one sense very much in the Puritan (or, more broadly speaking, New England) tradition. It encouraged man to be severe with himself and to aspire. Like Puritanism, it saw all things, both great and small, as interrelated. But, unlike Puritanism, it was a doctrine that preached self-confidence and saw man not as a damned soul, but as a source of spiritual richness. It proclaimed that the intellectual life was not a constant poring over dead books, but a living tradition that could be renewed by every man's individual insight. It was a call to man to achieve not material, but spiritual greatness.

BOSTON AND CAMBRIDGE: THE BRAHMINS

A Brahmin is, literally, a member of the very highest caste of Hindu society. The Boston and Cambridge authors—James Russell Lowell, Henry Wadsworth Longfellow, Oliver Wendell Holmes—are sometimes called "Brahmins" because they were, in a sense, high-caste New Englanders, socially important men for whom literature was an accomplishment as well as a vocation. All were polished poets, popular in England as well as in America. Longfellow, in fact, was one of the two or three most popular poets in English of his day. Each of these three Brahmins had successful careers outside literature: Longfellow as a teacher of foreign languages, Lowell as a teacher and diplomat, Holmes as a scientist, doctor, and teacher of anatomy. As poets they were also teachers, and their poetry was valued for the moral lessons it taught, such as Longfellow's famous admonition, "Life is real, life is earnest,/ And the grave is not its goal," or Holmes's call, "Build thee more stately mansions, O my soul." All three, because of their urbanity, wit, scholarship, and technical skill, won from Europeans respect for American literature.

THE DISSENTERS

While Lowell, Longfellow, and Holmes were not swept away by the fervor of the transcendentalists, they nevertheless responded and paid tribute to Emerson's power to inspire and awaken. It remained for the two great fiction writers of the time—Nathaniel Hawthorne and Herman Melville—to enter a serious dissent to transcendentalist optimism and to stress the presence of evil in the universe. As Melville wrote in an appreciation of Hawthorne, "Certain it is that this great power of blackness in him derives its force from its appeals to the Calvinistic sense of Innate Depravity and Original Sin, from whose visitations, in some shape or other, no deeply thinking mind is always and wholly free. For, in certain moods, no man can weigh this world without throwing in something, somehow like Original Sin, to strike the uneven balance." (For a discussion of Calvinism and the concept of innate depravity, see page 3.) Both Melville and Hawthorne were concerned with striking the uneven balance, with giving due weight to the "power of blackness." In their stories and novels, they gave powerful expression to their dissenting view as they wrestled with the central riddle of existence, the presence of evil in a world of good intentions. And, like other writers before and after, they pointed to the discrepancy between American ideals and realities.

Certainly, as the years passed, as a sense of foreboding possessed many men, as the conflict between North and South began more and more to seem inevitable, the insistence of these two writers on the power of blackness seemed to have a greater relevance than Emerson's call to individual greatness. With the coming of the War Between the States, the flowering of New England, this joyous youthful period in the intellectual and cultural life of the nation, was over. The nation no longer responded to Emerson's call to individual greatness or his prediction of national greatness. Instead it reflected Melville's dark lines: "I muse upon my country's ills—/ The tempest bursting from the waste of Time/ On the world's fairest hope linked with man's foulest crime."

RALPH WALDO EMERSON

(1803–1882)

"I gain my point, gain all points," Emerson said, "whenever I can reach the young man with any statement that teaches him his own worth." As lecturer and writer, Emerson inspired generation after generation of the young, teaching them to search for greatness within themselves. Although he was a notably shy man, his presence on the lecture platform was remarkable. His contemporary James Russell Lowell recalls how the young men of his day "used to walk in from the country to the Masonic Temple . . . through the crisp winter night and listen to that thrilling voice of his, so charged with subtle meaning and subtle music, as shipwrecked men on a raft [listened] to the hail that came with unhoped-for food and rescue." It was from the dull, the ordinary, the mediocre that Emerson rescued his listeners. He said, "There is a time in every man's education when he arrives at the conviction that envy is ignorance, that imitation is suicide; that he must take himself for better or worse as his portion. . . . The power which resides in him is new in nature, and none but he knows what that is which he can do, nor does he know until he has tried. . . . Trust thyself: every heart vibrates to that iron string." In "Self-Reliance," a famous essay, Emerson continued, "What I must do is all that concerns me, not what people think. . . . It is easy in the world to live after the world's opinion; it is easy in solitude to live after your own; but the great man is he who in the midst of the crowd keeps with perfect sweetness the independence of solitude." Emerson called on all who would listen to respond from the very depths of their natures to every different situation. He condemned systems of thought which forced men into intellectual conformity. "A foolish consistency is the hobgoblin of little minds. . . . With consistency a great soul simply has nothing to do. He may as well concern himself with his shadow on the wall. Speak what you think now in hard words and tomorrow speak what tomorrow thinks in hard words again, though it contradict everything you said today." Emerson's championship of inconsistency has led some critics to call him a shallow thinker, but they overlook the fact that Emerson was not seeking to formulate a precisely logical system. Instead he sought to arouse men to their own capacities and to make each man recognize that there was within himself something of God. As James Russell Lowell commented, Emerson was essentially a poet, and it was the power of his words that led to an intellectual awakening in this country.

Emerson's childhood was spent in poverty. His father, a minister, died when Emerson was eight, and at times the family did not have enough to eat. When Emerson went to Harvard, he worked as the president's messenger and waited on tables. After graduation, he taught at a girls' school and eventually decided to become a minister, although with some misgivings. In his *Journal,* he wrote, "I deliberately dedicate my time, my talents, and my hopes to the Church. . . . I cannot dissemble that my abilities are below my ambition. . . . I have, or had, a strong imagination, and . . . a keen relish for the beauties of poetry. The exercise which the practice of composition gives to this faculty is the cause of my immoderate fondness for writing. . . . My reasoning faculty is proportionately weak. . . ." He also noted "an inability to lead and unwillingness to follow the current conversation. . . ."

In 1832, Emerson renounced his pulpit in the Second (Unitarian) Church of Boston because he had come to feel increasingly uneasy as a minister of formal religion. His health was poor, and he was troubled in spirit. Two of his gifted younger brothers had died. Death had also claimed his beautiful wife after scarcely a year of marriage. The distinctive attitudes of his later years were not yet formed; he sensed many problems but few answers. He read the poets and philosophers of many nations but had not yet arrived at what he called "the integrity of your own mind." Late that same year he sailed for Europe. There he was stirred by St. Peter's Cathedral in Rome and delighted by the botanical garden in Paris, but the most fruitful events of his trip took place in England, where he met writers such as William Wordsworth, Walter Savage Landor, and Thomas Carlyle. Carlyle, in particular, with his adaptations of German philosophy, preoccupation with individual greatness, and search for a positive attitude toward life, was a lasting influence on Emerson. When Emerson returned to America, he moved to Concord, Massachusetts, and began to write *Nature.* As in many of his works, he argued that the only way to God is through trusting in the divinity that is in all of us. He believed that nature, like man's individual mind, is part of one spiritual reality which he called the Oversoul, or God. Because the individual and the external world of nature surrounding him are both parts of a single spiritual whole, men can find the way to God by opening themselves to the benign influence of the open fields, the trees, and the ponds.

Like Carlyle, his English friend, and Henry Thoreau, his protegé, Emerson was a transcendentalist, a believer in and seeker for a higher, deeper truth than that which is revealed through the senses or by logical analysis (see page 163). This search for a higher truth runs through all his work and is reflected in his style. He tended to circle around an idea, developing it and refining it in a series of memorable sentences. Often a reader remembers Emerson's sentences more easily than he does the implications of the work as a whole. Strung together like carefully shaped jewels, these sentences are the results of Emerson's quest for spiritual truth, and they appeal as much to a reader's sense of beauty as to his intellect. In works such as *Representative Men, English Traits,* and the two series of *Essays,* Emerson used as avenues toward the truth many ideas he found in his wide reading of English and German writers and philosophers and of Oriental religious writings.

In Concord, Emerson devoted his days to walking, keeping a journal, and preparing lectures, which he later revised and published as essays. He lectured throughout the East and Middle West, often traveling under difficult conditions to fulfill his engagements. Once, he noted in his *Journal,* he traveled and lectured in Wisconsin when the weather was twenty degrees below zero. Another time he rode forty-eight miles in a buggy from Kalamazoo, Michigan, to deliver a lecture in Grand Rapids. At home he lived quietly, but his revolutionary ideas, expressed in powerful addresses such as "The American Scholar," drew to Concord scores of troubled searchers for enlightenment. As he grew older, Emerson's radical optimism softened. He became more aware of human limitations, of the power of fate and experience. In old age, he came to be regarded as a benevolent gray-haired sage, a composer of inspiring mottoes. But earlier in life, he had been widely feared as a disturber of established ideas and institutions. Emerson's emphasis on the direct working of divine inspiration and the essential divinity of all men had disturbed leaders of the older generation such as John Quincy Adams, who thought that Emerson weakened the authority of the church and threatened the stability of society. But these doctrines gave younger men an intoxicating sense of human possibilities and made Emerson the central spokesman of his age. It was his stirring call to greatness that led James Russell Lowell to pay tribute to him and note "how much the country's intellectual emancipation was due to the stimulus of his teaching and example, how constantly he had kept burning the beacon of an ideal life above our lower region of turmoil."

The American Scholar

In the summer of 1837, less than a year after *Nature* was published, Emerson was invited to give the annual Phi Beta Kappa Oration at Harvard. He had short notice—another man had declined the invitation—but he had long been considering the ideas that were to establish him as the leading figure in the intellectual revolution of New England. Those who were present in the church opposite Harvard Yard that August afternoon have described the mixture of enthusiasm and consternation, wonder and grim silence evident in the large audience. Oliver Wendell Holmes wrote of it, "This grand oration was our intellectual Declaration of Independence." Carlyle wrote Emerson, "I could have wept to read that speech; the clear high melody of it went tingling through my heart."

MR. PRESIDENT AND GENTLEMEN: I greet you on the recommencement of our literary year. Our anniversary is one of hope, and, perhaps, not enough of labor. We do not meet for games of strength or skill, for the recitation of histories, tragedies, and odes, like the ancient Greeks; for parliaments of love and poesy, like the Troubadours;[1] nor for the advancement of science, like our contemporaries in the British and European capitals. Thus far, our holiday has been simply a friendly sign of the survival of the love of letters amongst a people too busy to give to letters any more. As such it is precious as the sign of an indestructible instinct. Perhaps the time is already come when it ought to be, and will be, something else; when the sluggard intellect of this continent will look from under its iron lids and fill the postponed expectation of the world with something better than the exertions of mechanical skill. Our day of dependence, our long apprenticeship to the learning of other lands, draws to a close. The millions that around us are rushing into life cannot always be fed on the sere remains of foreign harvests. Events, actions arise, that must be sung, that will sing themselves. Who can doubt that poetry will revive and lead in a new age, as the star in the constellation Harp,[2] which now flames in our zenith, astronomers announce, shall one day be the polestar for a thousand years?

In this hope I accept the topic which not only usage but the nature of our association seem to prescribe to this day—the AMERICAN SCHOLAR. Year by year we come up hither to read one more chapter of his biography. Let us inquire what light new days and events have thrown on his character and his hopes.

It is one of those fables which out of an unknown antiquity convey an unlooked-

---

[1] **Troubadours:** medieval poets of southern France, northern Italy, and eastern Spain who held poetic contests and sang of chivalry and love.

[2] **Harp:** the constellation Lyra.

for wisdom, that the gods, in the beginning, divided Man into men, that he might be more helpful to himself; just as the hand was divided into fingers, the better to answer its end.

The old fable covers a doctrine ever new and sublime; that there is One Man—present to all particular men only partially, or through one faculty; and that you must take the whole society to find the whole man. Man is not a farmer, or a professor, or an engineer, but he is all. Man is priest, and scholar, and statesman, and producer, and soldier. In the *divided* or social state these functions are parceled out to individuals, each of whom aims to do his stint of the joint work, whilst each other performs his. The fable implies that the individual, to possess himself, must sometimes return from his own labor to embrace all the other laborers. But, unfortunately, this original unit, this fountain of power, has been so distributed to multitudes, has been so minutely subdivided and peddled out, that it is spilled into drops, and cannot be gathered. The state of society is one in which the members have suffered amputation from the trunk, and strut about so many walking monsters—a good finger, a neck, a stomach, an elbow, but never a man.

Man is thus metamorphosed into a thing, into many things. The planter, who is Man sent out into the field to gather food, is seldom cheered by any idea of the true dignity of his ministry.[1] He sees his bushel and his cart, and nothing beyond, and sinks into the farmer, instead of Man on the farm. The tradesman scarcely ever gives an ideal worth to his work, but is ridden by the routine of his craft, and the soul is subject to dollars. The priest becomes a form; the attorney a statute book; the mechanic a machine; the sailor a rope of the ship.

In this distribution of functions the scholar is the delegated intellect. In the right state he is *Man Thinking*. In the degenerate state, when the victim of society,

he tends to become a mere thinker, or still worse, the parrot of other men's thinking.

In this view of him, as Man Thinking, the theory of his office [2] is contained. Him Nature solicits with all her placid, all her monitory pictures; him the past instructs; him the future invites. Is not indeed every man a student, and do not all things exist for the student's behoof? And, finally, is not the true scholar the only true master? But the old oracle said, "All things have two handles: beware of the wrong one." In life, too often, the scholar errs with mankind and forfeits his privilege. Let us see him in his school, and consider him in reference to the main influences he receives.

I. The first in time and the first in importance of the influences upon the mind is that of nature. Every day, the sun; and, after sunset, Night and her stars. Ever the winds blow; ever the grass grows. Every day, men and women, conversing—beholding and beholden. The scholar is he of all men whom this spectacle most engages. He must settle its value in his mind. What is nature to him? There is never a beginning, there is never an end, to the inexplicable continuity of this web of God, but always circular power returning into itself. Therein it resembles his own spirit, whose beginning, whose ending, he never can find—so entire, so boundless. Far too as her splendors shine, system on system shooting like rays, upward, downward, without center, without circumference—in the mass and in the particle, Nature hastens to render account of herself to the mind. Classification begins. To the young mind everything is individual, stands by itself. By and by, it finds how to join two things and see in them one nature; then three, then three thousand; and so, tyrannized over by its own unifying instinct, it goes on tying things together, diminishing anomalies, discovering roots running under ground whereby contrary and remote things cohere and flower out

---

[1] **ministry:** here, calling or occupation.

[2] **office:** here, the duty of his position.

from one stem. It presently learns that since the dawn of history there has been a constant accumulation and classifying of facts. But what is classification but the perceiving that these objects are not chaotic, and are not foreign, but have a law which is also a law of the human mind? The astronomer discovers that geometry, a pure abstraction of the human mind, is the measure of planetary motion. The chemist finds proportions and intelligible method throughout matter; and science is nothing but the finding of analogy, identity, in the most remote parts. The ambitious soul sits down before each refractory [1] fact; one after another reduces all strange constitutions,[2] all new powers, to their class and their law, and goes on forever to animate the last fiber of organization, the outskirts of nature, by insight.

Thus to him, to this schoolboy under the bending dome of day, is suggested that he and it proceed from one root; one is leaf and one is flower; relation, sympathy, stirring in every vein. And what is that root? Is not that the soul of his soul? A thought too bold; a dream too wild. Yet when this spiritual light shall have revealed the law of more earthly natures—when he has learned to worship the soul, and to see that the natural philosophy that now is, is only the first gropings of its gigantic hand, he shall look forward to an ever expanding knowledge as to a becoming creator. He shall see that nature is the opposite of the soul, answering to it part for part. One is seal and one is print. Its beauty is the beauty of his own mind. Its laws are the laws of his own mind. Nature then becomes to him the measure of his attainments. So much of nature as he is ignorant of, so much of his own mind does he not yet possess. And, in fine, the ancient precept, "Know thyself," and the modern precept, "Study nature," become at last one maxim.

___

[1] **refractory:** unyielding.

[2] **constitutions:** here, physical compositions or make-ups.

II. The next great influence into the spirit of the scholar is the mind of the Past —in whatever form, whether of literature, of art, of institutions, that mind is inscribed. Books are the best type of the influence of the past, and perhaps we shall get at the truth—learn the amount of this influence more conveniently—by considering their value alone.

The theory of books is noble. The scholar of the first age received into him the world around; brooded thereon; gave it the new arrangement of his own mind, and uttered it again. It came into him life; it went out from him truth. It came to him short-lived actions; it went out from him immortal thoughts. It came to him business; it went from him poetry. It was dead fact; now, it is quick thought. It can stand, and it can go. It now endures, it now flies, it now inspires. Precisely in proportion to the depth of mind from which it issued, so high does it soar, so long does it sing.

Or, I might say, it depends on how far the process had gone of transmuting life into truth. In proportion to the completeness of the distillation, so will the purity and imperishableness of the product be. But none is quite perfect. As no air pump can by any means make a perfect vacuum, so neither can any artist entirely exclude the conventional, the local, the perishable from his book, or write a book of pure thought that shall be as efficient in all respects to a remote posterity as to contemporaries, or rather to the second age. Each age, it is found, must write its own books; or rather, each generation for the next succeeding. The books of an older period will not fit this.

Yet hence arises a grave mischief. The sacredness which attaches to the act of creation, the act of thought, is transferred to the record. The poet chanting was felt to be a divine man: henceforth the chant is divine also. The writer was a just and wise spirit: henceforward it is settled the book is perfect; as love of the hero corrupts into worship of his statue. Instantly the book becomes noxious: the guide is a tyrant. The sluggish and perverted mind of the multitude, slow to open to the incursions of Reason, having once so opened, having once received this book, stands upon it, and makes an outcry if it is disparaged. Colleges are built on it. Books are written on it by thinkers, not by Man Thinking; by men of talent, that is, who start wrong, who set out from accepted dogmas, not from their own sight of principles. Meek young men grow up in libraries, believing it their duty to accept the views which Cicero,[1] which Locke,[2] which Bacon,[3] have given; forgetful that Cicero, Locke, and Bacon were only young men in libraries when they wrote these books.

Hence, instead of Man Thinking, we have the bookworm. Hence the book-learned class, who value books, as such; not as related to nature and the human constitution, but as making a sort of Third Estate with the world and the soul. Hence the restorers of readings, the emendators, the bibliomaniacs of all degrees.[4]

Books are the best of things, well used; abused, among the worst. What is the right use? What is the one end which all means go to effect? They are for nothing but to inspire. I had better never see a book than to be warped by its attraction clean out of my own orbit, and made a satellite instead of a system. The one thing in the world, of value, is the active soul. This every man is entitled to; this every man contains within him, although in almost all men obstructed and as yet unborn. The soul active sees absolute truth and utters truth, or creates. In this action it is genius; not the privilege of here and

there a favorite, but the sound estate of every man. In its essence it is progressive. The book, the college, the school of art, the institution of any kind, stop with some past utterance of genius. This is good, say they—let us hold by this. They pin me down. They look backward and not forward. But genius looks forward: the eyes of man are set in his forehead, not in his hind-head: man hopes: genius creates. Whatever talents may be, if the man create not, the pure efflux[5] of the Deity is not his—cinders and smoke there may be, but not yet flame. There are creative manners, there are creative actions, and creative words; manners, actions, words, that is, indicative of no custom or authority, but springing spontaneous from the mind's own sense of good and fair.

On the other part, instead of being its own seer, let it receive from another mind its truth, though it were in torrents of light, without periods of solitude, inquest, and self-recovery, and a fatal disservice is done. Genius is always sufficiently the enemy of genius by overinfluence. The literature of every nation bears me witness. The English dramatic poets have Shakespearized now for two hundred years.

Undoubtedly there is a right way of reading, so it be sternly subordinated. Man Thinking must not be subdued by his instruments. Books are for the scholar's idle times. When he can read God directly, the hour is too precious to be wasted in other men's transcripts of their readings. But when the intervals of darkness come, as come they must—when the sun is hid and the stars withdraw their shining—we repair to the lamps which were kindled by their ray, to guide our steps to the East again, where the dawn is. We hear, that we may speak. The Arabian proverb says, "A fig tree, looking on a fig tree, becometh fruitful."

It is remarkable, the character of the pleasure we derive from the best books. They impress us with the conviction that

---

[1] **Cicero:** Marcus Tullius Cicero (106–43 B.C.), Roman orator, essayist, and philosopher.

[2] **Locke:** John Locke (1632–1704), English philosopher and political thinker.

[3] **Bacon:** Francis Bacon (1561–1626), English essayist and proponent of scientific thought.

[4] **Hence . . . degrees:** All these are men who value a book for some reason other than what it says or who are more concerned with details than the whole. **Restorers** and **emendators** refer to scholars who do research on a literary work in order to restore it to the author's original text. **Bibliomaniacs** refers to book collectors who have allowed their avocation to become a passion.

[5] **efflux:** a flowing out.

one nature wrote and the same reads. We read the verses of one of the great English poets, of Chaucer, of Marvell, of Dryden,[1] with the most modern joy—with a pleasure, I mean, which is in great part caused by the abstraction of all *time* from their verses. There is some awe mixed with the joy of our surprise, when this poet, who lived in some past world, two or three hundred years ago, says that which lies close to my own soul, that which I also had well-nigh thought and said. But[2] for the evidence thence afforded to the philosophical doctrine of the identity of all minds, we should suppose some preestablished harmony, some foresight of souls that were to be, and some preparation of stores for their future wants, like the fact observed in insects, who lay up food before death for the young grub they shall never see.

I would not be hurried by any love of system, by any exaggeration of instincts, to underrate the Book. We all know that as the human body can be nourished on any food, though it were boiled grass and the broth of shoes, so the human mind can be fed by any knowledge. And great and heroic men have existed who had almost no other information than by the printed page. I only would say that it needs a strong head to bear that diet. One must be an inventor to read well. As the proverb says, "He that would bring home the wealth of the Indies must carry out the wealth of the Indies." There is then creative reading as well as creative writing. When the mind is braced by labor and invention, the page of whatever book we read becomes luminous with manifold allusion. Every sentence is doubly significant, and the sense of our author is as broad as the world. We then see, what is always true, that as the seer's hour of vision is short and rare among heavy days and months, so is its record, perchance, the least part of his volume. The discerning will read, in his Plato[3] or Shakespeare, only that least part—only the authentic utterances of the oracle—all the rest he rejects, were it never so many times Plato's and Shakespeare's.

Of course there is a portion of reading quite indispensable to a wise man. History and exact science he must learn by laborious reading. Colleges, in like manner, have their indispensable office—to teach elements. But they can only highly serve us when they aim not to drill, but to create; when they gather from far every ray of various genius to their hospitable halls, and by the concentrated fires, set the hearts of their youth on flame. Thought and knowledge are natures in which apparatus and pretension avail nothing. Gowns[4] and pecuniary foundations, though of towns of gold, can never countervail the least sentence or syllable of wit.[5] Forget this, and our American colleges will recede in their public importance whilst they grow richer every year.

III. There goes in the world a notion that the scholar should be a recluse, a valetudinarian—as unfit for any handiwork or public labor as a penknife for an ax. The so-called "practical men" sneer at speculative men, as if, because they speculate or *see*,[6] they could do nothing. I have heard it said that the clergy—who are always, more universally than any other class, the scholars of their day—are addressed as women; that the rough, spontaneous conversation of men they do not hear, but only a mincing and diluted speech. They are often virtually disfranchised; and indeed there are advocates for their celibacy. As far as this is true of the studious classes, it is not just and wise. Action is with the scholar subordinate, but it is essential. Without it he is not yet man. Without it thought can never ripen into truth. Whilst the world hangs before

---

[1] **Chaucer . . . Dryden:** Geoffrey Chaucer (1340?–1400), Andrew Marvell (1621–1678), John Dryden (1631–1700).

[2] **But:** here, except.

[3] **Plato:** Greek philosopher (427–347 B.C.).

[4] **Gowns:** caps and gowns worn by professors at academic ceremonies.

[5] **wit:** here, wisdom.

[6] **speculate . . . see:** "speculate" is from the Latin, "to observe."

the eye as a cloud of beauty, we cannot even see its beauty. Inaction is cowardice, but there can be no scholar without the heroic mind. The preamble of thought, the transition through which it passes from the unconscious to the conscious, is action. Only so much do I know, as I have lived. Instantly we know whose words are loaded with life, and whose not.

The world—this shadow of the soul, or *other me*—lies wide around. Its attractions are the keys which unlock my thoughts and make me acquainted with myself. I run eagerly into this resounding tumult. I grasp the hands of those next me, and take my place in the ring to suffer and to work, taught by an instinct that so shall the dumb abyss be vocal with speech. I pierce its order; I dissipate its fear; I dispose of it within the circuit of my expanding life. So much only of life as I know by experience, so much of the wilderness have I vanquished and planted, or so far have I extended my being, my dominion. I do not see how any man can afford, for the sake of his nerves and his nap, to spare any action in which he can partake. It is pearls and rubies to his discourse. Drudgery, calamity, exasperation, want, are instructors in eloquence and wisdom. The true scholar grudges every opportunity of action past by as a loss of power. It is the raw material out of which the intellect molds her splendid products. A strange process too, this by which experience is converted into thought, as a mulberry leaf[1] is converted into satin. The manufacture goes forward at all hours.

The actions and events of our childhood and youth are now matters of calmest observation. They lie like fair pictures in the air. Not so with our recent actions—with the business which we now have in hand. On this we are quite unable to speculate. Our affections as yet circulate through it. We no more feel or know it than we feel the feet, or the hand, or the brain of our body. The new deed is yet a part of life— remains for a time immersed in our unconscious life. In some contemplative hour it detaches itself from the life like a ripe fruit, to become a thought of the mind. Instantly it is raised, transfigured; the corruptible has put on incorruption.[2] Henceforth it is an object of beauty, however base its origin and neighborhood. Observe too the impossibility of antedating this act. In its grub state, it cannot fly, it cannot shine, it is a dull grub. But suddenly, without observation, the selfsame thing unfurls beautiful wings, and is an angel of wisdom. So is there no fact, no event, in our private history, which shall not, sooner or later, lose its adhesive, inert form, and astonish us by soaring from our body into the empyrean. Cradle and infancy, school and playground, the fear of boys, and dogs, and ferules,[3] the love of little maids and berries, and many another fact that once filled the whole sky, are gone already; friend and relative, profession and party, town and country, nation and world, must also soar and sing.

Of course, he who has put forth his total strength in fit actions has the richest return of wisdom. I will not shut myself out of this globe of action, and transplant an oak into a flowerpot, there to hunger and pine; nor trust the revenue of some single faculty, and exhaust one vein of thought, much like those Savoyards,[4] who, getting their livelihood by carving shepherds, shepherdesses, and smoking Dutchmen, for all Europe, went out one day to the mountain to find stock, and discovered that they had whittled up the last of their pine trees. Authors we have, in numbers, who have written out their vein, and who, moved by a commendable prudence, sail for Greece or Palestine, follow the trapper into the prairie, or ramble round Algiers, to replenish their merchantable stock.

[2] **the corruptible . . . incorruption:** "For this corruptible must put on incorruption." I Corinthians 15:53.

[3] **ferules:** rulers, sometimes used for punishing children.

[4] **Savoyards:** natives of Savoy, in Italy.

[1] **mulberry leaf:** Silkworms are fed on mulberry leaves.

If it were only for a vocabulary, the scholar would be covetous of action. Life is our dictionary. Years are well spent in country labors; in town; in the insight into trades and manufactures; in frank intercourse with many men and women; in science; in art; to the one end of mastering in all their facts a language by which to illustrate and embody our perceptions. I learn immediately from any speaker how much he has already lived through the poverty or the splendor of his speech. Life lies behind us as the quarry from whence we get tiles and copestones for the masonry of today. This is the way to learn grammar. Colleges and books only copy the language which the field and the workyard made.

But the final value of action, like that of books, and better than books, is that it is a resource. That great principle of Undulation in nature that shows itself in the inspiring and expiring of the breath; in desire and satiety; in the ebb and flow of the sea; in day and night; in heat and cold; and, as yet more deeply ingrained in every atom and every fluid, is known to us under the name of Polarity—these "fits of easy transmission and reflection," as Newton[1] called them, are the law of nature because they are the law of spirit.

The mind now thinks, now acts, and each fit[2] reproduces the other. When the artist has exhausted his materials, when the fancy no longer paints, when thoughts are no longer apprehended and books are a weariness—he has always the resource *to live*. Character is higher than intellect. Thinking is the function. Living is the functionary. The stream retreats to its source. A great soul will be strong to live, as well as strong to think. Does he lack organ or medium to impart his truths? He can still fall back on this elemental force of living them. This is a total act. Thinking is a partial act. Let the grandeur of justice shine in his affairs. Let the beauty of affec-

tion cheer his lowly roof. Those "far from fame," who dwell and act with him, will feel the force of his constitution in the doings and passages of the day better than it can be measured by any public and designed display. Time shall teach him that the scholar loses no hour which the man lives. Herein he unfolds the sacred germ of his instinct, screened from influence. What is lost in seemliness is gained in strength. Not out of those on whom systems of education have exhausted their culture comes the helpful giant to destroy the old or to build the new, but out of unhandseled[3] savage nature; out of terrible Druids and Berserkers[4] come at last Alfred[5] and Shakespeare.

I hear therefore with joy whatever is beginning to be said of the dignity and necessity of labor to every citizen. There is virtue yet in the hoe and the spade, for learned as well as for unlearned hands. And labor is everywhere welcome; always we are invited to work; only be this limitation observed, that a man shall not for the sake of wider activity sacrifice any opinion to the popular judgments and modes of action.

I have now spoken of the education of the scholar by nature, by books, and by action. It remains to say somewhat of his duties.

They are such as become Man Thinking. They may all be comprised in self-trust. The office of the scholar is to cheer, to raise, and to guide men by showing them facts amidst appearances. He plies the slow, unhonored, and unpaid task of observation. Flamsteed and Herschel,[6] in their glazed observatories, may catalogue the stars with the praise of all men, and the

[1] **Newton:** Sir Isaac Newton (1561–1626), the English mathematician and scientist who formulated the laws of motion and gravity.

[2] **fit:** here, phase.

[3] **unhandseled:** here, raw or primitive.

[4] **Druids . . . Berserkers:** Celtic priests and Norse warriors, representing the Celtic and Scandinavian strains in the British people.

[5] **Alfred:** Alfred the Great (849–899), English king who defeated the Danish invaders.

[6] **Flamsteed . . . Herschel:** John Flamsteed (1646–1719) and Sir Frederick Herschel (1738–1822), noted British astronomers.

results being splendid and useful, honor is sure. But he, in his private observatory, cataloguing obscure and nebulous stars of the human mind, which as yet no man has thought of as such—watching days and months sometimes for a few facts; correcting still his old records—must relinquish display and immediate fame. In the long period of his preparation he must betray often an ignorance and shiftlessness in popular arts, incurring the disdain of the able who shoulder him aside. Long he must stammer in his speech; often forego the living for the dead. Worse yet, he must accept—how often!—poverty and solitude. For the ease and pleasure of treading the old road, accepting the fashions, the education, the religion of society, he takes the cross of making his own, and, of course, the self-accusation, the faint heart, the frequent uncertainty and loss of time, which are the nettles and tangling vines in the way of the self-relying and self-directed; and the state of virtual hostility in which he seems to stand to society, and especially to educated society. For all this loss and scorn, what offset? He is to find consolation in exercising the highest functions of human nature. He is one who raises himself from private considerations and breathes and lives on public and illustrious thoughts. He is the world's eye. He is the world's heart. He is to resist the vulgar prosperity that retrogrades ever to barbarism by preserving and communicating heroic sentiments, noble biographies, melodious verse, and the conclusions of history. Whatsoever oracles the human heart, in all emergencies, in all solemn hours, has uttered as its commentary on the world of actions—these he shall receive and impart. And whatsoever new verdict Reason from her inviolable seat pronounces on the passing men and events of today—this he shall hear and promulgate.

These being his functions, it becomes him to feel all confidence in himself, and to defer never to the popular cry. He and he only knows the world. The world of any moment is the merest appearance.

Some great decorum, some fetish of a government, some ephemeral trade, or war, or man, is cried up by half mankind and cried down by the other half, as if all depended on this particular up or down. The odds are that the whole question is not worth the poorest thought which the scholar has lost in listening to the controversy. Let him not quit his belief that a popgun is a popgun, though the ancient and honorable of the earth affirm it to be the crack of doom. In silence, in steadiness, in severe abstraction, let him hold by himself; add observation to observation, patient of neglect, patient of reproach, and bide his own time—happy enough if he can satisfy himself alone that this day he has seen something truly. Success treads on every right step. For the instinct is sure that prompts him to tell his brother what he thinks. He then learns that in going down into the secrets of his own mind he has descended into the secrets of all minds. He learns that he who has mastered any law in his private thoughts is master to that extent of all men whose language he speaks, and of all into whose language his own can be translated. The poet, in utter solitude remembering his spontaneous thoughts and recording them, is found to have recorded that which men in crowded cities find true for them also. The orator distrusts at first the fitness of his frank confessions, his want of knowledge of the persons he addresses, until he finds that he is the complement of his hearers—that they drink his words because he fulfills for them their own nature; the deeper he dives into his privatest, secretest presentiment, to his wonder he finds this is the most acceptable, most public, and universally true. The people delight in it; the better part of every man feels, This is my music; this is myself.

In self-trust all the virtues are comprehended. Free should the scholar be—free and brave. Free even to the definition of freedom, "without any hindrance that does not arise out of his own constitution." Brave; for fear is a thing which a

Emerson's home in Concord, Massachusetts.

scholar by his very function puts behind him. Fear always springs from ignorance. It is a shame to him if his tranquillity, amid dangerous times, arise from the presumption that like children and women his is a protected class; or if he seek a temporary peace by the diversion of his thoughts from politics or vexed questions, hiding his head like an ostrich in the flowering bushes, peeping into microscopes, and turning rhymes, as a boy whistles to keep his courage up. So is the danger a danger still; so is the fear worse. Manlike let him turn and face it. Let him look into its eye and search its nature, inspect its origin— see the whelping of this lion—which lies no great way back; he will then find in himself a perfect comprehension of its nature and extent; he will have made his hands meet on the other side, and can henceforth defy it and pass on superior. The world is his who can see through its pretension. What deafness, what stone-blind custom, what overgrown error you behold is there only by sufferance—by your sufferance. See it to be a lie, and you have already dealt it its mortal blow.

Yes, we are the cowed—we the trustless. It is a mischievous notion that we are come late into nature; that the world was finished a long time ago. As the world was plastic and fluid in the hands of God, so it is ever to so much of his attributes as we bring to it. To ignorance and sin, it is flint. They adapt themselves to it as they may; but in proportion as a man has any-

thing in him divine, the firmament flows before him and takes his signet and form. Not he is great who can alter matter, but he who can alter my state of mind. They are the kings of the world who give the color of their present thought to all nature and all art, and persuade men by the cheerful serenity of their carrying the matter, that this thing which they do is the apple which the ages have desired to pluck, now at last ripe, and inviting nations to the harvest. The great man makes the great thing. Wherever Macdonald sits, there is the head of the table.[1] Linnæus [2] makes botany the most alluring of studies, and wins it from the farmer and the herb-woman; Davy,[3] chemistry; and Cuvier,[4] fossils. The day is always his who works in it with serenity and great aims. The unstable estimates of men crowd to him whose mind is filled with a truth, as the heaped waves of the Atlantic follow the moon.

For this self-trust, the reason is deeper than can be fathomed—darker than can be enlightened. I might not carry with me the feeling of my audience in stating my own belief. But I have already shown the ground of my hope, in adverting to the doctrine that man is one. I believe man has been wronged; he has wronged himself. He has almost lost the light that can lead him back to his prerogatives. Men are become of no account. Men in history, men in the world of today, are bugs, are spawn, and are called "the mass" and "the herd." In a century, in a millennium, one or two men; that is to say, one or two approximations to the right state of every man. All the rest behold in the hero or the poet their own green and crude being—

[1] **Wherever ... table:** an adaptation of an old proverb.
[2] **Linnæus:** Karl von Linne (1707–1778), usually referred to by the Latinized name Linnæus, a Swedish botanist who was the founder of the modern system of classifying plants.
[3] **Davy:** Sir Humphry Davy (1778–1829), English chemist.
[4] **Cuvier:** Baron Georges Léopold de Cuvier (1769–1832), French paleontologist and founder of comparative anatomy.

ripened; yes, and are content to be less, so *that* may attain to its full stature. What a testimony, full of grandeur, full of pity, is borne to the demands of his own nature by the poor clansman, the poor partisan, who rejoices in the glory of his chief. The poor and the low find some amends to their immense moral capacity for their acquiescence in a political and social inferiority. They are content to be brushed like flies from the path of a great person, so that justice shall be done by him to that common nature which it is the dearest desire of all to see enlarged and glorified. They sun themselves in the great man's light, and feel it to be their own element. They cast the dignity of man from their downtrod selves upon the shoulders of a hero, and will perish to add one drop of blood to make that great heart beat, those giant sinews combat and conquer. He lives for us, and we live in him.

Men, such as they are, very naturally seek money or power; and power because it is as good as money—the "spoils," so-called, "of office." And why not? for they aspire to the highest, and this, in their sleepwalking, they dream is highest. Wake them and they shall quit the false good and leap to the true, and leave governments to clerks and desks. This revolution is to be wrought by the gradual domestication of the idea of Culture. The main enterprise of the world for splendor, for extent, is the upbuilding of a man. Here are the materials strewn along the ground. The private life of one man shall be a more illustrious monarchy, more formidable to its enemy, more sweet and serene in its influence to its friend, than any kingdom in history. For a man, rightly viewed, comprehendeth the particular natures of all men. Each philosopher, each bard, each actor has only done for me, as by a delegate, what one day I can do for myself. The books which once we valued more than the apple of the eye, we have quite exhausted. What is that but saying that we have come up with the point of view which the universal mind took through the eyes of one scribe; we have been that

man, and have passed on. First, one, then another, we drain all cisterns, and waxing greater by all these supplies, we crave a better and more abundant food. The man has never lived that can feed us ever. The human mind cannot be enshrined in a person who shall set a barrier on any one side to this unbounded, unboundable empire. It is one central fire, which, flaming now out of the lips of Etna,[1] lightens the capes of Sicily, and now out of the throat of Vesuvius,[2] illuminates the towers and vineyards of Naples. It is one light which beams out of a thousand stars. It is one soul which animates all men.

But I have dwelt perhaps tediously upon this abstraction of the Scholar. I ought not to delay longer to add what I have to say of nearer reference to the time and to this country.

Historically, there is thought to be a difference in the ideas which predominate over successive epochs, and there are data for marking the genius of the Classic, of the Romantic, and now of the Reflective or Philosophical age. With the views I have intimated of the oneness or the identity of the mind through all individuals, I do not much dwell on these differences. In fact, I believe each individual passes through all three. The boy is a Greek;[3] the youth, romantic; the adult, reflective. I deny not, however, that a revolution in the leading idea may be distinctly enough traced.

Our age is bewailed as the age of Introversion. Must that needs be evil? We, it seems, are critical; we are embarrassed with second thoughts; we cannot enjoy anything for hankering to know whereof the pleasure consists; we are lined with eyes; we see with our feet; the time is infected with Hamlet's unhappiness—

"Sicklied o'er with the pale cast of thought."

[1] **Etna:** a volcano in Sicily.
[2] **Vesuvius:** a volcano near Naples, Italy.
[3] **The boy . . . Greek:** referring to the classical age of ancient Greece.

It is so bad then? Sight is the last thing to be pitied. Would we be blind? Do we fear lest we should outsee nature and God, and drink truth dry? I look upon the discontent of the literary class as a mere announcement of the fact that they find themselves not in the state of mind of their fathers, and regret the coming state as untried; as a boy dreads the water before he has learned that he can swim. If there is any period one would desire to be born in, is it not the age of Revolution; when the old and the new stand side by side and admit of being compared; when the energies of all men are searched by fear and by hope; when the historic glories of the old can be compensated by the rich possibilities of the new era? This time, like all times, is a very good one, if we but know what to do with it.

I read with some joy of the auspicious signs of the coming days, as they glimmer already through poetry and art, through philosophy and science, through church and state.

One of these signs is the fact that the same movement which effected the elevation of what was called the lowest class in the state assumed in literature a very marked and as benign an aspect. Instead of the sublime and beautiful, the near, the low, the common was explored and poetized. That which had been negligently trodden under foot by those who were harnessing and provisioning themselves for long journeys into far countries is suddenly found to be richer than all foreign parts. The literature of the poor, the feelings of the child, the philosophy of the street, the meaning of the household life, are the topics of the time. It is a great stride. It is a sign—is it not?—of new vigor when the extremities are made active, when currents of warm life run into the hands and the feet. I ask not for the great, the remote, the romantic; what is doing in Italy or Arabia; what is Greek art, or Provençal minstrelsy; [1] I embrace

the common, I explore and sit at the feet of the familiar, the low. Give me insight into today, and you may have the antique and future worlds. What would we really know the meaning of? The meal in the firkin; [2] the milk in the pan; the ballad in the street; the news of the boat; the glance of the eye; the form and the gait of the body—show me the ultimate reason of these matters; show me the sublime presence of the highest spiritual cause lurking, as always it does lurk, in these suburbs and extremities of nature; let me see every trifle bristling with the polarity that ranges it instantly on an eternal law; and the shop, the plough, and the ledger referred to the like cause by which light undulates and poets sing—and the world lies no longer a dull miscellany and lumber room, but has form and order; there is no trifle, there is no puzzle, but one design unites and animates the farthest pinnacle and the lowest trench.

This idea has inspired the genius of Goldsmith, Burns, Cowper,[3] and, in a newer time, of Goethe, Wordsworth, and Carlyle.[4] This idea they have differently followed and with various success. In contrast with their writing, the style of Pope, of Johnson, of Gibbon,[5] looks cold and pedantic. This writing is blood-warm. Man is surprised to find that things near are not less beautiful and wondrous than things remote. The near explains the far. The drop is a small ocean. A man is related to all nature. This perception of the worth of the vulgar is fruitful in discoveries. Goethe, in this very thing the most modern of the moderns, has shown

[1] **Provençal minstrelsy:** Provence in southeastern France was a center of the troubadours.

[2] **firkin:** a wooden bowl.

[3] **Goldsmith . . . Cowper:** Oliver Goldsmith (1728–1794), Robert Burns (1759–1796), William Cowper (1731–1800), British poets who wrote of everyday life.

[4] **Goethe . . . Carlyle:** Johann Wolfgang von Goethe (1749–1832), William Wordsworth (1770–1850), Thomas Carlyle (1795–1881), leading writers of the nineteenth century.

[5] **Pope . . . Gibbon:** Alexander Pope (1688–1794), Samuel Johnson (1709–1784), Edward Gibbon (1737–1794), leading English writers of the eighteenth century, known for their polished, intricate styles.

us, as none ever did, the genius of the ancients.

There is one man of genius who has done much for this philosophy of life, whose literary value has never yet been rightly estimated—I mean Emanuel Swedenborg.[1] The most imaginative of men, yet writing with the precision of a mathematician, he endeavored to engraft a purely philosophical Ethics on the popular Christianity of his time. Such an attempt of course must have difficulty which no genius could surmount. But he saw and showed the connection between nature and the affections of the soul. He pierced the emblematic or spiritual character of the visible, audible, tangible world. Especially did his shade-loving muse hover over and interpret the lower parts of nature; he showed the mysterious bond that allies moral evil to the foul material forms, and has given in epical parables a theory of insanity, of beasts, of unclean and fearful things.

Another sign of our times, also marked by an analogous political movement, is the new importance given to the single person. Everything that tends to insulate the individual—to surround him with barriers of natural respect, so that each man shall feel the world is his, and man shall treat with man as a sovereign state with a sovereign state—tends to true union as well as greatness. "I learned," said the melancholy Pestalozzi,[2] "that no man in God's wide earth is either willing or able to help any other man." Help must come from the bosom alone. The scholar is that man who must take up into himself all the ability of the time, all the contributions of the past, all the hopes of the future. He must be a university of knowledges. If there be one lesson more than another which should pierce his ear, it is, The world is nothing, the man is all; in your-

self is the law of all nature, and you know not yet how a globule of sap ascends; in yourself slumbers the whole of Reason; it is for you to know all; it is for you to dare all. Mr. President and Gentlemen, this confidence in the unsearched might of man belongs, by all motives, by all prophecy, by all preparation, to the American Scholar. We have listened too long to the courtly muses of Europe. The spirit of the American freeman is already suspected to be timid, imitative, tame. Public and private avarice make the air we breathe thick and fat. The scholar is decent, indolent, complacent. See already the tragic consequence. The mind of this country, taught to aim at low objects, eats upon itself. There is no work for any but the decorous and the complacent. Young men of the fairest promise, who begin life upon our shores, inflated by the mountain winds, shined upon by all the stars of God, find the earth below not in unison with these, but are hindered from action by the disgust which the principles on which business is managed inspire, and turn drudges, or die of disgust, some of them suicides. What is the remedy? They did not yet see, and thousands of young men as hopeful now crowding to the barriers for the career do not yet see, that if the single man plant himself indomitably on his instincts, and there abide, the huge world will come round to him. Patience—patience; with the shades of all the good and great for company; and for solace the perspective of your own infinite life; and for work the study and the communication of principles, the making those instincts prevalent, the conversion of the world. Is it not the chief disgrace in the world, not to be a unit—not to be reckoned one character—not to yield that peculiar fruit which each man was created to bear, but to be reckoned in the gross, in the hundred, or the thousand, of the party, the section, to which we belong; and our opinion predicted geographically, as the north, or the south? Not so, brothers and friends—please God, ours shall not be so. We will walk on our own feet; we will

[1] **Swedenborg:** Emanuel Swedenborg (1688–1772), Swedish mystic and theologian who influenced Emerson's theory of the correspondence between the natural world and the world of the spirit.

[2] **Pestalozzi:** Johann Heinrich Pestalozzi (1746–1827), Swiss educational reformer.

work with our own hands; we will speak our own minds. The study of letters shall be no longer a name for pity, for doubt, and for sensual indulgence. The dread of man and the love of man shall be a wall of defense and a wreath of joy around all. A nation of men will for the first time exist, because each believes himself inspired by the Divine Soul which also inspires all men.

FOR STUDY AND DISCUSSION

1. Why do you think Oliver Wendell Holmes called this selection "our intellectual Declaration of Independence"? Find passages in the selection to support your answer.

2. What, according to Emerson, is the relation of the scholar to other men? What is the scholar's role in the state? Why does Emerson define the scholar as "Man Thinking"?

3. Why does Emerson say that "the ancient precept, 'Know thyself,' and the modern precept, 'Study nature,' become at last one maxim"?

4. What influence, according to Emerson, do books have on the scholar? How may this influence be misused? Does Emerson think a scholar should live apart from the busy world to pursue his duties? Why or why not? What, in Emerson's view, is the relationship between thought and action?

5. According to Emerson, what are the scholar's duties? What does Emerson mean by saying that these duties "may all be comprised in self-trust"? In what ways can scholars be great men who can change the world?

6. Explain the distinction Emerson makes between appearance and reality. What does he regard as real? What does he think is mere appearance? Explain the statement, "Let him [the scholar] not quit his belief that a popgun is a popgun, though the ancient and honorable of the earth affirm it to be the crack of doom."

7. How does Emerson describe his own time? Do you think his description also fits our time? Why or why not? What signs does Emerson see that the times are improving? Do you see similar signs today? If so, what are these contemporary signs?

8. Study or read aloud the portion of the last paragraph beginning, "If there be one lesson more than another . . ." Point out some of the phrases that, in your opinion, are particularly effective as oratory.

9. Give a title to each of the three numbered sections in the selection. How are these sections related to each other?

10. One of Emerson's basic ideas is the interrelationship of all things. Find passages in "The American Scholar" that express or are influenced by this idea.

11. Emerson has sometimes been called the philosopher of democracy. Find passages in "The American Scholar" that bear out this title.

12. Do you think this essay is of value only to scholars? Why or why not?

LANGUAGE AND VOCABULARY

Emerson is a master not only of the thought-provoking sentence but also of the thought-provoking word. Discuss the meaning and implications of each of the italicized words, and tell why, in your opinion, Emerson chose each of these words rather than more familiar and more easily understood words.

1. "the *sluggard* intellect of this continent . . ."

2. "the *sere* remains of foreign harvests."

3. "Man is thus *metamorphosed* into a thing . . ."

4. "Nature . . . with all her placid, all her *monitory* pictures . . ."

5. "the scholar should be a *recluse,* a *valetudinarian* . . ."

6. "this he shall hear and *promulgate.*"

FOR COMPOSITION

1. Write a composition in which you discuss the meaning and implications of one of the following quotations from "The American Scholar." Indicate whether you agree or disagree with whichever of these implications you select, and give reasons based on your reading and experience for your agreement or disagreement.

a. " 'All things have two handles; beware of the wrong one.' "

b. "Books are the best things, well used; abused, among the worst."

c. " 'He that would bring home the wealth of the Indies must carry out the wealth of the Indies.' "

d. "One must be an inventor to read well."

2. Write a composition in which you describe the kind of school or college which Emerson would have looked upon as ideal. Base your description on ideas that you have gained from studying "The American Scholar."

The Concord Hymn

Emerson wrote the following hymn for the dedication, on July 4, 1837, of a monument commemorating the Minute Men, who signaled the beginning of the Revolutionary War by fighting off the British at the Battle of Concord.

By the rude bridge that arched the flood,
　Their flag to April's breeze unfurled,
Here once the embattled farmers stood,
　And fired the shot heard round the world.

The foe long since in silence slept;　5
　Alike the conqueror silent sleeps;
And Time the ruined bridge has swept
　Down the dark stream which seaward creeps.

On this green bank, by this soft stream,
　We set today a votive stone;　10
That memory may their deed redeem,
　When, like our sires, our sons are gone.

Spirit, that made those heroes dare
　To die and leave their children free,
Bid Time and Nature gently spare　15
　The shaft we raise to them and thee.

Voluntaries III

In an age of fops and toys,
Wanting wisdom, void of right,
Who shall nerve heroic boys
To hazard all in Freedom's fight—
Break sharply off their jolly games,　5
Forsake their comrades gay
And quit proud homes and youthful dames
For famine, toil, and fray?
Yet on the nimble air benign
Speed nimbler messages,　10
That waft the breath of grace divine
To hearts in sloth and ease.
So nigh is grandeur to our dust,
So near is God to man,
When duty whispers low, *Thou must,*　15
The youth replies, *I can.*

Brahma

Of all Emerson's poems, "Brahma" most clearly shows Emerson's involvement with Oriental theology and philosophy. In the Hindu sacred writings, Brahma is the supreme soul of the universe, absolute and eternal, from which all things spring, to which all things return, and in which all contradictions are resolved. Many readers were puzzled by the poem. Emerson answered them in a remark to his daughter: "If you tell them to say Jehovah instead of Brahma, they will not feel any perplexity."

If the red slayer think he slays,
　Or if the slain think he is slain,
They know not well the subtle ways
　I keep, and pass, and turn again.

Far or forgot to me is near;　5
　Shadow and sunlight are the same;
The vanished gods to me appear;
　And one to me are shame and fame.

They reckon ill who leave me out;
　When me they fly, I am the wings;　10
I am the doubter and the doubt,
　And I the hymn the Brahmin° sings.

The strong gods pine for my abode,
　And pine in vain the sacred Seven;°
But thou, meek lover of the good!　15
　Find me, and turn thy back on heaven.

12. **Brahmin:** here, Hindu priest. 14. **sacred Seven:** the greatest Hindu saints.

Hamatreya

"Hamatreya" is a New England version of a passage from the *Vishnu Purana,* one of the sacred books of the Hindus. The passage tells of the great kings of the world who disappeared with their kingdoms.

Bulkeley, Hunt, Willard, Hosmer, Meriam, Flint,°
Possessed the land which rendered to their toil
Hay, corn, roots, hemp, flax, apples, wool and wood.
Each of these landlords walked amidst his farm,
Saying, "'Tis mine, my children's and my names.   5
How sweet the west wind sounds in my own trees!
How graceful climb those shadows on my hill!
I fancy these pure waters and the flags
Know me, as does my dog: we sympathize;
And, I affirm, my actions smack of the soil."   10

Where are these men? Asleep beneath their grounds:
And strangers, fond as they, their furrows plow.
Earth laughs in flowers, to see her boastful boys
Earth-proud, proud of the earth which is not theirs;
Who steer the plow, but cannot steer their feet   15
Clear of the grave.
They added ridge to valley, brook to pond,
And sighed for all that bounded their domain;
"This suits me for a pasture; that's my park;
We must have clay, lime, gravel, granite-ledge,   20
And misty lowland, where to go for peat.
The land is well,—lies fairly to the south.
'Tis good, when you have crossed the sea and back,
To find the sitfast° acres where you left them."
Ah! the hot owner sees not Death, who adds   25
Him to his land, a lump of mold the more.
Hear what the Earth says:

EARTH–SONG

"Mine and yours;
Mine, not yours.
Earth endures;   30
Stars abide—
Shine down in the old sea;
Old are the shores;
But where are old men?
I who have seen much,   35
Such have I never seen.

---

1. **Bulkeley ... Flint:** early settlers of Concord.   24. **sitfast:** well-established.

"The lawyer's deed
Ran sure,
In tail,°
To them, and to their heirs   40
Who shall succeed,
Without fail,
Forevermore.

"Here is the land,
Shaggy with wood,   45
With its old valley,
Mound and flood.
But the heritors?—
Fled like the flood's foam.
The lawyer, and the laws,   50
And the kingdom,
Clean swept herefrom.

"They called me theirs,
Who so controlled me;
Yet every one   55
Wished to stay, and is gone,
How am I theirs,
If they cannot hold me,
But I hold them?"

When I heard the Earth-song,   60
I was no longer brave;
My avarice cooled
Like lust in the chill of the grave.

39. **In tail:** entail, referring to the inheritance of property.

FOR STUDY AND DISCUSSION

1. In "The Concord Hymn," in what ways was the shot "heard round the world"? Explain the appeal made in the last stanza. Read the first and last stanzas aloud. What consonant sounds predominate in the first stanza? in the last? How does the effect of the sound in these two stanzas differ?

2. In "Voluntaries III," what is Emerson's opinion of his own time? How does it compare with your opinion of our own time? What is meant by "our dust" in line 13? Several lines of this poem are often quoted. Which lines do you think they are? Why?

3. Point out the opposites that are united in "Brahma." Explain the last two lines of the poem. In what ways do the beliefs expressed in this poem serve as background for Emerson's discussion of the nature and obligations of the American scholar? Find quotations to support your answer.

4. In line 1 of "Hamatreya," why do you think Emerson substituted Concord farmers for the great kings of the world? Why does he have the farmers say, in line 10, "my actions smack of the soil"? What feelings about the earth are expressed in this poem? Is the point of view of this poem closer to the point of view of "Brahma" or of "Voluntaries III"? Give reasons to support your answer.

5. How do the poems by Emerson which you have read reveal his range and variety as a poet? Which poems reflect Emerson's role as a public figure? Which reveal his philosophy? Which express private moods?

HENRY DAVID THOREAU
(1817–1862)

It was no accident that Emerson's young friend Thoreau wrote *Walden, or, Life in the Woods*. Like Emerson, Thoreau believed that nature is a reflection of an inner spiritual reality. His life was spent in the pursuit of the essentials of reality and of experiences that would bring him close to these essentials. He went to Walden so that he could strip his life of inessential things. At the end of his two-year stay he had learned "that if one advances confidently in the direction of his dreams, and endeavors to live the life which he has imagined, he will meet with a success unexpected in common hours. He will put some things behind, will pass an invisible boundary. . . . In proportion as he simplifies his life, the laws of the universe will appear less complex, and solitude will not be solitude, nor poverty poverty, nor weakness weakness." In pursuit of his dreams—that is, of an inner reality—he was the self-reliant nonconformist that Emerson urged all men to be. "If a man does not keep pace with his companions," Thoreau wrote, "perhaps it is because he hears a different drummer. Let him keep step to the music which he hears, however measured or far away." During his stay at Walden, he had one striking clash with organized society. To show his disapproval of the Mexican war and slavery, he refused to pay taxes and, as a result, he spent a night in jail. Out of this incident came the famous essay, "Civil Disobedience." Thoreau has sometimes been criticized for being out of step with other men, but those who have heard his music have judged it one of the most valuable strains ever created by an American.

Thoreau was born and spent most of his early life in Concord. His father had financial troubles—he once went bankrupt—and Thoreau sometimes had patches on the clothes he wore at Harvard College. Upon graduation, he made little attempt to restore the family fortunes. Indeed, to his fellow townsmen his career must have seemed odd for a Harvard graduate. For a time he taught school, and he helped in the family business of making pencils. Skilled at all sorts of odd jobs, he worked as a general handyman and gardener at the Emerson house, and served for a short period as the town surveyor of Concord. He was a great walker. Hikes of twenty or thirty miles a day were easy for this seemingly frail young man. Occasionally he made excursions—to the Maine woods, to Cape Cod, to Canada—but most of his interests centered in and around Concord. "I have traveled a good deal in Concord," he said, and he wrote to his mother, "Methinks I should be content to sit at the back door in Concord, under the poplar tree, henceforth forever." In 1839, he and his brother John took a trip on the Concord and Merrimack Rivers. Ten years later he wrote about the trip in *A Week on the Concord and Merrimack Rivers*. Of the thousand copies printed of this, his first book, only 219 were sold. The rest were returned to the author, who wrote wryly in his journal, "I have now a library of nearly nine hundred volumes, over seven hundred of which I wrote myself." Like Emerson, he gave lectures which he later revised as essays, but his lectures were not nearly as popular as Emerson's. Bitterly he remarked that "whatever succeeded with an audience was bad."

Probably the greatest influence on Thoreau's adult life was Emerson, who encouraged the younger man to keep a regular journal and to write essays and poetry. But Thoreau was a good deal more than a disciple of Emerson. He was very much his own man who lived as he pleased and achieved greatness in his own fashion. In Thoreau's later years, Emerson felt that the two were growing more and more apart, and he wrote, "All his resources of wit and invention are lost to me, year after year." In a talk at Thoreau's funeral, he lamented that a man who might have been "engineering for all America . . . was the captain of a huckleberry party." Today, it seems clear that Emerson was mistaken. Thoreau's sense of the economy of his life has been justified by his book *Walden,* which now seems worth more than a great deal of social engineering.

Where I Lived,
and What I Lived For

FROM *Walden*

On July 4, 1845, when Thoreau was twenty-eight, he went to live in the woods by Walden Pond. Later he wrote, "I went to the woods because I wished to live deliberately, to front only the essential facts of life and see if I could not learn what it had to teach." He thought of this experiment in living as "exploring the farthest Indies," or searching the depths of his own soul. In 1847, he left Walden Pond "for as good a reason as I went there. Perhaps it seemed to me that I had several more lives to live and could not spare any more time for that one."

Like all great literature, *Walden* helps us to live our lives. It does not urge us, as some have thought, to build a cabin in the woods and live a simple life. It is concerned with the condition of our souls, not the location of our bodies. *Walden* is an interesting book if it is read simply as an account of life at the pond. It is doubly interesting if the reader understands that it is written metaphorically, that Thoreau constantly uses happenings in the woods as a kind of secret code to relate his real story, the story of his dealings with the "Celestial Empire" of the spirit. The two years he spent at the pond are condensed in the book into a single year. That year begins in the fullness of summer, passes into the seasons of fall and of frost and death in nature, and concludes in celebration of the awakening of the spirit in the ever reviving green of spring.

AT A CERTAIN season of our life we are accustomed to consider every spot as the possible site of a house. I have thus surveyed the country on every side within a dozen miles of where I live. In imagination I have bought all the farms in succession, for all were to be bought, and I knew their price. I walked over each farmer's premises, tasted his wild apples, discoursed on husbandry [1] with him, took his farm at his price, at any price, mortgaging it to him in my mind; even put a higher price on it—took everything but a deed of it—took his word for his deed, for I dearly love to

[1] **husbandry:** farming.

talk—cultivated it, and him too to some extent, I trust, and withdrew when I had enjoyed it long enough, leaving him to carry it on. This experience entitled me to be regarded as a sort of real-estate broker by my friends. Wherever I sat, there I might live, and the landscape radiated from me accordingly. What is a house but a *sedes,* a seat?—better if a country seat. I discovered many a site for a house not likely to be soon improved, which some might have thought too far from the village, but to my eyes the village was too far from it. Well, there I might live, I said; and there I did live, for an hour, a summer and a winter life; saw how I could let the years run off, buffet the winter through, and see the spring come in. The future inhabitants of this region, wherever they may place their houses, may be sure that they have been anticipated. An afternoon sufficed to lay out the land into orchard, wood lot, and pasture, and to decide what fine oaks or pines should be left to stand before the door, and whence each blasted tree could be seen to the best advantage; and then I let it lie, fallow perchance, for a man is rich in proportion to the number of things which he can afford to let alone.

My imagination carried me so far that I even had the refusal of several farms—the refusal was all I wanted—but I never got my fingers burned by actual possession. The nearest that I came to actual possession was when I bought the Hollowell place, and had begun to sort my seeds, and collected materials with which to make a wheelbarrow to carry it on or off with; but before the owner gave me a deed of it, his wife—every man has such a wife—changed her mind and wished to keep it, and he offered me ten dollars to release him. Now, to speak the truth, I had but ten cents in the world, and it surpassed my arithmetic to tell if I was that man who had ten cents, or who had a farm, or ten dollars, or all together. However, I let him keep the ten dollars and the farm too, for I had carried it far enough; or rather, to be generous, I sold him the farm for just what I gave for it, and, as he was not a rich man, made him a present of ten dollars, and still had my ten cents, and seeds, and materials for a wheelbarrow left. I found thus that I had been a rich man without any damage to my poverty. But I retained the landscape, and I have since annually carried off what it yielded without a wheelbarrow. With respect to landscapes—

"I am monarch of all I *survey,*
    My right there is none to dispute." [1]

I have frequently seen a poet withdraw, having enjoyed the most valuable part of a farm, while the crusty farmer supposed that he had got a few wild apples only. Why, the owner does not know it for many years when a poet has put his farm in rhyme, the most admirable kind of invisible fence, has fairly impounded it, milked it, skimmed it, and got all the cream, and left the farmer only the skimmed milk.

The real attractions of the Hollowell farm, to me, were its complete retirement, being about two miles from the village, half a mile from the nearest neighbor, and separated from the highway by a broad field; its bounding on the river, which the owner said protected it by its fogs from frosts in the spring, though that was nothing to me; the gray color and ruinous state of the house and barn, and the dilapidated fences, which put such an interval between me and the last occupant; the hollow and lichen-covered apple trees, gnawed by rabbits, showing what kind of neighbors I should have; but above all, the recollection I had of it from my earliest voyages up the river, when the house was concealed behind a dense grove of red maples, through which I heard the house-dog bark. I was in haste to buy it, before the proprietor finished getting out some rocks, cutting down the hollow apple trees, and grubbing up some young birches which had sprung up in the pasture, or, in short, had made any more of his im-

[1] **"I . . . dispute":** from Cowper's poem, "Imaginary Verses of Alexander Selkirk." Selkirk was the original of Robinson Crusoe.

translation I have seen makes sheer nonsense of the passage—"When you think of getting a farm turn it thus in your mind, not to buy greedily; nor spare your pains to look at it, and do not think it enough to go round it once. The oftener you go there the more it will please you, if it is good." I think I shall not buy greedily, but go round and round it as long as I live, and be buried in it first, that it may please me the more at last.

The present was my next experiment of this kind, which I purpose to describe more at length, for convenience putting the experience of two years into one. As I have said, I do not propose to write an ode to dejection,[3] but to brag as lustily as chanticleer[4] in the morning, standing on his roost, if only to wake my neighbors up.

When first I took up my abode in the woods, that is, began to spend my nights as well as days there, which, by accident, was on Independence Day, or the Fourth of July, 1845, my house was not finished for winter, but was merely a defence against the rain, without plastering or chimney, the walls being of rough, weather-stained boards, with wide chinks, which made it cool at night. The upright white hewn studs and freshly planed door and window casings gave it a clean and airy look, especially in the morning, when its timbers were saturated with dew, so that I fancied that by noon some sweet gum would exude from them. To my imagination it retained throughout the day more or less of this auroral character, reminding me of a certain house on a mountain which I had visited a year before. This was an airy and unplastered cabin, fit to entertain a traveling god, and where a goddess might trail her garments. The winds which passed over my dwelling were such as sweep over the ridges of mountains, bearing the broken strains, or celestial parts only, of terrestrial music. The morning wind forever blows, the poem of crea-

provements. To enjoy these advantages I was ready to carry it on; like Atlas,[1] to take the world on my shoulders—I never heard what compensation he received for that—and do all those things which had no other motive or excuse but that I might pay for it and be unmolested in my possession of it; for I knew all the while that it would yield the most abundant crop of the kind I wanted, if I could only afford to let it alone. But it turned out as I have said.

All that I could say, then, with respect to farming on a large scale—I have always cultivated a garden—was that I had had my seeds ready. Many think that seeds improve with age. I have no doubt that time discriminates between the good and the bad; and when at last I shall plant, I shall be less likely to be disappointed. But I would say to my fellows, once for all, As long as possible live free and uncommitted. It makes but little difference whether you are committed to a farm or the county jail.

Old Cato, whose "De Re Rustica" is my "Cultivator,"[2] says—and the only

---

[1] **Atlas:** In Greek mythology. Atlas is a Titan condemned to support the world on his shoulders.

[2] **Old . . . "Cultivator":** Marcus Porcius Cato (234–149 B.C.), Roman patriot and the author of *About Country Matters,* a book about farm management.

[3] **ode . . . dejection:** a reference to Samuel Taylor Coleridge's poem, "Dejection: an Ode."

[4] **chanticleer:** the rooster.

tion is uninterrupted; but few are the ears that hear it. Olympus [1] is but the outside of the earth everywhere.

The only house I had been the owner of before, if I except a boat, was a tent, which I used occasionally when making excursions in the summer, and this is still rolled up in my garret; but the boat, after passing from hand to hand, has gone down the stream of time. With this more substantial shelter about me, I had made some progress toward settling in the world. This frame, so slightly clad, was a sort of crystallization around me, and reacted on the builder. It was suggestive somewhat as a picture in outlines. I did not need to go outdoors to take the air, for the atmosphere within had lost none of its freshness. It was not so much within-doors as behind a door where I sat, even in the rainiest weather. The Harivansa [2] says, "An abode without birds is like a meat without seasoning." Such was not my abode, for I found myself suddenly neighbor to the birds; not by having imprisoned one, but having caged myself near them. I was not only nearer to some of those which commonly frequent the garden and the orchard, but to those wilder and more thrilling songsters of the forest which never, or rarely, serenade a villager—the wood thrush, the veery, the scarlet tanager, the field sparrow, the whippoorwill, and many others.

I was seated by the shore of a small pond, about a mile and a half south of the village of Concord and somewhat higher than it, in the midst of an extensive wood between that town and Lincoln, and about two miles south of that our only field known to fame, Concord Battle Ground; but I was so low in the woods that the opposite shore, half a mile off, like the rest covered with wood, was my most distant horizon. For the first week, whenever I looked out on the pond it impressed me like a tarn high up on the side of a mountain, its bottom far above the surface of other lakes, and, as the sun arose, I saw it throwing off its nightly clothing of mist, and here and there, by degrees, its soft ripples or its smooth reflecting surface was revealed, while the mists, like ghosts, were stealthily withdrawing in every direction into the woods, as at the breaking up of some nocturnal conventicle. [3] The very dew seemed to hang upon the trees later into the day than usual, as on the sides of mountains.

This small lake was of most value as a neighbor in the intervals of a gentle rainstorm in August, when, both air and water being perfectly still, but the sky overcast, midafternoon had all the serenity of evening, and the wood thrush sang around, and was heard from shore to shore. A lake like this is never smoother than at such a time; and the clear portion of the air above it being shallow and darkened by clouds, the water, full of light and reflections, becomes a lower heaven itself so much the more important. From a hilltop nearby, where the wood had been recently cut off, there was a pleasing vista southward across the pond, through a wide indentation in the hills which form the shore there, where their opposite sides sloping toward each other suggested a stream flowing out in that direction through a wooded valley, but stream there was none. That way I looked between and over the near green hills to some distant and higher ones in the horizon, tinged with blue. Indeed, by standing on tiptoe I could catch a glimpse of some of the peaks of the still bluer and more distant mountain ranges in the northwest, those true-blue coins from heaven's own mint, and also of some portion of the village. But in other directions, even from this point, I could not see over or beyond the woods which surrounded me. It is well to have some water in your neighborhood, to give buoyancy to and float the earth. One value even of the smallest well is that when you look into it you see that earth is not continent but insular. This is as important as that it

---

[1] **Olympus:** in Greek mythology, the mountain where the gods live.

[2] **Harivansa:** a Sanskrit poem.

[3] **conventicle:** secret meeting.

keeps butter cool. When I looked across the pond from this peak toward the Sudbury meadows,[1] which in time of flood I distinguished elevated perhaps by a mirage in their seething valley, like a coin in a basin, all the earth beyond the pond appeared like a thin crust insulated and floated even by this small sheet of intervening water, and I was reminded that this on which I dwelt was but *dry land*.

Though the view from my door was still more contracted, I did not feel crowded or confined in the least. There was pasture enough for my imagination. The low shrub oak plateau to which the opposite shore arose stretched away toward the prairies of the West and the steppes of Tartary,[2] affording ample room for all the roving families of men. "There are none happy in the world but beings who enjoy freely a vast horizon"—said Damodara,[3] when his herds required new and larger pastures.

Both place and time were changed, and I dwelt nearer to those parts of the universe and to those eras in history which had most attracted me. Where I lived was as far off as many a region viewed nightly by astronomers. We are wont to imagine rare and delectable places in some remote and more celestial corner of the system, behind the constellation of Cassiopeia's Chair, far from noise and disturbance. I discovered that my house actually had its site in such a withdrawn, but forever new and unprofaned, part of the universe. If it were worth the while to settle in those parts near to the Pleiades or the Hyades, to Aldebaran or Altair,[4] then I was really there, or at an equal remoteness from the life which I had left behind, dwindled and twinkling with as fine a ray to my nearest neighbor, and to be seen only in moonless nights by him. Such was that part of creation where I had squatted—

"There was a shepherd that did live,
    And held his thoughts as high
As were the mounts whereon his flocks
    Did hourly feed him by."

What should we think of the shepherd's life if his flocks always wandered to higher pastures than his thoughts?

Every morning was a cheerful invitation to make my life of equal simplicity, and I may say innocence, with Nature herself. I have been as sincere a worshiper of Aurora[5] as the Greeks. I got up early and bathed in the pond; that was a religious exercise, and one of the best things which I did. They say that characters were engraven on the bathing tub of King Tching-thang to this effect: "Renew thyself completely each day; do it again, and again, and forever again." I can understand that. Morning brings back the heroic ages. I was as much affected by the faint hum of a mosquito making its invisible and unimaginable tour through my apartment at earliest dawn, when I was sitting with door and windows open, as I could be by any trumpet that ever sang of fame. It was Homer's requiem; itself an Iliad and Odyssey in the air, singing its own wrath and wanderings.[6] There was something cosmical about it; a standing advertisement, till forbidden, of the everlasting vigor and fertility of the world. The morning, which is the most memorable season of the day, is the awakening hour. Then there is least somnolence in us; and for an hour, at least, some part of us awakes which slumbers all the rest of the day and night. Little is to be expected of that day, if it can be called a day, to which we are not awakened by our Genius,[7] but by the mechanical nudgings of some servitor, are not awakened by our own newly acquired force and aspirations from within, accompanied by the undulations of celestial music, instead of factory bells, and a

---

[1] **Sudbury meadows:** the land adjoining the Sudbury River.

[2] **steppes of Tartary:** vast plains in Russia and Mongolia.

[3] **Damodara:** an eleventh-century Sanskrit poet.

[4] **Pleides ... Altair:** distant stars and constellations.

[5] **Aurora:** the Greek goddess of the dawn.

[6] **wrath and wanderings:** in the *Iliad,* Homer sings Achilles's wrath; in the *Odyssey,* of Odysseus' wanderings.

[7] **Genius:** guardian spirit.

fragrance filling the air—to a higher life than we fell asleep from; and thus the darkness bear its fruit, and prove itself to be good, no less than the light. That man who does not believe that each day contains an earlier, more sacred, and auroral hour than he has yet profaned, has despaired of life, and is pursuing a descending and darkening way. After a partial cessation of his sensuous life, the soul of man, or its organs rather, are reinvigorated each day, and his Genius tries again what noble life it can make. All memorable events, I should say, transpire in morning time and in a morning atmosphere. The Vedas [1] say, "All intelligences awake with the morning." Poetry and art, and the fairest and most memorable of the actions of men, date from such an hour. All poets and heroes, like Memnon,[2] are the children of Aurora, and emit their music at sunrise. To him whose elastic and vigorous thought keeps pace with the sun, the day is a perpetual morning. It matters not what the clocks say or the attitudes and labors of men. Morning is when I am awake and there is a dawn in me. Moral reform is the effort to throw off sleep. Why is it that men give so poor an account of their day if they have not been slumbering? They are not such poor calculators. If they had not been overcome with drowsiness, they would have performed something. The millions are awake enough for physical labor; but only one in a million is awake enough for effective intellectual exertion, only one in a hundred millions to a poetic or divine life. To be awake is to be alive. I have never yet met a man who was quite awake. How could I have looked him in the face?

We must learn to reawaken and keep ourselves awake, not by mechanical aids, but by an infinite expectation of the dawn, which does not forsake us in our soundest sleep. I know of no more encouraging fact than the unquestionable ability of man to elevate his life by a conscious endeavor.

It is something to be able to paint a particular picture, or to carve a statue, and so to make a few objects beautiful; but it is far more glorious to carve and paint the very atmosphere and medium through which we look, which morally we can do. To affect the quality of the day, that is the highest of arts. Every man is tasked to make his life, even in its details, worthy of the contemplation of his most elevated and critical hour. If we refused, or rather used up, such paltry information as we get, the oracles would distinctly inform us how this might be done.

I went to the woods because I wished to live deliberately, to front only the essential facts of life, and see if I could not learn what it had to teach, and not, when I came to die, discover that I had not lived. I did not wish to live what was not life, living is so dear; nor did I wish to practice resignation, unless it was quite necessary. I wanted to live deep and suck out all the marrow of life, to live so sturdily and Spartan-like as to put to rout all that was not life, to cut a broad swath and shave close, to drive life into a corner, and reduce it to its lowest terms, and, if it proved to be mean, why then to get the whole and genuine meanness of it, and publish its meanness to the world; or if it were sublime, to know it by experience, and be able to give a true account of it in my next excursion. For most men, it appears to me, are in a strange uncertainty about it, whether it is of the devil or of God, and have *somewhat hastily* concluded that it is the chief end of man here to "glorify God and enjoy him forever." [3]

Still we live meanly, like ants; though the fable tells us that we were long ago changed into men; like pygmies we fight with cranes; it is error upon error, and clout upon clout, and our best virtue has for its occasion a superfluous and evitable [4] wretchedness. Our life is frittered away by detail. An honest man has hardly

[1] **Vedas:** sacred writings of the Hindus.

[2] **Memnon:** The statue of Memnon, son of Aurora, at Thebes made a harplike sound at dawn.

[3] **"glorify God . . . forever":** the answer to the first question in the Westminster (Presbyterian) Shorter Catechism.

[4] **evitable:** avoidable.

need to count more than his ten fingers, or in extreme cases he may add his ten toes, and lump the rest. Simplicity, simplicity, simplicity! I say, let your affairs be as two or three, and not a hundred or a thousand; instead of a million count half a dozen, and keep your accounts on your thumbnail. In the midst of this chopping sea of civilized life, such are the clouds and storms and quicksands and thousand-and-one items to be allowed for, that a man has to live, if he would not founder and go to the bottom and not make his port at all, by dead reckoning,[1] and he must be a great calculator indeed who succeeds. Simplify, simplify. Instead of three meals a day, if it be necessary eat but one; instead of a hundred dishes, five; and reduce other things in proportion. Our life is like a German Confederacy,[2] made up of petty states, with its boundary forever fluctuating, so that even a German cannot tell you how it is bounded at any moment. The nation itself, with all its so-called internal improvements, which, by the way, are all external and superficial, is just such an unwieldy and overgrown establishment, cluttered with furniture and tripped up by its own traps, ruined by luxury and heedless expense, by want of calculation and a worthy aim, as the million households in the land; and the only cure for it, as for them, is in a rigid economy, a stern and more than Spartan simplicity of life and elevation of purpose. It lives too fast. Men think that it is essential that the nation have commerce, and export ice, and talk through a telegraph, and ride thirty miles an hour, without a doubt, whether *they* do or not; but whether we should live like baboons or like men is a little uncertain. If we do not get out sleepers,[3] and forge rails, and devote days and nights to the work, but go to tinkering upon our *lives* to improve *them,* who will build railroads? And if railroads are not built, how shall we get to Heaven in season? But if we stay at home and mind our business, who will want railroads? We do not ride on the railroad; it rides upon us. Did you ever think what those sleepers are that underlie the railroad? Each one is a man, an Irishman,[4] or a Yankee man. The rails are laid on them, and they are covered with sand, and the cars run smoothly over them. They are sound sleepers, I assure you. And every few years a new lot is laid down and run over; so that, if some have the pleasure of riding on a rail, others have the misfortune to be ridden upon. And when they run over a man that is walking in his sleep, a supernumerary sleeper in the wrong position, and wake him up, they suddenly stop the cars, and make a hue and cry about it, as if this were an exception. I am glad to know that it takes a gang of men for every five miles to keep the sleepers down and level in their beds as it is, for this is a sign that they may sometime get up again.

Why should we live with such hurry and waste of life? We are determined to be starved before we are hungry. Men say that a stitch in time saves nine, and so they take a thousand stitches today to save nine tomorrow. As for *work,* we haven't any of any consequence. We have the Saint Vitus's dance, and cannot possibly keep our heads still. If I should only give a few pulls at the parish bell rope, as for a fire, that is, without setting the bell,[5] there is hardly a man on his farm in the outskirts of Concord, notwithstanding that press of engagements which was his excuse so many times this morning, nor a boy, nor a woman, I might almost say, but would forsake all and follow that sound, not mainly to save property from the flames, but, if we will confess the truth, much more to see it burn, since burn it must, and we, be it known, did not set it on fire—or to see it put out, and have a

---

[1] **dead reckoning:** a system of navigating without the aid of the stars.

[2] **German Confederacy:** Germany from 1815 to 1866 was a loose union of thirty-eight independent states.

[3] **sleepers:** railway ties.

[4] **Irishman:** Irish laborers were brought to Concord in the 1840's to help build a railroad.

[5] **without . . . bell:** that is, without pulling the bell upside down, as for a church service.

hand in it, if that is done as handsomely; yes, even if it were the parish church itself. Hardly a man takes a half-hour's nap after dinner, but when he wakes he holds up his head and asks, "What's the news?" as if the rest of mankind had stood his sentinels. Some give directions to be waked every half-hour, doubtless for no other purpose; and then, to pay for it, they tell what they have dreamed. After a night's sleep the news is as indispensable as the breakfast. "Pray tell me anything new that has happened to a man anywhere on this globe"—and he reads it over his coffee and rolls, that a man has had his eyes gouged out this morning on the Wachito River;[1] never dreaming the while that he lives in the dark unfathomed mammoth cave of this world, and has but the rudiment of an eye himself.

For my part, I could easily do without the post office. I think that there are very few important communications made through it. To speak critically, I never received more than one or two letters in my life—I wrote this some years ago— that were worth the postage. The penny-post is, commonly, an institution through which you seriously offer a man that penny for his thoughts which is so often safely offered in jest. And I am sure that I never read any memorable news in a newspaper. If we read of one man robbed, or murdered, or killed by accident, or one house burned, or one vessel wrecked, or one steamboat blown up, or one cow run over on the Western Railroad, or one mad dog killed, or one lot of grasshoppers in the winter—we never need read of another. One is enough. If you are acquainted with the principle, what do you care for a myriad instances and applications? To a philosopher all *news*, as it is called, is gossip, and they who edit and read it are old women over their tea. Yet not a few are greedy after this gossip. There was such a rush, as I hear, the other day at one of the offices to learn the for-

eign news by the last arrival, that several large squares of plate glass belonging to the establishment were broken by the pressure—news which I seriously think a ready wit might write a twelvemonth, or twelve years, beforehand with sufficient accuracy. As for Spain, for instance, if you know how to throw in Don Carlos and the Infanta, and Don Pedro[2] and Seville and Granada, from time to time in the right proportions—they may have changed the names a little since I saw the papers—and serve up a bullfight when other entertainments fail, it will be true to the letter, and give us as good an idea of the exact state or ruin of things in Spain as the most succinct and lucid reports under this head in the newspapers: and as for England, almost the last significant scrap of news from that quarter was the revolution of 1649;[3] and if you have learned the history of her crops for an average year, you never need attend to that thing again, unless your speculations are of a merely pecuniary character. If one may judge who rarely looks into the newspapers, nothing new does ever happen in foreign parts, a French revolution not excepted.

What news! how much more important to know what that is which was never old! "Kieou-he-yu (great dignitary of the state of Wei) sent a man to Khoung-tseu to know his news.[4] Khoung-tseu caused the messenger to be seated near him, and questioned him in these terms: What is your master doing? The messenger answered with respect: My master desires to diminish the number of his faults, but he cannot come to the end of them. The messenger being gone, the philosopher remarked: What a worthy messenger! What a worthy messenger!" The preacher, instead of vexing the ears of drowsy farmers on their day of rest at

---

[1] **Wachito River:** the Ouachita River in Arkansas, where gouging was a common form of fighting.

[2] **Don Carlos . . . Don Pedro:** principal figures in a Spanish civil war, then raging.

[3] **revolution of 1649:** the Puritan Revolution led by Cromwell against Charles I.

[4] **"Kieou-he-yu . . . news":** from the *Analects* of Confucius.

the end of the week—for Sunday is the fit conclusion of an ill-spent week, and not the fresh and brave beginning of a new one—with this one other draggle-tail of a sermon, should shout with thundering voice, "Pause! Avast! Why so seeming fast, but deadly slow?"

Shams and delusions are esteemed for soundest truths, while reality is fabulous. If men would steadily observe realities only, and not allow themselves to be deluded, life, to compare it with such things as we know, would be like a fairy tale and the Arabian Nights' Entertainments. If we respected only what is inevitable and has a right to be, music and poetry would resound along the streets. When we are unhurried and wise, we perceive that only great and worthy things have any permanent and absolute existence, that petty fears and petty pleasures are but the shadow of the reality. This is always exhilarating and sublime. By closing the eyes and slumbering, and consenting to be deceived by shows, men establish and confirm their daily life of routine and habit everywhere, which still is built on purely illusory foundations. Children, who play life, discern its true law and relations more clearly than men, who fail to live it worthily, but who think that they are wiser by experience, that is, by failure. I have read in a Hindu book that "there was a king's son, who, being expelled in infancy from his native city, was brought up by a forester, and, growing up to maturity in that state, imagined himself to belong to the barbarous race with which he lived. One of his father's ministers having discovered him, revealed to him what he was, and the misconception of his character was removed, and he knew himself to be a prince. So soul," continues the Hindu philosopher, "from the circumstances in which it is placed, mistakes its own character, until the truth is revealed to it by some holy teacher, and then it knows itself to be *Brahme*." [1] I perceive that we in-

[1] **Brahme:** in the Hindu religion, the great soul of the universe of which everything else is a part. Emerson's poem, "Brahma," develops this concept.

habitants of New England live this mean life that we do because our vision does not penetrate the surface of things. We think that that *is* which *appears* to be. If a man should walk through this town and see only the reality, where, think you, would the "mill-dam" [2] go to? If he should give us an account of the realities he beheld there, we should not recognize the place in his description. Look at a meeting house, or a courthouse, or a jail, or a shop, or a dwelling house, and say what that thing really is before a true gaze, and they would all go to pieces in your account of them. Men esteem truth remote, in the outskirts of the system, behind the farthest star, before Adam and after the last man. In eternity there is indeed something true and sublime. But all these times and places and occasions are now and here. God himself culminates in the present moment, and will never be more divine in the lapse of all the ages. And we are enabled to apprehend at all what is sublime and noble only by the perpetual instilling and drenching of the reality that surrounds us. The universe constantly and obediently answers to our conceptions; whether we travel fast or slow, the track is laid for us. Let us spend our lives in conceiving then. The poet or the artist never yet had so fair and noble a design but some of his posterity at least could accomplish it.

Let us spend one day as deliberately as Nature, and not be thrown off the track by every nutshell and mosquito's wing that falls on the rails. Let us rise early and fast, or break fast, gently and without perturbation; let company come and let company go, let the bells ring and the children cry—determined to make a day of it. Why should we knock under and go with the stream? Let us not be upset and overwhelmed in that terrible rapid and whirlpool called a dinner, situated in the meridian shallows. Weather this danger and you are safe, for the rest of the way is down hill. With unrelaxed nerves, with morning vigor, sail by it, looking another

[2] **"mill-dam":** the business center of Concord.

way, tied to the mast like Ulysses.[1] If the engine whistles, let it whistle till it is hoarse for its pains. If the bell rings, why should we run? We will consider what kind of music they are like. Let us settle ourselves, and work and wedge our feet downward through the mud and slush of opinion, and prejudice, and tradition, and delusion, and appearance, that alluvion [2] which covers the globe, through Paris and London, through New York and Boston and Concord, through Church and State, through poetry and philosophy and religion, till we come to a hard bottom and rocks in place, which we can call *reality,* and say, This is, and no mistake; and then begin, having a *point d'appui,*[3] below freshet and frost and fire, a place where you might found a wall or a state, or set a lamppost safely, or perhaps a gauge, not a Nilometer, but a Realometer, that future ages might know how deep a freshet of shams and appearances had gathered from time to time. If you stand right fronting and face to face to a fact, you will see the sun glimmer on both its surfaces, as if it were a cimeter,[4] and feel its sweet edge dividing you through the heart and marrow, and so you will happily conclude your mortal career. Be it life or death, we crave only reality. If we are really dying, let us hear the rattle in our throats and feel cold in the extremities; if we are alive, let us go about our business.

Time is but the stream I go a-fishing in. I drink at it; but while I drink I see the sandy bottom and detect how shallow it is. Its thin current slides away, but eternity remains. I would drink deeper; fish in the sky, whose bottom is pebbly with stars. I cannot count one. I know not the first letter of the alphabet. I have always been

[1] **tied . . . Ulysses:** According to Homer's *Odyssey,* Ulysses had his men lash him to a mast so that he would not succumb to the sirens' song and be shipwrecked on the rocks.
[2] **alluvion:** soil, sand, or similar material deposited by running water.
[3] *point d'appui:* a French phrase meaning "a point of support."
[4] **cimeter:** a saber with a curved blade, usually spelled *scimitar.*

regretting that I was not as wise as the day I was born. The intellect is a cleaver; it discerns and rifts [5] its way into the secret of things. I do not wish to be any more busy with my hands than is necessary. My head is hands and feet. I feel all my best faculties concentrated in it. My instinct tells me that my head is an organ for burrowing, as some creatures use their snout and forepaws, and with it I would mine and burrow my way through these hills. I think that the richest vein is somewhere hereabouts; so by the divining rod [6] and thin rising vapors I judge; and here I will begin to mine.

[5] **rifts:** here, cuts.
[6] **divining rod:** a forked stick that is supposed to indicate the presence of water or metal underground.

FOR STUDY AND DISCUSSION

1. Thoreau says of the Hollowell farm that he "knew all the while that it would yield the most abundant crop of the kind I wanted." What kind of crop does he mean?

2. Why did Thoreau go to the woods to live? What significance is there in the date Thoreau began to live at Walden?

3. Thoreau places great emphasis on the particular place where his cabin is situated and on the view he has from this place. Describe the view. Why does he value it? (In answering this question, consider the sentence, "I discovered that my house actually had its site in such a withdrawn, but forever new and unprofaned, part of the universe.")

4. Why does Thoreau consider the morning an especially important part of the day? Do you agree or disagree? Why?

5. What are some of Thoreau's objections to the way most people live? Why does he say that "we live meanly, like ants"? What other comparisons does he use to express his objections? What reasons does he usually give for his objection? Why does he say, "Simplicity, simplicity!"? Can you imagine reaching a stage in life when you would agree with Thoreau? Why or why not?

6. How does Thoreau evaluate the daily news? Do you agree or disagree? Why or why not?

7. Thoreau writes, "Shams and delusions are esteemed for soundest truths, while reality is fabulous." What does Thoreau mean by

"shams and delusions"? What does he consider reality to be?

8. Compare Thoreau's use of the word "Brahme" (page 192) with Emerson's poem "Brahma" (page 180). Do Emerson and Thoreau agree about what is real and what is false? Explain. What does Thoreau mean by a "Realometer"?

9. Study the last paragraph of the selection. Are the comparisons Thoreau uses effective? Why or why not?

10. Do you agree with the statement, "Like all great books, *Walden* teaches us how to live"? Why or why not?

11. If you were asked to choose five or six adjectives to describe Thoreau's character, which adjectives would you choose? Give reasons, based on your study of the selection, to defend your choices.

FOR COMPOSITION

1. Write a composition in which you discuss Thoreau's relevance to our time. Consider the following points: Is Thoreau's general point of view a good one for our time? Has the growth of an industrial society made his point of view outmoded? How much of what he specifically says is important to people living today? how much is irrelevant? Do you think that reading *Walden* might change your own life or the life of anyone you know?

2. Write a composition in which you discuss your agreement or disagreement with one of the following statements from the selection. Tell why you agree or disagree.

    a. "A man is rich in proportion to the number of things which he can afford to let alone."

    b. "Time is but the stream I go a-fishing in. I drink at it; but while I drink I see the sandy bottom and detect how shallow it is. Its thin current slides away, but eternity remains."

    c. "Why should we live with such hurry and waste of life? We are determined to be starved before we are hungry. Men say that a stitch in time saves nine, and so they take a thousand stitches today to save nine tomorrow. As for *work,* we haven't any of any consequence."

    d. "If men would steadily observe realities only, and not allow themselves to be deluded, life, to compare it with such things as we know, would be like a fairy tale and the Arabian Nights' Entertainments."

FROM THE *Journals*

April 16, 1852

As I TURNED round the corner of Hubbard's Grove, saw a woodchuck, the first of the season, in the middle of the field, six or seven rods from the fence which bounds the wood, and twenty rods distant. I ran along the fence and cut him off, or rather overtook him, though he started at the same time. When I was only a rod and a half off, he stopped, and I did the same; then he ran again, and I ran up within three feet of him, when he stopped again, the fence being between us. I squatted down and surveyed him at my leisure. His eyes were dull black and rather inobvious, with a faint chestnut iris, with but little expression and that more of resignation than of anger. The general aspect was a coarse grayish brown, a sort of grisel. A lighter brown next the skin, then black or very dark brown and tipped with whitish rather loosely. The head between a squirrel and a bear, flat on the top and dark brown, and darker still or black on the tip of the nose. The whiskers black, two inches long. The ears very small and roundish, set far back and nearly buried in the fur. Black feet, with long and slender claws for digging. It appeared to tremble, or perchance shivered with cold. When I moved, it gritted its teeth quite loud, sometimes striking the under jaw against the other chatteringly, sometimes grinding one jaw on the other, yet as if more from instinct than anger. Whichever way I turned, that way it headed. I took a twig a foot long and touched its snout, at which it started forward and bit the stick, lessening the distance between us to two feet, and still it held all the ground it gained. I played with it tenderly awhile with the stick, trying to open its gritting jaws. Ever its long in-cisors, two above and two below, were presented. But I thought it would go to sleep if I stayed long enough. It did not sit upright as sometimes, but *standing* on its forefeet with its head down, i.e., half sitting, half standing. We sat looking at one another about half an hour, till we began to feel mesmeric [1] influences. When I was tired, I moved away, wishing to see him run, but I could not start him. He would not stir as long as I was looking at him or could see him. I walked round him; he turned as fast and fronted me still. I sat down by his side within a foot. I talked to him *quasi* forest lingo, baby talk, at any rate in a conciliatory tone, and thought that I had some influence on him. He gritted his teeth less. I chewed check-erberry leaves and presented them to his nose at last without a grit; though I saw that by so much gritting of the teeth he had worn them rapidly and they were covered with a fine white powder, which, if you measured it thus, would have made his anger terrible. He did not mind any noise I might make. With a little stick I lifted one of his paws to examine it, and held it up at pleasure. I turned him over to see what color he was beneath (darker or more purely brown), though he turned himself back again sooner than I could have wished. His tail was also all brown, though not very dark, rat-tail-like, with loose hairs standing out on all sides like a caterpillar brush. He had a rather mild look. I spoke to him kindly. I reached checkerberry leaves to his mouth. I stretched my hands over him, though he turned up his head and still gritted a little. I laid my hand on him, but immediately took it off again, instinct not being wholly overcome. If I had had a few fresh bean leaves, thus in advance of the season, I am sure I should have tamed him com-pletely. It was a frizzly tail. His is a humble, terrestrial color like the par-tridge's, well concealed where dead wiry grass rises above darker brown or chest-nut dead leaves—a modest color. If I had had some food, I should have ended with stroking him at my leisure. Could easily have wrapped him in my handker-chief. He was not fat nor particularly lean. I finally had to leave him without seeing him move from the place. A large, clumsy, burrowing squirrel. *Arctomys,* bearmouse. I respect him as one of the natives. He lies there, by his color and habits so natu-ralized amid the dry leaves, the withered grass, and the bushes. A sound nap, too, he has enjoyed in his native fields, the past winter. I think I might learn some wisdom of him. His ancestors have lived here longer than mine. He is more thoroughly acclimated and naturalized than I. Bean leaves the red man raised for him, but he can do without them.

March 5, 1853

The Secretary of the Association for the Advancement of Science requests me, as he probably has thousands of others, by a printed circular letter from Washington the other day, to fill the blank against cer-tain questions, among which the most im-portant one was what branch of science I was specially interested in, using the term *science* in the most comprehensive sense possible. Now, though I could state to a select few that department of human inquiry which engages me, and should be rejoiced at an opportunity to do so, I felt that it would be to make myself the laugh-ingstock of the scientific community to describe or attempt to describe to them that branch of science which specially interests me, inasmuch as they do not be-lieve in a science which deals with the higher law. So I was obliged to speak to their condition and describe to them that poor part of me which alone they can un-derstand. The fact is I am a mystic, a transcendentalist, and a natural philoso-pher [2] to boot. Now I think of it, I should have told them at once that I was a trans-cendentalist. That would have been the

---

[1] **mesmeric:** hypnotic.

[2] **natural philosopher:** scientist.

shortest way of telling them that they would not understand my explanations.

How absurd that, though I probably stand as near to nature as any of them, and am by constitution as good an observer as most, yet a true account of my relation to nature should excite their ridicule only! If it had been the secretary of an association of which Plato or Aristotle was the president, I should not have hesitated to describe my studies at once and particularly.

December 28, 1852

It is worth the while to apply what wisdom one has to the conduct of his life, surely. I find myself oftenest wise in little things and foolish in great ones. That I may accomplish some particular petty affair well, I live my whole life coarsely. A broad margin of leisure is as beautiful in a man's life as in a book. Haste makes waste, no less in life than in housekeeping. Keep the time, observe the hours of the universe, not of the cars. What are threescore years and ten hurriedly and coarsely lived to moments of divine leisure in which your life is coincident with the life of the universe? We live too fast and coarsely, just as we eat too fast, and do not know the true savor of our food. We consult our will and understanding and the expectation of men, not our genius. I can impose upon myself tasks which will crush me for life and prevent all expansion, and this I am but too inclined to do.

One moment of life costs many hours, hours not of business but of preparation and invitation. Yet the man who does not betake himself at once and desperately to sawing is called a loafer, though he may be knocking at the doors of heaven all the while, which shall surely be opened to him. That aim in life is highest which requires the highest and finest discipline. How much, what infinite, leisure it requires, as of a lifetime, to appreciate a single phenomenon! You must camp down beside it as for life, having reached your land of promise, and give yourself wholly to it. It must stand for the whole world to you, symbolical of all things. The least partialness is your own defect of sight and cheapens the experience fatally. Unless the humming of a gnat is as the music of the spheres, and the music of the spheres is as the humming of a gnat, they are naught to me. It is not communications to serve for a history—which are sciences—but the great story itself, that cheers and satisfies us.

FOR STUDY AND DISCUSSION

1. Describe Thoreau's attitude toward the woodchuck. Is it that of a scientist, a sentimentalist about animals, or neither of these? Why do you think Thoreau says, "I think I might learn some wisdom" from the woodchuck?

2. Do you agree with Thoreau's statement that he finds himself "oftenest wise in little things and foolish in great ones"? Why or why not?

3. In what respects might Thoreau claim to be a scientist? In what ways is he unlike a scientist? What does he mean by "a science which deals with the higher law"? Describe Thoreau's attitude toward scientists.

4. Why does Thoreau value leisure? How does he think a person can gain leisure time? Study the second paragraph of the journal entry for December 28, 1852. Find passages in the selection from *Walden* that express the same or similar thoughts.

FOR COMPOSITION

Some writers who keep journals intend them for eventual publication. Others keep them simply as a record of their daily lives. Still others value them primarily as a rich source of ideas that are jotted down as they occur and that are later developed in an essay, poem, or story.

Keep a journal for a week, making an entry for each day. You may wish to record daily events, ideas you have thought of, and reactions to books, motion pictures, and television programs. You may also wish to set down observations about the human and animal life around you. Try to make your journal as revealing of your personality as Thoreau's journal was of his.

JAMES RUSSELL LOWELL
(1819–1891)

When Lowell was a student at Harvard, he would sometimes break off a serious discussion in Harvard Yard, leap over a stone column, crow like a rooster, and then pick up the conversation where he had left off. His brilliance and versatility matched his exuberance. William Dean Howells, the novelist who succeeded him as editor of the *Atlantic Monthly,* said of him, "He did not . . . make one impression on me but a thousand impressions, which I should seek in vain to embody in a single presentment." Poet, professor, critic, editor, diplomat, Lowell made a literary reputation early in his life. Before he was thirty, he had published several collections of lyric poems; *The Vision of Sir Launfal,* a long narrative poem; *A Fable for Critics,* and *The Biglow Papers,* the first series of his political satires expressed in Yankee dialect. During the remainder of his life he continued to write much poetry and many essays on literary and political subjects. He was one of America's most respected men of letters. Yet in his old age, he wrote: "I feel that my life has been mainly wasted—that I have thrown away more than most men ever had." He felt that he had devoted too much of his time to teaching and editing, that his brilliance enabled him to write too easily and copiously, and that his poems lacked the intensity of great poetry. Today he is remembered primarily not for his most serious and ambitious works, but for some of the poems he tossed off which reveal his human sympathies, and his exuberance.

A minister's son, Lowell was born in Elmwood, the family mansion on "Tory Row" in Cambridge, Massachusetts. After his graduation from Harvard College in 1838, he attended Harvard Law School but showed little interest in the practice of law. In 1839 he met Maria White, whom he married four years later. Under her influence he became involved in abolitionism and other social movements. He served for a time as an editorial writer for the *Pennsylvania Freeman,* an abolitionist magazine, and contributed articles to other periodicals. With the publication of the first series of *The Biglow Papers* in 1848, his talent for satire and dialect verse became evident. The same year he wrote *A Fable for Critics,* which was published anonymously, although many literary men were aware of or guessed the author's identity. Although this racy, almost flippant poem was practically improvised, "so rapidly was it written," it has proven remarkably durable. Some of its lines are quoted today in critical studies of authors whom Lowell has described in a few choice phrases.

After his wife's death in 1853, Lowell's instinctively conservative and aristocratic temperament became apparent. He praised the early ministers of New England as "a recognized aristocracy." In an influential essay on Thoreau, he expressed his disdain for Thoreau's romantic trust in the self and for his reliance on the companionship of the woods and "the society of musquashes." In 1855, Lowell succeeded Longfellow as Smith Professor of Modern Languages at Harvard. He was active in the founding of the *Atlantic Monthly* (now the *Atlantic*) in 1857 and served as its first editor. The most important publications of his later years are collections of genial and learned literary essays, with titles such as *Among My Books* and *My Study Windows*. Toward the end of his life, he served as minister to England and, as Washington Irving did, as minister to Spain.

The Courtin'

For *The Biglow Papers* Lowell created the character of Hosea Biglow, an uneducated but shrewd New England farmer who speaks in a rich Yankee dialect. This poem is one of the few inclusions in *The Biglow Papers* which is not satirical.

God makes sech nights, all white an' still
    Fur 'z you can look or listen,
Moonshine an' snow on field an' hill,
    All silence an' all glisten.

Zekle crep' up quite unbeknown   5
    An' peeked in thru' the winder,
An' there sot Huldy all alone,
    'ith no one nigh to hender.°

A fireplace filled the room's one side
    With half a cord o' wood in—   10
There warn't no stoves (tell comfort died)
    To bake ye to a puddin'.

The wa'nut logs shot sparkles out
    Towards the pootiest,° bless her,
An' leetle flames danced all about   15
    The chiny on the dresser.

Agin the chimbley crook-necks° hung,
    An' in amongst 'em rusted
The ole queen's-arm° thet gran'ther Young
    Fetched back f'om Concord busted.   20

The very room, coz she was in,
    Seemed warm f'om floor to ceilin',
An' she looked full ez rosy agin
    Ez the apples she was peelin'.

'Twas kin' o' kingdom-come to look   25
    On sech a blessed cretur,
A dogrose° blushin' to a brook
    Ain't modester nor sweeter.

He was six foot o' man, A 1,
    Clear grit an' human natur'.   30
None couldn't quicker pitch a ton
    Nor dror a furrer straighter.

He'd sparked it with full twenty gals,
    Hed squired 'em, danced 'em, druv 'em,
Fust this one, an' then thet, by spells—   35
    All is, he couldn't love 'em.

But long o' her his veins 'ould run
    All crinkly like curled maple,
The side she breshed felt full o' sun
    Ez a south slope in Ap'il.   40

    8. **hender:** hinder. 14. **pootiest:** prettiest. 17. **crook-necks:** gourds. 19. **queen's-arm:** a musket used in the Revolutionary War. 27. **dogrose:** a plant with pink flowers.

She thought no v'ice hed sech a swing
    Ez hisn in the choir;
My! when he made Ole Hunderd° ring,
    She *knowed* the Lord was nigher.

An' she'd blush scarlit, right in prayer,   45
    When her new meetin'-bonnet
Felt somehow thru' its crown a pair
    O' blue eyes sot upun it.

Thet night, I tell ye, she looked *some!*
    She seemed to 've gut a new soul,   50
For she felt sartin-sure he'd come,
    Down to her very shoe-sole.

She heered a foot, an' knowed it tu,
    A-raspin' on the scraper,—
All ways to once her feelin's flew   55
    Like sparks in burnt-up paper.

He kin' o' l'itered on the mat,
    Some doubtfle o' the sekle,°
His heart kep' goin' pity-pat,
    But hern went pity Zekle.   60

An' yit she gin her cheer a jerk
    Ez though she wished him furder,
An' on her apples kep' to work,
    Parin' away like murder.

"You want to see my Pa, I s'pose?"   65
    "Wal . . . no . . . I come dasignin'"—
"To see my Ma? She's sprinklin' clo'es
    Agin to-morrer's i'nin'."

To say why gals acts so or so,
    Or don't,'ould be persumin';   70
Mebby to mean *yes* an' say *no*
    Comes nateral to women.

He stood a spell on one foot fust,
    Then stood a spell on t'other,
An' on which one he felt the wust   75
    He couldn't ha' told ye nuther.

Says he, "I'd better call agin!"
    Says she, "Think likely, Mister."
Thet last word pricked him like a pin,
    An' . . . Wal, he up an' kist her.   80

When Ma bimeby upon 'em slips,
    Huldy sot pale ez ashes,
All kin' o' smily roun' the lips
    An' teary roun' the lashes.

For she was jes' the quiet kind   85
    Whose naturs never vary,
Like streams that keep a summer mind
    Snowhid in Jenooary.

The blood clost roun' her heart felt glued
    Too tight for all expressin',   90
Tell mother see how metters stood,
    An' gin 'em both her blessin'.

Then her red come back like the tide
    Down to the Bay o' Fundy,
An' all I know is they was cried°   95
    In meetin' come nex' Sunday.

43. **Ole Hunderd:** the tune to which Psalm 100 was sung. 58. **sekle:** sequel.

95. **they was cried:** the banns (that is, the announcement of their approaching marriage) were read in church.

FOR STUDY AND DISCUSSION

1. Is the description of beauty in the first stanza appropriate to a rural New Englander? Why or why not? What would this poem gain or lose if it were translated into standard English?

2. Certain rhymes in the poem depend on the use of dialect. One example is the "natur'-straighter" rhyme in the eighth stanza. Point out four other examples. Read aloud the stanzas in which these examples occur.

3. A number of comparisons in the poem are particularly suited to the speech of a rural New Englander. For example, in lines 27–28 the color of Huldy's skin is compared to a dog-rose, a flower of the area. Find several other comparisons that strike you as giving the flavor of New England speech.

4. What in your opinion is Lowell's attitude toward the characters in the poem? Does he make them broadly comical, as rural characters are sometimes portrayed in comic strips and motion pictures? Or does he treat them realistically and sympathetically? Give reasons for your answer.

LANGUAGE AND VOCABULARY

A writer using dialect must find spellings that adequately convey the special pronunciations of a particular region. However, he must not make his spellings too difficult for the reader to understand. If he is a good writer, he is very much aware of the spoken language and tries to find spellings that show how people actually speak, not how they are supposed to speak.

Find ten words in "The Courtin'" that are spelled to show dialect pronunciations. Draw three columns on your paper. In the first column, write the words as Lowell spells them. In the second column, give the standard spelling. In the third column, spell the words to show how you or a friend pronounce them. Listen carefully before writing. Do not write "hundred" when you actually say "hunert."

FROM *A Fable for Critics*

In *A Fable for Critics,* a literary critic explains to Apollo, the god of poetry, what the American writers of Lowell's time are like. Since the poem was published anonymously, Lowell was able to satirize himself as well as other writers.

[*Emerson*] There comes Emerson first, whose rich words, every one,
Are like gold nails in temples to hang trophies on,
Whose prose is grand verse, while his verse, the Lord knows,
Is some of it pr– No, 'tis not even prose;
I'm speaking of meters; some poems have welled   5
From those rare depths of soul that have ne'er been excelled;
They're not epics, but that doesn't matter a pin,
In creating, the only hard thing's to begin;
A grass-blade's no easier to make than an oak;
If you've once found the way, you've achieved the grand stroke;   10
In the worst of his poems are mines of rich matter,
But thrown in a heap with a crash and a clatter;
Now it is not one thing nor another alone
Makes a poem, but rather the general tone,
The something pervading, uniting the whole,   15
The before unconceived, unconceivable soul,
So that just in removing this trifle or that, you
Take away, as it were, a chief limb of the statue;
Roots, wood, bark, and leaves singly perfect may be,
But, clapt hodge-podge together, they don't make a tree.   20

But to come back to Emerson (whom, by the way
I believe we left waiting)—his is, we may say,
A Greek head on right Yankee shoulders, whose range
Has Olympus° for one pole, for t'other the Exchange;

24. **Olympus:** a symbol of Emerson's idealism, while the Exchange, where things are bought and sold, symbolizes his practicality.

He seems, to my thinking (although I'm afraid 25
The comparison must, long ere this, have been made),
A Plotinus-Montaigne,° where the Egyptian's gold mist
And the Gascon's shrewd wit cheek-by-jowl coexist;
All admire, and yet scarcely six converts he's got
To I don't (nor they either) exactly know what; 30
For though he builds glorious temples, 'tis odd
He leaves never a doorway to get in a god.
'Tis refreshing to old-fashioned people like me
To meet such a primitive Pagan as he,
In whose mind all creation is duly respected 35
As parts of himself—just a little projected;
And who's willing to worship the stars and the sun,
A convert to—nothing but Emerson.
So perfect a balance there is in his head,
That he talks of things sometimes as if they were dead; 40
Life, nature, love, God, and affairs of that sort,
He looks at as merely ideas; in short,
As if they were fossils stuck round in a cabinet,
Of such vast extent that our earth's a mere dab in it;
Composed just as he is inclined to conjecture her, 45
Namely, one part pure earth, ninety-nine parts pure lecturer;
You are filled with delight at his clear demonstration,
Each figure, word, gesture, just fits the occasion,
With the quiet precision of science he'll sort 'em,
But you can't help suspecting the whole a *post mortem.*° . . . 50

[*Bryant*] There is Bryant, as quiet, as cool, and as dignified,
As a smooth silent iceberg, that never is ignified,
Save when by·reflection 'tis kindled o' nights
With a semblance of flame by the chill northern lights.
He may rank (Griswold° says so) first bard of your nation, 55
(There's no doubt that he stands in supreme iceolation)
Your topmost Parnassus° he may set his heel on,
But no warm applauses come, peal following peal on—
He's too smooth and too polished to hang any zeal on. . . .
If he stir you at all, it is just, on my soul, 60
Like being stirred up with the very North Pole. . . .

[*Whittier*] There is Whittier, whose swelling and vehement heart
Strains the strait-breasted drab of the Quaker apart,
And reveals the live man, still supreme and erect,
Underneath the bemummying° wrappers of sect; 65

---

27. **Plotinus-Montaigne:** Plotinus (205–270), an Egyptian philosopher; and Michel Eyquem
de Montaigne, a French essayist from Gascony, represent the strains of idealism and down-to-
earth skepticism in Emerson's thought.   50. *post mortem:* an examination of a human body
after death.   55. **Griswold:** American critic and editor of Lowell's day, represented in the
poem as leading the poets up to Apollo.   57. **Parnassus** (pär·nas'əs): mountain in Greece,
sacred to Apollo and the Muses.   65. **bemummying** (bi·mum'ə·ing): stifling.

There was ne'er a man born who had more of the swing
Of the true lyric bard and all that kind of thing;
And his failures arise (though he seems not to know it)
From the very same cause that has made him a poet—
A fervor of mind which knows no separation   70
'Twixt simple excitement and pure inspiration. . . .
Then his grammar's not always correct, nor his rhymes,
And he's prone to repeat his own lyrics sometimes,
Not his best, though, for those are struck off at white heats
When the heart in his breast like a trip hammer beats,   75
And can ne'er be repeated again any more
Than they could have been carefully plotted before. . . .

[*Hawthorne*] There is Hawthorne, with genius so shrinking and rare
That you hardly at first see the strength that is there;
A frame so robust, with a nature so sweet,   80
So earnest, so graceful, so solid, so fleet,
Is worth a descent from Olympus° to meet;
'Tis as if a rough oak that for ages had stood,
With his gnarled bony branches like ribs of the wood,
Should bloom after cycles of struggle and scathe,°   85
With a single anemone° trembly and rathe.°. . .
When Nature was shaping him, clay was not granted
For making so full-sized a man as she wanted,
So, to fill out her model, a little she spared
From some finer-grained stuff for a woman prepared,   90
And she could not have hit a more excellent plan
For making him fully and perfectly man. . . .

[*Poe and Longfellow*] There comes Poe, with his raven, like Barnaby
    Rudge,°
Three fifths of him genius and two fifths sheer fudge,
Who talks like a book of iambs and pentameters,°   95
In a way to make people of common sense damn meters,
Who has written some things quite the best of their kind,
But the heart somehow seems all squeezed out by the mind,
Who—but heyday! What's this? Messieurs Mathews° and Poe,
You mustn't fling mud balls at Longfellow so,   100
Does it make a man worse that his character's such
As to make his friends love him (as you think) too much?
Why, there is not a bard at this moment alive
More willing than he that his fellows should thrive;
While you are abusing him thus, even now   105
He would help either one of you out of a slough;

82. **Olympus:** mountain in Greece, home of the gods.   85. **scathe:** misfortune.   86. **anemone** (ə·nem'ə·nē): a flowering herb.   **rathe:** early in the season.   93. **Barnaby Rudge:** a crazed youth in Dickens's novel of that name, who had a pet raven; see page 123 for Poe's "The Raven."   95. **iambs . . . pentameters:** metrical terms. The *iamb* is a foot consisting of a short syllable followed by a long one; *pentameter* is a line having five metrical feet (see page 116). 99. **Mathews:** an editor and critic of the time who, like Poe, wrote severe criticism of Longfellow.

You may say that he's smooth and all that till you're hoarse,
But remember that elegance also is force;
After polishing granite as much as you will,
The heart keeps its tough old persistency still;   110
Deduct all you can, *that* still keeps you at bay,
Why, he'll live till men weary of Collins and Gray.°. . .

[*Holmes*] There's Holmes, who is matchless among you for wit,
A Leyden jar° always full charged, from which flit
The electrical tingles of hit after hit;   115
In long poems 'tis painful sometimes, and invites
A thought of the way the new telegraph writes,
Which pricks down its little sharp sentences spitefully,
As if you'd got more than you'd title to rightfully,
And you find yourself hoping its wild father lightning   120
Would flame in for a second and give you a fright'ning. . . .

[*Lowell*] There is Lowell, who's striving Parnassus to climb
With a whole bale of *isms* tied together with rhyme; . . .
His lyre has some chords that would ring pretty well,
But he'd rather by half make a drum of the shell,   125
And rattle away till he's old as Methusalem,°
At the head of a march to the last new Jerusalem.

112. **Collins . . . Gray:** well-known English poets of the eighteenth century.   114. **Leyden** (līd'n) **jar:** an electricity condenser that can give strong shocks.   126. **Methusalem** (mə·thōō'-zə·ləm): Methuselah, oldest man in the Bible (Genesis 5:27).

Apollo, god of poetry, stands in the center
of this Greek vase of the fifth century B.C.

FOR STUDY AND DISCUSSION

1. Judging from the excerpts you have read, would you say that *A Fable for Critics* is basically a serious or a humorous poem? Why? In your opinion, is Lowell trying to be fair to the authors he is discussing, or is he only making fun of them? Give details from the poem to support your answer.

2. The line "Three fifths of him genius and two fifths sheer fudge" is a famous description of Poe. In your opinion, what is meant by this line? Do you agree or disagree with the description? Why?

3. What is Lowell's estimate of Emerson? Why does he call Emerson "a primitive Pagan"? Explain Lowell's comment that Emerson's work is like a *post mortem* (line 50). After reading "The American Scholar," do you agree or disagree?

4. Why do you think Lowell chose to write this work of criticism in verse rather than in prose? What changes might Lowell have made, either in his style or his judgments of other poets, if he had decided to write a prose critical essay instead of his *Fable?*

METER AND RHYME SCHEME

You have already encountered the *iamb*, the most common kind of poetic foot or unit of rhythm (see page 116). Lowell's poem, "The Courtin'," uses iambic meter. Other poems, such as *A Fable for Critics,* have a different rhythm. (Read a stanza of each poem. Notice how the obviously different rhythms give each poem a different pace and therefore a different effect.) In addition to iambic meter, there are three other basic kinds of meter used in English and American poetry:

Trochaic meter. The foot called the trochee is the opposite of the iamb. A trochee consists of a stressed syllable followed by an unstressed syllable. Poe's "The Raven" is written in trochaic meter: "Once up/ on a/ midnight/ dreary/ while I/ pondered/ weak and/ weary"

Anapestic meter. The anapest consists of two unstressed syllables followed by a stressed syllable. Generally, a poem using anapestic meter has a gay tripping sound. *A Fable for Critics* is written in anapestic meter. Occasionally an iambic foot is substituted for an anapestic foot. Note that the first foot of the following line from *A Fable* is an iamb instead of an anapest: "So per/ fect a bal/ ance there is/ in his head."

Dactylic meter. The dactyl is the opposite of the anapest. It consists of a stressed syllable followed by two unstressed syllables, as in the following line by the English poet, Thomas Hood: "Take her up/ tenderly." Karl Shapiro and Robert Beum, two contemporary American poets who have written extensively on poetic meters, comment: "Of the four basic meters, dactylic undoubtedly strikes our ear as the most artificial." Dactylic meter is often found in jingles, nursery rhymes, and light verse.

The rhythm of a line of poetry is usually described in terms of its meter and its length. As you have already seen (page 116), blank verse consists of unrhymed *iambic pentameter:* that is, each line contains five iambic feet. The terms describing the number of feet in a line are *monometer* (one foot), *dimeter* (two feet), *trimeter* (three feet), *tetrameter* (four feet), *pentameter* (five feet), and *hexameter* (six feet). The first line of "The Courtin'" is written in iambic tetrameter. That is, the line consists of four iambs. The second line is iambic trimeter. *A Fable for Critics* is written in anapestic tetrameter.

Rhyme scheme, the pattern of rhymes in a poem, is a technical feature of poetry that is often as important as meter. The rhyme scheme of a poem is usually described by using the letter *a* to represent the first rhyme sound and repeating the same letter to indicate each repetition of this rhyme. The letter *b* represents the second rhyme sound, the letter *c* the third rhyme sound, and so forth. For example, the rhyme scheme of the first stanza of "The Courtin'" is *abab.*

1. Describe the meter of the following lines of poetry in terms of meter and line length. (Example—"The Courtin'," line 9: iambic tetrameter.)

  a. "The Bells," line 14 (page 120).
  b. "To a Waterfowl," line 4 (page 112).
  c. "The Concord Hymn," line 15 (page 180).
  d. "The Courtin'," line 12 (page 198).
  e. "The Experience," line 7 (page 21).

2. Give the rhyme scheme of the following excerpts from poems. (Example—"The Courtin'," lines 36–40: *abab.*)

  a. "Brahma," lines 1–4 (page 180).
  b. "To a Waterfowl," lines 1–4 (page 112).
  c. "The Concord Hymn," lines 1–8 (page 180).
  d. "The Experience," lines 1–6 (page 21).
  e. "To Helen," lines 1–5 (page 119).

HENRY
WADSWORTH
LONGFELLOW
(1807–1882)

No other American poet, not even Robert Frost, has matched Henry Wadsworth Longfellow's popularity at the height of his career. During his lifetime, his poetry was admired throughout Europe and translated into twenty-four languages. In America, he was the poet who was everywhere read and everywhere quoted. His seventy-fifth birthday was observed in schoolrooms throughout the land. After his death, a bust of Longfellow was placed in the Poet's Corner of Westminster Abbey, which contains the tombs or monuments of such famous English poets as Chaucer, Shakespeare, and Milton. Longfellow was the first American poet to be so honored.

The son of a Maine lawyer, Longfellow was a descendant of John Alden, who came to America on the *Mayflower* and is a principal character in one of Longfellow's most popular poems, *The Courtship of Miles Standish*. Although Longfellow had literary ambitions early in life, his father warned him, "There is not wealth enough in this country to afford encouragement to merely literary men." When Longfellow graduated from Bowdoin College in 1825, he accepted a professorship in modern languages at Bowdoin and spent three happy years in Europe preparing himself for his duties. In his journal, Longfellow wrote that "the Old World" was for him "a kind of Holy Land." He devoted only a small portion of his time to serious study in Germany. The remainder was passed in leisurely travel in France and Italy and in Spain, where he met his boyhood idol, Washington Irving. Although the ostensible purpose of his European tour was the study of languages, his real interest was in Europe's romantic past, which he recreated in poems such as "The Skeleton in Armor."

A dandy with a fondness for bright colors in ties and waistcoats, Longfellow cut a distinctive figure at Bowdoin. In 1836, he became Smith Professor of Modern Languages at Harvard. Meanwhile, he was establishing a reputation as a poet. In 1839, his first collection of poems, *Voices of the Night,* was published and sold 43,000 copies. *Ballads and Other Poems,* a second collection published in 1842, proved just as popular. A year later, Longfellow's marriage to Frances Appleton, the daughter of a rich Boston merchant, brought him Craigie House on Cambridge's Brattle Street as a wedding present. Its spacious, inviting study, where Longfellow wrote some of his best-known poems, is preserved to this day. After eighteen years at Harvard, he resigned his professorship, stating that the responsibilities of teaching were "a great hand laid on all the strings of my lyre, stopping their vibration." His life was quiet and serene. He was surrounded by friends from the literary and scholarly world of

Cambridge and Boston and sustained by an admiring public. The great calamity of these years was the death of his wife in a fire. Longfellow's familiar beard was grown to cover scars left by the burns he suffered in trying to save her.

Longfellow's poetry is remarkably varied in form and subject. He wrote ballads and other simple poems on popular subjects, such as "The Wreck of the Hesperus," "Paul Revere's Ride," and "The Village Blacksmith." Some of his poems, like "The Beleaguered City" and "The Belfry of Bruges," are filled with a romantic fascination with the past ages of Europe. His three long narrative poems, *Evangeline, The Song of Hiawatha,* and *The Courtship of Miles Standish,* all have American settings but are romantically remote from the life of his times. After the death of his wife, Longfellow took refuge from his sorrow in translating Dante's *Divine Comedy.* The sonnets he wrote as prefaces for the three parts of his translation reflect the sad, mellow mood of his last years.

The Arsenal at Springfield

In 1843, while on his wedding trip, Longfellow visited the United States arsenal at Springfield, Massachusetts. Mrs. Longfellow, examining the gun barrels that were stacked against the walls, said that they looked like an organ on which Death might play. Several months later, at her urging, Longfellow wrote the following poem.

This is the Arsenal. From the floor to ceiling,
　　Like a huge organ, rise the burnished arms;
But from their silent pipes no anthem pealing
　　Startles the villages with strange alarms.

Ah! what a sound will rise, how wild and dreary,　　　　　5
　　When the death angel touches those swift keys!
What loud lament and dismal Miserere°
　　Will mingle with their awful symphonies!

I hear even now the infinite fierce chorus,
　　The cries of agony, the endless groan,　　　　　　　　10
Which, through the ages that have gone before us,
　　In long reverberations reach our own.

On helm and harness rings the Saxon hammer,
　　Through Cimbric° forest roars the Norseman's song,
And loud, amid the universal clamor,　　　　　　　　　15
　　O'er distant deserts sounds the Tatar° gong.

7. **Miserere** (miz'ə·râr'ē): the first word in the Latin version of the psalm beginning "Have mercy upon me, O Lord!"　14. **Cimbric** (sim'brik): referring to the Cimbri, a tribe of Norsemen destroyed by the Romans.　16. **Tatar** (tä'tər): The Tatars (commonly spelled Tartar), a race of savage Orientals, swept over Asia and most of Europe in the thirteenth century.

I hear the Florentine,° who from his palace
   Wheels out his battle bell with dreadful din,
And Aztec° priests upon their teocallis°
   Beat the wild war drums made of serpent's skin;   20

The tumult of each sacked and burning village;
   The shout that every prayer for mercy drowns;
The soldiers' revels in the midst of pillage;
   The wail of famine in beleaguered° towns;

The bursting shell, the gateway wrenched asunder,   25
   The rattling musketry, the clashing blade;
And ever and anon, in tones of thunder,
   The diapason° of the cannonade.

Is it, O man, with such discordant noises,
   With such accursèd instruments as these,   30
Thou drownest Nature's sweet and kindly voices,
   And jarrest the celestial harmonies?

Were half the power, that fills the world with terror,
   Were half the wealth, bestowed on camps and courts,
Given to redeem the human mind from error,   35
   There were no need of arsenals nor forts:

The warrior's name would be a name abhorrèd!
   And every nation, that should lift again
Its hands against a brother, on its forehead
   Would wear forevermore the curse of Cain!°   40

Down the dark future, through long generations,
   The echoing sounds grow fainter and then cease;
And like a bell, with solemn, sweet vibrations,
   I hear once more the voice of Christ say, "Peace!"

Peace! and no longer from its brazen portals   45
   The blast of War's great organ shakes the skies!
But beautiful as songs of the immortals,
   The holy melodies of love arise.

---

17. **Florentine** (flôr′ən·tēn): The soldiers of Florence, Italy, in medieval times actually wheeled a great bell out into the battlefield.   19. **Aztec:** a native race of Mexicans, found and later practically exterminated by the Spaniards.   **teocallis** (tē′ə·kal′ez): flat-topped pyramids of worship.   24. **beleaguered:** blockaded.   28. **diapason** (dī′ə·pā′sən): in music, the entire range of tones of an instrument.   40. **Cain:** a son of Adam and Eve, who was cursed because he slew his brother Abel (Genesis 4).

The Tide Rises, the Tide Falls

The tide rises, the tide falls,
The twilight darkens, the curlew° calls;
Along the sea sands damp and brown
The traveler hastens toward the town,
   And the tide rises, the tide falls.   5

Darkness settles on roofs and walls,
But the sea, the sea in the darkness calls;
The little waves, with their soft white hands,
Efface the footprints in the sands,
   And the tide rises, the tide falls.   10

The morning breaks; the steeds in their stalls
Stamp and neigh as the hostler calls;
The day returns, but nevermore
Returns the traveler to the shore,
   And the tide rises, the tide falls.   15

2. **curlew** (kûr′lo͞o): a large shore bird found in Europe and North America.

The Skeleton in Armor

"Speak! speak! thou fearful guest!
Who, with thy hollow breast,
Still in rude armor drest,
  Comest to daunt me!
Wrapt not in Eastern balms,   5
But with thy fleshless palms
Stretched, as if asking alms,
  Why dost thou haunt me?"

Then from those cavernous eyes
Pale flashes seemed to rise,   10
As when the Northern skies
  Gleam in December;
And, like the water's flow
Under December's snow,
Came a dull voice of woe   15
  From the heart's chamber.

"I was a Viking old!
My deeds, though manifold,
No Skald° in song has told,
  No Saga° taught thee!   20

Take heed that in thy verse
Thou dost the tale rehearse,°
Else dread a dead man's curse;
  For this I sought thee.

"Far in the Northern Land,   25
By the wild Baltic's strand,
I, with my childish hand,
  Tamed the gerfalcon;°
And, with my skates fast-bound,
Skimmed the half-frozen Sound,   30
That the poor whimpering hound
  Trembled to walk on.

"Oft to his frozen lair
Tracked I the grisly bear,
While from my path the hare   35
  Fled like a shadow;
Oft through the forest dark
Followed the werewolf's° bark,
Until the soaring lark
  Sang from the meadow.   40

19. **Skald:** an old Scandinavian poet. 20. **Saga:** a medieval Scandinavian story.

22. **rehearse:** here, tell. 28. **gerfalcon:** an Arctic falcon. 38. **werewolf:** a person changed into a wolf.

"But when I older grew,
Joining a corsair's° crew,
O'er the dark sea I flew
  With the marauders.
Wild was the life we led;   45
Many the souls that sped,
Many the hearts that bled,
  By our stern orders.

"Many a wassail-bout°
Wore the long winter out;   50
Often our midnight shout
  Set the cocks crowing,
As we the Berserk's° tale
Measured in cups of ale,
Draining the oaken pail   55
  Filled to o'erflowing.

"Once as I told in glee°
Tales of the stormy sea,
Soft eyes did gaze on me,
  Burning yet tender;   60
And as the white stars shine
On the dark Norway pine,
On that dark heart of mine
  Fell their soft splendor.

"I wooed the blue-eyed maid,   65
Yielding, yet half afraid,
And in the forest's shade
  Our vows were plighted.
Under its loosened vest
Fluttered her little breast,   70
Like birds within their nest
  By the hawk frighted.

"Bright in her father's hall
Shields gleamed upon the wall,
Loud sang the minstrels all,   75
  Chanting his glory;
When of old Hildebrand
I asked his daughter's hand,
Mute did the minstrels stand
  To hear my story.   80

"While the brown ale he quaffed,
Loud then the champion laughed,
And as the wind gusts waft
  The sea foam brightly,
So the loud laugh of scorn   85
Out of those lips unshorn,
From the deep drinking-horn
  Blew the foam lightly.

"She was a Prince's child,
I but a Viking wild,   90
And though she blushed and smiled,
  I was discarded!
Should not the dove so white
Follow the sea mew's° flight?
Why did they leave that night   95
  Her nest unguarded?

"Scarce had I put to sea,
Bearing the maid with me,
Fairest of all was she
  Among the Norsemen!   100
When on the white seastrand,°
Waving his armèd hand,
Saw we old Hildebrand,
  With twenty horsemen.

"Then launched they to the blast,   105
Bent like a reed each mast,
Yet we were gaining fast,
  When the wind failed us;
And with a sudden flaw
Came round the gusty Skaw,°   110
So that our foe we saw
  Laugh as he hailed us.

"And as to catch the gale
Round veered the flapping sail,
'Death!' was the helmsman's hail,   115
  'Death without quarter!'
Midships with iron keel
Struck we her ribs of steel;
Down her black hulk did reel
  Through the black water!   120

42. **corsair:** pirate. 49. **wassail-bout:** drinking
session. 53. **Berserk:** legendary Norse warrior who
fought like a madman. 57. **glee:** song.

94. **sea mew:** sea gull. 101. **seastrand:** seashore.
110. **Skaw:** Cape Skagen in Denmark.

"As with his wings aslant,
Sails the fierce cormorant,
Seeking some rocky haunt,
    With his prey laden—
So toward the open main,   125
Beating to sea again,
Through the wild hurricane,
    Bore I the maiden.

"Three weeks we westward bore,
And when the storm was o'er,   130
Cloudlike we saw the shore
    Stretching to leeward;
There for my lady's bower
Built I the lofty tower,
Which, to this very hour,   135
    Stands looking seaward.

"There lived we many years;
Time dried the maiden's tears;
She had forgot her fears,
    She was a mother;   140

Death closed her mild blue eyes;
Under that tower she lies;
Ne'er shall the sun arise
    On such another!

"Still grew my bosom then,   145
Still as a stagnant fen!
Hateful to me were men,
    The sunlight hateful!
In the vast forest here,
Clad in my warlike gear,   150
Fell I upon my spear,
    Oh, death was grateful!

"Thus, seamed with many scars,
Bursting these prison bars,
Up to its native stars   155
    My soul ascended!
There from the flowing bowl
Deep drinks the warrior's soul,
Skoal!° to the Northland! skoal!"
    Thus the tale ended.   160

159. *Skoal:* a Scandinavian drinking toast.

FOR STUDY AND DISCUSSION

THE ARSENAL AT SPRINGFIELD

1. The comparison between the arsenal and an organ is basic to the poem. In what two ways is the organ a fitting instrument with which to compare the arsenal?

2. What different ages and parts of the world are mentioned in the poem? How does the review of times and places strengthen Longfellow's point?

3. Point out the use of onomatopoeia (see page 122) in stanzas 4 and 7. In what other stanzas is the use of sound devices especially important?

THE TIDE RISES, THE TIDE FALLS

1. Why do you think Longfellow made the traveler a vague figure? How would the poem be different if more information about the traveler were given?

2. The refrain, "And the tide rises, the tide falls," occurs three times. What is the effect of this repetition?

3. Would you call "The Tide Rises, the Tide Falls" a sad poem? Why or why not?

THE SKELETON IN ARMOR

1. This poem was written following a discovery near Fall River, Massachusetts, of a man's skeleton clothed in armor. Longfellow imagined the man to have been a Viking seafarer. What sense of Viking life do you get from this poem? Give details from the poem to support your answer.

2. In your opinion, does this poem give primarily the impression of a wicked life or simply of a full, vigorous life? Do you think Longfellow approved or disapproved of the Viking? Find lines in the poem to support your opinion.

LANGUAGE AND VOCABULARY

In line 53 of "The Skeleton in Armor," the word *Berserk* is used in its original form. Today the word is generally used as an adjective to describe madness. Give the original meaning and one or more later meanings of the following words from the same poem: *wassail, minstrel, gusty* (and the related word, *gusto*), *saga.*

Divina Commedia

I

Oft have I seen at some cathedral door
A laborer, pausing in the dust and heat,
Lay down his burden, and with reverent feet
Enter, and cross himself, and on the floor
Kneel to repeat his paternoster° o'er;   5
Far off the noises of the world retreat;
The loud vociferations of the street
Become an undistinguishable roar.
So, as I enter here from day to day,
And leave my burden at this minster° gate   10
Kneeling in prayer, and not ashamed to pray,
The tumult of the time disconsolate,
To inarticulate murmurs dies away,
While the eternal ages watch and wait.

II

How strange the sculptures that adorn these towers!
This crowd of statues, in whose folded sleeves
Birds build their nests; while canopied with leaves
Parvis° and portal bloom like trellised bowers,
And the vast minster seems a cross of flowers!   5
But fiends and dragons on the gargoyled eaves°
Watch the dead Christ between the living thieves,
And, underneath, the traitor Judas lowers!
Ah! from what agonies of heart and brain,
What exultations trampling on despair,   10
What tenderness, what tears, what hate of wrong,
What passionate outcry of a soul in pain,
Uprose this poem° of the earth and air,
This medieval miracle of song!

III

I enter, and I see thee in the gloom
Of the long aisles, O poet saturnine!°
And strive to make my steps keep pace with thine.
The air is filled with some unknown perfume;

I. 5. **paternoster** (pā′tə·nos′tər): the Lord's Prayer.   10. **minster:** church: here used figuratively for Dante's *Divine Comedy*.
II. 4. **Parvis:** a court or portico in front of a church.   6. **gargoyled eaves:** The tops of the walls of medieval churches were often decorated with carvings of fantastic creatures.
13. **poem:** Dante's *The Divine Comedy*.
III. 2. **poet saturnine:** Dante, who wrote with somber gravity.

The congregation of the dead make room   5
For thee to pass; the votive tapers° shine;
Like rooks that haunt Ravenna's° groves of pine
The hovering echoes fly from tomb to tomb.
From the confessionals° I hear arise
Rehearsals° of forgotten tragedies,   10
And lamentations from the crypts below;
And then a voice celestial that begins
With the pathetic words, "Although your sins
As scarlet be," and ends with "as the snow."

6. **votive tapers:** consecrated candles. 7. **Ravenna:** the city in Italy where Dante was buried. 9. **confessionals:** small enclosures where priests hear confessions. 10. **Rehearsals:** here, retellings.

FOR STUDY AND DISCUSSION

1. These sonnets were written after the death of Longfellow's wife. In your opinion, do the poems reflect his grief at her death? Give details from all three poems to support your answer.

2. What does the cathedral in these three sonnets symbolize? In your opinion, is the symbol appropriate? Why or why not?

3. Explain the third line of the third sonnet. Explain the words with which the celestial voice begins and ends in the last two lines of this sonnet.

4. Which sonnet do you prefer? Why?

THE SONNET

The sonnet is one of the most demanding of all poetic forms, yet poets have come to it again and again. One reason for the sonnet's popularity is that most poets welcome a testing of their artistic resources and, like athletes or chess players, often perform best when they are most obliged to follow rules. The sonnet form offers certain advantages. As the American poets Karl Shapiro and Robert Beum point out, "The fourteen lines of a sonnet . . . offer room for the full development of a single, but perhaps impressively subtle, imaginative, and complete idea. A sonnet is large enough to allow the poet to set forth a problem and then go on to solve it (or find it insoluble); to present a situation and then interpret it . . ."

There are two principal kinds of sonnets: the Italian and the English (sometimes called the Elizabethan) sonnet. Both kinds consist of fourteen lines written in iambic pentameter; that is, each line has ten syllables, which are alternately unstressed and stressed (see page

116). The English sonnet is made up of three *quatrains* (groups of four lines) rhyming *abab* and a concluding *couplet* (two rhymed lines). Usually the quatrains each state the same essential idea in three different ways, while the final couplet resolves or sums up the idea. The most famous examples of the English sonnet are those by William Shakespeare.

The Italian sonnet consists of a group of eight lines called an *octave* followed by a group of six lines called a *sestet*. The octave of a sonnet usually poses a problem or presents an idea that is solved or developed in the last six lines. The three sonnets by Longfellow that you have just read are Italian sonnets. Usually the rhyme scheme of an Italian sonnet separates the octave from the sestet and unifies each of the two parts. Notice that in Longfellow's first sonnet there are only four rhymes, two used in the octave and two in the sestet. The rhyme scheme of the octave is *abba abba,* which is the rhyme scheme commonly used in the octave of an Italian sonnet. Such a rhyme scheme helps make the reader aware that all the lines belong to one part of the poem. In a similar fashion, the rhyme scheme of the sestet—*cdcdcd*—indicates that these six lines form a group separate from the octave.

1. In the first sonnet from "Divina Commedia," the octave deals with the laborer, while the sestet shifts to the "I" of the poem. Describe the shift in thought from the octave to the sestet in the second and third sonnets.

2. Examine the rhyme schemes of the second and third sonnets. Are they exactly the same as the rhyme scheme of the first? If there are differences, describe them. Do the rhyme schemes of the second and third sonnets also serve to separate the octave from the sestet? Explain.

JOHN GREENLEAF WHITTIER

(1807–1892)

"I am a *man*," wrote Whittier to a biographer, "and not a mere versemaker." For much of his life, Whittier was deeply involved in public affairs. Tall, eager, dressed in Quaker black, he was a notable antislavery speaker. At times he was splattered with eggs from angry crowds. Once in Concord, New Hampshire, he was assaulted by a mob and shot at. In Philadelphia, the office of a paper that he edited was burned. His activities were not limited to antislavery agitation, however. He served a term in the Massachusetts legislature and was a lobbyist for a number of causes, including woman suffrage, fair treatment of the Indians, and care for the blind.

Like other New England poets of his day, Whittier was admired as one of the "Fireside Poets," writers whose verse was read aloud around the fireplace. Other fireside poets such as Longfellow came from well-to-do families, attended good colleges, and went on to prosperous careers. Unlike them, Whittier came from a poor family, was largely self-taught, and remained poor most of his life.

Whittier was born in a Haverhill, Massachusetts, farmhouse which his ancestor, Thomas Whittier, had built in 1688. His family had been Quakers for several generations. He started to learn the cobbler's trade and was a schoolteacher for a year, but most of his life before the War Between the States was spent as an antislavery agitator and an editor of reform journals. He wrote many political poems. The most notable of these, "Ichabod," expresses the disappointment of many New Englanders with Daniel Webster for supporting compromise with the South, particularly with Webster's support of the Fugitive Slave Act. But as the War Between the States approached, Whittier withdrew from political activity and retired to his home in the quiet town of Amesbury, Massachusetts, a few miles down the Merrimack River from his native Haverhill. There he wrote his best poetry, works that convey the savor of rural New England with touching directness. Using the little he earned to support his mother and sisters, he never married. Only after the publication of *Snowbound* in 1866 did he have enough money to live comfortably.

In the last years of his life, Whittier became a national figure. His seventieth birthday was celebrated by a famous dinner in Boston at which Mark Twain told a story about three Nevada tramps who passed themselves off as Longfellow, Holmes, and Emerson. On Whittier's eightieth birthday, the entire nation paid homage to the former agitator's literary achievements, which pictured a simple but civilized way of life that seemed, even then in 1887, already lost.

FROM *Snowbound*

A WINTER IDYLL

The sun that brief December day
Rose cheerless over hills of gray,
And, darkly circled, gave at noon
A sadder light than waning moon.
Slow tracing down the thickening sky   5
Its mute and ominous prophecy,
A portent seeming less than threat,
It sank from sight before it set.
A chill no coat, however stout,
Of homespun stuff could quite shut out,
A hard, dull bitterness of cold,   11
   That checked, mid-vein, the circling
     race
   Of lifeblood in the sharpened face,
The coming of the snowstorm told.
The wind blew east: we heard the roar   15
Of Ocean on his wintry shore,
And felt the strong pulse throbbing there
Beat with low rhythm our inland air.

Meanwhile we did our nightly chores—
Brought in the wood from out of doors,
Littered the stalls, and from the mows   21
Raked down the herd's-grass for the cows;
Heard the horse whinnying for his corn;
And, sharply clashing horn on horn,
Impatient down the stanchion rows   25
The cattle shake their walnut bows;
While, peering from his early perch
Upon the scaffold's pole of birch,
The cock his crested helmet bent
And down his querulous challenge sent.

Unwarmed by any sunset light   31
The gray day darkened into night,
A night made hoary with the swarm
And whirl-dance of the blinding storm,
As zigzag, wavering to and fro,   35
Crossed and recrossed the winged snow:
And ere the early bedtime came,
The white drift piled the window frame,
And through the glass the clothesline
    posts
Looked in like tall and sheeted ghosts.   40

So all night long the storm roared on:
The morning broke without a sun;
In tiny spherule° traced with lines
Of Nature's geometric signs,
In starry flake and pellicle,°   45
All day the hoary meteor fell;
And, when the second morning shone,
We looked upon a world unknown,
On nothing we could call our own.
Around the glistening wonder bent   50
The blue walls of the firmament,
No cloud above, no earth below—
A universe of sky and snow!
The old familiar sights of ours
Took marvelous shapes; strange domes
    and towers   55
Rose up where sty or corncrib stood,
Or garden wall, or belt of wood;
A smooth white mound the brush pile
    showed,
A fenceless drift what once was road;
The bridle post an old man sat   60
With loose-flung coat and high cocked hat;
The wellcurb had a Chinese roof;°
And even the long sweep, high aloof,
In its slant splendor, seemed to tell
Of Pisa's leaning miracle.°   65

A prompt, decisive man, no breath
Our father wasted: "Boys, a path!"
Well pleased (for when did farmer boy
Count such a summons less than joy?)
Our buskins° on our feet we drew;   70
   With mittened hands, and caps drawn
    low,
   To guard our necks and ears from snow,
We cut the solid whiteness through.
And, where the drift was deepest, made
A tunnel walled and overlaid   75
   With dazzling crystal: we had read
Of rare Aladdin's° wondrous cave,

43. **spherule:** a little sphere. 45. **pellicle** (pel′i-kəl): a thin film. 62. **wellcurb ... roof:** When asked how this could be, Whittier explained that a board had been placed across the curb to hold the bucket and that this gave the roof effect. 65. **Pisa's** (pē′säz) ... **miracle:** a famous slanting tower in Pisa, Italy. 70. **buskins:** boots similar to the high-heeled boots worn by ancient Greek actors. 77. **Aladdin:** the youth in the *Arabian Nights* who discovered great treasure in a cave through the power of a magical lamp.

And to our own his name we gave,
With many a wish the luck were ours
To test his lamp's supernal powers.   80
We reached the barn with merry din,
And roused the prisoned brutes within.
The old horse thrust his long head out,
And grave with wonder gazed about;
The cock his lusty greeting said,   85
And forth his speckled harem led;
The oxen lashed their tails, and hooked,
And mild reproach of hunger looked;
The hornèd patriarch of the sheep,   89
Like Egypt's Amun° roused from sleep,
Shook his sage head with gesture mute,
And emphasized with stamp of foot.

All day the gusty north wind bore
The loosening drift its breath before;
Low circling round its southern zone,   95
The sun through dazzling snow-mist shone.
No church bell lent its Christian tone
To the savage air, no social smoke
Curled over woods of snow-hung oak.
A solitude made more intense   100
By dreary-voicèd elements,
The shrieking of the mindless wind,
The moaning tree boughs swaying blind,
And on the glass the unmeaning beat
Of ghostly finger tips of sleet.   105
Beyond the circle of our hearth
No welcome sound of toil or mirth
Unbound the spell, and testified
Of human life and thought outside.
We minded that the sharpest ear   110
The buried brooklet could not hear,
The music of whose liquid lip
Had been to us companionship,
And, in our lonely life, had grown
To have an almost human tone.   115

As night drew on, and, from the crest
Of wooded knolls that ridged the west,
The sun, a snow-blown traveler, sank
From sight beneath the smothering bank,
We piled with care our nightly stack   120
Of wood against the chimney back—

90. **Egypt's Amun:** an Egyptian god frequently
represented with a ram's head; usually spelled Amon
or Ammon.

The oaken log, green, huge, and thick,
And on its top the stout backstick;
The knotty forestick laid apart,
And filled between with curious art   125
The ragged brush; then, hovering near,
We watched the first red blaze appear,
Heard the sharp crackle, caught the gleam
On whitewashed wall and sagging beam,
Until the old, rude-furnished room   130
Burst, flowerlike, into rosy bloom;
While radiant with a mimic flame
Outside the sparkling drift became,
And through the bare-boughed lilac tree
Our own warm hearth seemed blazing
    free.   135
The crane and pendent trammels° showed,
The Turks' heads° on the andirons glowed;
While childish fancy, prompt to tell
The meaning of the miracle,

136. **crane . . . trammels:** Trammels are adjustable
pothooks that are hung on a swinging arm (crane) attached to the hearth.   137. **Turks' heads:** The design of the top of the andiron resembled a Turkish
cap.

Shook beam and rafter as it passed,
The merrier up its roaring draft
The great throat of the chimney laughed;
The house dog on his paws outspread   165
Laid to the fire his drowsy head,
The cat's dark silhouette on the wall
A couchant° tiger's seemed to fall;
And, for the winter fireside meet,
Between the andirons' straddling feet,
The mug of cider simmered slow,   171
The apples sputtered in a row.
And, close at hand, the basket stood
With nuts from brown October's wood.

What matter how the night behaved? 175
What matter how the north wind raved?
Blow high, blow low, not all its snow
Could quench our hearthfire's ruddy
        glow. . . .
We sped the time with stories old,   179
Wrought puzzles out, and riddles told,
Or stammered from our schoolbook lore
"The Chief of Gambia's golden shore."°. . .

Whispered the old rhyme: *"Under the
        tree*   140
When fire outdoors burns merrily,
There the witches are making tea."

The moon above the eastern wood
Shone at its full; the hill range stood
Transfigured in the silver flood,   145
Its blown snows flashing cold and keen,
Dead white, save where some sharp ravine
Took shadow, or the somber green
Of hemlocks turned to pitchy black
Against the whiteness at their back.   150
For such a world and such a night
Most fitting that unwarming light,
Which only seemed where'er it fell
To make the coldness visible.
Shut in from all the world without,   155
We sat the clean-winged hearth° about,
Content to let the north wind roar
In baffled rage at pane and door,
While the red logs before us beat
The frost line back with tropic heat;   160
And ever, when a louder blast

THE FATHER

Our father rode again his ride
On Memphremagog's° wooded side;
Sat down again to moose and samp°   185
In trapper's hut and Indian camp. . . .
We shared the fishing off Boar's Head,°
The chowder on the sand beach made,
Dipped by the hungry, steaming hot,   189
With spoons of clamshell from the pot.
We heard the tales of witchcraft old,
And dream and sign and marvel told
To sleepy listeners as they lay
Stretched idly on the salted hay,
Adrift along the winding shores,   195
    When favoring breezes deigned to blow
    The square sail of the gundalow,°
And idle lay the useless oars.

156. **clean-winged hearth:** A turkey wing was used for a hearth broom.

168. **couchant:** lying down.   182. **"The . . . shore":** a line from a popular poem of the day called "The African Chief." This shows the interest in antislavery in Whittier's boyhood.   184. **Memphremagog** (mem′frə·mā′gog): a lake between Vermont and Canada.   185. **samp:** boiled Indian corn. 187. **Boar's Head:** a point on the coast north of Salisbury, Massachusetts.   197. **gundalow:** a variant of *gondola,* a heavy, flat-bottomed barge or boat.

THE MOTHER

Our mother, while she turned her wheel
Or ran the new-knit stocking heel.   200
Told how the Indian hordes came down
At midnight on Cocheco° town,
And how her own great-uncle bore
His cruel scalp-mark to fourscore.
Recalling, in her fitting phrase   205
  So rich and picturesque and free,
  (The common unrhymed poetry
Of simple life and country ways),
The story of her early days—
She made us welcome to her home;   210
Old hearths grew wide to give us room;
We stole with her a frightened look
At the gray wizard's conjuring-book,
The fame whereof went far and wide
Through all the simple countryside;   215
We heard the hawks at twilight play,
The boat horn on Piscataqua,°
The loon's weird laughter far away;
We fished her little trout brook, knew
What flowers in wood and meadow grew,
What sunny hillsides autumn-brown   221
She climbed to shake the ripe nuts down,
Saw where in sheltered cove and bay
The duck's black squadron anchored lay,
And heard the wild geese calling loud 225
Beneath the gray November cloud. . . .

THE UNCLE

Our uncle,° innocent of books,
Was rich in lore of fields and brooks,
The ancient teachers never dumb
Of Nature's unhoused lyceum.°   230
In moons and tides and weather wise,
He read the clouds as prophecies,
And foul or fair could well divine,
By many an occult hint and sign,
Holding the cunning-warded keys°   235

202. **Cocheco** (kō·chē′kō): Indian name for Dover, New Hampshire. 217. **Piscataqua** (pis·kat′ə-kwô): a river between Maine and New Hampshire. The rhyme shows that Whittier gave it a rustic pronunciation. 227. **Our uncle:** Moses, the bachelor brother of Whittier's father. 230. **lyceum:** originally an area in which the Greek philosopher Aristotle lectured, now ordinarily used to indicate any lecture hall. 235. **cunning-warded keys:** keys with notches nicely adjusted to fit different locks.

To all the woodcraft mysteries;
Himself to Nature's heart so near
That all her voices in his ear
Of beast or bird had meanings clear.
A simple, guileless, childlike man,   240
Content to live where life began;
Strong only on his native grounds,
The little world of sights and sounds
Whose girdle was the parish bounds. . . .

THE AUNT

Next, the dear aunt,° whose smile of cheer
And voice in dreams I see and hear—   246
The sweetest woman ever Fate
Perverse denied a household mate,
Who, lonely, homeless, not the less
Found peace in love's unselfishness,   250
And welcome wheresoe'er she went,
A calm and gracious element,
Whose presence seemed the sweet income
And womanly atmosphere of home—
Called up her girlhood memories,   255
The huskings and the apple bees,
The sleigh rides and the summer sails,
Weaving through all the poor details
And homespun warp° of circumstance
A golden woof-thread of romance. . . .   260

THE ELDER SISTER

There, too, our elder sister° plied
Her evening task the stand beside;
A full, rich nature, free to trust,
Truthful and almost sternly just,
Impulsive, earnest, prompt to act,   265
And make her generous thought a fact,
Keeping with many a light disguise
The secret of self-sacrifice.
A heart sore tried! thou hast the best   269
That Heaven itself could give thee—rest,
Rest from all bitter thoughts and things!
  How many a poor one's blessing went
  With thee beneath the low green tent
Whose curtain never outward swings!

245. **the dear aunt:** Aunt Mercy, his mother's sister, who always made her home with the Whittiers. 259–60. **warp:** the threads lengthwise in a loom, crossed by the **weft** or **woof,** the filling thread carried by the shuttle. 261. **elder sister:** Mary, who died five years before the poem was written.

THE YOUNGER SISTER

As one who held herself a part   275
Of all she saw, and let her heart
  Against the household bosom lean,
Upon the motley-braided mat
Our youngest° and our dearest sat. . . .
The chill weight of the winter snow   280
  For months upon her grave has lain;
And now, when summer south winds blow
  And brier and harebell bloom again,
I tread the pleasant paths we trod,
I see the violet-sprinkled sod   285
Whereon she leaned, too frail and weak
The hillside flowers she loved to seek,
Yet following me where'er I went
With dark eyes full of love's content.
The birds are glad; the brier rose fills 290
The air with sweetness; all the hills
Stretch green to June's unclouded sky;
But still I wait with ear and eye
For something gone which should be nigh,
A loss in all familiar things,   295
In flower that blooms, and bird that
  sings. . . .

THE SCHOOLMASTER

Brisk wielder of the birch and rule,
The master of the district school
Held at the fire his favored place;
Its warm glow lit a laughing face   300
Fresh-hued and fair, where scarce ap-
  peared
The uncertain prophecy of beard.
He teased the mitten-blinded cat,
Played cross pins on my uncle's hat,
Sang songs, and told us what befalls   305
In classic Dartmouth's college halls.

Born the wild Northern hills among,
From whence his yeoman father wrung
By patient toil subsistence scant,
Not competence and yet not want,   310
He early gained the power to pay
His cheerful, self-reliant way;
Could doff at ease his scholar's gown

279. **Our youngest:** Elizabeth, the unmarried sister, who kept house for Whittier until she died, about
a year before the poem was written. As she too possessed some poetic gift, the brother and sister were
most congenial, and the poet's mourning for her is
feelingly expressed.

To peddle wares from town to town;
Or through the long vacation's reach   315
In lonely lowland districts teach,
Where all the droll experience found
At stranger hearths in boarding round,
The moonlit skater's keen delight,
The sleigh drive through the frosty night,
The rustic party, with its rough   321
Accompaniment of blindman's buff,
And whirling plate, and forfeits paid,
His winter task a pastime made.
Happy the snow-locked homes wherein
He tuned his merry violin,   326
Or played the athlete in the barn,
Or held the good dame's winding yarn,
Or mirth-provoking versions told
Of classic legends rare and old,   330
Wherein the scenes of Greece and Rome
Had all the commonplace of home,
And little seemed at best the odds
'Twixt Yankee peddlers and old gods.

At last the great logs, crumbling low, 335
Sent out a dull and duller glow,
The bull's-eye watch that hung in view,
Ticking its weary circuit through,
Pointed with mutely warning sign
Its black hand to the hour of nine.   340
That sign the pleasant circle broke:
My uncle ceased his pipe to smoke,
Knocked from its bowl the refuse gray
And laid it tenderly away;
Then roused himself to safely cover   345
The dull red brands with ashes over.
And while, with care, our mother laid
The work aside, her steps she stayed
One moment, seeking to express
Her grateful sense of happiness   350
For food and shelter, warmth and health,
And love's contentment more than wealth,
With simple wishes (not the weak,
Vain prayers which no fulfillment seek,
But such as warm the generous heart,   355
O'erprompt to do with Heaven its part)
That none might lack, that bitter night,
For bread and clothing, warmth and light.

Within our beds awhile we heard
The wind that round the gables roared,
With now and then a ruder shock,   361
Which made our very bedsteads rock.

We heard the loosened clapboards tossed,
The board nails snapping in the frost;
And on us, through the unplastered wall.
Felt the light-sifted snowflakes fall.   366
But sleep stole on, as sleep will do
When hearts are light and life is new;
Faint and more faint the murmurs grew,
Till in the summerland of dreams   370
They softened to the sound of streams,
Low stir of leaves, and dip of oars,
And lapsing waves on quiet shores.

Next morn we wakened with the shout
   Of merry voices high and clear;   375
   And saw the teamsters drawing near
To break the drifted highways out.
Down the long hillside treading slow
We saw the half-buried oxen go,   379
Shaking the snow from heads uptossed,
Their straining nostrils white with frost.
Before our door the straggling train
Drew up, an added team to gain.
The elders threshed their hands a-cold,
   Passed, with the cider mug, their jokes
   From lip to lip; the younger folks   386
Down the loose snowbanks, wrestling,
   rolled,
Then toiled again the cavalcade
   O'er windy hill, through clogged ravine,
   And woodland paths that wound be-
     tween   390
Low dropping pine boughs winterweighed.
From every barn a team afoot,
At every house a new recruit,
Where, drawn by Nature's subtlest law,
Haply the watchful young men saw   395
Sweet doorway pictures of the curls
And curious eyes of merry girls,
Lifting their hands in mock defense
Against the snowball's compliments,
And reading in each missive tossed   400
The charm with Eden never lost.

We heard once more the sleigh bells'
   sound;
   And, following where the teamsters led,
The wise old Doctor went his round,
Just pausing at our door to say,   405
In the brief autocratic way
Of one who, prompt at Duty's call,
Was free to urge her claim on all,

That some poor neighbor sick abed
At night our mother's aid would need.   410
For, one in generous thought and deed,
   What mattered in the sufferer's sight
   The Quaker matron's inward light,
The Doctor's mail of Calvin's creed?°
All hearts confess the saints elect   415
   Who, twain in faith, in love agree,
And melt not in an acid sect
   The Christian pearl of charity!

So days went on: a week had passed
Since the great world was heard from last.
The Almanac we studied o'er,   421
Read and reread our little store
Of books and pamphlets, scarce a score;
One harmless novel, mostly hid
From younger eyes, a book forbid,   425
And poetry (or good or bad,
A single book was all we had). . . .
At last the floundering carrier bore
The village paper to our door.
Lo! broadening outward as we read,   430
To warmer zones the horizon spread;
In panoramic length unrolled
We saw the marvels that it told. . . .

Welcome to us its week-old news,
Its corner for the rustic Muse,   435

414. **Calvin's creed:** The doctor was a follower of
Calvin, a sixteenth-century Swiss religious reformer.

Its monthly gauge of snow and rain,
Its record, mingling in a breath
The wedding bell and dirge of death;
Jest, anecdote, and lovelorn tale,
The latest culprit sent to jail;   440
Its hue and cry of stolen and lost,
Its vendue° sales and goods at cost,
    And traffic calling loud for gain.
We felt the stir of hall and street,
The pulse of life that round us beat;   445
The chill embargo of the snow
Was melted in the genial glow;
Wide swung again our ice-locked door,
And all the world was ours once more!

442. **vendue** (ven·dōō): auction.

FOR STUDY AND DISCUSSION

1. What sounds does Whittier use to convey the quality of the oncoming storm? What details are used to convey the unreal quality of the scene after the snowfall? What details are used near the end of the poem to show the quickening of life?

2. What have you learned from *Snowbound* about life in rural New England during the time of Whittier's boyhood? Which details, in your opinion, are special to that area and time? Which details are typical of all country life?

3. Would you call the Whittier family, as it is portrayed in this poem, a happy family? Why or why not? What is Whittier's attitude toward the schoolmaster? In what ways has the life of a teacher changed since the time of the poem?

4. Whittier wrote *Snowbound* when he was nearly sixty. What does the poem reveal of his feelings about his childhood?

5. In your opinion, is Whittier more skillful in describing scenery or people? Give details to support your answer.

IMAGERY

One of a writer's most important resources in establishing contact with his readers is his ability to appeal to the senses—that is, to create word pictures or *images*. Imagery depends on a world that reader and writer share, the world of physical sensations. "No ideas but in things," a modern poet has written (page 652); and by using images, a writer can call up in the reader's mind the particular way a thing looks, feels, or sounds. Imagery is particularly important to poetry, which often deals with private, special experiences. By using good, sharp images, a poet can establish a common ground between his own special experiences and the experience of any reader.

Whittier's *Snowbound,* for example, deals with scenes and a way of life that may be unfamiliar to many readers. Vivid images help bridge the gap between poet and reader. Notice how, in the first four lines of the poem, the use of visual imagery (the most common type) enables the reader to see how particular things looked on a particular day. Each of the italicized phrases creates a word picture.

> "The sun that brief December day
> *Rose cheerless* over *hills of gray,*
> And, *darkly circled,* gave at noon
> A *sadder light than waning moon.*"

Later images convey the feel of the cold weather ("A hard, dull bitterness of cold") and the sound of the wind ("The wind blew east: we heard the roar/ Of Ocean on his wintry shore"). The sharp images in *Snowbound* create an impression of shared experience and thus point up one of literature's chief values, the gift of many lives that it makes to the reader.

1. Find six images in *Snowbound.* Only two of these should be visual images.

2. Find two images in a prose work by each of the following authors: William Bradford, Edgar Allan Poe, Washington Irving, Henry David Thoreau.

OLIVER WENDELL HOLMES

(1809–1894)

For Oliver Wendell Holmes—poet, essayist, novelist, and professor of medicine —the practice of literature was essentially an avocation rather than a vocation, the natural result of his brilliant versatility. Most of his poetry, as sparkling and graceful as his conversation, is light or occasional. Only rarely, in a few poems such as "The Chambered Nautilus," did he feel that he had written profoundly. The main effort of his life he devoted to science, which he described as being "the true successor of the men of old who brought down the light of heaven to men." About his poems he was modest. He wrote to James Russell Lowell, "Though they are for the most part to poetry as the beating of a drum or the tinkling of a triangle is to the harmony of a band, yet it is not everybody who can get their limited significance out of these humble instruments." Many generations of readers have been delighted by Holmes's verse, and as long as readers turn to poetry for amusement as well as graver purposes, his work will continue to find admirers. Along with the English writers Edward Lear and Lewis Carroll, and the modern American poet Ogden Nash, Holmes is one of the most distinguished writers of light verse in English. His verse, like theirs, may be "light," but it is not flimsy. Instead, it is the result of a deft, careful technique and is genuinely imaginative as well—the work of the poetic imagination in its less serious moments.

Like his contemporary James Russell Lowell, Holmes was the son of a Cambridge minister. When he was a law student at Harvard, he read in a newspaper that the frigate *Constitution,* the victor of a famous sea battle in the War of 1812, was about to be destroyed. As a protest, he wrote "Old Ironsides," his first famous poem, and saved the ship. After a short time, Holmes changed from law to the study of medicine. He stayed almost two years in Paris studying the new French medical techniques and spent his vacations traveling throughout Europe. In 1838 he became professor of anatomy at Dartmouth College and seven years later accepted a post at Harvard, where he taught for thirty-five years and for five years served as dean of the Medical School. As a lecturer on anatomy and physiology, he was notable for imparting to his students his own excitement and delight in these subjects. He was a pioneer in surgical methods. Among the innovations he advocated were the use of anesthesia and the importance of antiseptic procedures in surgery. His paper on "The Contagiousness of Puerperal Fever" is regarded as an important work of medical research.

Despite his teaching responsibilities, Holmes found time to write three novels on medical subjects, several books of essays, books about his travels, a critical study of Emerson, and many poems. Until his late forties he was known principally as a physician and teacher and as a writer of verse for special occasions, such as the annual reunion of his Harvard class of 1829. His wit and charm made him a leading spirit of the Saturday Club, a group of Boston and Cambridge writers, scientists, and political leaders that met once a month for a session of good talk, which often lasted into the early morning hours. In 1857, Holmes and his friends founded a magazine, *The Atlantic Monthly,* and James Russell Lowell, its first editor, asked Holmes to contribute. For the *Atlantic,* Holmes wrote a series of essays—in which poems such as "Contentment" and "The Chambered Nautilus" were interwoven— that revolved around conversations at the breakfast table of a boarding house. These essays, collected as *The Autocrat of the Breakfast Table,* made both Holmes and the magazine famous. Later, Holmes wrote two further collections of table talk, *The Professor at the Breakfast Table* and *The Poet at the Breakfast Table.* Today, many readers find these conversations dated. But the poems that salt these essays continue to stimulate and entertain. They are a reminder of the little physician to whom a friend remarked, "Holmes, you are intellectually the most alive man I ever knew." Holmes replied, "I am, I am! From the crown of my head to the sole of my foot, I'm alive, I'm alive!"

The Height of the Ridiculous

I wrote some lines once on a time
  In wondrous merry mood,
And thought, as usual, men would say
  They were exceeding good.

They were so queer, so very queer,   5
  I laughed as I would die;
Albeit, in the general way,
  A sober man am I.

I called my servant, and he came;
  How kind it was of him   10
To mind a slender man like me,
  He of the mighty limb!

"These to the printer," I exclaimed,
  And, in my humorous way,
I added (as a trifling jest),   15
  "There'll be the devil° to pay."

He took the paper, and I watched,
  And saw him peep within;
At the first line he read, his face
  Was all upon the grin.   20

He read the next; the grin grew broad,
  And shot from ear to ear;
He read the third; a chuckling noise
  I now began to hear.

The fourth; he broke into a roar;   25
  The fifth; his waistband split;
The sixth; he burst five buttons off,
  And tumbled in a fit.

Ten days and nights, with sleepless eye,
  I watched that wretched man,   30
And since, I never dare to write
  As funny as I can.

16. **devil:** a printer's apprentice is called a "printer's devil."

[OLIVER WENDELL HOLMES CONTINUED ON PAGE 231]

Landscape Painters
of the American Wilderness

The Romantic movement in early nineteenth-century art was concerned more with emotional attitudes and freedom of expression than with problems of style. In Europe, though, the spirit of this movement was often tinged with melancholy and rebellion, whereas in America it was generally optimistic, based on a feeling of close kinship between man and the vast wilderness of the American continent. It was the grandeur of this raw, untamed country that inspired a new type of landscape painting in America during the 1840's, the first phase of which is referred to as the "Hudson River School."

The pioneer of this new landscape school was Thomas Cole, an artist who had taught himself to paint after coming to America from England at the age of seventeen. As a young man in the 1820's, Cole journeyed on foot along the Hudson River and through the Catskill mountains into upper New England, sketching views which he later elaborated in large oil paintings. His landscapes sold well, and he was soon recognized as the leading landscape painter in the country.

One of Cole's most ambitious projects was a series of five allegorical landscapes entitled *The Course of Empire,* with which he intended to represent the history of civilization. PLATE 2 reproduces the first picture in this series: *The Savage State,* which shows primitive man hunting in the wilderness with bow and arrow. The cluster of tents at the upper right, shown in detail in PLATE 3, represents man's first achievement in community living. (The other four pictures in the series show the course of civilization from an agricultural stage to the thriving of a great city, the wartime burning of the city, and the desolate end of civilization, in which the city is shown in ruins at sunset.) Such melodramatic landscapes reveal Cole as a romantic idealist, but also as an acute observer of nature. He based most of his details on drawings he had made of certain views along the Hudson or in the Catskills.

One of the first artists to recognize Cole's talent was Asher B. Durand, the leading engraver in America during the 1820's. Inspired by Cole's landscapes, Durand soon gave up engraving to become a painter himself, and shortly thereafter left New York City to explore the wilderness as Cole had done before him. Durand's best-known landscape is a picture of the Catskill forest called *Kindred Spirits* (PLATE 1), which he painted as a memorial to Cole in 1849, a year after his friend died. The two figures standing at the edge of a cliff represent Cole and the poet William Cullen Bryant, two "kindred spirits" who felt the same deep bond with nature. If you examine some of the details in this picture—especially the branches of the tree at the top—you can see the precision of outline that Durand had developed earlier as an engraver.

The influence of the Hudson River School continued into the 1850's, but American landscape painting soon took a radically different turn in the work of a young artist from New Haven named Frederick Edwin Church. Church studied with Thomas Cole but soon developed a unique style of his own, which combined a remarkable skill of hand with a fascination for many of the recent discoveries of science—the physics of light, the electrical laws of atmosphere, the biological principles of growth and change. PLATE 4, a painting based on various landscapes he observed and sketched as a member of two scientific expeditions to South America, shows one of Church's spectacular demonstrations of the effect of light on atmosphere.

Another important painter of the American wilderness was Albert Bierstadt. Born in Germany, he immigrated to America as a child, and then returned to his native country as a young man to study art for four years. Shortly after he returned to the United States, Bierstadt joined a federal expedition assigned to map an overland wagon route to the Pacific Ocean, his first of many trips to the Far West. The large oil paintings he later developed from his sketches on these trips established him as Frederick Church's chief rival in painting grandiose showpieces. *Merced River, Yosemite Valley* (PLATE 5) exemplifies his rather dry but theatrical style. Note the systematic arrangement of scenery almost like props on a stage, each form lighter in tone than the one in front of it.

Of all American landscape paintings done just after the War Between the States, the most well known today is not a spectacular panorama of the wilderness, but a pastoral scene of lush, cultivated farmland, called *Peace and Plenty* (PLATE 6). This huge canvas is the work of George Inness, a largely self-taught artist who originally painted in the tight, detailed manner of the Hudson River School. Partly as the result of several trips to Europe, where Inness watched some of the leading French landscape painters at work, he learned how to broaden his brushstroke and soften his tonal effects. In *Peace and Plenty* the sweeping panoramic view of the Hudson River School remains, but the forms of the landscape become blurred under a gentle glow of light, creating a more idyllic and intimate mood.

PLATE 1. ASHER B. DURAND (1796–1886): *Kindred Spirits*. 1849. Oil on canvas, 44 x 36 inches. (Collection of New York Public Library)

PLATE 2. THOMAS COLE (1801–1848): *The Savage State* from *The Course of Empire Series.*
1836. Oil on canvas, 39 x 63 inches. (New York Historical Association)

PLATE 3. Detail from PLATE 2.

227

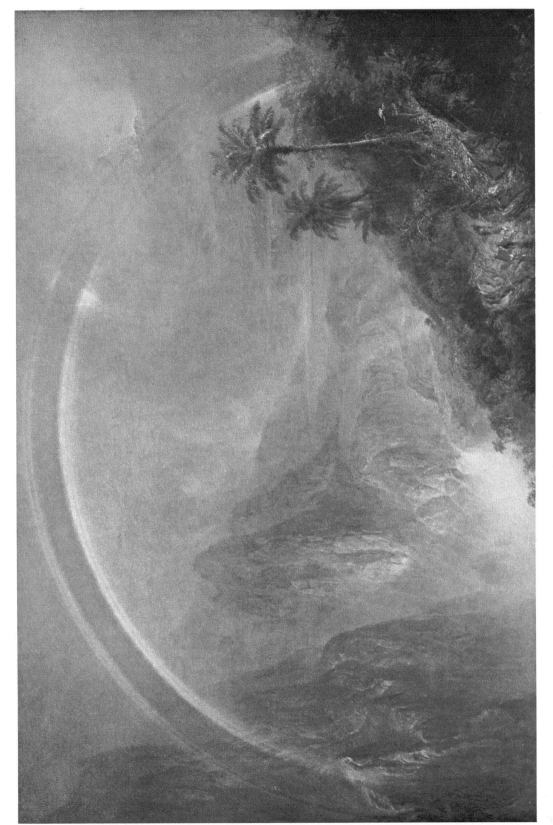

PLATE 4. FREDERICK E. CHURCH (1826–1900): *Rainy Season in the Tropics.* 1866. Oil on canvas, 55 x 84 inches. (Collection of Mr. and Mrs. J. William Middendorf II)

PLATE 5. ALBERT BIERSTADT (1830–1902): *Merced River, Yosemite Valley.* 1866. Oil on canvas, 36 x 50 inches. (The Metropolitan Museum of Art, New York, Gift of the sons of William Paton, 1909)

229

PLATE 6. GEORGE INNESS (1825–1894): *Peace and Plenty.* 1865. Oil on canvas, $77\frac{5}{8}$ x $112\frac{3}{8}$ inches. (The Metropolitan Museum of Art, New York, Gift of George A. Hearn, 1894)

230

Contentment

Little I ask; my wants are few;
   I only wish a hut of stone
(A *very plain* brown stone will do)
   That I may call my own;
And close at hand is such a one,   5
In yonder street that fronts the sun.

Plain food is quite enough for me;
   Three courses are as good as ten;
If nature can subsist on three,
   Thank Heaven for three. Amen!   10
I always thought cold victual nice;
My *choice* would be vanilla ice.

I care not much for gold or land;
   Give me a mortgage here and there,
Some good bank stock, some note of hand,
   Or trifling railroad share—   16
I only ask that Fortune send
A *little* more than I shall spend.

Honors are silly toys, I know,
   And titles are but empty names;   20
I would, *perhaps,* be Plenipo,°
   But only near St. James;°
I'm very sure I should not care
To fill our Gubernator's° chair.

Jewels are baubles; 'tis a sin   25
   To care for such unfruitful things;
One good-sized diamond in a pin,
   Some, *not so large,* in rings,
A ruby, and a pearl, or so,
Will do for me; I laugh at show.   30

My dame should dress in cheap attire;
   (Good heavy silks are never dear);
I own perhaps I *might* desire
   Some shawls of true Cashmere,
Some marrowy crepes of China silk,   35
Like wrinkled skins on scalded milk.

I would not have the horse I drive
   So fast that folks must stop and stare;
An easy gait—two forty-five—
   Suits me; I do not care;   40
Perhaps, for just a *single spurt,*
Some seconds less would do no hurt.

Of pictures, I should like to own
   Titians and Raphaels three or four,
I love so much their style and tone;   45
   One Turner, and no more,
(A landscape—foreground golden dirt—
The sunshine painted with a squirt.)

Of books but few—some fifty score
   For daily use, and bound for wear;   50
The rest upon an upper floor;
   Some *little* luxury *there*
Of red morocco's° gilded gleam
And vellum° rich as country cream.

Busts, cameos, gems—such things as
   these,   55
   Which others often show for pride,
I value for their power to please,
   And selfish churls° deride;
One Stradivarius, I confess,   59
Two Meerschaums, I would fain possess.

Wealth's wasteful tricks I will not learn,
   Nor ape the glittering upstart fool;
Shall not carved tables serve my turn,
   But *all* must be of buhl?°
Give grasping pomp its double share,   65
I ask but *one* recumbent chair.

Thus humble let me live and die,
   Nor long for Midas' golden touch;
If Heaven more generous gifts deny,
   I shall not miss them *much*—   70
Too grateful for the blessing lent
Of simple tastes and mind content!

21. **Plenipo:** Ambassador Plenipotentiary (with full powers). 22. **St. James:** the Court of St. James's in London. 24. **Gubernator:** governor.

53. **morocco:** a fine grade of leather. 54. **vellum:** either a rich calfskin binding or an expensive grade of paper; probably the latter. 58. **churls:** surly fellows. 64. **buhl** (bōōl): decoration in which tortoise shell, yellow metal, white metal, etc., are inlaid in furniture, making scrolls and other designs.

The Chambered Nautilus

The nautilus is a snail-like creature that lives in a shell which it creates by its own secretions. In the paragraph immediately preceding this poem in *The Autocrat of the Breakfast Table,* Holmes refers to "the series of enlarging compartments successively dwelt in by the animal that inhabits the shell, which is built in a dwindling spiral."

This is the ship of pearl, which, poets feign,
   Sails the unshadowed main—
   The venturous bark that flings
On the sweet summer wind its purpled wings
In gulfs enchanted, where the Siren° sings,   5
   And coral reefs lie bare,
Where the cold sea-maids rise to sun their streaming hair.

Its webs of living gauze no more unfurl;
   Wrecked is the ship of pearl!
   And every chambered cell,   10
Where its dim dreaming life was wont to dwell,
As the frail tenant shaped his growing shell,
   Before thee lies revealed—
Its irised ceiling rent, its sunless crypt unsealed!

Year after year beheld the silent toil   15
   That spread his lustrous coil;
   Still, as the spiral grew,
He left the past year's dwelling for the new,
Stole with soft step its shining archway through,
   Built up its idle door,   20
Stretched in his last-found home, and knew the old no more.

Thanks for the heavenly message brought by thee,
   Child of the wandering sea,
   Cast from her lap, forlorn!
From thy dead lips a clearer note is born   25

5. **Siren:** In classical mythology the sirens were sea nymphs near the west coast of Italy who lured mariners to their deaths by singing enchanting songs.

Than ever Triton° blew from wreathèd horn!
  While on mine ears it rings,
Through the deep caves of thought I hear a voice that sings:

Build thee more stately mansions, O my soul,
  As the swift seasons roll!   30
  Leave thy low-vaulted past!
Let each new temple, nobler than the last,
Shut thee from heaven with a dome more vast,
  Till thou at length art free,
Leaving thine outgrown shell by life's unresting sea!   35

26. **Triton** (trīt′n): ancient sea god whose lower part resembled a fish. He is usually represented as blowing a trumpet made of a seashell.

FOR STUDY AND DISCUSSION

THE HEIGHT OF THE RIDICULOUS

1. One device that is very common in American humor is exaggeration. How does Holmes use this device?

2. In your opinion is the pun in line 16 meant to be funny? What does this pun tell you about the narrator of the poem?

3. Do you consider this a funny poem? Why or why not?

CONTENTMENT

1. How does this poem make use of irony (see page 49)?

2. Compare the opening lines of each stanza with the closing lines. How do they differ? How does the effect of the poem depend upon this difference?

3. How do you think Thoreau would have reacted to this poem?

THE CHAMBERED NAUTILUS

1. This poem makes a comparison between the nautilus and the human soul. Explain this comparison.

2. In this poem, Holmes follows a regular pattern of rhyme. Do the rhymes seem to come easily and naturally in the third stanza, or do you think Holmes had to arrange his words awkwardly in order to carry out the rhyme scheme? Explain.

STANZA FORMS

As you have learned in studying Longfellow's sonnets (page 212), a poet may choose to place restrictions on himself in order to exhibit his skill. Sometimes a poet may invent an intricate stanza pattern of his own instead of following a common pattern. If you examine the stanza form of "The Chambered Nautilus," you will find that each stanza consists of seven lines. The first, fourth, and fifth lines of each stanza are written in iambic pentameter; the second, third, and sixth lines are iambic trimeter; while the seventh line, longer than the others and thus giving each stanza an effect of finality, is iambic hexameter. (For a discussion of meter, see page 204.) The rhyme scheme of each stanza, *aabbbcc,* is also rather intricate. Following this complex pattern forced Holmes occasionally to write an awkward line, but generally he has exhibited considerable technical skill.

As a reader of poetry, you should be aware of how a poet uses stanza form to mold his poem and give it a definite shape, both on the printed page and as it is read aloud. Pay particular attention to the length and rhythm of each line in a stanza and to the stanza's rhyme scheme. Examine the poem to see whether the poet uses the same stanza form throughout the poem.

Describe the stanza form of the following poems in terms of meter, line length, and rhyme scheme: "To a Waterfowl" (page 112), "To Helen" (page 119), and "The Height of the Ridiculous" (page 222).

FOR COMPOSITION

Compare "To a Waterfowl" and "The Chambered Nautilus." Show how both poems make use of comparisons. State which poem you like better and why.

New England Men of Letters

During its "Renaissance" and even before, New England was rich in men of letters. These authors were part of a general cultural awakening. They were highly aware of each other's existence and wrote with the assurance that their fellow New Englanders would be interested in their works.

Early figures. One of the most influential early New England writers was the Unitarian minister, William Ellery Channing. In his sermons and writings Channing stressed the God that is within all men: "The only God . . . is the God whose image dwells within our own souls." Regarding the physical world as "the outer garment of God," he celebrated the beauty of New England mountains, forests, and lakes. In an essay entitled "Remarks on National Literature," he called for great American writers who would embody a belief in "the essential equality of all human beings." Thus Channing anticipated ideas that were later developed in the writings of Emerson, Thoreau, and Whitman.

Richard Henry Dana, Jr., produced an early American classic in *Two Years Before the Mast* (1840). While a college student, Dana was forced to drop his studies because of failing eyesight. In 1834, he signed up as a common seaman on the brig *Pilgrim.* His account of his adventures has held its place ever since as a stirring, realistic tale of life at sea. In depicting the brutality of discipline in the merchant marine, he aroused public indignation at the injustices suffered by sailors.

Transcendentalists. Among the writers who gathered around Emerson at Concord, belonged to the Transcendental Club, and contributed to the *Dial* magazine, was the educator Bronson Alcott. Today Alcott is best known as the father of Louisa May Alcott, author of *Little Women.* In his own day Alcott was well known as an educational reformer whose ideas anticipated many modern educational practices. Margaret Fuller, along with Emerson an editor of the *Dial* and a leading champion of women's rights, wrote *Woman in the Nineteenth Century,* a book arguing for the full development of women as individuals. A series of articles for the New York *Tribune* established her as an important literary critic. Orestes Brownson, another member of the Transcendental Club, was later a convert to Roman Catholicism. An influential magazine editor, he is today regarded as an important American philosopher.

Historians. Three Bostonians who wrote in the middle of the nineteenth century are among America's greatest historians. Their works are remarkable not only for their fine command of detail but for the literary skill with which they bring the past to life. The greatest of them, Francis Parkman, struggled for many years to overcome his own infirmities in order to write *France and England in North America* (page 332). William Hicking Prescott made a study of Spanish ventures on the American continent; *A History of the Conquest of Mexico* is considered his masterpiece. John Lothrop Motley, the last of this trio, is best known for *The Rise of the Dutch Republic,* an account of the Dutch struggle for freedom against the Spanish Empire.

NATHANIEL HAWTHORNE
(1804–1864)

Emerson, the romantic prophet who believed in the profound possibilities of each human being, himself confessed that he had not given enough weight to one major aspect of human experience. "I could never give much reality to evil," he admitted. To Nathaniel Hawthorne, evil was very real indeed—not only the evil which lurks in dark alleys and in unavoidable catastrophes, but also the evil within man. The doctrine of original sin, so important to his Puritan ancestors, was never very far from Hawthorne's view of life. Born in Salem, Massachusetts, where, a century before, women had been hanged as witches, he wrote, "I felt it almost a destiny to make Salem my home." The first of Hawthorne's American forebears was a stern judge, well known for his persecution of the Quakers. That man's son, John Hathorne, was active in prosecuting suspected witches and committed about one hundred of them to jail. Of these men, Hawthorne wrote, "I take shame upon myself for their sakes and pray that any curse incurred by them . . . may be now and henceforth removed." In Hawthorne's view, unlike that of the Puritans, evil was found primarily in man's behavior toward man. For him, the greatest sinners were men so concerned with themselves that they coldly denied their sympathy to their fellow human beings. He saw evil as a force that leaves its mark on generation after generation, and in his stories and novels he traced the effects of its corrupting presence.

Hawthorne's father was a sea captain. Lost at sea when Hawthorne was only four, he left a widow and three children. Despite the family's reduced income, Hawthorne managed to attend Bowdoin College from which he was graduated in 1825. Among his friends there were Henry Wadsworth Longfellow, a classmate, and Franklin Pierce, who had graduated a year earlier and was to become the fourteenth President of the United States. After graduation, Hawthorne returned to his mother's house where he lived quietly for twelve years. During these "twelve dark years," as he called them, he wrote during the day and at night roamed the streets of Salem. In 1837 he described these years to Longfellow: "By some witchcraft or other . . . I have been carried apart from the main current of life and find it impossible to get back again . . . I have secluded myself from society. . . . I have not lived, but only dreamed about living." From time to time he did find relief from his seclusion; he visited friends and toured New England. But most of his time he devoted to developing his skill as a writer. He wrote an unsuccessful novel—*Fanshawe,* published in 1828, a number of stories that he destroyed, and a group of other stories that were first published anonymously in magazines and collected as the first volume of *Twice-*

Told Tales (1837). The next year he met and became engaged to Sophia Peabody, who helped him escape from his self-created prison and rejoin "the main current of life." From 1839 to 1841 he had a job in the Boston Custom House. In April, 1841, he began to live and work at Brook Farm, an experiment in communal living carried on by social reformers and transcendentalists, admirers and disciples of Emerson. Hawthorne found the farm work unpleasant, and he was unimpressed with schemes for reform that would not, he thought, change a wicked world into a good one. After seven months, he left. Years later, he used his experience as the basis of *The Blithedale Romance,* a novel that reflects his skepticism about the possibility of making men better by changing the conditions of their lives. In 1842, the year he married Sophia, he published the second volume of *Twice-Told Tales,* which was warmly praised by Edgar Allan Poe.

For a few years Hawthorne was able to support himself by his writing. He and Sophia moved into the Old Manse at Concord, where Emerson and Thoreau were neighbors but not close friends. In 1846, Hawthorne published a further collection of short stories, *Mosses from an Old Manse,* and accepted a political appointment as surveyor at the Salem Custom House. When the Whig party turned Hawthorne's friends out of office in 1849, he lost his job. During the next year, he gave his full energy to writing and published *The Scarlet Letter,* generally considered one of the three or four greatest American novels of the nineteenth century. Hawthorne never wrote another long work as complex and intense, as beautifully crafted in its use of words and details to achieve an effect, as this tale of four people entangled in the consequences of a sin. *The Scarlet Letter* made Hawthorne's literary reputation, and he was widely praised as a writer of distinction and originality. In the next few years he published another novel, *The House of the Seven Gables,* a fourth collection of short stories, and two books for children. Still he could not make a good living at writing. Then President Franklin Pierce temporarily relieved his old college friend of financial worries by appointing him American consul at Liverpool, England. Hawthorne held this post until 1857, when a change in political administration once again cost him a job. The last years of his life were uneasy ones, filled with concern over dwindling funds and made feverish by an attempt to complete a last novel. He was deeply troubled by the outbreak of the War Between the States. On a particularly bitter day in January, 1864, he wrote, "I have fallen into a quagmire of disgust and despondency with respect to literary matters. I am tired of my own thoughts and fancies, and my own mode of expressing them." He feared that the creative vigor of his earlier years was gone, a fear which an examination of his unfinished novels tends to confirm. In May, 1864, during a trip to New Hampshire, he died in his sleep.

In Hawthorne, Poe recognized a writer who calculated details and effects as precisely as he. But Hawthorne's work, unlike Poe's, is charged with a profound moral significance. His skill as a writer saves his better stories from being thinly disguised fables, mere excuses for moralizing. Their moral awareness, as complex as their artistry, led the poet T. S. Eliot to praise Hawthorne for "the firmness . . . of the genuine artist. In consequence, the observation of moral life . . . has solidity, has permanence, the permanence of art. It will always be of use . . . The work of Hawthorne . . . is truly a criticism of the Puritan morality, of the transcendental morality, and of the world which Hawthorne knew."

Dr. Heidegger's Experiment

THAT VERY singular man, old Dr. Heidegger, once invited four venerable friends to meet him in his study. There were three white-bearded gentlemen, Mr. Medbourne, Colonel Killigrew, and Mr. Gascoigne, and a withered gentlewoman, whose name was the Widow Wycherly. They were all melancholy old creatures, who had been unfortunate in life, and whose greatest misfortune it was that they were not long ago in their graves. Mr. Medbourne, in the vigor of his age, had been a prosperous merchant, but had lost his all by a frantic speculation and was now little better than a mendicant. Colonel Killigrew had wasted his best years, and his health and substance, in the pursuit of sinful pleasures, which had given birth to a brood of pains, such as the gout and divers other torments of soul and body. Mr. Gascoigne was a ruined politician, a man of evil fame, or at least had been so till time had buried him from the knowledge of the present generation and made him obscure instead of infamous. As for the Widow Wycherly, tradition tells us that she was a great beauty in her day; but, for a long while past, she had lived in deep seclusion, on account of certain scandalous stories which had prejudiced the gentry of the town against her. It is a circumstance worth mentioning that each of these three old gentlemen, Mr. Medbourne, Colonel Killigrew, and Mr. Gascoigne, were early lovers of the Widow Wycherly, and had once been on the point of cutting each other's throats for her sake. And, before proceeding further, I will merely hint that Dr. Heidegger and all his four guests were sometimes thought to be a little beside themselves— as is not unfrequently the case with old people, when worried either by present troubles or woeful recollections.

"My dear old friends," said Dr. Heidegger, motioning them to be seated, "I am desirous of your assistance in one of those little experiments with which I amuse myself here in my study."

If all stories were true, Dr. Heidegger's study must have been a very curious place. It was a dim, old-fashioned chamber, festooned with cobwebs and besprinkled with antique dust. Around the walls stood several oaken bookcases, the lower shelves of which were filled with rows of gigantic folios [1] and black-letter quartos,[2] and the upper with little parchment-covered duodecimos.[3] Over the central bookcase was a bronze bust of Hippocrates,[4] with which, according to some authorities, Dr. Heidegger was accustomed to hold consultations in all difficult cases of his practice. In the obscurest corner of the room stood a tall and narrow oaken closet, with its door ajar, within which doubtfully appeared a skeleton. Between two of the bookcases hung a looking glass, presenting its high and dusty plate within a tarnished gilt frame. Among many wonderful stories related of this mirror, it was fabled that the spirit of all the doctor's deceased patients dwelt within its verge and would stare him in the face whenever he looked thitherward. The opposite side of the chamber was ornamented with the full-length portrait of a young lady, arrayed in the faded magnificence of silk, satin, and brocade, and with a visage as faded as her dress. Above half a century ago, Dr. Heidegger had been on the point of marriage with this young lady; but being affected with some slight disorder, she had swallowed one of her lover's prescriptions and died on the bridal

---

[1] **folios:** books from twelve to twenty inches in height.

[2] **quartos:** books about nine and one-half by twelve and one-half inches.

[3] **duodecimos** (dōo'ō·des'ə·mōz): small volumes, about five by eight inches.

[4] **Hippocrates** (hi·pok'rə·tēz): (460?–377? B.C.) a Greek physician.

evening. The greatest curiosity of the study remains to be mentioned; it was a ponderous folio volume, bound in black leather, with massive silver clasps. There were no letters on the back, and nobody could tell the title of the book. But it was well known to be a book of magic; and once, when a chambermaid had lifted it, merely to brush away the dust, the skeleton had rattled in its closet, the picture of the young lady had stepped one foot upon the floor, and several ghastly faces had peeped forth from the mirror; while the brazen head of Hippocrates frowned and said, "Forbear!"

Such was Dr. Heidegger's study. On the summer afternoon of our tale, a small round table, as black as ebony, stood in the center of the room, sustaining a cut-glass vase of beautiful form and elaborate workmanship. The sunshine came through the window, between the heavy festoons of two faded damask curtains, and fell directly across this vase; so that a mild splendor was reflected from it on the ashen visages of the five old people who sat around. Four champagne glasses were also on the table.

"My dear old friends," repeated Dr. Heidegger, "may I reckon on your aid in performing an exceedingly curious experiment?"

Now Dr. Heidegger was a very strange old gentleman, whose eccentricity had become the nucleus for a thousand fantastic stories. Some of these fables, to my shame be it spoken, might possibly be traced back to my own veracious self; and if any passages of the present tale should startle the reader's faith, I must be content to bear the stigma of a fictionmonger.

When the doctor's four guests heard him talk of his proposed experiment, they anticipated nothing more wonderful than the murder of a mouse in an air pump, or the examination of a cobweb by the microscope, or some similar nonsense, with which he was constantly in the habit of pestering his intimates. But, without waiting for a reply, Dr. Heidegger hobbled across the chamber and returned with the same ponderous folio, bound in black leather, which common report affirmed to be a book of magic. Undoing the silver clasps, he opened the volume and took from among its black-letter pages a rose, or what was once a rose, though now the green leaves and crimson petals had assumed one brownish hue, and the ancient flower seemed ready to crumble to dust in the doctor's hands.

"This rose," said Dr. Heidegger, with a sigh, "this same withered and crumbling flower, blossomed five and fifty years ago. It was given me by Sylvia Ward, whose portrait hangs yonder; and I meant to wear it in my bosom at our wedding. Five and fifty years it has been treasured between the leaves of this old volume. Now, would you deem it possible that this rose of half a century could ever bloom again?"

"Nonsense!" said the Widow Wycherly, with a peevish toss of her head. "You might as well ask whether an old woman's wrinkled face could ever bloom again."

"See!" answered Dr. Heidegger.

He uncovered the vase and threw the rose into the water which it contained. At first, it lay lightly on the surface of the fluid, appearing to imbibe none of its moisture. Soon, however, a singular change began to be visible. The crushed and dried petals stirred and assumed a deepening tinge of crimson, as if the flower were reviving from a deathlike slumber; the slender stalk and twigs of foliage became green; and there was the rose of half a century, looking as fresh as when Sylvia Ward had first given it to her lover. It was scarcely full blown; for some of its delicate red leaves curled modestly around its moist bosom, within which two or three dewdrops were sparkling.

"That is certainly a very pretty deception," said the doctor's friends; carelessly, however, for they had witnessed greater miracles at a conjurer's show; "pray how was it effected?"

"Did you never hear of the 'Fountain of Youth'?" asked Dr. Heidegger, "which Ponce de Leon,[1] the Spanish adventurer, went in search of two or three centuries ago?"

"But did Ponce de Leon ever find it?" said the Widow Wycherly.

"No," answered Dr. Heidegger, "for he never sought it in the right place. The famous Fountain of Youth, if I am rightly informed, is situated in the southern part of the Floridian peninsula, not far from Lake Macaco. Its source is overshadowed

[1] **Ponce de Leon** (pons' dǝ lē'ǝn): (1460?–1521) Spanish discoverer of Florida.

by several gigantic magnolias, which, though numberless centuries old, have been kept as fresh as violets by the virtues of this wonderful water. An acquaintance of mine, knowing my curiosity in such matters, has sent me what you see in the vase."

"Ahem!" said Colonel Killigrew, who believed not a word of the doctor's story; "and what may be the effect of this fluid on the human frame?"

"You shall judge for yourself, my dear colonel," replied Dr. Heidegger; "and all of you, my respected friends, are welcome to so much of this admirable fluid as may restore to you the bloom of youth. For my own part, having had much trouble in growing old, I am in no hurry to grow young again. With your permission, therefor, I will merely watch the progress of the experiment."

While he spoke, Dr. Heidegger had been filling the four champagne glasses with the water of the Fountain of Youth. It was apparently impregnated with an effervescent gas, for little bubbles were continually ascending from the depths of the glasses and bursting in silvery spray at the surface. As the liquor diffused a pleasant perfume, the old people doubted not that it possessed cordial and comfortable properties; and though utter skeptics as to its rejuvenescent power, they were inclined to swallow it at once. But Dr. Heidegger besought them to stay a moment.

"Before you drink, my respectable old friends," said he, "it would be well that, with the experience of a lifetime to direct you, you should draw up a few general rules for your guidance, in passing a second time through the perils of youth. Think what a sin and shame it would be if, with your peculiar advantages, you should not become patterns of virtue and wisdom to all the young people of the age!"

The doctor's four venerable friends made him no answer, except by a feeble and tremulous laugh; so very ridiculous was the idea that, knowing how closely repentance treads behind the steps of error, they should ever go astray again.

"Drink, then," said the doctor, bowing. "I rejoice that I have so well selected the subjects of my experiment."

With palsied hands, they raised the glasses to their lips. The liquor, if it really possessed such virtues as Dr. Heidegger imputed to it, could not have been bestowed on four human beings who needed it more woefully. They looked as if they had never known what youth or pleasure was, but had been the offspring of Nature's dotage, and always the gray, decrepit, sapless, miserable creatures who now sat stooping round the doctor's table, without life enough in their souls or bodies to be animated even by the prospect of growing young again. They drank off the water and replaced their glasses on the table.

Assuredly there was an almost immediate improvement in the aspect of the party, not unlike what might have been produced by a glass of generous wine, together with a sudden glow of cheerful sunshine brightening over all their visages at once. There was a healthful suffusion on their cheeks, instead of the ashen hue that had made them look so corpselike. They gazed at one another and fancied that some magic power had really begun to smooth away the deep and sad inscriptions which Father Time had been

so long engraving on their brows. The Widow Wycherly adjusted her cap, for she felt almost like a woman again.

"Give us more of this wondrous water!" cried they, eagerly. "We are younger—but we are still too old! Quick—give us more!

"Patience, patience!" quoth Dr. Heidegger, who sat watching the experiment with philosophic coolness. "You have been a long time growing old. Surely, you might be content to grow young in half an hour! But the water is at your service."

Again he filled their glasses with the liquor of youth, enough of which still remained in the vase to turn half the old people in the city to the age of their own grandchildren. While the bubbles were yet sparkling on the brim, the doctor's four guests snatched their glasses from the table and swallowed the contents at a single gulp. Was it delusion? Even while the draft was passing down their throats, it seemed to have wrought a change on their whole systems. Their eyes grew clear and bright; a dark shade deepened among their silvery locks, they sat around the table, three gentlemen of middle age, and a woman hardly beyond her buxom prime.

"My dear widow, you are charming!" cried Colonel Killigrew, whose eyes had been fixed upon her face, while the shadows of age were flitting from it like darkness from the crimson daybreak.

The fair widow knew, of old, that Colonel Killigrew's compliments were not always measured by sober truth; so she started up and ran to the mirror, still dreading that the ugly visage of an old woman would meet her gaze. Meanwhile, the three gentlemen behaved in such a manner as proved that the water of the Fountain of Youth possessed some intoxicating qualities; unless, indeed, their exhilaration of spirits were merely a lightsome dizziness caused by the sudden removal of the weight of years. Mr. Gascoigne's mind seemed to run on political topics, but whether relating to the past, present, or future could not easily be determined, since the same ideas and phrases have been in vogue these fifty years. Now he rattled forth full-throated sentences about patriotism, national glory, and the people's right; now he muttered some perilous stuff or other, in a sly and doubtful whisper, so cautiously that even his own conscience could scarcely catch the secret; and now, again, he spoke in measured accents and a deeply deferential tone, as if a royal ear were listening to his well-turned periods. Colonel Killigrew all this time had been trolling forth a jolly bottle song and ringing his glass in symphony with the chorus, while his eyes wandered toward the buxom figure of the Widow Wycherly. On the other side of the table, Mr. Medbourne was involved in a calculation of dollars and cents, with which was strangely intermingled a project for supplying the East Indies with ice, by harnessing a team of whales to the polar icebergs.

As for the Widow Wycherly, she stood before the mirror curtsying and simpering to her own image and greeting it as the friend whom she loved better than all the world beside. She thrust her face close to the glass, to see whether some long-remembered wrinkle or crow's-foot had indeed vanished. She examined whether the snow had so entirely melted from her hair that the venerable cap could be safely thrown aside. At last, turning briskly

away, she came with a sort of dancing step to the table.

"My dear old doctor," cried she, "pray favor me with another glass!"

"Certainly, my dear madam, certainly!" replied the complaisant doctor; "See! I have already filled the glasses."

There, in fact, stood the four glasses, brimful of this wonderful water, the delicate spray of which, as it effervesced from the surface, resembled the tremulous glitter of diamonds. It was now so nearly sunset that the chamber had grown duskier than ever; but a mild and moonlike splendor gleamed from within the vase, and rested alike on the four guests and on the doctor's venerable figure. He sat in a high-backed, elaborately carved oaken armchair, with a gray dignity of aspect that might have well befitted that very Father Time whose power had never been disputed save by this fortunate company. Even while quaffing the third draft of the Fountain of Youth, they were almost awed by the expression of his mysterious visage.

But the next moment, the exhilarating gush of young life shot through their veins. They were now in the happy prime of youth. Age, with its miserable train of cares and sorrows and diseases, was remembered only as the trouble of a dream, from which they had joyously awaked. The fresh gloss of the soul, so early lost, and without which the world's successive scenes had been but a gallery of faded pictures, again threw its enchantment over all their prospects. They felt like new-created beings in a new-created universe.

"We are young! We are young!" they cried exultingly.

Youth, like the extremity of age, had effaced the strongly marked characteristics of middle life and mutually assimilated them all. They were a group of merry youngsters, almost maddened with the exuberant frolicsomeness of their years. The most singular effect of their gaiety was an impulse to mock the infirmity and decrepitude of which they had so lately been the victims. They laughed loudly at their old-fashioned attire, the wide-skirted coats and flapped waistcoats of the young men, and the ancient cap and gown of the blooming girl. One limped across the floor like a gouty grandfather; one set a pair of spectacles astride of his nose and pretended to pore over the black-letter pages of the book of magic; a third seated himself in an armchair and strove to imitate the venerable dignity of Dr. Heidegger. Then all shouted mirthfully and leaped about the room. The Widow Wycherly—if so fresh a damsel could be called a widow—tripped up to the doctor's chair, with a mischievous merriment in her rosy face.

"Doctor, you dear old soul," cried she, "get up and dance with me!" And then the four young people laughed louder than ever, to think what a queer figure the poor old doctor would cut.

"Pray excuse me," answered the doctor quietly. "I am old and rheumatic, and my dancing days were over long ago. But either of these gay young gentlemen will be glad of so pretty a partner."

"Dance with me, Clara!" cried Colonel Killigrew.

"No, no, I will be her partner!" shouted Mr. Gascoigne.

"She promised me her hand, fifty years ago!" exclaimed Mr. Medbourne.

They all gathered round her. One caught both her hands in his passionate grasp—another threw his arm about her waist—the third buried his hand among the glossy curls that clustered beneath the widow's cap. Blushing, panting, struggling, chiding, laughing, her warm breath fanning each of their faces by turns, she strove to disengage herself, yet still remained in their triple embrace. Never was there a livelier picture of youthful rivalship, with bewitching beauty for the prize. Yet, by a strange deception, owing to the duskiness of the chamber and the antique dresses which they still wore, the tall mirror is said to have reflected the figures of the three old, gray, withered grandsires ridiculously contending for the skinny ugliness of a shriveled grandam.

But they were young: their burning passions proved them so. Inflamed to madness by the coquetry of the girl-widow, who neither granted nor quite withheld her favors, the three rivals began to interchange threatening glances. Still keeping hold of the fair prize, they grappled fiercely at one another's throats. As they struggled to and fro, the table was overturned, and the vase dashed into a thousand fragments. The precious Water of Youth flowed in a bright stream across the floor, moistening the wings of a butterfly, which, grown old in the decline of summer, had alighted there to die. The insect fluttered lightly through the chamber and settled on the snowy head of Dr. Heidegger.

"Come, come, gentlemen!—come, Madam Wycherly," exclaimed the doctor, "I really must protest against this riot."

They stood still and shivered; for it seemed as if gray Time were calling them back from their sunny youth, far down into the chill and darksome vale of years. They looked at old Dr. Heidegger, who sat in his carved armchair, holding the rose of half a century, which he had rescued from among the fragments of the shattered vase. At the motion of his hand, the four rioters resumed their seats; the more readily because their violent exertions had wearied them, youthful though they were.

"My poor Sylvia's rose!" ejaculated Dr. Heidegger, holding it in the light of the

sunset clouds; "it appears to be fading again."

And so it was. Even while the party were looking at it, the flower continued to shrivel up, till it became as dry and fragile as when the doctor had first thrown it into the vase. He shook off the few drops of moisture which clung to its petals.

"I love it as well thus as in its dewy freshness," observed he, pressing the withered rose to his withered lips. While he spoke, the butterfly fluttered down from the doctor's snowy head and fell upon the floor.

His guests shivered again. A strange chillness, whether of the body or spirit they could not tell, was creeping gradually over them all. They gazed at one another, and fancied that each fleeting moment snatched away a charm, and left a deepening furrow where none had been before. Was it an illusion? Had the changes of a lifetime been crowded into so brief a space, and were they now four aged people, sitting with their old friend Dr. Heidegger?

"Are we grown old again, so soon?" cried they, dolefully.

In truth they had. The Water of Youth possessed merely a virtue more transient than that of wine. The delirium which it created had effervesced away. Yes! they were old again. With a shuddering impulse that showed her a woman still, the widow clasped her skinny hands before her face and wished that the coffin lid were over it, since it could be no longer beautiful.

"Yes, friends, ye are old again," said Dr. Heidegger, "and lo! the Water of Youth is all lavished on the ground. Well —I bemoan it not; for if the fountain gushed at my very doorstep, I would not stoop to bathe my lips in it—no, though its delirium were for years instead of moments. Such is the lesson ye have taught me!"

But the doctor's four friends had taught no such lesson to themselves. They resolved forthwith to make a pilgrimage to Florida, and quaff at morning, noon, and night, from the Fountain of Youth.

FOR STUDY AND DISCUSSION

1. Describe Dr. Heidegger's four guests. What do they have in common? Why did the author choose these particular characters as subjects for the experiment?

2. The third paragraph of the story describes Dr. Heidegger's study. What does this description tell the reader about Dr. Heidegger? What kind of a story does this paragraph lead the reader to expect? For example, does it lead him to expect a realistic story?

3. Why does Dr. Heidegger refrain from drinking the water? How does his refusal to act in this case emphasize his role as an observer of other people's actions? Does his refusal to drink seem wise or foolish?

4. What advice does the doctor give his friends before they drink? What is their reaction to his advice? In the light of what happens, is their reaction wise or foolish?

5. Describe the incident involving the mirror that occurs toward the end of the story. Do you feel that this incident adds to or detracts from the effectiveness of the story as a whole?

6. Explain the lesson which the four guests teach Dr. Heidegger. Can this lesson be stated as a general rule? Do you agree or disagree with the lesson?

LANGUAGE AND VOCABULARY

Explain the meaning of each of the following excerpts from the story and show how they add to the story's effectiveness. Be sure you know the meaning of each of the italicized words.

"time had . . . made him *obscure* instead of *infamous*." (Mr. Gascoigne)

"a very strange old gentleman, whose *eccentricity* had become the *nucleus* for a thousand fantastic stories." (Dr. Heidegger)

"its *rejuvenescent* power . . ." (the water)

"gray, *decrepit, sapless,* miserable creatures . . ." (the four guests)

FOR COMPOSITION

Defend or attack the following statement: "Dr. Heidegger's Experiment" illustrates a passage from Ecclesiastes—"Vanity of vanities . . . vanity of vanities; all is vanity." Before you write, consider all possible meanings of the words *vanity* and *vain*. For example, a man can be called "vain," or it can be said that he lived his life "in vain."

The Minister's Black Veil

A Parable

THE SEXTON stood in the porch of Milford meeting house, pulling busily at the bell rope. The old people of the village came stooping along the street. Children with bright faces tripped merrily beside their parents, or mimicked a graver gait, in the conscious dignity of their Sunday clothes. Spruce bachelors looked sidelong at the pretty maidens and fancied that the Sabbath sunshine made them prettier than on weekdays. When the throng had mostly streamed into the porch, the sexton began to toll the bell, keeping his eye on the Reverend Mr. Hooper's door. The first glimpse of the clergyman's figure was the signal for the bell to cease its summons.

"But what has good Parson Hooper got upon his face?" cried the sexton in astonishment.

All within hearing immediately turned about and beheld the semblance of Mr. Hooper, pacing slowly his meditative way toward the meeting house. With one accord they started, expressing more wonder than if some strange minister were coming to dust the cushions of Mr. Hooper's pulpit.

"Are you sure it is our parson?" inquired Goodman [1] Gray of the sexton.

"Of a certainty it is good Mr. Hooper," replied the sexton. "He was to have exchanged pulpits with Parson Shute, of Westbury; but Parson Shute sent to excuse himself yesterday, being to preach a funeral sermon."

The cause of so much amazement may appear sufficiently slight. Mr. Hooper, a gentlemanly person of about thirty, though

[1] **Goodman:** a title of address similar to "Mr."

still a bachelor was dressed with due clerical neatness, as if a careful wife had starched his band and brushed the weekly dust from his Sunday's garb. There was but one thing remarkable in his appearance. Swathed about his forehead, and hanging down over his face, so low as to be shaken by his breath, Mr. Hooper had on a black veil. On a nearer view it seemed to consist of two folds of crepe, which entirely concealed his features, except the mouth and chin, but probably did not intercept his sight, further than to give a darkened aspect to all living and inanimate things. With this gloomy shade before him, good Mr. Hooper walked onward at a slow and quiet pace, stooping somewhat and looking on the ground, as is customary with abstracted men, yet nodding kindly to those of his parishioners who still waited on the meeting house steps. But so wonder-struck were they that his greeting hardly met with a return.

"I can't really feel as if good Mr. Hooper's face was behind that piece of crepe," said the sexton.

"I don't like it," muttered an old woman, as she hobbled into the meeting house. "He has changed himself into something awful, only by hiding his face."

"Our parson has gone mad!" cried Goodman Gray, following him across the threshold.

A rumor of some unaccountable phenomenon had preceded Mr. Hooper into the meeting house and set all the congregation astir. Few could refrain from twisting their heads toward the door; many stood upright and turned directly about; while several little boys clambered upon the seats and came down again with a terrible racket. There was a general bustle, a rustling of the women's gowns and shuffling of the men's feet, greatly at variance with that hushed repose which should attend the entrance of the minister. But Mr. Hooper appeared not to notice the perturbation of his people. He entered with an almost noiseless step, bent his head mildly to the pews on each side, and bowed as he passed his oldest parishioner, a white-haired great-grandsire, who occupied an armchair in the center of the aisle. It was strange to observe how slowly this venerable man became conscious of something singular in the appearance of his pastor. He seemed not fully to partake of the prevailing wonder, till Mr. Hooper had ascended the stairs and showed himself in the pulpit, face to face with his congregation, except for the black veil. That mysterious emblem was never once withdrawn. It shook with his measured breath, as he gave out the psalm; it threw its obscurity between him and the holy page, as he read the Scriptures; and while he prayed, the veil lay heavily on his uplifted countenance. Did he seek to hide it from the dread Being whom he was addressing?

Such was the effect of this simple piece of crepe, that more than one woman of delicate nerves was forced to leave the meeting house. Yet perhaps the pale-faced congregation was almost as fearful a sight to the minister as his black veil to them.

Mr. Hooper had the reputation of a good preacher, but not an energetic one: he strove to win his people heavenward by mild, persuasive influences, rather than to drive them thither by the thunders of the Word. The sermon which he now delivered was marked by the same characteristics of style and manner as the general series of his pulpit oratory. But there was something, either in the sentiment of the discourse itself, or in the imagination of the auditors, which made it greatly the most powerful effort that they had ever heard from their pastor's lips. It was tinged, rather more darkly than usual, with the gentle gloom of Mr. Hooper's temperament. The subject had reference to secret sin, and those sad mysteries which we hide from our nearest and dearest, and would fain conceal from our own consciousness, even forgetting that the Omniscient [1] can detect them. A subtle power was breathed into his words. Each

member of the congregation, the most innocent girl, and the man of hardened breast, felt as if the preacher had crept upon them, behind his awful veil, and discovered their hoarded iniquity of deed or thought. Many spread their clasped hands on their bosoms. There was nothing terrible in what Mr. Hooper said, at least, no violence; and yet, with every tremor of his melancholy voice, the hearers quaked. An unsought pathos came hand in hand with awe. So sensible were the audience of some unwonted attribute in their minister that they longed for a breath of wind to blow aside the veil, almost believing that a stranger's visage would be discovered, though the form, gesture, and voice were those of Mr. Hooper.

At the close of the services, the people hurried out with indecorous confusion, eager to communicate their pent-up amazement and conscious of lighter spirits the moment they lost sight of the black veil. Some gathered in little circles, huddled closely together, with their mouths all whispering in the center; some went homeward alone, wrapt in silent meditation; some talked loudly and profaned the Sabbath day with ostentatious laughter. A few shook their sagacious heads, intimating that they could penetrate the mystery; while one or two affirmed that there was no mystery at all, but only that Mr. Hooper's eyes were so weakened by the midnight lamp as to require a shade. After a brief interval, forth came good Mr. Hooper also, in the rear of his flock. Turning his veiled face from one group to another, he paid due reverence to the hoary heads, saluted the middle-aged with kind dignity as their friend and spiritual guide, greeted the young with mingled authority and love, and laid his hands on the little children's heads to bless them. Such was always his custom on the Sabbath day. Strange and bewildered looks repaid him for his courtesy. None, as on former occasions, aspired to the honor of walking by their pastor's side. Old Squire Saunders, doubtless by an accidental lapse of memory, neglected to invite Mr. Hooper

---

[1] **the Omniscient:** God, in his all-knowing aspect.

to his table, where the good clergyman had been wont to bless the food almost every Sunday since his settlement. He returned, therefore, to the parsonage, and, at the moment of closing the door, was observed to look back upon the people, all of whom had their eyes fixed upon the minister. A sad smile gleamed faintly from beneath the black veil and flickered about his mouth, glimmering as he disappeared.

"How strange," said a lady, "that a simple black veil such as any woman might wear on her bonnet should become such a terrible thing on Mr. Hooper's face!"

"Something must surely be amiss with Mr. Hooper's intellects," observed her husband, the physician of the village. "But the strangest part of the affair is the effect of this vagary, even on a sober-minded man like myself. The black veil, though it covers only our pastor's face, throws its influence over his whole person and makes him ghostlike from head to foot. Do you not feel it so?"

"Truly do I," replied the lady; "and I would not be alone with him for the world. I wonder he is not afraid to be alone with himself!"

"Men sometimes are so," said her husband.

The afternoon service was attended with similar circumstances. At its conclusion, the bell tolled for the funeral of a young lady. The relatives and friends were assembled in the house, and the more distant acquaintances stood about the door, speaking of the good qualities of the deceased, when their talk was interrupted by the appearance of Mr. Hooper, still covered with his black veil. It was now an appropriate emblem. The clergyman stepped into the room where the corpse was laid and bent over the coffin, to take a last farewell of his deceased parishioner. As he stooped, the veil hung straight down from his forehead, so that, if her eyelids had not been closed forever, the dead maiden might have seen his face. Could Mr. Hooper be fearful of her glance, that he so hastily caught back the black veil? A person who watched the interview between the dead and living scrupled not to affirm that, at the instant when the clergyman's features were disclosed, the corpse had slightly shuddered, rustling the shroud and muslin cap, though the countenance retained the composure of death. A superstitious old woman was the only witness of this prodigy. From the coffin Mr. Hooper passed into the chamber of the mourners, and thence to the head of the staircase, to make the funeral prayer. It was a tender and heart-dissolving prayer, full of sorrow, yet so imbued with celestial hopes that the music of a heavenly harp, swept by the fingers of the dead, seemed faintly to be heard among the saddest accents of the minister. The people trembled, though they but darkly understood him when he prayed that they, and himself, and all of mortal race, might be ready, as he trusted this young maiden had been, for the dreadful hour that should snatch the veil from their faces. The bearers went heavily forth, and the mourners followed, saddening all the street, with the dead before them, and Mr. Hooper in his black veil behind.

"Why do you look back?" said one in the procession to his partner.

"I had a fancy," replied she, "that the minister and the maiden's spirit were walking hand in hand."

"And so had I, at the same moment," said the other.

That night, the handsomest couple in Milford village were to be joined in wedlock. Though reckoned a melancholy man, Mr. Hooper had a placid cheerfulness for such occasions, which often excited a sympathetic smile where livelier merriment would have been thrown away. There was no quality of his disposition which made him more beloved than this. The company at the wedding awaited his arrival with impatience, trusting that the strange awe, which had gathered over him throughout the day, would now be dispelled. But such was not the result. When Mr. Hooper came, the first thing that their eyes rested on was the same horrible black veil, which had added deeper gloom to the funeral and could portend nothing but evil to the wedding. Such was its immediate effect on the guests that a cloud seemed to have rolled duskily from beneath the black crepe and dimmed the light of the candles. The bridal pair stood up before the minister. But the bride's cold fingers quivered in the tremulous hand of the bridegroom, and her deathlike paleness caused a whisper that the maiden who had been buried a few hours before was come from her grave to be married. If ever another wedding were so dismal, it was that famous one where they tolled the wedding knell.[1] After performing the ceremony, Mr. Hooper raised a glass of wine to his lips, wishing happiness to the new-married couple in a strain of mild pleasantry that ought to have brightened the features of the guests, like a cheerful gleam from the hearth. At that instant, catching a glimpse of his figure in the looking glass, the black veil involved his own spirit in the horror with which it overwhelmed all others. His frame shuddered, his lips grew white, he spilt the untasted wine upon the carpet, and rushed forth into the darkness. For the Earth, too, had on her Black Veil.

The next day, the whole village of Milford talked of little else than Parson Hooper's black veil. That, and the mystery concealed behind it, supplied a topic for discussion between acquaintances meeting in the street and good women gossiping at their open windows. It was the first item of news that the tavernkeeper told to his guests. The children babbled of it on their way to school. One imitative little imp covered his face with an old black handkerchief, thereby so affrighting his playmates that the panic seized himself, and he well-nigh lost his wits by his own waggery.[2]

It was remarkable that of all the busybodies and impertinent people in the parish, not one ventured to put the plain question to Mr. Hooper, wherefore he did this thing. Hitherto, whenever there appeared the slightest call for such interference, he had never lacked advisers, nor shown himself averse to be guided by their judgment. If he erred at all, it was by so painful a degree of self-distrust that even the mildest censure would lead him to consider an indifferent action as a crime. Yet, though so well acquainted with this amiable weakness, no individual among his parishioners chose to make the black veil a subject of friendly remonstrance. There was a feeling of dread, neither plainly confessed nor carefully concealed, which caused each to shift the responsibility upon another, till at length it was found expedient to send a deputation of the church, in order to deal with Mr. Hooper about the mystery before it should grow into a scandal. Never did an embassy so ill discharge its duties. The minister received them with friendly courtesy but became silent after they were seated, leaving to his visitors the whole burden of introducing their important business. The topic, it might be supposed, was obvious enough. There was the black veil swathed round Mr. Hooper's forehead, and concealing every feature above his placid mouth, on which, at times, they could perceive the glimmering of a melancholy smile. But that piece of crepe, to their imagination, seemed to hang down before his heart, the symbol of a fearful secret between him and them. Were the veil but cast aside, they might speak freely of it, but not till then. Thus they sat a considerable time, speechless, confused, and shrinking uneasily from Mr. Hooper's eye, which they felt to be fixed upon them with an invisible glance. Finally, the deputies returned abashed to their constituents, pronouncing the matter too weighty to be handled, except by a council of the churches, if, indeed, it might not require a general synod.[3]

But there was one person in the village unappalled by the awe with which the

<hr>

[1] **"If . . . knell":** a reference to Hawthorne's story, "The Wedding Knell."

[2] **waggery:** mischievousness.

[3] **synod:** an ecclesiastical council.

black veil had impressed all beside herself. When the deputies returned without an explanation, or even venturing to demand one, she, with the calm energy of her character, determined to chase away the strange cloud that appeared to be settling round Mr. Hooper, every moment more darkly than before. As his plighted wife, it should be her privilege to know what the black veil concealed. At the minister's first visit, therefore, she entered upon the subject with a direct simplicity, which made the task easier both for him and her. After he had seated himself, she fixed her eyes steadfastly upon the veil, but could discern nothing of the dreadful gloom that had so overawed the multitude: it was but a double fold of crepe, hanging down from his forehead to his mouth, and slightly stirring with his breath.

"No," said she aloud, and smiling, "there is nothing terrible in this piece of crepe, except that it hides a face which I am always glad to look upon. Come, good sir, let the sun shine from behind the cloud. First lay aside your black veil: then tell me why you put it on."

Mr. Hooper's smile glimmered faintly.

"There is an hour to come," said he, "when all of us shall cast aside our veils. Take it not amiss, beloved friend, if I wear this piece of crepe till then."

"Your words are a mystery, too," returned the young lady. "Take away the veil from them, at least."

"Elizabeth, I will," said he, "so far as my vow may suffer me. Know, then, this veil is a type and a symbol, and I am bound to wear it ever, both in light and darkness, in solitude and before the gaze of multitudes, and as with strangers, so with my familiar friends. No mortal eye will see it withdrawn. This dismal shade must separate me from the world: even you, Elizabeth, can never come behind it!"

"What grievous affliction hath befallen you," she earnestly inquired, "that you should thus darken your eyes forever?"

"If it be a sign of mourning," replied Mr. Hooper, "I, perhaps, like most other mortals, have sorrows dark enough to be typified by a black veil."

"But what if the world will not believe that it is the type of an innocent sorrow?" urged Elizabeth. "Beloved and respected as you are, there may be whispers that you hide your face under the consciousness of secret sin. For the sake of your holy office, do away this scandal!"

The color rose into her cheeks as she intimated the nature of the rumors that were already abroad in the village. But Mr. Hooper's mildness did not forsake him. He even smiled again—that same sad smile, which always appeared like a faint glimmering of light, proceeding from the obscurity beneath the veil.

"If I hide my face for sorrow, there is cause enough," he merely replied; "and if I cover it for secret sin, what mortal might not do the same?"

And with this gentle but unconquerable obstinacy did he resist all her entreaties. At length Elizabeth sat silent. For a few moments she appeared lost in thought, considering, probably, what new methods might be tried to withdraw her lover from so dark a fantasy, which, if it had no other meaning, was perhaps a symptom of mental disease. Though of a firmer character than his own, the tears rolled down her cheeks. But in an instant, as it were, a new feeling took the place of sorrow: her eyes were fixed insensibly on the black veil when, like a sudden twilight in the air, its terrors fell around her. She arose and stood trembling before him.

"And do you feel it then, at last?" said he mournfully.

She made no reply, but covered her eyes with her hand and turned to leave the room. He rushed forward and caught her arm.

"Have patience with me, Elizabeth!" cried he, passionately. "Do not desert me, though this veil must be between us here on earth. Be mine, and hereafter there shall be no veil over my face, no darkness between our souls! It is but a mortal veil— it is not for eternity! O! you know not how lonely I am, and how frightened, to be alone behind my black veil. Do not leave me in this miserable obscurity forever!"

"Lift the veil but once, and look me in the face," said she.

"Never! It cannot be!" replied Mr. Hooper.

"Then farewell!" said Elizabeth.

She withdrew her arm from his grasp and slowly departed, pausing at the door to give one long, shuddering gaze that seemed almost to penetrate the mystery of the black veil. But, even amid his grief, Mr. Hooper smiled to think that only a material emblem had separated him from happiness, though the horrors which it shadowed forth must be drawn darkly between the fondest of lovers.

From that time no attempts were made to remove Mr. Hooper's black veil or, by a direct appeal, to discover the secret which it was supposed to hide. By persons who claimed a superiority to popular prejudice, it was reckoned merely an eccentric whim, such as often mingles with the sober actions of men otherwise rational and tinges them all with its own semblance of insanity. But with the multitude, good Mr. Hooper was irreparably a bugbear. [1] He could not walk the street with any peace of mind, so conscious was he that the gentle and timid would turn aside to avoid him, and that others would make it a point of hardihood to throw themselves in his way. The impertinence of the latter class compelled him to give up his customary walk at sunset to the burial ground; for when he leaned pensively over the gate, there would always be faces behind the gravestones, peeping at his black veil. A fable went the rounds that the stare of the dead people drove him thence. It grieved him, to the very depth of his kind heart, to observe how the children fled from his approach, breaking up their merriest sports, while his melancholy figure was yet afar off. Their instinctive dread caused him to feel more strongly than aught else that a preternatural horror was interwoven with the threads of the

black crepe. In truth, his own antipathy to the veil was known to be so great that he never willingly passed before a mirror, nor stooped to drink at a still fountain, lest, in its peaceful bosom, he should be affrighted by himself. This was what gave plausibility to the whispers that Mr. Hooper's conscience tortured him for some great crime too horrible to be entirely concealed, or otherwise than so obscurely intimated. Thus, from beneath the black veil, there rolled a cloud into the sunshine, and ambiguity of sin or sorrow, which enveloped the poor minister, so that love or sympathy could never reach him. It was said that ghost and fiend consorted with him there. With self-shudderings and outward terrors, he walked continually in its shadow, groping darkly within his own soul or gazing through a medium that saddened the whole world. Even the lawless wind, it was believed, respected his dreadful secret and never blew aside the veil.

[1] **bugbear:** object of dread.

But still good Mr. Hooper sadly smiled at the pale visages of the worldly throng as he passed by.

Among all its bad influences, the black veil had the one desirable effect of making its wearer a very efficient clergyman. By the aid of his mysterious emblem—for there was no other apparent cause—he became a man of awful power over souls that were in agony for sin. His converts always regarded him with a dread peculiar to themselves, affirming, though but figuratively, that before he brought them to celestial light they had been with him behind the black veil. Its gloom, indeed, enabled him to sympathize with all dark affections. Dying sinners cried aloud for Mr. Hooper, and would not yield their breath till he appeared; though ever, as he stooped to whisper consolation, they shuddered at the veiled face so near their own. Such were the terrors of the black veil, even when Death had bared his visage! Strangers came long distances to attend service at his church, with the mere idle purpose of gazing at his figure, because it was forbidden them to behold his face. But many were made to quake ere they departed! Once, during Governor Belcher's [1] administration, Mr. Hooper was appointed to preach the election sermon.[2] Covered with his black veil, he stood before the chief magistrate, the council, and the representatives, and wrought so deep an impression that the legislative measures of that year were characterized by all the gloom and piety of our earliest ancestral sway.

In this manner Mr. Hooper spent a long life, irreproachable in outward act, yet shrouded in dismal suspicions; kind and loving, though unloved and dimly feared; a man apart from men, shunned in their health and joy, but ever summoned to their aid in mortal anguish. As years wore on, shedding their snows above his sable

[1] **Governor Belcher:** Jonathan Belcher (1682–1757), royal governor of the Massachusetts Bay Colony, 1730–41.
[2] **election sermon:** It was a great honor for a minister to be chosen to make this formal address.

veil, he acquired a name throughout the New England churches, and they called him Father Hooper. Nearly all his parishioners, who were of mature age when he was settled, had been borne away by many a funeral: he had one congregation in the church, and a more crowded one in the churchyard; and having wrought so late into the evening, and done his work so well, it was now good Father Hooper's turn to rest.

Several persons were visible by the shaded candlelight, in the death chamber of the old clergyman. Natural connections he had none. But there was the decorously grave, though unmoved physician, seeking only to mitigate the last pangs of the patient whom he could not save. There were the deacons, and other eminently pious members of his church. There, also, was the Reverend Mr. Clark, of Westbury, a young and zealous divine, who had ridden in haste to pray by the bedside of the expiring minister. There was the nurse, no hired handmaiden of death, but one whose calm affection had endured thus long in secrecy, in solitude, amid the chill of age, and would not perish, even at the dying hour. Who, but Elizabeth! And there lay the hoary head of good Father Hooper upon the death pillow, with the black veil still swathed about his brow, and reaching down over his face, so that each more difficult gasp of his faint breath caused it to stir. All through life that piece of crepe had hung between him and the world: it had separated him from cheerful brotherhood and woman's love and kept him in that saddest of all prisons, his own heart; and still it lay upon his face, as if to deepen the gloom of his darksome chamber and shade him from the sunshine of eternity.

For some time previous, his mind had been confused, wavering doubtfully between the past and the present and hovering forward, as it were, at intervals, into the indistinctness of the world to come. There had been feverish turns, which tossed him from side to side and wore away what little strength he had. But in his most convulsive struggles, and in the wildest vagaries of his intellect, when no other thought retained its sober influence, he still showed an awful solicitude lest the black veil should slip aside. Even if his bewildered soul could have forgotten, there was a faithful woman at his pillow, who, with averted eyes, would have covered that aged face, which she had last beheld in the comeliness of manhood. At length the death-stricken old man lay quietly in the torpor of mental and bodily exhaustion, with an imperceptible pulse and breath that grew fainter and fainter, except when a long, deep, and irregular inspiration seemed to prelude the flight of his spirit.

The minister of Westbury approached the bedside.

"Venerable Father Hooper," said he, "the moment of your release is at hand. Are you ready for the lifting of the veil that shuts in time from eternity?"

Father Hooper at first replied merely by a feeble motion of his head; then, apprehensive, perhaps, that his meaning might be doubtful, he exerted himself to speak.

"Yea," said he, in faint accents, "my soul hath a patient weariness until that veil be lifted."

"And is it fitting," resumed the Reverend Mr. Clark, "that a man so given to prayer, of such a blameless example, holy in deed and thought, so far as mortal judgment may pronounce; is it fitting that a father in the church should leave a shadow on his memory that may seem to blacken a life so pure? I pray you, my venerable brother, let not this thing be! Suffer us to be gladdened by your triumphant aspect as you go to your reward. Before the veil of eternity be lifted, let me cast aside this black veil from your face!"

And thus speaking, the Reverend Mr. Clark bent forward to reveal the mystery of so many years. But, exerting a sudden energy that made all the beholders stand aghast, Father Hooper snatched both his hands from beneath the bedclothes and pressed them strongly on the black veil, resolute to struggle if the minister of Westbury would contend with a dying man.

"Never!" cried the veiled clergyman. "On earth, never!"

"Dark old man!" exclaimed the affrighted minister, "with what horrible crime upon your soul are you now passing to the judgment?"

Father Hooper's breath heaved; it rattled in his throat; but, with a mighty effort, grasping forward with his hands, he caught hold of life and held it back till he should speak. He even raised himself in bed; and there he sat, shivering with the arms of death around him, while the black veil hung down, awful, at that last moment, in the gathered terrors of a lifetime. And yet the faint, sad smile, so often there, now seemed to glimmer from its obscurity and linger on Father Hooper's lips.

"Why do you tremble at me alone?" cried he, turning his veiled face round the circle of pale spectators. "Tremble also at each other! Have men avoided me, and women shown no pity, and children screamed and fled, only for my black veil? What but the mystery which it obscurely typifies has made this piece of crepe so awful? When the friend shows his inmost heart to his friend; the lover to his best beloved; when man does not vainly shrink from the eye of his Creator, loathsomely treasuring up the secret of his sin; then deem me a monster for the symbol beneath which I have lived, and die! I look around me, and, lo! on every visage a Black Veil!"

While his auditors shrank from one another, in mutual affright, Father Hooper fell back upon his pillow, a veiled corpse, with a faint smile lingering on the lips. Still veiled, they laid him in his coffin, and a veiled corpse they bore him to the grave. The grass of many years has sprung up and withered on that grave, the burial stone is moss-grown, and good Mr. Hooper's face is dust; but awful is still the thought that it moldered beneath the Black Veil!

COMMENTARY

The plot of "The Minister's Black Veil" is rather simple and seemingly straightforward, but the underlying pattern of the story is more intricate than it may seem. One good way of approaching this pattern is to consider the consequences of the veil and the way in which these consequences are set forth.

One of the most obvious consequences of the veil is the change in Reverend Hooper's position in the community. When he first wears the veil at a Sunday service, it creates consternation and dismay among his congregation. At the very beginning of the story, a contrast is set up between the gloom of the veil and the cheerfulness of the Sunday morning. ("Children with bright faces tripped merrily beside their parents. . . . Spruce bachelors looked sidelong at the pretty maidens and fancied that the Sabbath sunshine made them prettier than on weekdays.") The sunny morning is a part of one aspect of human experience, but the veil represents a much more dreadful aspect. As a result of wearing the veil, Hooper becomes a man apart, isolated from love and sympathy, suspected and even feared by his fellows. Yet, strangely enough, the veil makes him a more effective minister. It gives him indefinable authority. His preaching takes on new power, and he displays a remarkable understanding of people who are troubled by sin. The veil makes Hooper a significant figure by *separating* him from the congregation. But, as the author remarks, "Perhaps the pale-faced congregation was almost as fearful a sight to the minister as his black veil to them." Whatever the veil signifies, its meaning seems to involve the congregation as much as it does Hooper. As he delivers his sermon on "secret sin," its effect on the congregation is remarkable. "Each member of the congregation, the most innocent girl, and the man of hardened breast, felt as if the preacher had crept upon them, behind his awful veil, and discovered their hoarded iniquity of deed or thought." The veil is in some way connected with "secret sin." It not only makes the Reverend Hooper different, but it also brings out the way in which he and his congregation are similar.

In speaking to Elizabeth, Hooper refers to the veil as "a type and a symbol." The veil both typifies and symbolizes the sorrow that comes from secret sin. (Whether the sin is specifically Hooper's is not clear.) Elsewhere in the story, the veil is called an "emblem," a symbol that is used to represent an abstract idea. Like many other symbols, the veil is an emotionally powerful way of presenting the idea.

On his deathbed at the conclusion of the story, the Reverend Hooper once again uses the verb "typifies" to explain the function of the veil, and again he makes reference to secret sin: "What but the mystery which it obscurely typifies has made this piece of crepe so awful? When the friend shows his inmost heart to his friend; the lover to his best beloved; when man does not vainly shrink from the eye of his Creator, loathsomely treasuring up the secret of his sin; then deem me a monster for the symbol beneath which I have lived, and die! I look around me, and lo! on every visage a Black Veil!"

Thus the veil has a double meaning and purpose. While it *conceals* Hooper's face, it *reveals* what the author regards as a truth that goes beneath the mere appearance of people and all the other surface truths that our senses convey. Hooper wears the veil to dramatize the isolation of man from man and of man from God, an isolation that is the result of sin. Perhaps the veil is a token of some particular sin that Hooper has committed. More important, the veil is a sign of man's state of sinful isolation and of the Reverend Hooper's penetration of this great truth and his sorrow over it.

1. What clues about the meaning of the black veil, other than those given in the Commentary, can you find? Explain the meaning of these clues.

2. Why do you think the author has Hooper officiate at both a funeral and a wedding on the day he first appears with the veil? How do the paragraphs describing Hooper's behavior at these two ceremonies add to your understanding of the veil's meaning?

3. Do you think that Hooper has actually committed a crime? In answering this question, you will have to define the word *crime*. How does your definition influence your answer?

4. At first Elizabeth refuses to see anything terrible about the veil. "But in an instant, as it were, a new feeling took the place of sorrow; her eyes were fixed insensibly on the black veil when, like a sudden twilight in the air, its terrors fell around her. She arose and stood trembling before him [Hooper]" (page 248). Explain this passage and Elizabeth's experience.

5. In old age, the minister becomes known as "Father Hooper." Does the community's attitude toward him change? If so, how? Do you think that familiarity with a particular sin or evil makes people indifferent to it? Give reasons for your answer. If possible, support your answer with examples from your reading or experience.

6. Do you agree or disagree with the interpretation of the story presented in the Commentary? Why?

ALLEGORY AND PARABLE

Basically, *allegory* refers to the representation of one thing by another. In the allegories illustrated in medieval tapestries, a unicorn frequently stands for purity and innocence. In a literary sense, an allegory is frequently a narrative in which characters or objects stand for abstract qualities or points of view. The most widely read allegory in English, John Bunyan's *The Pilgrim's Progress,* tells of a Christian's journey to the Celestial City, during which he meets such characters as Hope, Shame, and Despair. In this case, the allegorical intention is obvious, but in other works the allegory is presented more subtly and indirectly. In Hawthorne's story "Young Goodman Brown," for example, the wife of the leading character is called Faith. This name suggests a moral quality which she possesses and which her husband unhappily loses in the course of the story. (*Allegory* is closely related to *symbol*. For a discussion of symbols, see page 520.)

A *parable* is a tale from which a moral can be drawn and which may or may not be allegorical. The most widely known parables are those found in the Bible.

"The Minister's Black Veil" is subtitled "A Parable." Is it also an allegory? Why or why not? Is the minister an allegorical character? Is his veil allegorical?

FOR COMPOSITION

1. Write a composition in which you agree or disagree with Hawthorne's view of the world as this view is revealed in "The Minister's Black Veil." Consider the following points: Do you place as high an importance on secret sin as Hawthorne? Do you agree with the phrase, "and lo! on every visage, a Black Veil"?

2. In commenting on "The Minister's Black Veil," Edgar Allan Poe calls it "a masterly composition" in which the obvious meaning conceals a deeper one that is delicately hinted at. "The moral put into the mouth of the dying minister will be supposed to convey the true import of the narrative; and that a crime of dark dye (having reference to the "young lady" [over whose funeral Hooper presides]) has been committed, is a point which only minds congenial with that of the author will perceive."

Write a composition in which you agree or disagree with Poe's interpretation that the story is really about "a crime of dark dye." Before you write, you may find it helpful to study all the details of the story and particularly those paragraphs describing the young lady's funeral. In your paper, consider the following points: Can both Poe's interpretation and the interpretation given in the Commentary be true? Does Poe's interpretation tell us more about Hawthorne or about Poe?

3. Professor Stanley T. Williams has written, "We can understand New England without Hawthorne; yet Hawthorne without New England we cannot comprehend. She was literally of his blood and brain; her scenes and her people form the stuff of his romances. . . ." Write a composition discussing Hawthorne as a representative New Englander.

HERMAN MELVILLE
(1819–1891)

In November 1856 Herman Melville visited Nathaniel Hawthorne, then American consul at Liverpool, England. On the second day of the visit, the two friends took a long walk and rested on the sand hills near Liverpool. As Hawthorne described the incident, "Melville . . . began to reason of Providence and futurity, and of everything that lies beyond human ken. . . . It is strange how he persists—and has persisted ever since I knew him, and probably long before—in wandering to and fro over these deserts [of the mind], as dismal and monotonous as the sand hills amid which we were sitting. He can neither believe nor be comfortable in his unbelief; and he is too honest and courageous not to try to do one or the other. If he were a religious man, he would be one of the most truly religious and reverential; he has a very high and noble nature, and better worth immortality than most of us."

Much of Melville's life was taken up with a search for belief, a quest for the meaning behind all experience. The possibility that there might be no final meaning, that beyond the stars and the limits of man's intelligence there is nothing to reconcile pleasure and suffering, reason and madness, man's aspirations and failures—this possibility troubled him deeply. With the French philosopher Pascal, he could say, "The eternal silence of these empty spaces terrifies me." Like Hawthorne, he was artistically involved with the presence of evil, but unlike his friend he lacked a sustaining faith that could serve as a framework for his art. In his fiction, he was reaching out, molding his ideas and experiences, but almost always leaving something unresolved. A final interpretation of Melville's major work eludes the reader as much as a final interpretation of life itself.

Melville was born in New York City and grew up in Albany, New York. When the death of his father left the family in difficult circumstances, Herman, at thirteen, was obliged to quit Albany Academy and become a bank clerk. Two months before his twentieth birthday, he became a sailor; his first berth was on the *St. Lawrence,* bound for Liverpool. During his second voyage, on the whaler *Acushnet,* Melville and a friend, perhaps tired of the hard life at sea, jumped ship in the Marquesa Islands where the ship had stopped for fresh food and water. On the island of Nukahiva, the two sailors came upon a valley inhabited by the Typees, a Polynesian tribe reputed to be cannibals. Although Melville experienced a few chills in their company, especially when presented with a mysterious dish of meat, he managed to survive half-guest, half-prisoner until he was able to leave on an old Australian whaler. Eventually he made his way to Hawaii, where he enlisted in the U.S. Navy. Melville detested naval service. The life was harsh and cruel, and the rigid discipline was a blow to his pride. In *White-Jacket* he vividly depicted the injustices suffered by the common sailor aboard a naval vessel and drew a comparison between the sailor's lot and the lot of man in general. "Oh shipmates and world-mates, all round! We the people suffer many abuses. Our gun-deck is full of complaints. In vain from Lieutenants do we appeal to the Captain; in vain—while on board our world-frigate —to the indefinite Navy Commissioners; so far out of sight aloft. Yet the worst of our evils we blindly inflict upon ourselves. . . . From the last ills no being can save another; therein each man must be his own savior."

When Melville was twenty-five, he went to live with his mother near Albany. During the next eight years, he produced seven books, most of them drawing on his own experiences. *Typee,* published in 1846, is an account of his stay with the islanders of Nukahiva. Because of its considerable success, Melville became known as "the man who lived among cannibals." Its sequel, *Omoo,* dealing with Melville's subsequent adventures in the South Seas, was equally popular. In 1846 he married and, settling in New York, became one of a group of writers calling themselves the "Knights of the Round Table." While in New York he wrote *Redburn,* an autobiographical novel, and *Mardi,* an allegory centering about a series of voyages to mythical islands. Neither book was very popular. But, as Melville's popularity was waning, he was reaching the height of his creative powers. He himself was aware of this. As he wrote to Hawthorne, "Three weeks have scarcely passed . . . that I have not unfolded within myself. But I feel that I am now come to the inmost leaf of the bulb, and that shortly the flower must fall to the mold." In 1851, his masterpiece *Moby Dick* was published, but it received little notice. Then his next novel, *Pierre,* was attacked by the critics. He was faced with the bitter knowledge that the more he gave of himself as an artist, the less he pleased his readers. Writing to Hawthorne while he was working on *Moby Dick,* he commented: "Try to get a living by the truth—and go to the Soup Societies [charitable soup kitchens]. . . . What I feel most moved to write, that is banned—it will not pay. Yet, altogether, write the *other* way I cannot." After the failure of *Pierre,* he wrote two more novels that drew little attention and *The Piazza Tales,* a collection containing two of his finest works, "Bartleby" and "Benito Cereno." In 1859, Mrs. Melville wrote her mother, "Herman has taken to writing poetry. You need not tell anyone, for you know how such things get around." Long seen as an incidental by-product of his genius, Melville's poems are now receiving increased respect and attention. His four volumes of verse were the only remaining works to be published during his lifetime. *Billy Budd,* his last piece of fiction and one of his greatest, was not published until thirty-three years after his death.

By 1866, Melville was earning so little as a writer that he was obliged to take a position as a customs inspector, a post he held for twenty years. At the time of his death, he was remembered chiefly as the author of two entertaining books about the South Seas. Only in the 1920's was *Moby Dick* discovered as an American classic and Melville hailed as one of the greatest of all American writers. Today *Moby Dick* is appreciated as (in the words of critic Alfred Kazin) "one of those books that try to bring in as much life as a writer can get both hands on. . . . It sweeps everything before it; it gives us the happiness that only great vigor inspires." In depicting the struggle of the proud, half-mad Captain Ahab and the gigantic white whale, the novel also develops a mighty theme, that of man's struggle against the conditions of his existence, the principles of order that govern the universe. Ahab meditates:

"If man will strike, strike through the mask! How can the prisoner reach outside except by thrusting through the wall? Sometimes I think there's naught beyond. But 'tis enough He [God] tasks me. . . . Who's over me? Truth hath no confines." *Moby Dick* is a masterpiece of protest and doubt, Melville's as well as Ahab's. There is reason to believe that Melville eventually attained a serene acceptance of man's lot, of the great blood tragedy he witnessed in the War Between the States, of his own years of drudgery in the customs house and the failure of his greatest work to win popular acclaim. But he is chiefly remembered for the great cry of protest he uttered in *Moby Dick*. "He says NO! in thunder: but the devil himself cannot make him say *yes*." Melville wrote these words about Hawthorne, but with even greater justice they describe his own incomparable achievement.

Malvern Hill

On July 1, 1862, in a battle fought on Malvern Hill, near Richmond, Virginia, Union forces under General George B. McClellan repulsed a Confederate Army led by General Robert E. Lee. Previously, in a battle known as the Seven Days, Lee, in defense of Richmond, defeated McClellan's army, which retreated to Malvern Hill.

Ye elms that wave on Malvern Hill
  In prime of morn and May,
Recall ye how McClellan's men
    Here stood at bay?
While deep within yon forest dim   5
  Our rigid comrades lay—
Some with the cartridge in their mouth,
Others with fixed arms lifted South—
    Invoking so
The cypress glades? Ah wilds of woe! 10

The spires of Richmond, late beheld
  Through rifts in musket-haze,
Were closed from view in clouds of dust
    On leaf-walled ways,   14
Where streamed our wagons in caravan;
  And the Seven Nights and Days

Of march and fast, retreat and fight,
  Pinched our grimed faces to ghastly
    plight—
    Does the elm wood
Recall the haggard beards of blood? 20

The battle-smoked flag, with stars
    eclipsed,
  We followed (it never fell!)—
In silence husbanded our strength—
    Received their yell;
Till on this slope we patient turned 25
  With cannon ordered well;
Reverse we proved was not defeat;
But ah, the sod what thousands meet!—
    Does Malvern Wood
Bethink itself, and muse and brood? 30

    We elms of Malvern Hill
      Remembered every thing;
    But sap the twig will fill:
    Wag the world how it will,
      Leaves must be green in Spring. 35

In the Prison Pen

Listless he eyes the palisades
    And sentries in the glare;
'Tis barren as a pelican-beach—
    But his world is ended there.

Nothing to do; and vacant hands   5
    Bring on the idiot-pain;
He tries to think—to recollect,
    But the blur is on his brain.

Around him swarm the plaining ghosts
    Like those on Virgil's shore—°   10
A wilderness of faces dim,
    And pale ones gashed and hoar.

A smiting sun. No shed, no tree;
    He totters to his lair—
A den that sick hands dug in earth   15
    Ere famine wasted there,

Or, dropping in his place, he swoons,
    Walled in by throngs that press,
Till forth from the throngs they bear him
        dead—
    Dead in his meagerness.   20

10. **Virgil's Shore:** In Book VI of Virgil's *Aeneid*, Aeneas encounters on the shore of Hades a crowd of tormented ghosts who were not buried with proper rites.

FOR STUDY AND DISCUSSION

1. There are two speakers or groups of speakers in "Malvern Hill." Who are they? To what questions in the first three stanzas is the final stanza an answer? The first three stanzas emphasize struggle and death. What does the last stanza emphasize? Describe your own response to the last line of the poem.

2. The first three stanzas of "Malvern Hill" contain two conflicting attitudes about war. The soldiers see both its glory and its ghastly bloodiness. Find lines conveying each of these attitudes. Does this conflict in attitude weaken or strengthen the poem? Explain.

3. Why do you think "In the Prison Pen" treats the situation of one prisoner rather than all the prisoners? Is the prisoner viewed primarily as part of a crowd or in isolation? What is the importance of this view to the poem as a whole?

4. Explain the last line of "In the Prison Pen." Why do you think it concludes with the word "meagerness"? How is this word related to the details given in the preceding lines of the poem?

Bartleby the Scrivener

A Story of Wall Street

I AM A RATHER elderly man. The nature of my avocations, for the last thirty years, has brought me into more than ordinary contact with what would seem an interesting and somewhat singular set of men, of whom as yet nothing, that I know of, has ever been written—I mean the law-copyists, or scriveners.[1] I have known very many of them, professionally and privately, and, if I pleased, could relate divers histories, at which good-natured gentlemen might smile, and sentimental souls might weep. But I waive the biographies of all other scriveners for a few passages in the life of Bartleby, who was a scrivener, the strangest I ever saw, or heard of. While, of other law-copyists, I might write the complete life, of Bartleby nothing of that sort can be done. I believe that no materials exist for a full and satisfactory biography of this man. It is an irreparable loss to literature. Bartleby was one of those beings of whom nothing is ascertainable, except from the original sources, and, in his case, those are very small. What my own astonished eyes saw of Bartleby, *that* is all I know of him, except, indeed, one vague report, which will appear in the sequel.

Ere introducing the scrivener, as he first appeared to me, it is fit I make some mention of myself, my *employés,* my business, my chambers, and general surroundings; because some such description is indispensable to an adequate understanding of the chief character about to be presented. Imprimis: I am a man who, from his youth upwards, has been filled with a profound conviction that the easiest way of life is the best. Hence, though I belong to a profession proverbially energetic and nervous, even to turbulence at times, yet nothing of that sort have I ever suffered to invade my peace. I am one of those unambitious lawyers who never addresses a jury, or in any way draws down public applause; but, in the cool tranquillity of a snug retreat, do a snug business among rich men's bonds, and mortgages, and title deeds. All who know me consider me an eminently *safe* man. The late John Jacob Astor,[2] a personage little given to poetic enthusiasm, had no hesitation in pronouncing my first grand point to be prudence; my next, method. I do not speak it in vanity, but simply record the fact that I was not unemployed in my profession by the late John Jacob Astor; a name which, I admit, I love to repeat; for it hath a rounded and orbicular sound to it, and rings like unto bullion. I will freely add that I was not insensible to the late John Jacob Astor's good opinion.

Some time prior to the period at which this little history begins, my avocations had been largely increased. The good old office, now extinct in the State of New York, of a Master in Chancery,[3] had been conferred upon me. It was not a very arduous office, but very pleasantly remunerative. I seldom lose my temper; much more seldom indulge in dangerous indignation at wrongs and outrages; but I must be permitted to be rash here and declare that I consider the sudden and violent abrogation of the office of Master in Chancery, by the new Constitution,[4] as a ——premature act; inasmuch as I had counted upon a life lease of the profits,

[1] **scriveners:** men who, before the invention of the typewriter, made copies of legal documents.

[2] **Astor:** John Jacob Astor (1763–1848), American millionaire, one of the most important businessmen of his time.

[3] **Master in Chancery:** A master in chancery serves as a judge or referee in an equity court, which renders judgment in cases not covered in courts of law. (Such matters as rewriting the terms of a contract or suing for failure to perform a service specifically mentioned in a contract are usually handled by an equity court.)

[4] **Constitution:** that is, the constitution of the State of New York.

whereas I only received those of a few short years. But this is by the way.

My chambers were upstairs, at No.— Wall Street. At one end, they looked upon the white wall of the interior of a spacious skylight shaft, penetrating the building from top to bottom.

This view might have been considered rather tame than otherwise, deficient in what landscape painters call "life." But, if so, the view from the other end of my chambers offered, at least, a contrast, if nothing more. In that direction, my windows commanded an unobstructed view of a lofty brick wall, black by age and everlasting shade; which wall required no spyglass to bring out its lurking beauties, but, for the benefit of all nearsighted spectators, was pushed up to within ten feet of my windowpanes. Owing to the great height of the surrounding buildings, and my chambers being on the second floor, the interval between this wall and mine not a little resembled a huge square cistern.

At the period just preceding the advent of Bartleby, I had two persons as copyists in my employment, and a promising lad as an office boy. First, Turkey; second, Nippers; third, Ginger Nut. These may seem names the like of which are not usually found in the Directory. In truth, they were nicknames, mutually conferred upon each other by my three clerks, and were deemed expressive of their respective persons or characters. Turkey was a short, pursy Englishman, of about my own age—that is, somewhere not far from sixty. In the morning, one might say, his face was of a fine florid hue, but after twelve o'clock, meridian—his dinner[1] hour—it blazed like a grate full of Christmas coals; and continued blazing—but, as it were, with a gradual wane—till six o'clock P.M., or thereabouts; after which, I saw no more of the proprietor of the face, which, gaining its meridian with the sun, seemed to set with it, to rise, culminate, and decline the following day,

with the like regularity and undiminished glory. There are many singular coincidences I have known in the course of my life, not the least among which was the fact that, exactly when Turkey displayed his fullest beams from his red and radiant countenance, just then, too, at that critical moment, began the daily period when I considered his business capacities as seriously disturbed for the remainder of the twenty-four hours. Not that he was absolutely idle, or averse to business, then; far from it. The difficulty was, he was apt to be altogether too energetic. There was a strange, inflamed, flurried, flighty recklessness of activity about him. He would be incautious in dipping his pen into his inkstand. All his blots upon my documents were dropped there after twelve o'clock meridian. Indeed, not only would he be reckless and sadly given to making blots in the afternoon, but, some days, he went further, and was rather noisy. At such times, too, his face flamed with augmented blazonry,[2] as if cannel coal had been heaped on anthracite. He made an unpleasant racket with his chair; spilled his sandbox; in mending his pens, impatiently split them all to pieces and threw them on the floor in a sudden passion; stood up and leaned over his table, boxing his papers about in a most indecorous manner, very sad to behold in an elderly man like him. Nevertheless, as he was in many ways a most valuable person to me, and all the time before twelve o'clock meridian was the quickest, steadiest creature, too, accomplishing a great deal of work in a style not easily to be matched—for these reasons, I was willing to overlook his eccentricities, though, indeed, occasionally I remonstrated with him. I did this very gently, however, because, though the civilest, nay, the blandest and most reverential of men in the morning, yet, in the afternoon, he was disposed upon provocation to be slightly rash with his tongue—in fact, insolent. Now, valuing his morning services as I

---

[1] **dinner:** here, the midday meal.

[2] **blazonry:** show, display.

did, and resolved not to lose them—yet, at the same time, made uncomfortable by his inflamed ways after twelve o'clock —and being a man of peace, unwilling by my admonitions to call forth unseemly retorts from him, I took upon me one Saturday noon (he was always worse on Saturdays) to hint to him, very kindly, that perhaps, now that he was growing old, it might be well to abridge his labors; in short, he need not come to my chambers after twelve o'clock, but, dinner over, had best go home to his lodgings and rest himself till teatime. But no; he insisted upon his afternoon devotions. His countenance became intolerably fervid as he oratorically assured me—gesticulating with a long ruler at the other end of the room— that if his services in the morning were useful, how indispensable, then, in the afternoon?

"With submission, sir," said Turkey, on this occasion, "I consider myself your right-hand man. In the morning I but marshal and deploy my columns;[1] but in the afternoon I put myself at their head and gallantly charge the foe, thus"—and he made a violent thrust with the ruler.

"But the blots, Turkey," intimated I.

"True; but, with submission, sir, behold these hairs! I am getting old. Surely, sir, a blot or two of a warm afternoon is not to be severely urged against gray hairs. Old age—even if it blot the page—is honorable. With submission, sir, we *both* are getting old."

This appeal to my fellow-feeling was hardly to be resisted. At all events, I saw that go he would not. So, I made up my mind to let him stay, resolving, nevertheless, to see to it that during the afternoon he had to do with my less important papers.

Nippers, the second on my list, was a whiskered, sallow, and, upon the whole, rather piratical-looking young man, of about five and twenty. I always deemed him the victim of two evil powers—ambition and indigestion. The ambition was

evinced by a certain impatience of the duties of a mere copyist, an unwarrantable usurpation of strictly professional affairs, such as the original drawing up of legal documents. The indigestion seemed betokened in an occasional nervous testiness and grinning irritability, causing the teeth to audibly grind together over mistakes committed in copying; unnecessary maledictions, hissed, rather than spoken, in the heat of business; and especially by a continual discontent with the height of the table where he worked. Though of a very ingenious, mechanical turn, Nippers could never get this table to suit him. He put chips under it, blocks of various sorts, bits of pasteboard, and at last went so far as to attempt an exquisite adjustment, by final pieces of folded blotting paper. But no invention would answer. If, for the sake of easing his back, he brought the table lid at a sharp angle well up toward his chin and wrote there like a man using the steep roof of a Dutch house for his desk, then he declared that it stopped the circulation in his arms. If now he lowered the table to his waistbands and stooped over it in writing, then there was a sore aching in his back. In short, the truth of the matter was, Nippers knew not what he wanted. Or, if he wanted anything, it was to be rid of a scrivener's table altogether. Among the manifestations of his diseased ambition was a fondness he had for receiving visits from certain ambiguous-looking fellows in seedy coats, whom he called his clients. Indeed, I was aware that not only was he, at times, considerable of a ward politician, but he occasionally did a little business at the Justices' courts and was not unknown on the steps of the Tombs.[2] I have good reason to believe, however, that one individual who called upon him at my chambers, and who, with a grand air, he insisted was his client, was no other than a dun,[3] and the alleged title deed, a bill. But, with all his failings, and the annoyances he caused me, Nippers,

[2] **the Tombs:** a jail in New York City.

[3] **dun:** one who presses for the payment of bad debts.

[1] **columns:** here, formations of troops.

like his compatriot Turkey, was a very useful man to me; wrote a neat, swift hand; and, when he chose, was not deficient in a gentlemanly sort of deportment. Added to this, he always dressed in a gentlemanly sort of way; and so, incidentally, reflected credit upon my chambers. Whereas, with respect to Turkey, I had much ado to keep him from being a reproach to me. His clothes were apt to look oily and smell of eating houses. He wore his pantaloons very loose and baggy in summer. His coats were execrable; his hat not to be handled. But while the hat was a thing of indifference to me, inasmuch as his natural civility and deference, as a dependent Englishman, always led him to doff it the moment he entered the room, yet his coat was another matter. Concerning his coats, I reasoned with him; but with no effect. The truth was, I suppose, that a man with so small an income could not afford to sport such a lustrous face and a lustrous coat at one and the same time. As Nippers once observed, Turkey's money went chiefly for red ink. One winter day, I presented Turkey with a highly respectable-looking coat of my own—a padded gray coat, of a most comfortable warmth, and which buttoned straight up from the knee to the neck. I thought Turkey would appreciate the favor and abate his rashness and obstreperousness of afternoons. But no; I verily believe that buttoning himself up in so downy and blanketlike a coat had a pernicious effect upon him—upon the same principle that too much oats are bad for horses. In fact, precisely as a rash, restive horse is said to feel his oats, so Turkey felt his coat. It made him insolent. He was a man whom prosperity harmed.

Though, concerning the self-indulgent habits of Turkey, I had my own private surmises, yet, touching Nippers, I was well persuaded that whatever might be his faults in other respects, he was, at least, a temperate young man. But, indeed, nature herself seemed to have been his vintner, and, at his birth, charged him so thoroughly with an irritable, brandy-like disposition, that all subsequent potations were needless. When I consider how, amid the stillness of my chambers, Nippers would sometimes impatiently rise from his seat, and stooping over his table, spread his arms wide apart, seize the whole desk, and move it, and jerk it, with a grim, grinding motion on the floor, as if the table were a perverse voluntary agent and vexing him, I plainly perceive that, for Nippers, brandy-and-water were altogether superfluous.

It was fortunate for me that owing to its peculiar cause—indigestion—the irritability and consequent nervousness of Nippers were mainly observable in the morning, while in the afternoon he was comparatively mild. So that, Turkey's paroxysms only coming on about twelve o'clock, I never had to do with their eccentricities at one time. Their fits relieved each other, like guards. When Nippers's was on, Turkey's was off; and vice versa. This was a good natural arrangement, under the circumstances.

Ginger Nut, the third on my list, was a lad some twelve years old. His father was a car-man, ambitious of seeing his son on the bench instead of a cart, before he died. So he sent him to my office, as student at law, errand boy, cleaner and sweeper, at the rate of one dollar a week. He had a little desk to himself; but he did not use it much. Upon inspection, the drawer exhibited a great array of the shells of various sorts of nuts. Indeed, to this quick-witted youth, the whole noble science of the law was contained in a nutshell. Not the least among the employments of Ginger Nut, as well as one which he discharged with the most alacrity, was his duty as cake and apple purveyor for Turkey and Nippers. Copying law papers being proverbially a dry, husky sort of business, my two scriveners were fain to moisten their mouths very often with Spitzenbergs,[1] to be had at the numerous stalls nigh the Custom House and post office.

[1] **Spitzenbergs:** a variety of apple, usually spelled "Spitzenburgs."

Also, they sent Ginger Nut very frequently for that peculiar cake—small, flat, round, and very spicy—after which he had been named by them. Of a cold morning, when business was but dull, Turkey would gobble up scores of these cakes, as if they were mere wafers—indeed, they sell them at the rate of six or eight for a penny—the scrape of his pen blending with the crunching of the crisp particles in his mouth. Rashest of all the fiery afternoon blunders and flurried rashnesses of Turkey, was his once moistening a ginger cake between his lips and clapping it on to a mortgage, for a seal. I came within an ace of dismissing him then. But he mollified me by making an oriental bow, and saying—

"With submission, sir, it was generous of me to find you in stationery on my own account."[1]

Now my original business—that of a conveyancer and title hunter, and drawer-up of recondite documents of all sorts—was considerably increased by receiving the master's office. There was now great work for scriveners. Not only must I push the clerks already with me, but I must have additional help.

In answer to my advertisement, a motionless young man one morning stood upon my office threshold, the door being open, for it was summer. I can see that figure now—pallidly neat, pitiably respectable, incurably forlorn! It was Bartleby.

After a few words touching his qualifications, I engaged him, glad to have among my corps of copyists a man of so singularly sedate an aspect, which I thought might operate beneficially upon the flighty temper of Turkey, and the fiery one of Nippers.

I should have stated before that ground-glass folding doors divided my premises into two parts, one of which was occupied by my scriveners, the other by myself. According to my humor, I threw open these doors, or closed them. I resolved to assign Bartleby a corner by the folding doors, but on my side of them, so as to have this quiet man within easy call, in case any trifling thing was to be done. I placed his desk close up to a small side window in that part of the room, a window which originally had afforded a lateral view of certain grimy backyards and bricks, but which, owing to subsequent erections, commanded at present no view at all, though it gave some light. Within three feet of the panes was a wall, and the light came down from far above, between two lofty buildings, as from a very small opening in a dome. Still further to a satisfactory arrangement, I procured a high green folding screen, which might entirely isolate Bartleby from my sight, though not remove him from my voice. And thus, in a manner, privacy and society were conjoined.

At first, Bartleby did an extraordinary quantity of writing. As if long famishing for something to copy, he seemed to gorge himself on my documents. There was no pause for digestion. He ran a day and night line, copying by sunlight and by candle-light. I should have been quite delighted with his application, had he been cheerfully industrious. But he wrote on silently, palely, mechanically.

It is, of course, an indispensable part of a scrivener's business to verify the accuracy of his copy, word by word. Where there are two or more scriveners in an office, they assist each other in this examination, one reading from the copy, the other holding the original. It is a very dull, wearisome, and lethargic affair. I can readily imagine that, to some sanguine temperaments, it would be altogether intolerable. For example, I cannot credit that the mettlesome poet, Byron,[2] would have contentedly sat down with Bartleby to examine a law document of, say, five

---

[1] **"it . . . account":** that is, "It was generous of me to supply you with stationery (the ginger cake used as a seal) at my own expense."

[2] **Byron:** George Gordon, Lord Byron (1788–1824), English poet famous for his adventurous life and tales.

hundred pages, closely written in a crimpy [1] hand.

Now and then, in the haste of business, it had been my habit to assist in comparing some brief document myself, calling Turkey or Nippers for this purpose. One object I had, in placing Bartleby so handy to me behind the screen, was to avail myself of his services on such trivial occasions. It was on the third day, I think, of his being with me, and before any necessity had arisen for having his own writing examined, that, being much hurried to complete a small affair I had in hand, I abruptly called to Bartleby. In my haste and natural expectancy of instant compliance, I sat with my head bent over the original on my desk, and my right hand sideways and somewhat nervously extended with the copy, so that, immediately upon emerging from his retreat, Bartleby might snatch it and proceed to business without the least delay.

In this very attitude did I sit when I called to him, rapidly stating what it was I wanted him to do—namely, to examine a small paper with me. Imagine my surprise, nay, my consternation, when, without moving from his privacy, Bartleby, in a singularly mild, firm voice, replied, "I would prefer not to."

I sat awhile in perfect silence, rallying my stunned faculties. Immediately it occurred to me that my ears had deceived me, or Bartleby had entirely misunderstood my meaning. I repeated my request in the clearest tone I could assume; but in quite as clear a one came the previous reply, "I would prefer not to."

"Prefer not to," echoed I, rising in high excitement and crossing the room with a stride. "What do you mean? Are you moonstruck? I want you to help me compare this sheet here—take it," and I thrust it toward him.

"I would prefer not to," said he.

I looked at him steadfastly. His face was leanly composed; his gray eye dimly calm. Not a wrinkle of agitation rippled

him. Had there been the least uneasiness, anger, impatience, or impertinence in his manner; in other words, had there been anything ordinarily human about him, doubtless I should have violently dismissed him from the premises. But as it was, I should have as soon thought of turning my pale plaster-of-Paris bust of Cicero out of doors. I stood gazing at him awhile as he went on with his own writing, and then reseated myself at my desk. This is very strange, thought I. What had one best do? But my business hurried me. I concluded to forget the matter for the present, reserving it for my future leisure. So calling Nippers from the other room, the paper was speedily examined.

A few days after this, Bartleby concluded four lengthy documents, being quadruplicates of a week's testimony taken before me in my High Court of Chancery. It became necessary to examine them. It was an important suit, and great accuracy was imperative. Having all things arranged, I called Turkey, Nippers, and Ginger Nut from the next room, meaning to place the four copies in the hands of my four clerks, while I should read from the original. Accordingly, Turkey, Nippers, and Ginger Nut had taken their seats in a row, each with his document in his hand, when I called to Bartleby to join this interesting group.

"Bartleby! quick, I am waiting."

I heard a slow scrape of his chair legs on the uncarpeted floor, and soon he appeared standing at the entrance of his hermitage.

"What is wanted?" said he, mildly.

"The copies, the copies," said I, hurriedly. "We are going to examine them. There——" and I held toward him the fourth quadruplicate.

"I would prefer not to," he said, and gently disappeared behind the screen.

For a few moments I was turned into a pillar of salt, standing at the head of my seated column of clerks. Recovering myself, I advanced toward the screen and demanded the reason for such extraordinary conduct.

[1] **crimpy:** wavy.

"*Why* do you refuse?"

"I would prefer not to."

With any other man I should have flown outright into a dreadful passion, scorned all further words, and thrust him ignominiously from my presence. But there was something about Bartleby that not only strangely disarmed me, but in a wonderful manner, touched and disconcerted me. I began to reason with him.

"These are your own copies we are about to examine. It is labor saving to you, because one examination will answer for your four papers. It is common usage. Every copyist is bound to help examine his copy. Is it not so? Will you not speak? Answer!"

"I prefer not to," he replied in a flutelike tone. It seemed to me that, while I had been addressing him, he carefully revolved every statement that I made; fully comprehended the meaning; could not gainsay the irresistible conclusion; but, at the same time, some paramount consideration prevailed with him to reply as he did.

"You are decided, then, not to comply with my request—a request made according to common usage and common sense?"

He briefly gave me to understand that on that point my judgment was sound. Yes: his decision was irreversible.

It is not seldom the case that when a man is browbeaten in some unprecedented and violently unreasonable way, he begins to stagger in his own plainest faith. He begins, as it were, vaguely to surmise that, wonderful as it may be, all the justice and all the reason is on the other side. Accordingly, if any disinterested persons are present, he turns to them for some reinforcement of his own faltering mind.

"Turkey," said I, "what do you think of this? Am I not right?"

"With submission, sir," said Turkey, in his blandest tone, "I think that you are."

"Nippers," said I, "what do *you* think of it?"

"I think I should kick him out of the office."

"Ginger Nut," said I, willing to enlist the smallest suffrage in my behalf, "what do *you* think of it?"

"I think, sir, he's a little *luny*," replied Ginger Nut, with a grin.

"You hear what they say," said I, turning toward the screen, "come forth and do your duty."

But he vouchsafed no reply. I pondered a moment in sore perplexity. But once more business hurried me. I determined again to postpone the consideration of this dilemma to my future leisure. With a little trouble we made out to examine the papers without Bartleby, though at every page or two Turkey deferentially dropped his opinion that this proceeding was quite out of the common; while Nippers, twitching in his chair with a dyspeptic nervousness, ground out, between his set teeth, occasional hissing maledictions against the stubborn oaf behind the screen. And for his (Nippers's) part, this was the first and the last time he would do another man's business without pay.

Meanwhile Bartleby sat in his hermitage, oblivious to everything but his own peculiar business there.

Some days passed, the scrivener being employed upon another lengthy work. His late remarkable conduct led me to regard his ways narrowly. I observed that he never went to dinner; indeed, that he never went anywhere. As yet I had never, of my personal knowledge, known him to be outside of my office. He was a perpetual sentry in the corner. At about eleven o'clock though, in the morning, I noticed that Ginger Nut would advance toward the opening in Bartleby's screen, as if silently beckoned thither by a gesture in-

---

[1] **nice:** precise.

visible to me where I sat. The boy would then leave the office, jingling a few pence, and reappear with a handful of ginger nuts, which he delivered in the hermitage, receiving two of the cakes for his trouble.

He lives, then, on ginger nuts, thought I; never eats a dinner, properly speaking; he must be a vegetarian, then; but no; he never eats even vegetables; he eats nothing but ginger nuts. My mind then ran on in reveries concerning the probable effects upon the human constitution of living entirely on ginger nuts. Ginger nuts are so called because they contain ginger as one of their peculiar constituents, and the final flavoring one. Now, what was ginger? A hot, spicy thing. Was Bartleby hot and spicy? Not at all. Ginger, then, had no effect upon Bartleby. Probably he preferred it should have none.

Nothing so aggravates an earnest person as a passive resistance. If the individual so resisted be of a not inhumane temper, and the resisting one perfectly harmless in his passivity, then, in the better moods of the former, he will endeavor charitably to construe to his imagination what proves impossible to be solved by his judgment. Even so, for the most part, I regarded Bartleby and his ways. Poor fellow! thought I, he means no mischief; it is plain he intends no insolence; his aspect sufficiently evinces that his eccentricities are involuntary. He is useful to me. I can get along with him. If I turn him away, the chances are he will fall in with some less indulgent employer, and then he will be rudely treated and perhaps driven forth miserably to starve. Yes. Here I can cheaply purchase a delicious self-approval. To befriend Bartleby, to humor him in his strange willfulness, will cost me little or nothing, while I lay up in my soul what will eventually prove a sweet morsel for my conscience. But this mood was not invariable with me. The passiveness of Bartleby sometimes irritated me. I felt strangely goaded on to encounter him in new opposition—to elicit some angry spark from him answerable to my own. But, indeed, I might as well have

essayed to strike fire with my knuckles against a bit of Windsor soap. But one afternoon the evil impulse in me mastered me, and the following little scene ensued:

"Bartleby," said I, "when those papers are all copied, I will compare them with you."

"I would prefer not to."

"How? Surely you do not mean to persist in that mulish vagary?"

No answer.

I threw open the folding doors nearby, and, turning upon Turkey and Nippers, exclaimed:

"Bartleby a second time says he won't examine his papers. What do you think of it, Turkey?"

It was afternoon, be it remembered. Turkey sat glowing like a brass boiler; his bald head steaming; his hands reeling among his blotted papers.

"Think of it?" roared Turkey, "I think I'll just step behind his screen, and black his eyes for him!"

So saying, Turkey rose to his feet and threw his arms into a pugilistic position. He was hurrying away to make good his promise, when I detained him, alarmed at the effect of incautiously rousing Turkey's combativeness after dinner.

"Sit down, Turkey," said I, "and hear what Nippers has to say. What do you think of it, Nippers? Would I not be justified in immediately dismissing Bartleby?"

"Excuse me, that is for you to decide, sir. I think his conduct quite unusual, and, indeed, unjust, as regards Turkey and myself. But it may only be a passing whim."

"Ah," exclaimed I, "you have strangely changed your mind, then—you speak very gently of him now."

"All beer," cried Turkey; "gentleness is effects of beer—Nippers and I dined together today. You see how gentle *I* am, sir. Shall I go and black his eyes?"

"You refer to Bartleby, I suppose. No, not today, Turkey," I replied; "pray, put up your fists."

I closed the doors and again advanced toward Bartleby. I felt additional incentives tempting me to my fate. I burned to be rebelled against again. I remembered that Bartleby never left the office.

"Bartleby," said I, "Ginger Nut is away; just step around to the post office, won't you? (it was but a three minutes' walk), and see if there is anything for me."

"I would prefer not to."

"You *will* not?"

"I *prefer* not."

I staggered to my desk and sat there in a deep study. My blind inveteracy [1] returned. Was there any other thing in which I could procure myself to be ignominiously repulsed by this lean, penniless wight?—my hired clerk? What added thing is there, perfectly reasonable, that he will be sure to refuse to do?

"Bartleby!"

No answer.

"Bartleby," in a louder tone.

No answer.

"Bartleby," I roared.

Like a very ghost, agreeably to the laws of magical invocation, at the third summons he appeared at the entrance of his hermitage.

"Go to the next room, and tell Nippers to come to me."

"I prefer not to," he respectfully and slowly said, and mildly disappeared.

"Very good, Bartleby," said I, in a quiet sort of serenely severe, self-possessed tone, intimating the unalterable purpose of some terrible retribution very close at hand. At the moment I half intended something of the kind. But upon the whole, as it was drawing toward my dinner hour, I thought it best to put on my hat and walk home for the day, suffering much from perplexity and distress of mind.

Shall I acknowledge it? The conclusion of this whole business was that it soon became a fixed fact of my chambers that a pale young scrivener, by the name of Bartleby, had a desk there; that he copied for me at the usual rate of four cents a folio (one hundred words); but he was permanently exempt from examining the

work done by him, that duty being transferred to Turkey and Nippers, out of compliment, doubtless, to their superior acuteness; moreover, said Bartleby was never, on any account, to be dispatched on the most trivial errand of any sort; and that even if entreated to take upon him such a matter, it was generally understood that he would "prefer not to"—in other words, that he would refuse point-blank.

As days passed on, I became considerably reconciled to Bartleby. His steadiness, his freedom from all dissipation, his incessant industry (except when he chose to throw himself into a standing revery behind his screen), his great stillness, his unalterableness of demeanor under all circumstances, made him a valuable acquisition. One prime thing was this—*he was always there*—first in the morning, continually through the day, and the last at night. I had a singular confidence in his honesty. I felt my most precious papers perfectly safe in his hands. Sometimes, to be sure, I could not, for the very soul of me, avoid falling into sudden spasmodic passions with him. For it was exceeding difficult to bear in mind all the time those strange peculiarities, privileges, and unheard-of exemptions, forming the tacit stipulations on Bartleby's part under which he remained in my office. Now and then, in the eagerness of dispatching pressing business, I would inadvertently summon Bartleby, in a short, rapid tone, to put his finger, say, on the incipient tie of a bit of red tape with which I was about compressing some papers. Of course, from behind the screen the usual answer, "I prefer not to," was sure to come; and then, how could a human creature, with the common infirmities of our nature, refrain from bitterly exclaiming upon such perverseness—such unreasonableness. However, every added repulse of this sort which I received only tended to lessen the probability of my repeating the inadvertence.

Here it must be said that, according to the custom of most legal gentlemen occupying chambers in densely populated

_____
[1] **inveteracy:** deeply rooted habit.

law buildings, there were several keys to my door. One was kept by a woman residing in the attic, which person weekly scrubbed and daily swept and dusted my apartments. Another was kept by Turkey for convenience's sake. The third I sometimes carried in my own pocket. The fourth I knew not who had.

Now, one Sunday morning I happened to go to Trinity Church to hear a celebrated preacher, and finding myself rather early on the ground I thought I would walk around to my chambers for a while. Luckily I had my key with me; but upon applying it to the lock, I found it resisted by something inserted from the inside. Quite surprised, I called out, when to my consternation a key was turned from within; and thrusting his lean visage at me and holding the door ajar, the apparition of Bartleby appeared in his shirt sleeves, and otherwise in a strangely tattered *déshabille,*[1] saying quietly that he was sorry, but he was deeply engaged just then, and —preferred not admitting me at present. In a brief word or two, he moreover added that perhaps I had better walk around the block two or three times, and by that time he would probably have concluded his affairs.

Now, the utterly unsurmised appearance of Bartleby tenanting my law chambers of a Sunday morning, with his cadaverously gentlemanly *nonchalance,* yet withal firm and self-possessed, had such a strange effect upon me that incontinently I slunk away from my own door and did as desired. But not without sundry twinges of impotent rebellion against the mild effrontery of this unaccountable scrivener. Indeed, it was his wonderful mildness chiefly, which not only disarmed me, but unmanned me as it were. For I consider that one, for the time, is somehow unmanned when he tranquilly permits his hired clerk to dictate to him and order him away from his own premises. Furthermore, I was full of uneasiness as to what

Bartleby could possibly be doing in my office in his shirt sleeves, and in an otherwise dismantled condition of a Sunday morning. Was anything amiss going on? Nay, that was out of the question. It was not to be thought of for a moment that Bartleby was an immoral person. But what could he be doing there?—copying? Nay again; whatever might be his eccentricities, Bartleby was an eminently decorous person. He would be the last man to sit down to his desk in any state approaching to nudity. Besides, it was Sunday; and there was something about Bartleby that forbade the supposition that he would by any secular occupation violate the proprieties of the day.

Nevertheless, my mind was not pacified; and full of a restless curiosity, at last I returned to the door. Without hindrance I inserted my key, opened it, and entered. Bartleby was not to be seen. I looked round anxiously, peeped behind his screen; but it was very plain that he was gone. Upon more closely examining the place, I surmised that for an indefinite period Bartleby must have eaten, dressed, and slept in my office, and that, too, without plate, mirror, or bed. The cushioned seat of a rickety old sofa in one corner bore the faint impress of a lean, reclining

[1] *déshabille:* a French word meaning "the state of being carelessly or only partially dressed."

form. Rolled away under his desk, I found a blanket; under the empty grate, a blacking box and brush; on a chair, a tin basin, with soap and a ragged towel; in a newspaper a few crumbs of ginger nuts and a morsel of cheese. Yes, thought I, it is evident enough that Bartleby has been making his home here, keeping bachelor's hall all by himself. Immediately then the thought came sweeping across me, what miserable friendlessness and loneliness are here revealed! His poverty is great; but his solitude, how horrible! Think of it. Of a Sunday, Wall Street is deserted as Petra; [1] and every night of every day it is an emptiness. This building, too, which of weekdays hums with industry and life, at nightfall echoes with sheer vacancy, and all through Sunday is forlorn. And here Bartleby makes his home; sole spectator of a solitude which he has seen all populous—a sort of innocent and transformed Marius [2] brooding among the ruins of Carthage!

For the first time in my life a feeling of overpowering stinging melancholy seized me. Before I had never experienced aught but a not unpleasing sadness. The bond of a common humanity now drew me irresistibly to gloom. A fraternal melancholy! For both I and Bartleby were sons of Adam. I remembered the bright silks and sparkling faces I had seen that day, in gala trim, swanlike down the Mississippi of Broadway; and I contrasted them with the pallid copyist, and thought to myself, Ah, happiness courts the light, so we deem the world is gay; but misery hides aloof, so we deem that misery there is none. These sad fancyings—chimeras, [3] doubtless, of a sick and silly brain—led on to other and more special thoughts, concerning the eccentricities of Bartleby. Presentiments of strange discoveries hovered

---

[1] **Petra:** the ruins of an ancient city in Jordan.
[2] **Marius:** Gaius Marius (155?–186 B.C.), a Roman general who won great victories over Carthage but who was banished from Rome for political reasons.
[3] **chimeras:** absurd or horrible imaginings. In Greek mythology, the chimera was a fire-breathing monster, part lion, part goat, and part serpent.

round me. The scrivener's pale form appeared to me laid out, among uncaring strangers, in its shivering winding sheet.

Suddenly I was attracted by Bartleby's closed desk, the key in open sight left in the lock.

I mean no mischief, seek the gratification of no heartless curiosity, thought I; besides, the desk is mine, and its contents, too, so I will make bold to look within. Everything was methodically arranged, the papers smoothly placed. The pigeon holes were deep, and removing the files of documents, I groped into their recesses. Presently I felt something there and dragged it out. It was an old bandanna handkerchief, heavy and knotted. I opened it, and saw it was a savings' bank.

I now recalled all the quiet mysteries which I had noted in the man. I remembered that he never spoke but to answer; that, though at intervals he had considerable time to himself, yet I had never seen him reading—no, not even a newspaper; that for long periods he would stand looking out, at his pale window behind the screen, upon the dead brick wall; I was quite sure he never visited any refectory or eating house; while his pale face clearly indicated that he never drank beer like Turkey, or tea and coffee even, like other men; that he never went anywhere in particular that I could learn; never went out for a walk, unless, indeed, that was the case at present; that he had declined telling who he was, or whence he came, or whether he had any relatives in the world; that though so thin and pale, he never complained of ill health. And more than all, I remembered a certain unconscious air of pallid—how shall I call it?—of pallid haughtiness, say, or rather an austere reserve about him, which had positively awed me into my tame compliance with his eccentricities, when I had feared to ask him to do the slightest incidental thing for me, even though I might know, from his long-continued motionlessness, that behind his screen he must be standing in one of those dead-wall reveries of his.

Revolving all these things, and coupling

them with the recently discovered fact that he made my office his constant abiding place and home, and not forgetful of his morbid moodiness; revolving all these things, a prudential feeling began to steal over me. My first emotions had been those of pure melancholy and sincerest pity; but just in proportion as the forlornness of Bartleby grew and grew to my imagination, did that same melancholy merge into fear, that pity into repulsion. So true it is, and so terrible, too, that up to a certain point the thought or sight of misery enlists our best affections; but, in certain special cases, beyond that point it does not. They err who would assert that invariably this is owing to the inherent selfishness of the human heart. It rather proceeds from a certain hopelessness of remedying excessive and organic ill. To a sensitive being, pity is not seldom pain. And when at last it is perceived that such pity cannot lead to effectual succor, common sense bids the soul be rid of it. What I saw that morning persuaded me that the scrivener was the victim of innate and incurable disorder. I might give alms to his body; but his body did not pain him; it was his soul that suffered, and his soul I could not reach.

I did not accomplish the purpose of going to Trinity Church that morning. Somehow, the things I had seen disqualified me for the time from church-going. I walked homeward, thinking what I would do with Bartleby. Finally, I resolved upon this—I would put certain calm questions to him the next morning, touching his history, etc., and if he declined to answer them openly and unreservedly (and I supposed he would prefer not), then to give him a twenty dollar bill over and above whatever I might owe him, and tell him his services were no longer required; but that if in any other way I could assist him, I would be happy to do so, especially if he desired to return to his native place, wherever that might be, I would willingly help to defray the expenses. Moreover, if, after reaching home, he found himself at any time in want of aid, a letter from him would be sure of a reply.

The next morning came.

"Bartleby," said I, gently calling to him behind his screen.

No reply.

"Bartleby," said I, in a still gentler tone, "come here; I am not going to ask you to do anything you would prefer not to do—I simply wish to speak to you."

Upon this he noiselessly slid into view.

"Will you tell me, Bartleby, where you were born?"

"I would prefer not to."

"Will you tell me *anything* about yourself?"

"I would prefer not to."

"But what reasonable objection can you have to speak to me? I feel friendly toward you."

He did not look at me while I spoke, but kept his glance fixed upon my bust of Cicero, which, as I then sat, was directly behind me, some six inches above my head.

"What is your answer, Bartleby," said I, after waiting a considerable time for a reply, during which his countenance remained immovable, only there was the faintest conceivable tremor of the white attenuated mouth.

"At present I prefer to give no answer," he said, and retired into his hermitage.

It was rather weak in me I confess, but his manner, on this occasion, nettled me. Not only did there seem to lurk in it a certain calm disdain, but his perverseness seemed ungrateful, considering the undeniable good usage and indulgence he had received from me.

Again I sat ruminating what I should do. Mortified as I was at his behavior, and resolved as I had been to dismiss him when I entered my office, nevertheless I strangely felt something superstitious knocking at my heart, and forbidding me to carry out my purpose, and denouncing me for a villain if I dared to breathe one bitter word against this forlornest of mankind. At last, familiarly drawing my chair behind his screen, I sat down and said:

"Bartleby, never mind, then, about revealing your history; but let me entreat you, as a friend, to comply as far as may be with the usages of this office. Say now, you will help to examine papers tomorrow or next day: in short, say now, that in a day or two you will begin to be a little reasonable:—say so, Bartleby."

"At present I would prefer not to be a little reasonable," was his mildly cadaverous reply.

Just then the folding doors opened, and Nippers approached. He seemed suffering from an unusually bad night's rest, induced by severer indigestion than common. He overheard those final words of Bartleby.

"*Prefer not,* eh?" gritted Nippers—"I'd *prefer* him, if I were you, sir," addressing me—"I'd *prefer* him; I'd give him preferences, the stubborn mule! What is it, sir, pray, that he *prefers* not to do now?"

Bartleby moved not a limb.

"Mr. Nippers," said I, "I'd prefer that you would withdraw for the present."

Somehow, of late, I had got into the way of involuntarily using this word "prefer" upon all sorts of not exactly suitable occasions. And I trembled to think that my contact with the scrivener had already and seriously affected me in a mental way. And what further and deeper aberration might it not yet produce? This apprehension had not been without efficacy in determining me to summary measures.

As Nippers, looking very sour and sulky, was departing, Turkey blandly and deferentially approached.

"With submission, sir," said he, "yesterday I was thinking about Bartleby here, and I think that if he would but prefer to take a quart of good ale every day, it would do much toward mending him and enabling him to assist in examining his papers."

"So you have got the word, too," said I, slightly excited.

"With submission, what word, sir," asked Turkey, respectfully crowding himself into the contracted space behind the screen, and by so doing, making me jostle

the scrivener. "What word, sir?"

"I would prefer to be left alone here," said Bartleby, as if offended at being mobbed in his privacy.

"*That's* the word, Turkey," said I—"*that's* it."

"Oh, *prefer?* oh yes—queer word. I never use it myself. But, sir, as I was saying, if he would but prefer——"

"Turkey," interrupted I, "you will please withdraw."

"Oh certainly, sir, if you prefer that I should."

As he opened the folding door to retire, Nippers at his desk caught a glimpse of me and asked whether I would prefer to have a certain paper copied on blue paper or white. He did not in the least roguishly accent the word *prefer*. It was plain that it involuntarily rolled from his tongue. I thought to myself, surely I must get rid of a demented man, who already has in some degree turned the tongues, if not the heads, of myself and clerks. But I thought it prudent not to break the dismission at once.

The next day I noticed that Bartleby did nothing but stand at his window in his dead-wall revery. Upon asking him why he did not write, he said that he had decided upon doing no more writing.

"Why, how now? what next?" exclaimed I, "do no more writing?"

"No more."

"And what is the reason?"

"Do you not see the reason for yourself?" he indifferently replied.

I looked steadfastly at him and perceived that his eyes looked dull and glazed. Instantly it occurred to me that his unexampled diligence in copying by his dim window for the first few weeks of his stay with me might have temporarily impaired his vision.

I was touched. I said something in condolence with him. I hinted that of course he did wisely in abstaining from writing for a while; and urged him to embrace that opportunity of taking wholesome exercise in the open air. This, however, he did not do. A few days after this, my other clerks being absent, and being in a great hurry to dispatch certain letters by the mail, I thought that, having nothing else earthly to do, Bartleby would surely be less inflexible than usual and carry these letters to the post office. But he blankly declined. So, much to my inconvenience, I went myself.

Still added days went by. Whether Bartleby's eyes improved or not, I could not say. To all appearances I thought they did. But when I asked him if they did, he vouchsafed no answer. At all events, he would do no copying. At last, in reply to my urgings, he informed me that he had permanently given up copying.

"What!" exclaimed I; "suppose your eyes should get entirely well—better than ever before—would you not copy then?"

"I have given up copying," he answered, and slid aside.

He remained as ever, a fixture in my chamber. Nay—if that were possible—he became still more of a fixture than before. What was to be done? He would do nothing in the office; why should he stay there? In plain fact, he had now become a millstone to me, not only useless as a necklace, but afflictive to bear. Yet I was sorry for him. I speak less than truth when I say that, on his own account, he occasioned me uneasiness. If he would but have named a single relative or friend, I would instantly have written and urged their taking the poor fellow away to some convenient retreat. But he seemed alone, absolutely alone in the universe. A bit of wreck in the mid-Atlantic. At length, necessities connected with my business tyrannized over all other considerations. Decently as I could, I told Bartleby that in six days' time he must unconditionally leave the office. I warned him to take measures, in the interval, for procuring some other abode. I offered to assist him in his endeavor, if he himself would but take the first step toward a removal. "And when you finally quit me, Bartleby," added I, "I shall see that you go not away entirely unprovided. Six days from this hour, remember."

At the expiration of that period, I peeped behind the screen, and lo! Bartleby was there.

I buttoned up my coat, balanced myself; advanced slowly toward him, touched his shoulder, and said, "The time has come; you must quit this place; I am sorry for you; here is money; but you must go."

"I would prefer not," he replied, with his back still toward me.

"You *must.*"

He remained silent.

Now I had an unbounded confidence in this man's common honesty. He had frequently restored to me sixpences and shillings carelessly dropped upon the floor, for I am apt to be very reckless in such shirt-button affairs. The proceeding, then, which followed will not be deemed extraordinary.

"Bartleby," said I, "I owe you twelve dollars on account; here are thirty-two; the odd twenty are yours—will you take it?" and I handed the bills toward him.

But he made no motion.

"I will leave them here, then," putting them under a weight on the table. Then taking my hat and cane and going to the door, I tranquilly turned and added— "After you have removed your things from these offices, Bartleby, you will of course lock the door—since everyone is now gone for the day but you—and if you please, slip your key underneath the mat, so that I may have it in the morning. I shall not see you again; so good-by to you. If, hereafter, in your new place of abode, I can be of any service to you, do not fail to advise me by letter. Good-by, Bartleby, and fare you well."

But he answered not a word; like the last column of some ruined temple, he remained standing mute and solitary in the middle of the otherwise deserted room.

As I walked home in a pensive mood, my vanity got the better of my pity. I could not but highly plume myself on my masterly management in getting rid of Bartleby. Masterly I call it, and such it must appear to any dispassionate thinker.

The beauty of my procedure seemed to consist in its perfect quietness. There was no vulgar bullying, no bravado of any sort, no choleric hectoring [1] and striding to and fro across the apartment, jerking out vehement commands for Bartleby to bundle himself off with his beggarly traps. Nothing of the kind. Without loudly bidding Bartleby depart—as an inferior genius might have done—I *assumed* the ground that depart he must; and upon that assumption built all I had to say. The more I thought over my procedure, the more I was charmed with it. Nevertheless, next morning, upon awakening, I had my doubts—I had somehow slept off the fumes of vanity. One of the coolest and wisest hours a man has is just after he awakes in the morning. My procedure seemed as sagacious as ever—but only in theory. How it would prove in practice—there was the rub. It was truly a beautiful thought to have assumed Bartleby's departure; but, after all, that assumption was simply my own, and none of Bartleby's. The great point was, not whether I had assumed that he would quit me, but whether he would prefer so to do. He was more a man of preferences than assumptions.

After breakfast, I walked downtown, arguing the probabilities pro and con. One moment I thought it would prove a miserable failure, and Bartleby would be found all alive at my office as usual; the next moment it seemed certain that I should find his chair empty. And so I kept veering about. At the corner of Broadway and Canal Street, I saw quite an excited group of people standing in earnest conversation.

"I'll take odds he doesn't," said a voice as I passed.

"Doesn't go?—done!" said I; "put up your money."

I was instinctively putting my hand in my pocket to produce my own, when I remembered that this was an election day. The words I had overheard bore no reference to Bartleby, but to the success or

---

[1] **choleric hectoring:** angry ranting.

nonsuccess of some candidate for the mayoralty. In my intent frame of mind, I had, as it were, imagined that all Broadway shared in my excitement and were debating the same question with me. I passed on, very thankful that the uproar of the street screened my momentary absent-mindedness.

As I had intended, I was earlier than usual at my office door. I stood listening for a moment. All was still. He must be gone. I tried the knob. The door was locked. Yes, my procedure had worked to a charm; he indeed must be vanished. Yet a certain melancholy mixed with this: I was almost sorry for my brilliant success. I was fumbling under the door mat for the key, which Bartleby was to have left there for me, when accidentally my knee knocked against a panel, producing a summoning sound, and in response a voice came to me from within—"Not yet; I am occupied."

It was Bartleby.

I was thunderstruck. For an instant I stood like the man who, pipe in mouth, was killed one cloudless afternoon long ago in Virginia, by summer lightning; at his own warm open window he was killed, and remained leaning out there upon the dreamy afternoon, till someone touched him, when he fell.

"Not gone!" I murmured at last. But again obeying that wondrous ascendancy which the inscrutable scrivener had over me, and from which ascendancy, for all my chafing, I could not completely escape, I slowly went downstairs and out into the street, and while walking round the block, considered what I should next do in this unheard-of perplexity. Turn the man out by an actual thrusting I could not; to drive him away by calling him hard names would not do; calling in the police was an unpleasant idea; and yet, permit him to enjoy his cadaverous triumph over me—this, too, I could not think of. What was to be done? or, if nothing could be done, was there anything further that I could *assume* in the matter? Yes, as before I had prospectively assumed that

Bartleby would depart, so now I might retrospectively assume that departed he was. In the legitimate carrying out of this assumption, I might enter my office in a great hurry, and pretending not to see Bartleby at all, walk straight against him as if he were air. Such a proceeding would in a singular degree have the appearance of a home-thrust. It was hardly possible that Bartleby could withstand such an application of the doctrine of assumptions. But upon second thought the success of the plan seemed rather dubious. I resolved to argue the matter over with him again.

"Bartleby," said I, entering the office with a quietly severe expression, "I am seriously displeased. I am pained, Bartleby. I had thought better of you. I had imagined you of such a gentlemanly organization that in any delicate dilemma a slight hint would suffice—in short, an assumption. But it appears I am deceived. Why," I added, unaffectedly starting, "you have not even touched that money yet," pointing to it, just where I had left it the evening previous.

He answered nothing.

"Will you, or will you not, quit me?" I now demanded in a sudden passion, advancing close to him.

"I would prefer *not* to quit you," he replied, gently emphasizing the *not*.

"What earthly right have you to stay here? Do you pay any rent? Do you pay my taxes? Or is this property yours?"

He answered nothing.

"Are you ready to go on and write now? Are your eyes recovered? Could you copy a small paper for me this morning? or help examine a few lines? or step round to the post office? In a word, will you do anything at all to give a coloring to your refusal to depart the premises?"

He silently retired into his hermitage.

I was now in such a state of nervous resentment that I thought it but prudent to check myself at present from further demonstrations. Bartleby and I were alone. I remembered the tragedy of the unfortunate Adams and the still more unfortunate Colt in the solitary office of the latter; and how poor Colt, being dreadfully incensed by Adams and imprudently permitting himself to get wildly excited, was at unawares hurried into his fatal act—an act which certainly no man could possibly deplore more than the actor himself. Often it had occurred to me in my ponderings upon the subject that had that altercation taken place in the public street, or at a private residence, it would not have terminated as it did. It was the circumstance of being alone in a solitary office, upstairs, of a building entirely unhallowed by humanizing domestic associations—an uncarpeted office, doubtless, of a dusty, haggard sort of appearance—this it must have been, which greatly helped to enhance the irritable desperation of the hapless Colt.

But when this old Adam of resentment rose in me and tempted me concerning Bartleby, I grappled him and threw him. How? Why, simply by recalling the divine injunction: "A new commandment give I unto you, that ye love one another." [1] Yes, this it was that saved me. Aside from higher considerations, charity often operates as a vastly wise and prudent principle—a great safeguard to its possessor. Men have committed murder for jealousy's sake, and anger's sake, and hatred's sake, and selfishness's sake, and spiritual pride's sake; but no man, that ever I heard of, ever committed a diabolical murder for sweet charity's sake. Mere self-interest, then, if no better motive can be enlisted, should, especially with high-tempered men, prompt all beings to charity and philanthropy. At any rate, upon the occasion in question, I strove to drown my exasperated feelings toward the scrivener by benevolently construing his conduct. Poor fellow, poor fellow! thought I, he don't mean anything; and besides, he has seen hard times, and ought to be indulged.

I endeavored, also, immediately to occupy myself and at the same time to comfort my despondency. I tried to fancy

[1] "A . . . another": John 13:24.

that in the course of the morning, at such time as might prove agreeable to him, Bartleby, of his own free accord, would emerge from his hermitage and take up some decided line of march in the direction of the door. But no. Half-past twelve o'clock came; Turkey began to glow in the face, overturn his inkstand, and become generally obstreperous; Nippers abated down into quietude and courtesy; Ginger Nut munched his noon apple; and Bartleby remained standing at his window in one of his profoundest dead-wall reveries. Will it be credited? Ought I to acknowledge it? That afternoon I left the office without saying one further word to him.

Some days now passed during which, at leisure intervals, I looked a little into "Edwards on the Will," [1] and "Priestley on Necessity." [2] Under the circumstances, those books induced a salutary feeling. Gradually I slid into the persuasion that these troubles of mine touching the scrivener had been all predestinated from eternity, and Bartleby was billeted upon me for some mysterious purpose of an all-wise Providence, which it was not for a mere mortal like me to fathom. Yes, Bartleby, stay there behind your screen, thought I; I shall persecute you no more; you are harmless and noiseless as any of these old chairs; in short, I never feel so private as when I know you are here. At last I see it, I feel it; I penetrate to the predestinated purpose of my life. I am content. Others may have loftier parts to enact; but my mission in this world, Bartleby, is to furnish you with office room for such period as you may see fit to remain.

I believe that this wise and blessed frame of mind would have continued with me, had it not been for the unsolicited and uncharitable remarks obtruded upon me by my professional friends who visited the rooms. But thus it often is, that the constant friction of illiberal minds wears out at last the best resolves of the more generous. Though to be sure, when I reflected upon it, it was not strange that people entering my office should be struck by the peculiar aspect of the unaccountable Bartleby, and so be tempted to throw out some sinister observations concerning him. Sometimes an attorney, having business with me, and calling at my office, and finding no one but the scrivener there, would undertake to obtain some sort of precise information from him touching my whereabouts; but without heeding his idle talk, Bartleby would remain standing immovable in the middle of the room. So after contemplating him in that position for a time, the attorney would depart, no wiser than he came.

Also, when a reference was going on, and the room full of lawyers and witnesses, and business driving fast, some deeply occupied legal gentleman present, seeing Bartleby wholly unemployed, would request him to run round to his (the legal gentleman's) office and fetch some papers for him. Thereupon, Bartleby would tranquilly decline, and yet remain idle as before. Then the lawyer would give a great stare and turn to me. And what could I say? At last I was made aware that all through the circle of my professional acquaintance, a whisper of wonder was running round, having reference to the strange creature I kept at my office. This worried me very much. And as the idea came upon me of his possibly turning out a long-lived man, and keep occupying my chambers, and denying my authority; and perplexing my visitors; and scandalizing my professional reputation; and casting a general gloom over the premises; keeping soul and body together to the last upon his savings (for doubtless he spent but half a dime a day), and in the end perhaps outlive me, and claim possession of my office by right of his perpetual occupancy: as all these dark anticipations crowded upon me more and more, and my friends continu-

---

[1] **"Edwards . . . Will":** Jonathan Edwards (page 24), author of *The Freedom of the Will* (1754).

[2] **"Priestley . . . Necessity":** Joseph Priestley (1733–1804), English clergyman, philosopher, and chemist who discovered oxygen.

ally intruded their relentless remarks upon the apparition in my room, a great change was wrought in me. I resolved to gather all my faculties together and forever rid me of this intolerable incubus.

Ere revolving any complicated project, however, adapted to this end, I first simply suggested to Bartleby the propriety of his permanent departure. In a calm and serious tone, I commended the idea to his careful and mature consideration. But, having taken three days to meditate upon it, he apprised me that his original determination remained the same; in short, that he still preferred to abide with me.

What shall I do? I now said to myself, buttoning up my coat to the last button. What shall I do? what ought I to do? what does conscience say I *should* do with this man, or, rather, ghost. Rid myself of him, I must; go, he shall. But how? You will not thrust him, the poor, pale, passive mortal—you will not thrust such a helpless creature out of your door? you will not dishonor yourself by such cruelty? No, I will not, I cannot do that. Rather would I let him live and die here, and then mason up his remains in the wall. What, then, will you do? For all your coaxing, he will not budge. Bribes he leaves under your own paperweight on your table; in short, it is quite plain that he prefers to cling to you.

Then something severe, something unusual must be done. What! surely you will not have him collared by a constable and commit his innocent pallor to the common jail? And upon what ground could you procure such a thing to be done?—a vagrant, is he? What! he a vagrant, a wanderer, who refuses to budge? It is because he will *not* be a vagrant, then, that you seek to count him *as* a vagrant. That is too absurd. No visible means of support: there I have him. Wrong again: for indubitably he *does* support himself, and that is the only unanswerable proof that any man can show of his possessing the means so to do. No more, then. Since he will not quit me, I must quit him. I will change my offices; I will move elsewhere, and give him fair notice that if I find him on my new premises I will then proceed against him as a common trespasser.

Acting accordingly, next day I thus addressed him: "I find these chambers too far from the City Hall; the air is unwholesome. In a word, I propose to remove my offices next week, and shall no longer require your services. I tell you this now, in order that you may seek another place."

He made no reply; and nothing more was said.

On the appointed day I engaged carts and men, proceeded to my chambers, and, having but little furniture, everything was removed in a few hours. Throughout, the scrivener remained standing behind the screen, which I directed to be removed the last thing. It was withdrawn; and, being folded up like a huge folio,[1] left him the motionless occupant of a naked room. I stood in the entry watching him a moment, while something from within me upbraided me.

I reentered, with my hand in my pocket —and—and my heart in my mouth.

"Good-by, Bartleby; I am going—good-by, and God some way bless you; and take that," slipping something in his hand. But it dropped upon the floor, and then—strange to say—I tore myself from him whom I had so longed to be rid of.

Established in my new quarters, for a day or two I kept the door locked, and started at every footfall in the passages. When I returned to my rooms, after any little absence, I would pause at the threshold for an instant and attentively listen, ere applying my key. But these fears were needless. Bartleby never came nigh me.

I thought all was going well, when a perturbed-looking stranger visited me, inquiring whether I was the person who had recently occupied rooms at No.—Wall Street.

Full of forebodings, I replied that I was.

"Then, sir," said the stranger, who

[1] **folio:** a large book.

proved a lawyer, "you are responsible for the man you left there. He refuses to do any copying; he refuses to do anything; he says he prefers not to; and he refuses to quit the premises."

"I am very sorry, sir," said I, with assumed tranquillity, but an inward tremor, "but, really, the man you allude to is nothing to me—he is no relation or apprentice of mine, that you should hold me responsible for him."

"In mercy's name, who is he?"

"I certainly cannot inform you. I know nothing about him. Formerly I employed him as a copyist; but he has done nothing for me now for some time past."

"I shall settle him, then—good morning, sir."

Several days passed, and I heard nothing more; and, though I often felt a charitable prompting to call at the place and see poor Bartleby, yet a certain squeamishness, of I know not what, withheld me.

All is over with him by this time, thought I at last, when, through another week, no further intelligence reached me. But, coming to my room the day after, I found several persons waiting at my door in a high state of nervous excitement.

"That's the man—here he comes," cried the foremost one, whom I recognized as the lawyer who had previously called upon me alone.

"You must take him away, sir, at once," cried a portly person among them, advancing upon me, and whom I knew to be the landlord of No.—Wall Street. "These gentlemen, my tenants, cannot stand it any longer; Mr. B——," pointing to the lawyer, "has turned him out of his room, and he now persists in haunting the building generally, sitting upon the banisters of the stairs by day, and sleeping in the entry by night. Everybody is concerned; clients are leaving the offices; some fears are entertained of a mob; something you must do, and that without delay."

Aghast at this torrent, I fell back before it, and would fain have locked myself in my new quarters. In vain I persisted that Bartleby was nothing to me—no more than to anyone else. In vain—I was the last person known to have anything to do with him, and they held me to the terrible account. Fearful, then, of being exposed in the papers (as one person present obscurely threatened), I considered the matter and, at length, said that if the lawyer would give me a confidential interview with the scrivener, in his (the lawyer's) own room, I would, that afternoon, strive my best to rid them of the nuisance they complained of.

Going upstairs to my old haunt, there was Bartleby silently sitting upon the banister at the landing.

"What are you doing here, Bartleby?" said I.

"Sitting upon the banister," he mildly replied.

I motioned him into the lawyer's room, who then left us.

"Bartleby," said I, "are you aware that you are the cause of great tribulation to me, by persisting in occupying the entry after being dismissed from the office?"

No answer.

"Now one of two things must take place. Either you must do something, or something must be done to you. Now what sort of business would you like to engage in? Would you like to reengage in copying for someone?"

"No; I would prefer not to make any change."

"Would you like a clerkship in a dry-goods store?"

"There is too much confinement about that. No, I would not like a clerkship; but I am not particular."

"Too much confinement," I cried, "why you keep yourself confined all the time!"

"I would prefer not to take a clerkship," he rejoined, as if to settle that little item at once.

"How would a bartender's business suit you? There is no trying of the eyesight in that."

"I would not like it at all; though, as I said before, I am not particular."

His unwonted wordiness inspirited me. I returned to the charge.

"Well, then, would you like to travel through the country collecting bills for the merchants? That would improve your health."

"No, I would prefer to be doing something else."

"How, then, would going as a companion to Europe, to entertain some young gentleman with your conversation—how would that suit you?"

"Not at all. It does not strike me that there is anything definite about that. I like to be stationary. But I am not particular."

"Stationary you shall be, then," I cried, now losing all patience and, for the first time in all my exasperating connection with him, fairly flying into a passion. "If you do not go away from these premises before night, I shall feel bound—indeed, I *am* bound—to—to—to quit the premises myself!" I rather absurdly concluded, knowing not with what possible threat to try to frighten his immobility into compliance. Despairing of all further efforts, I was precipitately leaving him, when a final thought occurred to me—one which had not been wholly unindulged before.

"Bartleby," said I, in the kindest tone I could assume under such exciting circumstances, "will you go home with me now—not to my office, but my dwelling—and remain there till we can conclude upon some convenient arrangement for you at our leisure? Come, let us start now, right away."

"No: at present I would prefer not to make any change at all."

I answered nothing; but, effectually dodging everyone by the suddenness and rapidity of my flight, rushed from the building, ran up Wall Street toward Broadway, and, jumping into the first omnibus, was soon removed from pursuit. As soon as tranquillity returned, I distinctly perceived that I had now done all that I possibly could, both in respect to the demands of the landlord and his tenants, and with regard to my own desire and sense of duty, to benefit Bartleby and shield him from rude persecution. I now strove to be entirely carefree and quies-

cent; and my conscience justified me in the attempt; though, indeed, it was not so successful as I could have wished. So fearful was I of being again hunted out by the incensed landlord and his exasperated tenants that, surrendering my business to Nippers for a few days, I drove about the upper part of the town and through the suburbs in my rockaway,[1] crossed over to Jersey City and Hoboken, and paid fugitive visits to Manhattanville and Astoria. In fact, I almost lived in my rockaway for the time.

When again I entered my office, lo, a note from the landlord lay upon the desk. I opened it with trembling hands. It informed me that the writer had sent to the police, and had Bartleby removed to the Tombs as a vagrant. Moreover, since I knew more about him than anyone else, he wished me to appear at that place and make a suitable statement of the facts. These tidings had a conflicting effect upon me. At first I was indignant; but, at last, almost approved. The landlord's energetic, summary disposition had led him to adopt a procedure which I do not think I would have decided upon myself; and yet, as a last resort under such peculiar circumstances, it seemed the only plan.

As I afterwards learned, the poor scrivener, when told that he must be conducted to the Tombs, offered not the slightest obstacle, but, in his pale unmoving way, silently acquiesced.

Some of the compassionate and curious bystanders joined the party; and headed by one of the constables arm in arm with Bartleby, the silent procession filed its way through all the noise, and heat, and joy of the roaring thoroughfares at noon.

The same day I received the note, I went to the Tombs, or, to speak more properly, the Halls of Justice. Seeking the right officer, I stated the purpose of my call, and was informed that the individual I described was, indeed, within. I then assured the functionary that Bartleby was a perfectly honest man, and greatly to be

---

[1] **rockaway:** a four-wheeled carriage.

compassionated, however unaccountably eccentric. I narrated all I knew, and closed by suggesting the idea of letting him remain in as indulgent confinement as possible, till something less harsh might be done—though, indeed, I hardly knew what. At all events, if nothing else could be decided upon, the almshouse must receive him. I then begged to have an interview.

Being under no disgraceful charge, and quite serene and harmless in all his ways, they had permitted him freely to wander about the prison, and, especially, in the inclosed grass-platted yards thereof. And so I found him there, standing all alone in the quietest of the yards, his face toward a high wall, while all around, from the narrow slits of the jail windows, I thought I saw peering out upon him the eyes of murderers and thieves.

"Bartleby!"

"I know you," he said, without looking round—"and I want nothing to say to you."

"It was not I that brought you here, Bartleby," said I, keenly pained at his implied suspicion. "And to you, this should not be so vile a place. Nothing reproachful attaches to you by being here. And see, it is not so sad a place as one might think. Look, there is the sky, and here is the grass."

"I know where I am," he replied, but would say nothing more, and so I left him.

As I entered the corridor again, a broad meatlike man, in an apron, accosted me, and jerking his thumb over his shoulder, said—"Is that your friend?"

"Yes."

"Does he want to starve? If he does, let him live on the prison fare, that's all."

"Who are you?" asked I, not knowing what to make of such an unofficially speaking person in such a place.

"I am the grub-man. Such gentlemen as have friends here hire me to provide them with something good to eat."

"Is this so?" said I, turning to the turn-key.

He said it was.

"Well, then," said I, slipping some silver into the grub-man's hands (for so they called him), "I want you to give particular attention to my friend there; let him have the best dinner you can get. And you must be as polite to him as possible."

"Introduce me, will you?" said the grub-man, looking at me with an expression which seemed to say he was all impatience for an opportunity to give a specimen of his breeding.

Thinking it would prove of benefit to the scrivener, I acquiesced; and, asking the grub-man his name, went up with him to Bartleby.

"Bartleby, this is a friend; you will find him very useful to you."

"Your sarvant, sir, your sarvant," said the grub-man, making a low salutation behind his apron. "Hope you find it pleasant here, sir; nice grounds—cool apartments—hope you'll stay with us some time—try to make it agreeable. What will you have for dinner today?"

"I prefer not to dine today," said Bartleby, turning away. "It would disagree with me; I am unused to dinners." So saying, he slowly moved to the other side of the enclosure and took up a position fronting the dead-wall.

"How's this?" said the grub-man, addressing me with a stare of astonishment. "He's odd, ain't he?"

"I think he is a little deranged," said I, sadly.

"Deranged? deranged is it? Well, now, upon my word, I thought that friend of yourn was a gentleman forger; they are always pale and genteel-like, them forgers. I can't help pity 'em—can't help it, sir. Did you know Monroe Edwards?" he added, touchingly, and paused. Then, laying his hand piteously on my shoulder, sighed, "he died of consumption at Sing-Sing. So you weren't acquainted with Monroe?"

"No, I was never socially acquainted with any forgers. But I cannot stop longer. Look to my friend yonder. You will not lose by it. I will see you again."

Some few days after this, I again obtained admission to the Tombs and went through the corridors in quest of Bartleby; but without finding him.

"I saw him coming from his cell not long ago," said a turnkey, "maybe he's gone to loiter in the yards."

So I went in that direction.

"Are you looking for the silent man?" said another turnkey, passing me. "Yonder he lies—sleeping in the yard there. 'Tis not twenty minutes since I saw him lie down."

The yard was entirely quiet. It was not accessible to the common prisoners. The surrounding walls, of amazing thickness, kept off all sounds behind them. The Egyptian character of the masonry weighed upon me with its gloom. But a soft imprisoned turf grew under foot. The heart of the eternal pyramids, it seemed, wherein by some strange magic, through the clefts, grass-seed dropped by birds had sprung.

Strangely huddled at the base of the wall, his knees drawn up, and lying on his side, his head touching the cold stones, I saw the wasted Bartleby. But nothing stirred. I paused; then went close up to him; stooped over, and saw that his dim eyes were open; otherwise he seemed profoundly sleeping. Something prompted me to touch him. I felt his hand, when a tingling shiver ran up my arm and down my spine to my feet.

The round face of the grub-man peered upon me now. "His dinner is ready. Won't he dine today, either? Or does he live without dining?"

"Lives without dining," said I, and closed the eyes.

"Eh!—He's asleep, ain't he?"

"With kings and counselors," [1] murmured I.

There would seem little need for proceeding further in this history. Imagination will readily supply the meager recital of poor Bartleby's interment. But, ere parting with the reader, let me say that if

this little narrative has sufficiently interested him to awaken curiosity as to who Bartleby was, and what manner of life he led prior to the present narrator's making his acquaintance, I can only reply that in such curiosity I fully share, but am wholly unable to gratify it. Yet here I hardly know whether I should divulge one little item of rumor, which came to my ear a few months after the scrivener's decease. Upon what basis it rested, I could never ascertain; and hence, how true it is I cannot now tell. But, inasmuch as this vague report has not been without a certain suggestive interest to me, however said, it may prove the same with some others; and so I will briefly mention it. The report was this: that Bartleby had been a subordinate clerk in the Dead Letter Office at Washington, from which he had been suddenly removed by a change in the administration. When I think over this rumor, hardly can I express the emotions which seize me. Dead letters! does it not sound like dead men? Conceive a man by nature and misfortune prone to a pallid hopelessness, can any business seem more fitted to heighten it than that of continually handling these dead letters, and assorting them for the flames? For by the cartload they are annually burned. Sometimes from out the folded paper the pale clerk takes a ring—the finger it was meant for, perhaps, molders in the grave; a bank-note sent in swiftest charity—he whom it would relieve, nor eats nor hungers any more; pardon for those who died despairing; hope for those who died unhoping; good tidings for those who died stifled by unrelieved calamities. On errands of life, these letters speed to death.

Ah, Bartleby! Ah, humanity!

[1] **kings and counselors:** a reference to Job 3:13–14. "...then had I been at rest, with kings and counselors of the earth, which built desolate places for themselves."

COMMENTARY

About Bartleby, the narrator remarks, "I believe that no materials exist for a full and satisfactory biography of this man." Bartleby seems to exist more as a shadow than as a person, but his shadow is an oddly long and disturbing one. Similarly, the story in which he makes his phantom appearance is wonderfully strange and suggestive, but difficult to pin down to a single specific meaning. While a number of interpretations have been offered by scholars and critics, no one interpretation seems predominant or completely satisfactory.

Some interpreters of "Bartleby" find its significance in the facts of Melville's life. A scrivener is a kind of writer, and Bartleby has often been regarded as representative of Melville himself, discouraged by the collapse of his popular reputation after the publication of his novel *Pierre*. Bartleby's isolation behind the screen is thus interpreted as a symbol of Melville's isolation from the reading public, and the scrivener's "I would prefer not to" is held to be a version of Melville's own declaration, "What I feel most moved to write, that is banned—it will not pay. Yet, altogether, write the *other* way I cannot." While the story may have grown out of Melville's feelings of isolation, the wealth of detail about the law office and the extended account of Bartleby's downward path to the Tombs seems to indicate that Melville did not intend the story to be merely a secret message about his state of mind. The story's significance seems more general, more about a basic human relationship, than it is autobiographical.

Even apart from a possible association with his creator, Bartleby is an arresting character. In his gradual withdrawal from human activity and even from life, he performs only a few rudimentary actions. He copies legal papers (his only positive action), he refuses to perform any other duty, and he survives for a time simply by remaining inert. In some societies, idiots are given a special honored place because of their defenselessness. Bartleby is somewhat like these men, stripped of the strength and cleverness that most men use to survive and reduced to a basic humanity. The process of his decline is made even more compelling by the narrator's involvement in it. More than half of "Bartleby" is concerned with what the narrator did or failed to do or thought about the scrivener. In interpreting the story, then, it is essential to give the narrator his proper place as one of the two chief actors. What kind of man is he?

He introduces himself as "a rather elderly man," a lawyer who has avoided the "proverbially energetic and nervous" aspects of his profession and has chosen "in the cool tranquillity of a snug retreat [to] do a snug business among rich men's bonds, and mortgages, and title deeds." With pride he remarks that he is considered "eminently *safe*," and the greatest satisfaction of his career is that his "prudence" won the approval of a business giant, John Jacob Astor. Obviously, the opinion of the world means a great deal to the lawyer. Perhaps his basic motives, those influencing his most important actions, and, above all, his crucial failure to act, are a desire to avoid trouble and to maintain his respectability. On the whole, he is a kindly man, more patient with Bartleby than other employers might have been. In his desire to be "safe" and in his rather mild good will toward his fellow man, he can be called an average man.

After hiring Bartleby, the narrator assigns "this quiet man" a corner of his own office and places between them a high folding screen that becomes a major factor in the story. The screen is as much a convenience to the narrator as it is to the scrivener. For reasons of his own, Bartleby remains behind it, largely hidden. The narrator hardly ever goes beyond it. Once, when Bartleby has given his usual reply to a request ("I would prefer not to"), the narrator, instead of walking behind the screen, goes in precisely the opposite direction to consult with Turkey and Nippers. Shortly thereafter, the narrator asks Bartleby to run several errands, and again Bartleby refuses. Not once during this scene does the narrator walk around the screen to face Bartleby. Later in the story, on the morning of Bartleby's dismissal, the narrator comes to the office to discover that Bartleby has not left the premises. Instead of confronting the man, the lawyer wanders the streets and on his return is in such a rage that he is in danger of performing some dreadful, irrevocable act. All that saves him is "the divine injunction: 'A new commandment give I unto you, that ye love one another.'" Yet the divine command to love is not sufficient to inspire the narrator to take positive action in penetrating the human barriers that lie between himself and Bartleby and which, in their way, are as difficult to bypass as the high folding screen. The narrator has sufficient charity only to refrain from hurting Bartleby, not to help him. Finally he resolves the situation in a typically evasive fashion, by moving to another office. Later, when he does try to help Bartleby, the scrivener, in jail, is on the point of permanent withdrawal from the human race.

Thus "Bartleby" can be interpreted as a story about a relationship between two men which fails for lack of human charity. Perhaps one reason for the story's haunting power is that it forces the reader, by reviewing his own actions and motives, to discover how little or how much he has in common with the "eminently *safe*" lawyer.

FOR STUDY AND DISCUSSION

1. In the first paragraph of the story, the narrator remarks that Bartleby's biography cannot be written since nothing is known of his past life. Now that you have read the story, does this remark assume a greater significance for you than it had at first? Would the story be better or worse if details were given about Bartleby's past?

2. Near the beginning of the story, three minor characters are introduced: Turkey, Nippers, and Ginger Nut. Describe them. What roles do they play in the story? How does the narrator's treatment of Turkey and Nippers prepare us for his early treatment of Bartleby?

3. What is it that Bartleby first refuses to do? Bartleby always replies, "I would prefer not to," instead of "I will not." What significance do you find in this fact?

4. What does the narrator find out about Bartleby's mode of living? Do you think it is possible for a person to live as Bartleby does? How does Melville make this mode of living believable?

5. The narrator first feels pity for Bartleby, then fear and repulsion. Account for his change of feelings. What is there about Bartleby that excites fear and repulsion?

6. How does the narrator explain Bartleby's refusal to do any more copying? Do you think that this explanation is the correct one?

7. What does the fact that Bartleby had worked at the dead letter office add to the story? Is it significant that the story is about a scrivener?

8. Explain the last line of the story.

9. What comments can you make about Bartleby's character? Do you agree with those who say he is deranged? Does he irritate you? Do you feel any sympathy with him at all?

LANGUAGE AND VOCABULARY

The following phrases and sentences are used to describe Bartleby or to provide clues to his significance as a character. Give their meaning and explain how they contribute to your understanding of the story. Look up words you do not know.

1. "pallidly neat, pitiably respectable, incurably forlorn!"
2. "sat in his hermitage . . ." [behind the screen]
3. "his aspect sufficiently evinces that his eccentricities are involuntary."
4. "the apparition of Bartleby appeared in his shirt sleeves . . ."
5. "this intolerable incubus."

FOR COMPOSITION

Write a composition in which you express your own attitudes toward Bartleby and the narrator. One standard by which you may wish to judge these men is the Golden Rule: "Do unto others as you would have others do unto you."

EMILY DICKINSON
(1830–1886)

In 1862, Thomas Wentworth Higginson, a minister, soldier, and influential literary figure, received four poems from a shy young woman who wanted to know if they were "alive." They were odd, intense works, obviously the product of a highly individual talent. Later, in a letter to Higginson, their author described herself as "small, like the wren" with hair "bold, like the chestnut burr" and "eyes, like the sherry in the glass, that the guest leaves." She lived with her father in Amherst, Massachusetts, and saw few people. Although Higginson carried on a lengthy correspondence with Emily Dickinson, he met her only twice and described her as "remote" and "unique." Her personality, almost as intense and highly charged as her poetry, made him uncomfortably tired. He wrote, "I was never with anyone who drained my nerve power so much. Without touching her, she drew from me. I am glad not to live near her." While she lived, only seven of her poems were published, all anonymously and some against her wishes. Although several of her friends urged her to publish, she seemed reluctant to thrust herself and her work before the public. Only four years after her death did Higginson and Mabel Loomis Todd, a neighbor of Emily, assemble a first selection of her poetry, which she had called "my letter to the world." Although the poems seemed somewhat strange to the readers of the day, they achieved some popularity. Gradually more of her work was published, until in 1955 a complete edition of her poems was brought out. Today it is obvious that Emily Dickinson is a poet of major stature and that the poems discovered after her death, tied neatly together in little blue packets, are a legacy beyond price.

Emily Dickinson rarely left Amherst, a small college town that preserved the sober church-centered ways of an older Puritan New England. Her father was a lawyer, a formidable man who dominated his family and who achieved some prominence in politics and was treasurer of Amherst College for forty years. To Emily he seemed an awesome figure, but she was capable of writing that he was "too busy with his briefs to notice what we do—he buys me many books, but begs me not to read them because he fears they joggle the mind." Growing up in Amherst, she was much like other girls her age. Her letters to her friends and her brother, away at school, are full of girlish wit and high spirits. But as she grew older, she became more reluctant to be drawn away from home, even for an hour at a time. In a letter to Higginson she wrote, "You ask of my companions: hills, sir, and the sundown, and a dog, as large as myself, that my father bought me."

As far as is known, there were few important outward events in Emily Dickinson's life. The year 1862, when she began her friendship with Higginson, seems to have been a turning point. In that year she wrote more poems than in any other, roughly a poem a day. In that year also, Charles Wadsworth, a Presbyterian minister and the man Emily loved, departed for San Francisco. Apparently she saw Wadsworth, an older man, only three or four times. Although he was kind to her, he did not return her love. It was about the time of his departure that she took to dressing entirely in white. During the last ten years of her life, she refused to leave her house and garden or to meet any strangers. In 1884 her health broke down, and two years later she died.

That Emily Dickinson lived an intense inner life her poetry leaves no doubt. In a letter to Higginson, she described her standards for judging poetry. "If I read a book and it makes my whole body so cold no fire can ever warm me, I know *that* is poetry. If I feel physically as if the top of my head were taken off, I know *that* is poetry. These are the only ways I know it. Is there any other way?" Many of her own poems seem to call for as deep a response. They are both traditional and unusual. Their great subject, the connection between the happenings of everyday life and the world of the spirit, relates them to the works of older New England writers. Their rhythms are based upon the rhythms of church hymns. But Emily Dickinson's mode of expression—concise, informal, often abrupt—is so personal that it seems to belong not to a particular tradition or period of time but especially and only to herself. Her vision and her experiences remain fresh in the poetry that so individually preserves them.

The Soul Selects Her Own Society

The soul selects her own society,
Then shuts the door;
On her divine majority
Obtrude no more.

Unmoved, she notes the chariot's pausing
At her low gate;   6
Unmoved, an emperor is kneeling
Upon her mat.

I've known her from an ample nation
Choose one;   10
Then close the valves of her attention
Like stone.

There Is No Frigate like a Book

There is no frigate like a book
    To take us lands away,
Nor any coursers° like a page
    Of prancing poetry.
This traverse may the poorest take   5
    Without oppress of toll;
How frugal is the chariot
    That bears a human soul!

3. **coursers** (kôr′sərz): swift horses.

A Word Is Dead

A word is dead
When it is said,
    Some say.
I say it just
Begins to live
    That day.

Some Keep the Sabbath

Some keep the Sabbath going to church;
  I keep it staying at home,
With a bobolink for a chorister,
  And an orchard for a dome.

Some keep the Sabbath in surplice;°   5
  I just wear my wings;
And instead of tolling the bell for church,
  Our little sexton sings.

God preaches—a noted clergyman—
  And the sermon is never long;   10
So instead of getting to heaven at last,
  I'm going all along!

5. **surplice** (sûr′plis): a white vestment worn by clergymen.

The Sky Is Low, the Clouds Are Mean

The sky is low, the clouds are mean,
A traveling flake of snow
Across a barn or through a rut
Debates if it will go.

A narrow wind complains all day   5
How someone treated him.
Nature, like us, is sometimes caught
Without her diadem.

My Life Closed Twice

My life closed twice before its close;
  It yet remains to see
If Immortality unveil
  A third event to me,

So huge, so hopeless to conceive,   5
  As these that twice befell.
Parting is all we know of heaven,
  And all we need of hell.

Faith Is a Fine Invention

Faith is a fine invention
For gentlemen who see;
But microscopes are prudent
In an emergency!

The Bustle in a House

The bustle in a house
The morning after death
Is solemnest of industries
Enacted upon earth—

The sweeping up the heart,   5
And putting love away
We shall not want to use again
Until eternity.

I Never Saw a Moor

I never saw a moor,
  I never saw the sea;
Yet know I how the heather looks,
  And what a wave must be.

I never spoke with God,   5
  Nor visited in heaven;
Yet certain am I of the spot
  As if the chart were given.

Renunciation Is a Piercing Virtue

Renunciation
Is a piercing virtue,
The letting go
A presence for an expectation—
Not now.   5

The putting out of eyes
Just sunrise,
Lest Day Day's great progenitor
Out-show.

Renunciation is the choosing   10
Against itself,
Itself to justify
Unto itself;
When larger function
Make that appear   15
Smaller, that sated vision
Here.

Success Is Counted Sweetest

Success is counted sweetest
By those who ne'er succeed.
To comprehend a nectar
Requires sorest need.

Not one of all the purple host   5
Who took the flag today
Can tell the definition,
So clear, of victory,

As he, defeated, dying,
On whose forbidden ear   10
The distant strains of triumph
Break, agonized and clear.

Because I Could Not Stop for Death

Because I could not stop for Death,
He kindly stopped for me;
The carriage held but just ourselves
And Immortality.

We slowly drove, he knew no haste,   5
And I had put away
My labor, and my leisure too,
For his civility.

We passed the school where children
played
At wrestling in a ring;   10
We passed the fields of gazing grain,
We passed the setting sun.

We paused before a house that seemed
A swelling of the ground;
The roof was scarcely visible,   15
The cornice but a mound.

Since then 'tis centuries; but each
Feels shorter than the day
I first surmised the horses' heads
Were toward eternity.   20

THE SOUL SELECTS HER OWN SOCIETY

1. This poem has many characteristics that are typical of Emily Dickinson's poetry. Therefore, the attitude of the poem, its striking use of words, its meter and devices of sound, all merit close examination. To what is the soul compared in each stanza of the poem? What does the phrase "divine majority" suggest about the soul?

2. Describe the stanza form used in this poem. (For a discussion of stanza form, see page 233.) Would you call the stanzas of this poem complex? Why or why not?

3. Poems may use approximate rhymes as well as exact rhymes. "Hat"-"fat" is an exact rhyme, but "hat"-"fit" and "hat"-"foot" are approximate rhymes. Show the use of both exact and approximate rhymes in this poem.

SIMILE AND METAPHOR

A good deal of the power and effectiveness of poetry, and of much prose also, depends on the use of striking comparisons that stimulate the imagination. The two most common figures of speech depending on comparison are the *simile* and the *metaphor*. In a simile, the comparison is made obvious by the use of a signal word such as *like* or *as*. A metaphor uses no such word. It usually takes the reader by surprise and is often more powerful than a simile. If you were to describe a girl by saying, "Her cheeks are *as* red *as* a rose," you would be using a simile. If, with the poet Thomas Campion, you were to say, "There is a garden in her face,/ Where roses and white lilies grow," you would be using a metaphor to express your thought. In the second example, the comparison between the girl's face and the vivid colors of a garden is implied rather than stated. When Henry Wadsworth Longfellow writes in "The Arsenal at Springfield" that "From the floor to the ceiling/ Like a huge organ, rise the burnished arms," he is using a simile. When Oliver Wendell Holmes in "Contentment" writes, "Honors are silly toys," he is using metaphor, an implied comparison, to express the thought that the honors of high office are of no greater consequence or value than children's toys. The conceits of Edward Taylor's poems (pages 20–22) are extended metaphors.

Sometimes the term *metaphor* is used in a wider sense than in the previous paragraph. Then it refers to all figures of speech, including the simile, that depend on comparisons. Robert Frost is using the word in this sense when he writes that basically poetry "is metaphor, saying one thing and meaning another. . . . Poetry is simply made of metaphor." Frost is underlining one of the most important qualities of poetry, its power to awaken the imagination in several ways: by appealing to the senses, by suggesting much in a few words, by showing similarities or relationships in apparently unlike things. Similes and metaphors work in the imagination in all these ways. One noted critic, Northrup Frye, has suggested that the effectiveness of similes and metaphors depends on "a desire to associate, and finally to identify, the human mind with what goes on outside it," because the only genuine joy you can have is in these rare moments when you feel that although we may know in part . . . we are also part of a whole." Metaphor and simile constantly point out that we are part of something larger than ourselves and that our minds can reach out and make brilliant discoveries, even in an ordinary, everyday world.

In her use of similes and metaphors, Emily Dickinson is one of the most original of poets.

1. To what is the soul compared throughout most of "The Soul Selects . . ."? Do you consider this extended metaphor appropriate or inappropriate to the poem's meaning? Why?

2. To what is the soul compared in line 11? Is this comparison a simile or a metaphor? What does it suggest?

3. In your opinion, is the simile in line 12 an effective one? How would the effect of this line be different if the word *stone* were changed to *iron?* That is, what does *stone* suggest that *iron* does not?

THERE IS NO FRIGATE LIKE A BOOK
A WORD IS DEAD/ THE SKY IS LOW
FAITH IS A FINE INVENTION
THE BUSTLE IN A HOUSE

1. In these five poems, were there any lines that surprised you? If so, which? Which lines did you consider particularly effective?

2. In "There Is No Frigate like a Book," why is poetry described as "prancing"? Why is the chariot called "frugal"? What is meant by the "chariot/ That bears a human soul"?

3. The first sentence of "A Word Is Dead" is in inverted order. Read this sentence in

normal order beginning with the third line. What does the sentence gain or lose in meaning? In what sense does a word "begin to live" after it has been said?

4. Describe the mood of "The Sky Is Low, the Clouds Are Mean." How is the last word, *diadem,* related to the rest of the poem?

5. In "Faith Is a Fine Invention," why do you think Emily Dickinson chose the word *invention* rather than, say, *creation?* If you were to state the meaning of this poem in your own words, what words would you use instead of *faith* and *microscopes?*

6. In "The Bustle in a House," why do you think that "bustle" is called an "industry"? Explain the metaphor in the second stanza. To what is the heart compared? Are the rhymes in this poem exact or approximate?

SOME KEEP THE SABBATH/ MY LIFE CLOSED
TWICE/ I NEVER SAW A MOOR
RENUNCIATION IS A PIERCING VIRTUE
SUCCESS IS COUNTED SWEETEST

1. Emily Dickinson has been described as the most unconventionally religious person in her family. What does "Some Keep the Sabbath" tell you of her religious attitudes? What, in line 6, does she mean by "wings"? Explain the meaning of the last two lines.

2. After reading "My Life Closed Twice," would you say that Emily Dickinson lived an intense inner life? Why or why not? What do you think she meant by the last two lines?

3. "I Never Saw a Moor" reveals more about Emily Dickinson's religious beliefs. What is the relationship between the first and second stanzas? What comparison is made?

4. Point out the definitions of renunciation that are given in "Renunciation Is a Piercing Virtue." Why is renunciation called "piercing"? What is meant by "Day Day's great progenitor/ Out-show"? The last stanza of the poem has an irregular rhythm. What emotions might this rhythm suggest?

5. "Success Is Counted Sweetest" is one of the few poems that Emily Dickinson allowed to be published in her lifetime. The first stanza consists of two statements with similar meanings. What is the principal difference between the two statements? What is meant in line 5 by "the purple host"? Why, in the last stanza, is the ear called "forbidden"? Why are the strains of triumph called "agonized"? Examine the rhymes in this poem. Which are exact rhymes and which approximate rhymes?

BECAUSE I COULD NOT STOP FOR DEATH

1. By studying a number of poems by Emily Dickinson, you have become acquainted with her special qualities. You will now gain much by making a special study of one of her most subtle poems to discover how these qualities combine in a poem that could have been written by no one else. What picture of Death emerges from "Because I Could Not Stop for Death"? What is meant by his "civility"?

2. Are the objects that are passed on this journey described specifically or vaguely? What would the poem gain or lose if they were described otherwise? Were there any adjectives you thought particularly surprising? If so, which?

3. Where does the journey described in the poem end? What is the first indication of this destination?

4. Point out the use of exact and approximate rhyme in this poem. Describe the stanza form.

5. Point out features—attitude, the use of language, the use of simile and metaphor, stanza form, rhyme—that this poem has in common with other poems by Emily Dickinson that you have read, features that make her a unique poet.

FOR COMPOSITION

1. Write a composition in which you express your agreement or disagreement with one or both of the following statements about Emily Dickinson. Use details from her poems to support your opinions.

"Emily Dickinson loved words ardently. Her feeling about them amounted to veneration and her selection of them was ritualistic."

"Miss Dickinson lived in a world of paradox, for, while her eye was microscopic, her imagination dealt with mysteries and grandeurs. Ribbons and immortality were mingled in her mind, which passed from one to the other with the speed of lightning."

2. Write a composition in which you compare the treatment of death in Emily Dickinson's "Because I Could Not Stop for Death" and Bryant's "Thanatopsis." Consider the following points: Which poem is for you the more moving experience? Which poem do you think is more sensible in its attitude toward death? Support your statements with details and phrases from the poems.

ANALYSIS AND COMPOSITION

The Flowering of New England

The selections you have just studied belong to a period that is generally considered one of the greatest in American literature. New England during the 1830's, '40's, and '50's was remarkable not only for the number of fine writers it produced but for its intellectual excitement, its aliveness to books and ideas. Emerson, more than any other man, was the catalyzing force who fired the young men of his age with intellectual ideals and aspirations. But no one man alone awakened New England. The "flowering of New England" ·was one of those rare periods when innumerable factors combined to produce a great cultural age.

FROM ASPIRATION TO DOUBT

The keynote of this period is one of affirmation—affirmation of the potentialities of the individual and of the possibilities for unlimited freedom and progress. However, as the century passed the halfway mark and the nation drew closer to war, the conflict between ideals and realities became increasingly apparent.

1. What ideals did the transcendentalists—Emerson and Thoreau—hold up to the young men of New England? Cite specific passages to support your answers. Find passages from the poetry of Longfellow, Holmes, and Whittier which hold up ideals to their readers. How do the stories by Hawthorne and Melville cast doubts on these ideals? Judging from her poetry, what do you think Emily Dickinson's attitude was toward Emerson's writings?

2. Discuss the differences in thought between Emerson and Hawthorne, supporting your points with passages from the works of these writers.

3. On August 31, 1842, Hawthorne noted in his Journal, "Mr. Thorow [Thoreau] dined with us yesterday. He is a singular character—a young man with much of wild original stuff still remaining in him; and so far as he is sophisticated, it is in a way and method of his own. . . . Mr. Thorow is a keen and delicate observer of nature—a genuine observer, which, I suspect, is almost as rare a character as even an original poet; and Nature, in return for his love, seems to adopt him as her special child, and shows him secrets which few others are allowed to witness. . . . With all this he has more than a tincture of literature—a deep and true taste for poetry, especially the elder poets. . . . On the whole I find him a healthy and wholesome man to know." What might Hawthorne have added later when his distaste for the transcendentalists deepened? What kind of journal entry might Emerson or Thoreau

have written after reading several of Hawthorne's stories or Melville's "Bartleby the Scrivener"?

The literature of this period made the nation and the world aware of New England as a region with its own special traditions and customs. New England writers filled places such as Boston, Concord, Salem, and Walden Pond with a thousand literary associations, and readers have come to think of these places as they think of the London of the Elizabethan Age and the Florence of Dante and Petrarch. The writing of New England shows how good literature reaches out for the specific and the universal at the same time.

1. What do you learn of New England places and people from the selections in this unit? Make a list of nouns and adjectives that, judging from their literature, you would use to describe New Englanders. Explain how Emerson, Thoreau, Whittier, and Emily Dickinson exemplify the New England tradition of "plain living and high thinking."

2. How did writers such as Emerson, Thoreau, Hawthorne, Melville, and Dickinson make use of the specific in reaching out for universal significance?

ROMANTICISM

All the writers in this unit can be regarded as Romantics. Review the discussion of the Romantic movement on pages 89–92. Then consider the following questions.

1. Which selections depend on an appeal to the emotions? Which show an interest in the picturesque and unusual?

2. What does Emerson and Thoreau's attitude to nature have in common with that of Bryant and Cooper? Before answering, you may wish to reread Bryant's poem "I Broke the Spell That Held Me Long" (page 113) and the descriptive passage from Cooper's *The Deerslayer* (page 149).

3. One characteristic of Romanticism is the interest in a national literary and cultural tradition. Oliver Wendell Holmes called Emerson's lecture "The American Scholar" the "American intellectual Declaration of Independence." One difference between the Declaration of Independence and Emerson's address is that the political document emphasizes the *rights* of individuals and Emerson's speech stresses the *responsibilities* of an intellectual group. Identify the challenges Emerson offered to American scholars and writers; characterize the type of person he called "Man Thinking." Which writers of the period, in your opinion, come closest to Emerson's ideal? Which writers most clearly meet Emerson's call for uniquely American men of letters?

AMERICAN CLASSICS

Earlier in this book, you studied the contrast between classicism and Romanticism. The writers in this unit can all be considered Romantic writers but they are also the "classic" American authors, men who created monumental literary works. The word *classic* is difficult to define, but the famous French critic, Charles Sainte-Beuve, wrote a definition that has been widely quoted: "A true classic . . . is an author who has enriched the human mind, increased its treasure and caused it to advance a step; who has discovered some moral and not equivocal truth, or revealed some eternal passion in that heart where all seemed known and discovered; who has expressed his thought, observations, or invention, in no matter what form, only provided it be broad and great, refined and sensible, sane and beautiful in itself; who has spoken to all in his own peculiar style, a style . . . new and old, easily contemporary with all time."

1. Which writers in this unit do you think meet Sainte-Beuve's requirements for a classic author? In what respects do they meet them?

2. Which other writers you have read meet the requirements of Sainte-Beuve's definition? Defend your choices.

FOR COMPOSITION: THE FORMS OF DISCOURSE

While Emerson is best known as an author who inspired men—in his own way, a master of persuasive prose—he was also a master of exposition. In order to persuade men to accept his ideas, he had first to set forth these ideas. For example, in "The American Scholar" he had to make clear to his listeners just what kind of distinction he drew between Man Thinking and the "mere thinker." The second, third, and fourth paragraphs of this address (see pages 167–68)—in which he draws this distinction—are a good example of Emerson's use of expository prose. Reread these paragraphs carefully.

1. What means does Emerson use to present his ideas? Does he rely chiefly on details, on comparisons, on examples, or on none of these? As a student of English, you have probably had a good deal of experience in writing expository compositions on many subjects. What means of presenting facts or ideas do you share with Emerson?

2. Write an expository composition explaining one of the key ideas in a selection by Emerson or Thoreau. For example, the distinction between Man Thinking and the thinker, the importance of nature to the scholar, or the following quotation from *Walden:* "Shams and delusions are esteemed for soundest truths, while reality is fabulous" (page 192).

ART AND LITERATURE

Landscape painting, though it seeks to capture the flavor of a particular place, yet involves personal interpretation on the part of the artist. After examining the landscapes by Durand and Bierstadt on pages 225 and 229, compare them with photographs (in magazines, an encyclopedia, or geography book) of the Hudson River area or the Yosemite Valley. Write a composition in which you describe the differences between the painters' interpretations and the camera's eye view of the same landscapes.

TRAGEDY AND RENEWAL

Word over all, beautiful as the sky,
Beautiful that war and all its deeds of carnage must in time be
   utterly lost,
That the hands of the sisters Death and Night incessantly softly
   wash again, and ever again, this soiled world:
For my enemy is dead, a man divine as myself is dead. . . .
                             WALT WHITMAN

From April 12, 1861, when Confederate forces fired on Fort Sumter,
until April 9, 1865, when Lee surrendered to Grant at Appomattox, the
nation was torn by the worst internal conflict it has experienced. In an
evocative passage, Walt Whitman described the War Between the States:
"that many-threaded drama, with its sudden and strange surprises, its con-
founding of prophecies, its moments of despair, the dread of foreign interference, the interminable campaigns, the bloody battles, the mighty and
cumbrous and green armies, the drafts and bounties [of money]—the immense money expenditure, like a heavy-pouring constant rain—with, over
the whole land, the last three years of the struggle, an unending, universal
mourning-wail of women, parents, orphans . . ." When peace came, the
nation was like a patient recovering from his first crucial illness, ready
again to lead a healthy life but beyond the optimism that was possible before
this great experience of pain. Once again the nation could prosper and
expand, could again proclaim its "Manifest Destiny" to spread from sea
to sea, but it could not again proclaim the possibilities of life and of the
individual man with the buoyancy of the transcendentalists. Professor
Robert Spiller has written, "The story of American literature from 1865
to 1895 is that of a vast adjustment to a new set of conditions for living. . . .
Throughout the Western world, as in the United States, literature began to
pay less attention to general ideas and more to the immediate facts of life."
One sign of this trend was the great interest, after the war, in "local

color"—the special qualities of a particular area. Sarah Orne Jewett and Mary E. Wilkins Freeman wrote about New England; George Washington Cable and Joel Chandler Harris wrote about the South; Edward Eggleston, about the Middle West. By 1894, one popular author could state, "Everybody writes 'local' stories nowadays; it is as natural as the whooping cough."

Part of this movement from ideas to facts, the rise of *realism* and *naturalism,* will be considered in the next unit. Here, several important features of the period of transition—the War Between the States and the years immediately following—will be considered.

LINCOLN AND LEE: THE LITERATURE OF GREAT MEN

Out of the conflict, two figures arose who came to symbolize both the heroism and the tragedy of the war. One was a former small-town lawyer who became one of the country's greatest presidents. The other was an aristocrat, the product of the South's Cavalier tradition (page 4), a military genius who displayed not only brilliance of mind but greatness of character in his conduct of the war. Of the two men, Lincoln was the more polished writer, the more conscious shaper of words. An eager reader and a keen student of oratory, Lincoln worked hard to improve his writing. His teacher, Mentor Graham, said of him that he sometimes strove for hours to arrive at "the best way of three to express an idea." Lee was not as eloquent a writer, and his words do not soar like Lincoln's. Yet the cadences of his writing reveal a man of strength and sensitivity who commanded devotion in the South and respect in the North.

The ruins of Richmond, Virginia (1865), as seen from across the James River.

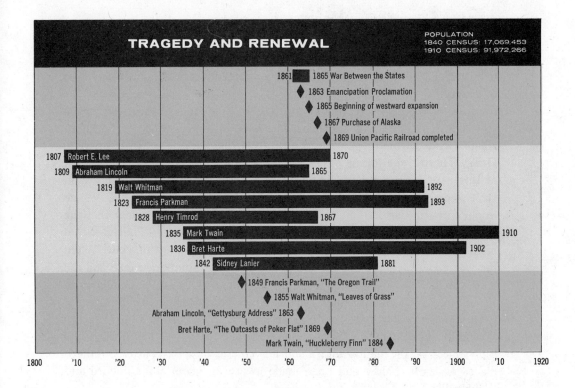

TRAGEDY AND RENEWAL

POPULATION
1840 CENSUS: 17,069,453
1910 CENSUS: 91,972,266

1861 [ ] 1865 War Between the States
1863 Emancipation Proclamation
1865 Beginning of westward expansion
1867 Purchase of Alaska
1869 Union Pacific Railroad completed

1807 Robert E. Lee 1870
1809 Abraham Lincoln 1865
1819 Walt Whitman 1892
1823 Francis Parkman 1893
1828 Henry Timrod 1867
1835 Mark Twain 1910
1836 Bret Harte 1902
1842 Sidney Lanier 1881

1849 Francis Parkman, "The Oregon Trail"
1855 Walt Whitman, "Leaves of Grass"
Abraham Lincoln, "Gettysburg Address" 1863
Bret Harte, "The Outcasts of Poker Flat" 1869
Mark Twain, "Huckleberry Finn" 1884

1800 '10 '20 '30 '40 '50 '60 '70 '80 '90 1900 '10 1920

THE POETRY OF THE WAR

Another significant part of the literature to come out of the war is the poetry written by two of America's greatest authors, Herman Melville and Walt Whitman. Wilfred Owen, an English poet of World War I, wrote of his own work, "My subject is war and the pity of war. The poetry is in the pity." These sentences are relevant to the war poetry of Melville and Whitman also. From such poems as "Malvern Hill" (page 256) and "Beat! Beat! Drums!" (page 319), the war emerges as a tragic, divisive event, a holocaust that struck the nation. As Melville wrote in retrospect, "All may go well for many a year,/ But who can think without a fear/ Of horrors that happen so?"

THE SOUTHERN LITERARY TRADITION: OLD AND NEW

While New England was experiencing an intellectual and literary resurgence (page 161), the South was creating its own literary tradition. Southerners were much aware that they were the inheritors of the Cavalier tradition. In 1843, one anonymous Southerner wrote: "A chivalrous daring —a spirit that may break but never bend—an estimate placed on individual honor which counts all else as dust in the balance—virtues such as these are the peculiar birthright of the Southern people. They hold them as a direct inheritance from that bold race of Cavaliers who emigrated from all parts of Europe and settled in the Southern colonies." Southern fiction depicted Southern society as one of the finest flowerings of civilization. Southern poetry vividly dramatized the Southerner's devotion to honor and his love of beauty.

Southern writers were drawn together by a strong sense of sharing a special way of life. This sense became even stronger when the Southern states seceded from the Union to form the Confederate states of America. Henry Timrod, the foremost poet of the Confederacy, celebrated the birth of this new nation and predicted a bright future for it. "Our happy land shall sleep/ In a repose as deep/ As if we lay intrenched behind/ Whole leagues of Russian ice and Arctic storm!" When it became clear that the Confederacy could not lead a happy, separate existence, Timrod wrote memorable poems about the war from the Southern point of view. When the war ended, Timrod memorialized the defeated Southern cause and the men who had died for it in his most famous poem, "Ode on the Confederate Dead" (page 305). It remained for another Southern writer to call attention to the Southern literary tradition as an important part of the national tradition. With such poems as "Song of the Chattahoochee," Sidney Lanier won the respect of the nation and made all Americans as aware of Southern places as, earlier, they had been made aware of Salem and Concord and Walden Pond by New England writers.

While both Timrod and Lanier were notable poets, most critics agree that the Southern literary tradition has found its finest expression in the twentieth century, in the works of such writers as William Faulkner (page 536), John Crowe Ransom (page 658), Katharine Anne Porter (page 559), Eudora Welty (page 599), and Thomas Wolfe (page 684). These are among the most distinguished poets, novelists, and essayists of our time. All have won a national and even an international fame. One has received a Nobel prize in literature. But all have written out of a deep sense of what it is to be a Southerner, part of a special region of the country with strong traditions and values.

WHITMAN: TRANSCENDENTALIST AND NATIONALIST

Whitman's importance as a poet of the war has already been considered. He is important as well as a poet who gave eloquent expression to transcendentalist beliefs and in many of his poems stressed the relationship between the outer world and the inner life. Whitman is also America's foremost nationalist poet, who reminded Americans again and again that they were a special people, creating new traditions, new literary and artistic forms, a completely new way of looking at the world. He stressed the relationship between the national spirit and the spirit of democracy: ". . . the genius of the United States is not best or most in its executives, or legislatures, nor

A California miner (about 1865).

in its ambassadors or authors or colleges or churches or parlors, nor even in its newspapers or inventors . . . but always most in the common people." After the divisive war, it was Whitman, more than any other writer, who expressed a sense of union, of one nation moving toward a future of greatness.

THE TRADITION OF THE FRONTIER

After the war, many Americans were looking not to the North or to the South, but to the West and its frontier, to give them a sense of national identity. Whitman celebrated the Western movement, the reaching out for new lands, new opportunities, and freedom, in his poem "Pioneers! O Pioneers!": "All the pulses of the world,/ Falling in they beat for us, with the Western movement beat,/ Holding single or together, steady moving to the front. . . ."

Forty years before the War Between the States, James Fenimore Cooper made important use of frontier types in his fiction (page 93). But Cooper's Natty Bumppo was an idealized frontiersman, the embodiment of the Romantic idea that the primitive man is the naturally good man. Later writers who used frontier types did not idealize them in the same way. Rather, they gave such types a larger-than-life quality. A frontiersman like Davy Crockett encouraged literary men to see Westerners as rough giants when he wrote of himself, "I'm that same David Crockett, fresh from the backwoods, half-horse, half-alligator, a little touched with the snapping turtle; can wade the Mississippi, leap the Ohio, ride a streak of lightning, slip without a scratch down a honey locust; can whip my weight in wildcats—and if any gentleman pleases, for a ten-dollar bill, he may throw in a panther." Over the years, the image of the West developed as a place where men grew taller, did bigger things, told bigger lies, made bigger jokes, than in the East. Many Americans began to regard Western attitudes and the Western way of doing things as being most truly American. The raw West was contrasted with the effete East, and a young boisterous America was held up against an aging, decadent Europe. When Mark Twain wrote a book about his trip to Europe and the Holy Land (page 350), he poked fun at older civilizations and delighted the country. When Bret Harte wrote his colorful, sentimental stories about gold-mining towns, he was hailed as the new genius of American letters (page 340).

The tradition of the frontier is important to American literature not only because a number of important writers (including Bret Harte and, above all, Mark Twain) have drawn on it. It is important also because it signaled a rebirth of the democratic ideal and provided a means for Americans to unite after a bloody, divisive struggle. It gave Americans an image that both Northerners and Southerners could share. The nation could move into the future thinking of itself as essentially Western: young, vital, boisterous.

Homesteaders were an important part of the movement westward. Through their efforts new farms and settlements were created out of undeveloped frontier land.

ABRAHAM
LINCOLN
(1809–1865)

Abraham Lincoln is one of the great tragic figures of America. Portraits of his face reflect the sorrow attending the most calamitous event in American history. The facts of his death symbolize the suffering of the time in which he lived. The grandeur of his words is a visible sign of the greatness to which America can rise.

In an autobiography written in 1859, Lincoln described himself as "in height, six feet four inches, nearly; lean in flesh, weighing on an average one hundred and eighty pounds; dark complexion, with coarse black hair and gray eyes. No other marks or brands recollected." He also told how he was born in Kentucky, moved to Indiana as a boy, learned to "read, write, and cipher to the rule of three," but "picked up" little other education, "was raised to farm work," came to Illinois when he was twenty-one, clerked in a store, served as a captain of volunteers in the Black Hawk War, first ran for public office in 1832, "and was beaten. . . . The next and three succeeding biennial elections I was elected to the legislature. . . . During this legislative period I studied law, and removed to Springfield to practice it. . . . I was losing interest in politics when the repeal of the Missouri Compromise aroused me." In 1858, the Lincoln-Douglas debates made Lincoln a national figure. In 1861, the former farmer, store clerk, and small-town lawyer became the sixteenth President of the United States. After his assassination, an old friend of his summed up Lincoln's greatness: "He had passed through all the grades of society when he reached the Presidency, and he had found common sense a sure reliance and he put it into practice. . . . Lincoln was a great common man."

Abraham Lincoln is known almost as well for his homely and comic utterances as for his grand ones. Once, when someone asked him how it felt to be President, he answered, "You have heard about the man tarred and feathered and ridden out of town on a rail? A man in the crowd asked him how he liked it, and his reply was that if it wasn't for the honor of the thing, he would much rather walk." Of a long-winded acquaintance he said, "He can compress more words into the smallest ideas of any man I ever met." In his more serious speeches and writings, Lincoln followed the advice he gave in his 1862 Message to Congress: "In times like the present, men should utter nothing for which they would not willingly be responsible through time and in eternity." His place in American literature is made secure by the two greatest political speeches ever written by an American.

Gettysburg Address

Before Lincoln spoke at the battlefields of Gettysburg on November 19, 1863, Edward Everett delivered a two-hour speech. Lincoln had told a reporter that his own address would be "short, short, short," and, in fact, it lasted hardly five minutes. These ten sentences have been called "one of the great American poems."

FOUR SCORE and seven years ago our fathers brought forth on this continent a new nation, conceived in liberty, and dedicated to the proposition that all men are created equal.

Now we are engaged in a great civil war, testing whether that nation, or any nation so conceived and so dedicated, can long endure. We are met on a great battlefield of that war. We have come to dedicate a portion of that field as a final resting place for those who here gave their lives that that nation might live. It is altogether fitting and proper that we should do this.

But in a larger sense we cannot dedicate, we cannot consecrate, we cannot hallow this ground. The brave men, living and dead, who struggled here, have consecrated it far above our poor power to add or detract. The world will little note nor long remember what we say here, but it can never forget what they did here. It is for us, the living, rather, to be dedicated here to the unfinished work which they who fought here have thus far so nobly advanced. It is rather for us to be here dedicated to the great task remaining before us—that from these honored dead we take increased devotion to that cause for which they gave the last full measure of devotion; that we here highly resolve that these dead shall not have died in vain; that this nation, under God, shall have a new birth of freedom; and that government of the people, by the people, for the people, shall not perish from the earth.

The Gettysburg Address—a portion of Lincoln's handwritten copy.

Letter to Mrs. Bixby

In this letter, Lincoln spoke through Mrs. Bixby to all families that had lost a man or a boy in the war.

*Washington
November 21, 1864*

DEAR MADAM: I have been shown in the files of the War Department a statement of the Adjutant General of Massachusetts that you are the mother of five sons who have died gloriously on the field of battle. I feel how weak and fruitless must be any words of mine which should attempt to beguile you from the grief of a loss so overwhelming. But I cannot refrain from tendering to you the consolation that may be found in the thanks of the Republic they died to save. I pray that our heavenly Father may assuage the anguish of your bereavement, and leave you only the cherished memory of the loved and lost, and the solemn pride that must be yours to have laid so costly a sacrifice upon the altar of freedom. Yours, very sincerely and respectfully,

ABRAHAM LINCOLN

*To Mrs. Bixby,
Boston, Massachusetts*

The Second Inaugural Address

The morning of Lincoln's second inauguration was cold and stormy, but at noon, as the procession moved from the White House, the sun came out. In the crowd were numerous wounded soldiers, a visible sign of the wounds the nation had suffered in the war. Of Lincoln's speech, the London *Spectator* later wrote, "We cannot read it without a renewed conviction that it is the noblest political document known to history, and should have for the nation and the statesmen he left behind him something of a sacred and almost prophetic character."

March 4, 1865

FELLOW COUNTRYMEN: At this second appearing to take the oath of the Presidential office, there is less occasion for an extended address than there was at the first. Then a statement, somewhat in detail, of a course to be pursued, seemed fitting and proper. Now, at the expiration of four years, during which public declarations have been constantly called forth on every point and phase of the great contest which still absorbs the attention and engrosses the energies of the nation, little that is new could be presented. The progress of our arms, upon which all else chiefly depends, is as well known to the public as to myself; and it is, I trust, reasonably satisfactory and encouraging to all. With high hope for the future, no prediction in regard to it is ventured.

On the occasion corresponding to this four years ago, all thoughts were anxiously directed to an impending civil war. All dreaded it—all sought to avert it. While the inaugural address was being delivered from this place, devoted altogether to saving the Union without war, insurgent agents were in the city seeking to destroy it without war—seeking to dissolve the Union, and divide effects, by negotiation. Both parties deprecated war; but one of them would make war rather than let the nation survive; and the other would accept war rather than let it perish. And the war came.

One eighth of the whole population were colored slaves, not distributed generally over the Union, but localized in the Southern part of it. These slaves constituted a peculiar and powerful interest. All knew that this interest was, somehow, the cause of the war. To strengthen, perpetuate, and extend this interest was the object for which the insurgents would rend the Union, even by war; while the government claimed no right to do more than to restrict the territorial enlargement of it.

Neither party expected for the war the magnitude or the duration which it has already attained. Neither anticipated that the cause of the conflict might cease with, or even before, the conflict itself should cease. Each looked for an easier triumph and a result less fundamental and astounding. Both read the same Bible, and pray to the same God; and each invokes His aid against the other. It may seem strange that any men should dare to ask a just God's assistance in wringing their bread from the sweat of other men's faces; but let us judge not, that we be not judged.[1] The prayers of both could not be answered—that of neither has been answered fully.

The Almighty has his own purposes. "Woe unto the world because of offenses! for it must needs to be that offenses come; but woe to that man by whom the offense cometh." [2] If we shall suppose that American slavery is one of those offenses which, in the province of God, must needs come, but which, having continued through His appointed time, He now wills to remove, and that He gives to both North and South this terrible war, as the woe due to those by whom the offense came, shall we discern therein any departure from those

[1] **judge . . . judged:** Matthew 7:1.
[2] **Woe . . . cometh:** Matthew 18:7.

divine attributes which the believers in a living God always ascribe to Him? Fondly do we hope—fervently do we pray—that this mighty scourge of war speedily pass away. Yet, if God wills that it continue until all the wealth piled by the bondman's two hundred and fifty years of unrequited toil shall be sunk, and until every drop of blood drawn with the lash shall be paid by another drawn with the sword, as was said three thousand years ago, still it must be said, "The judgments of the Lord are true and righteous altogether." [1]

With malice toward none; with charity for all; with firmness in the right, as God gives us to see the right, let us strive on to finish the work we are in; to bind up the nation's wounds; to care for him who shall have borne the battle, and for his widow and his orphan—to do all which may achieve and cherish a just and lasting peace among ourselves, and with all nations.

[1] "The . . . altogether": Psalms 19:9.

FOR STUDY AND DISCUSSION

1. The Gettysburg Address has been called the greatest speech ever written by an American, yet, strangely enough, Lincoln's audience paid it little attention. What qualities in the Address might an audience miss when first hearing it? Do you think that it is more effective when it is spoken or read? Why?

2. If you were to choose one sentence of the Gettysburg Address as a key sentence, which would you choose? Show how the remainder of the address develops the ideas in that sentence.

3. The letter to Mrs. Bixby is both an official and a personal letter to a bereaved mother. Explain how Lincoln avoids the stilted phrases of most official letters and gives the impression that he is speaking not only to Mrs. Bixby but to all those who have lost loved ones in the war.

4. One of Lincoln's gifts was the ability to put into simple words the profound feelings that often defeat attempts at expression. Find passages in the Second Inaugural Address that have become part of the creed of our nation.

5. The Gettysburg Address and the Second Inaugural Address are great oratory partly because of Lincoln's masterful use of rhythm. Read aloud passages from the two addresses in which you consider the rhythm to be especially effective.

LANGUAGE AND VOCABULARY

Denotation refers to the strictly literal meaning of a word, its dictionary definition. *Connotation* refers to the implications and associations that the word has. For example, the denotation of *Gettysburg* is simply a town in Pennsylvania, but to many people *Gettysburg* is a word rich in connotations, since one of the most famous battles of the War Between the States took place there. To a Southerner, *Gettysburg* may call to mind the gallant charge led by General Pickett against the Northern forces. To a Northerner, *Gettysburg* may connote the steadfast valor of the Northern troops against fierce onslaughts. Thus to many people *Gettysburg* has not only a simple denotative meaning but rich emotional overtones as well. A good writer or speaker chooses his words carefully, keeping in mind not only their denotations but the emotions which may be produced by their connotations.

Discuss the connotations of the following italicized words from Lincoln's addresses. What emotions do you think he was trying to produce in his listeners?

1. "our *fathers* brought forth on this continent a new nation, conceived in liberty and *dedicated* to the proposition that all men are *created* equal."

2. "we cannot *dedicate,* we cannot *consecrate,* we cannot *hallow* this ground."

3. "Both parties deprecated war; but one of them would make war rather than let the nation *survive;* and the other would accept war rather than let it *perish.*"

4. "With *malice* toward none, with *charity* for all; with *firmness* in the *right,* as God gives us to see the right, let us *strive* on to finish the *work* we are in . . . ."

FOR COMPOSITION

Study the discussion of persuasive writing on page 29. Then write an analysis of either the Gettysburg Address or the Second Inaugural Address in terms of (1) the speaker, (2) the audience, (3) the occasion, and (4) the means of persuasion.

ROBERT E. LEE

(1807–1870)

In 1852, when Robert E. Lee was forty-five years old, he was appointed super-intendent of the United States Military Academy at West Point. He had already made a fine record for himself as a staff officer in the Mexican War. General Winfield Scott had given credit for the victory at Veracruz largely to Lee's "skill, valor, and undaunted energy." As a member of one of the most esteemed families of Virginia and the husband of a descendant of Martha Washington, as the possessor of one of the best military minds of his time, and as a soldier who in the Mexican War had risen from captain to colonel, Lee could expect a brilliant future in the Army of the United States.

In 1861, after Fort Sumter was fired upon, Lee was offered the command of the Federal Army. He refused, "stating, as candidly and as courteously as I could, that, though opposed to secession and deprecating war, I could take no part in an invasion of the Southern States." When he learned that Virginia had seceded from the Union, he was in a drugstore paying a bill. He told the druggist, "I am one of those dull creatures that cannot see the good of secession." Nevertheless he could not refuse to serve his beloved state. On April 23, 1861, he assumed command of the Virginia forces. At first, Lee served mainly as military advisor to Jefferson Davis, but in time his abilities made him the leading military figure of the South. The strategy of his campaigns has been admired and studied ever since. One of his biographers has written that Lee's greatness consisted of the ability "to look calmly beyond the dangers and perils of his immediate front to the situation in the whole theater of war, that power, in short, which takes Lee out of the ranks of the good ordinary and places him in the select band of the supreme generals." If he had a fault, it was his tendency to place too great a trust in his subordinates, who sometimes failed him.

Lee was not only a great but a greatly loved military leader. On two occasions before his troops began a charge, they shouted, "Lee to the rear," seized the reins of his horse, and forced him to a place of safety. On the sad day when he rode back from Appomattox after surrendering to Grant, soldiers crowded around him and cheered him. He told them, "Men, we have fought through this war together. I have done the best I could for you. My heart is too full to say more." Lee is in the uniquely American tradition of statesmen-writers. His writings have a place in our literature not only because of his achievements but because of what they reveal of the man.

Letter to His Son

January 23, 1861

I RECEIVED Everett's *Life of Washington*[1] which you sent me, and enjoyed its perusal. How his spirit would be grieved could he see the wreck of his mighty labors! I will not, however, permit myself to believe, until all ground of hope is gone, that the fruit of his noble deeds will be destroyed, and that his precious advice and virtuous example will so soon be forgotten by his countrymen. As far as I can judge by the papers, we are between a state of anarchy and civil war. May God avert both of these evils from us! I fear that mankind will not for years be sufficiently Christianized to bear the absence of restraint and force. I see that four states[2] have declared themselves out of the Union; four more will apparently follow their example. Then, if the border states are brought into the gulf of revolution, one half of the country will be arrayed against the other. I must try and be patient and await the end, for I can do nothing to hasten or retard it.

The South, in my opinion, has been aggrieved by the acts of the North, as you say. I feel the aggression and am willing to take every proper step for redress. It is the principle I contend for, not individual or private benefit. As an American citizen, I take great pride in my country, her prosperity and institutions, and would defend any state if her rights were invaded. But I can anticipate no greater calamity for the country than a dissolution of the Union. It would be an accumulation of all the evils we complain of, and I am willing to sacrifice everything but honor for its preservation. I hope, therefore, that all constitutional means will be exhausted before there is a resort to force. Secession is nothing but revolution. The framers of our Constitution never exhausted so much labor, wisdom, and forbearance in its formation, and surrounded it with so many guards and securities, if it was intended to be broken by every member of the Confederacy at will. It was intended for "perpetual union," so expressed in the preamble, and for the establishment of a government, not a compact, which can only be dissolved by revolution or the consent of all the people in convention assembled. It is idle to talk of secession. Anarchy would have been established, and not a government, by Washington, Hamilton, Jefferson, Madison, and the other patriots of the Revolution. . . . Still, a Union that can only be maintained by swords and bayonets, and in which strife and civil war are to take the place of brotherly love and kindness, has no charm for me. I shall mourn for my country and for the welfare and progress of mankind. If the Union is dissolved, and the government disrupted, I shall return to my native state and share the miseries of my people; and, save in defense, will draw my sword on none.

Letter to General Scott

In the following letter to General Winfield Scott, Chief of Staff of the Army, Lee resigned his commission. The innate courtesy and considerateness that underlay Lee's character shine through this formal document.

Arlington, Virginia
April 20, 1861

G ENERAL: Since my interview with you on the 18th inst., I have felt that I ought no longer to retain my commission in the

[1] **Everett's *Life of Washington*:** Edward Everett (1794–1865), noted American orator who spoke at Gettysburg before Lincoln delivered his famous address.

[2] **four states:** South Carolina, Mississippi, Florida, Alabama.

army. I therefore tender my resignation, which I request you will recommend for acceptance. It would have been presented at once but for the struggle it has cost me to separate myself from a service to which I have devoted the best years of my life, and all the ability I possessed.

During the whole of that time—more than a quarter of a century—I have experienced nothing but kindness from my superiors and a most cordial friendship from my comrades. To no one, General, have I been as much indebted as to yourself for uniform kindness and consideration, and it has always been my ardent desire to merit your approbation. I shall carry to the grave the most grateful recollections of your kind consideration, and your name and fame shall always be dear to me.

Save in defense of my native state, I never desire again to draw my sword.

Be pleased to accept my most earnest wishes for the continuance of your happiness and prosperity, and believe me, most truly yours,

R. E. LEE

Farewell to the Army of Northern Virginia

Headquarters
Army of Northern Virginia
April 10, 1865

AFTER FOUR YEARS of arduous service, marked by unsurpassed courage and fortitude, the Army of Northern Virginia has been compelled to yield to overwhelming numbers and resources.

I need not tell the survivors of so many hard-fought battles who have remained steadfast to the last that I have consented to this result from no distrust of them; but feeling that valor and devotion could accomplish nothing that would compensate for the loss that must have attended the continuance of the contest, I determined to avoid the useless sacrifice of those whose past services have endeared them to their countrymen. By the terms of the agreement, officers and men can return to their homes and remain until exchanged.

You may take with you the satisfaction that proceeds from the consciousness of duty faithfully performed, and I earnestly pray that a merciful God will extend to you His blessing and protection.

With an unceasing admiration of your constancy and devotion to your country, and a grateful remembrance of your kind and generous consideration of myself, I bid you all an affectionate farewell.

R. E. LEE, GENERAL

FOR STUDY AND DISCUSSION

1. What beliefs did Lee hold about secession? Judging from his letter to his son, what were his reasons for deciding finally to uphold the secessionists? What passages show his devotion to his native state?

In the letter, Lee refers to George Washington's "precious advice." To what passages in Washington's Farewell Address might Lee be referring?

2. Like Lincoln's letter to Mrs. Bixby, Lee's letter to General Scott is an official letter. Do you think that it reveals Lee as a person as well as an official? Explain.

3. Why do you think that Lee's farewell to his army is considered a great document in American history? How is it possible for a man to be great though apparently he has failed? In your opinion, what qualities of literary greatness does this document have?

4. Do you find any points of resemblance between Lee and Lincoln? What was the greatest difference between them?

FOR COMPOSITION

Write a composition in which you compare Lincoln and Lee as great Americans and as writers. Discuss their similarities and differences. Consider which was the better writer and support your opinion with reasons based on a careful reading of the selections.

HENRY TIMROD
(1828–1867)

In 1860, Henry Timrod published a first collection of poetry, but most of the poems were pale imitations of the English nature poet, William Wordsworth. Then the advent of the War Between the States provided Timrod with a mighty theme, and his poems grew in power and majesty. With works such as "Ode on the Confederate Dead," "Charleston," "A Cry to Arms," and "Carolina," Timrod became known as "the Laureate of the Confederacy." In a study of Southern poets, Professor E. W. Parks has written of Timrod: "Although sincerity and throbbing emotion beat through his words in passionate undertones, the passion never carries the verse into formlessness of thought or reference. Instead an almost classic coolness and restraint appears, from first to last, in his war poems . . . his best poems combine a clear distinction of line with a sense of rounded completeness."

The son of a bookseller, Timrod was born in Charleston, South Carolina, studied for a year and a half at the University of Georgia, then supported himself by tutoring the children of wealthy planters' families. It was a poor living, barely augmented by contributing to *Russell's Magazine,* a Southern literary journal edited by Paul Hamilton Hayne.

When the War broke out, Timrod enlisted in the Confederate Army, but in less than a year he was mustered out because of poor health. Unable to serve as a soldier, he placed his literary talent at the disposal of the Confederate cause. For a time he worked as a war correspondent and reported on the battle of Shiloh. All the while Timrod was writing poems that expressed the hopes and fears, the fortitude and militant spirit of the Confederacy, especially of his own beloved state. ("The despot treads thy sacred sands,/ Thy pines give shelter to his bands,/ Thy sons stand by with idle hands,/ Carolina! . . . Girt with such wills to do and bear,/ Assured in right, and mailed in prayer,/ Thou wilt not bow thee to despair,/ Carolina!")

In 1864, Timrod began to edit a newspaper in Columbia, South Carolina, but when Sherman's army captured and burned Columbia in February, 1865, Timrod was left destitute. The remaining years of his life were spent in poverty and increasing ill health. After his death, his poems were collected in a volume edited by his friend and fellow poet, Hayne.

Ode on the Confederate Dead

*Sung at the occasion of decorating the graves of the Confederate dead at
Magnolia Cemetery, Charleston, S.C., 1867.*

Sleep sweetly in your humble graves,
  Sleep, martyrs of a fallen cause;
Though yet no marble column craves
  The pilgrim here to pause.

In seeds of laurel in the earth   5
  The blossom of your fame is blown,
And somewhere, waiting for its birth,
  The shaft is in the stone!

Meanwhile, behalf the tardy years
  Which keep in trust your storied tombs,
Behold! your sisters bring their tears,   11
  And these memorial blooms.

Small tributes! but your shades will smile
  More proudly on these wreaths today,
Than when some cannon-molded pile   15
  Shall overlook this bay.

Stoop, angels, hither from the skies!
  There is no holier spot of ground
Than where defeated valor lies,
  By mourning beauty crowned!   20

Charleston

Charleston, South Carolina, the most important port in the South, depended
heavily on its trade with Europe. During the War Between the States, it was blockaded by Northern ships.

Calm as that second summer which precedes
  The first fall of the snow,
In the broad sunlight of heroic deeds,
  The city bides the foe.

As yet, behind their ramparts, stern and proud,   5
  Her bolted thunders sleep—
Dark Sumter,° like a battlemented cloud
  Looms o'er the solemn deep.

No Calpe° frowns from lofty cliff or scar
  To guard the holy strand;   10
But Moultrie° holds in leash her dogs of war
  Above the level sand.

7. **Sumter:** Fort Sumter is in Charleston harbor. 9. **Calpe:** an old name for the rock of
Gibraltar. The fort at Gibraltar has been traditionally the last outpost of western Europe on
the Mediterranean. 11. **Moultrie:** Fort Moultrie, like Fort Sumter, is located in Charleston
harbor.

And down the dunes a thousand guns lie couched,
    Unseen, beside the flood—
Like tigers in some Orient jungle crouched   15
    That wait and watch for blood.

Meanwhile, through streets still echoing with trade,
    Walk grave and thoughtful men,
Whose hands may one day wield the patriot's blade
    As lightly as the pen.   20

And maidens, with such eyes as would grow dim
    Over a bleeding hound,
Seem each one to have caught the strength of him
    Whose sword she sadly bound.

Thus girt without and garrisoned at home,   25
    Day patient following day,
Old Charleston looks from roof and spire and dome,
    Across her tranquil bay.

Ships, through a hundred foes, from Saxon lands
    And spicy Indian ports,   30
Bring Saxon steel and iron to her hands,
    And summer to her courts.

But still, along yon dim Atlantic line,
    The only hostile smoke
Creeps like a harmless mist above the brine,   35
    From some frail floating oak.

Shall the spring dawn, and she, still clad in smiles,
    And with an unscathed brow,
Rest in the strong arms of her palm-crowned isles,
    As fair and free as now?   40

We know not; in the temple of the Fates
    God has inscribed her doom;
And, all untroubled in her faith, she waits
    The triumph or the tomb.

FOR STUDY AND DISCUSSION

1. In "Ode on the Confederate Dead" the poet divides his attention between two groups. What is his feeling about each of these groups? In line 8, what does Timrod imply will happen in the future?

2. The "Ode on the Confederate Dead" honors "defeated valor." Do you share Timrod's high estimate of courage that is maintained even in the face of overwhelming defeat? Explain.

3. Show how in the first four stanzas of "Charleston" Timrod creates a sense of a war that seems very far away, yet very near. What similes does he employ to create a feeling of suspense? How is Timrod's love for Charleston reflected in this poem? Why does he refer to the city as "untroubled in her faith" (line 43)?

SIDNEY LANIER
(1842–1881)

"Music is Love in search of a word," Sidney Lanier wrote in his poem "The Symphony." Both poet and musician, Lanier sought to unite the two arts so that his poems would be a more explicit music and a more sensuously emotional speech. Several of his poems, most notably "The Symphony" and "The Marshes of Glynn," have been compared in their structure to musical compositions. In his influential critical work, *The Science of English Poetry,* Lanier developed a theory that analyzed poetry in terms of music and maintained that the principal difference between music and verse is "the difference between the scale of tones used in music and the scale of tones used by the human speaking voice." To a large extent, Lanier's poetry supports his poetic theory. While several of his poems have sometimes been criticized for a vagueness of meaning, his poetry is almost always effective and sometimes powerful music.

Born and raised in Macon, Georgia, Lanier showed an early talent for music. Teaching himself to play the flute, he became an ardent amateur musician. Until he entered Oglethorpe University at the age of fourteen, his education was irregular. He read a great deal of English romantic poetry and the novels of Sir Walter Scott, and became an admirer of the ideals of chivalry. After his graduation from the University, he worked there for a while as a tutor, but his choice of career was uncertain. While he himself was attracted to the arts of music and poetry, his father expected him to follow a more practical profession and study law. Then, when the War Between the States broke out, he enlisted in the Confederate Army. Captured near the end of the war, he spent five months in a Federal prison. These months of captivity had on his already fragile constitution an effect from which it never recovered. After the war, Lanier worked as a bookkeeper and clerk and then as a teacher. In 1869 he became a lawyer, but his poor health prevented him from having a large practice. He died of tuberculosis before reaching the age of forty.

It was during the war that Lanier decided he had a vocation for poetry, and in the years that followed, his poems began to appear in a number of magazines. In 1867, he published *Tiger-Lilies,* a novel based on his war experiences. When the Peabody Symphony Orchestra was organized in Baltimore in 1873, Lanier received an appointment as first flutist. By now he was beginning to acquire some fame as a poet and as a literary spokesman of the new South. In 1876, the appearance in *Lippincott's Magazine* of two of his most important poems, "Corn" and "The Symphony," convinced many readers that a talent not simply of regional but of national importance had emerged. That same year, Lanier was chosen to write the words for a cantata to be sung at the Philadelphia Centennial Exhibition. But as Lanier's poetic powers developed, his health grew worse. For a time he lived in Florida, then he returned to Baltimore to become a lecturer on literature, first at the Peabody Institute, then at Johns Hopkins University. In December, 1880—eight months before his death—"A Ballad of Trees and the Master" appeared in a magazine. The following month he began a series of lectures on the English novel at Johns Hopkins. By August, his health was so bad that he was forced to move to the mountains of North Carolina where, on September 7, he died.

Song of the Chattahoochee

The Chattahoochee River winds through Lanier's native state of Georgia.

Out of the hills of Habersham,°
Down the valleys of Hall,°
I hurry amain° to reach the plain,
Run the rapid and leap the fall,
Split at the rock and together again,   5
Accept my bed, or narrow or wide,
And flee from folly on every side
With a lover's pain to attain the plain
   Far from the hills of Habersham,
   Far from the valleys of Hall.   10

All down the hills of Habersham,
All through the valleys of Hall,
The rushes cried, *Abide, abide,*
The willful waterweeds held me thrall,°
The laving laurel turned my tide,   15
The ferns and the fondling grass said *Stay,*
The dewberry dipped for to work delay,
And the little reeds sighed, *Abide, abide,*
   Here in the hills of Habersham,
   Here in the valleys of Hall.   20

High o'er the hills of Habersham,
Veiling the valleys of Hall,
The hickory told me manifold
Fair tales of shade, the poplar tall
Wrought me her shadowy self to hold,   25
The chestnut, the oak, the walnut, the
   pine,

Overleaning, with flickering meaning and
   sign,
Said, *Pass not, so cold, these manifold*
   Deep shades of the hills of Habersham,
   These glades in the valleys of Hall.   30

And oft in the hills of Habersham,
And oft in the valleys of Hall,
The white quartz shone, and the smooth
   brook-stone
Did bar me of passage with friendly brawl,
   And many a luminous jewel lone   35
—Crystals clear or a-cloud with mist,
Ruby, garnet, and amethyst—
Made lures with the lights of streaming
   stone
   In the clefts of the hills of Habersham,
   In the beds of the valleys of Hall.   40
But oh, not the hills of Habersham,
And oh, not the valleys of Hall
Avail: I am fain° for to water the plain.
Downward the voices of Duty call—
Downward, to toil and be mixed with the
   main;°   45
The dry fields burn, and the mills are to
   turn,
And a myriad flowers mortally yearn,
And the lordly main from beyond the plain
   Calls o'er the hills of Habersham,
   Calls through the valleys of Hall.   50

1–2. **Habersham** and **Hall**: counties in Georgia.
3. **amain** (ə·mān'): at full speed. 14. **thrall** (thrôl): enslaved.

43. **I . . . fain**: poetic for "I desire" or "I wish."
45. **main**: poetic for the sea.

A Ballad of Trees and the Master

This poem is a striking and original retelling of Christ's experience in the Garden of Gethsemane, the scene of His agony and arrest. It has been set to music several times and is often sung by church choirs.

Into the woods my Master went,
Clean forspent, forspent.°
Into the woods my Master came,
Forspent with love and shame.
But the olives they were not blind to Him,   5
The little gray leaves were kind to Him:
The thorn tree had a mind° to Him
When into the woods He came.

Out of the woods my Master went,
And He was well content.   10
Out of the woods my Master came,
Content with death and shame.°
When Death and Shame would woo Him last,
From under the trees they drew Him last:
'Twas on a tree they slew him—last   15
When out of the woods He came.

2. **clean . . . forspent:** wholly exhausted. 7. **had a mind:** probably, regarded him kindly.
12. **Content . . . shame:** In other words, He was now willing to accept death on the cross.

FOR STUDY AND DISCUSSION

SONG OF THE CHATTAHOOCHEE

1. What is the mood of this poem? Is there only one mood throughout the poem, or is there a shift in mood? What comparison with man's life is implied in the last stanza?

2. Describe the stanza pattern of this poem. (For a discussion of stanza pattern, see page 233.) Would this poem seem as unified if it lacked an intricate stanza pattern? Explain. How does Lanier vary the refrain of the poem?

3. Find examples of alliteration and internal rhyme in the poem. What other devices of sound help to create a musical effect? (See pages 122 and 669 for discussions of sound devices.)

A BALLAD OF TREES AND THE MASTER

1. Describe the changing relationship of the master to the trees. How is the repeated mention of trees brought to a climax at the end of the poem?

2. Notice the repetition of "last" in the second stanza. What is the effect of this repetition? How does the third use of the word "last" differ from the first two uses?

LANGUAGE AND VOCABULARY

The word *Chattahoochee,* like many American place names, is Indian in origin. Other names, like *New York,* are adaptations of English names. Still others honor specific people. Using various reference works, report on the origin of the following American place names. (Two reference books are especially helpful: H. L. Mencken, *The American Language,* 4th edition; and Mitford M. Matthews, *A Dictionary of Americanisms.*)

Albany, New York
Chicago, Illinois
Cincinnati, Ohio
Louisiana
Massachusetts
Niagara Falls
Omaha, Nebraska
Pittsburgh, Pennsylvania
Pottawatomie County, Kansas
Sing Sing, New York

WALT WHITMAN
(1819–1892)

In 1855, a book of poems appeared that was like no poetry that had appeared before. Called *Leaves of Grass,* the book was the work of a strikingly original talent. The poems were sometimes declamatory and oratorical, sometimes quiet and meditative, at times almost embarrassingly sensuous, at other times dizzying in their abstractions and intellectual assumptions. These poems surged with life, and if their exuberance was sometimes tiring and they sometimes seemed to consist of an endless series of details, they were almost always compelling in their bold, electric use of language. They were exhilarating and exhausting at the same time, like a fiercely contested game, or a conversation with an immensely vital person. When Ralph Waldo Emerson read the poems, he wrote Whitman, "I greet you at the beginning of a great career, which yet must have had a long foreground somewhere for such a start."

Part of Whitman's "foreground," to which Emerson referred, lay in the poet's childhood; another part lay in his reading of Emerson. A carpenter's son, Whitman grew up on Long Island among Quakers, who were accustomed at their religious meetings to speak up about their feelings and experiences. As one literary historian has written, "The essential fact is that he lived as a child and youth among men and women who took inspiration with the utmost seriousness, believing that, no matter how simple and unlearned was the voice that spoke of God, what was said was worthy of regard and should never be suppressed. He was familiar with the distinction which every Quaker made between the 'I' which did the daily business of life, and the 'soul' which, feeling a concern to report on the inner life of the spirit, might speak out . . . in the language of inspiration, a language usually rhythmic." As a young man, Whitman heard Emerson lecture and read his essays, and they strengthened his own sense that his innermost thoughts were intimately connected with the basic workings of the universe.

Whitman was thirty-five when the first edition of *Leaves of Grass* appeared. His previous published writings had given little warning of the appearance of a major poet. He had written some awkward conventional poems, some undistinguished magazine articles, and a moralistic novel, *Franklin Evans, or the Inebriate: A Tale of the Times.* He had been a good reporter and a good editor of the Brooklyn *Daily Eagle,* from which he was fired because he was too vehement an advocate of the antislavery cause. A notebook he kept in the late 1840's reveals that he read widely, and that he was slowly, haltingly, in rhapsodic prose and rough poetry, shaping the themes and working toward the style of *Leaves of Grass*. It is generally believed that a trip to New Orleans and a three-month stay in that city, a period of his life about which little is definitely known, was important to his artistic development. Several biographers have imagined that an unhappy love affair in New Orleans was the emotional crisis that brought Whitman to poetic greatness, but there is no evidence of such an affair. It is almost certain that his long trip to New Orleans, during which he traveled on the Ohio and Mississippi Rivers and saw great stretches of countryside, gave him the sense of America's vastness and variety that pervades a great deal of his poetry.

In his preface to the first edition of *Leaves of Grass,* Whitman issued a call for greatness in American poetry. He himself, he implied, was the first truly American poet. Others were to follow. "The Americans of all nations at any time upon the earth have probably the fullest poetical nature. The United States themselves are essentially the greatest poem. . . . Here is not merely a nation but a teeming nation of nations. Here is action . . . magnificently moving in vast masses. Here is the hospitality which forever indicates heroes." Whitman's poetry celebrated the American masses, but it also celebrated the individual, the great man standing apart from the masses. As he wrote in a poem that first appeared in the 1867 edition of his great book, "One's-self I sing, a simple separate person,/ Yet utter the word Democratic, the word En-Masse." In his poetry, Whitman could make a sudden transition from a vast list of different kinds of people to a quiet, sensitive passage dealing with the most private emotions. He did not seem to feel that he was creating an incongruous effect. He sought to unite different objects, feelings, and beliefs rather than to make philosophic, logical, or moral distinctions. He wished to encompass the universe, and with his bursts of enthusiasm and genius, he often convinces the reader that he has succeeded.

In 1856 and in 1860, Whitman brought out further editions of *Leaves of Grass* in which he included additional poems and revised the poems that had appeared in the first edition. He worked as editor of the Brooklyn *Daily Times* and assisted his father as a carpenter. In December, 1862, Whitman learned that his brother had been wounded in the war, and he journeyed South to nurse him. For eight days he stayed with the troops in the battle area and carried away an unforgettable picture of war's suffering and desolation. Until 1867, he served as a volunteer nurse in Washington, spending every moment he could among the wounded. He helped dress their wounds, distributed gifts, wrote letters home, and did what he could to comfort the men. In 1865 and 1866, he published two pamphlets containing his war poems, *Drum-Taps* and *Sequel to Drum-Taps*. These poems, including his great elegy on Lincoln's death, "When Lilacs Last in the Dooryard Bloomed," were included in the 1867 edition of *Leaves of Grass.*

Leaves of Grass, as it turned out, was Whitman's chief occupation, his life's work. He wrote several prose works—*Democratic Vistas,* a restatement of his faith in American democracy already expressed in the preface to *Leaves of Grass,* and *Specimen Days*—but most of his time was taken up with building and reshaping his great monument to himself. In the 1871 edition, "Passage to India" was added. In the 1891 edition, he wrote a touching farewell to his own poetic imagination:

> "Good-by my Fancy!
> Farewell dear mate, dear love!
> I'm going away, I know not where,
> Or to what fortune, or whether I may ever see you again,
> So good-by my Fancy."

Earlier, in 1888, he had written a final prose commentary on his aims and achievement, "A Backward Glance O'er Traveled Roads." In that work, he noted that his poetic experiments had not had the acceptance he had hoped-for. "I have not gained the acceptance of my own time, but have fallen back on fond dreams of the future . . . from the worldly and business point of view *Leaves of Grass* has been a failure." But he was satisfied that he had been true to his purpose: to show "that the crowning growth of the United States is to be spiritual and heroic. To help start and favor that growth . . . is the beginning, middle, and final purpose of my poems." And he declared, "my volume is a candidate for the future." Thus far, the future has given Whitman an uneven treatment. He has been attacked for the looseness and repetitiveness of his verse, for his inconsistencies, and for his failure to make logical distinctions. But most critics recognize that at his best Whitman is one of the great poets of the world, that *Leaves of Grass* contains masterpieces, and that the personality behind the poetry—"affectionate, haughty, electrical"—is one of the most arresting ever to appear on the printed page.

FROM *Song of Myself*

"Song of Myself" is Whitman's essential poem, related to his other poems as the hub of a wheel is related to the spokes. It is Whitman's application of Emerson's advice, "Know thyself: every heart vibrates to that iron string." The various sections of this long poem are not always clearly related to each other, but what unites them all is the personality and soul of the poet, reaching out, discovering, exploring himself and, through himself, the world.

1

I celebrate myself, and sing myself,
And what I assume you shall assume,
For every atom belonging to me as good belongs to you.

I loaf and invite my soul,
I lean and loaf at my ease observing a spear of summer grass.   5

My tongue, every atom of my blood, formed from this soil, this air,
Born here of parents born here from parents the same, and their parents
     the same,
I, now thirty-seven years old in perfect health begin,
Hoping to cease not till death.

Creeds and schools in abeyance,   10
Retiring back a while sufficed at what they are, but never forgotten,°
I harbor for good or bad, I permit to speak at every hazard,
Nature without check with original energy.

11. **Creeds . . . forgotten:** Creeds and schools for a while sufficed, but are now retiring to the back of the poet's mind.

A child said *What is the grass?* fetching it to me with full hands,
How could I answer the child? I do not know what it is any more than he.   15

I guess it must be the flag of my disposition, out of hopeful green stuff woven.

Or I guess it is the handkerchief of the Lord,
A scented gift and remembrancer designedly dropped,
Bearing the owner's name someway in the corners, that we may see and re-
   mark, and say *Whose?*

Or I guess the grass is itself a child, the produced babe of the vegetation.

Or I guess it is a uniform hieroglyphic,   21
And it means, Sprouting alike in broad zones and narrow zones,
Growing among black folks as among white,
Kanuck, Tuckahoe, Congressman, Cuff, I give the same, I receive them the
   same.

And now it seems to me the beautiful uncut hair of graves.   25

Tenderly will I use you curling grass,
It may be you transpire from the breasts of young men,
It may be if I had known them I would have loved them,
It may be you are from old people, or from offspring taken soon out of their
   mothers' laps,
And here you are the mothers' laps.   30

This grass is very dark to be from the white heads of old mothers,
Darker than the colorless beards of old men,
Dark to come from under the faint red roofs of mouths.
O I perceive after all so many uttering tongues,
And I perceive they do not come from the roofs of mouths for nothing. 35

I wish I could translate the hints about the dead young men and women,
And the hints about old men and mothers, and the offspring taken soon out
   of their laps.

What do you think has become of the young and old men?
And what do you think has become of the women and children?

They are alive and well somewhere,   40
The smallest sprout shows there is really no death,
And if ever there was it led forward life, and does not wait at the end to
   arrest it,
And ceased the moment life appeared.
All goes onward and outward, nothing collapses,
And to die is different from what anyone supposed, and luckier.   45

·I believe a leaf of grass is no less than the journey-work of the stars,
And the pismire° is equally perfect, and a grain of sand, and the egg of the
    wren,
And the tree toad is a chef-d'œuvre° for the highest,
And the running blackberry° would adorn the parlors of heaven,
And the narrowest hinge in my hand puts to scorn all machinery,   50
And the cow crunching with depressed head surpasses any statue,
And a mouse is miracle enough to stagger sextillions of infidels. . . .

33

I understand the large hearts of heroes,
The courage of present times and all times,
How the skipper saw the crowded and rudderless wreck of the steamship,
    and Death chasing it up and down the storm,   55
How he knuckled tight and gave not back an inch, and was faithful of days
    and faithful of nights,
And chalked in large letters on a board, *Be of good cheer, we will not desert
    you;*
How he followed with them and tacked° with them three days and would
    not give it up,
How he saved the drifting company at last,
How the lank loose-gowned women looked when boated from the side of
    their prepared graves,   60
How the silent old-faced infants and the lifted sick, and the sharp-lipped
    unshaved men;
All this I swallow, it tastes good, I like it well, it becomes mine,
I am the man, I suffered, I was there. . . .

35

Would you hear of an old-time sea fight?°
Would you learn who won by the light of the moon and stars?   65
List to the yarn, as my grandmother's father the sailor told it to me.

Our foe was no skulk in his ship I tell you (said he),
His was the surly English pluck, and there is no tougher or truer, and never
    was, and never will be;
Along the lowered eve he came horribly raking us.

    47. **pismire:** ant. 48. **chef-d'œuvre:** masterpiece. 49. **running blackberry:** the black-
berry sends out runners in the ground. 58. **tacked:** navigated by making a series of turns
into the wind. 64. **Would . . . sea fight:** Whitman is speaking of the famous sea battle during
the Revolutionary War between the *Bonhomme Richard,* under the command of John Paul
Jones, and the British warship *Serapis.*

We closed with him, the yards entangled, the cannon touched, 70
My captain lashed fast with his own hands.

We had received some eighteen pound shots under the water,
On our lower gun deck two large pieces had burst at the first fire, killing
    all around and blowing up overhead.

Fighting at sundown, fighting at dark,
Ten o'clock at night, the full moon well up, our leaks on the gain, and five
    feet of water reported, 75

The master-at-arms° loosing the prisoners confined in the afterhold to give
    them a chance for themselves.

The transit to and from the magazine° is now stopped by the sentinels,
They see so many strange faces they do not know whom to trust.

Our frigate takes fire,
The other asks if we demand quarter? 80
If our colors are struck and the fighting done?

Now I laugh content, for I hear the voice of my little captain,
We have not struck, he composedly cries, *we have just begun our part of
    the fighting.*

Only three guns are in use,
One is directed by the captain himself against the enemy's mainmast, 85
Two well served with grape and canister° silence his musketry and clear
    his decks.

The tops alone second the fire of this little battery, especially the main-
    top,
They hold out bravely during the whole of the action.

Not a moment's cease,
The leaks gain fast on the pumps, the fire eats toward the powder maga-
    zine. 90

One of the pumps has been shot away, it is generally thought we are sinking.

Serene stands the little captain,
He is not hurried, his voice is neither high nor low,
His eyes give more light to us than our battle lanterns.

Toward twelve there in the beams of the moon they surrender to us. 95

---

76. **master-at-arms:** petty officer assigned to police duty.   77. **magazine:** a storeroom where
ammunition and explosives are kept.   86. **grape and canister:** kinds of shot that are packed
in cannon balls and scatter when fired.

36

Stretched and still lies the midnight,
Two great hulls motionless on the breast of the darkness,
Our vessel riddled and slowly sinking, preparations to pass to the one we
   have conquered,
The captain on the quarter-deck coldly giving his orders through a counte-
   nance white as a sheet,
Nearby the corpse of the child that served in the cabin,   100
The dead face of an old salt with long white hair and carefully curled whis-
   kers,
The flames spite of all that can be done flickering aloft and below,
The husky voices of the two or three officers yet fit for duty,
Formless stacks of bodies and bodies by themselves, dabs of flesh upon
   the masts and spars,
Cut of cordage, dangle of rigging, slight shock of the soothe of waves,   105
Black and impassive guns, litter of powder parcels, strong scent,
A few large stars overhead, silent and mournful shining,
Delicate sniffs of sea breeze, smells of sedgy grass and fields by the shore,
   death messages given in charge to survivors,
The hiss of the surgeon's knife, the gnawing teeth of his saw,
Wheeze, cluck, swash of falling blood, short wild scream, and long, dull,
   tapering groan,   110
These so, these irretrievable.

52

The spotted hawk swoops by and accuses me, he complains of my gab and
   my loitering.

I too am not a bit tamed, I too am untranslatable,
I sound my barbaric yawp over the roofs of the world.

The last scud of day holds back for me,   115
It flings my likeness after the rest and true as any on the shadowed wilds,
It coaxes me to the vapor and the dusk.

I depart as air, I shake my white locks at the runaway sun,
I effuse° my flesh in eddies, and drift it in lacy jags.

I bequeath myself to the dirt to grow from the grass I love,   120
If you want me again look for me under your boot soles.

You will hardly know who I am or what I mean,
But I shall be good health to you nevertheless,
And filter and fiber your blood.

Failing to fetch me at first keep encouraged,   125
Missing me one place search another,
I stop somewhere waiting for you.

   119. **effuse:** pour out, exude.

FOR STUDY AND DISCUSSION

1. Do you like or dislike the person you meet in this poem? Why? Why do you think "Song of Myself" has been called Whitman's essential poem?

2. You have probably recognized that "Song of Myself" is different from most poems you have read. Describe some of the ways it is different.

3. Do you think that if "Song of Myself" were run together as a series of prose paragraphs instead of being divided into verse lines, it would be considered poetry? Why or why not?

4. Whitman shared Emerson's belief in the interrelation of all things. Find passages that express this idea.

5. As a poet, Whitman was particularly aware of the wonders of the five senses. Find examples in "Song of Myself" of his enjoyment of each of the senses.

6. What evidence do you find in "Song of Myself" that Whitman worked as a reporter? In your opinion, would Walt Whitman have made a good short-story writer? Give reasons for your answer.

7. In "Song of Myself," Whitman not only writes a new kind of poetry but also helps his readers to understand what kind of poetry he is creating. One example is lines 12–13, which indicate his intention to let his poetry flow naturally. Find other lines that are indications of Whitman's intentions. Do you think he succeeds in carrying out these intentions? Explain.

FREE VERSE

Free verse is verse without a regular pattern of meter and usually without rhyme. (For discussions of meter, see pages 116 and 204.) While Whitman was not the first poet to write free verse, it was he who more than any other poet established free verse as an important, acceptable kind of poetic rhythm. In poems such as "Song of Myself," "When Lilacs Last in the Dooryard Bloomed," "Passage to India," and "Out of the Cradle Endlessly Rocking," Whitman showed that free verse can be a medium for great poetry.

In adapting this loose, irregular form (which some critics complain is not really poetry at all), Whitman strove to create a new, peculiarly American kind of poetry. He wished to free poetry of the restraints set on it by Old World conventions. A poem, he thought, should develop as naturally as a tree or a flower. Its rhythms should not be imposed by a metrical pattern but should grow out of the poet's ideas and feelings. Whitman compared free verse to an ocean: "Its verses are the liquid, billowy waves, ever rising and falling, perhaps sunny and smooth, perhaps wild with storm, always moving, always alike in their nature as rolling waves, but hardly any two alike in size or measure [meter] . . ." Later poets writing in free verse—such as Carl Sandburg (page 626), Wallace Stevens (page 647), and William Carlos Williams (page 652)—owe a great deal to Whitman's pioneering efforts.

T. S. Eliot, a poet who wrote a good deal of free verse, said that no verse is really free "for the man who wants to do a good job." For the skilled poet, free verse is not a means of escaping the responsibilities of craftsmanship but of meeting them in a different way. As Karl Shapiro and Robert Beum point out, free verse is not simply prose divided into poetic lines. "Good free verse is always more concentrated and almost always less direct than prose."

LANGUAGE AND VOCABULARY

The words that Whitman chooses are almost always vigorous and sometimes startling. Many of his unusual words startle by their very simplicity. These are not long and learned words but sturdy, homely words that reflect his interest in the simple pursuits of everyday life. Two examples are the following italicized words: "I guess it is the *handkerchief* of the Lord" (line 17), and "And the narrowest *hinge* in my hand puts to scorn all machinery" (line 50).

Find five other examples of Whitman's use of homely words. Then, on the basis of the examples presented, discuss the suitability of such words in poetry. In your discussion, consider the following questions:

1. Are some words naturally "poetic" and other words naturally "unpoetic"?

2. Does a surprising word or phrase always improve the quality of a poem?

3. Are long, learned words out of place in a poem?

4. To what extent does the choice of words in a poem depend on the poem's subject matter?

5. To what extent does the choice of words in a poem reflect the poet's personality?

Mannahatta

Whitman loved old Indian names. He called his native Long Island "Paumanok," and to New York City he gave the name "Mannahatta." The name is perpetuated in Manhattan Island, which is the heart of the city today.

I was asking for something specific and perfect for my city,
Whereupon lo! upsprang the aboriginal° name.

Now I see what there is in a name,° a word, liquid, sane, unruly, musical, self-sufficient,
I see that the word of my city is that word from of old,
Because I see that word nested in nests of water bays, superb,⠀⠀⠀⠀⠀5
Rich, hemmed thick all around with sailships and steamships, an island sixteen miles long, solid-founded,
Numberless crowded streets, high growths of iron, slender, strong, light, splendidly uprising toward clear skies,
Tides swift and ample, well loved by me, toward sundown,
The flowing sea currents, the little islands, larger adjoining islands, the heights, the villas,
The countless masts, the white shore steamers, the lighters, the ferryboats, the black sea steamers well modeled,⠀⠀⠀⠀⠀10
The downtown streets, the jobbers' houses of business, the houses of business of the ship merchants and money brokers, the river streets,
Immigrants arriving, fifteen or twenty thousand in a week.
The carts hauling goods, the manly race of drivers of horses, the brown-faced sailors.
The summer air, the bright sun shining, and the sailing clouds aloft,
The winter snows, the sleigh bells, the broken ice in the river, passing along up or down with the flood tide or ebb tide,⠀⠀⠀⠀⠀15
The mechanics of the city, the masters, well formed, beautiful-faced, looking you straight in the eyes,
Trottoirs° thronged, vehicles, Broadway, the women, the shops and shows,
A million people—manners free and superb—open voices—hospitality—the most courageous and friendly young men,
City of hurried and sparkling waters! city of spires and masts!
City nested in bays! my city!⠀⠀⠀⠀⠀20

2. **aboriginal** (ab′ə·rij′ə·nəl): first.⠀3. **what . . . name:** Whitman here comments playfully on the famous lines in Shakespeare's *Romeo and Juliet* (Act II, Scene ii): "Oh, be some other name!/ What's in a name? That which we call a rose/ By any other name would smell as sweet."
17. **Trottoirs** (trä·twär′): sidewalks (French).

When I Heard the Learned Astronomer

When I heard the learned astronomer,
When the proofs, the figures, were ranged in columns before me,
When I was shown the charts and diagrams, to add, divide, and measure them,
When I sitting heard the astronomer where he lectured with much applause in the lecture room,
How soon unaccountable I became tired and sick, 5
Till rising and gliding out I wandered off by myself,
In the mystical moist night air, and from time to time,
Looked up in perfect silence at the stars.

Beat! Beat! Drums!

Beat! beat! drums!—blow! bugles! blow!
Through the windows—through doors—burst like a ruthless force,
Into the solemn church, and scatter the congregation,
Into the school where the scholar is studying;
Leave not the bridegroom quiet—no happiness must he have now with his bride, 5
Nor the peaceful farmer any peace, ploughing his field or gathering his grain,
So fierce you whirr and pound you drums—so shrill you bugles blow.

Beat! beat! drums!—blow! bugles! blow!
Over the traffic of cities—over the rumble of wheels in the streets;
Are beds prepared for sleepers at night in the houses? no sleepers must sleep in those beds, 10
No bargainers' bargains by day—no brokers or speculators—would they continue?
Would the talkers be talking? would the singer attempt to sing?
Would the lawyer rise in the court to state his case before the judge?
Then rattle quicker, heavier drums—you bugles wilder blow.

Beat! beat! drums!—blow! bugles! blow! 15
Make no parley—stop for no expostulation,
Mind not the timid—mind not the weeper or prayer,
Mind not the old man beseeching the young man,
Let not the child's voice be heard, nor the mother's entreaties,
Make even the trestles to shake the dead where they lie awaiting the hearses, 20
So strong you thump O terrible drums—so loud you bugles blow.

MANNAHATTA

1. What varied aspects of the city appeal to Whitman? Compare Whitman's picture of New York with cities you know. Judging from the poem, in what respects have cities changed since Whitman's time? In what respects have they remained the same? Do you think the passage of time has made the poem old-fashioned, or do you think that Whitman so captures the essential qualities of a large city that the poem remains modern?

2. Some critics of Whitman's poetry have accused him of piling detail on detail without organization or progression. Do you think this criticism applies to "Mannahatta"? Is the poem merely a random collection of details, or do the details combine to make a unified work of art?

WHEN I HEARD THE LEARNED ASTRONOMER

1. What ironical meaning does "learned" have in this poem?

2. Can you sum up the meaning of this poem in a sentence or two? What attitude toward knowledge does the astronomer represent? How does the poet disagree with this attitude? Is the meaning of this poem clear without being directly stated? Explain.

3. Compare Whitman's poem with your summary. Which is the more powerful statement? Why?

BEAT! BEAT! DRUMS!

1. What effects of the war are especially emphasized? Which of these effects seem to you the most devastating?

2. "Beat! Beat! Drums!" has a somewhat different rhythm from the other poems by Whitman you have read. Read aloud part of another poem by Whitman. Then read aloud the first section of "Beat! Beat! Drums!" How would you describe the difference in rhythm? Is the rhythm of "Beat! Beat! Drums!" appropriate to the poem's meaning? Illustrate your answer with references to specific lines. In the light of this comparison, would you say that Whitman, despite the fact that his poems are in free verse, was skilled in using poetic rhythms? Explain.

When Lilacs Last in the Dooryard Bloomed

Walt Whitman was at home in Brooklyn, visiting his family, when news came of President Lincoln's assassination on Good Friday, 1865. By Monday, Whitman was back in Washington. He witnessed the somber procession of thirty thousand battle-worn veterans passing slowly with banners furled and rifles reversed as the many bands sounded the dead march. Lilacs, then in full bloom in Washington, were heaped about the coffin as it lay in the rotunda of the Capitol. Later, in the funeral train carrying it to burial in Springfield, Illinois, the coffin would pass through Baltimore, Philadelphia, New York, Buffalo, Cleveland, and Chicago. Whitman expressed his personal grief at the nation's loss in "When Lilacs Last in the Dooryard Bloomed."

1

When lilacs last in the dooryard bloomed,
And the great star early dropped in the western sky in the night,
I mourned, and yet shall mourn with ever-returning spring.

Ever-returning spring, trinity sure to me you bring,
Lilac blooming perennial and drooping star in the west,°   5
And thought of him I love.

5. **drooping . . . west:** Venus, the western star.

2

O powerful western fallen star!
O shades of night—O moody, tearful night!
O great star disappeared—O the black murk that hides the star!
O cruel hands that hold me powerless—O helpless soul of me!   10
O harsh surrounding cloud that will not free my soul.

3

In the dooryard fronting an old farmhouse near the white-washed palings,
Stands the lilac-bush tall-growing with heart-shaped leaves of rich green,
With many a pointed blossom rising delicate, with the perfume strong I love,
With every leaf a miracle—and from this bush in the dooryard,   15
With delicate-colored blossoms and heart-shaped leaves of rich green,
A sprig with its flower I break.

4

In the swamp in secluded recesses,
A shy and hidden bird is warbling a song.

Solitary the thrush,°   20
The hermit withdrawn to himself, avoiding the settlements,
Sings by himself a song.
Song of the bleeding throat,
Death's outlet song of life (for well dear brother I know,
If thou wast not granted to sing thou would'st surely die).   25

5

Over the breast of the spring, the land, amid cities,
Amid lanes and through old woods, where lately the violets peeped from the
    ground, spotting the gray debris,
Amid the grass in the fields each side of the lanes, passing the endless grass,
Passing the yellow-speared wheat, every grain from its shroud in the dark-
    brown fields uprisen,
Passing the apple-tree blows of white and pink in the orchards,   30
Carrying a corpse to where it shall rest in the grave,
Night and day journeys a coffin.

6

Coffin that passes through lanes and streets,
Through day and night with the great cloud darkening the land,
With the pomp of the inlooped flags with the cities draped in black,   35
With the show of the States themselves as of crepe-veiled women standing,
With processions long and winding and the flambeaus° of the night,
With the countless torches lit, with the silent sea of faces and the unbared
    heads

20. **thrush:** The hermit thrush is noted for its beautiful song.   37. **flambeaus:** torches.

With the waiting depot, the arriving coffin, and the somber faces,
With dirges through the night, with the thousand voices rising strong and
    solemn,   40
With all the mournful voices of the dirges poured around the coffin,
The dim-lit churches and the shuddering organs—where amid these you
    journey,
With the tolling tolling bells' perpetual clang,
Here, coffin that slowly passes,
I give you my sprig of lilac.   45

7

(Nor for you, for one alone,
Blossoms and branches green to coffins all I bring,
For fresh as the morning, thus would I chant a song for you O sane and
    sacred death.
All over bouquets of roses,
O death, I cover you over with roses and early lilies,   50
But mostly and now the lilac that blooms the first,
Copious I break, I break the sprigs from the bushes,
With loaded arms I come, pouring for you,
For you and the coffins all of you O death.)

8

O western orb sailing the heaven,   55
Now I know what you must have meant as a month since I walked,
As I walked in silence the transparent shadowy night,
As I saw you had something to tell as you bent to me night after night,
As you drooped from the sky low down as if to my side (while the other
    stars all looked on),
As we wandered together the solemn night (for something I know not what
    kept me from sleep),   60
As the night advanced, and I saw on the rim of the west how full you were
    of woe,
As I stood on the rising ground in the breeze in the cool transparent night,
As I watched where you passed and was lost in the netherward black of the
    night,
As my soul in its trouble dissatisfied sank, as where you sad orb,
Concluded, dropped in the night, and was gone.   65

9

Sing on there in the swamp,
O singer bashful and tender, I hear your notes, I hear your call,
I hear, I come presently, I understand you,
But a moment I linger, for the lustrous star has detained me,
The star my departing comrade holds and detains me.   70

10

O how shall I warble myself for the dead one there I loved?
And how shall I deck my song for the large sweet soul that has gone?
And what shall my perfume be for the grave of him I love?

Sea winds blown from east and west,
Blown from the Eastern sea and blown from the Western sea, till there on
    the prairies meeting,   75
These and with these and the breath of my chant,
I'll perfume the grave of him I love.

11

O what shall I hang on the chamber walls?
And what shall the pictures be that I hang on the walls,
To adorn the burial house of him I love?   80

Pictures of growing spring and farms and homes,
With the Fourth-month° eve at sundown, and the gray smoke lucid and
    bright,
With floods of the yellow gold of the gorgeous, indolent, sinking sun, burn-
    ing, expanding the air,
With the fresh sweet herbage under foot, and the pale green leaves of the
    trees prolific,
In the distance the flowing glaze, the breast of the river, with a wind-dapple
    here and there,   85
With ranging hills on the banks, with many a line against the sky, and
    shadows,
And the city at hand with dwellings so dense, and stacks of chimneys,
And all the scenes of life and the workshops, and the workmen homeward
    returning.

12

Lo, body and soul—this land,
My own Manhattan with spires, and the sparkling and hurrying tides, and
    the ships,   90
The varied and ample land, the South and the North in the light, Ohio's
    shores and flashing Missouri,
And ever the far-spreading prairies covered with grass and corn.

Lo, the most excellent sun so calm and haughty,
The violet and purple morn with just-felt breezes,
The gentle soft-born measureless light,   95
The miracle spreading bathing all, the fulfilled noon,
The coming eve delicious, the welcome night and the stars,
Over my cities shining all, enveloping man and land.

82. **Fourth-month:** April, when Lincoln was killed.

13

Sing on, sing on you gray-brown bird,
Sing from the swamps, the recesses, pour your chant from the bushes, 100
Limitless out of the dusk, out of the cedars and pines.

Sing on dearest brother, warble your reedy song,
Loud human song, with voice of uttermost woe.
O liquid and free and tender!
O wild and loose to my soul—O wondrous singer, 105
You only I hear—yet the star holds me (but will soon depart),
Yet the lilac with mastering odor holds me.

14

Now while I sat in the day and looked forth,
In the close of the day with its light and the fields of spring, and the farmers
    preparing their crops,
In the large unconscious scenery of my land with its lakes and forests, 110
In the heavenly aerial beauty (after the perturbed winds and the storms),
Under the arching heavens of the afternoon swift-passing, and the voices of
    children and women,
The many-moving sea tides, and I saw the ships how they sailed,
And the summer approaching with richness, and the fields all busy with
    labor,
And the infinite separate houses, how they all went on, each with its meals
    and minutia° of daily usages, 115
And the streets how their throbbings throbbed, and the cities pent—lo,
    then and there,
Falling upon them all and among them all, enveloping me with the rest,
Appeared the cloud, appeared the long black trail,
And I knew death, its thought, and the sacred knowledge of death.

Then with the knowledge of death as walking one side of me, 120
And the thought of death close-walking the other side of me,
And I in the middle as with companions, and as holding the hands of com-
    panions,
I fled forth to the hiding receiving night that talks not,
Down to the shores of the water, the path by the swamp in the dimness,
To the solemn shadowy cedars and ghostly pines so still. 125

And the singer so shy to the rest received me,
The gray-brown bird I know received us comrades three,
And he sang the carol of death, and a verse for him I love.

From deep secluded recesses,
From the fragrant cedars and the ghostly pines so still, 130
Came the carol of the bird.

115. **minutia:** small details; usually spelled "minutiae."

And the charm of the carol rapt me,
As I held as if by their hands my comrades in the night,
And the voice of my spirit tallied the song of the bird.

Come lovely and soothing death,   135
Undulate round the world, serenely arriving, arriving,
In the day, in the night, to all, to each,
Sooner or later delicate death.

Praised be the fathomless universe,
For life and joy, and for objects and knowledge curious,   140
And for love, sweet love—but praise! praise! praise!
For the sure-enwinding arms of cool-enfolding death.

Dark mother always gliding near with soft feet,
Have none chanted for thee a chant of fullest welcome?
Then I chant it for thee, I glorify thee above all,   145
I bring thee a song that when thou must indeed come, come unfalteringly.

Approach strong deliveress,
When it is so, when thou hast taken them I joyously sing the dead,
Lost in the loving floating ocean of thee,
Laved in the flood of thy bliss O death.   150

From me to thee glad serenades,
Dances for thee I propose saluting thee, adornments and feastings for thee,
And the sights of the open landscape and the high-spread sky are fitting,
And life and the fields, and the huge and thoughtful night.

The night in silence under many a star,   155
The ocean shore and the husky whispering wave whose voice I know,
And the soul turning to thee O vast and well-veiled death,
And the body gratefully nestling close to thee.

Over the treetops I float thee a song,
Over the rising and sinking waves, over the myriad fields and the prairies
wide,   160
Over the dense-packed cities all and the teeming wharves and ways,
I float this carol with joy, with joy to thee O death.

15

To the tally of my soul,
Loud and strong kept up the gray-brown bird,
With pure deliberate notes spreading filling the night.   165

Loud in the pines and cedars dim,
Clear in the freshness moist and the swamp perfume,
And I with my comrades there in the night.

While my sight that was bound in my eyes unclosed,
As to long panoramas of visions.   170

And I saw askant° the armies,
I saw as in noiseless dreams hundreds of battle flags,
Borne through the smoke of the battles and pierced with missiles I saw them,
And carried hither and yon through the smoke, and torn and bloody,
And at last but a few shreds left on the staffs (and all in silence),   175
And the staffs all splintered and broken.

I saw battle corpses, myriads of them,
And the white skeletons of young men, I saw them,
I saw the debris and debris of all the slain soldiers of the war,
But I saw they were not as was thought,   180
They themselves were fully at rest, they suffered not,
The living remained and suffered, the mother suffered,
And the wife and the child and the musing comrade suffered,
And the armies that remained suffered.

16

Passing the visions, passing the night,   185
Passing, unloosing the hold of my comrades' hands,
Passing the song of the hermit bird and the tallying song of my soul,
Victorious song, death's outlet song, yet varying ever-altering song,
As low and wailing, yet clear the notes, rising and falling, flooding the night,
Sadly sinking and fainting, as warning and warning, and yet again bursting
    with joy,   190
Covering the earth and filling the spread of the heaven,
As that powerful psalm in the night I heard from recesses,
Passing, I leave thee lilac with heart-shaped leaves,
I leave thee there in the dooryard, blooming, returning with spring.

I cease from my song for thee,   195
From my gaze on thee in the west, fronting the west, communing with thee,
O comrade lustrous with silver face in the night.

Yet each to keep and all, retrievements out of the night,
The song, the wondrous chant of the gray-brown bird,
And the tallying chant, the echo aroused in my soul,   200
With the lustrous and drooping star with the countenance full of woe,
With the holders holding my hand nearing the call of the bird,
Comrades mine and I in the midst, and their memory ever to keep, for the
    dead I loved so well,
For the sweetest, wisest soul of all my days and lands—and this for his dear
    sake,
Lilac and star and bird twined with the chant of my soul,   205
There in the fragrant pines and the cedars dusk and dim.

171. **askant:** distrustfully.

COMMENTARY

"When Lilacs Last in the Dooryard Bloomed" is an expression of Whitman's bereavement at Lincoln's death. Yet like many elegies, it is concerned with not just a single death, even of so great a man as Lincoln, but with the questions raised by death for the living. Three symbols dominate the poem: the lilacs that surrounded Lincoln's coffin; Venus, the western star; and a singing bird, the hermit thrush. Since lilacs bloom in the spring, the season of rebirth, the first symbol is a reminder both of life and death. The tragic quality of the assassination is heightened when it is contrasted to the time of year when all nature quickens with life. The lilacs emphasize the idea that, in the midst of life, death comes as an intruder.

Before Lincoln's death Whitman had thought that the western star, the second symbol of the poem, was a good omen for all Americans. For several March evenings after Lincoln's second inauguration, this star had shone so large and clear that Whitman had taken it as a sign of the ending of the war. Later he came to see it as a premonition of Lincoln's death. In the second section of the poem, the star becomes a symbol of the loss of a great man. ("O great star disappeared . . .")

The third symbol, the hermit thrush, is introduced in the fourth section of the poem. Representing the poet singing his elegy, the bird is described as "solitary . . . withdrawn to himself." Like the bird, the poet expresses a private sorrow. His work is not a public announcement but the solitary grieving of one man for another.

After the introduction of the basic symbols in the first four sections of the poem, Whitman describes the passage of Lincoln's coffin across the country. Notice the emphasis on new life springing out of "the gray debris" left by winter, on the new wheat, every grain rising "from its shroud in the dark-brown fields." Even the "long and winding" processions that mourn Lincoln are signs of life and accentuate the stillness of death. In the seventh section of the poem, Whitman states that his tribute is not made to Lincoln alone but to "coffins all" (to all who have died) and to death itself. The phrase "sane and sacred death" is the first hint that the poem will turn away from a mood of grief to one of resignation and an understanding of death's role in the universe. In section 8, the poem returns to thoughts of grief and mourning, symbolized by the western star from which—in section 9—the poet is summoned by the thrush, singing a woeful yet comforting song. The conflict between these symbols is resolved by Whitman's identification with the bird as he asks himself what sort of elegy he should write for Lincoln: "O how shall I warble myself for the dead one" (line 71). His answer is that he will present images of sundown on a wonderful spring day, scenes teeming with the life of the city and countryside. Sundown is a time of respite, a kind of halfway point between day and night, motion and rest. Whitman is at a similar halfway point as he moves from awareness of life to knowledge of death (see lines 120–25).

Once Whitman has decided on the kind of song appropriate for Lincoln's death, he is free to join the thrush's carol in celebration of *"lovely and soothing death,"* the *"strong deliveress"* from life's pain (see lines 135 and 147). Caught up in the song, the poet sees "as in noiseless dreams" the terrible slaughter of the war, only recently ended. But now he is able to accept these visions of slaughter because he perceives that death is not what it seemed. Only those who remain alive suffer, but the dead are "fully at rest, they suffered not" (see lines 177–84).

In the last section of the poem, Whitman has passed through his period of grief, sustained by the thrush's carol and his new understanding of death. Looking ahead to other experiences, he prepares to break off his elegy (lines 195–97). Here he comes closest to a personal reference to Lincoln, "the sweetest, wisest soul of all my days and lands" (line 204). In the final lines he pulls together the diverse strands of the poem: "Lilac and star and bird twined with the chant of my soul,/ There in the fragrant pines and the cedars dusk and dim."

The three dominant symbols of the poem have passed with Whitman through the dark night of his grief. Now they and what they represent—the riddle of death in the midst of life—are "twined with the chant of my soul," reconciled through the new depth of the poet's understanding.

FOR STUDY AND DISCUSSION

1. Find lines in the poem that make an appeal to the senses. Which senses are appealed to most?

2. What are the principal symbols in sections 13 and 14? Is each of these symbols developed to the same extent in these sections? Which of the symbols becomes dominant? Why?

3. Point out the use of devices of sound in the poem. (For discussions of devices of sound, see pages 122 and 669.) Does the use of such devices heighten the poem's emotional effect? Explain.

4. Study the thrush's carol in section 14. What is its mood? Explain how Whitman uses the connotations of words such as *soothing, serenely,* and *delicate* to establish mood. Point out other words in the carol that are important because of their connotations.

5. Read aloud the first section of "Lilacs," then read aloud "Beat! Beat! Drums!" Describe the difference in rhythm of these poems. In what ways does this difference emphasize the difference in meaning?

6. One device Whitman frequently uses in his poems is the *catalogue,* a list of details that shows the largeness and variety of his subject. "Mannahatta," for example, is mostly a catalogue of the sights of New York City. Point out Whitman's use of the catalogue in "Lilacs." Why is this device particularly suitable to Whitman's kind of poetry and to his claim in "Song of Myself" that he allows nature to speak "without check with original energy"? Find other lines in the selections by Whitman

that, in expressing his purpose as a poet, indicate why he is fond of using the catalogue.

7. "Song of Myself" was written near the beginning of Whitman's career as a poet. "Lilacs" was written many years later. Would you conclude, after reading these two poems, that Whitman had changed greatly as a man or as a poet? Explain. What effect might the War Between the States have had on him?

FOR COMPOSITION

1. In his Preface to the 1855 edition of *Leaves of Grass,* Whitman describes the kind of great poets America needs. The following sentences are quotations from that description.

"The American poets are to enclose old and new, for America is a race of races. . . . His spirit responds to his country's spirit . . . he incarnates its geography and natural rivers and lakes . . . To him enter the essences of the real things and past and present events."

"Nothing out of its place is good and nothing in its place is bad. He [the poet] bestows on every object or quality its fit proportions neither more nor less. He is the arbiter of the diverse and he is the key. He is the equalizer of his age and land."

"The art of art, the glory of expression and the sunshine of the light of letters is simplicity. Nothing is better than simplicity . . . nothing can make up for excess or the lack of definiteness."

". . . but folks expect of the poet to indicate more than the beauty and dignity which always attach to dumb real objects [such as forests, mountains, rivers, animals, fishes, and birds]; they expect him to indicate the path between reality and their souls."

Write a composition in which you state your agreement or disagreement with any of the ideas expressed above. Base your opinion on your own reading of poetry, and support your arguments with examples from poems that you consider great. Then consider the following question: Does Whitman live up to his own description?

2. "Camerado, this is no book;/ Who touches this, touches a man" wrote Whitman of *Leaves of Grass.* Write a composition in which you give your impressions of this man. Use supporting examples from Whitman's poems.

FROM *Specimen Days*

Specimen Days is a kind of autobiography, a collection of reminiscences about Whitman's early years, his encounters with other literary men, his reactions to important events. Some of the most interesting sections are about his experiences during the War Between the States.

BATTLE OF BULL RUN, JULY, 1861

ALL THIS SORT of feeling [1] was destined to be arrested and reversed by a terrible shock—the battle of first Bull Run—certainly, as we now know it, one of the most singular fights on record. (All battles, and their results, are far more matters of accident than is generally thought; but this was throughout a casualty, a chance. Each side supposed it had won, till the last moment. One had, in point of fact, just the same right to be routed as the other. By a fiction, or series of fictions, the national forces at the last moment exploded in a panic and fled from the field.) The defeated troops commenced pouring into Washington over the Long Bridge [2] at daylight on Monday, 22d—day drizzling all through with rain. The Saturday and Sunday of the battle (20th, 21st) had been parched and hot to an extreme—the dust, the grime and smoke, in layers, sweated in, followed by other layers again sweated in, absorbed by those excited souls—their clothes all saturated with the clay powder filling the air—stirred up everywhere on the dry roads and trodden fields by the

regiments, swarming wagons, artillery, etc.—all the men with this coating of murk and sweat and rain, now recoiling back, pouring over the Long Bridge—a horrible march of twenty miles, returning to Washington baffled, humiliated, panic-struck. Where are the vaunts, and the proud boasts with which you went forth? Where are your banners, and your bands of music, and your ropes to bring back your prisoners? Well, there isn't a band playing—and there isn't a flag but clings ashamed and lank to its staff.

The sun rises, but shines not. The men appear, at first sparsely and shamefaced enough, then thicker, in the streets of Washington—appear in Pennsylvania Avenue, and on the steps and basement entrances. They come along in disorderly mobs, some in squads, stragglers, companies. Occasionally, a rare regiment, in perfect order, with its officers (some gaps, dead, the true braves) marching in silence, with lowering faces, stern, weary to sinking, all black and dirty, but every man with his musket, and stepping alive; but these are the exceptions. Sidewalks of Pennsylvania Avenue, Fourteenth Street, etc., crowded, jammed with citizens, clerks, everybody, lookers-on; women in the windows, curious expressions from faces, as those swarms of dirt-covered returned soldiers there (will they never end?) move by; but nothing said, no comments (half our lookers-on secesh [3] of the most venomous kind—they say nothing; but the devil snickers in their faces). During the forenoon Washington gets all-over motley with these defeated soldiers—queer-looking objects, strange eyes and faces, drenched (the steady rain drizzles on all day) and fearfully worn, hungry, haggard, blistered in the feet. Good people (but not over-many of them either) hurry up something for their grub. They put wash kettles on the fire, for soup, for coffee. They set tables on the sidewalks—wagonloads of bread are purchased, swiftly cut

---

[1] **feeling:** No major battle had yet been fought, and the North was confident that it could gain an easy victory over the South.

[2] **Long Bridge:** the bridge over the Potomac. The battle took place about twenty-five miles from Washington, D.C.

[3] **secesh:** secessionists.

in stout chunks. Here are two aged ladies, beautiful, the first in the city for culture and charm; they stand with store of eating and drink at an improvised table of rough plank, and give food, and have the store replenished from their house every half-hour all that day; and there in the rain they stand, active, silent, white-haired, and give food, though the tears stream down their cheeks, almost without intermission, the whole time. Amid the deep excitement, crowds and motion, and desperate eagerness, it seems strange to see many, very many, of the soldiers sleeping—in the midst of all, sleeping sound. They drop down anywhere, on the steps of houses, up close by the basements or fences, on the sidewalk, aside on some vacant lot, and deeply sleep. A poor seventeen- or eighteen-year-old boy lies there, on the stoop of a grand house; he sleeps so calmly, so profoundly. Some clutch their muskets firmly even in sleep. Some in squads; comrades, brothers, close together—and on them, as they lie, sulkily drips the rain.

As afternoon passed, and evening came, the streets, the barrooms, knots everywhere, listeners, questioners, terrible

yarns, bugaboo, masked batteries, our regiment all cut up, etc.—stories and storytellers, windy, bragging, vain centers of street crowds. Resolution, manliness, seem to have abandoned Washington. The principal hotel, Willard's, is full of shoulder straps [1]—thick, crushed, creeping with shoulder straps. (I see them, and must have a word with them. There you are, shoulder straps! But where are your companies? Where are your men? Incompetents! Never tell me of chances of battle, of getting strayed, and the like. I think this is your work, this retreat, after all. Sneak, blow, put on airs there in Willard's sumptuous parlors and barrooms, or anywhere—no explanation shall save you. Bull Run is your work; had you been half or one-tenth worthy your men, this would never have happened.)

Meantime, in Washington, among the great persons and their entourage, a mixture of awful consternation, uncertainty, rage, shame, helplessness, and stupefying disappointment. The worst is not only imminent, but already here. In a few hours —perhaps before the next meal—the secesh generals, with their victorious hordes, will be upon us. The dream of humanity, the vaunted Union we thought so strong, so impregnable—lo! it seems already smashed like a china plate. One bitter, bitter hour—perhaps proud America will never again know such an hour. She must pack and fly—no time to spare. Those white palaces—the dome-crowned Capitol there on the hill, so stately over the trees—shall they be left—or destroyed first? For it is certain that the talk among certain of the magnates and officers and clerks and officials everywhere, for twenty-four hours in and around Washington after Bull Run, was loud and undisguised for yielding out and out, and substituting the Southern rule, and Lincoln promptly abdicating and departing. If the secesh officers and forces had immediately followed, and by a bold Napoleonic movement had entered Washington the first

[1] **shoulder straps:** officers.

day (or even the second), they could have had things their own way, and a powerful faction North to back them. One of our returning colonels expressed in public that night, amid a swarm of officers and gentlemen in a crowded room, the opinion that it was useless to fight, that the Southerners had made their title clear, and that the best course for the national government to pursue was to desist from any further attempt at stopping them, and admit them again to the lead, on the best terms they were willing to grant. Not a voice was raised against this judgment, amid that large crowd of officers and gentlemen. (The fact is, the hour was one of the three or four of those crises we had then and afterward, during the fluctuations of four years, when human eyes appeared at least just as likely to see the last breath of the Union as to see it continue.)

DOWN AT THE FRONT

FALMOUTH, VA., *opposite Fredericksburg,*[1] *December 21, 1862*—Begin my visits among the camp hospitals in the Army of the Potomac. Spend a good part of the day in a large brick mansion on the banks of the Rappahannock, used as a hospital since the battle—seems to have received only the worst cases. Outdoors, at the foot of a tree, within ten yards of the front of the house, I notice a heap of amputated feet, legs, arms, hands, etc., a full load for a one-horse cart. Several dead bodies lie near, each covered with its brown woolen blanket. In the dooryard, toward the river, are fresh graves, mostly of officers, their names on pieces of barrel staves or broken boards, stuck in the dirt. (Most of these bodies were subsequently taken up and transported north to their friends.) The large mansion is quite crowded upstairs and down, everything impromptu, no system, all bad enough, but I have no doubt the best that can be done; all the wounds pretty bad, some

[1] **Fredericksburg:** On December 13, 1862, the Union Army suffered a bad defeat at the Battle of Fredericksburg.

frightful, the men in their old clothes, unclean and bloody. Some of the wounded are rebel soldiers and officers, prisoners. One, a Mississippian, a captain, hit badly in leg, I talked with some time; he asked me for papers, which I gave him. (I saw him three months afterward in Washington, with his leg amputated, doing well.) I went through the rooms, downstairs and up. Some of the men were dying. I had nothing to give at that visit, but wrote a few letters to folks home, mothers, etc. Also talked to three or four, who seemed most susceptible to it, and needing it.

FRANCIS
PARKMAN
(1823–1893)

While a student at Harvard, Francis Parkman made a trip to the woods of northern New Hampshire and saw clearly the theme of his life's work. He would write "the history of the American forest. . . . My theme fascinated me, and I was haunted with wilderness images night and day." What Parkman wrote was not simply an account of a wilderness but a story of how men overcame that wilderness and of how two great social orders, English and French, colonized the wilderness and strove with each other for final possession. His massive work called *France and England in North America* is generally regarded as the most vivid and compelling long historical narrative ever written by an American.

The son of a minister and grandson of a rich merchant, Parkman was born on Boston's Beacon Hill. As a boy he was an admirer of Cooper's woodsman hero, Natty Bumppo, and on summer vacations from Harvard, he began visiting the scenes of Indian battles. After college he made the arduous trip west he describes in *The Oregon Trail.* In preparation for the trip, Parkman became an expert woodsman, horseman, and rifleman. His feats were remarkable for so frail a man. With a Boston friend, Quincy Shaw, he made a seventeen-hundred-mile trip along the Oregon Trail, spent several months with a band of Ogillalah Indians, and, principally through good luck, managed to avoid any encounters with hostile Indians. At times on the trip, Parkman was so ill he could not ride.

In 1848, Parkman began *The Conspiracy of Pontiac,* a preliminary study of the conflict between France and England in the New World. It was published in 1851. Then Parkman began to collect materials for his longer, more detailed narrative. During the War Between the States, Parkman bitterly resented being unfit to fight, but his bitterness did not prevent him from completing the first volume of his epic history and publishing it in 1865. In all, *France and England in North America* ran to seven parts published in thirteen volumes, the last part being published in 1892. Parkman had a passion for accuracy. To see what they were really like, he insisted on traveling to the places where the historic events he wrote about had occurred. He made several trips to Europe and Canada to study colonial papers, and he hired copyists to work for him in London and Paris. For a long time, he waited for permission to examine a collection of documents of a French archivist, and after gaining access to these papers, he completely rewrote his volume, *La Salle and the Discovery of the Great West.* His aim as a writer of history was "to imbue himself with the life and spirit of the time."

A wiry little man who walked with chin thrust forward and scorned all kinds of softness, Parkman waged an unending battle against chronic ill health. His eyesight was poor; he had arthritis in his left knee; and he was afflicted with mental illness which he called "the enemy" and which put him through long periods of depression. For years after his wife's death, he was unable to read more than a few hours at a time or to get more than two hours' sleep at night. To write at all he needed a special machine. But his ailments did not prevent him from making long trips to gather material or from keeping steadfastly at his monumental task. For Parkman, civilization, if it were to survive, had to produce strength rather than softness, had to conquer adversity as he himself had conquered his ailments. In men, the virtues he prized most were courage, patriotism, and self-control. He wrote of Indians who bore no resemblance to the noble redmen of Cooper. They were the wild and treacherous foes of his heroes, the white explorers who seemed great to Parkman because they had the power of will to prevail over natural hardships and savage enemies.

The Hardihood of La Salle

FROM *La Salle and the Discovery of the Great West*

In another historical work, *The Conspiracy of Pontiac,* Parkman discusses La Salle's achievement: "Conspicuous in the annals of Canada stands the memorable name of Robert Cavelier de La Salle, the man who, beyond all his compeers, contributed to expand the boundary of French empire in the west. La Salle commanded at Fort Frontenac, erected near the outlet of Lake Ontario, on its northern shore, and then forming the most advanced military outpost of the colony. . . . He had resolved to complete the achievement of Father Marquette, to trace the unknown Mississippi to its mouth, to plant the standard of his king in the newly discovered regions, and found colonies. . . ."

"He led his followers to the banks of the river now called the St. Joseph. . . . Thence he pushed on into the unknown region of Illinois, and now dangers and difficulties began to thicken about him. Indians threatened hostility; his men lost heart. clamored, grew mutinous, and repeatedly deserted; and worse than all, nothing was heard of the vessel which had been sent back to Canada for necessary supplies. Weeks wore on, and doubt ripened into certainty. She had foundered among the storms of these wilderness oceans. . . . In this disastrous crisis, La Salle embraced a resolution characteristic of his intrepid temper. Leaving his men in charge of a subordinate at a fort which he had built on the river Illinois, he turned his face again towards Canada." The selection following picks up La Salle's story as he heads north.

LA SALLE well knew what was before him, and nothing but necessity spurred him to this desperate journey. He says that, unless the articles lost in the *Griffin* [1] were replaced without delay, the expedition would be retarded a full year, and he and his associates consumed by its expenses. "Therefore," he writes to one of them, "though the thaws of approaching spring greatly increased the difficulty of the way, interrupted as it was everywhere by marshes and rivers, to say nothing of the length of the journey, which is about five hundred leagues in a direct line, and the danger of meeting Indians of four or five different nations, through whose country we were to pass, as well as an Iroquois army, which we knew was coming that way; though we must suffer all the time from hunger; sleep on the open

[1] *Griffin:* La Salle's vessel.

ground, and often without food; watch by night and march by day, loaded with baggage, such as blanket, clothing, kettle, hatchet, gun, powder, lead, and skins to make moccasins; sometimes pushing through thickets, sometimes climbing rocks covered with ice and snow, sometimes wading whole days through marshes where the water was waist-deep or even more, at a season when the snow was not entirely melted—though I knew all this, it did not prevent me from resolving to go on foot to Fort Frontenac, to learn for myself what had become of my vessel, and bring back the things we needed."

The winter had been a severe one; and when, an hour after leaving the fort, he and his companions reached the still water of Peoria Lake,[1] they found it sheeted with ice from shore to shore. They carried their canoes up the bank, made two rude sledges, placed the light vessels upon them, and dragged them to the upper end of the lake, where they encamped. In the morning, they found the river still covered with ice, too weak to bear them and too strong to permit them to break a way for the canoes. They spent the whole day in carrying them through the woods, toiling knee-deep in saturated snow. Rain fell in

[1] **Peoria Lake:** on the Illinois River in central Illinois.

floods, and they took shelter at night in a deserted Indian hut.

In the morning, the third of March, they dragged their canoes half a league farther; then launched them and, breaking the ice with clubs and hatchets, forced their way slowly up the stream. Again their progress was barred, and again they took to the woods, toiling onward till a tempest of moist, half-liquid snow forced them to bivouac for the night. A sharp frost followed, and in the morning the white waste around them was glazed with a dazzling crust. Now, for the first time, they could use their snowshoes. Bending to their work, dragging their canoes, which glided smoothly over the polished surface, they journeyed on hour after hour and league after league, till they reached at length the great town of the Illinois, still void of its inhabitants.

It was a desolate and lonely scene: the river gliding dark and cold between its banks of rushes; the empty lodges, covered with crusted snow; the vast white meadows; the distant cliffs, bearded with shining icicles; and the hills wrapped in forests, which glittered from afar with the icy incrustations that cased each frozen twig. Yet there was life in the savage landscape. The men saw buffalo wading in the snow, and they killed one of them. More than this: they discovered the tracks of moccasins. They cut rushes by the edge of the river, piled them on the bank, and set them on fire, that the smoke might attract the eyes of savages roaming near.

On the following day, while the hunters were smoking the meat of the buffalo, La Salle went out to reconnoiter, and presently met three Indians, one of whom proved to be Chassagoac, the principal chief of the Illinois.[1] La Salle brought them to his bivouac, feasted them, gave them a red blanket, a kettle, and some knives and hatchets, made friends with them, promised to restrain the Iroquois from attacking them, told them that he was on his way to the settlements to bring arms and ammunition to defend them against their enemies, and, as the result of these advances, gained from the chief a promise that he would send provisions to Tonty's[2] party at Fort Crèvecœur.[3]

After several days spent at the deserted town, La Salle prepared to resume his journey. Before his departure, his attention was attracted to the remarkable cliff of yellow sandstone, now called Starved Rock, a mile or more above the village— a natural fortress, which a score of resolute white men might make good against a host of savages; and he soon afterwards sent Tonty an order to examine it and make it his stronghold in case of need.

On the fifteenth, the party set out again, carried their canoes along the bank of the river as far as the rapids above Ottawa; then launched them and pushed their way upward, battling with the floating ice, which, loosened by a warm rain, drove down the swollen current in sheets. On the eighteenth, they reached a point some miles below the site of Joliet and here found the river once more completely closed. Despairing of farther progress by water, they hid their canoes on an island and struck across the country for Lake Michigan.

It was the worst of all seasons for such a journey. The nights were cold, but the sun was warm at noon, and the half-thawed prairie was one vast tract of mud, water, and discolored, half-liquid snow. On the twenty-second, they crossed marshes and inundated meadows, wading to the knee, till at noon they were stopped by a river, perhaps the Calumet. They made a raft of hardwood timber, for there was no other, and shoved themselves across. On the next day, they could see Lake Michigan dimly glimmering beyond the waste of woods; and, after crossing three swollen streams, they reached it at evening. On the twenty-fourth, they followed its shore, till, at nightfall, they arrived at the fort, which they had built in the autumn at the mouth of the St. Joseph. Here La Salle found Chapelle and Leblanc, the two men whom he had sent from hence to Michillimackinac,[4] in search of the *Griffin*. They reported that they had made the circuit of the lake, and had neither seen her nor heard tidings of her. Assured of her fate, he ordered them to rejoin Tonty at Fort Crèvecœur; while he pushed onward with his party through the unknown wild of southern Michigan.

"The rain," says La Salle, "which lasted all day, and the raft we were obliged to make to cross the river, stopped us till noon of the twenty-fifth, when we continued our march through the woods, which was so interlaced with thorns and brambles that in two days and a half our clothes were all torn and our faces so covered with blood that we hardly knew each other. On the twenty-eighth, we found the woods more open and began to fare better, meeting a good deal of game, which after this rarely failed us; so that we no longer carried provisions with us, but

[1] The same whom Hennepin calls Chassagouasse. He was brother of the chief, Nicanopé, who, in his absence, had feasted the French on the day after the nocturnal council with Monso. Chassagoac was afterward baptized by Membré or Ribourde, but soon relapsed into the superstitions of his people, and died, as the former tells us, "doubly a child of perdition." [Author's note.]

[2] **Tonty:** Henri de Tonty, La Salle's lieutenant.

[3] **Fort Crèvecœur:** on the Illinois River just below Lake Peoria.

[4] **Michillimackinac:** now shortened to Mackinac, the strait in northern Michigan between Lake Michigan and Lake Huron.

made a meal of roast meat wherever we happened to kill a deer, bear, or turkey. These are the choicest feasts on a journey like this; and till now we had generally gone without them, so that we had often walked all day without breakfast.

"The Indians do not hunt in this region, which is debatable ground between five or six nations who are at war, and, being afraid of each other, do not venture into these parts, except to surprise each other, and always with the greatest precaution and all possible secrecy. The reports of our guns and the carcasses of the animals we killed soon led some of them to find our trail. In fact, on the evening of the twenty-eighth, having made our fire by the edge of a prairie, we were surrounded by them; but as the man on guard waked us, and we posted ourselves behind trees with our guns, these savages, who are called Wapoos, took us for Iroquois, and thinking that there must be a great many of us, because we did not travel secretly, as they do when in small bands, they ran off without shooting their arrows and gave the alarm to their comrades, so that we were two days without meeting anybody."

La Salle guessed the cause of their fright; and, in order to confirm their delusion, he drew with charcoal, on the trunks of trees from which he had stripped the bark, the usual marks of an Iroquois war party, with signs for prisoners and for scalps, after the custom of those dreaded warriors. This ingenious artifice, as will soon appear, was near proving the destruction of the whole party. He also set fire to the dry grass of the prairies over which he and his men had just passed, thus destroying the traces of their passage. "We practiced this device every night, and it answered very well so long as we were passing over an open country; but, on the thirtieth, we got into great marshes, flooded by the thaws, and were obliged to cross them in mud or water up to the waist; so that our tracks betrayed us to a band of Mascoutins, who were out after Iroquois. They followed us through these marshes during the three days we were crossing them; but we made no fire at night, contenting ourselves with taking off our wet clothes and wrapping ourselves in our blankets on some dry knoll, where we slept till morning. At last, on the night of the second of April, there came a hard frost, and our clothes, which were drenched when we took them off, froze stiff as sticks, so that we could not put them on in the morning without making a fire to thaw them. The fire betrayed us to the Indians, who were encamped across the marsh; and they ran towards us with loud cries, till they were stopped halfway by a stream so deep that they could not get over, the ice which had formed in the night not being strong enough to bear them. We went to meet them, within gunshot; and whether our firearms frightened them, or whether they thought us more numerous than we were, or whether they really meant us no harm, they called out, in the Illinois language, that they had taken us for Iroquois, but now saw that we were friends and brothers; whereupon, they went off as they came, and we kept on our way till the fourth, when two of my men fell ill and could not walk."

In this emergency, La Salle went in search of some watercourse by which they might reach Lake Erie, and soon came upon a small river, which was probably the Huron. Here, while the sick men rested, their companions made a canoe. There were no birch trees; and they were forced to use elm bark, which at that early season would not slip freely from the wood until they loosened it with hot water. Their canoe being made, they embarked in it and for a time floated prosperously down the stream, when at length the way was barred by a matted barricade of trees fallen across the water. The sick men could now walk again, and, pushing eastward through the forest, the party soon reached the banks of the Detroit.[1]

La Salle directed two of the men to make a canoe and go to Michillimackinac,

[1] **Detroit:** the Detroit River.

the nearest harborage. With the remaining two, he crossed the Detroit on a raft and, striking a direct line across the country, reached Lake Erie, not far from Point Pelée.[1] Snow, sleet, and rain pelted them with little intermission; and when, after a walk of about thirty miles, they gained the lake, the Mohegan and one of the Frenchmen were attacked with fever and spitting of blood. Only one man now remained in health. With his aid, La Salle made another canoe and, embarking the invalids, pushed for Niagara. It was Easter Monday when they landed at a cabin of logs above the cataract, probably on the spot where the *Griffin* was built. Here several of La Salle's men had been left the year before, and here they still remained. They told him woeful news. Not only had he lost the *Griffin* and her lading of ten thousand crowns in value, but a ship from France, freighted with his goods, valued at more than twenty-two thousand livres, had been totally wrecked at the mouth of the St. Lawrence; and, of twenty hired men on their way from Europe to join him, some had been detained by his enemy, the Intendant Duchesneau,[2] while all but four of the remainder, being told that he was dead, had found means to return home.

His three followers were all unfit for travel: he alone retained his strength and spirit. Taking with him three fresh men at Niagara, he resumed his journey, and on the sixth of May descried, looming through floods of rain, the familiar shores of his seigniory[3] and the bastioned walls of Fort Frontenac. During sixty-five days, he had toiled almost incessantly, traveling, by the course he took, about a thousand miles through a country beset with every form of peril and obstruction; "the

most arduous journey," says the chronicler, "ever made by Frenchmen in America." Such was Cavelier de la Salle. In him, an unconquerable mind held at its service a frame of iron, and tasked it to the utmost of its endurance. The pioneer of western pioneers was no rude son of toil, but a man of thought, trained amid arts and letters.[4]

He had reached his goal; but for him there was neither rest nor peace. Man and Nature seemed in arms against him. His agents had plundered him; his creditors had seized his property; and several of his canoes, richly laden, had been lost in the rapids of the St. Lawrence. He hastened to Montreal, where his sudden advent caused great astonishment; and where, despite his crippled resources and damaged credit, he succeeded, within a week, in gaining the supplies which he required and the needful succors for the forlorn band on the Illinois. He had returned to Fort Frontenac and was on the point of embarking for their relief, when a blow fell upon him more disheartening than any that had preceded. On the twenty-second of July, two *voyageurs*,[5] Messier and Laurent, came to him with a letter from Tonty, who wrote that soon after La Salle's departure nearly all the men had deserted, after destroying Fort Crèvecœur, plundering the magazine, and throwing into the river all the arms, goods, and stores which they could not carry off. The messengers who brought this letter were speedily followed by two of the *habitants*[6] of Fort Frontenac, who had been trading on the lakes, and who, with a fidelity

---

[1] **Point Pelée:** in Ontario, about forty-five miles southeast of Detroit.

[2] **Intendant Duchesneau:** An intendant was a high official responsible only to the king. Jacques Duchesneau, Intendant of New France from 1675 to 1682, was an enemy of La Salle.

[3] **seigniory:** his own territory, granted under a feudal system of apportioning land.

[4] A Rocky Mountain trapper, being complimented on the hardihood of himself and his companions, once said to the writer, "That's so; but a gentleman of the right sort will stand hardship better than anybody else." The history of Arctic and African travel, and the military records of all time, are a standing evidence that a trained and developed mind is not the enemy, but the active and powerful ally, of constitutional hardihood. The culture that enervates instead of strengthening is always a false or a partial one. [Author's note.]

[5] *voyageurs:* boatmen who carried men and supplies between remote outposts.

[6] *habitants:* farmers.

which the unhappy La Salle rarely knew how to inspire, had traveled day and night to bring him their tidings. They reported that they had met the deserters, and that, having been reinforced by recruits gained at Michillimackinac and Niagara, they now numbered twenty men.[1] They had destroyed the fort on the St. Joseph,[2] seized a quantity of furs belonging to La Salle at Michillimackinac, and plundered the magazine at Niagara. Here they had separated, eight of them coasting the south side of Lake Ontario to find harborage at Albany, a common refuge at that time of this class of scoundrels; while the remaining twelve, in three canoes, made for Fort Frontenac along the north shore, intending to kill La Salle as the surest means of escaping punishment.

He lost no time in lamentation. Of the few men at his command, he chose nine of the trustiest, embarked with them in canoes, and went to meet the marauders. After passing the Bay of Quinté,[3] he took his station, with five of his party, at a point of land suited to his purpose, and detached the remaining four to keep watch. In the morning, two canoes were discovered, approaching without suspicion, one of them far in advance of the other. As the foremost drew near, La Salle's canoe darted out from under the leafy shore; two of the men handling the paddles, while he, with the remaining two, leveled their

guns at the deserters and called on them to surrender. Astonished and dismayed, they yielded at once; while two more, who were in the second canoe, hastened to follow their example. La Salle now returned to the fort with his prisoners, placed them in custody, and again set forth. He met the third canoe upon the lake at about six o'clock in the evening. His men vainly plied their paddles in pursuit. The mutineers reached the shore, took post among rocks and trees, leveled their guns, and showed fight. Four of La Salle's men made a circuit to gain their rear and dislodge them, on which they stole back to their canoe and tried to escape in the darkness. They were pursued and summoned to yield; but they replied by aiming their guns at their pursuers, who instantly gave them a volley, killed two of them, and captured the remaining three. Like their companions, they were placed in custody at the fort to await the arrival of Count Frontenac.[4]

[In *The Conspiracy of Pontiac*, Parkman describes the outcome of La Salle's adventure: "Once more he stood before Count Frontenac, and once more bent all his resources and all his credit to gain means for the prosecution of his enterprise. He succeeded. With his little flotilla of canoes, he left his fort at the outlet of Lake Ontario, and slowly retraced those interminable waters and lines of forest-bounded shore which had grown drearily familiar to his eyes. Fate at length seemed tired of the conflict with so stubborn an adversary. All went prosperously with the voyagers. They passed the lakes in safety, crossed the rough portage to the waters of the Illinois, followed its winding channel, and descended the turbid eddies of the Mississippi, received with various welcome by the scattered tribes who dwelt along its banks. Now the waters grew bitter to the taste; now the trampling of the surf was heard; and now the broad ocean opened upon their sight, and their goal

[1] When La Salle was at Niagara, in April, he had ordered Dautray, the best of the men who had accompanied him from the Illinois, to return thither as soon as he was able. Four men from Niagara were to go with him, and he was to rejoin Tonty with such supplies as that post could furnish. Dautray set out accordingly, but was met on the lakes by the deserters, who told him that Tonty was dead, and seduced his men. Dautray himself seems to have remained true; at least, he was in La Salle's service immediately after and was one of his most trusted followers. He was of good birth, being the son of Jean Bourdon, a conspicuous personage in the early period of the colony; and his name appears on official records as Jean Bourdon, Sieur d'Autray. [Author's note.]

[2] **fort . . . St. Joseph:** Fort Miamis at the southeastern end of Lake Michigan.

[3] **Bay of Quinté:** about fifty miles west of Fort Frontenac.

[4] **Count Frontenac:** Louis de Buade de Frontenac (1620–1698), Governor of French Canada from 1672 to 1682 and from 1689 to 1698.

was won. On the ninth of April, 1682 . . . La Salle took formal possession of the vast valley of the Mississippi, in the name of Louis the Great, King of France and Navarre."]

1. Why does Parkman have a high regard for La Salle? What qualities in La Salle most appealed to Parkman? Notice that much of the narrative is quoted from La Salle's own account. What kind of impression do you get of La Salle from the way he describes his arduous adventures?

2. To what extent does Parkman make direct comments about La Salle's character? To what extent does he show La Salle's character through the man's own actions? Which method do you consider more effective? Give reasons for your answer.

3. What elements of conflict and drama make Parkman's narrative naturally exciting? What devices does Parkman use to make the narrative even more exciting? Cite passages to support your answer.

4. Parkman is highly regarded for his ability to make history come alive by his effective use of detail. Select a paragraph in which you think this skill is particularly displayed and point out the details that give the narrative a vivid quality.

5. Parkman stresses the fact that La Salle was a man "trained amid arts and letters." Do you agree with Parkman's estimate of the value of La Salle's education in his life as a pioneer? Why or why not?

LANGUAGE AND VOCABULARY

As you have learned (page 300), words may have an emotional force that depends not so much on their strict literal meanings—their denotations—as on their connotations, the associations and implications they convey. Words may also be *honorific* or *derogatory* to show approval or disapproval. For example, a candidate running for high office may be called a "statesman" (an honorific word showing approval) or a "demagogue" (a derogatory word showing disapproval). Parkman, who approved of La Salle, might have called him "bold," but other historians, who did not approve of the explorer, might instead have called him "rash" or "headstrong." A good reader is aware of

how writers use words to influence feelings or opinions.

State whether the following italicized words and phrases from the selection are honorific or derogatory; then substitute a word or phrase that gives the opposite effect from the one Parkman intended. (*Example:* "This ingenious *artifice*" [page 336]: honorific; sly trick.)

1. "Such was the Cavalier de La Salle. In him, an *unconquerable* mind held at its service a frame of *iron* . . . The *pioneer* of western pioneers was no *rude son of toil,* but a man of thought . . ." (Page 337.)

2. "Man and Nature seemed in arms against him. His agents had *plundered* him . . ." (Page 337.)

3. "Here they had separated, eight of them coasting the south side of Lake Ontario to find harborage at Albany, a common refuge at that time for *this class of scoundrels* . . ." (Page 338.)

4. "a natural fortress, which a score of *resolute* white men might make good against a host of *savages* . . ." (Page 335.)

FOR COMPOSITION

The art of writing a dramatic, exciting historical narrative is a difficult one, yet clearly Parkman has mastered it. Two methods he uses to add interest to his narrative are emphasizing elements of conflict (La Salle against nature, La Salle against his enemies), and choosing vivid specific details. (Parkman does not simply state that La Salle's journey was dangerous. Instead, in the first paragraph of the selection, he gives details to show just how dangerous it was.)

Write a historical account of three or four paragraphs based on your reading or study of history in which you use Parkman's methods—giving specific details of description to add interest to the narrative. You may wish to write on one of the following topics:

The landing of the Pilgrims

Washington crossing the Delaware to surprise the Hessians at Trenton

The burning of Washington during the War of 1812

A moment of danger during the Rogers and Clark expedition

The reaction in New England to Daniel Webster's speech supporting the Compromise of 1850

Pickett's charge during the Battle of Gettysburg

BRET HARTE
(1836–1902)

In 1868, a short story appeared in the second issue of a San Francisco magazine, the *Overland Monthly*. Called "The Luck of Roaring Camp," it was by the magazine's young editor, Bret Harte. When copies of the magazine arrived in the East, the effect of the story was sensational. Here, New Yorkers and Bostonians felt, was real Western literature with authentic details of a mining camp and its colorful citizens. Further issues of the *Overland Monthly* had other stories by Bret Harte: "Tennessee's Partner," "The Idyll of Red Gulch," "Brown of Calaveras." A poem written in Western dialect, "Plain Language from Truthful James," proved enormously popular. Within a few years, Bret Harte was a famous writer, and when, in 1871, he left San Francisco for Boston, he was greeted as a genius, the great voice of the Far West. Today, it is difficult to imagine the excitement created by Bret Harte's writings when they first appeared. The striking characters Harte introduced into fiction—the rough miner with a heart of gold, the gambler willing to risk all on the turn of a card, the innocent young schoolmarm from New England—have figured in countless stories, motion pictures, and television plays. Yet no later writer has given more vitality to these characters than Bret Harte did in his early stories.

Francis Bret Harte was an Easterner, born in Albany, New York, who went West in 1854. For a while, he was a schoolteacher in La Grange, California. He also worked as a pharmacist, a miner, a Wells Fargo messenger, and a printer. Eventually he made the transition from setting type to writing and contributed to a number of San Francisco magazines. He became a leading figure in a group of Western writers and journalists that included Mark Twain. Later, in a letter to the writer Thomas Bailey Aldrich, Twain gave credit to Bret Harte for having "trimmed and trained and schooled me patiently, until he changed me from an awkward utterer of coarse grotesquenesses to a writer of paragraphs and chapters that have found a certain favor in the eyes of even some of the very decentest people in the land. . . ."

After Harte's triumphal return East, he continued to write a few more stories (notably "The Outcasts of Poker Flat") that were as good as the ones he had written out West, but for the most part his writing had lost its freshness. Much of his later work was written according to formula: dull flat re-creations of the characters and situations he had introduced in his earlier stories. As his literary powers and fame declined, he began a diplomatic career, serving as a United States consul in Prussia and Scotland. Finally he settled in London where he remained until his death.

The Outcasts of Poker Flat

As Mr. John Oakhurst, gambler, stepped into the main street of Poker Flat on the morning of the twenty-third of November, 1850, he was conscious of a change in its moral atmosphere since the preceding night. Two or three men, conversing earnestly together, ceased as he approached and exchanged significant glances. There was a Sabbath lull in the air, which, in a settlement unused to Sabbath influences, looked ominous.

Mr. Oakhurst's calm, handsome face betrayed small concern in these indications. Whether he was conscious of any predisposing cause was another question. "I reckon they're after somebody," he reflected; "likely it's me." He returned to his pocket the handkerchief with which he had been whipping away the red dust of Poker Flat from his neat boots, and quietly discharged his mind of any further conjecture.

In point of fact, Poker Flat was "after somebody." It had lately suffered the loss of several thousand dollars, two valuable horses, and a prominent citizen. It was experiencing a spasm of virtuous reactions, quite as lawless and ungovernable as any of the acts that had provoked it. A secret committee had determined to rid the town of all improper persons. This was done permanently in regard to two men who were then hanging from the boughs of a sycamore in the gulch, and temporarily in the banishment of certain other objectionable characters. I regret to say that some of these were ladies. It is but due to the sex, however, to state that their impropriety was professional, and it was only in such easily established standards of evil that Poker Flat ventured to sit in judgment.

"The Outcasts of Poker Flat" by Bret Harte. Reprinted by permission of Houghton Mifflin Company.

Mr. Oakhurst was right in supposing that he was included in this category. A few of the committee had urged hanging him as a possible example and a sure method of reimbursing themselves from his pockets of the sums he had won from them. "It's agin justice," said Jim Wheeler, "to let this yer young man from Roaring Camp—an entire stranger—carry away our money." But a crude sentiment of equity residing in the breasts of those who had been fortunate enough to win from Mr. Oakhurst overruled this narrower local prejudice.

Mr. Oakhurst received his sentence with philosophic calmness, none the less coolly that he was aware of the hesitation of his judges. He was too much of a gambler not to accept fate. With him life was at best an uncertain game, and he recognized the usual percentage in favor of the dealer.

A body of armed men accompanied the deported wickedness of Poker Flat to the outskirts of the settlement. Besides Mr. Oakhurst, who was known to be a coolly desperate man, and for whose intimidation the armed escort was intended, the expatriated party consisted of a young woman familiarly known as "The Duchess"; another who had won the title of "Mother Shipton"; [1] and "Uncle Billy," a suspected sluice robber [2] and confirmed drunkard. The cavalcade provoked no comments from the spectators, nor was any word uttered by the escort. Only when the gulch which marked the uttermost limit of Poker Flat was reached, the leader spoke briefly and to the point. The exiles were forbidden to return at the peril of their lives.

As the escort disappeared, their pent-up feelings found vent in a few hysterical tears from the Duchess, some bad lan-

---

[1] **"Mother Shipton":** The original Mother Shipton was supposed to have been a notorious English witch.

[2] **sluice robber:** Miners separated gold ore from other material by running water over it through channels called *sluices*. Sluice robbing was considered a particularly cowardly way of stealing gold.

guage from Mother Shipton, and a Parthian [1] volley of expletives from Uncle Billy. The philosophic Oakhurst alone remained silent. He listened calmly to Mother Shipton's desire to cut somebody's heart out, to the repeated statements of the Duchess that she would die in the road, and to the alarming oaths that seemed to be bumped out of Uncle Billy as he rode forward. With the easy good humor characteristic of his class, he insisted upon exchanging his own riding horse, "Five-Spot," for the sorry mule which the Duchess rode. But even this act did not draw the party into any closer sympathy. The young woman adjusted her somewhat draggled plumes with a feeble, faded coquetry; Mother Shipton eyed the possessor of Five-Spot with malevolence, and Uncle Billy included the whole party in one sweeping anathema.

The road to Sandy Bar—a camp that, not having as yet experienced the regenerating influences of Poker Flat, consequently seemed to offer some invitation to the emigrants—lay over a steep mountain range. It was distant a day's severe travel. In that advanced season the party soon passed out of the moist, temperate regions of the foothills into the dry, cold, bracing air of the Sierras. The trail was

[1] **Parthian:** The Parthians were an ancient people who, when retreating during a battle, were supposed to have turned around to shoot their arrows at the enemy.

narrow and difficult. At noon the Duchess, rolling out of her saddle upon the ground, declared her intention of going no farther, and the party halted.

The spot was singularly wild and impressive. A wooded amphitheater, surrounded on three sides by precipitous cliffs of naked granite, sloped gently toward the crest of another precipice that overlooked the valley. It was, undoubtedly, the most suitable spot for a camp, had camping been advisable. But Mr. Oakhurst knew that scarcely half the journey to Sandy Bar was accomplished, and the party were not equipped or provisioned for delay. This fact he pointed out to his companions curtly, with a philosophic commentary on the folly of "throwing up their hand before the game was played out." But they were furnished with liquor, which in this emergency stood them in place of food, fuel, rest, and prescience. In spite of his remonstrances, it was not long before they were more or less under its influence. Uncle Billy passed rapidly from a bellicose state into one of stupor, the Duchess became maudlin, and Mother Shipton snored. Mr. Oakhurst alone remained erect, leaning against a rock, calmly surveying them.

Mr. Oakhurst did not drink. It interfered with a profession which required coolness, impassiveness, and presence of mind, and, in his own language, he "couldn't afford it." As he gazed at his recumbent fellow exiles, the loneliness begotten of his pariah trade, his habits of life, his very vices, for the first time seriously oppressed him. He bestirred himself in dusting his black clothes, washing his hands and face, and other acts characteristic of his studiously neat habits, and for a moment forgot his annoyance. The thought of deserting his weaker and more pitiable companions never perhaps occurred to him. Yet he could not help feeling the want of that excitement which, singularly enough, was most conducive to that calm equanimity for which he was notorious. He looked at the gloomy walls that rose a thousand feet sheer above the circling pines around him, at the sky ominously clouded, at the valley below, already deepening into shadow; and, doing so, suddenly he heard his own name called.

A horseman slowly ascended the trail. In the fresh, open face of the newcomer Mr. Oakhurst recognized Tom Simson, otherwise known as "The Innocent," of Sandy Bar. He had met him sometime before over a "little game" and had, with perfect equanimity, won the entire fortune—amounting to some forty dollars—of that guileless youth. After the game was finished, Mr. Oakhurst drew the youthful speculator behind the door and thus addressed him: "Tommy, you're a good little man, but you can't gamble worth a cent. Don't try it over again." He then handed him his money back, pushed him gently from the room, and so made a devoted slave of Tom Simson.

There was a remembrance of this in his boyish and enthusiastic greeting of Mr. Oakhurst. He had started, he said, to go to Poker Flat to seek his fortune. "Alone?" No, not exactly alone; in fact (a giggle), he had run away with Piney Woods. Didn't Mr. Oakhurst remember Piney? She that used to wait on the table at the Temperance House? They had been engaged a long time, but old Jake Woods had objected, and so they had run away, and were going to Poker Flat to be married, and here they were. And they were tired out, and how lucky it was they had found a place to camp, and company. All this the Innocent delivered rapidly, while Piney, a stout, comely damsel of fifteen, emerged from behind the pine tree, where she had been blushing unseen, and rode to the side of her lover.

Mr. Oakhurst seldom troubled himself with sentiment, still less with propriety; but he had a vague idea that the situation was not fortunate. He retained, however, his presence of mind sufficiently to kick Uncle Billy, who was about to say something, and Uncle Billy was sober enough to recognize in Mr. Oakhurst's kick a superior power that would not bear trifling. He then endeavored to dissuade Tom Simson from delaying further, but in vain. He even pointed out the fact that there was no provision, nor means of making a camp. But, unluckily, the Innocent met this objection by assuring the party that he was provided with an extra mule loaded with provisions, and by the discovery of a rude attempt at a log house near the trail. "Piney can stay with Mrs. Oakhurst," said the Innocent, pointing to the Duchess, "and I can shift for myself."

Nothing but Mr. Oakhurst's admonishing foot saved Uncle Billy from bursting into a roar of laughter. As it was, he felt compelled to retire up the canyon until he could recover his gravity. There he confided the joke to the tall pine trees, with many slaps of his leg, contortions of his face, and the usual profanity. But when he returned to the party, he found them seated by a fire—for the air had grown strangely chill and the sky overcast—in apparently amicable conversation. Piney was actually talking in an impulsive girlish fashion to the Duchess, who was listening with an interest and animation she had not shown for many days. The Innocent was holding forth, apparently with equal effect, to Mr. Oakhurst and Mother Shipton, who was actually relaxing into amiability. "Is this yer a d——d picnic?"

said Uncle Billy, with inward scorn, as he surveyed the sylvan group, the glancing firelight, and the tethered animals in the foreground. Suddenly an idea mingled with the alcoholic fumes that disturbed his brain. It was apparently of a jocular nature, for he felt impelled to slap his leg again and cram his fist into his mouth.

As the shadows crept slowly up the mountain, a slight breeze rocked the tops of the pine trees and moaned through their long and gloomy aisles. The ruined cabin, patched and covered with pine boughs, was set apart for the ladies. As the lovers parted, they unaffectedly exchanged a kiss, so honest and sincere that it might have been heard above the swaying pines. The frail Duchess and the malevolent Mother Shipton were probably too stunned to remark upon this last evidence of simplicity, and so turned without a word to the hut. The fire was replenished, the men lay down before the door, and in a few minutes were asleep.

Mr. Oakhurst was a light sleeper. Toward morning he awoke benumbed and cold. As he stirred the dying fire, the wind, which was now blowing strongly, brought to his cheek that which caused the blood to leave it—snow!

He started to his feet with the intention of awakening the sleepers, for there was no time to lose. But, turning to where Uncle Billy had been lying, he found him

gone. A suspicion leaped to his brain, and a curse to his lips. He ran to the spot where the mules had been tethered—they were no longer there. The tracks were already rapidly disappearing in the snow.

The momentary excitement brought Mr. Oakhurst back to the fire with his usual calm. He did not waken the sleepers. The Innocent slumbered peacefully, with a smile on his good-humored, freckled face; the virgin Piney slept beside her frailer sisters as sweetly as though attended by celestial guardians; and Mr. Oakhurst, drawing his blanket over his shoulders, stroked his mustaches and waited for the dawn. It came slowly in a whirly mist of snowflakes that dazzled and confused the eye. What could be seen of the landscape appeared magically changed. He looked over the valley and summed up the present and future in two words, "Snowed in!"

A careful inventory of the provisions, which, fortunately for the party, had been stored within the hut, and so escaped the felonious fingers of Uncle Billy, disclosed the fact that with care and prudence, they might last ten days longer. "That is," said Mr. Oakhurst *sotto voce* [1] to the Innocent, "if you're willing to board us. If you ain't —and perhaps you'd better not—you can wait till Uncle Billy gets back with provisions." For some occult reason, Mr. Oakhurst could not bring himself to disclose Uncle Billy's rascality, and so offered the hypothesis that he had wandered from the camp and had accidentally stampeded the animals. He dropped a warning to the Duchess and Mother Shipton, who of course knew the facts of their associate's defection. "They'll find out the truth about us *all* when they find out anything," he added significantly, "and there's no good frightening them now."

Tom Simson not only put all his worldly store at the disposal of Mr. Oakhurst, but seemed to enjoy the prospect of their enforced seclusion. "We'll have a good camp for a week, and then the snow'll melt, and

[1] *sotto voce* (sot′ō vō′che): in an undertone (Italian).

we'll all go back together." The cheerful gaiety of the young man and Mr. Oakhurst's calm infected the others. The Innocent, with the aid of pine boughs, extemporized a thatch for the roofless cabin, and the Duchess directed Piney in the rearrangement of the interior with a taste and tact that opened the blue eyes of that provincial maiden to their fullest extent. "I reckon now you're used to fine things at Poker Flat," said Piney. The Duchess turned away sharply to conceal something that reddened her cheeks through their professional tint, and Mother Shipton requested Piney not to "chatter." But when Mr. Oakhurst returned from a weary search for the trail, he heard the sound of happy laughter echoed from the rocks. He stopped in some alarm, and his thoughts first naturally reverted to the whisky, which he had prudently cached. "And yet it don't somehow sound like whisky," said the gambler. It was not until he caught sight of the blazing fire through the still blind storm, and the group around it, that he settled to the conviction that it was "square fun."

Whether Mr. Oakhurst had cached his cards with the whisky as something debarred the free access of the community, I cannot say. It was certain that, in Mother Shipton's words, he "didn't say 'cards' once" during that evening. Haply the time was beguiled by an accordion, produced somewhat ostentatiously by Tom Simson from his pack. Notwithstanding some difficulties attending the manipulation of this instrument, Piney Woods managed to pluck several reluctant melodies from its keys, to an accompaniment by the Innocent on a pair of bone castanets. But the crowning festivity of the evening was reached in a rude camp-meeting hymn, which the lovers, joining hands, sang with great earnestness and vociferation. I fear that a certain defiant tone and Covenanters' [1] swing to its chorus, rather than

---

[1] **Covenanters:** in seventeenth-century Scotland, adherents of the Presbyterian Covenant to resist the rule of the Anglican churches.

American Legends

The drama of the westward thrust toward the Pacific generated legendary tales. Certain names sprang into prominence and were talked about by the pioneers. It was the kind of talk that breeds legends.

Several real persons became entwined in folklore. One was Jonathan Chapman, who traveled through the wilderness regions of Ohio and Indiana with a bag of seeds and became known as "Johnny Appleseed." The riverboatman Mike Fink became known for his bragging and brawling. Davy Crockett became a legend after the publication of *A Narrative of the Life of David Crockett of the State of Tennessee.*

Later, tales were invented about completely imaginary characters. Pecos Bill was a southwestern Hercules. He could kill a deer by running him to exhaustion. He could hug a bear to death. He once rode a cyclone to Texas when the country needed rain. The Hercules of the Northwestern lumberjacks was Paul Bunyan. With the help of Babe, the Blue Ox, he cut down trees by the quarter section, drained lakes, and changed the flow of great rivers. He once swam straight up a column of rain and turned it off. Down South there was John Henry, the steel-driving man of the railroad construction gangs who worked himself to death winning a stone-drilling contest against a steam drill.

America was creating myths of its own, tales that would express its adventurous spirit, its sense of humor, and its striving for something larger than life.

any devotional quality, caused it speedily to infect the others, who at last joined in the refrain:

"I'm proud to live in the service of the Lord,
And I'm bound to die in His army."

The pines rocked, the storm eddied and whirled above the miserable group, and the flames of their altar leaped heavenward, as if in token of the vow.

At midnight the storm abated, the rolling clouds parted, and the stars glittered keenly above the sleeping camp. Mr. Oakhurst, whose professional habits had enabled him to live on the smallest possible amount of sleep, in dividing the watch with Tom Simson, somehow managed to take upon himself the greater part of that duty. He excused himself to the Innocent by saying that he had "often been a week without sleep." "Doing what?" asked Tom. "Poker!" replied Oakhurst sententiously. "When a man gets a streak of luck, he don't get tired. The luck gives in first. Luck," continued the gambler reflectively, "is a mighty queer thing. All you know about it for certain is that it's bound to change. And it's finding out when it's going to change that makes you. We've had a streak of bad luck since we left Poker Flat—you come along, and slap, you get into it, too. If you can hold your cards right along, you're all right. For," added the gambler, with cheerful irrelevance,

"I'm proud to live in the service of the Lord,
And I'm bound to die in His army."

The third day came, and the sun, looking through the white-curtained valley, saw the outcasts dividing their slowly decreasing store of provisions for the morning meal. It was one of the peculiarities of that mountain climate that its rays diffused a kindly warmth over the wintry landscape, as if in regretful commiseration of the past. But it revealed drift on drift of snow piled high around the hut—a hopeless, uncharted, trackless sea of white

lying below the rocky shores to which the castaways still clung. Through the marvelously clear air the smoke of the pastoral village of Poker Flat rose miles away. Mother Shipton saw it and, from a remote pinnacle of her rocky fastness, hurled in that direction a final malediction. It was her last vituperative attempt and, perhaps for that reason, was invested with a certain degree of sublimity. It did her good, she privately informed the Duchess. "Just you go out there and cuss, and see." She then set herself to the task of amusing "the child," as she and the Duchess were pleased to call Piney. Piney was no chicken, but it was a soothing and original theory of the pair thus to account for the fact that she didn't swear and wasn't improper.

When night crept up again through the gorges, the reedy notes of the accordion rose and fell in fitful spasms and long-drawn gasps by the flickering campfire. But music failed to fill entirely the aching void left by insufficient food, and a new diversion was proposed by Piney—storytelling. Neither Mr. Oakhurst nor his female companions caring to relate their personal experiences, this plan would have failed too, but for the Innocent. Some months before he had chanced upon a stray copy of Mr. Pope's [1] ingenious translation of the *Iliad*. He now proposed to narrate the principal incidents of that poem—having thoroughly mastered the argument and fairly forgotten the words—in the current vernacular of Sandy Bar. And so, for the rest of that night, the Homeric demigods again walked the earth. Trojan bully and wily Greek wrestled in the winds, and the great pines in the canyon seemed to bow to the wrath of the son of Peleus.[2] Mr. Oakhurst listened with great satisfaction. Most especially was he interested in the fate of "Ashheels," as the Innocent persisted in denominating the "swift-footed Achilles."

[1] **Mr. Pope's:** Alexander Pope, an English poet (1688–1744).
[2] **son of Peleus** (pē'lūs): Achilles (ə·kil'ēz), a character in Homer's *Iliad*.

So, with small food and much of Homer and the accordion, a week passed over the heads of the outcasts. The sun again forsook them, and again from leaden skies the snowflakes were sifted over the land. Day by day closer around them drew the snowy circle, until at last they looked from their prison over drifted walls of dazzling white that towered twenty feet above their heads. It became more and more difficult to replenish their fires, even from the fallen trees beside them, now half-hidden in the drifts. And yet no one complained. The lovers turned from the dreary prospect and looked into each other's eyes, and were happy. Mr. Oakhurst settled himself coolly to the losing game before him. The Duchess, more cheerful than she had been, assumed the care of Piney. Only Mother Shipton—once the strongest of the party—seemed to sicken and fade. At midnight on the tenth day, she called Oakhurst to her side. "I'm going," she said, in a voice of querulous weakness, "but don't say anything about it. Don't waken the kids. Take the bundle from under my head, and open it." Mr. Oakhurst did so. It contained Mother Shipton's rations for the last week, untouched. "Give 'em to the child," she said, pointing to the sleeping Piney. "You've starved yourself," said the gambler. "That's what they call it," said the woman querulously, as she lay down

again and, turning her face to the wall, passed quietly away.

The accordion and the bones were put aside that day, and Homer was forgotten. When the body of Mother Shipton had been committed to the snow, Mr. Oakhurst took the Innocent aside and showed him a pair of snowshoes, which he had fashioned from the old packsaddle. "There's one chance in a hundred to save her yet," he said, pointing to Piney: "but it's there," he added, pointing toward Poker Flat. "If you can reach there in two days, she's safe." "And you?" asked Tom Simson. "I'll stay here," was the curt reply.

The lovers parted with a long embrace. "You are not going, too?" said the Duchess, as she saw Mr. Oakhurst apparently waiting to accompany him. "As far as the canyon," he replied. He turned suddenly and kissed the Duchess, leaving her pallid face aflame and her trembling limbs rigid with amazement.

Night came, but not Mr. Oakhurst. It brought the storm again and the whirling snow. Then the Duchess, feeding the fire, found someone had quietly piled beside the hut enough fuel to last a few days longer. The tears rose to her eyes, but she hid them from Piney.

The women slept but little. In the morning, looking into each other's faces, they read their fate. Neither spoke, but Piney, accepting the position of the stronger, drew near and placed her arm around the Duchess's waist. They kept this attitude for the rest of the day. That night the storm reached its greatest fury and, rending asunder the protecting vines, invaded the very hut.

Toward morning they found themselves unable to feed the fire, which gradually died away. As the embers slowly blackened, the Duchess crept closer to Piney and broke the silence of many hours: "Piney, can you pray?" "No, dear," said Piney simply. The Duchess, without knowing exactly why, felt relieved and, putting her head upon Piney's shoulder, spoke no more. And so reclining, the younger and purer pillowing the head of her soiled sister upon her virgin breast, they fell asleep.

The wind lulled as if it feared to waken them. Feathery drifts of snow, shaken from the long pine boughs, flew like white-winged birds and settled about them as they slept. The moon through the rifted clouds looked down upon what had been the camp. But all human stain, all trace of earthly travail, was hidden beneath the spotless mantle mercifully flung from above.

They slept all that day and the next, nor did they waken when voices and foot-steps broke the silence of the camp. And when pitying fingers brushed the snow from their wan faces, you could scarcely have told from the equal peace that dwelt upon them which was she that had sinned. Even the law of Poker Flat recognized this and turned away, leaving them still locked in each other's arms.

But at the head of the gulch, on one of the largest pine trees, they found the deuce of clubs pinned to the bark with a bowie knife. It bore the following, written in pencil in a firm hand:

BENEATH THIS TREE
LIES THE BODY
OF
JOHN OAKHURST,
WHO STRUCK A STREAK OF BAD LUCK
ON THE 23D OF NOVEMBER, 1850,
AND
HANDED IN HIS CHECKS
ON THE 7TH DECEMBER, 1850.

And pulseless and cold, with a Derringer [1] by his side and a bullet in his heart, though still calm as in life, beneath the snow lay he who was at once the strongest and yet the weakest of the outcasts of Poker Flat.

[1] **Derringer:** a small pistol.

FOR STUDY AND DISCUSSION

1. Do you think that this story, more than most, is dependent upon a particular setting? Could the story have happened only in a par-ticular time at a particular place? Explain.

2. What do you learn about the moral code of the old West from this story? Why did the citizens suddenly decide to clean up Poker Flat? Why did they banish Oakhurst instead of hanging him?

3. In your opinion, are the characters in this story treated realistically? Do all their actions seem "in character"? In answering this question, consider the following incidents: Uncle Billy's desertion; Oakhurst returning to Tom Simson the money he lost in gambling; the Duchess asking, "Piney, can you pray?" and feeling relieved at the answer; Mother Shipton handing Oakhurst the bundle of food.

4. Explain the last statement in the story that Oakhurst "was at once the strongest and yet the weakest of the outcasts of Poker Flat."

5. Despite the story's essential seriousness, there are a number of humorous touches. Give examples of these. Which examples can be called "regional humor"—that is, humor de-pending on the characteristics of a particular region?

LANGUAGE AND VOCABULARY

Bret Harte's characterization depends a good deal on the use of precise adjectives and nouns to describe his characters. Define the following italicized words and show how they deepen your understanding of the characters described.

1. "[Uncle Billy's] *felonious* fingers . . ."
2. "the *malevolent* Mother Shipton . . ."
3. "[Oakhurst's] profession which required coolness, *impassiveness,* and presence of mind . . ."
4. "that calm *equanimity* for which he [Oak-hurst] was notorious . . ."
5. "that *guileless* youth." (Tom)

FOR COMPOSITION

While today "The Outcasts of Poker Flat" may seem familiar and similar to other stories about mining towns which it influenced, the reaction to the story when it was first pub-lished was quite different. In a brief composi-tion describe two imaginary reactions to the story, two short reviews: one, the reaction of a nineteenth-century New England lady after reading the story as first published in a maga-zine; the other, the reaction of a present-day reader who prides himself on his sophistication and his realistic point of view.

MARK TWAIN
(1835–1910)

Mark Twain, so beloved a figure in his lifetime that the writer Upton Sinclair called him "the uncrowned king of America," once explained in a letter that he liked to write about "boy-life on the Mississippi" because that phase of his life was dear to him and not because he was unfamiliar with other sides of life. At various times, he went on, he had been a soldier, a miner, a reporter, a Mississippi riverboat pilot, a journeyman printer, and a lecturer. Twain's personality was as complex as his experience was many-sided, and his work can be appreciated on many levels. Millions of readers have been delighted by his account of his career as a riverboat pilot in *Life on the Mississippi* and of his Western adventures in *Roughing It*. Young readers are fascinated by *The Adventures of Tom Sawyer,* perhaps the most popular book for young people ever written. The bitter pessimism of his later works—*The Mysterious Stranger, What Is Man?,* and "The Man Who Corrupted Hadleyburg"— is disquieting when it is set against the buoyant love of life in the earlier books. In these last works, Twain questions the meaning of existence and finds no answer. But most students of Twain agree that his finest book, rich and deep in its view of life and beautiful in its use of vernacular English, is *The Adventures of Huckleberry Finn,* a work that, like Shakespeare's tragedies or *Don Quixote* or *Gulliver's Travels* or the *Odyssey,* reaches out beyond the limitations of time and place and touches what is most human in the readers of any age or country.

Samuel Langhorne Clemens, who was to become famous under the pen name "Mark Twain," spent his boyhood in Hannibal, Missouri, a small town on the west bank of the Mississippi River. In his *Autobiography* he describes the town as a place where "everyone was poor but didn't know it; and everybody was comfortable and did know it." When he was twelve, his father died, and the following year, Sam was apprenticed to a printer. Like Whitman, Bret Harte, and other printers of the day, Clemens became a journalist as well, contributing humorous pieces to various papers. In 1857, he began to work as a Mississippi riverboat pilot, a profession that he "loved far better than any I have followed since, and I took a measureless pride in it. The reason is plain: a pilot, in those days, was the only unfettered and entirely independent human being that lived in the earth. . . . The moment that the boat was underway in the river, she was under the sole and unquestioned control of the pilot."

In 1861, Clemens traveled with his brother to Nevada, where he caught the mining fever. Eventually he became a reporter, first in Virginia City, then in San Francisco, and in addition to his regular work, he wrote sketches that were imitations of the work of dialect humorists. In 1863, he met Artemus Ward, the most popular dialect humorist of the time, who encouraged the twenty-eight-year-old reporter to seek a wider audience. Clemens began to write pieces for Eastern newspapers, using the pseudonym "Mark Twain," a term used by pilots to gauge the depth of the river. After his story "The Celebrated Jumping Frog of Calaveras County" appeared in the New York *Saturday Press* in November, 1865, he began to acquire a national reputation. From Artemus Ward, he learned how effective a humorist could be on a lecture platform, and on his return in 1866 from a trip to Hawaii, he gave his first lectures in San Francisco. At this point in his career, Samuel Clemens was simply a promising young writer and lecturer. But after a trip to Europe and the Holy Land as correspondent for the San Francisco *Alta California,* and the publication of a best seller about the trip *(The Innocents Abroad),* Mark Twain was a famous literary name. Twain once told a biographer, "When I began to lecture, and in my earlier writings, my sole idea was to make comic capital out of everything I saw and heard." Now the events of his life were to shape him into something more than a comedian.

In 1870, the "Wild Humorist of the Pacific Slope," as Twain labeled himself in his San Francisco days, married Olivia Langdon, a serious, idealistic, semi-invalid young lady, who was the daughter of the richest businessman in Elmira, New York. From then on, Twain was an Easterner. With the help of Olivia's father, he became part owner of the Buffalo (New York) *Express* but soon found this position disagreeable, and in 1873, he settled down in Hartford, Connecticut, to the life of a free-lance writer. In the previous year, *Roughing It,* an enormous success, had been published. Twain became the friend of William Dean Howells, editor of the *Atlantic Monthly* and the most influential man of letters of his time. Both his wife "Livy" and Howells saw the possibilities inherent in the gifted Westerner, and they urged him on to greater things.

Twain's Easternization and Livy's influence on his work have been debated by many biographers and critics. Some maintain that Twain's wife tamed and weakened his genius, and that if it had not been for his removal from the West and Livy's restrictions, he would have written more masterpieces. Other students of Twain hold that without Livy as a disciplining influence, he would not have been capable of serious, sustained work. In his letters, Twain referred to his wife's censorship of passages that she considered in poor taste, but these references are to some extent part of a family joke. Twain enjoyed playing the role of a henpecked husband, the Westerner of uncertain manners dominated by a "respectable" Eastern wife.

Mark Twain was sometimes uncomfortable in the East, but at the same time he wished to be judged by its literary standards. When he sent the first installment of "Old Times on the Mississippi" (later to be incorporated into *Life on the Mississippi)* to the *Atlantic Monthly,* Howells asked for more, advising him, "Don't write *at* any supposed *Atlantic* audience, but yarn it off as if into my sympathetic ear." Twain replied, "It isn't the *Atlantic* audience that distresses me; for *it* is the only audience that I sit down before in perfect serenity (for the simple reason that it don't require a 'humorist' to paint himself stripèd and stand on his head every fifteen minutes.)" Nevertheless, the "Wild Humorist" in him sometimes broke out. One of the most famous occasions was his speech at a dinner honoring Whittier in which he told of an encounter with a miner who claimed he had met three tramps, "littrey men" named Longfellow, Emerson, and Holmes: "Mr. Emerson was a seedy little bit of a chap—red-headed. Mr. Holmes was fat as a balloon—he weighed as much as three hundred, and had double chins all the way down to his stomach. Mr. Longfellow was built like a prize fighter." Many people were scandalized, and Twain wrote a letter of abject apology to the three authors.

Professor Lewis Leary has written of "the character called Mark Twain who was the inspired creation of a talented man named Samuel L. Clemens," and it is difficult to separate Twain the public figure from Twain the artist. Yet his literary achievement is of tremendous importance. Despite the fact that he wrote much that is of minor or fleeting interest, he also produced a number of works that have enormously enriched American literature. Twain's chief claim to literary greatness, of course, is *The Adventures of Huckleberry Finn*. Ernest Hemingway wrote, "All modern American literature comes from one book by Mark Twain called *Huckleberry Finn*.... There was nothing before. There has been nothing as good since." Most readers would disagree with the last two sentences, but would share Hemingway's feeling that *Huckleberry Finn* is one of the supreme masterpieces of American literature.

The Buffalo That Climbed a Tree

FROM *Roughing It*

In 1861, when Mark Twain's older brother Orion was appointed secretary to the territorial governor of Nevada, Mark traveled to Nevada with him. In *Roughing It* he describes the trip west.

WE CAME to the shallow, yellow, muddy South Platte,[1] with its low banks and its scattering flat sandbars and pygmy islands—a melancholy stream straggling through the center of the enormous flat plain, and only saved from being impossible to find with the naked eye by its sentinel rank of scattering trees standing on either bank. The Platte was "up," they said—which made me wish I could see it when it was down, if it could look any sicker and sorrier. They said it was a dangerous stream to cross, now, because its quicksands were liable to swallow up horses, coach, and passengers if an attempt was made to ford it. But the mails had to go, and we made the attempt. Once or twice in midstream the wheels sunk into the yielding sands so threateningly that we half believed we had dreaded and avoided the sea all our lives to be shipwrecked in a "mud-wagon" in the middle of a desert at last. But we dragged through and sped away toward the setting sun.

Next morning just before dawn, when about five hundred and fifty miles from St. Joseph,[2] our mud-wagon broke down. We were to be delayed five or six hours, and therefore we took horses, by invitation, and joined a party who were just starting on a buffalo hunt. It was noble sport galloping over the plain in the dewy freshness of the morning, but our part of the hunt ended in disaster and disgrace, for a wounded buffalo bull chased the

---

[1] **Platte:** a river running through Nebraska.

"The Buffalo That Climbed a Tree" from Chapter VII of *Roughing It* by Mark Twain. Reprinted by permission of Harper & Row, Publishers.

[2] **St. Joseph:** a town in western Missouri that, in the middle of the nineteenth century, was an important jumping-off point for the long trip west.

passenger Bemis nearly two miles, and then he forsook his horse and took to a lone tree. He was very sullen about the matter for some twenty-four hours, but at last he began to soften little by little, and finally he said:

"Well, it was not funny, and there was no sense in those gawks making themselves so facetious over it. I tell you I was angry in earnest for a while. I should have shot that long gangly lubber [1] they called Hank, if I could have done it without crippling six or seven other people—but of course I couldn't, the old 'Allen' 's [2] so confounded comprehensive. I wish those loafers had been up in the tree; they wouldn't have wanted to laugh so. If I had had a horse worth a cent—but no, the minute he saw that buffalo bull wheel on him and give a bellow, he raised straight up in the air and stood on his heels. The saddle began to slip, and I took him round the neck and laid close to him, and began to pray. Then he came down and stood up on the other end awhile, and the bull actually stopped pawing sand and bellowing to contemplate the inhuman spectacle. Then the bull made a pass at him and uttered a bellow that sounded perfectly frightful, it was so close to me, and that seemed to literally prostrate my horse's reason, and make a raving distracted maniac of him, and I wish I may die if he didn't stand on his head for a quarter of a minute and shed tears. He was absolutely out of his mind—he was, as sure as truth itself, and he really didn't know what he was doing. Then the bull came charging at us, and my horse dropped down on all fours and took a fresh start—and then for the next ten minutes he would actually throw one handspring after another so fast that the bull began to get unsettled, too, and didn't know where to start in—and so he stood there sneezing, and shoveling dust over his back, and bellowing every now and then, and thinking he had got a

fifteen-hundred-dollar circus horse for breakfast, certain. Well, I was first out on his neck—the horse's, not the bull's—and then underneath, and next on his rump, and sometimes head up, and sometimes heels—but I tell you it seemed solemn and awful to be ripping and tearing and carrying on so in the presence of death, as you might say. Pretty soon the bull made a snatch for us and brought away some of my horse's tail (I suppose, but do not know, being pretty busy at the time), but *something* made him hungry for solitude and suggested to him to get up and hunt for it. And then you ought to have seen that spider-legged old skeleton go! and you ought to have seen the bull cut out after him, too—head down, tongue out, tail up, bellowing like everything, and actually mowing down the weeds, and tearing up the earth, and boosting up the sand like a whirlwind! By George, it was a hot race! I and the saddle were back on the rump, and I had the bridle in my teeth and holding on to the pommel [3] with both hands. First we left the dogs behind; then we passed a jackass-rabbit; then we overtook a coyote, and were gaining on an antelope when the rotten girths let go and threw me about thirty yards off to the left, and as the saddle went down over the horse's rump he gave it a lift with his heels that sent it more than four hundred yards up in the air, I wish I may die in a minute if he didn't. I fell at the foot of the only solitary tree there was in nine counties adjacent (as any creature could see with the naked eye), and the next second I had hold of the bark with four sets of nails and my teeth, and the next second after that I was astraddle of the main limb and blaspheming my luck in a way that made my breath smell of brimstone. I *had* the bull, now, if he did not think of *one* thing. But that one thing I dreaded. I dreaded it very seriously. There was a possibility that the bull might not think of it, but there were greater chances that he would. I made up

---

[1] **lubber:** awkward person.
[2] **Allen:** a shotgun.

[3] **pommel:** a knob or horn at the front of the saddle.

my mind what I would do in case he did. It was a little over forty feet to the ground from where I sat. I cautiously unwound the lariat from the pommel of my saddle——"

"Your *saddle?* Did you take your saddle up in the tree with you?"

"Take it up in the tree with me? Why, how you talk! Of course I didn't. No man could do that. It *fell* in the tree when it came down."

"Oh—exactly."

"Certainly. I unwound the lariat, and fastened one end of it to the limb. It was the very best green rawhide, and capable of sustaining tons. I made a slip noose in the other end, and then hung it down to see the length. It reached down twenty-two feet—halfway to the ground. I then loaded every barrel of the Allen with a double charge. I felt satisfied. I said to myself, if he never thinks of that one thing that I dread, all right—but if he does, all right anyhow—I am fixed for him. But don't you know that the very thing a man dreads is the thing that always happens? Indeed it is so. I watched the bull, now, with anxiety—anxiety which no one can conceive of who has not been in such a situation and felt that at any moment death might come. Presently a thought came into the bull's eye. I knew it! said I—if my nerve fails now, I am lost. Sure enough, it was just as I had dreaded, he started in to climb the tree——"

"What, the bull?"

"Of course—who else?"

"But a bull can't climb a tree."

"He can't, can't he? Since you know so much about it, did you ever see a bull try?"

"No! I never dreamed of such a thing."

"Well, then, what is the use of your talking that way, then? Because you never saw a thing done, is that any reason why it can't be done?"

"Well, all right—go on. What did you do?"

"The bull started up, and got along well for about ten feet, then slipped and slid back. I breathed easier. He tried it again— got up a little higher—slipped again. But he came at it once more, and this time he was careful. He got gradually higher and higher, and my spirits went down more and more. Up he came—an inch at a time—with his eyes hot, and his tongue hanging out. Higher and higher—hitched his foot over the stump of a limb, and looked up, as much as to say, 'You are my meat, friend.' Up again—higher and higher, and getting more excited the closer he got. He was within ten feet of me! I took a long breath—and then said I, 'It is now or never.' I had the coil of the lariat all ready; I paid it out slowly, till it hung right over his head; all of a sudden I let go of the slack and the slip noose fell fairly round his neck! Quicker than lightning I out with the Allen and let him have it in the face. It was an awful roar, and must have scared the bull out of his senses. When the smoke cleared away, there he was, dangling in the air, twenty foot from the ground, and going out of one convulsion into another faster than you could count! I didn't stop to count, any-how—I shinned down the tree and shot for home."

"Bemis, is all that true, just as you have stated it?"

"I wish I may rot in my tracks and die the death of a dog if it isn't."

"Well, we can't refuse to believe it, and we don't. But if there were some proofs——"

"Proofs! Did I bring back my lariat?"

"No."

"Did I bring back my horse?"

"No."

"Did you ever see the bull again?"

"No."

"Well, then, what more do you want? I never saw anybody as particular as you are about a little thing like that."

I made up my mind that if this man was not a liar he only missed it by the skin of his teeth.

[STUDY AIDS FOLLOW ON PAGE 367]

Mark Twain and the Public Reading

"His Grandfather's Old Ram"
FROM HIS *Autobiography*

WHAT IS CALLED a "reading," as a public platform entertainment, was first essayed by Charles Dickens, I think. He had made it very popular at home, and he made it so acceptable and so popular in America that his houses were crowded everywhere, and in a single season he earned two hundred thousand dollars. I heard him once during that season; it was in Steinway Hall, in December, and it made the fortune of my life—not in dollars, I am not thinking of dollars; it made the real fortune of my life in that it made the happiness of my life; on that day I called at the St. Nicholas Hotel to see my Quaker City Excursion shipmate, Charley Langdon, and was introduced to a sweet and timid and lovely young girl, his sister.[1] The family went to the Dickens reading, and I accompanied them. It was forty years ago; from that day to this, the sister has never been out of my mind nor heart.

Mr. Dickens read scenes from his printed books. From my distance he was a small and slender figure, rather fancifully dressed, and striking and picturesque in appearance. He wore a black velvet coat with a large and glaring red flower in the buttonhole. He stood under a red upholstered shed behind whose slant was a row of strong lights—just such an arrangement as artists use to concentrate a strong

---

[1] **sister:** Olivia Langdon, whom Mark Twain later married.

"Mark Twain and the Public Reading" ("His Grandfather's Old Ram") from Chapter 35 of *The Autobiography of Mark Twain*, edited by Charles Neider, copyright © 1959 by The Mark Twain Company. Reprinted by permission of Harper & Row, Publishers.

---

light upon a great picture. Dickens's audience sat in a pleasant twilight, while he performed in the powerful light cast upon him from the concealed lamps. He read with great force and animation, in the lively passages, and with stirring effect. It will be understood that he did not merely read but also acted. . . .

I had never tried reading as a trade, and I wanted to try it. . . . It was ghastly! At least in the beginning. I had selected my readings well enough but had not studied them. I supposed it would only be necessary to do like Dickens—get out on the platform and read from the book. I did that and made a botch of it. Written things are not for speech; their form is literary; they are stiff, inflexible, and will not lend themselves to happy and effective delivery with the tongue—where their purpose is to merely entertain, not instruct; they have to be limbered up, broken up, colloquialized, and turned into the common forms of unpremeditated talk—otherwise they will bore the house, not entertain it. After a week's experience with the book, I laid it aside and never carried it to the platform again; but meantime I had memorized those pieces, and in delivering them from the platform they soon transformed themselves into flexible talk, with all their obstructing preciseness and formalities gone out of them for good.

One of the readings which I used was part of an extravagant chapter in dialect from *Roughing It* which I entitled "His Grandfather's Old Ram." After I had memorized it, it began to undergo changes on the platform, and it continued to edit and revise itself night after night until, by and by, from dreading to begin on it before an audience, I came to like it and enjoy it. I never knew how considerable the changes had been when I finished the season's work; I never knew until ten or eleven years later, when I took up that book in a parlor in New York one night to read that chapter to a dozen friends, of the two sexes, who had asked for it. It *wouldn't read*—that is, it wouldn't read aloud. I struggled along with it for five minutes and then gave it up and said I should have to tell the tale as best I might from memory. It turned out that my memory was equal to the emergency; it reproduced the platform form of the story pretty faithfully after that interval of years. I still remember that form of it, I think, and I wish to recite it here, so that the reader may compare it with the story as told in *Roughing It,* if he pleases, and note how different the spoken version is from the written and printed version.

The idea of the tale is to exhibit certain bad effects of a good memory: the sort of memory which is too good, which remembers everything and forgets nothing, which has no sense of proportion and can't tell an important event from an unimportant one but preserves them all, states them all, and thus retards the progress of a narrative, at the same time making a tangled, inextricable confusion of it and intolerably wearisome to the listener. The historian of "His Grandfather's Old Ram" had that kind of a memory. He often tried to communicate that history to his comrades, the other surface miners, but he could never complete it because his memory defeated his every attempt to march a straight course; it persistently threw remembered details in his way that had nothing to do with the tale; these unrelated details would interest him and sidetrack him; if he came across a name or a family or any other thing that had nothing to do with his tale, he would diverge from his course to tell about the person who owned that name or explain all about that family—with the result that as he plodded on, he always got further and further from his grandfather's memorable adventure with the ram, and finally went to sleep before he got to the end of the story, and so did his comrades. Once he did manage to approach so nearly to the end, apparently, that the boys were filled with an eager hope; they believed that at last they were going to find out all about the grandfather's adventure and what it was that had happened. After the usual preliminaries, the historian said:

"Well, as I was a-sayin', he bought that old ram from a feller up in Siskiyou County and fetched him home and turned him loose in the medder, and next morning he went down to have a look at him, and accident'ly dropped a ten-cent piece in the grass and stooped down—so—and was a-fumblin' around in the grass to git it, and the ram he was a-standin' up the slope taking notice; but my grandfather wasn't taking notice, because he had his back to the ram and was int'rested about the dime. Well, there he was, as I was a-sayin', down at the foot of the slope a-bendin' over—so—fumblin' in the grass, and the ram he was up there at the top of the slope, and Smith—Smith was a-standin' there—no, not jest there, a little further away—fifteen foot perhaps— well, my grandfather was a-stoopin' way down—so—and the ram was up there observing, you know, and Smith he . . . (musing) . . . the ram he bent his head down, so . . . Smith of Calaveras . . . no, no it couldn't ben Smith of Calaveras— I remember now that he—b'George it was Smith of Tulare County—'course it was, I remember it now perfectly plain.

"Well, Smith he stood just there, and my grandfather he stood just here, you know, and he was a-bendin' down just so, fumblin' in the grass, and when the old ram see'd him in that attitude, he took it fur an invitation—and here he come! down the slope thirty mile an hour and his eye full of business. You see, my grandfather's back being to him, and him stooping down like that, of course he—why sho! it *warn't* Smith of Tulare at all, it was Smith of Sacramento—my goodness, how did I ever come to get them Smiths mixed like that—why, Smith of Tulare was jest a nobody, but Smith of Sacramento—why the Smiths of Sacramento come of the best Southern blood in the United States; there warn't ever any better blood south of the line than the Sacramento Smiths. Why look here, one of them married a Whitaker! I reckon that gives you an idea of the kind of society the Sacramento Smiths could 'sociate around in; there ain't no better blood than that Whitaker blood; I reckon anybody'll tell you that.

"Look at Mariar Whitaker—there was a girl for you! Little? Why yes, she was little, but what of that? Look at the heart of her—had a heart like a bullock—just as good and sweet and lovely and generous as the day is long; if she had a thing and you wanted it, you could have it—have it and welcome. . . . She had a glass eye, and she used to lend it to Flora Ann Baxter that hadn't any, to receive company with; well she was pretty large, and it didn't fit; it was a number seven, and she was excavated for a fourteen, and so that eye wouldn't lay still; every time she winked, it would turn over. It was a beautiful eye and set her off admirable, because it was a lovely pale blue on the front side—the side you look out of—and it was gilded on the back side; didn't match the other eye, which was one of them browny-yellery eyes and tranquil and quiet, you know, the way that kind of eyes are; but that warn't any matter—they worked together all right and plenty picturesque. When Flora Ann winked, that blue-and-gilt eye would whirl over, and the other one stand still, and as soon as she begun to get excited, that hand-made eye would give a whirl and then go on a-whirlin' faster and faster, and a-flashin' first blue and then yaller and then blue and then yaller, and when it got to whizzing and flashing like that, the oldest man in the world couldn't keep up with the expression on that side of her face. Flora Ann Baxter married a Hogadorn. I reckon that lets you understand what kind of blood she was—old Maryland Eastern Shore blood; not a better family in the United States than the Hogadorns.

"Sally—that's Sally Hogadorn—Sally married a missionary, and they went off carrying the good news to the cannibals out in one of them way-off islands round the world in the middle of the ocean somers, and they et her; et him too, which was irregular; it warn't the custom to eat the missionary, but only the family, and when they see what they had done they was dreadful sorry about it, and when the relations sent down there to fetch away the things, they said so—said so right out —said they was sorry, and 'pologized, and said it shouldn't happen again; said 'twas an accident.

"Accident! now that's foolishness; there ain't no such thing as an accident; there ain't nothing happens in the world but what's ordered just so by a wiser Power than us, and it's always fur a good purpose; we don't know what the good purpose was, sometimes—and it was the same with the families that was short a missionary and his wife. But that ain't no matter, and it ain't any of our business; all that concerns us is that it was a special providence and it had a good intention. No, sir, there ain't no such thing as an accident. Whenever a thing happens that you think is an accident, you make up your mind it ain't no accident at all—it's a special providence.

"You look at my Uncle Lem—what do you say to that? That's all I ask you—you just look at my Uncle Lem and talk to me about accidents! It was like this: one day my Uncle Lem and his dog was downtown, and he was a-leanin' up against a scaffolding—sick, or drunk, or somethin' —and there was an Irishman with a hod of bricks up the ladder along about the third story, and his foot slipped and down he come, bricks and all, and hit a stranger fair and square and knocked the everlasting aspirations out of him; he was ready for the coroner in two minutes. Now then, people said it was an accident.

"Accident! there warn't no accident about it; 'twas a special providence, and had a mysterious, noble intention back of it. The idea was to save that Irishman. If the stranger hadn't been there, that Irishman would have been killed. The people said 'special providence—sho! the dog was there—why didn't the Irishman fall on the dog? Why warn't the dog app'inted?' Fer a mighty good reason— the dog would 'a' seen him a-comin'; you can't depend on no dog to carry out a special providence. You couldn't hit a dog with an Irishman because—lemme see, what was that dog's name . . . (musing) . . . oh, yes, Jasper—and a mighty good dog too; he wa'n't no common dog, he wa'n't no mongrel; he was a composite. A composite dog is a dog that's made up of all the valuable qualities that's in the dog breed—kind of a syndicate; and a mongrel is made up of the riffraff that's left over. That Jasper was one of the most wonderful dogs you ever see. Uncle Lem got him of the Wheelers. I reckon you've heard of the Wheelers; ain't no better blood south of the line than the Wheelers.

"Well, one day Wheeler was a-meditating and dreaming around in the carpet factory, and the machinery made a snatch at him, and first you know he was a-meandering all over that factory, from the garret to the cellar, and everywhere, at such another gait as—why, you couldn't even see him; you could only hear him whiz when he went by. Well, you know a person can't go through an experience like that and arrive back home the way he was when he went. No, Wheeler got wove up into thirty-nine yards of best three-ply carpeting. The widder was sorry, she was uncommon sorry, and loved him and done the best she could fur him in the circumstances, which was unusual. She took the whole piece—thirty-nine yards—and she wanted to give him proper and honorable burial, but she couldn't bear to roll him up; she took and spread him out full length and said she wouldn't have it any other way. She wanted to buy a tunnel for him, but there wasn't any tunnel for sale, so she boxed him in a beautiful box and stood it on the hill on a pedestal twenty-one foot high, and so it was monument and grave together, and economical—sixty foot high —you could see it from everywhere—and she painted on it. 'To the loving memory of thirty-nine yards best three-ply carpeting containing the mortal remainders of Millington G. Wheeler go thou and do likewise.' "

At this point the historian's voice be-

gan to wobble and his eyelids to droop with weariness and he fell asleep; and so from that day to this, we are still in ignorance; we don't know whether the old grandfather ever got the ten-cent piece out of the grass; we haven't any idea what it was that happened or whether anything happened at all.

Upon comparing the above with the original in *Roughing It,* I find myself unable to clearly and definitely explain why the one can be effectively *recited* before an audience and the other can't; there is a reason, but it is too subtle for adequate conveyance by the lumbering vehicle of words; I sense it but cannot express it; it is as elusive as an odor, pungent, pervasive, but defying analysis. I give it up. I merely know that the one version will recite, and the other won't.

By reciting I mean, of course, delivery from memory; neither version can be read effectively from the book. There are plenty of good reasons why this should be so, but there is one reason which is sufficient by itself, perhaps: in reading from the book you are telling another person's tale at second hand; you are a mimic and not the person involved; you are an artificiality, not a reality; whereas in telling the tale without the book, you absorb the character and presently become the man himself, just as is the case with the actor.

The greatest actor would not be able to carry his audience by storm with a book in his hand; reading from the book renders the nicest shadings of delivery impossible. I mean those studied fictions which seem to be the impulse of the moment and which are so effective; such as, for instance, fictitious hesitancies for the right word, fictitious unconscious pauses, fictitious unconscious side remarks, fictitious unconscious embarrassments, fictitious unconscious emphases placed upon the wrong word with a deep intention back of it—these and all the other artful fictive [1]

[1] **fictive:** referring to fiction; hence, creative, imaginative.

shades which give to a recited tale the captivating naturalness of an impromptu narration can be attempted by a book reader and are attempted, but they are easily detectable as artifice, and although the audience may admire their cleverness and their ingenuity as artifice, they only get at the intellect of the house, they don't get at its heart; and so the reader's success lacks a good deal of being complete.

When a man is reading from a book on the platform, he soon realizes that there is one powerful gun in his battery of artifice that he can't work with an effect proportionate to its caliber: that is the *pause* —that impressive silence, that eloquent silence, that geometrically progressive silence which often achieves a desired effect where no combination of words howsoever felicitous could accomplish it. The pause is not of much use to the man who is reading from a book because he cannot know what the exact length of it ought to be; he is not the one to determine the measurement—the audience must do that for him. He must perceive by their faces when the pause has reached the proper length, but his eyes are not on the faces, they are on the book; therefore he must determine the proper length of the pause by guess; he cannot guess with exactness, and nothing but exactness, absolute exactness, will answer.

The man who recites without the book has all the advantage; when he comes to an old familiar remark in his tale which he has uttered nightly for a hundred nights— a remark preceded or followed by a pause —the faces of the audience tell him when to end the pause. For one audience the pause will be short, for another a little longer, for another a shade longer still; the performer must vary the length of the pause to suit the shades of difference between audiences. These variations of measurement are so slight, so delicate, that they may almost be compared with the shadings achieved by Pratt and Whitney's ingenious machine which measures the five-millionth part of an inch. An audience is that machine's twin; it can measure a pause down to that vanishing fraction. . . .

In "His Grandfather's Old Ram" a pause has place; it follows a certain remark, and Mrs. Clemens and Clara,[1] when we were on our way around the world, would afflict themselves with my whole performance every night when there was no sort of necessity for it in order that they might watch the house when that pause came; they believed that by the effect they could accurately measure the high or low intelligence of the audience. I know better, but it was not in my interest to say so. When the pause was right, the effect was sure; when the pause was wrong in length, by the five-millionth of an inch, the laughter was only mild, never a crash. That passage occurs in "His Grandfather's Old Ram" where the question under discussion is whether the falling of the Irishman on the stranger was an accident or was a special providence. If it was a special providence and if the sole purpose of it was to save the Irishman, why was it necessary to sacrifice the stranger? "The dog was there. Why didn't he fall on the dog? Why warn't the dog app'inted? Becuz *the dog would 'a' seen him a-comin'.*" That last remark was the one the family waited for. A pause *after* the remark was absolutely necessary with any and all audiences because no man, howsoever intelligent he may be, can instantly adjust his mind to a new and unfamiliar, and yet for a moment or two apparently plausible, logic, which recognizes in a dog an instrument too indifferent to pious restraint and too alert in looking out for his own personal interest to be safely depended upon in an emergency requiring self-sacrifice for the benefit of another, even when the command comes from on high.

[1] **Clara:** Twain's daughter.

[STUDY AIDS FOLLOW ON PAGE 367]

AMERICAN PAINTING

Mystics and Realists

By the 1860's, two important currents were developing in American painting. One was a mystical, poetic interpretation of landscape in the romantic tradition of earlier painters such as Washington Allston (page 151). The other was a new type of realism, based on a careful study of figures, objects, and, sometimes, landscapes—but quite different from the meticulously detailed panoramas of the Hudson River School.

The first of these new currents can be seen in the paintings of Albert Pinkham Ryder, a self-taught artist who spent most of his career secluded in his New York studio. If we compare Ryder's small picture *The Forest of Arden* (PLATE 1) with the sweeping landscapes of the Hudson River School, his highly simplified style seems almost primitive. Such a landscape, a romantic version of an English woodland, is pure invention. Yet Ryder's dreamlike scene has a reality all its own, for even the clouds appear so dense and solid that we can't help feeling their physical presence. To create this effect, Ryder built up crusty surfaces of thick pigment and then added layers of color glazes thinned out with varnish. But unfortunately, he reworked his canvases too many times, causing the surfaces to crack eventually and the colors to lose their freshness.

Another painter of poetic landscapes was Ryder's contemporary Ralph Albert Blakelock. *Moonlight* (PLATE 2) shows one of Blakelock's typical scenes that he based on memories of his travels through the West, where he had lived in Indian encampments of the sort shown at the left in this picture. Blakelock probably had no particular place in mind here; what mattered most to him in such a picture was its mood. Like Ryder, he created a variety of paint textures and used glazes of pigment and varnish to produce deep, resonant tones. But notice that Blakelock's forms are more detailed, especially the foliage silhouetted against the sky.

The new approach to realism, the other main current in this period of American art, can be found in several different types of paintings. In *Steelworkers—Noontime* (PLATE 3) by Thomas P. Anshutz, for example, we see a genre painting in the tradition of George Caleb Bingham's *Raftsmen Playing Cards* (page 152). But here the setting is in the heart of an industrial city rather than in the wilderness. Anshutz has depicted a typical urban scene: a group of husky factory workers relaxing outdoors under the midday sun. Notice how he has grouped the figures so that they lead our eye across the front of the picture-space toward the right, thus counterbalancing the perspective lines of the factory which plunge into the distance at the left.

In PLATE 4, *John Biglen in a Single Scull,* by Anshutz's teacher Thomas Eakins, we see a forceful close-up of a human figure in a casual outdoor setting, a picture which seems to combine qualities of both portraiture and genre painting. Curiously enough, Eakins intended this oil painting to be a preparatory study for a *horizontally* shaped watercolor, in which more of the boat and river would be shown. The vertical format of the oil, however, makes a more powerful impression because of the way Biglen's body seems to fill the space. And notice how Eakins painted the sky, applying the pigment in thick slabs, so that this plain area seems almost as solid as the form of the figure. Eakins's choice of such ordinary subjects for his pictures won him very few patrons among the wealthier people in Philadelphia, where he spent most of his life. Moreover, the frankness with which he portrayed human character was unacceptable to an age that demanded flattery. Yet this painter, who was largely unappreciated in his own lifetime, is regarded today as one of the greatest in American history.

During the 1870's, another Philadelphia artist, named William Harnett, began to devote his time entirely to painting *still lifes*—pictures which represent simple, ordinary objects such as books and baskets of fruit. Harnett brought to still-life painting the kind of "fool-the-eye" realism that he had admired in the "deceptions" of Charles Willson Peale and his sons. In *Music and Good Luck* (PLATE 5), for example, through extremely subtle handling of tones, he made trivial details extraordinarily significant— details such as rust stains on a wooden door and a tear in a piece of sheet music, which we would scarcely be aware of in real life.

Among American painters in the second half of the nineteenth century only Winslow Homer rivaled Eakins in power and originality. But unlike Eakins, Homer had the good fortune to be recognized as a great artist during his own lifetime. In fact, by his mid-twenties, before he had done much painting at all, Homer was already well known to the general public as the leading illustrator for *Harper's Weekly.* The disciplines he learned in drawing for crude black-and-white woodblock reproduction contributed later to the forcefulness of his larger compositions on canvas. *Searchlight: Harbor Entrance, Santiago de Cuba* (PLATE 6), one of Homer's later works, represents the Cuban fortification where the Spanish navy had been defeated three years earlier in the Spanish-American War. The simplicity and strength of this picture's design point toward the more abstract work of later American painters of the 1920's and 1930's.

PLATE 1. ALBERT PINKHAM RYDER (1847–1917): *The Forest of Arden.* About 1897. Oil on canvas, 19 x 15 inches. (The Metropolitan Museum of Art, New York, Bequest of Stephen C. Clark, 1960)

361

PLATE 2. RALPH ALBERT BLAKELOCK (1847–1919): *Moonlight*. About 1885. Oil on canvas, 27¼ x 32¼ inches. (The Brooklyn Museum)

362

PLATE 3. THOMAS P. ANSHUTZ (1815–1912): *Steel Workers—Noontime*. About 1880. Oil on canvas, 17 x 24 inches. (Collection of Dr. and Mrs. Irving F. Burton)

363

PLATE 4. THOMAS EAKINS (1844–1916): *John Biglen in a Single Scull*. 1874. Oil on canvas, 24 x 15½ inches. (Yale University Art Gallery, New Haven, Connecticut, Whitney Collection of Sporting Art)

PLATE 5. WILLIAM M. HARNETT (1848–1892): *Music and Good Luck*. 1888. Oil on canvas, 40 x 30 inches. (The Metropolitan Museum of Art, New York, Wolfe Fund, 1963)

PLATE 6. WINSLOW HOMER (1836–1910): *Searchlight: Harbor Entrance, Santiago de Cuba.* 1901. Oil on canvas, $30\frac{1}{2}$ x $50\frac{1}{2}$ inches. (The Metropolitan Museum of Art, New York, Gift of George A. Hearn, 1906)

THE BUFFALO THAT CLIMBED A TREE

FOR STUDY AND DISCUSSION

1. At what point do you first become suspicious of Bemis's story? At what point are your suspicions confirmed?

2. Part of the humor of the selection lies in the way Bemis tells his story as if he meant it to be believed. Find details that seem to indicate that he is taking pains to lend plausibility to the story. In your opinion, does Bemis really think he will be believed? Why does he pretend to think so?

3. This selection is exciting as well as funny. Do the excitement and humor go hand in hand? That is, does the story become funnier as it becomes more exciting? Explain. What motion pictures or television plays have you seen in which the humor depends partly on suspense or thrills?

4. The effect of humor and excitement is gained partly through the use of colorful and vivid phrases. Point out some of these phrases.

5. Mark Twain is America's most famous humorist. What is characteristically American about the humor of this selection? What does it have in common with tales you may have read about Paul Bunyan, Pecos Bill, or Davy Crockett?

LANGUAGE AND VOCABULARY

Like James Russell Lowell in "The Courtin'" (see page 198), Mark Twain is telling a tale in dialect. But while Lowell's narrator is a New England farmer, Bemis is apparently a Midwesterner and is speaking in an obviously different dialect. Cite passages from this selection by Twain that are similar to the passages in "The Courtin'" given below. Then discuss any differences you find between the two dialects. (*Example:* "My! when he made Ole Hunderd ring . . ." [Find any interjection used by Twain]: "By George, it was a hot race!")

1. "But long o' her his veins 'ould run/ All crinkly like curled maple . . ." (Find the description of a sensation or emotion.)

2. "The side she breshed felt full o' sun/ Ez a south slope in Ap'il." (Find an extravagant simile.)

3. "He was six foot o'man, A 1 . . ." (Find a description of a man.)

4. "An' yit she gin her cheer a jerk." (Find a description of an action.)

5. "Says he, 'I'd better call agin!'/ Says she, 'Think likely, Mister.'" (Find a short dialogue between two characters.)

MARK TWAIN AND THE PUBLIC READING

FOR STUDY AND DISCUSSION

1. Why did Mark Twain find his first public reading experiences "ghastly"? What did he discover about the reactions of an audience to a recitation of selections that were originally intended to be read silently?

2. Explain how the story of "His Grandfather's Old Ram" happens to have so many characters.

3. Why does Mark Twain say that it is essential to pause after the remark, "Becuz the dog would 'a' seen him a-comin'"? If you were giving a public reading of "His Grandfather's Old Ram," at what other places in the story would you pause for effect?

4. Compare the humor of "His Grandfather's Old Ram" with the humor of "The Buffalo That Climbed a Tree." Which piece depends more on exaggeration? Which piece depends more on the peculiarities of the narrator? Which piece do you think is funnier? Why?

5. On the basis of what you have learned from this selection and from comparing other selections in this book (for example, Lincoln's Gettysburg Address and his letter to Mrs. Bixby), discuss the difference between prose that is meant to be read silently and prose that is meant to be spoken. What kind of sentences and paragraphs are especially effective when spoken? In adapting an essay or story for a public reading, what kind of changes would you make?

FOR COMPOSITION

Write a composition in which you compare Mark Twain with one or two modern American humorists—James Thurber, for example (page 695). In your composition, consider the following questions: What attitudes and humorous devices, if any, do these humorists have in common? Can any of the writers be considered "typically American" humorists? If so, what are the qualities of "typically American" humor? (See page 369 for a discussion of American humor.)

The Private History of a Campaign That Failed

YOU HAVE HEARD from a great many people who did something in the war.[1] Is it not fair and right that you listen a little moment to one who started out to do something in it, but didn't? Thousands entered the war, got just a taste of it, and then stepped out again permanently. These, by their very numbers, are respectable and are therefore entitled to a sort of a voice—not a loud one but a modest one, not a boastful one but an apologetic one. They ought not to be allowed much space among better people—people who did something. I grant that, but they ought at least to be allowed to state why they didn't do anything and also to explain the process by which they didn't do anything. Surely this kind of light must have a sort of value.

Out West there was a good deal of confusion in men's minds during the first months of the great trouble—a good deal of unsettledness, of leaning first this way, then that, then the other way. It was hard for us to get our bearings. I call to mind an instance of this. I was piloting on the Mississippi when the news came that South Carolina had gone out of the Union on the 20th of December, 1860. My pilot mate was a New Yorker. He was strong for the union; so was I. But he would not listen to me with any patience; my loyalty was smirched, to his eye, because my father had owned slaves. I said in palliation[2] of this dark fact that I had heard my father say, some years before he died, that slavery was a great wrong and that he

[1] **war:** the War Between the States.
[2] **palliation:** extenuation.

"The Private History of a Campaign That Failed" by Mark Twain. Reprinted by permission of Harper & Row, Publishers.

would free the solitary slave he then owned if he could think it right to give away the property of the family when he was so straitened in means. My mate retorted that a mere impulse was nothing—anybody could pretend to a good impulse, and went on decrying my Unionism and libeling my ancestry. A month later the secession atmosphere had considerably thickened on the Lower Mississippi and I became a rebel; so did he. We were together in New Orleans the 26th of January, when Louisiana went out of the Union. He did his full share of the rebel shouting but was bitterly opposed to letting me do mine. He said that I came of bad stock—of a father who had been willing to set slaves free. In the following summer he was piloting a Federal gunboat and shouting for the Union again and I was in the Confederate army. I held his note for some borrowed money. He was one of the most upright men I ever knew but he repudiated that note without hesitation because I was a rebel and the son of a man who owned slaves.

In that summer of 1861 the first wash of the wave of war broke upon the shores of Missouri. Our state was invaded by the Union forces. They took possession of St. Louis, Jefferson Barracks, and some other points. The Governor, Claib Jackson, issued his proclamation calling out fifty thousand militia to repel the invader.

I was visiting in the small town where my boyhood had been spent, Hannibal, Marion County. Several of us got together in a secret place by night and formed ourselves into a military company. One Tom Lyman, a young fellow of a good deal of spirit but of no military experience, was made captain; I was made second lieutenant. We had no first lieutenant; I do not know why; it was long ago. There were fifteen of us. By the advice of an innocent connected with the organization, we called ourselves the Marion Rangers. I do not remember that anyone found fault with the name. I did not; I thought it sounded quite well. The young fellow who proposed this title was perhaps a fair sample of the kind of stuff we were made of. He was young, ignorant, good-natured, well-meaning, trivial, full of romance, and given to reading chivalric novels and singing forlorn love ditties. He had some pathetic little nickel-plated aristocratic instincts and detested his name, which was Dunlap; detested it partly because it was nearly as common in that region as Smith but mainly because it had a plebeian sound to his ear. So he tried to ennoble it by writing it in this way: *d'Unlap.* That contented his eye but left his ear unsatisfied, for people gave the new name the same old pronunciation—emphasis on the front end of it. He then did the bravest thing that can be imagined, a thing to make one shiver when one remembers how the world is given to resenting shams and affectations, he began to write his name so: *d'Un Lap.* And he waited patiently through the long storm of mud that was flung at this work of art and he had his reward at last, for he lived to see that name accepted and the emphasis put where he wanted it by people who had known him all his life, and to whom the tribe of Dunlaps had been as familiar as the rain and the sunshine for forty years. So sure of victory at last is the courage that can wait. He said he had found by consulting some ancient French chronicles that the name was rightly and originally written d'Un Lap, and said that if it were translated into English it would mean Peterson: *Lap,* Latin, or Greek, he said, for stone or rock, same as the French *pierre,* that is to say, Peter: *d',* of or from; *un,* a or one; hence, d'Un Lap, of or from a stone or a Peter; that is to say, one who is the son of a stone, the son of a Peter—Peterson. Our militia company were not learned and the explanation confused them; so they called him Peterson Dunlap. He proved useful to us in his way; he named our camps for us and he generally struck a name that was "no slouch," as the boys said.

That is one sample of us. Another was Ed Stevens, son of the town jeweler, trim-built, handsome, graceful, neat as a cat; bright, educated, but given over entirely

Mark Twain and American Humor

When Twain began to write the humorous stories and sketches that made him famous, he was able to draw on a rich tradition. American humorists had long pleased their fellow countrymen with their sharp renderings of dialects, their vivid language, and their soaring exaggerations. Mark Twain himself commented: "To string incongruities together in a wandering and sometimes purposeless way, and seem innocently aware that they are absurdities, is the basis of American art." A humorous story, Mark Twain maintained, "is strictly a work of art, high and delicate art—and only an artist can tell it."

One of the beginnings of this art was the Southwestern tradition of yarnspinning. Able storytellers were particularly admired in frontier America, and men such as Abraham Lincoln and Davy Crockett became famous partly because of their ability to tell a good, funny story. The flavor of such stories was caught in Thomas Bangs Thorpe's "The Big Bear of Arkansas." When the bear was finally killed, Thorpe's backwoods storyteller commented: " 'Twould astonish you to know how big he was: I made a *bedspread of his skin* and the way it used to cover my bar mattress and leave several feet on each side to tuck up would have delighted you. It was in fact a creation bar, and if it had lived in Samson's time, and had met him in a fair fight, it would have licked him in the twinkling of a dice-box."

to fun. There was nothing serious in life to him. As far as he was concerned, this military expedition of ours was simply a holiday. I should say that about half of us looked upon it in the same way; not consciously, perhaps, but unconsciously. We did not think; we were not capable of it. As for myself, I was full of unreasoning joy to be done with turning out of bed at midnight and four in the morning for a while, grateful to have a change, new scenes, new occupations, a new interest. In my thoughts that was as far as I went; I did not go into the details; as a rule one doesn't at twenty-four.

Another sample was Smith, the blacksmith's apprentice. This vast donkey had some pluck, of a slow and sluggish nature, but a soft heart; at one time he would knock a horse down for some impropriety and at another he would get homesick and cry. However, he had one ultimate credit to his account which some of us hadn't; he stuck to the war and was killed in battle at last.

Jo Bowers, another sample, was a huge, good-natured, flax-headed lubber, lazy, sentimental, full of harmless brag, a grumbler by nature; an experienced, industrious, ambitious, and often quite picturesque liar and yet not a successful one, for he had had no intelligent training but was allowed to come up just any way. This life was serious enough to him, and seldom satisfactory. But he was a good fellow, anyway, and the boys all liked him. He was made orderly sergeant; Stevens was made corporal.

These samples will answer—and they are quite fair ones. Well, this herd of cattle started for the war. What could you expect of them? They did as well as they knew how but, really, what was justly to be expected of them? Nothing, I should say. That is what they did.

We waited for a dark night, for caution and secrecy were necessary; then toward midnight we stole in couples and from various directions to the Griffith place, beyond the town; from that point we set out together on foot. Hannibal lies at the extreme southeastern corner of Marion County, on the Mississippi River; our objective point was the hamlet of New London, ten miles away, in Ralls County.

The first hour was all fun, all idle nonsense and laughter. But that could not be kept up. The steady trudging came to be like work, the play had somehow oozed out of it, the stillness of the woods and the somberness of the night began to throw a depressing influence over the spirits of the boys, and presently the talking died out and each person shut himself up in his own thoughts. During the last half of the second hour nobody said a word.

Now we approached a log farmhouse where, according to report, there was a guard of five Union soldiers. Lyman called a halt and there, in the deep gloom of the overhanging branches, he began to whisper a plan of assault upon that house, which made the gloom more depressing than it was before. It was a crucial moment; we realized with a cold suddenness that here was no jest—we were standing face to face with actual war. We were equal to the occasion. In our response there was no hesitation, no indecision: we said that if Lyman wanted to meddle with those soldiers, he could go ahead and do it, but if he waited for us to follow him, he would wait a long time.

Lyman urged, pleaded, tried to shame us, but it had no effect. Our course was plain, our minds were made up: we would flank the farmhouse—go out around. And that was what we did.

We struck into the woods and entered upon a rough time, stumbling over roots, getting tangled in vines and torn by briers. At last we reached an open place in a safe region and sat down, blown and hot, to cool off and nurse our scratches and bruises. Lyman was annoyed but the rest of us were cheerful; we had flanked the farmhouse, we had made our first military movement and it was a success; we had nothing to fret about, we were feeling just the other way. Horseplay and laughing began again; the expedition was become a holiday frolic once more.

Then we had two more hours of dull trudging and ultimate silence and depression; then about dawn we straggled into New London, soiled, heel-blistered, fagged with our little march, and all of us except Stevens in a sour and raspy humor and privately down on the war. We stacked our shabby old shotguns in Colonel Ralls's barn and then went in a body and breakfasted with that veteran of the Mexican War. Afterward he took us to a distant meadow, and there in the shade of a tree we listened to an old-fashioned speech from him, full of gunpowder and glory, full of that adjective-piling, mixed metaphor and windy declamation which were regarded as eloquence in that ancient time and that remote region; and then he swore us on the Bible to be faithful to the State of Missouri and drive all invaders from her soil, no matter whence they might come or under what flag they might march. This mixed us considerably and we could not make out just what service we were embarked in, but Colonel Ralls, the practiced politician and phrase-juggler, was not similarly in doubt; he knew quite clearly that he had invested us in the cause of the Southern Confederacy. He closed the solemnities by belting around me the sword which his neighbor, Colonel Brown, had worn at Buena

Vista and Molino del Rey; [1] and he accompanied this act with another impressive blast.

Then we formed in line of battle and marched four miles to a shady and pleasant piece of woods on the border of the far-reaching expanses of a flowery prairie. It was an enchanting region for war—our kind of war.

We pierced the forest about half a mile and took up a strong position, with some low, rocky, and wooded hills behind us and a purling, limpid creek in front. Straightway half the command were in swimming and the other half fishing. The ass with the French name gave this position a romantic title but it was too long, so the boys shortened and simplified it to Camp Ralls.

We occupied an old maple-sugar camp, whose half-rotted troughs were still propped against the trees. A long corncrib served for sleeping quarters for the battalion. On our left, half a mile away, were Mason's farm and house, and he was a friend to the cause. Shortly after noon the farmers began to arrive from several directions with mules and horses for our use, and these they lent us for as long as the war might last, which they judged would be about three months. The animals were of all sizes, all colors, and all breeds. They were mainly young and frisky, and nobody in the command could stay on them long at a time, for we were town boys and ignorant of horsemanship. The creature that fell to my share was a very small mule, and yet so quick and active that it could throw me without difficulty, and it did this whenever I got on it. Then it would bray—stretching its neck out, laying its ears back, and spreading its jaws till you could see down to its works. It was a disagreeable animal in every way. If I took it by the bridle and tried to lead it off the grounds, it would sit down and brace back and no one could budge it. However,

[1] **Buena Vista . . . Molino del Rey:** two Mexican cities where American forces won important victories in the Mexican War.

like a railroad bridge. His size enabled him to reach all about, and as far as he wanted to, with his head; so he was always biting Bowers's legs. On the march, in the sun, Bowers slept a good deal, and as soon as the horse recognized that he was asleep he would reach around and bite him on the leg. His legs were black and blue with bites. This was the only thing that could ever make him swear but this always did; whenever his horse bit him he always swore, and of course Stevens, who laughed at everything, laughed at this and would even get into such convulsions over it as to lose his balance and fall off his horse; and 'then Bowers, already irritated by the pain of the horse bite, would resent the laughter with hard language, and there would be a quarrel; so that horse made no end of trouble and bad blood in the command.

However, I will get back to where I was —our first afternoon in the sugar camp. The sugar troughs came very handy as horse troughs and we had plenty of corn to fill them with. I ordered Sergeant Bowers to feed my mule, but he said that if I reckoned he went to war to be a dry nurse to a mule it wouldn't take me very long to find out my mistake. I believed that this was insubordination but I was full of uncertainties about everything military, and so I let the thing pass and went and ordered Smith, the blacksmith's apprentice, to feed the mule; but he merely gave me a large, cold, sarcastic grin, such as an ostensibly seven-year-old horse gives you when you lift his lip and find he is fourteen, and turned his back on me. I then went to the captain and asked if it were not right and proper and military for me to have an orderly. He said it was but as there was only one orderly in the corps, it was but right that he himself should have Bowers on his staff. Bowers said he wouldn't serve on anybody's staff, and if anybody thought he could make him, let him try it. So, of course, the thing had to be dropped; there was no other way.

Next, nobody would cook; it was considered a degradation; so we had no

I was not entirely destitute of military resources and I did presently manage to spoil this game, for I had seen many a steamboat aground in my time and knew a trick or two which even a grounded mule would be obliged to respect. There was a well by the corncrib; so I substituted thirty fathom of rope for the bridle, and fetched him home with the windlass.[1]

I will anticipate here sufficiently to say that he did learn to ride after some days' practice, but never well. We could not learn to like our animals; they were not choice ones and most of them had annoying peculiarities of one kind or another. Stevens's horse would carry him, when he was not noticing, under the huge excrescences which form on the trunks of oak trees, and wipe him out of the saddle; in this way Stevens got several bad hurts. Sergeant Bowers's horse was very large and tall, with slim, long legs, and looked

[1] **windlass:** a device for hauling or lifting by cranking a rope around a drum or barrel.

dinner. We lazied the rest of the pleasant afternoon away, some dozing under the trees, some smoking cob pipes and talking sweethearts and war, some playing games. By late suppertime all hands were famished, and to meet the difficulty all hands turned to on an equal footing and gathered wood, built fires, and cooked the meal. Afterward everything was smooth for a while; then trouble broke out between the corporal and the sergeant, each claiming to rank the other. Nobody knew which was the higher office; so Lyman had to settle the matter by making the rank of both officers equal. The commander of an ignorant crew like that has many troubles and vexations which probably do not occur in the regular army at all. However, with the song-singing and yarn-spinning around the campfire, everything presently became serene again, and by and by we raked the corn down level in one end of the crib and all went to bed on it, tying a horse to the door, so that he would neigh if anyone tried to get in.[1]

We had some horsemanship drill every forenoon; then, afternoons, we rode off here and there in squads a few miles and visited the farmers' girls, and had a youthful good time and got an honest good dinner or supper, and then home again to camp, happy and content.

For a time life was idly delicious, it was perfect; there was nothing to mar it. Then came some farmers with an alarm one day. They said it was rumored that the enemy were advancing in our direction from over Hyde's prairie. The result was a sharp

stir among us, and general consternation. It was a rude awakening from our pleasant trance. The rumor was but a rumor—nothing definite about it; so in the confusion we did not know which way to retreat. Lyman was for not retreating at all in these uncertain circumstances, but he found that if he tried to maintain that attitude he would fare badly, for the command were in no humor to put up with insubordination. So he yielded the point and called a council of war, to consist of himself and the three other officers; but the privates made such a fuss about being left out that we had to allow them to remain, for they were already present and doing the most of the talking too. The question was, which way to retreat; but all were so flurried that nobody seemed to have even a guess to offer. Except Lyman. He explained in a few calm words that, inasmuch as the enemy were approaching from over Hyde's prairie, our course was simple: all we had to do was not to retreat *toward* him; any other direction would answer our needs perfectly. Everybody saw in a moment how true this was, and how wise, so Lyman got a great many compliments. It was now decided that we should fall back on Mason's farm.

---

[1] It was always my impression that that was what the horse was there for and I know that it was also the impression of at least one other of the command, for we talked about it at the time and admired the military ingenuity of the device; but when I was out West three years ago, I was told by Mr. A. G. Fuqua, a member of our company, that the horse was his, that the leaving him tied at the door was a matter of mere forgetfulness, and that to attribute it to intelligent invention was to give him quite too much credit. In support of his position he called my attention to the suggestive fact that the artifice was not employed again. I had not thought of that before. [Author's note.]

It was after dark by this time and as we could not know how soon the enemy might arrive, it did not seem best to try to take the horses and things with us; so we only took the guns and ammunition, and started at once. The route was very rough and hilly and rocky, and presently the night grew very black and rain began to fall; so we had a troublesome time of it, struggling and stumbling along in the dark, and soon some person slipped and fell, and then the next person behind stumbled over him and fell, and so did the rest, one after the other; and then Bowers came, with the keg of powder in his arms, while the command were all mixed together, arms and legs, on the muddy slope, and so he fell, of course, with the keg, and this started the whole detachment down the hill in a body, and they landed in the brook at the bottom in a pile, and each that was undermost pulling the hair and scratching and biting those that were on top of him, and those that were being scratched and bitten scratching and biting the rest in their turn, and all saying they would die before they would ever go to war again if they ever got out of this brook this time and the invader might rot for all they cared, and the country along with him— and all such talk as that, which was dismal to hear and take part in, in such smothered, low voices, and such a grisly dark place and so wet, and the enemy, maybe, coming any moment.

The keg of powder was lost, and the guns too; so the growling and complaining continued straight along while the brigade pawed around the pasty hillside and slopped around in the brook hunting for these things; consequently we lost considerable time at this, and then we heard a sound and held our breath and listened, and it seemed to be the enemy coming, though it could have been a cow, for it had a cough like a cow; but we did not wait but left a couple of guns behind and struck out for Mason's again as briskly as we could scramble along in the dark. But we got lost presently among the rugged little ravines and wasted a deal of

time finding the way again, so it was after nine when we reached Mason's stile at last; and then before we could open our mouths to give the countersign several dogs came bounding over the fence with great riot and noise, and each of them took a soldier by the slack of his trousers and

began to back away with him. We could not shoot the dogs without endangering the persons they were attached to; so we had to look on helpless at what was perhaps the most mortifying spectacle of the war. There was light enough and to spare, for the Masons had now run out on the porch with candles in their hands. The old man and his son came and undid the dogs without difficulty, all but Bowers's; but they couldn't undo his dog, they didn't know his combination; he was of the bull kind and seemed to be set with a Yale time-lock, but they got him loose at last with some scalding water, of which Bowers got his share and returned thanks. Peterson Dunlap afterward made up a fine name for this engagement, and also for the night march which preceded it, but both have long ago faded out of my memory.

We now went into the house and they began to ask us a world of questions, whereby it presently came out that we did not know anything concerning who or what we were running from; so the old gentleman made himself very frank and said we were a curious breed of soldiers and guessed we could be depended on to end up the war in time, because no government could stand the expense of the shoe leather we should cost it trying to follow us around. "Marion *Rangers!* good name, b'gosh!" said he. And wanted to know why we hadn't had a picket guard at the place where the road entered the prairie, and why we hadn't sent out a scouting party to spy out the enemy and bring us an account of his strength, and so on, before jumping up and stampeding out of a strong position upon a mere vague rumor —and so on, and so forth, till he made us all feel shabbier than the dogs had done, not half so enthusiastically welcome. So we went to bed shamed and low-spirited, except Stevens. Soon Stevens began to devise a garment for Bowers which could be made to automatically display his battle scars to the grateful or conceal them from the envious, according to his occasions, but Bowers was in no humor for this, so there was a fight and when it was over Stevens had some battle scars of his own to think about.

Then we got a little sleep. But after all we had gone through, our activities were not over for the night, for about two o'clock in the morning we heard a shout of warning from down the lane, accompanied by a chorus from all the dogs, and in a moment everybody was up and flying around to find out what the alarm was about. The alarmist was a horseman who gave notice that a detachment of Union soldiers was on its way from Hannibal with orders to capture and hang any bands like ours which it could find, and said we had no time to lose. Farmer Mason was in a flurry this time himself. He hurried us out of the house with all haste, and sent one of his slaves with us to show us where to hide ourselves and our telltale guns among the ravines half a mile away. It was raining heavily.

We struck down the lane, then across some rocky pasture land which offered good advantages for stumbling; consequently we were down in the mud most of the time, and every time a man went down he blackguarded the war and the people that started it and everybody connected with it, and gave himself the master dose of all for being so foolish as to go into it. At last we reached the wooded mouth of a ravine, and there we huddled ourselves under the streaming trees and sent the

slave back home. It was a dismal and heartbreaking time. We were like to be drowned with the rain, deafened with the howling wind and the booming thunder, and blinded by the lightning. It was indeed a wild night. The drenching we were getting was misery enough, but a deeper misery still was the reflection that the halter might end us before we were a day older. A death of this shameful sort had not occurred to us as being among the possibilities of war. It took the romance all out of the campaign and turned our dreams of glory into a repulsive nightmare. As for doubting that so barbarous an order had been given, not one of us did that.

The long night wore itself out at last, and then the slave came to us with the news that the alarm had manifestly been a false one and that breakfast would soon be ready. Straightway we were lighthearted again, and the world was bright and life as full of hope and promise as ever—for we were young then. How long ago that was! Twenty-four years.

The mongrel child of philology named the night's refuge Camp Devastation and no soul objected. The Masons gave us a Missouri country breakfast in Missourian abundance, and we needed it: hot biscuits, hot "wheat bread," prettily crisscrossed in a lattice pattern on top, hot corn pone, fried chicken, bacon, coffee, eggs, milk, buttermilk, etc., and the world may be confidently challenged to furnish the equal of such a breakfast, as it is cooked in the South.

We stayed several days at Mason's, and after all these years the memory of the dullness and stillness and lifelessness of that slumberous farmhouse still oppresses my spirit as with a sense of the presence of death and mourning. There was nothing to do, nothing to think about; there was no interest in life. The male part of the household were away in the fields all day, the women were busy and out of our sight; there was no sound but the plaintive wailing of a spinning wheel, forever moaning out from some distant room, the most lonesome sound in nature, a sound steeped and sodden with homesickness and the emptiness of life. The family went to bed about dark every night, and as we were not invited to intrude any new customs we naturally followed theirs. Those nights were a hundred years long to youths accustomed to being up till twelve. We lay awake and miserable till that hour every time, and grew old and decrepit waiting through the still eternities for the clock strikes. This was no place for town boys. So at last it was with something very like joy that we received news that the enemy were on our track again. With a new birth of the old warrior spirit we sprang to our places in line of battle and fell back on Camp Ralls.

Captain Lyman had taken a hint from Mason's talk, and he now gave orders that our camp should be guarded against surprise by the posting of pickets. I was ordered to place a picket at the forks of the road in Hyde's prairie. Night shut down black and threatening. I told Sergeant Bowers to go out to that place and stay till midnight and, just as I was expecting, he said he wouldn't do it. I tried to get others to go but all refused. Some excused themselves on account of the weather, but the rest were frank enough to say they wouldn't go in any kind of weather. This kind of thing sounds odd now, and impossible, but there was no surprise in it at the time. On the contrary, it seemed a perfectly natural thing to do. There were scores of little camps scattered over Missouri where the same thing was happening. These camps were composed of young men who had been born and reared to a sturdy independence, and who did not know what it meant to be ordered around by Tom, Dick, and Harry, whom they had known familiarly all their lives in the village or on the farm. It is quite within the probabilities that this same thing was happening all over the South. James Redpath recognized the justice of this assumption and furnished the following instance in support of it. During a short stay in East Tennessee he was in a citizen colonel's tent one day talking, when a big private appeared at the door and, without salute or other circumlocution, said to the colonel:

"Say, Jim, I'm a-goin' home for a few days."

"What for?"

"Well, I hain't be'en there for a right smart while and I'd like to see how things is comin' on."

"How long are you going to be gone?"

" 'Bout two weeks."

"Well, don't be gone longer than that, and get back sooner if you can."

That was all, and the citizen officer resumed his conversation where the private had broken it off. This was in the first months of the war, of course. The camps in our part of Missouri were under Brigadier General Thomas H. Harris. He was a townsman of ours, a first-rate fellow and well liked, but we had all familiarly known him as the sole and modest-salaried operator in our telegraph office, where he had to send about one dispatch a week in ordinary times and two when there was a rush of business; consequently, when he appeared in our midst one day on the wing, and delivered a military command of some sort in a large military fashion, nobody was surprised at the response which he got from the assembled soldiery:

"Oh, now, what'll you take to *don't*, Tom Harris?"

It was quite the natural thing. One might justly imagine that we were hopeless material for war. And so we seemed in our ignorant state, but there were those among us who afterward learned the grim trade, learned to obey like machines, became valuable soldiers; fought all through the war, and came out at the end with excellent records. One of the very boys who refused to go out on picket duty that night and called me an ass for thinking he would expose himself to danger in such a foolhardy way, had become distinguished for intrepidity before he was a year older.

I did secure my picket that night, not by authority but by diplomacy. I got Bowers to go by agreeing to exchange ranks with him for the time being, and go along and stand the watch with him as his subordinate. We stayed out there a couple of dreary hours in the pitchy darkness and the rain, with nothing to modify the dreariness but Bowers's monotonous growlings at the war and the weather; then we began to nod and presently found it next to impossible to stay in the saddle, so we gave up the tedious job and went back to the camp without waiting for the relief guard. We rode into camp without interruption or objection from anybody and the enemy could have done the same, for there were no sentries. Everybody was asleep; at midnight there was nobody to send out another picket, so none was sent. We never tried to establish a watch at night again, as far as I remember, but we generally kept a picket out in the daytime.

In that camp the whole command slept on the corn in the big corncrib and there was usually a general row before morning, for the place was full of rats and they would scramble over the boys' bodies and faces, annoying and irritating everybody, and now and then they would bite someone's toe, and the person who owned the toe would start up and magnify his English and begin to throw corn in the dark. The ears were half as heavy as bricks and when they struck they hurt. The persons struck would respond and inside of five minutes every man would be locked in a death grip with his neighbor. There was a grievous deal of blood shed in the corncrib but this was all that was spilt while I was in the war. No, that is not quite true. But for one circumstance it would have been all. I will come to that now.

Our scares were frequent. Every few days rumors would come that the enemy were approaching. In these cases we always fell back on some other camp of ours; we never stayed where we were. But the rumors always turned out to be false, so at last even we began to grow indifferent to them. One night a slave was sent to our corncrib with the same old warning, the enemy was hovering in our neighborhood. We all said let him hover. We resolved to stay still and be comfortable. It was a fine warlike resolution, and no doubt we all felt the stir of it in our veins—for a moment. We had been having a very jolly time that was full of horseplay and schoolboy hilarity but that cooled down now, and presently the fast-waning fire of forced jokes and forced laughs died out altogether and the company became silent. Silent and nervous. And soon uneasy—worried—apprehensive. We had said we would stay and we were committed. We could have been persuaded to go but there was nobody brave enough to suggest it. An almost noiseless movement presently began in the dark by a general but unvoiced impulse. When the movement was completed each man knew that he was not the only person who had crept to the front wall and had his eye at a crack between the logs. No, we were all there, all there with our hearts in our throats and staring out toward the sugar troughs where the forest footpath came through. It was late and there was a deep woodsy stillness everywhere. There was a veiled moonlight, which was only just strong enough to enable us to mark the general shape of objects. Presently a muffled sound caught our ears and we recognized it as the hoofbeats of a horse or horses. And right away a figure appeared in the forest path; it could have been made of smoke, its mass

had so little sharpness of outline. It was a man on horseback and it seemed to me that there were others behind him. I got hold of a gun in the dark, and pushed it through a crack between the logs, hardly knowing what I was doing, I was so dazed with fright. Somebody said "Fire!" I pulled the trigger. I seemed to see a hundred flashes and hear a hundred reports; then I saw the man fall down out of the saddle. My first feeling was of surprised gratification; my first impulse was an apprentice-sportsman's impulse to run and pick up his game. Somebody said, hardly audibly, "Good—we've got him!—wait for the rest." But the rest did not come. We waited—listened—still no more came. There was not a sound, not the whisper of a leaf; just perfect stillness, an uncanny kind of stillness which was all the more uncanny on account of the damp, earthy, late-night smells now rising and pervading it. Then, wondering, we crept stealthily out and approached the man. When we got to him the moon revealed him distinctly. He was lying on his back with his arms abroad, his mouth was open and his chest heaving with long gasps, and his white shirtfront was all splashed with blood. The thought shot through me that I was a murderer, that I had killed a man, a man who had never done me any harm. That was the coldest sensation that ever went through my marrow. I was down by him in a moment, helplessly stroking his forehead, and I would have given anything then—my own life freely—to make him again what he had been five minutes before. And all the boys seemed to be feeling in the same way; they hung over him, full of pitying interest, and tried all they could to help him and said all sorts of regretful things. They had forgotten all about the enemy, they thought only of this one forlorn unit of the foe. Once my imagination persuaded me that the dying man gave me a reproachful look out of his shadowy eyes, and it seemed to me that I could rather he had stabbed me than done that. He muttered and mumbled like a dreamer in his sleep about his wife and his child, and I thought with a new despair, "This thing that I have done does not end with him; it falls upon *them* too, and they never did me any harm, any more than he."

In a little while the man was dead. He was killed in war, killed in fair and legitimate war, killed in battle, as you may say, and yet he was as sincerely mourned by the opposing force as if he had been their brother. The boys stood there a half-hour sorrowing over him and recalling the details of the tragedy, and wondering who he might be and if he were a spy, and saying that if it were to do over again they would not hurt him unless he attacked them first. It soon came out that mine was not the only shot fired; there were five others, a division of the guilt which was a great relief to me since it in some degree lightened and diminished the burden I was carrying. There were six shots fired at once but I was not in my right mind at the time, and my heated imagination had magnified my one shot into a volley.

The man was not in uniform and was not armed. He was a stranger in the country, that was all we ever found out about him. The thought of him got to preying upon me every night; I could not get rid of it. I could not drive it away, the taking of that unoffending life seemed such a wanton thing. And it seemed an epitome of war, that all war must be just that—the killing of strangers against whom you feel no personal animosity, strangers whom in other circumstances you would help if you found them in trouble, and who would help you if you needed it. My campaign was spoiled. It seemed to me that I was not rightly equipped for this awful business, that war was intended for men and I for a child's nurse. I resolved to retire from this avocation of sham soldiership while I could save some remnant of my self-respect. These morbid thoughts clung to me against reason, for at bottom I did not believe I had touched that man. The law of probabilities decreed me guiltless of his blood, for in all my small experience with guns I had never hit anything I had tried to hit and I knew I had done my best to hit him. Yet there was no solace in the thought. Against a diseased imagination demonstration goes for nothing.

The rest of my war experience was of a piece with what I have already told of it. We kept monotonously falling back upon one camp or another and eating up the farmers and their families. They ought to have shot us; on the contrary, they were as hospitably kind and courteous to us as if we had deserved it. In one of these camps we found Ab Grimes, an Upper Mississippi pilot who afterward became famous as a daredevil rebel spy, whose career bristled with desperate adventures. The look and style of his comrades suggested that they had not come into the war to play and their deeds made good the conjecture later. They were fine horsemen and good revolver shots, but their favorite arm was the lasso. Each had one at his pommel and could snatch a man out of the saddle with it every time, on a full gallop, at any reasonable distance.

In another camp the chief was a fierce and profane old blacksmith of sixty and he had furnished his twenty recruits with gigantic homemade bowie knives, to be swung with two hands like the *machetes* of the Isthmus.[1] It was a grisly spectacle

---

[1] *machetes . . .* **Isthmus:** heavy knives used for cutting through foliage and for fighting by the natives of tropical America, including the Isthmus of Panama.

to see that earnest band practicing their murderous cuts and slashes under the eye of that remorseless old fanatic.

The last camp which we fell back upon was in a hollow near the village of Florida where I was born, in Monroe County. Here we were warned one day that a Union colonel was sweeping down on us with a whole regiment at his heel. This looked decidedly serious. Our boys went apart and consulted; then we went back and told the other companies present that the war was a disappointment to us and we were going to disband. They were getting ready themselves to fall back on some place or other, and we were only waiting for General Tom Harris, who was expected to arrive at any moment, so they tried to persuade us to wait a little while but the majority of us said no, we were accustomed to falling back and didn't need any of Tom Harris's help, we could get along perfectly well without him and save time, too. So about half of our fifteen, including myself, mounted and left on the instant; the others yielded to persuasion and stayed—stayed through the war.

An hour later we met General Harris on the road, with two or three people in his company, his staff probably, but we could not tell; none of them were in uniform; uniforms had not come into vogue among us yet. Harris ordered us back but we told him there was a Union colonel coming with a whole regiment in his wake and it looked as if there was going to be a disturbance, so we had concluded to go home. He raged a little but it was of no use, our minds were made up. We had done our share, had killed one man, exterminated one army, such as it was; let him go and kill the rest and that would end the war. I did not see that brisk young general again until last year; then he was wearing white hair and whiskers.

In time I came to know that Union colonel whose coming frightened me out of the war and crippled the Southern cause to that extent—General Grant. I came within a few hours of seeing him when he was as unknown as I was myself;

at a time when anybody could have said, "Grant?—Ulysses S. Grant? I do not remember hearing the name before." It seems difficult to realize that there was once a time when such a remark could be rationally made but there *was,* and I was within a few miles of the place and the occasion too, though proceeding in the other direction.

The thoughtful will not throw this war paper of mine lightly aside as being valueless. It has this value: it is a not unfair picture of what went on in many and many a militia camp in the first months of the rebellion, when the green recruits were without discipline, without the steadying and heartening influence of trained leaders, when all their circumstances were new and strange and charged with exaggerated terrors, and before the invaluable experience of actual collision in the field had turned them from rabbits into soldiers. If this side of the picture of that early day has not before been put into history, then history has been to that degree incomplete, for it had and has its rightful place there. There was more Bull Run [1] material scattered through the early camps of this country than exhibited itself at Bull Run. And yet it learned its trade presently and helped to fight the great battles later. I could have become a soldier myself if I had waited. I had got part of it learned, I knew more about retreating than the man that invented retreating.

[1] **Bull Run:** a creek in Virginia that was the scene of two famous Southern victories in the War Between the States. For Walt Whitman's description of the aftermath of the first battle of Bull Run, see page 329.

FOR STUDY AND DISCUSSION

1. What kind of a "history" does the first paragraph lead you to expect? In what way is the selection, as the first paragraph predicts it will be, "apologetic"? How does this "private history" differ from most public histories of wars and campaigns (aside from the obvious differences that public histories generally do not deal with such a small group of men as the Marion Rangers)?

2. What attitudes toward the issues involved in the War Between the States does Twain show in his account of the changing opinions of his pilot mate? Contrast this attitude with the attitudes of Lincoln and Lee toward the issues of the war. Why do you think Twain deals so lightheartedly with these issues?

3. Twain gives four "samples" of the men that constituted the Marion Rangers. Describe these men. From these samples, which the author says are "quite fair ones," do you expect that the Rangers will perform deeds of exceptional daring and heroism? Explain.

4. Colonel Ralls is called "a practiced politician and phrase-juggler." What aspect of the war does he represent? Do you think there are men like Colonel Ralls in all wars? Explain.

5. Mark Twain comments about Captain Lyman's problems: "The commander of an ignorant crew like that has many troubles and vexations which probably do not occur in the regular army at all." What "troubles and vexations" arise because of a lack of discipline? Which arise because of a lack of military experience? Can the Marion Rangers really be considered as part of an army? Why or why not?

6. Describe the change in mood that occurs near the end of the selection. How does the author's view of combat change?

7. Twain writes, "In a little while the man was dead. He was killed in war, killed in a legitimate war, killed in battle, as you may say, and yet he was as sincerely mourned by the opposing force as if he had been their brother." Might these sentences be applied to the entire War Between the States? Explain.

8. Would you classify "A Short History of a Campaign That Failed" as a basically humorous selection? Explain. Do you think Mark Twain had a humorous or serious purpose, or both, in writing it?

9. Point out sentences in the selection that illustrate Mark Twain's knack of turning a phrase for humorous effect.

10. If you were asked to choose five words to describe Mark Twain as a writer, which words would you choose? Select details from the Twain selections to support your choice.

LANGUAGE AND VOCABULARY

Mark Twain's account of Dunlap's attempts to change his name so that it might have a less "plebeian sound" reflects a common tendency in human beings to seek or invent names that will make them, their occupations, or their actions more attractive. Some proper names, like Dunlap's, have been changed to make them appear more aristocratic. By the same token, the unpleasant reality of acts such as a dictator's murder of his political opponents can be glossed over by an evasive term like "the elimination of unreliable elements."

On the basis of the names and terms you invent for the following situations, discuss the need to examine all pretentious terms to discover what they really mean. Is this need especially important today? Explain.

1. A young man named Floyd Peckham wants to become a movie star. He thinks he should change his name. Suggest several names he might choose.

2. Someone in your school wants to become class president. Because he does not have much chance of winning against more popular candidates, he argues that he is the only one really qualified for the job and that therefore his name alone should be placed on the ballot. Naturally he does not want his proposal to be called "doing away with free elections." What more evasive term might he invent?

FOR COMPOSITION

Fred Lewis Pattee has belittled Mark Twain's importance as a thinker and stated that Twain's chief claim to literary eminence is that he "made the common people laugh. Who in all the history of literature has done more?" One of the charges Professor Pattee makes against Twain is that the author failed to respond to the tragic grandeur of the War Between the States: "What of Mark Twain during the Gethsemane of his nation, when hundreds of thousands of his generation were dead upon the battlefields of the South that had been his home? Not a word in all his works . . . save a humorous exaggeranza describing his desertion from the colors."

Do you think that "The Private History of a Campaign That Failed" should be described as a "humorous exaggeranza"? Or can it be argued that this selection, lighthearted as it may seem, has its moments of deep tragedy and is basically serious in purpose? Write a composition in which you agree or disagree with Professor Pattee's evaluation of the selection. Support your position with details from the work.

Tragedy and Renewal

One characteristic that the unit you have just studied shares with the first unit in this book is its response to a great, overshadowing event in American history. A number of the selections in the first unit reflect the American struggle for independence; some of the selections in this unit reflect a bitter internal conflict, the War Between the States. While literature is always, in some sense, a response to life, this response is usually quite different from that seen in written history. In such a tremendous experience as the War Between the States, however, history and literature share a common ground. The "Gettysburg Address" is both a great historical and literary event. But while historians usually approach a war in terms of its causes and of the great battles that were fought, the literary man sees it as a great tragic event, full of universal meaning.

TRAGEDY: LIFE AND LITERATURE

In the preceding unit, you observed a gradual change in the American temper from an affirmation of the ideals of human and social perfectibility to a dark awareness of national realities. This clash between ideals and realities came to a dramatic test in the bloody conflict that has been called our first major national tragedy. Look up the words *tragedy* and *tragic* in the dictionary. Consider how these words can be applied not only to the drama (see page 751) but to life itself. Then discuss the following questions.

1. How may Lincoln and Lee be regarded as tragic heroes? Cite passages from selections by these two men which reveal their own recognition of the war's tragic nature.

2. Contrast the selections by Lincoln and Lee with the more consciously literary treatment of the war in the poems of Timrod and Whitman. What liberty in organizing their material did Whitman and Timrod have which Lincoln and Lee lacked? How might an historical account of the blockade of Charleston differ from Timrod's poem "Charleston"? What impression of Lincoln do you get from his own writings? How does this impression of Lincoln differ from that which you get from reading "When Lilacs Last in the Dooryard Bloomed"? How do these differences point up the difference between life and literature?

3. The memory of a bloody event such as the War Between the States was painful to many people. Yet instead of trying to forget about the war, writers returned to it again and again. Why do you think writers showed a special concern for such a tragic event? Why do great writers, artists, and

composers continually confront the painful and the tragic? Does such a poem as "When Lilacs Last in the Dooryard Bloomed" arouse only sad, painful thoughts in the reader?

REAFFIRMATION OF IDEALS

The period after the war was not only one in which Americans confronted and tried to understand what they had been through, but one in which they reaffirmed democratic ideals. Two great writers—Whitman and Twain—are especially noteworthy as prophets, spokesmen, and representatives of American democracy.

1. Cite passages that show Whitman's belief in the common man, in the innate goodness of the individual, in the great destiny of the United States. Cite lines in which Whitman relates himself to his readers and to all Americans.

2. Bernard De Voto, a distinguished biographer of Mark Twain, wrote about Twain:

"No doubt his first importance in . . . [American] literature is the democratizing effect of his work. It is a concretely liberating effect, and therefore different in kind from Whitman's vision of democracy, which can hardly be said to have been understood by or to have found a response among any considerable number of Americans. Mark Twain was the first great writer who was also a popular writer, and that in itself is important. Much more important is the implicit and explicit democracy of his books. They are the first American literature of the highest rank which portrays the ordinary bulk of Americans, expresses them, accepts their values, and delineates their hopes, fears, decencies, and indecencies as from within. . . . He is mid-nineteenth-century American democracy finding its first major voice in literature, ultimately its strongest voice. In him the literature of democracy becomes more robust than it had been before . . ."

Discuss the "implicit and explicit democracy" in Mark Twain's works. Support your statements with specific references to selections. Consider the following points: What is significantly democratic about Twain's subject matter? about the characters he portrays? about the picture he presents of himself? How is Twain's humor markedly democratic in contrast to the more aristocratic humor of Washington Irving or William Byrd?

THE SOUTHERN TRADITION

The Southern literary tradition has had its finest flowering in the twentieth century, in writers such as William Faulkner, Eudora Welty, John Crowe Ransom, and Thomas Wolfe. Henry Timrod and Sidney Lanier, however, are also fine representatives of that tradition. Reread the discussions of the Southern tradition on pages 4 and 293. Then compare the work of Timrod and Lanier with the work of earlier Southerners such as William Byrd (page 13) and Edgar Allan Poe (page 117). How does each of these writers support the Southern tradition as described in the unit introduction?

In a famous essay called "The Significance of the Frontier in American History," the historian Frederick Jackson Turner developed the concept of the frontier as a tremendously important element in American life and culture. Calling the frontier "the line of most rapid and effective Americanization," he wrote, "To the frontier the American intellect owes its striking characteristics. That coarseness and strength combined with acuteness and inquisitiveness; that practical, inventive turn of mind, quick to find expedients; that masterful grasp of material things, lacking in the artistic but powerful to effect great ends; that restless, nervous energy, that dominant individualism, working for good and evil, and withal that buoyancy and exuberance which comes with freedom—these are the traits of the frontier, or traits called out elsewhere because of the existence of the frontier."

1. Which of the traits identified by Professor Turner are revealed in the selections by Bret Harte and Mark Twain? Which of these traits do Harte and Twain lack? Judging from their writings, which author would you say belongs more fully to the tradition of the frontier, Twain or Harte? Which other writers in this unit show the influences of this tradition?

2. Explain how the following American writers show (or fail to show) the influence of the frontier tradition: Benjamin Franklin, James Fenimore Cooper, Washington Irving, Henry David Thoreau, Nathaniel Hawthorne.

3. Discuss the influence of the frontier tradition on the following aspects of modern America: politics, entertainment, rural life, city life.

FOR COMPOSITION: THE USE OF DIALOGUE

If you were to contrast the use of dialogue in Poe's "The Fall of the House of Usher" and Twain's "The Buffalo That Climbed a Tree," you would find that Poe's characters speak in a very literary dialect while Twain's character Bemis speaks a dialect of a particular region. Twain once remarked, "No one can talk the quartz dialect correctly without learning it with pick and shovel and drill and fuse." By this he meant that to re-create realistic dialect (or dialogue), you must observe actual speech and learn to distinguish fine differences in pronunciation, word choice, and grammatical usage.

After observing your own speech and that of those around you, write a short narrative with dialogue in which you use what you have observed. You may wish to have your narrative include a conversation between persons speaking more than one dialect. Be sure that your use of dialect is based on your own observations, not on reading or television watching.

ART AND LITERATURE

One of the chief devices of expository writing is comparison and contrast. The paintings on pages 361–66 represent two trends in American art, "a mystical, poetic interpretation of landscape" and "a new type of realism." Write a composition contrasting a painting by Ryder or Blakelock with one by Anshutz or Eakins, and point out the differences between these two types of paintings.

THE TRIUMPH
OF REALISM

"I understand that a man is born into the world with his own pair of eyes, and he is not at all responsible for his vision—he is merely responsible for his personal honesty. To keep close to this personal honesty is my supreme ambition."

STEPHEN CRANE

America, toward the end of the nineteenth century, was an exciting country to live in. It was still growing, still prospering, the most powerful nation in the Western hemisphere and about to become a major power among the nations of the world. By the 1890's the frontier was gone and with it the Old West, although the tradition of the frontier is still a powerful force in our society. The process of expansion changed from that of pushing into new territory to that of settling and developing those areas. While the United States was still predominantly an agricultural nation, industry was becoming a more and more important part of the country. New inventions—the telephone, the electric light, the Bessemer steel process—were changing the lives of Americans. The United States was still the land of opportunity to hundreds of thousands of immigrants, who fled from poverty in their native lands. Men such as Andrew Carnegie and John D. Rockefeller, who began with only a few dollars, built up great personal fortunes. Millions of Americans dreamed of matching their success.

Once again, the dreams of Americans did not always match the reality of their lives. Industrial workers in cities worked long hours at backbreaking jobs and lived in poverty and squalor. Farmers were afraid that the market prices set on their crops would be too low to meet their expenses and that it would be necessary for them to go heavily into debt. Many men were uncertain of their place in society, fearful that they were caught up in large, impersonal forces beyond their control.

We have seen how the struggle between ideals and realities shaped the intellectual life and the literature of the nation in other periods: how with the

The telephone was one of the many new inventions that changed the lives of Americans in the late nineteenth century. Above, the General Exchange in New York.

Romantic movement there came a renewed belief in the individual and the possibilities of life (page 89); how the approach of the War Between the States made the skepticism of Hawthorne and Melville more meaningful than Emerson's optimism (page 164); and how, after the War, another kind of ideal, the image of the American as a boisterous frontiersman, became important to a country seeking to heal its wounds and see itself as a healthy, growing nation (page 295). Now realism, a literary and intellectual movement that has often been contrasted with Romanticism, led poets and novelists, not to imagine life as it could be, but to examine life as it was actually lived and to record what they saw around them as honestly as they could.

REALISM

Realism can be defined as the depiction of life as most people live and know it. The realistic writer is concerned with recording the details of ordinary life, with showing the reader not generally but precisely how ordinary life is lived. *Ordinary* is a key word in any discussion of realism. Many realistic writers, in their search for subject matter, tend to avoid the unusual or out-of-the-way and deliberately concentrate on the typical and the average. Yet because of these writers' close observation of life and their ability to record precisely what they have observed, they are able to reveal much to the average reader that he has not gleaned from his own experience. Some realistic writers regard their work as being similar to the job of the scientist—to observe, to record, to analyze. William Dean Howells (page 350), the most influential literary man of his time and a strong defender of realism, declared that the realistic writer cannot regard any aspect of life as being "unworthy of notice, any more than the scientist can declare a fact of the material world beneath the dignity of his inquiry." One term that is often used in connection with realism is "slice of life." The realistic writer takes a slice of the real world and examines it in almost the same way that a scientist examines a specimen under a microscope.

The concern with life as it is really lived brought into literature new kinds of subject matter, scenes, and characters that Romantic writers had generally avoided. The realistic writers dealt with factories and slums, workmen, bosses, corrupt politicians, petty criminals, and social outcasts. They wrote about reformers, political agitators, shopkeepers, businessmen, the rising middle class, and slum dwellers. The realists offered stark descriptions of the hardships and poverty that were often a part of farm lives. It was impossible to write about life in America at the end of the nineteenth century without dealing with all of these new subjects. They were here to stay as a part of the whole new range of life that forms the writer's material.

Some literary scholars regard realism as an outgrowth and integral part of the Romantic movement. But the realistic writers at the end of the nineteenth century saw themselves as being in revolt against an outworn Romantic movement. Late nineteenth-century Romantic writers bitterly attacked realism on the ground that it dealt only with the sordid or the trivial, and thus debased literature. As one Romantic writer charged, "All this worship of the vulgar, the commonplace, and the insignificant is the last stage of vulgarity, hopelessness, and decadence." Readers complained that realistic fiction depressed them; what they wanted from their reading was not gloom but hopefulness. To such critics, Howells replied that the search for truth in literature could never be debasing; it was always uplifting. The Romantic movement, Howells stated, had lost the vigor it had had at "the beginning of the century when romance was making the same fight against effete classicism which realism is making today against effete romanticism." The realist "finds nothing insignificant. . . . He feels in every nerve the equality of things and the unity of men; his soul is exalted, not by vain shows and shadows and ideals, but by realities, in which alone the truth lives."

But, Howells cautioned, realism must not degenerate into a mere recording of facts. It must pursue a deeper and a higher reality. "When realism becomes false to life, when it heaps up facts merely, realism will perish too."

INFLUENCES ON AMERICAN REALISM

While American realistic writers had to fight their own battles and develop their own standards of judgment, they were influenced by the work of European writers they admired, notably the French writers Stendhal, Honoré de Balzac, and Gustave Flaubert. They were also influenced by the intellectual currents of the time, particularly the great interest in science and the scientific method. In the latter part of the nineteenth century, this method, which had led to so many advances in knowledge and to inventions that were changing everyone's life, seemed to consist principally of two steps: gathering the facts carefully, and drawing conclusions from them. If such a method had been so successful in other fields, writers asked themselves, why couldn't it be applied to literature? Thus, as you have already seen, some writers regarded themselves as scientists, conducting investigations into human problems.

Another important influence of science on literature was Charles Darwin's theory of evolution and natural selection. Many writers and intellectuals felt that if Darwin was right, if plants and animals had developed into more complex organisms through the survival of the fittest, then all traditional morality was meaningless and the only moral law that ruled the world was "the law of the jungle." Man was caught up in a savage struggle, the victim of turbulent forces he could not control. This view of the universe led to a development of realism called *naturalism*.

NATURALISM

Naturalism has been defined as an extreme kind of realism, one which does not simply pursue the truth wherever the search may lead, but which begins with a view of the universe and man's place in it and imposes this view on literary works. The naturalistic writer sees man as a creature that is acted upon by nature, the result of the forces of heredity and environment. As one of the characters in a novel by Theodore Dreiser remarks, "All of us are more or less pawns. We're moved about like chessmen by circumstances over which we have no control." The European writer who most influenced the American naturalists is the French novelist Émile Zola, who

"Departure for America." By the 1890's millions from all over Europe, the Near East, and the Orient had left their homes to emigrate to the United States.

An immigrant family arriving in New York. The constantly rising influx of new-comers helped develop the United States into a major industrial power.

wrote a famous series of novels, the Rougon-Macquart novels, showing how hereditary traits influenced the lives of the members of one family. The most highly regarded American naturalist writers are Dreiser, Frank Norris, and Stephen Crane (page 391).

THE RANGE OF REALISM

It might seem that the movement toward realism would produce only dull works about commonplace people. But, as always in the history of literature, the imagination of the artist goes beyond the generalizations of the literary theorist. At his best, the realist has been concerned with the whole of life, not with just the surface of it. He has produced intensely personal works as well as broad studies of a changing society. He has concentrated on moments of great psychological significance in addition to depicting the unexciting times of an ordinary man. Poets such as Edwin Arlington Robinson (page 480) and Edgar Lee Masters (page 487) ranged the spectrum of emotion and presented compressed, unforgettable portraits of morally significant characters of the period. Realistic and naturalistic novelists such as Willa Cather (page 491) and Stephen Crane (page 391) produced works that are notable not only for their fidelity to life but also for the depth of their insight and the artistry of their style.

The best realistic writers could agree with the advice that the great American novelist Henry James gave to the other novelists of his time: "All life belongs to you, and do not listen to . . . those who would shut you up into corners of it and tell you that it is only here and there that art inhabits. . . . There is no impression of life, no manner of seeing and feeling it, to which the plan of the novelist may not offer a place."

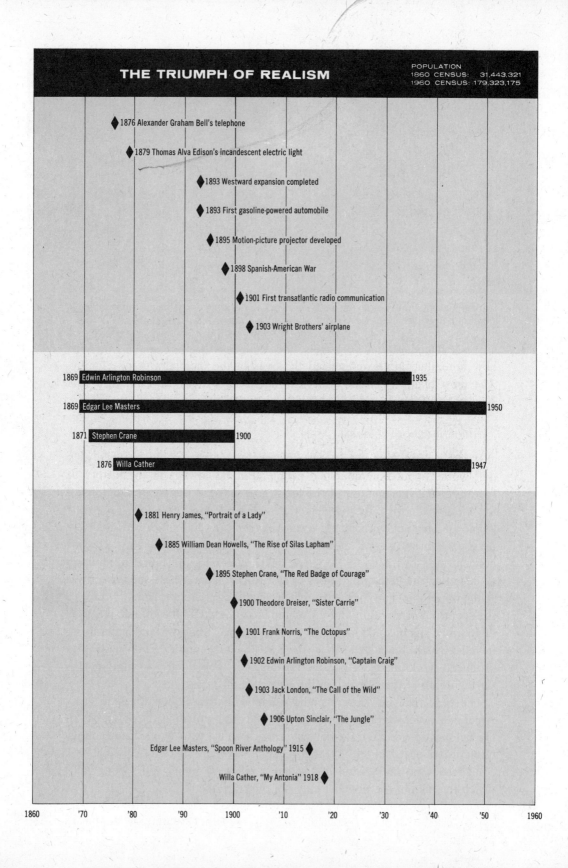

THE TRIUMPH OF REALISM

POPULATION
1860 CENSUS: 31,443,321
1960 CENSUS: 179,323,175

1876 Alexander Graham Bell's telephone

1879 Thomas Alva Edison's incandescent electric light

1893 Westward expansion completed

1893 First gasoline-powered automobile

1895 Motion-picture projector developed

1898 Spanish-American War

1901 First transatlantic radio communication

1903 Wright Brothers' airplane

1869 Edwin Arlington Robinson 1935

1869 Edgar Lee Masters 1950

1871 Stephen Crane 1900

1876 Willa Cather 1947

1881 Henry James, "Portrait of a Lady"

1885 William Dean Howells, "The Rise of Silas Lapham"

1895 Stephen Crane, "The Red Badge of Courage"

1900 Theodore Dreiser, "Sister Carrie"

1901 Frank Norris, "The Octopus"

1902 Edwin Arlington Robinson, "Captain Craig"

1903 Jack London, "The Call of the Wild"

1906 Upton Sinclair, "The Jungle"

Edgar Lee Masters, "Spoon River Anthology" 1915

Willa Cather, "My Antonia" 1918

1860 '70 '80 '90 1900 '10 '20 '30 '40 '50 1960

STEPHEN CRANE
(1871–1900)

Although Stephen Crane's boyhood ambition was to become a big-league baseball player, he cared enough about literature to lose a tooth defending his criticism of Tennyson's poetry. The son of a Methodist minister, Crane spent some months at Lafayette College and later at Syracuse University, but he seemed more interested in sports and card playing than in his studies. He went to New York determined "to recover from college." Barely able to support himself by free-lance newspaper work, he drew from his experiences of life in the New York slums to write his first novel, *Maggie: A Girl of the Streets.* No publisher would accept *Maggie,* and when Crane printed the novel at his own expense, he found that no bookseller would stock it. He might have given up writing if he had not had the encouragement of Hamlin Garland (page 476), who helped him sell a short story and introduced him to the influential novelist and critic William Dean Howells (page 386). Garland also gave Crane the money to pay for the typing of his second novel, *The Red Badge of Courage.*

The success of this book, which Ernest Hemingway has called "a boy's long dream of war" and which is remarkable for its depiction of men's reactions to the crises of battle, established Crane's reputation. He then set out to experience the violence and anger he had imagined in his book and restlessly roamed the globe as a reporter and special correspondent. He toured the West, barely escaped being murdered in Mexico, and journeyed all the way to Greece to report the Greco-Turkish War. In Greece Crane first witnessed actual combat and found that his experiences confirmed his intuitive understanding of war. With relief he observed, *"The Red Badge* is all right." Later he covered the Spanish-American War in Cuba and in Puerto Rico with a reckless unconcern for his own safety. One of the finest stories to come out of his own experiences of danger is "The Open Boat." Crane had sailed for Cuba with a group of Cuban revolutionaries a year before America had declared war on Spain. His boat, possibly a victim of sabotage, sank off the Florida coast, and a peril-filled day and night in a ten-foot dinghy followed. Out of the experience, Crane selected and interpreted events to shape a work of art. In the story, he makes no mention of the sailor he himself saved from the raging surf. Other stories that added to Crane's reputation are "The Blue Hotel," "The Bride Comes to Yellow Sky," "A Mystery of Heroism," and "An Experiment in Misery." Two interesting longer tales are *George's Mother* and *The Monster.*

The last months of Crane's life were spent in England, where he moved into an immense manor house. By this time he had acquired an international reputation, and he moved in the society of such writers as Henry James and Joseph Conrad. At twenty-eight, fatally ill with tuberculosis, he was taken to a sanatorium in Germany where he died, five months before his twenty-ninth birthday.

The best of Crane's writing reflects the heroism of his life. His irony comes from his awareness of the absurd way life plays with human expectations. His works contain many arresting images, often daubed with strong colors, that reflect his desire to capture transitory moments of the greatest intensity. His poetry, like his fiction, is very personal and original. It is moody and vivid, symbolic yet stripped to essentials, and it anticipates the free verse of the twentieth century.

War Is Kind

Do not weep, maiden, for war is kind.
Because your lover threw wild hands toward the sky
And the affrighted steed ran on alone,
Do not weep.
War is kind.   5

   Hoarse, booming drums of the regiment,
   Little souls who thirst for fight,
   These men were born to drill and die.
   The unexplained glory flies above them,
   Great is the battle-god, great, and his kingdom—   10
   A field where a thousand corpses lie.

Do not weep, babe, for war is kind.
Because your father tumbled in the yellow trenches,
Raged at his breast, gulped and died,
Do not weep.   15
War is kind.

   Swift blazing flag of the regiment,
   Eagle with crest of red and gold,
   These men were born to drill and die.
   Point for them the virtue of slaughter,   20
   Make plain to them the excellence of killing
   And a field where a thousand corpses lie.

Mother whose heart hung humble as a button
On the bright splendid shroud of your son,
Do not weep.
War is kind.   25

"War Is Kind" from *Stephen Crane: An Omnibus*, edited by Robert Wooster Stallman. Reprinted by permission of Alfred A. Knopf, Inc.

The Book of Wisdom

I met a seer.
He held in his hands
The book of wisdom.
"Sir," I addressed him,
"Let me read."   5
"Child——" he began.
"Sir," I said,
"Think not that I am a child,
For already I know much
Of that which you hold;   10
Aye, much."

He smiled.
Then he opened the book
And held it before me.
Strange that I should have grown so suddenly blind.   15

Think as I Think

"Think as I think," said a man,
"Or you are abominably wicked;
You are a toad."
And after I had thought of it,
I said, "I will, then, be a toad."   5

FOR STUDY AND DISCUSSION

1. How do stanzas 2 and 4 of "War Is Kind" differ in tone and rhythm from the rest of the poem? In your opinion, are the contrasting images in the last stanza a successful conclusion to the poem? Defend your answer.

2. Crane's poems often make a statement, which is followed by a contradiction and then a turning. Where is the turning in "The Book of Wisdom"? What is ironic about the poem?

3. In "Think as I Think," why does the narrator say that he will be a toad? This poem implies a point of view about conformity and nonconformity. Do you agree or disagree with it? Would the poem be more effective if it had stated its point of view directly? Explain.

4. What can you tell about Crane's attitudes from his poems? from his manner of expression? Do you think he approved of Whitman's full, direct statements? Explain.

FREE VERSE

Crane's free verse is quite different from Whitman's. (For a discussion of Whitman's free verse, see page 317.) Read aloud a passage from Whitman's "Song of Myself" and a poem by Crane, and consider the following questions: In terms of line length and rhythm, how does Crane's free verse differ from Whitman's? Which poet is more freely emotional? Which poet is more indirect and ironic? How are the differences in line length and rhythm related to the emotional qualities of the two poets? Find a passage by Crane that is most like Whitman's verse. Find a passage that is quite different from Whitman.

"The Book of Wisdom" from *Stephen Crane: An Omnibus,* edited by Robert Wooster Stallman. Reprinted by permission of Alfred A. Knopf, Inc.
"Think as I Think" from *Stephen Crane: An Omnibus,* edited by Robert Wooster Stallman. Reprinted by permission of Alfred A. Knopf, Inc.

The Red Badge of Courage

One of Stephen Crane's greatest achievements in *The Red Badge of Courage* was to show what battle is really like. When at twenty-one years of age he had finished the first draft of his novel, he wrote to a friend that he couldn't be sure that his facts were real and therefore he would have to write it all over again. He went to Virginia to talk with veterans of the war, concluded nearly thirty years before, and spent the summer of 1893 revising his work. He took time off for football with his nieces and later explained that he had learned from the game much of what he knew about the war. "The psychology is the same," he said. "The opposite team is an enemy tribe." Crane's work of rewriting and probing more deeply into his imagination was thorough enough so that, after he returned from the war between Greece and Turkey, he was able to tell the great Polish-English novelist, Joseph Conrad, "My picture of war was all right! I have found it as I imagined it." Later Conrad was to praise Crane's achievement in *The Red Badge of Courage* as that of "an artist, a man not of experience but a man inspired, a seer with a gift for rendering the significant on the surface of things and with an incomparable insight into primitive emotions, who, in order to give us the image of war, had looked profoundly into his own breast."

Scholars have discovered that the battle scenes described in *The Red Badge of Courage* are based primarily on Chancellorsville, the great Confederate victory in the wilderness near the Rappahannock River in the spring of 1863. Crane also relied on his old teacher's stories of the route of the 34th New York at Antietam a year earlier, but he never identifies the battle nor explains the higher strategy of the generals. What we get is the ordinary soldier's experience of the battle, of any battle.

CHAPTER 1

THE COLD passed reluctantly from the earth, and the retiring fogs revealed an army stretched out on the hills, resting. As the landscape changed from brown to green, the army awakened and began to tremble with eagerness at the noise of rumors. It cast its eyes upon the roads, which were growing from long troughs of liquid mud to proper thoroughfares. A river, amber-tinted in the shadow of its banks, purled at the army's feet; and at night, when the stream had become of a sorrowful blackness, one could see across it the red, eyelike gleam of hostile campfires set in the low brows of distant hills.

Once a certain tall soldier developed virtues and went resolutely to wash a shirt. He came flying back from a brook waving his garment bannerlike. He was swelled with a tale he had heard from a reliable friend, who had heard it from a truthful cavalryman, who had heard it from his trustworthy brother, one of the orderlies at division headquarters. He adopted the important air of a herald [1] in red and gold.

"We're goin' t' move t'morrah—sure," he said pompously to a group in the company street. "We're goin' 'way up the river, cut across, an' come around in behint 'em."

[1] **herald:** In former times, a herald was an officer, dressed in special clothes, who had the special duties of carrying messages between opposing armies, carrying challenges, and arranging tournaments.

To his attentive audience he drew a loud and elaborate plan of a very brilliant campaign. When he had finished, the blue-clothed men scattered into small arguing groups between the rows of squat brown huts. A Negro teamster who had been dancing upon a cracker box with the hilarious encouragement of twoscore soldiers was deserted. He sat mournfully down. Smoke drifted lazily from a multitude of quaint chimneys.

"It's a lie! that's all it is—a thunderin' lie!" said another private loudly. His smooth face was flushed, and his hands were thrust sulkily into his trousers pockets. He took the matter as an affront to him. "I don't believe the derned old army's ever going to move. We're set. I've got ready to move eight times in the last two weeks, and we ain't moved yet."

The tall soldier felt called upon to defend the truth of a rumor he himself had introduced. He and the loud one came near to fighting over it.

A corporal began to swear before the assemblage. He had just put a costly board floor in his house, he said. During the early spring he had refrained from adding extensively to the comfort of his environment because he had felt that the army might start on the march at any moment. Of late, however, he had been impressed that they were in a sort of eternal camp.

Many of the men engaged in a spirited debate. One outlined in a peculiarly lucid manner all the plans of the commanding general. He was opposed by men who advocated that there were other plans of campaign. They clamored at each other, numbers making futile bids for the popular attention. Meanwhile, the soldier who had fetched the rumor bustled about with much importance. He was continually assailed by questions.

"What's up, Jim?"

"Th' army's goin' t' move."

"Ah, what yeh talkin' about? How yeh know it is?"

"Well, yeh kin b'lieve me er not, jest as yeh like. I don't care a hang."

There was much food for thought in the manner in which he replied. He came near to convincing them by disdaining to produce proofs. They grew much excited over it.

There was a youthful private who listened with eager ears to the words of the tall soldier and to the varied comments of his comrades. After receiving a fill of discussions concerning marches and attacks, he went to his hut and crawled through an intricate hole that served it as a door. He wished to be alone with some new thoughts that had lately come to him.

He lay down on a wide bunk that stretched across the end of the room. In the other end, cracker boxes were made to serve as furniture. They were grouped about the fireplace. A picture from an illustrated weekly was upon the log walls, and three rifles were paralleled on pegs. Equipments hung on handy projections, and some tin dishes lay upon a small pile of firewood. A folded tent was serving as a roof. The sunlight, without, beating upon it, made it glow a light yellow shade. A small window shot an oblique square of whiter light upon the cluttered floor. The smoke from the fire at times neglected the clay chimney and wreathed into the room, and this flimsy chimney of clay and sticks made endless threats to set ablaze the whole establishment.

The youth was in a little trance of astonishment. So they were at last going to fight. On the morrow, perhaps, there would be a battle, and he would be in it. For a time he was obliged to labor to make himself believe. He could not accept with assurance an omen that he was about to mingle in one of those great affairs of the earth.

He had, of course, dreamed of battles all his life—of vague and bloody conflicts that had thrilled him with their sweep and fire. In visions he had seen himself in many struggles. He had imagined peoples secure in the shadow of his eagle-eyed prowess. But awake he had regarded battles as crimson blotches on the pages of the past. He had put them as things of the bygone with his thought-images of heavy crowns and high castles. There was a portion of the world's history which he had regarded as the time of wars, but it, he thought, had been long gone over the horizon and had disappeared forever.

From his home his youthful eyes had looked upon the war in his own country with distrust. It must be some sort of a play affair. He had long despaired of witnessing a Greeklike struggle. Such would be no more, he had said. Men were better, or more timid. Secular and religious education had effaced the throat-grappling instinct, or else firm finance held in check the passions.

He had burned several times to enlist. Tales of great movements shook the land. They might not be distinctly Homeric, but there seemed to be much glory in them. He had read of marches, sieges, conflicts, and he had longed to see it all. His busy mind had drawn for him large pictures extravagant in color, lurid with breathless deeds.

But his mother had discouraged him. She had affected to look with some contempt upon the quality of his war ardor and patriotism. She could calmly seat herself and with no apparent difficulty give him many hundreds of reasons why he was of vastly more importance on the farm than on the field of battle. She had had certain ways of expression that told him that her statements on the subject came from a deep conviction. Moreover, on her side, was his belief that her ethical motive in the argument was impregnable.

At last, however, he had made firm rebellion against this yellow light thrown upon the color of his ambitions. The newspapers, the gossip of the village, his own picturings, had aroused him to an uncheckable degree. They were in truth fighting finely down there. Almost every day the newspapers printed accounts of a decisive victory.

One night, as he lay in bed, the winds had carried to him the clangoring of the church bell as some enthusiast jerked the rope frantically to tell the twisted news of a great battle. This voice of the people rejoicing in the night had made him shiver in a prolonged ecstasy of excitement. Later, he had gone down to his mother's room and had spoken thus: "Ma, I'm going to enlist."

"Henry, don't you be a fool," his mother had replied. She had then covered her face with the quilt. There was an end to the matter for that night.

Nevertheless, the next morning he had gone to a town that was near his mother's farm and had enlisted in a company that was forming there. When he had returned home, his mother was milking the brindle cow. Four others stood waiting. "Ma, I've enlisted," he had said to her diffidently. There was a short silence. "The Lord's will be done, Henry," she had finally replied, and had then continued to milk the brindle cow.

When he had stood in the doorway with his soldier's clothes on his back, and with the light of excitement and expectancy in his eyes almost defeating the glow of regret for the home bonds, he had seen two tears leaving their trails on his mother's scarred cheeks.

Still, she had disappointed him by saying nothing whatever about returning with his shield or on it.[1] He had privately primed himself for a beautiful scene. He had prepared certain sentences which he thought could be used with touching effect. But her words destroyed his plans. She had doggedly peeled potatoes and addressed him as follows: "You watch out, Henry, an' take good care of yerself in this here fighting business—you watch out, an' take good care of yerself. Don't go a-thinkin' you can lick the hull rebel army at the start, because yeh can't. Yer jest one little feller amongst a hull lot of others, and yeh've got to keep quiet an' do what they tell yeh. I know how you are, Henry.

[1] with . . . it: Spartan women were supposed to have told their sons or husbands to return either with their shields or on them—that is, either victorious or dead.

"I've knet yeh eight pair of socks, Henry, and I've put in all yer best shirts, because I want my boy to be jest as warm and comf'able as anybody in the army. Whenever they get holes in 'em, I want yeh to send 'em right-away back to me, so's I kin dern 'em.

"An' allus be careful an' choose yer comp'ny. There's lots of bad men in the army, Henry. The army makes 'em wild, and they like nothing better than the job of leading off a young feller like you, as ain't never been away from home much and has allus had a mother, an' a-learning 'em to drink and swear. Keep clear of them folks, Henry. I don't want yeh to ever do anything, Henry, that yeh would be 'shamed to let me know about. Jest think as if I was a-watchin' yeh. If yeh keep that in yer mind allus, I guess yeh'll come out about right.

"Yeh must allus remember yer father, too, child, an' remember he never drunk a drop of licker in his life, and seldom swore a cross oath.

"I don't know what else to tell yeh, Henry, excepting that yeh must never do no shirking, child, on my account. If so be a time comes when yeh have to be kilt or do a mean thing, why, Henry, don't think of anything 'cept what's right, because there's many a woman has to bear up 'ginst sech things these times, and the Lord'll take keer of us all.

"Don't forgit about the socks and the shirts, child; and I've put a cup of blackberry jam with yer bundle, because I know yeh like it above all things. Goodby, Henry. Watch out, and be a good boy."

He had, of course, been impatient under the ordeal of this speech. It had not been quite what he expected, and he had borne it with an air of irritation. He departed feeling vague relief.

Still, when he had looked back from the gate, he had seen his mother kneeling among the potato parings. Her brown face, upraised, was stained with tears, and her spare form was quivering. He bowed his head and went on, feeling suddenly ashamed of his purposes.

From his home he had gone to the seminary [1] to bid adieu to many schoolmates. They had thronged about him with wonder and admiration. He had felt the gulf now between them and had swelled with calm pride. He and some of his fellows who had donned blue were quite overwhelmed with privileges for all of one afternoon, and it had been a very delicious thing. They had strutted.

A certain light-haired girl had made vivacious fun at his martial spirit, but there was another and darker girl whom he had gazed at steadfastly, and he thought she grew demure and sad at sight of his blue and brass. As he had walked down the path between the rows of oaks, he had turned his head and detected her at a window watching his departure. As he perceived her, she had immediately begun to stare up through the high tree branches at the sky. He had seen a good deal of flurry and haste in her movement as she changed her attitude. He often thought of it.

On the way to Washington his spirit had soared. The regiment was fed and caressed at station after station until the youth had believed that he must be a hero. There was a lavish expenditure of bread and cold meats, coffee, and pickles and cheese. As he basked in the smiles of the girls and was patted and complimented by the old men, he had felt growing within him the strength to do mighty deeds of arms.

After complicated journeyings with many pauses, there had come months of monotonous life in a camp. He had had the belief that real war was a series of death struggles with small time in between for sleep and meals; but since his regiment had come to the field the army had done little but sit still and try to keep warm.

He was brought then gradually back to his old ideas. Greeklike struggles would be no more. Men were better, or more timid. Secular and religious educa-

[1] **seminary:** here, the local secondary school.

tion had effaced the throat-grappling instinct, or else firm finance held in check the passions.

He had grown to regard himself merely as a part of a vast blue demonstration. His province was to look out, as far as he could, for his personal comfort. For recreation he could twiddle his thumbs and speculate on the thoughts which must agitate the minds of the generals. Also, he was drilled and drilled and reviewed, and drilled and drilled and reviewed.

The only foes he had seen were some pickets [1] along the river bank. They were a sun-tanned, philosophical lot, who sometimes shot reflectively at the blue pickets. When reproached for this afterward, they usually expressed sorrow, and swore by their gods that the guns had exploded without their permission. The youth, on guard duty one night, conversed across

[1] **pickets:** sentries.

the stream with one of them. He was a slightly ragged man, who spat skillfully between his shoes and possessed a great fund of bland and infantile assurance. The youth liked him personally.

"Yank," the other had informed him, "yer a right dum good feller." This sentiment, floating to him upon the still air, had made him temporarily regret war.

Various veterans had told him tales. Some talked of gray, bewhiskered hordes who were advancing with relentless curses and chewing tobacco with unspeakable valor; tremendous bodies of fierce soldiery who were sweeping along like the Huns.[2] Others spoke of tattered and eternally hungry men who fired despondent powders. "They'll charge through hell's fire an' brimstone t' git a holt on a haversack,[3] an' sech stomachs ain't a-lastin' long," he was told. From the stories, the youth imagined the red, live bones sticking out through slits in the faded uniforms.

Still, he could not put a whole faith in veterans' tales, for recruits were their prey. They talked much of smoke, fire, and blood, but he could not tell how much might be lies. They persistently yelled, "Fresh fish!" [4] at him, and were in no wise to be trusted.

However, he perceived now that it did not greatly matter what kind of soldiers he was going to fight, so long as they fought, which fact no one disputed. There was a more serious problem. He lay in his bunk pondering upon it. He tried to mathematically prove to himself that he would not run from a battle.

Previously he had never felt obliged to wrestle too seriously with this question. In his life he had taken certain things for granted, never challenging his belief in ultimate success, and bothering little about means and roads. But here he was confronted with a thing of moment. It had

[2] **Huns:** a tribe of Asiatic barbarians who ravaged Europe in the fifth century.

[3] **haversack:** a canvas bag in which the soldier carried his provisions.

[4] **"Fresh fish":** a raw recruit (slang).

suddenly appeared to him that perhaps in a battle he might run. He was forced to admit that as far as war was concerned he knew nothing of himself.

A sufficient time before he would have allowed the problem to kick its heels at the outer portals of his mind, but now he felt compelled to give serious attention to it.

A little panic-fear grew in his mind. As his imagination went forward to a fight, he saw hideous possibilities. He contemplated the lurking menaces of the future and failed in an effort to see himself standing stoutly in the midst of them. He recalled his visions of broken-bladed glory, but in the shadow of the impending tumult he suspected them to be impossible pictures.

He sprang from the bunk and began to pace nervously to and fro. "Good Lord, what's th' matter with me?" he said aloud.

He felt that in this crisis his laws of life were useless. Whatever he had learned of himself was here of no avail. He was an unknown quantity. He saw that he would again be obliged to experiment as he had in early youth. He must accumulate information of himself, and meanwhile he resolved to remain close upon his guard lest those qualities of which he knew nothing should everlastingly disgrace him. "Good Lord!" he repeated in dismay.

After a time the tall soldier slid dexterously through the hole. The loud private followed. They were wrangling.

"That's all right," said the tall soldier as he entered. He waved his hand expressively. "You can believe me or not, jest as you like. All you got to do is to sit down and wait as quiet as you can. Then pretty soon you'll find out I was right."

His comrade grunted stubbornly. For a moment he seemed to be searching for a formidable reply. Finally he said: "Well, you don't know everything in the world, do you?"

"Didn't say I knew everything in the world," retorted the other sharply. He began to stow various articles snugly into his knapsack.

The youth, pausing in his nervous walk, looked down at the busy figure. "Going to be a battle, sure, is there, Jim?" he asked.

"Of course there is," replied the tall soldier. "Of course there is. You jest wait 'til tomorrow, and you'll see one of the biggest battles ever was. You jest wait."

"Thunder!" said the youth.

"Oh, you'll see fighting this time, my boy, what'll be regular out-and-out fighting," added the tall soldier, with the air of a man who is about to exhibit a battle for the benefit of his friends.

"Huh!" said the loud one from a corner.

"Well," remarked the youth, "like as not this story'll turn out jest like them others did."

"Not much it won't," replied the tall soldier, exasperated. "Not much it won't. Didn't the cavalry all start this morning?" He glared about him. No one denied his statement. "The cavalry started this morning," he continued. "They say there ain't hardly any cavalry left in camp. They're going to Richmond, or some place, while we fight all the Johnnies.[1] It's some dodge like that. The regiment's got orders, too. A feller what seen 'em go to headquarters told me a little while ago. And they're raising blazes all over camp—anybody can see that."

"Shucks!" said the loud one.

The youth remained silent for a time. At last he spoke to the tall soldier. "Jim!"

"What?"

"How do you think the reg'ment 'll do?"

"Oh, they'll fight all right, I guess, after they once get into it," said the other with cold judgment. He made a fine use of the third person. "There's been heaps of fun poked at 'em because they're new, of course, and all that; but they'll fight all right, I guess."

"Think any of the boys 'll run?" persisted the youth.

---

[1] **Johnnies:** Johnny Rebs, or Confederate soldiers.

"Oh, there may be a few of 'em run, but there's them kind in every regiment, 'specially when they first goes under fire," said the other in a tolerant way. "Of course it might happen that the hull kit-and-boodle [1] might start and run, if some big fighting came first-off, and then again they might stay and fight like fun. But you can't bet on nothing. Of course they ain't never been under fire yet, and it ain't likely they'll lick the hull rebel army all-to-oncet the first time; but I think they'll fight better than some, if worse than others. That's the way I figger. They call the reg'ment 'Fresh fish' and everything; but the boys come of good stock, and most of 'em 'll fight like sin after they oncet git shootin'," he added, with a mighty emphasis on the last four words.

"Oh, you think you know——" began the loud soldier with scorn.

The other turned savagely upon him. They had a rapid altercation, in which they fastened upon each other various strange epithets.

The youth at last interrupted them. "Did you ever think you might run yourself, Jim?" he asked. On concluding the sentence he laughed as if he had meant to aim a joke. The loud soldier also giggled.

The tall private waved his hand. "Well," said he profoundly, "I've thought it might get too hot for Jim Conklin in some of them scrimmages,[2] and if a whole lot of boys started and run, why, I s'pose I'd start and run. And if I once started to run, I'd run like the devil, and no mistake. But if everybody was a-standing and a-fighting, why, I'd stand and fight. Be jiminey, I would. I'll bet on it."

"Huh!" said the loud one.

The youth of this tale felt gratitude for these words of his comrade. He had feared that all of the untried men possessed a great and correct confidence. He now was in a measure reassured.

[1] **kit-and-boodle:** the whole lot.
[2] **scrimmages:** here, skirmishes.

CHAPTER 2

THE NEXT MORNING the youth discovered that his tall comrade had been the fast-flying messenger of a mistake. There was much scoffing at the latter by those who had yesterday been firm adherents of his views, and there was even a little sneering by men who had never believed the rumor. The tall one fought with a man from Chatfield Corners and beat him severely.

The youth felt, however, that his problem was in no wise lifted from him. There was, on the contrary, an irritating prolongation. The tale had created in him a great concern for himself. Now, with the newborn question in his mind, he was compelled to sink back into his old place as part of a blue demonstration.

For days he made ceaseless calculations, but they were all wondrously unsatisfactory. He found that he could establish nothing. He finally concluded that the only way to prove himself was to go into the blaze, and then figuratively to watch his legs to discover their merits and faults. He reluctantly admitted that he could not sit still and with a mental slate and pencil derive an answer. To gain it, he must have blaze, blood, and danger, even as a chemist requires this, that, and the other. So he fretted for an opportunity.

Meanwhile he continually tried to measure himself by his comrades. The tall soldier, for one, gave him some assurance. This man's serene unconcern dealt him a measure of confidence, for he had known him since childhood, and from his intimate knowledge he did not see how he could be capable of anything that was beyond him, the youth. Still, he thought that his comrade might be mistaken about himself. Or, on the other hand, he might be a man heretofore doomed to peace and obscurity, but, in reality, made to shine in war.

The youth would have liked to have discovered another who suspected himself.

A sympathetic comparison of mental notes would have been a joy to him.

He occasionally tried to fathom [1] a comrade with seductive sentences. He looked about to find men in the proper mood. All attempts failed to bring forth any statement which looked in any way like a confession to those doubts which he privately acknowledged in himself. He was afraid to make an open declaration of his concern, because he dreaded to place some unscrupulous confidant upon the high plane of the unconfessed, from which elevation he could be derided.

In regard to his companions his mind wavered between two opinions, according to his mood. Sometimes he inclined to believing them all heroes. In fact, he usually admitted in secret the superior development of the higher qualities in others. He could conceive of men going very insignificantly about the world bearing a load of courage unseen, and, although he had known many of his comrades through boyhood, he began to fear that his judgment of them had been blind. Then, in other moments, he flouted these theories, and assured himself that his fellows were all privately wondering and quaking.

His emotions made him feel strange in the presence of men who talked excitedly of a prospective battle as of a drama they were about to witness, with nothing but eagerness and curiosity apparent in their faces. It was often that he suspected them to be liars.

He did not pass such thoughts without severe condemnation of himself. He dinned reproaches at times. He was convicted by himself of many shameful crimes against the gods of traditions.

In his great anxiety his heart was continually clamoring at what he considered the intolerable slowness of the generals. They seemed content to perch tranquilly on the river bank, and leave him bowed down by the weight of a great problem. He wanted it settled forthwith. He could not long bear such a load, he said. Sometimes his anger at the commanders reached an acute stage, and he grumbled about the camp like a veteran.

One morning, however, he found himself in the ranks of his prepared regiment. The men were whispering speculations and recounting the old rumors. In the gloom before the break of the day their uniforms glowed a deep purple hue. From across the river the red eyes were still peering. In the eastern sky there was a yellow patch like a rug laid for the feet of the coming sun; and against it, black and patternlike, loomed the gigantic figure of the colonel on a gigantic horse.

From off in the darkness came the trampling of feet. The youth could occasionally see dark shadows that moved like monsters. The regiment stood at rest for what seemed a long time. The youth grew impatient. It was unendurable the way these affairs were managed. He wondered how long they were to be kept waiting.

As he looked all about him and pondered upon the mystic gloom, he began to believe that at any moment the ominous distance might be aflare, and the rolling crashes of an engagement come to his ears. Staring once at the red eyes across the river, he conceived them to be growing larger, as the orbs [2] of a row of dragons advancing. He turned toward the colonel and saw him lift his gigantic arm and calmly stroke his mustache.

At last he heard from along the road at the foot of the hill the clatter of a horse's galloping hoofs. It must be the coming of orders. He bent forward, scarce breathing. The exciting clickety-click, as it grew louder and louder, seemed to be beating upon his soul. Presently a horseman with jangling equipment drew rein before the colonel of the regiment. The two held a short, sharp-worded conversation. The men in the foremost ranks craned their necks.

As the horseman wheeled his animal and galloped away, he turned to shout over

[1] **fathom:** here, question.

[2] **orbs:** here, eyes.

his shoulder, "Don't forget that box of cigars!" The colonel mumbled in reply. The youth wondered what a box of cigars had to do with war.

A moment later the regiment went swinging off into the darkness. It was now like one of those moving monsters wending with many feet. The air was heavy, and cold with dew. A mass of wet grass, marched upon, rustled like silk.

There was an occasional flash and glimmer of steel from the backs of all these huge crawling reptiles. From the road came creakings and grumblings as some surly guns were dragged away.

The men stumbled along still muttering speculations. There was a subdued debate. Once a man fell down, and as he reached for his rifle a comrade, unseeing, trod upon his hand. He of the injured fingers swore bitterly and aloud. A low, low, tittering laugh went among his fellows.

Presently they passed into a roadway and marched forward with easy strides. A dark regiment moved before them, and from behind also came the tinkle of equipments on the bodies of marching men.

The rushing yellow of the developing day went on behind their backs. When the sunrays at last struck full and mellowingly upon the earth, the youth saw that the landscape was streaked with two long, thin, black columns which disappeared on the brow of a hill in front and rearward vanished in a wood. They were like two serpents crawling from the cavern of the night.

The river was not in view. The tall soldier burst into praises of what he thought to be his powers of perception.

Some of the tall one's companions cried with emphasis that they, too, had evolved the same thing, and they congratulated themselves upon it. But there were others who said that the tall one's plan was not the true one at all. They persisted with other theories. There was a vigorous discussion.

The youth took no part in them. As he walked along in careless line he was engaged with his own eternal debate. He could not hinder himself from dwelling upon it. He was despondent and sullen, and threw shifting glances about him. He looked ahead, often expecting to hear from the advance the rattle of firing.

But the long serpents crawled slowly from hill to hill without bluster of smoke. A dun-colored cloud of dust floated away to the right. The sky overhead was of a fairy blue.

The youth studied the faces of his companions, ever on the watch to detect kindred emotions. He suffered disappointment. Some ardor of the air which was causing the veteran commands to move with glee—almost with song—had infected the new regiment. The men began to speak of victory as of a thing they knew. Also, the tall soldier received his vindication. They were certainly going to come around in behind the enemy. They expressed commiseration for that part of the army which had been left upon the river bank, felicitating themselves upon being a part of a blasting host.

The youth, considering himself as separated from the others, was saddened by the blithe and merry speeches that went from rank to rank. The company wags all made their best endeavors. The regiment tramped to the tune of laughter.

The blatant soldier often convulsed whole files by his biting sarcasms aimed at the tall one.

And it was not long before all the men seemed to forget their mission. Whole brigades grinned in unison, and regiments laughed.

A rather fat soldier attempted to pilfer a horse from a dooryard. He planned to load his knapsack upon it. He was escaping with his prize when a young girl rushed from the house and grabbed the animal's mane. There followed a wrangle. The young girl, with pink cheeks and shining eyes, stood like a dauntless statue.

The observant regiment, standing at rest in the roadway, whooped at once, and entered whole-souled upon the side of the maiden. The men became so engrossed in this affair that they entirely ceased to remember their own large war. They jeered the piratical private, and called attention to various defects in his personal appearance; and they were wildly enthusiastic in support of the young girl.

To her, from some distance, came bold advice. "Hit him with a stick."

There were crows and catcalls showered upon him when he retreated without the horse. The regiment rejoiced at his downfall. Loud and vociferous congratulations were showered upon the maiden, who stood panting and regarding the troops with defiance.

At nightfall the column broke into regimental pieces, and the fragments went into the fields to camp. Tents sprang up like strange plants. Campfires, like red, peculiar blossoms, dotted the night.

The youth kept from intercourse with his companions as much as circumstances would allow him. In the evening he wandered a few paces into the gloom. From this little distance the many fires, with the black forms of men passing to and fro before the crimson rays, made weird and satanic effects.

He lay down in the grass. The blades pressed tenderly against his cheek. The moon had been lighted and was hung in a treetop. The liquid stillness of the night enveloping him made him feel vast pity for himself. There was a caress in the soft winds; and the whole mood of the darkness, he thought, was one of sympathy for himself in his distress.

He wished, without reserve, that he was at home again making the endless rounds from the house to the barn, from the barn to the fields, from the fields to the barn, from the barn to the house. He remembered he had often cursed the brindle cow and her mates, and had sometimes flung milking stools. But, from his present point of view, there was a halo of happiness about each of their heads, and he would have sacrificed all the brass buttons on the continent to have been enabled to return to them. He told himself that he was not formed for a soldier. And he mused seriously upon the radical differences between himself and those men who were dodging implike around the fires.

As he mused thus, he heard the rustle of grass and, upon turning his head, discovered the loud soldier. He called out, "Oh, Wilson!"

The latter approached and looked down. "Why, hello, Henry; is it you? What you doing here?"

"Oh, thinking," said the youth.

The other sat down and carefully lighted his pipe. "You're getting blue, my boy. You're looking thundering peeked.[1] What the dickens is wrong with you?"

"Oh, nothing," said the youth.

The loud soldier launched then into the subject of the anticipated fight. "Oh, we've got 'em now!" As he spoke his boyish face was wreathed in a gleeful smile, and his voice had an exultant ring. "We've got 'em now. At last, by the eternal thunders, we'll lick 'em good!"

"If the truth was known," he added, more soberly, *"they've* licked *us* about every clip up to now; but this time—this time—we'll lick 'em good!"

"I thought you was objecting to this march a little while ago," said the youth coldly.

"Oh, it wasn't that," explained the other. "I don't mind marching, if there's going to be fighting at the end of it. What I hate is this getting moved here and moved there, with no good coming of it, as far as I can see, excepting sore feet and damned short rations."

"Well, Jim Conklin says we'll get a plenty of fighting this time."

"He's right for once, I guess, though I can't see how it come. This time we're in for a big battle, and we've got the best end of it, certain sure. Gee rod! how we will thump 'em!"

He arose and began to pace to and fro excitedly. The thrill of his enthusiasm made him walk with an elastic step. He was sprightly, vigorous, fiery in his belief in success. He looked into the future with

---

[1] **peeked:** peaked, or sickly.

clear, proud eyes, and he swore with the air of an old soldier.

The youth watched him for a moment in silence. When he finally spoke, his voice was as bitter as dregs. "Oh, you're going to do great things, I s'pose!"

The loud soldier blew a thoughtful cloud of smoke from his pipe. "Oh, I don't know," he remarked with dignity; "I don't know. I s'pose I'll do as well as the rest. I'm going to try like thunder." He evidently complimented himself upon the modesty of this statement.

"How do you know you won't run when the time comes?" asked the youth.

"Run?" said the loud one; "run?—of course not!" He laughed.

"Well," continued the youth, "lots of good-a-nough men have thought they was going to do great things before the fight, but when the time come they skedaddled."

"Oh, that's all true, I s'pose," replied the other; "but I'm not going to skedaddle. The man that bets on my running will lose his money, that's all." He nodded confidently.

"Oh, shucks!" said the youth. "You ain't the bravest man in the world, are you?"

"No, I ain't," exclaimed the loud soldier indignantly; "and I didn't say I was the bravest man in the world, neither. I said I was going to do my share of fighting—that's what I said. And I am, too. Who are you, anyhow? You talk as if you thought you was Napoleon Bonaparte." He glared at the youth for a moment, and then strode away.

The youth called in a savage voice after his comrade: "Well, you needn't git mad about it!" But the other continued on his way and made no reply.

He felt alone in space when his injured comrade had disappeared. His failure to discover any mite of resemblance in their viewpoints made him more miserable than before. No one seemed to be wrestling with such a terrific personal problem. He was a mental outcast.

He went slowly to his tent and stretched himself on a blanket by the side of the snoring tall soldier. In the darkness he saw visions of a thousand-tongued fear that would babble at his back and cause him to flee, while others were going coolly about their country's business. He admitted that he would not be able to cope with this monster. He felt that every nerve in his body would be an ear to hear the voices, while other men would remain stolid and deaf.

And as he sweated with the pain of these thoughts, he could hear low, serene sentences. "I'll bid five." "Make it six." "Seven." "Seven goes."

He stared at the red, shivering reflection of a fire on the white wall of his tent until, exhausted and ill from the monotony of his suffering, he fell asleep.

CHAPTER 3

WHEN ANOTHER NIGHT came the columns, changed to purple streaks, filed across two pontoon bridges.[1] A glaring fire wine-tinted the waters of the river. Its rays, shining upon the moving masses of troops, brought forth here and there sudden gleams of silver or gold. Upon the other shore a dark and mysterious range of hills was curved against the sky. The insect voices of the night sang solemnly.

After this crossing the youth assured himself that at any moment they might be suddenly and fearfully assaulted from the caves of the lowering woods. He kept his eyes watchfully upon the darkness.

But his regiment went unmolested to a camping place, and its soldiers slept the brave sleep of wearied men. In the morning they were routed out with early energy and hustled along a narrow road that led deep into the forest.

It was during this rapid march that the regiment lost many of the marks of a new command.

The men had begun to count the miles upon their fingers, and they grew tired.

[1] **pontoon bridges:** temporary bridges supported on floats.

"Sore feet an' damned short rations, that's all," said the loud soldier. There were perspiration and grumblings. After a time they began to shed their knapsacks. Some tossed them unconcernedly down; others hid them carefully, asserting their plans to return for them at some convenient time. Men extricated themselves from thick shirts. Presently few carried anything but their necessary clothing, blankets, haversacks, canteens, and arms and ammunition. "You can now eat and shoot," said the tall soldier to the youth. "That's all you want to do."

There was sudden change from the ponderous infantry of theory to the light and speedy infantry of practice. The regiment, relieved of a burden, received a new impetus. But there was much loss of valuable knapsacks and, on the whole, very good shirts.

But the regiment was not yet veteran-like in appearance. Veteran regiments in the army were likely to be very small aggregations of men. Once, when the command had first come to the field, some perambulating veterans, noting the length of their column, had accosted them thus: "Hey, fellers, what brigade is that?" And when the men had replied that they formed a regiment and not a brigade, the older soldiers had laughed, and said, "O Gawd!"

Also, there was too great a similarity in the hats. The hats of a regiment should properly represent the history of headgear for a period of years. And, moreover, there were no letters of faded gold speaking from the colors. They were new and beautiful, and the color bearer habitually oiled the pole.

Presently the army again sat down to think. The odor of the peaceful pines was in the men's nostrils. The sound of monotonous ax blows rang through the forest, and the insects, nodding upon their perches, crooned like old women. The youth returned to his theory of a blue demonstration.

One gray dawn, however, he was kicked in the leg by the tall soldier, and then, before he was entirely awake, he found himself running down a wood road in the midst of men who were panting from the first effects of speed. His canteen banged rhythmically upon his thigh, and his haversack bobbed softly. His musket bounced a trifle from his shoulder at each stride and made his cap feel uncertain upon his head.

He could hear the men whisper jerky sentences: "Say—what's all this—about?" "What th' thunder—we—skedaddlin' this way fer?" "Billie—keep off m' feet. Yeh run—like a cow." And the loud soldier's shrill voice could be heard: "What th' devil they in sich a hurry for?"

The youth thought the damp fog of early morning moved from the rush of a great body of troops. From the distance came a sudden spatter of firing.

He was bewildered. As he ran with his comrades he strenuously tried to think, but all he knew was that if he fell down those coming behind would tread upon him. All his faculties seemed to be needed to guide him over and past obstructions. He felt carried along by a mob.

The sun spread disclosing rays, and, one by one, regiments burst into view like armed men just born of the earth. The youth perceived that the time had come. He was about to be measured. For a moment he felt in the face of his great trial like a babe, and the flesh over his heart seemed very thin. He seized time to look about him calculatingly.

But he instantly saw that it would be impossible for him to escape from the regiment. It enclosed him. And there were iron laws of tradition and law on four sides. He was in a moving box.

As he perceived this fact, it occurred to him that he had never wished to come to the war. He had not enlisted of his free will. He had been dragged by the merciless government. And now they were taking him out to be slaughtered.

The regiment slid down a bank and wallowed across a little stream. The mournful current moved slowly on, and from the water, shaded black, some white bubble eyes looked at the men.

As they climbed the hill on the farther side artillery began to boom. Here the youth forgot many things as he felt a sudden impulse of curiosity. He scrambled up the bank with a speed that could not be exceeded by a bloodthirsty man.

He expected a battle scene.

There were some little fields girded and squeezed by a forest. Spread over the grass and in among the tree trunks, he could see knots and waving lines of skirmishers who were running hither and thither and firing at the landscape. A dark battle line lay upon a sunstruck clearing that gleamed orange color. A flag fluttered.

Other regiments floundered up the bank. The brigade was formed in line of battle, and after a pause started slowly through the woods in the rear of the receding skirmishers, who were continually melting into the scene to appear again farther on. They were always busy as bees, deeply absorbed in their little combats.

The youth tried to observe everything. He did not use care to avoid trees and branches, and his forgotten feet were constantly knocking against stones or getting entangled in briers. He was aware that these battalions with their commotions were woven red and startling into the gentle fabric of softened greens and

browns. It looked to be a wrong place for a battlefield.

The skirmishers in advance fascinated him. Their shots into thickets and at distant and prominent trees spoke to him of tragedies—hidden, mysterious, solemn.

Once the line encountered the body of a dead soldier. He lay upon his back staring at the sky. He was dressed in an awkward suit of yellowish brown. The youth could see that the soles of his shoes had been worn to the thinness of writing paper, and from a great rent in one the dead foot projected piteously. And it was as if fate had betrayed the soldier. In death it exposed to his enemies that poverty which in life he had perhaps concealed from his friends.

The ranks opened covertly to avoid the corpse. The invulnerable dead man forced a way for himself. The youth looked keenly at the ashen face. The wind raised the tawny beard. It moved as if a hand were stroking it. He vaguely desired to walk around and around the body and stare; the impulse of the living to try to read in dead eyes the answer to the Question.

During the march the ardor which the youth had acquired when out of view of the field rapidly faded to nothing. His curiosity was quite easily satisfied. If an intense scene had caught him with its wild swing as he came to the top of the bank, he might have gone roaring on. This advance upon Nature was too calm. He had opportunity to reflect. He had time in which to wonder about himself and to attempt to probe his sensations.

Absurd ideas took hold upon him. He thought that he did not relish the landscape. It threatened him. A coldness swept over his back, and it is true that his trousers felt to him that they were no fit for his legs at all.

A house standing placidly in distant fields had to him an ominous look. The shadows of the woods were formidable. He was certain that in this vista there lurked fierce-eyed hosts. The swift thought came to him that the generals did not know what they were about. It was all a trap. Suddenly those close forests would bristle with rifle barrels. Ironlike brigades would appear in the rear. They were all going to be sacrificed. The generals were stupids. The enemy would presently swallow the whole command. He glared about him, expecting to see the stealthy approach of his death.

He thought that he must break from the ranks and harangue his comrades. They must not all be killed like pigs; and he was sure it would come to pass unless they were informed of these dangers. The generals were idiots to send them marching into a regular pen. There was but one pair of eyes in the corps. He would step forth and make a speech. Shrill and passionate words came to his lips.

The line, broken into moving fragments by the ground, went calmly on through fields and woods. The youth looked at the men nearest him and saw, for the most part, expressions of deep interest, as if they were investigating something that had fascinated them. One or two stepped with overvaliant airs as if they were already plunged into war. Others walked as upon thin ice. The greater part of the untested men appeared quiet and absorbed. They were going to look at war, the red animal—war, the blood-swollen god. And they were deeply engrossed in this march.

As he looked, the youth gripped his outcry at his throat. He saw that even if the men were tottering with fear they would laugh at his warning. They would jeer him, and, if practicable, pelt him with missiles. Admitting that he might be wrong, a frenzied declamation of the kind would turn him into a worm.

He assumed, then, the demeanor of one who knows that he is doomed alone to unwritten responsibilities. He lagged, with tragic glances at the sky.

He was surprised presently by the young lieutenant of his company, who began heartily to beat him with a sword, calling out in a loud and insolent voice: "Come, young man, get up into ranks there. No skulking 'll do here." He

mended his pace with suitable haste. And he hated the lieutenant, who had no appreciation of fine minds. He was a mere brute.

After a time the brigade was halted in the cathedral light of a forest. The busy skirmishers were still popping. Through the aisles of the wood could be seen the floating smoke from their rifles. Sometimes it went up in little balls, white and compact.

During this halt many men in the regiment began erecting tiny hills in front of them. They used stones, sticks, earth, and anything they thought might turn a bullet. Some built comparatively large ones, while others seemed content with little ones.

This procedure caused a discussion among the men. Some wished to fight like duelists, believing it to be correct to stand erect and be, from their feet to their foreheads, a mark. They said they scorned the devices of the cautious. But the others scoffed in reply, and pointed to the veterans on the flanks who were digging at the ground like terriers. In a short time there was quite a barricade along the regimental fronts. Directly, however, they were ordered to withdraw from that place.

This astounded the youth. He forgot his stewing over the advance movement. "Well, then, what did they march us out here for?" he demanded of the tall soldier. The latter with calm faith began a heavy explanation, although he had been compelled to leave a little protection of stones and dirt to which he had devoted much care and skill.

When the regiment was aligned in another position each man's regard for his safety caused another line of small intrenchments. They ate their noon meal behind a third one. They were moved from this one also. They were marched from place to place with apparent aimlessness.

The youth had been taught that a man became another thing in a battle. He saw his salvation in such a change. Hence this waiting was an ordeal to him. He was in a fever of impatience. He considered that there was denoted a lack of purpose on the part of the generals. He began to complain to the tall soldier. "I can't stand this much longer," he cried. "I don't see what good it does to make us wear out our legs for nothin'." He wished to return to camp, knowing that this affair was a blue demonstration; or else to go into a battle and discover that he had been a fool in his doubts, and was, in truth, a man of traditional courage. The strain of present circumstances he felt to be intolerable.

The philosophical tall soldier measured a sandwich of cracker [1] and pork and swallowed it in a nonchalant manner. "Oh, I suppose we must go reconnoitering around the country jest to keep 'em from getting too close, or to develop 'em, or something."

"Huh!" said the loud soldier.

"Well," cried the youth, still fidgeting, "I'd rather do anything 'most than go tramping 'round the country all day doing no good to nobody and jest tiring ourselves out."

"So would I," said the loud soldier. "It ain't right. I tell you if anybody with any sense was a-runnin' this army it——"

"Oh, shut up!" roared the tall private. "You little fool. You little damn' cuss. You ain't had that there coat and them pants on for six months, and yet you talk as if——"

"Well, I wanta do some fighting anyway," interrupted the other. "I didn't come here to walk. I could 'ave walked to home—'round an 'round the barn, if I jest wanted to walk."

The tall one, red-faced, swallowed another sandwich as if taking poison in despair.

But gradually, as he chewed, his face became again quiet and contented. He could not rage in fierce argument in the presence of such sandwiches. During his meals he always wore an air of blissful contemplation of the food he had swallowed. His spirit seemed then to be communing with the viands.

1 **cracker:** here, hardtack.

He accepted new environment and circumstance with great coolness, eating from his haversack at every opportunity. On the march he went along with the stride of a hunter, objecting to neither gait nor distance. And he had not raised his voice when he had been ordered away from three little protective piles of earth and stone, each of which had been an engineering feat worthy of being made sacred to the name of his grandmother.

In the afternoon the regiment went out over the same ground it had taken in the morning. The landscape then ceased to threaten the youth. He had been close to it and become familiar with it.

When, however, they began to pass into a new region, his old fears of stupidity and incompetence reassailed him, but this time he doggedly let them babble. He was occupied with his problem, and in his desperation he concluded that the stupidity did not greatly matter.

Once he thought he had concluded that it would be better to get killed directly and end his troubles. Regarding death thus out of the corner of his eye, he conceived it to be nothing but rest, and he was filled with a momentary astonishment that he should have made an extraordinary commotion over the mere matter of getting killed. He would die; he would go to some place where he would be understood. It was useless to expect appreciation of his profound and fine senses from such men as the lieutenant. He must look to the grave for comprehension.

The skirmish fire increased to a long clattering sound. With it was mingled faraway cheering. A battery spoke.

Directly the youth would see the skirmishers running. They were pursued by the sound of musketry fire. After a time the hot, dangerous flashes of the rifles were visible. Smoke clouds went slowly and insolently across the fields like observant phantoms. The din became crescendo, like the roar of an oncoming train.

A brigade ahead of them and on the right went into action with a rending roar. It was as if it had exploded. And thereafter it lay stretched in the distance behind a long gray wall, that one was obliged to look twice at to make sure that it was smoke.

The youth, forgetting his neat plan of getting killed, gazed spellbound. His eyes grew wide and busy with the action of the scene. His mouth was a little ways open.

Of a sudden he felt a heavy and sad hand laid upon his shoulder. Awakening from his trance of observation he turned and beheld the loud soldier.

"It's my first and last battle, old boy," said the latter, with intense gloom. He was quite pale and his girlish lip was trembling.

"Eh?" murmured the youth in great astonishment.

"It's my first and last battle, old boy," continued the loud soldier. "Something tells me——"

"What?"

"I'm a gone coon this first time and— and I w-want you to take these here things —to—my—folks." He ended in a quavering sob of pity for himself. He handed the youth a little packet done up in a yellow envelope.

"Why, what the devil——" began the youth again.

But the other gave him a glance as from the depths of a tomb, and raised his limp hand in a prophetic manner and turned away.

CHAPTER 4

THE BRIGADE was halted in the fringe of a grove. The men crouched among the trees and pointed their restless guns out at the fields. They tried to look beyond the smoke.

Out of this haze they could see running men. Some shouted information and gestured as they hurried.

The men of the new regiment watched and listened eagerly, while their tongues ran on in gossip of the battle. They mouthed rumors that had flown like birds out of the unknown.

"They say Perry has been driven in with big loss."

"Yes, Carrott went t' th' hospital. He said he was sick. That smart lieutenant is commanding 'G' Company. Th' boys say they won't be under Carrott no more if they all have t' desert. They allus knew he was a——"

"Hannises' batt'ry is took."

"It ain't either. I saw Hannises' batt'ry off on th' left not more'n fifteen minutes ago."

"Well——"

"Th' general, he ses he is goin't' take th' hull cammand of th' 304th when we go inteh action, an' then he ses we'll do sech fightin'. as never another one reg'ment done."

"They say we're catchin' it over on th' left. They say th' enemy driv' our line inteh a devil of a swamp an' took Hannises' batt'ry."

"No sech thing. Hannises' batt'ry was 'long here 'bout a minute ago."

"That young Hasbrouck, he makes a good off'cer. He ain't afraid 'a nothin'.'"

"I met one of th' 148th Maine boys an' he ses his brigade fit th' hull rebel army fer four hours over on th' turnpike road an' killed about five thousand of 'em. He ses one more sech fight as that an' th' war 'll be over."

"Bill wasn't scared either. No, sir! It wasn't that. Bill ain't a-gittin' scared easy. He was jest mad, that's what he was. When that feller trod on his hand, he up an' sed that he was willin' t' give his hand t' his country, but he be dumbed if he was goin' t' have every dumb bushwacker [1] in th' kentry walkin' 'round on it. So he went t' th' hospital disregardless of th' fight. Three fingers was crunched. Th' dern doctor wanted t' amputate 'm, an' Bill, he raised a helluva row, I hear. He's a funny feller."

The din in front swelled to a tremendous chorus. The youth and his fellows were frozen to silence. They could see a flag

---

[1] **bushwacker:** here, Confederate guerrilla fighters.

that tossed in the smoke angrily. Near it were the blurred and agitated forms of troops. There came a turbulent stream of men across the fields. A battery changing position at a frantic gallop scattered the stragglers right and left.

A shell screaming like a storm banshee [1] went over the huddled heads of the reserves. It landed in the grove and, exploding redly, flung the brown earth. There was a little shower of pine needles.

Bullets began to whistle among the branches and nip at the trees. Twigs and leaves came sailing down. It was as if a thousand axes, wee and invisible, were being wielded. Many of the men were constantly dodging and ducking their heads.

The lieutenant of the youth's company was shot in the hand. He began to swear so wondrously that a nervous laugh went along the regimental line. The officer's profanity sounded conventional. It relieved the tightened senses of the new men. It was as if he had hit his fingers with a tack hammer at home.

He held the wounded member carefully away from his side so that the blood would not drip upon his trousers.

The captain of the company, tucking his sword under his arm, produced a handkerchief and began to bind with it the lieutenant's wound. And they disputed as to how the binding should be done.

The battle flag in the distance jerked about madly. It seemed to be struggling to free itself from an agony. The billowing smoke was filled with horizontal flashes.

Men running swiftly emerged from it. They grew in numbers until it was seen that the whole command was fleeing. The flag suddenly sank down as if dying. Its motion as it fell was a gesture of despair.

Wild yells came from behind the walls of smoke. A sketch in gray and red dissolved into a moblike body of men who galloped like wild horses.

The veteran regiments on the right and

[1] **banshee:** an Irish spirit whose wailing was supposed to foretell death.

left of the 304th immediately began to jeer. With the passionate song of the bullets and the banshee shrieks of shells were mingled loud catcalls and bits of facetious advice concerning places of safety.

But the new regiment was breathless with horror. "Gawd! Saunders 's got crushed!" whispered the man at the youth's elbow. They shrank back and crouched as if compelled to await a flood.

The youth shot a swift glance along the blue ranks of the regiment. The profiles were motionless, carven; and afterward he remembered that the color sergeant was standing with his legs apart, as if he expected to be pushed to the ground.

The following throng went whirling around the flank. Here and there were officers carried along on the stream like exasperated chips. They were striking about them with their swords and with their left fists, punching every head they could reach. They cursed like highwaymen.

A mounted officer displayed the furious anger of a spoiled child. He raged with his head, his arms, and his legs.

Another, the commander of the brigade, was galloping about bawling. His hat was gone and his clothes were awry. He resembled a man who has come from bed to go to a fire. The hoofs of his horse often threatened the heads of the running men, but they scampered with singular fortune. In this rush they were apparently all deaf and blind. They heeded not the largest and longest of the oaths that were thrown at them from all directions.

Frequently over this tumult could be heard the grim jokes of the critical veterans; but the retreating men apparently were not even conscious of the presence of an audience.

The battle reflection that shone for an instant in the faces on the mad current made the youth feel that forceful hands from heaven would not have been able to have held him in place if he could have got intelligent control of his legs.

There was an appalling imprint upon these faces. The struggle in the smoke had pictured an exaggeration of itself on the bleached cheeks and in the eyes wild with one desire.

The sight of this stampede exerted a floodlike force that seemed able to drag sticks and stones and men from the ground. They of the reserves had to hold on. They grew pale and firm, and red and quaking.

The youth achieved one little thought in the midst of this chaos. The composite monster which had caused the other troops to flee had not then appeared. He resolved to get a view of it, and then he thought he might very likely run better than the best of them.

CHAPTER 5

THERE WERE moments of waiting. The youth thought of the village street at home before the arrival of the circus parade on a day in the spring. He remembered how he had stood, a small, thrillful boy, prepared to follow the dingy lady upon the white horse or the band in its faded chariot. He saw the yellow road, the lines of expectant people, and the sober houses. He particularly remembered an old fellow who used to sit upon a cracker box in front of the store and feign to despise such exhibitions. A thousand details of color and form surged in his mind. The old fellow upon the cracker box appeared in middle prominence.

Someone cried, "Here they come!"

There was rustling and muttering among the men. They displayed a feverish desire to have every possible cartridge ready to their hands. The boxes were pulled around into various positions and adjusted with great care. It was as if seven hundred new bonnets were being tried on.

The tall soldier, having prepared his rifle, produced a red handkerchief of some kind. He was engaged in knitting it about his throat with exquisite attention to its position, when the cry was repeated up and down the line in a muffled roar of sound.

"Here they come! Here they come!" Gun locks clicked.

Across the smoke-infested fields came a brown swarm of running men who were giving shrill yells. They came on, stooping and swinging their rifles at all angles. A flag, tilted forward, sped near the front.

As he caught sight of them, the youth was momentarily startled by a thought that perhaps his gun was not loaded. He stood trying to rally his faltering intellect so that he might recollect the moment when he had loaded, but he could not.

A hatless general pulled his dripping horse to a stand near the colonel of the 304th. He shook his fist in the other's face. "You've got to hold 'em back!" he shouted, savagely; "you've got to hold 'em back!"

In his agitation the colonel began to stammer. "A-all r-right, General, all right, by Gawd! We-we'll do our—we-we'll d-d-do—do our best, General." The general made a passionate gesture and galloped away. The colonel, perchance to relieve his feelings, began to scold like a wet parrot. The youth, turning swiftly to make sure that the rear was unmolested, saw the commander regarding his men in a highly resentful manner, as if he regretted above everything his association with them.

The man at the youth's elbow was mumbling, as if to himself: "Oh, we're in for it now! Oh, we're in for it now!"

The captain of the company had been pacing excitedly to and fro in the rear. He coaxed in schoolmistress fashion, as to a congregation of boys with primers. His talk was an endless repetition. "Reserve your fire, boys—don't shoot till I tell you—save your fire—wait till they get close up—don't be damned fools——"

Perspiration streamed down the youth's face, which was soiled like that of a weeping urchin. He frequently, with a nervous movement, wiped his eyes with his coat sleeve. His mouth was still a little ways open.

He got the one glance at the foe-swarming field in front of him and instantly ceased to debate the question of his piece being loaded. Before he was ready to begin—before he had announced to himself that he was about to fight—he threw the obedient, well-balanced rifle into position and fired a first wild shot. Directly he was working at his weapon like an automatic affair.

He suddenly lost concern for himself and forgot to look at a menacing fate. He became not a man but a member. He felt that something of which he was a part—a regiment, an army, a cause, or a country—was in a crisis. He was welded into a common personality which was dominated by a single desire. For some moments he could not flee, no more than a little finger can commit a revolution from a hand.

If he had thought the regiment was about to be annihilated, perhaps he could have amputated himself from it. But its noise gave him assurance. The regiment was like a firework that, once ignited, proceeds superior to circumstances until its blazing vitality fades. It wheezed and banged with a mighty power. He pictured the ground before it as strewn with the discomfited.

There was a consciousness always of the presence of his comrades about him. He felt the subtle battle brotherhood more potent even than the cause for which they were fighting. It was a mysterious fraternity born of the smoke and danger of death.

He was at a task. He was like a carpenter who has made many boxes, making still another box, only there was furious haste in his movements. He, in his thought, was careering off in other places, even as the carpenter who as he works whistles and thinks of his friend or his enemy, his home or a saloon. And these jolted dreams were never perfect to him afterward, but remained a mass of blurred shapes.

Presently he began to feel the effects of the war atmosphere—a blistering sweat, a sensation that his eyeballs were about to crack like hot stones. A burning roar filled his ears.

Following this came a red rage. He developed the acute exasperation of a pestered animal, a well-meaning cow worried by dogs. He had a mad feeling against his rifle, which could only be used against one life at a time. He wished to rush forward and strangle with his fingers. He craved a power that would enable him to make a world-sweeping gesture and brush all back. His impotency appeared to him and made his rage into that of a driven beast.

Buried in the smoke of many rifles, his anger was directed not so much against men whom he knew were rushing toward him as against the swirling battle phantoms which were choking him, stuffing their smoke robes down his parched throat. He fought frantically for respite for his senses, for air, as a babe being smothered attacks the deadly blankets.

There was a blare of heated rage mingled with a certain expression of intentness on all faces. Many of the men were making low-toned noises with their mouths, and these subdued cheers, snarls, imprecations, prayers, made a wild, barbaric song that went as an undercurrent of sound, strange and chantlike with the resounding chords of the war march. The man at the youth's elbow was babbling. In it there was something soft and tender like the monologue of a babe. The tall soldier was swearing in a loud voice. From his lips came a black procession of curious oaths. Of a sudden another broke out in a querulous way like a man who has mislaid his hat. "Well, why don't they support us? Why don't they send supports? Do they think——"

The youth in his battle sleep heard this as one who dozes hears.

There was a singular absence of heroic poses. The men bending and surging in their haste and rage were in every impossible attitude. The steel ramrods [1] clanked and clanged with incessant din as the men pounded them furiously into the

---

[1] **ramrods:** rods used to insert the cartridge in muzzle-loading firearms.

hot rifle barrels. The flaps of the cartridge boxes were all unfastened, and bobbed idiotically with each movement. The rifles, once loaded, were jerked to the shoulder and fired without apparent aim into the smoke or at one of the blurred and shifting forms which, upon the field before the regiment, had been growing larger and larger like puppets under a magician's hand.

The officers, at their intervals, rearward, neglected to stand in picturesque attitudes. They were bobbing to and fro roaring directions and encouragements. The dimensions of their howls were extraordinary. They expended their lungs with prodigal wills. And often they nearly stood upon their heads in their anxiety to observe the enemy on the other side of the tumbling smoke.

The lieutenant of the youth's company had encountered a soldier who had fled screaming at the first volley of his comrades. Behind the lines these two were acting a little isolated scene. The man was blubbering and staring with sheeplike eyes at the lieutenant, who had seized him by the collar and was pommeling him. He drove him back into the ranks with many blows. The soldier went mechanically, dully, with his animal-like eyes upon the officer. Perhaps there was to him a divinity expressed in the voice of the other—stern, hard, with no reflection of fear in it. He tried to reload his gun, but his shaking hands prevented. The lieutenant was obliged to assist him.

The men dropped here and there like bundles. The captain of the youth's company had been killed in an early part of the action. His body lay stretched out in the position of a tired man resting, but upon his face there was an astonished and sorrowful look, as if he thought some friend had done him an ill turn. The babbling man was grazed by a shot that made the blood stream widely down his face. He clapped both hands to his head. "Oh!" he said, and ran. Another grunted suddenly as if he had been struck by a club in the stomach. He sat down and gazed ruefully. In his eyes there was mute, indefinite reproach. Farther up the line a man, standing behind a tree, had had his knee joint splintered by a ball. Immediately he had dropped his rifle and gripped the tree with both arms. And there he remained, clinging desperately and crying for assistance that he might withdraw his hold upon the tree.

At last an exultant yell went along the quivering line. The firing dwindled from an uproar to a last vindictive popping. As the smoke slowly eddied away, the youth saw that the charge had been repulsed. The enemy were scattered into reluctant groups. He saw a man climb to the top of the fence, straddle the rail, and fire a parting shot. The waves had receded, leaving bits of dark débris upon the ground.

Some in the regiment began to whoop frenziedly. Many were silent. Apparently they were trying to contemplate themselves.

After the fever had left his veins, the youth thought that at last he was going to suffocate. He became aware of the foul atmosphere in which he had been struggling. He was grimy and dripping like a laborer in a foundry. He grasped his canteen and took a long swallow of the warmed water.

A sentence with variations went up and down the line. "Well, we've helt 'em back. We've helt 'em back; derned if we haven't." The men said it blissfully, leering at each other with dirty smiles.

The youth turned to look behind him and off to the right and off to the left. He experienced the joy of a man who at last finds leisure in which to look about him.

Under foot there were a few ghastly forms motionless. They lay twisted in fantastic contortions. Arms were bent and heads were turned in incredible ways. It seemed that the dead men must have fallen from some great height to get into such positions. They looked to be dumped out upon the ground from the sky.

From a position in the rear of the grove a battery was throwing shells over it. The flash of the guns startled the youth at first. He thought they were aimed directly at him. Through the trees he watched the black figures of the gunners as they worked swiftly and intently. Their labor seemed a complicated thing. He wondered how they could remember its formula in the midst of confusion.

The guns squatted in a row like savage chiefs. They argued with abrupt violence. It was a grim powwow. Their busy servants ran hither and thither.

A small procession of wounded men were going drearily toward the rear. It was a flow of blood from the torn body of the brigade.

To the right and to the left were the dark lines of other troops. Far in front he thought he could see lighter masses protruding in points from the forest. They were suggestive of unnumbered thousands.

Once he saw a tiny battery go dashing along the line of the horizon. The tiny riders were beating the tiny horses.

From a sloping hill came the sound of cheerings and clashes. Smoke welled slowly through the leaves.

Batteries were speaking with thunderous oratorical effort. Here and there were flags, the red in the stripes dominating. They splashed bits of warm color upon the dark lines of troops.

The youth felt the old thrill at the sight of the emblem. They were like beautiful birds strangely undaunted in a storm.

As he listened to the din from the hillside, to a deep pulsating thunder that came from afar to the left, and to the lesser clamors which came from many directions, it occurred to him that they were fighting, too, over there, and over there, and over there. Heretofore he had supposed that all the battle was directly under his nose.

As he gazed around him the youth felt a flash of astonishment at the blue pure sky and the sun gleamings on the trees and fields. It was surprising that Nature had gone tranquilly on with her golden process in the midst of so much devilment.

CHAPTER 6

THE YOUTH awakened slowly. He came gradually back to a position from which he could regard himself. For moments he had been scrutinizing his person in a dazed way as if he had never before seen himself. Then he picked up his cap from the ground. He wriggled in his jacket to make a more comfortable fit and, kneeling, relaced his shoe. He thoughtfully mopped his reeking [1] features.

So it was all over at last! The supreme trial had been passed. The red, formidable difficulties of war had been vanquished.

He went into an ecstasy of self-satisfaction. He had the most delightful sensations of his life. Standing as if apart from himself, he viewed that last scene. He perceived that the man who had fought thus was magnificent.

He felt that he was a fine fellow. He saw himself even with those ideals which he had considered as far beyond him. He smiled in deep gratification.

Upon his fellows he beamed tenderness and good will. "Gee! ain't it hot, hey?" he said affably to a man who was polishing his streaming face with his coat sleeves.

"You bet!" said the other, grinning sociably. "I never seen sech dumb hotness." He sprawled out luxuriously on the ground. "Gee, yes! An' I hope we don't have no more fightin' till a week from Monday."

There were some handshakings and deep speeches with men whose features were familiar, but with whom the youth now felt the bonds of tied hearts. He helped a cursing comrade to bind up a wound of the shin.

But, of a sudden, cries of amazement broke out along the ranks of the new regiment. "Here they come ag'in! Here they come ag'in!" The man who had sprawled upon the ground started up and said, "Gosh!"

The youth turned quick eyes upon the

---

[1] **reeking:** here, perspiring.

field. He discerned forms begin to swell in masses out of a distant wood. He again saw the tilted flag speeding forward.

The shells, which had ceased to trouble the regiment for a time, came swirling again and exploded in the grass or among the leaves of the trees. They looked to be strange war flowers bursting into fierce bloom.

The men groaned. The luster faded from their eyes. Their smudged countenances now expressed a profound dejection. They moved their stiffened bodies slowly and watched in sullen mood the frantic approach of the enemy. The slaves toiling in the temple of this god began to feel rebellion at his harsh tasks.

They fretted and complained each to each. "Oh, say, this is too much of a good thing! Why can't somebody send us supports?"

"We ain't never goin' to stand this second banging. I didn't come here to fight the hull damn' rebel army."

There was one who raised a doleful cry. "I wish Bill Smithers had trod on my hand, insteader me treddin' on his'n." The sore joints of the regiment creaked as it painfully floundered into position to repulse.

The youth stared. Surely, he thought, this impossible thing was not about to happen. He waited as if he expected the enemy to suddenly stop, apologize, and retire bowing. It was all a mistake.

But the firing began somewhere on the regimental line and ripped along in both directions. The level sheets of flame developed great clouds of smoke that tumbled and tossed in the mild wind near the ground for a moment, and then rolled through the ranks as through a gate. The clouds were tinged an earthlike yellow in the sunrays and in the shadow were a sorry blue. The flag was sometimes eaten and lost in this mass of vapor, but more often it projected, sun-touched, resplendent.

Into the youth's eyes there came a look that one can see in the orbs of a jaded horse. His neck was quivering with nervous weakness and the muscles of his arms felt numb and bloodless. His hands, too, seemed large and awkward as if he were wearing invisible mittens. And there was a great uncertainty about his knee joints.

The words that comrades had uttered previous to the firing began to recur to him. "Oh, say, this is too much of a good thing! What do they take us for—why don't they send supports? I didn't come here to fight the hull damned rebel army."

He began to exaggerate the endurance, the skill, and the valor of those who were coming. Himself reeling from exhaustion, he was astonished beyond measure at such persistency. They must be machines of steel. It was very gloomy struggling against such affairs, wound up perhaps to fight until sundown.

He slowly lifted his rifle, and, catching a glimpse of the thickspread field, he blazed at a cantering cluster. He stopped then and began to peer as best he could through the smoke. He caught changing views of the ground covered with men who were all running like pursued imps and yelling.

To the youth it was an onslaught of redoubtable dragons. He became like the man who lost his legs at the approach of the red and green monster. He waited in a sort of a horrified, listening attitude. He seemed to shut his eyes and wait to be gobbled.

A man near him who up to this time had been working feverishly at his rifle suddenly stopped and ran with howls. A lad whose face had borne an expression of exalted courage, the majesty of him who dares give his life, was, at an instant, smitten abject.[1] He blanched like one who has come to the edge of a cliff at midnight and is suddenly made aware. There was a revelation. He, too, threw down his gun and fled. There was no shame in his face. He ran like a rabbit.

Others began to scamper away through

[1] **smitten abject:** struck down to a groveling position—that is, filled with fear.

the smoke. The youth turned his head, shaken from his trance by this movement as if the regiment was leaving him behind. He saw the few fleeting forms.

He yelled then with fright and swung about. For a moment, in the great clamor, he was like a proverbial chicken. He lost the direction of safety. Destruction threatened him from all points.

Directly he began to speed toward the rear in great leaps. His rifle and cap were gone. His unbuttoned coat bulged in the wind. The flap of his cartridge box bobbed wildly, and his canteen, by its slender cord, swung out behind. On his face was all the horror of those things which he imagined.

The lieutenant sprang forward bawling. The youth saw his features wrathfully red, and saw him make a dab with his sword. His one thought of the incident was that the lieutenant was a peculiar creature to feel interested in such matters upon this occasion.

He ran like a blind man. Two or three times he fell down. Once he knocked his shoulder so heavily against a tree that he went headlong.

Since he had turned his back upon the fight, his fears had been wondrously magnified. Death about to thrust him between the shoulder blades was far more dreadful than death about to smite him between the eyes. When he thought of it later, he conceived the impression that it is better to view the appalling than to be merely within hearing. The noises of the battle were like stones; he believed himself liable to be crushed.

As he ran on, he mingled with others. He dimly saw men on his right and on his left, and he heard footsteps behind him. He thought that all the regiment was fleeing, pursued by these ominous crashes.

In his flight the sound of these following footsteps gave him his one meager relief. He felt vaguely that death must make a first choice of the men who were nearest; the initial morsels for the dragons would be then those who were following him. So he displayed the zeal of an insane sprinter in his purpose to keep them in the rear. There was a race.

As he, leading, went across a little field, he found himself in a region of shells. They hurtled over his head with long wild screams. As he listened, he imagined them to have rows of cruel teeth that grinned at him. Once one lit before him, and the livid lightning of the explosion effectually barred the way in his chosen direction. He groveled on the ground and then, springing up, went careering off through some bushes.

He experienced a thrill of amazement when he came within view of a battery in action. The men there seemed to be in conventional moods, altogether unaware of the impending annihilation. The battery was disputing with a distant antagonist, and the gunners were wrapped in admiration of their shooting. They were continually bending in coaxing postures over the guns. They seemed to be patting them on the back and encouraging them with words. The guns, stolid and undaunted, spoke with dogged valor.

The precise gunners were coolly enthusiastic. They lifted their eyes every chance to the smoke-wreathed hillock from whence the hostile battery addressed them. The youth pitied them as he ran. Methodical idiots! Machinelike fools! The refined joy of planting shells in the midst of the other battery's formation would appear a little thing when the infantry came swooping out of the woods.

The face of a youthful rider, who was jerking his frantic horse with an abandon of temper he might display in a placid barnyard, was impressed deeply upon his mind. He knew that he looked upon a man who would presently be dead.

Too, he felt a pity for the guns, standing, six good comrades, in a bold row.

He saw a brigade going to the relief of its pestered fellows. He scrambled upon a wee hill and watched it sweeping finely, keeping formation in difficult places. The blue of the line was crusted with steel color, and the brilliant flags projected. Officers were shouting.

This sight also filled him with wonder. The brigade was hurrying briskly to be gulped into the infernal mouths of the war god. What manner of men were they, anyhow? Ah, it was some wondrous breed! Or else they didn't comprehend—the fools.

A furious order caused commotion in the artillery. An officer on a bounding horse made maniacal motions with his arms. The teams went swinging up from the rear, the guns were whirled about, and the battery scampered away. The cannon with their noses poked slantingly at the ground grunted and grumbled like stout men, brave but with objections to hurry.

The youth went on, moderating his pace since he had left the place of noises.

Later he came upon a general of division seated upon a horse that pricked its ears in an interested way at the battle. There was a great gleaming of yellow and patent leather about the saddle and bridle. The quiet man astride looked mouse-colored upon such a splendid charger.

A jingling staff [1] was galloping hither and thither. Sometimes the general was surrounded by horsemen, and at other times he was quite alone. He looked to be much harassed. He had the appearance of a businessman whose market is swinging up and down.

The youth went slinking around this spot. He went as near as he dared, trying to overhear words. Perhaps the general, unable to comprehend chaos, might call upon him for information. And he could tell him. He knew all concerning it. Of a surety the force was in a fix, and any fool could see that if they did not retreat while they had opportunity—why——

He felt that he would like to thrash the general, or at least approach and tell him in plain words exactly what he thought him to be. It was criminal to stay calmly in one spot and make no effort to stay destruction. He loitered in a fever of eagerness for the division commander to apply to him.

As he warily moved about, he heard the general call out irritably: "Tompkins, go over an' see Taylor, an' tell him not t' be in such an all-fired hurry; tell him t' halt his brigade in th' edge of th' woods; tell him t' detach a reg'ment—say I think th' center 'll break if we don't help it out some; tell him t' hurry up."

A slim youth on a fine chestnut horse caught these swift words from the mouth of his superior. He made his horse bound into a gallop almost from a walk in his haste to go upon his mission. There was a cloud of dust.

A moment later the youth saw the general bounce excitedly in his saddle.

"Yes, by heavens, they have!" The officer leaned forward. His face was aflame with excitement. "Yes, by heavens, they've held 'im! They've held 'im!"

He began to blithely roar at his staff: "We'll wallop 'im now. We'll wallop 'im now. We've got 'em sure." He turned suddenly upon an aide: "Here—you—Jones—quick—ride after Tompkins—see Taylor—tell him t' go in—everlastingly—like blazes—anything."

As another officer sped his horse after the first messenger, the general beamed upon the earth like a sun. In his eyes was a desire to chant a paean.[2] He kept repeating, "They've held 'em, by heavens!"

His excitement made his horse plunge, and he merrily kicked and swore at it. He held a little carnival of joy on horseback.

[1] **staff:** here, the officers on the general's staff.

[2] **paean:** a song of triumph.

1. Study the first paragraph of the novel. What picture does it give of the army?

2. What does the flashback in the first chapter reveal of Henry and his ambitions? Why is he disappointed in his mother's farewell to him? What is he most concerned about in this chapter?

3. What aspect of military life and of war is represented by the incident concerning the box of cigars in Chapter 2? (Remember that the youth "wondered what a box of cigars had to do with war.") What other incidents in the first six chapters represent this side of war?

4. Besides Henry Fleming, two other soldiers play a prominent part in the chapters you have read. What are they called? Why do you think they are not referred to by their names? What is Henry usually called by the author? Why do you think Crane is slow to disclose his hero's full name and rarely uses it to refer to him?

5. What are Henry's feelings about his comrades? How does he feel particularly about the tall soldier and the loud soldier? Do you think they are typical soldiers? Do they remind you of other soldiers you have read about? If so, who? Are they much different from other soldiers you have read about—for example, Ulysses or Brutus or George Washington? Explain the differences.

6. Study the description of the dead soldier in Chapter 3. What details are emphasized? How are these details related to the general picture Crane seems to be giving of war and of life itself? Can the description be called ironic? Explain.

7. Describe Henry's changes of feeling about war and about the army in the first four chapters. How can you explain these changes? Would you call Henry a particularly changeable or empty-headed person, or do you think that his reactions are typical of most recruits? Defend your answer.

8. Contrast Henry's behavior in the first and second attacks. Account for the difference.

9. What were Henry's feelings as he ran away? What details does he notice? How, in your opinion, is this episode related to Crane's depiction of war and battles generally?

10. The phrase "blue demonstration" is used a number of times. What significance does this phrase have for Henry? How is it related to his own idea of himself as an individual with the power to make his own choices and decisions?

CHAPTER 7

THE YOUTH cringed as if discovered in a crime. By heavens, they had won after all! The imbecile [1] line had remained and become victors. He could hear cheering.

He lifted himself upon his toes and looked in the direction of the fight. A yellow fog lay wallowing on the treetops. From beneath it came the clatter of musketry. Hoarse cries told of an advance.

He turned away amazed and angry. He felt that he had been wronged.

He had fled, he told himself, because annihilation approached. He had done a good part in saving himself, who was a little piece of the army. He had considered the time, he said, to be one in which it was the duty of every little piece to rescue itself if possible. Later the officers could fit the little pieces together again, and make a battle front. If none of the little pieces were wise enough to save themselves from the flurry of death at such a time, why, then, where would be the army? It was all plain that he had proceeded according to very correct and commendable rules. His actions had been sagacious things. They had been full of strategy. They were the work of a master's legs.

Thoughts of his comrades came to him. The brittle blue line had withstood the blows and won. He grew bitter over it. It seemed that the blind ignorance and stupidity of those little pieces had betrayed him. He had been overturned and crushed by their lack of sense in holding the position, when intelligent deliberation would have convinced them that it was impossible. He, the enlightened man who looks afar in the dark, had fled because of his superior perceptions and knowledge. He felt a great anger against his comrades. He knew it could be proved that they had been fools.

He wondered what they would remark when later he appeared in camp. His mind heard howls of derision. Their destiny

[1] **imbecile:** here, powerless.

would not enable them to understand his sharper point of view.

He began to pity himself acutely. He was ill used. He was trodden beneath the feet of an iron injustice. He had proceeded with wisdom and from the most righteous motives under heaven's blue only to be frustrated by hateful circumstances.

A dull, animal-like rebellion against his fellows, war in the abstract, and fate grew within him. He shambled along with bowed head, his brain in a tumult of agony and despair. When he looked loweringly up, quivering at each sound, his eyes had the expression of those of a criminal who thinks his guilt and his punishment great, and knows that he can find no words.

He went from the fields into a thick woods, as if resolved to bury himself. He wished to get out of hearing of the crackling shots which were to him like voices.

The ground was cluttered with vines and bushes, and the trees grew close and spread out like bouquets. He was obliged to force his way with much noise. The creepers, catching against his legs, cried out harshly as their sprays were torn from the barks of trees. The swishing saplings tried to make known his presence to the world. He could not conciliate the forest. As he made his way, it was always calling out protestations. When he separated embraces of trees and vines, the disturbed foliages waved their arms and turned their face leaves toward him. He dreaded lest these noisy motions and cries should bring men to look at him. So he went far, seeking dark and intricate places.

After a time the sound of musketry grew faint and the cannon boomed in the distance. The sun, suddenly apparent, blazed among the trees. The insects were making rhythmical noises. They seemed to be grinding their teeth in unison. A woodpecker stuck his impudent head around the side of a tree. A bird flew on lighthearted wing.

Off was the rumble of death. It seemed now that Nature had no ears.

This landscape gave him assurance. A fair field holding life. It was the religion of peace. It would die if its timid eyes were compelled to see blood. He conceived Nature to be a woman with a deep aversion to tragedy.

He threw a pine cone at a jovial squirrel, and he ran with chattering fear. High in a treetop he stopped, and, poking his head cautiously from behind a branch, looked down with an air of trepidation.

The youth felt triumphant at this exhibition. There was the law, he said. Nature had given him a sign. The squirrel, immediately upon recognizing danger, had taken to his legs without ado. He did not stand stolidly baring his furry belly to the missile, and die with an upward glance at the sympathetic heavens. On the contrary, he had fled as fast as his legs could carry him; and he was but an ordinary squirrel, too—doubtless no philosopher of his race. The youth wended, feeling that Nature was of his mind. She reinforced his argument with proofs that lived where the sun shone.

Once he found himself almost into a swamp. He was obliged to walk upon bog tufts and watch his feet to keep from the oily mire. Pausing at one time to look about him he saw, out at some black water, a small animal pounce in and emerge directly with a gleaming fish.

The youth went again into the deep thickets. The brushed branches made a noise that drowned the sounds of cannon. He walked on, going from obscurity into promises of a greater obscurity.

At length he reached a place where the high, arching boughs made a chapel. He softly pushed the green doors aside and entered. Pine needles were a gentle brown carpet. There was a religious half-light.

Near the threshold he stopped, horror-stricken at the sight of a thing.

He was being looked at by a dead man who was seated with his back against a columnlike tree. The corpse was dressed in a uniform that once had been blue, but was now faded to a melancholy shade of green. The eyes, staring at the youth, had changed to the dull hue to be seen on the side of a dead fish. The mouth was open. Its red had changed to an appalling yellow. Over the gray skin of the face ran little ants. One was trundling some sort of a bundle along the upper lip.

The youth gave a shriek as he confronted the thing. He was for moments turned to stone before it. He remained staring into the liquid-looking eyes. The dead man and the living man exchanged a long look. Then the youth cautiously put one hand behind him and brought it against a tree. Leaning upon this he retreated, step by step, with his face still toward the thing. He feared that if he turned his back the body might spring up and stealthily pursue him.

The branches, pushing against him, threatened to throw him over upon it. His unguided feet, too, caught aggravatingly in brambles; and with it all he received a subtle suggestion to touch the corpse. As he thought of his hand upon it, he shuddered profoundly.

At last he burst the bonds which had fastened him to the spot and fled, unheeding the underbrush. He was pursued by a sight of the black ants swarming greedily upon the gray face and venturing horribly near to the eyes.

After a time he paused, and, breathless and panting, listened. He imagined some strange voice would come from the dead throat and squawk after him in horrible menaces.

The trees about the portals of the chapel moved soughingly in a soft wind. A sad silence was upon the little guarding edifice.

CHAPTER 8

THE TREES began softly to sing a hymn of twilight. The sun sank until slanted bronze rays struck the forest. There was a lull in the noises of insects as if they had bowed their beaks and were making a devotional pause. There was silence save for the chanted chorus of the trees.

Then, upon this stillness, there suddenly broke a tremendous clangor of sounds. A crimson roar came from the distance.

The youth stopped. He was transfixed by this terrific medley of all noises. It was as if worlds were being rended. There was the ripping sound of musketry and the breaking crash of the artillery.

His mind flew in all directions. He conceived the two armies to be at each other panther-fashion. He listened for a time. Then he began to run in the direction of the battle. He saw that it was an ironical thing for him to be running thus toward that which he had been at such pains to avoid. But he said, in substance, to himself that if the earth and the moon were about to clash, many persons would doubtless plan to get upon the roofs to witness the collision.

As he ran, he became aware that the forest had stopped its music, as if at last becoming capable of hearing the foreign sounds. The trees hushed and stood motionless. Everything seemed to be listening to the crackle and clatter and ear-shaking thunder. The chorus pealed over the still earth.

It suddenly occurred to the youth that the fight in which he had been was, after all, but perfunctory popping. In the hearing of this present din he was doubtful if he had seen real battle scenes. This uproar explained a celestial battle; it was tumbling hordes a-struggle in the air.

Reflecting, he saw a sort of a humor in the point of view of himself and his fellows during the late encounter. They had taken themselves and the enemy very seriously and had imagined that they were deciding the war. Individuals must have supposed that they were cutting the letters of their names deep into everlasting tablets of brass, or enshrining their reputations forever in the hearts of their countrymen, while, as to fact, the affair would appear in printed reports under a meek and immaterial title. But he saw that it was good, else, he said, in battle everyone would surely run save forlorn hopes and their ilk.

He went rapidly on. He wished to come to the edge of the forest that he might peer out.

As he hastened, there passed through his mind pictures of stupendous conflicts. His accumulated thought upon such subjects was used to form scenes. The noise was as the voice of an eloquent being, describing.

Sometimes the brambles formed chains and tried to hold him back. Trees, confronting him, stretched out their arms and forbade him to pass. After its previous hostility this new resistance of the forest filled him with a fine bitterness. It seemed that Nature could not be quite ready to kill him.

But he obstinately took roundabout ways, and presently he was where he could see long gray walls of vapor where lay battle lines. The voices of cannon shook him. The musketry sounded in long irregular surges that played havoc with his ears. He stood regardant [1] for a moment. His eyes had an awestruck expression. He gawked in the direction of the fight.

Presently he proceeded again on his forward way. The battle was like the grinding of an immense and terrible machine to him. Its complexities and powers, its grim processes, fascinated him. He must go close and see it produce corpses.

He came to a fence and clambered over it. On the far side, the ground was littered with clothes and guns. A newspaper, folded up, lay in the dirt. A dead soldier was stretched with his face hidden in his arm. Farther off there was a group of four or five corpses keeping mournful company. A hot sun had blazed upon the spot.

In this place the youth felt that he was an invader. This forgotten part of the battleground was owned by the dead men, and he hurried, in the vague apprehension that one of the swollen forms would rise and tell him to be gone.

He came finally to a road from which he could see in the distance dark and agitated bodies of troops, smoke-fringed. In the lane was a blood-stained crowd streaming to the rear. The wounded men were cursing, groaning, and wailing. In the air, always, was a mighty swell of sound that, it seemed, could sway the earth. With the courageous words of the artillery and the spiteful sentences of the musketry mingled red cheers. And from this region of noises came the steady current of the maimed.

One of the wounded men had a shoeful of blood. He hopped like a schoolboy in a game. He was laughing hysterically.

One was swearing that he had been shot in the arm through the commanding general's mismanagement of the army. One was marching with an air imitative of some sublime drum major. Upon his features was an unholy mixture of merriment and agony. As he marched he sang a bit of doggerel [2] in a high and quavering voice:

"Sing a song 'a vic'try,
    A pocketful 'a bullets,
Five an' twenty dead men
    Baked in a—pie."

Parts of the procession limped and staggered to this tune.

Another had the gray seal of death already upon his face. His lips were curled in hard lines and his teeth were clinched. His hands were bloody from where he had pressed them upon his wound. He seemed to be awaiting the moment when he should pitch headlong. He stalked like the specter of a soldier, his eyes burning with the power of a stare into the unknown.

There were some who proceeded sullenly, full of anger at their wounds and ready to turn upon anything as an obscure cause.

An officer was carried along by two privates. He was peevish. "Don't joggle so, Johnson, yeh fool," he cried. "Think

---

[1] **regardant:** looking backward.

[2] **doggerel:** awkward trivial verse, usually comic.

m' leg is made of iron? If yeh can't carry me decent, put me down an' let someone else do it."

He bellowed at the tottering crowd who blocked the quick march of his bearers. "Say, make way there, can't yeh? Make way, dickens take it all."

They sulkily parted and went to the roadsides. As he was carried past, they made pert remarks to him. When he raged in reply and threatened them, they told him to be damned.

The shoulder of one of the tramping bearers knocked heavily against the spectral soldier who was staring into the unknown.

The youth joined this crowd and marched along with it. The torn bodies expressed the awful machinery in which the men had been entangled.

Orderlies and couriers occasionally broke through the throng in the roadway, scattering wounded men right and left, galloping on followed by howls. The melancholy march was continually disturbed by the messengers, and sometimes by bustling batteries that came swinging and thumping down upon them, the officers shouting orders to clear the way.

There was a tattered man, fouled with dust, blood and powder stain from hair to shoes, who trudged quietly at the youth's side. He was listening with eagerness and much humility to the lurid descriptions of a bearded sergeant. His lean features wore an expression of awe and admiration. He was like a listener in a country store to wondrous tales told among the sugar barrels. He eyed the storyteller with unspeakable wonder. His mouth was agape in yokel [1] fashion.

The sergeant, taking note of this, gave pause to his elaborate history while he administered a sardonic comment. "Be keerful, honey, you'll be a-ketchin' flies," he said.

The tattered man shrank back abashed.

After a time he began to sidle near to the youth and in a different way try to

make him a friend. His voice was gentle as a girl's voice and his eyes were pleading. The youth saw with surprise that the soldier had two wounds, one in the head, bound with a blood-soaked rag, and the other in the arm, making that member dangle like a broken bough.

After they had walked together for some time, the tattered man mustered sufficient courage to speak. "Was pretty good fight, wa'n't it?" he timidly said. The youth, deep in thought, glanced up at the bloody and grim figure with its lamblike eyes. "What?"

"Was pretty good fight, wa'n't it?"

"Yes," said the youth shortly. He quickened his pace.

But the other hobbled industriously after him. There was an air of apology in his manner, but he evidently thought that he needed only to talk for a time, and the youth would perceive that he was a good fellow.

"Was pretty good fight, wa'n't it?" he began in a small voice, and then he achieved the fortitude to continue. "Dern me if I ever see fellers fight so. Laws, how they did fight! I knowed th' boys 'd like when they oncet got square at it. Th' boys ain't had no fair chancet up t' now, but this time they showed what they was. I knowed it 'd turn out this way. Yeh can't lick them boys. No, sir! They're fighters, they be."

He breathed a deep breath of humble admiration. He had looked at the youth for encouragement several times. He received none, but gradually he seemed to get absorbed in his subject.

"I was talkin' 'cross pickets with a boy from Georgie, oncet, an' that boy, he ses, 'Your fellers 'll all run like hell when they oncet hearn a gun,' he ses. 'Mebbe they will,' I ses, 'but I don't b'lieve none of it,' I ses; 'an' b'jiminey,' I ses back t' 'um, 'mebbe your fellers 'll all run like hell when they oncet hearn a gun,' I ses. He larfed. Well, they didn't run t'day, did they, hey? No, sir! They fit, an' fit, an' fit."

His homely face was suffused with a

[1] **yokel:** a contemptuous term for a country person.

light of love for the army which was to him all things beautiful and powerful.

After a time he turned to the youth. "Where yeh hit, ol' boy?" he asked in a brotherly tone.

The youth felt instant panic at this question, although at first its full import was not borne in upon him.

"What?" he asked.

"Where yeh hit?" repeated the tattered man.

"Why," began the youth, "I—I—that is—why—I——"

He turned away suddenly and slid through the crowd. His brow was heavily flushed, and his fingers were picking nervously at one of his buttons. He bent his head and fastened his eyes studiously upon the button as if it were a little problem.

The tattered man looked after him in astonishment.

CHAPTER 9

THE YOUTH fell back in the procession until the tattered soldier was not in sight. Then he started to walk on with the others.

But he was amid wounds. The mob of men was bleeding. Because of the tattered soldier's question he now felt that his shame could be viewed. He was continually casting sidelong glances to see if the men were contemplating the letters of guilt he felt burned into his brow.

At times he regarded the wounded soldiers in an envious way. He conceived persons with torn bodies to be peculiarly happy. He wished that he, too, had a wound, a red badge of courage.

The spectral soldier was at his side like a stalking reproach. The man's eyes were still fixed in a stare into the unknown. His gray, appalling face had attracted attention in the crowd, and men, slowing to his dreary pace, were walking with him. They were discussing his plight, questioning him and giving him advice. In a dogged way he repelled them, signing to them to go on and leave him alone.

The shadows of his face were deepening and his tight lips seemed holding in check the moan of great despair. There could be seen a certain stiffness in the movements of his body, as if he were taking infinite care not to arouse the passion of his wounds. As he went on, he seemed always looking for a place, like one who goes to choose a grave.

Something in the gesture of the man as he waved the bloody and pitying soldiers away made the youth start as if bitten. He yelled in horror. Tottering forward he laid a quivering hand upon the man's arm. As the latter slowly turned his waxlike features toward him, the youth screamed:

"Gawd! Jim Conklin!"

The tall soldier made a little commonplace smile. "Hello, Henry," he said.

The youth swayed on his legs and glared strangely. He stuttered and stammered. "Oh, Jim—oh, Jim—oh, Jim——"

The tall soldier held out his gory hand. There was a curious red and black combination of new blood and old blood upon it. "Where yeh been, Henry?" he asked. He continued in a monotonous voice, "I thought mebbe yeh got keeled over. There's been thunder t' pay t'day. I was worryin' about it a good deal."

The youth still lamented. "Oh, Jim—oh, Jim—oh, Jim——"

"Yeh know," said the tall soldier, "I was out there." He made a careful gesture. "An', Lord, what a circus! An', b'jiminey, I got shot—I got shot. Yes, b'jiminey, I got shot." He reiterated this fact in a bewildered way, as if he did not know how it came about.

The youth put forth anxious arms to assist him, but the tall soldier went firmly on as if propelled. Since the youth's arrival as a guardian for his friend, the other wounded men had ceased to display much interest. They occupied themselves again in dragging their own tragedies toward the rear.

Suddenly, as the two friends marched on, the tall soldier seemed to be overcome by a terror. His face turned to a semblance of gray paste. He clutched the youth's arm and looked all about him, as if dreading to be overheard. Then he began to speak in a shaking whisper:

"I tell yeh what I'm 'fraid of, Henry— I'll tell yeh what I'm 'fraid of. I'm 'fraid I'll fall down—an' then yeh know— them damned artillery wagons—they like as not 'll run over me. That's what I'm 'fraid of——"

The youth cried out to him hysterically: "I'll take care of yeh, Jim! I'll take care of yeh! I swear t' Gawd I will!"

"Sure—will yeh, Henry?" the tall soldier beseeched.

"Yes—yes—I tell yeh—I'll take care of yeh, Jim!" protested the youth. He could not speak accurately because of the gulpings in his throat.

But the tall soldier continued to beg in a lowly way. He now hung babelike to the youth's arm. His eyes rolled in the wildness of his terror. "I was allus a good friend t' yeh, wa'n't I, Henry? I've allus been a pretty good feller, ain't I? An' it ain't much t' ask, is it? Jest t' pull me along outer th' road? I'd do it fer you, wouldn't I, Henry?"

He paused in piteous anxiety to await his friend's reply.

The youth had reached an anguish where the sobs scorched him. He strove to express his loyalty, but he could only make fantastic gestures.

However, the tall soldier seemed suddenly to forget all those fears. He became again the grim, stalking specter of a soldier. He went stonily forward. The youth wished his friend to lean upon him, but the other always shook his head and strangely protested. "No—no—no—leave me be—leave me be——"

His look was fixed again upon the unknown. He moved with mysterious purpose, and all of the youth's offers he brushed aside. "No—no—leave me be— leave me be——"

The youth had to follow.

Presently the latter heard a voice talking softly near his shoulders. Turning, he saw that it belonged to the tattered soldier.

"Ye'd better take 'im outa th' road, pardner. There's a batt'ry comin' helitywhoop down th' road an' he'll git runned over. He's a goner anyhow in about five minutes—yeh kin see that. Ye'd better take 'im outa th' road. Where th' blazes does he git his stren'th from?"

"Lord knows!" cried the youth. He was shaking his hands helplessly.

He ran forward presently and grasped the tall soldier by the arm. "Jim! Jim!" he coaxed, "come with me."

The tall soldier weakly tried to wrench himself free. "Huh," he said vacantly. He stared at the youth for a moment. At last he spoke as if dimly comprehending. "Oh! Inteh th' fields? Oh!"

He started blindly through the grass.

The youth turned once to look at the lashing riders and jouncing guns of the battery. He was startled from this view by a shrill outcry from the tattered man.

"Gawd! He's runnin'!"

Turning his head swiftly, the youth saw his friend running in a staggering and stumbling way toward the little clump of bushes. His heart seemed to wrench itself almost free from his body at this sight. He made a noise of pain. He and the tattered man began a pursuit. There was a singular race.

When he overtook the tall soldier he began to plead with all the words he could find. "Jim—Jim—what are you doing— what makes you do this way—you'll hurt yerself."

The same purpose was in the tall soldier's face. He protested in a dulled way, keeping his eyes fastened on the mystic place of his intentions. "No—no—don't tech me—leave me be—leave me be——"

The youth, aghast and filled with wonder at the tall soldier, began quaveringly to question him. "Where yeh goin', Jim? What you thinking about? Where you going? Tell me, won't you, Jim?"

The tall soldier faced about as upon relentless pursuers. In his eyes there was a great appeal. "Leave me be, can't yeh? Leave me be fer a minnit."

The youth recoiled. "Why, Jim," he said, in a dazed way, "what's the matter with you?"

The tall soldier turned and, lurching dangerously, went on. The youth and the tattered soldier followed, sneaking as if whipped, feeling unable to face the stricken man if he should again confront them. They began to have thoughts of a solemn ceremony. There was something ritelike in these movements of the doomed soldier. And there was a resemblance in him to a devotee of a mad religion, blood-sucking, muscle-wrenching, bone-crushing. They were awed and afraid. They hung back lest he have at command a dreadful weapon.

At last, they saw him stop and stand motionless. Hastening up, they perceived that his face wore an expression telling that he had at last found the place for which he had struggled. His spare figure was erect; his bloody hands were quietly at his side. He was waiting with patience for something that he had come to meet. He was at the rendezvous. They paused and stood, expectant.

There was a silence.

Finally, the chest of the doomed soldier began to heave with a strained motion. It increased in violence until it was as if an animal was within and was kicking and tumbling furiously to be free.

This spectacle of gradual strangulation made the youth writhe, and once as his friend rolled his eyes, he saw something in them that made him sink wailing to the ground. He raised his voice in a last supreme call.

"Jim—Jim—Jim——"

The tall soldier opened his lips and spoke. He made a gesture. "Leave me be—don't tech me—leave me be——"

There was another silence while he waited.

Suddenly, his form stiffened and straightened. Then it was shaken by a prolonged ague. He stared into space. To the two watchers there was a curious and profound dignity in the firm lines of his awful face.

He was invaded by a creeping strangeness that slowly enveloped him. For a moment the tremor of his legs caused him to dance a sort of hideous hornpipe. His arms beat wildly about his head in expression of implike enthusiasm.

His tall figure stretched itself to its full height. There was a slight rending sound. Then it began to swing forward, slow and straight, in the manner of a falling tree. A swift muscular contortion made the left shoulder strike the ground first.

The body seemed to bounce a little way from the earth. "God!" said the tattered soldier.

The youth had watched, spellbound, this ceremony at the place of meeting. His face had been twisted into an expression of every agony he had imagined for his friend.

He now sprang to his feet and, going closer, gazed upon the pastelike face. The mouth was opened and the teeth showed in a laugh.

As the flap of the blue jacket fell away

from the body, he could see that the side looked as if it had been chewed by wolves.

The youth turned, with sudden, livid rage, toward the battlefield. He shook his fist. He seemed about to deliver a philippic.[1]

"Hell——"

The red sun was pasted in the sky like a wafer.

CHAPTER 10

THE TATTERED MAN stood musing.

"Well, he was reg'lar jim-dandy fer nerve, wa'n't he," said he finally in a little awestruck voice. "A reg'lar jim-dandy." He thoughtfully poked one of the docile hands with his foot. "I wonner where he got 'is stren'th from? I never seen a man do like that before. It was a funny thing. Well, he was a reg'lar jim-dandy."

The youth desired to screech out his grief. He was stabbed, but his tongue lay dead in the tomb of his mouth. He threw himself again upon the ground and began to brood.

The tattered man stood musing.

"Look-a-here, pardner," he said, after a time. He regarded the corpse as he spoke. "He's up an' gone, ain't 'e, an' we might as well begin t' look out fer ol' number one. This here thing is all over. He's up an' gone, ain't 'e? An' he's all right here. Nobody won't bother 'im. An' I must say I ain't enjoying any great health m'self these days."

The youth, awakened by the tattered soldier's tone, looked quickly up. He saw that he was swinging uncertainly on his legs and that his face had turned to a shade of blue.

"Good Lord!" he cried, "you ain't goin' t'—not you, too."

The tattered man waved his hand. "Nary die," he said. "All I want is some pea soup an' a good bed. Some pea soup," he repeated dreamfully.

[1] **philippic:** a bitter verbal attack. The word originally referred to the speeches of the Greek orator Demosthenes against Philip, King of Macedon.

The youth arose from the ground. "I wonder where he came from. I left him over there." He pointed. "And now I find 'im here. And he was coming from over there, too." He indicated a new direction. They both turned toward the body as if to ask of it a question.

"Well," at length spoke the tattered man, "there ain't no use in our stayin' here an' tryin' t' ask him anything."

The youth nodded an assent wearily. They both turned to gaze for a moment at the corpse.

The youth murmured something.

"Well, he was a jim-dandy, wa'n't 'e?" said the tattered man as if in response.

They turned their backs upon it and started away. For a time they stole softly, treading with their toes. It remained laughing there in the grass.

"I'm commencin' t' feel pretty bad," said the tattered man, suddenly breaking one of his little silences. "I'm commencin' t' feel pretty damn' bad."

The youth groaned. "O Lord!" He wondered if he was to be the tortured witness of another grim encounter.

But his companion waved his hand reassuringly. "Oh, I'm not goin' t' die yit! There too much dependin' on me fer me t' die yit. No, sir! Nary die! I can't! Ye'd oughta see th' swad [2] a' chil'ren I've got, an' all like that."

The youth, glancing at his companion, could see by the shadow of a smile that he was making some kind of fun.

As they plodded on, the tattered soldier continued to talk. "Besides, if I died, I wouldn't die th' way that feller did. That was th' funniest thing. I'd jest flop down, I would. I never seen a feller die th' way that feller did.

"Yeh know Tom Jamison, he lives next door t' me up home. He's a nice feller, he is, an' we was allus good friends. Smart, too. Smart as a steel trap. Well, when we was a-fightin' this afternoon, all-of-a-sudden he begin t' rip up an' cuss an' beller at me. 'Yer shot, yeh blamed infernal!'—he

[2] **swad:** group (slang).

swear horrible—he ses t' me. I put up m' hand t' m' head an' when I looked at m' fingers, I seen, sure 'nough, I was shot. I give a holler an' begin t' run, but b'fore I could git away another one hit me in th' arm an' whirl' me clean 'round. I got skeared when they was all a-shootin' b'hind me an' I run t' beat all, but I cotch it pretty bad. I've an idee I'd a' been fightin' yit, if t'wasn't fer Tom Jamison."

Then he made a calm announcement: "There's two of 'em—little ones—but they're beginnin' t' have fun with me now. I don't b'lieve I kin walk much furder."

They went slowly on in silence. "Yeh look pretty peek-ed yerself," said the tattered man at last. "I bet yeh 've got a worser one than yeh think. Ye'd better take keer of yer hurt. It don't do t' let sech things go. It might be inside mostly, an' them plays thunder. Where is it located?" But he continued his harangue without waiting for a reply. "I see' a feller git hit plum in th' head when my reg'ment was a-standin' at ease oncet. An' everybody yelled out to 'im: Hurt, John? Are yeh hurt much? 'No,' ses he. He looked kinder surprised, an' he went on tellin' 'em how he felt. He sed he didn't feel nothin'. But, by dad, th' first thing that feller knowed he was dead. Yes, he was dead—stone dead. So, yeh wanta watch out. Yeh might have some queer kind 'a hurt yerself. Yeh can't never tell. Where is your'n located?"

The youth had been wriggling since the introduction of this topic. He now gave a cry of exasperation and made a furious motion with his hand. "Oh, don't bother me!" he said. He was enraged against the tattered man, and could have strangled him. His companions seemed ever to play intolerable parts. They were ever upraising the ghost of shame on the stick of their curiosity. He turned toward the tattered man as one at bay. "Now, don't bother me," he repeated with desperate menace.

"Well, Lord knows I don't wanta bother anybody," said the other. There was a little accent of despair in his voice as he replied, "Lord knows I've gota 'nough m' own t' tend to."

The youth, who had been holding a bitter debate with himself and casting glances of hatred and contempt at the tattered man, here spoke in a hard voice. "Good-by," he said.

The tattered man looked at him in gaping amazement. "Why—why, pardner, where yeh goin'?" he asked unsteadily. The youth, looking at him, could see that he, too, like that other one, was beginning to act dumb and animal-like. His thoughts seemed to be floundering about in his head. "Now—now—look—a—here, you Tom Jamison—now—I won't have this—this here won't do. Where—where yeh goin'?"

The youth pointed vaguely. "Over there," he replied.

"Well, now look—a—here—now," said the tattered man, rambling on in idiot fashion. His head was hanging forward and his words were slurred. "This thing won't do, now, Tom Jamison. It won't do. I know yeh, yeh pigheaded devil. Yeh wanta go trompin' off with a bad hurt. It ain't right—now—Tom Jamison—it ain't. Yeh wanta leave me take keer of yeh, Tom Jamison. It ain't—right—it ain't —fer yeh t' go —trompin' off—with a bad hurt—it ain't—ain't—ain't right—it ain't."

In reply the youth climbed a fence and started away. He could hear the tattered man bleating plaintively.

Once he faced about angrily. "What?"

"Look—a—here, now, Tom Jamison— now—it ain't——"

The youth went on. Turning at a distance, he saw the tattered man wandering about helplessly in the field.

He now thought that he wished he was dead. He believed that he envied those men whose bodies lay strewn over the grass of the fields and on the fallen leaves of the forest.

The simple questions of the tattered man had been knife thrusts to him. They asserted a society that probes pitilessly at secrets until all is apparent. His late companion's chance persistency made him feel that he could not keep his crime concealed in his bosom. It was sure to be brought plain by one of those arrows which cloud the air and are constantly pricking, discovering, proclaiming those things which are willed to be forever hidden. He admitted that he could not defend himself against this agency. It was not within the power of vigilance.

CHAPTER 11

HE BECAME AWARE that the furnace roar of the battle was growing louder. Great brown clouds had floated to the still heights of air before him. The noise, too, was approaching. The woods filtered men and the fields became dotted.

As he rounded a hillock, he perceived that the roadway was now a crying mass of wagons, teams, and men. From the heaving tangle issued exhortations, commands, imprecations.[1] Fear was sweeping it all along. The cracking whips bit and horses plunged and tugged. The white-topped wagons strained and stumbled in their exertions like fat sheep.

The youth felt comforted in a measure by this sight. They were all retreating. Perhaps, then, he was not so bad after all. He seated himself and watched the terror-stricken wagons. They fled like soft, ungainly animals. All the roarers and lashers served to help him to magnify the dangers and horrors of the engagement that he might try to prove to himself that the thing with which men could charge him was in truth a symmetrical act. There was an amount of pleasure to him in watching the wild march of this vindication.

Presently the calm head of a forward-going column of infantry appeared in the road. It came swiftly on. Avoiding the obstructions gave it the sinuous movement of a serpent. The men at the head butted mules with their musket stocks. They prodded teamsters indifferent to all howls. The men forced their way through parts of the dense mass by strength. The blunt head of the column pushed. The raving teamsters swore many strange oaths.

The commands to make way had the ring of a great importance in them. The men were going forward to the heart of the din. They were to confront the eager rush of the enemy. They felt the pride of their onward movement when the remainder of the army seemed trying to dribble down this road. They tumbled teams about with a fine feeling that it was no matter so long as their column got to the front in time. This importance made their faces grave and stern. And the backs of the officers were very rigid.

As the youth looked at them the black weight of his woe returned to him. He felt that he was regarding a procession of chosen beings. The separation was as great to him as if they had marched with weapons of flame and banners of sunlight. He could never be like them. He could have wept in his longings.

He searched about in his mind for an adequate malediction[2] for the indefinite cause, the thing upon which men turn the words of final blame. It—whatever it was —was responsible for him, he said. There lay the fault.

The haste of the column to reach the battle seemed to the forlorn young man to be something much finer than stout fighting. Heroes, he thought, could find excuses in that long seething lane. They could retire with perfect self-respect and make excuses to the stars.

He wondered what those men had eaten that they could be in such haste to force their way to grim chances of death. As he watched, his envy grew until he thought that he wished to change lives with one of them. He would have liked to have used a tremendous force, he said, throw off himself and become a better. Swift pictures of himself, apart, yet in himself, came to him —a blue desperate figure leading lurid charges with one knee forward and a broken blade high—a blue, determined figure standing before a crimson and steel

---

[1] **exhortations . . . imprecations:** pleas, commands, and curses.

[2] **malediction:** curse.

assault, getting calmly killed on a high place before the eyes of all. He thought of the magnificent pathos of his dead body.

These thoughts uplifted him. He felt the quiver of war desire. In his ears, he heard the ring of victory. He knew the frenzy of a rapid successful charge. The music of the trampling feet, the sharp voices, the clanking arms of the column near him made him soar on the red wings of war. For a few moments he was sublime.

He thought that he was about to start for the front. Indeed, he saw a picture of himself, dust-stained, haggard, panting, flying to the front at the proper moment to seize and throttle the dark, leering witch of calamity.

Then the difficulties of the thing began to drag at him. He hesitated, balancing awkwardly on one foot.

He had no rifle; he could not fight with his hands, said he resentfully to his plan. Well, rifles could be had for the picking. They were extraordinarily profuse.

Also, he continued, it would be a miracle if he found his regiment. Well, he could fight with any regiment.

He started forward slowly. He stepped as if he expected to tread upon some explosive thing. Doubts and he were struggling.

He would truly be a worm if any of his comrades should see him returning thus, the marks of his flight upon him. There was a reply that the intent fighters did not care for what happened rearward, saving that no hostile bayonets appeared there. In the battle-blur his face would in a way be hidden, like the face of a cowled man.

But then he said that his tireless fate would bring forth, when the strife lulled for a moment, a man to ask of him an explanation. In imagination he felt the scrutiny of his companions as he painfully labored through some lies.

Eventually, his courage expended itself upon these objections. The debates drained him of his fire.

He was not cast down by this defeat of his plan, for, upon studying the affair carefully, he could not but admit that the objections were very formidable.

Furthermore, various ailments had begun to cry out. In their presence he could not persist in flying high with the wings of war; they rendered it almost impossible for him to see himself in a heroic light. He tumbled headlong.

He discovered that he had a scorching thirst. His face was so dry and grimy that he thought he could feel his skin crackle. Each bone of his body had an ache in it, and seemingly threatened to break with each movement. His feet were like two sores. Also, his body was calling for food. It was more powerful than a direct hunger. There was a dull, weightlike feeling in his stomach, and, when he tried to walk, his head swayed and he tottered. He could not see with distinctness. Small patches of green mist floated before his vision.

While he had been tossed by many emotions, he had not been aware of ailments. Now they beset him and made clamor. As he was at last compelled to pay attention to them, his capacity for self-hate was multiplied. In despair, he declared that he was not like those others. He now conceded it to be impossible that he should ever become a hero. He was a craven loon. Those pictures of glory were piteous things. He groaned from his heart and went staggering off.

A certain mothlike quality within him kept him in the vicinity of the battle. He had a great desire to see, and to get news. He wished to know who was winning.

He told himself that, despite his unprecedented suffering, he had never lost his greed for a victory, yet, he said, in a half-apologetic manner to his conscience, he could not but know that a defeat for the army this time might mean many favorable things for him. The blows of the enemy would splinter regiments into fragments. Thus, many men of courage, he considered, would be obliged to desert the colors and scurry like chickens. He would appear as one of them. They would be sullen brothers in distress, and he could then easily believe he had not run any farther or faster than they. And if he himself could believe in his virtuous perfection, he conceived that there would be small trouble in convincing all others.

He said, as if in excuse for this hope, that previously the army had encountered great defeats and in a few months had shaken off all blood and tradition of them, emerging as bright and valiant as a new one; thrusting out of sight the memory of disaster, and appearing with the valor and confidence of unconquered legions. The shrilling voices of the people at home would pipe dismally for a time, but various generals were usually compelled to listen to these ditties. He of course felt no compunctions for proposing a general as a sacrifice. He could not tell who the chosen for the barbs might be, so he could center no direct sympathy upon him. The people were afar and he did not conceive public opinion to be accurate at long range. It was quite probable they would hit the wrong man who, after he had recovered from his amazement, would perhaps spend the rest of his days in writing replies to the songs of his alleged failure. It would be very unfortunate, no doubt, but in this case a general was of no consequence to the youth.

In a defeat there would be a roundabout vindication of himself. He thought it would prove, in a manner, that he had fled early because of his superior powers of perception. A serious prophet upon predicting a flood should be the first man to climb a tree. This would demonstrate that he was indeed a seer.

A moral vindication was regarded by the youth as a very important thing. Without salve, he could not, he thought, wear the sore badge of his dishonor through life. With his heart continually assuring him that he was despicable, he could not exist without making it, through his actions, apparent to all men.

If the army had gone gloriously on, he would be lost. If the din meant that now his army's flags were tilted forward, he was a condemned wretch. He would be compelled to doom himself to isolation. If the men were advancing, their indifferent feet were trampling upon his chances for a successful life.

As these thoughts went rapidly through his mind, he turned upon them and tried to thrust them away. He denounced himself as a villain. He said that he was the most unutterably selfish man in existence. His mind pictured the soldiers who would place their defiant bodies before the spear of the yelling battle fiend, and as he saw their dripping corpses on an imagined field, he said that he was their murderer.

Again he thought that he wished he was dead. He believed that he envied a corpse. Thinking of the slain, he achieved a great contempt for some of them, as if they were guilty for thus becoming lifeless. They might have been killed by lucky chances, he said, before they had had opportunities to flee or before they had been really tested. Yet they would receive laurels from tradition. He cried out bitterly that their crowns were stolen and their robes of glorious memories were shams. However, he still said that it was a great pity he was not as they.

A defeat of the army had suggested itself to him as a means of escape from the consequences of his fall. He considered now, however, that it was useless to think of such a possibility. His education had been that success for that mighty blue machine was certain; that it would make victories as a contrivance turns out buttons. He presently discarded all his speculations in the other direction. He returned to the creed of soldiers.

When he perceived again that it was not possible for the army to be defeated, he tried to bethink him of a fine tale which he could take back to his regiment and with it turn the expected shafts of derision.

But, as he mortally feared these shafts, it became impossible for him to invent a tale he felt he could trust. He experimented with many schemes, but threw them aside one by one as flimsy. He was quick to see vulnerable places in them all.

Furthermore, he was much afraid that some arrow of scorn might lay him mentally low before he could raise his protecting tale.

He imagined the whole regiment saying: "Where's Henry Fleming? He run, didn't 'e? Oh, my!" He recalled various persons who would be quite sure to leave him no peace about it. They would doubtless question him with sneers and laugh at his stammering hesitation. In the next engagement they would try to keep watch of him to discover when he would run.

Wherever he went in camp, he would encounter insolent and lingeringly cruel stares. As he imagined himself passing near a crowd of comrades, he could hear some one say, "There he goes!"

Then, as if the heads were moved by one muscle, all the faces were turned toward him with wide, derisive grins. He seemed to hear someone make a humorous remark in a low tone. At it the others all crowed and crackled. He was a slang phrase.

CHAPTER 12

THE COLUMN that had butted stoutly at the obstacles in the roadway was barely out of the youth's sight before he saw dark waves of men come sweeping out of the woods and down through the fields. He knew at once that the steel fibers had been washed from their hearts. They were bursting from their coats and their equipments as from entanglements. They charged down upon him like terrified buffaloes.

Behind them blue smoke curled and clouded above the treetops, and through the thickets he could sometimes see a distant pink glare. The voices of the cannon were clamoring in interminable chorus.

The youth was horror-stricken. He stared in agony and amazement. He forgot that he was engaged in combating the universe. He threw aside his mental pamphlets on the philosophy of the retreated and rules for the guidance of the damned.

The fight was lost. The dragons were coming with invincible strides. The army, helpless in the matted thickets and blinded by the overhanging night, was going to be swallowed. War, the red animal, war, the blood-swollen god, would have bloated full.

Within him something bade to cry out. He had the impulse to make a rallying speech, to sing a battle hymn, but he could only get his tongue to call into the air: "Why—why—what—what's th' matter?"

Soon he was in the midst of them. They were leaping and scampering all about him. Their blanched faces shone in the dusk. They seemed, for the most part, to be very burly men. The youth turned from one to another of them as they galloped along. His incoherent questions were lost. They were heedless of his appeals. They did not seem to see him.

They sometimes gabbled insanely. One huge man was asking of the sky: "Say, where de plank road? Where de plank road!" It was as if he had lost a child. He wept in his pain and dismay.

Presently, men were running hither and thither in all ways. The artillery booming, forward, rearward, and on the flanks, made jumble of ideas of direction. Landmarks had vanished into the gathered gloom. The youth began to imagine that he had got into the center of the tremendous quarrel, and he could perceive no way out of it. From the mouths of the fleeing men came a thousand wild questions, but no one made answers.

The youth, after rushing about and throwing interrogations at the heedless bands of retreating infantry, finally clutched a man by the arm. They swung around face to face.

"Why—why——" stammered the youth, struggling with his balking tongue.

The man screamed: "Let go me! Let go me!" His face was livid and his eyes were rolling uncontrolled. He was heaving and panting. He still grasped his rifle, perhaps having forgotten to release his hold upon it. He tugged frantically, and the youth, being compelled to lean forward, was dragged several paces.

"Let go me! Let go me!"

"Why—why——" stuttered the youth.

"Well, then!" bawled the man in a lurid rage. He adroitly and fiercely swung his rifle. It crushed upon the youth's head. The man ran on.

The youth's fingers had turned to paste upon the other's arm. The energy was smitten from his muscles. He saw the flaming wings of lightning flash before his vision. There was a deafening rumble of thunder within his head.

Suddenly his legs seemed to die. He sank writhing to the ground. He tried to arise. In his efforts against the numbing pain he was like a man wrestling with a creature of the air.

There was a sinister struggle.

Sometimes he would achieve a position half erect, battle with the air for a moment, and then fall again, grabbing at the grass. His face was of a clammy pallor. Deep groans were wrenched from him.

At last, with a twisting movement, he got upon his hands and knees, and from thence, like a babe trying to walk, to his feet. Pressing his hands to his temples, he went lurching over the grass.

He fought an intense battle with his body. His dulled senses wished him to swoon and he opposed them stubbornly, his mind portraying unknown dangers and mutilations if he should fall upon the field. He went tall-soldier fashion. He imagined secluded spots where he could fall and be unmolested. To search for one he strove against the tide of his pain.

Once he put his hand to the top of his head and timidly touched the wound. The scratching pain of the contact made him draw a long breath through his clinched teeth. His fingers were dabbled with blood. He regarded them with a fixed stare.

Around him he could hear the grumble of jolted cannon as the scurrying horses were lashed toward the front. Once a young officer on a besplashed charger nearly ran him down. He turned and watched the mass of guns, men, and horses sweeping in a wide curve toward a gap in a fence. The officer was making excited motions with a gauntleted [1] hand. The guns followed the teams with an air of unwillingness, of being dragged by the heels.

Some officers of the scattered infantry were cursing and railing like fishwives. Their scolding voices could be heard above the din. Into the unspeakable jumble in the roadway rode a squadron of cavalry. The faded yellow of their facings [2] shone bravely. There was a mighty altercation.

The artillery were assembling as if for a conference.

The blue haze of evening was upon the field. The lines of forest were long purple shadows. One cloud lay along the western sky partly smothering the red.

As the youth left the scene behind him, he heard the guns suddenly roar out. He imagined them shaking in black rage. They belched and howled like brass devils guarding a gate. The soft air was filled with the tremendous remonstrance. With it came the shattering peal of opposing infantry. Turning to look behind him, he could see sheets of orange light illumine the shadowy distance. There were subtle and sudden lightnings in the far air. At times he thought he could see heaving masses of men.

He hurried on in the dusk. The day had faded until he could barely distinguish place for his feet. The purple darkness was filled with men who lectured and jabbered. Sometimes he could see them gesticulating against the blue and somber sky. There seemed to be a great ruck [3] of men and munitions spread about in the forest and in the fields.

The little narrow roadway now lay lifeless. There were overturned wagons like sun-dried boulders. The bed of the former torrent was choked with the bodies

[1] **gauntleted:** covered with a gauntlet, a long heavy glove.

[2] **facings:** the cuffs, collar, and trimmings of a uniformed coat.

[3] **ruck:** crowd.

of horses and splintered parts of war machines.

It had come to pass that his wound pained him but little. He was afraid to move rapidly, however, for a dread of disturbing it. He held his head very still and took many precautions against stumbling. He was filled with anxiety, and his face was pinched and drawn in anticipation of the pain of any sudden mistake of his feet in the gloom.

His thoughts, as he walked, fixed intently upon his hurt. There was a cool, liquid feeling about it and he imagined blood moving slowly down under his hair. His head seemed swollen to a size that made him think his neck to be inadequate.

The new silence of his wound made much worriment. The little blistering voices of pain that had called out from his scalp were, he thought, definite in their expression of danger. By them he believed that he could measure his plight. But when they remained ominously silent, he became frightened and imagined terrible fingers that clutched into his brain.

Amid it he began to reflect upon various incidents and conditions of the past. He bethought him of certain meals his mother had cooked at home, in which those dishes of which he was particularly fond had occupied prominent positions. He saw the spread table. The pine walls of the kitchen were glowing in the warm light from the stove. Too, he remembered how he and his companions used to go from the schoolhouse to the bank of a shaded pool. He saw his clothes in disorderly array upon the grass of the bank. He felt the swash of the fragrant water upon his body. The leaves of the overhanging maple rustled with melody in the wind of youthful summer.

He was overcome presently by a dragging weariness. His head hung forward and his shoulders were stooped as if he were bearing a great bundle. His feet shuffled along the ground.

He held continuous arguments as to whether he should lie down and sleep at some near spot or force himself on until he reached a certain haven. He often tried to dismiss the question, but his body persisted in rebellion and his senses nagged at him like pampered babies.

At last he heard a cheery voice near his shoulder: "Yeh seem t' be in a pretty bad way, boy?"

The youth did not look up, but he assented with thick tongue. "Uh!"

The owner of the cheery voice took him firmly by the arm. "Well," he said, with a round laugh, "I'm goin' your way. Th' hull gang is goin' your way. An' I guess I kin give yeh a lift." They began to walk like a drunken man and his friend.

As they went along, the man questioned the youth and assisted him with the replies like one manipulating the mind of a child. Sometimes he interjected anecdotes. "What reg'ment do yeh b'long teh? Eh? What's that? Th' 304th N' York? Why, what corps is that in? Oh, it is? Why, I thought they wasn't engaged t'day— they're 'way over in th' center. Oh, they was, eh? Well, pretty nearly everybody got their share 'a fightin' t'day. By dad, I give myself up fer dead any number 'a times. There was shootin' here an' shootin' there, an' hollerin' here an' hollerin' there, in th' damn' darkness, until I couldn't tell t' save m' soul which side I was on. Sometimes I thought I was sure 'nough from Ohier, an' other times I could a' swore I was from th' bitter end of Florida. It was th' most mixed up dern thing I ever see. An' these here hull woods is a reg'lar mess. It'll be a miracle if we find our reg'ments t'night. Pretty soon, though, we'll meet a-plenty of guards an' provost-guards, an' one thing an' another. Ho! there they go with an off'cer, I guess. Look at his hand a-draggin'. He's got all th' war he wants, I bet. He won't be talkin' so big about his reputation an' all when they go t' sawin' off his leg. Poor feller! My brother's got whiskers jest like that. How did yeh git 'way over here, anyhow? Your reg'ment is a long way from here, ain't it? Well, I guess we can find it. Yeh know there was a boy killed in my comp'ny t'day that I thought th' world an' all of.

Jack was a nice feller. By ginger, it hurt like thunder t' see ol' Jack jest git knocked flat. We was a-standin' purty peaceable fer a spell, 'though there was men runnin' ev'ry way all 'round us, an' while we was a-standin' like that, 'long come a big fat feller. He began t' peck at Jack's elbow, an' he ses: 'Say, where 's th' road t' th' river?' An' Jack, he never paid no attention, an' th' feller kept on a-peckin' at his elbow an' sayin': 'Say, where's th' road t' th' river?' Jack was a-lookin' ahead all th' time tryin' t' see th' Johnnies comin' through th' woods, an' he never paid no attention t' this big fat feller fer a long time, but at last he turned 'round an' he ses: 'Ah, go t' hell an' find th' road t' th' river!' An' jest then a shot slapped him bang on th' side th' head. He was a sergeant, too. Them was his last words. Thunder, I wish we was sure 'a findin' our reg'ments t'night. It's goin' t' be long huntin'. But I guess we kin do it."

In the search which followed, the man of the cheery voice seemed to the youth to possess a wand of a magic kind. He threaded the mazes of the tangled forest with a strange fortune. In encounters with guards and patrols he displayed the keenness of a detective and the valor of a gamin.[1] Obstacles fell before him and became of assistance. The youth, with his chin still on his breast, stood woodenly by while his companion beat ways and means out of sullen things.

The forest seemed a vast hive of men buzzing about in frantic circles, but the cheery man conducted the youth without mistakes, until at last he began to chuckle with glee and self-satisfaction. "Ah, there yeh are! See that fire?"

The youth nodded stupidly.

"Well, there's where your reg'ment is. An' now, good-by, ol' boy, good luck t' yeh."

A warm and strong hand clasped the youth's languid fingers for an instant, and then he heard a cheerful and audacious whistling as the man strode away. As he

[1] **gamin:** street urchin.

who had so befriended him was thus passing out of his life, it suddenly occurred to the youth that he had not once seen his face.

CHAPTER 13

THE YOUTH went slowly toward the fire indicated by his departed friend. As he reeled, he bethought him of the welcome his comrades would give him. He had a conviction that he would soon feel in his sore heart the barbed missiles of ridicule. He had no strength to invent a tale; he would be a soft target.

He made vague plans to go off into the deeper darkness and hide, but they were all destroyed by the voices of exhaustion and pain from his body. His ailments, clamoring, forced him to seek the place of food and rest, at whatever cost.

He swung unsteadily toward the fire. He could see the forms of men throwing black shadows in the red light, and as he went nearer it became known to him in some way that the ground was strewn with sleeping men.

Of a sudden he confronted a black and monstrous figure. A rifle barrel caught some glinting beams. "Halt! Halt!" He was dismayed for a moment, but he presently thought that he recognized the nervous voice. As he stood tottering before the rifle barrel, he called out: "Why, hello, Wilson, you—you here?"

The rifle was lowered to a position of caution, and the loud soldier came slowly forward. He peered into the youth's face. "That you, Henry?"

"Yes it's—it's me."

"Well, well, ol' boy," said the other, "by ginger, I'm glad t' see yeh! I give yeh up fer a goner. I thought yeh was dead sure enough." There was husky emotion in his voice.

The youth found that now he could barely stand upon his feet. There was a sudden sinking of his forces. He thought he must hasten to produce his tale to protect him from the missiles already at the lips of his redoubtable [1] comrades. So, staggering before the loud soldier, he began: "Yes, yes. I've—I've had an awful time. I've been all over. Way over on th' right. Ter'ble fightin' over there. I had an awful time. I got separated from th' reg'-ment. Over on th' right, I got shot. In th' head. I never see sech fightin'. Awful time. I don't see how I could a' got separated from th' reg'ment. I got shot, too."

His friend had stepped forward quickly. "What? Got shot? Why didn't yeh say so first? Poor ol' boy, we must—hol' on a minnit; what am I doin'. I'll call Simpson."

Another figure at that moment loomed in the gloom. They could see that it was the corporal. "Who yeh talkin' to, Wilson?" he demanded. His voice was anger-toned. "Who yeh talkin' to? Yeh th' derndest sentinel—why—hello, Henry, you here? Why, I thought you was dead four hours ago! Great Jerusalem, they keep turnin' up every ten minutes or so! We thought we'd lost forty-two men by straight count, but if they keep on a-comin' this way, we'll git th' comp'ny all back by mornin' yit. Where was yeh?"

"Over on th' right. I got separated"—began the youth with considerable glibness.

But his friend had interrupted hastily. "Yes, an' he got shot in th' head an' he's in a fix, an' we must see t' him right away." He rested his rifle in the hollow of his left arm and his right around the youth's shoulder.

"Gee, it must hurt like thunder!" he said.

The youth leaned heavily upon his friend. "Yes, it hurts—hurts a good deal," he replied. There was a faltering in his voice.

"Oh," said the corporal. He linked his arm in the youth's and drew him forward. "Come on, Henry. I'll take keer 'a yeh."

As they went on together the loud private called out after them: "Put 'im t' sleep in my blanket, Simpson. An'—hol' on a minnit—here's my canteen. It's full 'a coffee. Look at his head by th' fire an' see how it looks. Maybe it's a pretty bad un. When I git relieved in a couple 'a minnits, I'll be over an' see t' him."

The youth's senses were so deadened that his friend's voice sounded from afar and he could scarcely feel the pressure of the corporal's arm. He submitted passively to the latter's directing strength. His head was in the old manner hanging forward upon his breast. His knees wobbled.

The corporal led him into the glare of the fire. "Now, Henry," he said, "let's have look at yer ol' head."

The youth sat down obediently, and the corporal, laying aside his rifle, began to fumble in the bushy hair of his comrade. He was obliged to turn the other's head so that the full flush of the firelight would beam upon it. He puckered his mouth with a critical air. He drew back his lips and whistled through his teeth when his fingers came in contact with the splashed blood and the rare wound.

"Ah, here we are!" he said. He awkwardly made further investigations. "Jest as I thought," he added, presently. "Yeh've been grazed by a ball. It's raised a queer lump jest as if some feller had lammed yeh on th' head with a club. It stopped a-bleedin' long time ago. Th' most about it is that in th' mornin' yeh'll feel that a number ten hat wouldn't fit yeh. An' your head 'll be all het up an' feel as dry as burnt pork. An' yeh may git a lot 'a other sicknesses, too, by mornin'. Yeh can't never tell. Still, I don't much think so. It's jest a damn' good belt on th' head, an' nothin' more. Now, you jest sit here an' don't move, while I go rout out th' relief. Then I'll send Wilson t' take keer 'a yeh."

The corporal went away. The youth remained on the ground like a parcel. He stared with a vacant look into the fire.

After a time he aroused, for some part, and the things about him began to take

---

[1] **redoubtable:** formidable.

form. He saw that the ground in the deep shadows was cluttered with men, sprawling in every conceivable posture. Glancing narrowly into the more distant darkness, he caught occasional glimpses of visages that loomed pallid and ghostly, lit with a phosphorescent glow. These faces expressed in their lines the deep stupor of the tired soldiers. They made them appear like men drunk with wine. This bit of forest might have appeared to an ethereal wanderer as a scene of the result of some frightful debauch.

On the other side of the fire the youth observed an officer asleep, seated bolt upright, with his back against a tree. There was something perilous in his position. Badgered by dreams, perhaps, he swayed with little bounces and starts, like an old, toddy-stricken grandfather in a chimney corner. Dust and stains were upon his face. His lower jaw hung down as if lacking strength to assume its normal position. He was the picture of an exhausted soldier after a feast of war.

He had evidently gone to sleep with his sword in his arms. These two had slumbered in an embrace, but the weapon had been allowed in time to fall unheeded to the ground. The brass-mounted hilt lay in contact with some parts of the fire.

Within the gleam of rose and orange light from the burning sticks were other soldiers, snoring and heaving, or lying deathlike in slumber. A few pairs of legs were stuck forth, rigid and straight. The shoes displayed the mud or dust of marches, and bits of rounded trousers, protruding from the blankets, showed rents and tears from hurried pitchings through the dense brambles.

The fire crackled musically. From it swelled light smoke. Overhead the foliage moved softly. The leaves, with their faces turned toward the blaze, were colored shifting hues of silver, often edged with red. Far off to the right, through a window in the forest, could be seen a handful of stars lying, like glittering pebbles, on the black level of the night.

Occasionally, in this low-arched hall, a soldier would arouse and turn his body to a new position, the experience of his sleep having taught him of uneven and objectionable places upon the ground under him. Or, perhaps, he would lift himself to a sitting posture, blink at the fire for an unintelligent moment, throw a swift glance at his prostrate companion, and then cuddle down again with a grunt of sleepy content.

The youth sat in a forlorn heap until his friend, the loud young soldier, came, swinging two canteens by their light strings. "Well, now, Henry, ol' boy," said the latter, "we'll have yeh fixed up in jest about a minnit."

He had the bustling ways of an amateur nurse. He fussed around the fire and stirred the sticks to brilliant exertions. He made his patient drink largely from the canteen that contained the coffee. It was to the youth a delicious draft. He tilted his head afar back and held the canteen long to his lips. The cool mixture went caressingly down his blistered throat. Having finished, he sighed with comfortable delight.

The loud young soldier watched his comrade with an air of satisfaction. He later produced an extensive handkerchief from his pocket. He folded it into a manner of bandage and soused water from the other canteen upon the middle of it. This crude arrangement he bound over the youth's head, tying the ends in a queer knot at the back of the neck.

"There," he said, moving off and surveying his deed, "yeh look like th' devil, but I bet yeh feel better."

The youth contemplated his friend with grateful eyes. Upon his aching and swelling head the cold cloth was like a tender woman's hand.

"Yeh don't holler ner say nothin'," remarked his friend approvingly. "I know I'm a blacksmith at takin' keer 'a sick folks, an' yeh never squeaked. Yer a good un, Henry. Most 'a men would a' been in th' hospital long ago. A shot in th' head ain't foolin' business."

The youth made no reply, but began to fumble with the buttons of his jacket.

"Well, come, now," continued his friend, "come on. I must put yeh t' bed an' see that yeh git a good night's rest."

The other got carefully erect, and the loud young soldier led him among the sleeping forms lying in groups and rows. Presently he stooped and picked up his blankets. He spread the rubber one upon the ground and placed the woolen one about the youth's shoulders.

"There now," he said, "lie down an' git some sleep."

The youth, with his manner of doglike obedience, got carefully down like a crone stooping. He stretched out with a murmur of relief and comfort. The ground felt like the softest couch.

But of a sudden he ejaculated: "Hol' on a minnit! Where you goin' t' sleep?"

His friend waved his hand impatiently. "Right down there by yeh."

"Well, but hol' on a minnit," continued the youth. "What yeh goin' t' sleep in? I've got your——"

The loud young soldier snarled: "Shet up an' go on t' sleep. Don't be makin' a damn' fool 'a yerself," he said severely.

After the reproof the youth said no more. An exquisite drowsiness had spread through him. The warm comfort of the blanket enveloped him and made a gentle languor. His head fell forward on his crooked arm and his weighted lids went slowly down over his eyes. Hearing a splatter of musketry from the distance, he wondered indifferently if those men sometimes slept. He gave a long sigh, snuggled down into his blanket, and in a moment was like his comrades.

FOR STUDY AND DISCUSSION

1. What is the significance of Henry's encounter with the squirrel in Chapter 7? Do you agree with Henry's philosophizing about this incident? Do you think that Crane intends the reader to agree? Explain.

2. Study the episode concerning Henry's encounter with the corpse in Chapter 7. What details are emphasized? Why do you think Crane has the trees that arch over the man resemble "the portals of [a] chapel"?

3. In Chapter 8, why does Henry feel he must approach the battle? What is the effect of the procession of wounded men on him?

4. Describe the encounter with Jim Conklin in Chapter 9. Cite details that particularly impressed you about this episode.

5. Chapter 9 concludes with the sentence "The red sun was pasted in the sky like a wafer." Why do you think Crane chose to make this his concluding sentence? What is its significance? Does it seem to you an appropriate ending for the chapter? Explain.

6. What in your opinion is the importance of the tattered man to the novel? Why does Henry desert him? Several critics have said that this desertion is Henry's most shameful act. Do you agree? Why or why not?

7. Describe the shifts in Henry's feelings and his changing resolutions in Chapter 11. Do these shifts make you think less of Henry, or do they make him a more sympathetic character? Give reasons for your answer.

8. How is Henry wounded? What is ironic about this episode? Do you blame Henry for not explaining how he was injured? Explain.

9. Contrast Henry's encounters with the tattered man and the cheerful man. How do these characters differ? What is the difference in their effect on Henry?

10. Compare Chapters 7–13 with the preceding chapters of the novel. How do these later chapters add to your understanding of Henry? How do they develop the view of war that is introduced in the earlier chapters?

CHAPTER 14

WHEN THE YOUTH awoke it seemed to him that he had been asleep for a thousand years, and he felt sure that he opened his eyes upon an unexpected world. Gray mists were slowly shifting before the first efforts of the sunrays. An impending splendor could be seen in the eastern sky. An icy dew had chilled his face, and immediately upon arousing he curled farther down into his blankets. He stared for a while at the leaves overhead, moving in a heraldic wind of the day.

The distance was splintering and blaring with the noise of fighting. There was in the sound an expression of a deadly persistency, as if it had not begun and was not to cease.

About him were the rows and groups of men that he had dimly seen the previous night. They were getting a last draft of sleep before the awakening. The gaunt, careworn features and dusty figures were made plain by this quaint light at the dawning, but it dressed the skin of the men in corpselike hues and made the tangled limbs appear pulseless and dead. The youth started up with a little cry when his eyes first swept over this motionless mass of men, thick-spread upon the ground, pallid, and in strange postures. His disordered mind interpreted the hall of the forest as a charnel place.[1] He believed for an instant that he was in the house of the dead, and he did not dare to move lest these corpses start up, squalling and squawking. In a second, however, he achieved his proper mind. He swore a complicated oath at himself. He saw that this somber picture was not a fact of the present, but a mere prophecy.

He heard then the noise of a fire crackling briskly in the cold air, and, turning his head, he saw his friend pottering busily about a small blaze. A few other figures moved in the fog, and he heard the hard cracking of ax blows.

Suddenly there was a hollow rumble of

drums. A distant bugle sang faintly. Similar sounds, varying in strength, came from near and far over the forest. The bugles called to each other like brazen game-cocks. The near thunder of the regimental drums rolled.

The body of men in the woods rustled. There was a general uplifting of heads. A murmuring of voices broke upon the air. In it there was much bass of grumbling oaths. Strange gods were addressed in condemnation of the early hours necessary to correct war. An officer's peremptory tenor rang out and quickened the stiffened movement of the men. The tangled limbs unraveled. The corpse-hued faces were hidden behind fists that twisted slowly in the eye sockets.

The youth sat up and gave vent to an enormous yawn. "Thunder!" he remarked petulantly. He rubbed his eyes and then, putting up his hand, felt carefully of the bandage over his wound. His friend, perceiving him to be awake, came from the fire. "Well, Henry, ol' man, how do yeh feel this mornin'?" he demanded.

The youth yawned again. Then he puckered his mouth to a little pucker. His head, in truth, felt precisely like a melon, and there was an unpleasant sensation at his stomach.

"Oh, Lord, I feel pretty bad," he said.

"Thunder!" exclaimed the other. "I hoped ye'd feel all right this mornin'. Let's see th' bandage—I guess it's slipped." He began to tinker at the wound in rather a clumsy way until the youth exploded.

"Gosh-dern it!" he said in sharp irritation; "you're the hangdest man I ever saw! You wear muffs on your hands. Why in good thunderation can't you be more easy? I'd rather you'd stand off an' throw guns at it. Now, go slow, an' don't act as if you was nailing down carpet."

He glared with insolent command at his friend, but the latter answered soothingly. "Well, well, come now, an' git some grub," he said. "Then, maybe, yeh'll feel better."

At the fireside the loud young soldier watched over his comrade's wants with tenderness and care. He was very busy

---

[1] **charnel place:** place for the dead.

marshaling the little black vagabonds of tin cups and pouring into them the streaming, iron-colored mixture from a small and sooty tin pail. He had some fresh meat, which he roasted hurriedly upon a stick. He sat down then and contemplated the youth's appetite with glee.

The youth took note of a remarkable change in his comrade since those days of camp life upon the river bank. He seemed no more to be continually regarding the proportions of his personal prowess. He was not furious at small words that pricked his conceits. He was no more a loud young soldier. There was about him now a fine reliance. He showed a quiet belief in his purposes and his abilities. And this inward confidence evidently enabled him to be indifferent to little words of other men aimed at him.

The youth reflected. He had been used to regarding his comrade as a blatant child with an audacity grown from his inexperience, thoughtless, headstrong, jealous, and filled with a tinsel courage. A swaggering babe accustomed to strut in his own dooryard. The youth wondered where had been born these new eyes; when his comrade had made the great discovery that there were many men who would refuse to be subjected by him. Apparently, the other had now climbed a peak of wisdom from which he could perceive himself as a very wee thing. And the youth saw that ever after it would be easier to live in his friend's neighborhood.

His comrade balanced his ebony coffee cup on his knee. "Well, Henry," he said, "what d'yeh think th' chances are? D'yeh think we'll wallop 'em?"

The youth considered for a moment. "Day-b'fore-yesterday," he finally replied, with boldness, "you would 'a' bet you'd lick the hull kit-an'-boodle all by yourself."

His friend looked a trifle amazed. "Would I?" he asked. He pondered. "Well, perhaps I would," he decided at last. He stared humbly at the fire.

The youth was quite disconcerted at this surprising reception of his remarks.

"Oh, no, you wouldn't either," he said, hastily trying to retrace.

But the other made a deprecating [1] gesture. "Oh, yeh needn't mind, Henry," he said. "I believe I was a pretty big fool in those days." He spoke as after a lapse of years.

There was a little pause.

"All th' officers say we've got th' rebs in a pretty tight box," said the friend, clearing his throat in a commonplace way. "They all seem t' think we've got 'em jest where we want 'em."

"I don't know about that," the youth replied. "What I seen over on th' right makes me think it was th' other way about. From where I was, it looked as if we was gettin' a good poundin' yestirday."

"D'yeh think so?" inquired the friend. "I thought we handled 'em pretty rough yestirday."

"Not a bit," said the youth. "Why, lord, man, you didn't see nothing of the fight. Why!" Then a sudden thought came to him. "Oh! Jim Conklin's dead."

His friend started. "What? Is he? Jim Conklin?"

The youth spoke slowly. "Yes. He's dead. Shot in th' side."

"Yeh don't say so. Jim Conklin . . . poor cuss!"

All about them were other small fires surrounded by men with their little black utensils. From one of these near came sudden sharp voices in a row. It appeared that two light-footed soldiers had been teasing a huge, bearded man, causing him to spill coffee upon his blue knees. The man had gone into a rage and had sworn comprehensively. Stung by his language, his tormentors had immediately bristled at him with a great show of resenting unjust oaths. Possibly there was going to be a fight.

The friend arose and went over to them, making pacific motions with his arms. "Oh, here, now, boys, what's th' use?" he said. "We'll be at th' rebs in less'n an

---

[1] **deprecating:** here, self-deprecating or expressing self-disapproval.

hour. What's th' good fightin' 'mong ourselves?"

One of the light-footed soldiers turned upon him red-faced and violent. "Yeh needn't come around here with yer preachin'. I s'pose yeh don't approve 'a fightin' since Charley Morgan licked yeh; but I don't see what business this here is 'a yours or anybody else."

"Well, it ain't," said the friend mildly. "Still I hate t' see——"

That was a tangled argument.

"Well, he——" said the two, indicating their opponent with accusative forefingers.

The huge soldier was quite purple with rage. He pointed at the two soldiers with his great hand, extended clawlike. "Well, they——"

But during this argumentative time the desire to deal blows seemed to pass, although they said much to each other. Finally the friend returned to his old seat. In a short while the three antagonists could be seen together in an amiable bunch.

"Jimmie Rogers ses I'll have t' fight him after th' battle t'day," announced the friend as he again seated himself. "He ses he don't allow no interferin' in his business. I hate t' see th' boys fightin' 'mong themselves."

The youth laughed. "Yer changed a good bit. Yeh ain't at all like yeh was. I remember when you an' that Irish feller ——" He stopped and laughed again.

"No, I didn't use t' be that way," said his friend thoughtfully. "That's true 'nough."

"Well, I didn't mean——" began the youth.

The friend made another deprecatory gesture. "Oh, yeh needn't mind, Henry."

There was another little pause.

"Th' reg'ment lost over half th' men yestirday," remarked the friend eventually. "I thought a course they was all dead, but, laws, they kep' a-comin' back last night until it seems, after all, we didn't lose but a few. They'd been scattered all over, wanderin' around in th' woods, fightin' with other reg'ments, an' everything. Jest like you done."

"So?" said the youth.

CHAPTER 15

THE REGIMENT was standing at order arms at the side of a lane, waiting for the command to march, when suddenly the youth remembered the little packet enwrapped in a faded yellow envelope which the loud young soldier with lugubrious words had entrusted to him. It made him start. He uttered an exclamation and turned toward his comrade.

"Wilson!"

"What?"

His friend, at his side in the ranks, was thoughtfully staring down the road. From some cause his expression was at that moment very meek. The youth, regarding him with sidelong glances, felt impelled to change his purpose. "Oh, nothing," he said.

His friend turned his head in some surprise. "Why, what was yeh goin' t' say?"

"Oh, nothing," repeated the youth.

He resolved not to deal the little blow. It was sufficient that the fact made him glad. It was not necessary to knock his friend on the head with the misguided packet.

He had been possessed of much fear of his friend, for he saw how easily questionings could make holes in his feelings. Lately, he had assured himself that the altered comrade would not tantalize him with a persistent curiosity, but he felt certain that during the first period of leisure his friend would ask him to relate his adventures of the previous day.

He now rejoiced in the possession of a small weapon with which he could prostrate his comrade at the first signs of a cross-examination. He was master. It would now be he who could laugh and shoot the shafts of derision.

The friend had, in a weak hour, spoken

with sobs of his own death. He had delivered a melancholy oration previous to his funeral, and had doubtless in the packet of letters presented various keepsakes to relatives. But he had not died, and thus he had delivered himself into the hands of the youth.

The latter felt immensely superior to his friend, but he inclined to condescension. He adopted toward him an air of patronizing good humor.

His self-pride was now entirely restored. In the shade of its flourishing growth he stood with braced and self-confident legs, and since nothing could now be discovered he did not shrink from an encounter with the eyes of judges, and allowed no thoughts of his own to keep him from an attitude of manfulness. He had performed his mistakes in the dark, so he was still a man.

Indeed, when he remembered his fortunes of yesterday and looked at them from a distance, he began to see something fine there. He had license to be pompous and veteranlike.

His panting agonies of the past he put out of his sight.

In the present, he declared to himself that it was only the doomed and the damned who roared with sincerity at circumstance. Few but they ever did it. A man with a full stomach and the respect of his fellows had no business to scold about anything that he might think to be wrong in the ways of the universe, or even with the ways of society. Let the unfortunates rail; the others may play marbles.

He did not give a great deal of thought to these battles that lay directly before him. It was not essential that he should plan his ways in regard to them. He had been taught that many obligations of a life were easily avoided. The lessons of yesterday had been that retribution was a laggard and blind. With these facts before him he did not deem it necessary that he should become feverish over the possibilities of the ensuing twenty-four hours. He could leave much to chance. Besides, a faith in himself had secretly blossomed. There was a little flower of confidence growing within him. He was now a man of experience. He had been out among the dragons, he said, and he assured himself that they were not so hideous as he had imagined them. Also, they were inaccurate; they did not sting with precision. A stout heart often defied and, defying, escaped.

And, furthermore, how could they kill him who was the chosen of gods and doomed to greatness?

He remembered how some of the men had run from the battle. As he recalled their terror-struck faces, he felt a scorn for them. They had surely been more fleet and more wild than was absolutely necessary. They were weak mortals. As for himself, he had fled with discretion and dignity.

He was aroused from this reverie by his friend, who, having hitched about nervously and blinked at the trees for a time, suddenly coughed in an introductory way, and spoke.

"Fleming!"

"What?"

The friend put his hand up to his mouth and coughed again. He fidgeted in his jacket.

"Well," he gulped, at last, "I guess yeh might as well give me back them letters." Dark, prickling blood had flushed into his cheeks and brow.

"All right, Wilson," said the youth. He loosened two buttons of his coat, thrust in his hand, and brought forth the packet. As he extended it to his friend, the latter's face was turned from him.

He had been slow in the act of producing the packet because during it he had been trying to invent a remarkable comment upon the affair. He could conjure nothing of sufficient point. He was compelled to allow his friend to escape unmolested with his packet. And for this he took unto himself considerable credit. It was a generous thing.

His friend at his side seemed suffering great shame. As he contemplated him, the youth felt his heart grow more strong and stout. He had never been compelled to blush in such manner for his acts; he was an individual of extraordinary virtues.

He reflected, with condescending pity: "Too bad! Too bad! The poor devil, it makes him feel tough!"

After this incident, and as he reviewed the battle pictures he had seen, he felt quite competent to return home and make the hearts of the people glow with stories of war. He could see himself in a room of warm tints telling tales to listeners. He could exhibit laurels. They were insignificant; still, in a district where laurels were infrequent, they might shine.

He saw his gaping audience picturing him as the central figure in blazing scenes. And he imagined the consternation and the ejaculations of his mother and the young lady at the seminary as they drank his recitals. Their vague feminine formula for beloved ones doing brave deeds on the field of battle without risk of life would be destroyed.

CHAPTER 16

A SPUTTERING of musketry was always to be heard. Later, the cannon had entered the dispute. In the fog-filled air their voices made a thudding sound. The reverberations were continued. This part of the world led a strange, battleful existence.

The youth's regiment was marched to relieve a command that had lain long in some damp trenches. The men took positions behind a curving line of rifle pits that had been turned up, like a large furrow, along the line of woods. Before them was a level stretch, peopled with short, deformed stumps. From the woods beyond came the dull popping of the skirmishers and pickets, firing in the fog. From the right came the noise of a terrific fracas.

The men cuddled behind the small embankment and sat in easy attitudes awaiting their turn. Many had their backs to the firing. The youth's friend lay down, buried his face in his arms, and, almost instantly, it seemed, he was in a deep sleep.

The youth leaned his breast against the brown dirt and peered over at the woods and up and down the line. Curtains of trees interfered with his ways of vision. He could see the low line of trenches but for a short distance. A few idle flags were perched on the dirt hills. Behind them were rows of dark bodies with a few heads sticking curiously over the top.

Always the noise of skirmishers came from the woods on the front and left, and the din on the right had grown to frightful proportions. The guns were roaring without an instant's pause for breath. It seemed that the cannon had come from all parts and were engaged in a stupendous wrangle. It became impossible to make a sentence heard.

The youth wished to launch a joke—a quotation from newspapers. He desired to say, "All quiet on the Rappahannock," [1] but the guns refused to permit even a comment upon their uproar. He never successfully concluded the sentence. But at last the guns stopped, and among the men in the rifle pits rumors again flew, like birds, but they were now for the most part black creatures who flapped their wings drearily near to the ground and refused to rise on any wings of hope. The men's faces grew doleful from the interpreting of omens. Tales of hesitation and uncertainty on the part of those high in place and responsibility came to their ears. Stories of disaster were borne into their minds with many proofs. This din of musketry on the right, growing like a released genie of sound, expressed and emphasized the army's plight.

The men were disheartened and began

---

[1] **All . . . Rappahannock:** a reference to "All quiet along the Potomac," a phrase common during the War Between the States. The Rappahannock River is in northeastern Virginia.

to mutter. They made gestures expressive of the sentence: "Ah, what more can we do?" And it could always be seen that they were bewildered by the alleged news and could not fully comprehend a defeat.

Before the gray mists had been totally obliterated by the sunrays, the regiment was marching in a spread column that was retiring carefully through the woods. The disordered, hurrying lines of the enemy could sometimes be seen down through the groves and little fields. They were yelling, shrill and exultant.

At this sight the youth forgot many personal matters and became greatly enraged. He exploded in loud sentences. "B'jiminey, we're generaled by a lot 'a lunkheads."

"More than one feller has said that t'day," observed a man.

His friend, recently aroused, was still very drowsy. He looked behind him until his mind took in the meaning of the movement. Then he sighed. "Oh, well, I s'pose we got licked," he remarked sadly.

The youth had a thought that it would not be handsome for him to freely condemn other men. He made an attempt to restrain himself, but the words upon his tongue were too bitter. He presently began a long and intricate denunciation of the commander of the forces.

"Mebbe, it wa'n't all his fault—not altogether. He did th' best he knowed. It's our luck t' git licked often," said his friend in a weary tone. He was trudging along with stooped shoulders and shifting eyes like a man who has been caned and kicked.

"Well, don't we fight like the devil? Don't we do all that men can?" demanded the youth loudly.

He was secretly dumbfounded at this sentiment when it came from his lips. For a moment his face lost its valor and he looked guiltily about him. But no one questioned his right to deal in such words, and presently he recovered his air of courage. He went on to repeat a statement he had heard going from group to group at the camp that morning. "The brigadier said he never saw a new reg'ment fight the way we fought yestirday, didn't he? And we didn't do better than many another reg'ment, did we? Well, then, you can't say it's th' army's fault, can you?"

In his reply, the friend's voice was stern. "'A course not," he said. "No man dare say we don't fight like th' devil. No man will ever dare say it. Th' boys fight like hell-roosters. But still—still, we don't have no luck."

"Well, then, if we fight like the devil an' don't ever whip, it must be the general's fault," said the youth grandly and decisively. "And I don't see any sense in fighting and fighting and fighting, yet always losing through some derned old lunkhead of a general."

A sarcastic man who was tramping at the youth's side then spoke lazily. "Mebbe yeh think yeh fit th' hull battle yestirday, Fleming," he remarked.

The speech pierced the youth. Inwardly he was reduced to an abject pulp by these chance words. His legs quaked privately. He cast a frightened glance at the sarcastic man.

"Why, no," he hastened to say in a conciliating voice, "I don't think I fought the whole battle yesterday."

But the other seemed innocent of any deeper meaning. Apparently, he had no information. It was merely his habit. "Oh!" he replied in the same tone of calm derision.

The youth, nevertheless, felt a threat. His mind shrank from going near to the danger, and thereafter he was silent. The significance of the sarcastic man's words took from him all loud moods that would make him appear prominent. He became suddenly a modest person.

There was low-toned talk among the troops. The officers were impatient and snappy, their countenances clouded with tales of misfortune. The troops, sifting through the forest, were sullen. In the youth's company once a man's laugh rang out. A dozen soldiers turned their faces quickly toward him and frowned with vague displeasure.

The noise of firing dogged their footsteps. Sometimes, it seemed to be driven a little way, but it always returned again with increased insolence. The men muttered and cursed, throwing black looks in its direction.

In a clear space the troops were at last halted. Regiments and brigades, broken and detached through their encounters with thickets, grew together again, and lines were faced toward the pursuing bark of the enemy's infantry.

This noise, following like the yellings of eager, metallic hounds, increased to a loud and joyous burst, and then, as the sun went serenely up the sky, throwing illuminating rays into the gloomy thickets, it broke forth into prolonged pealings. The woods began to crackle as if afire.

"Whoop-a-dadee," said a man, "here we are! Everybody fightin'. Blood an' destruction."

"I was willin' t' bet they'd attack as soon as th' sun got fairly up," savagely asserted the lieutenant who commanded the youth's company. He jerked without mercy at his little mustache. He strode to and fro with dark dignity in the rear of his men, who were lying down behind whatever protection they had collected.

A battery had trundled into position in the rear and was thoughtfully shelling the distance. The regiment, unmolested as yet, awaited the moment when the gray shadows of the woods before them should be slashed by the lines of flame. There was much growling and swearing.

"Good Gawd," the youth grumbled, "we're always being chased around like rats! It makes me sick. Nobody seems to know where we go or why we go. We just get fired around from pillar to post and get licked here and get licked there, and nobody knows what it's done for. It makes a man feel like a damn' kitten in a bag. Now, I'd like to know what the eternal thunders we was marched into these woods for anyhow, unless it was to give the rebs a regular pot shot at us. We came in here and got our legs all tangled up in these cussed briers, and

then we begin to fight and the rebs had an easy time of it. Don't tell me it's just luck! I know better. It's this derned old——"

The friend seemed jaded, but he interrupted his comrade with a voice of calm confidence. "It'll turn out all right in th' end," he said.

"Oh, the devil it will! You always talk like a dog-hanged parson. Don't tell me! I know——"

At this time there was an interposition [1] by the savage-minded lieutenant, who was obliged to vent some of his inward dissatisfaction upon his men. "You boys shut right up! There's no need 'a your wastin' your breath in long-winded arguments about this an' that an' th' other. You've been jawin' like a lot 'a old hens. All you've got t' do is t' fight, an' you'll get plenty 'a that t' do in about ten minutes. Less talkin' an' more fightin' is what's best for you boys. I never saw sech gabbling jackasses."

He paused, ready to pounce upon any man who might have the temerity to reply. No words being said, he resumed his dignified pacing.

"There's too much chin music an' too little fightin' in this war, anyhow," he said to them, turning his head for a final remark.

The day had grown more white, until the sun shed his full radiance upon the thronged forest. A sort of a gust of battle came sweeping toward that part of the line where lay the youth's regiment. The front shifted a trifle to meet it squarely. There was a wait. In this part of the field there passed slowly the intense moments that precede the tempest.

A single rifle flashed in a thicket before the regiment. In an instant it was joined by many others. There was a mighty song of clashes and crashes that went sweeping through the woods. The guns in the rear, aroused and enraged by shells that had been thrown burrlike [2] at them, suddenly involved themselves in a hideous

---

[1] **interposition:** here, interruption.
[2] **burrlike:** prickly as a burr.

altercation with another band of guns. The battle roar settled to a rolling thunder, which was a single, long explosion.

In the regiment there was a peculiar kind of hesitation denoted in the attitudes of the men. They were worn, exhausted, having slept but little and labored much. They rolled their eyes toward the advancing battle as they stood awaiting the shock. Some shrank and flinched. They stood as men tied to stakes.

CHAPTER 17

THIS ADVANCE of the enemy had seemed to the youth like a ruthless hunting. He began to fume with rage and exasperation. He beat his foot upon the ground and scowled with hate at the swirling smoke that was approaching like a phantom flood. There was a maddening quality in this seeming resolution of the foe to give him no rest, to give him no time to sit down and think. Yesterday he had fought and had fled rapidly. There had been many adventures. For today he felt that he had earned opportunities for contemplative repose. He could have enjoyed portraying to uninitiated listeners various scenes at which he had been a witness or ably discussing the processes of war with other proved men. Too it was important that he should have time for physical recuperation. He was sore and stiff from his experiences. He had received his fill of all exertions, and he wished to rest.

But those other men seemed never to grow weary; they were fighting with their old speed. He had a wild hate for the relentless foe. Yesterday, when he had imagined the universe to be against him, he had hated it, little gods and big gods; today he hated the army of the foe with the same great hatred. He was not going to be badgered of his life, like a kitten chased by boys, he said. It was not well to drive men into final corners; at those moments they could all develop teeth and claws.

He leaned and spoke into his friend's ear. He menaced the woods with a gesture. "If they keep on chasing us, by Gawd, they'd better watch out. Can't stand *too* much."

The friend twisted his head and made a calm reply. "If they keep on a-chasin' us they'll drive us all inteh th' river."

The youth cried out savagely at this statement. He crouched behind a little tree, with his eyes burning hatefully and his teeth set in a curlike snarl. The awkward bandage was still about his head, and upon it, over his wound, there was a spot of dry blood. His hair was wondrously tousled, and some straggling, moving locks hung over the cloth of the bandage down toward his forehead. His jacket and shirt were open at the throat, and exposed his young bronzed neck. There could be seen spasmodic gulpings at his throat.

His fingers twined nervously about his rifle. He wished that it was an engine of annihilating power. He felt that he and his companions were being taunted and derided from sincere convictions that they were poor and puny. His knowledge of his inability to take vengeance for it made his rage into a dark and stormy specter that possessed him and made him dream of abominable cruelties. The tormentors were flies sucking insolently at his blood, and he thought that he would have given his life for a revenge of seeing their faces in pitiful plights.

The winds of battle had swept all about the regiment, until the one rifle, instantly followed by others, flashed in its front. A moment later the regiment roared forth its sudden and valiant retort. A dense wall of smoke settled slowly down. It was furiously slit and slashed by the knifelike fire from the rifles.

To the youth the fighters resembled animals tossed for a death struggle into a dark pit. There was a sensation that he and his fellows, at bay, were pushing back, always pushing fierce onslaughts of creatures who were slippery. Their beams of crimson seemed to get no purchase upon the bodies of their foes; the latter seemed to evade them with ease and come through, between, around, and about with unopposed skill.

When, in a dream, it occurred to the youth that his rifle was an impotent stick, he lost sense of everything but his hate, his desire to smash into pulp the glittering smile of victory which he could feel upon the faces of his enemies.

The blue smoke-swallowed line curled and writhed like a snake stepped upon. It swung its ends to and fro in an agony of fear and rage.

The youth was not conscious that he was erect upon his feet. He did not know the direction of the ground. Indeed, once he even lost the habit of balance and fell heavily. He was up again immediately. One thought went through the chaos of his brain at the time. He wondered if he had fallen because he had been shot. But the suspicion flew away at once. He did not think more of it.

He had taken up a first position behind the little tree, with a direct determination to hold it against the world. He had not deemed it possible that his army could that day succeed, and from this he felt the ability to fight harder. But the throng had surged in all ways, until he lost directions and locations, save that he knew where lay the enemy.

The flames bit him, and the hot smoke broiled his skin. His rifle barrel grew so hot that ordinarily he could not have borne it upon his palms; but he kept on stuffing cartridges into it, and pounding them with his clanking, bending ramrod. If he aimed at some changing form through the smoke, he pulled his trigger with a fierce grunt, as if he were dealing a blow of the fist with all his strength.

When the enemy seemed falling back before him and his fellows, he went instantly forward, like a dog who, seeing his foes lagging, turns and insists upon being pursued. And when he was compelled to retire again, he did it slowly, sullenly, taking steps of wrathful despair.

Once he, in his intent hate, was almost alone, and was firing, when all those near him had ceased. He was so engrossed in his occupation that he was not aware of a lull.

He was recalled by a hoarse laugh and a sentence that came to his ears in a voice of contempt and amazement. "Yeh infernal fool, don't yeh know enough t' quit when there ain't anything t' shoot at? Good Gawd!"

He turned then and, pausing with his rifle thrown half into position, looked at the blue line of his comrades. During this moment of leisure they seemed all to be engaged in staring with astonishment at him. They had become spectators. Turning to the front again he saw, under the lifted smoke, a deserted ground.

He looked bewildered for a moment. Then there appeared upon the glazed vacancy of his eyes a diamond point of intelligence. "Oh," he said, comprehending.

He returned to his comrades and threw himself upon the ground. He sprawled like a man who had been thrashed. His flesh seemed strangely on fire, and the sounds of the battle continued in his ears. He groped blindly for his canteen.

The lieutenant was crowing. He seemed drunk with fighting. He called out to the youth: "By heavens, if I had ten thousand wildcats like you I could tear th' stomach outa this war in less'n a week!" He puffed out his chest with large dignity as he said it.

Some of the men muttered and looked at the youth in awestruck ways. It was plain that as he had gone on loading and firing and cursing without the proper intermission, they had found time to regard him. And they now looked upon him as a war devil.

The friend came staggering to him. There was some fright and dismay in his voice. "Are yeh all right, Fleming? Do yeh feel all right? There ain't nothin' th' matter with yeh, Henry, is there?"

"No," said the youth with difficulty. His throat seemed full of knobs and burrs.

These incidents made the youth ponder.

It was revealed to him that he had been a barbarian, a beast. He had fought like a pagan who defends his religion. Regarding it, he saw that it was fine, wild, and, in some ways, easy. He had been a tremendous figure, no doubt. By this struggle he had overcome obstacles which he had admitted to be mountains. They had fallen like paper peaks, and he was now what he called a hero. And he had not been aware of the process. He had slept and, awakening, found himself a knight.

He lay and basked in the occasional stares of his comrades. Their faces were varied in degrees of blackness from the burned powder. Some were utterly smudged. They were reeking with perspiration, and their breaths came hard and wheezing. And from these soiled expanses they peered at him.

"Hot work! Hot work!" cried the lieutenant deliriously. He walked up and down, restless and eager. Sometimes his voice could be heard in a wild, incomprehensible laugh.

When he had a particularly profound thought upon the science of war he always unconsciously addressed himself to the youth.

There was some grim rejoicing by the men. "By thunder, I bet this army'll never see another new reg'ment like us!"

"You bet!

'A dog, a woman, an' a walnut tree,
Th' more yeh beat 'em, th' better they be!'

That's like us."

"Lost a piler men, they did. If an' ol' woman swep' up th' woods she'd git a dustpanful."

"Yes, an' if she'll come around ag'in in 'bout an' hour she'll git a pile more."

The forest still bore its burden of clamor. From off under the trees came the rolling clatter of the musketry. Each distant thicket seemed a strange porcupine with quills of flame. A cloud of dark smoke, as from smoldering ruins, went up toward the sun, now bright and gay in the blue, enameled sky.

CHAPTER 18

THE RAGGED LINE had respite for some minutes, but during its pause the struggle in the forest became magnified until the trees seemed to quiver from the firing and the ground to shake from the rushing of the men. The voices of the cannon were mingled in a long and interminable row. It seemed difficult to live in such an atmosphere. The chests of the men strained for a bit of freshness, and their throats craved water.

There was one, shot through the body, who raised a cry of bitter lamentation when came this lull. Perhaps he had been calling out during the fighting also, but at that time no one had heard him. But now the men turned at the woeful complaints of him upon the ground.

"Who is it? Who is it?"

"It's Jimmie Rogers. Jimmie Rogers."

When their eyes first encountered him there was a sudden halt, as if they feared to go near. He was thrashing about in the grass, twisting his shuddering body into many strange postures. He was screaming loudly. This instant's hesitation seemed to fill him with a tremendous, fantastic contempt, and he damned them in shrieked sentences.

The youth's friend had a geographical illusion concerning a stream, and he obtained permission to go for some water. Immediately canteens were showered upon him. "Fill mine, will yeh?" "Bring me some, too." "And me, too." He departed, laden. The youth went with his friend, feeling a desire to throw his heated body onto the stream and, soaking there, drink quarts.

They made a hurried search for the supposed stream, but did not find it. "No water here," said the youth. They turned without delay and began to retrace their steps.

From their position as they again faced toward the place of the fighting, they could of course comprehend a greater amount of the battle than when their visions had been blurred by the hurling smoke of the line. They could see dark stretches winding along the land, and on one cleared space there was a row of guns making gray clouds, which were filled with large flashes of orange-colored flame. Over some foliage they could see the roof of a house. One window, glowing a deep murder red, shone squarely through the leaves. From the edifice a tall leaning tower of smoke went far into the sky.

Looking over their own troops, they saw mixed masses slowly getting into regular form. The sunlight made twinkling points of the bright steel. To the rear there was a glimpse of a distant roadway as it curved over a slope. It was crowded with retreating infantry. From all the interwoven forest arose the smoke and bluster of the battle. The air was always occupied by a blaring.

Near where they stood shells were flip-flapping and hooting. Occasional bullets buzzed in the air and spanged into tree trunks. Wounded men and other stragglers were slinking through the woods.

Looking down an aisle of the grove, the youth and his companion saw a jangling general and his staff almost ride upon a wounded man, who was crawling on his hands and knees. The general reined strongly at his charger's opened and foamy mouth and guided it with dexterous horsemanship past the man. The latter scrambled in wild and torturing haste. His strength evidently failed him as he reached a place of safety. One of his arms suddenly weakened, and he fell, sliding over upon his back. He lay stretched out, breathing gently.

A moment later the small, creaking cavalcade was directly in front of the two soldiers. Another officer, riding with the skillful abandon of a cowboy, galloped his horse to a position directly before the general. The two unnoticed foot soldiers made a little show of going on, but they lingered near in the desire to overhear the conversation. Perhaps, they thought, some great inner historical things would be said.

The general, whom the boys knew as the commander of their division, looked at the other officer and spoke coolly, as if he were criticising his clothes. "Th' enemy's formin' over there for another charge," he said. "It'll be directed against Whiterside, an' I fear they'll break through there unless we work like thunder t' stop them."

The other swore at his restive horse, and then cleared his throat. He made a gesture toward his cap. "It'll be hell t' pay stoppin' them," he said shortly.

"I presume so," remarked the general. Then he began to talk rapidly and in a lower tone. He frequently illustrated his words with a pointing finger. The two infantrymen could hear nothing until finally he asked: "What troops can you spare?"

The officer who rode like a cowboy reflected for an instant. "Well," he said, "I had to order in th' 12th to help th' 76th, an' I haven't really got any. But there's th' 304th. They fight like a lot 'a mule drivers. I can spare them best of any."

The youth and his friend exchanged glances of astonishment.

The general spoke sharply. "Get 'em ready, then. I'll watch developments from here, an' send you word when t' start them. It'll happen in five minutes."

As the other officer tossed his fingers toward his cap and, wheeling his horse, started away, the general called out to him in a sober voice: "I don't believe many of your mule drivers will get back."

The other shouted something in reply. He smiled.

With scared faces, the youth and his companion hurried back to the line.

These happenings had occupied an incredibly short time, yet the youth felt that in them he had been made aged. New eyes were given to him. And the most startling thing was to learn suddenly that he was very insignificant. The officer spoke of the regiment as if he referred to a broom. Some part of the woods needed sweeping perhaps, and he merely indicated a broom in a tone properly indifferent to its fate. It was war, no doubt, but it appeared strange.

As the two boys approached the line, the lieutenant perceived them and swelled with wrath. "Fleming—Wilson—how long does it take yeh to git water, anyhow—where yeh been to."

But his oration ceased as he saw their eyes, which were large with great tales. "We're goin' t' charge—we're goin' t' charge!" cried the youth's friend, hastening with his news.

"Charge?" said the lieutenant. "Charge? Well, b'Gawd! Now; this is real fightin'." Over his soiled countenance there went a boastful smile. "Charge? Well, b'Gawd!"

A little group of soldiers surrounded the two youths. "Are we, sure 'nough? Well, I'll be derned! Charge? What fer? What at? Wilson, you're lyin'."

"I hope to die," said the youth, pitching his tones to the key of angry remonstrance. "Sure as shooting, I tell you."

And his friend spoke in reinforcement. "Not by a blame sight, he ain't lyin'. We heard 'em talkin'."

They caught sight of two mounted figures a short distance from them. One was the colonel of the regiment and the other was the officer who had received orders from the commander of the division. They were gesticulating at each other. The soldier, pointing at them, interpreted the scene.

One man had a final objection: "How could yeh hear 'em talkin'?" But the men, for a large part, nodded, admitting that previously the two friends had spoken truth.

They settled back into reposeful attitudes with airs of having accepted the matter. And they mused upon it, with a hundred varieties of expression. It was an engrossing thing to think about. Many tightened their belts carefully and hitched at their trousers.

A moment later the officers began to bustle among the men, pushing them into a more compact mass and into a better alignment. They chased those that straggled and fumed at a few men who seemed to show by their attitudes that they had decided to remain at that spot. They were like critical shepherds struggling with sheep.

Presently, the regiment seemed to draw itself up and heave a deep breath. None of the men's faces were mirrors of large thoughts. The soldiers were bended and stooped like sprinters before a signal. Many pairs of glinting eyes peered from the grimy faces toward the curtains of the deeper woods. They seemed to be engaged in deep calculations of time and distance.

They were surrounded by the noises of the monstrous altercation between the two armies. The world was fully interested in other matters. Apparently, the regiment had its small affair to itself.

The youth, turning, shot a quick, inquiring glance at his friend. The latter returned to him the same manner of look. They were the only ones who possessed an inner knowledge. "Mule drivers—hell t' pay—don't believe many will get back." It was an ironical secret. Still, they saw no hesitation in each other's faces, and they nodded a mute and unprotesting assent when a shaggy man near them said in a meek voice: "We'll git swallowed."

CHAPTER 19

THE YOUTH stared at the land in front of him. Its foliage now seemed to veil powers and horrors. He was unaware of the machinery of orders that started the charge, although from the corners of his eyes he saw an officer, who looked like a boy a-horseback, come galloping, waving his hat. Suddenly he felt a straining and heaving among the men. The line fell slowly forward like a toppling wall, and, with a convulsive gasp that was intended for a cheer, the regiment began its journey. The youth was pushed and jostled for a moment before he understood the movement at all, but directly he lunged ahead and began to run.

He fixed his eye upon a distant and prominent clump of trees where he had concluded the enemy were to be met, and he ran toward it as toward a goal. He had believed throughout that it was a mere question of getting over an unpleasant matter as quickly as possible, and he ran desperately, as if pursued for a murder. His face was drawn hard and tight with the stress of his endeavor. His eyes were fixed in a lurid glare. And with his soiled and disordered dress, his red and inflamed features surmounted by the dingy rag with its spot of blood, his wildly swinging rifle and banging accouterments, he looked to be an insane soldier.

As the regiment swung from its position out into a cleared space, the woods and thickets before it awakened. Yellow flames leaped toward it from many directions. The forest made a tremendous objection.

The line lurched straight for a moment. Then the right wing sprung forward; it in turn was surpassed by the left. Afterward the center careered to the front until the regiment was a wedge-shaped mass, but an instant later the opposition of the bushes, trees, and uneven places on the ground split the command and scattered it into detached clusters.

The youth, light-footed, was unconsciously in advance. His eyes still kept note of the clump of trees. From all places near it the clannish yell of the enemy could be heard. The little flames of rifles leaped from it. The song of the bullets was in the air, and shells snarled among the treetops. One tumbled directly into the middle of a hurrying group and exploded in crimson fury. There was an instant's spectacle of a man, almost over it, throwing up his hands to shield his eyes.

Other men, punched by bullets, fell in grotesque agonies. The regiment left a coherent trail of bodies.

They had passed into a clearer atmosphere. There was an effect like a revelation in the new appearance of the landscape. Some men working madly at a battery were plain to them, and the opposing infantry's lines were defined by the gray walls and fringes of smoke.

It seemed to the youth that he saw everything. Each blade of the green grass was bold and clear. He thought that he was aware of every change in the thin, transparent vapor that floated idly in sheets. The brown or gray trunks of the trees showed each roughness of their surfaces. And the men of the regiment, with their starting eyes and sweating faces, running madly, or falling, as if thrown headlong, into queer, heaped-up corpses —all were comprehended. His mind took a mechanical but firm impression, so that afterward everything was pictured and explained to him, save why he himself was there.

But there was a frenzy made from this furious rush. The men, pitching forward insanely, had burst into cheerings, moblike and barbaric, but tuned in strange keys that can arouse the dullard and the stoic.[1] It made a mad enthusiasm that, it seemed, would be incapable of checking itself before granite and brass. There was the delirium that encounters despair and death and is heedless and blind to the odds. It is a temporary but sublime absence of selfishness. And because it was of this order was the reason, perhaps, why the youth wondered, afterward, what reasons he could have had for being there.

Presently the straining pace ate up the energies of the men. As if by agreement, the leaders began to slacken their speed. The volleys directed against them had had a seeming windlike effect. The regiment snorted and blew. Among some stolid trees it began to falter and hesitate. The men, staring intently, began to wait for some of the distant walls of smoke to move and disclose to them the scene. Since much of their strength and their

[1] **stoic:** one who is indifferent to pleasure or pain.

breath had vanished, they returned to caution. They were become men again.

The youth had a vague belief that he had run miles, and he thought, in a way, that he was now in some new and unknown land.

The moment the regiment ceased its advance the protesting splutter of musketry became a steadied roar. Long and accurate fringes of smoke spread out. From the top of a small hill came level belchings of yellow flame that caused an inhuman whistling in the air.

The men, halted, had opportunity to see some of their comrades dropping with moans and shrieks. A few lay under foot, still or wailing. And now for an instant the men stood, their rifles slack in their hands, and watched the regiment dwindle. They appeared dazed and stupid. This spectacle seemed to paralyze them, overcome them with a fatal fascination. They stared woodenly at the sights and, lowering their eyes, looked from face to face. It was a strange pause, and a strange silence.

Then, above the sounds of the outside commotion, arose the roar of the lieutenant. He strode suddenly forth, his infantile features black with rage.

"Come on, yeh fools!" he bellowed. "Come on! Yeh can't stay here. Yeh must come on." He said more, but much of it could not be understood.

He started rapidly forward, with his head turned toward the men. "Come on," he was shouting. The men stared with blank and yokel-like eyes at him. He was obliged to halt and retrace his steps. He stood then with his back to the enemy and delivered gigantic curses into the faces of the men. His body vibrated from the weight and force of his imprecations. And he could string oaths with the facility of a maiden who strings beads.

The friend of the youth aroused. Lurching suddenly forward and dropping to his knees, he fired an angry shot at the persistent woods. This action awakened the men. They huddled no more like sheep. They seemed suddenly to bethink them of their weapons, and at once commenced firing. Belabored [1] by their officers, they began to move forward. The regiment, involved like a cart involved in mud and muddle, started unevenly with many jolts and jerks. The men stopped now every few paces to fire and load, and in this manner moved slowly on from trees to trees.

The flaming opposition in their front grew with their advance until it seemed that all forward ways were barred by the thin leaping tongues, and off to the right an ominous demonstration could sometimes be dimly discerned. The smoke lately generated was in confusing clouds that made it difficult for the regiment to proceed with intelligence. As he passed through each curling mass, the youth wondered what would confront him on the farther side.

The command went painfully forward until an open space interposed between them and the lurid lines. Here, crouching and cowering behind some trees, the men clung with desperation, as if threatened by a wave. They looked wild-eyed and as if amazed at this furious disturbance they had stirred. In the storm there was an ironical expression of their importance. The faces of the men, too, showed a lack of a certain feeling of responsibility for being there. It was as if they had been driven. It was the dominant animal failing to remember in the supreme moments the forceful causes of various superficial qualities. The whole affair seemed incomprehensible to many of them.

As they halted thus, the lieutenant again began to bellow profanely. Regardless of the vindictive threats of the bullets, he went about coaxing, berating, and bedamning. His lips, that were habitually in a soft and childlike curve, were now writhed into unholy contortions. He swore by all possible deities.

Once he grabbed the youth by the arm. "Come on, yeh lunkhead!" he roared. "Come on! We'll all git killed if we stay here. We've on'y got t' go across that lot.

[1] **Belabored:** here, yelled at.

An' then"—the remainder of his idea disappeared in a blue haze of curses.

The youth stretched forth his arm. "Cross there?" His mouth was puckered in doubt and awe.

"Certainly. Jest 'cross th' lot! We can't stay here," screamed the lieutenant. He poked his face close to the youth and waved his bandaged hand. "Come on!" Presently he grappled with him as if for a wrestling bout. It was as if he planned to drag the youth by the ear on to the assault.

The private felt a sudden unspeakable indignation against his officer. He wrenched fiercely and shook him off.

"Come on yerself, then," he yelled. There was a bitter challenge in his voice.

They galloped together down the regimental front. The friend scrambled after them. In front of the colors the three men began to bawl: "Come on! come on!" They danced and gyrated like tortured savages.

The flag, obedient to these appeals, bended its glittering form and swept toward them. The men wavered in indecision for a moment, and then with a long, wailful cry the dilapidated regiment surged forward and began its new journey.

Over the field went the scurrying mass. It was a handful of men splattered into the faces of the enemy. Toward it instantly sprang the yellow tongues. A vast quantity of blue smoke hung before them. A mighty banging made ears valueless.

The youth ran like a madman to reach the woods before a bullet could discover him. He ducked his head low, like a football player. In his haste his eyes almost closed, and the scene was a wild blur. Pulsating saliva stood at the corners of his mouth.

Within him, as he hurled himself forward, was born a love, a despairing fondness for this flag which was near him. It was a creation of beauty and invulnerability. It was a goddess, radiant, that bended its form with an imperious gesture to him. It was a woman, red and white, hating and loving, that called him with the voice of his hopes. Because no harm could come to it he endowed it with power. He kept near, as if it could be a saver of lives, and an imploring cry went from his mind.

In the mad scramble he was aware that the color sergeant flinched suddenly, as if struck by a bludgeon. He faltered and then became motionless, save for his quivering knees.

He made a spring and a clutch at the pole. At the same instant his friend grabbed it from the other side. They jerked at it, stout and furious, but the color sergeant was dead, and the corpse would not relinquish its trust. For a moment there was a grim encounter. The dead man, swinging with bended back, seemed to be obstinately tugging, in ludicrous and awful ways, for the possession of the flag.

It was past in an instant of time. They wrenched the flag furiously from the dead man, and, as they turned again, the corpse swayed forward with bowed head. One arm swung high, and the curved hand fell with heavy protest on the friend's unheeding shoulder.

CHAPTER 20

WHEN THE two youths turned with the flag they saw that much of the regiment had crumbled away, and the dejected remnant was coming back. The men, having hurled themselves in projectile fashion, had presently expended their forces. They slowly retreated, with their faces still toward the spluttering woods, and their hot rifles still replying to the din. Several officers were giving orders, their voices keyed to screams.

"Where in hell yeh goin'?" the lieutenant was asking in a sarcastic howl. And a red-bearded officer, whose voice of triple brass [1] could plainly be heard, was commanding: "Shoot into 'em! Shoot into 'em, Gawd damn their souls!" There was

[1] **triple brass:** used here to mean great strength or power.

a melée of screeches, in which the men were ordered to do conflicting and impossible things.

The youth and his friend had a small scuffle over the flag. "Give it t' me!" "No, let me keep it!" Each felt satisfied with the other's possession of it, but each felt bound to declare, by an offer to carry the emblem, his willingness to further risk himself. The youth roughly pushed his friend away.

The regiment fell back to the stolid trees. There it halted for a moment to blaze at some dark forms that had begun to steal upon its track. Presently it resumed its march again, curving among the tree trunks. By the time the depleted regiment had again reached the first open space they were receiving a fast and merciless fire. There seemed to be mobs all about them.

The greater part of the men, discouraged, their spirits worn by the turmoil, acted as if stunned. They accepted the pelting of the bullets with bowed and weary heads. It was of no purpose to strive against walls. It was of no use to batter themselves against granite. And from this consciousness that they had attempted to conquer an unconquerable thing there seemed to arise a feeling that they had been betrayed. They glowered with bent brows, but dangerously, upon some of the officers, more particularly upon the red-bearded one with the voice of triple brass.

However, the rear of the regiment was fringed with men, who continued to shoot irritably at the advancing foes. They seemed resolved to make every trouble. The youthful lieutenant was perhaps the last man in the disordered mass. His forgotten back was toward the enemy. He had been shot in the arm. It hung straight and rigid. Occasionally he would cease to remember it and be about to emphasize an oath with a sweeping gesture. The multiplied pain caused him to swear with incredible power.

The youth went along with slipping, uncertain feet. He kept watchful eyes rearward. A scowl of mortification and rage was upon his face. He had thought of a fine revenge upon the officer who had referred to him and his fellows as mule drivers. But he saw that it could not come to pass. His dreams had collapsed when the mule drivers, dwindling rapidly, had wavered and hesitated on the little clearing and then had recoiled. And now the retreat of the mule drivers was a march of shame to him.

A dagger-pointed gaze from without his blackened face was held toward the enemy, but his greater hatred was riveted upon the man who, not knowing him, had called him a mule driver.

When he knew that he and his comrades had failed to do anything in successful ways that might bring the little pangs of a kind of remorse upon the officer, the youth allowed the rage of the baffled to possess him. This cold officer upon a monument, who dropped epithets unconcernedly down, would be finer as a dead man, he thought. So grievous did he think it that he could never possess the secret right to taunt truly in answer.

He had pictured red letters of curious revenge. "We *are* mule drivers, are we?" And now he was compelled to throw them away.

He presently wrapped his heart in the cloak of his pride and kept the flag erect. He harangued his fellows, pushing against their chests with his free hand. To those he knew well he made frantic appeals, beseeching them by name. Between him and the lieutenant, scolding and near to losing his mind with rage, there was felt a subtle fellowship and equality. They supported each other in all manner of hoarse, howling protests.

But the regiment was a machine run down. The two men babbled at a forceless thing. The soldiers who had heart to go slowly were continually shaken in their resolves by a knowledge that comrades were slipping with speed back to the lines. It was difficult to think of reputation when others were thinking of skins. Wounded men were left crying on this black journey.

The smoke fringes and flames blustered always. The youth, peering once through a sudden rift in a cloud, saw a brown mass of troops, interwoven and magnified until they appeared to be thousands. A fierce-hued flag flashed before his vision.

Immediately, as if the uplifting of the smoke had been prearranged, the discovered troops burst into a rasping yell and a hundred flames jetted toward the retreating band. A rolling gray cloud again interposed as the regiment doggedly replied. The youth had to depend again upon his misused ears, which were trembling and buzzing from the melée of musketry and yells.

The way seemed eternal. In the clouded haze men became panic-stricken with the thought that the regiment had lost its path and was proceeding in a perilous direction. Once the men who headed the wild procession turned and came pushing back against their comrades, screaming that they were being fired upon from points which they had considered to be toward their own lines. At this cry a hysterical fear and dismay beset the troops. A soldier, who heretofore had been ambitious to make the regiment into a wise little band that would proceed calmly amid the huge-appearing difficulties, suddenly sank down and buried his face in his arms with an air of bowing to a doom. From another a shrill lamentation rang out filled with profane allusions to a general. Men ran hither and thither, seeking with their eyes roads of escape. With serene regularity, as if controlled by a schedule, bullets buffed into the men.

The youth walked stolidly into the midst of the mob, and with his flag in his hands took a stand as if he expected an attempt to push him to the ground. He unconsciously assumed the attitude of the color bearer in the fight of the preceding day. He passed over his brow a hand that trembled. His breath did not come freely. He was choking during this small wait for the crisis.

His friend came to him. "Well, Henry, I guess this is good-by—John."

"Oh, shut up, you damned fool!" replied the youth, and he would not look at the other.

The officers labored like politicians to beat the mass into a proper circle to face the menaces. The ground was uneven and torn. The men curled into depressions and fitted themselves snugly behind whatever would frustrate a bullet.

The youth noted with vague surprise that the lieutenant was standing mutely with his legs far apart and his sword held in the manner of a cane. The youth wondered what had happened to his vocal organs that he no more cursed.

There was something curious in this little intent pause of the lieutenant. He was like a babe which, having wept its fill, raises its eyes and fixes upon a distant toy. He was engrossed in this contemplation, and the soft underlip quivered from self-whispered words.

Some lazy and ignorant smoke curled slowly. The men, hiding from the bullets, waited anxiously for it to lift and disclose the plight of the regiment.

The silent ranks were suddenly thrilled by the eager voice of the youthful lieutenant bawling out: "Here they come! Right on to us, b'Gawd!" His further words were lost in a roar of wicked thunder from the men's rifles.

The youth's eyes had instantly turned in the direction indicated by the awakened and agitated lieutenant, and he had seen the haze of treachery disclosing a body of soldiers of the enemy. They were so near that he could see their features. There was a recognition as he looked at the types of faces. Also he perceived with dim amazement that their uniforms were rather gay in effect, being light gray, accented with a brilliant-hued facing. Too, the clothes seemed new.

These troops had apparently been going forward with caution, their rifles held in readiness, when the youthful lieutenant had discovered them and their movement had been interrupted by the volley from the blue regiment. From the moment's glimpse, it was derived that they had been unaware of the proximity of their dark-suited foes or had mistaken the direction. Almost instantly they were shut utterly from the youth's sight by the smoke from the energetic rifles of his companions. He strained his vision to learn the accomplishment of the volley, but the smoke hung before him.

The two bodies of troops exchanged blows in the manner of a pair of boxers. The fast angry firings went back and forth. The men in blue were intent with the despair of their circumstances and they seized upon the revenge to be had at close range. Their thunder swelled loud and valiant. Their curving front bristled with flashes and the place resounded with the clangor of their ramrods. The youth ducked and dodged for a time and achieved a few unsatisfactory views of the enemy. There appeared to be many of them and they were replying swiftly. They seemed moving toward the blue regiment, step by step. He seated himself gloomily on the ground with his flag between his knees.

As he noted the vicious, wolflike temper of his comrades, he had a sweet thought that if the enemy was about to swallow the regimental broom as a large prisoner, it could at least have the consolation of going down with bristles forward.

But the blows of the antagonist began to grow more weak. Fewer bullets ripped the air, and finally, when the men slackened to learn of the fight, they could see only dark, floating smoke. The regiment lay still and gazed. Presently some chance whim came to the pestering blur, and it began to coil heavily away. The men saw a ground vacant of fighters. It would have been an empty stage if it were not for a few corpses that lay thrown and twisted into fantastic shapes upon the sward.

At sight of this tableau, many of the men in blue sprang from behind their covers and made an ungainly dance of joy. Their eyes burned and a hoarse cheer of elation broke from their dry lips.

It had begun to seem to them that events were trying to prove that they were impotent. These little battles had evidently endeavored to demonstrate that the men could not fight well. When on the verge of submission to these opinions, the small duel had showed them that the proportions were not impossible, and by it they had revenged themselves upon their misgivings and upon the foe.

The impetus of enthusiasm was theirs again. They gazed about them with looks of uplifted pride, feeling new trust in the grim, always confident weapons in their hands. And they were men.

CHAPTER 21

PRESENTLY THEY KNEW that no fighting threatened them. All ways seemed once more opened to them. The dusty blue lines of their friends were disclosed a short distance away. In the distance there were many colossal noises, but in all this part of the field there was a sudden stillness.

They perceived that they were free. The depleted band drew a long breath of relief and gathered itself into a bunch to complete its trip.

In this last length of journey the men began to show strange emotions. They hurried with nervous fear. Some who had been dark and unfaltering in the grimmest moments now could not conceal an anxiety that made them frantic. It was perhaps that they dreaded to be killed in insignificant ways after the times for proper military deaths had passed. Or, perhaps, they thought it would be too ironical to get killed at the portals of safety. With backward looks of perturbation, they hastened.

As they approached their own lines there was some sarcasm exhibited on the part of a gaunt and bronzed regiment that lay resting in the shade of trees. Questions were wafted to them.

"Where th' hell yeh been?"

"What yeh comin' back fer?"

"Why didn't yeh stay there?"

"Was it warm out there, sonny?"

"Goin' home now, boys?"

One shouted in taunting mimicry: "Oh, mother, come quick an' look at th' sojers!"

There was no reply from the bruised and battered regiment, save that one man made broadcast challenges to fist fights and the red-bearded officer walked rather near and glared in great swashbuckler style at a tall captain in the other regiment. But the lieutenant suppressed the man who wished to fist fight, and the tall captain, flushing at the little fanfare of the red-bearded one, was obliged to look intently at some trees.

The youth's tender flesh was deeply stung by these remarks. From under his creased brows he glowered with hate at the mockers. He meditated upon a few revenges. Still, many in the regiment hung their heads in criminal fashion, so that it came to pass that the men trudged with sudden heaviness, as if they bore upon their bended shoulders the coffin of their honor. And the youthful lieutenant, recollecting himself, began to mutter softly in black curses.

They turned when they arrived at their old position to regard the ground over which they had charged.

The youth in this contemplation was smitten with a large astonishment. He discovered that the distances, as compared with the brilliant measurings of his mind, were trivial and ridiculous. The stolid trees, where much had taken place, seemed incredibly near. The time, too, now that he reflected, he saw to have been short. He wondered at the number of emotions and events that had been crowded into such little spaces. Elfin [1] thoughts must have exaggerated and enlarged everything, he said.

It seemed, then, that there was bitter justice in the speeches of the gaunt and bronzed veterans. He veiled a glance of disdain at his fellows who strewed the ground, choking with dust, red from perspiration, misty-eyed, disheveled.

They were gulping at their canteens, fierce to wring every mite of water from them, and they polished at their swollen and watery features with coat sleeves and bunches of grass.

However, to the youth there was a considerable joy in musing upon his performances during the charge. He had had very little time previously in which to appreciate himself, so that there was now much satisfaction in quietly thinking of his actions. He recalled bits of color that in the flurry had stamped themselves unawares upon his engaged senses.

As the regiment lay heaving from its hot exertions, the officer who had named them as mule drivers came galloping along the line. He had lost his cap. His tousled hair streamed wildly, and his face was dark with vexation and wrath. His temper was displayed with more clearness by the way in which he managed his horse. He jerked and wrenched savagely at his bridle, stopping the hard-breathing animal with a furious pull near the colonel of the regiment. He immediately exploded in reproaches which came unbidden to the ears of the men. They were suddenly alert, being always curious about black words between officers.

"Oh, thunder, MacChesnay, what an awful bull [2] you made of this thing!" began the officer. He attempted low tones, but his indignation caused certain of the men to learn the sense of his words. "What an awful mess you made! Good Lord, man, you stopped about a hundred feet this side of a very pretty success! If your men had gone a hundred feet farther you would have made a great charge, but as it is— what a lot of mud diggers you've got anyway!"

The men, listening with bated breath, now turned their curious eyes upon the colonel. They had a ragamuffin interest in this affair.

The colonel was seen to straighten his form and put one hand forth in oratorical fashion. He wore an injured air; it was as

---

[1] **Elfin:** elfish; here, mischievous.

[2] **bull:** blunder (slang).

if a deacon had been accused of stealing. The men were wiggling in an ecstasy of excitement.

But of a sudden the colonel's manner changed from that of a deacon to that of a Frenchman. He shrugged his shoulders. "Oh, well, general, we went as far as we could," he said calmly.

"As far as you could? Did you, b'Gawd?" snorted the other. "Well, that wasn't very far, was it?" he added, with a glance of cold contempt into the other's eyes. "Not very far, I think. You were intended to make a diversion in favor of Whiterside. How well you succeeded your own ears can now tell you." He wheeled his horse and rode stiffly away.

The colonel, bidden to hear the jarring noises of an engagement in the woods to the left, broke out in vague damnations.

The lieutenant, who had listened with an air of impotent rage to the interview, spoke suddenly in firm and undaunted tones. "I don't care what a man is—whether he is a general or what—if he says th' boys didn't put up a good fight out there he's a damned fool."

"Lieutenant," began the colonel, severely, "this is my own affair, and I'll trouble you——"

The lieutenant made an obedient gesture. "All right, colonel, all right," he said. He sat down with an air of being content with himself.

The news that the regiment had been reproached went along the line. For a time the men were bewildered by it. "Good thunder!" they ejaculated, staring at the vanishing form of the general. They conceived it to be a huge mistake.

Presently, however, they began to believe that in truth their efforts had been called light. The youth could see this conviction weigh upon the entire regiment until the men were like cuffed and cursed animals, but withal rebellious.

The friend, with a grievance in his eye, went to the youth. "I wonder what he does want," he said. "He must think we went out there an' played marbles! I never see sech a man!"

The youth developed a tranquil philosophy for these moments of irritation. "Oh, well," he rejoined, "he probably didn't see nothing of it at all and got mad as blazes and concluded we were a lot of sheep, just because we didn't do what he wanted done. It's a pity old Grandpa Henderson got killed yestirday—he'd have known that we did our best and fought good. It's just our awful luck, that's what."

"I should say so," replied the friend. He seemed to be deeply wounded at an injustice. "I should say we did have awful luck! There's no fun in fightin' fer people when everything yeh do—no matter what—ain't done right. I have a notion t' stay behind next time an' let 'em take their ol' charge an' go t' th' devil with it."

The youth spoke soothingly to his comrade. "Well, we both did good. I'd like to see the fool what'd say we both didn't do as good as we could!"

"Of course we did," declared the friend stoutly. "An' I'd break th' feller's neck if he was as big as a church. But we're all right, anyhow, for I heard one feller say that we two fit th' best in th' reg'ment, an' they had a great argument 'bout it. Another feller, 'a course, he had t' up an' say it was a lie—he seen all what was goin' on an' he never seen us from th' beginnin' t' th' end. An' a lot more struck in an' ses it wasn't a lie—we did fight like thunder, an' they give us quite a send-off. But this is what I can't stand—these everlastin' ol' soldiers, titterin' an' laughin', an' then that general, he's crazy."

The youth exclaimed with sudden exasperation: "He's a lunkhead! He makes me mad. I wish he'd come along next time. We'd show 'im what——"

He ceased because several men had come hurrying up. Their faces expressed a bringing of great news.

"O Flem, yeh jest oughta heard!" cried one, eagerly.

"Heard what?" said the youth.

"Yeh jest oughta heard!" repeated the other, and he arranged himself to tell his tidings. The others made an excited circle.

"Well, sir, th' colonel met your lieutenant right by us—it was damnedest thing I ever heard––an' he ses: 'Ahem! ahem!' he ses. 'Mr. Hasbrouck!' he ses, 'by th' way, who was that lad what carried th' flag?' he ses. There, Flemin', what d' yeh think 'a that? 'Who was th' lad what carried th' flag?' he ses, an' th' lieutenant, he speaks up right away: 'That's Flemin', an' he's a jimhickey,' he ses, right away. What? I say he did. 'A jimhickey,' he ses—those 'r his words. He did, too. I say he did. If you kin tell this story better than I kin, go ahead an' tell it. Well, then, keep yer mouth shet. Th' lieutenant, he ses: 'He's a jimhickey,' an' th' colonel, he ses: 'Ahem! ahem! he is, indeed, a very good man t' have, ahem! He kep' th' flag 'way t' th' front. I saw 'im. He's a good un,' ses th' colonel. 'You bet,' ses th' lieutenant, 'he an' a feller named Wilson was at th' head 'a th' charge, an' howlin' like Indians all th' time,' he ses. 'Head a' th' charge all th' time,' he ses. 'A feller named Wilson,' he ses. There, Wilson, m'boy, put that in a letter an' send it hum t' yer mother, hay? 'A feller named Wilson,' he ses. An' th' colonel, he ses: 'Were they, indeed? Ahem! ahem! My sakes!' he ses. 'At th' head a' th' reg'ment?' he ses. 'They were,' ses th' lieutenant. 'My sakes!' ses th' colonel. He ses: 'Well, well, well,' he ses, 'those two babies?' 'They were,' ses th' lieutenant. 'Well, well,' ses th' colonel, 'they deserve t' be major-generals,' he ses. 'They deserve t' be major-generals.'"

The youth and his friend had said: "Huh!" "Yer lyin', Thompson." "Oh, go t' blazes!" "He never sed it." "Oh, what a lie!" "Huh!" But despite these youthful scoffings and embarrassments, they knew that their faces were deeply flushing from thrills of pleasure. They exchanged a secret glance of joy and congratulation.

They speedily forgot many things. The past held no pictures of error and disappointment. They were very happy, and their hearts swelled with grateful affection for the colonel and the youthful lieutenant.

CHAPTER 22

WHEN THE WOODS again began to pour forth the dark-hued masses of the enemy the youth felt serene self-confidence. He smiled briefly when he saw men dodge and duck at the long screechings of shells that were thrown in giant handfuls over them. He stood, erect and tranquil, watching the attack begin against a part of the line that made a blue curve along the side of an adjacent hill. His vision being unmolested by smoke from the rifles of his companions, he had opportunities to see parts of the hard fight. It was a relief to perceive at last from whence came some of these noises which had been roared into his ears.

Off a short way he saw two regiments fighting a little separate battle with two other regiments. It was in a cleared space, wearing a set-apart look. They were blazing as if upon a wager, giving and taking tremendous blows. The firings were incredibly fierce and rapid. These intent regiments apparently were oblivious of all larger purposes of war, and were slugging each other as if at a matched game.

In another direction he saw a magnificent brigade going with the evident intention of driving the enemy from a wood. They passed in out of sight and presently there was a most awe-inspiring racket in the wood. The noise was unspeakable. Having stirred this prodigious uproar, and, apparently, finding it too prodigious, the brigade, after a little time, came marching airily out again with its fine formation in nowise disturbed. There were no traces of speed in its movements. The brigade was jaunty and seemed to point a proud thumb at the yelling wood.

On a slope to the left there was a long row of guns, gruff and maddened, denouncing the enemy, who, down through the woods, were forming for another attack in the pitiless monotony of conflicts. The round red discharges from the guns made a crimson flare and a high, thick smoke. Occasional glimpses could be caught of groups of the toiling artillery-men. In the rear of this row of guns stood a house, calm and white, amid bursting shells. A congregation of horses, tied to a long railing, were tugging frenziedly at their bridles. Men were running hither and thither.

The detached battle between the four regiments lasted for some time. There chanced to be no interference, and they settled their dispute by themselves. They struck savagely and powerfully at each other for a period of minutes, and then the lighter-hued regiments faltered and drew back, leaving the dark-blue lines shouting. The youth could see the two flags shaking with laughter amid the smoke remnants.

Presently there was a stillness, pregnant with meaning. The blue lines shifted and changed a trifle and stared expectantly at the silent woods and fields before them. The hush was solemn and churchlike, save for a distant battery that, evidently unable to remain quiet, sent a faint rolling thunder over the ground. It irritated, like the noises of unimpressed boys. The men imagined that it would prevent their perched ears from hearing the first words of the new battle.

Of a sudden the guns on the slope roared out a message of warning. A splut-tering sound had begun in the woods. It swelled with amazing speed to a profound clamor that involved the earth in noises. The splitting crashes swept along the lines until an interminable roar was developed. To those in the midst of it, it became a din fitted to the universe. It was the whirring and thumping of gigantic machinery, com-plications among the smaller stars. The youth's ears were filled up. They were in-capable of hearing more.

On an incline over which a road wound, he saw wild and desperate rushes of men perpetually backward and forward in riot-ous surges. These parts of the opposing armies were two long waves that pitched upon each other madly at dictated points.

To and fro they swelled. Sometimes, one side by its yells and cheers would pro-claim decisive blows, but a moment later the other side would be all yells and cheers. Once the youth saw a spray of light forms go in houndlike leaps toward the waving blue lines. There was much howling, and presently it went away with a vast mouthful of prisoners. Again, he saw a blue wave dash with such thunder-ous force against a gray obstruction that it seemed to clear the earth of it and leave nothing but trampled sod. And always in their swift and deadly rushes to and fro the men screamed and yelled like maniacs.

Particular pieces of fence or secure po-sitions behind collections of trees were wrangled over, as gold thrones or pearl bedsteads. There were desperate lunges at these chosen spots seemingly every in-stant, and most of them were bandied like light toys between the contending forces. The youth could not tell from the battle flags flying like crimson foam in many directions which color of cloth was win-ning.

His emaciated [1] regiment bustled forth with undiminished fierceness when its time came. When assaulted again by bul-lets, the men burst out in a barbaric cry of rage and pain. They bent their heads in aims of intent hatred behind the pro-jected hammers of their guns. Their ram-rods clanged loud with fury as their eager arms pounded the cartridges into the rifle barrels. The front of the regiment was a smoke-wall penetrated by the flashing points of yellow and red.

Wallowing in the fight, they were in an astonishingly short time resmudged. They surpassed in stain and dirt all their pre-vious appearances. Moving to and fro with strained exertion, jabbering the while, they were, with their swaying bodies, black faces, and glowing eyes, like strange and ugly fiends jigging heavily in the smoke.

[1] **emaciated:** here, greatly reduced in size and strength.

The lieutenant, returning from a tour after a bandage, produced from a hidden receptacle of his mind new and portentous [1] oaths suited to the emergency. Strings of expletives he swung lashlike over the backs of his men, and it was evident that his previous efforts had in nowise impaired his resources.

The youth, still the bearer of the colors, did not feel his idleness. He was deeply absorbed as a spectator. The crash and swing of the great drama made him lean forward, intent-eyed, his face working in small contortions. Sometimes he prattled, words coming unconsciously from him in grotesque exclamations. He did not know that he breathed; that the flag hung silently over him, so absorbed was he.

A formidable line of the enemy came within dangerous range. They could be seen plainly—tall, gaunt men with excited faces running with long strides toward a wandering fence.

At sight of this danger the men suddenly ceased their cursing monotone. There was an instant of strained silence before they threw up their rifles and fired a plumping volley at the foes. There had been no order given; the men, upon recognizing the menace, had immediately let drive their flock of bullets without waiting for word of command.

But the enemy were quick to gain the protection of the wandering line of fence. They slid down behind it with remarkable celerity, and from this position they began briskly to slice up the blue men.

These latter braced their energies for a great struggle. Often, white clenched teeth shone from the dusky faces. Many heads surged to and fro, floating upon a pale sea of smoke. Those behind the fence frequently shouted and yelped in taunts and gibelike [2] cries, but the regiment maintained a stressed silence. Perhaps, at this new assault, the men recalled the fact that they had been named mud diggers, and it made their situation thrice bitter. They

were breathlessly intent upon keeping the ground and thrusting away the rejoicing body of the enemy. They fought swiftly and with a despairing savageness denoted in their expressions.

The youth had resolved not to budge whatever should happen. Some arrows of scorn that had buried themselves in his heart had generated strange and unspeakable hatred. It was clear to him that his final and absolute revenge was to be achieved by his dead body lying, torn and guttering,[3] upon the field. This was to be a poignant retaliation upon the officer who had said "mule drivers," and later "mud diggers," for in all the wild graspings of his mind for a unit responsible for his sufferings and commotions he always seized upon the man who had dubbed him wrongly. And it was his idea, vaguely formulated, that his corpse would be for those eyes a great and salt reproach.

The regiment bled extravagantly. Grunting bundles of blue began to drop. The orderly sergeant of the youth's company was shot through the cheeks. Its supports being injured, his jaw hung afar down, disclosing in the wide cavern of his mouth a pulsing mass of blood and teeth. And with all he made attempts to cry out. In his endeavor there was a dreadful earnestness, as if he conceived that one great shriek would make him well.

The youth saw him presently go rearward. His strength seemed in nowise impaired. He ran swiftly, casting wild glances for succor.

Others fell down about the feet of their companions. Some of the wounded crawled out and away, but many lay still, their bodies twisted into impossible shapes.

The youth looked once for his friend. He saw a vehement young man, powder-smeared and frowzled,[4] whom he knew to be him. The lieutenant, also, was unscathed in his position at the rear. He had continued to curse, but it was now

---

[1] **portentous:** here, frightful.
[2] **gibelike:** jeering.
[3] **guttering:** here, bleeding heavily.
[4] **frowzled:** disheveled.

with the air of a man who was using his last box of oaths.

For the fire of the regiment had begun to wane and drip. The robust voice, that had come strangely from the thin ranks, was growing rapidly weak.

CHAPTER 23

THE COLONEL came running along back of the line. There were other officers following him. "We must charge'm!" they shouted. "We must charge'm!" they cried with resentful voices, as if anticipating a rebellion against this plan by the men.

The youth, upon hearing the shouts, began to study the distance between him and the enemy. He made vague calculations. He saw that to be firm soldiers they must go forward. It would be death to stay in the present place, and with all the circumstances to go backward would exalt too many others. Their hope was to push the galling foes away from the fence.

He expected that his companions, weary and stiffened, would have to be driven to this assault, but as he turned toward them he perceived with a certain surprise that they were giving quick and unqualified expressions of assent. There was an ominous, clanging overture to the charge when the shafts of the bayonets rattled upon the rifle barrels. At the yelled words of command the soldiers sprang forward in eager leaps. There was new and unexpected force in the movement of the regiment. A knowledge of its faded and jaded condition made the charge appear like a paroxysm, a display of the strength that comes before a final feebleness. The men scampered in insane fever of haste, racing as if to achieve a sudden success before an exhilarating fluid should leave them. It was a blind and despairing rush by the collection of men in dusty and tattered blue, over a green sward and under a sapphire sky, toward a fence, dimly outlined in smoke, from behind which spluttered the fierce rifles of enemies.

The youth kept the bright colors to the front. He was waving his free arm in furious circles, the while shrieking mad calls and appeals, urging on those that did not need to be urged, for it seemed that the mob of blue men hurling themselves on the dangerous group of rifles were again grown suddenly wild with an enthusiasm of unselfishness. From the many firings starting toward them, it looked as if they would merely succeed in making a great sprinkling of corpses on the grass between their former position and the fence. But they were in a state of frenzy, perhaps because of forgotten vanities, and it made an exhibition of sublime recklessness. There was no obvious questioning, nor figurings, nor diagrams. There was, apparently, no considered loophole. It appeared that the swift wings of their desires would have shattered against the iron gates of the impossible.

He himself felt the daring spirit of a savage, religion-mad. He was capable of profound sacrifices, a tremendous death. He had no time for dissections, but he knew that he thought of the bullets only as things that could prevent him from reaching the place of his endeavor. There were subtle flashings of joy within him that thus should be his mind.

He strained all his strength. His eyesight was shaken and dazzled by the tension of thought and muscle. He did not see anything excepting the mist of smoke gashed by the little knives of fire, but he knew that in it lay the aged fence of a vanished farmer protecting the snuggled bodies of the gray men.

As he ran, a thought of the shock of contact gleamed in his mind. He expected a great concussion when the two bodies

of troops crashed together. This became a part of his wild battle madness. He could feel the onward swing of the regiment about him, and he conceived of a thunderous, crushing blow that would prostrate the resistance and spread consternation and amazement for miles. The flying regiment was going to have a catapultian [1] effect. This dream made him run faster among his comrades, who were giving vent to hoarse and frantic cheers.

But presently he could see that many of the men in gray did not intend to abide the blow. The smoke, rolling, disclosed men who ran, their faces still turned. These grew to a crowd, who retired stubbornly. Individuals wheeled frequently to send a bullet at the blue wave.

But at one part of the line there was a grim and obdurate group that made no movement. They were settled firmly down behind posts and rails. A flag, ruffled and fierce, waved over them and their rifles dinned fiercely.

The blue whirl of men got very near, until it seemed that in truth there would be a close and frightful scuffle. There was an expressed disdain in the opposition of the little group that changed the meaning of the cheers of the men in blue. They became yells of wrath, directed, personal. The cries of the two parties were now in sound an interchange of scathing insults.

They in blue showed their teeth; their eyes shone all white. They launched themselves as at the throats of those who stood resisting. The space between dwindled to an insignificant distance.

The youth had centered the gaze of his soul upon that other flag. Its possession would be high pride. It would express bloody minglings, near blows. He had a gigantic hatred for those who made great difficulties and complications. They caused it to be as a craved treasure of mythology, hung amid tasks and contrivances of danger.

He plunged like a mad horse at it. He was resolved it should not escape if wild blows and darings of blows could seize it. His own emblem, quivering and aflare, was winging toward the other. It seemed there would shortly be an encounter of strange beaks and claws, as of eagles.

The swirling body of blue men came to a sudden halt at close and disastrous range and roared a swift volley. The group in gray was split and broken by this fire, but its riddled body still fought. The men in blue yelled again and rushed in upon it.

The youth, in his leapings, saw, as through a mist, a picture of four or five men stretched upon the ground or writhing upon their knees with bowed heads as if they had been stricken by bolts from the sky. Tottering among them was the rival color bearer, who the youth saw had been bitten vitally by the bullets of the last formidable volley. He perceived this man fighting a last struggle, the struggle of one whose legs are grasped by demons. It was a ghastly battle. Over his face was the bleach of death, but set upon it were the dark and hard lines of desperate purpose. With this terrible grin of resolution he hugged his precious flag to him and was stumbling and staggering in his design to go the way that led to safety for it.

But his wounds always made it seem that his feet were retarded, held, and he fought a grim fight, as with invisible ghouls fastened greedily upon his limbs. Those in advance of the scampering blue men, howling cheers, leaped at the fence. The despair of the lost was in his eyes as he glanced back at them.

The youth's friend went over the obstruction in a tumbling heap and sprang at the flag as a panther at prey. He pulled at it and, wrenching it free, swung up its red brilliancy with a mad cry of exultation even as the color bearer, gasping, lurched over in a final throe and, stiffening convulsively, turned his dead face to the ground. There was much blood upon the grass blades.

[1] **catapultian:** referring to a catapult, an ancient military machine used to hurl heavy missiles.

[CONTINUED ON PAGE 471]

Americans Abroad

During the second half of the nineteenth century, while Eakins and Homer were forming powerful styles out of their own native experience, other American painters were being attracted to Europe by exciting new developments in the world of art. Most of these painters went abroad to study in famous art academies or in studio classes supervised by painters of international renown. But once there, some found life in Europe so stimulating that they lingered on for many years. A few even settled abroad permanently as American expatriates.

One of these expatriates was James A. McNeill Whistler, an American-born painter who had grown up mainly in St. Petersburg, Russia. Whistler returned to America as a youth, stayed a few years, and then, at the age of eighteen, decided to study painting in Paris. During the next two decades he established a reputation, first in Paris and then in London, as an outstanding painter of exquisite decorative compositions.

Whistler was one of the first Western painters to appreciate and collect Japanese art. Through a careful study of Japanese woodblock color prints, he learned to simplify his compositions—to combine a few large, boldly silhouetted shapes with delicately toned passages of open space. Look, for example, at his painting *Old Battersea Bridge* (PLATE 1), a London scene on the Thames. To call attention to its harmonies of color, which he likened to harmonies of sound in music, Whistler later retitled this picture *Nocturne in Blue and Gold.*

Another famous European art center was the German city of Munich. There, within five years, a young man from St. Louis named William Merritt Chase developed from a promising artist into a remarkably skilled one. Upon returning to America in 1878, Chase opened a spacious studio in New York, which soon became a well-known meeting place for artists and students. His extraordinary collection of pictures, sumptuous furnishings, and exotic knickknacks from Europe can be seen in his painting entitled *In the Studio* (PLATE 2).

The first woman to figure prominently in the history of both American and European art was a Philadelphian named Mary Cassatt, who went to

463

Europe in her early twenties and remained there the rest of her life. When she settled in Paris in 1873, Mary Cassatt began to participate in an exciting new movement called "Impressionism," a movement formed by a small group of young French painters who were fascinated with the color of light and with the changing aspects of everyday life. She herself was mainly interested in painting scenes of women and children, such as *The Boating Party* (PLATE 3), which shows a mother and child on a Mediterranean excursion. This large oil of the early 1890's shows how much Cassatt was influenced by the bold patterns and clear colors of Japanese prints. By comparing PLATES 1 and 3 you can see how differently Mary Cassatt and Whistler made use of this same source of inspiration.

One of the most widely celebrated American painters of this period was John Singer Sargent. Like Whistler and Mary Cassatt, Sargent spent most of his life in Europe. Eventually making London his headquarters, as Whistler had done before him, Sargent developed an extraordinary reputation as a painter of fashionable portraits. A good example of his fluid, virtuoso style is his double portrait, *Mr. and Mrs. Isaac Newton Phelps Stokes* (PLATE 4), which he painted in 1897. Sargent began this painting as a portrait of Mrs. Stokes alone, posing her in evening dress next to a small round table. But when she arrived for her sixth sitting (or "standing") in tennis clothes, her cheeks flushed from her morning walk, Sargent decided then and there to rub out what he had already painted and pose her just as she was. He intended to replace the table with a Great Dane owned by one of his friends, so that Mrs. Stokes could be portrayed with her right hand patting the dog's head. But when it was learned that the dog would not be available, Mr. Stokes jokingly offered to take its place. To his great surprise, Sargent accepted the offer and proceeded to paint him into the picture in two sittings. Mrs. Stokes's radiant beauty proved more elusive, for Sargent was not satisfied with her portrait until she had posed twenty-eight times.

Like Mary Cassatt, Maurice Prendergast and Childe Hassam were also both strongly influenced by French Impressionism. The lives of these two men were curiously similar: both were born in Massachusetts in 1859, both went to Paris in 1886, and both eventually returned to America. But their styles of painting were completely different. Prendergast was more attracted to the Impressionists' rich, bright colors than to their tonal effects of light and atmosphere. In his later paintings, such as *Ponte della Paglia* (PLATE 5), which shows people crossing a busy Venetian bridge, he transformed whole scenes into lively patterns of bright color-patches, creating a decorative quality somewhat like the sparkle of inlaid stones in a mosaic.

Hassam, on the other hand, was interested mainly in capturing the soft visual effects of light and atmosphere. After returning to America, he devoted many of his pictures to scenes like the one in PLATE 6, *Late Afternoon, New York: Winter,* a view of a New York City street during a snowfall.

PLATE 1. JAMES A. MCNEILL WHISTLER (1834–1903): *Nocturne in Blue and Gold: Old Battersea Bridge*. 1877. Oil on canvas, $26\frac{1}{4}$ x $19\frac{3}{4}$ inches. (Reproduced by courtesy of the Trustees, The Tate Gallery, London)

PLATE 2. WILLIAM MERRITT CHASE (1849–1916): *In the Studio.* 1880–83. Oil on canvas, 76 x 52 inches. (The Brooklyn Museum)

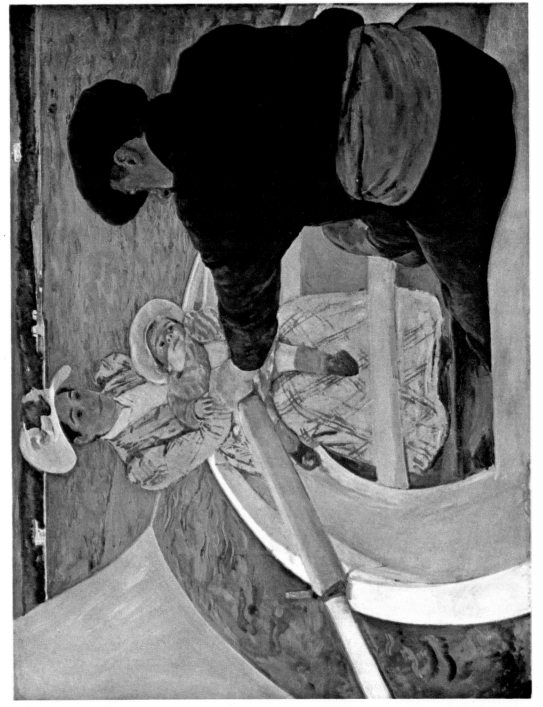

PLATE 3. MARY CASSATT (1845–1926): *The Boating Party.* About 1893. Oil on canvas, $35\frac{1}{2}$ x $46\frac{1}{4}$ inches. (National Gallery of Art, Washington, D.C., Chester Dale Collection)

PLATE 4. JOHN SINGER
SARGENT (1856–1925):
*Mr. and Mrs. Isaac New-
ton Phelps Stokes*. 1897.
Oil on canvas, 84¼ x 39¾
inches. (The Metropolitan
Museum of Art, New York,
Bequest of Edith Minturn
Stokes, 1938)

468

PLATE 5. MAURICE PRENDERGAST (1861–1924): *Ponte della Paglia*. 1899. Oil on canvas, 28 x 23 inches. (The Phillips Collection, Washington, D.C.)

PLATE 6. CHILDE HASSAM (1859–1935): *Late Afternoon, New York: Winter*. 1900. Oil on canvas, 37¼ x 29⅛ inches. (The Brooklyn Museum)

At the place of success there began more wild clamorings of cheers. The men gesticulated and bellowed in an ecstasy. When they spoke, it was as if they considered their listener to be a mile away. What hats and caps were left to them they often slung high in the air.

At one part of the line four men had been swooped upon, and they now sat as prisoners. Some blue men were about them in an eager and curious circle. The soldiers had trapped strange birds, and there was an examination. A flurry of fast questions was in the air.

One of the prisoners was nursing a superficial wound in the foot. He cuddled it, baby-wise, but he looked up from it often to curse with an astonishing utter abandon straight at the noses of his captors. He consigned them to red regions; he called upon the pestilential wrath of strange gods. And with it all he was singularly free from recognition of the finer points of the conduct of prisoners of war. It was as if a clumsy clod had trod upon his toe and he conceived it to be his privilege, his duty, to use deep, resentful oaths.

Another, who was a boy in years, took his plight with great calmness and apparent good nature. He conversed with the men in blue, studying their faces with his bright and keen eyes. They spoke of battles and conditions. There was an acute interest in all their faces during this exchange of viewpoints. It seemed a great satisfaction to hear voices from where all had been darkness and speculation.

The third captive sat with a morose countenance. He preserved a stoical and cold attitude. To all advances he made one reply without variation, "Ah, go t' hell!"

The last of the four was always silent and, for the most part, kept his face turned in unmolested directions. From the views the youth received he seemed to be in a state of absolute dejection. Shame was upon him, and with it profound regret that he was, perhaps, no more to be counted in the ranks of his fellows. The youth could detect no expression that would allow him to believe that the other was giving a thought to his narrowed future, the pictured dungeons, perhaps, and starvations and brutalities, liable to the imagination. All to be seen was shame for captivity and regret for the right to antagonize.

After the men had celebrated sufficiently, they settled down behind the old rail fence, on the opposite side to the one from which their foes had been driven. A few shot perfunctorily at distant marks.

There was some long grass. The youth nestled in it and rested, making a convenient rail support the flag. His friend, jubilant and glorified, holding his treasure with vanity, came to him there. They sat side by side and congratulated each other.

CHAPTER 24

THE ROARINGS that had stretched in a long line of sound across the face of the forest began to grow intermittent and weaker. The stentorian [1] speeches of the artillery continued in some distant encounter, but the crashes of the musketry had almost ceased. The youth and his friend of a sudden looked up, feeling a deadened form of distress at the waning of these noises, which had become a part of life. They could see changes going on among the troops. There were marchings this way and that way. A battery wheeled leisurely. On the crest of a small hill was the thick gleam of many departing muskets.

The youth arose. "Well, what now, I wonder?" he said. By his tone he seemed to be preparing to resent some new monstrosity in the way of dins and smashes.

---

[1] stentorian: very loud. In the *Iliad,* Stentor, a Greek herald, is described as having the voice of fifty men.

He shaded his eyes with his grimy hand and gazed over the field.

His friend also arose and stared. "I bet we're goin' t' git along out of this an' back over th' river," said he.

"Well, I swan!" said the youth.

They waited, watching. Within a little while the regiment received orders to retrace its way. The men got up grunting from the grass, regretting the soft repose. They jerked their stiffened legs and stretched their arms over their heads. One man swore as he rubbed his eyes. They all groaned "O Lord!" They had as many objections to this change as they would have had to a proposal for a new battle.

They trampled slowly back over the field across which they had run in a mad scamper.

The regiment marched until it had joined its fellows. The reformed brigade, in column, aimed through a wood at the road. Directly they were in a mass of dust-covered troops and were trudging along in a way parallel to the enemy's lines as these had been defined by the previous turmoil.

They passed within view of a stolid white house and saw in front of it groups of their comrades lying in wait behind a neat breastwork. A row of guns were booming at a distant enemy. Shells thrown in reply were raising clouds of dust and splinters. Horsemen dashed along the line of intrenchments.

At this point of its march the division curved away from the field and went winding off in the direction of the river. When the significance of this movement had impressed itself upon the youth, he turned his head and looked over his shoulder toward the trampled and débris-strewed ground. He breathed a breath of new satisfaction. He finally nudged his friend. "Well, it's all over," he said to him.

His friend gazed backward. "B'Gawd, it is," he assented. They mused.

For a time the youth was obliged to reflect in a puzzled and uncertain way. His mind was undergoing a subtle change. It took moments for it to cast off its battleful ways and resume its accustomed course of thought. Gradually his brain emerged from the clogged clouds, and at last he was enabled to more closely comprehend himself and circumstance.

He understood then that the existence of shot and countershot was in the past. He had dwelt in a land of strange, squalling upheavals and had come forth. He had been where there was red of blood and black of passion, and he was escaped. His first thoughts were given to rejoicings at this fact.

Later he began to study his deeds, his failures, and his achievements. Thus, fresh from scenes where many of his usual machines of reflection had been idle, from where he had proceeded sheeplike, he struggled to marshal all his acts.

At last they marched before him clearly. From this present viewpoint he was enabled to look upon them in spectator fashion and to criticize them with some correctness, for his new condition had already defeated certain sympathies.

Regarding his procession of memory he felt gleeful and unregretting, for in it his public deeds were paraded in great and shining prominence. Those performances which had been witnessed by his fellows marched now in wide purple and gold, having various deflections.[1] They went gaily with music. It was pleasure to watch these things. He spent delightful minutes viewing the gilded images of memory.

He saw that he was good. He recalled with a thrill of joy the respectful comments of his fellows upon his conduct.

Nevertheless, the ghost of his flight from the first engagement appeared to him and danced. There were small shoutings in his brain about these matters. For a moment he blushed, and the light of his soul flickered with shame.

A specter of reproach came to him. There loomed the dogging memory of the

[1] **deflections:** here, shades.

tattered soldier—he who, gored by bullets and faint for blood, had fretted concerning an imagined wound in another; he who had loaned his last of strength and intellect for the tall soldier; he who, blind with weariness and pain, had been deserted in the field.

For an instant a wretched chill of sweat was upon him at the thought that he might be detected in the thing. As he stood persistently before his vision, he gave vent to a cry of sharp irritation and agony.

His friend turned. "What's the matter, Henry?" he demanded. The youth's reply was an outburst of crimson oaths.

As he marched along the little branch-hung roadway among his prattling companions, this vision of cruelty brooded over him. It clung near him always and darkened his view of these deeds in purple and gold. Whichever way his thoughts turned, they were followed by the somber phantom of the desertion in the fields. He looked stealthily at his companions, feeling sure that they must discern in his face evidences of this pursuit. But they were plodding in ragged array, discussing with quick tongues the accomplishments of the late battle.

"Oh, if a man should come up an' ask me, I'd say we got a dum good lickin'."

"Lickin'—in yer eye! We ain't licked, sonny. We're going down here aways, swing aroun', an' come in behint 'em."

"Oh, hush, with your comin' in behint 'em. I've seen all 'a that I wanta. Don't tell me about comin' in behint——"

"Bill Smithers, he ses he'd rather been in ten hundred battles than been in that heluva hospital. He ses they got shootin' in th' night-time, an' shells dropped plum among 'em in th' hospital. He ses sech hollerin' he never see."

"Hasbrouck? He's th' best off'cer in this here reg'ment. He's a whale."

"Didn't I tell yeh we'd come aroun' in behint 'em? Didn't I tell yeh so? We——"

"Oh, shet yer mouth!"

For a time this pursuing recollection of the tattered man took all elation from the youth's veins. He saw his vivid error, and he was afraid that it would stand before him all his life. He took no share in the chatter of his comrades, nor did he look at them or know them, save when he felt sudden suspicion that they were seeing his thoughts and scrutinizing each detail of the scene with the tattered soldier.

Yet gradually he mustered force to put the sin at a distance. And at last his eyes seemed to open to some new ways. He found that he could look back upon the brass and bombast of his earlier gospels [1] and see them truly. He was gleeful when he discovered that he now despised them.

With this conviction came a store of assurance. He felt a quiet manhood, non-assertive but of sturdy and strong blood. He knew that he would no more quail before his guides wherever they should point. He had been to touch the great death and found that, after all, it was but the great death. He was a man.

So it came to pass that as he trudged from the place of blood and wrath his soul changed. He came from hot plow-shares [2] to prospects of clover tranquilly, and it was as if hot plowshares were not. Scars faded as flowers.

It rained. The procession of weary soldiers became a bedraggled train, despondent and muttering, marching with churning effort in a trough of liquid brown mud under a low, wretched sky. Yet the youth smiled, for he saw that the world was a world for him, though many discovered it to be made of oaths and walking sticks. He had rid himself of the red sickness of battle. The sultry nightmare was in the past. He had been an animal blistered and sweating in the heat and pain of war. He turned now with a lover's thirst to images of tranquil skies, fresh meadows, cool brooks—an existence of soft and eternal peace.

Over the river a golden ray of sun came through the hosts of leaden rain clouds.

[1] **gospels:** here, beliefs.

[2] **hot plowshares:** here, swords, and thus war in general (see the Old Testament, Isaiah 2:4).

1. What change has come over Wilson, the loud soldier? In what way does his behavior form a contrast to Henry's?

2. What is the tone of the following passage from the novel?

"He had been slow in the act of producing the packet because during it he had been trying to invent a remarkable comment upon the affair. He could conjure up nothing of sufficient point. He was compelled to allow his friend to escape unmolested with his packet. And for this he took unto himself considerable credit. It was a generous thing." (Page 441.)

Does this passage make you sympathetic toward Henry? Why or why not? Find two other passages, in other chapters, that have the same tone.

3. Account for Henry's bravery in Chapter 17. Do you think his behavior in this chapter is a sign of any great change in his character? Give reasons for your answer.

4. What is the effect on Henry of his over-hearing the conversation between his colonel and the general? What does the conversation reveal of the difference between the way in which a general experiences a war and the way in which a private soldier experiences it.

5. How and why did Henry Fleming become a hero in the last of the fighting? Do you think that Henry became a better man through this experience? Give reasons to support your answer.

6. The last of the many transformations of Henry Fleming occurs after his regiment has marched away from the battlefield. How has he changed? What has he learned about war and life itself? In answering this question, consider the following sentence: "He had been to touch the great death and found that, after all, it was but the great death."

7. Study the next-to-last paragraph of the novel. What do you think is the significance of Henry's turning "to images of tranquil skies, fresh meadows, cool brooks—an existence of soft and eternal peace"? In your opinion, should this passage be accepted at face value, or does it have an ironic undertone? Explain.

8. How may the last sentence of the novel be contrasted to the last sentence of Chapter 9? Do you think this last sentence is an appropriate conclusion to the novel? Why or why not?

THE NOVEL AS A WHOLE

1. One veteran of the War Between the States called this novel "a vicious satire upon American soldiers and American armies." Do you agree? Why or why not?

2. Crane's original title was *Private Fleming: His Various Battles*. Do you prefer this to the final title? Explain.

3. One of the major themes of the novel is the relationship of the individual to the group. Give an account of Henry's changing feelings about his regiment. Explain how these feelings are related to the more general theme.

4. Crane's expressive use of color has often been admired. There is a notable use of the color red in Chapter 9. What other uses are made of this color? Cite the uses of other colors. What are they meant to express?

5. *The Red Badge of Courage* has been criticized for lacking a plot: that is, for being just a loosely strung together collection of episodes. Do you think this criticism is justified? If not, explain how, in your opinion, all the episodes are connected. Into how many stages would you divide the plot? Why? If you think the criticism is justified, tell why the episodes fail to hang together.

6. Would you call *The Red Badge of Courage* a realistic or a naturalistic novel? (Before answering you may wish to review the discussion of realism and naturalism on pages 386–89.) Naturalism, as you have learned, depends on a view of human character and destiny. As Crane wrote of his novel *Maggie: A Girl of the Streets*, "... it tries to show that environment is a tremendous thing in the world and frequently shapes lives regardless." To what extent is Henry shaped by his environment, the stresses of war and combat? To what extent does he rise above environment? How do irony and esthetic distance (see below) influence your judgment of Henry?

ESTHETIC DISTANCE

One of the problems a writer of fiction must deal with is *esthetic distance*. That is, he must decide how much distance must be placed between the reader and the characters, particularly the main character. In a story or novel that is told by the main character, there is obviously very little distance. In a story told by a subsidiary character (such as "The Fall of the House of Usher"), there is more distance, and it is easier for the reader to stand aside from the main character and to judge him. In a story or novel told in the third person, there is usually even more distance. In some stories or novels written in the third person, however, where all the events are seen from the point of view of one character, the distance between the reader and the character is usually small. The reader tends to sympathize with that character and to agree with his reactions. In some cases, a casual reader may overlook certain signs—the wording of particular phrases and sentences—that indicate the author is giving an ironic presentation of the character's thoughts and feelings. Keeping in mind two problems related to distance—point of view (page 604) and irony (page 49)—consider the distance between the reader and Henry Fleming. To what extent should a reader sympathize with Henry? To what extent should he stand aside and judge him? Find specific passages that indicate Crane is treating Henry's thoughts and feelings ironically. You have already discussed the fact that Crane usually refers to his hero as "the youth" rather than by his name. How is this fact related to the problem of distance in the novel?

STYLE

One critic of the novel criticized its style, noting "the violent straining after effect in the mere unusual association of words, in the forced and distorted use of adjectives." He also attacked the "absurd similes." Another critic defended the style, stating that most of the expressions attacked "seemed to me admirable and picturesque." Study the italicized phrases below, which are among the expressions that the first critic found particularly objectionable. With which critic do you agree in general? Would you want to attack or defend any passage in particular? If so, why? What do you learn about Crane's use of language and images by studying these passages? For example, does Crane use images merely to appeal to the senses, or do his images also express moods and ideas?

1. "A brigade ahead of them and on the right went into action *with a rending roar*. It was as if it had exploded."
2. "The lieutenant of the youth's company was shot in the hand. He began to swear so wondrously that a nervous laugh went along the regimental line. The officer's profanity sounded conventional. It relieved the tightened senses of the new man. *It was as if he had hit his fingers with a tack hammer at home.*"

3. "Another [officer] was galloping about *bawling*. His hat was gone and his clothes were awry. *He resembled a man who has come from bed to go to a fire.*"
4. "There was a *blare of heated rage* . . ."
5. "The youth had reached an anguish where *the sobs scorched him.*"
6. *"They were ever upraising the ghost of shame on the stick of their curiosity."*
7. "The *new silence of his wound* made much worriment."
8. "The distance *was splintering* and blaring with the noise of fighting."
9. "began to *mutter softly in black curses.*"

FOR COMPOSITION

1. When *The Red Badge of Courage* first appeared, its readers were most impressed with what the American novelist Harold Frederic called its "tremendously effective battle painting." Discuss in a composition Crane's depiction of battle and of the experiences of men caught up in a battle. In your composition, consider one or more of the following contrasts, citing passages from the novel to support your points.
   a. Henry's ideas about war before he has actually been in a battle and his ideas about war at the end of the novel
   b. battle as experienced by privates and as experienced by generals
   c. battles as they appear in history books as a series of moves and countermoves and as they seem to the combatants
2. Consider the importance of the subordinate characters in *The Red Badge of Courage,* particularly the tall soldier, the loud soldier, the tattered man, and the cheerful man. What effect do these characters have on Henry? How are they sometimes used to contrast with Henry? How are they used to bring out the author's view of battle and war?
3. Some critics believe that *The Red Badge of Courage* is an account of a young man's progress toward moral perfection and of his victory over weakness and selfishness. Others maintain that the novel is instead a record of the changing delusions of a green farm boy whose actions and thoughts are determined by the grotesque and insane world of battle. State your own interpretation of the novel. Consider whether either of the interpretations summarized gives a satisfactory account of the novel. Support your own interpretation with reference to specific passages.

Realists and Naturalists

After the War Between the States, with industrialization and the growth of cities and large corporations, there developed a new outlook in American literature (see pages 385–86). In the new realistic mood of American prose, writers looked about and wrote about what they observed. Some writers found much to criticize in our changing society. Others sought to record an older society that was already beginning to pass away. Among the most outstanding writers of the period were:

William Dean Howells. Howells was not the greatest of our writers, but few writers ever dominated a generation as he did. As the editor of the *Atlantic Monthly,* he was the constant defender and encourager of realistic writers. In his book *Criticism and Fiction,* he developed a credo that other writers might follow. His own work as a pioneer of realism began with the novel, *A Modern Instance.* This book was followed by *The Rise of Silas Lapham* (1885), a story of a newly rich businessman who sought social acceptance from Boston society. These novels offer an impressively accurate picture of middle-class America of Howells' time.

Sarah Orne Jewett. Maine was the setting of Miss Jewett's sketches and stories. Impressed by the decay that struck Maine coastal towns when their days as active seaports were ended, she took the effects of this change as one of her chief subjects. She is best remembered for her volume of stories, *The Country of the Pointed Firs,* which is notable for its sympathetic portrayal of the simple lives of her Maine neighbors.

Hamlin Garland. Garland grew up in the prairie regions of Iowa and the Dakotas during the late nineteenth century. As an adult he saw prairie life in a fresh light. "All the gilding of farm life melted away. The hard and bitter realities came back on me with a flood . . . no splendor of cloud, no grace of sunset could conceal the poverty of these people." His short stories, collected in *Main Traveled Roads* (1891), dealt with the harsh farm life of the prairie region which he called the "Middle Border." His autobiography, *A Son of the Middle Border,* is an excellent picture of the late West.

Frank Norris. Norris died at thirty-two, perhaps before reaching the height of his powers. Inspired by the French realist Émile Zola, Norris produced several remarkable novels. *McTeague* is a story of poverty and greed in San Francisco. *The Octopus* is about the struggle between California wheat farmers and the railroads. *The Pit* deals with high finance and speculation on the Chicago wheat exchange.

Theodore Dreiser. Dreiser, whose novels extend into the modern period, lived to see his talents mature. His long encyclopedic novels have been criticized for their clumsy style and for their indiscriminate piling of detail on detail. They have also been praised for the power of their vision of life. By many critics, Dreiser is regarded as a major American writer. His important first novel, *Sister Carrie,* is concerned with a poor country girl's rise to success as an actress in New York. His most important novel is probably *An American Tragedy.*

THE AMERICAN NOVEL

A novel can be defined as a prose narrative that is longer than a short story. Some novels are very long, some barely longer than a long story. Set beside Tolstoy's *War and Peace,* which runs to more than fifteen hundred pages, Stephen Crane's *The Red Badge of Courage* seems very short indeed. But all novels are more complex, more ambitious undertakings than stories. In a novel, a writer can do more than in a story, and he must make more elaborate plans to achieve what he undertakes. Often a novel introduces many more characters than a short story, and many novels give a much more detailed picture of the society in which the characters move. A novel also enables the writer to make a more powerful statement about the world or the universe than does a short story. To reduce Melville's *Moby Dick*—his " 'No' in thunder" —to short-story length would be like compressing an electrical storm to a single burst of static. While a short story generally reveals a writer's artistry—his mastery of form and detail—a novel reveals, in addition, the size of his vision and his ability to deal with complex situations. Many of the short-story writers represented in this book are also fine novelists. In the following pages, we will consider what they and other writers have done to develop the American novel.

THE BEGINNINGS
OF THE AMERICAN NOVEL

In the last decade of the eighteenth century, two novels appeared that were to indicate several important directions that the American novel would take. One, *Modern Chivalry,* was by a Pennsylvania politician and judge, Hugh Henry Brackenridge. Modeled on Cervantes' *Don Quixote,* Brackenridge's novel tells of the travels through Pennsylvania of Captain John Farrago and his servant, Teague O'Regan. A journey through some part of

this country was to be an important element in later novels which exposed and commented upon a particular segment of American life. The scrapes which Teague gets into and from which he is rescued by Farrago give the author many opportunities to comment on society, especially on the problems facing the new American democracy. At one point Brackenridge cautions, "The demagogue is the first great destroyer of the Constitution by deceiving the people. . . . He is an aristocrat and seeks after more power than is just. He will never rest short of despotic rule."

Several years later, a very different kind of novel appeared. Charles Brockden Brown's *Wieland* was influenced by English novels like Horace Walpole's *The Castle of Otranto.* These novels, involving mysterious plots, melodramatic characters, and elements of suspense and horror, are known as Gothic novels, and Brown is generally regarded as the first "American Gothic" novelist. *Wieland* is about the tragic experiments of a ventriloquist who persuades others that they are hearing mysterious voices. One literary historian has commented that *"Wieland* derives its strength not merely from the exploitation of sensation, but from the blending of the Gothic method with philosophical, psychological, and moral implications to create a powerful, even if unbalanced, book." Using grotesque characters and situations to explore moral problems is a characteristic of many later American novels, from Nathaniel Hawthorne's *The House of the Seven Gables* to William Faulkner's *Light in August.*

THE GREAT EARLY NOVELISTS

While Brackenridge and Brown produced works that are considered significant by literary historians, their novels are rarely read today. Many years were to pass before America was to produce a novelist of real importance, one whose novels were admired by Americans and Europeans alike and who, because he created one of the great characters of literature, is still read today. In 1823, *The Pioneers* by James Fenimore Cooper, the first of five *Leatherstocking Tales* dealing with the frontiersman Natty Bumppo (see page 93), was published. In depicting Bumppo, the "natural man" who serves as a bond between the innocent ways of the forest and the complex ways of society, Cooper created one of the significant character types of American literature.

Five years after *The Pioneers,* Nathaniel Hawthorne's first novel, *Fanshawe,* appeared. The author regarded this work as a failure, and it is rarely read today. Many years later—in 1845—Hawthorne produced one of the masterpieces of American literature, *The Scarlet Letter.* Unlike Cooper's novels of adventure, *The Scarlet Letter* is a compact, intricately worked out story of how the lives of four people are affected by one sin. Carefully constructed and written, *The Scarlet Letter* is as notable for its artistry as for its psychological and moral depth. It showed later novelists—among them, Henry James and Willa Cather—what an American writer could accomplish when he set out not only to write a serious, morally complex novel but also a carefully shaped work of art in which hardly one word, one detail is wasted.

Hawthorne's friend Herman Melville (page 254) produced a very different novel. *Moby Dick* is a large, sprawling piece of work. No one would call it perfectly constructed, but many readers prize it above all other American novels for its tumultuous grapplings with the meaning of life and for its profoundly posed questions about man and his place in the universe. *Moby Dick,* as an exploration of the technique and form of the novel, probably has had little influence on subsequent novelists. It is a unique work of genius. But its example has encouraged modern novelists to wrestle with the same ques-

tions that tormented Melville, perhaps in the hope that such gigantic doubts would inspire in them an eloquence comparable to his.

POSTWAR NOVELISTS

Mark Twain, the greatest prose writer to emerge in America in the decade after the War Between the States, did not publish his masterpiece, *The Adventures of Huckleberry Finn,* until 1884. During his own lifetime, Mark Twain was known primarily as a humorist and a lecturer, a beloved public figure. Today his reputation rests on a small part of his work, notably *The Adventures of Tom Sawyer, Life on the Mississippi, Roughing It,* and above all, *Huckleberry Finn.* Ernest Hemingway wrote, "All modern American literature comes from one book by Mark Twain called *Huckleberry Finn."* It was the example of this novel that influenced writers such as Hemingway and Sherwood Anderson to develop a simple, flexible style based on common speech rhythms. And the story of the relationship between Huck the boy and Jim the runaway slave is one of the most moving and profound told by an American.

As realism came to dominate American writing (page 386), novelists turned more and more to close observation of the world they knew. William Dean Howells, influential as a magazine editor and critic, was also one of the foremost novelists of the period. Novels such as *The Rise of Silas Lapham* display minute observation of specific sections of society and of the interaction between different social levels. Henry James, who lived much of his life in England and wrote as much about the English as about Americans, spent his artistic life striving to make the novel a more sensitive, more subtle, more complex instrument for exploring the life around him (page 500). In his novels *Daisy Miller, Washington Square,* and *The American,* and in complex later works, including *The Ambassadors* and *The Wings of the Dove,* he probed not only social complexities but the mysteries of the individual personality.

Stephen Crane's *The Red Badge of Courage* is an outstanding example of the realistic novel (page 394). Although Crane lived to complete other novels and some fine short stories, his early death is one of the tragedies of American literature. Another important realistic writer is Frank Norris, whose novel *The Octopus* deals with the bitter commercial war between wheat farmers and the railroads, and whose *McTeague* carefully traces the degenerating effects of greed on one man. Regarded by some critics as a giant among realistic writers, Theodore Dreiser wrote long, detailed novels, among them *Sister Carrie* and *An American Tragedy*.

Three women novelists practiced the art of the realistic novel in a more restrained, subtle manner than either Dreiser or Norris. Willa Cather wrote of Nebraska farmers and of men and women caught by the limitations that society placed on them (page 491). Among the best of her finely crafted novels are *O Pioneers, My Ántonia, The Professor's House,* and *Death Comes for the Archbishop.* Ellen Glasgow, a member of a distinguished Virginia family, wrote about the contrast between the old and new South in works such as *Barren Ground* and *Vein of Iron.* Edith Wharton, a New Yorker and a friend of Henry James, wrote about the wealthy "aristocracy" of American cities in *The House of Mirth* and *The Age of Innocence. Ethan Frome,* set in isolated New England farm country, is perhaps her best-known book, although her least typical.

THE MODERN AMERICAN NOVEL

There have been a number of outstanding American novelists since World War I. Three of the most important—Ernest Hemingway (page 521), William Faulkner (page 536), and F. Scott Fitzgerald (page 550)—are discussed in the biographical introductions to their stories. Another important postwar novelist, Sinclair Lewis, caricatured some of the crudities of postwar life in *Main Street* and *Babbitt.* In *Arrowsmith* and *Dodsworth* he gave two American types, the scientist and the businessman, more sympathetic treatment. John Dos Passos in *Manhattan Transfer* and in his trilogy of novels called *U.S.A.* used experimental techniques to capture the movement of a city and of the entire country. Thornton Wilder wrote several distinguished novels including one—*The Bridge of San Luis Rey*—that won him a Pulitzer prize (page 744). Pearl Buck, winner of a Nobel prize, wrote *The Good Earth,* a remarkable study of a Chinese family. John Steinbeck (page 575), who received a Pulitzer prize for *The Grapes of Wrath,* was also awarded a Nobel prize. Thomas Wolfe's novels (page 684) have been praised for their poetry and vitality and have been criticized for their shapelessness. His first novel, *Look Homeward, Angel,* is probably his best. John P. Marquand's novels about old New England families, notably *The Late George Apley,* won him a reputation as a social satirist. Robert Penn Warren, also a poet and critic, is an important Southern novelist. Among his best novels are *Night Rider* and *All the King's Men.*

More recent writers who have produced important novels are J. D. Salinger (*The Catcher in the Rye*), John Knowles (*A Separate Peace*), Saul Bellow (*The Adventures of Augie March*), John Updike (*The Centaur, On the Farm*), and Ralph Ellison (*The Invisible Man*). All these writers continue to build on the base that Hawthorne, Melville, and Twain created. All continue to make the American novel a vital, changing form. It is impossible to predict what directions the novel will take in the future. But it is almost certain that American novelists will continue to produce exciting, challenging works—unsettling in their commentaries on society, deeply moving in their probings of the individual personality, exhilarating in their explorations of the novel as an artistic form.

EDWIN ARLINGTON ROBINSON
(1869–1935)

Edwin Arlington Robinson's poems about Richard Cory and the other inhabitants of Tilbury Town are bitter poems, but their biting quality is leavened by a restrained style and a wry appreciation of life's ironies. In a memoir published shortly after the death of his old friend, Robert Frost wrote that "any poet, to resemble him in the least, would have to resemble him in that grazing closeness to the spiritual realities." Frost also noted that Robinson's "outer seriousness" was balanced by an "inner humor," and he spoke of Robinson's "happy skill. His theme was unhappiness itself, but his skill was as happy as it was playful."

Edwin Arlington Robinson grew up in Gardiner, Maine, a town on the Kennebec River which became the Tilbury Town of his poetry. Gardiner had once been an active center of shipping. Robinson's father had been a prosperous timber merchant, but after his death, the family suddenly found itself poor. Two promising older brothers died young, and their mother's death was preceded by a long and painful illness. Robinson's poems grew out of his response to his family and his region, a land of suddenly diminished opportunities, of large old-fashioned houses, and of lonely dreamers who had once been prosperous and happy. In later life Robinson returned to Gardiner only three times: when he attended the funerals of his brothers and when he came to Maine in 1925 to receive an honorary degree from Bowdoin College.

After two years at Harvard, Robinson was forced to leave college because of his family's dwindling fortunes. He found his way to New York City, the "town down the river," where he lived in Greenwich Village, a quarter that has been the home of many artists and writers. In those years he was so poor that he often could pack all his possessions into one suitcase. He was a slight, shy man with little talent for practical affairs, but with great sympathy for those who were dispossessed, lonely, and troubled. The poet and anthologist Louis Untermeyer wrote of him, "His talk, like his expression, was colorless. All the color was in his verse. The attention and affection that most men reserve for their families, homes, friends, and careers, Robinson gave to his poetry. After Robinson's death, one magazine commented that for him, the craft of poetry had played the part of wife, children, job, and recreation."

When Robinson began publishing his poetry in the 1890's, there were few good American poets and almost no audience for him. He had to pay for the printing of his first two books, *The Torrent and the Night Before* and *The Children of the*

Night. Friends secretly subsidized the publication of *Captain Craig,* his third book, and former President Theodore Roosevelt used his influence to effect the publication of a fourth, *The Town Down the River.* When Robinson's poetry was discovered by Roosevelt, the poet was working underground inspecting loads of construction materials in an uncompleted subway. Roosevelt secured Robinson a clerkship in the New York Custom House, an action that recalls an earlier use of political patronage on Nathaniel Hawthorne's behalf (page 236). From now on, Robinson's worst financial difficulties were over. After 1911, he customarily spent his summers at the MacDowell Colony for artists in New Hampshire, and in the last years of his life, his books earned enough money to support him. He received the Pulitzer prize for poetry three times, in 1922, 1925, and 1928, and in the 1920's he was generally regarded as the greatest living American poet.

During the modern American poetic revival that began in the second decade of the century, Robinson was hailed as the foremost figure of the "New Poetry," but he had little in common with other figures of the revival such as Carl Sandburg and Amy Lowell. He had begun writing poetry long before most of them, and the forms he worked in were traditional, not experimental. Many of his poems are sonnets, and a great many are written in tight stanza forms. The poems most popular in his own lifetime were his long narratives about the court of King Arthur: *Merlin, Lancelot,* and *Tristram.* He was a master of the dramatic monologue, a form perfected earlier by the English poet Robert Browning. Robert Frost summed up Robinson's contribution to American poetry by writing that his old friend had "stayed content with the old way to be new."

Richard Cory

Whenever Richard Cory went downtown,
    We people on the pavement looked at him:
He was a gentleman from sole to crown,
    Clean-favored, and imperially slim.

And he was always quietly arrayed,   5
    And he was always human when he talked;
But still he fluttered pulses when he said,
    "Good morning," and he glittered when he walked.

And he was rich—yes, richer than a king—
    And admirably schooled in every grace: 10
In fine, we thought that he was everything
    To make us wish that we were in his place.

So on we worked, and waited for the light,
    And went without the meat, and cursed the bread;
And Richard Cory, one calm summer night,   15
    Went home and put a bullet through his head.

Miniver Cheevy

Miniver Cheevy, child of scorn,
    Grew lean while he assailed the seasons;
He wept that he was ever born,
    And he had reasons.

Miniver loved the days of old   5
    When swords were bright and steeds were prancing;
The vision of a warrior bold
    Would set him dancing.

Miniver sighed for what was not,
    And dreamed, and rested from his labors;   10
He dreamed of Thebes° and Camelot,°
    And Priam's° neighbors.

Miniver mourned the ripe renown
    That made so many a name so fragrant;
He mourned Romance, now on the town,°   15
    And Art, a vagrant.

Miniver loved the Medici,°
    Albeit° he had never seen one;
He would have sinned incessantly
    Could he have been one.   20

Miniver cursed the commonplace
    And eyed a khaki suit with loathing;
He missed the medieval grace
    Of iron clothing.

Miniver scorned the gold he sought,   25
    But sore annoyed was he without it;
Miniver thought, and thought, and thought,
    And thought about it.

Miniver Cheevy, born too late,
    Scratched his head and kept on thinking;   30
Miniver coughed, and called it fate,
    And kept on drinking.

---

11. **Thebes** (thēbz): a famous city of ancient Greece. **Camelot** (kam'ə·lot): the city of King Arthur and the Knights of the Round Table. 12. **Priam** (prī'əm): the king of Troy during the time the Greeks were besieging it. 15. **on the town:** on public relief. 17. **Medici** (med'ə·chē): the leading family of Florence, Italy, during the fifteenth and sixteenth centuries. 18. **Albeit** (ôl·bē'it): although.

Mr. Flood's Party

Old Eben Flood, climbing alone one night
Over the hill between the town below
And the forsaken upland hermitage
That held as much as he should ever know
On earth again of home, paused wearily.   5
The road was his with not a native near;
And Eben, having leisure, said aloud,
For no man else in Tilbury Town to hear:

"Well, Mr. Flood, we have the harvest moon
Again, and we may not have many more;   10
The bird is on the wing, the poet° says,
And you and I have said it here before.
Drink to the bird." He raised up to the light
The jug that he had gone so far to fill,
And answered huskily: "Well, Mr. Flood,   15
Since you propose it, I believe I will."

Alone, as if enduring to the end
A valiant armor of scarred hopes outworn,
He stood there in the middle of the road
Like Roland's ghost° winding a silent horn.   20
Below him, in the town among the trees,
Where friends of other days had honored him,
A phantom salutation of the dead
Rang thinly till old Eben's eyes were dim.

Then, as a mother lays her sleeping child   25
Down tenderly, fearing it may awake,
He set the jug down slowly at his feet
With trembling care, knowing that most things break;
And only when assured that on firm earth
It stood, as the uncertain lives of men   30
Assuredly did not, he paced away,
And with his hand extended paused again:

"Well, Mr. Flood, we have not met like this
In a long time; and many a change has come
To both of us, I fear, since last it was   35
We had a drop together. Welcome home!"

---

11. **poet:** Edward Fitzgerald in his translation of *The Rubáiyát of Omar Khayyám.*   20. **Roland's ghost:** Roland was a legendary hero who, in leading the forces of Charlemagne against the Saracens at Roncevalles, blew his horn for help before he died. Robinson may also have had in mind the hero of Robert Browning's poem, "Childe Roland to the Dark Tower Came."

Convivially returning with himself,
Again he raised the jug up to the light;
And with an acquiescent quaver said:
"Well, Mr. Flood, if you insist, I might.   40

"Only a very little, Mr. Flood—
For auld lang syne.° No more, sir; that will do."
So, for the time, apparently it did,
And Eben evidently thought so too;
For soon amid the silver loneliness   45
Of night he lifted up his voice and sang,
Secure, with only two moons listening,
Until the whole harmonious landscape rang—

"For auld lang syne." The weary throat gave out,
The last word wavered; and the song being done,   50
He raised again the jug regretfully
And shook his head, and was again alone.
There was not much that was ahead of him,
And there was nothing in the town below—
Where strangers would have shut the many doors   55
That many friends had opened long ago.

    42. **auld lang syne:** old times.

For a Dead Lady

No more with overflowing light
Shall fill the eyes that now are faded,
Nor shall another's fringe with night
Their woman-hidden world as they did.
No more shall quiver down the days   5
The flowing wonder of her ways,
Whereof no language may requite
The shifting and the many-shaded.

The grace, divine, definitive,
Clings only as a faint forestalling;   10
The laugh that love could not forgive
Is hushed, and answers to no calling;

The forehead and the little ears
Have gone where Saturn° keeps the years;
The breast where roses could not live   15
Has done with rising and with falling.

The beauty, shattered by the laws
That have creation in their keeping,
No longer trembles at applause,
Or over children that are sleeping;   20
And we who delve in beauty's lore
Know all that we have known before
Of what inexorable cause
Makes Time so vicious in his reaping.

14. **Saturn:** Saturn was the Roman god of seedtime and harvest. His emblem was the sickle.
Robinson seems to identify him with Father Time.

FOR STUDY AND DISCUSSION

RICHARD CORY

1. Explain what is meant by "he glittered when he walked." Explain the meaning of lines 13–14. How do these lines emphasize the difference between Cory and the other townspeople?

2. Why do you think Robinson used the pronoun "we" rather than the pronoun "I" throughout the poem? That is, why does he describe the reaction of a group of people to Richard Cory rather than the reaction of one sensitive individual? (To answer this question, it may help to reread the poem, substituting "I" wherever "we" occurs.)

3. What was your reaction to the last line of the poem? Do you think, judging from all the details that precede this line, that your reaction was the one Robinson was building toward? Explain. Why do you think Robinson does not supply a reason for Cory's final act?

MINIVER CHEEVY

1. How do the rhymes in this poem add to the amusing effect? Point out rhymes that you think are especially effective.

2. Explain how the lines "He missed the medieval grace/ Of iron clothing" reveal Robinson's attitude toward Miniver Cheevy. Cite other lines in the poem which reveal this attitude.

3. In your opinion, what conditions in modern life may produce men like Richard Cory and Miniver Cheevy?

MR. FLOOD'S PARTY

1. What does the first stanza reveal of Mr. Flood's circumstances? Read aloud the lines that are most revealing.

2. How is the precise place where Mr. Flood stops important to the poem? How do the first and last stanzas bring out this importance?

3. Why do you think Mr. Flood is compared to "Roland's ghost" in the third stanza? Do you think this simile and the line "A valiant armor of scarred hopes outworn" are appropriate to Mr. Flood? Explain. How do they make of him something more than an inebriated old man?

4. Many poets have found it difficult to write natural-sounding dialogue in a strict metrical pattern. Do you think Robinson overcomes this difficulty? Cite lines to support your answer.

5. Explain how pathos and humor are combined in "Miniver Cheevy" and "Mr. Flood's Party." Judging from these poems, would you say that humor and pathos are compatible in the same literary work, or do they tend to cancel each other out?

FOR A DEAD LADY

1. Explain lines 3 and 4. What is the antecedent of "they" in line 4?

2. What do you think was the relationship between the speaker and the lady? In answering this question, consider especially the line "The laugh that love could not forgive."

3. What word makes the last line of the poem particularly personal and forceful?

FOR COMPOSITION

Robinson shares a number of qualities with good modern short-story writers, particularly the ability to create interesting situations and striking characters. Yet he chose to be a poet, rather than a writer of fiction, perhaps because he believed that he could express more in a poem than in a story. In a brief composition, consider the differences between the short narrative or dramatic poem and the short story. What would a poem such as "Richard Cory" or "Miniver Cheevy" lose if it were adapted as a story? Would it gain anything?

Henry Adams

Born to one of the most respected families of Boston and of America, Henry Adams commented that in the game of life, "Probably no child, born in the year [1838] held better cards than he." Yet perhaps, he speculated, his strong sense of tradition had been an inadequate preparation for life in a changing world. "What could become of such a child of the seventeenth and eighteenth centuries when he should wake up to find himself required to play the game of the twentieth?"

Adams became a teacher at Harvard University and an eminent historian and writer. His most important work, *The Education of Henry Adams,* is a valuable record of a man of intellect trying to understand the changes around him. In this autobiography, written in the third person, Adams told of his encounter with a machine that symbolized the new age for him. At the Paris Exposition of 1900, Adams visited the hall of dynamos: "As he grew accustomed to the great gallery of machines, he [Adams] began to feel the forty-foot dynamos as a moral force, much as the early Christians felt the Cross. The planet itself felt less impressive in its old-fashioned, deliberate . . . revolution than this huge wheel. . . . Before the end, one began to pray to it; inherited instinct taught the natural expression of man before silent and infinite force. Among the thousand symbols of ultimate energy, the dynamo was not so human as some, but it was the most expressive."

In this famous passage Henry Adams set forth a memorable symbol for the new mechanized age.

EDGAR LEE MASTERS
(1869–1950)

Edgar Lee Masters was born in Kansas but grew up in southern Illinois, the same country where, forty years earlier, Lincoln had been a storekeeper, lawyer, and aspiring politician. In Masters' boyhood, the Middle West was not greatly changed from what it had been in the days of the pioneers. As a boy Masters knew Lincoln's old law partner, William Herndon. Later he recalled his grandfather's tales of wolf hunts in Tennessee, prairie schooners, and camp meetings held in the forest. After a brief stay at Knox College, Masters studied law in his father's law office in Lewiston, Illinois. He wrote many poems in traditional forms, imitating Poe, Keats, and Shelley. As a young man with literary ambitions, he found small-town life oppressive. In his autobiography he wrote, "I feel that no poet in English or American history had a harder life than mine was in the beginning at Lewiston among a people whose flesh and vibrations were better calculated to poison, to pervert, and even to kill a sensitive nature." When he was twenty-three, he moved to Chicago where he became the partner of a leading criminal lawyer and built up a large law practice. In his spare time, he wrote poems, plays, and essays, but none of his work attracted much attention.

In 1914, William Marion Reedy, an editor friend of Masters, gave him a copy of *Epigrams from the Greek Anthology*. The *Greek Anthology* is a collection of short Greek poems, many of them epitaphs that, in a few pointed lines, sum up the span of a man's life. These poems gave Masters the idea of writing their Middle Western counterparts, uncovering the wasted lives he had known in the small towns of southern Illinois. Instead of the traditional forms and meters he had used in his previous poetry, Masters chose to write his epitaphs in free verse, a form enjoying a revival in the work of Carl Sandburg and other contributors to the Chicago magazine *Poetry* (page 637). The epitaphs for the citizens of Spoon River are varied. A few of the inhabitants of the graveyard on the hill had lived full lives and were content, but far more were the bitter, frustrated victims of spiritual isolation. When *Spoon River Anthology* appeared, it was enthusiastically praised by some reviewers, bitterly attacked by others, and soon became a best seller. In drawing attention to the private tragedies of small Middle Western towns, it prepared the way for fiction writers such as Sinclair Lewis and Sherwood Anderson. Today *Spoon River Anthology* is regarded as an American classic. While the *Anthology* contains many fine individual poems, its full force is revealed only after it is read in its entirety, as it relentlessly lays open life after wasted life.

In 1920, Masters was able to give up the practice of law and devote himself entirely to literature. He wrote books of poetry, novels, biographies, and his autobiography, *Across Spoon River,* at the pace of about a book a year. None of his other books was nearly as successful as his *Anthology* or is as highly regarded. Yet, because of this single achievement, his place as an American poet and chronicler of the small town is secure.

Seth Compton

When I died, the circulating library
Which I built up for Spoon River,
And managed for the good of inquiring minds,
Was sold at auction on the public square,
As if to destroy the last vestige   5
Of my memory and influence.
For those of you who could not see the virtue
Of knowing Volney's *Ruins*° as well as Butler's *Analogy,*°
And *Faust*° as well as *Evangeline,*°
Were really the power in the village,   10
And often you asked me,
"What is the use of knowing the evil in the world?"
I am out of your way now, Spoon River,
Choose your own good and call it good.
For I could never make you see   15
That no one knows what is good
Who knows not what is evil;
And no one knows what is true
Who knows not what is false.

8. **Volney's *Ruins:*** a work on the philosophy of history by Constantine Volney (1757–1820), a French writer. **Butler's *Analogy:*** religious writings of an English bishop, Joseph Butler (1692–1752). 9. ***Faust*** (foust): a drama by the German poet Johann von Goethe (gœ′tə) (1749–1832). ***Evangeline:*** a poem by Longfellow.

Flossie Cabanis

From Bindle's opera house in the village
To Broadway is a great step.
But I tried to take it, my ambition fired
When sixteen years of age,
Seeing "East Lynne"° played here in the village   5
By Ralph Barrett, the coming
Romantic actor, who enthralled my soul.
True, I trailed back home, a broken failure,
When Ralph disappeared in New York,
Leaving me alone in the city—   10
But life broke him also.
In all this place of silence
There are no kindred spirits.
How I wish Duse° could stand amid the pathos
Of these quiet fields   15
And read these words.

5. **"East Lynne":** a melodrama popular in the early years of this century. 14. **Duse** (do͞o′zā): Eleonora Duse (1859–1924), a great Italian actress.

Petit, the Poet

Seeds in a dry pod, tick, tick, tick,
Tick, tick, tick, like mites in a quarrel—
Faint iambics that the full breeze wakens—
But the pine tree makes a symphony thereof.
Triolets, villanelles, rondels, rondeaus,   5
Ballades° by the score with the same old thought:
The snows and the roses of yesterday are vanished;°
And what is love but a rose that fades?
Life all around me here in the village:
Tragedy, comedy, valor and truth,   10
Courage, constancy, heroism, failure—

5–6. **Triolets ... Ballades:** different types of poems with intricate patterns. Often these poems are on trivial subjects but display considerable technical skill. 7. **The ... vanished:** "Where are the snows of yesteryear?" is a famous line in "The Ballade of the Dead Ladies" by François Villon (1431–?) as translated by Dante Gabriel Rossetti.

"Flossie Cabanis" from *Spoon River Anthology* by Edgar Lee Masters, published by The Macmillan Company, 1914, 1942. Reprinted by permission of Ellen C. Masters.
"Petit, the Poet" from *Spoon River Anthology* by Edgar Lee Masters, published by The Macmillan Company, 1914, 1942. Reprinted by permission of Ellen C. Masters.

EDGAR LEE MASTERS   489

All in the loom, and oh what patterns!
Woodlands, meadows, streams and rivers—
Blind to all of it all my life long.
Triolets, villanelles, rondels, rondeaus,   15
Seeds in a dry pod, tick, tick, tick,
Tick, tick, tick, what little iambics,
While Homer and Whitman roared in the pines?

FOR STUDY AND DISCUSSION

1. What do you think Seth Compton meant by "no one knows what is good/ Who knows not what is evil"? In what way is this statement a criticism of the people of Spoon River? Do you agree or disagree with Compton's point of view? Explain.

2. Why did Flossie Cabanis wish that Eleonora Duse might read her epitaph? Read the poem aloud. Are there any changes in rhythm to emphasize emotional changes? What, in your opinion, is the best way to read the last three lines of the poem?

3. How is the phrase "seeds in a dry pod" related to Petit, the Poet's life? What do the pine trees represent to Petit? What do Homer and Whitman mean to him? In what ways was Whitman unlike Petit? (Before answering, you may wish to reread some of Whitman's poems.) Read "Petit, the Poet" aloud. Do you think the rhythm of the poem is appropriate to Petit's personality and accomplishments? Explain.

4. Like Whitman and Crane, Masters wrote in free verse (see pages 317 and 393). Do you think he avoided rhyme and regular meters because he thought free verse was most appropriate to his subject matter? Give reasons for your answer.

FOR COMPOSITION

1. Choose a character whom you know from your reading of a short story, novel, or play. In the manner of Edgar Lee Masters, write a free verse epitaph for this character.

2. Compare Robinson's Tilbury Town with Masters' Spoon River, as these towns are portrayed in the authors' poetry. In your composition, consider the following questions: What do these towns have in common? Would you care to live in either town? What do Robinson's and Masters' poetry reveal of small-town life near the turn of the century? In what ways have small towns changed since then?

WILLA CATHER
(1873–1947)

Willa Cather was born in the hills of western Virginia. When she was ten, her family moved to a farm on the vast plains of Nebraska. There she found the materials for many of her novels: the land, open to the sky, rolling without interruption throughout the varying seasons to the distant horizons; the people—Slavic, Scandinavian, German, and old American stock—living in sod-roofed dugouts and bare farmhouses and trying to preserve the old moral and cultural values in an age of raw materialism. A critic has written of the importance of this period of her life: "Her enduring values were the values of this society, but they were not merely pioneer and agrarian values. There was a touch of Europe in Nebraska everywhere during her girlhood, and much of her distinctive literary culture was to be drawn from it. . . . It was in this world, with its accumulation of many cultures . . . that Willa Cather learned to appreciate the American novelist Henry James and at the same time to see in the pioneer society of the West a culture and a distinction of its own. Her first two years there, she wrote later, were the most important to her as a writer."

Willa Cather borrowed books in French and German from her neighbors and was taught Greek and Latin by a storekeeper called Uncle Billy Drucker. She attended the University of Nebraska, where she supported herself by doing newspaper work, and after her graduation in 1895, she got a job with the Pittsburgh *Daily Leader.* Later she became a high school teacher of English. In the years following college, her stories began to appear in national magazines, and in 1905 she published a collection of short stories, *The Troll Garden,* which included "The Sculptor's Funeral." In 1906, she went to New York where she worked as managing editor of *McClure's Magazine.* Then, at thirty-nine, she resigned to be able to give her full energy to writing a series of novels shaped by her idyllic memories of her prairie childhood, notably *O Pioneers!, The Song of the Lark,* and *My Ántonia.* Not all her memories of life on the prairies were happy ones, however, as such stories as "The Sculptor's Funeral" and "A Wagner Matinee" attest. Even in her happiest novels, a dark note intruded, in Alfred Kazin's words, an awareness of "thousands of farm women suffering alone in their kitchens, living in a strange world amidst familiar scenes, wearing their lives out with endless chores and fears." In such novels as *A Lost Lady* and *The Professor's House,* she traces the dilemma of individuals who move in societies too small for their aspirations.

In her late novels—*Death Comes to the Archbishop* and *Shadows on the Rock*—she turned her attention to the older Catholic cultures of the Southwest and of

French colonial Quebec. All her novels are marked by an awareness of sounds and colors, of landscape, and of the changing seasons. The characters that drew her greatest sympathy were artists, priests, and women of moral sensitivity—people who stand for spiritual values in a world overly concerned with getting ahead and accumulating money.

The Sculptor's Funeral

A GROUP of the townspeople stood on the station siding of a little Kansas town, awaiting the coming of the night train, which was already twenty minutes overdue. The snow had fallen thick over everything; in the pale starlight the line of bluffs across the wide, white meadows south of the town made soft, smoke-colored curves against the clear sky. The men on the siding stood first on one foot and then on the other, their hands thrust deep into their trousers pockets, their overcoats open, their shoulders screwed up with the cold; and they glanced from time to time toward the southeast, where the railroad track wound along the river shore. They conversed in low tones and moved about restlessly, seeming uncertain as to what was expected of them. There was but one of the company who looked as if he knew exactly why he was there, and he kept conspicuously apart; walking to the far end of the platform, returning to the station door, then pacing up the track again, his chin sunk in the high collar of his overcoat, his burly shoulders drooping forward, his gait heavy and dogged. Presently he was approached by a tall, spare, grizzled man clad in a faded Grand Army [1] suit, who shuffled

[1] **Grand Army:** the Grand Army of the Republic (or G.A.R.), an organization of veterans of the War Between the States.

"The Sculptor's Funeral" from *Youth and the Bright Medusa* by Willa Cather. Reprinted by permission of Alfred A. Knopf, Inc.

out from the group and advanced with a certain deference, craning his neck forward until his back made the angle of a jackknife three quarters open.

"I reckon she's a-goin' to be pretty late again tonight, Jim," he remarked in a squeaky falsetto. "S'pose it's the snow?"

"I don't know," responded the other man with a shade of annoyance, speaking from out an astonishing cataract of red beard that grew fiercely and thickly in all directions.

The spare man shifted the quill toothpick he was chewing to the other side of his mouth. "It ain't likely that anybody from the East will come with the corpse, I s'pose," he went on reflectively.

"I don't know," responded the other, more curtly than before.

"It's too bad he didn't belong to some lodge or other. I like an order funeral myself. They seem more appropriate for people of some repytation," the spare man continued, with an ingratiating concession in his shrill voice, as he carefully placed his toothpick in his vest pocket. He always carried the flag at the G.A.R. funerals in the town.

The heavy man turned on his heel, without replying, and walked up the siding. The spare man rejoined the uneasy group. "Jim's ez full ez a tick, ez ushel," he commented commiseratingly.

Just then a distant whistle sounded, and there was a shuffling of feet on the platform. A number of lanky boys, of all ages, appeared as suddenly and slimily as eels wakened by the crack of thunder; some came from the waiting room, where they had been warming themselves by the red stove, or half asleep on the slat benches; others uncoiled themselves from baggage trucks or slid out of express wagons. Two clambered down from the driver's seat of a hearse that stood backed up against the siding. They straightened their stooping shoulders and lifted their heads, and a flash of momentary animation kindled their dull eyes at that cold, vibrant scream, the worldwide call for men. It stirred them like the note of a trumpet; just as it had often stirred the man who was coming home tonight, in his boyhood.

The night express shot, red as a rocket, from out the eastward marshlands and wound along the river shore under the long lines of shivering poplars that sentineled the meadows, the escaping steam hanging in gray masses against the pale sky and blotting out the Milky Way. In a moment the red glare from the headlight streamed up the snow-covered track before the siding and glittered on the wet, black rails. The burly man with the disheveled red beard walked swiftly up the platform toward the approaching train, uncovering his head as he went. The group of men behind him hesitated, glanced questioningly at one another, and awkwardly followed his example. The train stopped, and the crowd shuffled up to the express car just as the door was thrown open, the man in the G.A.R. suit thrusting his head forward with curiosity. The express messenger appeared in the doorway, accompanied by a young man in a long ulster [1] and traveling cap.

"Are Mr. Merrick's friends here?" inquired the young man.

The group on the platform swayed uneasily. Philip Phelps, the banker, responded with dignity: "We have come to take charge of the body. Mr. Merrick's father is very feeble and can't be about."

"Send the agent out here," growled the express messenger, "and tell the operator to lend a hand."

The coffin was got out of its rough box and down on the snowy platform. The townspeople drew back enough to make room for it and then formed a close semicircle about it, looking curiously at the palm leaf [2] which lay across the black cover. No one said anything. The baggage man stood by his truck, waiting to get at the trunks. The engine panted heavily, and the fireman dodged in and out among the wheels with his yellow torch and long oilcan, snapping the spindle boxes. The young Bostonian, one of the dead sculptor's pupils, who had come with the body, looked about him helplessly. He turned to the banker, the only one of that black, uneasy, stoop-shouldered group who seemed enough of an individual to be addressed.

"None of Mr. Merrick's brothers are here?" he asked uncertainly.

The man with the red beard for the first time stepped up and joined the others. "No, they have not come yet; the family is scattered. The body will be taken directly to the house." He stooped and took hold of one of the handles of the coffin.

"Take the long hill road up, Thompson, it will be easier on the horses," called the liveryman as the undertaker snapped the door of the hearse and prepared to mount to the driver's seat.

Laird, the red-bearded lawyer, turned again to the stranger: "We didn't know whether there would be anyone with him or not," he explained. "It's a long walk, so you'd better go up in the hack." He pointed to a single battered conveyance, but the young man replied stiffly: "Thank you, but I think I will go up with the hearse. If you don't object," turning to the undertaker, "I'll ride with you."

They clambered up over the wheels and drove off in the starlight up the long, white hill toward the town. The lamps in the still village were shining from under the low, snow-burdened roofs; and beyond, on every side, the plains reached out into emptiness, peaceful and wide as the soft sky itself, and wrapped in a tangible, white silence.

When the hearse backed up to a wooden

[1] **ulster:** overcoat.

[2] **palm leaf:** a symbol of achievement.

sequious solemnity as she turned to the banker: "The parlor is ready, Mr. Phelps."

The bearers carried the coffin along the narrow boards, while the undertaker ran ahead with the coffin rests. They bore it into a large, unheated room that smelled of dampness and disuse and furniture polish, and set it down under a hanging lamp ornamented with jingling glass prisms and before a "Rogers group" [1] of John Alden and Priscilla, wreathed with smilax.[2] Henry Steavens stared about him with the sickening conviction that there had been a mistake and that he had somehow arrived at the wrong destination. He looked at the clover-green Brussels,[3] the fat plush upholstery, among the hand-painted china plaques and panels and vases, for some mark of identification—for something that might once conceivably have belonged to Harvey Merrick. It was not until he recognized his friend in the crayon portrait of a little boy in kilts and curls, hanging above the piano, that he felt willing to let any of these people approach the coffin.

"Take the lid off, Mr. Thompson; let me see my boy's face," wailed the elder woman between her sobs. This time Steavens looked fearfully, almost beseechingly, into her face, red and swollen under its masses of strong, black, shiny hair. He flushed, dropped his eyes, and then, almost incredulously, looked again. There was a kind of power about her face —a kind of brutal handsomeness, even; but it was scarred and furrowed by violence, and so colored and coarsened by fiercer passions that grief seemed never to have laid a gentle finger there. The long nose was distended and knobbed at the end, and there were deep lines on either side of it; her heavy, black brows almost met across her forehead, her teeth

[1] **"Rogers group":** Plaster reproductions of statuette groups by John Rogers, often with historical or sentimental themes, were common in late nineteenth-century American homes.
[2] **smilax:** a delicate twining plant with green leaves.
[3] **Brussels:** a patterned carpet.

sidewalk before a naked, weather-beaten frame house, the same composite, ill-defined group that had stood upon the station siding was huddled about the gate. The front yard was an icy swamp, and a couple of warped planks, extending from the sidewalk to the door, made a sort of rickety footbridge. The gate hung on one hinge, and was opened wide with difficulty. Steavens, the young stranger, noticed that something black was tied to the knob of the front door.

The grating sound made by the casket, as it was drawn from the hearse, was answered by a scream from the house; the front door was wrenched open, and a tall, corpulent woman rushed out bareheaded into the snow and flung herself upon the coffin, shrieking: "My boy, my boy! And this is how you've come home to me!"

As Steavens turned away and closed his eyes with a shudder of unutterable repulsion, another woman, also tall, but flat and angular, dressed entirely in black, darted out of the house and caught Mrs. Merrick by the shoulders, crying sharply: "Come, come, mother; you mustn't go on like this!" Her tone changed to one of ob-

were large and square, and set far apart—teeth that could tear. She filled the room; the men were obliterated, seemed tossed about like twigs in an angry water, and even Steavens felt himself being drawn into the whirlpool.

The daughter—the tall, rawboned woman in crepe, with a mourning comb in her hair which curiously lengthened her long face, sat stiffly upon the sofa, her hands, conspicuous for their large knuckles, folded in her lap, her mouth and eyes drawn down, solemnly awaiting the opening of the coffin. Near the door stood a mulatto woman, evidently a servant in the house, with a timid bearing and an emaciated face pitifully sad and gentle. She was weeping silently, the corner of her calico apron lifted to her eyes, occasionally suppressing a long, quivering sob. Steavens walked over and stood beside her.

Feeble steps were heard on the stairs, and an old man, tall and frail, odorous of pipe smoke, with shaggy, unkempt gray hair and a dingy beard, tobacco-stained about the mouth, entered uncertainly. He went slowly up to the coffin and stood rolling a blue cotton handkerchief between his hands, seeming so pained and embarrassed by his wife's orgy of grief that he had no consciousness of anything else.

"There, there, Annie, dear, don't take on so," he quavered timidly, putting out a shaking hand and awkwardly patting her elbow. She turned and sank upon his shoulder with such violence that he tottered a little. He did not even glance toward the coffin, but continued to look at her with a dull, frightened, appealing expression, as a spaniel looks at the whip. His sunken cheeks slowly reddened and burned with miserable shame. When his wife rushed from the room, her daughter strode after her with set lips. The servant stole up to the coffin, bent over it for a moment, and then slipped away to the kitchen, leaving Steavens, the lawyer, and the father to themselves. The old man stood looking down at his dead son's face. The sculptor's splendid head seemed

even more noble in its rigid stillness than in life. The dark hair had crept down upon the wide forehead; the face seemed strangely long, but in it there was not that repose we expect to find in the faces of the dead. The brows were so drawn that there were two deep lines above the beaked nose, and the chin was thrust forward defiantly. It was as though the strain of life had been so sharp and bitter that death could not at once relax the tension and smooth the countenance into perfect peace—as though he were still guarding something precious, which might even yet be wrested from him.

The old man's lips were working under his stained beard. He turned to the lawyer with timid deference: "Phelps and the rest are comin' back to set up with Harve, ain't they?" he asked. "Thank'ee Jim, thankee." He brushed the hair back gently from his son's forehead. "He was a good boy, Jim; always a good boy. He was ez gentle ez a child and the kindest of 'em all—only we didn't none of us ever onderstand him." The tears trickled slowly down his beard and dropped upon the sculptor's coat.

"Martin, Martin! Oh, Martin! come here," his wife wailed from the top of the stairs. The old man started timorously: "Yes, Annie, I'm coming." He turned away, hesitated, stood for a moment in miserable indecision; then reached back and patted the dead man's hair softly, and stumbled from the room.

"Poor old man, I didn't think he had any tears left. Seems as if his eyes would have gone dry long ago. At his age nothing cuts very deep," remarked the lawyer.

Something in his tone made Steavens glance up. While the mother had been in the room, the young man had scarcely seen anyone else; but now, from the moment he first glanced into Jim Laird's florid face and bloodshot eyes, he knew that he had found what he had been heartsick at not finding before—the feeling, the understanding, that must exist in someone, even here.

The man was red as his beard, with

features swollen and blurred by dissipation, and a hot, blazing blue eye. His face was strained—that of a man who is controlling himself with difficulty—and he kept plucking at his beard with a sort of fierce resentment. Steavens, sitting by the window, watched him turn down the glaring lamp, still its jangling pendants with an angry gesture, and then stand with his hands locked behind him, staring down into the master's face. He could not help wondering what link there had been between the porcelain vessel and so sooty a lump of potter's clay.

From the kitchen an uproar was sounding; when the dining-room door opened, the import of it was clear. The mother was abusing the maid for having forgotten to make the dressing for the chicken salad which had been prepared for the watchers. Steavens had never heard anything in the least like it; it was injured, emotional, dramatic abuse, unique and masterly in its excruciating cruelty, as violent and unrestrained as had been her grief of twenty minutes before. With a shudder of disgust, the lawyer went into the dining room and closed the door into the kitchen.

"Poor Roxy's getting it now," he remarked when he came back. "The Merricks took her out of the poorhouse years ago; and if her loyalty would let her, I guess the poor old thing could tell tales that would curdle your blood. She's the mulatto woman who was standing in here a while ago, with her apron to her eyes. The old woman is a fury; there never was anybody like her. She made Harvey's life a hell for him when he lived at home; he was so sick ashamed of it. I never could see how he kept himself sweet."

"He was wonderful," said Steavens slowly, "wonderful; but until tonight I have never known how wonderful."

"That is the eternal wonder of it, anyway; that it can come even from such a dung heap as this," the lawyer cried, with a sweeping gesture which seemed to indicate much more than the four walls within which they stood.

"I think I'll see whether I can get a little air. The room is so close I am beginning to feel rather faint," murmured Steavens, struggling with one of the windows. The sash was stuck, however, and would not yield, so he sat down dejectedly and began pulling at his collar. The lawyer came over, loosened the sash with one blow of his red fist, and sent the window up a few inches. Steavens thanked him, but the nausea which had been gradually climbing into his throat for the last half hour left him with but one desire—a desperate feeling that he must get away from this place with what was left of Harvey Merrick. Oh, he comprehended well enough now the quiet bitterness of the smile that he had seen so often on his master's lips!

Once when Merrick returned from a visit home, he brought with him a singularly feeling and suggestive bas-relief [1] of a thin, faded old woman, sitting and sewing something pinned to her knee; while a full-lipped, full-blooded little urchin, his trousers held up by a single gallows,[2] stood beside her, impatiently twitching her gown to call her attention to a butterfly he had caught. Steavens, impressed by the tender and delicate modeling of the thin, tired face, had asked him if it were his mother. He remembered the dull flush that had burned up in the sculptor's face.

The lawyer was sitting in a rocking chair beside the coffin, his head thrown back and his eyes closed. Steavens looked at him earnestly, puzzled at the line of the chin, and wondering why a man should conceal a feature of such distinction under that disfiguring shock of beard. Suddenly, as though he felt the young sculptor's keen glance, Jim Laird opened his eyes.

"Was he always a good deal of an oyster?" [3] he asked abruptly. "He was terribly shy as a boy."

---

[1] **bas-relief** (bä´ri·lēf´): a type of sculpture in which the figures are a part of the background and project only slightly from it; a coin is an example of one type of relief.

[2] **gallows** (gal´əs): suspender (colloquial).

[3] **oyster:** a shy, quiet person (slang).

"Yes, he was an oyster, since you put it so," rejoined Steavens. "Although he could be very fond of people, he always gave one the impression of being detached. He disliked violent emotion; he was reflective, and rather distrustful of himself—except, of course, as regarded his work. He was sure enough there. He distrusted men pretty thoroughly and women even more, yet somehow without believing ill of them. He was determined, indeed, to believe the best; but he seemed afraid to investigate."

"A burnt dog dreads the fire," said the lawyer grimly, and closed his eyes.

Steavens went on and on, reconstructing that whole miserable boyhood. All this raw, biting ugliness had been the portion of the man whose mind was to become an exhaustless gallery of beautiful impressions—so sensitive that the mere shadow of a poplar leaf flickering against a sunny wall would be etched and held there forever. Surely, if ever a man had the magic word in his finger tips, it was Merrick. Whatever he touched, he revealed its holiest secret; liberated it from enchantment and restored it to its pristine loveliness. Upon whatever he had come in contact with, he had left a beautiful record of the experience—a sort of ethereal signature; a scent, a sound, a color that was his own.

Steavens understood now the real tragedy of his master's life; neither love nor wine, as many had conjectured; but a blow which had fallen earlier and cut deeper than anything else could have done—a shame not his, and yet so unescapably his, to hide in his heart from his very boyhood. And without—the frontier warfare; the yearning of a boy, cast ashore upon a desert of newness and ugliness and sordidness, for all that is chastened and old, and noble with traditions.

At eleven o'clock the tall, flat woman in black announced that the watchers were arriving, and asked them to "step into the dining room." As Steavens rose, the lawyer said dryly: "You go on—it'll be a good experience for you. I'm not equal to that crowd tonight; I've had twenty years of them."

As Steavens closed the door after him, he glanced back at the lawyer, sitting by the coffin in the dim light, with his chin resting on his hand.

The same misty group that had stood before the door of the express car shuffled into the dining room. In the light of the kerosene lamp, they separated and became individuals. The minister, a pale, feeble-looking man with white hair and blond chin whiskers, took his seat beside a small side table, and placed his Bible upon it. The Grand Army man sat down behind the stove and tilted his chair back comfortably against the wall, fishing his quill toothpick from his waistcoat pocket. The two bankers, Phelps and Elder, sat off in a corner behind the dinner table, where they could finish their discussion of the new usury law [1] and its effect on chattel [2] security loans. The real-estate agent, an old man with a smiling, hypocritical face, soon joined them. The coal and lumber dealer and the cattle shipper sat on opposite sides of the hard coal burner, their feet on the nickelwork. Steavens took a book from his pocket and began to read. The talk around him ranged through various topics of local interest while the house was quieting down. When it was clear that the members of the family were in bed, the Grand Army man hitched his shoulders and, untangling his long legs, caught his heels on the rounds of his chair.

"S'pose there'll be a will, Phelps?" he queried in his weak falsetto.

The banker laughed disagreeably, and began trimming his nails with a pearl-handled pocketknife.

"There'll scarcely be any need for one, will there?" he queried in his turn.

The restless Grand Army man shifted his position again, getting his knees still nearer his chin. "Why, the ole man says

[1] **usury** (yōo′zhər·ē) **law:** a law regulating the amount of interest that can be charged on a loan. In modern usage the term *usury* means an excessive rate of interest.

[2] **chattel:** any item of property except real estate.

Harve's done right well lately," he chirped.

The other banker spoke up. "I reckon he means by that Harve ain't asked him to mortgage any more farms lately, so as he could go on with his education."

"Seems like my mind don't reach back to a time when Harve wasn't bein' edycated," tittered the Grand Army man.

There was a general chuckle. The minister took out his handkerchief and blew his nose sonorously. Banker Phelps closed his knife with a snap. "It's too bad the old man's sons didn't turn out better," he remarked with reflective authority. "They never hung together. He spent money enough on Harve to stock a dozen cattle farms, and he might as well have poured it into Sand Creek. If Harve had stayed at home and helped nurse what little they had, and gone into stock on the old man's bottom farm, they might all have been well fixed. But the old man had to trust everything to tenants and was cheated right and left."

"Harve never could have handled stock none," interposed the cattleman. "He hadn't it in him to be sharp. Do you remember when he bought Sander's mules for eight-year-olds, when everybody in town knew that Sander's father-in-law give 'em to his wife for a wedding present eighteen years before, an' they was full-grown mules then?"

The company laughed discreetly, and the Grand Army man rubbed his knees with a spasm of childish delight.

"Harve never was much account for anything practical, and he shore was never fond of work," began the coal and lumber dealer. "I mind the last time he was home; the day he left, when the old man was out to the barn helpin' his hand hitch up to take Harve to the train, and Cal Moots was patchin' up the fence; Harve, he come out on the step and sings out, in his ladylike voice: 'Cal Moots, Cal Moots! Please come cord my trunk.'"

"That's Harve for you," approved the Grand Army man. "I kin hear him howlin' yet, when he was a big feller in long pants and his mother used to whale him with

a rawhide in the barn for lettin' the cows git foundered in the cornfield when he was drivin' 'em home from pasture. He killed a cow of mine that-a-way onct—a pure Jersey and the best milker I had, an' the ole man had to put up for her. Harve, he was watchin' the sun set acrost the marshes when the anamile got away."

"Where the old man made his mistake was in sending the boy East to school," said Phelps, stroking his goatee and speaking in a deliberate, judicial tone. "There was where he got his head full of nonsense. What Harve needed, of all people, was a course in some first-class Kansas City business college."

The letters were swimming before Steavens's eyes. Was it possible that these men did not understand, that the palm on the coffin meant nothing to them? The very name of their town would have remained forever buried in the postal guide had it not been now and again mentioned in the world in connection with Harvey Merrick's. He remembered what his master had said to him on the day of his death, after the congestion of both lungs had shut off any probability of recovery, and the sculptor had asked his pupil to send his body home. "It's not a pleasant place to be lying while the world is moving and doing and bettering," he had said with a feeble smile, "but it rather seems as though we ought to go back to the place we came from, in the end. The townspeople will come in for a look at me; and after they have had their say, I shan't have much to fear from the judgment of God!"

The cattleman took up the comment. "Forty's young for a Merrick to cash in; they usually hang on pretty well. Probably he helped it along with whisky."

"His mother's people were not long lived, and Harvey never had a robust constitution," said the minister mildly. He would have liked to say more. He had been the boy's Sunday school teacher, and had been fond of him; but he felt that he was not in a position to speak. His own sons had turned out badly, and it was not a year since one of them had made his last trip home in the express car, shot in a gambling house in the Black Hills.

"Nevertheless, there is no disputin' that Harve frequently looked upon the wine when it was red, also variegated, and it shore made an oncommon fool of him," moralized the cattleman.

Just then the door leading into the parlor rattled loudly, and everyone started involuntarily, looking relieved when only Jim Laird came out. The Grand Army man ducked his head when he saw the spark in his blue, bloodshot eye. They were all afraid of Jim; he was a drunkard, but he could twist the law to suit his client's needs as no other man in all western Kansas could do, and there were many who tried. The lawyer closed the door behind him, leaned back against it, and folded his arms, cocking his head a little to one side. When he assumed this attitude in the courtroom, ears were always pricked up, as it usually foretold a flood of withering sarcasm.

"I've been with you gentlemen before," he began in a dry, even tone, "when you've sat by the coffins of boys born and raised in this town; and, if I remember rightly, you were never any too well satisfied when you checked them up. What's the matter anyhow? Why is it that reputable young men are as scarce as millionaires in Sand City? It might almost seem to a stranger that there was some way something the matter with your progressive town. Why did Ruben Sayer, the brightest young lawyer you ever turned out, after he had come home from the university as straight as a die, take to drinking and forge a check and shoot himself? Why did Bill Merrit's son die of the shakes in a saloon in Omaha? Why was Mr. Thomas's son, here, shot in a gambling house? Why did young Adams burn his mill to beat the insurance companies, and go to the pen?"

The lawyer paused and unfolded his arms, laying one clenched fist quietly on the table. "I'll tell you why. Because you drummed nothing but money and knavery into their ears from the time they wore knickerbockers; because you carped away at them as you've been carping here tonight, holding our friends Phelps and Elder up to them for their models, as our grandfathers held up George Washington and John Adams. But the boys were young, and raw at the business you put them to, and how could they match coppers with such artists as Phelps and Elder? You wanted them to be successful rascals; they were only unsuccessful ones —that's all the difference. There was only one boy ever raised in this borderland between ruffianism and civilization who didn't come to grief, and you hated Harvey Merrick more for winning out than you hated all the other boys who got under the wheels. Lord, Lord, how you did hate him! Phelps, here, is fond of saying that he could buy and sell us all out any time he's a mind to; but he knew Harve wouldn't have given a tinker's dam for his bank and all his cattle farms put together; and a lack of appreciation, that way, goes hard with Phelps.

"Old Nimrod thinks Harve drank too much; and this from such as Nimrod and me!

"Brother Elder says Harve was too free with the old man's money—fell short in filial consideration, maybe. Well, we can all remember the very tone in which brother Elder swore his own father was a liar, in the county court; and we all know that the old man came out of that partnership with his son as bare as a sheared lamb. But maybe I'm getting personal, and I'd better be driving ahead at what I want to say."

The lawyer paused a moment, squared his heavy shoulders, and went on: "Harvey Merrick and I went to school together, back East. We were dead in earnest, and we wanted you all to be proud of us some day. We meant to be great men. Even I, and I haven't lost my sense of humor, gentlemen, I meant to be a great man. I came back here to practice, and I found you didn't in the least

Henry James and the Art of Fiction

One of the best writers of his age, Henry James was important to later novelists not only for his fine novels but also for the example he set as a literary artist. James was dedicated to enlarging the range of the novel, to making it a more suitable instrument for tracing the subtleties of the human mind and the complexities of social relationships. He was equally dedicated to the novel as an art form, to shaping his novels so that every word, every detail, would contribute to the whole. He maintained that the form of a novel should be organic, not mechanical. In his essay "The Art of Fiction" he wrote: "I cannot imagine composition existing in a series of blocks, nor conceive, in any novel worth discussing at all, of a passage of description that is not in its intention narrative, a passage of dialogue that is not in its intention descriptive . . ."

James counseled the young novelist to follow no set formula in writing. "A novel is in its broadest definition a personal, a direct impression of life. . . . But there will be no intensity at all, and therefore no value, unless there is freedom to feel or say." He cautioned against superficiality and called for the novelist to explore and take advantage "of the magnificence of the form that is open to him, which offers to sight so few restrictions and such innumerable opportunities. . . . Remember that your first duty is to be as complete as possible—to make as perfect a work. Be generous and delicate and pursue the prize."

want me to be a great man. You wanted me to be a shrewd lawyer—oh, yes! Our veteran here wanted me to get him an increase of pension, because he had dyspepsia; Phelps wanted a new county survey that would put the widow Wilson's little bottom farm inside his south line; Elder wanted to lend money at five percent a month, and get it collected; and Stark here wanted to wheedle old women up in Vermont into investing their annuities in real-estate mortgages that are not worth the paper they are written on. Oh, you needed me hard enough, and you'll go on needing me!

"Well, I came back here and became the damned shyster you wanted me to be. You pretend to have some sort of respect for me; and yet you'll stand up and throw mud at Harvey Merrick, whose soul you couldn't dirty and whose hands you couldn't tie. Oh, you're a discriminating lot of Christians! There have been times when the sight of Harvey's name in some Eastern paper has made me hang my head like a whipped dog; and, again, times when I liked to think of him off there in the world, away from all this hog wallow, climbing the big, clean upgrade he'd set for himself.

"And we? Now that we've fought and lied and sweated and stolen, and hated as only the disappointed strugglers in a bitter, dead little Western town know how to do, what have we got to show for it? Harvey Merrick wouldn't have given one sunset over your marshes for all you've got put together, and you know it. It's not for me to say why, in the inscrutable wisdom of God, a genius should ever have been called from this place of hatred and bitter waters; but I want this Boston man to know that the drivel he's been hearing here tonight is the only tribute any truly great man could have from such a lot of sick, sidetracked, burntdog, land-poor sharks as the here-present financiers of Sand City—upon which town may God have mercy!"

The lawyer thrust out his hand to Steavens as he passed him, caught up his overcoat in the hall, and had left the house before the Grand Army man had time to lift his ducked head and crane his long neck about at his fellows.

Next day Jim Laird was drunk and unable to attend the funeral services. Steavens called twice at his office, but was compelled to start East without seeing him. He had a presentiment that he would hear from him again, and left his address on the lawyer's table; but if Laird found it, he never acknowledged it. The thing in him that Harvey Merrick had loved must have gone underground with Harvey Merrick's coffin; for it never spoke again, and Jim got the cold he died of driving across the Colorado mountains to defend one of Phelps's sons, who had got into trouble out there by cutting government timber.

FOR STUDY AND DISCUSSION

1. What important character is introduced in the first paragraph of the story? How is his importance emphasized?

2. Does the author's treatment of the characters who appear in the beginning of the story (before the arrival of the train) seem sympathetic or unsympathetic? Give details to support your answer. Is the impression made by the setting in the first ten paragraphs or so of the story agreeable or disagreeable? Explain.

3. After the train arrives, the story is told primarily through the point of view of Henry Steavens. How does the use of this point of view influence your attitude toward the other characters? Give three examples of Steavens's reactions and tell how they influence your own reactions. (For a discussion of point of view in fiction, see page 604.)

4. What impression is given of Harvey Merrick's sister, mother, and father? What details of appearance help give this impression? Do the actions of these characters support the impression? Why or why not?

5. Explain Jim Laird's remark, "A burnt dog dreads the fire" (page 497). What does this remark imply about Harvey Merrick's early years?

6. How do the remarks of the two bankers, the Grand Army man, the cattle dealer, and the coal and lumber dealer help characterize the town? How do they help you understand Harvey Merrick? Do these remarks increase or decrease your sympathy for Merrick? Explain.

7. The sculptor had anticipated what his funeral would be like. Explain his words: "... after they have had their say, I shan't have much to fear from the judgment of God!" What do you think of his decision to be buried in this town?

8. What use does Willa Cather make of Jim Laird in the story? How would the story be different without him? How does he influence your feelings about Harvey Merrick and the town? Do you think his outburst about the townspeople is a fitting climax to the story? Why do you think the story concludes with a detail about his death?

9. You have already discussed the use of setting in the beginning of the story. Now give six other examples of the use of setting to influence your reaction or to deepen your understanding of the town and its people, particularly Merrick's relatives.

10. The struggle of a sensitive individual against a hostile environment is a familiar subject in literature. In what other literary works have you encountered it? Why do you think Harvey Merrick gained a victory over his environment while other characters you have read about went down in defeat?

FOR COMPOSITION

1. The descriptions of the Merrick house, particularly the living room, tell a great deal about the inhabitants (and about a former inhabitant—Harvey Merrick). Study these descriptions. Then write a description of a house or a room so that a perceptive reader will know from reading it the kind of person or persons who live there.

2. As you have seen, the fact that much of "The Sculptor's Funeral" is told from Steavens's point of view is important in determining the reader's attitude toward the townspeople and Harvey Merrick. Write a composition in which you show how your attitude might be different if the story were told from the point of view of Merrick's mother, Merrick's teacher, or Banker Phelps. As a conclusion, to show the difference in point of view, rewrite one paragraph or short episode in the story from the point of view you have chosen.

The Triumph of Realism

One of the unifying themes of this book has been the continuing conflict between ideals and realities in American life and literature. Literature is a way of organizing and evaluating the materials of life, and American writers of different periods have tended to organize their materials in different ways, both in terms of their attitudes toward life and society and in terms of their literary theories and attitudes. In previous units, you have seen how a Romantic view of life stressed the ideal of human perfection, and how Romantic theories of life and literature encouraged such different writers as Thoreau, Bryant, and Poe to use nature as a symbol, both of good and evil. You have seen also how a trial by war led to a reinstatement of American ideals in such writers as Whitman and Twain and to a richer appreciation of the frontiersman and of frontier life. The writers in the unit you have just studied mark a triumph of realism over Romanticism. As you have learned from the unit introduction (page 385), some scholars consider realism an outgrowth and part of the Romantic movement, but the realistic writers themselves saw Romanticism as an outworn approach to literature. They considered themselves a new school of writers, one which revitalized literature by bringing it closer to actual life.

THE CONFLICT BETWEEN APPEARANCE AND ACTUALITY

The writers in this unit were concerned with the contrast between the actual and the potential, between fact and wish. All of them dramatized the conflict between appearance and actuality (or between ideals and realities): appearance of life and the hard facts beneath this appearance.

1. Discuss how each of the following works deals with the theme of conflict between appearance and actuality (or between ideals and realities): *The Red Badge of Courage,* "Miniver Cheevy," "Richard Cory," "Seth Compton," "The Sculptor's Funeral."

2. Cite examples of irony in the selections in the unit. Why is irony an important device of these writers? (See page 49 for a discussion of irony.)

REALISM OF METHOD

One writer has differentiated "realism of fact" from "realism of method." Realistic subject matter and realistic style are not necessarily the same thing. Perhaps by contrasting a Romantic story, "The Fall of the House of Usher," and a realistic story, "The Sculptor's Funeral," some characteristics of the realistic style can be identified.

1. Compare two descriptions of rooms: the paragraph in "The Fall of the House of Usher" beginning "The room in which I found myself . . ." (page 129); and the paragraph from "The Sculptor's Funeral" beginning "The bearers carried the coffin . . ." (page 494). Which passage has more unusual words? Which passage relies more heavily on adjectives and adverbs? Which has longer, more complex sentences? What connection is there between choice of words and sentences and the effect of each description?

2. Compare the description of Usher (page 129) with the description of Jim Laird (pages 495–96). What is the difference between the different kinds of details presented? Compare the dialogue. In which story is the dialogue closer to real speech?

4. What conclusions can you draw about the realistic style from these comparisons?

5. Compare a Romantic poem such as Bryant's "To a Water Fowl" with a realistic poem such as "Mr. Flood's Party." Find differences in the choice of words and details.

Now that you have compared "The Fall of the House of Usher" and "The Sculptor's Funeral," apply what you have learned in your own writing.

1. Write two versions of a description, the first as Poe might have written it, the second as a realist would write it.

2. Write a dialogue between Usher and the narrator of the story as Stephen Crane or Willa Cather might have written it.

REALISM AND NATURALISM

Review the discussion of naturalism on page 388 and the discussion question on *The Red Badge of Courage* relating to realism and naturalism (page 474). Then discuss the following questions.

1. Émile Zola, the French naturalist writer, wrote, "We [the naturalists] consider that man cannot be separated from his surroundings, that he is completed by his clothes, his house, his city, and his country; and hence we shall not note a single phenomenon of his brain or heart without looking for the causes or the consequences in his surroundings." To what extent can this quotation be applied to the selections in this unit? Cite passages to support your answer.

2. Both realistic and naturalistic fiction have been criticized as being excessively gloomy, of dealing only with dull and miserable lives. The American poet and newspaper columnist Eugene Field poked fun at such writing. In one of his columns he imagined a conversation between the Russian novelist Leo Tolstoy and the American realist Hamlin Garland:

" 'From bad, humanity goes to worse. Its condition becomes harder and harder all the time. This barren country about us will eventually be cultivated, these trees felled, these mountains quarried, these plains plowed and irrigated.'

" 'And all involves more labor, more suffering, more sorrow?'

" 'That will be the harvest of realism,' continued the "younger genius" [Garland]. 'There will be more sweat, more sore feet, more lame backs, more callous hands, more evil smells, a greater destitution of socks, and a vaster plenitude of patched pants than the philosophy of veritism [realism] even dreams of these days.'

" 'And we shall not be here to enjoy these miseries and the telling of them! It is this thought that makes our lot more wretched.' "

Does Field's satire of realism and naturalism seem effective to you, or does it seem to miss the point? Explain.

3. The French realist Guy de Maupassant observed that "the realist, if he is an artist, will seek not to give us a banal photography of life but a vision of it that is fuller, sharper, more convincing than reality itself." To achieve such a "vision" the realist not only uses sharply observed, precisely recorded details but also vivid, powerful images. *The Red Badge of Courage* is especially noteworthy for its use of startling images (page 475). Cite particularly effective images in "The Sculptor's Funeral," in "Mr. Flood's Party," in "Miniver Cheevy."

FOR COMPOSITION: THE FORMS OF DISCOURSE

When you first started to write narratives, you may have been content with simply telling what happened. Later you learned to describe settings and characters. Through studying short stories you learned that it is more effective to reveal a character through actions and dialogue than simply to state what he is like. You learned also that a good writer organizes his narratives and tries to make every word count. From studying the writers in this unit, you have probably become aware of the importance of using convincing details, details that give the impression of real lives being led in a real world.

Give five examples from the selections in this unit of the effective use of convincing details. Then write a narrative (fiction or nonfiction) in which you use some of the techniques that you have learned from studying the writers represented in this unit.

ART AND LITERATURE

1. While the realistic movement in writing was developing in American literature, a number of American painters in the second half of the nineteenth century were responding to the influence of a school of French painting called Impressionism. Stephen Crane's style has sometimes been called "impressionist." What similarity is there between Crane's descriptions of battle in *The Red Badge of Courage* and the use of color and detail in the Impressionist paintings by Mary Cassatt, Maurice Prendergast, and Childe Hassam shown on pages 467, 469, and 470?

2. Probably the most important realistic school of painters in the United States was the "Ash Can School." Study the paintings by the members of this school on pages 569–72. Then write a composition comparing one or more of these paintings to the realistic literature you have read. Pay special attention to choice of subject matter and choice of details.

AMERICA AND THE MODERN WORLD

"And then came the Great War [World War I]. . . It was terrific in its physical aspects—bodies mangled, the young manhood of England, Germany, and France blown away or bled white, a great nation like Germany humiliated in the end. . . .

"You, my son, did not get into the War. You were too young. . . . Just the same you are not at all the same man you would have been but for the War.

"Of course there were other forces at work—the flowering of the industrial age, speeded up, no doubt, by the War.

"Thousands of men, everywhere, jerked out of the old individualistic life—plenty of machinery to jerk them out fast, machinery to kill them in masses like cattle—hurled into a new mass life." *

SHERWOOD ANDERSON *in a letter to his son*

During the twentieth century, the United States has been involved in two World Wars, wars that tore Europe apart, that at first made America draw off by itself, but that eventually made it more firmly than ever a part of the Western world, its destinies closely tied to those of Europe. In the end, America became the leader of the West, the most powerful nation in the world, faced with problems and responsibilities it had never dreamed of facing in the nineteenth century. In the second decade of our century, the critic and scholar Van Wyck Brooks wrote a book called *America's Coming of Age,* in which he foresaw a time of cultural greatness for the country. In the 1960's, a political columnist parodied this title by calling his book *America's Coming of Middle Age.* Not only the two World Wars but a great

* From *Letters of Sherwood Anderson,* edited by H. M. Jones and Walter Rideout, copyright 1953 by Eleanor Anderson. Reprinted by permission of Little, Brown and Company.

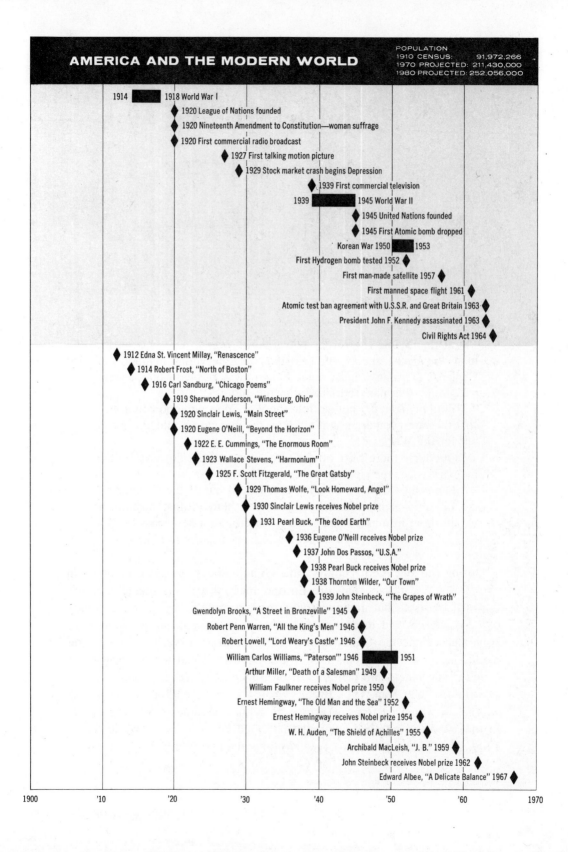

AMERICA AND THE MODERN WORLD

POPULATION
1910 CENSUS: 91,972,266
1970 PROJECTED: 211,430,000
1980 PROJECTED: 252,056,000

1914 ■ 1918 World War I
1920 League of Nations founded
1920 Nineteenth Amendment to Constitution—woman suffrage
1920 First commercial radio broadcast
1927 First talking motion picture
1929 Stock market crash begins Depression
1939 First commercial television
1939 ■ 1945 World War II
1945 United Nations founded
1945 First Atomic bomb dropped
Korean War 1950 ■ 1953
First Hydrogen bomb tested 1952
First man-made satellite 1957
First manned space flight 1961
Atomic test ban agreement with U.S.S.R. and Great Britain 1963
President John F. Kennedy assassinated 1963
Civil Rights Act 1964

1912 Edna St. Vincent Millay, "Renascence"
1914 Robert Frost, "North of Boston"
1916 Carl Sandburg, "Chicago Poems"
1919 Sherwood Anderson, "Winesburg, Ohio"
1920 Sinclair Lewis, "Main Street"
1920 Eugene O'Neill, "Beyond the Horizon"
1922 E. E. Cummings, "The Enormous Room"
1923 Wallace Stevens, "Harmonium"
1925 F. Scott Fitzgerald, "The Great Gatsby"
1929 Thomas Wolfe, "Look Homeward, Angel"
1930 Sinclair Lewis receives Nobel prize
1931 Pearl Buck, "The Good Earth"
1936 Eugene O'Neill receives Nobel prize
1937 John Dos Passos, "U.S.A."
1938 Pearl Buck receives Nobel prize
1938 Thornton Wilder, "Our Town"
1939 John Steinbeck, "The Grapes of Wrath"
Gwendolyn Brooks, "A Street in Bronzeville" 1945
Robert Penn Warren, "All the King's Men" 1946
Robert Lowell, "Lord Weary's Castle" 1946
William Carlos Williams, "Paterson'" 1946 ■ 1951
Arthur Miller, "Death of a Salesman" 1949
William Faulkner receives Nobel prize 1950
Ernest Hemingway, "The Old Man and the Sea" 1952
Ernest Hemingway receives Nobel prize 1954
W. H. Auden, "The Shield of Achilles" 1955
Archibald MacLeish, "J. B." 1959
John Steinbeck receives Nobel prize 1962
Edward Albee, "A Delicate Balance" 1967

1900　'10　'20　'30　'40　'50　'60　1970

Job hunters of the 1930's. The effect of the Great Depression was widespread. Many millions of Americans found themselves unemployed and often homeless.

economic depression—a time when millions of Americans were uprooted from their places in society—forced the nation into maturity, into a period when it could no longer dream of greatness but had to face the problems that greatness had thrust upon it.

THE CONTINUITY OF AMERICAN LITERATURE

Two themes have dominated this survey of American literature, themes that draw together American literary works from colonial times to the present and make them part of a process of national development and self-realization. The first theme is the ceaseless conflict between ideals and realities in the intellectual life of the nation and its literature, of the gradual modification of both ideals and of realities as the nation grew, solved old problems, and faced new ones. The second is the continual striving by American writers to create a significant and distinctive national literature.

The first of these two themes probably will never be entirely resolved. Americans are constantly aware of the gap between their ideals and the realities of the national life, the social problems that confront contemporary America and give direction to many of its writers. But few countries in the history of civilization have been so concerned with the gap between the ideal of a national life and the realities of life as most Americans know them. And few countries have maintained such a relentless effort to close the gap.

To the second theme, there has been a clear resolution. In 1820, Sydney Smith could pose the sarcastic question, "In the four quarters of the globe, who reads an American book?" (page 88). In 1959, the *London Times Literary Supplement,* one of the most influential journals in the English-speaking world, published a special report on *The American Imagination.* In the report, the *Times* acknowledged, "But in fact it is true to say that the flowering of the American imagination has been the chief event in the sphere of living art since the end of the First World War." Modern American writers, such as Ernest Hemingway, William Faulkner, and Thornton Wilder, have caught the imagination of Frenchmen, Germans, Englishmen, and shaped their view of life. From a minor development of English literature, American writing has become a distinctive and leading branch of the literature of the world.

FRAGMENTATION IN MODERN LIFE

Certain tendencies against which American writers had previously protested became more pronounced after World War I. As you have seen (page 388), some Americans in the latter part of the nineteenth century felt that they were caught up in vast forces over which they had little or no control. They felt isolated from their fellow Americans, from the corporations for which they worked, and from the universe at large. Then, in the 1920's, life was characterized by an accelerating *fragmentation* of society. Many individuals felt, more strongly than ever, that they were no longer bound to each other by traditional standards of conduct or by the structure of their society. Economically, the emphasis on mass production and giant corporations widened the gulf between workers and their employers. Many Americans became disillusioned with the nation's political life. They no longer felt that they could respect the nation's leaders or that there was a close, necessary connection between themselves and their government. Some Americans with literary or artistic ambitions became convinced that they could not develop their talents in America and went to France to seek artistic fulfillment. Men had a sense of floating in a void as fragments of a society that had been blown into bits and pieces and was no longer whole. When the Depression struck America, the sense of fragmentation became even more intense. Americans cast about desperately for the basic values that would make them feel they were part of some larger whole—an American tradition.

THE RESPONSE OF MODERN LITERATURE

The work of American writers since World War I reflects both the fragmentation of American life and the attempt to find meanings that will pull society together. F. Scott Fitzgerald and Ernest Hemingway wrote about the wanderings of a "lost generation," searching at home and abroad for stable values in a "jazz age." Sherwood Anderson, like Edgar Lee Masters and Edwin Arlington Robinson, explored the life of small towns. He found them to be not stable, closely knit communities, but places of loneliness, frustration, and even terror. Eugene O'Neill transformed the American theater with his harsh questionings, his tumultuous grapplings with fate. Poets such as Carl Sandburg, William Carlos Williams, and E. E. Cummings experimented with forms that would express modern

Sinclair Lewis, the first American to receive a Nobel Prize for Literature.

moods and the modern view of the world. Wallace Stevens, one of our finest poets, came to believe that it was the job of the poet to bring order out of a chaotic reality and thus make life bearable.

Other writers turned back to traditional values. In *Our Town,* Thornton Wilder looked back to a New England of almost idyllic simplicity. William Faulkner celebrated the traditional values of the rural South, of men who pay respect to animals and to the land that gives them all life. Van Wyck Brooks undertook a monumental search through American literary history for a "usable past," a cultural tradition that would support Americans as they looked toward the future.

American literature today is still searching for values, still looking for a way to bring ideals and realities together. Out of this quest, notable literary works are still being produced. No one can predict with certainty what direction American literature will take in the future. But the words of one of our best poets are as good a prediction and summation as any. This survey began with the opening of Robert Frost's "The Gift Outright" (page 1). The remainder of the poem is one man's view of the struggle of Americans, writers included, to realize themselves.

> "Something we were withholding made us weak
> Until we found out that it was ourselves
> We were withholding from the land of living,
> And forthwith found salvation in surrender.
> Such as we were we gave ourselves outright
> (The deed of gift was many deeds of war)
> To the land vaguely realizing westward,
> But still unstoried, artless, unenhanced,
> Such as she was, such as she would become."

MODERN SHORT STORIES

Art imposes some kind of arrangement or order on life. A painting of a man may exaggerate certain of his features and de-emphasize others by way of suggesting his personality through his appearance. Music deliberately excludes most sounds and concentrates on only a few, which it arranges in certain patterns. A poem may bring out striking and unexpected similarities between two objects and thus establish a new relationship between these objects. All these are evidences of the human mind arranging the material of human experience—choosing, excluding, comparing, exaggerating, de-emphasizing—to create order, patterns, and forms.

Because fiction, of all literature, seems most closely to recreate real life and the raw material of experience, some readers may not be aware of how the writer shapes this experience and charges it with meaning that ordinary life often lacks. Such readers will miss a great deal. As in all of art, much of the meaning of fiction depends on what order the writer gives to his material. And of the kinds of fiction—novel, novella, short story—probably the short story illustrates most clearly the importance of order and form.

It was Edgar Allan Poe who, more than any other critic, made writers and readers aware of the short story as a special form. Poe stated that each story should achieve "a certain and unique effect," and that every detail of the story should contribute to that effect (page 138). "If his [the writer's] initial sentence tends not to the outbringing of this effect, then he has failed in his first step. In the whole composition there should be no word written, of which the tendency, direct or indirect, is not to the one preestablished design." Since Poe's day, American writers, while almost always arranging their details to work toward one predominant effect, have achieved a remarkable variety of effects within the compressed short-story form. Twentieth-century American writers, highly skilled in the short-story form, have won recognition for the modern American short story as a distinctive contribution to world literature.

To appreciate fully the short-story writer's artistry, you should be aware of the elements of a story and of how these elements work together. In the following pages, you will encounter discussions of the elements of the short story: *plot* (pages 520, 558, and 566), *character* (page 548), *theme* (page 549), *point of view* (page 604), and *style* (page 611). These discussions will help you answer two questions that you should keep in mind as you read all short stories: (1) What is the predominant effect of the story? (2) How does the author achieve this effect?

SHERWOOD
ANDERSON
(1876–1941)

Winesburg, Ohio, Anderson's best-known work, has a short introduction explaining what his characters have in common: they are all "grotesques." Grotesques, according to Anderson, seize on one "truth," an idea or an ambition, and allow it to become an obsession. In their single-minded passion for an overriding idea, they lead lonely, possessed lives, cut off from those who pursue other "truths" or have a more balanced view of life. Anderson managed to make his grotesques into symbols of the American village. Other writers saw the village or small town as a snug, secure community bound together by common traditions and attitudes. Anderson saw it as an unhappy place full of isolated, despairing souls leading hidden lives. He was one of the first modern writers to deal with a significant American figure: the man whose life is tragically warped by his dreams and ambitions.

Sherwood Anderson's father was a harness maker who was slowly put out of work as his craft became obsolete. The Andersons had seven children, and Sherwood, the third, was obliged to help support the rest. Leaving school after a year of high school, he was known around Clyde, Ohio, where he grew up, as "Jobby" because of the variety of odd jobs he held. He led a grueling life before coming to Chicago at the age of twenty-four to work in an advertising agency. Eventually he moved to Elyria, Ohio, and began his own business as the manufacturer of a product called "Roof-fix." The business went badly, and one day, sick of responsibilities, growing debts, and the painful effort of conforming to the demands imposed by his ambitions, he fled. Four days later he was found in Cleveland in a state of collapse. He later wrote about his attempted escape. To him it meant flight from the stifling conformities of the business world, a search for artistic freedom and the life of the imagination.

After a time he returned to Chicago and took a job writing advertisements. He met Chicago intellectuals and writers, among them Theodore Dreiser and Carl Sandburg, who encouraged him to write. His early novels, *Windy McPherson's Son* and *Marching Men,* were hailed as the appearance of an original talent. All the while he was sifting his experiences in small Ohio towns. Edgar Lee Masters' *Spoon River Anthology* (page 487) suggested to him the possibility of writing a prose equivalent of this work, a collection of short stories all about people living in the same town and tied together by one character, a reporter who appears in most of the stories. When *Winesburg, Ohio* appeared in 1919, it established Anderson as an important writer. This book, with its effective use of simple language and its glimpses beneath the surfaces of isolated lives, showed the way to younger men who wanted to write simply and truthfully about the life they knew. Anderson became a literary celebrity sought out by aspiring writers, including Ernest Hemingway and William Faulkner, whose careers he aided. He wrote a number of fine short stories, collected in *The Triumph of the Egg, Horses and Men,* and *Death in the Woods and Other Stories,* and wrote several novels that met with varying success. The last years of his life were spent in Virginia as a farmer and newspaper editor.

The Egg

M Y FATHER was, I am sure, intended by nature to be a cheerful, kindly man. Until he was thirty-four years old he worked as a farm hand for a man named Thomas Butterworth whose place lay near the town of Bidwell, Ohio. He had then a horse of his own and on Saturday evenings drove into town to spend a few hours in social intercourse with other farm hands. In town he drank several glasses of beer and stood about in Ben Head's saloon—crowded on Saturday evenings with visiting farm hands. Songs were sung and glasses thumped on the bar. At ten o'clock father drove home along a lonely country road, made his horse comfortable for the night and himself went to bed, quite happy in his position in life. He had at that time no notion of trying to rise in the world.

It was in the spring of his thirty-fifth year that father married my mother, then a country schoolteacher, and in the following spring I came wriggling and crying into the world. Something happened to the two people. They became ambitious. The American passion for getting up in the world took possession of them.

It may have been that mother was responsible. Being a schoolteacher she had no doubt read books and magazines. She had, I presume, read of how Garfield, Lincoln, and other Americans rose from poverty to fame and greatness and as I lay beside her—in the days of her lying-in—she may have dreamed that I would some day rule men and cities. At any rate she induced father to give up his place as a farm hand, sell his horse and embark on an independent enterprise of his own. She was a tall silent woman with a long nose and troubled gray eyes. For herself she wanted nothing. For father and myself she was incurably ambitious.

The first venture into which the two people went turned out badly. They rented ten acres of poor stony land on Griggs's Road, eight miles from Bidwell, and launched into chicken raising. I grew into boyhood on the place and got my first impressions of life there. From the beginning they were impressions of disaster and if, in my turn, I am a gloomy man inclined to see the darker side of life, I attribute it to the fact that what should have been for me the happy joyous days of childhood were spent on a chicken farm.

One unversed in such matters can have no notion of the many and tragic things that can happen to a chicken. It is born out of an egg, lives for a few weeks as a tiny fluffy thing such as you will see pictured on Easter cards, then becomes hideously naked, eats quantities of corn and meal bought by the sweat of your father's brow, gets diseases called pip, cholera, and other names, stands looking with stupid eyes at the sun, becomes sick and dies. A few hens and now and then a rooster, intended to serve God's mysterious ends, struggle through to maturity. The hens lay eggs out of which come other chickens and the dreadful cycle is thus made complete. It is all unbelievably complex. Most philosophers must have been raised on chicken farms. One hopes for so much from a chicken and is so dreadfully disillusioned. Small chickens, just setting out on the journey of life, look so bright and alert and they are in fact so dreadfully stupid. They are so much like people they mix one up in one's judgments of life. If disease does not kill them they wait until your expectations are thoroughly aroused and then walk under the wheels of a wagon—to go squashed and dead back to their maker. Vermin infest their youth, and fortunes must be spent for curative powders. In later life I have seen how a literature has been built up on the subject of fortunes to be made out of the raising of chickens. It is intended to be read by the gods who have just eaten of the tree of the knowledge [1] of good and evil. It is a hopeful literature and declares that much may be done by simple ambitious people who own a few hens. Do not be led astray by it. It was not written for you. Go hunt for gold on the frozen hills of Alaska, put your faith in the honesty of a politician, believe if you will that the world is daily growing better and that good will triumph over evil, but do not read and believe the literature that is written concerning the hen. It was not written for you.

I, however, digress. My tale does not primarily concern itself with the hen. If correctly told it will center on the egg. For ten years my father and mother struggled to make our chicken farm pay and then they gave up that struggle and began another. They moved into the town of Bidwell, Ohio, and embarked in the res-

taurant business. After ten years of worry with incubators that did not hatch, and with tiny—and in their own way lovely—balls of fluff that passed on into semi-naked pullethood and from that into dead henhood, we threw all aside and packing our belongings on a wagon drove down Griggs's Road toward Bidwell, a tiny caravan of hope looking for a new place from which to start on our upward journey through life.

We must have been a sad-looking lot, not, I fancy, unlike refugees fleeing from a battlefield. Mother and I walked in the road. The wagon that contained our goods had been borrowed for the day from Mr. Albert Griggs, a neighbor. Out of its sides stuck the legs of cheap chairs and at the back of the pile of beds, tables, and boxes filled with kitchen utensils was a crate of live chickens, and on top of that the baby carriage in which I had been wheeled about in my infancy. Why we stuck to the baby carriage I don't know. It was unlikely other children would be born and the wheels were broken. People who have

[1] **tree ... knowledge:** an allusion to the third chapter of Genesis.

SHERWOOD ANDERSON   513

few possessions cling tightly to those they have. That is one of the facts that make life so discouraging.

Father rode on top of the wagon. He was then a bald-headed man of forty-five, a little fat and from long association with mother and the chickens he had become habitually silent and discouraged. All during our ten years on the chicken farm he had worked as a laborer on neighboring farms and most of the money he had earned had been spent for remedies to cure chicken diseases, on Wilmer's White Wonder Cholera Cure or Professor Bidlow's Egg Producer or some other preparations that mother found advertised in the poultry papers. There were two little patches of hair on father's head just above his ears. I remember that as a child I used to sit looking at him when he had gone to sleep in a chair before the stove on Sunday afternoons in the winter. I had at that time already begun to read books and have notions of my own and the bald path that led over the top of his head was, I fancied, something like a broad road, such a road as Caesar might have made on which to lead his legions out of Rome and into the wonders of an unknown world. The tufts of hair that grew above father's ears were, I thought, like forests. I fell into a half-sleeping, half-waking state and dreamed I was a tiny thing going along the road into a far beautiful place where there were no chicken farms and where life was a happy eggless affair.

One might write a book concerning our flight from the chicken farm into town. Mother and I walked the entire eight miles —she to be sure that nothing fell from the wagon and I to see the wonders of the world. On the seat of the wagon beside father was his greatest treasure. I will tell you of that.

On a chicken farm where hundreds and even thousands of chickens come out of eggs surprising things sometimes happen. Grotesques are born out of eggs as out of people. The accident does not often occur—perhaps once in a thousand births.

A chicken is, you see, born that has four legs, two pairs of wings, two heads or what not. The things do not live. They go quickly back to the hand of their maker that has for a moment trembled. The fact that the poor little things could not live was one of the tragedies of life to father. He had some sort of notion that if he could but bring into henhood or roosterhood a five-legged hen or a two-headed rooster his fortune would be made. He dreamed of taking the wonder about to county fairs and of growing rich by exhibiting it to other farm hands.

At any rate he saved all the little monstrous things that had been born on our chicken farm. They were preserved in alcohol and put each in its own glass bottle. These he had carefully put into a box and on our journey into town it was carried on the wagon seat beside him. He drove the horses with one hand and with the other clung to the box. When we got to our destination the box was taken down at once and the bottles removed. All during our days as keepers of a restaurant in the town of Bidwell, Ohio, the grotesques in their little glass bottles sat on a shelf back of the counter. Mother sometimes protested but father was a rock on the subject of his treasure. The grotesques were, he declared, valuable. People, he said, liked to look at strange and wonderful things.

Did I say that we embarked in the restaurant business in the town of Bidwell, Ohio? I exaggerated a little. The town itself lay at the foot of a low hill and on the shore of a small river. The railroad did not run through the town and the station was a mile away to the north at a place called Pickleville. There had been a cider mill and pickle factory at the station, but before the time of our coming they had both gone out of business. In the morning and in the evening busses came down to the station along a road called Turner's Pike from the hotel on the main street of Bidwell. Our going to the out-of-the-way place to embark in the restaurant business was mother's idea. She

PICKLEVILLE

talked of it for a year and then one day went off and rented an empty store building opposite the railroad station. It was her idea that the restaurant would be profitable. Traveling men, she said, would be always waiting around to take trains out of town and town people would come to the station to await incoming trains. They would come to the restaurant to buy pieces of pie and drink coffee. Now that I am older I know that she had another motive in going. She was ambitious for me. She wanted me to rise in the world, to get into a town school and become a man of the towns.

At Pickleville father and mother worked hard as they always had done. At first there was the necessity of putting our place into shape to be a restaurant. That took a month. Father built a shelf on which he put tins of vegetables. He painted a sign on which he put his name in large red letters. Below his name was the sharp command—"EAT HERE"—that was so seldom obeyed. A showcase was bought and filled with cigars and tobacco. Mother scrubbed the floor and the walls of the room. I went to school in the town and was glad to be away from the farm and from the presence of the discouraged, sad-looking chickens. Still I was not very joyous. In the evening I walked home from school along Turner's Pike and re-

membered the children I had seen playing in the town schoolyard. A troop of little girls had gone hopping about and singing. I tried that. Down along the frozen road I went hopping solemnly on one leg. "Hippity Hop To The Barber Shop," I sang shrilly. Then I stopped and looked doubtfully about. I was afraid of being seen in my gay mood. It must have seemed to me that I was doing a thing that should not be done by one who, like myself, had been raised on a chicken farm where death was a daily visitor.

Mother decided that our restaurant should remain open at night. At ten in the evening a passenger train went north past our door followed by a local freight. The freight crew had switching to do in Pickleville and when the work was done they came to our restaurant for hot coffee and food. Sometimes one of them ordered a fried egg. In the morning at four they returned north-bound and again visited us. A little trade began to grow up. Mother slept at night and during the day tended the restaurant and fed our boarders while father slept. He slept in the same bed mother had occupied during the night and I went off to the town of Bidwell and to school. During the long nights, while mother and I slept, father cooked meats that were to go into sandwiches for the lunch baskets of our boarders. Then an idea in regard to getting up in the world came into his head. The American spirit took hold of him. He also became ambitious.

In the long nights when there was little to do father had time to think. That was his undoing. He decided that he had in the past been an unsuccessful man because he had not been cheerful enough and that in the future he would adopt a cheerful outlook on life. In the early morning he came upstairs and got into bed with mother. She woke and the two talked. From my bed in the corner I listened.

It was father's idea that both he and mother should try to entertain the people who came to eat at our restaurant. I cannot now remember his words, but he gave the impression of one about to become in some obscure way a kind of public entertainer. When people, particularly young people from the town of Bidwell, came into our place, as on very rare occasions they did, bright entertaining conversation was to be made. From father's words I gathered that something of the jolly innkeeper effect was to be sought. Mother must have been doubtful from the first, but she said nothing discouraging. It was father's notion that a passion for the company of himself and mother would spring up in the breasts of the younger people of the town of Bidwell. In the evening bright happy groups would come singing down Turner's Pike. They would troop shouting with joy and laughter into our place. There would be song and festivity. I do not mean to give the impression that father spoke so elaborately of the matter. He was as I have said an uncommunicative man. "They want some place to go. I tell you they want some place to go," he said over and over. That was as far as he got. My own imagination has filled in the blanks.

For two or three weeks this notion of father's invaded our house. We did not talk much, but in our daily lives tried earnestly to make smiles take the place of glum looks. Mother smiled at the boarders and I, catching the infection, smiled at our cat. Father became a little feverish in his anxiety to please. There was no doubt, lurking somewhere in him, a touch of the spirit of the showman. He did not waste much of his ammunition on the railroad men' he served at night but seemed to be waiting for a young man or woman from Bidwell to come in to show what he could do. On the counter in the restaurant there was a wire basket kept always filled with eggs, and it must have been before his eyes when the idea of being entertaining was born in his brain. There was something prenatal about the way eggs kept themselves connected with the development of his idea. At any rate an egg ruined his new impulse in life. Late one night I was awakened by a roar of anger coming from father's throat. Both

mother and I sat upright in our beds. With trembling hands she lighted a lamp that stood on a table by her head. Downstairs the front door of our restaurant went shut with a bang and in a few minutes father tramped up the stairs. He held an egg in his hand and his hand trembled as though he were having a chill. There was a half-insane light in his eyes. As he stood glaring at us I was sure he intended throwing the egg at either mother or me. Then he laid it gently on the table beside the lamp and dropped on his knees beside mother's bed. He began to cry like a boy and I, carried away by his grief, cried with him. The two of us filled the little upstairs room with our wailing voices. It is ridiculous, but of the picture we made I can remember only the fact that mother's hand continually stroked the bald path that ran across the top of his head. I have forgotten what mother said to him and how she induced him to tell her of what had happened downstairs. His explanation also has gone out of my mind. I remember only my own grief and fright and the shiny path over father's head glowing in the lamplight as he knelt by the bed.

As to what happened downstairs. For some unexplainable reason I know the story as well as though I had been a witness to my father's discomfiture. One in time gets to know many unexplainable things. On that evening young Joe Kane, son of a merchant of Bidwell, came to Pickleville to meet his father, who was expected on the ten o'clock evening train from the South. The train was three hours late and Joe came into our place to loaf about and to wait for its arrival. The local freight train came in and the freight crew were fed. Joe was left alone in the restaurant with father.

From the moment he came into our place the Bidwell young man must have been puzzled by my father's actions. It was his notion that father was angry at him for hanging around. He noticed that the restaurant keeper was apparently disturbed by his presence and he thought of going out. However, it began to rain and

he did not fancy the long walk to town and back. He bought a five-cent cigar and ordered a cup of coffee. He had a newspaper in his pocket and took it out and began to read. "I'm waiting for the evening train. It's late," he said apologetically.

For a long time father, whom Joe Kane had never seen before, remained silently gazing at his visitor. He was no doubt suffering from an attack of stage fright. As so often happens in life he had thought so much and so often of the situation that now confronted him that he was somewhat nervous in its presence.

For one thing, he did not know what to do with his hands. He thrust one of them nervously over the counter and shook hands with Joe Kane. "How-de-do," he said. Joe Kane put his newspaper down and stared at him. Father's eye lighted on the basket of eggs that sat on the counter and he began to talk. "Well," he began hesitatingly, "well, you have heard of Christopher Columbus, eh?" He seemed to be angry. "That Christopher Columbus was a cheat," he declared emphatically. "He talked of making an egg stand on its end. He talked, he did, and then he went and broke the end of the egg."

My father seemed to his visitor to be beside himself at the duplicity of Christopher Columbus. He muttered and swore.

He declared it was wrong to teach children that Christopher Columbus was a great man when, after all, he cheated at the critical moment. He had declared he would make an egg stand on end and then when his bluff had been called he had done a trick. Still grumbling at Columbus, father took an egg from the basket on the counter and began to walk up and down. He rolled the egg between the palms of his hands. He smiled genially. He began to mumble words regarding the effect to be produced on an egg by the electricity that comes out of the human body. He declared that without breaking its shell and by virtue of rolling it back and forth in his hands he could stand the egg on its end. He explained that the warmth of his hands and the gentle rolling movement he gave the egg created a new center of gravity, and Joe Kane was mildly interested. "I have handled thousands of eggs," father said. "No one knows more about eggs than I do."

He stood the egg on the counter and it fell on its side. He tried the trick again and again, each time rolling the egg between the palms of his hands and saying the words regarding the wonders of electricity and the laws of gravity. When after a half hour's effort he did succeed in making the egg stand for a moment he looked up to find that his visitor was no

From Poe to Anderson

In his review of Hawthorne's *Twice-Told Tales,* Edgar Allan Poe made a basic statement about the art of the short story. "A skillful literary artist has construed a tale . . . he combines such events as may best aid him in establishing . . . [a] preconceived effect . . ." (see pages 138 and 510).

As the short story developed, many critics required craftsmanship above all else from writers. The most popular stories were usually those with clever plots and tricky endings. A number of writers, however, felt that the American short story was in danger of becoming an empty form. Some of these began to write stories in which plot was less important, stories that revealed character or conveyed a mood. Sherwood Anderson described as follows his own efforts to widen the range of the short-story form:

"Our writers, our storytellers, in wrapping life up into neat little packages were only betraying life . . . for a long time . . . I was almost universally condemned by the critics. My stories, it seemed, had no definite ends. . . . I was called vague. . . . It seems I could not get a formula and stick to it. . . . For ten or fifteen years after I had written and published the Winesburg stories, I was compelled to make my living outside the field of writing."

Today it seems clear that Anderson's stories are the beginnings of the modern American short story— a more open form adhering to no formula.

longer watching. By the time he had succeeded in calling Joe Kane's attention to the success of his effort the egg had again rolled over and lay on its side.

Afire with the showman's passion and at the same time a good deal disconcerted by the failure of his first effort, father now took the bottles containing the poultry monstrosities down from their place on the shelf and began to show them to his visitor. "How would you like to have seven legs and two heads like this fellow?" he asked, exhibiting the most remarkable of his treasures. A cheerful smile played over his face. He reached over the counter and tried to slap Joe Kane on the shoulder as he had seen men do in Ben Head's saloon when he was a young farm hand and drove to town on Saturday evenings. His visitor was made a little ill by the sight of the body of the terribly deformed bird floating in the alcohol in the bottle and got up to go. Coming from behind the counter father took hold of the young man's arm and led him back to his seat. He grew a little angry and for a moment had to turn his face away and force himself to smile. Then he put the bottles back on the shelf. In an outburst of generosity he fairly compelled Joe Kane to have a fresh cup of coffee and another cigar at his expense. Then he took a pan and, filling it with vinegar taken from a jug that sat beneath the counter, he declared himself about to do a new trick. "I will heat this egg in this pan of vinegar," he said. "Then I will put it through the neck of a bottle without breaking the shell. When the egg is inside the bottle it will resume its normal shape and the shell will become hard again. Then I will give the bottle with the egg in it to you. You can take it about with you wherever you go. People will want to know how you got the egg in the bottle. Don't tell them. Keep them guessing. That is the way to have fun with this trick."

Father grinned and winked at his visitor. Joe Kane decided that the man who confronted him was mildly insane but harmless. He drank the cup of coffee that had been given him and began to read his paper again. When the egg had been heated in vinegar father carried it on a spoon to the counter and going into a back room got an empty bottle. He was angry because his visitor did not watch him as he began to do his trick, but nevertheless went cheerfully to work. For a long time he struggled, trying to get the egg to go through the neck of the bottle. He put the pan of vinegar back on the stove, intending to reheat the egg, then picked it up and burned his fingers. After a second bath in the hot vinegar the shell of the egg had been softened a little but not enough for his purpose. He worked and worked and a spirit of desperate determination took possession of him. When he thought that at last the trick was about to be consummated the delayed train came in at the station and Joe Kane started to go nonchalantly out at the door. Father made a last desperate effort to conquer the egg and make it do the thing that would establish his reputation as one who knew how to entertain guests who came into his restaurant. He worried the egg. He attempted to be somewhat rough with it. He swore and the sweat stood out on his forehead. The egg broke under his hand. When the contents spurted over his clothes, Joe Kane, who had stopped at the door, turned and laughed.

A roar of anger rose from my father's throat. He danced and shouted a string of inarticulate words. Grabbing another egg from the basket on the counter, he threw it, just missing the head of the young man as he dodged through the door and escaped.

Father came upstairs to mother and me with an egg in his hand. I do not know what he intended to do. I imagine he had some idea of destroying it, of destroying all eggs, and that he intended to let mother and me see him begin. When, however, he got into the presence of mother something happened to him. He laid the egg gently on the table and dropped on his knees by the bed as I have already explained. He later decided to close the restaurant for the night and to come upstairs and get into bed. When he did so he blew out the light and after much muttered conversation both he and mother went to sleep. I suppose I went to sleep also, but my sleep was troubled. I awoke at dawn and for a long time looked at the egg that lay on the table. I wondered why eggs had to be and why from the egg came the hen who again laid the egg. The question got into my blood. It has stayed there, I imagine, because I am the son of my father. At any rate, the problem remains unsolved in my mind. And that, I conclude, is but another evidence of the complete and final triumph of the egg— at least as far as my family is concerned.

FOR STUDY AND DISCUSSION

1. The narrator remarks of his parents, "The American passion for getting up in the world took possession of them." How did this passion change the lives of the narrator and his family? In what way was the narrator's mother responsible for this passion? In your opinion, does this passion lead more often to happiness or unhappiness?

2. According to the narrator, what are the difficulties involved in running a chicken farm? Do you think that another family might have made a success of the farm? Why or why not?

3. The narrator describes at length the way his family appeared during their move to Bidwell, Ohio. What does this description tell you about the family? How are they like "refugees fleeing from a battlefield"? What is their "battlefield"?

4. What do you think of the father's methods of popularizing his restaurant? Do you think other methods might have made it popular, or was the business a hopeless one?

5. The narrator refers to the "little monstrous things" that his father has preserved in alcohol as "grotesques." In terms of Anderson's own definition of a "grotesque" (see biographical introduction), in what way can the father also be called a "grotesque"?

6. How is the final scene of the story similar to a slapstick comedy? Can this scene be described as sad and funny at the same time? Explain. Tell about comedies you have read or seen that are essentially sad underneath the fun.

PLOT

Any work of literature that tells a story— be it a novel, a short story, a play, or a narrative poem—has a *plot;* that is, a pattern growing out of the events of the work and out of the order in which they are told. A plot can be regarded as a kind of skeleton that the writer fills out by using well-drawn, convincing *characters* (see page 548), an effective *point of view* (page 604), a vivid *setting* (page 587), and a distinctive *style* (page 611). These other elements—character, point of view, setting, and style—determine to some extent the impression a work of fiction makes on the reader, but the basic shape of a story or novel depends on its skeleton or plot.

Most plots involve *conflict,* both external and internal. A plot concerned primarily with external conflict may pit a character against other characters or against his environment. A plot concerned primarily with internal conflict may depict a character's struggle with his own weaknesses or show how conflicting desires or ambitions pull him in opposite directions. While conflict, in some form, is essential to almost all plots, many modern short stories subordinate conflict to *revelation.* These stories move toward some insight into a character or into his relationship with other characters, or sometimes into the writer's view of the world.

The order in which events are told and the emphasis that is given to different events are as much a part of the plot as the events themselves. Some stories use a straightforward chronological order: events are presented in the order in which they happen. Other stories begin in the middle and tell what has previously happened by means of flashbacks. Still others continually shift from the present to the past and back again. (A good example of such a story is "The Jilting of Granny Weatherall," page 560.) Even in a story in which the events are presented chronologically, some events are emphasized more than others. Just as a sightseeing bus may stop to examine an important landmark and then go on quickly to the next important sight, so a story may linger over one event and pass lightly over less important ones. In discussing emphasis, some critics make a distinction between *scene* and *summary.* A summary does not stop to linger but moves on quickly. ("Before I knew it, my school days were over.") A scene examines an event at length and presents it vividly. ("Gaunt

and sour-faced, he stood before me. 'What do you want?' I said.")

1. Is the conflict in "The Egg" primarily external or internal? Explain. In your opinion, are the events of this story arranged primarily to develop a conflict or to move toward a revelation? Explain your answer with reference to passages in the text.

2. What events in "The Egg" are summarized? What is the important scene in the story? Why do you think Anderson has arranged his story so that it consists of a long summary leading up to one important scene?

UNDERSTANDING SYMBOLS

A *symbol* is an event, a character, or an object that is used in a work of art to stand for something else, usually an idea, and thus can be a powerful tool for deepening the meaning of a work. In a poem, for example, a description of a rose may be used to suggest the idea of beauty. Because a rose withers quickly, it may also symbolize the idea of beauty's impermanence. Both these ideas, beauty and beauty's impermanence, can be suggested by the same symbol in the same poem. Because the two ideas are linked to a specific object, they possess an emotional power they might otherwise not have.

An extremely suggestive symbol, an egg, is used in Anderson's story. Because an egg can symbolize birth, it can also symbolize the idea of life. Because the process of birth is concealed within a shell, an egg can also symbolize the mystery of life. Because the shell is easily broken, an egg can symbolize life's fragility. An egg, then, is a potentially powerful symbol because it touches upon issues that are basic to life.

1. To understand the last paragraph of "The Egg," you must understand how the egg is used as a symbol. What ideas does the egg symbolize in this paragraph? Why does the boy wonder about eggs? What does Anderson mean by the "triumph of the egg," a phrase he thought important enough to use as the title of a short-story collection?

2. Find at least three other passages in this story in which an egg is used symbolically. In each case, explain the idea symbolized by the egg.

3. Explain the symbolic significance of the chicken farm. To do so, you will have to study the fifth and tenth paragraphs of the story.

ERNEST HEMINGWAY
(1898–1961)

Ernest Hemingway is probably the most widely imitated American writer of the twentieth century. Few writers of our time have escaped a confrontation with him and the acceptance or rejection of his influence. The art of fiction has gained new life from techniques he perfected—a deceptively simple, rhythmic prose that is admirably suited to depicting moments of action and the rapid, terse dialogue that reflects the nature of Hemingway's characters quietly standing up to the pain of life. Hemingway has made two major contributions other than technique to American literature. The first of these is a vision of life both as a kind of perpetual battlefield where everyone is eventually wounded and as a game with almost formal moves. The second is the "Hemingway hero," a man for whom it is a point of honor to suffer with grace and dignity, and who, though sensing that defeat is inevitable, plays the game well.

Ernest Hemingway was born in Oak Park, Illinois, a suburb of Chicago. His father was a doctor who loved the out-of-doors and took his son on hunting and fishing trips in northern Michigan. At Oak Park High School he was an athlete, but he also worked on the school newspaper and published stories in the literary magazine. In 1917, when he graduated, the United States had already entered World War I. Hemingway wanted to enlist and fight in Europe, but his father prevented him from doing so. Instead he got a job as a cub reporter on the Kansas City *Star*. In 1918 he joined a Red Cross ambulance corps and was sent to the Italian front. He was severely wounded by an artillery shell and for three months lay convalescing in a hospital in Milan. He then returned to Illinois. Thereafter, his thoughts circled about the significance of his wound, and he also came to discover the many ways a man can be wounded in peacetime as well as on a battlefront.

For the next year or so he made his living at newspaper work. He became a friend of Sherwood Anderson and, with the older man's encouragement, kept trying to write poems and short stories. He spent his spare time in gymnasiums, boxing and watching boxers, fascinated by this sport where man is tested through pain and danger. Later he discovered bullfighting and wrote *Death in the Afternoon,* a book exploring the significance of the duel between man and animal.

In 1921, he got a job as a roving correspondent with the Toronto *Star* and left for Europe. There, chiefly in Paris, he met other American young men of his generation who had left the United States in the belief that they would find personal and artistic fulfillment in an older civilization. As a newspaperman, Hemingway traveled through

Europe and the Near East, finding material that would later serve him as a writer of fiction. In Paris, he fell under the influence of Gertrude Stein, who had outraged many readers with her experiments in language. (Her line, "A rose is a rose is a rose," is still held up as the ultimate absurdity of experimental writing.) Miss Stein sought to gain her effects by the use of simple language, rhythm, and repetition. Hemingway worked hard under her tutelage, bringing stories to her for criticism and making changes as she suggested. Later he rebelled against her, but he never denied that she had helped his art.

Hemingway's earliest two books were privately published in Paris. *In Our Time,* a collection of short stories published in 1925, was his first book to reach a general audience. The perceptive critic Edmund Wilson saw in these early books the debut of a gifted young writer, but it took the publication of *The Sun Also Rises* (1926) to give Hemingway a wide audience. This novel, about a group of English and American expatriates hunting for sensations that would let them forget the pain attending life, gave everyone a new phrase to describe the men who had fought in World War I and who had become disillusioned with the war's ideals: "the lost generation." In his next novel, *A Farewell to Arms,* Hemingway wrote about the war itself and a romance growing out of it. His description of the retreat from Caporetto is a famous episode in the novel. All the while, he was writing brilliant short stories which later were collected in *Men Without Women* and *Winner Take Nothing.*

With each book Hemingway's personal fame grew. He was regarded as the original hero of his stories, a big tough man hunting in Africa, deep-sea fishing, and following the bullfight. As a hero who lived dangerously and gracefully, he became the embodiment of the attitudes made popular by his writing. In the thirties he covered the Spanish Civil War as a foreign correspondent. Out of this experience came his most popular novel, *For Whom the Bell Tolls.* The title of this book is taken from John Donne's famous meditation: "Any man's death diminishes me, because I am involved in mankind, and therefore never send to know for whom the bell tolls; it tolls for thee." Both the novel and its title reflect Hemingway's growing commitment to larger issues. Instead of concentrating on the ordeals of personal existence, Hemingway and his hero, Robert Jordan, are "involved with mankind," concerned not only with individual fate but with the lot of humanity. In *The Old Man and the Sea,* the last notable work published during his lifetime, Hemingway returned to his old theme, the testing of the individual, but, in the old man's calm acceptance of his fate, gave it a new dignity.

In 1954, Ernest Hemingway was awarded the Nobel prize for literature. *A Moveable Feast,* his posthumously published memoir of his early days in Paris, is regarded by some readers as one of his best works. Since his death, it seems clearer than ever that Hemingway's best work has the concise intensity of fine poetry and that his artistic quest for the fewest and best words was similar to that of many poets. In his book about hunting big game, *The Green Hills of Africa,* he described this quest: to find "how far prose can be carried if any one is serious enough and has enough luck. There is a fourth and fifth dimension that can be gotten. . . . It is much more difficult than poetry. It is a prose that has never been written. But it can be written, without tricks and without cheating. With nothing that will go bad afterwards."

Big Two-Hearted River

"Big Two-Hearted River" is the concluding story of *In Our Time,* a collection of short stories mostly about Nick Adams. Earlier in the book, Nick has been gravely wounded while fighting on the Italian front. Now he returns to the Michigan woods where he and his father hunted and fished before the war.

PART I

THE TRAIN went on up the track out of sight, around one of the hills of burnt timber. Nick sat down on the bundle of canvas and bedding the baggage man had pitched out of the door of the baggage car. There was no town, nothing but the rails and the burned-over country. The thirteen saloons that had lined the one street of Seney had not left a trace. The foundations of the Mansion House hotel stuck up above the ground. The stone was chipped and split by the fire. It was all that was left of the town of Seney. Even the surface had been burned off the ground.

Nick looked at the burned-over stretch of hillside, where he had expected to find the scattered houses of the town and then walked down the railroad track to the bridge over the river. The river was there. It swirled against the log spiles [1] of the bridge. Nick looked down into the clear, brown water, colored from the pebbly bottom, and watched the trout keeping themselves steady in the current with wavering fins. As he watched them they changed their positions by quick angles, only to hold steady in the fast water again. Nick watched them a long time.

He watched them holding themselves with their noses into the current, many trout in deep, fast-moving water, slightly distorted as he watched far down through the glassy convex surface of the pool, its surface pushing and swelling smooth against the resistance of the log-driven piles of the bridge. At the bottom of the pool were the big trout. Nick did not see them at first. Then he saw them at the bottom of the pool, big trout looking to hold themselves on the gravel bottom in a varying mist of gravel and sand, raised in spurts by the current.

Nick looked down into the pool from the bridge. It was a hot day. A kingfisher flew up the stream. It was a long time since Nick had looked into a stream and seen trout. They were very satisfactory. As the shadow of the kingfisher moved up the stream, a big trout shot upstream in a long angle, only his shadow marking the angle, then lost his shadow as he came through the surface of the water, caught the sun, and then, as he went back into the stream under the surface, his shadow seemed to float down the stream with the current, unresisting, to his post under the bridge where he tightened facing up into the current.

Nick's heart tightened as the trout moved. He felt all the old feeling.

He turned and looked down the stream. It stretched away, pebbly-bottomed with shallows and big boulders and a deep pool as it curved away around the foot of a bluff.

Nick walked back up the ties to where his pack lay in the cinders beside the railway track. He was happy. He adjusted the pack harness around the bundle, pulling straps tight, slung the pack on his back, got his arms through the shoulder straps and took some of the pull off his shoulders by leaning his forehead against the wide band of the tumpline. [2] Still, it

[1] **spiles:** upright supports.

[2] **tumpline:** a sling formed by a strap slung over the forehead or chest, used by one carrying a pack on his back or hauling game.

was too heavy. It was much too heavy. He had his leather rod-case in his hand and leaning forward to keep the weight of the pack high on his shoulders he walked along the road that paralleled the railway track, leaving the burned town behind in the heat, and then turned off around a hill with a high, fire-scarred hill on either side onto a road that went back into the country. He walked along the road feeling the ache from the pull of the heavy pack. The road climbed steadily. It was hard work walking uphill. His muscles ached and the day was hot, but Nick felt happy. He felt he had left everything behind, the need for thinking, the need to write, other needs. It was all back of him.

From the time he had gotten down off the train and the baggage man had thrown his pack out of the open car door things had been different. Seney was burned, the country was burned over and changed, but it did not matter. It could not all be burned. He knew that. He hiked along the road, sweating in the sun, climbing to cross the range of hills that separated the railway from the pine plains.

The road ran on, dipping occasionally, but always climbing. Nick went on up. Finally the road after going parallel to the burnt hillside reached the top. Nick leaned back against a stump and slipped out of the pack harness. Ahead of him, as far as he could see, was the pine plain. The burned country stopped off at the left with the range of hills. On ahead islands of dark pine trees rose out of the plain. Far off to the left was the line of the river. Nick followed it with his eye and caught glints of the water in the sun.

There was nothing but the pine plain ahead of him, until the far blue hills that marked the Lake Superior height of land. He could hardly see them, faint and far away in the heat-light over the plain. If he looked too steadily they were gone. But if he only half looked they were there, the far-off hills of the height of land.

Nick sat down against the charred stump and smoked a cigarette. His pack balanced on the top of the stump, harness holding ready, a hollow molded in it from his back. Nick sat smoking, looking out over the country. He did not need to get his map out. He knew where he was from the position of the river.

As he smoked, his legs stretched out in front of him, he noticed a grasshopper walk along the ground and up onto his woolen sock. The grasshopper was black. As he had walked along the road, climbing, he had started many grasshoppers from the dust. They were all black. They were not the big grasshoppers with yellow and black or red and black wings whirring out from their black wing-sheathing as they fly up. These were just ordinary hoppers, but all a sooty black in color. Nick had wondered about them as he walked, without really thinking about them. Now, as he watched the black hopper that was nibbling at the wool of his sock with its fourway lip, he realized that they had all turned black from living in the burned-over land. He realized that the fire must have come the year before, but the grasshoppers were all black now. He wondered how long they would stay that way.

Carefully he reached his hand down and took hold of the hopper by the wings. He turned him up, all his legs walking in the air, and looked at his jointed belly. Yes, it was black too, iridescent where the back and head were dusty.

"Go on, hopper," Nick said, speaking out loud for the first time. "Fly away somewhere."

He tossed the grasshopper up into the air and watched him sail away to a charcoal stump across the road.

Nick stood up. He leaned his back against the weight of his pack where it rested upright on the stump and got his arms through the shoulder straps. He stood with the pack on his back on the brow of the hill looking out across the country, toward the distant river, and then struck down the hillside away from the road. Underfoot the ground was good walking. Two hundred yards down the hillside the fire line stopped. Then it was sweet fern, growing ankle high, to walk through, and clumps of jack pines; a long undulating country with frequent rises and descents, sandy underfoot and the country alive again.

Nick kept his direction by the sun. He knew where he wanted to strike the river and he kept on through the pine plain, mounting small rises to see other rises ahead of him and sometimes from the top of a rise a great solid island of pines off to his right or his left. He broke off some sprigs of the heathery sweet fern, and put them under his pack straps. The chafing crushed it and he smelled it as he walked.

He was tired and very hot, walking across the uneven, shadeless pine plain. At any time he knew he could strike the river by turning off to his left. It could not be more than a mile away. But he kept on toward the north to hit the river as far upstream as he could go in one day's walking.

For some time as he walked Nick had been in sight of one of the big islands of pine standing out above the rolling high ground he was crossing. He dipped down and then as he came slowly up to the crest of the ridge he turned and made toward the pine trees.

There was no underbrush in the island of pine trees. The trunks of the trees went straight up or slanted toward each other. The trunks were straight and brown without branches. The branches were high above. Some interlocked to make a solid shadow on the brown forest floor. Around the grove of trees was a bare space. It was brown and soft underfoot as Nick walked on it. This was the overlapping of the pine needle floor, extending out beyond the width of the high branches. The trees had grown tall and the branches moved high, leaving in the sun this bare space they had once covered with shadow. Sharp at the edge of this extension of the forest floor commenced the sweet fern.

Nick slipped off his pack and lay down in the shade. He lay on his back and

looked up into the pine trees. His neck and back and the small of his back rested as he stretched. The earth felt good against his back. He looked up at the sky, through the branches, and then shut his eyes. He opened them and looked up again. There was a wind high up in the branches. He shut his eyes again and went to sleep.

Nick woke stiff and cramped. The sun was nearly down. His pack was heavy and the straps painful as he lifted it on. He leaned over with the pack on and picked up the leather rod-case and started out from the pine trees across the sweet fern swale, toward the river. He knew it could not be more than a mile.

He came down a hillside covered with stumps into a meadow. At the edge of the meadow flowed the river. Nick was glad to get to the river. He walked upstream through the meadow. His trousers were soaked with the dew as he walked. After the hot day, the dew had come quickly and heavily. The river made no sound. It was too fast and smooth. At the edge of the meadow, before he mounted to a piece of high ground to make camp, Nick looked down the river at the trout rising. They were rising to insects come from the swamp on the other side of the stream when the sun went down. The trout jumped out of water to take them. While Nick walked through the little stretch of meadow alongside the stream, trout had jumped high out of water. Now as he looked down the river, the insects must be settling on the surface, for the trout were feeding steadily all down the stream. As far down the long stretch as he could see, the trout were rising, making circles all down the surface of the water, as though it were starting to rain.

The ground rose, wooded and sandy, to overlook the meadow, the stretch of river and the swamp. Nick dropped his pack and rod-case and looked for a level piece of ground. He was very hungry and he wanted to make his camp before he cooked. Between two jack pines, the ground was quite level. He took the ax out of the pack and chopped out two projecting roots. That leveled a piece of ground large enough to sleep on. He smoothed out the sandy soil with his hand and pulled all the sweet fern bushes by their roots. His hands smelled good from the sweet fern. He smoothed the uprooted earth. He did not want anything making lumps under the blankets. When he had the ground smooth, he spread his three blankets. One he folded double, next to the ground. The other two he spread on top.

With the ax he slit off a bright slab of pine from one of the stumps and split it into pegs for the tent. He wanted them long and solid to hold in the ground. With the tent unpacked and spread on the ground, the pack, leaning against a jack-pine, looked much smaller. Nick tied the rope that served the tent for a ridge-pole to the trunk of one of the pine trees and pulled the tent up off the ground with the other end of the rope and tied it to the other pine. The tent hung on the rope like a canvas blanket on a clothesline. Nick poked a pole he had cut up under the back

peak of the canvas and then made it a tent by pegging out the sides. He pegged the sides out taut and drove the pegs deep, hitting them down into the ground with the flat of the ax until the rope loops were buried and the canvas was drum tight.

Across the open mouth of the tent Nick fixed cheesecloth to keep out mosquitoes. He crawled inside under the mosquito bar with various things from the pack to put at the head of the bed under the slant of the canvas. Inside the tent the light came through the brown canvas. It smelled pleasantly of canvas. Already there was something mysterious and homelike. Nick was happy as he crawled inside the tent. He had not been unhappy all day. This was different though. Now things were done. There had been this to do. Now it was done. It had been a hard trip. He was very tired. That was done. He had made his camp. He was settled. Nothing could touch him. It was a good place to camp. He was there, in the good place. He was in his home where he had made it. Now he was hungry.

He came out, crawling under the cheesecloth. It was quite dark outside. It was lighter in the tent.

Nick went over to the pack and found, with his fingers, a long nail in a paper sack of nails, in the bottom of the pack. He drove it into the pine tree, holding it close

and hitting it gently with the flat of the ax. He hung the pack up on the nail. All his supplies were in the pack. They were off the ground and sheltered now.

Nick was hungry. He did not believe he had ever been hungrier. He opened and emptied a can of pork and beans and a can of spaghetti into the frying pan.

"I've got a right to eat this kind of stuff, if I'm willing to carry it," Nick said. His voice sounded strange in the darkening woods. He did not speak again.

He started a fire with some chunks of pine he got with the ax from a stump. Over the fire he stuck a wire grill, pushing the four legs down into the ground with his boot. Nick put the frying pan on the grill over the flames. He was hungrier. The beans and spaghetti warmed. Nick stirred them and mixed them together. They began to bubble, making little bubbles that rose with difficulty to the surface. There was a good smell. Nick got out a bottle of tomato catchup and cut four slices of bread. The little bubbles were coming faster now. Nick sat down beside the fire and lifted the frying pan off. He poured about half the contents out into the tin plate. It spread slowly on the plate. Nick knew it was too hot. He poured on some tomato catchup. He knew the beans and spaghetti were still too hot. He looked at the fire, then at the tent, he was not going to spoil it all by burning his tongue. For years he had never enjoyed fried bananas because he had never been able to wait for them to cool. His tongue was very sensitive. He was very hungry. Across the river in the swamp, in the almost dark, he saw a mist rising. He looked at the tent once more. All right. He took a full spoonful from the plate.

He ate the whole plateful before he remembered the bread. Nick finished the second plateful with the bread, mopping the plate shiny. He had not eaten since a cup of coffee and a ham sandwich in the station restaurant at St. Ignace.[1] It had

been a very fine experience. He had been that hungry before, but had not been able to satisfy it. He could have made camp hours before if he had wanted to. There were plenty of good places to camp on the river. But this was good.

Nick tucked two big chips of pine under the grill. The fire flared up. He had forgotten to get water for the coffee. Out of the pack he got a folding canvas bucket and walked down the hill, across the edge of the meadow, to the stream. The other bank was in the white mist. The grass was wet and cold as he knelt on the bank and dipped the canvas bucket into the stream. It bellied and pulled hard in the current. The water was ice cold. Nick rinsed the bucket and carried it full up to the camp. Up away from the stream it was not so cold.

Nick drove another big nail and hung up the bucket full of water. He dipped the coffee pot half full, put some more chips under the grill onto the fire and put the pot on. He could not remember which way he made coffee. He could remember an argument about it with Hopkins, but not which side he had taken. He decided to bring it to a boil. He remembered now that was Hopkins's way. He had once argued about everything with Hopkins. While he waited for the coffee to boil, he opened a small can of apricots. He liked to open cans. He emptied the can of apricots out into a tin cup. While he watched the coffee on the fire, he drank the juice syrup of the apricots, carefully at first to keep from spilling, then meditatively, sucking the apricots down. They were better than fresh apricots.

The coffee boiled as he watched. The lid came up and coffee and grounds ran down the side of the pot. Nick took it off the grill. It was a triumph for Hopkins. He put sugar in the empty apricot cup and poured some of the coffee out to cool. It was too hot to pour and he used his hat to hold the handle of the coffee pot. He would not let it steep in the pot at all. Not the first cup. It should be straight Hopkins all the way. Hop deserved that. He was a very serious

---

[1] **St. Ignace** (ig′nas): a town on the northern shore of the Straits of Mackinac.

coffee drinker. He was the most serious man Nick had ever known. Not heavy, serious. That was a long time ago. Hopkins spoke without moving his lips. He had played polo. He made millions of dollars in Texas. He had borrowed carfare to go to Chicago, when the wire came that his first big well had come in. He could have wired for money. That would have been too slow. They called Hop's girl the Blonde Venus. Hop did not mind because she was not his real girl. Hopkins said very confidently that none of them would make fun of his real girl. He was right. Hopkins went away when the telegram came. That was on the Black River.[1] It took eight days for the telegram to reach him. Hopkins gave away his .22 caliber Colt automatic pistol to Nick. He gave his camera to Bill. It was to remember him always by. They were all going fishing again next summer. The Hop Head was rich. He would get a yacht and they would all cruise along the north shore of Lake Superior. He was excited but serious. They said good-by and all felt bad. It broke up the trip. They never saw Hopkins again. That was a long time ago on the Black River.

Nick drank the coffee, the coffee according to Hopkins. The coffee was bitter. Nick laughed. It made a good ending to the story. His mind was starting to work. He knew he could choke it because he was tired enough. He spilled the coffee out of the pot and shook the grounds loose into the fire. He lit a cigarette and went inside the tent. He took off his shoes and trousers, sitting on the blankets, rolled the shoes up inside the trousers for a pillow and got in between the blankets.

Out through the front of the tent he watched the glow of the fire, when the night wind blew on it. It was a quiet night. The swamp was perfectly quiet. Nick stretched under the blanket comfortably. A mosquito hummed close to his ear. Nick sat up and lit a match. The mosquito

---

[1] **Black River:** a stream in the northern part of the Lower Peninsula of Michigan.

was on the canvas, over his head. Nick moved the match quickly up to it. The mosquito made a satisfactory hiss in the flame. The match went out. Nick lay down again under the blanket. He turned on his side and shut his eyes. He was sleepy. He felt sleep coming. He curled up under the blanket and went to sleep.

PART II

In the morning the sun was up and the tent was starting to get hot. Nick crawled out under the mosquito netting stretched across the mouth of the tent, to look at the morning. The grass was wet on his hands as he came out. He held his trousers and his shoes in his hands. The sun was just up over the hill. There was the meadow, the river and the swamp. There were birch trees in the green of the swamp on the other side of the river.

The river was clear and smoothly fast in the early morning. Down about two hundred yards were three logs all the way across the stream. They made the water smooth and deep above them. As Nick watched, a mink crossed the river on the logs and went into the swamp. Nick was excited. He was excited by the early morning and the river. He was really too hurried to eat breakfast, but he knew he must. He built a little fire and put on the coffee pot.

While the water was heating in the pot he took an empty bottle and went down over the edge of the high ground to the meadow. The meadow was wet with dew and Nick wanted to catch grasshoppers for bait before the sun dried the grass. He found plenty of good grasshoppers. They were at the base of the grass stems. Sometimes they clung to a grass stem. They were cold and wet with the dew, and could not jump until the sun warmed them. Nick picked them up, taking only the medium-sized brown ones, and put them into the bottle. He turned over a log and just under the shelter of the edge were several hundred hoppers. It was a grasshopper lodging house. Nick put about fifty of the medium browns into the bottle. While he was picking up the hoppers the others warmed in the sun and commenced to hop away. They flew when they hopped. At first they made one flight and stayed stiff when they landed, as though they were dead.

Nick knew that by the time he was through with breakfast they would be as lively as ever. Without dew in the grass it would take him all day to catch a bottle full of good grasshoppers and he would have to crush many of them, slamming at them with his hat. He washed his hands at the stream. He was excited to be near it. Then he walked up to the tent. The hoppers were already jumping stiffly in the grass. In the bottle, warmed by the sun, they were jumping in a mass. Nick put in a pine stick as a cork. It plugged the mouth of the bottle enough, so the hoppers could not get out and left plenty of air passage.

He had rolled the log back and knew he could get grasshoppers there every morning.

Nick laid the bottle full of jumping grasshoppers against a pine trunk. Rapidly he mixed some buckwheat flour with water and stirred it smooth, one cup of flour, one cup of water. He put a handful of coffee in the pot and dipped a lump of grease out of a can and slid it sputtering across the hot skillet. On the smoking skillet he poured smoothly the buckwheat batter. It spread like lava, the grease spitting sharply. Around the edges the buckwheat cake began to firm, then brown, then crisp. The surface was bubbling slowly to porousness. Nick pushed under the browned under surface with a fresh pine chip. He shook the skillet sideways and the cake was loose on the surface. I won't try and flop it, he thought. He slid the chip of clean wood all the way under the cake, and flopped it over onto its face. It sputtered in the pan.

When it was cooked Nick regreased the skillet. He used all the batter. It made another big flapjack and one smaller one.

Nick ate a big flapjack and a smaller one, covered with apple butter. He put apple butter on the third cake, folded it over twice, wrapped it in oiled paper and put it in his shirt pocket. He put the apple butter jar back in the pack and cut bread for two sandwiches.

In the pack he found a big onion. He sliced it in two and peeled the silky outer skin. Then he cut one half into slices and made onion sandwiches. He wrapped them in oiled paper and buttoned them in the other pocket of his khaki shirt. He turned the skillet upside down on the grill, drank the coffee, sweetened and yellow brown with the condensed milk in it, and tidied up the camp. It was a good camp.

Nick took his fly rod out of the leather rod-case, jointed it, and shoved the rod-case back into the tent. He put on the reel and threaded the line through the guides. He had to hold it from hand to hand, as he threaded it, or it would slip back through its own weight. It was a heavy, double-tapered fly line. Nick had paid eight dollars for it a long time ago. It was made heavy to lift back in the air and come forward flat and heavy and straight to make it possible to cast a fly which has no weight. Nick opened the aluminum leader box. The leaders were coiled between the damp flannel pads. Nick had wet the pads at the water cooler on the train up to St. Ignace. In the damp pads the gut leaders had softened and Nick unrolled one and tied it by a loop at the end to the heavy fly line. He fastened a hook on the end of the leader. It was a small hook; very thin and springy.

Nick took it from his hook book, sitting with the rod across his lap. He tested the knot and the spring of the rod by pulling the line taut. It was a good feeling. He was careful not to let the hook bite into his finger.

He started down to the stream, holding his rod, the bottle of grasshoppers hung from his neck by a thong tied in half hitches around the neck of the bottle. His landing net hung by a hook from his belt. Over his shoulder was a long flour sack tied at each corner into an ear. The cord went over his shoulder. The sack flapped against his legs.

Nick felt awkward and professionally happy with all his equipment hanging from him. The grasshopper bottle swung against his chest. In his shirt the breast pockets bulged against him with the lunch and his fly book.

He stepped into the stream. It was a shock. His trousers clung tight to his legs. His shoes felt the gravel. The water was a rising cold shock.

Rushing, the current sucked against his legs. Where he stepped in, the water was over his knees. He waded with the current. The gravel slid under his shoes. He looked down at the swirl of water below each leg and tipped up the bottle to get a grasshopper.

The first grasshopper gave a jump in the neck of the bottle and went out into the water. He was sucked under in the whirl by Nick's right leg and came to the surface a little way down stream. He floated rapidly, kicking. In a quick circle, breaking the smooth surface of the water, he disappeared. A trout had taken him.

Another hopper poked his face out of the bottle. His antennæ wavered. He was getting his front legs out of the bottle to jump. Nick took him by the head and held him while he threaded the slim hook under his chin, down through his thorax and into the last segments of his abdomen. The grasshopper took hold of the hook with his front feet, spitting tobacco juice on it. Nick dropped him into the water.

Holding the rod in his right hand he let out line against the pull of the grasshopper in the current. He stripped off line from the reel with his left hand and let it run free. He could see the hopper in the little waves of the current. It went out of sight.

There was a tug on the line. Nick pulled against the taut line. It was his first strike. Holding the now living rod across the current, he brought in the line with his left hand. The rod bent in jerks, the trout

pumping against the current. Nick knew it was a small one. He lifted the rod straight up in the air. It bowed with the pull.

He saw the trout in the water jerking with his head and body against the shifting tangent of the line in the stream.

Nick took the line in his left hand and pulled the trout, thumping tiredly against the current, to the surface. His back was mottled the clear, water-over-gravel color, his side flashing in the sun. The rod under his right arm, Nick stooped, dipping his right hand into the current. He held the trout, never still, with his moist right hand, while he unhooked the barb from his mouth, then dropped him back into the stream.

He hung unsteadily in the current, then settled to the bottom beside a stone. Nick reached down his hand to touch him, his arm to the elbow under water. The trout was steady in the moving stream, resting on the gravel, beside a stone. As Nick's fingers touched him, touched his smooth, cool, underwater feeling he was gone, gone in a shadow across the bottom of the stream.

He's all right, Nick thought. He was only tired.

He had wet his hand before he touched the trout, so he would not disturb the delicate mucus that covered him. If a trout was touched with a dry hand, a white fungus attacked the unprotected spot. Years before when he had fished crowded streams, with fly fishermen ahead of him and behind him, Nick had again and again come on dead trout, furry with white fungus, drifted against a rock, or floating belly up in some pool. Nick did not like to fish with other men on the river. Unless they were of your party, they spoiled it.

He wallowed down the stream, above his knees in the current, through the fifty yards of shallow water above the pile of logs that crossed the stream. He did not rebait his hook and held it in his hand as he waded. He was certain he could catch small trout in the shallows, but he did not want them. There would be no big trout in the shallows this time of day.

Now the water deepened up his thighs sharply and coldly. Ahead was the smooth dammed-back flood of water above the logs. The water was smooth and dark; on the left, the lower edge of the meadow; on the right the swamp.

Nick leaned back against the current and took a hopper from the bottle. He threaded the hopper on the hook and spat on him for good luck. Then he pulled several yards of line from the reel and tossed the hopper out ahead onto the fast, dark water. It floated down toward the logs, then the weight of the line pulled the bait under the surface. Nick held the rod in his right hand, letting the line run out through his fingers.

There was a long tug. Nick struck and the rod came alive and dangerous, bent double, the line tightening, coming out of water, tightening, all in a heavy, dangerous, steady pull. Nick felt the moment when the leader would break if the strain increased and let the line go.

The reel ratcheted into a mechanical shriek as the line went out in a rush. Too fast. Nick could not check it, the line rushing out, the reel note rising as the line ran out.

With the core of the reel showing, his heart feeling stopped with the excitement, leaning back against the current that mounted icily his thighs, Nick thumbed the reel hard with his left hand. It was awkward getting his thumb inside the fly reel frame.

As he put on pressure the line tightened into sudden hardness and beyond the logs a huge trout went high out of water. As he jumped, Nick lowered the tip of the rod. But he felt, as he dropped the tip to ease the strain, the moment when the strain was too great; the hardness too tight. Of course, the leader had broken. There was no mistaking the feeling when all spring left the line and it became dry and hard. Then it went slack.

His mouth dry, his heart down, Nick reeled in. He had never seen so big a

trout. There was a heaviness, a power not to be held, and then the bulk of him, as he jumped. He looked as broad as a salmon.

Nick's hand was shaky. He reeled in slowly. The thrill had been too much. He felt, vaguely, a little sick, as though it would be better to sit down.

The leader had broken where the hook was tied to it. Nick took it in his hand. He thought of the trout somewhere on the bottom, holding himself steady over the gravel, far down below the light, under the logs, with the hook in his jaw. Nick knew the trout's teeth would cut through the snell [1] of the hook. The hook would imbed itself in his jaw. He'd bet the trout was angry. Anything that size would be angry. That was a trout. He had been solidly hooked. Solid as a rock. He felt like a rock, too, before he started off. He was a big one. He was the biggest one I ever heard of.

Nick climbed out onto the meadow and stood, water running down his trousers and out of his shoes, his shoes squelchy. He went over and sat on the logs. He did not want to rush his sensations any.

He wriggled his toes in the water, in his shoes, and got out a cigarette from his breast pocket. He lit it and tossed the match into the fast water below the logs. A tiny trout rose at the match, as it swung around in the fast current. Nick laughed. He would finish the cigarette.

[1] **snell:** a short line of gut by which the hook is attached to the line.

He sat on the logs, smoking, drying in the sun, the sun warm on his back, the river shallow ahead entering the woods, curving into the woods, shallows, light glittering, big water-smooth rocks, cedars along the bank and white birches, the logs warm in the sun, smooth to sit on, without bark, gray to the touch; slowly the feeling of disappointment left him. It went away slowly, the feeling of disappointment that came sharply after the thrill that made his shoulders ache. It was all right now. His rod lying out on the logs, Nick tied a new hook on the leader, pulling the gut tight until it grimped [1] into itself in a hard knot.

He baited up, then picked up the rod and walked to the far end of the logs to get into the water, where it was not too deep. Under and beyond the logs was a deep pool. Nick walked around the shallow shelf near the swamp shore until he came out on the shallow bed of the stream.

On the left, where the meadow ended and the woods began, a great elm tree was uprooted. Gone over in a storm, it lay back into the woods, its roots clotted with dirt, grass growing in them, rising a solid bank beside the stream. The river cut to the edge of the uprooted tree. From where Nick stood he could see deep channels, like ruts, cut in the shallow bed of the stream by the flow of the current. Pebbly where he stood and pebbly and full of boulders beyond; where it curved near the tree roots, the bed of the stream was marly and between the ruts of deep water green weed fronds swung in the current.

Nick swung the rod back over his shoulder and forward, and the line, curving forward, laid the grasshopper down on one of the deep channels in the weeds. A trout struck and Nick hooked him.

Holding the rod far out toward the uprooted tree and sloshing backward in the current, Nick worked the trout, plunging, the rod bending alive, out of the danger of the weeds into the open river. Holding the rod, pumping alive against the current,

Nick brought the trout in. He rushed, but always came, the spring of the rod yielding to the rushes, sometimes jerking under water, but always bringing him in. Nick eased downstream with the rushes. The rod above his head he led the trout over the net, then lifted.

The trout hung heavy in the net, mottled trout back and silver sides in the meshes. Nick unhooked him; heavy sides, good to hold, big undershot jaw, and slipped him, heaving and big sliding, into the long sack that hung from his shoulders in the water.

Nick spread the mouth of the sack against the current and it filled, heavy with water. He held it up, the bottom in the stream, and the water poured out through the sides. Inside at the bottom was the big trout, alive in the water.

Nick moved downstream. The sack out ahead of him sunk heavy in the water, pulling from his shoulders.

It was getting hot, the sun hot on the back of his neck.

Nick had one good trout. He did not care about getting many trout. Now the stream was shallow and wide. There were trees along both banks. The trees of the left bank made short shadows on the current in the forenoon sun. Nick knew there were trout in each shadow. In the afternoon, after the sun had crossed toward the hills, the trout would be in the cool shadows on the other side of the stream.

The very biggest ones would lie up close to the bank. You could always pick them up there on the Black. When the sun was down they all moved out into the current. Just when the sun made the water blinding in the glare before it went down, you were liable to strike a big trout anywhere in the current. It was almost impossible to fish then, the surface of the water was blinding as a mirror in the sun. Of course, you could fish upstream, but in a stream like the Black, or this, you had to wallow against the current and in a deep place, the water piled up on you. It was no fun to fish upstream with this much current.

Nick moved along through the shallow

[1] **grimped:** drew up.

stretch watching the banks for deep holes. A beech tree grew close beside the river, so that the branches hung down into the water. The stream went back in under the leaves. There were always trout in a place like that.

Nick did not care about fishing that hole. He was sure he would get hooked in the branches.

It looked deep though. He dropped the grasshopper so the current took it under water, back in under the overhanging branch. The line pulled hard and Nick struck. The trout threshed heavily, half out of water in the leaves and branches. The line was caught. Nick pulled hard and the trout was off. He reeled in and holding the hook in his hand, walked down the stream.

Ahead, close to the left bank, was a big log. Nick saw it was hollow; pointing up river the current entered it smoothly, only a little ripple spread each side of the log. The water was deepening. The top of the hollow log was gray and dry. It was partly in the shadow.

Nick took the cork out of the grasshopper bottle and a hopper clung to it. He picked him off, hooked him and tossed him out. He held the rod far out so that the hopper on the water moved into the current flowing into the hollow log. Nick lowered the rod and the hopper floated in. There was a heavy strike. Nick swung the rod against the pull. It felt as though he were hooked into the log itself, except for the live feeling.

He tried to force the fish out into the current. It came, heavily.

The line went slack and Nick thought the trout was gone. Then he saw him, very near, in the current, shaking his head, trying to get the hook out. His mouth was clamped shut. He was fighting the hook in the clear flowing current.

Looping in the line with his left hand, Nick swung the rod to make the line taut and tried to lead the trout toward the net, but he was gone, out of sight, the line pumping. Nick fought him against the current, letting him thump in the water against

the spring of the rod. He shifted the rod to his left hand, worked the trout upstream, holding his weight, fighting on the rod, and then let him down into the net. He lifted him clear of the water, a heavy half circle in the net, the net dripping, unhooked him and slid him into the sack.

He spread the mouth of the sack and looked down in at the two big trout alive in the water.

Through the deepening water, Nick waded over to the hollow log. He took the sack off, over his head, the trout flopping as it came out of water, and hung it so the trout were deep in the water. Then he pulled himself up on the log and sat, the water from his trousers and boots running down into the stream. He laid his rod down, moved along to the shady end of the log and took the sandwiches out of his pocket. He dipped the sandwiches in the cold water. The current carried away the crumbs. He ate the sandwiches and dipped his hat full of water to drink, the water running out through his hat just ahead of his drinking.

It was cool in the shade, sitting on the log. He took a cigarette out and struck a match to light it. The match sunk into the gray wood, making a tiny furrow. Nick leaned over the side of the log, found a hard place and lit the match. He sat smoking and watching the river.

Ahead the river narrowed and went into a swamp. The river became smooth and deep and the swamp looked solid with cedar trees, their trunks close together, their branches solid. It would not be possible to walk through a swamp like that. The branches grew so low. You would have to keep almost level with the ground to move at all. You could not crash through the branches. That must be why the animals that lived in swamps were built the way they were, Nick thought.

He wished he had brought something to read. He felt like reading. He did not feel like going on into the swamp. He looked down the river. A big cedar slanted all the way across the stream. Beyond that the river went into the swamp.

Nick did not want to go in there now. He felt a reaction against deep wading with the water deepening up under his armpits, to hook big trout in places impossible to land them. In the swamp the banks were bare, the big cedars came together overhead, the sun did not come through, except in patches; in the fast deep water, in the half light, the fishing would be tragic. In the swamp fishing was a tragic adventure. Nick did not want it. He did not want to go down the stream any further today.

He took out his knife, opened it and stuck it in the log. Then he pulled up the sack, reached into it and brought out one of the trout. Holding him near the tail, hard to hold, alive, in his hand, he whacked him against the log. The trout quivered, rigid. Nick laid him on the log in the shade and broke the neck of the other fish the same way. He laid them side by side on the log. They were fine trout.

Nick cleaned them, slitting them from the vent to the tip of the jaw. All the insides and the gills and tongue came out in one piece. They were both males; long gray-white strips of milt, smooth and clean. All the insides clean and compact, coming out all together. Nick tossed the offal ashore for the minks to find.

He washed the trout in the stream. When he held them back up in the water they looked like live fish. Their color was not gone yet. He washed his hands and dried them on the log. Then he laid the trout on the sack spread out on the log, rolled them up in it, tied the bundle and put it in the landing net. His knife was still standing, blade stuck in the log. He cleaned it on the wood and put it in his pocket.

Nick stood up on the log, holding his rod, the landing net hanging heavy, then stepped into the water and splashed ashore. He climbed the bank and cut up into the woods, toward the high ground. He was going back to camp. He looked back. The river just showed through the trees. There were plenty of days coming when he could fish the swamp.

COMMENTARY

If a person were to read "Big Two-Hearted River" without having read other works by Hemingway, he might be puzzled by the story and even more puzzled by critics who think that "Big Two-Hearted River" is one of Hemingway's best, most important stories. At first the surface events of this story—making camp, catching trout, and so forth—may seem boring and unimportant. But these events are primarily reflections of other events existing on a deeper level of the story, like the trout hiding at the bottom of the river.

Nick, you must recall, had been gravely wounded while fighting on the Italian front. The reader is told little about Nick's troubles in this story, but sentences like "His mind was starting to work. He knew that he could choke it because he was tired enough" show that Nick is deeply troubled. Physically, perhaps, he has recovered from his wound, but in other ways the wound is still a part of him that he is trying to escape. Like the country in northern Michigan that he first walks through, he has been burned over, and he has to be very careful not to put himself under any sort of a mental strain. Physical effort seems to afford him relief.

As we read, we begin to realize that although Nick has left the Italian front, in a sense he has not escaped from the battlefield. The town of Seney has been burned to the ground as if it had been the site of a battle. So violent has been its destruction that all the grasshoppers in the area are black. The trout that Nick catches are casualties in a kind of battle as are the grasshoppers he uses as bait. Violence and death are present even in upper Michigan.

Very early in the story Hemingway describes Nick lingering on the railroad bridge, looking down at the river swirling against the log-driven piles. In the midst of the devastated countryside, the river still contains living fish. The symbolic importance of this fact to Nick is suggested by two sentences: "It was a long time since Nick had looked into a stream and seen trout. They were very satisfactory."

Nick feels he can live safely only on the level of sensations. He can find pleasure in eating spaghetti and beans and drinking coffee, but he must not think of Hopkins, who taught him how to prepare coffee, because memories of Hopkins might lead to other, more dangerous memories. Restricting his awareness to physical sensations gives him both pleasure and a feeling of security. Furthermore, he can take pride in performing simple, physically demanding tasks. A passage characteristic of Hemingway's best writing depicts Nick's level of awareness and his feeling of achievement.

"Now things were done. There had been this to do. Now it was done. It had been a hard trip. He was very tired. That was done. He had made his camp. He was settled. Nothing could touch him. It was a good place to camp. He was there, in the good place. He was in his home where he had made it."

This passage may seem absurdly simple, even childish, but studying it carefully will reveal its artfulness. The rhythm of the sentences and the repetition of words and phrases, such as "done," "place," "it was," and "he was," give this passage an almost hypnotic quality and vividly convey Nick's fatigue and his almost sullen avoidance of any significant or complicated thought.

On the second day Nick makes very careful preparations for fishing and he fishes well, but he overextends himself and loses the biggest trout he has ever seen. All this time Nick has been fishing in one part of the river, where the water is bright and clear. Now he sees the river narrow and go into the swamp. "Nick did not want to go in there now. He felt a reaction against deep wading with the water deepening up under his armpits ... In the swamp fishing was a tragic adventure. Nick did not want it. He did not want to go down the stream any further today." Nick retreats, as previously he has retreated from memories of Hopkins. He cleans the fish and prepares to go back to camp. "There were plenty of days coming when he could fish the swamp."

FOR STUDY AND DISCUSSION

1. What is the significance of the title of this story? Why does Nick retreat from the swamp? Why does he see fishing there as a "tragic adventure"?

2. What is the symbolic significance of the fact, referred to in the Commentary, that in the midst of the devastated countryside, the river still contains living fish?

3. At what point in the story do you first become aware that something is wrong with Nick? Why?

4. Find passages in this story that convey a sense of pleasure in purely physical sensations. Hemingway has a reputation for being able to convey precisely how a thing looks or how it feels. Do you think he deserves this reputation? Explain your answer.

5. Judging from this story, what do you gather Hemingway considered important in life? What kinds of skills did he think it was important for a man to have? How did he think a man should face life? Support your answers with details from this story.

6. Do you think that Nick will be able to fish in the swamp some day? Why or why not?

FOR COMPOSITION

1. The Commentary of this story states: "At first the surface events of this story . . . may seem boring and unimportant. But these events are primarily reflections of other events existing on a deeper level of the story, like the trout hiding at the bottom of the river." Write a composition in which you agree or disagree with this statement. Give details from the story to support your case.

2. "Big Two-Hearted River" grows in meaning if it is related to the other stories of *In Our Time*. Study this collection. Discuss Nick Adams's development as a character. What does he learn about life and about his own times? What do the vignettes which appear between the stories contribute to your understanding of Nick's times?

WILLIAM FAULKNER

(1897–1962)

William Faulkner once said in an interview that in writing his novel *Sartoris* he became aware of his true subject: "I discovered that my little postage stamp of native soil was worth writing about and that I would never live long enough to exhaust it, and that by sublimating the actual with the apocryphal I would have complete liberty to use whatever talent I might have to its actual top. It opened up a gold mine of people, as I created a cosmos of my own." The fictional cosmos Faulkner created is Yoknapatawpha County, and it does have a reality of its own. Most students of Faulkner know, for example, that it is in northern Mississippi, that it consists of 2,400 square miles and some 15,000 persons, and that the county seat is Jefferson. More important, Faulkner has charged what happens there with a significance that only literature can infuse. Slowly, with the appearance of each novel and story, he filled in the history of the county. This is also the history of a society, the decisions it faces, the directions in which it is drawn, its effort to maintain its traditions and code of honor, and the threat posed by a new kind of man lacking a code or any sense of order except what can be found in the credit and debit columns of a ledger. Faulkner has written of his county with such a mastery of social and psychological detail that he has made it seem an actual part of the Deep South, but he has also imagined a sequence of events that has the basic moral quality of a parable.

William Faulkner was born near Oxford, Mississippi. John Cullum, a friend of Faulkner, remembers him as a "quiet, dreamy-eyed boy" who liked to listen to stories about hunting. "He did not ask too many questions as most young town boys do. He just seemed to enjoy walking around in the woods and observing the things that he saw." At the time, said Cullum, "we never thought that this . . . boy would remember every detail of all he heard and saw and would some day weave these memories into stories . . ."

After the fifth grade, Faulkner attended school only occasionally, but he read a good deal—especially French and modern English poetry—and took several courses at the University of Mississippi, in Oxford. During World War I he went to Canada and joined the Royal Flying Corps, in which he was made a lieutenant. After the Armistice he returned to Oxford and entered the University. He attended classes on and off for two years, and meanwhile supported himself as a carpenter and house painter and later as university postmaster. Faulkner continued as postmaster until October, 1924, when, according to his own account, he resigned "by mutual consent on part of two inspectors: accused of throwing all incoming mail into garbage can. How disposed of outgoing mail never proved. Inspectors foiled."

In December, 1924, William Faulkner went to New Orleans, where he met Sherwood Anderson. There Faulkner wrote his first novel, *Soldier's Pay,* and Anderson agreed to recommend it to a publisher on condition that he did not have to read it first. Before the novel's publication in 1926, Faulkner spent some unhappy months in New York and most of a year in Europe; then he returned to Oxford, Mississippi. He moved into an old house that he renovated himself, and lived there most of the rest of his life.

Once back home, Faulkner began to write the novels and short stories that many critics regard as among the most important by an American writer of the twentieth century. His first notable work, *The Sound and the Fury,* appeared in 1929. Concerned with the ruin of the Compson family over several generations, it requires and deserves several careful readings. The opening portion is told through Benjy, an idiot who lacks all sense of time and constantly jumbles together the past and present. Only in the final section does Faulkner show the balanced, lucid style he uses when he feels it is appropriate to his subject. Many of Faulkner's works make similar demands on the reader, but these demands are rarely unreasonable. The involved syntax, the sudden shifts in time and subject matter, and the frequent use of symbols reflect the dark, confused emotions of his characters and the growing disorder that surrounds them. Only a few of the characters manage to escape disorder by following simple, natural occupations—farming and hunting—and by respecting the life-giving soil and all living things. After *The Sound and the Fury* other important works followed: *As I Lay Dying, The Hamlet, Light in August, Absalom, Absalom,* and *Go Down Moses.*

In the thirties and early forties, Faulkner was regarded primarily as an eccentric writer who might possibly occupy a minor place in American literature. By 1945, his novels were nearly out of print. Only gradually was he recognized as a major writer. Critics such as Robert Penn Warren and Malcolm Cowley wrote essays that penetrated his surface oddities to discover his underlying greatness: an intense concern with issues not simply peculiar to the South but involving all humanity; a tremendous variety of stories and situations, ranging from earthy comedy to deep tragedy; and, at best, an enormous power of expression. Before his death Faulkner was regarded by many as the greatest living American novelist. When he was awarded the Nobel prize in 1949, he made a famous statement about his own work and all literature:

"I feel that this award was made not to me as a man, but to my work—a life's work in the agony and sweat of the human spirit, not for glory and least of all for profit, but to create out of the materials of the human spirit something which did not exist before. So this award is only mine in trust. . . . I decline to accept the end of man. . . . I believe that man will not merely endure; he will prevail. He is immortal, not because he alone among creatures has an inexhaustible voice, but because he has a soul, a spirit capable of compassion and sacrifice and endurance. The poet's, the writer's, duty is to write about these things. It is his privilege to help man endure by lifting his heart, by reminding him of the courage and honor and hope and pride and compassion and pity and sacrifice which have been the glory of his past."

Race at Morning

I WAS in the boat when I seen him. It was jest dust-dark; I had jest fed the horses and clumb back down the bank to the boat and shoved off to cross back to camp when I seen him, about half a quarter up the river, swimming; jest his head above the water, and it no more than a dot in that light. But I could see that rocking chair he toted on it and I knowed it was him, going right back to that canebrake in the fork of the bayou where he lived all year until the day before the season opened, like the game wardens had give him a calendar, when he would clear out and disappear, nobody knowed where, until the day after the season closed. But here he was, coming back a day ahead of time, like maybe he had got mixed up and was using last year's calendar by mistake. Which was jest too bad for him, because me and Mister Ernest would be setting on the horse right over him when the sun rose tomorrow morning.

So I told Mister Ernest and we et supper and fed the dogs, and then I holp Mister Ernest in the poker game, standing behind his chair until about ten o'clock, when Roth Edmonds said, "Why don't you go to bed, boy?"

"Or if you're going to set up," Willy Legate said, "why don't you take a spelling book to set up over? He knows every cuss word in the dictionary, every poker hand in the deck and every whisky label in the distillery, but he can't even write his name. Can you?" he says to me.

"I don't need to write my name down," I said. "I can remember in my mind who I am."

"You're twelve years old," Walter Ewell said. "Man to man now, how many

days in your life did you ever spend in school?"

"He ain't got time to go to school," Willy Legate said. "What's the use in going to school from September to middle of November, when he'll have to quit then to come in here and do Ernest's hearing for him? And what's the use in going back to school in January, when in jest eleven months it will be November fifteenth again and he'll have to start all over telling Ernest which way the dogs went?"

"Well, stop looking into my hand, anyway," Roth Edmonds said.

"What's that? What's that?" Mister Ernest said. He wore his listening button in his ear all the time, but he never brought the battery to camp with him because the cord would bound to get snagged ever time we run through a thicket.

"Willy says for me to go to bed!" I hollered.

"Don't you never call nobody 'mister'?" Willy said.

"I call Mister Ernest 'mister,' " I said.

"All right," Mister Ernest said. "Go to bed then. I don't need you."

"That ain't no lie," Willy said. "Deaf or no deaf, he can hear a fifty-dollar raise [1] if you don't even move your lips."

So I went to bed, and after a while Mister Ernest come in and I wanted to tell him again how big them horns looked even half a quarter away in the river. Only I would 'a' had to holler, and the only time Mister Ernest agreed he couldn't hear was when we would be setting on Dan, waiting for me to point which way the dogs was going. So we jest laid down, and it wasn't no time Simon was beating the bottom of the dishpan with the spoon, hollering, "Raise up and get your four-o'clock coffee!" and I crossed the river in the dark this time, with the lantern, and fed Dan and Roth Edmondziz horse. It was going to be a fine day, cold and bright; even in the dark I could see the white frost on the leaves and bushes—jest

---

[1] **fifty-dollar raise:** a reference to raising the bet in poker.

exactly the kind of day that big old son of a gun laying up there in that brake would like to run.

Then we et, and set the stand-holder across for Uncle Ike McCaslin to put them on the stands where he thought they ought to be, because he was the oldest one in camp. He had been hunting deer in these woods for about a hundred years, I reckon, and if anybody would know where a buck would pass, it would be him. Maybe with a big old buck like this one, that had been running the woods for what would amount to a hundred years in a deer's life, too, him and Uncle Ike would sholy manage to be at the same place at the same time this morning—provided, of course, he managed to git away from me and Mister Ernest on the jump. Because me and Mister Ernest was going to git him.

Then me and Mister Ernest and Roth Edmonds sent the dogs over, with Simon holding Eagle and the other old dogs on leash because the young ones, the puppies, wasn't going nowhere until Eagle let them, nohow. Then me and Mister Ernest and Roth saddled up, and Mister Ernest got up and I handed him up his pump gun and let Dan's bridle go for him to git rid of the spell of bucking he had to git shut of ever morning until Mister Ernest hit him between the ears with the gun barrel. Then Mister Ernest loaded the gun and give me the stirrup, and I got up behind him and we taken the fire road up toward the bayou, the four big dogs dragging Simon along in front with his single-barrel britch-loader slung on a piece of plow line across his back, and the puppies moiling[1] along in ever'body's way. It was light now and it was going to be jest fine; the east already yellow for the sun and our breaths smoking in the cold still bright air until the sun would come up and warm it, and a little skim of ice in the ruts, and ever leaf and twig and switch and even the frozen clods frosted over, waiting to sparkle like a rain-

[1] **moiling:** struggling.

bow when the sun finally come up and hit them. Until all my insides felt light and strong as a balloon, full of that light cold strong air, so that it seemed to me like I couldn't even feel the horse's back I was straddle of—jest the hot strong muscles moving under the hot strong skin, setting up there without no weight atall, so that when old Eagle struck and jumped, me and Dan and Mister Ernest would go jest like a bird, not even touching the ground. It was jest fine. When that big old buck got killed today, I knowed that even if he had put it off another ten years, he couldn't 'a' picked a better one.

And sho enough, as soon as we come to the bayou we seen his foot in the mud where he had come up out of the river last night, spread in the soft mud like a cow's foot, big as a cow's, big as a mule's, with Eagle and the other dogs laying into the leash rope now until Mister Ernest told me to jump down and help Simon hold them. Because me and Mister Ernest knowed exactly where he would be—a little canebrake island in the middle of the bayou, where he could lay up until whatever doe or little deer the dogs had happened to jump could go up or down the bayou in either direction and take the dogs on away, so he could steal out and creep back down the bayou to the river and swim it, and leave the country like he always done the day the season opened.

Which is jest what we never aimed for him to do this time. So we left Roth on his horse to cut him off and turn him over Uncle Ike's standers if he tried to slip back down the bayou, and me and Simon, with the leashed dogs, walked on up the bayou until Mister Ernest on the horse said it was fur enough; then turned up into the woods about half a quarter above the brake because the wind was going to be south this morning when it riz, and turned down toward the brake, and Mister Ernest give the word to cast them, and we slipped the leash and Mister Ernest give me the stirrup again and I got up.

Old Eagle had done already took off because he knowed where that old son of a gun would be laying as good as we did, not making no racket atall yet, but jest boring on through the buck vines with the other dogs trailing along behind him, and even Dan seemed to know about that buck, too, beginning to souple up [1] and jump a little through the vines, so that I taken my holt on Mister Ernest's belt already before the time had come for Mister Ernest to touch him. Because when we got strung out, going fast behind a deer, I wasn't on Dan's back much of the time nohow, but mostly jest strung out from my holt on Mister Ernest's belt, so that Willy Legate said that when we was going through the woods fast, it looked like Mister Ernest had a boy-size pair of empty overalls blowing out of his hind pocket.

So it wasn't even a strike, it was a jump. Eagle must 'a' walked right up behind him or maybe even stepped on him while he was laying there still thinking it was day after tomorrow. Eagle jest throwed his head back and up and said, "There he goes," and we even heard the buck crashing through the first of the cane. Then all the other dogs was hollering behind him, and Dan give a squat to jump, but it was against the curb [2] this time, not jest the snaffle,[3] and Mister Ernest let him down into the bayou and swung him around the brake and up the other bank. Only he never had to say, "Which way?" because I was already pointing past his shoulder, freshening my holt on the belt jest as Mister Ernest touched Dan with that big old rusty spur on his nigh heel, because when Dan felt it he would go off jest like a stick of dynamite, straight through whatever he could bust and over or under what he couldn't, over it like a bird or under it crawling on his knees like a mole or a big coon, with Mister Ernest still on him because he had the saddle to hold on to, and me still there because I had Mister Ernest to hold on to; me and Mister Ernest not

riding him, but jest going along with him, provided we held on. Because when the jump come, Dan never cared who else was there neither; I believe to my soul he could 'a' cast and run them dogs by hisself, without me or Mister Ernest or Simon or nobody.

That's what he done. He had to; the dogs was already almost out of hearing. Eagle must 'a' been looking right up that big son of a gun's tail until he finally decided he better git on out of there. And now they must 'a' been getting pretty close to Uncle Ike's standers, and Mister Ernest reined Dan back and held him, squatting and bouncing and trembling like a mule having his tail roached,[4] while we listened for the shots. But never none come, and I hollered to Mister Ernest we better go on while I could still hear the dogs, and he let Dan off, but still there wasn't no shots, and now we knowed the race had done already passed the standers,[5] like that old son of a gun actually was a hant, like Simon and the other field hands said he was, and we busted out of a thicket, and sho enough there was Uncle Ike and Willy standing beside his foot in a soft patch.

"He got through us all," Uncle Ike said. "I don't know how he done it. I just had a glimpse of him. He looked big as a elephant, with a rack on his head you could cradle a yellin' calf in. He went right on down the ridge. You better get on, too; that Hog Bayou camp might not miss him."

So I freshened my holt and Mister Ernest touched Dan again. The ridge run due south; it was clear of vines and bushes so we could go fast, into the wind, too, because it had riz now, and now the sun was up, too; though I hadn't had time to notice it, bright and strong and level through the woods, shining and sparking like a rainbow on the frosted leaves. So we would hear the dogs again any time

[1] **souple up:** loosen up.
[2] **curb:** a bit with a chain or strap which is pulled to restrain the horse.
[3] **snaffle:** a plain, jointed bridle bit.

[4] **roached.** trimmed.
[5] **standers:** members of a hunting party whose duty it is to stand while the game is driven within shooting range of them.

now as the wind got up; we could make time now, but still holding Dan back to a canter, because it was either going to be quick, when he got down to the standers from that Hog Bayou camp eight miles below ourn, or a long time, in case he got by them, too. And sho enough, after a while we heard the dogs; we was walking Dan now to let him blow [1] a while, and we heard them, the sound coming faint up the wind, not running now, but trailing because the big son of a gun had decided a good piece back, probably, to put a end to this foolishness, and picked hisself up and soupled out and put about a mile between hisself and the dogs—until he run up on them other standers from that camp below. I could almost see him stopped behind a bush, peeping out and saying, "What's this? What's this? Is this whole durn country full of folks this morning?" Then looking back over his shoulder at where old Eagle and the others was hollering along after him while he decided how much time he had to decide what to do next.

Except he almost shaved it too fine. We heard the shots; it sounded like a war. Old Eagle must 'a' been looking right up his tail again and he had to bust on through the best way he could. "Pow, pow, pow, pow" and then "Pow, pow, pow, pow," like it must 'a' been three or four ganged right up on him before he had time even to swerve, and me hollering, "No! No! No! No!" because he was ourn. It was our beans and oats he et and our brake he laid in; we had been watching him every year, and it was like we had raised him, to be killed at last on our jump, in front of our dogs, by some strangers that would probably try to beat the dogs off and drag him away before we could even git a piece of the meat.

"Shut up and listen," Mister Ernest said. So I done it and we could hear the dogs; not just the others, but Eagle too, not trailing no scent now and not baying no downed meat neither, but running hot

on sight long after the shooting was over. I jest had time to freshen my holt. Yes, sir, they was running on sight. Like Willy Legate would say, if Eagle jest had a drink of whisky he would ketch that deer; going on, done already gone when we broke out of the thicket and seen the fellers that had done the shooting, five or six of them, squatting and crawling around, looking at the ground and the bushes, like maybe if they looked hard enough, spots of blood would bloom out on the stalks and leaves like frogstools or hawberries,[2] with old Eagle still in hearing and still telling them that what blood they found wasn't coming out of nothing in front of him.

"Have any luck, boys?" Mister Ernest said.

"I think I hit him," one of them said. "I know I did. We're hunting blood now."

"Well, when you find him, blow your horn and I'll come back and tote him in to camp for you," Mister Ernest said.

So we went on, going fast now because the race was almost out of hearing again, going fast, too, like not jest the buck, but the dogs, too, had took a new leash on life from all the excitement and shooting.

We was in strange country now because we never had to run this fur before, we had always killed before now; now we had come to Hog Bayou that runs into the river a good fifteen miles below our camp. It had water in it, not to mention a mess of down trees and logs and such, and Mister Ernest checked Dan again, saying, "Which way?" I could just barely hear them, off to the east a little, like the old son of a gun had give up the idea of Vicksburg or New Orleans, like he first seemed to have, and had decided to have a look at Alabama, maybe, since he was already up and moving; so I pointed and we turned up the bayou hunting for a crossing, and maybe we could 'a' found one, except that I reckon Mister Ernest decided we never had time to wait.

---

[1] **blow:** breathe less hard.

[2] **hawberries:** small red fruits of the hawthorn, a spiny shrub.

We come to a place where the bayou had narrowed down to about twelve or fifteen feet, and Mister Ernest said, "Look out, I'm going to touch him" and done it; I didn't even have time to freshen my holt when we was already in the air, and then I seen the vine—it was a loop of grapevine nigh as big as my wrist, looping down right across the middle of the bayou—and I thought he seen it, too, and was jest waiting to grab it and fling it up over our heads to go under it, and I know Dan seen it because he even ducked his head to jump under it. But Mister Ernest never seen it atall until it skun back along Dan's neck and hooked under the head of the saddle horn, us flying on through the air, the loop of the vine gitting tighter and tighter until something somewhere was going to have to give. It was the saddle girth. It broke, and Dan going on and scrabbling up the other bank bare nekkid except for the bridle, and me and Mister Ernest and the saddle, Mister Ernest still setting in the saddle holding the gun, and me still holding onto Mister Ernest's belt, hanging in the air over the bayou in the tightened loop of that vine like in the drawed-back loop of a big rubber-banded slingshot, until it snapped back and shot us back

across the bayou and flang us clear, me still holding onto Mister Ernest's belt and on the bottom now, so that when we lit I would 'a' had Mister Ernest and the saddle both on top of me if I hadn't climb fast around the saddle and up Mister Ernest's side, so that when we landed, it was the saddle first, then Mister Ernest, and me on top, until I jumped up, and Mister Ernest still laying there with jest the white rim of his eyes showing.

"Mister Ernest!" I hollered, and then clumb down to the bayou and scooped my cap full of water and clumb back and throwed it in his face, and he opened his eyes and laid there on the saddle cussing me.

"Dawg it," he said, "why didn't you stay behind where you started out?"

"You was the biggest!" I said. "You would 'a' mashed me flat!"

"What do you think you done to me?" Mister Ernest said. "Next time, if you can't stay where you start out, jump clear. Don't climb up on top of me no more. You hear?"

"Yes, sir," I said.

So he got up then, still cussing and holding his back, and clumb down to the water and dipped some in his hand onto his face and neck and dipped some more up and drunk it, and I drunk some, too, and clumb back and got the saddle and the gun, and we crossed the bayou on the down logs. If we could jest ketch Dan; not that he would have went them fifteen miles back to camp, because, if anything, he would have went on by hisself to try to help Eagle ketch that buck. But he was about fifty yards away, eating buck vines, so I brought him back, and we taken Mister Ernest's galluses and my belt and the whang [1] leather loop off Mister Ernest's horn and tied the saddle back on Dan. It didn't look like much, but maybe it would hold.

"Provided you don't let me jump him through no more grapevines without hollering first," Mister Ernest said.

[1] **whang:** a buckskin thong.

"Yes, sir," I said. "I'll holler first next time—provided you'll holler a little quicker when you touch him next time, too." But it was all right; we jest had to be a little easy getting up. "Now which-a-way?" I said. Because we couldn't hear nothing now, after wasting all this time. And this was new country, sho enough. It had been cut over and growed up in thickets we couldn't 'a' seen over even standing up on Dan.

But Mister Ernest never even answered. He jest turned Dan along the bank of the bayou where it was a little more open and we could move faster again, soon as Dan and us got used to that homemade cinch strop and got a little confidence in it. Which jest happened to be east, or so I thought then, because I never paid no particular attention to east then because the sun—I don't know where the morning had went, but it was gone, the morning and the frost, too—was up high now, even if my insides had told me it was past dinner-time.

And then we heard him. No, that's wrong; what we heard was shots. And that was when we realized how fur he had come, because the only camp we knowed about in that direction was the Holly-knowe camp, and Hollyknowe was ex-actly twenty-eight miles from Van Dorn, where me and Mister Ernest lived—jest the shots, no dogs nor nothing. If old Eagle was still behind him and the buck was still alive, he was too wore out now to even say, "Here he comes."

"Don't touch him!" I hollered. But Mister Ernest remembered that cinch strop, too, and he jest let Dan off the snaffle. And Dan heard them shots, too, picking his way through the thickets, hopping the vines and logs when he could and going under them when he couldn't. And sho enough, it was jest like before—two or three men squatting and creeping among the bushes, looking for blood that Eagle had done already told them wasn't there. But we never stopped this time, jest trotting on by with Dan hopping and dodg-ing among the brush and vines dainty as a

dancer. Then Mister Ernest swung Dan until we was going due north.

"Wait!" I hollered. "Not this way."

But Mister Ernest jest turned his face back over his shoulder. It looked tired, too, and there was a smear of mud on it where that ere grapevine had snatched him off the horse.

"Don't you know where he's heading?" he said. "He's done done his part, give everybody a fair open shot at him, and now he's going home, back to that brake in our bayou. He ought to make it exactly at dark."

And that's what he was doing. We went on. It didn't matter to hurry now. There wasn't no sound nowhere; it was that time in the early afternoon in November when don't nothing move or cry, not even birds, the peckerwoods and yellowhammers and jays, and it seemed to me like I could see all three of us—me and Mister Ernest and Dan—and Eagle, and the other dogs, and that big old buck, moving through the quiet woods in the same direction, headed for the same place, not running now but walking, that had all run the fine race the

best we knowed how, and all three of us now turned like on a agreement to walk back home, not together in a bunch because we didn't want to worry or tempt one another, because what we had all three spent this morning doing was no play-acting jest for fun, but was serious, and all three of us was still what we was— that old buck that had to run, not because he was skeered, but because running was what he done the best and was proudest at; and Eagle and the dogs that chased him, not because they hated or feared him, but because that was the thing they done the best and was proudest at; and me and Mister Ernest and Dan, that run him not because we wanted his meat, which would be too tough to eat anyhow, or his head to hang on a wall, but because now we could go back and work hard for eleven months making a crop, so we would have the right to come back here next November—all three of us going back home now, peaceful and separate, but still side by side, until next year, next time.

Then we seen him for the first time. We was out of the cut-over now; we could even 'a' cantered, except that all three of us was long past that, and now you could tell where west was because the sun was already halfway down it. So we was walking, too, when we come on the dogs—the puppies and one of the old ones—played out, laying in a little wet swag, panting, jest looking up at us when we passed, but not moving when we went on. Then we come to a long open glade, you could see about half a quarter, and we seen the three other old dogs and about a hundred yards ahead of them Eagle, all walking, not making no sound; and then suddenly, at the fur end of the glade, the buck hisself getting up from where he had been resting for the dogs to come up, getting up without no hurry, big, big as a mule, tall as a mule, and turned without no hurry still, and the white underside of his tail for a second or two more before the thicket taken him.

It might 'a' been a signal, a good-by, a farewell. Still walking, we passed the other three old dogs in the middle of the glade, laying down, too, now jest where they was when the buck vanished, and not trying to get up neither when we passed; and still that hundred yards ahead of them, Eagle, too, not laying down, because he was still on his feet, but his legs was spraddled and his head was down; maybe jest waiting until we was out of sight of his shame, his eyes saying plain as talk when we passed, "I'm sorry, boys, but this here is all."

Mister Ernest stopped Dan. "Jump down and look at his feet," he said.

"Ain't nothing wrong with his feet," I said. "It's his wind has done give out."

"Jump down and look at his feet," Mister Ernest said.

So I done it, and while I was stooping over Eagle I could hear the pump gun go, "Snick-cluck. Snick-cluck. Snick-cluck" three times, except that I never thought nothing then. Maybe he was jest running the shells through to be sho it would work when we seen him again or maybe to make sho they was all buckshot. Then I got up again, and we went on, still walking; a little west of north now, because when we seen his white flag that second or two before the thicket hid it, it was on a beeline for that notch in the bayou. And it was evening, too, now. The wind had done dropped and there was a edge to the air and the sun jest touched the tops of the trees now, except jest now and then, when it found a hole to come almost level through onto the ground. And he was taking the easiest way, too, now, going straight as he could. When we seen his foot in the soft places he was running for a while at first after his rest. But soon he was walking, too, like he knowed, too, where Eagle and the dogs was.

And then we seen him again. It was the last time—a thicket, with the sun coming through a hole onto it like a searchlight. He crashed jest once; then he was standing there broadside to us, not twenty yards away, big as a statue and red as gold in the sun, and the sun sparking on the tips of his horns—they was twelve of them—so

that he looked like he had twelve lighted candles branched around his head, standing there looking at us while Mister Ernest raised the gun and aimed at his neck, and the gun went, "Click. Snick-cluck. Click. Snick-cluck. Click. Snick-cluck" three times, and Mister Ernest still holding the gun aimed while the buck turned and give one long bound, the white underside of tail like a blaze of fire, too, until the thicket and the shadows put it out; and Mister Ernest laid the gun slow and gentle back across the saddle in front of him, saying quiet and peaceful, and not much louder than jest breathing, "Dawg, dawg."

Then he jogged me with his elbow and we got down, easy and careful because of that ere cinch strop, and he reached into his vest and taken out one of the cigars. It was busted where I had fell on it, I reckon, when we hit the ground. He throwed it away and taken out the other one. It was busted, too, so he bit off a hunk of it to chew and throwed the rest away. And now the sun was gone even from the tops of the trees and there wasn't nothing left but a big red glare in the west.

"Don't worry," I said. "I ain't going to tell them you forgot to load your gun. For that matter, they don't need to know we ever seed him."

"Much oblige," Mister Ernest said. There wasn't going to be no moon tonight neither, so he taken the compass off the whang leather loop in his buttonhole and handed me the gun and set the compass on a stump and stepped back and looked at it. "Just about the way we're headed now," he said, and taken the gun from me and opened it and put one shell in the britch and taken up the compass, and I taken Dan's reins and we started, with him in front with the compass in his hand.

And after a while it was full dark; Mister Ernest would have to strike a match ever now and then to read the compass, until the stars come out good and we could pick out one to follow, because I said, "How fur do you reckon it is?" and he said, "A little more than one box of matches." So we used a star when we could, only we couldn't see it all the time because the woods was too dense and we would git a little off until he would have to spend another match. And now it was good and late, and he stopped and said, "Get on the horse."

"I ain't tired," I said.

"Get on the horse," he said. "We don't want to spoil him."

Because he had been a good feller ever since I had knowed him, which was even before that day two years ago when maw went off with the Vicksburg roadhouse feller and the next day pap didn't come home neither, and on the third one Mister Ernest rid Dan up to the door of the cabin on the river he let us live in, so pap could work his piece of land and run his fish line, too, and said, "Put that gun down and come on here and climb up behind."

So I got in the saddle even if I couldn't reach the stirrups, and Mister Ernest taken the reins and I must 'a' went to sleep, because the next thing I knowed a buttonhole of my lumberjack was tied to the saddle horn with that ere whang cord off the compass, and it was good and late now and we wasn't fur, because Dan was already smelling water, the river. Or maybe it was the feed lot itself he smelled, because we struck the fire road not a quarter below it, and soon I could see the river, too, with the white mist laying on it soft and still as cotton. Then the lot, home; and up yonder in the dark, not no piece akchully, close enough to hear us unsaddling and shucking corn prob'ly, and sholy close enough to hear Mister Ernest blowing his horn at the dark camp for Simon to come in the boat and git us, that old buck in his brake in the bayou; home, too, resting, too, after the hard run, waking hisself now and then, dreaming of dogs behind him or maybe it was the racket we was making would wake him, but not neither of them for more than jest a little while before sleeping again.

Then Mister Ernest stood on the bank blowing until Simon's lantern went bobbing down into the mist; then we clumb down to the landing and Mister Ernest blowed again now and then to guide Simon, until we seen the lantern in the mist, and then Simon and the boat; only it looked like ever time I set down and got still, I went back to sleep, because Mister Ernest was shaking me again to git out

and climb the bank into the dark camp, until I felt a bed against my knees and tumbled into it.

Then it was morning, tomorrow; it was all over now until next November, next year, and we could come back. Uncle Ike and Willy and Walter and Roth and the rest of them had come in yestiddy, soon as Eagle taken the buck out of hearing and they knowed that deer was gone, to pack up and be ready to leave this morning for Yoknapatawpha, where they lived, until it would be November again and they could come back again.

So, as soon as we et breakfast, Simon run them back up the river in the big boat to where they left their cars and pickups, and now it wasn't nobody but jest me and Mister Ernest setting on the bench against the kitchen wall in the sun; Mister Ernest smoking a cigar—a whole one this time that Dan hadn't had no chance to jump him through a grapevine and bust. He hadn't washed his face neither where that vine had throwed him into the mud. But that was all right, too; his face usually did have a smudge of mud or tractor grease or beard stubble on it, because he wasn't jest a planter; he was a farmer, he worked as hard as ara one of his hands and tenants—which is why I knowed from the very first that we would git along, that I wouldn't have no trouble with him and he wouldn't have no trouble with me, from that very first day when I woke up and maw had done gone off with that Vicksburg roadhouse feller without ever waiting to cook breakfast, and the next morning pap was gone, too, and it was almost night the next day when I heard a horse coming up and I taken the gun that I had already throwed a shell into the britch when pap never came home last night, and stood in the door while Mister Ernest rid up and said, "Come on. Your paw ain't coming back neither."

"You mean he give me to you?" I said.

"Who cares?" he said. "Come on. I brought a lock for the door. We'll send the pickup back tomorrow for whatever you want."

So I come home with him and it was all right, it was jest fine—his wife had died about three years ago—without no women to worry us or take off in the middle of the night with a durn Vicksburg roadhouse jake without even waiting to cook breakfast. And we would go home this afternoon, too, but not jest yet; we always stayed one more day after the others left because Uncle Ike always left what grub they hadn't et, and the rest of the homemade corn whisky he drunk and that town whisky of Roth Edmondziz he called Scotch that smelled like it come out of a old bucket of roof paint; setting in the sun for one more day before we went back home to git ready to put in next year's crop of cotton and oats and beans and hay; and across the river yonder, behind the wall of trees where the big woods started, that old buck laying up today in the sun, too—resting today, too, without nobody to bother him until next November.

So at least one of us was glad it would be eleven months and two weeks before he would have to run that fur that fast again. So he was glad of the very same thing we was sorry of, and so all of a sudden I thought about how maybe planting and working and then harvesting oats and cotton and beans and hay wasn't jest something me and Mister Ernest done three hundred and fifty-one days to fill in the time until we could come back hunting again, but it was something we had to do, and do honest and good during the three hundred and fifty-one days, to have the right to come back into the big woods and hunt for the other fourteen; and the fourteen days that old buck run in front of dogs wasn't jest something to fill his time until the three hundred and fifty-one when he didn't have to, but the running and the risking in front of guns and dogs was something he had to do for fourteen days to have the right not to be bothered for the other three hundred and fifty-one. And so the hunting and the farming wasn't two different things atall—they was jest the other side of each other.

"Yes," I said. "All we got to do now is put in that next year's crop. Then November won't be no time away atall."

"You ain't going to put in the crop next year," Mister Ernest said. "You're going to school."

So at first I didn't even believe I had heard him. "What?" I said. "Me? Go to school?"

"Yes," Mister Ernest said. "You must make something out of yourself."

"I am," I said. "I'm doing it now. I'm going to be a hunter and a farmer like you."

"No," Mister Ernest said. "That ain't enough any more. Time was when all a man had to do was just farm eleven and a half months, and hunt the other half. But not now. Now just to belong to the farming business and the hunting business ain't enough. You got to belong to the business of mankind."

"Mankind?" I said.

"Yes," Mister Ernest said. "So you're going to school. Because you got to know why. You can belong to the farming and hunting business and you can learn the difference between what's right and what's wrong, and do right. And that used to be enough—just to do right. But not now.

You got to know why it's right and why it's wrong, and be able to tell the folks that never had no chance to learn it; teach them how to do what's right, not just because they know it's right, but because they know now why it's right because you just showed them, told them, taught them why. So you're going to school."

"It's because you been listening to that durn Will Legate and Walter Ewell!" I said.

"No," Mister Ernest said.

"Yes!" I said. "No wonder you missed that buck yestiddy, taking ideas from the very fellers that let him git away, after me and you had run Dan and the dogs durn nigh clean to death! Because you never even missed him! You never forgot to load that gun! You had done already unloaded it a purpose! I heard you!"

"All right, all right," Mister Ernest said. "Which would you rather have? His bloody head and hide on the kitchen floor yonder and half his meat in a pickup truck on the way to Yoknapatawpha County, or him with his head and hide and meat still together over yonder in that brake, waiting for next November for us to run him again?"

"And git him, too," I said. "We won't even fool with no Willy Legate and Walter Ewell next time."

"Maybe," Mister Ernest said.

"Yes," I said.

"Maybe," Mister Ernest said. "The best word in our language, the best of all. That's what mankind keeps going on: Maybe. The best days of his life ain't the ones when he said 'Yes' beforehand: they're the ones when all he knew to say was 'Maybe.' He can't say 'Yes' until afterward because he not only don't know it until then, he don't want to know 'Yes' until then. . . . Step in the kitchen and make me a toddy. Then we'll see about dinner."

"All right," I said. I got up. "You want some of Uncle Ike's corn or that town whisky of Roth Emondziz?"

"Can't you say Mister Roth or Mister Edmonds?" Mister Ernest said.

"Yes, sir," I said. "Well, which do you want? Uncle Ike's corn or that ere stuff of Roth Edmondziz?"

FOR STUDY AND DISCUSSION

1. In the first sentence of the story, who or what is meant by "him"?

2. How do the morning preparations make clear what is going on? Why do you think Faulkner left the subject of the story vague up to this point?

3. What sensory pleasures of the hunt are depicted in this story? Give details to support your answer. In what way do these pleasures give value to the life of farming and hunting?

4. What details show Mr. Ernest to be a wise and experienced hunter? Identify Dan and Eagle. What evidence is there that these two enjoy the hunt as much as their master?

5. How do the hunters set about cornering the buck? How does the buck elude them? Why does the boy holler "No! No! No! No!" when he thinks the buck has been shot?

6. Mr. Ernest says of the buck: "He's done done his part, give everybody a fair open shot at him, and now he's going home . . ." What does this sentence reveal about Mr. Ernest's code of honor? How is it related to his aiming at the buck with an empty gun?

7. Only near the end of the story does the reader learn about the boy's past and the way he and Mr. Ernest came together. Why do you think Faulkner delays so long in revealing these details? How would the story be different if these details had been presented at the beginning? Is it important that the reader learns about Mr. Ernest's past actions *only* after learning about Mr. Ernest's treatment of the buck? Why or why not?

8. Why does Mr. Ernest insist that the boy go to school?

CHARACTER

Much of a story's effectiveness may depend on how well the characters are presented. Even if the plot is well constructed, a reader may not become emotionally involved in the story unless he can respond to its characters. He must be able to like or dislike them, to be happy for them or feel pity for them, to judge them morally. Not all characters in a story are developed to the same degree. For example, the reader, after finishing "Race at

Morning," probably feels that he knows Mr. Ernest a good deal better than he knows Uncle Ike McCaslin. In some stories, character development is more subtle and detailed than in others. The boy in "Race at Morning," for example, is presented more distinctly than the boy in "The Egg." However, "The Egg" is not necessarily an inferior story on this account. The character of the boy is presented as fully as necessary to carry out that story's design, as is true of any good story. "Race at Morning" requires a more fully drawn character, one for whom the reader feels a close sympathy. The boy in "Race at Morning" may be terribly lazy, but Faulkner does not present this trait. A story about a hard-hearted landlord will show him victimizing his tenants but will probably not show his kindness to his own wife and children or present testimony from the occasional cripple he helps across the road.

Generally a writer develops a character in one or more of the following ways: (1) through the character's actions, (2) through the character's thoughts and speeches, (3) through a physical description of the character, (4) through showing the opinions other characters have about him, (5) through a direct statement about him telling what the writer thinks of him. Modern writers generally avoid the last method. They prefer to show the character in action and have the reader form his own opinion.

1. Which of the methods described above are used to develop the characters of Mr. Ernest and the boy? Cite details.

2. What does the reader learn about such minor characters as Willy Legate and Walter Ewell? Explain how a character such as Willy Legate is used to bring out by contrast the qualities of Mr. Ernest.

THEME

Theme may be defined as the *idea behind a story,* the unspoken comment growing out of every sentence, every detail, every character, every event. In some stories, the theme is closely related to moments of revelation. Often, in the best stories, the theme is difficult to state. It is as complex as the story itself. However, making a rough statement of the theme will usually help a reader to understand a story; and finding and interpreting significant passages is a good method of arriving at the theme.

1. "Race at Morning" is basically not about hunting; it is about a way of life and how it is changing. The theme of this story grows out of a presentation of this way of life. How is the following passage related to the theme?

". . . and so all of a sudden I thought about how maybe planting and working and then harvesting oats and cotton and beans and hay wasn't jest something . . . to fill in the time until we could come back hunting again, but it was something we had to do, and do honest and good during the three hundred and fifty-one days, to have the right to come back into the big woods and hunt for the other fourteen . . . And so the hunting and the farming wasn't two different things atall—they was jest the other side of each other." (Page 547.)

2. Why do you think the story is called "Race at Morning" rather than "Hunt at Morning"?

3. When Mister Ernest tells the boy that the boy must go to school, he explains:

"Time was when all a man had to do was just farm eleven and a half months, and hunt the other half. But not now. Now just to belong to the farming business and the hunting business ain't enough. You got to belong to the business of mankind. . . . You can belong to the farming and hunting business and you can learn the difference between what's right and what's wrong, and do right. And that used to be enough—just to do right. But not now. You got to know why it's right and why it's wrong, and be able to tell the folks that never had no chance to learn . . ." (Pages 547–48.)

How are the ideas that Mr. Ernest expresses different from the ideas in the passages quoted in the first question? Do Mr. Ernest's ideas contradict the ideas expressed earlier, or do they simply qualify them? Explain.

FOR COMPOSITION

Write a paragraph or two in which you state the theme of "Race at Morning" in your own words. Give details from the story to support your statement. Do not rely simply on the passages quoted above. Reread the story to find your own details. (One question to ponder: How is the story's theme related to Mister Ernest's deliberately emptying his gun before taking aim at the buck?)

F. SCOTT FITZGERALD

(1896–1940)

To some readers, F. Scott Fitzgerald's life is a kind of parable—the story of a writer who dreams of becoming rich and famous, succeeds, and is then destroyed by his dream; who realizes his gifts early and burns out early. This vision of Fitzgerald is too simple to encompass the complicated, divided man he actually was, and it does little justice to his best writing. Yet it touches on the reasons why he fascinates those who read him. In his stories and novels Fitzgerald managed to include all the hectic charm of the 1920's, that period of "flaming youth" and wild parties, of postwar disillusion with ideals and of obsession with sensations, of defiance of convention and aspiration for personal fulfillment. The titles of his short-story collections, *Flappers and Philosophers, Tales of the Jazz Age,* and *All the Sad Young Men,* recall the flavor of that era even for readers who never lived through it. More than any other writer, Fitzgerald responded to the spirit of that time and made literature of it. When the stock market crash of 1929 put an end to this period, he recorded the aftermath—the morning after the wild party.

Francis Scott Key Fitzgerald was born in St. Paul, Minnesota, to a family with social pretensions but not enough money to live up to them. Even as a boy he was noted for his charm and good looks and traveled in the best circles, but he was aware of the gap between himself and the rich. The glamour of the rich became an important fact in his life. In "The Rich Boy" he wrote, "They possess and enjoy early, and it does something to them . . . in a way that, unless you were born rich, it is very difficult to understand." He thought that by his gifts and hard work he could join this charmed circle, and he wrote about other ambitious youths and young men who are obsessed with sharing the special magic of the rich.

In 1913 Fitzgerald entered Princeton University, where he failed in his principal ambition of making the football team. Nevertheless, he was a very popular undergraduate and gained early fame as a writer for the student drama society. In 1917, after the United States entered World War I, he accepted a commission in the army but did not serve overseas. In 1918, at an officer's dance in Alabama, he met and fell in love with Zelda Sayre, a Montgomery belle. Discharged from the army, he came to New York to try to earn enough money to persuade Zelda to marry him. All he could find was a job at an advertising agency at a miserable salary. After three months, he returned to St. Paul to rewrite a novel he had completed in the army. *This Side of Paradise* was published in 1920 and was an enormous success. Fitzgerald, only twenty-four years old, became an important literary figure, the voice of the young men and women of the "jazz age." His short stories were published in popular magazines; he turned them out quickly for large sums of money. Once again living in New York, he was able to persuade Zelda to come North to marry him.

The Fitzgeralds were a dazzling couple. They lived on Long Island, in Rome and Paris, and on the Riviera. They gave and attended spectacular parties. They drove, drank, and spent recklessly. Through it all Fitzgerald managed to find the time to write story after story, some of them among his best and some damaged by a relentless need for productivity. Although he later commented, "I had been only a mediocre caretaker of most of the things left in my hands, even of my talent," he did make a serious attempt to live up to his gifts. An increasingly divided view of the rich pervaded his work. He was still fascinated by them, but more and more he came to distrust them and his own ambition to be one of them. The most notable product of these years is *The Great Gatsby,* a novel some critics consider one of the best written in the twentieth century.

In 1930, Zelda Fitzgerald suffered a nervous breakdown, and from then on she spent most of her time in sanatoriums. Fitzgerald was obliged to find money to pay her bills; in addition, he had run up considerable debts. He worked feverishly at his writing, trying to put his life in order and to earn more than he owed. But in the world of the Depression, the concerns of the twenties seemed dated and naive. In 1935, *Tender Is the Night,* a novel that many admirers of Fitzgerald's work regard as his finest novel, was published; it sold few copies. To earn money he went to Hollywood, where he was treated as a dim figure from the past and given hack writing jobs. He has described his state of mind during these years in several disturbing, memorable essays. In 1940, he died of a heart attack. That Fitzgerald continued growing as a writer to the very end is attested to by his final, unfinished novel, *The Last Tycoon.*

The Baby Party

WHEN JOHN ANDROS felt old he found solace in the thought of life continuing through his child. The dark trumpets of oblivion were less loud at the patter of his child's feet or at the sound of his child's voice babbling mad non sequiturs [1] to him over the telephone. The latter in-

---

[1] **non sequiturs** (non sek′wə·tərz): disconnected, illogical statements.

cident occurred every afternoon at three when his wife called the office from the country, and he came to look forward to it as one of the vivid minutes of his day.

He was not physically old, but his life had been a series of struggles up a series of rugged hills, and here at thirty-eight, having won his battles against ill-health and poverty, he cherished less than the usual number of illusions. Even his feeling about his little girl was qualified. She had interrupted his rather intense love affair with his wife, and she was the reason for their living in a suburban town, where they paid for country air with endless servant troubles and the weary merry-go-round of the commuting train.

It was little Ede as a definite piece of youth that chiefly interested him. He liked to take her on his lap and examine minutely her fragrant, downy scalp and her eyes with their irises of morning blue. Having paid this homage John was content that the nurse should take her away. After ten minutes the very vitality of the child irritated him; he was inclined to lose his temper when things were broken, and one Sunday afternoon when she had disrupted a bridge game by permanently hiding up the ace of spades, he had made a scene that had reduced his wife to tears.

This was absurd and John was ashamed of himself. It was inevitable that such things would happen, and it was impossible that little Ede should spend all her indoor hours in the nursery upstairs when she was becoming, as her mother said, more nearly a "real person" every day.

She was two and a half, and this afternoon, for instance, she was going to a baby party. Grown-up Edith, her mother, had telephoned the information to the office, and little Ede had confirmed the business by shouting "I yam going to a *pantry!*" into John's unsuspecting left ear.

"Drop in at the Markeys' when you get home, won't you, dear?" resumed her mother. "It'll be funny. Ede's going to be all dressed up in her new pink dress——"

The conversation terminated abruptly with a squawk which indicated that the telephone had been pulled violently to the floor. John laughed and decided to get an early train out; the prospect of a baby party in someone else's house amused him.

"What a peach of a mess!" he thought humorously. "A dozen mothers, and each one looking at nothing but her own child. All the babies breaking things and grabbing at the cake, and each mamma going home thinking about the subtle superiority of her own child to every other child there."

He was in a good humor today—all the things in his life were going better than they had ever gone before. When he got off the train at his station, he shook his head at an importunate taxi man and began to walk up the long hill toward his house through the crisp December twilight. It was only six o'clock but the moon was out, shining with proud brilliance on the thin sugary snow that lay over the lawns.

As he walked along drawing his lungs full of cold air his happiness increased, and the idea of a baby party appealed to him more and more. He began to wonder how Ede compared to other children of her own age, and if the pink dress she was to wear was something radical and mature. Increasing his gait, he came in sight of his own house, where the lights of a defunct Christmas tree still blossomed in the window, but he continued on past the walk. The party was at the Markeys' next door.

As he mounted the brick step and rang the bell, he became aware of voices inside, and he was glad he was not too late. Then he raised his head and listened—the voices were not children's voices, but they were loud and pitched high with anger; there were at least three of them and one, which rose as he listened to a hysterical sob, he recognized immediately as his wife's.

"There's been some trouble," he thought quickly.

Trying the door, he found it unlocked and pushed it open.

The baby party began at half past four, but Edith Andros, calculating shrewdly that the new dress would stand out more sensationally against vestments already rumpled, planned the arrival of herself and little Ede for five. When they appeared, it was already a flourishing affair. Four baby girls and nine baby boys, each one curled and washed and dressed with all the care of a proud and jealous heart, were dancing to the music of a phonograph. Never more than two or three were dancing at once, but as all were continually in motion running to and from their mothers for encouragement, the general effect was the same.

As Edith and her daughter entered, the music was temporarily drowned out by a sustained chorus, consisting largely of the word *cute* and directed toward little Ede, who stood looking timidly about and fingering the edges of her pink dress. She was not kissed—this is the sanitary age—but she was passed along a row of mammas, each one of whom said "cu-u-ute" to her and held her pink little hand before passing her on to the next. After some encouragement and a few mild pushes she was absorbed into the dance, and became an active member of the party.

Edith stood near the door talking to Mrs. Markey, and keeping one eye on the tiny figure in the pink dress. She did not care for Mrs. Markey; she considered her both snippy and common, but John and Joe Markey were congenial and went in together on the commuting train every morning, so the two women kept up an elaborate pretense of warm amity. They were always reproaching each other for "not coming to see me," and they were always planning the kind of parties that began with "You'll have to come to dinner with us soon, and we'll go in to the theater," but never matured further.

"Little Ede looks perfectly darling," said Mrs. Markey, smiling and moistening her lips in a way that Edith found particularly repulsive. "So *grown-up*—I can't *believe* it!"

Edith wondered if "little Ede" referred to the fact that Billy Markey, though several months younger, weighed almost five pounds more. Accepting a cup of tea, she took a seat with two other ladies on a divan and launched into the real business of the afternoon, which of course lay in relating the recent accomplishments and insouciances of her child.

An hour passed. Dancing palled and the babies took to sterner sport. They ran into the dining room, rounded the big table, and essayed the kitchen door, from which they were rescued by an expeditionary force of mothers. Having been rounded up they immediately broke loose and, rushing back to the dining room, tried the familiar swinging door again. The word "overheated" began to be used, and small white brows were dried with small white handkerchiefs. A general attempt to make the babies sit down began, but the babies squirmed off laps with peremptory cries of "Down! Down!" and the rush into the fascinating dining room began anew.

This phase of the party came to an end with the arrival of refreshments, a large cake with two candles, and saucers of vanilla ice cream. Billy Markey, a stout laughing baby with red hair and legs somewhat bowed, blew out the candles, and placed an experimental thumb on the white frosting. The refreshments were distributed, and the children ate, greedily but without confusion—they had behaved remarkably well all afternoon. They were modern babies who ate and slept at regular hours, so their dispositions were good, and their faces healthy and pink—such a peaceful party would not have been possible thirty years ago.

After the refreshments a gradual exodus began. Edith glanced anxiously at her watch—it was almost six, and John had not arrived. She wanted him to see Ede with the other children—to see how dignified and polite and intelligent she was, and how the only ice-cream spot on her dress was some that had dropped from her chin when she was joggled from behind.

"You're a darling," she whispered to her child, drawing her suddenly against her knee. "Do you know you're a darling? Do you *know* you're a darling?"

Ede laughed. "Bow-wow," she said suddenly.

"Bow-wow?" Edith looked around. "There isn't any bow-wow."

"Bow-wow," repeated Ede. "I want a bow-wow."

Edith followed the small pointing finger.

"That isn't a bow-wow, dearest, that's a teddy bear."

"Bear?"

"Yes, that's a teddy bear, and it belongs to Billy Markey. You don't want Billy Markey's teddy bear, do you?"

Ede did want it.

She broke away from her mother and approached Billy Markey, who held the toy closely in his arms. Ede stood regarding him with inscrutable eyes, and Billy laughed.

Grown-up Edith looked at her watch again, this time impatiently.

The party had dwindled until, besides Ede and Billy, there were only two babies remaining—and one of the two remained only by virtue of having hidden himself under the dining-room table. It was selfish of John not to come. It showed so little pride in the child. Other fathers had come, half a dozen of them, to call for their wives, and they had stayed for a while and looked on.

There was a sudden wail. Ede had obtained Billy's teddy bear by pulling it forcibly from his arms, and on Billy's attempt to recover it, she had pushed him casually to the floor.

"Why, Ede!" cried her mother, repressing an inclination to laugh.

Joe Markey, a handsome, broad-shouldered man of thirty-five, picked up his son and set him on his feet. "You're a fine fellow," he said jovially. "Let a girl knock you over! You're a fine fellow."

"Did he bump his head?" Mrs. Markey returned anxiously from bowing the next to last remaining mother out the door.

"No-o-o-o," exclaimed Markey. "He bumped something else, didn't you, Billy? He bumped something else."

Billy had so far forgotten the bump that he was already making an attempt to recover his property. He seized a leg of the bear which projected from Ede's enveloping arms and tugged at it but without success.

"No," said Ede emphatically.

Suddenly, encouraged by the success of her former half-accidental maneuver, Ede dropped the teddy bear, placed her hands on Billy's shoulders and pushed him backward off his feet.

This time he landed less harmlessly; his head hit the bare floor just off the rug with a dull hollow sound, whereupon he drew in his breath and delivered an agonized yell.

Immediately the room was in confusion.

With an exclamation Markey hurried to his son, but his wife was first to reach the injured baby and catch him up into her arms.

"Oh, *Billy,*" she cried, "what a terrible bump! She ought to be spanked."

Edith, who had rushed immediately to her daughter, heard this remark, and her lips came sharply together.

"Why, Ede," she whispered perfunctorily, "you bad girl!"

Ede put back her little head suddenly and laughed. It was a loud laugh, a triumphant laugh with victory in it and challenge and contempt. Unfortunately it was also an infectious laugh. Before her mother realized the delicacy of the situation, she too had laughed, an audible, distinct laugh not unlike the baby's, and partaking of the same overtones.

Then, as suddenly, she stopped.

Mrs. Markey's face had grown red with anger, and Markey, who had been feeling the back of the baby's head with one finger, looked at her, frowning.

"It's swollen already," he said with a note of reproof in his voice. "I'll get some witch-hazel."

But Mrs. Markey had lost her temper. "I don't see anything funny about a child being hurt!" she said in a trembling voice.

Little Ede meanwhile had been looking at her mother curiously. She noted that her own laugh had produced her mother's, and she wondered if the same cause would always produce the same effect. So she chose this moment to throw back her head and laugh again.

To her mother the additional mirth added the final touch of hysteria to the situation. Pressing her handkerchief to her mouth she giggled irrepressibly. It was more than nervousness—she felt that in a peculiar way she was laughing with her child—they were laughing together.

It was in a way a defiance—those two against the world.

While Markey rushed upstairs to the bathroom for ointment, his wife was walking up and down rocking the yelling boy in her arms.

"Please go home!" she broke out suddenly. "The child's badly hurt, and if you haven't the decency to be quiet, you'd better go home."

"Very well," said Edith, her own temper rising. "I've never seen any one make such a mountain out of——"

"Get out!" cried Mrs. Markey frantically. "There's the door, get out—I never want to see you in our house again. You or your brat either!"

Edith had taken her daughter's hand and was moving quickly toward the door, but at this remark she stopped and turned around, her face contracting with indignation.

"Don't you dare call her that!"

Mrs. Markey did not answer but continued walking up and down, muttering to herself and to Billy in an inaudible voice.

Edith began to cry.

"I will get out!" she sobbed, "I've never heard anybody so rude and c-common in my life. I'm glad your baby did get pushed down—he's nothing but a f-fat little fool anyhow."

Joe Markey reached the foot of the stairs just in time to hear this remark.

"Why, Mrs. Andros," he said sharply, "can't you see the child's hurt? You really ought to control yourself."

"Control m-myself!" exclaimed Edith brokenly. "You better ask her to c-control herself. I've never heard anybody so c-common in my life."

"She's insulting me!" Mrs. Markey was now livid with rage. "Did you hear what she said, Joe? I wish you'd put her out. If she won't go, just take her by the shoulders and put her out!"

"Don't you dare touch me!" cried Edith. "I'm going just as quick as I can find my c-coat!"

Blind with tears she took a step toward the hall. It was just at this moment that the door opened and John Andros walked anxiously in.

"What's the matter? Why, what's the matter?"

"They're—they're putting me out!" she wailed, collapsing against him. "He'd just

started to take me by the shoulders and put me out. I want my coat!"

"That's not true," objected Markey hurriedly. "Nobody's going to put you out." He turned to John. "Nobody's going to put her out," he repeated. "She's——"

"What do you mean 'put her out'?" demanded John abruptly. "What's all this talk, anyhow?"

"Oh, let's go!" cried Edith. "I want to go. They're so *common*, John!"

"Look here!" Markey's face darkened. "You've said that about enough. You're acting sort of crazy."

"They called Ede a brat!"

For the second time that afternoon little Ede expressed emotion at an inopportune moment. Confused and frightened at the shouting voices, she began to cry, and her tears had the effect of conveying that she felt the insult in her heart.

"What's the idea of this?" broke out John. "Do you insult your guests in your own house?"

"It seems to me it's your wife that's done the insulting!" answered Markey crisply. "In fact, your baby there started all the trouble."

John gave a contemptuous snort. "Are you calling names at a little baby?" he inquired. "That's a fine manly business!"

"Don't talk to him, John," insisted Edith. "Find my coat!"

"You must be in a bad way," went on John angrily, "if you have to take out your temper on a helpless little baby."

"I never heard anything so twisted in my life," shouted Markey. "If that wife of yours would shut her mouth for a minute——"

"Wait a minute! You're not talking to a woman and child now——"

There was an incidental interruption. Edith had been fumbling on a chair for her coat, and Mrs. Markey had been watching her with hot, angry eyes. Suddenly she laid Billy down on the sofa, where he immediately stopped crying and pulled himself upright, and coming into the hall she quickly found Edith's coat and handed it to her without a word. Then she went back to the sofa, picked up Billy, and rocking him in her arms looked again at Edith with hot, angry eyes. The interruption had taken less than a minute.

"Your wife comes in here and begins shouting around about how common we are!" burst out Markey violently. "Well, if we're so common, you'd better stay away! And, what's more, you'd better get out now!"

Again John gave a short, contemptuous laugh.

"You're not only common," he returned, "you're evidently an awful bully—when there's any helpless women and children around." He felt for the knob and swung the door open. "Come on, Edith."

Taking up her daughter in her arms, his wife stepped outside and John, still looking contemptuously at Markey, started to follow.

"Wait a minute!" Markey took a step forward; he was trembling slightly, and two large veins on his temple were suddenly full of blood. "You don't think you can get away with that, do you? With me?"

Without a word John walked out the door, leaving it open.

Edith, still weeping, had started for home. After following her with his eyes until she reached her own walk, John turned back toward the lighted doorway where Markey was slowly coming down the slippery steps. He took off his overcoat and hat, tossed them off the path onto the snow. Then, sliding a little on the iced walk, he took a step forward.

At the first blow, they both slipped and fell heavily to the sidewalk, half rising then, and again pulling each other to the ground. They found a better foothold in the thin snow to the side of the walk and rushed at each other, both swinging wildly and pressing out the snow into a pasty mud underfoot.

The street was deserted, and except for their short tired gasps and the padded sound as one or the other slipped down into the slushy mud, they fought in silence, clearly defined to each other by

the full moonlight as well as by the amber glow that shone out of the open door. Several times they both slipped down together, and then for a while the conflict threshed about wildly on the lawn.

For ten, fifteen, twenty minutes they fought there senselessly in the moonlight. They had both taken off coats and vests at some silently agreed-upon interval and now their shirts dripped from their backs in wet pulpy shreds. Both were torn and bleeding and so exhausted that they could stand only when by their position they mutually supported each other—the impact, the mere effort of a blow, would send them both to their hands and knees.

But it was not weariness that ended the business, and the very meaninglessness of the fight was a reason for not stopping. They stopped because once when they were straining at each other on the ground, they heard a man's footsteps coming along the sidewalk. They had rolled somehow into the shadow, and when they heard these footsteps they stopped fighting, stopped moving, stopped breathing, lay huddled together like two boys playing Indian until the footsteps had passed. Then, staggering to their feet, they looked at each other like two drunken men.

"I'll be darned if I'm going on with this thing any more," cried Markey thickly.

"I'm not going on any more either," said John Andros. "I've had enough of this thing."

Again they looked at each other, sulkily this time, as if each suspected the other of urging him to a renewal of the fight. Markey spat out a mouthful of blood from a cut lip; then he cursed softly and, picking up his coat and vest, shook off the snow from them in a surprised way, as if their comparative dampness was his only worry in the world.

"Want to come in and wash up?" he asked suddenly.

"No, thanks," said John. "I ought to be going home—my wife'll be worried."

He too picked up his coat and vest and

then his overcoat and hat. Soaking wet and dripping with perspiration, it seemed absurd that less than half an hour ago he had been wearing all these clothes.

"Well—good night," he said hesitantly.

Suddenly they both walked toward each other and shook hands. It was no perfunctory handshake: John Andros's arm went around Markey's shoulder, and he patted him softly on the back for a little while.

"No harm done," he said brokenly.

"No—you?"

"No, no harm done."

"Well," said John Andros after a minute, "I guess I'll say good night."

"Good night."

Limping slightly and with his clothes over his arm, John Andros turned away. The moonlight was still bright as he left the dark patch of trampled ground and walked over the intervening lawn. Down at the station, half a mile away, he could hear the rumble of the seven o'clock train.

"But you must have been crazy," cried Edith brokenly. "I thought you were going to fix it all up there and shake hands. That's why I went away."

"Did you want us to fix it up?"

"Of course not, I never want to see them again. But I thought of course that was what you were going to do." She was touching the bruises on his neck and back with iodine as he sat placidly in a hot bath. "I'm going to get the doctor," she said insistently. "You may be hurt internally."

He shook his head. "Not a chance," he answered. "I don't want this to get all over town."

"I don't understand yet how it all happened."

"Neither do I." He smiled grimly. "I guess these baby parties are pretty rough affairs."

"Well, one thing—" suggested Edith hopefully, "I'm certainly glad we have beefsteak in the house for tomorrow's dinner."

"Why?"

"For your eye, of course. Do you know I came within an ace of ordering veal? Wasn't that the luckiest thing?"

Half an hour later, dressed except that his neck would accommodate no collar, John moved his limbs experimentally before the glass. "I believe I'll get myself in better shape," he said thoughtfully. "I must be getting old."

"You mean so that next time you can beat him?"

"I did beat him," he announced. "At least, I beat him as much as he beat me. And there isn't going to be any next time. Don't you go calling people common any more. If you get in any trouble, you just take your coat and go home. Understand?"

"Yes, dear," she said meekly. "I was very foolish and now I understand."

Out in the hall, he paused abruptly by the baby's door.

"Is she asleep?"

"Sound asleep. But you can go in and peek at her—just to say good night."

They tiptoed in and bent together over the bed. Little Ede, her cheeks flushed with health, her pink hands clasped tight together, was sleeping soundly in the cool, dark room. John reached over the railing of the bed and passed his hand lightly over the silken hair.

"She's asleep," he murmured in a puzzled way.

"Naturally, after such an afternoon."

"Miz Andros," the maid's stage whisper floated in from the hall, "Mr. and Miz Markey downstairs an' want to see you. Mr. Markey he's all cut up in pieces, ma'am. His face look like a roast beef. An' Miz Markey she 'pear mighty mad."

"Why, what incomparable nerve!" exclaimed Edith. "Just tell them we're not home. I wouldn't go down for anything in the world."

"You most certainly will." John's voice was hard and set.

"What?"

"You'll go down right now, and, what's more, whatever that other woman does, you'll apologize for what you said this afternoon. After that you don't ever have to see her again."

"Why—John, I can't."

"You've got to. And just remember that she probably hated to come over here just twice as much as you hate to go downstairs."

"Aren't you coming? Do I have to go alone?"

"I'll be down—in just a minute."

John Andros waited until she had closed the door behind her; then he reached over into the bed and, picking up his daughter, blankets and all, sat down in the rocking chair holding her tightly in his arms. She moved a little, and he held his breath, but she was sleeping soundly, and in a moment she was resting quietly in the hollow of his elbow. Slowly he bent his head until his cheek was against her bright hair. "Dear little girl," he whispered. "Dear little girl, dear little girl."

John Andros knew at length what it was he had fought for so savagely that evening. He had it now, he possessed it forever, and for some time he sat there rocking very slowly to and fro in the darkness.

FOR STUDY AND DISCUSSION

1. While at the office John Andros reflects that the party will be "a peach of a mess." What besides the conduct of the children may he be thinking about?

2. How does Fitzgerald prepare us for the quarrel between the two mothers? What details of characterization presented early in the story reveal the mothers' dislike of each other?

3. This story clearly illustrates the rule that almost all plots develop out of one or more conflicts. Describe the conflict between the Andros and Markey families; the conflict between John Andros and his wife near the end of the story; the conflicting attitudes that John Andros has towards Ede; and the conflict in Edith Andros when, after the fight, she tells John, "But you must have been crazy. I thought you were going to fix it all up there and shake hands," and then "I never want to see them again." How are all these conflicts related?

4. Do you think that John and Edith Andros are silly people, or do you feel that what happened to them could happen to anyone? Why? What basic human qualities do John and Edith display?

5. The story refers to "the very meaninglessness of the fight." Why is the fight called meaningless? What details are used to bring out its strangeness? The fight ends when Andros and Markey hide after they hear someone coming. What does this action reveal about their attitudes toward the fight?

6. Explain the last paragraph of the story. What does Andros realize he had been fighting for? Why does he feel that he now possesses it?

PLOT: THE FLASHBACK

A *flashback* is a passage in a story or novel —or a scene in a play or motion picture—that depicts an event that happened earlier. A story about a victim of amnesia, for example, may use a flashback to show an event in the victim's past. Flashbacks may be used for a number of reasons. Often a writer may choose to capture the reader's attention by beginning with a particularly interesting event and gradually telling what happened earlier. (The Latin term usually used to refer to this method of narration is *in medias res,* "in the middle of things.") Sometimes, when a story is told in the first person, a flashback may be used to present an event that the narrator did not witness but only learned about later. A flashback also may be used to emphasize the importance of a particular event or to prepare the reader for the event by showing its results.

1. Which event in "The Baby Party" is presented in a flashback?

2. How is the importance of this event emphasized? What results of the event are shown before the event itself is presented?

3. Are flashbacks used in any television plays or motion pictures that you have recently seen? If so, tell about the events that were presented in flashback. Why do you think this method of presentation was used?

FOR COMPOSITION

Write a brief story using the flashback technique. You may wish to begin in the present, then present an event or events that happened earlier, and finally conclude your story in the present.

KATHERINE
ANNE PORTER
(1894–   )

When Katherine Anne Porter's first collection of short stories was reprinted some twenty years after World War I and little more than a year before America's entry into World War II, she added a preface that was both a statement of purpose and of faith:

". . . all the conscious and recollected years of my life have been lived to this day under the heavy threat of world catastrophe, and most of the energies of my mind and spirit have been spent in the effort to grasp the meaning of those threats, to trace them to their sources and to understand the logic of this majestic and terrible failure of the life of man in the Western world. In the face of such shape and weight of present misfortune, the voice of the individual artist may seem perhaps of no more consequence than the whirring of a cricket in the grass; but the arts do live continuously, and they live literally by faith; their names and their shapes and their uses and their basic meanings survive unchanged in all that matters through times of interruption, diminishment, neglect; they outlive governments and creeds and the societies, even the very civilizations that produced them. They cannot be destroyed altogether because they represent the substance of faith and the only reality."

Through the years Miss Porter has held true to her faith in the art of literature. She has worked hard at perfecting a few works. Edmund Wilson, among others, has recognized that "she is an absolutely first-rate artist" writing "English of a purity and precision almost unique in contemporary fiction."

Katherine Anne Porter was born at Indian Creek, Texas. Her family was a large one with deep roots in the South, particularly in southern Texas and Louisiana. One of her ancestors was Daniel Boone. On the various occasions—births, christenings, confirmations, marriages, deaths—on which her family met, family stories were told and retold. A sense of the family as a community with its own outlook and traditions and a solid residue of love that one can draw on and return to pervades many of her stories. Such families, it once was clear, had histories that went far into the past and would go as far into the future. Yet, after World War I, these proud, solid families seemed to belong to an old order that was slowly passing. Some of Miss Porter's stories recreate the old order, others deal with the crises of individuals who must cope with the disappearance of order. A number of her stories have heroes or heroines who find themselves in places far from home—in Mexico or Europe—

with a sense of being cast adrift, unable to see a pattern beneath events or seeing it all too clearly and despising it.

Miss Porter was educated in Southern convent schools. She began to write "as soon as I learned to form letters on paper," but published nothing until she was over thirty. She has written that she learned her art in isolation, thus prolonging her development but saving her from "discipleship, personal influences, and membership in groups." To support herself, she performed a number of workaday writing tasks such as reviewing books and rewriting manuscripts, and has described the income of these years as "a sorry living. . . . Without the help of devoted friends I should have perished many times over." In 1930, the publication of *Flowering Judas,* a collection of short stories, gained her a small devoted readership. Her next major book, *Pale Horse, Pale Rider,* was not published until 1939. By this time she was recognized as an important writer, and serious readers awaited the appearance of her first novel, scheduled to appear in 1942. It did not appear until many years later.

In 1944 *The Leaning Tower,* a collection of seven short stories and a novella, added to her high reputation. Miss Porter continued to support herself with a variety of jobs, and occasionally went to Hollywood to write for the motion pictures. In 1962, her long-awaited novel, *Ship of Fools,* was published and was a great popular success, finally gaining its author a wide audience. In 1966, Miss Porter won the National Book Award for her *Collected Short Stories.*

The Jilting of Granny Weatherall

SHE FLICKED her wrist neatly out of Doctor Harry's pudgy careful fingers and pulled the sheet up to her chin. The brat ought to be in knee breeches. Doctoring around the country with spectacles on his nose! "Get along now, take your schoolbooks and go. There's nothing wrong with me."

Doctor Harry spread a warm paw like a cushion on her forehead where the forked green vein danced and made her eyelids twitch. "Now, now, be a good girl, and we'll have you up in no time."

"That's no way to speak to a woman nearly eighty years old just because she's down. I'd have you respect your elders, young man."

"Well, Missy, excuse me." Doctor Harry patted her cheek. "But I've got to warn you, haven't I? You're a marvel, but you must be careful or you're going to be good and sorry."

"Don't tell me what I'm going to be. I'm on my feet now, morally speaking. It's Cornelia. I had to go to bed to get rid of her."

Her bones felt loose, and floated around in her skin, and Doctor Harry floated like a balloon around the foot of the bed. He floated and pulled down his waistcoat and swung his glasses on a cord. "Well, stay where you are, it certainly can't hurt you."

"Get along and doctor your sick," said Granny Weatherall. "Leave a well woman alone. I'll call for you when I want you. . . . Where were you forty years ago when I pulled through milk-leg and double pneumonia? You weren't even born. Don't let Cornelia lead you on," she shouted, because Doctor Harry appeared to float up to the ceiling and out. "I pay my own bills, and I don't throw my money away on nonsense!"

She meant to wave good-by, but it was too much trouble. Her eyes closed of themselves, it was like a dark curtain drawn around the bed. The pillow rose and floated under her, pleasant as a hammock in a light wind. She listened to the leaves rustling outside the window. No, somebody was swishing newspapers: no, Cornelia and Doctor Harry were whispering together. She leaped broad awake, thinking they whispered in her ear.

"She was never like this, *never* like this!" "Well, what can we expect?" "Yes, eighty years old. . . ."

Well, and what if she was? She still had ears. It was like Cornelia to whisper around doors. She always kept things secret in such a public way. She was always being tactful and kind. Cornelia was dutiful; that was the trouble with her. Dutiful and good: "So good and dutiful," said Granny, "that I'd like to spank her." She saw herself spanking Cornelia and making a fine job of it.

"What'd you say, Mother?"

Granny felt her face tying up in hard knots.

"Can't a body think, I'd like to know?"

"I thought you might want something."

"I do. I want a lot of things. First off, go away and don't whisper."

She lay and drowsed, hoping in her sleep that the children would keep out and let her rest a minute. It had been a long day. Not that she was tired. It was always pleasant to snatch a minute now and then. There was always so much to be done, let me see: tomorrow.

Tomorrow was far away and there was nothing to trouble about. Things were finished somehow when the time came; thank God there was always a little margin over for peace: then a person could spread out the plan of life and tuck in the edges orderly. It was good to have everything clean and folded away, with the hair

brushes and tonic bottles sitting straight on the white embroidered linen: the day started without fuss and the pantry shelves laid out with rows of jelly glasses and brown jugs and white stone-china jars with blue whirligigs and words painted on them: coffee, tea, sugar, ginger, cinnamon, allspice: and the bronze clock with the lion on top nicely dusted off. The dust that lion could collect in twenty-four hours! The box in the attic with all those letters tied up, well, she'd have to go through that tomorrow. All those letters —George's letters and John's letters and her letters to them both—lying around for the children to find afterward made her uneasy. Yes, that would be tomorrow's business. No use to let them know how silly she had been once.

While she was rummaging around she found death in her mind and it felt clammy and unfamiliar. She had spent so much time preparing for death there was no need for bringing it up again. Let it take care of itself now. When she was sixty she had felt very old, finished, and went around making farewell trips to see her children and grandchildren, with a secret in her mind: This is the very last of your mother, children! Then she made her will and came down with a long fever. That was all just a notion like a lot of other things, but it was lucky too, for she had once for all got over the idea of dying for a long time. Now she couldn't be worried. She hoped she had better sense now. Her father had lived to be one hundred and two years old and had drunk a noggin of strong hot toddy on his last birthday. He told the reporters it was his daily habit, and he owed his long life to that. He had made quite a scandal and was very pleased about it. She believed she'd just plague Cornelia a little.

"Cornelia! Cornelia!" No footsteps, but a sudden hand on her cheek. "Bless you, where have you been?"

"Here, Mother."

"Well, Cornelia, I want a noggin of hot toddy."

"Are you cold, darling?"

"I'm chilly, Cornelia. Lying in bed stops the circulation. I must have told you that a thousand times."

Well, she could just hear Cornelia telling her husband that Mother was getting a little childish and they'd have to humor her. The thing that most annoyed her was that Cornelia thought she was deaf, dumb, and blind. Little hasty glances and tiny gestures tossed around her and over her head saying, "Don't cross her, let her have her way, she's eighty years old," and she sitting there as if she lived in a thin glass cage. Sometimes Granny almost made up her mind to pack up and move back to her own house where nobody could remind her every minute that she was old. Wait, wait, Cornelia, till your own children whisper behind your back!

In her day she had kept a better house and had got more work done. She wasn't too old yet for Lydia to be driving eighty miles for advice when one of the children jumped the track, and Jimmy still dropped in and talked things over: "Now, Mammy, you've a good business head, I want to know what you think of this? . . ." Old. Cornelia couldn't change the furniture around without asking. Little things, little things! They had been so sweet when they were little. Granny wished the old days were back again with the children young and everything to be done over. It had been a hard pull, but not too much for her. When she thought of all the food she had cooked, and all the clothes she had cut and sewed, and all the gardens she had made—well, the children showed it. There they were, made out of her, and they couldn't get away from that. Sometimes she wanted to see John again and point to them and say, Well, I didn't do so badly, did I? But that would have to wait. That was for tomorrow. She used to think of him as a man, but now all the children were older than their father, and he would be a child beside her if she saw him now. It seemed strange and there was something wrong in the idea. Why, he couldn't possibly recognize her. She had

fenced in a hundred acres once, digging the post holes herself and clamping the wires with just a boy to help. That changed a woman. John would be looking for a young woman with the peaked Spanish comb in her hair and the painted fan. Digging post holes changed a woman. Riding country roads in the winter when women had their babies was another thing: sitting up nights with sick horses and sick children and hardly ever losing one. John, I hardly ever lost one of them! John would see that in a minute, that would be something he could understand, she wouldn't have to explain anything!

It made her feel like rolling up her sleeves and putting the whole place to rights again. No matter if Cornelia was determined to be everywhere at once, there were a great many things left undone on this place. She would start tomorrow and do them. It was good to be strong enough for everything, even if all you made melted and changed and slipped under your hands, so that by the time you finished you almost forgot what you were working for. What was it I set out to do? she asked herself intently, but she could not remember. A fog rose over the valley, she saw it marching across the creek swallowing the trees and moving up the hill like an army of ghosts. Soon it would be at the near edge of the orchard, and then it was time to go in and light the lamps. Come in, children, don't stay out in the night air.

Lighting the lamps had been beautiful. The children huddled up to her and breathed like little calves waiting at the bars in the twilight. Their eyes followed the match and watched the flame rise and settle in a blue curve, then they moved away from her. The lamp was lit, they didn't have to be scared and hang on to Mother any more. Never, never, never more. God, for all my life I thank Thee. Without Thee, my God, I could never have done it. Hail, Mary, full of grace.

I want you to pick all the fruit this year and see that nothing is wasted. There's always someone who can use it. Don't let good things rot for want of using. You waste life when you waste good food. Don't let things get lost. It's bitter to lose things. Now, don't let me get to thinking, not when I am tired and taking a little nap before supper. . . .

The pillow rose about her shoulders and pressed against her heart and the memory was being squeezed out of it: oh, push down the pillow, somebody: it would smother her if she tried to hold it. Such a fresh breeze blowing and such a green day with no threats in it. But he had not come, just the same. What does a woman do when she has put on the white veil and set out the white cake for a man and he doesn't come? She tried to remember. No, I swear he never harmed me but in that. He never harmed me but in that . . . and what if he did? There was the day, the day, but a whirl of dark smoke rose and covered it, crept up and over into the bright field where everything was planted so carefully in orderly rows. That was hell, she knew hell when she saw it. For sixty years she had prayed against remembering him and against losing her soul in the deep pit of hell, and now the two things were mingled in one and the thought of him was a smoky cloud from hell that moved and crept in her head when she had just got rid of Doctor Harry and was trying to rest a minute. Wounded vanity, Ellen, said a sharp voice in the top of her mind. Don't let your wounded vanity get the upper hand of you. Plenty of girls get jilted. You were jilted, weren't you? Then stand up to it. Her eyelids wavered and let in streamers of blue-gray light like tissue paper over her eyes. She must get up and pull the shades down or she'd never sleep. She was in bed again and the shades were not down. How could that happen? Better turn over, hide from the light, sleeping in the light gave you nightmares. "Mother, how do you feel now?" and a stinging wetness on her forehead. But I don't like having my face washed in cold water!

Hapsy? George? Lydia? Jimmy? No, Cornelia, and her features were swollen and full of little puddles. "They're coming, darling, they'll all be here soon." Go wash your face, child, you look funny.

Instead of obeying, Cornelia knelt down and put her head on the pillow. She seemed to be talking but there was no sound. "Well, are you tongue-tied? Whose birthday is it? Are you going to give a party?"

Cornelia's mouth moved urgently in strange shapes. "Don't do that, you bother me, daughter."

"Oh, no, Mother. Oh, no. . . ."

Nonsense. It was strange about children. They disputed your every word. "No what, Cornelia?"

"Here's Doctor Harry."

"I won't see that boy again. He just left five minutes ago."

"That was this morning, Mother. It's night now. Here's the nurse."

"This is Doctor Harry, Mrs. Weatherall. I never saw you look so young and happy!"

"Ah, I'll never be young again—but I'd be happy if they'd let me lie in peace and get rested."

She thought she spoke up loudly, but no one answered. A warm weight on her forehead, a warm bracelet on her wrist, and a breeze went on whispering, trying to tell her something. A shuffle of leaves in the everlasting hand of God, He blew on them and they danced and rattled. "Mother, don't mind, we're going to give you a little hypodermic." "Look here, daughter, how do ants get in this bed? I saw sugar ants yesterday." Did you send for Hapsy too?

It was Hapsy she really wanted. She had to go a long way back through a great many rooms to find Hapsy standing with a baby on her arm. She seemed to herself to be Hapsy also, and the baby on Hapsy's arm was Hapsy and himself and herself, all at once, and there was no surprise in the meeting. Then Hapsy melted from within and turned flimsy as gray gauze and the baby was a gauzy shadow, and Hapsy came up close and said, "I thought you'd never come," and looked at her very searchingly and said, "You haven't changed a bit!" They leaned forward to kiss, when Cornelia began whispering from a long way off, "Oh, is there anything you want to tell me? Is there anything I can do for you?"

Yes, she had changed her mind after sixty years and she would like to see George. I want you to find George. Find him and be sure to tell him I forgot him. I want him to know I had my husband just the same and my children and my house like any other woman. A good house too and a good husband that I loved and fine children out of him. Better than I hoped for even. Tell him I was given back everything he took away and more. Oh, no, oh, God, no, there was something else besides the house and the man and the children. Oh, surely they were not all? What was it? Something not given back. . . . Her breath crowded down under her ribs and grew into a monstrous frightening shape with cutting edges; it bored up into her head, and the agony was unbelievable: Yes, John, get the Doctor now, no more talk, my time has come.

When this one was born it should be the last. The last. It should have been born first, for it was the one she had truly wanted. Everything came in good time. Nothing left out, left over. She was strong, in three days she would be as well as ever. Better. A woman needed milk in her to have her full health.

"Mother, do you hear me?"

"I've been telling you——"

"Mother, Father Connolly's here."

"I went to Holy Communion only last week. Tell him I'm not so sinful as all that."

"Father just wants to speak to you."

He could speak as much as he pleased. It was like him to drop in and inquire about her soul as if it were a teething baby, and then stay on for a cup of tea and a round of cards and gossip. He always had a funny story of some sort, usually about an Irishman who made his little mistakes and confessed them, and the point lay in some absurd thing he would blurt out in the confessional showing his struggles between native piety and original sin. Granny felt easy about her soul. Cornelia, where are your manners? Give Father Connolly a chair. She had her secret comfortable understanding with a few favorite saints who cleared a straight road to God for her. All as surely signed and sealed as the papers for the new Forty Acres. Forever . . . heirs and assigns forever. Since the day the wedding cake was not cut, but thrown out and wasted. The whole bottom dropped out of the world, and there she was blind and sweating with nothing under her feet and the walls falling away. His hand had caught her under the breast, she had not fallen, there was the freshly polished floor with the green rug on it, just as before. He had cursed like a sailor's parrot and said, "I'll kill him for you." Don't lay a hand on him, for my sake leave something to God. "Now, Ellen, you must believe what I tell you. . . ."

So there was nothing, nothing to worry about any more, except sometimes in the night one of the children screamed in a nightmare, and they both hustled out shaking and hunting for the matches and calling, "There, wait a minute, here we are!" John, get the doctor now, Hapsy's time has come. But there was Hapsy standing by the bed in a white cap. "Cornelia, tell Hapsy to take off her cap. I can't see her plain."

Her eyes opened very wide and the room stood out like a picture she had seen somewhere. Dark colors with the shadows rising toward the ceiling in long angles. The tall black dresser gleamed with nothing on it but John's picture, enlarged from a little one, with John's eyes very black when they should have been blue. You never saw him, so how do you know how he looked? But the man insisted the copy was perfect, it was very rich and handsome. For a picture, yes, but it's not my husband. The table by the bed had a linen cover and a candle and a crucifix.

The light was blue from Cornelia's silk lampshades. No sort of light at all, just frippery. You had to live forty years with kerosene lamps to appreciate honest electricity. She felt very strong and she saw Doctor Harry with a rosy nimbus around him.

"You look like a saint, Doctor Harry, and I vow that's as near as you'll ever come to it."

"She's saying something."

"I heard you, Cornelia. What's all this carrying-on?"

"Father Connolly's saying——"

Cornelia's voice staggered and bumped like a cart in a bad road. It rounded corners and turned back again and arrived nowhere. Granny stepped up in the cart very lightly and reached for the reins, but a man sat beside her and she knew him by his hands, driving the cart. She did not look in his face, for she knew without seeing, but looked instead down the road where the trees leaned over and bowed to each other and a thousand birds were singing a Mass. She felt like singing too, but she put her hand in the bosom of her dress and pulled out a rosary, and Father Connolly murmured Latin in a very solemn voice and tickled her feet.[1] My God, will you stop that nonsense? I'm a married woman. What if he did run away and leave me to face the priest by myself? I found another a whole world better. I wouldn't have exchanged my husband for anybody except St. Michael[2] himself, and you may tell him that for me with a thank you in the bargain.

Light flashed on her closed eyelids, and a deep roaring shook her. Cornelia, is that lightning? I hear thunder. There's going to be a storm. Close all the windows. Call the children in. . . . "Mother, here we are, all of us." "Is that you, Hapsy?" "Oh, no, I'm Lydia. We drove as fast as we could." Their faces drifted above her, drifted

[1] **tickled her feet:** Father Connolly is administering the last rites of the Church.

[2] **St. Michael:** the great prince of all the angels. In paintings he is pictured as a handsome young man.

away. The rosary fell out of her hands and Lydia put it back. Jimmy tried to help, their hands fumbled together, and Granny closed two fingers around Jimmy's thumb. Beads wouldn't do, it must be something alive. She was so amazed her thoughts ran round and round. So, my dear Lord, this is my death and I wasn't even thinking about it. My children have come to see me die. But I can't, it's not time. Oh, I always hated surprises. I wanted to give Cornelia the amethyst set —Cornelia, you're to have the amethyst set, but Hapsy's to wear it when she wants, and, Doctor Harry, do shut up. Nobody sent for you. Oh, my dear Lord, do wait a minute. I meant to do something about the Forty Acres, Jimmy doesn't need it and Lydia will later on, with that worthless husband of hers. I meant to finish the altar cloth and send six bottles of wine to Sister Borgia for her dyspepsia. I want to send six bottles of wine to Sister Borgia, Father Connolly, now don't let me forget.

Cornelia's voice made short turns and tilted over and crashed. "Oh, Mother, oh, Mother, oh, Mother. . . ."

"I'm not going, Cornelia. I'm taken by surprise. I can't go."

You'll see Hapsy again. What about her? "I thought you'd never come." Granny made a long journey outward, looking for Hapsy. What if I don't find her? What then? Her heart sank down and down, there was no bottom to death, she couldn't come to the end of it. The blue light from Cornelia's lampshade drew into a tiny point in the center of her brain, it flickered and winked like an eye, quietly it fluttered and dwindled. Granny lay down within herself, amazed and watchful, staring at the point of light that was herself; her body was now only a deeper mass of shadow in an endless darkness and this darkness would curl around the light and swallow it up. God, give a sign!

For the second time there was no sign. Again no bridegroom and the priest in the house. She could not remember any other sorrow because this grief wiped them all away. Oh, no, there's nothing more cruel than this—I'll never forgive it. She stretched herself with a deep breath and blew out the light.

FOR STUDY AND DISCUSSION

1. Why is "Weatherall" a good name for the main character? Cite examples from the story to show that life has not been "too much for her."

2. Identify the following characters and tell whether they are related primarily to Granny's "present" or to her "past": Cornelia, John, Doctor Harry, George, Father Connolly. What roles do these characters play in Granny's life and her thoughts?

3. "She had spent so much time preparing for death there was no need for bringing it up again." Explain this sentence. How had Granny spent her time preparing for death?

4. Describe the jilting. Why is it so important to Granny? How is it related to the last paragraph of the story? Why do you think Miss Porter gives such a vague account of this important event?

5. Miss Porter uses figurative language to convey Granny's state of mind. For example, to Granny "Doctor Harry floated like a balloon around the foot of the bed." Find five other examples in this story of figurative language used to convey a state of mind.

PLOT: ORDER OF EVENTS

As you know (page 558), a writer may arrange the events of a story in straightforward chronological order or may use some other order, perhaps introducing a flashback at some point, as in "The Baby Party." In "The Jilting of Granny Weatherall," the order of events may at first seem confusing. There is a constant shifting from the present to the past, reflecting Granny's state of mind. As an old lady on her deathbed, she tends to live in the past, but various events (visits by her daughter, the doctor, and the priest) constantly bring her back to the present. After studying the story, you will see a plan behind the apparent confusion: Miss Porter has deliberately chosen a particular order of events in order to create a particular effect.

Make two charts showing the events in the story. In the first chart show the events as they would be presented if the story were told in straight chronological order. (Begin with Granny as a young girl, and end with Granny on her deathbed.) In the second chart show the events in the order in which they are presented in the story. (Begin with Granny being examined by Doctor Harry, and end with Granny blowing out the light.) Explain why the author presented the events of the story in the order that they appear on the second chart. For example, why is the reader told about Cornelia before he is told about John?

LANGUAGE AND VOCABULARY

Indicating shifts from Granny's present to her past might have been difficult if the English language had not provided a means of indicating subtle distinctions in tense. This story, like almost all stories, is told in the past tense, which is used to describe events happening "now." When Granny begins to remember events in her past, the tense shifts to past perfect, a shift signaled by the use of the helping verb "had." While a passage dealing with Granny's past may begin in the past perfect tense, however, this tense is not used throughout the passage. Instead, the passage usually reverts to the past tense for two reasons: (1) to show that Granny is now living mentally in the past, and (2) to avoid the awkward sentences that usually result from the frequent use of past perfect verbs.

Analyze the following paragraphs to show how shifts in tense indicate shifts in time. Show also how tense is used to indicate that certain sentences represent Granny Weatherall's thoughts, as if her thoughts were being directly quoted.

"It made her feel like rolling up her sleeves and putting the whole place to rights again. No matter if Cornelia was determined to be everywhere at once, there were a great many things left undone on this place. She would start tomorrow and do them."

"Lighting the lamps had been beautiful. The children huddled up to her and breathed like little calves waiting at the bars in the twilight. Their eyes followed the match and watched the flame rise and settle in a blue curve, then they moved away from her. The lamp was lit, they didn't have to be scared and hang on to Mother any more. Never, never, never more. God, for all my life I thank Thee."

AMERICAN PAINTING

Realism and Abstraction

By the opening of the twentieth century, several new movements had developed in European painting, causing quite a stir in the world of art. These movements proclaimed the artist's privilege to express his ideas and feelings simply through color and design, without having to follow closely the visual appearances of nature. But in America, at the same time, the most progressive young painters were less concerned with the new European art than with their own observations of everyday life in the streets, parks, and harbors of the big cities. During this period a powerful school of realism was flourishing in American literature—the "Chicago School" of Theodore Dreiser, Edgar Lee Masters, Carl Sandburg, and Sherwood Anderson. Just as these four writers had worked for many years as newspaper reporters, so had three talented painters in Philadelphia—George Luks, John Sloan, and William Glackens—begun their careers as newspaper illustrators. It was through their early experience as journalists that these writers and artists learned to observe city life "in the raw."

In their spare time Luks, Sloan, and Glackens studied painting under a brilliant artist-teacher named Robert Henri, who encouraged them to draw their subjects from their everyday experiences. Unfortunately, their pictures of dingy streets and backyard slums horrified the critics and the public, both in Philadelphia and later in New York, where Henri and his friends moved around 1900. One of the New York critics sarcastically referred to them as the "Ash Can School." Finally, in 1907, when the National Academy of Design rejected one of Luks's paintings for exhibition because of its "vulgarity," the four artists decided to hold a show of their own. Inviting four other painters to join them, they called themselves "The Eight Americans," a label by which these artists are still known even though they never exhibited as a group again.

What bothered the critics most about George Luks's paintings were his portraits of coal miners, slum dwellers, and other "common" people. But even when Luks chose a subject that was socially acceptable, the critics were disturbed by his gusty, robust style: for it did not conform to the kind of genteel portraiture which was then fashionable. Note, for example, that in his *Otis Skinner as Colonel Bridau* (PLATE 1), there are no fussy details or "pretty" decorative effects—simply bold sweeps of the brush and well-placed accents of color, which make this characterization of a great American actor unusually forceful and vivid.

Despite the outcry against "vulgarity," many of the Ash Can School genre paintings were quite gentle and lyrical in mood. Look, for instance, at John Sloan's *The Wake of the Ferry* (PLATE 2). Almost immediately we identify ourselves with the lone figure standing at the rail in a quiet mood of reverie. Sloan has combined the figure with the rail, the post, and other shapes to form a framework of dark tones which leads our eye up to the softer, closer harmonies of dusky grays and gray-blues beyond.

Equally lyrical were many of William Glackens's paintings. In *Central Park in Winter* (PLATE 3), even the trees seem to bend to the same gentle rhythms as do the people below, who are strolling idly through the park. Note particularly Glackens's keen observation of the typical poses and gestures of children at play.

Another "realist" from this period was a somewhat younger painter named George Bellows, who had been strongly influenced by the Ash Can School. Today Bellows is best known for his dynamic pictures showing memorable scenes from prize fights—such as the moment when Firpo, the gigantic challenger from Argentina, knocked Jack Dempsey, the heavy-weight champion, through the ropes into the laps of the ringside reporters (PLATE 4). To dramatize the action, Bellows has set up two powerful diagonal lines in the center of the composition: one leading down the left side of Firpo's body, and the other down the referee's right arm, both converging on the sprawling figure of Dempsey as he hurtles out of the ring.

Today it is difficult to understand why these American realists were so severely criticized, especially when we compare their paintings with the far more radical work of many European painters from the same period. *Side-Wheeler, II* (PLATE 5), for instance, is a "Cubist" painting by an American-born artist named Lyonel Feininger, who as a youth had emigrated to Germany. This complex type of painting, in which the visible world is fractured into geometric patterns, was developed originally by a small group of artists in Paris just before Feininger went there to study in 1913. In *Side-Wheeler, II* even the smoke and sky are broken up into angular planes, which intersect one another with almost crushing force.

Feininger's picture, however, seems relatively quiet in comparison with the clangorous colors and crowded, vibrating patterns of Marsden Hartley's *Number 46* (PLATE 6), one of several abstract compositions that Hartley painted while living in Berlin at the beginning of World War I. The flag shapes suggest military symbols, but Hartley himself maintained that he had intended them merely as abstract arrangements of shapes and colors, with no allusions to actual objects whatsoever.

PLATE 1. GEORGE LUKS (1867–1933): *Otis Skinner as Colonel Bridau*. 1919. Oil on canvas, 52 x 44 inches. (The Phillips Collection, Washington, D.C.)

PLATE 2. JOHN SLOAN (1871–1951): *The Wake of the Ferry*. 1907. Oil on canvas, 26 x 32 inches. (The Phillips Collection, Washington, D.C.)

PLATE 3. WILLIAM J. GLACKENS (1870–1938): *Central Park in Winter.* 1905. Oil on canvas, 25 x 30 inches. (The Metropolitan Museum of Art, New York, George A. Hearn Fund, 1921)

PLATE 4. GEORGE W. BELLOWS (1882–1925): *Dempsey and Firpo.* 1924. Oil on canvas, 51 x 63¼ inches. (Collection of the Whitney Museum of American Art, New York)

572

PLATE 5. LYONEL FEININGER (1871–1956): *Side-Wheeler, II*. 1913. Oil on canvas. $31\frac{1}{2}$ x $35\frac{3}{4}$ inches. (The Detroit Institute of Arts)

PLATE 6. MARSDEN HARTLEY (1877–1943): *Number 46*. About 1914. Oil on canvas, 39 x $31\frac{1}{4}$ inches. (Albright-Knox Art Gallery, Buffalo, Philip Kirwen Fund)

JOHN
STEINBECK
(1902–1968)

When John Steinbeck was awarded the Nobel prize for literature in 1962, the Swedish Literary Academy in announcing the award cited the author's "great feeling for nature, for the tilled soil, the wasteland, the mountains and the ocean coasts . . . in the midst of, and beyond, the world of human beings." The Academy also noted "a strain of grim humor which to some extent redeems his often cruel . . . motif" and a sympathy for "the oppressed, the misfits, the distressed." Much of Steinbeck's work is marked by a conflict between his feeling for nature and his sympathy for men. With the detachment of a scientist, he can view his characters as living on a purely animal level, moved by forces which they can hardly understand or control. But at times there flickers in his work a vision of man striving toward wisdom and, even under the cruelest circumstances, retaining a measure of dignity.

Steinbeck was born in Salinas, California, the son of a county treasurer and a schoolteacher. Much of his early work is concerned with the prosperous ranches of the Salinas Valley and with the wild Monterey coast where he lived for a time. After graduating from high school, he attended Stanford University and devoted special attention to the study of marine biology. He worked at many jobs. Until the publication of *Tortilla Flat* in 1935, his writing earned him little money. In 1937 he published a best-selling novel, *Of Mice and Men,* which was made into a successful Broadway play and a motion picture. Moved by the plight of the "Okies"—Oklahoma farmers who, unable to make a living from their land, migrated to California to seek jobs as fruit pickers—he wrote *The Grapes of Wrath,* a sensational best seller which was awarded the Pulitzer prize and made Steinbeck one of the most widely known writers of our time. A shy man, he escaped from his public by leading a marine biology expedition to the Galápagos Islands. Later, with E. F. Ricketts, another member of the party, he described the expedition in *The Sea of Cortez.*

A number of Steinbeck's later works have locales other than California. *The Moon Is Down* deals with the Nazi occupation of a Scandinavian village; *The Pearl* tells of the tragedy of a Mexican fisherman; and *The Winter of Our Discontent* is concerned with the moral choices confronting a citizen of a New England town. *East of Eden,* a long ambitious novel published in 1952, has been praised for its originality and called Steinbeck's finest novel. It has also been criticized as a work that falls far short of its pretensions. One of Steinbeck's most popular books is *Travels with Charley,* an account of the author's tour of America with his dog Charley.

Flight

ABOUT FIFTEEN MILES below Monterey, on the wild coast, the Torres family had their farm, a few sloping acres above a cliff that dropped to the brown reefs and to the hissing white waters of the ocean. Behind the farm the stone mountains stood up against the sky. The farm buildings huddled like the clinging aphids [1] on the mountain skirts, crouched low to the ground as though the wind might blow them into the sea. The little shack, the rattling, rotting barn were gray-bitten with sea salt, beaten by the damp wind until they had taken on the color of the granite hills. Two horses, a red cow and a red calf, half a dozen pigs and a flock of lean, multicolored chickens stocked the place. A little corn was raised on the sterile slope, and it grew short and thick under the wind, and all the cobs formed on the landward sides of the stalks.

Mama Torres, a lean, dry woman with ancient eyes, had ruled the farm for ten years, ever since her husband tripped over a stone in the field one day and fell full length on a rattlesnake. When one is bitten on the chest there is not much that can be done.

Mama Torres had three children, two undersized black ones of twelve and fourteen, Emilio [2] and Rosy, whom Mama kept fishing on the rocks below the farm when the sea was kind and when the truant officer was in some distant part of Monterey County. And there was Pepé, [3] the tall smiling son of nineteen, a gentle, affectionate boy, but very lazy. Pepé had a tall head, pointed at the top, and from its peak coarse black hair grew down like a thatch all around. Over his smiling little eyes Mama cut a straight bang so he could see. Pepé had sharp Indian cheekbones and an eagle nose, but his mouth was as sweet and shapely as a girl's mouth, and his chin was fragile and chiseled. He was loose and gangling, all legs and feet and wrists, and he was very lazy. Mama thought him fine and brave, but she never told him so. She said, "Some lazy cow must have got into thy father's family, else how could I have a son like thee." And she said, "When I carried thee, a sneaking lazy coyote came out of the brush and looked at me one day. That must have made thee so."

Pepé smiled sheepishly and stabbed at the ground with his knife to keep the blade sharp and free from rust. It was his inheritance, that knife, his father's knife. The long heavy blade folded back into the black handle. There was a button on the handle. When Pepé pressed the button, the blade leaped out ready for use. The knife was with Pepé always, for it had been his father's knife.

One sunny morning when the sea below the cliff was glinting and blue and the white surf creamed on the reef, when even the stone mountains looked kindly, Mama Torres called out the door of the shack, "Pepé, I have a labor for thee."

There was no answer. Mama listened. From behind the barn she heard a burst of laughter. She lifted her full long skirt and walked in the direction of the noise.

Pepé was sitting on the ground with his back against a box. His white teeth glistened. On either side of him stood the two black ones, tense and expectant. Fifteen feet away a redwood post was set in the ground. Pepé's right hand lay limply in his lap, and in the palm the big black knife rested. The blade was closed back into the handle. Pepé looked smiling at the sky.

Suddenly Emilio cried, "Ya!"

Pepé's wrist flicked like the head of a snake. The blade seemed to fly open in midair, and with a thump the point dug into the redwood post, and the black

---

[1] **aphids** (ā'fidz): small insects that live on plants and suck their juices.

[2] **Emilio** (ā·mēl'yō).

[3] **Pepé** (pā·pā').

handle quivered. The three burst into excited laughter. Rosy ran to the post and pulled out the knife and brought it back to Pepé. He closed the blade and settled the knife carefully in his listless palm again. He grinned self-consciously at the sky.

"Ya!"

The heavy knife lanced out and sunk into the post again. Mama moved forward like a ship and scattered the play.

"All day you do foolish things with the knife, like a toy baby," she stormed. "Get up on thy huge feet that eat up shoes. Get up!" She took him by one loose shoulder and hoisted at him. Pepé grinned sheepishly and came halfheartedly to his feet. "Look!" Mama cried. "Big lazy, you must catch the horse and put on him thy father's saddle. You must ride to Monterey. The medicine bottle is empty. There is no salt. Go thou now, Peanut! Catch the horse."

A revolution took place in the relaxed figure of Pepé. "To Monterey, me? Alone? Sí, Mama."

She scowled at him. "Do not think, big sheep, that you will buy candy. No, I will give you only enough for the medicine and the salt."

Pepé smiled. "Mama, you will put the hatband on the hat?"

She relented then. "Yes, Pepé. You may wear the hatband."

His voice grew insinuating. "And the green handkerchief, Mama?"

"Yes, if you go quickly and return with no trouble, the silk green handkerchief will go. If you make sure to take off the handkerchief when you eat so no spot may fall on it."

"Sí, Mama. I will be careful. I am a man."

"Thou? A man? Thou art a peanut."

He went into the rickety barn and brought out a rope, and he walked agilely enough up the hill to catch the horse.

When he was ready and mounted before the door, mounted on his father's saddle that was so old that the oaken frame showed through torn leather in many places, then Mama brought out the round black hat with the tooled leather band, and she reached up and knotted the green silk handkerchief about his neck. Pepé's blue denim coat was much darker than his jeans, for it had been washed much less often.

Mama handed up the big medicine bottle and the silver coins. "That for the medicine," she said, "and that for the salt. That for a candle to burn for the papa. That for *dulces* [1] for the little ones. Our friend Mrs. Rodriguez [2] will give you dinner and maybe a bed for the night. When you go to the church, say only ten paternosters [3] and only twenty-five Ave Marias. [4] Oh! I know, big coyote. You would sit there flapping your mouth over Aves all day while you looked at the candles and the holy pictures. That is not good devotion to stare at the pretty things."

The black hat, covering the high pointed head and black thatched hair of Pepé, gave him dignity and age. He sat the rangy horse well. Mama thought how handsome he was, dark and lean and tall. "I would not send thee now alone, thou little one, except for the medicine," she said softly. "It is not good to have no medicine, for who knows when the toothache will come, or the sadness of the stomach. These things are."

"*Adiós*, Mama," Pepé cried. "I will come back soon. You may send me often alone. I am a man."

"Thou art a foolish chicken."

He straightened his shoulders, flipped the reins against the horse's shoulder, and rode away. He turned once and saw that they still watched him, Emilio and Rosy and Mama. Pepé grinned with pride and gladness and lifted the tough buckskin horse to a trot.

---

[1] *dulces* (dōol'sās): sweets.

[2] **Rodriguez** (rô·drē'gās).

[3] **ten paternosters** (pā´ tə·nos'tərz): ten repetitions of the Lord's Prayer.

[4] **Ave Marias** (ä'vä mə·rē'əz): prayers to the Virgin Mary, beginning "Hail, Mary."

When he had dropped out of sight over a little dip in the road, Mama turned to the black ones, but she spoke to herself. "He is nearly a man now," she said. "It will be a nice thing to have a man in the house again." Her eyes sharpened on the children. "Go to the rocks now. The tide is going out. There will be abalones [1] to be found." She put the iron hooks into their hands and saw them down the steep trail to the reefs. She brought the smooth stone metate [2] to the doorway and sat grinding her corn to flour and looking occasionally at the road over which Pepé had gone. The noonday came and then the afternoon, when the little ones beat the abalones on a rock to make them tender and Mama patted the *tortillas* to make them thin. They ate their dinner as the red sun was plunging down toward the ocean. They sat on the doorsteps and watched a big white moon come over the mountaintops.

Mama said, "He is now at the house of our friend Mrs. Rodriguez. She will give him nice things to eat and maybe a present."

Emilio said, "Someday I, too, will ride to Monterey for medicine. Did Pepé come to be a man today?"

Mama said wisely, "A boy gets to be a man when a man is needed. Remember this thing. I have known boys forty years old because there was no need for a man."

Soon afterward they retired, Mama in her big oak bed on one side of the room, Emilio and Rosy in their boxes full of straw and sheepskins on the other side of the room.

The moon went over the sky and the surf roared on the rocks. The roosters crowed the first call. The surf subsided to a whispering surge against the reef. The moon dropped toward the sea. The roosters crowed again.

The moon was near down to the water when Pepé rode on a winded horse to his home flat. His dog bounced out and circled the horse, yelping with pleasure. Pepé slid off the saddle to the ground. The weathered little shack was silver in the moonlight and the square shadow of it was black to the north and east. Against the east the piling mountains were misty with light; their tops melted into the sky.

Pepé walked wearily up the three steps and into the house. It was dark inside. There was a rustle in the corner.

Mama cried out from her bed. "Who comes? Pepé, is it thou?"

"*Sí,* Mama."

"Did you get the medicine?"

"*Sí,* Mama."

"Well, go to sleep, then. I thought you would be sleeping at the house of Mrs. Rodriguez." Pepé stood silently in the dark room. "Why do you stand there, Pepé? Did you drink wine?"

"*Sí,* Mama."

"Well, go to bed then and sleep out the wine."

His voice was tired and patient, but very firm. "Light the candle, Mama. I must go away into the mountains."

"What is this, Pepé? You are crazy." Mama struck a sulfur match and held the little blue burr until the flame spread up the stick. She set light to the candle on the floor beside her bed. "Now, Pepé, what is this you say?" She looked anxiously into his face.

He was changed. The fragile quality seemed to have gone from his chin. His mouth was less full than it had been, the lines of the lips were straighter, but in his eyes the greatest change had taken place. There was no laughter in them any more, nor any bashfulness. They were sharp and bright and purposeful.

He told her in a tired monotone, told her everything just as it had happened. A few people came into the kitchen of Mrs. Rodriguez. There was wine to drink. Pepé drank wine. The little quarrel—the man started toward Pepé and then the knife—it went almost by itself. It flew,

---

[1] **abalones** (ab´ə·lō′nēz): large shellfish.
[2] **metate** (mā·tä′tä): a stone used in the southwestern United States for grinding cereal seeds.

it darted before Pepé knew it. As he talked, Mama's face grew stern, and it seemed to grow more lean. Pepé finished. "I am a man now, Mama. The man said names to me I could not allow."

Mama nodded. "Yes, thou art a man, my poor little Pepé. Thou art a man. I have seen it coming on thee. I have watched you throwing the knife into the post, and I have been afraid." For a moment her face had softened, but now it grew stern again. "Come! We must get you ready. Go. Awaken Emilio and Rosy. Go quickly."

Pepé stepped over to the corner where his brother and sister slept among the sheepskins. He leaned down and shook them gently. "Come, Rosy! Come, Emilio! The Mama says you must arise."

The little black ones sat up and rubbed their eyes in the candlelight. Mama was out of bed now, her long black skirt over her nightgown. "Emilio," she cried. "Go up and catch the other horse for Pepé. Quickly, now! Quickly." Emilio put his legs in his overalls and stumbled sleepily out the door.

"You heard no one behind you on the road?" Mama demanded.

"No, Mama. I listened carefully. No one was on the road."

Mama darted like a bird about the room. From a nail on the wall she took a canvas water bag and threw it on the floor. She stripped a blanket from her bed and rolled it into a tight tube and tied the ends with string. From a box beside the stove she lifted a flour sack half full of black stringy jerky. "Your father's black coat, Pepé. Here, put it on."

Pepé stood in the middle of the floor watching her activity. She reached behind the door and brought out the rifle, a long 38–56, worn shiny the whole length of the barrel. Pepé took it from her and held it in the crook of his elbow. Mama brought a little leather bag and counted the cartridges into his hand. "Only ten left," she warned. "You must not waste them."

Emilio put his head in the door. " '*Qui 'st 'l caballo,*[1] Mama."

"Put on the saddle from the other horse. Tie on the blanket. Here, tie the jerky to the saddle horn."

Still Pepé stood silently watching his mother's frantic activity. His chin looked hard, and his sweet mouth was drawn and thin. His little eyes followed Mama about the room almost suspiciously.

Rosy asked softly, "Where goes Pepé?"

Mama's eyes were fierce. "Pepé goes on a journey. Pepé is a man now. He has a man's thing to do."

Pepé straightened his shoulders. His mouth changed until he looked very much like Mama.

At last the preparation was finished. The loaded horse stood outside the door. The water bag dripped a line of moisture down the bay shoulder.

The moonlight was being thinned by the dawn, and the big white moon was near down to the sea. The family stood by the shack. Mama confronted Pepé. "Look, my son! Do not stop until it is dark again. Do not sleep even though you are tired. Take care of the horse in order that he may not stop of weariness. Remember to be careful with the bullets— there are only ten. Do not fill thy stomach with jerky or it will make thee sick. Eat a little jerky and fill thy stomach with grass. When thou comest to the high mountains, if thou seest any of the dark

---

[1] *'Qui 'st 'l caballo* (kēst'l kä·bä′yō): Here is the horse (colloquial Spanish).

watching men, go not near to them nor try to speak to them. And forget not thy prayers." She put her lean hands on Pepé's shoulders, stood on her toes and kissed him formally on both cheeks, and Pepé kissed her on both cheeks. Then he went to Emilio and Rosy and kissed both of their cheeks.

Pepé turned back to Mama. He seemed to look for a little softness, a little weakness in her. His eyes were searching, but Mama's face remained fierce. "Go now," she said. "Do not wait to be caught like a chicken."

Pepé pulled himself into the saddle. "I am a man," he said.

It was the first dawn when he rode up the hill toward the little canyon which let a trail into the mountains. Moonlight and daylight fought with each other, and the two warring qualities made it difficult to see. Before Pepé had gone a hundred yards, the outlines of his figure were misty; and long before he entered the canyon, he had become a gray, indefinite shadow.

Mama stood stiffly in front of her doorstep, and on either side of her stood Emilio and Rosy. They cast furtive glances at Mama now and then.

When the gray shape of Pepé melted into the hillside and disappeared, Mama relaxed. She began the high, whining keen [1] of the death wail. "Our beautiful— our brave," she cried. "Our protector, our son is gone." Emilio and Rosy moaned beside her. "Our beautiful—our brave, he is gone." It was the formal wail. It rose to a high piercing whine and subsided to a moan. Mama raised it three times and then she turned and went into the house and shut the door.

Emilio and Rosy stood wondering in the dawn. They heard Mama whimpering in the house. They went out to sit on the cliff above the ocean. They touched shoulders. "When did Pepé come to be a man?" Emilio asked.

"Last night," said Rosy. "Last night in Monterey." The ocean clouds turned red with the sun that was behind the mountains.

"We will have no breakfast," said Emilio. "Mama will not want to cook." Rosy did not answer him. "Where is Pepé gone?" he asked.

Rosy looked around at him. She drew her knowledge from the quiet air. "He has gone on a journey. He will never come back."

"Is he dead? Do you think he is dead?"

Rosy looked back at the ocean again. A little steamer, drawing a line of smoke, sat on the edge of the horizon. "He is not dead," Rosy explained. "Not yet."

Pepé rested the big rifle across the saddle in front of him. He let the horse walk up the hill and he didn't look back. The stony slope took on a coat of short brush so that Pepé found the entrance to a trail and entered it.

When he came to the canyon opening, he swung once in his saddle and looked back, but the houses were swallowed in the misty light. Pepé jerked forward again. The high shoulder of the canyon closed in on him. His horse stretched out its neck and sighed and settled to the trail.

It was a well-worn path, dark soft leaf-mold earth strewn with broken pieces of sandstone. The trail rounded the shoulder of the canyon and dropped steeply into the bed of the stream. In the shallows the water ran smoothly, glinting in the first morning sun. Small round stones on the bottom were as brown as rust with sun moss. In the sand along the edges of the stream the tall, rich wild mint grew, while in the water itself the cress,[2] old and tough, had gone to heavy seed.

The path went into the stream and emerged on the other side. The horse sloshed into the water and stopped. Pepé dropped his bridle and let the beast drink of the running water.

Soon the canyon sides became steep

[1] **keen:** a lamentation, or dirge, for the dead.

[2] **cress** (or **watercress**): an edible white-flowered plant that grows in clear running water.

and the first giant sentinel redwoods guarded the trail, great round red trunks bearing foliage as green and lacy as ferns. Once Pepé was among the trees, the sun was lost. A perfumed and purple light lay in the pale green of the underbrush. Gooseberry bushes and blackberries and tall ferns lined the stream, and overhead the branches of the redwoods met and cut off the sky.

Pepé drank from the water bag, and he reached into the flour sack and brought out a black string of jerky. His white teeth gnawed at the string until the tough meat parted. He chewed slowly and drank occasionally from the water bag. His little eyes were slumberous and tired, but the muscles of his face were hard-set. The earth of the trail was black now. It gave up a hollow sound under the walking hoof-beats.

The stream fell more sharply. Little waterfalls splashed on the stones. Five-fingered ferns hung over the water and dropped spray from their finger tips. Pepé rode half over his saddle, dangling one leg loosely. He picked a bay leaf from a tree beside the way and put it into his mouth for a moment to flavor the dry jerky. He

held the gun loosely across the pommel.

Suddenly he squared in his saddle, swung the horse from the trail and kicked it hurriedly up behind a big redwood tree. He pulled up the reins tight against the bit to keep the horse from whinnying. His face was intent and his nostrils quivered a little.

A hollow pounding came down the trail, and a horseman rode by, a fat man with red cheeks and a white stubble beard. His horse put down his head and blubbered at the trail when it came to the place where Pepé had turned off. "Hold up!" said the man, and he pulled up his horse's head.

When the last sound of the hoofs died away, Pepé came back into the trail again. He did not relax in the saddle any more. He lifted the big rifle and swung the lever to throw a shell into the chamber, and then he let down the hammer to half cock.

The trail grew very steep. Now the redwood trees were smaller and their tops were dead, bitten dead where the· wind reached them. The horse plodded on; the sun went slowly overhead and started down toward the afternoon.

Where the stream came out of a side canyon, the trail left it. Pepé dismounted and watered his horse and filled up his water bag. As soon as the trail had parted from the stream, the trees were gone and only the thick brittle sage and manzanita [1] and the chaparral [2] edged the trail. And the soft black earth was gone, too, leaving only the light tan broken rock for the trail bed. Lizards scampered away into the brush as the horse rattled over the little stones.

Pepé turned in his saddle and looked back. He was in the open now: he could be seen from a distance. As he ascended the trail the country grew more rough and terrible and dry. The way wound about the bases of great square rocks. Little gray rabbits skittered in the brush. A bird made a monotonous high creaking. East-

[1] **manzanita** (man′ za·nē′tə): shrubs.
[2] **chaparral** (chap′ə·ral′): a thicket of shrubs or dwarf trees.

ward the bare rock mountaintops were pale and powder-dry under the dropping sun. The horse plodded up and up the trail toward the little V in the ridge which was the pass.

Pepé looked suspiciously back every minute or so, and his eyes sought the tops of the ridges ahead. Once, on a white barren spur, he saw a black figure for a moment; but he looked quickly away, for it was one of the dark watchers. No one knew who the watchers were, nor where they lived, but it was better to ignore them and never to show interest in them. They did not bother one who stayed on the trail and minded his own business.

The air was parched and full of light dust blown by the breeze from the eroding mountains. Pepé drank sparingly from his bag and corked it tightly and hung it on the horn again. The trail moved up the dry shale hillside, avoiding rocks, dropping under clefts, climbing in and out of old water scars. When he arrived at the little pass he stopped and looked back for a long time. No dark watchers were to be seen now. The trail behind was empty. Only the high tops of the redwoods indicated where the stream flowed.

Pepé rode on through the pass. His little eyes were nearly closed with weariness, but his face was stern, relentless, and manly. The high mountain wind coasted sighing through the pass and whistled on the edges of the big blocks of broken granite. In the air, a red-tailed hawk sailed over close to the ridge and screamed angrily. Pepé went slowly through the broken jagged pass and looked down on the other side.

The trail dropped quickly, staggering among broken rock. At the bottom of the slope there was a dark crease, thick with brush, and on the other side of the crease a little flat, in which a grove of oak trees grew. A scar of green grass cut across the flat. And behind the flat another mountain rose, desolate with dead rocks and starving little black bushes. Pepé drank from the bag again, for the air was so dry that it encrusted his nostrils and burned

his lips. He put the horse down the trail. The hoofs slipped and struggled on the steep way, starting little stones that rolled off into the brush. The sun was gone behind the westward mountain now, but still it glowed brilliantly on the oaks and on the grassy flat. The rocks and the hillsides still sent up waves of the heat they had gathered from the day's sun.

Pepé looked up to the top of the next dry withered ridge. He saw a dark form against the sky, a man's figure standing on top of a rock, and he glanced away quickly not to appear curious. When a moment later he looked up again, the figure was gone.

Downward the trail was quickly covered. Sometimes the horse floundered for footing, sometimes set his feet and slid a little way. They came at last to the bottom where the dark chaparral was higher than Pepé's head. He held up his rifle on one side and his arm on the other to shield his face from the sharp brittle fingers of the brush.

Up and out of the crease he rode, and up a little cliff. The grassy flat was before him, and the round comfortable oaks. For a moment he studied the trail down which he had come, but there was no movement and no sound from it. Finally he rode out over the flat, to the green streak, and at the upper end of the damp he found a little spring welling out of the earth and dropping into a dug basin before it seeped out over the flat.

Pepé filled his bag first, and then he let the thirsty horse drink out of the pool. He led the horse to the clump of oaks, and in the middle of the grove, fairly protected from sight on all sides, he took off the saddle and the bridle and laid them on the ground. The horse stretched his jaws sideways and yawned. Pepé knotted the lead rope about the horse's neck and tied him to a sapling among the oaks, where he could graze in a fairly large circle.

When the horse was gnawing hungrily at the dry grass, Pepé went to the saddle and took a black string of jerky from the sack and strolled to an oak tree on the edge of the grove, from under which he could watch the trail. He sat down in the crisp dry oak leaves and automatically felt for his big black knife to cut the jerky, but he had no knife. He leaned back on his elbow and gnawed at the tough strong meat. His face was blank, but it was a man's face.

The bright evening light washed the eastern ridge, but the valley was darkening. Doves flew down from the hills to the spring, and the quail came running out of the brush and joined them, calling clearly to one another.

Out of the corner of his eye Pepé saw a shadow grow out of the bushy crease. He turned his head slowly. A big spotted wildcat was creeping toward the spring, belly to the ground, moving like thought.

Pepé cocked his rifle and edged the muzzle slowly around. Then he looked apprehensively up the trail and dropped the hammer again. From the ground beside him he picked an oak twig and threw it toward the spring. The quail flew up with a roar and the doves whistled away. The big cat stood up; for a long moment he looked at Pepé with cold yellow eyes, and then fearlessly walked back into the gulch.

The dusk gathered quickly in the deep valley. Pepé muttered his prayers, put his head down on his arm and went instantly to sleep.

The moon came up and filled the valley with cold blue light, and the wind swept rustling down from the peaks. The owls worked up and down the slopes looking for rabbits. Down in the brush of the gulch a coyote gabbled. The oak trees whispered softly in the night breeze.

Pepé started up, listening. His horse had whinnied. The moon was just slipping behind the western ridge, leaving the valley in darkness behind it. Pepé sat tensely gripping his rifle. From far up the trail he heard an answering whinny and the crash of shod hoofs on the broken rock. He jumped to his feet, ran to his horse and led it under the trees. He threw on the saddle and cinched it tight for the steep trail, caught the unwilling head and forced the bit into the mouth. He felt the saddle to make sure the water bag and the sack of jerky were there. Then he mounted and turned up the hill.

It was velvet-dark. The horse found the entrance to the trail where it left the flat, and started up, stumbling and slipping on the rocks. Pepé's hand rose up to his head. His hat was gone. He had left it under the oak tree.

The horse had struggled far up the trail when the first change of dawn came into the air, a steel grayness as light mixed thoroughly with dark. Gradually the sharp snaggled edge of the ridge stood out above them, rotten granite tortured and eaten by the winds of time. Pepé had dropped his reins on the horn, leaving direction to the horse. The brush grabbed at his legs in the dark until one knee of his jeans was ripped.

Gradually the light flowed down over the ridge. The starved brush and rocks stood out in the half-light, strange and lonely in high perspective. Then there came warmth into the light. Pepé drew up and looked back, but he could see nothing in the darker valley below. The sky turned blue over the coming sun. In the waste of the mountainside, the poor dry brush grew only three feet high. Here and there, big outcroppings of unrotted granite stood up like moldering houses. Pepé relaxed a little. He drank from his water bag and bit off a piece of jerky. A single eagle flew over, high in the light.

Without warning Pepé's horse screamed and fell on its side. He was almost down before the rifle crash echoed up from the valley. From a hole behind the struggling shoulder, a stream of bright crimson blood pumped and stopped and pumped and stopped. The hoofs threshed on the ground. Pepé lay half-stunned beside the horse. He looked slowly down the hill. A piece of sage clipped off beside his head and another crash echoed up from side to side of the canyon. Pepé flung himself frantically behind a bush.

He crawled up the hill on his knees and one hand. His right hand held the rifle up off the ground and pushed it ahead of him. He moved with the instinctive care of an animal. Rapidly he wormed his way toward one of the big outcroppings of granite on the hill above him. Where the brush was high he doubled up and ran; but where the cover was slight he wriggled forward on his stomach, pushing the rifle ahead of him. In the last little distance there was no cover at all. Pepé poised and then he darted across the space and flashed around the corner of the rock.

He leaned panting against the stone. When his breath came easier he moved along behind the big rock until he came to a narrow split that offered a thin section of vision down the hill. Pepé lay on his stomach and pushed the rifle barrel through the slit and waited.

The sun reddened the western ridges now. Already the buzzards were settling down toward the place where the horse lay. A small brown bird scratched in the dead sage leaves directly in front of the rifle muzzle. The coasting eagle flew back toward the rising sun.

Pepé saw a little movement in the brush far below. His grip tightened on the gun. A little brown doe stepped daintily out on the trail and crossed it and disappeared into the brush again. For a long time Pepé

waited. Far below he could see the little flat and the oak trees and the slash of green. Suddenly his eyes flashed back at the trail again. A quarter of a mile down there had been a quick movement in the chaparral. The rifle swung over. The front sight nestled in the V of the rear sight. Pepé studied for a moment and then raised the rear sight a notch. The little movement in the brush came again. The sight settled on it. Pepé squeezed the trigger. The explosion crashed down the mountain and up the other side, and came rattling back. The whole side of the slope grew still. No more movement. And then a white streak cut into the granite of the slit and a bullet whined away and a crash sounded up from below. Pepé felt a sharp pain in his right hand. A sliver of granite was sticking out from between his first and second knuckles and the point protruded from his palm. Carefully he pulled out the sliver of stone. The wound bled evenly and gently. No vein or artery was cut.

Pepé looked into a little dusty cave in the rock and gathered a handful of spider web, and he pressed the mass into the cut, plastering the soft web into the blood. The flow stopped almost at once.

The rifle was on the ground. Pepé picked it up, levered a new shell into the chamber. And then he slid into the brush on his stomach. Far to the right he crawled, and then up the hill, moving slowly and carefully, crawling to cover and resting and then crawling again.

In the mountains the sun is high in its arc before it penetrates the gorges. The hot face looked over the hill and brought instant heat with it. The white light beat on the rocks and reflected from them and rose up quivering from the earth again, and the rocks and bushes seemed to quiver behind the air.

Pepé crawled in the general direction of the ridge peak, zigzagging for cover. The deep cut between his knuckles began to throb. He crawled close to a rattlesnake before he saw it, and when it raised its dry head and made a soft beginning whir, he backed up and took another way. The quick gray lizards flashed in front of him, raising a tiny line of dust. He found another mass of spider web and pressed it against his throbbing hand.

Pepé was pushing the rifle with his left hand now. Little drops of sweat ran to the ends of his coarse black hair and rolled down his cheeks. His lips and tongue were growing thick and heavy. His lips writhed to draw saliva into his mouth. His little dark eyes were uneasy and suspicious. Once when a gray lizard paused in front of him on the parched ground and turned its head sideways, he crushed it flat with a stone.

When the sun slid past noon he had not gone a mile. He crawled exhaustedly a last hundred yards to a patch of high sharp manzanita, crawled desperately, and when the patch was reached he wriggled in among the tough gnarly trunks and dropped his head on his left arm. There was little shade in the meager brush, but there was cover and safety. Pepé went to sleep as he lay and the sun beat on his back. A few little birds hopped close to him and peered and hopped away. Pepé squirmed in his sleep and he raised and dropped his wounded hand again and again.

The sun went down behind the peaks and the cool evening came, and then the dark. A coyote yelled from the hillside. Pepé started awake and looked about with misty eyes. His hand was swollen and heavy; a little thread of pain ran up the inside of his arm and settled in a pocket in his armpit. He peered about and then stood up, for the mountains were black and the moon had not yet risen. Pepé stood up in the dark. The coat of his father pressed on his arm. His tongue was swollen until it nearly filled his mouth. He wriggled out of the coat and dropped it in the brush, and then he struggled up the hill, falling over rocks and tearing his way through the brush. The rifle knocked against stones as he went. Little dry avalanches of gravel and shattered stone went whispering down the hill behind him.

After a while the old moon came up and showed the jagged ridgetop ahead of him. By moonlight Pepé traveled more easily. He bent forward so that his throbbing arm hung away from his body. The journey uphill was made in dashes and rests, a frantic rush up a few yards and then a rest. The wind coasted down the slope, rattling the dry stems of the bushes.

The moon was at meridian when Pepé came at last to the sharp backbone of the ridgetop. On the last hundred yards of the rise no soil had clung under the wearing winds. The way was on solid rock. He clambered to the top and looked down on the other side. There was a draw like the last below him, misty with moonlight, brushed with dry struggling sage and chaparral. On the other side the hill rose up sharply and at the top the jagged rotten teeth of the mountain showed against the sky. At the bottom of the cut the brush was thick and dark.

Pepé stumbled down the hill. His throat was almost closed with thirst. At first he tried to run, but immediately he fell and rolled. After that he went more carefully. The moon was just disappearing behind the mountains when he came to the bottom. He crawled into the heavy brush, feeling with his fingers for water. There was no water in the bed of the stream, only damp earth. Pepé laid his gun down and scooped up a handful of mud and put it in his mouth, and then he spluttered and scraped the earth from his tongue with his finger, for the mud drew at his mouth like a poultice. He dug a hole in the stream bed with his fingers, dug a little basin to catch water; but before it was very deep his head fell forward on the damp ground and he slept.

The dawn came and the heat of the day fell on the earth, and still Pepé slept. Late in the afternoon his head jerked up. He looked slowly around. His eyes were slits of weariness. Twenty feet away in the heavy brush a big tawny mountain lion stood looking at him. Its long thick tail waved gracefully; its ears were erect with interest, not laid back dangerously. The lion squatted down on its stomach and watched him.

Pepé looked at the hole he had dug in the earth. A half-inch of muddy water had collected in the bottom. He tore the sleeve from his hurt arm, with his teeth ripped out a little square, soaked it in the water and put it in his mouth. Over and over he filled the cloth and sucked it.

Still the lion sat and watched him. The evening came down but there was no movement on the hills. No birds visited the dry bottom of the cut. Pepé looked occasionally at the lion. The eyes of the yellow beast drooped as though he were about to sleep. He yawned and his long thin red tongue curled out. Suddenly his head jerked around and his nostrils quivered. His big tail lashed. He stood up and slunk like a tawny shadow into the thick brush.

A moment later Pepé heard the sound, the faint far crash of horses' hoofs on gravel. And he heard something else, a high whining yelp of a dog.

Pepé took his rifle in his left hand and he glided into the brush almost as quietly as the lion had. In the darkening evening he crouched up the hill toward the next ridge. Only when the dark came did he stand up. His energy was short. Once it was dark he fell over the rocks and slipped to his knees on the steep slope, but he moved on and on up the hill, climbing and scrambling over the broken hillside.

When he was far up toward the top, he lay down and slept for a little while. The withered moon, shining on his face, awakened him. He stood up and moved up the hill. Fifty yards away he stopped and turned back, for he had forgotten his rifle. He walked heavily down and poked about in the brush, but he could not find his gun. At last he lay down to rest. The pocket of pain in his armpit had grown more sharp. His arm seemed to swell out and fall with every heartbeat. There was no position lying down where the heavy arm did not press against his armpit.

With the effort of a hurt beast, Pepé got up and moved again toward the top of the ridge. He held his swollen arm away from his body with his left hand. Up the steep hill he dragged himself, a few steps and a rest, and a few more steps. At last he was nearing the top. The moon showed the uneven sharp back of it against the sky.

Pepé's brain spun in a big spiral up and away from him. He slumped to the ground and lay still. The rock ridgetop was only a hundred feet above him.

The moon moved over the sky. Pepé half turned on his back. His tongue tried to make words, but only a thick hissing came from between his lips.

When the dawn came, Pepé pulled himself up. His eyes were sane again. He drew his great puffed arm in front of him and looked at the angry wound. The black line ran up from his wrist to his armpit. Automatically he reached in his pocket for the big black knife, but it was not there. His eyes searched the ground. He picked up a sharp blade of stone and scraped at the wound, sawed at the proud flesh and then squeezed the green juice out in big drops. Instantly he threw back his head and whined like a dog. His whole right side shuddered at the pain, but the pain cleared his head.

In the gray light he struggled up the last slope to the ridge and crawled over and lay down behind a line of rocks. Below him lay a deep canyon exactly like the last, waterless and desolate. There was no flat, no oak trees, not even heavy brush in the bottom of it. And on the other side a sharp ridge stood up, thinly brushed with starving sage, littered with broken granite. Strewn over the hill there were giant outcroppings, and on the top the granite teeth stood out against the sky.

The new day was light now. The flame of the sun came over the ridge and fell on Pepé where he lay on the ground. His coarse black hair was littered with twigs and bits of spider web. His eyes had retreated back into his head. Between his lips the tip of his black tongue showed.

He sat up and dragged his great arm into his lap and nursed it, rocking his body and moaning in his throat. He threw back his head and looked up into the pale sky. A big black bird circled nearly out of sight, far to the left another was sailing near.

He lifted his head to listen, for a familiar sound had come to him from the valley he had climbed out of; it was the crying yelp of hounds, excited and feverish, on a trail.

Pepé bowed his head quickly. He tried to speak rapid words but only a thick hiss came from his lips. He drew a shaky cross on his breast with his left hand. It was a long struggle to get to his feet. He crawled slowly and mechanically to the top of a big rock on the ridge peak. Once there, he arose slowly, swaying to his feet, and stood erect. Far below he could see the dark brush where he had slept. He braced his feet and stood there, black against the morning sky.

There came a ripping sound at his feet. A piece of stone flew up and a bullet droned off into the next gorge. The hollow crash echoed up from below. Pepé looked down for a moment and then pulled himself straight again.

His body jarred back. His left hand fluttered helplessly toward his breast. The second crash sounded from below. Pepé swung forward and toppled from the rock. His body struck and rolled over and over, starting a little avalanche. And when at last he stopped against a bush, the avalanche slid slowly down and covered up his head.

FOR STUDY AND DISCUSSION

1. Describe three impressions that you get of the Torres family life from the first few paragraphs. Support each impression with details from the story. What admirable qualities do you find in Mama? Why do you think Pepé's laziness is emphasized?

2. Do you think that Mama and Pepé choose the right way of meeting Pepé's situation? Why or why not? How does Pepé's behavior on his return from Monterey and on his flight support Mama's idea of what changes a boy into a man?

3. Is the story more or less interesting because you never see the pursuers or know anything about them? What is the first indication of real danger? Trace the events in the story that make Pepé's situation increasingly hopeless.

4. How is Pepé reduced to the level of an animal? How does he manage to retain his dignity as a human being? Does the ending satisfy you? Why or why not?

5. How do the encounters with the wildcat and the mountain lion help suggest Pepé's reduction to the brute level? Cite other details that suggest this reduction.

SETTING

Setting—specific place and time—is rarely the most important element of a story, but it almost always influences the story's events, either directly or indirectly. A story must have an appropriate setting. For example, it is difficult to imagine a tender love story taking place in a butcher shop, or a duel to the death taking place in the reading room of a library. Setting also plays a part in determining the characters of a story. Just as we are all products of our environment, so a good author shows how his characters are shaped by their environment. In some stories, setting is particularly important in building atmosphere or in expressing the author's view of the world. A harsh setting, for example, may reflect the author's view that the world is harsh, and the events in the story will reflect the same point of view.

1. How are Mama and Pepé shaped by their environment?

2. What kind of story does the description of the setting in the first paragraph lead you to expect? Explain.

3. Describe the changing nature of the country through which Pepé rides. How are these changes related to his chances of escape?

4. In what respects would this story be different if it took place in a city slum?

5. Do the various details of setting in this story confirm or contradict the description of Steinbeck's point of view in the first paragraph of the biographical introduction (page 575)? Defend your answer.

FOR COMPOSITION

Write a description of a setting that might serve as the first paragraph of a story. Then explain what kind of a story you intend to write and why your descriptive paragraph is an appropriate introduction.

THIS IS GOOD SHIT

STEPHEN VINCENT BENÉT
(1898–1943)

Stephen Vincent Benét's best works are the stories and poems which recreate traditions and events that have formed this nation and its people, and which explore what it means to be an American. His most famous work, "The Devil and Daniel Webster," was recognized from the time of its publication as a classic blending of history and folklore into a legend that transcends a particular time and place. This short story has been made into a one-act play, a motion picture, an opera, and a television play. It seems likely that "The Devil and Daniel Webster" will remain a part of the American tradition, like the tales which grew up about Davy Crockett and Mike Fink (page 345), and which transformed them from historical persons into legendary figures.

Benét was born in Bethlehem, Pennsylvania, the son of an army colonel, whose father and grandfather were also army officers. Benét's father was a cultivated man who loved poetry and encouraged his sons to write. Two other Benét children besides Stephen, William Rose and Laura, became well-known writers. Stephen himself published his first volume of poetry (*Five Men and Pompey*) when he was only seventeen and his second collection (*Young Adventure*) three years later, after he had graduated from Yale. William Rose Benét once wrote of his brother that "poetry was from the first a bright valor in his blood." In 1921 Stephen married Rosemary Carr, a writer with whom he later collaborated on *A Book for Americans.*

During the early part of his career, Benét depended for a living on the several novels he published and on the stories he wrote for popular magazines. Dissatisfied with these works, he longed for the leisure to write a long narrative poem based on his father's collection of old military records. A Guggenheim fellowship enabled him to begin this work in 1926. The result, *John Brown's Body,* became a best seller, won a Pulitzer prize in 1929, and is acknowledged as a minor American classic. Louis Untermeyer commented, "Benét . . . proved that a long narrative poem if skillfully blended could hold attention as easily as a novel. . . . If no single passage contains that unanalyzable but unmistakable quality which permeates great poetry, the originality of the work, the vigor of its portraits, the interpolated lyrics, and the unflagging pace reveal an unusually rich talent." In the 1930's Benét wrote a number of stories which make American dialects into a kind of poetry. One of the best of these is "Johnny Pye and the Fool-killer." *Western Star,* his uncompleted narrative poem about the colonization of America, was published after his death in 1943.

The Devil and
Daniel Webster

IT'S A STORY they tell in the border country, where Massachusetts joins Vermont and New Hampshire.

Yes, Dan'l Webster's dead—or, at least, they buried him. But every time there's a thunderstorm around Marshfield,[1] they say you can hear his rolling voice in the hollows of the sky. And they say that if you go to his grave and speak loud and clear, "Dan'l Webster—Dan'l Webster!" the ground'll begin to shiver and the trees begin to shake. And after a while you'll hear a deep voice saying, "Neighbor, how stands the Union?" Then you better answer: the Union stands as she stood, rock-bottomed and copper-sheathed, one and indivisible, or he's liable to rear right out of the ground. At least, that's what I was told when I was a youngster.

You see, for a while, he was the biggest man in the country. He never got to be President, but he was the biggest man. There were thousands that trusted in him right next to God Almighty, and they told stories about him and all the things that belonged to him that were like the stories of patriarchs and such. They said when he stood up to speak, stars and stripes came right out in the sky, and once he spoke against a river and made it sink into the ground. They said when he walked the woods with his fishing rod, Killall, the trout would jump out of the streams right into his pockets, for they knew it was no use putting up a fight against him; and, when he argued a case, he could turn on the harps of the blessed and the shaking of the earth underground. That was the kind of man he was, and his big farm up at Marshfield was suitable to him. The chickens he raised were all white meat down through the drumsticks, the cows were tended like children, and the big ram he called Goliath [2] had horns with a curl like a morning-glory vine and could butt through an iron door. But Dan'l wasn't one of your gentlemen farmers; he knew all the ways of the land, and he'd be up by candlelight to see that the chores got done. A man with a mouth like a mastiff, a brow like a mountain, and eyes like burning anthracite—that was Dan'l Webster in his prime. And the biggest case he argued never got written down in the books, for he argued it against the devil, nip and tuck, and no holds barred. And this is the way I used to hear it told:

There was a man named Jabez Stone, lived at Cross Corners, New Hampshire. He wasn't a bad man to start with, but he was an unlucky man. If he planted corn, he got borers; [3] if he planted potatoes, he got blight.[4] He had good enough land, but it didn't prosper him; he had a decent wife and children, but the more children he had, the less there was to feed them. If stones cropped up in his neighbor's field, boulders boiled up in his; if he had a horse with the spavins,[5] he'd trade it for one with the staggers [6] and give something extra. There's some folks bound to be like that, apparently. But one day Jabez Stone got sick of the whole business.

He'd been plowing that morning and he'd just broke the plowshare on a rock that he could have sworn hadn't been

[2] **Goliath** (gə·lī′əth): a famous giant in the Bible (1 Samuel, 17), who was slain by the young David.
[3] **borers:** a corn-destroying insect.
[4] **blight:** a plant disease.
[5] **spavins** (spav′inz): a disease of the leg bone that causes a horse to limp.
[6] **staggers:** a disease that causes a horse to reel or fall down.

STEPHEN VINCENT BENÉT   589

there yesterday. And, as he stood looking at the plowshare, the off horse began to cough—that ropy kind of cough that means sickness and horse doctors. There were two children down with the measles, his wife was ailing, and he had a whitlow [1] on his thumb. It was about the last straw for Jabez Stone. "I vow," he said, and he looked around him kind of desperate—"I vow it's enough to make a man want to sell his soul to the devil! And I would, too, for two cents!"

Then he felt a kind of queerness come over him at having said what he'd said; though, naturally, being a New Hampshireman, he wouldn't take it back. But, all the same, when it got to be evening and, as far as he could see, no notice had been taken, he felt relieved in his mind, for he was a religious man. But notice is always taken, sooner or later, just like the Good Book says. And, sure enough, the next day, about suppertime, a soft-spoken, dark-dressed stranger drove up in a handsome buggy and asked for Jabez Stone.

Well, Jabez told his family it was a lawyer, come to see him about a legacy. But he knew who it was. He didn't like the looks of the stranger, nor the way he smiled with his teeth. They were white teeth, and plentiful—some say they were filed to a point, but I wouldn't vouch for that. And he didn't like it when the dog took one look at the stranger and ran away howling, with his tail between his legs. But having passed his word, more or less, he stuck to it, and they went out behind the barn and made their bargain. Jabez Stone had to prick his finger to sign, and the stranger lent him a silver pen. The wound healed clean, but it left a little white scar.

After that, all of a sudden, things began to pick up and prosper for Jabez Stone. His cows got fat and his horses sleek, his crops were the envy of the neighborhood, and lightning might strike all over the valley, but it wouldn't strike his barn. Pretty soon, he was one of the prosperous people of the county; they asked him to stand for selectman,[2] and he stood for it; there began to be talk of running him for state senate. All in all, you might say the Stone family was as happy and contented as cats in a dairy. And so they were, except for Jabez Stone.

He'd been contented enough, the first few years. It's a great thing when bad luck turns; it drives most other things out of your head. True, every now and then, especially in rainy weather, the little white scar on his finger would give him a twinge.

And once a year, punctual as clockwork, the stranger with the handsome buggy would come driving by. But the sixth year, the stranger lighted, and, after that, his peace was over for Jabez Stone.

The stranger came up through the lower field, switching his boots with a cane—they were handsome black boots, but Jabez Stone never liked the look of them,

[1] whitlow: an inflamed sore.

[2] selectman: one of a board of officers chosen annually in some New England towns to transact public business.

particularly the toes. And, after he'd passed the time of day, he said, "Well, Mr. Stone, you're a hummer! It's a very pretty property you've got here, Mr. Stone."

"Well, some might favor it and others might not," said Jabez Stone, for he was a New Hampshireman.

"Oh, no need to decry your industry!" said the stranger, very easy, showing his teeth in a smile. "After all, we know what's been done, and it's been according to contract and specifications. So when—ahem—the mortgage falls due next year, you shouldn't have any regrets."

"Speaking of that mortgage, mister," said Jabez Stone, and he looked around for help to the earth and the sky, "I'm beginning to have one or two doubts about it."

"Doubts?" said the stranger, not quite so pleasantly.

"Why, yes," said Jabez Stone. "This being the U.S.A. and me always having been a religious man." He cleared his throat and got bolder. "Yes, sir," he said, "I'm beginning to have considerable doubts as to that mortgage holding in court."

"There's courts and courts," said the stranger, clicking his teeth. "Still, we might as well have a look at the original document." And he hauled out a big black pocketbook, full of papers. "Sherwin, Slater, Stevens, Stone," he muttered. "I, Jabez Stone, for a term of seven years—Oh, it's quite in order, I think."

But Jabez Stone wasn't listening, for he saw something else flutter out of the black pocketbook. It was something that looked like a moth, but it wasn't a moth. And as Jabez Stone stared at it, it seemed to speak to him in a small sort of piping voice, terrible small and thin, but terrible human.

"Neighbor Stone!" it squeaked. "Neighbor Stone! Help me! I beg you, help me!"

But before Jabez Stone could stir hand or foot, the stranger whipped out a big bandanna handkerchief, caught the creature in it, just like a butterfly, and started tying up the ends of the bandanna.

"Sorry for the interruption," he said. "As I was saying——"

But Jabez Stone was shaking all over like a scared horse.

"That's Miser Stevens' voice!" he said, in a croak. "And you've got him in your handkerchief!"

The stranger looked a little embarrassed.

"Yes, I really should have transferred him to the collecting box," he said with a simper, "but there were some rather unusual specimens there and I didn't want them crowded. Well, well, these little contretemps [1] will occur."

"I don't know what you mean by contertan," said Jabez Stone, "but that was Miser Stevens' voice! And he ain't dead! You can't tell me he is! He was just as spry and mean as a woodchuck, Tuesday!"

"In the midst of life—" [2] said the stranger, kind of pious. "Listen!" Then a bell began to toll in the valley, and Jabez Stone listened, with the sweat running down his face. For he knew it was tolled for Miser Stevens and that he was dead.

"These long-standing accounts," said the stranger with a sigh; "one really hates to close them. But business is business."

He still had the bandanna in his hand, and Jabez Stone felt sick as he saw the cloth struggle and flutter.

"Are they all as small as that?" he asked hoarsely.

"Small?" said the stranger. "Oh, I see what you mean. Why, they vary." He measured Jabez Stone with his eyes, and his teeth showed. "Don't worry, Mr. Stone," he said. "You'll go with a very good grade. I wouldn't trust you outside the collecting box. Now, a man like Dan'l Webster, of course—well, we'd have to build a special box for him, and even at that, I imagine the wingspread would as-

---

[1] **contretemps** (kôṅ·trə·täṅ′): an embarrassing situation. Note Stone's pronunciation of the word in the next paragraph.

[2] **In . . . life:** The remainder of this quotation is "we are in death." This is part of the burial service in the *Book of Common Prayer*.

tonish you. He'd certainly be a prize. I wish we could see our way clear to him. But, in your case, as I was saying——"

"Put that handkerchief away!" said Jabez Stone, and he began to beg and to pray. But the best he could get at the end was a three years' extension, with conditions.

But till you make a bargain like that, you've got no idea of how fast four years can run. By the last months of those years, Jabez Stone's known all over the state and there's talk of running him for governor— and it's dust and ashes in his mouth. For every day, when he gets up, he thinks, "There's one more night gone," and every night when he lies down, he thinks of the black pocketbook and the soul of Miser Stevens, and it makes him sick at heart. Till, finally, he can't bear it any longer, and, in the last days of the last year, he hitches up his horse and drives off to seek Dan'l Webster. For Dan'l Webster was born in New Hampshire, only a few miles from Cross Corners, and it's well known that he has a particular soft spot for old neighbors.

It was early in the morning when he got to Marshfield, but Dan'l was up already, talking Latin to the farm hands and wrestling with the ram, Goliath, and trying out a new trotter and working up speeches to make against John C. Calhoun.[1] But when he heard a New Hampshireman had come to see him, he dropped everything else he was doing, for that was Dan'l's way. He gave Jabez Stone a breakfast that five men couldn't eat, went into the living history of every man and woman in Cross Corners, and finally asked him how he could serve him.

Jabez Stone allowed that it was a kind of mortgage case.

"Well, I haven't pleaded a mortgage case in a long time, and I don't generally plead now, except before the Supreme Court," said Dan'l, "but if I can, I'll help you."

"Then I've got hope for the first time in ten years," said Jabez Stone, and told him the details.

Dan'l walked up and down as he listened, hands behind his back, now and then asking a question, now and then plunging his eyes at the floor, as if they'd bore through it like gimlets.[2] When Jabez Stone had finished, Dan'l puffed out his cheeks and blew. Then he turned to Jabez Stone, and a smile broke over his face like the sunrise over Monadnock.[3]

"You've certainly given yourself the devil's own row to hoe, Neighbor Stone," he said, "but I'll take your case."

"You'll take it?" said Jabez Stone, hardly daring to believe.

"Yes," said Dan'l Webster. "I've got about seventy-five other things to do and the Missouri Compromise[4] to straighten out, but I'll take your case. For if two New Hampshiremen aren't a match for the devil, we might as well give the country back to the Indians."

Then he shook Jabez Stone by the hand and said, "Did you come down here in a hurry?"

"Well, I admit I made time," said Jabez Stone.

"You'll go back faster," said Dan'l Webster, and he told 'em to hitch up Constitution and Constellation to the carriage. They were matched grays with one white forefoot, and they stepped like greased lightning.

Well, I won't describe how excited and pleased the whole Stone family was to have the great Dan'l Webster for a guest, when they finally got there. Jabez Stone had lost his hat on the way, blown off. when they overtook a wind, but he didn't take much account of that. But after supper he sent the family off to bed, for he had most particular business with Mr. Webster. Mrs. Stone wanted them to sit in the

---

[1] **John C. Calhoun:** the great orator for the South, as Webster was for the North.

[2] **gimlets:** small tools used for drilling.

[3] **Monadnock** (mō·nad'nok): the highest mountain in southern New Hampshire.

[4] **Missouri Compromise:** an act passed by Congress in 1820 in an attempt to settle the dispute about slavery in the newly formed Western states.

front parlor, but Dan'l Webster knew front parlors and said he preferred the kitchen. So it was there they sat, waiting for the stranger, with a jug on the table between them and a bright fire on the hearth—the stranger being scheduled to show up on the stroke of midnight, according to specification.

Well, most men wouldn't have asked for better company than Dan'l Webster and a jug. But with every tick of the clock Jabez Stone got sadder and sadder. His eyes roved round, and though he sampled the jug, you could see he couldn't taste it. Finally, on the stroke of 11:30, he reached over and grabbed Dan'l Webster by the arm.

"Mr. Webster, Mr. Webster!" he said, and his voice was shaking with fear and a desperate courage. "For God's sake, Mr. Webster, harness your horses and get away from this place while you can!"

"You've brought me a long way, neighbor, to tell me you don't like my company," said Dan'l Webster, quite peaceable, pulling at the jug.

"Miserable wretch that I am!" groaned Jabez Stone. "I've brought you a devilish way, and now I see my folly. Let him take me if he wills. I don't hanker after it, I must say, but I can stand it. But you're the Union's stay and New Hampshire's pride! He mustn't get you, Mr. Webster! He mustn't get you!"

Dan'l Webster looked at the distracted man, all gray and shaking in the firelight, and laid a hand on his shoulder.

"I'm obliged to you, Neighbor Stone," he said gently. "It's kindly thought of. But there's a jug on the table and a case in hand. And I never left a jug or a case half finished in my life."

And just at that moment there was a sharp rap on the door.

"Ah," said Dan'l Webster, very coolly, "I thought your clock was a trifle slow, Neighbor Stone." He stepped to the door and opened it. "Come in!" he said.

The stranger came in—very dark and tall he looked in the firelight. He was carrying a box under his arm—a black, japanned [1] box with little air holes in the lid. At the sight of the box, Jabez Stone gave a low cry and shrank into a corner of the room.

"Mr. Webster, I presume," said the stranger very polite, but with his eyes glowing like a fox's deep in the woods.

"Attorney of record for Jabez Stone," said Dan'l Webster, but his eyes were glowing too. "Might I ask your name?"

"I've gone by a good many," said the stranger carelessly. "Perhaps Scratch will do for the evening. I'm often called that in these regions."

Then he sat down at the table and poured himself a drink from the jug. The liquor was cold in the jug, but it came steaming into the glass.

"And now," said the stranger, smiling and showing his teeth, "I shall call upon you, as a law-abiding citizen, to assist me in taking possession of my property."

Well, with that the argument began—and it went hot and heavy. At first, Jabez Stone had a flicker of hope, but when he saw Dan'l Webster being forced back at point after point, he just sat scrunched in his corner, with his eyes on that japanned box. For there wasn't any doubt as to the deed or the signature—that was the worst of it. Dan'l Webster twisted and turned and thumped his fist on the table, but he couldn't get away from that. He offered to compromise the case; the stranger wouldn't hear of it. He pointed out the property had increased in value, and state senators ought to be worth more; the stranger stuck to the letter of the law. He was a great lawyer, Dan'l Webster, but we know who's the King of Lawyers, as the Good Book tells us, and it seemed as if, for the first time, Dan'l Webster had met his match.

Finally, the stranger yawned a little. "Your spirited efforts on behalf of your client do you credit, Mr. Webster," he said, "but if you have no more arguments to adduce, I'm rather pressed for time—" and Jabez Stone shuddered.

[1] **japanned:** lacquered.

STEPHEN VINCENT BENÉT   593

Dan'l Webster's brow looked dark as a thundercloud. "Pressed or not, you shall not have this man!" he thundered. "Mr. Stone is an American citizen, and no American citizen may be forced into the service of a foreign prince. We fought England for that in '12 [1] and we'll fight all hell for it again!"

"Foreign?" said the stranger. "And who calls me a foreigner?"

"Well, I never yet heard of the dev—of your claiming American citizenship," said Dan'l Webster with surprise.

"And who with better right?" said the stranger, with one of his terrible smiles. "When the first wrong was done to the first Indian, I was there. When the first slaver put out for the Congo, I stood on her deck. Am I not in your books and stories and beliefs, from the first settlements on? Am I not spoken of, still, in every church in New England? 'Tis true the North claims me for a Southerner, and the South for a Northerner, but I am neither. I am merely an honest American like yourself—and of the best descent—for, to tell the truth, Mr. Webster, though I don't like to boast of it, my name is older in this country than yours."

"Aha!" said Dan'l Webster, with the veins standing out in his forehead. "Then I stand on the Constitution! I demand a trial for my client!"

"The case is hardly one for an ordinary court," said the stranger, his eyes flickering. "And, indeed, the lateness of the hour——"

"Let it be any court you choose, so it is an American judge and an American jury!" said Dan'l Webster in his pride. "Let it be the quick [2] or the dead; I'll abide the issue!"

"You have said it," said the stranger, and pointed his finger at the door. And with that, and all of a sudden, there was a rushing of wind outside and a noise of footsteps. They came, clear and distinct,

through the night. And yet, they were not like the footsteps of living men.

"In God's name, who comes by so late?" cried Jabez Stone, in an ague of fear.

"The jury Mr. Webster demands," said the stranger, sipping at his boiling glass. "You must pardon the rough appearance of one or two; they will have come a long way."

And with that the fire burned blue and the door blew open and twelve men entered, one by one.

If Jabez Stone had been sick with terror before, he was blind with terror now. For there was Walter Butler, the Loyalist, who spread fire and horror through the Mohawk Valley in the times of the Revolution; and there was Simon Girty, the renegade, who saw white men burned at the stake and whooped with the Indians to see them burn. His eyes were green, like a catamount's, and the stains on his hunting shirt did not come from the blood of the deer. King Philip [3] was there, wild and proud as he had been in life, with the great gash in his head that gave him his death wound, and cruel Governor Dale,[4] who broke men on the wheel. There was Morton of Merry Mount, who so vexed the Plymouth Colony, with his flushed, loose, handsome face and his hate of the godly. There was Teach, the bloody pirate, with his black beard curling on his breast. The Reverend John Smeet, with his strangler's hands and his Geneva gown,[5] walked as daintily as he had to the gallows. The red print of the rope was still around his neck, but he carried a perfumed handkerchief in one hand. One and all, they came into the room with the fires of hell still upon them, and the stranger named their names and their deeds as

[1] **'12:** the War of 1812, partially caused by the impressing of Americans into the British navy.
[2] **quick:** living.

[3] **King Philip:** an Indian chief who organized an uprising against the white settlers in 1675, and was killed the following year.
[4] **Governor Dale:** English Deputy-Governor of Virginia, 1611–16, whose severe laws caused the colonists to call these the "years of slavery."
[5] **Geneva gown:** minister's robe.

they came, till the tale of twelve was told. Yet the stranger had told the truth—they had all played a part in America.

"Are you satisfied with the jury, Mr. Webster?" said the stranger mockingly, when they had taken their places.

The sweat stood upon Dan'l Webster's brow, but his voice was clear.

"Quite satisfied," he said. "Though I miss General Arnold from the company."

"Benedict Arnold is engaged upon other business," said the stranger, with a glower. "Ah, you asked for a justice, I believe."

He pointed his finger once more, and a tall man, soberly clad in Puritan garb, with the burning gaze of the fanatic, stalked into the room and took his judge's place.

"Justice Hathorne is a jurist of experience," said the stranger. "He presided at certain witch trials once held in Salem. There were others who repented of the business later, but not he."

"Repent of such notable wonders and undertakings?" said the stern old justice. "Nay, hang them—hang them all!" And he muttered to himself in a way that struck ice into the soul of Jabez Stone.

Then the trial began, and, as you might expect, it didn't look anyways good for the defense. And Jabez Stone didn't make much of a witness in his own behalf. He took one look at Simon Girty and screeched, and they had to put him back in his corner in a kind of swoon.

It didn't halt the trial, though; the trial went on, as trials do. Dan'l Webster had faced some hard juries and hanging judges in his time, but this was the hardest he'd ever faced, and he knew it. They sat there with a kind of glitter in their eyes, and the stranger's smooth voice went on and on. Every time he'd raise an objection, it'd be "Objection sustained," but whenever Dan'l objected, it'd be "Objection denied." Well, you couldn't expect fair play from a fellow like this Mr. Scratch.

It got to Dan'l in the end, and he began to heat, like iron in the forge. When he got up to speak, he was going to flay that stranger with every trick known to the law, and the judge and jury too. He didn't care if it was contempt of court or what would happen to him for it. He didn't care any more what happened to Jabez Stone. He just got madder and madder, thinking of what he'd say. And yet, curiously enough, the more he thought about it, the less he was able to arrange his speech in his mind.

Till, finally, it was time for him to get up on his feet, and he did so, all ready to bust out with lightnings and denunciations. But before he started, he looked over the judge and jury for a moment, such being his custom. And he noticed the glitter in their eyes was twice as strong as before, and they all leaned forward. Like hounds just before they get the fox, they looked, and the blue mist of evil in the room thickened as he watched them. Then he saw what he'd been about to do, and he wiped his forehead, as a man might who's just escaped falling into a pit in the dark.

For it was him they'd come for, not only Jabez Stone. He read it in the glitter of their eyes and in the way the stranger hid his mouth with one hand. And if he fought them with their own weapons, he'd fall into their power; he knew that, though he couldn't have told you how. It was his own anger and horror that burned in their eyes; and he'd have to wipe that out or the case was lost. He stood there for a moment, his black eyes burning like anthracite. And then he began to speak.

He started off in a low voice, though you could hear every word. They say he could call on the harps of the blessed when he chose. And this was just as simple and easy as a man could talk. But he didn't start out by condemning or reviling. He was talking about the things that make a country a country, and a man a man.

And he began with the simple things that everybody's known and felt—the freshness of a fine morning when you're young, and the taste of food when you're hungry, and the new day that's every day when you're a child. He took them up and he turned them in his hands. They were good things for any man. But without freedom, they sickened. And when he talked of those enslaved, and the sorrows of slavery, his voice got like a big bell. He talked of the early days of America and the men who had made those days. It wasn't a spread-eagle speech, but he made you see it. He admitted all the wrong that had ever been done. But he showed how, out of the wrong and the right, the suffering and the starvations, something new had come. And everybody had played a part in it, even the traitors.

Then he turned to Jabez Stone and showed him as he was—an ordinary man who'd had hard luck and wanted to change it. And, because he'd wanted to change it, now he was going to be punished for all eternity. And yet there was good in Jabez Stone, and he showed that good. He was hard and mean, in some ways, but he was a man. There was sadness in being a man, but it was a proud thing too. And he showed what the pride of it was till you couldn't help feeling it. Yes, even in hell, if a man was a man, you'd know it. And he wasn't pleading for any one person any more, though his voice rang like an organ. He was telling the story and the failures and the endless journey of mankind. They got tricked and trapped and bamboozled, but it was a great journey. And no demon that was ever foaled could know the inwardness of it—it took a man to do that.

The fire began to die on the hearth and the wind before morning to blow. The light was getting gray in the room when Dan'l Webster finished. And his words came back at the end to New Hampshire ground, and the one spot of land that each man loves and clings to. He painted a picture of that, and to each one of that jury he spoke of things long forgotten. For his voice could search the heart, and that was his gift and his strength. And to one, his voice was like the forest and its secrecy, and to another like the sea and the storms of the sea; and one heard the cry of his

lost nation in it, and another saw a little harmless scene he hadn't remembered for years. But each saw something. And when Dan'l Webster finished, he didn't know whether or not he'd saved Jabez Stone. But he knew he'd done a miracle. For the glitter was gone from the eyes of judge and jury, and, for the moment, they were men again, and knew they were men.

"The defense rests," said Dan'l Webster, and stood there like a mountain. His ears were still ringing with his speech, and he didn't hear anything else till he heard Judge Hathorne say, "The jury will retire to consider its verdict."

Walter Butler rose in his place and his face had a dark, gay pride on it.

"The jury has considered its verdict," he said, and looked the stranger full in the eye. "We find for the defendant, Jabez Stone."

With that, the smile left the stranger's face, but Walter Butler did not flinch.

"Perhaps 'tis not strictly in accordance with the evidence," he said, "but even the damned may salute the eloquence of Mr. Webster."

With that, the long crow of a rooster split the gray morning sky, and judge and jury were gone from the room like a puff of smoke and as if they had never been there. The stranger turned to Dan'l Webster, smiling wryly. "Major Butler was always a bold man," he said. "I had not thought him quite so bold. Nevertheless, my congratulations, as between two gentlemen."

"I'll have that paper first, if you please," said Dan'l Webster, and he took it and tore it into four pieces. It was queerly warm to the touch. "And now," he said, "I'll have you!" and his hand came down like a bear trap on the stranger's arm. For he knew that once you bested anybody like Mr. Scratch in fair fight, his power on you was gone. And he could see that Mr. Scratch knew it too.

The stranger twisted and wriggled, but he couldn't get out of that grip. "Come, come, Mr. Webster," he said, smiling palely. "This sort of thing is ridic—ouch! —is ridiculous. If you're worried about the costs of the case, naturally, I'd be glad to pay——"

"And so you shall!" said Dan'l Webster, shaking him till his teeth rattled. "For you'll sit right down at that table and draw up a document, promising never to bother Jabez Stone nor his heirs or assigns [1] nor any other New Hampshire-man till doomsday! For any hades we want to raise in this state, we can raise ourselves, without assistance from strangers."

"Ouch!" said the stranger. "Ouch! Well, they never did run very big to the barrel, but—ouch!—I agree!"

So he sat down and drew up the document. But Dan'l Webster kept his hand on his coat collar all the time.

"And, now, may I go?" said the stranger, quite humble, when Dan'l'd seen the document was in proper and legal form.

"Go?" said Dan'l, giving him another shake. "I'm still trying to figure out what I'll do with you. For you've settled the costs of the case, but you haven't settled with me. I think I'll take you back to Marshfield," he said, kind of reflective. "I've got a ram there named Goliath that can butt through an iron door. I'd kind of

like to turn you loose in his field and see what he'd do."

Well, with that the stranger began to beg and to plead. And he begged and he pled so humble that finally Dan'l, who was naturally kindhearted, agreed to let him go. The stranger seemed terrible grateful for that and said, just to show they were friends, he'd tell Dan'l's fortune before leaving. So Dan'l agreed to that, though he didn't take much stock in fortunetellers ordinarily.

But, naturally, the stranger was a little different. Well, he pried and he peered at the lines in Dan'l's hands. And he told him one thing and another that was quite remarkable. But they were all in the past.

"Yes, all that's true, and it happened," said Dan'l Webster. "But what's to come in the future?"

The stranger grinned, kind of happily, and shook his head. "The future's not as you think it," he said. "It's dark. You have a great ambition, Mr. Webster."

"I have," said Dan'l firmly, for everybody knew he wanted to be President.

"It seems almost within your grasp," said the stranger, "but you will not attain it. Lesser men will be made President and you will be passed over."

"And, if I am, I'll still be Daniel Webster," said Dan'l. "Say on."

"You have two strong sons," said the stranger, shaking his head. "You look to found a line. But each will die in war and neither reach greatness."

"Live or die, they are still my sons," said Dan'l Webster. "Say on."

"You have made great speeches," said the stranger. "You will make more."

"Ah," said Dan'l Webster.

"But the last great speech you make will turn many of your own against you," said the stranger. "They will call you Ichabod; [2] they will call you by other

---

[1] **assigns:** persons who inherit money or property.

[2] **Ichabod** (ik′ə·bod): the title of Whittier's poem criticizing Webster's speech of March 7, 1850, in which Webster denounced the Abolitionists. Because of his speech many Northerners considered Webster a traitor. Ichabod is a Hebrew name meaning "where is the glory?" or "the glory is departed."

names. Even in New England some will say you have turned your coat and sold your country, and their voices will be loud against you till you die."

"So it is an honest speech, it does not matter what men say," said Dan'l Webster. Then he looked at the stranger and their glances locked.

"One question," he said. "I have fought for the Union all my life. Will I see that fight won against those who would tear it apart?"

"Not while you live," said the stranger, grimly, "but it will be won. And after you are dead, there are thousands who will fight for your cause, because of words that you spoke."

"Why, then, you long-barreled, slab-sided, lantern-jawed, fortunetelling note-shaver!" said Dan'l Webster, with a great roar of laughter, "be off with you to your own place before I put my mark on you! For, by the thirteen original colonies I'd go to the Pit itself to save the Union!"

And with that he drew back his foot for a kick that would have stunned a horse. It was only the tip of his shoe that caught the stranger, but he went flying out of the door with his collecting box under his arm.

"And now," said Dan'l Webster, seeing Jabez Stone beginning to rouse from his swoon, "let's see what's left in the jug, for it's dry work talking all night. I hope there's pie for breakfast, Neighbor Stone."

But they say that whenever the devil comes near Marshfield, even now, he gives it a wide berth. And he hasn't been seen in the state of New Hampshire from that day to this. I'm not talking about Massachusetts or Vermont.

FOR STUDY AND DISCUSSION

1. Do the first three paragraphs of this story prepare you for a realistic story, one that you can accept as literally true? Explain. Which details prepare the reader for the kind of story it turns out to be? Is Daniel Webster presented strictly as a historical person?

2. In what ways can the three main characters—Jabez Stone, Daniel Webster, and Mr. Scratch—be called typical New England men? What do you learn about New Englanders from this story?

3. On what grounds does the stranger claim American citizenship? What criticism of American policies of the past is implied? What facts make the case go against Webster at first?

4. How is suspense increased by the entrance of the jury? Why was the judge particularly chosen for the stranger's side of the case? What indicates that court procedure was unfair?

5. What made Webster change the tone of his speech? Why was his speech a masterpiece of appeal to such a jury? Why is the speech described rather than quoted directly?

6. How is the stranger an amusing figure? How is he a frightening one? Why do you think that Benét has the stranger speak mainly in legal and business terms, as one who is interested chiefly in the lawful acquisition of property? In what ways can the speech of the stranger be described as ironic?

7. Would you describe the tone of this story as serious or humorous? Or can you think of a better description?

LANGUAGE AND VOCABULARY

The atmosphere of New England is established in this story partly by an occasional use of New England dialect. For example, Daniel Webster is referred to as "Dan'l" and it is said of him that he may "rear up" out of the ground. Find other examples of dialect in the story. Why do you think Benét does not make heavier use of dialect? Compare the use of dialect in this story with the dialect in Lowell's "The Courtin'" (page 198). Which is more difficult to understand?

FOR COMPOSITION

Write a composition in which you compare "The Devil and Daniel Webster" with Washington Irving's "The Devil and Tom Walker." Consider the following points: the importance of setting in the two stories (see page 587), the character of the devil in each story, and the characters and fates of Tom Walker and Jabez Stone. (If Daniel Webster had been defending Tom Walker, do you think he could have secured an acquittal?)

EUDORA WELTY

(1909–   )

Eudora Welty, like her fellow Mississippian William Faulkner, has a vivid sense of detail. Her characters move against a rich background of pine-clad hills, red clay farms, cotton fields, ramshackle houses with rusting Chevrolets in the dooryard, and little towns drowsing in the sun. The people in her world are united by a common core of shared beliefs and attitudes, and everyone has a strong sense of his own position in the social scheme. Miss Welty's quiet gaze misses nothing. The ludicrous and pathetic are noted down as impartially as the brave. Compassion and tolerance pervade her work. Her best stories are often like poems and spring out of the same lyrical impulse to praise or wonder at the world. Sinclair Lewis once said of her, "Her writing is as clear . . . as the Gettysburg Address."

Eudora Welty was born in Jackson, Mississippi, the daughter of a president of a large insurance company. She was raised in comfortable circumstances, went to school and college in Mississippi, and then transferred to the University of Wisconsin. After she graduated, she went to New York where she entered Columbia University to study advertising. Unable to find a steady job in New York in the middle of the Depression, she returned to Jackson in 1931 where she spent the next nine years in a variety of jobs. One of the most interesting was with the Works Projects Administration, a federal agency created to provide jobs during the Depression. As "Junior Publicity Agent," she was sent all over the state to publicize the projects sponsored by the agency. She spoke to "everybody" from flood victims to the Key Brothers, "who stayed up in an airplane longer than anybody else up to then." During these years she began to take pictures of Mississippi subjects and wrote of them as well. Both on film and in her stories, she tried always to catch the same fugitive thing, the mysterious atmosphere of place and the meanings half divulged by the expressions and gestures of people she met. In 1936 her first published story appeared in a small magazine, and since then her reputation has climbed steadily. Her short stories and novels have won her international recognition, and her own country has awarded her many honors. For a time she taught in the English Department at Smith College.

Miss Welty's short stories have been collected in *A Curtain of Green and Other Stories* (1941), *The Wide Net* (1943), *The Golden Apples* (1949), and *The Bride of Inisfallen* (1955). Her longer works of fiction include *Delta Wedding* (1946) and *The Ponder Heart* (1954).

A Visit of Charity

IT WAS MIDMORNING—a very cold, bright day. Holding a potted plant before her, a girl of fourteen jumped off the bus in front of the Old Ladies' Home, on the outskirts of town. She wore a red coat, and her straight yellow hair was hanging down loose from the pointed white cap all the little girls were wearing that year. She stopped for a moment beside one of the prickly dark shrubs with which the city had beautified the Home, and then proceeded slowly toward the building, which was of whitewashed brick and reflected the winter sunlight like a block of ice. As she walked vaguely up the steps she shifted the small pot from hand to hand; then she had to set it down and remove her mittens before she could open the heavy door.

"I'm a Campfire Girl. . . . I have to pay a visit to some old lady," she told the nurse at the desk. This was a woman in a white uniform who looked as if she were cold; she had close-cut hair which stood up on the very top of her head exactly like a sea wave. Marian, the little girl, did not tell her that this visit would give her a minimum of only three points in her score.

"Acquainted with any of our residents?" asked the nurse. She lifted one eyebrow and spoke like a man.

"With any old ladies? No—but—that is, any of them will do," Marian stammered. With her free hand she pushed her hair behind her ears, as she did when it was time to study Science.

The nurse shrugged and rose. "You have a nice *multiflora cineraria* [1] there,"

[1] *multiflora cineraria* (mul′ti·flō′rə sin′ə·rā′-ri·ə): a potted plant of the aster family.

she remarked as she walked ahead down the hall of closed doors to pick out an old lady.

There was loose, bulging linoleum on the floor. Marian felt as if she were walking on the waves, but the nurse paid no attention to it. There was a smell in the hall like the interior of a clock. Everything was silent until, behind one of the doors, an old lady of some kind cleared her throat like a sheep bleating. This decided the nurse. Stopping in her tracks, she first extended her arm, bent her elbow, and leaned forward from the hips—all to examine the watch strapped to her wrist; then she gave a loud double-rap on the door.

"There are two in each room," the nurse remarked over her shoulder.

"Two what?" asked Marian without thinking. The sound like a sheep's bleating almost made her turn around and run back.

One old woman was pulling the door open in short, gradual jerks, and when she saw the nurse a strange smile forced her old face dangerously awry. Marian, suddenly propelled by the strong, impatient arm of the nurse, saw next the side-face of another old woman, even older, who was lying flat in bed with a cap on and a counterpane drawn up to her chin.

"Visitor," said the nurse, and after one more shove she was off up the hall.

Marian stood tongue-tied; both hands held the potted plant. The old woman, still with that terrible, square smile (which was a smile of welcome) stamped on her bony face, was waiting. . . . Perhaps she said something. The old woman in bed said nothing at all, and she did not look around.

Suddenly Marian saw a hand, quick as a bird claw, reach up in the air and pluck the white cap off her head. At the same time, another claw to match drew her all the way into the room, and the next moment the door closed behind her.

"My, my, my," said the old lady at her side.

Marian stood enclosed by a bed, a washstand and a chair; the tiny room had altogether too much furniture. Everything smelled wet—even the bare floor. She held onto the back of the chair, which was wicker and felt soft and damp. Her heart beat more and more slowly, her hands got colder and colder, and she could not hear whether the old women were saying anything or not. She could not see them very clearly. How dark it was! The window shade was down, and the only door was shut. Marian looked at the ceiling. . . . It was like being caught in a robbers' cave, just before one was murdered.

"Did you come to be our little girl for a while?" the first robber asked.

Then something was snatched from Marian's hand—the little potted plant.

"Flowers!" screamed the old woman. She stood holding the pot in an undecided way. "Pretty flowers," she added.

Then the old woman in bed cleared her throat and spoke. "They are not pretty," she said, still without looking around, but very distinctly.

Marian suddenly pitched against the chair and sat down in it.

"Pretty flowers," the first old woman insisted. "Pretty—pretty . . ."

Marian wished she had the little pot

back for just a moment—she had forgotten to look at the plant herself before giving it away. What did it look like?

"Stinkweeds," said the other old woman sharply. She had a bunchy white forehead and red eyes like a sheep. Now she turned them toward Marian. The fogginess seemed to rise in her throat again, and she bleated, "Who—are—you?"

To her surprise, Marian could not remember her name. "I'm a Campfire Girl," she said finally.

"Watch out for the germs," said the old woman like a sheep, not addressing anyone.

"One came out last month to see us," said the first old woman.

A sheep or a germ? wondered Marian dreamily, holding onto the chair.

"Did not!" cried the other old woman.

"Did so! Read to us out of the Bible, and we enjoyed it!" screamed the first.

"Who enjoyed it!" said the woman in bed. Her mouth was unexpectedly small and sorrowful, like a pet's.

"We enjoyed it," insisted the other. "You enjoyed it—I enjoyed it."

"We all enjoyed it," said Marian, without realizing that she had said a word.

The first old woman had just finished

putting the potted plant high, high on the top of the wardrobe, where it could hardly be seen from below. Marian wondered how she had ever succeeded in placing it there, how she could ever have reached so high.

"You mustn't pay any attention to old Addie," she now said to the little girl. "She's ailing today."

"Will you shut your mouth?" said the woman in bed. "I am not."

"You're a story."

"I can't stay but a minute—really, I can't," said Marian suddenly. She looked down at the wet floor and thought that if she were sick in here they would have to let her go.

With much to-do the first old woman sat down in a rocking chair—still another piece of furniture!—and began to rock. With the fingers of one hand she touched a very dirty cameo pin on her chest. "What do you do at school?" she asked.

"I don't know . . ." said Marian. She tried to think but she could not.

"Oh, but the flowers are beautiful," the old woman whispered. She seemed to rock faster and faster; Marian did not see

how anyone could rock so fast.

"Ugly," said the woman in bed.

"If we bring flowers—" Marian began, and then fell silent. She had almost said that if Campfire Girls brought flowers to the Old Ladies' Home, the visit would count one extra point, and if they took a Bible with them on the bus and read it to the old ladies, it counted double. But the old woman had not listened, anyway; she was rocking and watching the other one, who watched back from the bed.

"Poor Addie is ailing. She has to take medicine—see?" she said, pointing a horny finger at a row of bottles on the table, and rocking so high that her black comfort shoes lifted off the floor like a little child's.

"I am no more sick than you are," said the woman in bed.

"Oh, yes you are!"

"I just got more sense than you have, that's all," said the other woman, nodding her head.

"That's only the contrary way she talks when *you all* come," said the first old lady with sudden intimacy. She stopped the rocker with a neat pat of her feet and leaned toward Marian. Her hand reached over—it felt like a petunia leaf, clinging and just a little sticky.

"Will you hush! Will you hush!" cried the other one.

Marian leaned back rigidly in her chair.

"When I was a little girl like you, I went to school and all," said the old woman in the same intimate, menacing voice. "Not here—another town. . . ."

"Hush!" said the sick woman. "You never went to school. You never came and you never went. You never were anything—only here. You never were born! You don't know anything. Your head is empty, your heart and hands and your old black purse are all empty, even that little old box that you brought with you you brought empty—you showed it to me. And yet you talk, talk, talk, talk, talk all the time until I think I'm losing my mind! Who are you? You're a stranger—a perfect stranger! Don't you know you're a stranger? Is it possible that they have actually done a thing like this to anyone—sent them in a stranger to talk, and rock, and tell away her whole long rigmarole? Do they seriously suppose that I'll be able to keep it up, day in, day out, night in, night out, living in the same room with a terrible old woman—forever?"

Marian saw the old woman's eyes grow bright and turn toward her. This old woman was looking at her with despair and calculation in her face. Her small lips suddenly dropped apart, and exposed a half-circle of false teeth with tan gums.

"Come here, I want to tell you something," she whispered. "Come here!"

Marian was trembling, and her heart nearly stopped beating altogether for a moment.

"Now, now, Addie," said the first old woman. "That's not polite. Do you know what's really the matter with old Addie today?" She, too, looked at Marian; one of her eyelids drooped low.

"The matter?" the child repeated stupidly. "What's the matter with her?"

"Why, she's mad because it's her birthday!" said the first old woman, beginning to rock again and giving a little crow as though she had answered her own riddle.

"It is not, it is not!" screamed the old woman in bed. "It is not my birthday, no one knows when that is but myself, and will you please be quiet and say nothing more, or I'll go straight out of my mind!" She turned her eyes toward Marian again, and presently she said in the soft, foggy voice, "When the worst comes to the worst, I ring this bell, and the nurse comes." One of her hands was drawn out from under the patched counterpane—a thin little hand with enormous black freckles. With a finger which would not hold still she pointed to a little bell on the table among the bottles.

"How old are you?" Marian breathed. Now she could see the old woman in bed very closely and plainly, and very abruptly, from all sides, as in dreams. She

wondered about her—she wondered for a moment as though there was nothing else in the world to wonder about. It was the first time such a thing had happened to Marian.

"I won't tell!"

The old face on the pillow, where Marian was bending over it, slowly gathered and collapsed. Soft whimpers came out of the small open mouth. It was a sheep that she sounded like—a little lamb. Marian's face drew very close, the yellow hair hung forward.

"She's crying!" She turned a bright, burning face up to the first old woman.

"That's Addie for you," the old woman said spitefully.

Marian jumped up and moved toward the door. For the second time, the claw almost touched her hair, but it was not quick enough. The little girl put her cap on.

"Well, it was a real visit," said the old woman, following Marian through the doorway and all the way out into the hall. Then from behind she suddenly clutched the child with her sharp little fingers. In an affected, high-pitched whine she cried, "Oh, little girl, have you a penny to spare for a poor old woman that's not got anything of her own? We don't have a thing in the world—not a penny for candy—not a thing! Little girl, just a nickel—a penny——"

Marian pulled violently against the old hands for a moment before she was free. Then she ran down the hall, without looking behind her and without looking at the nurse, who was reading *Field & Stream* at her desk. The nurse, after another triple motion to consult her wrist watch, asked automatically the question put to visitors in all institutions: "Won't you stay and have dinner with *us?*"

Marian never replied. She pushed the heavy door open into the cold air and ran down the steps.

Under the prickly shrub she stooped and quickly, without being seen, retrieved a red apple she had hidden there.

Her yellow hair under the white cap, her scarlet coat, her bare knees all flashed in the sunlight as she ran to meet the big bus rocketing through the street.

"Wait for me!" she shouted. As though at an imperial command, the bus ground to a stop.

She jumped on and took a big bite out of the apple.

FOR STUDY AND DISCUSSION

1. What is Marian's motive in making her "visit of charity"? Are her intentions really charitable? Cite details from the story to support your answer.

2. Describe the nurse. How is her character an indication of the way the old ladies are treated at the home? In answering this question, consider especially the nurse's remark, "There are two in each room," and Marian's question, "Two what?"

3. "Empty . . . empty . . . empty," one old lady says of the other. What is she talking about? How can the word "empty" be applied to the lives of both women?

4. Find at least three figures of speech that emphasize Marian's feeling of being trapped in the room with the old ladies.

5. Why does Marian flee from the room? Can it be said that in one way she is closer to accepting the two old ladies as human beings than is the nurse who invites her to stay for dinner? Explain.

6. Do you think that the last sentence of the story is a good conclusion? Explain your answer. What does this sentence indicate about Marian?

7. In what way is this story humorous? In what way is it terribly serious?

POINT OF VIEW

Point of view refers to the position in which a reader is placed in relation to the story. Just as a playgoer may watch a play from many different vantage points—close to the stage, from the balcony, sometimes (as in Elizabethan times) from the stage itself—so the reader of a story can be made to view the action from different vantage points. A good writer is aware of the importance of point of view and will calculate just where he wants to place his reader.

Basically, a story can be told in three ways: (1) in the third person by an omniscient observer who tells what happens and comments on the action, (2) in the third person by a detached observer who merely records what happens and makes no comments, (3) in the first person by one of the characters of the story. Of course, writers have worked out many variations of these three basic points of view. For example, a story can be told in the third person but through the awareness of one of the characters. ("John knew this was the big day. He swallowed nervously. He felt an elbow digging into his side.") A story may be told in the first person by someone who primarily observes and comments on what happens, as in "The Fall of the House of Usher." In such a story the point of view is close to that of the omniscient observer (as in "The Devil and Daniel Webster"), although such a narrator cannot go into the minds of other characters.

Like style, point of view is an important device that a writer uses to indicate his attitude toward the characters and events of a story, and to persuade the reader to share his attitude. In judging a story, a careful reader will consider its point of view and decide whether the writer has chosen the best possible way of telling the story. (A concept closely related to point of view is *esthetic distance,* discussed on page 474.)

1. From which of the three basic points of view is "A Visit of Charity" told? Where does the story depart from this point of view? Do you think these departures hurt the effect of the story? Why or why not?

2. Study the first two paragraphs of the story. How close does Miss Welty bring you to the main character? Where do you first learn the character's name? What other details help establish a distance between reader and character?

3. How would the effect of this story be different if it were told in the first person by Marian? by one of the old ladies? Compare the points of view of "A Visit of Charity" and "Race at Morning." Why do you think Faulkner's story is told in the first person, and Miss Welty's in the third person?

FOR COMPOSITION

Compare "A Visit of Charity" with "The Egg" to show how both stories use humor for serious purposes.

SHIRLEY
JACKSON
(1919–1965)

Readers became electrically aware of Shirley Jackson when they read her story "The Lottery" in the *New Yorker*. "The Lottery" provoked hundreds of letters from readers and was one of the most discussed stories ever to appear in that magazine. In a precise style which was capable of disturbing nuances, she veered suddenly from the reassuringly familiar to something which is horrible exactly because it too is somehow familiar. In her novels, *Hangsaman, The Bird's Nest, The Haunting of Hill House,* and *We Have Always Lived in the Castle,* she continued to explore areas that lie just around the corner of a familiar street, just beyond the normal range of vision. She wrote about the dark underside of the human personality and mysterious events that provide glimpses into the relationship between the routine and the bizarre. Critics and book reviewers rarely dismiss Miss Jackson's work as mere "horror stories." There is something about these books that makes them seem terribly relevant to the modern world.

Shirley Jackson was born in San Francisco and spent most of her early life in California. She came East to attend Syracuse University, where she met Stanley Edgar Hyman, now a literary critic who teaches at Bennington College. The Hymans lived in a rural Vermont community. Of their life together, Shirley Jackson commented, "Our major exports are books and children, both of which we produce in abundance." People meeting Shirley Jackson were puzzled by the discrepancy between this cheerful, humorous housewife and the chilling stories and novels that she published. In addition to her studies of the savage, the frightening, and the inexplicable, she wrote two funny, happy books about her family, *Life Among the Savages* and *Raising Demons*. These books are as sunny as her novels are shadowy. They share with her more disturbing work the craftsmanship that marks all her writing.

Shirley Jackson died of heart failure when she was forty-six. In an essay about his late wife, Stanley Hyman wrote, "Shirley Jackson wrote in a variety of forms and styles because she was, like everyone else, a complex human being, confronting the world in many different roles and moods. She tried to express as much of herself as possible in her work, and to express each aspect as fully as possible. . . . I think that the future will find her powerful visions of suffering and inhumanity increasingly significant and meaningful . . . if she used the resources of supernatural terror, it was to provide metaphors for the all-too-real terrors of the natural."

The Lottery

THE MORNING of June 27th was clear and sunny, with the fresh warmth of a full-summer day; the flowers were blossoming profusely, and the grass was richly green. The people of the village began to gather in the square, between the post office and the bank, around ten o'clock; in some towns there were so many people that the lottery took two days and had to be started on June 26th, but in this village, where there were only about three hundred people, the whole lottery took only about two hours, so it could begin at ten o'clock in the morning and still be through in time to allow the villagers to get home for noon dinner.

The children assembled first, of course. School was recently over for the summer, and the feeling of liberty sat uneasily on most of them; they tended to gather together quietly for a while before they broke into boisterous play, and their talk was still of the classroom and the teacher, of books and reprimands. Bobby Martin had already stuffed his pockets full of stones, and the other boys soon followed his example, selecting the smoothest and roundest stones; Bobby and Harry Jones and Dickie Delacroix—the villagers pronounced this name "Dellacroy"—eventually made a great pile of stones in one corner of the square and guarded it against the raids of the other boys. The girls stood aside, talking among themselves, looking over their shoulders at the boys, and the very small children rolled in the dust or clung to the hands of their older brothers or sisters.

Soon the men began to gather, surveying their own children, speaking of plant-

ing and rain, tractors and taxes. They stood together, away from the pile of stones in the corner, and their jokes were quiet and they smiled rather than laughed. The women, wearing faded house dresses and sweaters, came shortly after their menfolk. They greeted one another and exchanged bits of gossip as they went to join their husbands. Soon the women, standing by their husbands, began to call to their children, and the children came reluctantly, having to be called four or five times. Bobby Martin ducked under his mother's grasping hand and ran, laughing, back to the pile of stones. His father spoke up sharply, and Bobby came quickly and took his place between his father and his oldest brother.

The lottery was conducted—as were the square dances, the teen-age club, the Halloween program—by Mr. Summers, who had time and energy to devote to civic activities. He was a round-faced, jovial man, and he ran the coal business; and people were sorry for him, because he had no children and his wife was a scold. When he arrived in the square, carrying the black wooden box, there was a murmur of conversation among the villagers, and he waved and called, "Little late today, folks." The postmaster, Mr. Graves, followed him, carrying a three-legged stool; and the stool was put in the center of the square, and Mr. Summers set the black box down on it. The villagers kept their distance, leaving a space between themselves and the stool, and when Mr. Summers said, "Some of you fellows want to give me a hand?" there was a hesitation before two men, Mr. Martin and his oldest son, Baxter, came forward to hold the box steady on the stool while Mr. Summers stirred up the papers inside it.

The original paraphernalia for the lottery had been lost long ago, and the black box now resting on the stool had been put into use even before Old Man Warner, the oldest man in town, was born. Mr. Summers spoke frequently to the villagers about making a new box, but no one liked to upset even as much tradition as was represented by the black box. There was a story that the present box had been made with some pieces of the box that had preceded it, the one that had been constructed when the first people settled down to make a village here. Every year, after the lottery, Mr. Summers began talking again about a new box, but every year the subject was allowed to fade off without anything's being done. The black box grew shabbier each year; by now it was no longer completely black but splintered badly along one side to show the original wood color, and in some places faded or stained.

Mr. Martin and his oldest son, Baxter, held the black box securely on the stool until Mr. Summers had stirred the papers thoroughly with his hand. Because so much of the ritual had been forgotten or discarded, Mr. Summers had been successful in having slips of paper substituted for the chips of wood that had been used for generations. Chips of wood, Mr. Summers had argued, had been all very well when the village was tiny, but now that the populaton was more than three hundred and likely to keep on growing, it was necessary to use something that would fit more easily into the black box. The night before the lottery, Mr. Summers and Mr. Graves made up the slips of paper and put them into the box, and it was then taken to the safe of Mr. Summers' coal company and locked up until Mr. Summers was ready to take it to the square next morning. The rest of the year, the box was put away, sometimes one place, sometimes another; it had spent one year in Mr. Graves's barn and another year underfoot in the post office, and sometimes it was set on a shelf in the Martin grocery and left there.

There was a great deal of fussing to be done before Mr. Summers declared the lottery open. There were the lists to make up—of heads of families, heads of households in each family, members of each household in each family. There was the proper swearing-in of Mr. Summers by the postmaster, as the official of the lottery; at one time, some people remembered, there had been a recital of some sort, performed by the official of the lottery, a perfunctory, tuneless chant that had been rattled off duly each year; some people believed that the official of the lottery used to stand just so when he said or sang it; others believed that he was supposed to walk among the people; but years and years ago this part of the ritual had been allowed to lapse. There had been, also, a ritual salute, which the official of the lottery had had to use in addressing each person who came up to draw from the box, but this also had changed with time, until now it was felt necessary only for the official to speak to each person approaching. Mr. Summers was very good at all this; in his clean white shirt and blue jeans, with one hand resting carelessly on the black box, he seemed very proper and important as he talked interminably to Mr. Graves and the Martins.

Just as Mr. Summers finally left off talking and turned to the assembled villagers, Mrs. Hutchinson came hurriedly along the path to the square, her sweater thrown over her shoulders, and slid into place in the back of the crowd. "Clean forgot what day it was," she said to Mrs. Delacroix, who stood next to her, and they both laughed softly. "Thought my old man was out back stacking wood," Mrs. Hutchinson went on, "and then I looked out the window and the kids was gone, and then I remembered it was the twenty-seventh and came a-running." She dried her hands on her apron, and Mrs. Delacroix said, "You're in time, though. They're still talking away up there."

Mrs. Hutchinson craned her neck to see through the crowd and found her husband and children standing near the front. She tapped Mrs. Delacroix on the arm as a farewell and began to make her way through the crowd. The people separated good-humoredly to let her through; two or three people said, in voices just loud enough to be heard across the crowd,

"Here comes your Mrs., Hutchinson," and "Bill, she made it after all." Mrs. Hutchinson reached her husband, and Mr. Summers, who had been waiting, said cheerfully, "Thought we were going to have to get on without you, Tessie." Mrs. Hutchinson said, grinning, "Wouldn't have me leave m'dishes in the sink, now, would you, Joe?" and soft laughter ran through the crowd as the people stirred back into position after Mrs. Hutchinson's arrival.

"Well, now," Mr. Summers said soberly, "guess we better get started, get this over with, so's we can go back to work. Anybody ain't here?"

"Dunbar," several people said. "Dunbar, Dunbar."

Mr. Summers consulted his list. "Clyde Dunbar," he said. "That's right. He's broke his leg, hasn't he? Who's drawing for him?"

"Me, I guess," a woman said, and Mr. Summers turned to look at her. "Wife draws for her husband," Mr. Summers said. "Don't you have a grown boy to do it for you, Janey?" Although Mr. Summers and everyone else in the village knew the answer perfectly well, it was the business of the official of the lottery to ask such questions formally. Mr. Summers waited with an expression of polite interest while Mrs. Dunbar answered.

"Horace's not but sixteen yet," Mrs. Dunbar said regretfully. "Guess I gotta fill in for the old man this year."

"Right," Mr. Summers said. He made a note on the list he was holding. Then he asked, "Watson boy drawing this year?"

A tall boy in the crowd raised his hand. "Here," he said. "I'm drawing for m'mother and me." He blinked his eyes nervously and ducked his head as several voices in the crowd said things like "Good fellow, Jack," and "Glad to see your mother's got a man to do it."

"Well," Mr. Summers said, "guess that's everyone. Old Man Warner make it?"

"Here," a voice said, and Mr. Summers nodded.

A sudden hush fell on the crowd as Mr. Summers cleared his throat and looked at the list. "All ready?" he called. "Now, I'll read the names—heads of families first—and the men come up and take a paper out of the box. Keep the paper folded in your hand without looking at it until everyone has had a turn. Everything clear?"

The people had done it so many times that they only half listened to the directions; most of them were quiet, wetting their lips, not looking around. Then Mr. Summers raised one hand high and said, "Adams." A man disengaged himself from the crowd and came forward. "Hi, Steve," Mr. Summers said, and Mr. Adams said, "Hi, Joe." They grinned at one another humorlessly and nervously. Then Mr. Adams reached into the black box and took out a folded paper. He held it firmly by one corner as he turned and went hastily back to his place in the crowd, where he stood a little apart from his family, not looking down at his hand.

"Allen," Mr. Summers said. "Anderson . . . Bentham."

"Seems like there's no time at all between lotteries any more," Mrs. Delacroix said to Mrs. Graves in the back row. "Seems like we got through with the last one only last week."

"Time sure goes fast," Mrs. Graves said.

"Clark . . . Delacroix."

"There goes my old man," Mrs. Delacroix said. She held her breath while her husband went forward.

"Dunbar," Mr. Summers said, and Mrs. Dunbar went steadily to the box while one of the women said, "Go on, Janey," and another said, "There she goes."

"We're next," Mrs. Graves said. She watched while Mr. Graves came around from the side of the box, greeted Mr. Summers gravely, and selected a slip of paper from the box. By now, all through the crowd there were men holding the small folded papers in their large hands, turning them over and over nervously. Mrs. Dunbar and her two sons stood together, Mrs. Dunbar holding the slip of paper.

"Harburt . . . Hutchinson."

"Get up there, Bill," Mrs. Hutchinson said, and the people near her laughed.

"Jones."

"They do say," Mr. Adams said to Old Man Warner, who stood next to him, "that over in the north village they're talking of giving up the lottery."

Old Man Warner snorted. "Pack of crazy fools," he said. "Listening to the young folks, nothing's good enough for them. Next thing you know, they'll be wanting to go back to living in caves, nobody work any more, live *that* way for a while. Used to be a saying about 'Lottery in June, corn be heavy soon.' First thing you know, we'd all be eating stewed chickweed and acorns. There's always been a lottery," he added petulantly. "Bad enough to see young Joe Summers up there joking with everybody."

"Some places have already quit lotteries," Mrs. Adams said.

"Nothing but trouble in that," Old Man Warner said stoutly. "Pack of young fools."

"Martin." And Bobby Martin watched his father go forward. "Overdyke . . . Percy."

"I wish they'd hurry," Mrs. Dunbar said to her older son. "I wish they'd hurry."

"They're almost through," her son said.

"You get ready to run tell Dad," Mrs. Dunbar said.

Mr. Summers called his own name and then stepped forward precisely and selected a slip from the box. Then he called, "Warner."

"Seventy-seventh year I been in the lottery," Old Man Warner said as he went through the crowd. "Seventy-seventh time."

"Watson." The tall boy came awkwardly through the crowd. Someone said, "Don't be nervous, Jack," and Mr. Summers said, "Take your time, son."

"Zanini."

After that, there was a long pause, a breathless pause, until Mr. Summers, holding his slip of paper in the air, said, "All right, fellows." For a minute, no one moved, and then all the slips of paper were opened. Suddenly, all the women began to speak at once, saying, "Who is it?" "Who's got it?" "Is it the Dunbars?" "Is it the Watsons?" Then the voices began to say, "It's Hutchinson. It's Bill." "Bill Hutchinson's got it."

"Go tell your father," Mrs. Dunbar said to her older son.

People began to look around to see the Hutchinsons. Bill Hutchinson was standing quiet, staring down at the paper in his hand. Suddenly, Tessie Hutchinson shouted to Mr. Summers, "You didn't give him time enough to take any paper he wanted. I saw you. It wasn't fair!"

"Be a good sport, Tessie," Mrs. Delacroix called, and Mrs. Graves said, "All of us took the same chance."

"Shut up, Tessie," Bill Hutchinson said.

"Well, everyone," Mr. Summers said, "that was done pretty fast, and now we've got to be hurrying a little more to get done in time." He consulted his next list. "Bill," he said, "you draw for the Hutchinson family. You got any other households in the Hutchinsons?"

"There's Don and Eva," Mrs. Hutchinson yelled. "Make *them* take their chance!"

"Daughters draw with their husbands' families, Tessie," Mr. Summers said gently. "You know that as well as anyone else."

"It wasn't *fair,*" Tessie said.

"I guess not, Joe," Bill Hutchinson said regretfully. "My daughter draws with her husband's family, that's only fair. And I've got no other family except the kids."

"Then, as far as drawing for families is concerned, it's you," Mr. Summers said in explanation, "and as far as drawing for households is concerned, that's you, too. Right?"

"Right," Bill Hutchinson said.

"How many kids, Bill?" Mr. Summers asked formally.

"Three," Bill Hutchinson said. "There's Bill, Jr., and Nancy, and little Dave. And Tessie and me."

"All right, then," Mr. Summers said. "Harry, you got their tickets back?"

Mr. Graves nodded and held up the slips of paper. "Put them in the box, then," Mr. Summers directed. "Take Bill's and put it in."

"I think we ought to start over," Mrs. Hutchinson said, as quietly as she could. "I tell you it wasn't *fair*. You didn't give him time enough to choose. *Everybody* saw that."

Mr. Graves had selected the five slips and put them in the box, and he dropped all the papers but those onto the ground, where the breeze caught them and lifted them off.

"Listen, everybody," Mrs. Hutchinson was saying to the people around her.

"Ready, Bill?" Mr. Summers asked, and Bill Hutchinson, with one quick glance around at his wife and children, nodded.

"Remember," Mr. Summers said, "take the slips and keep them folded until each person has taken one. Harry, you help little Dave." Mr. Graves took the hand of the little boy, who came willingly with him up to the box. "Take a paper out of the box, Davy," Mr. Summers said. Davy put his hand into the box and laughed. "Take just one paper," Mr. Summers said. "Harry, you hold it for him." Mr. Graves took the child's hand and removed the folded paper from the tight fist and held it while little Dave stood next to him and looked up at him wonderingly.

"Nancy next," Mr. Summers said. Nancy was twelve, and her school friends breathed heavily as she went forward, switching her skirt, and took a slip daintily from the box. "Bill, Jr.," Mr. Summers said, and Billy, his face red and

his feet overlarge, nearly knocked the box over as he got a paper out. "Tessie," Mr. Summers said. She hesitated for a minute, looking around defiantly, and then set her lips and went up to the box. She snatched a paper out and held it behind her.

"Bill," Mr. Summers said, and Bill Hutchinson reached into the box and felt around bringing his hand out at last with the slip of paper in it.

The crowd was quiet. A girl whispered, "I hope it's not Nancy," and the sound of the whisper reached the edges of the crowd.

"It's not the way it used to be," Old Man Warner said clearly. "People ain't the way they used to be."

"All right," Mr. Summers said, "open the papers. Harry, you open little Dave's."

Mr. Graves opened the slip of paper, and there was a general sigh through the crowd as he held it up and everyone could see that it was blank. Nancy and Bill, Jr., opened theirs at the same time, and both beamed and laughed, turning around to the crowd and holding their slips of paper above their heads.

"Tessie," Mr. Summers said. There was a pause, and then Mr. Summers looked at Bill Hutchinson, and Bill unfolded his paper and showed it. It was blank.

"It's Tessie," Mr. Summers said, and his voice was hushed. "Show us her paper, Bill."

Bill Hutchinson went over to his wife and forced the slip of paper out of her hand. It had a black spot on it, the black spot Mr. Summers had made the night before with the heavy pencil in the coal-company office. Bill Hutchinson held it up, and there was a stir in the crowd.

"All right, folks," Mr. Summers said. "Let's finish quickly."

Although the villagers had forgotten the ritual and lost the original black box, they still remembered to use stones. The pile of stones the boys had made earlier was ready; there were stones on the ground with the blowing scraps of paper that had come out of the box. Mrs. Delacroix selected a stone so large she had to pick it up with both hands and turned to Mrs. Dunbar. "Come on," she said. "Hurry up."

Mrs. Dunbar had small stones in both hands, and she said, gasping for breath, "I can't run at all. You'll have to go ahead and I'll catch up with you."

The children had stones already, and someone gave little Davy Hutchinson a few pebbles.

Tessie Hutchinson was in the center of a cleared space by now, and she held her hands out desperately as the villagers moved in on her. "It isn't fair," she said. A stone hit her on the side of the head.

Old Man Warner was saying, "Come on, come on, everyone." Steve Adams was in the front of the crowd of villagers, with Mrs. Graves beside him.

"It isn't fair, it isn't right," Mrs. Hutchinson screamed, and then they were upon her.

FOR STUDY AND DISCUSSION

1. What kind of story do the first three paragraphs lead you to expect? Why do you think the story begins as it does?

2. Notice that the lottery is taking place in other towns over an unspecified area. What is the effect of the remark that in this town they could "be through in time to allow the villagers to get home for noon dinner"?

3. "The lottery was conducted—as were the square dances, the teen-age club, the Halloween program—by Mr. Summers . . ." Why is the lottery listed with these other activities?

4. Does the way in which each member of the Hutchinson family makes the final drawing add to our understanding of the individuals? If so, how? What is the effect of having Nancy and Bill, Jr., laugh at their own blank slips without thinking further?

5. At what point do you have an inkling that something dreadful is going to happen? What details increase your sense of foreboding? What details seem horrible only later?

6. Although the lottery is imaginary, what does the story tell us about customs and attitudes that are quite real?

STYLE

A French writer once said, "The style is the man." In all aspects of life there are styles —in clothing, in behavior, in playing basketball or golf. In writing, style usually refers to an author's choice of words, the length and kinds of sentences used, and the relation of those sentences to each other. Ernest Hemingway's short words and sentences and his rhythmic use of language, for example, make for a highly individual style that has been much admired and imitated. Thornton Wilder has a reputation as a stylist because of the appropriateness and distinction of his words and phrases.

A number of contemporary fiction writers deliberately choose a quiet, unobtrusive style. There is little about the style of "The Lottery" that calls attention to itself. Yet a close study of this story reveals the importance of style as an element in the art of fiction.

1. Compare the first sentence of "The Lottery" with the following rewritten versions. How might the story be different if it were rewritten in either of these styles?

June 27th was a sunny day. It was warm. The flowers were in bloom. The grass was a nice shade of green.

June 27th, ah! what a glorious day it was! Just the beginning of a glorious summer, the panoply of flowers making an ornate pattern against the quiet, rich green of the grass, stationed modestly below its more colorful neighbors.

2. Rewrite the last three paragraphs of the story in a different style. Which version do you consider more effective in terms of the story as a whole? Why?

FOR COMPOSITION

For a long time Miss Jackson refused to discuss this story. Finally, some twelve years after it was written, she remarked to an interviewer that she had been on her way to the market one day when it occurred to her to wonder how it might be if human sacrifice were practiced in our society. Once home, she began to write "The Lottery."

Write a composition in which you show how the author's remark referred to above might point to an interpretation of the story. Discuss also the extent to which the story may be considered a criticism of our society and the extent to which it may be a commentary on mankind in general.

MODERN POETRY

A completely satisfactory definition of poetry probably will never be written. Poets have a way of going beyond the boundaries of definition, of proving that all creation is within their range. Walt Whitman showed that good poems do not have to be written in formal meter (page 317). Twentieth-century poets have shown that good poems can be written on subjects that nineteenth-century readers considered "unpoetic"—a train, for example.

Yet certain statements do provide clues to the nature of poetry and point the way to the special territory that poetry holds apart from other kinds of writing. The English poet and critic Samuel Taylor Coleridge called poetry "the best words in their best order." Matthew Arnold, another English poet, defined poetry as "simply the most beautiful, impressive, and widely effective mode of saying things." Both definitions point to one of poetry's most important characteristics: that it is a kind of writing in which *every word counts*. Probably more than any other kind of writer, a poet pays close attention to the exact weight and meaning of each word. Thus poetry has sometimes been called "charged language," and Ralph Waldo Emerson described it as teaching "the enormous force of a few words."

Words are important to a poet in another way. They are not only a means of compressing his meaning but also of unlocking the imagination. "A poet," W. H. Auden wrote, "is, before anything else, a person who is passionately in love with language." Poets are fascinated by words, by their sound, their look, and their power of suggestion. To many poets, a word is not simply a group of letters or the name of something but a world of its own.

In addition to words, poets are also aware of the physical objects and the people around them, and, as Whitman did, they respond to the great events of their time. Poets tell us much about our environment, about qualities and relationships that less observant or imaginative people miss. Modern American poetry is especially notable for its precise observations of the "things of this world" (as Richard Wilbur has called them), for celebrating the delight of being a part of the physical universe.

In the pages that follow, you will encounter poems that demonstrate both the modern American poet's fascination with words and his strong responses to the world around him. You will read poems that show a desire to experiment with new forms and that test the resources of traditional forms, such as the sonnet. Some critics regard the twentieth century as a golden age of American poetry. As you explore the depth and variety of twentieth-century American poetry, keep in mind Coleridge's definition: "the best words in their best order."

ROBERT FROST
(1874–1963)

In January 1961, at the inauguration of President John Fitzgerald Kennedy, a blinding sun made it difficult for the eighty-six-year-old Robert Frost to make out the manuscript he had brought to read to the nation. Instead he spoke a poem from memory with the skill and assurance he had learned during his many years on the lecture platform. It was appropriate that Robert Frost, of all American poets, should be chosen to participate in President Kennedy's inauguraton. In his old age, Frost was honored beyond all living poets since the days of Longfellow and Whittier. In 1947, Oxford and Cambridge Universities gave him honorary degrees. The United States Senate passed resolutions to commemorate his seventy-fifth and eighty-fifth birthdays. In an age when poetry had, on the whole, become the concern of a relatively few enthusiasts, Frost was a genuinely popular figure, regarded by the nation as one of its wise old men. But, as with any beloved figure, there is the danger of forgetting the real, complex individual underneath. And in the case of a great poet, there is the further danger of overlooking or misunderstanding the specific poems he has written. While some of Frost's poems express joy, many others—including some of his greatest—are dark confrontations with the pain and struggle and mystery of life.

This poet of New England was born in San Francisco, the son of a Southern sympathizer who named him Robert Lee Frost. After his father died, the boy was taken to Lawrence, Massachusetts, by his mother. Mrs. Frost made a living by teaching school, and Robert helped out by working during his vacations from the time he was twelve. When he graduated from Lawrence High School, he was valedictorian of his class, a distinction he shared with Elinor White, whom he later married. After high school, he entered Dartmouth College but left after less than two months, then spent his time assisting his mother in the classroom, and later working in a mill. In 1894, his first poem was published. By this time, Frost already knew that he was a poet and that any other occupation would be only a means to live and write poetry. In autumn of 1894, he visited Elinor, who was attending college, to show her his poems. To Elinor, Robert seemed an impractical young man who was not making a steady living. Feeling rebuffed, Frost wandered through Maryland, Virginia and North Carolina, "scalded by denial of worth . . . doing minor jobs for bread, breaking his pride all the way" (as one biographer has written). That Christmas, Robert and Elinor were reconciled, and a year later they were married.

Frost's grandfather made it possible for Robert to attend Harvard University, but after nearly two years he left. He later wrote, "Harvard had taken me away from the question of whether I could write or not." By this time he was in his middle twenties and about to become a father. At this crucial point in Frost's life, Elinor appealed to his grandfather to buy them a farm in West Derry, New Hampshire. The grandfather, knowing that Frost's principal concern was poetry, asked, "Shall I give you a year? Will you settle down if I give you a year to try this out?" Frost replied, "Give me twenty." As it turned out, he spent ten long years on the "thirty acres, rather run down and poor, but with orchard, fields, pasture, woodland, and spring." He arranged his schedule to accommodate his poetry, milking his cows at midnight so that he could devote the late evening hours to writing poems. Not a great farmer, he was forced into part-time teaching to support his growing family. But these trying years were the making of the poet, and they shaped much of what he was to write.

In 1912, Frost sold his farm. An unknown poet at the age of thirty-eight, he sailed to England with his family, to seek the recognition he had failed to find in America. Gradually he came to know a number of English and American poets and was able to arrange for the publication of his first collection, *A Boy's Will*. His second book, *North of Boston*, published when he was forty, was widely acclaimed, especially for its quiet assurance in turning living speech into poetry.

When Frost returned to the United States in 1915, he found himself an established poet. He continued to publish regularly for the rest of his life. He also taught at various colleges, primarily Amherst, but always he was wary about the effect that academic surroundings might have on his poetry. The many brightly colored academic hoods, which he received on being awarded honorary degrees, he had cut up and made into crazy quilts.

Frost once wrote that poetry "begins in delight and ends in wisdom." Writing poetry for him was as much fun as it was art, and he thought that a good part of the fun and the art came from following certain definite rules. He had little sympathy with free verse poets. But he also felt that too much planning would spoil a poem, that good poems come unexpectedly. Poetry, he wrote, "inclines to impulse, it assumes direction with the first line laid down, and ends in a clarification of life . . . in a momentary stay against confusion."

Much of the strength of Frost's poetry springs from the strength of the man. He had the courage and the determination to follow his own course in the world, to remain true to his poetry despite years of obscurity and hardship. And despite personal tragedies—the death of wife and children—his spirit remained unbroken, and his later poetry reflects his refusal to turn his back on the world and retreat into a private grief. Randall Jarrell, the American poet and critic, wrote of Frost, "Frost is that rare thing, a complete or representative poet, and not one of the brilliant partial poets who do justice . . . to a portion of reality, and leave the rest of things forlorn. When you know Frost's poems you know surprisingly well how the world seemed to one man, and what it was to seem that way. . . ." And Frost himself has described his own life in several of his most famous lines:

> "And were an epitaph to be my story
> I'd have a short one ready for my own.
> I would have written of me on my stone:
> I had a lover's quarrel with the world."

The Pasture

I'm going out to clean the pasture spring;
I'll only stop to rake the leaves away
(And wait to watch the water clear, I may):
I shan't be gone long—You come too.

I'm going out to fetch the little calf   5
That's standing by the mother. It's so young,
It totters when she licks it with her tongue.
I shan't be gone long—You come too.

The Road Not Taken

Two roads diverged in a yellow wood,
And sorry I could not travel both
And be one traveler, long I stood
And looked down one as far as I could
To where it bent in the undergrowth;   5

Then took the other, as just as fair,
And having perhaps the better claim,
Because it was grassy and wanted wear;
Though as for that the passing there
Had worn them really about the same,   10

And both that morning equally lay
In leaves no step had trodden black.
Oh, I kept the first for another day!
Yet knowing how way leads on to way,
I doubted if I should ever come back.   15

I shall be telling this with a sigh
Somewhere ages and ages hence:
Two roads diverged in a wood, and I—
I took the one less traveled by
And that has made all the difference.   20

Stopping by Woods on a Snowy Evening

Whose woods these are I think I know.
His house is in the village though;
He will not see me stopping here
To watch his woods fill up with snow.

My little horse must think it queer   5
To stop without a farmhouse near
Between the woods and frozen lake
The darkest evening of the year.

He gives his harness bells a shake
To ask if there is some mistake.   10
The only other sound's the sweep
Of easy wind and downy flake.

The woods are lovely, dark, and deep,
But I have promises to keep,
And miles to go before I sleep,   15
And miles to go before I sleep.

Nothing Gold Can Stay

Nature's first green is gold,
Her hardest hue to hold.
Her early leaf's a flower;
But only so an hour.
Then leaf subsides to leaf.   5
So Eden sank to grief,
So dawn goes down to day.
Nothing gold can stay.

Fire and Ice

Some say the world will end in fire,
Some say in ice.
From what I've tasted of desire
I hold with those who favor fire.
But if it had to perish twice,   5
I think I know enough of hate
To say that for destruction ice
Is also great
And would suffice.

Mending Wall

Something there is that doesn't love a wall,
That sends the frozen ground swell under it,
And spills the upper boulders in the sun;
And makes gaps even two can pass abreast.
The work of hunters is another thing: 5
I have come after them and made repair
Where they have left not one stone on a stone,
But they would have the rabbit out of hiding,
To please the yelping dogs. The gaps I mean,
No one has seen them made or heard them made,   10
But at spring mending time we find them there.
I let my neighbor know beyond the hill;
And on a day we meet to walk the line
And set the wall between us once again.
We keep the wall between us as we go.   15
To each the boulders that have fallen to each.
And some are loaves and some so nearly balls
We have to use a spell to make them balance:
"Stay where you are until our backs are turned!"
We wear our fingers rough with handling them.   20
Oh, just another kind of outdoor game,
One on a side. It comes to little more:
There where it is we do not need the wall:
He is all pine and I am apple orchard.
My apple trees will never get across   25
And eat the cones under his pines, I tell him.
He only says, "Good fences make good neighbors."
Spring is the mischief in me, and I wonder
If I could put a notion in his head:
"*Why* do they make good neighbors? Isn't it   30
Where there are cows? But here there are no cows.
Before I built a wall I'd ask to know
What I was walling in or walling out,
And to whom I was like to give offense.
Something there is that doesn't love a wall,   35
That wants it down." I could say "Elves" to him,
But it's not elves exactly, and I'd rather
He said it for himself. I see him there
Bringing a stone grasped firmly by the top
In each hand, like an old stone savage armed.   40
He moves in darkness as it seems to me,
Not of woods only and the shade of trees.
He will not go behind his father's saying,
And he likes having thought of it so well
He says again, "Good fences make good neighbors."   45

Acquainted with the Night

I have been one acquainted with the night.
I have walked out in rain—and back in rain.
I have outwalked the furthest city light.

I have looked down the saddest city lane.
I have passed the watchman on his beat   5
And dropped my eyes, unwilling to explain.

I have stood still and stopped the sound of feet
When far away an interrupted cry
Came over houses from another street,

But not to call me back or say good-by;   10
And further still at an unearthly height,
One luminary clock against the sky

Proclaimed the time was neither wrong nor right.
I have been one acquainted with the night.

The Silken Tent

She is as in a field a silken tent
At midday when a sunny summer breeze
Has dried the dew and all its ropes relent,
So that in guys° it gently sways at ease,
And its supporting central cedar pole,   5
That is its pinnacle to heavenward
And signifies the sureness of the soul,
Seems to owe naught to any single cord,
But strictly held by none, is loosely bound
By countless silken ties of love and thought   10
To everything on earth the compass round,
And only by one's going slightly taut
In the capriciousness of summer air
Is of the slightest bondage made aware.

4. **guys:** steadying ropes.

It Bids Pretty Fair

The play seems out for an almost infinite run.
Don't mind a little thing like the actors fighting.
The only thing I worry about is the sun.
We'll be all right if nothing goes wrong with the lighting.

Provide, Provide

The witch that came (the withered hag)
To wash the steps with pail and rag,
Was once the beauty Abishag,°

The picture pride of Hollywood.
Too many fall from great and good   5
For you to doubt the likelihood.

Die early and avoid the fate.
Or if predestined to die late,
Make up your mind to die in state.

Make the whole stock exchange your
    own!   10
If need be occupy a throne,
Where nobody can call *you* crone.

Some have relied on what they knew;
Others on being simply true.   14
What worked for them might work for you.

No memory of having starred
Atones for later disregard,
Or keeps the end from being hard.

Better to go down dignified
With boughten friendship at your side   20
Than none at all. Provide, provide!

3. **Abishag:** in the Bible, a beautiful young woman
who was a servant to the aged King David. See
I Kings 1:3–4.

FOR STUDY AND DISCUSSION

THE PASTURE

1. This poem appears as an introduction to Frost's collected poems. How is it an appropriate introduction to a book of poems, particularly one by Frost?

2. Frost once defined poetry as "metaphor, saying one thing and meaning another, saying one thing in terms of another." How may this definition of poetry be applied to "The Pasture"?

3. "The Pasture" has been interpreted as a love poem. Does this interpretation seem convincing to you? Why or why not?

THE ROAD NOT TAKEN

1. What details of the poem lead you to believe that it is more than a simple account of a journey? What is the significance of the traveler's choice?

2. How might this poem be applied to your own life?

STOPPING BY WOODS ON A SNOWY EVENING

1. This poem is one of the most discussed short lyrics of the twentieth century. What do you see in the poem that might lead critics to read many implications into it? What interpretation do you give the poem? Consider especially the journey which the traveler is on, the impatient shake that the horse gives his harness bells, and the suggestive quality of the last stanza.

2. Read aloud the third stanza. What impresses you most about its sound and rhythm? Is there any contrast in sounds?

3. Why do you think the final stanza ends with a repetition of a line? What is the effect of the repetition?

NOTHING GOLD CAN STAY

1. Explain the first line of this poem. How is the last line related to the rest of the poem?

How does the meaning of "gold" deepen when it is used a second time?

2. In its use of specific objects, what does this poem have in common with other poems by Frost?

FIRE AND ICE

1. What kind of person does the speaker of this poem seem to be? (For example, does he seem very young or romantic?)

2. Explain the difference between "fire" and "ice" as the words are used in the poem.

3. Would you have preferred a stronger word than *suffice* at the end of the poem? Why or why not?

4. Frost wrote of Edwin Arlington Robinson's poetry that an outer seriousness was balanced by an inner humor. Is the balance the same in Frost? Explain.

MENDING WALL

1. Characterize the speaker of this poem. How does his personality come out in the first line? (To answer this question, consider the effect of changing the line to "Nature wreaks an awesome wrath on walls.")

2. To what might "whom" in line 34 refer? Might it have more than one possible reference? Explain.

3. Notice that the first line is repeated later in the poem. How does its meaning change in line 35?

4. Explain the difference in attitude between the speaker and his neighbor. Why does it seem to the speaker that his neighbor "moves in darkness"? What is the significance of the fact that the neighbor's favorite saying, "Good fences make good neighbors," was spoken by his father?

ACQUAINTED WITH THE NIGHT

1. The first line of this poem is also its last line. How is the meaning of the line deepened when it is repeated? In what other poems does Frost use the device of repetition to enrich the meaning of a poem?

2. Explain the meaning of line 13. Have you ever experienced a time "that was neither wrong nor right"? Explain.

THE SILKEN TENT

1. This poem is built around a single extended simile. Explain how the simile is developed. Does the comparison made in the poem seem to you an appropriate one? Why or why not?

2. Review the discussion of the sonnet on page 212. Is "The Silken Tent" an Italian or an English sonnet, or neither? Is the rhyme scheme of this sonnet an important clue to how the poem is organized or divided into parts? Considering the advantages of the sonnet form, why do you think Frost chose to make this poem a sonnet?

IT BIDS PRETTY FAIR

1. Explain the basic metaphor of the poem. How do the details of the poem develop the metaphor?

2. Compare this poem with "Fire and Ice." What attitudes do the two poems have in common? Is there anything humorous about this poem? If so, what?

PROVIDE, PROVIDE

1. Why do you think Frost calls the former movie star Abishag (aside from finding a rhyme for "hag")? How does this name widen the implications of the poem?

2. How seriously do you take the advice of this poem? Does the attitude of this poem seem similar or different from the attitudes of "Fire and Ice" and "Nothing Gold Can Stay"?

3. Now that you have read a number of poems by Frost, describe the personality that emerges from these poems. Discuss some of Frost's outstanding characteristics: his humor, the simplicity of his language, the precision of his observation of specific things, his gift for memorable phrases, his use of repetition, the suggestive way he uses objects such as a leaf and events such as a journey.

FOR COMPOSITION

During the last twenty years of his life, Frost was America's most beloved poet. His works were cherished as fine lyrical utterances expressing a love of nature and rural life and containing the shrewd wisdom of the country man. In recent years, several critics have pointed out that there is a dark pessimistic side to Frost's poetry that is overlooked by many readers who wish to preserve their idea of Frost as a "lovable poet." Write a composition in which you examine the claim that a dark side—an awareness of pain and cruelty and tragedy as an unavoidable part of living—is a characteristic of Frost's poetry. Use specific references to poems and lines to support your general statements.

The Death of the Hired Man

Mary sat musing on the lamp flame at the table,
Waiting for Warren. When she heard his step,
She ran on tiptoe down the darkened passage
To meet him in the doorway with the news
And put him on his guard. "Silas is back."   5
She pushed him outward with her through the door
And shut it after her. "Be kind," she said.
She took the market things from Warren's arms
And set them on the porch, then drew him down
To sit beside her on the wooden steps.   10

"When was I ever anything but kind to him?
But I'll not have the fellow back," he said.
"I told him so last haying, didn't I?
'If he left then,' I said, 'that ended it.'
What good is he? Who else will harbor him   15
At his age for the little he can do?
What help he is there's no depending on.
Off he goes always when I need him most.
He thinks he ought to earn a little pay,
Enough at least to buy tobacco with,   20
So he won't have to 'beg and be beholden.'
'All right,' I say, 'I can't afford to pay
Any fixed wages, though I wish I could.'
'Someone else can.' 'Then someone else will have to.'
I shouldn't mind his bettering himself   25
If that was what it was. You can be certain,
When he begins like that, there's someone at him
Trying to coax him off with pocket money—
In haying time, when any help is scarce.
In winter he comes back to us. I'm done."   30

"Sh! not so loud: he'll hear you," Mary said.

"I want him to: he'll have to soon or late."

"He's worn out. He's asleep beside the stove.
When I came up from Rowe's I found him here,
Huddled against the barn door fast asleep,   35
A miserable sight, and frightening, too—
You needn't smile—I didn't recognize him—
I wasn't looking for him—and he's changed.
Wait till you see."

"Where did you say he'd been?"

"He didn't say. I dragged him to the house,   40
And gave him tea, and tried to make him smoke.
I tried to make him talk about his travels.
Nothing would do: he just kept nodding off."

"What did he say? Did he say anything?"

"But little."

   "Anything? Mary, confess   45
He said he'd come to ditch the meadow for me."

"Warren!"

   "But did he? I just want to know."

"Of course he did. What would you have him say?
Surely you wouldn't grudge the poor old man
Some humble way to save his self-respect.   50
He added, if you really care to know,
He meant to clear the upper pasture, too.
That sounds like something you have heard before?
Warren, I wish you could have heard the way
He jumbled everything. I stopped to look   55
Two or three times—he made me feel so queer—
To see if he was talking in his sleep.
He ran on Harold Wilson—you remember—
The boy you had in haying four years since.
He's finished school, and teaching in his college.   60
Silas declares you'll have to get him back.
He says they two will make a team for work:
Between them they will lay this farm as smooth!
The way he mixed that in with other things.
He thinks young Wilson a likely lad, though daft   65
On education—you know how they fought
All through July under the blazing sun,
Silas up on the cart to build the load,
Harold along beside to pitch it on."

"Yes, I took care to keep well out of earshot."   70

"Well, those days trouble Silas like a dream.
You wouldn't think they would. How some things linger!
Harold's young college boy's assurance piqued him.
After so many years he still keeps finding
Good arguments he sees he might have used.   75
I sympathize. I know just how it feels
To think of the right thing to say too late.

Harold's associated in his mind with Latin.
He asked me what I thought of Harold's saying
He studied Latin like the violin   80
Because he liked it—that an argument!
He said he couldn't make the boy believe
He could find water with a hazel prong°—
Which showed how much good school had ever done him.
He wanted to go over that. But most of all   85
He thinks if he could have another chance
To teach him how to build a load of hay——"

"I know, that's Silas' one accomplishment.
He bundles every forkful in its place,
And tags and numbers it for future reference,   90
So he can find and easily dislodge it
In the unloading. Silas does that well.
He takes it out in bunches like big birds' nests.
You never see him standing on the hay
He's trying to lift, straining to lift himself."   95

"He thinks if he could teach him that, he'd be
Some good perhaps to someone in the world.
He hates to see a boy the fool of books.
Poor Silas, so concerned for other folk,
And nothing to look backward to with pride,   100
And nothing to look forward to with hope,
So now and never any different."

Part of a moon was falling down the west,
Dragging the whole sky with it to the hills.
Its light poured softly in her lap. She saw   105
And spread her apron to it. She put out her hand
Among the harplike morning-glory strings,
Taut with the dew from garden bed to eaves,
As if she played unheard the tenderness
That wrought on him beside her in the night.   110
"Warren," she said, "he has come home to die:
You needn't be afraid he'll leave you this time."

"Home," he mocked gently.

                              "Yes, what else but home?
It all depends on what you mean by home.
Of course he's nothing to us, any more   115
Than was the hound that came a stranger to us
Out of the woods, worn out upon the trail."

---

83. **find . . . prong:** a common belief that a proper location for a well can be ascertained
by walking around holding in front of one a forked twig of a single season's growth. The twig
is supposed to bend down at the point where water is to be found under the surface.

"Home is the place where, when you have to go there,
They have to take you in."

                          "I should have called it
Something you somehow haven't to deserve." 120

Warren leaned out and took a step or two,
Picked up a little stick, and brought it back
And broke it in his hand and tossed it by.
"Silas has better claim on us, you think,
Than on his brother? Thirteen little miles 125
As the road winds would bring him to his door.
Silas has walked that far no doubt today.
Why didn't he go there? His brother's rich,
A somebody—director in the bank."

"He never told us that."

                           "We know it though." 130

"I think his brother ought to help, of course.
I'll see to that if there is need. He ought of right
To take him in, and might be willing to—
He may be better than appearances.
But have some pity on Silas. Do you think 135
If he'd had any pride in claiming kin
Or anything he looked for from his brother,
He'd keep so still about him all this time?"

"I wonder what's between them."

                           "I can tell you.
Silas is what he is—we wouldn't mind him— 140
But just the kind that kinsfolk can't abide.
He never did a thing so very bad.
He don't know why he isn't quite as good
As anyone. He won't be made ashamed
To please his brother, worthless though he is." 145

"*I* can't think Si ever hurt anyone."

"No, but he hurt my heart the way he lay
And rolled his old head on that sharp-edged chair back.
He wouldn't let me put him on the lounge.
You must go in and see what you can do. 150
I made the bed up for him there tonight.
You'll be surprised at him—how much he's broken.
His working days are done; I'm sure of it."

"I'd not be in a hurry to say that."

"I haven't been. Go, look, see for yourself.   155
But, Warren, please remember how it is:
He's come to help you ditch the meadow.
He has a plan. You mustn't laugh at him.
He may not speak of it, and then he may.
I'll sit and see if that small sailing cloud   160
Will hit or miss the moon."

                  It hit the moon.
Then there were three, making a dim row,
The moon, the little silver cloud, and she.

Warren returned—too soon, it seemed to her,
Slipped to her side, caught up her hand and waited.   165

"Warren?" she questioned.

               "Dead," was all he answered.

FOR STUDY AND DISCUSSION

1. What do you learn about the situation of the poem from the first ten lines? What conclusions can you draw about Mary and Warren from these lines? Why?

2. What sort of man was Silas? In answering, consider his relation to his brother and to Harold Wilson as well as to Mary and Warren.

3. Although most of the poem is conversation, there are two passages of description. What do lines 103–110 and lines 161–163 add to the poem? Why do you think Mary is grouped with the moon and cloud in line 163?

4. Describe the relationship between Warren and Mary. Why do you think Frost chose to tell of Silas's death through a conversation rather than to write directly about Silas?

5. What do you learn of New England farm life from this poem? How would the poem be different if the setting were a large city?

BLANK VERSE

Frost has written that in English "there are virtually but two meters, strict iambic and loose iambic." Capable himself of drawing a remarkable range of effects from iambic meter (see page 116), he stated, "The possibilities for tune from the dramatic tones of meaning struck across the rigidity of a limited meter are endless." Among his finest achievements as a craftsman in verse is his use of meter in blank verse poems. Review the discussion of blank verse on page 116. Then consider the following questions.

1. Compare "Mending Wall" with "Thanatopsis" (page 114). Which poem seems closer to the rhythm of conversation? Which poem has more departures from strict iambic pentameter?

2. Are there any lines in "Mending Wall" or in "Death of the Hired Man" that seem unnatural, as if Frost had introduced an awkward construction simply for the sake of keeping to his meter? (The line "Something there is that doesn't love a wall" might be rearranged as "There is something that doesn't love a wall.") Explain.

3. "The Death of the Hired Man" could be rewritten in prose as a short story. What qualities does it gain by being written in blank verse? Cite passages in which you think the rhythm is particularly effective.

FOR COMPOSITION

Write a composition in which you examine Frost's use of opposing points of view in "Mending Wall" and "Death of the Hired Man." Do you think that in either poem he advocates one or the other view? For example, is the reader meant to sympathize with Warren or Mary?

CARL SANDBURG
(1878–1967)

Among the ten definitions of poetry offered by Carl Sandburg are: "Poetry is a projection across silence of cadences arranged to break the silence with definite intentions of echoes, syllables, wave lengths," and "Poetry is the opening and closing of a door, leaving those who look through to guess what is seen during a moment." Some of Sandburg's poetry can certainly be considered a breaking of silence, a bold, resonant projection that echoes in the mind. But other poems are as delicate as the fleeting view caught between "the opening and closing of a door." He can sing loud songs about the violent contrasts of large cities, he can assert confidently that "The people will live on," and he can also capture sudden moments of beauty that come when least expected. He has been praised as the poet who most effectively captures the varied qualities of the Middle West and whose poems, to be most fully appreciated, must be read with a Middle Western accent.

Carl Sandburg was born in Galesburg, Illinois, of Swedish immigrant parents. Sandburg's father changed his name from Johnson to distinguish himself from the many other Johnsons who worked for the railroad. After leaving school at thirteen, Carl had a hard time supporting himself. He helped in a barber shop, worked as a harvest hand, and tried bricklaying, dishwashing, and house painting before he volunteered for the Spanish-American War. An army friend interested him in entering Lombard College in Galesburg. At Lombard, he edited the literary magazine and was captain of the football team. After college, he was a reporter for the Chicago *Daily News.*

In 1914, Sandburg began to make a name for himself with poems that were published in *Poetry* magazine, rough yet tender free verse about Chicago and its working people. His first book, *Chicago Poems,* was published in 1916 and attracted a good deal of attention. He was praised as one of the most energetic and original new poets of the time. Other collections of poetry followed rapidly.

Sandburg is as well known as a biographer of Abraham Lincoln as he is as a poet. For thirty years he collected material about Lincoln, until the Lincoln room in his house could hold no more and the overflow had to be stored in a barn. He typed the two volumes of *Abraham Lincoln: The War Years* in his attic. During the final years of his work on Lincoln, he supported himself by going on tours, reciting poetry and singing folk songs. In the late 1930's, he was considered one of America's leading folk singers, and his anthology, *The American Songbag,* is an important collection of folk songs.

Carl Sandburg's seventy-fifth birthday was proclaimed "Carl Sandburg Day" by the governor of Illinois, and on that occasion Sandburg was presented with a decoration by the king of Sweden. On the hundred and fiftieth anniversary of Lincoln's birthday, Sandburg addressed a joint session of Congress. During the last years of his life, he lived on a farm in North Carolina where he wrote poetry and an autobiography called *Always the Young Strangers*.

Chicago

Hog Butcher for the World,
Toolmaker, Stacker of Wheat,
Player with Railroads and the Nation's Freight Handler;
Stormy, husky, brawling,
City of the Big Shoulders: 5

They tell me you are wicked and I believe them, for I have seen your painted
  women under the gas lamps luring the farm boys.
And they tell me you are crooked and I answer: Yes, it is true I have seen
  the gunman kill and go free to kill again.
And they tell me you are brutal and my reply is: On the faces of women and
  children I have seen the marks of wanton hunger.
And having answered so I turn once more to those who sneer at this my city,
  and I give them back the sneer and say to them:
Come and show me another city with lifted head singing so proud to be
  alive and coarse and strong and cunning.   10
Flinging magnetic curses amid the toil of piling job on job, here is a tall bold
  slugger set vivid against the little soft cities;
Fierce as a dog with tongue lapping for action, cunning as a savage pitted
  against the wilderness,
        Bareheaded,
        Shoveling,
        Wrecking,   15
        Planning,
        Building, breaking, rebuilding,
Under the smoke, dust all over his mouth, laughing with white teeth,
Under the terrible burden of destiny laughing as a young man laughs,
Laughing even as an ignorant fighter laughs who has never lost a battle, 20
Bragging and laughing that under his wrist is the pulse, and under his ribs
  the heart of the people,
              Laughing!
Laughing the stormy, husky, brawling laughter of Youth, half-naked, sweat-
  ing, proud to be Hog Butcher, Toolmaker, Stacker of Wheat, Player with
  Railroads and Freight Handler to the Nation.

The Harbor

Passing through huddled and ugly walls
By doorways where women
Looked from their hunger-deep eyes,
Haunted with shadows of hunger-hands,
Out from the huddled and ugly walls,   5
I came sudden, at the city's edge,
On a blue burst of lake,
Long lake waves breaking under the sun
On a spray-flung curve of shore;
And a fluttering storm of gulls,   10
Masses of great gray wings
And flying white bellies
Veering and wheeling free in the open.

Grass

Pile the bodies high at Austerlitz° and Waterloo.°
Shovel them under and let me work—
    I am the grass; I cover all.

And pile them high at Gettysburg
And pile them high at Ypres° and Verdun.°   5

Shovel them under and let me work.
Two years, ten years, and passengers ask the conductor:
    What place is this?
    Where are we now?

    I am the grass.   10
    Let me work.

1. **Austerlitz and Waterloo:** sites of battles of the Napoleonic Wars.   5. **Ypres** (ē′pr′, popularly, wī′pûrz) **and Verdun:** sites of battles of World War I.

Nocturne in a Deserted Brickyard

Stuff of the moon
Runs on the lapping sand
Out to the longest shadows
Under the curving willows,
And round the creep of the wave line,   5
Fluxions° of yellow and dusk on the waters
Make a wide dreaming pansy of an old pond in the night.

6. **Fluxions** (fluk′shunz): motions.

CARL SANDBURG   629

EDNA
ST. VINCENT
MILLAY
(1892–1950)

Edna St. Vincent Millay was the most popular and characteristic poetic voice of the 1920's. Her reputation was made by "Renascence," a remarkable poem to be written by a nineteen-year-old girl, and her subsequent poetry gave delight to a great many readers. Since her death, her poetry has been somewhat out of fashion. Her poems have been criticized for their direct, rather uncomplicated outpouring of emotion, very different from the complex formulations of poets such as Wallace Stevens, John Crowe Ransom, and Robert Lowell (pages 647, 658, and 676). Yet so distinguished a critic as Edmund Wilson has come to her defense. He has called her one of the great poets of the century, and has said that "in giving supreme expression to profoundly felt personal experience, she was able to identify herself with more general human experience and stand forth as spokesman for the human spirit. . . ." Miss Millay's poetry is traditionally romantic. Among her favorite forms are the sonnet and the simple ballad, and her favorite subjects include love, the inevitability of death, the beauty of nature. If readers rarely find in her poems the mingling of intellect and passion that characterizes much of the best modern poetry, they nevertheless find power and beauty of expression.

A red-haired, green-eyed tomboy, Edna Millay grew up on the shores of Penobscot Bay in Maine. After graduating from Vassar College, she moved to New York's Greenwich Village, where she soon became a leading figure. In an affectionate essay about her, Edmund Wilson has said that she was an immensely exciting person to know. "She was one of those women whose features are not perfect and who in their moments of dimness may not seem even pretty, but who, excited by the blood or the spirit, become almost supernaturally beautiful . . . her reading of poetry was thrilling. She pronounced every syllable distinctly; she gave every sound its value." During her Village days, she wrote poetic plays for the Provincetown Players, a famous experimental theater that was the first to produce Eugene O'Neill's plays. She published several very popular volumes of lyric poems. When she gave public readings, she was able to command large fees. After a number of hectic years in New York and Paris, she married Eugene Boissevain, a Dutch importer who lived in New York. Except for summers in Maine, she lived quietly at "Steepletop"— a farm in Austerlitz, New York—for the last twenty-five years of her life. Her later poems, generally somber and without the emotional exhilaration of her earlier poems, reflect both a growing awareness of social ills and a troubled inner life.

Euclid alone has looked on Beauty bare

Euclid° alone has looked on Beauty bare.
Let all who prate of Beauty hold their peace,
And lay them prone upon the earth and cease
To ponder on themselves, the while they stare
At nothing, intricately drawn nowhere   5
In shapes of shifting lineage; let geese
Gabble and hiss, but heroes seek release
From dusty bondage into luminous air.

O blinding hour, O holy, terrible day,
When first the shaft into his vision shone   10
Of light anatomized!° Euclid alone
Has looked on Beauty bare. Fortunate they
Who, though once only and then but far away,
Have heard her massive sandal set on stone.

1. **Euclid:** Greek mathematician of the third century B.C., who developed the basic principles of geometry. 11. **anatomized:** analyzed.

Lament

Listen, children:
Your father is dead.
From his old coats
I'll make you little jackets;
I'll make you little trousers   5
From his old pants.
There'll be in his pockets
Things he used to put there,
Keys and pennies
Covered with tobacco;   10
Dan shall have the pennies
To save in his bank;
Anne shall have the keys
To make a pretty noise with.
Life must go on,   15
And the dead be forgotten;
Life must go on,
Though good men die;
Anne, eat your breakfast;
Dan, take your medicine;   20
Life must go on;
I forget just why.

Renascence

All I could see from where I stood
Was three long mountains and a wood;
I turned and looked another way,
And saw three islands in a bay.
So with my eyes I traced the line   5
Of the horizon, thin and fine,
Straight around till I was come
Back to where I'd started from;
And all I saw from where I stood
Was three long mountains and a wood.   10
Over these things I could not see;
These were the things that bounded me;
And I could touch them with my hand,
Almost, I thought, from where I stand.

And all at once things seemed so small   15
My breath came short, and scarce at all.
But, sure, the sky is big, I said;
Miles and miles above my head;
So here upon my back I'll lie
And look my fill into the sky.   20
And so I looked, and, after all,

The sky was not so very tall.
The sky, I said, must somewhere stop,
And—sure enough!—I see the top!
The sky, I thought, is not so grand;   25
I 'most could touch it with my hand!
And, reaching up my hand to try,
I screamed to feel it touch the sky.

I screamed, and—lo!—Infinity
Came down and settled over me;   30
Forced back my scream into my chest,
Bent back my arm upon my breast,
And, pressing of the Undefined
The definition on my mind,
Held up before my eyes a glass   35
Through which my shrinking sight did pass
Until it seemed I must behold
Immensity made manifold;
Whispered to me a word whose sound
Deafened the air for worlds around,   40
And brought unmuffled to my ears
The gossiping of friendly spheres,
The creaking of the tented sky,
The ticking of Eternity.

I saw and heard, and knew at last   45
The How and Why of all things, past
And present, and forevermore.
The universe, cleft to the core,
Lay open to my probing sense   49
That, sick'ning, I would fain pluck thence
But could not—nay! But needs must suck
At the great wound, and could not pluck
My lips away till I had drawn
All venom out.—Ah, fearful pawn!
For my omniscience paid I toll   55
In infinite remorse of soul.
All sin was of my sinning, all
Atoning mine, and mine the gall
Of all regret. Mine was the weight
Of every brooded wrong, the hate   60
That stood behind each envious thrust,
Mine every greed, mine every lust.
And all the while for every grief,
Each suffering, I craved relief
With individual desire—   65
Craved all in vain! And felt fierce fire
About a thousand people crawl;
Perished with each—then mourned for all!
A man was starving in Capri;
He moved his eyes and looked at me;   70

I felt his gaze, I heard his moan,
And knew his hunger as my own.
I saw at sea a great fog bank
Between two ships that struck and sank;
A thousand screams the heavens smote;
And every scream tore through my throat.
No hurt I did not feel, no death   77
That was not mine; mine each last breath
That, crying, met an answering cry
From the compassion that was I.   80
All suffering mine, and mine its rod;
Mine, pity like the pity of God.
Ah, awful weight! Infinity
Pressed down upon the finite Me!
My anguished spirit, like a bird,   85
Beating against my lips I heard;
Yet lay the weight so close about
There was no room for it without.
And so beneath the weight lay I
And suffered death, but could not die.   90

Long had I lain thus, craving death,
When quietly the earth beneath
Gave way, and inch by inch, so great
At last had grown the crushing weight,
Into the earth I sank till I   95
Full six feet under ground did lie,
And sank no more,—there is no weight
Can follow here, however great.
From off my breast I felt it roll,
And as it went my tortured soul   100
Burst forth and fled in such a gust
That all about me swirled the dust.

Deep in the earth I rested now
Cool is its hand upon the brow
And soft its breast beneath the head   105
Of one who is so gladly dead.
And all at once, and over all,
The pitying rain began to fall;
I lay and heard each pattering hoof
Upon my lowly, thatchèd roof,   110
And seemed to love the sound far more
Than ever I had done before.
For rain it hath a friendly sound
To one who's six feet underground;
And scarce the friendly voice or face: 115
A grave is such a quiet place.

The rain, I said, is kind to come
And speak to me in my new home.

I would I were alive again
To kiss the fingers of the rain,   120
To drink into my eyes the shine
Of every slanting silver line,
To catch the freshened, fragrant breeze
From drenched and dripping apple trees.
For soon the shower will be done,   125
And then the broad face of the sun
Will laugh above the rain-soaked earth
Until the world with answering mirth
Shakes joyously, and each round drop
Rolls, twinkling, from its grass-blade top.
How can I bear it; buried here,   131
While overhead the sky grows clear
And blue again after the storm?
O, multicolored, multiform
Belovèd beauty over me,   135
That I shall never, never see
Again! Spring silver, autumn gold,
That I shall never more behold!
Sleeping your myriad magics through,
Close-sepulchered away from you!   140
O God, I cried, give me new birth,
And put me back upon the earth!
Upset each cloud's gigantic gourd
And let the heavy rain, down poured
In one big torrent, set me free,   145
Washing my grave away from me!

I ceased; and, through the breathless
    hush
That answered me, the far-off rush
Of herald wings came whispering
Like music down the vibrant string   150
Of my ascending prayer, and—crash!
Before the wild wind's whistling lash
The startled storm clouds reared on high
And plunged in terror down the sky,
And the big rain in one black wave   155
Fell from the sky and struck my grave.

I know not how such things can be
I only know there came to me
A fragrance such as never clings
To aught save happy living things;   160
A sound as of some joyous elf
Singing sweet songs to please himself,
And, through and over everything,
A sense of glad awakening.
The grass, a-tiptoe at my ear,   165

Whispering to me I could hear;
I felt the rain's cool finger tips
Brushed tenderly across my lips,
Laid gently on my sealèd sight,
And all at once the heavy night   170
Fell from my eyes and I could see—
A drenched and dripping apple tree,
A last long line of silver rain,
A sky grown clear and blue again.
And as I looked a quickening gust   175
Of wind blew up to me and thrust
Into my face a miracle
Of orchard breath, and with the smell—
I know not how such things can be!—
I breathed my soul back into me.   180

Ah! Up then from the ground sprang I
And hailed the earth with such a cry
As is not heard save from a man
Who has been dead, and lives again.
About the trees my arms I wound;   185
Like one gone mad I hugged the ground;
I raised my quivering arms on high;
I laughed and laughed into the sky,
Till at my throat a strangling sob
Caught fiercely, and a great heartthrob
Sent instant tears into my eyes;   191
O God, I cried, no dark disguise
Can e'er hereafter hide from me
Thy radiant identity!
Thou canst not move across the grass 195
But my quick eyes will see Thee pass,
Nor speak, however silently,
But my hushed voice will answer Thee.
I know the path that tells Thy way
Through the cool eve of every day;   200
God, I can push the grass apart
And lay my finger on Thy heart!

The world stands out on either side
No wider than the heart is wide;   204
Above the world is stretched the sky—
No higher than the soul is high.
The heart can push the sea and land
Farther away on either hand;
The soul can split the sky in two,   209
And let the face of God shine through.
But East and West will pinch the heart
That cannot keep them pushed apart;
And he whose soul is flat—the sky
Will cave in on him by and by.

EDNA ST. VINCENT MILLAY   633

EUCLID ALONE HAS LOOKED ON BEAUTY BARE

1. Why is *Beauty* capitalized? Which phrases in the poem carry out this idea of beauty?

2. Why is the day described as "holy" and "terrible"? In what way did Euclid have a vision of "light anatomized"? Why do you think this poem refers to a mathematician such as Euclid rather than to a poet such as Shakespeare or to a painter such as Rembrandt?

LAMENT

1. What seems to be the attitude of the speaker in the early part of the poem? At what point do you realize that she has a very different attitude?

2. What is the emotional effect of the short lines and sentences of the poem? (To answer this question, it may help to read the poem aloud.)

RENASCENCE

1. What mood is created in the first section of the poem? Point out details that contribute to this mood. How does the mood change in the second section?

2. What does the poet mean by saying that "Infinity" settled over her? Describe the experience that results. What causes the poet to imagine herself dead?

3. Show how the rain is used as a transition between the sixth and seventh sections. How is the rain responsible for a change in the mood of the poem?

4. What images are used to describe the poet's renascence? Which do you think are most effective? Study the description of natural things in lines 165–78 and compare it with the list of things in the first section of the poem. Why do you think the later passage is more detailed?

5. Compare the first and last sections of the poem. What is the difference in tone and point of view? In what way does the poet's experience of death and rebirth deepen her understanding?

6. Make a list of words that are capitalized in the poem (other than ordinary proper nouns like *Capri*). Why do you think the poet capitalizes these words? How would the effect of the poem be different if these words had been left uncapitalized?

THE SONNET

Study the discussion of the sonnet on page 212 and compare "Euclid alone has looked on Beauty bare" with Longfellow's three sonnets and Frost's "The Silken Tent" (page 618). Is Miss Millay's sonnet more like Longfellow's or Frost's? Is it an English or an Italian sonnet? What clues support your answer? How closely is the content of "Euclid" related to its form?

LANGUAGE AND VOCABULARY

Although the language of "Renascence" is on the whole very simple and straightforward, there are words in the poem that some dictionaries would label *archaic* and that might, at first glance, seem out of place in the poem. How can you justify the choice of each of the following italicized words? (If you are not familiar with the label *archaic,* look it up in a good unabridged dictionary. Look up any of the following italicized words which you do not understand.)

1. "That, sick'ning, I would *fain* pluck thence
    But could not—*nay!* But *needs* must suck . . ." (Lines 50–51)

2. "Close-*sepulchered* away from you!" (line 140)

3. "To *aught* save happy living things . . ." (line 160)

FOR COMPOSITION

1. "Renascence" is about an emotional event in the poet's life, an inner experience that deepened her awareness and understanding. Write a composition about a similar event in your life. (If you wish, the event can be an imaginary one.)

2. "The world stands out on either side/ No wider than the heart is wide" ("Renascence," lines 203–04) are among Edna St. Vincent Millay's most often quoted lines of poetry. Write a composition in which you discuss the meaning and impact of these lines. Consider the following points: What makes the lines memorable? How do the verses that follow (lines 205–14) deepen the meaning of the lines? What is the emotional impact of the lines when they are read as a climax to all that has gone before in the poem?

E. E. CUMMINGS
(1894–1962)

The first thing a reader new to E. E. Cummings's poems will probably notice about them is their unusual arrangement on the page. Cummings was a painter as well as a poet, and in his attempts to make poetry a fresh experience for the reader, he used visual as well as verbal devices. He wanted the reader to see each poem as a new creation—not simply as a stale ordinary piece of work that had been shaped in a perfectly expected way by thousands of years of tradition. After a reader has become accustomed to the striking features of Cummings's poems, he will notice several things: Cummings is often a more traditional poet than may at first appear, and has worked adroitly with a number of traditional forms, particularly the sonnet. Also, Cummings's poems appeal to the ear as much as to the eye; his visual devices do not disguise a lack of feeling for the sound of words. Third, although Cummings was an experimentalist in his use of words and forms, the ideas behind his poems are usually straightforward and even old-fashioned. He believed in romantic love and individualism and hated standardization and conformity. He had little use for the mass of men but was delighted by the promise inherent in individual man. Once he wrote that in exploring two cities, he made "the discovery . . . that all groups, gangs, and collectivities—no matter how apparently disparate—are fundamentally alike; and that what makes any world go round is not the trivial difference between a Somerville and a Cambridge, but the immeasurable difference between either of them and individuality." His unusual poetic devices—the avoidance of capital letters, the minimizing of punctuation, the altering of normal sentence order—are intended to jolt the reader into a fresh awareness of life's immense possibilities and of one individual, Cummings, who is discovering these possibilities and communicating that discovery to others.

Edward Estlin Cummings was born in Cambridge, Massachusetts, the son of a Harvard teacher who later became a Unitarian minister. After receiving two degrees from Harvard University, he enlisted in a voluntary ambulance corps that served in France during World War I. Because of a censor's mistake, Cummings spent three months in a French detention camp. His book, *The Enormous Room*, published in 1922, gives an account of his sentencing and imprisonment. After his release, he volunteered for service as a private in the United States Infantry. Although his lifelong hatred of war and of authority was nourished by his wartime experiences, he did not regret having served. "World War I," he told his biographer, Charles Norman, "was the great experience of my generation."

After the Armistice, Cummings studied painting in Paris and later settled in New York's Greenwich Village, the home of many artists and writers, including Edna St. Vincent Millay. In 1923, *Tulips and Chimneys,* his first book of poems, was published. Many other volumes followed, including *is 5* (referring to the fact that, to a poet, two plus two may not always equal four), *XAIPE* (Greek for *rejoice*), and one collection without a title. Among Cummings's other works are *EIMI* (Greek for *I am*), a travel book expressing his outrage at the regimentation of individuals in the Soviet Union, and *i: six nonlectures,* a series of talks he delivered as the Charles Eliot Norton Visiting Professor at Harvard.

During the latter part of his life, Cummings gave many readings of his own poetry. Once, during a reading at Bennington College, his audience surprised him by reciting one of his poems in unison. Throughout his life, he continued to draw and to paint in watercolors. He was an independent man who spoke out about his likes and dislikes. His actions as well as his writings were a testimony to his belief that

"—when skies are hanged and oceans drowned,
the single secret will still be man"

if there are any heavens

if there are any heavens my mother will(all by herself)have
one. It will not be a pansy heaven nor
a fragile heaven of lilies-of-the-valley but
it will be a heaven of blackred roses

my father will be(deep like a rose   5
tall like a rose)

standing near my

(swaying over her
silent)
with eyes which are really petals and see   10

nothing with the face of a poet really which
is a flower and not a face with
hands
which whisper
This is my beloved my   15

                        (suddenly in sunlight
he will bow,

& the whole garden will bow)

sweet spring

"sweet spring is your
time is my time is our
time for springtime is lovetime
and viva sweet love"

(all the merry little birds are   5
flying in the floating in the
very spirits singing in
are winging in the blossoming)

lovers go and lovers come
awandering awondering   10
but any two are perfectly
alone there's nobody else alive

(such a sky and such a sun
i never knew and neither did you
and everybody never breathed   15
quite so many kinds of yes)

not a tree can count his leaves
each herself by opening
but shining who by thousands mean
only one amazing thing   20

(secretly adoring shyly
tiny winging darting floating
merry in the blossoming
always joyful selves are singing)

"sweet spring is your   25
time is my time is our
time for springtime is lovetime
and viva sweet love"

The "New Poetry"

In October 1912, Harriet Monroe, a Chicago patron of the arts, began to publish *Poetry: A Magazine of Verse*. Its purpose was "to give poetry her own place, her own voice." *Poetry* was a literary storm center and a fulfillment of Miss Monroe's hopes. Attracting what was most vital in American verse, *Poetry* became known as the home of the "new poetry."

In its early issues, *Poetry* introduced its readers to Imagism. The Imagists—Ezra Pound, Amy Lowell, and others—sought to renew poetry by a more precise use of language. Their principles are a valuable guide to much modern poetry:

1. "To use the language of common speech but to employ always the *exact* word . . ."
2. "To create new rhythms. . . . We do not insist upon free verse as the only method of writing poetry. We fight for it as a principle of liberty . . ."
3. "To allow absolute freedom in the choice of subject . . ."
4. "To present an image . . . poetry should render particulars exactly and not deal in vague generalities . . ."
5. "To produce poetry that is hard and clear . . ."
6. "Finally, most of us believe that concentration is of the very essence of poetry."

The Imagists made an early effort to bring freshness and precision to poetry. Later poets—including William Carlos Williams, Marianne Moore, Elizabeth Bishop, and Richard Wilbur—owe a great deal to them.

since feeling is first

since feeling is first
who pays any attention
to the syntax° of things
will never wholly kiss you;

wholly to be a fool   5
while Spring is in the world

my blood approves,
and kisses are a better fate
than wisdom
lady i swear by all flowers. Don't cry   10
—the best gesture of my brain is less than
your eyelids' flutter which says

we are for each other: then
laugh, leaning back in my arms
for life's not a paragraph   15

And death i think is no parenthesis

3. **syntax:** word order in a sentence.

FOR STUDY AND DISCUSSION

IF THERE ARE ANY HEAVENS

1. Because of the way Cummings has designed this poem to appear on the printed
page, the reader is forced to read actively,
not passively, so that he almost helps to create
the poem as he reads. What details of the
visual arrangement of the poem seem to you
particularly effective? How do they influence
your reading of the poem? Why do you think
the poem has no commas and only a single
period? What effect is gained by the place-
ment of "nothing" (line 11) and "hands"
(line 13)?

2. What is the significance of Cummings's
comparing his father to a rose? What do you
think Cummings sees as the difference between roses and lilies-of-the-valley and pan-
sies?

3. In a letter to his editor, Cummings called

certain of his works "picture poems." What
do you think he meant? Can this term be applied to any of the poems by Cummings which
you have read?

4. In an essay called "A Poet's Advice,"
Cummings defined a poet as "somebody who
feels, and expresses his feelings through
words." This, he said, was harder than it
sounded because "A lot of people think or
believe or know they feel—but that's thinking
or believing or knowing; not feeling. And
poetry is feeling—not knowing or believing or
thinking. . . . As for expressing nobody-but-
yourself in words, that means working just a
little harder than anybody who isn't a poet
can possibly imagine." How might this statement be applied to the poems you have read
by Cummings?

SWEET SPRING

1. How would you describe the rhythm of
this poem? Does the rhythm seem appropriate
to the mood? Why or why not?

2. How does the use of quotation marks
and parentheses help make the poem a picture
on the page?

3. What is the effect of the second stanza
of the poem? Do you think Cummings could
have achieved the same effect by writing normal sentences? Explain.

SINCE FEELING IS FIRST

1. Why does Cummings take a dim view of
those who are concerned with syntax? Do
you think his own syntax is careless? What
is the effect of his departure from normal word
order?

2. Explain the last two lines of the poem.
To what previous line are they related most
closely?

FOR COMPOSITION

According to Cummings's biographer,
Charles Norman, Cummings did not care
for Robert Frost's poetry. Once Cummings
said to Norman, "You know, I ought to like
Frost. After all, we're both New Englanders."
He asked Norman to read several poems by
Frost. Finally he said, "Would you like to
know what *I* think? They lack intensity."

Write a composition in which you attack or
defend Cummings's opinion of Frost's poetry.
Or write a dialogue between the two poets in
which they argue for their different views of
poetry.

AMERICAN PAINTING

The 1920's and Early 1930's

On February 17, 1913, a huge exhibition of both American and European art opened in New York at the 69th Regiment Armory. Organized by a committee of American painters, the "Armory Show" was the most important single exhibition ever held in the United States, for it introduced the American public to the revolutionary movements in art which had been developing in Europe over the past thirty years.

The influence of European modernism upon American painters varied considerably from one artist to another. A few, like Feininger and Hartley (page 568), had participated directly in the original Cubist and Expressionist movements during their many years abroad. Others made trips to Europe but then developed their styles in America, adapting European ideas to suit their own needs. Still others, who remained in America all their lives, seem to have been unaffected by the new styles imported from abroad.

John Marin belongs to the second of these groups. Although exposed to Cubism and other modern movements while in Paris, he managed to assimilate these influences while developing an extremely personal style. Marin was a master of watercolor; with a very few strokes of the brush he could suggest the explosive energies of a great American city—the "warring, pushing, pulling forces" which he felt were present among New York's huge skyscrapers. For example, in *The Singer Building, 1921* (PLATE 1), notice how Marin's brushwork has made the skyscraper appear to set off powerful vibrations in the space around it as it thrusts upward into the sky.

Charles Demuth also developed a highly original style after returning to America from Paris. In his pictures of the 1920's, such as *I Saw the Figure 5 in Gold* (PLATE 2), Demuth created the illusion of flat planes intersecting one another at different angles, somewhat as in Cubist paintings. But notice that he did not allow these planes to break up or distort the main forms: the number 5 projecting out toward us is shown completely intact in each of three different sizes. Demuth attempted here to paint what his friend the poet William Carlos Williams had described in words: a vision of the figure 5 gleaming in gold on the side of a red firetruck speeding through a dark, rainy city.

One American painter of this period who seems to have been unusually free of foreign influences was Charles Burchfield. Primarily a watercolorist, Burchfield drew his subject matter from the regions he knew best—those around Salem, Ohio, and Buffalo, New York. But unlike the painters of the Ash Can School, Burchfield often concentrated on buildings and streets rather than on people. *Ice Glare* (PLATE 3), for instance, shows a winter streetcrossing in Buffalo, where tumble-down frame houses are bordered by austere brick factories. The only real sign of life here is a tree at the upper left, seemingly trying to free itself from its squalid surroundings. As for the black car, it somehow has more the presence of a coffin than of an automobile. A pall of soot lies over the whole scene, except where snow and light on the ice have bleached it white. Yet out of this bleakness, Burchfield has extracted a harsh beauty, perhaps by the way he has handled the light and the sharp-edged shadows it casts across the ice.

Edward Hopper, like Marin and Demuth, received his training both in America and Europe. Like Marin, he exhibited in the Armory Show. Perhaps his most famous oil is *Early Sunday Morning* (PLATE 4), in which he typifies small-town America somewhat as Sinclair Lewis had done in his novel *Main Street.* Yet Hopper's picture has none of Lewis's social satire. Nor is there caricature of the sort found in Burchfield's *Ice Glare.* Hopper's forms are more solid than Burchfield's, his composition more simplified and compact. Here too the light is important, but in a quieter way: it passes slowly across the shopfronts in long shadows, evoking a mood of stillness, isolation, and loneliness.

Another veteran of the Armory Show who was influenced by Cubism was Charles Sheeler. From 1918 on, Sheeler exhibited regularly not only as a painter but also as a photographer, and in 1927 he was commissioned to photograph the Ford Plant at River Rouge, Michigan. A few years later he used his photographs of this site as source material for paintings of modern industrial scenes, such as *American Landscape* (PLATE 5). Like Hopper, Sheeler was essentially a realist. Yet pictures such as this one have a cool, abstract quality as well; for in real life, nature is never quite so spic-and-span, so neatly composed, or so clearly outlined as it is shown here.

Marin, Demuth, and Sheeler belonged to a small group of artists who exhibited at a New York gallery owned and run by Alfred Stieglitz, one of America's pioneer photographers of the early twentieth century. Another distinguished member of this group was the painter Georgia O'Keeffe, who married Stieglitz in 1924. Her smooth, highly simplified style is similar to Demuth's and Sheeler's, but usually it is not as impersonal. In *Brooklyn Bridge* (PLATE 6), for instance, the two pointed arches and tinted spaces of sky, which suggest stained glass windows in a cathedral, create a lyrical, poetic mood.

640

PLATE 1. JOHN MARIN (1870–1953): *The Singer Building, 1921*. Watercolor, $26\frac{1}{2}$ x $21\frac{5}{8}$ inches. (Philadelphia Museum of Art, The Alfred Stieglitz Collection)

PLATE 2. CHARLES DEMUTH (1883–1935): *I Saw the Figure 5 in Gold*. 1928. Oil on composition board, 36 x 29¾ inches. (The Metropolitan Museum of Art, New York, The Alfred Stieglitz Collection, 1949)

PLATE 3. CHARLES E. BURCHFIELD (1893–1967): *Ice Glare*. 1933. Watercolor, 30¾ x 24¾ inches. (Collection of the Whitney Museum of American Art, New York)

Plate 4. EDWARD HOPPER (1882–1967): *Early Sunday Morning.* 1930. Oil on canvas, 35 x 60 inches. (Collection of the Whitney Museum of American Art, New York)

PLATE 5. CHARLES SHEELER (1883–): *American Landscape*. 1930. Oil on canvas, 24 x 31 inches. (Collection, The Museum of Modern Art, New York, Gift of Abby Aldrich Rockefeller)

645

PLATE 6. GEORGIA O'KEEFFE (1887–   ): *Brooklyn Bridge*. 1949. Oil on canvas, 48 x 36 inches. (Private Collection, New York)

WALLACE
STEVENS
(1879–1955)

When Wallace Stevens first read his poems in public, he was heard to remark, "I wonder what the boys at the office would think of this." Stevens's office was at the Accident and Indemnity Company of Hartford, Connecticut, where he worked for over forty years and rose to the position of vice-president. The delicacy and elegance of Stevens's poems have been widely praised. Often, they are flamboyant. Thus, "Bantams in the Pine-Woods" begins with the often quoted lines: "Chieftain Iffucan of Azcan in caftan/ Of tan with henna hackles, halt!" Some of his poems have striking titles, such as "The Comedian as the Letter C," "Le Monocle de Mon Oncle," and "The Sense of the Sleight-of-Hand Man." Many of his poems luxuriate in the resources of language, in the effects that can be gained by novel words and various combinations of sounds.

Of the two parts of his life, Stevens commented, "I prefer to think I'm just a man, not a poet part time, businessman the rest." Poetry was important to Stevens because he regarded it as a way of letting the imagination organize reality—"things as they are"—of giving shape and meaning to his surroundings. He wrote that the role of the poet "is to help people live their lives. He [the poet] has immensely to do with giving life whatever savor it possesses. He has to do with whatever the imagination and the senses have made of the world." Stevens believed poetry was the supreme way of organizing and giving meaning to life. Without poetry's power to confront and change reality, he thought, human beings are poor indeed; but sustained by this power, man is able bravely to face the dark. One of the chief sources of poetry's power, he wrote, was in its words. "The deepening need for words to express our thoughts and feelings . . . makes us listen to words when we hear them, loving them and feeling them, makes us search the sound of them, for a finality, a perfection, an unalterable vibration, which it is only within the power of the acutest poet to give them." Stevens himself was a master of words.

Wallace Stevens was born in Reading, Pennsylvania, and studied at Harvard University under the philosopher George Santayana. After Harvard, he attended New York Law School. His first collection of poems, *Harmonium,* was not published until 1923, when he was forty-four. Although *Harmonium* is today regarded as one of the most important books of poetry of the twentieth century, it sold only about a hundred copies at the time. Perhaps discouraged by its reception, Stevens wrote little for several years, and a dozen years passed before the appearance of a second collection. But during the latter part of his life, he was highly productive and published four more major collections of verse. Much of Stevens's early poetry is marked by an exotic vocabulary, tropical luxuriance of color, and an opulence of sound. *Harmonium* as a whole was full of what Stevens called "the essential gaudiness of poetry." Later his verse became simpler and more direct, essentially a poetry of statement. But from the beginning until the end, Stevens remained loyal to his great subject, the role of the human imagination in "pressing back against the pressure of reality" and helping us to live our lives.

Disillusionment of Ten O'Clock

The houses are haunted
By white nightgowns.
None are green,
Or purple with green rings,
Or green with yellow rings,   5
Or yellow with blue rings.
None of them are strange,
With socks of lace
And beaded ceintures.°
People are not going   10
To dream of baboons and periwinkles.°
Only, here and there, an old sailor,
Drunk and asleep in his boots,
Catches tigers
In red weather.   15

9. **ceintures:** belts or girdles. 11. **periwinkles:** salt-water snails with cone-shaped shells marked with dark spiral bands.

The Emperor of Ice Cream

Call the roller of big cigars,
The muscular one, and bid him whip
In kitchen cups concupiscent° curds.°
Let the wenches dawdle in such dress
As they are used to wear, and let the boys   5
Bring flowers in last month's newspapers.
Let be be finale of seem.
The only emperor is the emperor of ice cream.

3. **concupiscent:** desirous. **curds:** coagulated parts of milk, here ice cream.

Take from the dresser of deal,°
Lacking the three glass knobs, that sheet   10
On which she embroidered fantails° once
And spread it so as to cover her face.
If her horny° feet protrude, they come
To show how cold she is, and dumb.
Let the lamp affix its beam.   15
The only emperor is the emperor of ice cream.

9. **deal:** fir or pine.   11. **fantails:** decorations resembling open fans.   13. **horny:** calloused.

FOR STUDY AND DISCUSSION

1. How can "Disillusionment of Ten O'Clock" be interpreted as a protest against conformity and a dull, unimaginative way of life? Explain the contrast between the white nightgowns and the nightgowns in other colors. Why are the people "not going/ To dream"? How is the sailor different from the other people? In what way is this poem about "disillusionment"?

2. "The Emperor of Ice Cream" is a difficult poem. Stevens himself refused to tie it down to a single rational meaning. However, it should be possible to approach the meaning and the emotional quality of the poem by establishing what is most clear about it and discussing the implications of its vague or puzzling aspects.

What occasion is being described in the poem? What seems to be the attitude of the poet toward the dead woman? What is the contrast between her present state and his memories of her? What is the significance of the boys bringing flowers "in last month's newspapers"? (Why not "today's newspapers"?)

The newspapers, the dead woman, and the ice cream all seem to point to the impermanence of events and objects and the necessity of change and death. Why then is "the only emperor . . . the emperor of ice cream"? (What quality of ice cream seems important to the poem?) What is the difference between "be" and "seem"? To which category do the newspapers and the woman, when alive, belong? In what sense is "be" the "finale of seem"? How is this line related to the death of the woman?

Domination of Black

At night, by the fire,
The colors of the bushes
And of the fallen leaves,
Repeating themselves,
Turned in the room,   5
Like the leaves themselves
Turning in the wind.
Yes: but the color of the heavy hemlocks
Came striding.
And I remembered the cry of the peacocks.   10

The colors of their tails
Were like the leaves themselves
Turning in the wind,
In the twilight wind.

WALLACE STEVENS   649

They swept over the room,   15
Just as they flew from the boughs of the hemlocks
Down to the ground.
I heard them cry—the peacocks.
Was it a cry against the twilight
Or against the leaves themselves   20
Turning in the wind,
Turning as the flames
Turned in the fire,
Turning as the tails of the peacocks
Turned in the loud fire,   25
Loud as the hemlocks
Full of the cry of the peacocks?
Or was it a cry against the hemlocks?

Out of the window,
I saw how the planets gathered   30
Like the leaves themselves
Turning in the wind.
I saw how the night came,
Came striding like the color of the heavy hemlocks.
I felt afraid.   35
And I remembered the cry of the peacocks.

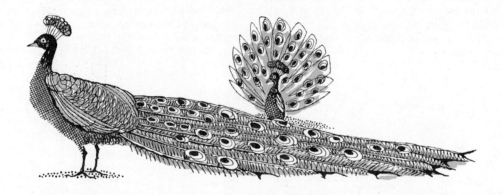

COMMENTARY

"Domination of Black" can be described as a poem about a man sitting at night watching a fire. The flames remind him of the color of fallen leaves, which in turn reminds him of bright-colored peacocks and their strange, harsh cry. Finally, after a passage of rapidly intensifying terror, the man looks out the window and perceives that even the planets turn like the fallen leaves in the wind. He is afraid because of his realization that all color and animation, all the qualities that give richness and life to the physical world, must yield to the darkness, just as a fire must eventually die out and leaves must fall from trees and, when they are most rich in color, crumble and vanish. The poem's effectiveness depends on the suggestive qualities of the objects—leaves, hemlocks, peacocks—that are included and on the emotional power of rhythm.

Although the poem does not follow any regular metrical pattern, Stevens's control of rhythm is very sure and very important to the poem's effect. The poem begins slowly and firmly; there is a definite pause at the end of each line. The reader is gradually pulled into a circular rhythm which increases in speed, revolving as the colors of the flames revolve around the walls of the room, "Like the leaves themselves/ Turning in the wind." This rhythm is broken by the heavy rhythm beginning in line 8, a rhythm which suggests the stride of the hemlocks into the room.

The second section of the poem begins by resuming the revolving rhythm of the opening lines, but this rhythm is soon replaced by a more forceful and urgent rhythm (in line 15), which suggests the birds sweeping through the room and the poet's rising terror. Then, in line 21, the circular movement is again picked up in a passage of increasing intensity which draws together in one powerful whirling motion the leaves, the flames, and the tails of the peacocks. Note that with the exception of line 24, the primary accents in lines 21–27 fall on the first and last syllables of the lines. The final line of this section also departs from this intense rhythm to indicate a pause. The poem has passed its emotional and rhythmic climax, and in the question "or was it the cry against the hemlocks?" it prepares to point up the meaning of the poem.

The final section begins rather briskly with a rhythm that is similar to the rhythm of the poem's opening lines. The poet looks out of the window at the planets beyond and perceives that they also turn like the flames and the leaves. As in the first stanza, the turning rhythm is broken (in line 34), this time by a powerful, pulsing rhythm which suggests the onrushing night and the fear of the poet.

In addition to his deft handling of rhythm, Stevens's skillful use of repetition is important. The phrase "Turning in the wind" (or a variant of it) is used several times with increasing forcefulness. Consider the effect of repeated words and sounds in the following passage:

"*Turning* in the wind,
Turning as the flames
Turned in the fire,
Turning as the tails of the peacocks
Turned in the loud fire,"

The poem grows out of a repetition of objects and themes which gradually develop in meaning. The fire, for example, seems at first warm and comforting and is compared to colored leaves pleasantly turning in the wind. But before long the wind has become the twilight wind and associated with the cry of the peacocks. And the fire is transformed into the rather ominous "loud fire" which is related to both the tails and the cry of peacocks.

Another notable change is in the significance of the title. It seems innocent and harmless at first, but gradually it gathers significance. By the end of the poem, black is the cause of both the fear of the poet and the cry of the peacocks. It is the color of the onrushing night which seems to threaten the continued existence of the universe itself.

FOR STUDY AND DISCUSSION

1. Discuss the implications and suggestive qualities of the most important objects in the poem: the leaves, the hemlocks, the peacocks. Why do you think Stevens chose to include hemlocks and not some other tree? Why peacocks and not some other bird? (Crows, for example, are noted for their raucous cries.) In answering, consider the sounds of "hemlocks" and "peacocks" as well as the connotations of these words.

2. Study lines 17–27. What do you think the cry of the peacocks means to the poet? Why might it be "a cry against the hemlocks" (line 28)?

3. Consider the effect of the word "striding" in the poem. How would the effect be different if Stevens had used another word, such as "rushing" or "hurtling" or "marching"?

WILLIAM CARLOS
WILLIAMS
(1883–1963)

In "A Sort of Song," William Carlos Williams wrote:

> "Compose. (No ideas
> but in things) Invent!
> Saxiphrage is my flower that splits
> the rocks"

It is significant that Williams should choose as his flower one that blooms in rocky places and that he should use as a kind of battle cry the phrase "no ideas but in things." In his poetry he continually tried to make his words true to the immediacy and uniqueness of simple, bare things. Clean and full of sharp movement, his poems achieve their meanings from a "continual and violent refreshing" of individual perception, in suddenly seeing the importance of simple objects and their relationships. He hated the abstractions that deaden experience. Unlike some modern poets, who seem to gain their heightened perception of the physical universe at the expense of human relationships, Williams was as alive to people as to things. He could write with equal warmth and freshness of a flower fighting its way through the hard winter ground and of a poor old woman "munching a plum on the street." He is one of the most likable of modern poets. One critic has written that a list of words characterizing Williams would include *"outspoken, good-hearted . . . generous . . . fresh, sympathetic, enthusiastic, spontaneous, open, impulsive, emotional, observant, curious, rash, courageous, undignified."* The same critic commented that he "has the honesty that consists in writing down the way things seem to you yourself, not the way that they really must be. . . ."

William Carlos Williams was a pediatrician as well as a poet. Once he said of his profession, "I take care of babies and try to make them grow. I enjoy it. Nothing is more appropriate to a man than an interest in babies." Educated at the University of Pennsylvania and in Germany at the University of Leipzig, he returned to practice medicine in his home town, Rutherford, New Jersey. Between patients he found time for poetry. He believed that his medical practice and his writing helped sustain each other. For a man who once said he worked at his profession day in and day out and wrote only when he had nothing better to do, he was remarkably prolific. In addition to a great deal of poetry, he wrote many essays, four novels, three collections of short stories, and an autobiography. One especially notable work is *In the American Grain,* a brilliant personal and lyrical interpretation of American heroes and history.

Perhaps Williams's single most important work is *Paterson,* a long poem in five parts that is his own modern version of an epic poem. *Paterson* centers on the poet's relationship to a modern city, his own neighboring industrial city at the falls of the Passaic River in New Jersey. The poet-protagonist wanders about the city, perceiving its present, remembering its past, and meditating upon his own life in it, until he is able to experience and understand all aspects of the city and, in a sense, to become the city. In all his poems, his use of forms is highly original and has influenced many younger poets. The rhythm of his best poems is subtle but sure. In his poorest poems, his use of rhythm and line length—the basic devices of the free verse poet—seems limp and haphazard, but in much of his fine work, the exact way the poem appears on the printed page seems essential to the poem's success. As Randall Jarrell comments, "We want to explain *why* Williams's free verse . . . is successful, not to make fools of ourselves by arguing that it isn't."

Love Song

Sweep the house clean,
hang fresh curtains
in the windows
put on a new dress
and come with me!   5

The elm is scattering
its little loaves
of sweet smells
from a white sky!

Who shall hear of us   10
in the time to come?

Let him say there was
a burst of fragrance
from black branches.

The Red Wheelbarrow

so much depends
upon

a red wheel
barrow

glazed with rain   5
water

beside the white
chickens

The Widow's Lament in Springtime

Sorrow is my own yard
where the new grass
flames as it has flamed
often before but not
with the cold fire   5
that closes round me this year.
Thirtyfive years
I lived with my husband.
The plumtree is white today
with masses of flowers.   10
Masses of flowers
loaded the cherry branches
and color some bushes
yellow and some red

but the grief in my heart   15
is stronger than they
for though they were my joy
formerly, today I notice them
and turned away forgetting.
Today my son told me   20
that in the meadows,
at the edge of the heavy woods
in the distance, he saw
trees of white flowers.
I feel that I would like   25
to go there
and fall into those flowers
and sink into the marsh near them.

FOR STUDY AND DISCUSSION

1. How does "Love Song" justify its title? How are the last three lines of the poem an answer to lines 10–11? Do you think it is important that the branches are black? Explain. Is it appropriate to speak of "sweet smells" as "little loaves"? Why or why not? Does this poem bear out a description of Williams as a poet of the suburbs?

2. Explain the first line of "The Red Wheelbarrow." How is this line related to the precise manner in which the image of the red wheelbarrow is conveyed? What is the importance of colors in this poem? This poem is without conventional rhyme or meter. Can you sense a particular rhythm in it?

3. How, in "The Widow's Lament in Springtime," is the metaphor in the first line developed? How are the flowers used to unite the poem? In what way is the time of year important? Read the poem aloud and compare the rhythm and pace of the last nine lines with the first six. Describe the difference.

FOR COMPOSITION

Write a composition in which you compare the use of specific objects in "Domination of Black" and William Carlos Williams's "The Widow's Lament in Springtime." In your composition, consider the following points, among others: Which poem makes the more suggestive use of objects? Which poem tends more to give an impression of objects having a specific independent existence of their own? (In other words, which poem is more concerned with the real physical world?) Which poem seems to you to have a greater emotional effect? Cite lines and phrases from the two poems to support your points.

MARIANNE MOORE

(1887–)

Marianne Moore is a lively woman who is fond of gay, elaborate hats and is fascinated by animals. From 1929 to 1966, she lived in Brooklyn, New York, on the fifth floor of a yellow brick building. ("At all events there is in Brooklyn/ something that makes me feel at home.") Once she wrote a poem about the Dodgers in the World Series, before the team forsook Brooklyn for Los Angeles. ("A neat bunt, please; a cloud breaker, a drive . . .")

Miss Moore's poems are difficult, usually because their thought is so compressed. At first reading, they may not seem to be poetry at all but simply intelligent speech filled with striking images. She herself has commented in an interview, "What I write . . . could only be called poetry because there is no other category in which to put it." Yet many readers, among them such distinguished poets as T. S. Eliot and W. H. Auden, are sure that Marianne Moore is one of the best and most original poets of our time. To get at the special kinds of pleasure that are available in Miss Moore's poetry, the reader must be prepared to read very carefully and to be alive to the way her poems move quickly from object to idea. For example, in a poem about a steamroller she will say, "You lack half wit. You crush all particles down/ into close conformity, and then walk back and forth on them." Thus she not only describes the way a steamroller acts but also makes a comment about the way some people think. While the form of her poems may at first be puzzling, careful reading will disclose delicate, understated patterns of rhyme and meter. Of her poetic practice, she has written, "I dislike the reversed order of words [i.e., poetic inversions; see page 861]; don't like to be impeded by an unnecessary capital at the beginning of every line . . . I like straight writing . . . an effect of flowing continuity. . . ." She has been called a master of the "light rhyme," rhyme that is unnoticeable until the reader looks for it but which enhances the musical effect. Quotations abound in her poetry, a result of her wide reading. Of this practice, she writes, " 'Why the many quotation marks?' I am asked. . . . When a thing has been said so well that it could not be said better, why paraphrase it? Hence my writing is, if not a cabinet of fossils, a kind of collection of flies in amber."

Miss Moore was born near St. Louis, Missouri. After graduating from Bryn Mawr College, she taught commercial subjects at the Indian School in Carlisle, Pennsylvania. Among her students was the great athlete Jim Thorpe. Later she was a librarian at a branch of the New York Public Library. During the 1920's, she was editor of *The Dial,* an important literary magazine of the period.

Advertisements are one of Miss Moore's many interests, and once she participated in an interesting experiment in advertising. The Ford Motor Company, in the process of developing a new car, asked Miss Moore to suggest possible names for it. Stimulated by the project, she thought of Ford Silver Sword, Hurricane Hirundo, Resilient Bullet, and Thunder Crester. Eventually, however, the Ford Company decided to name the new car after Henry Ford's son Edsel. The car itself proved to be a commercial failure.

Miss Moore has continued to be a productive poet throughout the years. She has written that she does not write "for money *or* fame. To earn a living is needful, but it can be done in routine ways. One writes because one has a burning desire to objectify what it is indispensable to one's happiness to express. . . ."

Poetry

I, too, dislike it: there are things that are important beyond all this fiddle.
  Reading it, however, with a perfect contempt for it, one discovers in
  it, after all, a place for the genuine.
     Hands that can grasp, eyes
     that can dilate, hair that can rise   5
       if it must, these things are important not because a

high-sounding interpretation can be put upon them but because they are
  useful. When they become so derivative as to become unintelligible,
  the same thing may be said for all of us, that we
     do not admire what   10
     we cannot understand: the bat
       holding on upside down or in quest of something to

eat, elephants pushing, a wild horse taking a roll, a tireless wolf under
  a tree, the immovable critic twitching his skin like a horse that feels a flea,
      the base-
     ball fan, the statistician—   15
       nor is it valid
         to discriminate against "business documents and

schoolbooks"; all these phenomena are important. One must make a distinction
  however: when dragged into prominence by half poets, the result is not poetry,
  nor till the poets among us can be   20
     "literalists° of
     the imagination"—above
       insolence and triviality and can present

21. **literalists:** persons who insist on the exact meaning of a word.

"Poetry" from *Collected Poems* by Marianne Moore, copyright 1935 by Marianne Moore; renewed © 1963 by Marianne Moore and T. S. Eliot. Reprinted by permission of The Macmillan Company.

656   AMERICA AND THE MODERN WORLD

for inspection, "imaginary gardens with real toads in them," shall we have
it. In the meantime, if you demand on the one hand   25
          the raw material of poetry in
              all its rawness and
          that which is on the other hand
              genuine, then you are interested in poetry.

What Are Years?

What is our innocence,
what is our guilt? All are
    naked, none is safe. And whence
is courage: the unanswered question,
the resolute doubt—   5
dumbly calling, deafly listening—that
in misfortune, even death,
        encourages others
        and in its defeat, stirs

    the soul to be strong? He   10
sees deep and is glad, who
    accedes to mortality
and in his imprisonment, rises
upon himself as
the sea in a chasm, struggling to be   15
free and unable to be,
        in its surrendering
        finds its continuing.

    So he who strongly feels,
behaves. The very bird,   20
    grown taller as he sings, steels
his form straight up. Though he is captive,
his mighty singing
says, satisfaction is a lowly
thing, how pure a thing is joy.   25
        This is mortality,
        this is eternity.

FOR STUDY AND DISCUSSION

1. Do you find the beginning of "Poetry"
surprising? Why do you think Miss Moore
states, "I, too, dislike it"? What is the significance of "too"? How does she discover in
poetry "a place for the genuine"? Much of the

poem is a discussion about what are proper
and improper subjects for poetry. What subjects that are usually considered inappropriate for poetry does Miss Moore contend
are appropriate? When is "the result . . . not
poetry"? Explain how "the raw material of
poetry in/ all its rawness and/ that which is on
the other hand/ genuine" interact in poetry.
This poem may at first seem to differ little from
prose. Read it aloud and point out how internal
rhyme and end rhyme are used to strengthen
its sound pattern.

2. In "What Are Years?" how does Miss
Moore answer the question "Whence is courage"? How does the comparison of the soul
to the sea in the second stanza help to answer
the question? Consider the central image in
the third stanza. In what ways does it parallel
the image of the sea in the second stanza?
What is the connection between the poem and
its title?

3. One essay about Miss Moore, borrowing a phrase from "Poetry" (lines 21–22), is
called "A Literalist of the Imagination." How
is this an appropriate phrase for Miss Moore's
achievement as a poet?

4. In "A Note on the Notes" in her *Collected Poems,* Miss Moore explains the necessity to identify the sources of some of her lines
by saying that "in anything I have written,
there have been lines in which the chief interest is borrowed. . . ." Miss Moore's practice
of imbedding quotations, usually altered and
adapted, into her poems is illustrated by lines
17–18 of "Poetry," in which a quotation from
the diary of the great Russian novelist Leo
Tolstoy is used: "Poetry is verse: prose is not
verse. Or else poetry is everything with the
exception of business documents and schoolbooks." Again, the phrase "literalists of the
imagination" is adapted from a work by the
Irish poet William Butler Yeats.

Miss Moore's practice of using quotations is
an integral part of many of her poems. In your
opinion, is this practice always bad or good?
In poems as special as Miss Moore's do you
think the appearance of quotations is justified?

JOHN CROWE RANSOM

(1888–   )

The most striking characteristic of John Crowe Ransom's poems is their manner: courtly, witty, ironical. Their half-mocking tone both conceals and points to a humane sympathy that is deeper than that of many poets who are more openly emotional. Ransom's former student and fellow poet, Randall Jarrell, has perceptively described Ransom's manner as "a way of handling sentiment or emotion without even seeming sentimental or overemotional. . . . He was writing in an age in which the most natural feeling of tenderness, happiness, or sorrow was likely to be called sentimental. . . ." Some of the words Ransom uses and the courteous conversational tone of his poems may give the impression of an old-fashioned gentleman; but his method of indicating emotion by half pretending it doesn't exist is thoroughly modern.

The son of a minister, John Crowe Ransom was born in Pulaski, Tennessee, and was educated at Vanderbilt University and later in England, as a Rhodes Scholar at Oxford University. He was a professor of English at Vanderbilt and later at Kenyon College in Gambier, Ohio. A notable teacher of poets, he has been an important member of the Southern Agrarians, a group which advocated a return to the traditional principles of the rural South. Many of the Agrarians were also poets and critics who contributed to the influential Southern literary magazine, *The Fugitive,* which Ransom helped found. As much as any man, Ransom has been responsible for the Southern literary renaissance of this century.

As a teacher and writer, Ransom has been involved with both criticism and poetry. Robert Frost once sent him a telegram reading, "Hope you quit that criticism stuff," but Ransom continued to believe in the value of critical standards and methods, of criticism's importance in defining the place of poetry in the modern world. When Ransom moved to Kenyon College, he established the *Kenyon Review,* which has been one of the most important literary and critical magazines of our time. His book *The New Criticism,* published in 1941, provided the name for the influential critical movement which stresses the close analysis of literary works, especially poems. He himself has advocated the view that poetry is a special way of knowing reality and that, as a mode of investigating the world, it is just as important as scientific investigation. Occasionally he has been accused of encouraging an overly intellectual approach to poetry. Some critics claim that his poems lose emotional force through their exaggerated pursuit of subtle insights. Many of Ransom's readers feel, however, that he has written a number of unforgettable poems of great originality.

Janet Waking

Beautifully Janet slept
Till it was deeply morning. She woke then
And thought about her dainty-feathered hen,
To see how it had kept.

One kiss she gave her mother,   5
Only a small one gave she to her daddy
Who would have kissed each curl of his shining baby;
No kiss at all for her brother.

"Old Chucky, Old Chucky!" she cried,
Running on little pink feet upon the grass   10
To Chucky's house, and listening. But alas,
Her Chucky had died.

It was a transmogrifying° bee
Came droning down on Chucky's old bald head
And sat and put the poison. It scarcely bled,   15
But how exceedingly

And purply did the knot
Swell with the venom and communicate
Its rigor! Now the poor comb stood up straight
But Chucky did not.   20

So there was Janet
Kneeling on the wet grass, crying her brown hen
(Translated far beyond the daughters of men)
To rise and walk upon it.

And weeping fast as she had breath   25
Janet implored us, "Wake her from her sleep!"
And would not be instructed in how deep
Was the forgetful kingdom of death.

13. **transmogrifying:** transforming, often in a humorous or grotesque way.

Bells for John Whiteside's Daughter

There was such speed in her little body,
And such lightness in her footfall,
It is no wonder that her brown study°
Astonishes us all.

Her wars were bruited° in our high window.   5
We looked among orchard trees and beyond.
Where she took arms against her shadow
Or harried unto the pond

The lazy geese, like a snow cloud
Dripping their snow on the green grass,   10
Tricking and stopping, sleepy and proud,
Who cried in goose, Alas,

For the tireless heart within the little
Lady with rod that made them rise
From their noon apple-dreams, and scuttle   15
Goose-fashion under the skies!

But now go the bells, and we are ready;
In one house we are sternly stopped
To say we are vexed at her brown study,
Lying so primly propped.   20

3. **brown study:** the state of being in deep thought. 5. **bruited:** reported.

FOR STUDY AND DISCUSSION

1. In "Janet Waking," why do you think the poet indicates that Janet slept "beautifully"? Explain the use of the word "deeply" in line 2. How do these words help establish a playful attitude toward Janet? How does Janet's character emerge in the second stanza? What is her feeling about Chucky's death? What feeling do you think Ransom intends the reader to have? Cite phrases from the poem to support your answer. Is "Janet Waking" basically a playful poem? Explain. (Before answering, you may wish to read the last stanza aloud.)

2. In "Bells for John Whiteside's Daughter" the emotional response of the poet is carefully restrained. Point out words and phrases that limit the emotion of the poem. Do you think this restraint conceals strong emotions? Why or why not? Would the poem be better or worse if it were openly emotional? Give reasons for your answer.

3. What phrases in "Bells" indicate the poet's unwillingness to accept the fact that the little girl is dead? How does the account of the girl in life, in the middle three stanzas, make her death more poignant? Consider the alliteration of "sternly stopped" and "primly propped." Do the sounds of these words make the poem more touching, or do they, by calling attention to themselves, have an inappropriately trivial effect?

ARCHIBALD
MacLEISH
(1892–   )

Archibald MacLeish has been praised for his mastery of many different kinds of poetry, both formal and experimental, and for the range of subject matter in his poetry. He has written some deeply personal poems, and he has also written poems expressing the dreams and aspirations of the nation. The poems for which he will be most remembered are perhaps those which flow most directly from his feelings and awareness as a private person rather than from his statements as a national spokesman. As the poet and anthologist Louis Untermeyer has commented, MacLeish is distinguished for "the discipline he imposes on the flow of suggestions, on the very chaos of the unconscious. . . ."

Archibald MacLeish was born in Illinois and attended Yale University. During World War I he served in France as an ambulance driver and later as an artillery captain. After the war, he attended Harvard Law School and was for a time a lawyer in Boston.

He once declared, "I date the beginning of my life from 1923." In that year, deciding to devote all his energies to the writing of poetry, he left the United States to join other American writers who were living in France—among them, Ernest Hemingway and F. Scott Fitzgerald. Like most of the others, he returned to America before the end of the twenties, settling in Farmington, Connecticut. By 1930 he had published seven collections of poetry, including *The Pot of Earth, Streets in the Moon, The Hamlet of A. MacLeish,* and *New Found Land.* One of his most ambitious works is the long poem, *Conquistador,* which won a Pulitzer prize in 1933 and which deals with the Spanish conquest of Mexico. In order to prepare himself to write this poem, MacLeish followed the route of Cortes in Mexico.

Until the middle of the 1930's, MacLeish was a believer in the value of poetry for its own sake apart from any social value it might have. In a famous poem about poetry, "Ars Poetica," he wrote, "A poem should not mean/ But be." But gradually he found himself more and more involved in public issues and public life. His collection *Public Speech,* published in 1937, contains poems that are simpler and more direct than many of his earlier poems. Seeking a wider audience for what he had to say, he wrote several radio plays. His message was one of faith in the individual and of resistance to the growing forces of dictatorship. In 1939, he became Librarian of Congress. During World War II, he was also Assistant Director of the Office of War Information, and he served for a year as Assistant Secretary of State. He was a close advisor to President Franklin D. Roosevelt.

In 1939, MacLeish became the Boylston Professor of Rhetoric and Oratory at Harvard, a position which was first filled by John Quincy Adams and which is one of the most honored professorial chairs in the United States. MacLeish's *Collected Poems: 1917–1952,* hailed by the poet Richard Eberhart as "a major achievement in American letters," won the Bollingen prize, a Pulitzer prize, and a National Book Award. His play *J. B.,* a modern version of the Biblical story of Job, was successfully produced on Broadway in 1958.

Eleven

And summer mornings the mute child, rebellious,
Stupid, hating the words, the meanings, hating
The Think now, Think, the Oh but Think! would leave
On tiptoe the three chairs on the verandah
And crossing tree by tree the empty lawn   5
Push back the shed door and upon the sill
Stand pressing out the sunlight from his eyes
And enter and with outstretched fingers feel
The grindstone and behind it the bare wall
And turn and in the corner on the cool   10
Hard earth sit listening. And one by one,
Out of the dazzled shadow in the room,
The shapes would gather, the brown plowshare, spades,
Mattocks,° the polished helves° of picks, a scythe
Hung from the rafters, shovels, slender tines°   15
Glinting across the curve of sickles—shapes
Older than men were, the wise tools, the iron
Friendly with earth. And sit there, quiet, breathing
The harsh dry smell of withered bulbs, the faint
Odor of dung, the silence. And outside   20
Beyond the half-shut door the blind leaves
And the corn moving. And at noon would come,
Up from the garden, his hard crooked hands
Gentle with earth, his knees still earth-stained, smelling
Of sun, of summer, the old gardener, like   25
A priest, like an interpreter, and bend
Over his baskets.
                And they would not speak:
They would say nothing. And the child would sit there
Happy as though he had no name, as though
He had been no one: like a leaf, a stem,   30
Like a root growing—

14. **Mattocks:** tools similar to a pick.   **helves:** handles.   15. **tines:** the prongs of a pitchfork.

"Eleven" from *Collected Poems of Archibald MacLeish 1917–1952.* Reprinted by permission of Houghton Mifflin Company.

The End of the World

Quite unexpectedly as Vasserot
The armless ambidextrian° was lighting
A match between his great and second toe
And Ralph the lion was engaged in biting
The neck of Madame Sossman while the drum   5
Pointed, and Teeny was about to cough
In waltz-time swinging Jocko by the thumb—
Quite unexpectedly the top blew off:

And there, there overhead, there, there, hung over
Those thousands of white faces, those dazed eyes,   10
There in the starless dark, the poise, the hover,
There with vast wings across the canceled skies,
There in the sudden blackness, the black pall°
Of nothing, nothing, nothing—nothing at all.

2. **ambidextrian:** a word normally used to describe a person who can use both hands equally well.   13. **pall:** a dark covering.

FOR STUDY AND DISCUSSION

ELEVEN

1. What sensory experiences are recalled in this poem? To how many senses does the poem appeal?

2. Characterize the child in this poem. Do you think he is actually "mute," that is, physically incapable of speech? In what sense is he "stupid"? Explain how the third line of the poem clarifies the adjectives *mute, rebellious,* and *stupid*.
What does the boy derive from the shapes "Older than men were"? Why, in the last two lines of the poem, is he compared to a leaf, a stem, and a root?

3. Why is the gardener compared to a priest? Why does MacLeish emphasize the fact that the gardener and the boy do not speak? Find lines in the earlier part of the poem that deepen the meaning of lines 28–29.

4. The last line of the poem breaks off abruptly. Why do you think MacLeish chose to make this line incomplete?

THE END OF THE WORLD

1. What is the scene of this poem, at first? How is this scene enlarged in the second part of the poem? Explain how the eighth line of the poem grows in significance.

2. Do you think the basic comparison of this poem is an appropriate one? What view of the world emerges from this comparison? Do you agree with this view? Why or why not?

3. Review the material on the sonnet (page 212). Show how MacLeish makes use of the traditional opposition between octave and sestet in an Italian sonnet.

FOR COMPOSITION

Recall sensory experiences that were important to you as a child, using words that will convey the exact quality of these experiences. (Note how in "Eleven" MacLeish is able to show how exactly the boy reacted to certain sensory experiences: "... and with outstretched fingers feel/ The grindstone and behind it the bare wall/ And turn and in the corner on the cool/ Hard earth sit listening.")

"The End of the World" from *Collected Poems of Archibald MacLeish 1917–1952*. Reprinted by permission of Houghton Mifflin Company.

COUNTEE
CULLEN
(1903–1946)

Of his poetry, Countee Cullen wrote, "Most things I write I do for the sheer love of the music in them. Somehow I find my poetry of itself treating of the Negro, of his joys and his sorrows—mostly of the latter—and of the heights and depths of emotion I feel as a Negro." In his concern with joys and sorrows, he was able to create a number of poems that are relevant to all men everywhere. The subjects with which he was most involved—death, the complexities of love, the difficulties and rewards of human relationships—are largely traditional subjects of poetry, and in his use of metrical forms, he was also largely traditional. The many sonnets he wrote are evidence of his technical mastery. At best, his skillful poems are the moving testament of a sensitive individual, one who "sorrowed at" all human ills and who made many illuminating comments about the pleasures and burdens of being human.

Countee Cullen was born in New York City, the son of a minister. When he was fourteen he wrote a poem that was reprinted in *Modern School Magazine*. Another poem written while Cullen was still in his teens won first prize in a contest held by the Federation of Women's Clubs. In 1925 he graduated from New York University, where he was a member of Phi Beta Kappa, and the following year he received a master's degree in English literature from Harvard University. For several years he was assistant editor of the magazine *Opportunity*. Then he won a Guggenheim fellowship, which enabled him to spend a year abroad. During the last eleven years of his life, he was a teacher of French in New York City.

While still in college, Cullen wrote the poems that were collected in his first book, *Color,* published in 1925. Over the years, other collections followed, including *Copper Sun* and *The Ballad of the Brown Girl*. His translation of *Medea,* a tragedy by the ancient Greek dramatist Euripides, was set to music by the distinguished American composer Virgil Thompson. Shortly before his death, Cullen selected what he considered his best poems to be included in his final collection, *On These I Stand*. His achievement as a poet has been praised by his fellow poet Alfred Kreymborg, who called him "an authentic poet some of whose lyrics vie with the finest in America." In addition to his poetry, Countee Cullen was the author of a children's fantasy about a cat (*My Lives and How I Lost Them*) and a novel (*One Way to Heaven*), and was the editor of *Caroling Dusk: An Anthology of Verse by Negro Poets*. His last published work was a play, *St. Louis Woman,* written in collaboration with Arna Bontemps.

Sonnet

Some for a little while do love, and some for long;
And some rare few forever and for aye;
Some for the measure of a poet's song,
And some the ribbon width of a summer's day.
Some on a golden crucifix do swear,   5
And some in blood do plight a fickle troth;
Some struck divinely mad may only stare,
And out of silence weave an iron oath.

So many ways love has none may appear
The bitter best, and none the sweetest worst;   10
Strange food the hungry have been known to bear,
And brackish water slakes an utter thirst.
It is a rare and tantalizing fruit
Our hands reach for, but nothing absolute.

Any Human to Another

The ills I sorrow at
Not me alone
Like an arrow,
Pierce to the marrow,
Through the fat   5
And past the bone.

Your grief and mine
Must intertwine
Like sea and river,
Be fused and mingle,   10
Diverse yet single,
Forever and forever.

Let no man be so proud
And confident,
To think he is allowed   15
A little tent
Pitched in a meadow
Of sun and shadow
All his little own.

Joy may be shy, unique,   20
Friendly to a few,
Sorrow never scorned to speak
To any who
Were false or true.

Your every grief   25
Like a blade
Shining and unsheathed
Must strike me down.
Of bitter aloes° wreathed,
My sorrow must be laid   30
On your head like a crown.

29. **aloes** (al'ōz): the leaves of the aloe plant, whose bitter dried juice is used as a drug.

FOR STUDY AND DISCUSSION

1. Does "Sonnet" divide naturally into two or four parts? How does the final couplet resolve the poem?

2. What, according to the poem, is the necessary relationship of "any human to another"? What unites them? Why in the final lines is sorrow compared to a crown? Why is it appropriate that the crown should be "wreathed" of "bitter aloes"? What, in Cullen's view, is the difference between joy and sorrow?

W. H. AUDEN
(1907–   )

It is difficult to decide whether Auden is more properly considered an English or an American poet. He spent the first thirty-two years of his life in England and during the 1930's was considered one of the leading English poets. However, since settling in America in 1939 (becoming an American citizen in 1946), he has shown in many of his poems that he takes his new nationality seriously. Poetically, he is important to the entire English-speaking world.

Wystan Hugh Auden's father was a doctor and professor of public health. As a boy, the poet's interests were entirely scientific. At Oxford University, he was the dominant figure in his circle of students, many of whom (such as Stephen Spender) became noted writers. In addition to his literary ability, Auden was a wonderful mimic who delighted in assuming comic roles. He was also a great walker and is remembered following his favorite route past the Oxford gas works and the city dump, talking incessantly and moving with large, ungainly strides.

Auden's early poetry began to appear while he was teaching school in England and Scotland. The poems of this period reflect his impatience with English middle-class society in the years between the two world wars. The worst of these poems reveal too great a straining at cleverness. Most of the best poems are exhilaratingly witty, with an intellectual drive that carries with it an emotional power. Two plays, written with Christopher Isherwood for the Group Theatre in London—*The Dog Beneath the Skin* and *The Ascent of F-6*—demonstrate Auden's gift for writing songs. Although Auden became concerned with social questions during the thirties, he was never deeply involved in politics.

An important reason for Auden's residence in the United States is the openness of this country, an absence of the strong and limiting European sense of tradition. To some extent, Auden must have felt that Europe near the end of the thirties was a society that was slowly dying, and that his residence in a young nation would bring with it new life. Since settling here, Auden's literary productivity has continued to be enormous, and much of his later work is explicitly religious in its significance. In one of his most famous poems, "September 1, 1939" he contemplates the moral state of the world, "the international wrong," and man's avoidance of the truth: "We must love one another or die." He has written three ambitious long poems: *For the Time Being,* a modern Christmas oratorio in which Auden explores the significance of the Nativity for modern man; *The Sea and the Mirror,* a discourse in poetic form on the relationship between life and art, which takes the form of a commentary on Shakespeare's *The Tempest;* and *The Age of Anxiety,* a work which presents four individuals attempting to find a way out of their spiritual dilemmas. In recent years, Auden's poetry has tended to become mellower, reflecting a spirit that is now less urgent in its denunciation of evil and a point of view that is as often gently humorous as it is satirical. His poetry has not lost its moral quality, however, nor has it abandoned its concern with the troubles of the modern world. In addition to poetry, Auden has published brilliant volumes of criticism and notable anthologies. He has been especially interested in the problems of writing librettos for opera. With his friend Chester Kallman, he wrote the words for Igor Stravinsky's opera, *The Rake's Progress*, and translated into English the librettos of Mozart's operas, *Don Giovanni* and *The Magic Flute*.

Auden's poetry has an immensely varied vitality. Reflecting a great number of influences, it reveals the poet's delight in experimenting with a multitude of forms and expressing himself in a wide range of tones, from satiric wit to simple reverence. His great concern has been with human life and with human love, the force that gives life meaning. He looks on poetry as a fundamentally serious undertaking, one that has its own special obligations.

Look, Stranger

Look, stranger, on this island now
The leaping light for your delight discovers,°
Stand stable here
And silent be,
That through the channels of the ear   5
May wander like a river
The swaying sound of the sea.

Here at the small field's ending pause
When the chalk wall falls to the foam, and its tall ledges
Oppose the pluck   10
And knock of the tide,
And the shingle° scrambles after the suck-
ing surf, and the gull lodges
A moment on its sheer side.

Far off like floating seeds the ships   15
Diverge on urgent voluntary errands;
And the full view
Indeed may enter
And move in memory as now these clouds do,
That pass the harbor mirror   20
And all the summer through the water saunter.

2. **discovers:** here, reveals.   12. **shingle:** gravel.

Law, Say the Gardeners

Law, say the gardeners, is the sun,
Law is the one
All gardeners obey
Tomorrow, yesterday, today.

Law is the wisdom of the old,   5
The impotent grandfathers shrilly scold;
The grandchildren put out a treble° tongue,
Law is the senses of the young.

Law, says the priest with a priestly look,
Expounding to an unpriestly people,   10
Law is the words in my priestly book,
Law is my pulpit and my steeple.

Law, says the judge as he looks down his
   nose,
Speaking clearly and most severely,
Law is as I've told you before,   15
Law is as you know I suppose,
Law is but let me explain it once more,
Law is The Law.

Yet law-abiding scholars write:
Law is neither wrong nor right,   20
Law is only crimes
Punished by places and by times,
Law is the clothes men wear
Anytime, anywhere,
Law is Good-morning and Good-night.   25

Others say, Law is our Fate;
Others say, Law is our State;
Others say, others say
Law is no more,
Law is gone away.   30

And always the loud angry crowd
Very angry and very loud
Law is We,
And always the soft idiot softly Me.

If we, dear, know we know no more   35
Than they about the law,
If I no more than you
Know what we should and should not do
Except that all agree
Gladly or miserably   40
That the law is
And that all know this,
If therefore thinking it absurd
To identify Law with some other word,
Unlike so many men   45
I cannot say Law is again,
No more than they can we suppress
The universal wish to guess
Or slip out of our own position
Into an unconcerned condition.   50

Although I can at least confine
Your vanity and mine
To stating timidly
A timid similarity,
We shall boast anyway: 55
Like love I say.

Like love we don't know where or why
Like love we can't compel or fly°
Like love we often weep
Like love we seldom keep.   60

7. **treble:** here, referring to a high-pitched, shrill sound.

58. **fly:** here, flee.

Epitaph on a Tyrant

Perfection, of a kind, was what he was after,
And the poetry he invented was easy to understand;
He knew human folly like the back of his hand,
And was greatly interested in armies and fleets;
When he laughed, respectable senators burst with laughter,   5
And when he cried, the little children died in the streets.

FOR STUDY AND DISCUSSION

LOOK, STRANGER

1. Does this poem appeal more to the eye or to the ear? Why?

2. Whom does Auden address as "stranger"? Why do you think he uses this word?

3. What does Auden mean by the "harbor mirror"? Why does he compare it to memory?

4. Consider Auden's choice of the word *saunter* at the end of the poem. Substitute other words close to *saunter* in meaning and explain how these substitutions would change the effect of the poem.

LAW, SAY THE GARDENERS

1. Explain what law means, according to the poem, to the gardener, to the old, to the young, to the priest, to the judge, and to the scholar. How are the definitions appropriate to these various groups?

2. Explain why the "soft idiot" says "softly Me" (line 34). How is the idiot contrasted to the "loud angry crowd"?

3. This poem might be divided into two parts. The first part, lines 1–34, shows that law means many different things to different people. The second part, building from this premise, explores what law should mean to the poet and the person whom he addresses as "dear." Why does his discussion of law in lines 35–50 prompt the poet to make his final statement "timidly"? Why does he make a contrast between "timid" and "boast" in lines 54–55?

4. This poem depends a good deal for its effect on logic, wit, and ingenious arguments. Yet it is also a love poem. Do you think that logic, wit, and ingenuity are out of place in a love poem? Why or why not?

EPITAPH ON A TYRANT

1. What kind of "perfection" do you think the tyrant sought?

2. In your opinion, what is meant by the "poetry" the tyrant invented? How is the fact related in the fifth line disturbing?

3. Do you think that Auden is writing about a particular tyrant or that he is making a comment on the nature of tyranny? Explain. To what tyrants you have read about might this poem be applied?

DEVICES OF SOUND

"Look, Stranger" is almost as heavily dependent on devices of sound as is Poe's "The Bells." One important device in the poem is *internal rhyme*—rhyme that occurs within a poetic line—as in line 9: "When the chalk *wall* falls to the foam, and its *tall* ledges." The poem also makes important use of *assonance, consonance*, and *alliteration* (see page 122).

1. Find examples of the use of sound devices in "Look, Stranger."

2. Compare the use of sound devices in this poem with their use in "The Bells." Which poem, in your opinion, uses these devices more successfully? Why? Which poem uses them less obviously, more subtly? Do you think subtlety is an advantage or a disadvantage in this kind of poem? Explain.

FOR COMPOSITION

"Law, Say the Gardeners" examines a large, general word in terms of what it means to specific groups. Write a composition in which you show how another such word, like "happiness" or "success," might mean different things to different people. Conclude with an explanation of what the word means to you.

THEODORE
ROETHKE
(1908–1963)

A dancing bear, an image Theodore Roethke used in a poem to express his attempts to master the graces of poetry, could well have been applied to the poet in a physical sense. He was a big blond man who was surprisingly agile on the tennis court and who was varsity tennis coach at several of the colleges where he taught. He once wrote that he had lived "very quietly and then foolishly and violently." His poetry reflects the different aspects of his life, especially the violence and strain and the struggle toward serenity and wisdom. Often his search for fulfillment was reflected in his poetry by an identification with plants, with the green peace of solidly rooted and slowly growing things. Among his most impressive achievements are a number of long poems "which try in their rhythms to catch the very movement of the mind itself, to trace the spiritual history of a protagonist . . . of all haunted and harried men. . . ."

Roethke was born in Saginaw, Michigan, and was educated at the University of Michigan and Harvard. His early experiences in a "beautiful greenhouse" owned by his father and uncle colored much of his poetry. Roethke began to write poetry seriously when he was at Harvard, where the encouragement of a teacher convinced him that he should follow his talent and vocation. For a good part of his life, he made a living by teaching writing at Bennington College, Pennsylvania State University, and the University of Washington. He wrote slowly, and it took him ten years to write enough poems for his slim first book, *Open House,* published in 1941. In 1954 he received the Pulitzer prize for *The Waking,* and in 1965 he was posthumously awarded the National Book Award for poetry for *The Far Field.*

Roethke wrote many compressed poems in tight stanza forms. These often give an impression of a violence that is under powerful control and show the acknowledged influence of the great modern Irish poet, William Butler Yeats. Roethke also wrote many long, highly personal and expressive poems in free verse. In these the flow of the lines often reflects the flow of his own aspiration to put himself "among the happy poets." Roethke knew that poetry "is shot through with appeals to the unconscious, to the fears and desires that go far back into childhood, into the imagination of the race." His own poetry made powerful use of such appeals. The poet Stanley Kunitz has noted the "ferocity of Roethke's imagination," and W. H. Auden has paid tribute to Roethke's rare achievement, "both to remember and to transform his humiliations into something beautiful."

Night Journey

Now as the train bears west,
Its rhythm rocks the earth,
And from my Pullman berth
I stare into the night
While others take their rest.   5
Bridges of iron lace,
A suddenness of trees,
A lap of mountain mist
All cross my line of sight,
Then a bleak wasted place,   10
And a lake below my knees.
Full on my neck I feel
The straining at a curve;
My muscles move with steel,
I wake in every nerve.   15
I watch a beacon swing
From dark to blazing bright;
We thunder through ravines
And gullies washed with light.
Beyond the mountain pass   20
Mist deepens on the pane;
We rush into a rain
That rattles double glass.
Wheels shake the roadbed stone,
The pistons jerk and shove,   25
I stay up half the night
To see the land I love.

"Night Journey" from *Words for the Wind* by Theodore Roethke, copyright 1940 by Theodore Roethke. Reprinted by permission of Doubleday & Company, Inc.

Elegy for Jane

(My student, thrown by a horse)

I remember the neckcurls, limp and damp as tendrils,
And her quick look, a sidelong pickerel smile;
And how, once startled into talk, the light syllables leaped for her,
And she balanced in the delight of her thought,
A wren, happy, tail into the wind,   5
Her song trembling the twigs and small branches.
The shade sang with her;
The leaves, their whispers turned to kissing;
And the mold sang in the bleached valleys under the rose.

Oh, when she was sad, she cast herself down into such a pure depth, 10
Even a father could not find her:
Scraping her cheek against straw;
Stirring the clearest water.

My sparrow, you are not here,
Waiting like a fern, making a spiney shadow.   15
The sides of wet stones cannot console me,
Nor the moss, wound with the last light.

If only I could nudge you from this sleep,
My maimed darling, my skittery pigeon.
Over this damp grave I speak the words of my love: 20
I, with no rights in this matter,
Neither father nor lover.

FOR STUDY AND DISCUSSION

1. In "Night Journey," what is the point of view of the poet in relation to the landscape? Cite lines appealing to various senses. How does the rhythm of the poem catch the impression of a moving train? What nouns and verbs are especially effective in conveying a sense of motion?

2. In "Elegy for Jane," how does the poet use images to convey his feeling for the girl? How is the contrast between life and death emphasized? Would you say that rhythm is an important element of this free verse poem? Explain your answer.

FOR COMPOSITION

Compare the treatment of death and mourning in "Elegy for Jane" and John Crowe Ransom's "Bells for John Whiteside's Daughter." Which poem is more openly emotional? Would you judge that one poem is a more effective statement of grief than the other, or do you think that the poems are equally effective in their different ways? Cite lines and phrases from the poems to support your general statements.

Ransom's poem uses a conventional meter while Roethke's poem is in free verse. In which poem is rhythm more important?

GWENDOLYN
BROOKS
(1917–   )

The poetry of Gwendolyn Brooks has been praised for deepening the significance of personal and social experiences so that these experiences become universal in their implication. She has also been praised for her "sense of form, which is basic . . . [and] remarkable." Many of her poems are concerned with a Negro community named Bronzeville, on the south side of Chicago. Her literary skill makes Bronzeville more than just a place on a map. This community, like all important literary places (Robinson's Tilbury Town and Masters' Spoon River, for example) becomes a testing ground of personality, a place where the raw material of experience is shaped by imagination and where the joys and trials of being human are both sung and judged. The qualities for which Miss Brooks's poetry are noted are (as one critic has pointed out) "boldness, invention, a daring to experiment, and a naturalness that does not scorn literature but absorbs it. . . ."

Gwendolyn Brooks was born in Topeka, Kansas, but has lived almost all of her life in Chicago. In 1936, she graduated from Wilson Junior College and then worked for several years as a typist. She married Henry Blakely in 1939 and has several children.

Her love for poetry began early. At the age of seven, she "began to put rhymes together," and when she was thirteen, one of her poems was published in a children's magazine. During her teens she contributed more than seventy-five poems to a Chicago newspaper. In 1941, she began to attend a class in writing poetry at the South Side Community Art Center, and several years later, her poems began to appear in *Poetry* and other magazines. Her first collection of poems, *A Street in Bronzeville,* was published in 1945. Four years later, *Annie Allen,* her second collection of poems, appeared. Called "essentially a novel," it is divided into three parts—"Notes from the Childhood and the Girlhood," "The Anniad," and "The Womanhood"—and tells the story of Annie's life through a series of poems. In 1950, *Annie Allen* was awarded a Pulitzer prize for poetry. A novel, *Maud Martha,* about a young Negro girl growing up in Chicago, published in 1953, was praised for its warmth and insights. In 1963, her *Selected Poems* appeared.

Miss Brooks has received a number of other awards and honors, including several Poetry Workshop Awards of the Midwest Writers' Conference, two Guggenheim Fellowships, an award from the American Academy of Arts and Letters, and the Eunice Tietjens Memorial Award given by *Poetry* magazine.

In Honor of David Anderson Brooks, My Father

July 30, 1883—November 21, 1959

A dryness is upon the house
My father loved and tended.
Beyond his firm and sculptured door
His light and lease have ended.

He walks the valleys, now—replies   5
To sun and wind forever.
No more the cramping chamber's chill,
No more the hindering fever.

Now out upon the wide clean air
My father's soul revives,   10
All innocent of self-interest
And the fear that strikes and strives.

He who was Goodness, Gentleness,
And Dignity is free,
Translates to public Love   15
Old private Charity.

Mrs. Small

Mrs. Small went to the kitchen for her pocketbook
And came back to the living room with a peculiar look
And the coffee pot.
Pocketbook. Pot.
Pot. Pocketbook.   5

The insurance man was waiting there
With superb and cared-for hair.
His face did not have much time.
He did not glance with sublime
Love upon the little plump tan woman   10
With the half-open mouth and the half-mad eyes
And the smile half-human
Who stood in the middle of the living-room floor planning apple pies
And graciously offering him a steaming coffee pot.
Pocketbook. Pot.   15

"Oh!" Mrs. Small came to her senses,
Peered earnestly through thick lenses,
Jumped terribly. This, too, was a mistake,
Unforgivable no matter how much she had to bake.
For there can be no whiter whiteness than this one: 20
An insurance man's shirt on its morning run.
This Mrs. Small now soiled
With a pair of brown
Spurts (just recently boiled)
Of the "very best coffee in town."   25

"The best coffee in town is what you make, Delphine! There is
    none dandier!"
Those were the words of the pleased Jim Small—
Who was no bandier of words at all.
Jim Small was likely to give you a good swat
When he was *not*   30
Pleased. He was, absolutely, no bandier.

"I don't know where my mind is this morning,"
Said Mrs. Small, scorning
Apologies! For there was so much
For which to apologize! Oh such   35
Mountains of things, she'd never get anything done
If she begged forgiveness for each one.

She paid him.

But apologies and her hurry would not mix.
The six   40
Daughters were a-yell, a-scramble, in the hall. The four
Sons (horrors) could not be heard any more.

No.
The insurance man would have to glare
Idiotically into her own sterile stare   45
A moment—then depart,
Leaving her to release her heart
And dizziness

And silence her six
And mix   50
Her spices and core
And slice her apples, and find her four.
Continuing her part
Of the world's business.

FOR STUDY AND DISCUSSION

1. In the poem in memory of her father, what qualities in her father does Miss Brooks admire? Why does she write that he "walks the valleys, now" (line 5)? Describe the contrasts in the poem between indoors and outdoors and, in the last two lines, between public and private. How are the two contrasts related?

2. Why is Mrs. Small's smile described as "half-human" and her eyes as "half-mad"? Are these adjectives a description of a woman driven to the point of madness by her troubles, or merely of a woman who, because of her many cares, is giving only half a mind to what she is doing? Or is there another reason for the adjectives? Why, near the end of the poem, is she left "to release her heart"? In what way is this poem about the failure of two fellow creatures to reach out and understand and love one another? (In answering this question, consider that neither Mrs. Small nor the salesman have much time and that the salesman is described as not glancing "with sublime/ Love upon the little plump tan woman . . .")

3. Does your attitude toward Mrs. Small change as you read the poem? Why or why not? What is your final attitude toward Mrs. Small?

ROBERT LOWELL

(1917–   )

Robert Lowell is regarded by many readers of poetry as the finest American poet of his generation. Most of his poetry is somber; some of it is harsh. Much of it reflects a personality tormented by the contradictions and evils of the modern world, as he sees it. Occasionally his poetry is overweighted with literary allusions and a violence of language that seems unjustified. At its finest, it is strikingly intense, the complex expression of a man of deep feeling and learning who is also a gifted poet.

Robert Lowell is a Boston Lowell. Amy Lowell (page 637), a poet writing earlier in the century, was a relative, and James Russell Lowell (page 197) was his grandfather's brother. Robert Lowell has described his boyhood in Boston as the son of a naval officer in his memoir, "91 Revere Street." He attended Harvard University for two years, then he moved on to Kenyon College, where he studied with John Crowe Ransom (page 658). His first slim book of poems, *The Land of Unlikeness,* appeared in 1944 but did not receive much attention. In 1946, his second collection, *Lord Weary's Castle,* convinced many readers that an important new poet was at work. This volume won a Pulitzer prize the following year. Four years later, a third book, *The Mills of the Kavanaughs,* containing a long story poem and several very fine dramatic monologues, was published. Almost all of Lowell's poetry published thus far had been written in tight traditional forms. He had written a number of sonnets and, in a number of longer poems, made the most original use in our time of the pentameter couplet. Many of the poems were preoccupied with the guilt which Lowell feels is embodied in the New England past and reflected in its present, a guilt which he, as a member of one of New England's oldest and most distinguished families, had inherited. ("Our fathers wrung their bread from stocks and stones/ And fenced their gardens with the Redman's bones.")

In his poems since *The Mills of the Kavanaughs,* Lowell has moved in the direction of less formal, more personal verse. His later poems, collected in *Life Studies* and *For the Union Dead,* are concerned more with the difficulties of Lowell's personal situation than with the burden of the past. He has tended to write more simply and has done a good deal of experimenting with free verse, although he still makes impressive use of traditional meters and rhyme. In the later poetry, as much as in the earlier, there is evidence of a formidable poetic technique, of a poet who trained himself rigorously in his craft, writing his early poems in blank verse to get the sense of them on paper and then rewriting them in rhymed couplets to tighten their structure.

Water

It was a Maine lobster town—
each morning boatloads of hands
pushed off for granite
quarries on the islands,

and left dozens of bleak   5
white frame houses stuck
like oyster shells
on a hill of rock,

and below us, the sea lapped
the raw little match-stick   10
mazes of a weir,°
where the fish for bait were trapped.

Remember? We sat on a slab of rock.
From this distance in time,
it seems the color   15
of iris, rotting and turning purpler,

but it was only
the usual gray rock
turning the usual green
when drenched by the sea.   20

The sea drenched the rock
at our feet all day,
and kept tearing away
flake after flake.

One night you dreamed   25
You were a mermaid clinging to a wharf-
    pile,
and trying to pull
off the barnacles with your hands.

We wished our two souls
might return like gulls   30
to the rock. In the end,
the water was too cold for us.

11. **weir** (wir): a fence placed in water in order to
trap fish.

FOR STUDY AND DISCUSSION

1. This poem is actually about a relationship between two people. What happened to
them? What does the last line of the poem contribute to your understanding of the relationship?

2. The fourth and fifth stanzas of the poem
are concerned with the color of a "slab of
rock." How is the color of the rock symbolically related to the relationship of the two
people?

3. How would you describe the tone and
mood of this poem? Cite details that contribute
to the tone and mood.

Hawthorne

Follow its lazy main street lounging
from the alms house° to Gallows Hill°
along a flat, unvaried surface
covered with wooden houses
aged by yellow drain   5
like the unhealthy hair of an old dog.
You'll walk to no purpose
in Hawthorne's Salem.

I cannot resilver the smudged plate.°

I drop to Hawthorne, the customs officer,°
measuring coal and mostly trying to keep
    warm—   11
to the stunted black schooner,
the dismal South-end dock,
the wharf-piles with their fungus of ice.
On State Street°   15
a steeple with a glowing dial-clock
measures the weary hours,
the merciless march of professional feet.

2. **alms house:** poorhouse. **Gallows Hill:** a hill in
Salem, Massachusetts, where nineteen supposed
witches were hanged. 9. **resilver ... plate:** Early
photographs were taken on a metal plate with a silver
coating. 10. **customs officer:** Hawthorne served as
a customs officer in Boston and in Salem (see page
236). 15. **State Street:** the principal street in the
business district of Boston.

Even this shy distrustful ego
sometimes walked on top of the blazing
   roof,   20
and felt those flashes
that char the discharged cells° of the brain.

Look at the faces—
Longfellow, Lowell, Holmes and Whittier!
Study the grizzled silver of their beards.
Hawthorne's picture,   26
however, has a blond mustache
and golden General Custer° scalp.
He looks like a Civil War officer.
He shines in the firelight. His hard   30
survivor's smile is touched with fire.
Leave him alone for a moment or two,
and you'll see him with his head
bent down, brooding, brooding,
eyes fixed on some chip,   35
some stone, some common plant,
the commonest thing,
as if it were the clue.
The disturbed eyes rise,
furtive, foiled, dissatisfied   40
from meditation on the true
and insignificant.

22. **discharged cells:** a reference to the cells of a battery. 28. **General Custer:** George Armstrong Custer (1839–1876), who served as a general in the War Between the States and whose troops were massacred by the Sioux at the Battle of the Little Big Horn, had flowing blond hair.

COMMENTARY

A good many American writers do not think of themselves as isolated figures striving only to express themselves. They are aware of themselves as part of a tradition which they must face up to and which they can help shape. As a member of an old New England family which has produced many distinguished men and women, including two important poets, Robert Lowell is probably more aware of tradition than most. His elegy "The Quaker Graveyard in Nantucket" shows a detailed knowledge of Melville's *Moby Dick*. He has written three poems about Jonathan Edwards and that divine's wrestling with the problems of good and evil. Like the novelist Henry James, who found in the works of Hawthorne a confirmation of his ambition to become a literary artist, Lowell too draws sustenance from Hawthorne's example. The poem "Hawthorne" is an attempt to explain why.

This poem, which shows detailed knowledge of Hawthorne's works, is a good example of how a poet can shape to his own purposes what he has found in his reading. The opening portions of the poem draw heavily on Hawthorne's writings, and even the later passages seem to have been developed from hints found in Hawthorne's work. Lowell's description of the meandering main street of Salem is based closely on a sentence in "The Custom House," the introductory essay to *The Scarlet Letter*. He added the reference to "yellow drain like the unhealthy hair of an old dog," cut out words he considered unnecessary, and subtly altered the rhythm.

The description of the lethargic customs officer at work in Boston is derived from a letter in which Hawthorne wrote his wife, "Your husband has been measuring coal all day, aboard a black little British schooner, in a dismal dock at the North end of the city. Most of the time he paced the deck to keep himself warm." Later in the letter Hawthorne mentions a church steeple near the Bunker Hill monument "with the dial of clock upon it, whereby I was enabled to measure the march of the weary hours." Lowell has sharpened the image of the schooner by making it "stunted" instead of merely "little," and he has made the clock more vivid. The image of "wharf-piles with their fungus of ice" is Lowell's own invention. His most notable change was to move the steeple to State Street, the center of Boston's business district, and to transport the dock to the South end. This shift enabled him to include not only Hawthorne's impression of the dreary progress of time, but also a suggestion of the dispiriting routines of those concerned only with material things.

Lowell's lines describing Hawthorne's walking on top of the blazing roof were probably based on the novelist's description of himself pacing the Custom House and developing the plot of *The Scarlet Letter*. Lowell's use of images drawn from photography, which originally required a silvered plate, was perhaps suggested by Hawthorne's describing his imagination at this time as "a tarnished mirror." The images of the flashes which burned into Hawthorne's brain and of the fire which touched "his hard survivor's smile" recall a passage in "The Custom House" telling how the glow of a coal fire helped to stimulate his creativity and to convert his imagined characters from pale "snow images into men and women."

Hawthorne's casual reference, in another part of the Custom House essay, to his picking Indian arrowheads from a field near the Old Manse in Concord seems particularly to have impressed Lowell. From this clue he constructed the powerful concluding stanza. Its intensity comes from the use of rhyme, the tightening of the rhythm, and from the force of repetition as we watch Hawthorne with head "bent down, brooding, brooding." It is in this last section of the poem that Hawthorne's significance to Lowell most clearly emerges. It is Hawthorne, the seeker, the artist who probes the commonplace objects of life ("some stone, some common plant,/ the commonest thing") to penetrate to the cosmic mystery behind them, who fascinates Lowell. Yet, as Lowell must admit, Hawthorne registered the mystery of life but not its solution. Always "The disturbed eyes rise, furtive, foiled, dissatisfied . . ." What Hawthorne (and with him Lowell) has observed—the hill where supposed witches were hung, the dreary streets of Salem, the "dismal South-end dock" in Boston, and State Street which bears "the merciless march of professional feet"—all the sights which shaped Hawthorne's tragic vision of life, these must remain the pieces of an unresolved puzzle that a poet or storyteller may use in his art but which he can never wholly explain.

FOR STUDY AND DISCUSSION

1. Explain the significance of the metaphor involving photography in line 9. What, do you think, are the implications of "the smudged plate"? What, for example, is on the plate? Can it be smudged in more ways than one?

2. Why does Lowell give Hawthorne a "hard/ survivor's smile"? Do you think the comparison to Custer is appropriate? Explain. Why does he contrast Hawthorne with "Longfellow, Lowell, Holmes and Whittier"?

3. Explain the phrase which Lowell gives great emphasis by placing it last: "The true/ and insignificant." What relation has this phrase to the underlying theme of the poem?

FOR COMPOSITION

Write a composition in which you consider how Robert Frost or Carl Sandburg might write a poem in which he confronts some great American writer of the past who has been especially important to him. Give reasons for the choice and indicate what quotations from the writer might be incorporated (perhaps in adapted form) into the poem. Indicate how Frost (or Sandburg) might draw his themes from a study of the work of the earlier writer. (You may prefer to write the poem itself, in the manner of Frost or Sandburg, instead of writing a description of it.)

RICHARD WILBUR
(1921–)

Of all modern American poets, Richard Wilbur is probably the most graceful and elegant. In reviewing Wilbur's second collection, Randall Jarrell called him "delicate, charming, and skillful. . . . His poems not only make you use, but make you eager to use, words like *attractive* and *appealing* and *engaging.*" Wilbur conceives of the poem as a window opening upon a part of the world, establishing a dynamic relationship between the mind of the poet and what is outside it. The subject of much of his poetry is suggested by the titles of two poems: " 'A World Without Objects Is a Sensible Emptiness' " and "Love Calls Us to the Things of This World." However, he is as much concerned with the technical qualities of a poem as with the relationships examined by it. He has said that a critic once labeled him as "one of the 'New Formalists,' and I will accept the label provided it be understood that to try to revive the force of rhyme and other formal devices, by reconciling them with experimental gains of the past several decades, is itself sufficiently experimental." Wilbur has been criticized for not being ambitious enough as a poet, for letting his taste and gift for elegant language set too great limits on his achievements. One critic wrote, "Mr. Wilbur never goes too far, but he never goes far enough," and imagined readers saying to him "in encouraging impatient voices: 'Come on, *take a chance!*'" Despite his limited range, however, Wilbur is one of our best poets and has written some of the most polished poetry of our time. His most recent poems are generally more pithy and more directly concerned with moral values than his earlier work. He dares now not only to observe and compare but to comment and advise.

The son of an artist, Richard Wilbur was born in New York City but grew up in rural northern New Jersey. He edited the student paper at Amherst College. While he was serving in Italy during World War II, he began to write poetry seriously. Of this focus of interest, he has commented, "One does not use poetry for its major purposes, as a means of organizing oneself and the world, until one's world somehow gets out of hand." After the war, he was a junior fellow and assistant professor of English at Harvard University. He now teaches at Wesleyan University in Middletown, Connecticut. In 1957, his collection, *Things of This World,* received both the Pulitzer prize and the National Book Award. In addition to his lyric poems, Mr. Wilbur has also published a verse translation of Molière's play *The Misanthrope,* and with Leonard Bernstein and Lillian Hellman he collaborated on the opera *Candide.*

Year's End

Now winter downs the dying of the year,
And night is all a settlement of snow;
From the soft street the rooms of houses show
A gathered light, a shapen atmosphere,
Like frozen-over lakes whose ice is thin   5
And still allows some stirring down within.

I've known the wind by water banks to shake
The late leaves down, which frozen where they fell
And held in ice as dancers in a spell,
Fluttered all winter long into a lake;   10
Graved on the dark in gestures of descent,
They seemed their own most perfect monument.

There was perfection in the death of ferns
Which laid their fragile cheeks against the stone
A million years. Great mammoths overthrown   15
Composedly have made their long sojourns,
Like palaces of patience, in the gray
And changeless lands of ice. And at Pompeii°

The little dog° lay curled and did not rise
But slept the deeper as the ashes rose   20
And found the people incomplete, and froze
The random hands, the loose unready eyes
Of men expecting yet another sun
To do the shapely thing they had not done.

These sudden ends of time must give us pause.   25
We fray into the future, rarely wrought
Save in the tapestries of afterthought.
More time, more time. Barrages of applause
Come muffled from a buried radio.
The New Year bells are wrangling with the snow.   30

18. **Pompeii** (pom·pā′): an ancient city in Italy which was destroyed by the eruption of a
volcano, Mount Vesuvius, in A.D. 79.   19. **little dog:** When the ruins of Pompeii were excavated in the nineteenth century, the skeleton of a dog was found in one of the larger buildings.

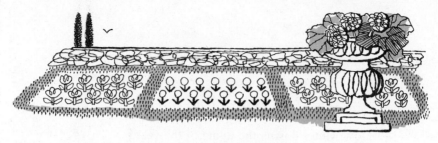

A Summer Morning

Her young employers, having got in late
From seeing friends in town
And scraped the right front fender on the gate,
Will not, the cook expects, be coming down.

She makes a quiet breakfast for herself.   5
The coffeepot is bright,
The jelly where it should be on the shelf.
She breaks an egg into the morning light,

Then, with the bread knife lifted, stands and hears
The sweet efficient sounds   10
Of thrush and catbird, and the snip of shears
Where, in the terraced backward of the grounds,

A gardener works before the heat of day.
He straightens for a view
Of the big house ascending stony-gray   15
Out of his beds° mosaic° with the dew.

His young employers having got in late,
He and the cook alone
Receive the morning on their old estate,
Possessing what the owners can but own.   20

16. **beds:** flowerbeds. **mosaic:** here, patterned, beaded.

FOR STUDY AND DISCUSSION

1. How is "Year's End" concerned with "the dying of the year"? How is the meaning of the season expressed in the simile in lines 5–6? What sense of winter and of death do you get from the second and third stanzas? What is the significance of the contrast between the sleeping dog and the "incomplete" people who were caught in the eruption of Pompeii? Why does the poet write that the ashes "froze" these people? Explain the phrase "sudden ends of time" in line 25. How do we "fray into the future"? The poem begins with the quietness of death. How does it end? Why is the radio in line 29 described as "buried"?

2. In "A Summer Morning," what advantage do the cook and gardener have over their young employers? Describe the difference between "possessing" and "owning." What details in the poem influence your attitude toward the employers and toward their servants? Why is it appropriate that the cook hears "The sweet *efficient* sounds" of the birds?

"A Summer Morning" from *Advice to a Prophet and Other Poems* by Richard Wilbur, © 1960 by Richard Wilbur. Reprinted by permission of Harcourt, Brace & World, Inc.

MODERN ESSAYS

The critic Alfred Kazin has called the essay "the open form." Of all kinds of writing, the essay allows the writer most freedom to pursue his thought in whatever direction he wishes. An essay may meander from idea to idea, held together only by a strong impression of the writer's personality or the distinction of an individual style. Or an essay may present a dense, closely reasoned argument that the reader must follow very carefully if he does not want to lose the train of thought. An essay can be written on any subject, the author's boyhood, the life and works of an important poet, a national issue, or the pleasures of eating roast pork.

What makes the essay a distinct kind of writing is that in it the author is speaking directly to the reader. The essayist, as Alfred Kazin wrote, "starts from the fact that he is himself, and there is nothing that he can say about himself that is more personal than what he thinks. The essay, as a form, is open enough to allow the writer to find the run of his argument. That is why the essay is so peculiarly modern a form, for it expresses the individual's wholly undetermined and freely discovered point of view." Even when the essayist chooses another person as his subject, as in Van Wyck Brooks's essay on Emily Dickinson (page 730), the reader is always aware of two presences, the subject of the essay and the writer, responding to and evaluating his subject.

The word *essay* comes from the French word *essai,* meaning "attempt." This term was first used to distinguish the essay from more formal, more elaborate kinds of discourse. Yet while an essay may be a relatively open kind of writing, it does not lack form altogether. It may be an "open form," but never a simple, haphazard collection of paragraphs or ideas. No matter how much an essay meanders, always there is some thread running through it, holding it together and giving it unity. An essayist, just as much as a poet or short-story writer, is a craftsman, working always to give his essay some final shape. The perceptive reader is equally aware of an essay's formal qualities. He reads not only to find out what is being said, but to appreciate how it is said and to perceive the underlying structure that holds an essay together and shapes it.

GENERAL ESSAYS

THOMAS WOLFE
(1900–1938)

Thomas Wolfe was a giant of a man (six feet six inches tall) with tremendous emotions and appetites, who acknowledged his own "intemperate excess, an almost insane hunger to devour the body of human experience." He was a feverishly energetic writer, amassing great piles of manuscript that his distinguished editor, Maxwell Perkins, helped him to trim and shape into his first novel, *Look Homeward, Angel.* As a writer, Wolfe has been criticized for his inability to know when to stop the mad rush of words and feelings that tears down all subtleties. Yet despite his failings, Wolfe has undeniable claims to literary importance. His was a considerable talent, even if sometimes misused, and it is difficult to read Wolfe's writings without experiencing moments of great power. Perhaps the best title for him is that given in a sympathetic critical study: *Angry Gulliver.*

Wolfe was born in Asheville, North Carolina, and attended the University of North Carolina. At first, his ambition was to be a dramatist, and after graduation from college he went to Harvard to study playwriting at a famous course conducted by George Pierce Baker, who had been the teacher of Eugene O'Neill. Gradually, Wolfe found that the drama was too confining for his talent. While teaching in New York, he wrote novels at night. Several publishers rejected Wolfe's enormous manuscripts until Perkins, discerning the talent beneath the wordage, worked with Wolfe for eight months to get a book into shape for publication. *Look Homeward, Angel,* an obviously autobiographical novel, was an enormous success and established Wolfe's literary reputation. In his thinly disguised depictions of his home town neighbors he offended a number of people. Lifelong friends suddenly became his enemies, and one old lady wrote him that she would not be sorry if his "big overgrown karkus [were] dragged across the public square." Always Wolfe had felt that because of his height and sensitivity, he was different from other men. Now he felt more isolated than ever. With Perkins's help, he published a second novel, *Of Time and the River.* Then, perhaps feeling that Perkins had played too great a role in determining the final shape of his novels, Wolfe went to another publisher and editor. The hero of Wolfe's first two novels was Eugene Gant, a character who, in height and ambitions, was very much like Wolfe himself. To demonstrate that he was much more than an autobiographical novelist, Wolfe created a new hero for his later work: George Webber, whose chief difference from Eugene Gant was that Webber was shorter. After

Wolfe's death, two novels about George Webber were published posthumously: *The Web and the Rock* (1939) and *You Can't Go Home Again* (1940). From time to time, parts of the manuscripts that Wolfe had left behind him were edited and published.

It is significant that in 1939, passages from Wolfe's novels were arranged as poems and published in *The Face of a Nation*. Wolfe once said. "I'd rather be a poet than anything else in the world. What I wouldn't give to be one." Many of his best passages have the eloquence and excitement of poetry, including the passage from *The Web and the Rock* that was inscribed on his tombstone: "Death bent to touch his chosen son with mercy, love, and pity, and put the seal of honor on him when he died."

Circus at Dawn

THERE WERE times in early autumn—in September—when the greater circuses would come to town—the Ringling Brothers, Robinson's, and Barnum and Bailey shows, and when I was a route-boy on the morning paper, on those mornings when the circus would be coming in, I would rush madly through my route in the cool and thrilling darkness that comes just before break of day, and then I would go back home and get my brother out of bed.

Talking in low excited voices we would walk rapidly back toward town under the rustle of September leaves, in cool streets just grayed now with that still, that unearthly and magical first light of day which seems suddenly to rediscover the great earth out of darkness, so that the earth emerges with an awful, a glorious sculptural stillness, and one looks out with a feeling of joy and disbelief, as the first men on this earth must have done, for to see this happen is one of the things that men will remember out of life forever and think of as they die.

At the sculptural still square where at one corner, just emerging into light, my father's shabby little marble shop stood with a ghostly strangeness and familiarity, my brother and I would "catch" the first streetcar of the day bound for the "depot" where the circus was—or sometimes we would meet someone we knew, who would give us a lift in his automobile.

Then, having reached the dingy, grimy, and rickety depot section, we would get out, and walk rapidly across the tracks of the station yard, where we could see great flares and steamings from the engines, and hear the crash and bump of shifting freight cars, the swift sporadic thunders of a shifting engine, the tolling of bells, the sounds of great trains on the rails.

And to all these familiar sounds, filled with their exultant prophecies of flight, the voyage, morning, and the shining cities—to all the sharp and thrilling odors of the trains—the smell of cinders, acrid smoke, of musty, rusty freight cars, the clean pine-board of crated produce, and the smells of fresh stored food—oranges, coffee, tangerines and bacon, ham, and flour and beef—there would be added now, with an unforgettable magic and familiarity, all the strange sounds and smells of the coming circus.

The gay yellow sumptuous-looking cars in which the star performers lived and slept, still dark and silent, heavily and powerfully still, would be drawn up in

long strings upon the tracks. And all around them the sounds of the unloading circus would go on furiously in the darkness. The receding gulf of lilac and departing night would be filled with the savage roar of the lions, the murderously sudden snarling of great jungle cats, the trumpeting of the elephants, the stamp of the horses, and with the musty, pungent, unfamiliar odor of the jungle animals: the tawny camel smells, and the smells of panthers, zebras, tigers, elephants, and bears.

Then, along the tracks, beside the circus trains, there would be the sharp cries and oaths of the circus men, the magical swinging dance of lanterns in the darkness, the sudden heavy rumble of the loaded vans and wagons as they were pulled along the flats[1] and gondolas,[2] and down the runways to the ground. And everywhere, in the thrilling mystery of darkness and awakening light, there would be the tremendous conflict of a confused, hurried, and yet orderly movement.

The great iron-gray horses, four and six to a team, would be plodding along the road of thick white dust to a rattling of chains and traces and the harsh cries of their drivers. The men would drive the animals to the river which flowed by beyond the tracks, and water them; and as

[1] **flats:** flatcars.
[2] **gondolas** (gon'də·ləz): railroad cars with sides and ends, but without tops.

first light came, one could see the elephants wallowing in the familiar river and the big horses going slowly and carefully down to drink.

Then, on the circus grounds, the tents were going up already with the magic speed of dreams. All over the place (which was near the tracks and the only space of flat land in the town that was big enough to hold a circus) there would be this fierce, savagely hurried, and yet orderly confusion. Great flares of gaseous circus light would blaze down on the seared and battered faces of the circus toughs as, with the rhythmic precision of a single animal—a human riveting machine—they swung their sledges at the stakes, driving a stake into the earth with the incredible instancy of accelerated figures in a motion picture. And everywhere, as light came, and the sun appeared, there would be a scene of magic, order, and of violence. The drivers would curse and talk their special language to their teams, there would be the loud, gasping, and uneven labor of a gasoline engine, the shouts and curses of the bosses, the wooden riveting of driven stakes, and the rattle of heavy chains.

Already in an immense cleared space of dusty beaten earth, the stakes were being driven for the main exhibition tent. And an elephant would lurch ponderously to the field, slowly lower his great swinging head at the command of a man who sat perched upon his skull, flourish his gray, wrinkled snout a time or two, and then solemnly wrap it around a tent pole big as the mast of a racing schooner. Then the elephant would back slowly away, dragging the great pole with him as if it were a stick of matchwood. . . .

Meanwhile, the circus food tent—a huge canvas top without concealing sides —had already been put up, and now we could see the performers seated at long trestled tables underneath the tent, as they ate breakfast. And the savor of the food they ate—mixed as it was with our strong excitement, with the powerful but wholesome smells of the animals, and with all the joy, sweetness, mystery, jubilant magic and glory of the morning and the coming of the circus—seemed to us to be of the most maddening and appetizing succulence of any food that we had ever known or eaten.

We could see the circus performers eating tremendous breakfasts, with all the savage relish of their power and strength: they ate big fried steaks, pork chops, rashers [1] of bacon, a half-dozen eggs, great slabs of fried ham and great stacks of wheat cakes which a cook kept flipping in the air with the skill of a juggler, and which a husky-looking waitress kept rushing to their tables on loaded trays held high and balanced marvelously on the fingers of a brawny hand. And above all the maddening odors of the wholesome and succulent food, there brooded forever the sultry and delicious fragrance—that somehow seemed to add a zest and sharpness to all the powerful and thrilling life of morning—of strong boiling coffee, which we could see sending off clouds of steam from an enormous polished urn, and which the circus performers gulped down, cup after cup.

And the circus men and women themselves—these star performers—were such fine-looking people, strong and handsome, yet speaking and moving with an almost stern dignity and decorum, that their lives seemed to us to be as splendid and wonderful as any lives on earth could be. There was never anything loose, rowdy, or tough in their comportment. . . .

Rather, these people in an astonishing way seemed to have created an established community which lived an ordered existence on wheels, and to observe with a stern fidelity unknown in towns and cities the decencies of family life. There would be a powerful young man, a handsome and magnificent young woman with blond hair and the figure of an Amazon,[2]

[1] **rashers:** thin slices.
[2] **Amazon:** a member of a legendary race of women warriors; used generally to describe a woman of great strength or size.

and a powerfully built, thickset man of middle age, who had a stern, lined, responsible-looking face and a bald head. They were probably the members of a trapeze team—the young man and woman would leap through space like projectiles, meeting the grip of the older man and hurtling back again upon their narrow perches, catching the swing of their trapeze in mid-air, and whirling thrice before they caught it, in a perilous and beautiful exhibition of human balance and precision.

But when they came into the breakfast tent, they would speak gravely yet courteously to other performers, and seat themselves in a family group at one of the long tables, eating their tremendous breakfast with an earnest concentration, seldom speaking to one another, and then gravely, seriously, and briefly.

And my brother and I would look at them with fascinated eyes; my brother would watch the man with the bald head for a while and then turn toward me, whispering:

"D-d-do you see that f-f-fellow there with the bald head? W-w-well, he's the heavy man," he whispered knowingly. "He's the one that c-c-c-catches them! That f-f-fellow's got to know his business! You know what happens if he m-m-misses, don't you?" said my brother.

"What?" I would say in a fascinated tone.

My brother snapped his fingers in the air.

"Over!" he said. "D-d-done for! W-w-why, they'd be d-d-d-dead before they knew what happened. Sure!" he said, nodding vigorously. "It's a f-f-f-fact! If he ever m-m-m-misses it's all over! That boy has g-g-g-got to know his s-s-s-stuff!" my brother said. "W-w-w-why," he went on in a low tone of solemn conviction, "it w-w-w-wouldn't surprise me at all if they p-p-p-pay him s-s-seventy-five or a hundred dollars a week! It's a fact!" my brother cried vigorously.

And we would turn our fascinated stares again upon these splendid and romantic creatures, whose lives were so different from our own, and whom we seemed to know with such familiar and affectionate intimacy. And at length, reluctantly, with full light come and the sun up, we would leave the circus grounds and start for home.

And somehow the memory of all we had seen and heard that glorious morning, and the memory of the food tent with its wonderful smells, would waken in us the pangs of such a ravenous hunger that we could not wait until we got home to eat. We would stop off in town at lunchrooms and, seated on tall stools before the counter, we would devour ham-and-egg sandwiches, hot hamburgers, red and pungent at their cores with coarse, spicy, sanguinary beef, coffee, glasses of foaming milk, and doughnuts, and then go home to eat up everything in sight upon the breakfast table.

FOR STUDY AND DISCUSSION

1. What three circus scenes are described? How does each scene help convey the special qualities that might be missing during other times of day?

2. From the boys' point of view, how does the behavior of the circus people differ from that of ordinary people?

3. Wolfe is sensitively aware of sights, sounds, and odors. Find descriptive phrases that you think are particularly effective in appealing to the senses.

4. Wolfe has written this essay from the point of view of an adult recreating his childhood experiences. Do you think adults or adolescents are more likely to see their childhood in true perspective or to romanticize it and distort the truth? Support your answer with examples from the essay and from your own experience.

LANGUAGE AND VOCABULARY

It is interesting to note various characteristics of Wolfe's style. In "Circus at Dawn," find two examples of each of these stylistic devices:

1. his piling up of detail after detail
2. his joining together of a number of clauses
3. his extravagant use of adjectives and adverbs such as "thrilling," "magical," and "powerfully"

What effect on the reader is Wolfe trying to create? Does his style contribute successfully to that effect?

FOR COMPOSITION

Write a paragraph on one of the following subjects, using one or more of the stylistic devices used in "Circus at Dawn."

1. An event in your life that is connected with particular sights and sounds
2. A description of a particular time of day
3. An event from your childhood that you now see from a different point of view

E. B. WHITE
(1899–)

E. B. White is regarded by many readers as one of the most distinguished essayists and stylists of our time. His friend James Thurber (page 695) has written of White's "silver and crystal sentences which had a ring like the ring of nobody else's sentences in the world." From his own advice to young writers, it is evident that White is above all a careful, patient writer. He counsels, "The approach to style is by way of plainness, simplicity, orderliness, sincerity." In a striking metaphor, he comments that a writer must be as alert and quick and as patient as a hunter: "Writing is, for most, laborious and slow. The mind travels faster than the pen; consequently, writing becomes a question of learning to make occasional wing shots, bringing down the bird of thought as it flashes by. A writer is a gunner, sometimes waiting in his blind for something to come in, sometimes roaming the countryside hoping to scare something up. Like other gunners, he must cultivate patience; he may have to work many covers to bring down one partridge." Like many supremely skillful sportsmen and athletes, White is not a flashy, but a deceptively simple, workman. Yet he is so sure in his craft that many of his seemingly casual sentences linger in the memory and gain rather than lose power when they are reread.

The son of an executive in a piano manufacturing company, Elwyn Brooks White grew up in Mount Vernon, New York. While attending Cornell University, he was editor of the Cornell *Daily Sun* and won an Associated Press Award for the best undergraduate editorial of the year. It was at Cornell that White acquired the nickname "Andy." As Thurber explained in an essay on his friend, "He went to Cornell, and it seems that every White who goes there is nicknamed Andy for the simple if rather faraway reason that the first president of the University was named Andrew White." For a number of years White was a staff member of *The New Yorker,* and he played a major part in shaping the distinctive style of that magazine. His essays and stories have been collected in *Quo Vadimus, One Man's Meat, The Second Tree from the Corner,* and *Points of My Compass.* In addition to being a fine essayist, White is a very skillful writer of light verse, which has been collected in *The Lady Is Cold* and *The Fox of Peapack.* He has written two popular books for children, *Stuart Little* and *Charlotte's Web,* and with his wife, Katherine S. White, he has edited *A Subtreasury of American Humor.* Since his retirement from *The New Yorker* staff, White has lived on a farm in Maine. Like one of his favorite subjects, Thoreau, he pursues simplicity in his life as well as in his writing.

Walden (June 1939)

*Miss Nims, take a letter
to Henry David Thoreau.*

DEAR HENRY: I thought of you the other afternoon as I was approaching Concord, doing fifty on Route 62. That is a high speed at which to hold a philosopher in one's mind, but in this century we are a nimble bunch.

On one of the lawns in the outskirts of the village, a woman was cutting the grass with a motorized lawn mower. What made me think of you was that the machine had rather got away from her, although she was game enough, and in the brief glimpse I had of the scene, it appeared to me that the lawn was mowing the lady. She kept a tight grip on the handles, which throbbed violently with every explosion of the one-cylinder motor, and as she steered around bushes and lurched along at a reluctant trot behind her impetuous servant, she looked like a puppy who had grabbed something that was too much for him. Concord hasn't changed much, Henry; the farm implements and the animals still have the upper hand.

I may as well admit that I was journeying to Concord with the deliberate intention of visiting your woods; for although I have never knelt at the grave of a philosopher nor placed wreaths on moldy poets, and have often gone a mile out of my way to avoid some place of historical interest, I have always wanted to see Walden Pond. The account which you left of your sojourn there is, you will be amused to learn, a document of increasing pertinence; each year it seems to gain a little

headway, as the world loses ground. We may all be transcendental [1] yet, whether we like it or not. As our common complexities increase, any tale of individual simplicity (and yours is the best written and the cockiest) acquires a new fascination; as our goods accumulate, but not our well-being, your report of an existence without material adornment takes on a certain awkward credibility.

My purpose in going to Walden Pond, like yours, was not to live cheaply or to live dearly there, but to transact some private business with the fewest obstacles. Approaching Concord, doing forty, doing forty-five, doing fifty, the steering wheel held snug in my palms, the highway held grimly in my vision, the crown of the road now serving me (on the right-hand curves), now defeating me (on the left-hand curves), I began to rouse myself from the stupefaction which a day's motor journey induces. It was a delicious evening, Henry, when the whole body is one sense, and imbibes delight through every pore, if I may coin a phrase. Fields were richly brown where the harrow, drawn by the stripped Ford, had lately sunk its teeth; pastures were green; and overhead the sky had that same everlasting great look which you will find on page 144 of the Oxford pocket edition.[2] I could feel the road entering me, through tire, wheel, spring, and cushion; shall I not have intelligence with earth too? Am I not partly leaves and vegetable mold myself?—a man of infinite horsepower, yet partly leaves.

Stay with me on 62, and it will take you into Concord. As I say, it was a delicious evening. The snake had come forth to die in a bloody S on the highway, the wheel upon its head, its bowels flat now and exposed. The turtle had come up too to cross the road and die in the attempt, its hard shell smashed under the rubber blow, its intestinal yearning (for the other

[1] **transcendental:** For a discussion of the transcendentalist philosophy, see page 163.
[2] **Oxford pocket edition:** an edition of Thoreau's *Walden*.

side of the road) forever squashed. There was a sign by the wayside which announced that the road had a "cotton surface." You wouldn't know what that is, but neither, for that matter, did I. There is a cryptic ingredient in many of our modern improvements—we are awed and pleased without knowing quite what we are enjoying. It is something to be traveling on a road with a cotton surface.

The civilization round Concord today is an odd distillation of city, village, farm, and manor. The houses, yards, fields look not quite suburban, not quite rural. Under the bronze beech and the blue spruce of the departed baron grazes the milch [1] goat of the heirs. Under the porte-cochère [2] stands the reconditioned station wagon; under the grape arbor sit the puppies for sale. (But why do men degenerate ever? What makes families run out?)

It was June and everywhere June was publishing her immemorial stanza; in the lilacs, in the syringa,[3] in the freshly edged paths and the sweetness of moist, beloved gardens, and the little wire wickets that preserve the tulips' front. Farmers were already moving the fruits of their toil into their yards, arranging the rhubarb, the asparagus, the strictly fresh eggs on the painted stands under the little shed roofs with the patent shingles. And though it was almost a hundred years since you had taken your ax and started cutting out your home on Walden Pond, I was interested to observe that the philosophical spirit was still alive in Massachusetts: in the center of a vacant lot, some boys were assembling the framework of the rude shelter, their whole mind and skill concentrated in the rather inauspicious helter-skelton of studs and rafters. They too were escaping from town, to live naturally, in a rich blend of savagery and philosophy.

That evening, after supper at the inn, I strolled out into the twilight to dream my shapeless transcendental dreams and see that the car was locked up for the night (first open the right front door, then reach over, straining, and pull up the handles of the left rear and the left front till you hear the click, then the handle of the right rear, then shut the right front but open it again, remembering that the key is still in the ignition switch, remove the key, shut the right front again with a bang, push the tiny keyhole cover to one side, insert key, turn, and withdraw). It is what we all do, Henry. It is called locking the car. It is said to confuse thieves and keep them from making off with the lap robe. Four doors to lock behind one robe. The driver himself never uses a lap robe, the free movement of his legs being vital to the operation of the vehicle; so that when he locks the car, it is a pure and unselfish act. I have in my life gained very little essential heat from lap robes, yet I have ever been at pains to lock them up.

The evening was full of sounds, some of which would have stirred your memory. The robins still love the elms of New England villages at sundown. There is enough of the thrush in them to make song inevitable at the end of day, and enough of the tramp to make them hang round the dwellings of men. A robin, like many another American, dearly loves a white house with green blinds. Concord is still full of them.

Your fellow townsmen were stirring abroad—not many afoot, most of them in their cars; and the sound which they made in Concord at evening was a rustling and a whispering. The sound lacks steadfastness and is wholly unlike that of a train. A train, as you know who lived so near the Fitchburg line, whistles once or twice sadly and is gone, trailing a memory in smoke, soothing to ear and mind. Automobiles, skirting a village green, are like flies that have gained the inner ear—they buzz, cease, pause, start, shift, stop, halt, brake, and the whole effect is a nervous polytone,[4] curiously disturbing.

[1] **milch:** giving milk.
[2] **porte-cochère** (pôrt′kō·shâr′): a carport.
[3] **syringa** (si·ring′gə): a large white or cream-colored flower.

[4] **polytone:** combination of sounds.

As I wandered along, the toc-toc of ping-pong balls drifted from an attic window. In front of the Reuben Brown house, a Buick was drawn up. At the wheel, motionless, his hat upon his head, a man sat, listening to Amos and Andy on the radio (it is a drama of many scenes and without an end). The deep voice of Andrew Brown, emerging from the car, although it originated more than two hundred miles away, was unstrained by distance. When you used to sit on the shore of your pond on Sunday morning, listening to the church bells of Acton and Concord, you were aware of the excellent filter of the intervening atmosphere. Science has attended to that, and sound now maintains its intensity without regard for distance. Properly sponsored, it goes on forever.

A fire engine, out for a trial spin, roared past Emerson's house, hot with readiness for public duty. Over the barn roofs the martins dipped and chittered. A swarthy daughter of an asparagus grower, in culottes,[1] shirt, and bandanna, pedaled past on her bicycle. It was indeed a delicious evening, and I returned to the inn (I believe it was your house once) to rock with the old ladies on the concrete veranda.

Next morning early I started afoot for Walden, out Main Street and down Thoreau, past the depot and the Minuteman Chevrolet Company. The morning was fresh, and in a bean field along the way, I flushed an agriculturalist, quietly studying his beans. Thoreau Street soon joined Number 126, an artery of the State. We number our highways nowadays, our speed being so great we can remember little of their quality or character and are lucky to remember their number. (Men have an indistinct notion that if they keep up this activity long enough, all will at length ride somewhere, in next to no time.) Your pond is on 126.

I knew I must be nearing your woodland retreat when the Golden Pheasant lunchroom came into view—Sealtest ice cream, toasted sandwiches, hot frankfurters, waffles, tonics, and lunches. Were I the proprietor, I should add rice, Indian meal, and molasses [2]—just for old time's sake. The Pheasant, incidentally, is for sale: a chance for some nature lover who wishes to set himself up beside a pond in the Concord atmosphere and live deliberately, fronting only the essential facts of life on Number 126. Beyond the Pheasant was a place called Walden Breezes, an oasis whose porch pillars were made of old green shutters sawed into lengths. On the porch was a distorting mirror, to give the traveler a comical image of himself, who had miraculously learned to gaze in an ordinary glass without smiling. Behind the Breezes, in a sun-parched clearing, dwelt your philosophical descendants in their trailers, each trailer the size of your hut, but all grouped together for the sake of congeniality. Trailer people leave the city, as you did, to discover solitude and in any weather, at any hour of the day or night, to improve the nick of time; but they soon collect in villages and get bogged deeper in the mud than ever. The camp behind Walden Breezes was just rousing itself to the morning. The ground was packed hard under the heel,

---

[1] **culottes** (kyōō·lots′): a woman's garment, which like a skirt, but is divided like trousers.

[2] **rice, Indian meal, and molasses:** the main ingredients of Thoreau's diet.

and the sun came through the clearing to bake the soil and enlarge the wry smile of cramped housekeeping. Cushman's bakery truck had stopped to deliver an early basket of rolls. A camp dog, seeing me in the road, barked petulantly. A man emerged from one of the trailers and set forth with a bucket to draw water from some forest tap.

Leaving the highway, I turned off into the woods toward the pond, which was apparent through the foliage. The floor of the forest was strewn with dried old oak leaves and *Transcripts*.[1] From beneath the flattened popcorn wrapper *(granum explosum)* peeped the frail violet. I followed a footpath and descended to the water's edge. The pond lay clear and blue in the morning light, as you have seen it so many times. In the shallows a man's waterlogged shirt undulated gently. A few flies came out to greet me and convoy me to your cove, past the No Bathing signs on which the fellows and the girls had scrawled their names. I felt strangely excited suddenly to be snooping around your premises, tiptoeing along watchfully, as though not to tread by mistake upon the intervening century. Before I got to the cove, I heard something which seemed to me quite wonderful: I heard your frog, a full, clear *troonk,* guiding me, still hoarse and solemn, bridging the years as the robins had bridged them in the sweetness of the village evening. But he soon quit, and I came on a couple of young boys throwing stones at him.

Your front yard is marked by a bronze tablet set in a stone. Four small granite posts, a few feet away, show where the house was. On top of the tablet was a pair of faded blue bathing trunks with a white stripe. Back of it is a pile of stones, a sort of cairn,[2] left by your visitors as a tribute, I suppose. It is a rather ugly little heap of stones, Henry. In fact, the hillside itself seems faded, browbeaten; a

few tall, skinny pines, bare of lower limbs, a smattering of young maples in suitable green, some birches and oaks, and a number of trees felled by the last big wind. It was from the bole [3] of one of these fallen pines, torn up by the roots, that I extracted the stone which I added to the cairn—a sentimental act in which I was interrupted by a small terrier from a nearby picnic group, who confronted me and wanted to know about the stone.

I sat down for a while on one of the posts of your house to listen to the bluebottles and the dragonflies. The invaded glade sprawled shabby and mean at my feet, but the flies were tuned to the old vibration. There were the remains of a fire in your ruins, but I doubt that it was yours; also two beer bottles trodden into the soil and become part of earth. A young oak had taken root in your house, and two or three ferns, unrolling like the ticklers at a banquet. The only other furnishings were a DuBarry pattern sheet,[4] a page torn from a picture magazine, and some crusts in wax paper.

Before I quit, I walked clear round the pond and found the place where you used to sit on the northeast side to get the sun in the fall, and the beach where you got sand for scrubbing your floor. On the eastern side of the pond, where the highway

[1] *Transcripts:* The *Evening Transcript* was a Boston newspaper.
[2] **cairn** (kârn): a pile of stones raised as a memorial or landmark.

[3] **bole:** trunk.
[4] **DuBarry pattern sheet:** a dress pattern.

borders it, the State has built dressing rooms for swimmers, a float with diving towers, drinking fountains of porcelain, and rowboats for hire. The pond is in fact a State Preserve, and carries a twenty-dollar fine for picking wild flowers, a decree signed in all solemnity by your fellow citizens Walter C. Wardwell, Erson B. Barlow, and Nathaniel I. Bowditch. There was a smell of creosote [1] where they had been building a wide wooden stairway to the road and the parking area. Swimmers and boaters were arriving; bodies plunged vigorously into the water and emerged wet and beautiful in the bright air. As I left, a boatload of town boys were splashing about in mid-pond, kidding and fooling, the young fellows singing at the tops of their lungs in a wild chorus:

"Amer-ica, Amer-ica, God shed his
  grace on thee,
And crown thy good with brotherhood
From sea to shi-ning sea!"

I walked back to town along the railroad, following your custom. The rails were expanding noisily in the hot sun, and on the slope of the roadbed, the wild grape and the blackberry sent up their creepers to the track.

The expense of my brief sojourn in Concord was:

Canvas shoes	$1.95	
Baseball bat	.25	gifts to
Left-handed fielder's		take back
glove	1.25	to a boy
Hotel and meals	4.25	
In all	$7.70	

As you see, this amount was almost what you spent for food for eight months. I cannot defend the shoes or the expenditure for shelter and food: they reveal a meanness and grossness in my nature which you would find contemptible. The baseball equipment, however, is the kind of impediment with which you were never on

[1] **creosote** (krē′ə·sōt): tar.

even terms. You must remember that the house where you practiced the sort of economy which I respect was haunted only by mice and squirrels. You never had to cope with a shortstop.

FOR STUDY AND DISCUSSION

1. What is the significance of the woman with the lawn mower that White encounters? (Remember that the mower is motorized.)

2. Explain why White says that Thoreau's book *Walden* each year "seems to gain a little headway, as the world loses ground." Throughout the essay there is a contrast between Thoreau's book and the "world"—or, the conditions of modern life. Cite details that develop this contrast.

3. White observes that "the philosophical spirit [is] still alive in Massachusetts." How does this observation apply to the group of boys who are "assembling the framework of the rude shelter"? In what ways are these boys like Thoreau?

4. What is White's attitude toward the trailer camp? What irony can you find in the paragraph dealing with the camp (page 692)?

5. Sum up White's attitude toward the modern world. To what extent is the attitude implied rather than stated? What means does White use to communicate his attitudes to the reader? To answer this question, you will have to consider the role of irony in the entire essay. Cite specific passages to support your answer.

6. Why do you think White has written this essay in the form of a letter addressed to Thoreau instead of addressing himself directly to the reader? In what way does the fact that the letter is dictated to a secretary, rather than written out by the author, symbolize White's position in the modern world? How does the last paragraph of the essay indicate this position?

FOR COMPOSITION

Do you think that Henry David Thoreau would sympathize with E. B. White or disagree with him? After studying the selections by Thoreau (pages 184 and 194), write a reply to White as Thoreau might have written it. Show what you think might be Thoreau's opinions about the changes that have taken place in the world in general and in Concord and Walden Pond in particular.

JAMES THURBER

(1894–1961)

During the last twenty or so years of his life, James Thurber was widely regarded as the best American humorist of his time. While readers laughed at his essays and stories, they were aware of another quality in much of his work, a vein of melancholy that threw the humor into relief and gave it an edge. The greatest American humorist, Mark Twain, once commented about his own writing that it was well received because basically he had something serious to say. Similarly, the poet T. S. Eliot described Thurber's work as "a form of humor which is also a way of saying something serious." Many of Thurber's best jokes and funniest passages are like little flares that highlight the pains of human existence. He had a wonderful appreciation of the tensions of everyday life, the misunderstandings and occasional hostilities that mark the relationship between men and women, the absurdities that arise out of trying to maintain dignity in a world that becomes ever more difficult to understand. He was a dedicated craftsman who rewrote as many as twenty-five times the works that embody his sad, funny point of view.

James Thurber grew up in Columbus, Ohio, and attended Ohio State University, from which he graduated in 1919. He worked as a newspaper reporter in Columbus, Paris, and New York. During the middle 1920's, he began to contribute humorous sketches to *The New Yorker* (his first was accepted after nineteen previous rejections), and in 1927 he was hired by Harold Ross, the remarkable editor and founder of that magazine whom Thurber has memorialized in *The Years with Ross*. A member of *The New Yorker's* staff in its early days remembers James Thurber as "a weirdly unorthodox young man, tall and gangling, with a cascading mop of hair which kept falling forward and almost obliterating his face," a talker with "magnificent fluency" and a "mad mimic ... especially fond of confusing deceptions on the telephone." In 1933, Thurber resigned from *The New Yorker's* staff, but he remained a contributor to the end of his life. Along with the work of his friend E. B. White (page 689), Thurber's writings are regarded as one of the distinctive contributions of *The New Yorker* to American literature.

It was White who was responsible for Thurber's second career as a cartoonist. Thurber had been in the habit of visiting his colleagues on *The New Yorker* staff and leaving doodles of men, women, and animals on their scratch pads. White first recognized the value of these doodles, saved some of them, furnished captions for them, and suggested they be printed as cartoons. The best-known collection of Thurber cartoons is *Men, Women, and Dogs*, which contains many drawings of bewildered people and patient, compassionate dogs. One famous series of cartoons is called "The War Between Men and Women." Several of Thurber's best collections of sketches and stories are *My Life and Hard Times, My World and Welcome to It,* and *The Beast in Me and Other Animals.* These include not only famous humorous works such as "The Secret Life of Walter Mitty," "You Could Look It Up," and "The Catbird Seat," but several fine serious stories such as "A Friend to Alexander," "One Is a Wanderer," and "The Whippoorwill." In addition, Thurber collaborated with his old college friend Elliot Nugent on *The Male Animal,* a comedy that was successfully produced twice on Broadway and adapted as a motion picture.

During the last years of his life, Thurber became completely blind, and in his final writing, humor was more heavily tinged with melancholy than ever before. But in one of his last collections, *Lanterns and Lances,* he made an eloquent statement of "The Case for Comedy" and humor in general:

> "As brevity is the soul of wit, form, it seems to me, is the heart of humor and the salvation of comedy. . . . It is up to our writers, in this era of Oral Culture, to bring back respect for form and for the innate stature and dignity of comedy. . . . The trend of the modern temper is toward gloom, resignation, and even surrender. . . . Well, we are still going on, and we have four decades left in this battered and bloody century. . . . It is high time that we came of age and realized that, like Emily Dickinson's hope, humor is a feathered thing that perches in the soul."

Home

This cartoon, entitled "Home," is typical of those drawn by Thurber for *The New Yorker.*

The Letters of
James Thurber

"Adams was a great letter writer of the type that is now almost extinct . . . his circle of friends was larger perhaps and more distinguished than that of any other American of his generation."

H. S. COMMAGER
on "Letters of Henry Adams." [1]

JAMES THURBER was a letter writer of the type that is now completely extinct. His circle of correspondents was perhaps no larger but it was easily more bewildered than that of any other American of his generation. Thurber laid the foundation for his voluminous correspondence during his Formative Period. In those years he wrote to many distinguished persons, none of whom ever replied, among them Admiral Schley, Young Barbarian, Senator Atlee Pomerene, June Caprice, and a man named Unglaub who played first base for the Washington Senators at the turn of the century. Unglaub, in Thurber's estimation, stood head and shoulders above all the rest of his correspondents and, indeed, he said so in his letter to McKinley. Thurber did not write as many letters as Henry Adams or John Jay Chapman [2] or some of the other boys whose correspondence has been published lately, but that is because he never set pen to paper after his forty-third year.

The effect of Thurber's letters on his generation was about the same as the effect of anybody's letters on any generation; that is to say, nil. It is only when a man's letters are published after his death that they have any effect and this effect is usually only on literary critics. Nobody else ever reads a volume of letters and anybody who says he does is a liar. A person may pick up a volume of correspondence now and then and read a letter here and there, but he never gets any connected idea of what the man is trying to say and soon abandons the book for the poems of John Greenleaf Whittier. This is largely because every man whose letters have ever been published was in the habit of writing every third one to a Mrs. Cameron or a Mrs. Winslow or a Miss Betch, the confidante of a lifetime, with whom he shared any number of gaily obscure little secrets. These letters all read like this: "Dear Puttums: I love what you say about Mooey! It's so devastatingly true! B—— dropped in yesterday (Icky was out at the time) and gave some sort of report on Neddy but I am afraid I didn't listen (*ut ediendam aut debendo!*).[3] He and Liddy are in Venice, I think I gathered, or Newport. What in the world do you suppose came over Buppa that Great Night? ? ? You, of course, were as splendidly consequent as ever (*in loco sporenti abadabba est*)—but I was deeply disappointed in Sig's reaction. All he can think of, poor fellow, is Margery's 'flight.' Remind me to tell you some day what Pet said about the Ordeal." These particular letters are sometimes further obscured by a series of explanatory editorial footnotes, such as "Probably Harry Boynton or his brother Norton," "A neighbor at Bar Harbor," "The late Edward J. Belcher," "Also sometimes lovingly referred to as Butty, a niece-in-law by his first marriage." In the end, as I say, one lays the book aside for "Snowbound" in order to get a feeling of reality before going to bed.

Thurber's letters from Europe during his long stay there in 1937 and 1938 (the

---

[1] **H. S. Commager . . . Adams:** a commentary by the American historian Henry Steele Commager (1902–) on a collection of letters by Henry Adams.

[2] **John Jay Chapman:** American writer and social commentator (1862–1933).

"The Letters of James Thurber" from *My World—and Welcome to It,* published by Harcourt, Brace & World, Inc., copyright © 1942 by James Thurber. Reprinted by permission of Helen Thurber.

[3] *ut . . . debendo:* the Latin quotations in this paragraph are apparently complete nonsense.

European Phase) are perhaps the least interesting of all those he, or anybody else, ever wrote. He seems to have had at no time any idea at all, either clear or vague, as to what was going on. A certain Groping, to be sure, is discernible, but it doesn't appear to be toward anything. All this may have been due in great part to the fact that he took his automobile to Europe with him and spent most of his time worrying about running out of gas. The gasoline gauge of his car had got out of order and sometimes registered "empty" when the tank was half full and "full" when it contained only two or three gallons. A stronger character would have had the gauge fixed or carried a five-gallon can of *essence* in the back of the car, thus releasing the mind for more mature and significant preoccupations, but not Thurber.

I have been unable to find any one of Thurber's many correspondents who saved any of his letters (Thurber himself kept carbons, although this is not generally known or cared about). "We threw them out when we moved," people would tell me, or "We gave them to the janitor's little boy." Thurber gradually became aware of this on his return to America (the Final Phase) because of the embarrassed silence that always greeted him when, at his friends' homes, he would say, "Why don't we get out my letters to you and read them aloud?" After a painful pause the subject was quickly changed,

usually by putting up the ping-pong table.

In his last years the once voluminous letter writer ceased writing letters altogether, and such communication as he maintained with the great figures of his time was over the telephone and consisted of getting prominent persons on the phone, making a deplorable sound with his lips, and hanging up. His continual but vain attempts to reach the former Barbara Hutton [1] by phone clouded the last years of his life but at the same time gave him something to do. His last words, to his wife, at the fag end of the Final Phase, were "Before they put up the ping-pong table, tell them I am not running out of gas." He was as wrong, and as mixed up, in this particular instance as he was in most others. I am not sure that we should not judge him too harshly.

[1] **Barbara Hutton:** a famous American millionairess.

FOR STUDY AND DISCUSSION

1. Why do you think the author refers to himself as "James Thurber" rather than as "I"? What relation does this have to the quotation by Commager? What sentences in the first paragraph are most closely related to the quotation? Do these sentences prepare you for a serious or a humourous essay? Explain.

2. What points is Thurber making about collections of letters and people who write commentaries about them? Do you think the "distinguished personalities" referred to in the first paragraph really existed? Why or why not?

3. Why do you think such words and phrases as "Formative Period," "European Phase," and "Groping" are capitalized?

4. Part of the humor of this essay comes from the incongruity between the dignified style and the facts that are being related. Cite five examples of incongruity in the essay.

FOR COMPOSITION

Write a brief essay imitating Thurber's manner and tone. You may wish to write about your work habits, your artistic talent, or your mechanical ability. Or, select a similar topic of your own choosing.

BIOGRAPHICAL ESSAYS

STEWART H.
HOLBROOK

(1893–1965)

Stewart Holbrook has written, "My only ambition as a writer is to put into books the figures and portions of American history that I think have been largely ignored, or badly treated." During his career as a writer, Mr. Holbrook published more than thirty-five books, including regional and business histories and biographies of pioneers and industrialists. His special talent for making history lively and entertaining without distorting the truth has made him one of America's most popular historians and biographers.

Holbrook was born in Vermont and spent his early years in that state and in New Hampshire where he attended Colebrook Academy. During World War I he saw action in Europe with an artillery unit. After the war, he worked in several logging camps and later as a writer and editor. As a reporter for the *Lumber News,* he covered forest fires, riots, and logging camp and sawmill strikes. In 1934 he decided to devote all his time to writing and resigned his job. His intimate knowledge of loggers and logging furnished him with the material for his first book, *Holy Old Mackinaw: A Natural History of the American Lumberjack* (1938), and for a later work, *Burning an Empire: America's Great Forest Fires* (1943). He has also written a biography of Ethan Allen (1940), *The Story of American Railroads* (1947), and *The Age of Moguls* (1953). One of Holbrook's most interesting works is *Lost Men of American History,* which explores the lives of little-known but highly individual figures out of America's past. One of the "lost men," for example, is Robert Gibbon Johnson, who ate a tomato in public to disprove the superstition that tomatoes contain a deadly poison. "The Beard of Joseph Palmer" is another study of an obscure figure from America's past, a stubborn man whose fight with barbers and with leading citizens has its humorous side but whose devotion to individual rights teaches a lesson to all Americans.

For many years, Holbrook lived in Portland, Oregon. However he returned to New England briefly to take up residence in Cambridge, Massachusetts. During that time he lectured at Harvard and Boston University. He once stated that he was very proud of what he called his "sole distinction," his election to the American Antiquarian Society.

The Beard of Joseph Palmer

ONE OF THE unsung but really great individualists who helped to make the United States a better and a safer place to live in was Joseph Palmer of Fitchburg and Harvard, Massachusetts, a man to be reckoned with in any discussion of the Bill of Rights. He is forgotten now, and this is bad forgetting, for Palmer was of a race of men that is now all but extinct. And his story, I think, is as heart-warming as it is improbable.

Palmer came to national attention because he was the victim of one of the strangest persecutions in history. Neither race nor religion played a part in Palmer's case, which with some reason might otherwise be termed *l'affaire Dreyfus*[1] of Fitchburg. It was brought about by the fact that Joe Palmer liked to wear a beard, one of the most magnificent growths ever seen in New England or, for that matter, in the United States; and what made this beard particularly heinous was that it was almost, if not quite, the only beard east of the Rocky Mountains, and possibly beyond.

One lone set of whiskers amid millions of smooth-shaven faces is something to contemplate, and Palmer paid dearly for his eccentricity. Indeed, one might say,

with but little stretch of imagination and metaphor, that it was Joe Palmer who carried the Knowledge of Whiskers through the dark ages of beardless America. He was born almost a century too late and seventy-five years too soon to wear whiskers with impunity. He was forty-two years old in 1830, when he moved from his nearby farm into the hustling village of Fitchburg. He came of sturdy old Yankee stock. His father had served in the Revolution, and Joe himself had carried a musket in 1812. He was married and had one son, Thomas.

When the beard first made its appearance isn't of record, but Joe was wearing it when he came to Fitchburg, and here, because of it, he immediately became the butt of cruel jokes and derision and, in time, the victim of downright persecution. But before relating the violence caused by Palmer's famous beard, it is imperative—if one is to comprehend the proceedings at all—to trace briefly the history of whiskers in America up to the time of the Palmer beard.

This continent was explored by men of many nationalities, almost all of them wearing whiskers. About Columbus and Amerigo Vespucci we are uncertain, since there are no authenticated contemporary portraits of them. But after them came a host of beards. Cortes,

[1] *l'affaire Dreyfus* (là'fâr' drā'fəs): "The Dreyfus Affair." Alfred Dreyfus was a French army officer who, in 1895, was unjustly convicted of treason and imprisoned. It was claimed that some of the army and court officials were prejudiced against Dreyfus because of his Jewish religion. When the French government failed to take action, the case attracted international attention, with protests pouring in from many countries. Finally, after some five years' delay and a change of government, Dreyfus was released and declared innocent.

"The Beard of Joseph Palmer" by Stewart Holbrook from *The American Scholar*, Volume 13, Number 4, Autumn, 1944, copyright © 1944 by the United Chapters of Phi Beta Kappa. Reprinted by permission of the publishers.

Ponce de León, Cartier, Champlain, Drake, Raleigh, Captain John Smith, De Soto—all sported whiskers of varying length and style. Little wonder the Indians thought them gods.

Then came the Pilgrims and the Puritans, bearded almost to a man when they arrived at The Rock and elsewhere. But the beards of the first settlers didn't last. American whiskers were reduced gradually in size until they were scarcely more than mild goatees, and soon disappeared entirely. By 1720 at the latest, American colonists were wholly free of facial hair. Try to find a Copley portrait, or a Ralph Earle [1] with a whisker in it. And the fighting men of the Revolution were beardless. Not a mustache or a suspicion of a mutton chop appeared on the faces of Washington, Gates, Greene, Knox. Even old John Stark and Israel Putnam were smooth-shaven, and so was the backwoods general Ethan Allen. It was the same with the other Patriots, and with the British also—Cornwallis, the Howes, Burgoyne. No signer of the Declaration had either beard or mustache.

And so it continued down the years. No President before Lincoln had any hair on his face. Until 1858 the cartoonists' conception of their own creature, Uncle Sam—otherwise much as he is today—was of a tall and lanky but smooth-shaven man. America did not really go hairy until the War Between the States was well under way.

Thus, when Joe Palmer came to town wearing a beard in 1830, whiskers had been virtually nonexistent for at least a hundred years. In spite of his hirsute oddity, Palmer was an honest, kindly man and a good citizen, deeply religious but tolerant, and a man of many intellectual interests. He was also quite immovable when it came to principles, which in his case included the right to wear a full, flowing beard.

[1] **Copley ... Earle:** John Singleton Copley (1738–1815) and Ralph Earle (1751–1801) were famous American portrait painters of the late eighteenth century.

Everywhere he went, small boys threw stones and shouted at him and made life miserable for his son, Tom. Women sniffed and crossed to the other side of the street when they saw him coming. Often the windows of his modest home were broken by unknown rowdies. Grown men jeered at him openly. The Reverend George Trask, local pastor, took him to task for his eccentricity, but Joe replied with exact Scriptural reasons—nay, commands—for beard-wearing. Old Doctor Williams told Joe to his face that he should "be prosecuted for wearing such a monstrosity." And when Joe went to Boston to attend literary and reform meetings, huge crowds "followed him the length of Tremont Street, jeering." He was present at the celebrated Chardon Street Convention [2] in 1840, and one has no difficulty locating him in Emerson's comment on that gathering:

"If the assembly was disorderly, it was picturesque. Madmen, madwomen, men with beards, Dunkers, Muggletonians, Come-outers, Groaners, Agrarians. Seventh-Day Baptists, Quakers, Abolitionists, Calvinists, Unitarians, and Philosophers—all came successively to the top, and seized their moment, if not their hour, wherein to chide, or pray, or preach, or protest."

By the time of this convention, Joe Palmer was a national character, made so by two events that had happened in quick succession in his home town of Fitchburg. In spite of the snubs of the congregation, Joe never missed a church service, but one Sunday he quite justifiably lost his usually serene temper. It was a Communion Sunday in 1830. Joe knelt with the rest, only to be publicly humiliated when the officiating clergyman ignored him, "passed him by with the communion bread and wine." Joe was cut to the quick. He rose up and strode to the communion table. He

[2] **Chardon Street Convention:** The meeting brought together various groups of religious and political reformers.

lifted the cup to his lips and took a mighty swig. Then: "I love my Jesus," he shouted in a voice loud with hurt and anger, "as well, and better, than any of you!" Then he went home.

A few days later, as he was coming out of the Fitchburg Hotel, he was seized by four men armed with shears, brush, soap, and razor. They told him that the sentiment of the town was that his beard should come off and they were going to do the job there and then. When Joe started to struggle, the four men threw him violently to the ground, seriously injuring his back and head. But Joe had just begun to fight. When they were about to apply the shears, he managed to get an old jackknife out of his pocket. He laid about him wildly, cutting two of his assailants in their legs, not seriously but sufficiently to discourage any barber work. When Joe stood up, hurt and bleeding, his gorgeous beard was intact.

Presently he was arrested, charged with "an unprovoked assault." Fined by Justice Brigham, he refused to pay. Matter of principle, he said. He was put in the city jail at Worcester, and there he remained for more than a year, part of the time in solitary confinement. Even here he had to fight for his whiskers, for once Jailor Bellows came with several men with the idea of removing the now-

famous beard. Joe threw himself at them and fought so furiously that the mob retreated without a hair. He also successfully repulsed at least two attempts by prisoners to shave him.

In the jail Joe wrote letters which he smuggled out a window to his son, who took them to the Worcester *Spy*. They were published and soon were being widely copied by other newspapers. In his letters the bearded prisoner stated that he was in jail not for assault but because he chose to wear whiskers—which was unquestionably the case. He complained of the food, of the quarters, and of the lack of any religious life behind the bars. People all over Massachusetts read these letters. They began to talk, and even to reflect. It wasn't long before the sheriff came to realize that he had a Tartar [1] and possibly a martyr on his hands. He went to Joe and told him to run along home and forget it—the fine and everything. No, said Joe. The jailor urged him to leave. His aged mother wrote him to come home. All in vain. Nothing could move the man who was now known as The Bearded Prisoner of Worcester.

Day after day he sat in his limbo, keeping an elaborate and pathetic journal of his persecutions. And time after time he told officers and worried magistrates that they had put him there, and they would have to take him out. "I won't walk one single step toward freedom!" he roared through the bars. Nor did he. He sat there in a chair like a whiskered Buddha until the desperate sheriff and jailors picked him up in his chair and carried him to the street.

Never again was violence attempted on Joe Palmer's beard, which by the time of his release, or rather his eviction, from jail, was a beard famous as far away as New York and Philadelphia. Free now, he soon became a minor figure in New England's intellectual ferment. A hater

[1] **Tartar** (or **Tatar**): a person from Tartary in Siberia; used in a general sense to indicate a captive who proves stronger than his captor.

of slavery, he went to Boston often for the meetings of Parker and Garrison,[1] contributing both time and money to the movement for abolition. He met Emerson, Thoreau, Alcott, Channing, and these men found him an odd but staunch character, the possessor of much good sense. He loathed liquor as much as he did slavery, and was active at Temperance meetings. He visited the communities at Brook Farm and Hopedale.

When Bronson Alcott and family,[2] with Charles Lane and a few others, bought a farm in Harvard, near Fitchburg, named it Fruitlands, and attempted to found the Con-Sociate Family, Joe Palmer was vastly interested. He donated a lot of fine old furniture and up-to-date farm implements to the colony. When he saw that Alcott's idiotic ideas about farming were going to bring famine to the group, he brought his own team and plow and turned up the soil. He was, in fact, the only sensible male in that wondrous experiment. (Joe Palmer appears in Louisa May Alcott's *Transcendental Wild Oats* as Moses White.)

Fruitlands had the distinction of being the worst-managed and shortest-lived of all American colonies. When the half-starved Alcotts and the others had moved away, Joe Palmer bought the farm and moved there with his wife and family. Here, for more than twenty years, he carried on a strange sort of community life of his own devising. He was widely known now and never lacked for company. Emerson and Thoreau visited him, and so did every reformer who passed through or operated in New England. The merely curious came to see the famous beard. The Palmers always had a pot of beans on the stove, plenty of bread in the butt'ry.[3] All were welcome to come and to stay,

so long as they had no trace of liquor about them.

In place of persecution, Joe now found himself something of a hero. The years crept on, and with them his great beard grew even more famously, spreading like a willow. A photograph taken at about this time shows a growth that makes Walt Whitman seem a beardless youth in comparison. And at last, many years before he died, the whiskers of all America came into their fullest glory. This second coming of the beard was sudden, an almost instantaneous wilderness of hair that covered the face of male America.

One cannot know with certainty the reason for this sudden era of whiskers; it can only be recorded. Lincoln, when elected, was smooth-shaven, but, when inaugurated, wore a beard. Grant, the lieutenant, had worn a tiny mustache; Grant, the general, had a full beard. Robert E. Lee went smooth of face to war, and was presently full-bearded. In 1860 Jeff Davis was clean of chin. He was soon wearing whiskers longer than Lincoln's. Nearly all of the generals of the War Between the States, on both sides, were peering out of whiskers by 1862, and so were their men. Stonewall Jackson grew a mighty beard. Custer

[1] **Parker and Garrison:** Theodore Parker (1810–1860) and William Lloyd Garrison (1805–1879) were leading figures in the movement for abolition of slavery.

[2] For more information on the Alcott family and Brook Farm, see pages 161, 163.

[3] **butt'ry** (or **buttery**): storeroom.

grew a unique combination beard and mustache, but it was General Ambrose E. Burnside who gave his name to a special type of whiskers.

The baseball players of the sixties and seventies, as depicted by the careful Currier & Ives,[1] had whiskers. Bankers grew a style all their own. Razors went into the discard, and vendors of quack beard-growers swarmed into the new market. The proper gift to a male was an elegant mustache cup. Manufacturers

of soap, patent medicines, and cough drops—notably cough drops—came out with one or more bearded faces on their labels. Whiskers, through some odd turn of the folkways, now were a sign of solid worth, a badge of integrity in every line of endeavor. If the poor barbers thought the end of things had arrived, it is easy to understand why.

As for old Joe Palmer, he was immensely happy, a true prophet who had lived to see his justification. Few prophets have been so fortunate. All over America, Joe Palmer knew, were now full beards, Van Dykes, goatees, galways, dundrearys, mutton chops, burnsides, fringe beards, and millions of stupendous mustaches of the over-Niagara type. Aye, the prophet had come into his own. Yet Joe was no

[1] **Currier & Ives:** an American printing firm noted for detailed and realistic lithographs of American scenes.

gloater. He seems to have remarked only once on the greatly changed styles of what men wore on their faces. That was when he met the same Reverend Trask who had so churlishly upbraided him many years before for wearing his beard. Trask himself was now wearing a luxuriant growth. Meeting him on a Fitchburg street one day, Joe stroked his own beard and remarked: "Knowest thou that thy redeemer liveth?"

Joe Palmer died in 1875, when beards were at their fullest, and was thus spared the dreadful sight of their withering and final disappearance. What happened during the thirty-five years following Joe's death would certainly have saddened him.

The whisker debacle of the last quarter of the nineteenth century has engrossed only a few of us minor social historians, but Mr. Lewis Gannett has charted the decline so graphically that little more research needs to be done. He used his alma mater, Harvard University, to demonstrate the mysterious rises and falls of male American hair; and his studies show that graduating classes of the 1860's were hairy as goats. The Class of 1870 had four beards. Two years later a good majority were wearing not beards but mustaches and burnsides. By 1890 beards and burnsides (sideburns are the same thing, only there isn't quite so much to them) were distinctly obsolete, and the mustache was at or nearing its peak.

Decline now followed with tragic speed. The Class of 1900 was without one beard, the first such crowd of sissies since the Mexican War. The last Harvard football mustache appeared in 1901, Mr. Gannett's chart shows, and the last Harvard baseball mustache in 1905. Since then Harvard men—except for a few professors—have been mostly smooth of chin and lip.

The White House witnessed a similar decline of hair. From Lincoln to Wilson, only one man without at least a mustache was elected to the Presidency. Grant had a beard, Hayes was positively hairy. Garfield fairly burgeoned with whiskers. Cleveland had a sizable mustache, Harrison a flowing beard, and both Theodore Roosevelt and Taft had mustaches. The lone smooth-shaven President during this entire period was McKinley.

Beginning with Wilson in 1912 and continuing to the present, no President has worn hair on his face. Many thought it was his beard that defeated Hughes,[1] and his was for years the only honest beard to wag on the once heavily whiskered Supreme Court.

Old Joe Palmer, then, died at exactly the right time, and he took some pains to make certain, no matter what styles frivolous men might adopt, that he was not wholly forgotten. In the old cemetery in North Leominster, not far from Fitchburg, is his monument, a rugged square stone as tall as a man; and on its front is an excellent medallion carving of Joe's head, with its noble beard flowing and rippling in white marble. Below the head appears a simple legend: "Persecuted for Wearing the Beard."

Joe Palmer's last home, the celebrated Fruitlands in nearby Harvard, has been restored with loving care as an historical showplace by Clara Endicott Sears—not so much in memory of Palmer as of the Alcotts. In this charming house, however, one may see old Joe's beautiful furniture, and a good photograph of the kindly yet

determined old gentleman who wished to be remembered only as the Redeemer of the Beard.

FOR STUDY AND DISCUSSION

1. How would you characterize Joseph Palmer as he is revealed in this essay? What points of view did Palmer hold? To what extent did his opinions and actions contribute to his persecution? Why does Holbrook think Palmer was a great individualist?

2. Why do you think Holbrook has chosen to write about a man's struggle to keep his beard rather than about a more important struggle for the rights of the individual? What point do you think he wishes to make?

3. "The Beard of Joseph Palmer" combines biography with history. Which part of the essay is primarily biographical? Which is primarily historical? Do you think that an essay based on either the biographical or the historical aspect would have been as interesting? Why or why not?

4. Find sentences in the essay that show that Holbrook is aware of the humorous side of Joseph Palmer's struggle. (For example, in writing that "it was Joe Palmer who carried the Knowledge of Whiskers through the dark ages of beardless America," Holbrook is using humorous exaggeration.)

LANGUAGE AND VOCABULARY

Explain how the italicized words help bring out the humorous aspect of Joseph Palmer's story. Look up any words you do not know.

1. "What made this beard particularly *heinous* . . ."
2. "He was born almost a century too late and seventy-five years too soon to wear whiskers with *impunity*."
3. "Day after day he sat in his *limbo* . . ."
4. "Reverend Trask who had so *churlishly* upbraided him many years before for wearing his beard."
5. "The whisker *debacle* of the last quarter of the nineteenth century . . ."

FOR COMPOSITION

In his essay, Holbrook mentions Emerson, Thoreau, and Whitman. Explain what Joseph Palmer has in common with these writers, citing passages from these writers to support your points.

[1] **Hughes:** Charles Evans Hughes, Chief Justice of the Supreme Court (1930–41), and candidate for President in 1916.

F. SCOTT
FITZGERALD
(1896–1940)

In 1936, F. Scott Fitzgerald (see biography on page 550) wrote for *Esquire* magazine a series of three articles telling how, at the age of thirty-nine, he had had a nervous breakdown, the result of "too much anger and too many tears." The first article describes how he had "cracked like an old plate." The third article, called "Pasting It Together," describes how he managed to survive the breakdown and the price he paid—an increased bitterness and a realization that "life would never be very pleasant again." What follows is the second article, "Handle with Care." The three articles were later published together posthumously under the collective title "The Crack-Up."

After the publication of these essays, Fitzgerald was rebuked for revealing so much of his personal life. He was particularly hurt that Ernest Hemingway "bawled me out for having been so public about what were essentially private affairs. . . ." Now, many years after their initial appearance, the articles have ceased to be embarrassingly personal and are valued for their revealing account of a crisis in the life of a gifted writer.

FROM *The Crack-Up*

March, 1936

IN A PREVIOUS article this writer told about his realization that what he had before him was not the dish that he had ordered for his forties. In fact—since he and the dish were one, he described himself as a cracked plate, the kind that one wonders whether it is worth preserving. Your editor thought that the article suggested too many aspects without regarding them closely, and probably many readers felt the same way—and there are always those to whom all self-revelation is contemptible, unless it ends with a noble thanks to the gods for the Unconquerable Soul. [1]

[1] **Unconquerable Soul:** a reference to lines from "Invictus," a poem by the British poet William Ernest Henley: "I thank whatever gods may be/ For my unconquerable soul/ . . . I am the master of my fate;/ I am the captain of my soul."

But I had been thanking the gods too long, and thanking them for nothing. I wanted to put a lament into my record, without even the background of the Euganean Hills [1] to give it color. There weren't any Euganean hills that I could see.

Sometimes, though, the cracked plate has to be retained in the pantry, has to be kept in service as a household necessity. It can never again be warmed on the stove nor shuffled with the other plates in the dishpan; it will not be brought out for company, but it will do to hold crackers late at night or to go into the ice box under leftovers . . .

Hence this sequel—a cracked plate's further history.

Now the standard cure for one who is sunk is to consider those in actual destitution or physical suffering—this is an all-weather beatitude for gloom in general and fairly salutary daytime advice for everyone. But at three o'clock in the morning, a forgotten package has the same tragic importance as a death sentence, and the cure doesn't work—and in a real dark night of the soul, it is always three o'clock in the morning, day after day. At that hour the tendency is to refuse to face things as long as possible by retiring into an infantile dream—but one is continually startled out of this by various contacts with the world. One meets these occasions as quickly and carelessly as possible and retires once more back into the dream, hoping that things will adjust themselves by some great material or spiritual bonanza. But as the withdrawal persists, there is less and less chance of the bonanza—one is not waiting for the fade-out of a single sorrow, but rather being an unwilling witness of an execution, the disintegration of one's own personality . . .

This phase comes to a dead end, eventually, and is succeeded by a vacuous quiet. In this you can try to estimate what has been sheared away and what is left. Only when this quiet came to me, did I realize that I had gone through two parallel experiences.

The first time was twenty years ago, when I left Princeton in junior year with a complaint diagnosed as malaria. It transpired, through an X ray taken a dozen years later, that it had been tuberculosis—a mild case, and after a few months of rest I went back to college. But I had lost certain offices, the chief one was the presidency of the Triangle Club,[2] a musical comedy idea, and also I dropped back a class. To me college would never be the same. There were to be no badges of pride, no medals, after all. It seemed on one March afternoon that I had lost every single thing I wanted.

Years later I realized that my failure as a big shot in college was all right—instead of serving on committees, I took a beating on English poetry; when I got the idea of what it was all about, I set about learning how to write. On Shaw's [3] principle that "If you don't get what you like, you better like what you get," it was a lucky break—at the moment it was a harsh and bitter business to know that my career as a leader of men was over.

Since that day I have not been able to fire a bad servant, and I am astonished and impressed by people who can. Some old desire for personal dominance was broken and gone. Life around me was a solemn dream, and I lived on the letters I wrote to a girl in another city. A man does not recover from such jolts—he becomes a different person and, eventually, the new person finds new things to care about.

The other episode parallel to my current situation took place after the war, when I had again overextended my flank. It was one of those tragic loves doomed for lack of money, and one day the girl closed it out on the basis of common sense. During a long summer of despair I wrote a

---

[1] **Euganean Hills:** In "Lines Written Among the Euganean Hills" (1818), the British poet Percy Bysshe Shelley attempts to conquer his despair.

[2] **Triangle Club:** a club at Princeton University that puts on an annual musical comedy.

[3] **Shaw:** George Bernard Shaw (1856–1950), Irish dramatist and essayist.

novel instead of letters, so it came out all right, but it came out all right for a different person. The man with the jingle of money in his pocket who married the girl a year later would always cherish an abiding distrust, an animosity, toward the leisure class—not the conviction of a revolutionist but the smoldering hatred of a peasant. In the years since then I have never been able to stop wondering where my friends' money came from.

For sixteen years I lived pretty much as this latter person, distrusting the rich, yet working for money with which to share their mobility and the grace that some of them brought into their lives. During this time I had plenty of the usual horses shot from under me—I remember some of their names—*Punctured Pride, Thwarted Expectation, Faithless, Show-off, Hard Hit, Never Again.* And after awhile I wasn't twenty-five, then not even thirty-five, and nothing was quite as good. But in all these years I don't remember a moment of discouragement. I saw honest men through moods of suicidal gloom—some of them gave up and died; others adjusted themselves and went on to a larger success than mine; but my morale never sank below the level of self-disgust when I had put on some unsightly personal show. Trouble has no necessary connection with discouragement—discouragement has a germ of its own, as different from trouble as arthritis is different from a stiff joint.

When a new sky cut off the sun last spring, I didn't at first relate it to what had happened fifteen or twenty years ago. Only gradually did a certain family resemblance come through—an overextension of the flank, a burning of the candle at both ends; a call upon physical resources that I did not command, like a man overdrawing at his bank. In its impact this blow was more violent than the other two, but it was the same in kind—a feeling that I was standing at twilight on a deserted range, with an empty rifle in my hands and the targets down. No problem set—simply

a silence with only the sound of my own breathing.

In this silence there was a vast irresponsibility toward every obligation, a deflation of all my values. A passionate belief in order, a disregard of motives or consequences in favor of guesswork and prophecy, a feeling that craft and industry would have a place in any world—one by one, these and other convictions were swept away. I saw that the novel, which at my maturity was the strongest and supplest medium for conveying thought and emotion from one human being to another, was becoming subordinated to a mechanical and communal art that, whether in the hands of Hollywood merchants or Russian idealists, was capable of reflecting only the tritest thought, the most obvious emotion. It was an art in which words were subordinate to images, where personality was worn down to the inevitable low gear of collaboration. As long past as 1930, I had a hunch that the talkies would make even the best-selling novelist as archaic as silent pictures. People still read, if only Professor Canby's book of the month [1]—but there was a rankling indignity, that to me had become almost an obsession, in seeing the power of the written word subordinated to another power, a more glittering, a grosser power . . .

I set that down as an example of what haunted me during the long night—this was something I could neither accept nor struggle against, something which tended to make my efforts obsolescent, as the chain stores have crippled the small merchant, an exterior force, unbeatable——

(I have the sense of lecturing now, looking at a watch on the desk before me and seeing how many more minutes——.)

Well, when I had reached this period of silence, I was forced into a measure that no one ever adopts voluntarily: I was impelled to think. God, was it difficult! The moving about of great secret trunks. In the first exhausted halt, I wondered whether I had ever thought. After a long time I came to these conclusions, just as I write them here:

(1) That I had done very little thinking, save within the problems of my craft. For twenty years a certain man had been my intellectual conscience. That was Edmund Wilson. [2]

(2) That another man represented my sense of the "good life," though I saw him once in a decade, and since then he might have been hung. He is in the fur business in the Northwest and wouldn't like his name set down here. But in difficult situations I had tried to think what *he* would have thought, how *he* would have acted.

(3) That a third contemporary [3] had been an artistic conscience to me—I had

not imitated his infectious style, because my own style, such as it is, was formed before he published anything, but there was an awful pull toward him when I was on a spot.

(4) That a fourth man [4] had come to dictate my relations with other people when these relations were successful: how to do, what to say. How to make people at least momentarily happy (in opposition to Mrs. Post's theories [5] of how to make everyone thoroughly uncomfortable with a sort of systematized vulgarity). This always confused me and made me want to go out and get drunk, but this man had seen the game, analyzed it, and beaten it, and his word was good enough for me.

(5) That my political conscience had scarcely existed for ten years save as an element of irony in my stuff. When I became again concerned with the system I should function under, it was a man much younger than myself [6] who brought it to me, with a mixture of passion and fresh air.

So there was not an "I" any more—not a basis on which I could organize my self-respect—save my limitless capacity for toil that it seemed I possessed no more. It was strange to have no self—to be like a little boy left alone in a big house, who knew that now he could do anything he wanted to do, but found that there was nothing that he wanted to do——

(The watch is past the hour and I have barely reached my thesis. I have some doubts as to whether this is of general interest, but if anyone wants more, there is plenty left and your editor will tell me. If you've had enough, say so—but not too loud, because I have the feeling that someone, I'm not sure who, is sound asleep—someone who could have helped me to keep my shop open.)

---

[1] **Professor . . . month:** Henry Seidel Canby (1871–1961), was an advisor to the Book of the Month Club.

[2] **Wilson:** Edmund Wilson (1895–), the distinguished critic, was a close friend of Fitzgerald.

[3] **third contemporary:** Ernest Hemingway (see page 521).

[4] **a fourth man:** Gerald Murphy, a wealthy American friend in France.

[5] **Mrs. Post's theories:** Emily Post (1873–1960) was the author of a famous book on etiquette.

[6] **man . . . myself:** Probably Budd Schulburg, the American novelist (1914–).

The Expatriates

After World War I, many young American writers and artists came to believe, in Malcolm Cowley's words, in "The idea of self-expression . . . the idea of liberty . . . the idea of changing place. . . . By expatriating himself, by living in Paris, Capri, or the South of France, the artist can break the Puritan shackles [of American life] freely, and be wholly creative." To be able to do just this and to learn at first hand the new ideas about literature, music, and art that were circulating there, many young writers and artists went to live in Paris.

On one occasion, Gertrude Stein, an older American living in Paris, said to Ernest Hemingway, "You are all a lost generation." When Hemingway used this phrase in his novel *The Sun Also Rises,* many other people began to think of these young Americans as a "lost generation." But they thought of themselves as a *liberated* generation, as a generation liberated by new artistic techniques, new ideas, and a free life. Their exuberance and exhilaration was reflected in their work. Although there was sometimes a hectic undertone to their work, in many ways this period of youth and nervous optimism was one of the great literary periods in America. But it was a period that could not last. As Malcolm Cowley noted, "It was an easy, quick, adventurous age, good to be young in; and yet on coming out of it one felt a sense of relief, as on coming out of a room too full of talk and people into the sunlight of winter streets."

FOR STUDY AND DISCUSSION

1. To what does Fitzgerald compare himself in the first paragraph? How does he develop the comparison in the third paragraph? Cite three other examples of Fitzgerald's use of comparisons to convey an idea or a state of mind.
2. What two specific experiences in his earlier life does Fitzgerald recount? How are they related to his present depression?
3. As a result of his "thinking," Fitzgerald decided that "there was not an 'I' any more." Explain this phrase. What influences contributed to this feeling?
4. Why does Fitzgerald think that the growth of the film industry is leading to the decline of the novel? Do you agree or disagree? Explain.
5. Fitzgerald's third essay, "Pasting It Together" (see page 706), describes his decision to make "some sort of clean break" with the past. "A clean break is something you cannot come back from; that is irretrievable because it makes the past cease to exist. So, since I could no longer fulfill the obligations that life had set for me or that I had set for myself, why not slay the empty shell who had been posturing as it for four years." He wrote, "I have now at last become a writer only. The man I had persistently tried to be became such a burden that I have 'cut him loose'. . . ." Judging from the selection you have read, describe what Fitzgerald tried to "cut loose" from.

LANGUAGE AND VOCABULARY

Explain how the italicized words deepen your understanding of Fitzgerald's state of mind. Look up any words you do not know.
1. "an all-weather *beatitude* for gloom . . ."
2. "*vacuous* quiet."
3. "that to me had become almost an *obsession* . . ."
4. "something which tended to make my efforts *obsolescent* . . ."

FOR COMPOSITION

This essay contains one of the most often quoted phrases in modern literature: "in a real dark night of the soul, it is always three o'clock in the morning." Explain what Fitzgerald means by this phrase. Then explore the psychological depth of the phrase by applying it to lives other than Fitzgerald's. Consider also whether the phrase applies to any stories, novels, or poems you have read.

AMERICAN PAINTING

The Great Depression: Regionalism and Social Protest

During the Depression years of the 1930's, American painters seem to have turned away from Europe as a source of inspiration. There were exceptions, of course, but by and large the modernist movements introduced by the Armory Show were now at least temporarily forgotten. The new battle cry was the rediscovery of America: its history, and the various types of people and culture in its many different regions. In art, this new attitude was expressed by a return to realism.

The most widely reproduced painting from this "regionalist" movement was Grant Wood's *American Gothic* (PLATE 1). Part of the appeal of this painting was its "period" flavor—the old-fashioned pose of the two figures and the Victorian Gothic house in the background. The figures represent the kind of rural types that had been popularized in novels of the preceding decade. And Wood's fastidious attention to the most minute details satisfied the average person's interest in literal realism.

There seems to be little in common between Wood's prim rural couple and the pitiful creatures in Reginald Marsh's picture *The Bowery* (PLATE 2), New York's famous "haven for homeless men." Both paintings, however, represent genuine aspects of our many-sided culture. In his picture Marsh used a fast-drying tempera medium instead of oil, building up his forms tone by tone with superimposed glazes of color. (You can distinguish some of these separate glazes in the tones of the pavement at the lower left and in those of the coat worn by the man who is pointing.) But though the figures in this painting are solidly constructed and crowded with realistic detail, the soft, flickering light that falls over the whole scene transforms it into a shadowy world of almost ghostlike images.

The hard years of the Depression produced a great deal of social protest in America. Among the most ardent crusaders against the inequities of the times was a young painter from Boston named Jack Levine, who chose subjects such as secret back-room "deals" between corrupt lawyers, politicians, and policemen (*The Feast of Pure Reason,* PLATE 3). Despite his choice of subject matter, Levine was essentially a traditional painter, thoroughly familiar with the work of the great European masters. By painting pictures of social protest he was simply trying "to bring the great tradition up to date." The reproduction in PLATE 3 gives you at least some idea of his lively handling of paint, as well as of the richness and thickness of the pigment itself. A subtle play between light and shadow brings the most important details into sharp focus and leaves the others purposely blurred.

The most outspoken champion of regionalism in American painting during the 1930's was Thomas Hart Benton of Missouri. As a young man Benton participated in the Cubist movement in Paris, but after World War I he rejected European modernism altogether, developing a more realistic style in order to portray various aspects of American life. The *Arts of the West, Mural #2* (PLATE 4), is one of a series of wall paintings, or murals, that celebrate our expanding frontier life. Such solid forms composed in deep space shocked many of Benton's contemporaries, who argued that a mural should always appear two-dimensional, that it should never seem to "punch a hole" in the wall. Benton paid little heed to his critics, however, and continued to work according to his own convictions.

Ben Shahn also painted pictures of social protest during the 1930's, but he relied more on understatement and irony than did Levine. His tempera painting *Handball* (PLATE 5), for example, contains none of Levine's gross characterization or heavily loaded paint textures, nor has it any of the melodrama of Benton's murals. The composition is trim and spare: six crisply patterned figures silhouetted against the light ground and the white handball court look like cutouts pasted on a page. Each figure seems isolated, yet all six are linked together by the hypnotic action of the game. Notice, incidentally, that Shahn has provided no markings on the ground to help us determine spatial intervals in depth. Furthermore, because of their brightly colored patterns, the distant billboards and brick buildings seem to press forward, thus distorting the perspective. It is only the varying sizes of the figures themselves that offer a clue to human scale in this vast, open, and impersonal urban space.

A feeling of resignation and acceptance rather than of protest seems to pervade Ivan Le Lorraine Albright's picture *That Which I Should Have Done I Did Not Do* (PLATE 6). The title gives us a clue to its theme: the tragedy of all mortal beings and material things. A funeral wreath hangs on a tall, coffinlike door which has been scarred and warped out of shape. At the far left, the puffy white hand of an old woman tenderly touches the elaborately carved surface of the door jamb. This odd blend of realism and fantasy perhaps can be best explained by Albright's own statement: "A picture is like a house wherein all things are to be found, both material and immaterial; it is a place wherein, side by side, rest decay and the sublime. . . ."

PLATE 1. GRANT WOOD (1892–1942): *American Gothic*. 1930. Oil on beaver board, $29\frac{7}{8}$ x $24\frac{7}{8}$ inches. (Courtesy of The Art Institute of Chicago)

PLATE 2. REGINALD MARSH (1898–1954): *The Bowery*. 1930. Tempera on canvas, 48 x 36 inches. (The Metropolitan Museum of Art, New York, Arthur H. Hearn Fund, 1932)

714

PLATE 3. JACK LEVINE (1915–): *The Feast of Pure Reason.* 1937. Oil on canvas, 42 x 48 inches. (On extended loan to The Museum of Modern Art from the United States WPA Art Program)

PLATE 4. THOMAS HART BENTON (1889–): *Arts of the West, Mural #2.* 1932. Tempera and oil, 8 x 13 feet. (The New Britain Museum of American Art, New Britain, Connecticut.)

716

PLATE 5. BEN SHAHN (1898–): *Handball.* 1939. Tempera on canvas, 24 x 33¼ inches. (Collection, The Museum of Modern Art, New York, Abby Aldrich Rockefeller Fund)

PLATE 6. IVAN LE LORRAINE
ALBRIGHT (1897–   ): *"That
Which I Should Have Done I Did
Not Do."* 1941. Oil on canvas,
97 x 36 inches. (Courtesy of The
Art Institute of Chicago)

718

JOHN UPDIKE

(1932–)

John Updike is recognized as one of the most brilliant of our younger writers. His early stories in *The New Yorker* have been praised for their fine craftsmanship. They have also been criticized for having smooth, highly polished surfaces that conceal an unwillingness to take chances and to deal with important subjects. But Updike has been expanding and deepening his art. In his novels and later short stories, he has explored some of the most basic issues of our times—questions of faith and unbelief, of the preservation of individual identity in an increasingly complex and mechanized society. With acute insight, he has portrayed characters reaching out and painfully attempting to communicate with others; to love, express love, and be loved in return. He has stated that an author should express the "complexity and ambiguity of life," and his stories, especially, show his skill at revealing depths of meaning in seemingly ordinary situations.

The only child of a high school mathematics teacher, Updike spent his boyhood in Shillington, Pennsylvania. In 1954 he graduated summa cum laude from Harvard University and then spent a year in Oxford, England, studying art at the Ruskin School of Drawing and Fine Art. Returning to the United States, he worked on the staff of *The New Yorker* until 1957, when he turned his full attention to writing poetry, short stories, and novels. He now lives in Connecticut with his wife and children. In 1958 his first book of poetry, *The Carpentered Hen and Other Tame Creatures,* appeared, to be followed by the novels *The Poorhouse Fair* and *Rabbit, Run* and a collection of short stories, *Pigeon Feathers.* His novel *The Centaur* won the National Book Award for fiction for 1963. More recently, he has written another novel, *On the Farm,* and has published a further collection of light verse.

In 1965, *Assorted Prose,* a collection of Updike's nonfiction, was published. Many of the works included are of minor interest: parodies, book reviews, short interviews written for the "Talk of the Town" section of *The New Yorker.* Two of the works are especially fine. One is an account of the retirement of the great hitter Ted Williams from the Boston Red Sox. The other work, far more personal and complex, deals with the author's boyhood and shows many of the qualities of his best fiction. Among other things, it is a study of loneliness. "My own sense of the abysses of childhood doesn't come at all from being . . . [a] father," Mr. Updike once said, "it comes from having *been* a child. We're all so curiously alone. But it's important to keep making signals through the glass."

The Dogwood Tree: Boyhood in the 1940's

WHEN I WAS BORN, my parents and my mother's parents planted a dogwood tree in the side yard of the large white house in which we lived throughout my boyhood. This tree, I learned quite early, was exactly my age; was, in a sense, me. But I never observed it closely, am not now sure what color its petals were; its presence was no more distinct than that of my shadow. The tree was my shadow, and had it died, had it ceased to occupy, each year with increasing volume and brilliance, its place in the side yard, I would have felt that a blessing like the blessing of light had been withdrawn from my life.

Though I cannot ask you to see it more clearly than I myself saw it, yet mentioning it seems to open the possibility of my boyhood home coming again to life. With a sweet damp rush the grass of our yard seems to breathe again on me. It is just cut. My mother is pushing the mower, to which a canvas catch is attached. My grandmother is raking up the loose grass in thick heaps, small green haystacks impregnated with dew, and my grandfather stands off to one side, smoking a cigar, elegantly holding the elbow of his right arm in the palm of his left hand while the blue smoke twists from under his mustache and dissolves in the heavy evening air, that misted, too-rich Pennsylvania air. My father is off, doing some duty in the town; he is a conscientious man, a schoolteacher and deacon, and also, somehow, a man of the streets. . . .

From "Boyhood in the 1940's" (abridged) by John Updike in *Five Boyhoods*, edited by Martin Levin, published by Doubleday & Co., Inc., copyright © 1962 by Martin Levin. Reprinted by permission of Martin Levin.

My boyhood was spent in a world made tranquil by two invisible catastrophes: the Depression and World War II. Between 1932, when I was born, and 1945, when we moved away, the town of Shillington changed, as far as I could see, very little. The vacant lot beside our home on Philadelphia Avenue remained vacant. The houses along the street were neither altered nor replaced. The high school grounds, season after season, continued to make a placid plain visible from our rear windows. The softball field, with its triptych backstop, was nearest us. A little beyond, on the left, were the school and its boiler house, built in the late 1920's of the same ochre brick. In the center a cinder track circumscribed the football field. At a greater distance there were the tennis courts and the poor farm fields and the tall double rows of trees marking the Poorhouse Lane. The horizon was the blue cloud, scarred by a gravel pit's orange slash, of Mount Penn, which overlooked the city of Reading.

A little gravel alley, too small to be marked with a street sign but known in the neighborhood as Shilling Alley, wound hazardously around our property and on down, past an untidy sequence of back buildings—chicken houses, barns out of plumb, a gunshop, a small lumber mill, a shack where a blind man lived, and the enchanted grotto of a garage whose cement floors had been waxed to the luster of ebony by oil drippings and in whose greasy-black depths a silver drinking fountain spurted the coldest water in the world, silver water so cold it made your front teeth throb—on down to Lancaster Avenue, the main street, where the trolley cars ran. All through those years, the trolley cars ran. All through those years Pappy Shilling, the surviving son of the landowner after whom the town was named, walked up and down Philadelphia Avenue with his thin cane and his snow-white bangs; a vibrating chain of perfect-Sunday-school-attendance pins dangled

from his lapel. Each autumn the horse-chestnut trees dropped their useless, treasurable nuts; each spring the dogwood tree put forth a slightly larger spread of blossoms; always the leaning walnut tree in our back yard fretted with the same black branches the view we had.

Within our house, too, there was little change. My grandparents did not die, though they seemed very old. My father continued to teach at the high school; he had secured the job shortly after I was born. No one else was born. I was an only child. A great many only children were born in 1932. I make no apologies. I do not remember ever feeling the space for a competitor within the house. The five of us already there locked into a star that would have shattered like crystal at the admission of a sixth. We had no pets. We fed Tommy [1] on the porch, but he was too wild to set foot in the kitchen, and only my grandmother, in a way wild herself, could touch him. Tommy came to us increasingly battered and once did not come at all. As if he had never existed: that was death. And then there was a squirrel, Tilly, that we fed peanuts to; she became very tame, and under the grape arbor would take them from our hands—the excitement of those tiny brown teeth shivering against my fingertips: life. But she, too, came from the outside, and returned to her tree, and did not dare intrude in our house.

The arrangement inside, which seemed to me so absolute, had been achieved, beyond the peripheries of my vision, drastically and accidentally. It may, at first, have been meant to be temporary. My father and grandfather were casualties of the early thirties. My father lost his job as a cable splicer with the telephone company; he and my mother had been living—for how long I have never understood—in boardinghouses and hotels throughout western Pennsylvania, in towns whose names (Hazelton, Altoona) even now make their faces light up with youth, a glow flowing out of the darkness preceding my birth. They lived through this darkness, and the details of the adventure that my mother recalls—her lonely closeted days, the games of solitaire, the novels by Turgenev,[2] the men sleeping and starving in the parks of Pittsburgh—seem to waken in her an unjust and unreasonable happiness that used to rouse jealousy in my childish heart. I remember waiting with her by a window for my father to return from weeks on the road. It is in the Shillington living room. My hands are on the radiator ridges, I can see my father striding through the hedge toward the grape arbor, I feel my mother's excitement beside me mingle with mine. But she says this cannot be; he had lost his job before I was born.

My grandfather came from farming people in the south of the county. He prospered, and prematurely retired; the large suburban house he bought to house his good fortune became his fortune's shell, the one fragment of it left him. The two men pooled their diminished resources of strength and property and, with their women, came to live together. I do not believe they expected this arrangement to last long. For all of them —for all four of my adult guardians— Shillington was a snag, a halt in a journey

---

[1] **Tommy:** a neighborhood cat.

[2] **Turgenev:** Ivan Turgenev (1818–1883), Russian novelist.

that had begun elsewhere. Only I belonged to the town. The accidents that had planted me here made uneasy echoes in the house, but, like Tilly and Tommy, their source was beyond my vision. . . .

I moved upward from grade to grade and birthday to birthday on a notched stick that itself was held perfectly steady. There was the movie house, and the playground, and the schools, and the grocery stores, and our yard, and my friends, and the horse-chestnut trees. My geography went like this: in the center of the world lay our neighborhood of Shillington. Around it there was greater Shillington, and around that, Berks County. Around Berks County there was the State of Pennsylvania, the best, the least eccentric, state in the Union. Around Pennsylvania, there was the United States, with a greater weight of people on the right and a greater weight of land on the left. For clear geometrical reasons, not all children could be born, like me, at the center of the nation. But that some children chose to be born in other countries and even continents seemed sad and fantastic. There was only one possible nation: mine. Above this vast, rectangular, slightly (the schoolteachers insisted) curved field of the blessed, there was the sky, and the flag, and, mixed up with both, Roosevelt.[1]

NOW

Roosevelt was for me the cap on a steadfast world, its emblem and crown. He was always there. Now he is a weakening memory, a semimyth; it has begun to seem fabulous—like an episode in a medieval chronicle—that the greatest nation in the world was led through the world's greatest war by a man who could not walk. Now the brick home of my boyhood is owned by a doctor, who has added an annex to the front, to contain his offices. The house was too narrow for its lot and its height; it had a pinched look from the front that used to annoy my mother. But

[1]**Roosevelt:** Franklin Delano Roosevelt (1882–1945), thirty-second President of the United States.

that thin white front with its eyes of green window sash and its mouth of striped awning had been a face to me; it has vanished. My dogwood tree still stands in the side yard, taller than ever, but the walnut tree out back has been cut down. My grandparents are dead. Pappy Shilling is dead. Shilling Alley has been straightened, and hardtopped, and rechristened Brobst Street. The trolley cars no longer run. The vacant lots across the town have been filled with new houses and stores. New homes have been built far out Philadelphia Avenue and all over the poorhouse property. The poorhouse has been demolished. The poorhouse dam and its groves have been trimmed into a town park. If I could go again into 117 Philadelphia Avenue, and look out the rear windows, I would see, beyond the football field and the cinder track, a new, two-million-dollar high school, and beyond it, where still stands one row of the double line of trees that marked the Poorhouse Lane, a gaudy depth of postwar housing and a Food Fair[2] like a hideous ark breasting an ocean of parked cars. Here, where wheat grew, loudspeakers unremittingly vomit commercials. It has taken me the shocks of many returnings, more and more widely spaced now, to learn, what seems simple enough, that change is the order of things. The immutability, the steadfastness, of the site of my boyhood was an exceptional effect, purchased for me at unimaginable cost by the paralyzing calamity of the Depression and the heroic external effort of the Second World War.

SCHOOLS

The elementary school was a big brick cube set in a square of black surfacing chalked and painted with the diagrams and runes of children's games. Wire fences guarded the neighboring homes from the playground. Whoever, at soccer, kicked the ball over the fence into Snitzy's yard had to bring it back. It was very terrible

[2] **Food Fair:** a chain of supermarkets.

to have to go into Snitzy's yard, but there was only one ball for each grade. Snitzy was a large dark old German who might give you the ball or lock you up in his garage, depending upon his mood. He did not move like other men; suddenly the air near you condensed, and his huge black hands were around your head.

I was a Crow. That is my chief memory of what went on inside the elementary school. In music class the singers were divided into three groups: Nightingales, Robins, and Crows. From year to year the names changed. Sometimes the Crows were Parrots. When visitors from the high school, or elsewhere "outside," came to hear us sing, the Crows were taken out of the room and sent upstairs to watch with the fifth grade an educational film about salmon fishing in the Columbia River. Usually there were only two of us, me and a girl from Philadelphia Avenue whose voice was in truth very husky. I never understood why I was a Crow, though it gave me a certain derisive distinction. As I heard it, I sang rather well, and my singing gives me pleasure still.

The other Crow was the first girl I kissed. I just did it, one day, walking back from school along the gutter where the water from the ice plant ran down, because somebody dared me to. And I continued to do it every day, when we reached that spot on the pavement, until a neighbor told my mother, and she, with a solemn weight that seemed unrelated to the airy act, forbade it.

I walked to school mostly with girls. It happened that the mothers of Philadelphia Avenue and, a block up, of Second Street, had borne female babies in 1932. These babies now teased me, the lone boy in their pack, by singing the new song, "Oh, Johnny, oh Johnny, how you can love!" and stealing my precious rubber-lined bookbag. The queen of these girls later became the May Queen of our senior class. She had freckles and thick pigtails and green eyes and her mother made her wear high-top shoes long after the rest of us had stopped. She had so much vitality

that on the way back from school her nose would start bleeding for no reason. We would be walking along over the wings of the maple seeds and suddenly she would tip her head back and rest it on a wall while someone ran and soaked a handkerchief in the ice-plant water and applied it to her streaming, narrow, crimson-shining nostrils. She was a Nightingale. I loved her deeply, and ineffectually.

My love for that girl carries through all those elementary-school cloakrooms; they always smelled of wet raincoats and rubbers. That tangy, thinly resonant, lonely smell: can love have a better envelope? Everything I did in grammar school was meant to catch her attention. I had a daydream wherein the stars of the music class were asked to pick partners and she, a Nightingale, picked me, a Crow. The teacher was shocked; the class buzzed. To their amazement I sang superbly; my voice, thought to be so ugly, in duet with hers was beautiful. Still singing, we led some sort of parade. In the world of reality, my triumph was getting her to slap me once. In the third grade. She was always slapping boys in those years; I could not quite figure out what they did. Pull her pigtails, untie her shoes, tease her (they called her "Pug")— this much I could see. But somehow there seemed to be under these offensive acts a current running the opposite way; for it was precisely the boys who were most hateful to her that she talked to solemnly at recess, and walked with after school, and whose names she wrote on the sides of her books. Without seeing this current, but deducing its presence, I tried to jump in; I entered a tussle she was having with a boy in homeroom before the bell. I pulled the bow at the back of her dress, and was slapped so hard that children at the other end of the hall heard the crack. I was overjoyed; the stain and pain on my face seemed a badge of initiation. But it was not; the distance between us remained as it was; I did not really want to tease her, I wanted to rescue her, and to be rescued by her. I lacked—and perhaps here the only child suffers a certain deprivation—that kink in the instincts on which childish courtship turns. He lacks a certain easy roughness with other children.

THREE BOYS

A, B, and *C,* I'll say, in case they care. *A* lived next door; he *loomed* next door, rather. He seemed immense—a great wallowing fatso stuffed with possessions; he was the son of a full-fashioned knitter. He seemed to have a beer-belly—solid, portentous, proud. After several generations beer-bellies may become congenital. Also his face had no features; it was just a blank ball on his shoulders. He used to call me "Ostrich," after Disney's Ollie Ostrich. My neck was not very long; the name seemed horribly unfair; it was its injustice that made me cry. But nothing I could say, or scream, would make him stop. And I still, now and then sometimes —in reading, say, a book review by one of the apple-cheeked savants of the quarterlies or one of the pious gremlins who manufacture puns for *Time*—get the old sensations: my ears close up, my eyes go warm, my chest feels thin as an eggshell, my voice churns silently in my stomach. From *A* I received my first impression of the smug, chinkless, irresistible *power* of stupidity; it is the most powerful force on earth. It says "Ostrich" often enough, and the universe crumbles.

A was more than a boy, he was a force-field that could manifest itself in many forms, that could take the wiry, disconsolate shape of wide-mouthed, tiny-eared boys who would now and then beat me up on the way back from school. I did not greatly mind being beaten up, though I resisted it. For one thing, it firmly involved me, at least during the beating, with the circumambient humanity that so often seemed evasive. Also, the boys who applied the beating were misfits, periodic flunkers, who wore knickers whose knees had lost the corduroy ribbing and men's shirts with the top button buttoned —this last an infallible sign of deep

poverty. So that I felt there was some justice, some condonable revenge, being applied with their fists to this little teacher's son. And then there was the delicious alarm of my mother and grandmother when I returned home bloody, bruised, and torn. My father took the attitude that it was making a boy of me, an attitude I dimly shared. He and I both were afraid of me becoming a sissy—he perhaps more afraid than I.

When I was eleven or so I met *B*. It was summer and I was down at the playground. He was pushing a little tank with moving rubber treads up and down the hills in the sandbox. It was a beautiful little toy, mottled with camouflage green;

patriotic manufacturers produced throughout the war millions of such authentic miniatures which we maneuvered with authentic, if miniature, hate. Drawn by the toy, I spoke to him; though taller and a little older than I, he had my dull straight brown hair and a look of being also alone. We became fast friends. He lived just up the street—toward the poorhouse, the east part of the street, from which the little winds of tragedy blew. He had just moved from the Midwest, and his mother was a widow. Besides wage war, we did many things together. We played marbles for days at a time, until one of us had won the other's entire coffee-canful. With jigsaws we cut out of plywood animals copied from comic books. We made movies by tearing the pages out of Big Little Books and coloring the drawings and pasting them in a strip, and winding them on toilet-paper spools, and making a cardboard carton a theater. We rigged up telephones, and racing wagons, and miniature cities, using orange crates and cigar boxes and peanut-butter jars and such potent debris. We loved Smokey Stover and were always saying "Foo." We had an intense spell of Monopoly. He called me "Uppy"—the only person who ever did so. I remember once, knowing he was coming down that afternoon to my house to play Monopoly, in order to show my joy I set up the board elaborately, with the Chance and Community Chest cards fanned painstakingly, like spiral staircases. He came into the room, groaned, "Uppy, what are you doing?" and impatiently scrabbled the cards together in a sensible pile. The older we got, the more the year between us told, and the more my friendship embarrassed him. We fought. Once, to my horror, I heard myself taunting him with the fact that he had no father. The unmentionable, the unforgivable. I suppose we patched things up, children do, but nothing was quite right after that. He had a long, pale, serious face, with buck teeth, and is probably an electronics engineer somewhere now, doing secret government work.

So through *B* I first experienced the pattern of friendship. There are three stages. First, acquaintance: we are new to each other, make each other laugh in surprise, and demand nothing beyond politeness. The death of the one would startle the other, no more. It is a pleasant stage, a stable stage; on austere rations of exposure it can live a lifetime, and the two parties to it always feel a slight gratification upon meeting, will feel vaguely confirmed in their human state. Then comes intimacy: now we laugh before two words of the joke are out of the other's mouth, because we know what he will say. Our whole two beings seem marvelously joined, from our toes to our heads, along tingling points of agreement; everything we venture is right, everything we put forth lodges in a corresponding socket in the frame of the other. The death of the one would grieve the other. To be

together is to enjoy a mounting excitement, a constant echo and amplification. It is an ecstatic and unstable stage, bound of its own agitation to tip into the third: revulsion. One or the other makes a misjudgment; presumes; puts forth that which does not meet agreement. Sometimes there is an explosion; more often the moment is swallowed in silence, and months pass before its nature dawns. Instead of dissolving, it grows. The mind, the throat, are clogged; forgiveness, forgetfulness, that have arrived so often, fail. Now everything jars and is distasteful; the betrayal, perhaps a tiny fraction in itself, has inverted the tingling column of agreement, made all pluses minuses. Everything about the other is hateful, despicable; yet he cannot be dismissed. We have confided in him too many minutes, too many words; he has those minutes and words as hostages, and his confidences are embedded in us where they cannot be scraped away, and even rivers of time cannot erode them completely, for there are indelible stains. Now—though the friends may continue to meet, and smile, as if they had never trespassed beyond acquaintance—the death of the one would please the other.

An unhappy pattern to which *C* is an exception. He was my friend before kindergarten, he is my friend still. I go to his home now, and he and his wife serve me and my wife with alcoholic drinks and slices of excellent cheese on crisp crackers, just as twenty years ago he served me with treats from his mother's refrigerator. He was a born host, and I a born guest. Also, he was intelligent. If my childhood's brain, when I look back at it, seems a primitive mammal, a lemur or shrew, his brain was an angel whose visitation was widely hailed as wonderful. When in school he stood to recite, his cool rectangular forehead glowed. He tucked his right hand into his left armpit and with his left hand mechanically tapped a pencil against his thigh. His answers were always correct. He beat me at spelling bees and, in another sort of competition, when we both collected Big Little Books, he outbid me for my supreme find (in the attic of a third boy), the first Mickey Mouse. I can still see that book, I wanted it so badly, its paper tan with age and its drawings done in Disney's primitive style, when Mickey's black chest is naked like a child's and his eyes are two nicked oblongs. Losing it was perhaps a lucky blow; it began to wean me away from any hope of ever having possessions.

C was fearless. He deliberately set fields on fire; he engaged in rock-throwing duels with tough boys. One afternoon he persisted in playing quoits with me although—as the hospital discovered that night—his appendix was nearly bursting. He was enterprising. He peddled magazine subscriptions door-to-door; he mowed neighbors' lawns; he struck financial bargains with his father. He collected stamps so well his collection blossomed into a stamp company that filled his room with steel cabinets and mimeograph machinery. He collected money—every time I went over to his house he would get out a little tin box and count the money in it for me: $27.50 one week, $29.95 the next, $30.90 the next—all changed into new bills nicely folded together. It was a strange ritual, whose meaning for me was: since he was

doing it, I didn't have to. His money made me richer. We read Ellery Queen and played chess and invented board games and discussed infinity together. In later adolescence, he collected records. He liked the Goodman quintets [1] but loved Fats Waller. [2] Sitting there in that room so familiar to me, where the machinery of the Shilco Stamp Company still crowded the walls and for that matter the tin box of money might still be hiding, while my pale friend grunted softly along with that dead dark angel on "You're Not the Only Oyster in the Stew," I felt, in the best sense, patronized. The perfect guest of the perfect host. What made it perfect was that we had both spent our entire lives in Shillington. . . .

ART

Leafing through a scrapbook my mother long ago made of my childhood drawings, I was greeted by one I had titled "Mr. Sun talking to Old Man Winter in his Office." Old Man Winter, a cloud with stick legs, and his host, a radiant ball with similar legs, sit at ease, both smiling, on two chairs that are the only furniture of the solar office. That the source of all light should have, somewhere, an office, suited my conception of an artist, who was someone who lived in a small town like Shillington, and who, equipped with pencils and paper, practiced his solitary trade as methodically as the dentist practiced his. And indeed, that is how it is at present with me.

Goethe—probably among others—says to be wary of our youthful wishes, for in maturity we are apt to get them. I go back, now, to Pennsylvania, and on one of the walls of the house in which my parents now live there hangs a photograph of myself as a boy. I am smiling, and staring with clear eyes at something in the corner of the room. I stand before that photograph, and am disappointed to receive no

[1] **Goodman quintets:** jazz records by the Benny Goodman quintet.
[2] **Fats Waller:** jazz pianist and composer.

flicker, not the shadow of a flicker, of approval, of gratitude. The boy continues to smile at the corner of the room, beyond me. That boy is not a ghost to me, he is real to me; it is I who am a ghost to him. I, in my present state, was one of the ghosts that haunted his childhood. Like some phantom conjured by this child from a glue bottle, I have executed his commands; acquired pencils, paper, and an office. Now I wait apprehensively for his next command, or at least a nod of appreciation, and he smiles through me, as if I am already transparent with failure.

He saw art—between drawing and writing he ignorantly made no distinction—as a method of riding a thin pencil line out of Shillington, out of time altogether, into an infinity of unseen and even unborn hearts. He pictured this infinity as radiant. How innocent! But his assumption here, like his assumptions on religion and politics, is one for which I had found no certain substitute. He loved blank paper and obedience to this love led me to a difficult artistic attempt. I reasoned thus: just as the paper is the basis for the marks upon it, might not events be contingent upon a never-expressed (because featureless) ground? Is the true marvel of Sunday skaters the pattern of their pirouettes or the fact that they are silently upheld? Blankness is not emptiness; we may skate upon an intense radiance we do not see because we see nothing else. And in fact there is a color, a quiet but tireless goodness that things at rest, like a brick wall or a small stone, seem to affirm. A wordless reassurance these things are pressing to give. An hallucination? To transcribe middleness with all its grits, bumps, and anonymities, in its fullness of satisfaction and mystery: is it possible or, in view of the suffering that violently colors the periphery and that at all moments threatens to move into the center, worth doing? Possibly not; but the horse-chestnut trees, the telephone poles, the porches, the green hedges recede to a calm point that in my subjective geography is still the center of the world.

END

I was walking down this Philadelphia Avenue one April and was just stepping over the shallow little rain gutter in the pavement that could throw you if you were on roller skates—though it had been years since I had been on roller skates—when from the semidetached house across the street a boy broke and ran. He was the youngest of six sons. All of his brothers were in the armed services, and five blue stars hung in his home's front window. He was several years older than I was, and used to annoy my grandparents by walking through our yard, down past the grape arbor, on his way to high school. On his long legs he was now running diagonally across the high-crowned street. I was the only other person out in the air. "Chonny!" he called. I was flattered to have him, so tall and grown, speak to me. "Did you hear?"

"No. What?"

"On the radio. The President is dead."

That summer the war ended, and that fall, suddenly mobile, we moved away from the big white house. We moved on Halloween night. As the movers were fitting the last pieces of our furniture, furniture that had not moved since I was born, into their truck, little figures dressed as ghosts and cats flitted in and out of the shadows of the street. A few rang our bell, and when my mother opened the door

they were frightened by the empty rooms they saw behind her, and went away without begging. When the last things had been packed, and the kitchen light turned off, and the doors locked, the three of us—my grandparents were already at the new house—got into the old Buick my father had bought—in Shillington we had never had a car, for we could walk everywhere—and drove up the street, east, toward the poorhouse and beyond. Somewhat self-consciously and cruelly dramatizing my grief, for I was thirteen and beginning to be cunning, I twisted and watched our house recede through the rear window. Moonlight momentarily caught in an upper pane; then the reflection passed, and the brightest thing was the white brick wall itself. Against the broad part where I used to play tennis with myself, the silhouette of the dogwood tree stood, confused with the shapes of the other bushes in our side yard but taller. I turned away before it would have disappeared from sight, and so it is that my shadow has always remained in one place.

FOR STUDY AND DISCUSSION

1. What is the importance of the dogwood tree to Updike? Why do you think he calls special attention to it in the title of the essay?

2. Describe Updike's attitudes toward Shillington, Pennsylvania, and toward his parents. Use specific details to support your answers.

3. What did Updike learn from his experiences with the girl he kissed and with friends *A, B,* and *C?* In what ways do you think these experiences shaped his character? If Updike had been your schoolmate, do you think you would have liked him? Why or why not? What is Updike's adult attitude toward himself as a boy?

4. Although this essay is divided into sections, each devoted to a different topic, several topics—principally the war and President Roosevelt—are referred to more than once. Explain how the recurrence of these topics helps unify the essay. What other recurring topics can you find?

5. Updike says that as a boy he "ignorantly made no distinction" between drawing and writing. How do you think his interest in art contributed to his development as a writer? Cite specific phrases and sentences to support your answer.

LANGUAGE AND VOCABULARY

One of the qualities for which Updike is noted is his careful style, his inventive, occasionally surprising, but almost always appropriate use of words. Discuss the choice of the italicized words below. Do any of them seem unusual or particularly inventive to you? Would you substitute more common words in some cases? Do you think that using these words makes Updike a better or a worse writer, a more or a less interesting stylist?

1. "the softball field, with its *triptych* backstop . . ."
2. "The *immutability,* the *steadfastness,* of the site of my boyhood was an exceptional effect, purchased for me at unimaginable cost . . ."
3. "a book review by one of the apple-cheeked *savants* of the quarterlies . . ."
4. "For one thing, it [the beating] firmly involved me, at least during the beating, with the *circumambient* humanity that so often seemed evasive."

FOR COMPOSITION

A distinctive feature of this essay is its vivid, loving descriptions of places that were an important part of Updike's boyhood. Write a short description from memory of a place that is, or was, an important part of your life. Choose your words and details carefully to show your attitude toward the place.

CRITICAL ESSAYS

VAN WYCK BROOKS

(1886–1963)

As a critic and cultural historian, Van Wyck Brooks was noted for several qualities: his concern with the problems of the artist in a materialistic society, his moral idealism and poetic vision of a society where the literary artist can achieve fulfillment, and his fine prose style, which is a sensitive expression of a highly individual point of view. Brooks's earlier books were attacks on the shortcomings of American civilization, a civilization that, in his view, repressed writers such as Henry James and Mark Twain, forcing the one to leave the United States and spend much of his creative life in England, and sapping the creative vitality of the second as he struggled to conform to the demands of a narrow-minded East (page 349). In his later work, Brooks undertook a reexamination of American life and literature of the nineteenth century. Where previously he had criticized America's past shortcomings, he now explored the American past for values it could offer contemporary America, defining and re-creating a rich literary tradition. As the critic Malcolm Cowley commented, what is important about Brooks's later writings is not only "his proof that in literature this country has long possessed a usable past. It is beyond this, his love of letters as an art and his integrity as a lonely scholar."

Van Wyck Brooks was born in Plainfield, New Jersey. In 1907 he was graduated from Harvard University, where he was one of the editors of the *Harvard Advocate*. After graduation, he spent a year and a half in England, writing articles for English newspapers and magazines. On returning to America, he wrote a number of important works, including *The Wine of the Puritans*, a critical appraisal of America's Puritan heritage; *The Ordeal of Mark Twain;* and *The Pilgrimage of Henry James*. An influential early work was *America's Coming of Age*, published in 1915, in which Brooks, like Emerson and Whitman before him, called upon the United States to overcome petty-mindedness and achieve literary and cultural greatness.

In the early 1930's Brooks began his monumental series, *Makers and Finders: A History of the Writer in America, 1800–1915*. The five books in the series are *The World of Washington Irving; The Flowering of New England, 1815–1865* (which won a Pulitzer prize); *The Times of Melville and Whitman; New England: Indian Summer, 1865–1915;* and *The Confident Years*. Together, these books are remarkable not only for the scholarship they display but for the skill with which they bring alive America's cultural past. Commenting on one book in the series, Edmund Wilson wrote, "He has put on the whole picture a color, a finish, a glaze like those of the best paintings of the period. . . ." If the books do have a fault, it is that Brooks's skill in coloring the past tends to make certain minor figures seem too important, too large a part of the national heritage. Nevertheless, *Makers and Finders* is one of the most important literary studies written by an American, a work that is made rich not only by its details but by its central vision, a vision of a "usable past" that all Americans can draw on as they face the future.

Emily Dickinson

THE DICKINSONS lived in the principal house in Amherst. A large, square, red-brick mansion that stood behind a hemlock hedge, with three gates accurately closed, it was a symbol of rural propriety and all the substantialities of western New England. Edward Dickinson, the lawyer, had always had his office in the village, and four times a day, in his broadcloth coat and beaver hat, with a gold-headed cane in his hand, he had passed through one of the gates, going or coming. A thin severe punctilious man who had once been a member of Congress, a friend of Daniel Webster [1] in his youth, a Calvinist [2] of the strictest persuasion, he was a pillar of Amherst College until his death in 1874. The college had been founded, largely by his father, to check the sort of errors that were spreading from Harvard, and he never abated his rigor in the interests of pleasure. He was said to have laughed on one occasion, but usually he was as cold and still as the white marble mantel in his parlor. The story was told in Amherst, however, that once he had rung the churchbell, as if to summon the people to a fire. The whole town came running, for he rang the bell excitedly. He wished to call attention to the sunset.

Next door, behind the hemlock hedge, another ample dwelling stood, suggesting in its style an Italian villa. Here lived the Squire's son Austin, once his partner, who kept open house for the college. While the Dickinson mansion was somewhat forbidding, with the stamp of the Squire's grim ways and his invalid wife, the villa was a center of Hampshire hospitality that shared its rolling lawns and charming garden. Olmsted had visited there, when he was planning Central Park, to examine the shrubs and trees, the plants and flowers; and distinguished guests at the college commencements and lecturers during the winter season were received and welcomed there as nowhere else. Emerson, Wendell Phillips,[3] and Beecher [4] had stayed in this house next door, and Samuel Bowles of the *Springfield Republican* was an intimate friend of all the Dickinsons. The *Republican* was a school for journalists, known far and wide, and travelers—Dickens and Kingsley [5] among them—constantly stopped at Springfield in order to have a chat with Samuel Bowles. His paper was a sovereign authority in Amherst, and he often drove

[1] **Daniel Webster:** American statesman and orator (1782–1852).
[2] **Calvinist:** a believer in the religious doctrines of the French theologian John Calvin (1509–1564), who emphasized man's depravity and God's sternness (see page 3).

"Emily Dickinson" from *A Chilmark Miscellany* by Van Wyck Brooks, copyright 1948 by E. P. Dutton & Co., Inc. Reprinted by permission of the publishers.

[3] **Wendell Phillips:** American abolitionist and social reformer (1811–1884).
[4] **Beecher:** Henry Ward Beecher (1813–1887), American clergyman famous for his powerful sermons; the brother of Harriet Beecher Stowe.
[5] **Kingsley:** Charles Kingsley (1819–1875), English novelist.

While her friends seldom saw her, and almost never face to face—for she spoke from the shadows of the hallway, as they sat in the parlor, or sometimes down the stairs—they were used to receiving little letters from her. These letters were also peculiar. Miss Dickinson rarely addressed the envelopes. Some other hand, perhaps her sister's, performed this office for her. More often the names of the person and town had been clipped from a printed paper and pasted together, as if it were a sort of violation to expose the strokes of her pen to the touch of the postman. The letters themselves were brief and cryptic, usually only a line or two: "Do you look out tonight?" for example. "The moon rides like a girl through a topaz town." Or "The frogs sing sweet today—they have such pretty, lazy times—how nice to be a frog." Or "Tonight the crimson children are playing in the West." Or "The lawn is full of south and the odors tangle, and I hear today for the first the river in the tree." Now and again, some fine phrase emerged from the silvery spray of words— "Not what the stars have done, but what they are to do, is what detains the sky." Sometimes her notes had a humorous touch: "Father steps like Cromwell [1] when he gets the kindlings," or "Mrs. S. gets bigger, and rolls down the lane to church like a reverend marble." But her messages often contained no words at all. She would lower baskets of goodies out of the window to children waiting below. At times, instead of a letter, she sent a poem, an odd little fragment of three or four lines, with a box of chocolate caramels or frosted cakes and a flower or a sprig of pine on top, heliotrope, perhaps, or an oleander blossom or a dandelion tied with a scarlet ribbon. Her letters were rhythmical, they scanned like the poems, and they were congested with images— every phrase was an image; while the poems themselves suggested nursery

[1] **Cromwell:** Oliver Cromwell (1599–1658), English statesman and general who led the Puritan revolution against Charles I and ruled England for nine years.

over for a call at the villa or the mansion, sometimes bringing manuscripts by well-known authors to show the Dickinson daughters before they were published. His favorite was Emily, who was older than Lavinia, but Emily usually "elfed it" when visitors came. She was always in the act of disappearing. Through the blinds of her western windows, overlooking the garden, she observed the hospitalities of the villa, and snatches of whatever was current in the books and talk of a college town, in the politics and thought of the moment, reached her when the guests had gone away. But even her oldest friends seldom saw her. While sometimes, in the evening, she flitted across the garden, she never left the place by day or night. To have caught a fleeting glimpse of her was something to boast of, and a young girl across the way who watched at night for a light at her window was thrilled if Miss Emily's shadow appeared for a moment. There were nursemaids who thought she was a witch. They frightened the children by uttering her name, as if there were something malign in Miss Dickinson's queerness.

rhymes or Dr. Watts's [1] hymns, broken up and filled with a strange new content. They might have struck unsympathetic readers as a sort of transcendental baby-talk. It was evident that Miss Dickinson had lost the art of communication, as the circle of her school friends understood it. She vibrated toward them, she put forth shy, impalpable tentacles, she instantly signalized with a verse or a note every event in their lives. But she did not speak the language of the world outside her, and one gathered that she did not wish to touch it. She was rapt in a private world of sensations and thoughts. It was even observed that her handwriting went through three distinct phases and that toward the end the letters never touched. Each character, separately formed, stood quite alone.

She had been a recluse since the early sixties, and her family surmised the reason. She had fallen in love with a married man, a Philadelphia clergyman, and had buried herself at home by way of refuge. When her supposed lover supposedly pursued her there, her sister dashed across to the house next door and exclaimed to their brother Austin's wife, "Sue, come! That man is here. Father and mother are away, and I am afraid Emily will go away with him." Such was the family legend, which may have been apocryphal. Undoubtedly, the clergyman came to see her, but probably only to call. Was he in love with Emily? Probably not. In any case, she did not go away. She withdrew from all activities outside the household, and her mind turned in upon itself. She had hitherto been eminently social, or as much so as her little world permitted. Born in 1830, in the red-brick mansion, she had grown up a lively girl who was always a center of attention. She was a capital mimic. She travestied the young-lady pieces, the "Battle of Prague" and others, which she played on the mahogany

piano, and her odd and funny stories enthralled her friends. Later they remembered that she placed bouquets of flowers in the pews of those she liked best, at church. Dancing and cardplaying were not allowed in Amherst, but Noah Webster's granddaughter, who lived there, evaded the prohibition on behalf of her circle. She held "P.O.M." meetings for the Poetry of Motion, and Emily Dickinson excelled in this branch of learning. She joined in picnics and walks over the Amherst hills with groups of boys and girls from the town and the college. They had "sugaring-off" parties and valentine parties, and they often climbed Mount Norwottuck where they found ferns and lady's-slippers; and sometimes they met at a brookside in the woods, where the boys went fishing and the girls made chowder. Emily was an ardent botanist. She knew the haunts of all the wild flowers in the region, and sometimes she scrambled alone through the forest, perhaps with her big dog Carlo. She was an expert cook. At home she baked the bread and boiled her father's puddings, but her father was difficult to please. He read "lonely and rigorous books," she said, on Sunday afternoons, fearing that anything else might "joggle the mind"; and Shakespeare, the Bible, and Dr. Watts's hymns were the reading that he chose for his daughter. He did not like her to work in the garden, or to make visits without him, and when she was too witty he left the table. At fifteen she could not tell the time: her father supposed he had taught her, but she had not understood him, and she did not dare to ask him again or ask anyone else who might have told him. Now and again, she rebelled. She smashed a plate or a teacup, and her friends and her brother found ways to provide her with books, hiding them in the box-bush that stood beside the front door or on the parlor piano, under the cover. In one way or another, she contrived to read most of the current authors, especially the Brontës and the Brownings, with Hawthorne, Coleridge, Irving, Keats, and Ruskin. One of her

[1] **Watts:** Isaac Watts (1674–1748), English hymn writer, some of whose hymns are still sung at church services today.

special favorites was Sir Thomas Browne,[1] and she loved the drollery of Dickens. For the rest, she read Heine in German and Emerson's poems, and Frank B. Sanborn's letters in the *Springfield Republican* kept her in the literary current. She was by no means passive in this house of duty. Once, at a funeral in Hadley, whither she had gone with her father in the family barouche,[2] she ran away for several hours with a young cousin from Worcester and drove back to Amherst in his buggy. At school, she declared her independence. She had been sent as a boarding pupil to Mary Lyon's seminary, where she had written her themes on the nature of sin. She had listened to lectures on total depravity as if, like most of the other girls, she had meant to be a missionary's wife; but when, one day, Miss Lyon asked all the girls to rise, all who wished to be Christians, Emily alone refused to do so. She had found that she could not share the orthodox faith. Otherwise her life went on, with a few journeys here and there, like that of any country lawyer's daughter. As a young girl, she had visited Boston. She remembered the concerts and Bunker Hill, the Chinese Museum and Mount Auburn; and later, on two occasions, she stayed in Cambridge, to receive some treatment for her eyes. When her father was serving his term in Congress, in 1854, she spent seven weeks in Washington with him. Her father's friends were struck by her charm and her wit. It was on her way home that she stopped at Philadelphia and received the sudden shock that had changed her life.

This was the whole of Miss Dickinson's story, so far as outward events were concerned, when Thomas Wentworth Higginson[3] entered the picture. Higginson had written an appeal in *The Atlantic,* addressed to the rising generation. Re-

membering the days of *The Dial,* when the hazel wand, waved over New England, had indicated hidden springs of talent in many a country town, he said that to find a "new genius" was an editor's greatest privilege. If any such existed who read *The Atlantic,* let him court the editor— "draw near him with soft approaches and mild persuasions." Higginson added a number of admonitions: "Charge your style with life . . . Tolerate no superfluities . . . There may be years of crowded passion in a word, and half a life in a sentence." This appeal was anonymous, but many of the Amherst people knew who wrote the articles in *The Atlantic,* for Sanborn's literary gossip kept them posted; and presently Colonel Higginson, who was living in Worcester, received an odd little letter. The letter was unsigned, but the writer sent four poems, and she placed in a separate envelope the signature "Emily Dickinson." She begged this distant friend to be her "master." The poems puzzled Higginson. While he felt a curious power in them, he was not prepared for a "new genius" who broke so many rules as this lady in Amherst, who punctuated with dashes only and seemed to have small use for rhyme and merely wished to know if she was "clear." She did not ask him to publish the poems, and he did not pass them on to the editor, but he wrote her a sympathetic letter that was followed by a long correspondence. She continued to send him poems at intervals, signing her notes "your gnome" and "your scholar," but, although she asked him again if he would be her "preceptor," and he offered her a number of suggestions, she never changed a line or a word to please him. In one note she said, "If I read a book and it makes my whole body so cold no fire can ever warm me, I know that is poetry. If I feel physically as if the top of my head were taken off, I know that is poetry. These are the only ways I know it. Is there any other way?" And once she replied, when he asked her for a photograph, "I had no portrait now, but am small, like the wren; and my hair is bold,

---

[1] **Sir Thomas Browne:** English writer (1605–1682) who is highly regarded for his ornate prose style.

[2] **barouche:** four-wheeled carriage with a folding top.

[3] **Thomas Wentworth Higginson:** See page 282.

like the chestnut burr; and my eyes like the sherry in the glass that the guest leaves." This feminine mystification piqued the colonel. He wrote, "You enshroud yourself in this fiery mist and I cannot reach you, but only rejoice in the rare sparkles of light." When she told him that her companions were the hills and the sundown, he replied that she ought to come to Boston: she would find herself at home at Mrs. Sargent's. At last, in 1870, he went to Amherst. After a brief delay, while he waited in the parlor, he heard a faint footstep in the hallway and a shy, little childlike creature glided in. She carried two daylilies, which she placed in his hand, saying, in a soft, breathless voice, "These are my introduction," adding in a whisper, "Forgive me if I am frightened. I never see strangers and hardly know what to say." She spoke of her household occupations and said that "people must have puddings," and she added a few detached enigmatic remarks. She seemed to the amiable Higginson as unique and remote as Undine or Mignon or Thekla.[1] But he was disturbed by the tension in the air and was glad he did not live too near this lady. There was something abnormal about her, he felt. He had never met anyone before who drained his nerve power so much.

At that time, Miss Dickinson was forty years old and had long since withdrawn from the world; and the friends who came to see her sister were used to the "hurrying whiteness" that was always just going through a door. She sometimes swept into the parlor, bowed and touched a hand or two, poised over the flowered Brussels carpet, and vanished like a ghost or an exhalation; but even these appearances had grown rarer and rarer. Only the neighbors' children really saw her. She had given up wearing colors and was always dressed in diaphanous white, with a cameo

[1] **Undine . . . Thekla:** Undine, in a romance of the same name, is a water sprite who fell in love with a mortal. In Goethe's *Wilhelm Meister's Apprenticeship*, Mignon is a mysterious Italian girl who falls in love with the hero. Thekla is a first-century saint about whom little is known.

pin that held the ruching together. She was decisive in manner, anything but frail. Her complexion was velvety white, her lips were red. Her hair was bound with a chestnut-colored snood, and when it was chilly she wore a little shoulder cape crocheted with soft white worsted run through with a ribbon. She often had a flower in her hand. She moved about in a sort of reverie, flitting "as quick as a trout" when she was disturbed. (This was one of her sister Lavinia's phrases.) The children knew her "high, surprised voice." They knew her dramatic way of throwing up her hands as she ended one of the stories she liked to tell them. She made them her fellow conspirators. They followed her upstairs and heard her comments on the guests she had left in the parlor. She would say, with finger on lip, as feminine callers left, "Listen! Hear them kiss, the traitors!" Or, peeping down the stairs, she would say of some man, "Look, dear, his face is as pretty as a cloth pink," or "His face is as handsome and meaningless as the full moon." She remarked, apropos of some scholarly person, "He has the facts, but not the phosphorescence of learning." She said that her own ideal caller was always just going out of sight, and that it made her shiver to hear people talk as if they were "taking all the clothes off their souls." She called herself the "cow lily," because of the orange lights in her hair and her eyes, and she observed that the housemaid moved about "in a calico sarcophagus." Once she said to her little niece, who was puzzled by her shy ways, "No one could ever punish a Dickinson by shutting her up alone." Meanwhile, her life went on with her flowers and her sister. She had a small conservatory, opening out of the dining room, a diminutive glass chamber with shelves around it; and there she grouped the ferns and the jasmine, the lilies and the heliotrope and the oxalis plants in their hanging baskets. She had a little watering pot, with a long slender spout that was like the antenna of an insect, and she sat up all night at times in winter to keep her flowers

from freezing. The garden was her special care, and occasionally one saw her at dusk through the gate, fluttering about the porch like a moth in the moonlight. When it was damp, she knelt on an old red army blanket that she had thrown on the ground, to reach the flowers. Usually, on summer evenings, she sat for a while with Lavinia on the side piazza, overlooking the flagged path that led to the villa. There stood the giant daphne odora,[1] moved out from the conservatory, and the two small oleanders in their tubs.

Meanwhile, since 1862, Miss Dickinson had been writing poems, although there were very few of her friends who knew it. They all knew the little rhymes she sent them with arbutus buds, but they did not know how seriously she pursued her writing, at night, beside the Franklin stove in the upstairs corner bedroom, in the light that often glimmered over the snow. From her window she had caught suggestions that gave her a picture, a fancy, an image. Perhaps a boy passed whistling, or a neighbor on her way to church, or a dog with feet "like intermittent plush"; or perhaps she knew that a traveling circus was going to pass in the early morning, and she sat up to watch the "Algerian procession." A dead fly on the

windowpane stirred her imagination, and once in the glare of a fire at night she saw a caterpillar measuring a leaf far down in the orchard. She saw the bluebirds darting round "with little dodging feet,"

"The motions of the dipping birds,
The lightning's jointed road;"

and all these observations went into her verses. She wrote on sheets of notepaper, which she sewed together, rolling and tying the bundles with a thread or a ribbon and tucking them away in the drawers of her bureau; although sometimes the back of an envelope served her as well. But, casual in this, she was anything but casual —she was a cunning workman—in her composition. Poetry was her solitaire and, so to speak, her journal, for, like Thoreau in Concord, she watched the motions of her mind, recording its ebbs and flows and the gleams that shot through it; and she labored over her phrases to make them right. Were they all her own? Were there echoes in them, or anything of the conventional, the rhetorical, the fat? Were they clear, were they exact, were they compact? She liked the common hymn-meters, and the meters of nursery jingles, which had been deeply ingrained in her mind as a child, and she seemed to take a rebellious joy in violating all their rules, fulfilling the traditional patterns while she

[1] **daphne odora:** a fragrant plant.

also broke them. She was always experimenting with her rhymes and her rhythms, sometimes adding extra syllables to break up their monotony, sometimes deliberately twisting a rhyme, as Emerson did, for the sake of harshness, to escape the mellifluous effect of conventional poems. Many of her pieces were like parodies of hymns, whose gentle glow in her mind had become heat lightning. For Emily Dickinson's light was quick. It was sudden, sharp and evanescent; and this light was the dry light that is closest to fire.

The visible setting of these poems was the New England countryside, the village, the garden, the household that she knew so well, a scene, the only scene she knew, that she invested with magic, so that the familiar objects become portents and symbols. Here were the hills, the changing seasons, the winter light, the light of spring, the bee, the mouse, the hummingbird, the cricket, the lonely houses off the road, the village inn, the lamppost that became, in the play of her fancy, sublime or droll; and with what gifts of observation she caught the traits of her birds and insects, of everything that crept or ran or flew—the snake "unbraiding in the sun," the robin's eyes, "like frightened beads," the umbrella of the bat that was "quaintly halved." She often seemed a little girl, amusing herself with childish whimsies, and, in fact, as the ward of her father, she

remained in some ways adolescent; and, as she dressed to the end in the fashion of her early youth, so she retained the imagery of the child in the household. But her whimsies sometimes turned into bold ideas. She saw the mountain, like her father, sitting "in his eternal chair"; her ocean had a "basement," like the house in Amherst, and her wind and snow swept the road like the brooms that she had been taught to use—the brooms of the breeze swept vale and tree and hill. A journey to the Day of Judgment struck her as a "buggy ride," and she saw a "schoolroom" in the sky. She domesticated the universe and read her own experience into the motions of nature and the world she observed. The sun rose in the East for her "a ribbon at a time," and the "housewife in the evening West" came back to "dust the pond." Clouds for her were "millinery," mountains wore bonnets, shawls, and sandals, eternity "rambled" with her, like her dog Carlo; the wind had fingers and combed the sky, and March walked boldly up and knocked like a neighbor. Volcanoes purred for her like cats, and she saw the planets "frisking about," her Providence kept a store on the village street, and she thought of death as coming with a broom and a dustpan. The moon slid down the stairs for her "to see who's there," and the grave for her was a little cottage where she could "lay the marble tea." One could not "fold a flood," she said, and "put it in a drawer," but she rolled up the months in mothballs and laid them away, as she had swept up the heart and put away love; and she saw hope, fear, time, future, and past as persons to rally, welcome, play with, flee, or tease.

The turns of fancy that marked these poems were sharp and unpredictable, and yet they were singularly natural—nothing was forced. Miss Dickinson lived in a world of paradox, for, while her eye was microscopic, her imagination dwelt with mysteries and grandeurs. Ribbons and immortality were mingled in her mind, which passed from one to the other with the speed of lightning, though she sometimes took a mischievous pleasure in extravagant combinations of thought, uniting the droll and the sublime, the trivial and the grand. There was in this an element of the characteristic American humor that liked to play with incongruities, and Miss Dickinson maintained in the poems of her later years the fun-loving spirit she had shown as a schoolgirl. To juxtapose the great and the small, in unexpected ways, had been one of her prime amusements as the wit of her circle, and this, like the laconic speech that also marked the Yankee, had remained an essential note of her style as a poet. "Shorter than a snake's delay," her poems were packed with meaning; and, swiftly as her images changed, they were scarcely able to keep the pace with which her mind veered from mood to mood, from faith to mockery, from mysticism to rationalism, through ecstasy, disillusion, anguish, joy. These poems were fairylike in their shimmer and lightness, they moved like bees upon a raft of air; and yet one felt behind them an energy of mind and spirit that only the rarest poets ever possessed. Was not Emily Dickinson's idiom the final proof that she possessed it? Her style, her stamp, her form were completely her own.

Such were the games of solitaire that

Miss Dickinson played in the silent room, as lonely as Jane Eyre, in her red-curtained alcove, dreaming over the book with its pictures of the arctic wastes and the rock that stood up in the sea of billow and spray. Miss Dickinson had only this "acre of a rock," and yet what a harvest it yielded of grape and maize. Having but a crumb, she was sovereign of them all, as she said quite truly; for her constant theme was deprivation, the "banquet of abstemiousness," and this sharpened as nothing else her perception of values. When the well's dry, we know the worth of water, and she felt that she knew victory because she knew defeat, she felt that she knew love because she had lost it. Certainly for all she missed she made up in intensity: where others merely glowed, she was incandescent.

FOR STUDY AND DISCUSSION

1. Brooks does not mention Emily Dickinson until the middle of the second paragraph. What details does he take up first? Why do you think he delays in introducing his principal character?

2. What do you learn about Emily Dickinson's relations with her relatives and friends? with Higginson? Judging by what you learn from this essay, how would you describe Emily Dickinson as a person?

3. At what point does the essay begin to deal primarily with Emily Dickinson as a poet rather than as a person? What is the relationship of this part of the essay to the earlier part?

4. Brooks's essay is in part an attempt to convey Emily Dickinson's *incandescence*. Explain this term as it is used in the essay. What details in the essay help to define the term?

5. Cite three examples of figurative language in the essay. Why do you think Brooks at times uses similes and metaphors rather than making direct statements about Emily Dickinson or her poetry?

FOR COMPOSITION

Write a composition in which you explain how the essay by Van Wyck Brooks can be related directly to certain poems by Emily Dickinson. Deal specifically with at least one poem by Miss Dickinson (pages 283–85).

JAMES BALDWIN
(1924–   )

As a writer, James Baldwin has shown a special talent for working outward from a special situation—his own or that of the characters in his novels—toward a universal moral significance. Although he is a sharp critic of American society, his is essentially (in Robert Frost's phrase) "a lover's quarrel with the world." In his novels, stories, and plays, he is true to the duty of an artist, as he sees it: to expose his fellow citizens to unpleasant realities, to "let us know that there is nothing stable under heaven," and to "drive to the heart of every answer and expose the question the answer hides."

James Baldwin was born in the Harlem section of New York City. After his graduation from De Witt Clinton High School in 1942, he worked for a while in defense plants. Then he moved to New York's Greenwich Village and worked as a handyman, office boy, and waiter by day while writing at night. Eventually he was able to publish book reviews in national magazines. While he was working on a novel, he met the famous writer Richard Wright, who helped the younger man get a Eugene F. Saxton Memorial Trust Award. Another literary award made it possible for Baldwin to go to Paris, where he stayed on and off for nearly ten years. While he was overseas, his first novel, *Go Tell It on the Mountain,* was published in 1952 and praised by many critics. In 1955, the publication of a collection of essays, *Notes of a Native Son,* led several reviewers to comment that perhaps Baldwin's true talent was as an essayist rather than as a writer of fiction. The essay ranged from a touching account of the death of Baldwin's father to a discussion of the "protest novel" in America. *Nobody Knows My Name,* published in 1961, added to Baldwin's reputation as an essayist.

As Baldwin indicated in several essays, his stay in Europe made him continually more aware of his identity as an American and of the qualities and attitudes that he shared with other Americans. He determined to return home and to involve himself in the affairs of his country. Since his return he has made a reputation not only as an important writer but as a prominent public figure. A television documentary about his childhood that he wrote and narrated has been broadcast nationally. He has appeared on a number of public affairs programs. The sociologist and writer Dr. Kenneth Clark has described Baldwin as "a little man, physically, with tremendous emotional and intellectual power. He radiates a nervous, sensitive involvement with all aspects of his environment."

The Creative Process

PERHAPS THE primary distinction of the artist is that he must actively cultivate that state which most men, necessarily, must avoid: the state of being alone. That all men *are,* when the chips are down, alone, is a banality—a banality because it is very frequently stated, but very rarely, on the evidence, believed. Most of us are not compelled to linger with the knowledge of our aloneness, for it is a knowledge that can paralyze all action in this world. There are, forever, swamps to be drained, cities to be created, mines to be exploited, children to be fed. None of these things can be done alone. But the conquest of the physical world is not man's only duty. He is also enjoined to conquer the great wilderness of himself. The precise role of the artist, then, is to illuminate that darkness, blaze roads through that vast forest, so that we will not, in all our doing, lose sight of its purpose, which is, after all, to make the world a more human dwelling place.

The state of being alone is not meant to bring to mind merely a rustic musing beside some silver lake. The aloneness of which I speak is much more like the aloneness of birth or death. It is like the fearful aloneness that one sees in the eyes of someone who is suffering, whom we cannot help. Or it is like the aloneness of love, the force and mystery that so many have extolled and so many have cursed, but which no one has ever understood or ever really been able to control. I put the matter this way, not out of any desire to create pity for the artist—God forbid!—but to suggest how nearly, after all, is his state the state of everyone, and in an attempt to make vivid his endeavor. The states of birth, suffering, love, and death are extreme states—extreme, universal, and inescapable. We all know this, but we would rather not know it. The artist is present to correct the delusions to which we fall prey in our attempts to avoid this knowledge.

It is for this reason that all societies have battled with that incorrigible disturber of the peace—the artist. I doubt that future societies will get on with him any better. The entire purpose of society is to create a bulwark against the inner and the outer chaos, in order to make life bearable and to keep the human race alive. And it is absolutely inevitable that when a tradition has been evolved, whatever the tradition is, the people, in general, will suppose it to have existed from before the beginning of time and will be most unwilling and indeed unable to conceive of any changes in it. They do not know how they will live without those traditions that have given them their identity. Their reaction, when it is suggested that they can or that they must, is panic. And we see this panic, I think, everywhere in the world today, from the streets of New Orleans to the grisly battleground of Algeria.[1] And a higher level of consciousness among the people is the only hope we have, now or in the future, of minimizing human damage.

The artist is distinguished from all other responsible actors in society—the politicians, legislators, educators, and scientists—by the fact that he is his own test tube, his own laboratory, working according to very rigorous rules, however unstated these may be, and cannot allow any consideration to supersede his responsibility to reveal all that he can possibly discover concerning the mystery of the human being. Society must accept some things as real; but he must always know that visible reality hides a deeper one, and that all our action and achievement rests on things unseen. A society must assume

[1] **Algeria:** In its last years as a French colony, Algeria waged a fierce struggle for independence.

that it is stable, but the artist must know, and he must let us know, that there is nothing stable under heaven. One cannot possibly build a school, teach a child, or drive a car without taking some things for granted. The artist cannot and must not take anything for granted, but must drive to the heart of every answer and expose the question the answer hides.

I seem to be making extremely grandiloquent claims for a breed of men and women historically despised while living and acclaimed when safely dead. But, in a way, the belated honor that all societies tender their artists proves the reality of the point I am trying to make. I am really trying to make clear the nature of the artist's responsibility to his society. The peculiar nature of this responsibility is that he must never cease warring with it, for its sake and for his own. For the truth, in spite of appearances and all our hopes, is that everything is always changing and the measure of our maturity as nations and as men is how well prepared we are to meet these changes and, further, to use them for our health.

Now, anyone who has ever been compelled to think about it—anyone, for example, who has ever been in love—knows that the one face that one can never see is one's own face. One's lover—or one's brother, or one's enemy—sees the face you wear, and this face can elicit the most extraordinary reactions. We do the things we do and feel what we feel essentially because we must—we are responsible for our actions, but we rarely understand them. It goes without saying, I believe, that if we understood ourselves better, we would damage ourselves less. But the barrier between oneself and one's knowledge of oneself is high indeed. There are so many things one would rather not know! We become social creatures because we cannot live any other way. But in order to become social, there are a great many other things that we must not become, and we are frightened, all of us, of those forces within us that perpetually menace our precarious security. Yet the

forces are there; we cannot will them away. All we can do is learn to live with them. And we cannot learn this unless we are willing to tell the truth about ourselves, and the truth about us is always at variance with what we wish to be. The human effort is to bring these two realities into a relationship resembling reconciliation. The human beings whom we respect the most, after all—and sometimes fear the most—are those who are most deeply involved in this delicate and strenuous effort, for they have the unshakable authority that comes only from having looked on and endured and survived the worst. That nation is healthiest which has the least necessity to distrust or ostracize or victimize these people—whom, as I say, we honor, once they are gone, because somewhere in our hearts we know that we cannot live without them.

The dangers of being an American artist are not greater than those of being an artist anywhere else in the world, but they are very particular. These dangers are produced by our history. They rest on the fact that in order to conquer this continent, the particular aloneness of which I speak—the aloneness in which one discovers that life is tragic, and therefore unutterably beautiful—could not be permitted. And that this prohibition is typical of all emergent nations will be proved, I have no doubt, in many ways during the next fifty years. This continent now is conquered, but our habits and our fears remain. And, in the same way that to become a social human being one modifies and suppresses and, ultimately, without great courage, lies to oneself about all one's interior, uncharted chaos, so have we, as a nation, modified and suppressed and lied about all the darker forces in our history. We know, in the case of the person, that whoever cannot tell himself the truth about his past is trapped in it, is immobilized in the prison of his undiscovered self. This is also true of nations. We know how a person, in such a paralysis, is unable to assess either his weaknesses or his strengths, and how frequently in-

The Literature of Minorities

Throughout the nineteenth century and part of the twentieth, wave after wave of immigrants arrived from Europe and Asia. Some came as laborers to build railroads and work in mines; others came as artisans and technicians, bringing valuable skills to the New World. Some came as political refugees, others as refugees from poverty and famine. One minority group came in shackles, brought over in slave ships from Africa. All these immigrants began life in this country as members of minority groups, but slowly they reached out to become part of the national life. Out of this experience some of these newcomers created a valuable literature.

Much of the early writing by members of minority groups was done in the original language of the group—in German, French, or Italian. Probably the most noteworthy American novel written in a foreign language is Ole Rolvaag's *Giants in the Earth,* which tells of the Norwegian settling of the northern plains. It deals not only with an external conflict against nature but with internal conflict, for the settlers struggled with their own sensitivity to survive in a harsh environment. Today another important American author writes in a foreign language. Isaac Bashevis Singer's novels and stories about the Jews in the ghettos of Poland and Russia are translated from the original Yiddish.

But most authors who deal with minorities write in English. They wish their works to be judged not as social documents but as works of art that have something important to say about individuals as well as groups. In *The Last Hurrah* and *The Edge of Sadness,* Edwin O'Connor writes about Irish-Americans. In *My Name Is Aram,* William Saroyan has written charmingly and poignantly of Armenians in California. Harry Mark Petrakis has written of Greek-Americans *(Pericles on Thirty-First Street).*

Today American readers are most aware of the literary work of two minority groups. Contemporary Jewish writers tend not only to probe Jewish problems but to use the Jew as a symbol for all of suffering humanity. Two of the most distinguished Jewish writers in America are Saul Bellow *(The Victim, The Adventures of Augie March)* and Bernard Malamud *(The Assistant, The Magic Barrel).* A number of outstanding Negro writers have also written with great power. In the 1940's Richard Wright made Americans violently aware of the Negro's dissatisfactions in his novel *Native Son* and his autobiography *Black Boy.* More recently, James Baldwin has emerged as a fine essayist (page 738) and novelist. Many critics consider Ralph Ellison's novel *Invisible Man,* a partly realistic, partly allegorical treatment of the Negro's situation in the United States, to be the finest American novel published in the last twenty years. A number of Negro writers have gained reputations as poets, including Countee Cullen, Langston Hughes, and Gwendolyn Brooks. All these writers are valued not simply as literary spokesmen for minority groups, but as authors who have vastly enriched our national literature.

James Baldwin lecturing to a group in Paris.

deed he mistakes the one for the other. And this, I think, we do. We are the strongest nation in the Western world, but this is not for the reasons that we think. It is because we have an opportunity that no other nation has of moving beyond the Old World concepts of race and class and caste, to create, finally, what we must have had in mind when we first began speaking of the New World. But the price of this is a long look backward whence we came and an unflinching assessment of the record. For an artist, the record of that journey is most clearly revealed in the personalities of the people the journey produced. Societies never know it, but the war of an artist with his society is a lover's war, and he does, at his best, what lovers do, which is to reveal the beloved to himself and, with that revelation, to make freedom real.

FOR STUDY AND DISCUSSION

1. What does Baldwin mean by "aloneness"? How is this concept particularly important to his discussion of the artist's situation?

2. Why does Baldwin say that "all societies have battled with that incorrigible disturber of the peace—the artist"? Why is the artist a "disturber of the peace"?

3. What claims does Baldwin make for the artist? Why does he say that the artist "must drive to the heart of every answer and explore the question the answer hides"? What, according to Baldwin, is the artist's responsibility to society?

4. What, according to Baldwin, are the particular dangers of being an artist in America? Do you agree or disagree? Explain. Can you think of any advantages that an artist in America might have over other artists? Can you think of any disadvantages that Baldwin does not mention?

5. In what ways is this essay an exploration of the basic relationship of all individuals to society?

LANGUAGE AND VOCABULARY

Find synonyms for the italicized words below. Discuss whether your synonyms clarify the meaning of Baldwin's sentences or make the meaning less precise.

1. "He [the artist] is also *enjoined* to conquer the great wilderness of himself." (Page 739.)

2. "That all men *are,* when the chips are down, alone, is a *banality* . . ." (Page 739.)

3. "The state of being alone is not meant to bring to mind merely a *rustic* musing beside some silver lake." (Page 739.)

4. "the *grisly* battleground of Algeria." (Page 739.)

5. "I seem to be making extremely *grandiloquent* claims . . ." (Page 740.)

FOR COMPOSITION

Baldwin writes, "That nation is healthiest which has the least necessity to distrust or ostracize or victimize these people—whom, as I say, we honor, once they are gone, because somewhere in our hearts we know that we cannot live without them." Referring to the essay, explain who is meant by "these people." Give a specific example based on your reading or personal experience. Then indicate whether you agree or disagree with James Baldwin's statement that we cannot live without such people. Be sure to give reasons to support your position.

THORNTON WILDER

(1897–   )

Thornton Wilder is one of the few living American writers to gain distinction both as a writer of fiction and as a dramatist. A novel and two plays by him have won Pulitzer prizes. Most of his works, both fiction and drama, share a concern that sets him apart from many contemporary American writers. Wilder seeks to go beneath situations and circumstances peculiar to a specific time, to touch what is most universal. Once he told an interviewer, "Literature is the orchestration of platitudes," the restatement of universally recognized truths. In a series of talks on nineteenth-century American writers, Wilder said that the American, being more than most persons "exposed to the awareness of vast distances and innumerable existences," is impelled to relate "every existing thing" to a central core of meaning, "to the All, to the Everywhere, to the Always." This concern with universal truths links Wilder with such nineteenth-century Americans as Emerson and Thoreau. However, unlike these writers, whose works are a free expression of ideas and emotions, Wilder has also learned a great deal from Latin poets such as Virgil and Horace. He is a classicist who measures his words carefully. Often the underlying ideas are only hinted at, and the emotions that propel a novel or play find open expression only in a few terse, crucial passages. Wilder's style has been praised for having the grace of poetry, but it is a grace that lends much of his work a deceptively placid surface. The reader must go beneath this surface, just as Wilder goes beneath the surface of everyday life, to discover the profound and deeply moving confrontation with the All, the Everywhere, and the Always, that marks Wilder's best work.

Thornton Wilder was born in Madison, Wisconsin. His father was a newspaper publisher who was active in politics and was appointed consul general in China when his son was nine years old. Much of Thornton's boyhood was spent in China. In an essay on Wilder, the critic Malcolm Cowley has described the author's boyhood: "He read widely, wrote plays for his sisters to act in cheesecloth robes, and used the margins of his notebooks for taking literary notes. 'Poor Thornton, poor Thornton,' his father used to say, 'he'll be a burden all his life.'" After graduation from high school in Berkeley, California (where his family had settled after returning from China), Wilder attended Oberlin College for two years and then went to Yale University, from which he graduated in 1920. The next year was spent in the study of archaeology at the American Academy in Rome. For seven years he was a teacher of French and housemaster at the Lawrenceville School in New Jersey. Later he taught at the University of Chicago and at Harvard University.

Wilder's first novel, *The Cabala,* grew out of notebooks he had kept during his year in Rome. It was written after friends at Yale had asked him why, after the great promise shown at college, he had not yet published. The novel received little attention. Wilder's second novel, *The Bridge of San Luis Rey,* was published in 1927. Somewhat to his surprise, it was hailed as a masterpiece, became a best seller, and is still generally regarded as Wilder's best novel. A later novel, *The Ides of March* (1948), dealing with Julius Caesar, was almost as popular and well received by the critics.

Wilder's full-length plays are *Our Town, The Merchant of Yonkers, The Skin of Our Teeth,* and *The Matchmaker.* Both *Our Town* and *The Skin of Our Teeth* have won Pulitzer prizes in drama. *The Matchmaker,* a revised version of *The Merchant of Yonkers,* was successfully produced on Broadway and was in turn adapted as the enormously popular musical comedy, *Hello, Dolly.* Mr. Wilder's interest in dramas goes beyond writing them. He has acted in little theater productions, and in a New York revival of *Our Town* he played the part of the Stage Manager.

A Platform and a
Passion or Two

Toward the end of the twenties I began to lose pleasure in going to the theater. I ceased to believe in the stories I saw presented there. When I did go it was to admire some secondary aspect of the play, the work of a great actor or director or designer. Yet at the same time the conviction was growing in me that the theater was the greatest of all the arts. I felt that something had gone wrong with it in my time and that it was fulfilling only a small part of its potentialities. I was filled with admiration for presentations of classical works by Max Reinhardt and Louis Jouvet and the Old Vic,[1] as I was by the best plays of my own time, like *Desire Under the Elms* and *The Front Page;*[2] but at heart I didn't believe a word of them. I was like a schoolmaster grading a paper; to each of these offerings I gave an A+, but the condition of mind of one grading a paper is not that of one being overwhelmed by an artistic creation. The response we make when we "believe" a work of the imagination is that of saying, "This is the way things are. I have always known it without being fully aware that I knew it. Now in the presence of this play or novel or poem (or picture or piece of music) I know that I know it." It is this form of knowledge which Plato[3] called "recollection." We have all murdered, in thought; and been murdered. We have all seen the ridiculous in estimable persons and in ourselves. We have all known terror as well as enchantment. Imaginative literature has nothing to say to those who do not recognize—who cannot be *reminded*—of such conditions. Of all the arts the theater is best endowed to awaken this recollection within us—to believe is

[1] **Max . . . Vic:** Max Reinhardt (1873–1943), Austrian theatrical producer and director; Louis Jouvet (1887–1951), French actor, producer, and director; the Old Vic, an English theatrical company famous for its productions of Shakespeare.

Preface to *Three Plays* by Thornton Wilder, copyright © 1957 by Thornton Wilder, originally published under the title "A Platform and a Passion or Two" in *Harper's* Magazine. Reprinted by permission of Harper & Row, Publishers.

[2] **Desire . . . Page:** *Desire Under the Elms* is a tragedy by the modern American dramatist Eugene O'Neill (see page 803). *The Front Page* is a modern American comedy by Ben Hecht and Charles MacArthur.

[3] **Plato:** Greek philosopher (427?–347? B.C.).

to say "yes"; but in the theaters of my time I did not feel myself prompted to any such grateful and self-forgetting acquiescence.

This dissatisfaction worried me. I was not ready to condemn myself as blasé and overfastidious, for I knew that I was still capable of belief. I believed every word of *Ulysses* and of Proust and of *The Magic Mountain*,[1] as I did of hundreds of plays when I read them. It was on the stage that imaginative narration became false. Finally, my dissatisfaction passed into resentment. I began to feel that the theater was not only inadequate, it was evasive; it did not wish to draw upon its deeper potentialities. I found the word for it: it aimed to be *soothing*. The tragic had no heat; the comic had no bite; the social criticism failed to indict us with responsibility. I began to search for the point where the theater had run off the track, where it had chosen—and been permitted—to become a minor art and an inconsequential diversion.

The trouble began in the nineteenth century and was connected with the rise of the middle classes—they wanted their theater soothing. There's nothing wrong with the middle classes in themselves. We know that now. The United States and Scandinavia and Germany are middle-class countries, so completely so that they have lost the very memory of their once despised and ludicrous inferiority (they had been inferior not only to the aristocracy but, in human dignity, to the peasantry). When a middle class is new, however, there is much that is wrong with it. When it is emerging from under the shadow of an aristocracy, from the myth and prestige of those well-born Higher-ups, it is alternately insecure and aggressively complacent. It must find its justification and reassurance in making money and displaying it. To this day, members

---

[1] *Ulysses . . . Mountain:* James Joyce's *Ulysses,* Marcel Proust's *Remembrance of Things Past,* and Thomas Mann's *The Magic Mountain* are considered by many readers to be the three most important novels written in the twentieth century.

of the middle classes in England, France, and Italy feel themselves to be a little ridiculous and humiliated. The prestige of aristocracies is based upon a dreary untruth that moral superiority and the qualifications for leadership are transmittable through the chromosomes, and the secondary lie, that the environment afforded by privilege and leisure tends to nurture the flowers of the spirit. An aristocracy, defending and fostering its lie, extracts from the arts only such elements as can further its interests, the aroma and not the sap, the grace and not the trenchancy. Equally harmful to culture is the newly arrived middle class. In the English-speaking world the middle classes came into power early in the nineteenth century and gained control over the theater. They were pious, law-abiding, and industrious. They were assured of eternal life in the next world and, in this, they were squarely seated on Property and the privileges that accompany it. They were attended by devoted servants who knew their place. They were benevolent within certain limits, but chose to ignore wide tracts of injustice and stupidity in the world about them; and they shrank from contemplating those elements within themselves that were ridiculous, shallow, and harmful. They distrusted the passions and tried to deny them. Their questions about the nature of life seemed to be sufficiently answered by the demonstration of financial status and by conformity to some clearly established rules of decorum. These were precarious positions; abysses yawned on either side. The air was loud with questions that must not be asked. These audiences fashioned a theater which could not disturb them. They thronged to melodrama (which deals with tragic possibilities in such a way that you know from the beginning that all will end happily) and to sentimental drama (which accords a total license to the supposition that the wish is father to the thought) and to comedies in which the characters were so represented that they always resembled someone else and not oneself. Between

An example of a box-set stage.

the plays that Sheridan [1] wrote in his twenties and the first works of Wilde and Shaw [2] there was no play of even moderate interest written in the English language. (Unless you happen to admire and except Shelley's *The Cenci*.[3]) These audiences, however, also thronged to Shakespeare. How did they shield themselves against his probing? How did they smother the theater—and with such effect that it smothers us still? The box set [4] was already there, the curtain, the proscenium, but not taken "seriously"—it was a convenience in view of the weather in northern countries. They took it seriously and emphasized and enhanced everything that thus removed, cut off, and boxed the action; they increasingly shut the play up into a museum showcase.

Let us examine why the box-set stage stifles the life in drama and why and how it militates against belief.

Every action which has ever taken place—every thought, every emotion—has taken place only once, at one moment in time and place. "I love you," "I rejoice," "I suffer," have been said and felt many billions of times, and never twice the same. Every person who has ever lived has lived an unbroken succession of unique occasions. Yet the more one is aware of this individuality in experience (innumerable! innumerable!) the more one becomes attentive to what these disparate moments have in common, to repetitive patterns. As an artist (or listener or beholder) which "truth" do you prefer—that of the isolated occasion, or that which includes and resumes the innumerable? Which truth is more worth telling? Every age differs in this. Is the Venus de Milo [5] "one woman"? Is the play *Macbeth* the story of "one destiny"? The theater is admirably fitted to tell both truths. It has one foot planted firmly in the particular, since each actor before us (even when he wears a mask!) is indubitably a living, breathing "one"; yet it tends and strains to exhibit a general truth since its relation to a specific "realistic" truth is confused and undermined by the fact that it is an accumulation of untruths, pre-

---

[1] **Sheridan:** Richard Brinsley Sheridan (1751–1816), Irish dramatist.

[2] **Wilde . . . Shaw:** Oscar Wilde (1856–1900), Irish poet, dramatist, and novelist; George Bernard Shaw (1856–1950), Irish dramatist and essayist.

[3] ***The Cenci:*** a blank verse tragedy by the English poet Percy Bysshe Shelley (1792–1822).

[4] **box set:** the kind of stage which is found in most theaters. The box-set stage requires the audience to assume that the stage is like a room with one wall removed.

[5] **Venus de Milo:** a famous statue of the goddess Venus found on the island of Milo.

tenses, and fiction. The novel is preeminently the vehicle of the unique occasion, the theater of the generalized one. It is through the theater's power to raise the exhibited individual action into the realm of idea and type and universal that it is able to evoke our belief. But power is precisely what those nineteenth-century audiences did not—dared not—confront. They tamed it and drew its teeth; squeezed it into that removed showcase. They loaded the stage with specific objects, because every concrete object on the stage fixes and narrows the action to one moment in time and place. (Have you ever noticed that in the plays of Shakespeare no one—except occasionally a ruler—ever sits down? There were not even chairs on the English or Spanish stages in the time of Elizabeth I.) So it was by a jugglery with time that the middle classes devitalized the theater. When you emphasize *place* in the theater, you drag down and limit and harness time to it. You thrust the action back into past time, whereas it is precisely the glory of the stage that it is always "now" there. Under such production methods the characters are all dead before the action starts. You don't have to pay deeply from your heart's participation. No great age in the theater ever attempted to capture the audiences' belief through this kind of specification and localization. I became dissatisfied with the theater because I was unable to lend credence to such childish attempts to be "real."

I began writing one-act plays that tried to capture not verisimilitude but reality. In *The Happy Journey to Trenton and Camden* four kitchen chairs represent an automobile and a family travels seventy miles in twenty minutes. Ninety years go by in *The Long Christmas Dinner*. In *Pullman Car Hiawatha* some more plain chairs serve as berths and we hear the very vital statistics of the towns and fields that passengers are traversing; we hear their thoughts; we even hear the planets over their heads. In Chinese drama a char-

The set of a Japanese No play.

acter, by straddling a stick, conveys to us that he is on horseback. In almost every No play [1] of the Japanese an actor makes a tour of the stage and we know that he is making a long journey. Think of the ubiquity that Shakespeare's stage afforded for the battle scenes at the close of *Julius Caesar* and *Antony and Cleopatra*. As we see them today what a cutting and hacking of the text takes place—what condescension, what contempt for his dramaturgy.

Our Town is not offered as a picture of life in a New Hampshire village; or as a speculation about the conditions of life after death (that element I merely took from Dante's *Purgatory*).[2] It is an attempt to find a value above all price for the smallest events in our daily life. I have made the claim as preposterous as possible, for I have set the village against the largest dimensions of time and place. The recurrent words in this play (few have noticed it) are "hundreds," "thousands," and "millions." Emily's joys and griefs, her algebra lessons and her birthday presents—what are they when we consider all the billions of girls who have lived, who are living, and who will live? Each indi-

[1] **No play:** the classic drama of Japan which is performed almost as a ritual.
[2] ***Purgatory:*** the first part of the Italian poet Dante's *Divine Comedy*.

Print from the first edition of Molière's
Le Misanthrope.

vidual's assertion to an absolute reality
can only be inner, very inner. And here
the method of staging finds its justification
—in the first two acts there are at least a
few chairs and tables; but when she re-
visits the earth and the kitchen to which
she descended on her twelfth birthday, the
very chairs and table are gone. Our claim,
our hope, our despair are in the mind—
not in things, not in "scenery." Molière
said that for the theater all he needed was
a platform and a passion or two. The
climax of this play needs only five square
feet of boarding and the passion to know
what life means to us.

The Matchmaker is an only slightly
modified version of *The Merchant of
Yonkers,* which I wrote in the year after
I had written *Our Town.* One way to
shake off the nonsense of the nineteenth-
century staging is to make fun of it. This
play parodies the stock-company plays
that I used to see at Ye Liberty Theatre,
Oakland, California, when I was a boy.
I have already read small theses in German comparing it with the great Austrian
original on which it is based. The scholars
are very bewildered. There is most of the
plot (except that our friend Dolly Levi [1]
is not in Nestroy's [2] play); there are some
of the tags; but it's all "about" quite different matters. My play is about the aspirations of the young (and not only of
the young) for a fuller, freer participation
in life. Imagine an Austrian pharmacist
going to the shelf to draw from a bottle
which he knows to contain a stinging corrosive liquid, guaranteed to remove warts
and wens; and imagine his surprise when
he discovers that it has been filled over-
night with very American birch-bark beer.

The Skin of Our Teeth begins, also, by
making fun of old-fashioned playwriting;
but the audience soon perceives that he is
seeing "two times at once." The Antrobus
family is living both in prehistoric times
and in a New Jersey commuters' suburb
today. Again, the events of our homely
daily life—this time the family life—are
depicted against the vast dimensions of
time and place. It was written on the eve
of our entrance into the war and under
strong emotion and I think it mostly
comes alive under conditions of crisis. It
has been often charged with being a book-
ish fantasia about history, full of rather
bloodless schoolmasterish jokes. But to
have seen it in Germany soon after the
war, in the shattered churches and beer-
halls that were serving as theaters, with
audiences whose price of admission meant
the loss of a meal and for whom it was of

[1] **Dolly Levi:** the title role in *The Matchmaker.*
[2] **Nestroy:** Johann Nestroy (1801–1862), Austrian
dramatist.

absorbing interest that there was a "recipe for grass soup that did not cause the diarrhea," was an experience that was not so cool. I am very proud that this year it has received a first and overwhelming reception in Warsaw. The play is deeply indebted to James Joyce's *Finnegans Wake*.[1] I should be very happy if, in the future, some author should feel similarly indebted to any work of mine. Literature has always more resembled a torch race than a furious dispute among heirs.

The theater has lagged behind the other arts in finding the "new ways" to express how men and women think and feel in our time. I am not one of the new dramatists we are looking for. I wish I were. I hope I have played a part in preparing the way for them. I am not an innovator but a rediscoverer of forgotten goods and I hope a remover of obtrusive bric-a-brac. And as I view the work of my contemporaries I seem to feel that I am exceptional in one thing—I give (don't I?) the impression of having enormously enjoyed it.

[1] *Finnegans Wake*: Joyce's last novel, an extremely difficult experimental work. Its verbal devices will probably continue to influence many writers.

FOR STUDY AND DISCUSSION

1. Thornton Wilder says that toward the end of the 1920's he lost pleasure in playgoing because he could no longer "believe" in what he saw there. In what sense does he use the word "believe" here? (In answering, consider Wilder's statement that "to believe is to say 'yes.'")

2. According to Wilder, how was the newly powerful middle class responsible for the great changes that took place in the theater in the nineteenth century? Describe these changes.

3. Why does Wilder say that the box-set stage "stifles the life in drama"? Do you think that television plays and motion pictures manage to escape the limitations of the box-set stage? Explain.

4. What do you learn from this essay about Wilder's aims as a dramatist and about the plays he has written? Explain what he means by, "I am not an innovator but a rediscoverer

of forgotten goods and I hope a remover of obtrusive bric-a-brac." Why, for example, does he feel it is necessary to remove much scenery, such as tables and chairs, from the stage?

5. Study Wilder's descriptions of melodrama, sentimental drama, and comedies. Apply these descriptions to plays, motion pictures, or television dramas you have seen. How accurate do you think Wilder's descriptions are? What do they imply about the limitations of melodrama and sentimental drama?

LANGUAGE AND VOCABULARY

Give the meaning of each of the italicized words. Consider not only the dictionary definition but also the meaning each word gains from its context.

1. "An aristocracy . . . extracts from the arts only such elements as can further its interests, the *aroma* and not the *sap,* the *grace* and not the *trenchancy.*" (Page 745.)

2. "I began writing one-act plays that tried to capture not *verisimilitude* but *reality.*" (Page 747.)

3. "Think of the *ubiquity* that Shakespeare's stage afforded for the battle scenes . . ." (Page 747.)

FOR COMPOSITION

1. "Literature has always more resembled a torch race than a furious dispute among heirs." Write a paper in which you discuss the meaning of these two comparisons. Explain why you agree or disagree with Wilder's point of view.

2. After you have read *Our Town* (page 755), you will probably wish to return to Wilder's essay and reread it as a commentary on his play. Write a composition in which you tell how "A Platform and a Passion or Two" has helped to explain Wilder's techniques and ideas in your understanding of *Our Town*. Consider the following points:

   a. The discussion of the limitations of the box set and the devices used in *Our Town* to overcome these limitations

   b. Wilder's intention "to capture not verisimilitude but reality"

   c. The description of *Our Town* on page 747, especially the statement that the play "is an attempt to find a value above all price for the smallest events in our daily life"

MODERN DRAMA

The word *drama* comes from the Greek word *dran,* which means "to do" or "to act." Besides being traditionally literary, the drama is a theatrical form. The dramatist does not usually write with the purpose of communicating directly with the individual reader, as do the fiction writer, poet, and essayist. Instead, the dramatist asks people of the theater—actors, director, scene designer, and so on—to communicate with him. The good dramatist is highly aware of the resources and limitations of his medium. He recognizes that he must tell his story in a different way from the novelist. Yet like other literary artists, he attempts to make his work meaningful in two ways: by careful use of words, and by careful attention to basic structure.

THE STRUCTURE OF DRAMA

The Greek philosopher Aristotle, in writing a treatise based on the plays of his time (the fifth century B.C.), defined drama as "an imitation of an action," a definition which has become the basis for almost all subsequent dramatic criticism. Aristotle's definition is more complicated than may at first appear, and it should be considered carefully.

To take the last word first, Aristotle meant by *action* not merely activity or exertion, but rather the direction the play moves in, the closely related series of events that make up the single momentum of a play. A play—at least, in Aristotle's terms—must have a *plot* with a beginning, middle, and end. Almost always, a plot involves *conflict,* either an outer conflict between the main character and other characters or an inner conflict in the mind of the main character, or both. Also, the plot must involve some kind of decision; the main character of a play must before too long make up his mind and choose to perform or not to perform some morally meaningful act. If there is no element of personal decision in a play—if the main character does not convince the audience that he, like us, is a rational creature capable of making moral choices—then the play tends to become meaningless, merely a series of events with no central moral relevance to tie them together.

To return to the first term in Aristotle's definition, *imitation* does not necessarily mean a close copying of real life. To imitate something is not always to reproduce it exactly; a painting is different from a photograph.

Like any other work of art, a play arranges the material of life in some kind of a pattern to bring out meaning and significance. All of us go to plays (or read them) so that we can, in some way, see reenacted the impulses or fears or aspirations of our society. And usually we respond to plays collectively, as an audience, rather than as strictly separate individuals. We should not criticize a play if it does not accurately reflect the details of our individual lives. The play should imitate what is going on in our souls as they represent the consciousness of a community.

TYPES OF DRAMA

Drama has traditionally been categorized under two main types: *tragedy* and *comedy*. Tragedy, said to come from the Greek word *tragoidia,* or "goat-song," apparently had its beginnings in the laments sung by primitive Greek actors dressed in goatskins. In any event, tragedy deals with a main character, or *protagonist,* who decides on a course of action against what the audience knows are impossible odds; he suffers as a result of his decision; and ultimately he perceives the discrepancy between his own objectives and the order of the universe, an order which will not permit him to achieve his goals. While this description hardly does justice to the sweeping implications of tragedy, it may suggest the sense of aspiration, agony, and comprehension that lies at the heart of it. Tragedy involves a net that tightens around the protagonist, in spite of and even because of his efforts to escape it. Because of the focus on the individual and his challenge of unbreakable cosmic laws, watching a great tragedy being performed (or reading it perceptively) can be a profoundly moving experience.

Comedy, on the other hand, allows for a solution to the struggle. The comic protagonist usually takes on odds that only appear to be insurmountable. The word *comedy* apparently comes from the Greek *komoidia,* which means a "festive song," and comedy still carries with it connotations of festivity. Through the centuries, comedy has focused its aim, not on man's confrontation with a cosmic order, but on the vices and follies of society. A comedy usually ends with a healthy, amicable armistice between the protagonist and society.

THE TWO LANGUAGES OF DRAMA: DIALOGUE AND STAGING

As a reader, you are forced to rely principally on a play's *dialogue* to learn what it is all about. But you should always keep in mind that drama uses a second language: the play's *staging* or stagecraft. Plays are designed to be performed by actors in theaters in front of audiences, and thus make use of what Aristotle called *spectacle*—all the visual devices that speak to the eye as the dialogue of a play speaks to the ear. The perceptive reader tries to recreate a performance of a play in his mind as he reads. He is aware of the chief devices of staging:

1. *Scenery.* The setting of a play is normally indicated by painted scenery that provides a visual frame for the action. Many modern plays use very detailed scenery to make the audience feel it is watching something that is actually taking place. Thornton Wilder's *Our Town* makes a dramatic point in just the opposite way, by using practically no scenery at all.

2. *Costume.* What a character wears, too, has particular significance in the theater. Since much information about a character must be communicated in a short time, costume becomes an essential statement of drama. For example, when the heroine of *Our Town* appears in a white dress (page 795), the costume tells us a good deal about the play's attitude toward death.

3. *Gesture and movement.* Greek dramatists had their choruses dance out their speeches in a series of highly stylized steps. Today a shrug or even a raised eyebrow, under the close scrutiny of a movie camera, can convey a world of feeling.

4. *Lighting.* In the modern theater, much is done to convey a mood or an atmosphere with lights. A comic scene may not seem half so funny if it is dimly lit, while a serious one can lose its emotional intensity if the lights are too bright. Lights can suggest a time or season, pinpoint an action, isolate a character, or rejuvenate an actress.

All these aspects of staging, the visual tools of the theater, can be used to great advantage to underscore the action of a play and to help the audience understand its structure and meaning. The perceptive reader receives similar help from a play's stage directions, which help him recreate a performance of the play in his mind.

THE DEVELOPMENT OF AMERICAN DRAMA:
REALISM AND EXPERIMENTALISM

Most critics of drama agree that American drama became a significant part of American literature only in the second decade of this century, when Eugene O'Neill (page 803) began to write plays. O'Neill's work exemplifies the two major trends of the modern American theater—the trend toward *realism* and the trend toward *experimentation.*

Like realistic novelists (page 478), realistic dramatists try to approach ordinary life as closely as possible. Theatrical realism, exemplified at its best in the plays of Norway's Henrik Ibsen, asks the audience to assume that the play is a "slice of life." The stage is assumed to be an ordinary room with one wall removed to permit the audience to eavesdrop on the action. The scenery is accurately representational, and the dialogue tries to imitate what people would actually say. Realistic drama asks us to scrutinize the world as it is and, sometimes, to reform it.

Eugene O'Neill's first plays were realistic, and in such plays as *Ah! Wilderness* and *The Iceman Cometh,* he returned to this kind of drama. His first Broadway success, *Beyond the Horizon* (page 804), is written within the conventions of the realistic theater, but even in this early play there is a reaching out beyond these conventions, an attempt to do more than simply present a photograph of farm life. Later, in such plays as *The Great God Brown, Strange Interlude,* and *Mourning Becomes Electra,* he experimented with many different ways of stretching the theater beyond the realistic frame. He had his characters wear masks; he reintroduced the Greek device of the chorus, a person or persons who comment on the action and showed, through "asides," what a character thinks as well as says. O'Neill's efforts opened the door for further experimentation, such as Elmer Rice's *The Adding Machine* and William Saroyan's *My Heart's in the Highlands.* Maxwell Anderson returned the use of dramatic verse to the stage in works such as *Elizabeth the Queen* and *Winterset.* In *Our Town* and *The Skin of Our Teeth,* Thornton Wilder rejected the conventions of the realistic theater and boldly confronted his audiences with the fact that a play is an imitation of life, a work to be performed by actors on a stage. Yet other important American dramatists—S. N. Behrman, Robert Sherwood, Clifford Odets, Sidney Kingsley, and Lillian Hellman—managed to work most effectively within the traditional limitations of realistic drama.

Three prominent American dramatists to emerge since World War II— Arthur Miller, Tennessee Williams, and Edward Albee—continue to reflect the pull between realism and experimentalism. Williams and Albee have written both realistic and experimental plays. Miller seems closest, in his aims and his concept of drama's role, to the realistic drama of Henrik Ibsen. But while *Death of a Salesman,* Miller's most powerful play, makes a searching examination of the values of contemporary society, it also makes extensive use of the devices of experimental theater. American dramatists today show a willingness to experiment, to break into the illusion of reality, or to go beyond surface reality to a deeper reality. More than ever before, the American theater seems ready to receive a new dramatic giant, someone who will use the gains of the experimental theater and make great literature out of them.

OUR TOWN

THORNTON WILDER

Thornton Wilder's work ranges in its subject matter all over time and space. He has written about the Republic of Rome (in *The Ides of March*) and Grover's Corners, New Hampshire (in *Our Town*), about Greece just before the birth of Christ (in *The Woman of Andros*), and the American Midwest during the 1930's (in *Heaven's My Destination*). But pervading all his work is the theme of the repetitive, cyclical nature of life—the idea that no matter who you are, or where or when you live, the patterns of existence are in many ways the same.

Although Wilder may not be as prolific as other major writers, he has always created work of polished intelligence and grace. His work for the theater, particularly, shows a bright, innovative use of the stage, and *Our Town* certainly has become one of the classic plays of the American theater. Thornton Wilder once wrote that "the theater is an art of many collaborators," all of whom may distort the playwright's original intentions. Consequently, the dramatist must "turn his attention to the laws of narration, its logic, and its deep necessity of presenting a unifying idea. . . ." Wilder's plays, especially *Our Town*, possess such an inner logic and adherence to a unifying idea. (For a more detailed account of Thornton Wilder's literary achievement, see page 743.)

Our Town may seem disarmingly easy to read. The language is simple and straightforward, the characters easily recognizable and uncomplicated, and the plot is immediately comprehensible. The subtlety and irony of the play, then, lie not so much in what goes on but rather in how it is presented onstage. When you read this play, try to imagine yourself in a theater, as a part of an audience, watching *Our Town* as it unfolds on a stage. Read the opening stage directions carefully, and consider what would be the reaction of an audience to a play that opens with "no curtain" and "no scenery." Consider also that the first character you encounter is called the "Stage Manager," someone who does not ordinarily appear before an audience, and that he begins the play in a most unusual way—by talking directly to the audience, announcing the cast of the play, and setting the scene. Later two trellises are pushed onstage, and the Stage Manager casually remarks, "There's some scenery for those who think they have to have scenery." Apparently, scenery is not very important to the play. There seem to be good reasons for the bareness of the stage and for the unconvincing bits of scenery that are occasionally used. As you read, be attentive to all the unusual characteristics of the staging and ask yourself what the reasons are behind them. Only then will you fully respond to this carefully conceived play.

Our Town

Characters

STAGE MANAGER

DR. GIBBS

JOE CROWELL, JR.

HOWIE NEWSOME

MRS. GIBBS

MRS. WEBB

GEORGE GIBBS

REBECCA GIBBS

WALLY WEBB

EMILY WEBB

PROFESSOR WILLARD

MR. WEBB

WOMAN IN THE BALCONY

TALL MAN AT BACK OF AUDITORIUM

LADY IN A BOX

SIMON STIMSON

MRS. SOAMES

CONSTABLE WARREN

SI CROWELL

SAM CRAIG

JOE STODDARD

PEOPLE OF THE TOWN

The entire play takes place in Grover's Corners, New Hampshire, 1901 to 1913.

ACT I

No curtain. No scenery. The audience, arriving, sees an empty stage in half-light.

Presently the STAGE MANAGER, *hat on and pipe in mouth, enters and begins placing a table and several chairs downstage left, and a table and chairs down-stage right. "Left" and "right" are from the point of view of the actor facing the audience. "Up" is toward the back wall.*

As the house lights go down, he has finished setting the stage and, leaning against the right proscenium [1] pillar, watches the late arrivals in the audience. When the auditorium is in complete darkness, he speaks.

STAGE MANAGER. This play is called *Our Town*. It was written by Thornton Wilder; produced and directed by A____ [or: produced by A____: directed by B____]. In it you will see Miss C____, Miss D____, Miss E____, and Mr. F____, Mr. G____, Mr. H____, and many others.

The name of the town is Grover's Corners, New Hampshire—just across the Massachusetts line: longitude forty-two degrees, forty minutes; latitude seventy degrees, thirty-seven minutes.

The first act shows a day in our town. The day is May 7, 1901. The time is just before dawn.

[*A rooster crows.*]

The sky is beginning to show some streaks of light over in the east there, behind our mount'in. The morning star always gets wonderful bright the minute before it has to go. (*He stares at it for a moment, then goes upstage.*)

Well, I'd better show you how our town lies. Up here (*That is, parallel with the back wall*) is Main Street. Way back there is the railway station; tracks go that way. Polish Town's across the tracks and some Canuck [2] families. (*Toward the left*) Over there is the Congregational

---

[1] **proscenium** (prō·sē′nē·əm): the small area on a stage in front of the curtain, where action takes place when the curtain is closed.

[2] **Canuck:** French-Canadian.

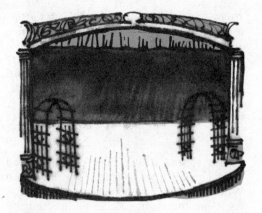

Church; across the street's the Presbyterian. Methodist and Unitarian are over there. Baptist is down in the holla by the river. Catholic Church is over beyond the tracks.

Here's the Town Hall and Post Office combined; jail's in the basement. Bryan [1] once made a speech from these steps here. Along here's a row of stores. Hitching posts and horse blocks in front of them. First automobile's going to come along in about five years—belonged to Banker Cartwright, our richest citizen . . . lives in the big white house up on the hill.

Here's the grocery store and here's Mr. Morgan's drugstore. Most everybody in town manages to look into those two stores once a day. Public school's over yonder. High school's still farther over. Quarter of nine mornings, noontimes, and three o'clock afternoons, the hull town can hear the yelling and screaming from those schoolyards. *(He approaches the table and chairs downstage right.)*

This is our doctor's house—Doc Gibbs's. This is the back door.

[*Two arched trellises are pushed out, one by each proscenium pillar.*]

There's some scenery for those who think they have to have scenery. There's a garden here. Corn . . . peas . . . beans

---

[1] **Bryan:** William Jennings Bryan (1860–1925). Democratic Presidential nominee in 1896, 1900, and 1908.

. . . hollyhocks . . . heliotrope . . . and a lot of burdock. *(Crosses the stage)*

In those days our newspaper come out twice a week—the Grover's Corners *Sentinel*—and this is Editor Webb's house. And this is Mrs. Webb's garden. Just like Mrs. Gibbs's, only it's got a lot of sunflowers, too. Right here—big butternut tree.

[*He returns to his place by the right proscenium pillar and looks at the audience for a minute.*]

Nice town, y'know what I mean? Nobody very remarkable ever come out of it—s'far as we know. The earliest tombstones in the cemetery up there on the mountain say 1670, 1680—they're Grovers and Cartwrights and Gibbses and Herseys—same names as are around here now.

Well, as I said, it's about dawn. The only lights on in town are in a cottage over by the tracks where a Polish mother's just had twins. And in the Joe Crowell house, where Joe Jr.'s getting up so as to deliver the paper. And in the depot, where Shorty Hawkins is gettin' ready to flag the five-forty-five for Boston.

[*A train whistle is heard. The* STAGE MANAGER *takes out his watch and nods.*]

Naturally, out in the country—all around —they've been lights on for some time, what with milkin's and so on. But town people sleep late.

So—another day's begun. There's Doc Gibbs comin' down Main Street now, comin' back from that baby case. And here's his wife comin' downstairs to get breakfast. Doc Gibbs died in 1930. The new hospital's named after him. Mrs. Gibbs died first—long time ago, in fact. She went out to visit her daughter, Rebecca, who married an insurance man in Canton, Ohio, and died there—pneumonia—but her body was brought back here. She's up in the cemetery there now, in with a whole mess of Gibbses and

Herseys—she was Julia Hersey 'fore she married Doc Gibbs in the Congregational Church over there.

In our town we like to know the facts about everybody.... That's Doc Gibbs. And there comes Joe Crowell, Jr., delivering Mr. Webb's *Sentinel*.

[DR. GIBBS *has been coming along Main Street from the left. At the point where he would turn to approach his house, he stops, sets down his—imaginary— black bag, takes off his hat, and rubs his face with fatigue, using an enormous handkerchief.* MRS. GIBBS *has entered her kitchen, gone through the motions of putting wood into a stove, lighting it, and preparing breakfast. Suddenly,* JOE CROWELL, JR., *starts down Main Street from the right, hurling imaginary newspapers into doorways.*]

JOE CROWELL, JR. Morning, Doc Gibbs.

DR. GIBBS. Morning, Joe.

JOE CROWELL, JR. Somebody been sick, Doc?

DR. GIBBS. No. Just some twins born over in Polish Town.

JOE CROWELL, JR. Do you want your paper now?

DR. GIBBS. Yes, I'll take it. Anything serious goin' on in the world since Wednesday?

JOE CROWELL, JR. Yessir. My schoolteacher, Miss Foster, 's getting married to a fella over in Concord.

DR. GIBBS. I declare. How do you boys feel about that?

JOE CROWELL, JR. Well, of course, it's none of my business—but I think if a person starts out to be a teacher, she ought to stay one.

DR. GIBBS. How's your knee, Joe?

JOE CROWELL, JR. Fine, Doc. I never think about it at all. Only like you said, it always tells me when it's going to rain.

DR. GIBBS. What's it telling you today? Goin' to rain?

JOE CROWELL, JR. No, sir.

DR. GIBBS. Sure?

JOE CROWELL, JR. Yessir.

DR. GIBBS. Knee ever make a mistake?

JOE CROWELL, JR. No, sir.

[JOE *goes off.* DR. GIBBS *stands reading his paper.*]

STAGE MANAGER. Here comes Howie Newsome delivering the milk.

[HOWIE NEWSOME *comes along Main Street, passes* DR. GIBBS, *comes down the center of the stage, leaves some bottles at* MRS. WEBB'S *back door, and crosses the stage to* MRS. GIBBS'S.]

HOWIE NEWSOME. Git-ap, Bessie. What's the matter with you? ... Morning, Doc.

DR. GIBBS. Morning, Howie.

HOWIE NEWSOME. Somebody sick?

DR. GIBBS. Pair of twins over to Mrs. Goruslawski's.

HOWIE NEWSOME. Twins, eh? This town's gettin' bigger every year.

DR. GIBBS. Going to rain, Howie?

HOWIE NEWSOME. No, no. Fine day— that'll burn through. Come on, Bessie.

DR. GIBBS. Hello, Bessie. (*He strokes her.*) How old is she, Howie?

HOWIE NEWSOME. Going on seventeen. Bessie's all mixed up about the route ever since the Lockharts stopped takin' their quart of milk every day. She wants to leave 'em a quart just the same—keeps scolding me the hull trip.

[*He reaches* MRS. GIBBS'S *back door. She is waiting for him.*]

MRS. GIBBS. Good morning, Howie.

HOWIE NEWSOME. Morning, Mrs. Gibbs. Doc's just comin' down the street.

MRS. GIBBS. Is he? Seems like you're late today.

HOWIE NEWSOME. Yes. Somep'n went wrong with the separator.[1] Don't know what 'twas.

[*He goes back to Main Street, clucks for Bessie, and goes off right.* DR. GIBBS *reaches his home and goes in.*]

---

[1] **separator:** a machine that separates cream from milk.

MRS. GIBBS. Everything all right?

DR. GIBBS. Yes. I declare—easy as kittens.

MRS. GIBBS. Bacon'll be ready in a minute. Set down and drink your coffee. Child-*run!* Child-*run!* Time to get up. George! Rebecca! . . . You can catch a couple hours' sleep this morning, can't you?

DR. GIBBS. Hm! . . . Mrs. Wentworth's coming at eleven. Guess I know what it's about, too. Her stummick ain't what it ought to be.

MRS. GIBBS. All told, you won't get more'n three hours' sleep. Frank Gibbs, I don't know what's goin' to become of you. I do wish I could get you to go away some place and take a rest. I think it would do you good.

MRS. WEBB. Emileeee! Time to get up! Wally! Seven o'clock!

MRS. GIBBS. I declare, you got to speak to George. Seems like something's come over him lately. He's no help to me at all. I can't even get him to cut me some wood.

DR. GIBBS. Is he sassy to you?

MRS. GIBBS. No. He just whines! All he thinks about is that baseball—George! Rebecca! You'll be late for school.

DR. GIBBS. M-m-m. . . .

MRS. GIBBS. George!

DR. GIBBS. George, look sharp!

GEORGE'S VOICE. Yes, Pa!

DR. GIBBS (*as he goes off the stage*). Don't you hear your mother calling you?

MRS. WEBB. Walleee! Emileee! You'll be late for school! Walleee! You wash yourself good or I'll come up and do it myself.

REBECCA GIBBS'S VOICE. Ma! What dress shall I wear?

MRS. GIBBS. Don't make a noise. Your father's been out all night and needs his sleep. I washed and ironed the blue gingham for you special.

REBECCA. Ma, I hate that dress.

MRS. GIBBS. Oh, hush up with you.

REBECCA. Every day I go to school dressed like a sick turkey.

MRS. GIBBS. Now, Rebecca, don't be

impossible. You always look *very* nice.

REBECCA. Mamma, George's throwing soap at me.

MRS. GIBBS. I'll come up and slap the both of you—that's what I'll do.

[*A factory whistle sounds. The children enter and take their places at the breakfast tables:* EMILY *and* WALLY WEBB; GEORGE *and* REBECCA GIBBS.]

STAGE MANAGER. We've got a factory in our town too—hear it? Makes blankets. Cartwrights own it and it brung 'em a fortune.

MRS. WEBB. Children! Now I won't have it. Breakfast is just as good as any other meal and I won't have you gobbling like wolves. It'll stunt your growth —that's a fact. Put away your book, Wally.

WALLY. Aw, Ma!

MRS. WEBB. You know the rule's well as I do—no books at table. As for me, I'd rather have my children healthy than bright!

EMILY. I'm both, Mamma; you know I am. I'm the brightest girl in school for my age. I have a wonderful memory.

MRS. WEBB. Eat your breakfast.

WALLY. I'm bright, too, when I'm looking at my stamp collection.

MRS. GIBBS. I'll speak to your father about it when he's rested. Seems to me twenty-five cents a week's enough for a boy your age. I declare I don't know how you spend it all.

GEORGE. Aw, Ma—I gotta lotta things to buy.

MRS. GIBBS. Strawberry phosphates— that's what you spend it on.

GEORGE. I don't see how Rebecca comes to have so much money. She has more'n a dollar.

REBECCA (*spoon in mouth, dreamily*). I've been saving it up gradual.

MRS. GIBBS. Well, dear, I think it's a good thing every now and then to spend some.

REBECCA. Mamma, do you know what I love most in the world—do you? Money!

MRS. GIBBS. Eat your breakfast.

[*The school bell is heard.*]

CHILDREN. Mamma, there's first bell. . . . I gotta hurry. . . . I don't want any more.

MRS. WEBB. Walk fast, but you don't have to run. Wally, pull up your pants at the knee. Stand up straight, Emily.

MRS. GIBBS. Tell Miss Foster I send her my best congratulations. Can you remember that?

REBECCA. Yes, Ma.

MRS. GIBBS. You look real nice, Rebecca. Pick up your feet.

ALL. Good-by.

[*The children from the two houses join at the center of the stage and go up to Main Street, then off left.* MRS. GIBBS *fills her apron with food for the chickens and comes down to the footlights.*]

MRS. GIBBS. Here, chick, chick, chick, . . . No, go away, you. Go away. . . . Here, chick, chick, chick. What's the matter with *you?* Fight, fight, fight— that's all you do. Hm . . . *you* don't belong to me. Where'd you come from? (*She shakes her apron.*) Oh, don't be so scared. Nobody's going to hurt you.

[MRS. WEBB *is sitting by her trellis, stringing beans.*]

Good Morning, Myrtle. How's your cold?

MRS. WEBB. Well, it's better; but I told Charles I didn't know as I'd go to choir practice tonight. Wouldn't be any use.

MRS. GIBBS. Just the same, you come to choir practice, Myrtle, and try it.

MRS. WEBB. Well, if I don't feel any worse than I do now I probably will. While I'm resting myself, I thought I'd string some of these beans.

MRS. GIBBS (*rolling up her sleeves as she crosses the stage for a chat*). Let me help you. Beans have been good this year.

MRS. WEBB. I've decided to put up forty quarts if it kills me. The children say they hate 'em, but I notice they're able to get 'em down all winter. (*Pause*)

MRS. GIBBS. Now, Myrtle. I've got to tell you something, because if I don't tell somebody I'll burst.

MRS. WEBB. Why, Julia Gibbs!

MRS. GIBBS. Here, give me some more of those beans. Myrtle, did one of those secondhand furniture men from Boston come to see you last Friday?

MRS. WEBB. No-o.

MRS. GIBBS. Well, he called on me. First I thought he was a patient wantin' to see Dr. Gibbs. 'N he wormed his way into my parlor, and, Myrtle Webb, he offered me three hundred and fifty dollars for Grandmother Wentworth's highboy,[1] as I'm sitting here!

MRS. WEBB. Why, Julia Gibbs!

MRS. GIBBS. He did! That old thing! Why, it was so big I didn't know where to put it, and I almost give it to Cousin Hester Wilcox.

MRS. WEBB. Well, you're going to take it, aren't you?

MRS. GIBBS. I don't know.

MRS. WEBB. You don't know—three hundred and fifty dollars! What's come over you?

MRS. GIBBS. Well, if I could get the Doctor to take the money and go away some place on a real trip, I'd sell it like that. Myrtle, ever since I was *that* high I've had the thought that I'd like to see Paris, France. I suppose I'm crazy.

MRS. WEBB. Oh, I know what you mean. How does the Doctor feel about it?

MRS. GIBBS. Well, I did beat about the bush a little and said that if I got a legacy—that's the way I put it—I'd make him take me somewhere.

MRS. WEBB. M-m-m. . . . What did he say?

MRS. GIBBS. You know how he is. I haven't heard a serious word out of him ever since I've known him. No, he said, it might make him discontented with Grover's Corners to go traipsin' about Europe; better let well enough alone, he says. Every two years he makes a trip to the battlefields of the Civil War; and

---

[1] **highboy:** tall chest of drawers.

that's enough treat for anybody, he says.

MRS. WEBB. Well, Mr. Webb just *admires* the way Dr. Gibbs knows everything about the Civil War. Mr. Webb's a good mind to give up Napoleon and move over to the Civil War, only Dr. Gibbs being one of the greatest experts in the country just makes him despair.

MRS. GIBBS. It's a fact! Dr. Gibbs is never so happy as when he's at Antietam or Gettysburg. The times I've walked over those hills, Myrtle, stopping at every bush and pacing it all out, like we was going to buy it.

MRS. WEBB. Well, if that secondhand man's really serious about buyin' it, Julia, you sell it. And then you'll get to see Paris, all right.

MRS. GIBBS. Oh, I'm sorry I mentioned it. Only it seems to me that once in your life before you die you ought to see a country where they don't talk and think in English and don't even want to.

[*The* STAGE MANAGER *returns to the center of the stage.*]

STAGE MANAGER. That'll do. That'll do. Thank you very much, ladies.

[MRS. GIBBS *and* MRS. WEBB *gather up their things, return into their homes, and disappear.*]

Now we're going to skip a few hours in the day at Grover's Corners. But before we go on, I want you to know some more things about the town—all kinds of things. So I've asked Professor Willard of our State University to come down here and sketch in a few details of our past history—kind of scientific account, you might say. Is Professor Willard here?

[PROFESSOR WILLARD, *a rural savant,*[1] *pince-nez*[2] *on a wide satin ribbon, enters from the right with some notes in his hand.*]

---

[1] **savant** (sə·vänt): scholar.
[2] **pince-nez** (pans′nā): old-fashioned eyeglasses that are clipped to the nose with a spring.

May I introduce Professor Willard of our university. A few brief notes, thank you, Professor—unfortunately our time is limited.

PROFESSOR WILLARD. Grover's Corners ... let me see ... Grover's Corners lies on the old Archeozoic granite of the Appalachian range. I may say it's some of the oldest land in the world. We're very proud of that. A shelf of Devonian basalt crosses it with vestiges of Mesozoic[3] shale, and some sandstone outcroppings; but that's all more recent: two hundred, three hundred million years old. Some highly interesting fossils have been found—I may say unique fossils—two miles out of town, in Silas Peckham's cow pasture. They can be seen at the museum in our university at any time.... Did you wish the meteorological conditions?

STAGE MANAGER. Thank you. We would.

PROFESSOR WILLARD. The mean precipitation is forty inches. The mean annual temperature is forty-three degrees, ranging between one hundred two degrees in the shade and thirty-eight degrees below zero in winter. The ... the ... uh ...

STAGE MANAGER. Thank you, Professor. And have you Professor Gruber's notes on the history of human life here?

PROFESSOR WILLARD. Hm ... yes ... anthropological data. Early Amerindian[4] stock. Cotahatchee[5] tribes ... no evidence before the tenth century of this era ... hm ... now entirely disappeared ... possible traces in three families. Migration toward the end of the seventeenth century of English brachycephalic[6] blue-eyed stock ... for the most part. Since

---

[3] **Archeozoic ... Mesozoic:** "Archeozoic" and "Mesozoic" refer to the geological eras when the layers of granite and shale were formed. "Devonian" refers to the period in the Paleozoic Era when the basalt was formed.
[4] **Amerindian:** pertaining to the American Indian.
[5] **Cotahatchee** (kō·tə·ha′chi).
[6] **brachycephalic** (brak′i·sə·fal′ik): short-headed, or broad-headed.

then some influx of Slav and Mediterranean types . . .

STAGE MANAGER. And the population, Professor Willard?

PROFESSOR WILLARD. Within the town limits, 2,640. The postal district brings in 507 more. Mortality and birth rates are constant; by MacPherson's gauge, 6.032.

STAGE MANAGER. Thank you *very* much, Professor. We're all very much obliged to you, I'm sure.

PROFESSOR WILLARD. Not at all, sir; not at all.

STAGE MANAGER. This way, Professor, and thank you again.

[*Exit* PROFESSOR WILLARD.]

Now the political and social report: Editor Webb. . . . Oh, Mr. Webb?

[MRS. WEBB *appears at her back door.*]

MRS. WEBB. He'll be here in a minute. . . . He just cut his hand while he was eatin' an apple.

STAGE MANAGER. Thank you, Mrs. Webb.

MRS. WEBB. Charles! Everybody's waitin'. (*Exit.*)

STAGE MANAGER. Mr. Webb is publisher and editor of the Grover's Corners *Sentinel.* That's our local paper, y'know.

[MR. WEBB *enters from his house, pulling on his coat. His finger is bound in a handkerchief.*]

MR. WEBB. Hm. . . . I don't have to tell you that we're run here by a board of selectmen.[1] All males vote at the age of twenty-one. Women vote indirect. We're lower middle class, sprinkling of professional men . . . ten percent illiterate laborers. Politically, we're eighty-six percent Republicans; six percent Democrats; four percent Socialists; rest, indifferent. Religiously, we're eighty-five percent Protestants; twelve percent Catholics; rest, indifferent. Do you want the poverty and insanity statistics?

STAGE MANAGER. Thank you, no. Have you any comments, Mr Webb?

MR. WEBB. Very ordinary town, if you ask me. Little better behaved than most. Probably a lot duller. But our young people here seem to like it well enough: ninety percent of 'em graduating from high school settle down right here to live—even when they've been away to college.

STAGE MANAGER. Thank you, Mr. Webb. Now, is there anyone in the audience who would like to ask Editor Webb anything about the town?

WOMAN IN THE BALCONY. Is there much drinking in Grover's Corners?

MR. WEBB. Well, ma'am, I wouldn't know what you'd call *much.* Satiddy nights the farm hands meet down in Ellery Greenough's stable and holler some. Fourth of July I've been known to taste a drop myself—and Decoration Day, of course. We've got one or two town drunks, but they're always having remorses every time an evangelist comes to town. No, ma'am, I'd say likker ain't a regular thing in the home here, except in the medicine chest. Right good for snake bite, y'know —always was.

TALL MAN AT BACK OF AUDITORIUM. Is there no one in town aware of——

STAGE MANAGER. Come forward, will you, where we can all hear you—what were you saying?

TALL MAN. Is there no one in town aware of social injustice and industrial inequality?

MR. WEBB. Oh, yes, everybody is— somethin' terrible. Seems like they spend most of their time talking about who's rich and who's poor.

TALL MAN. Then why don't they do something about it?

MR. WEBB. Well, we're ready to listen to everybody's suggestion as to how you can see that the diligent and sensible'll rise to the top and the lazy and quarrelsome sink to the bottom. We'll listen

---

[1] **board of selectmen:** a board of officers elected annually.

to anybody. Meantime, until that's settled, we try to take care of those that can't help themselves, and those that can we leave alone. Are there any more questions?

LADY IN A BOX. Oh, Mr. Webb? Mr. Webb, is there any culture or love of beauty in Grover's Corners?

MR. WEBB. Well, ma'am, there ain't much—not in the sense you mean. Come to think of it, there's some girls that play the piano at high school commencement; but they ain't happy about it. Yes, and I see where my daughter's been made to read *The Merchant of Venice* over to the school. Seems all pretty remote to 'em, y'know what I mean. No, ma'am, there isn't much culture; but maybe this is the place to tell you that we've got a lot of pleasures of a kind here: we like the sun comin' up over the mountain in the morning, and we all notice a good deal about the birds. We pay a lot of attention to them, and trees and plants. And we watch the change of the seasons: yes, everybody knows about them. But those other things—you're right, ma'am—there ain't much. *Robinson Crusoe* and the Bible; and Handel's "Largo," [1] we all know that; and Whistler's "Mother"—those are just about as far as we go.

LADY IN A BOX. So I thought. Thank you, Mr. Webb.

STAGE MANAGER. All right! All right! Thank you, everybody.

[MR. WEBB *retires.*]

We'll go back to the town now. It's middle of the afternoon. All 2,642 have had their dinners, and all the dishes have been washed. There's an early-afternoon calm in our town: a buzzin' and a hummin' from the school buildings; only a few buggies on Main Street—the horses dozing at the hitching posts; you all remember what it's like. Doc Gibbs is in his office, tapping people and making

[1] **Handel's "Largo":** an orchestral piece from *Xerxes*, an oratorio by George Frederic Handel (1685–1759).

them say "Ah." Mr. Webb's cuttin' his lawn over there; one man in ten thinks it's a privilege to push his own lawn mower.

No, Sir. It's later than I thought. There are the children coming home from school already.

[EMILY WEBB *comes sedately down Main Street, carrying some schoolbooks. There are some signs that she is imagining herself to be a lady of striking elegance. Her father's movements to and fro with the lawn mower bring him into her vicinity.*]

EMILY. I *can't*, Lois. I've got to go home and help my mother. I *promised.*

MR. WEBB. Emily, walk simply. Who do you think you are today?

EMILY. Papa, you're terrible. One minute you tell me to stand up straight, and the next minute you call me names. I just don't listen to you. (*She gives him an abrupt kiss.*)

MR. WEBB. Golly, I never got a kiss from such a great lady before.

[*He goes out of sight.* EMILY *leans over and picks some flowers by the gate of her house.* GEORGE GIBBS *comes careening down Main Street. He is throwing a ball up to dizzy heights and waiting to catch it again. This sometimes requires his taking six steps backward.*]

GEORGE. Excuse me, Mrs. Forrest.

STAGE MANAGER (*as* MRS. FORREST). Go out and play in the fields, young man. You got no business playing baseball on Main Street.

GEORGE. Awfully sorry, Mrs. Forrest. . . . Hello, Emily.

EMILY. H'lo.

GEORGE. You made a fine speech in class.

EMILY. Well . . . I was really ready to make a speech about the Monroe Doctrine, but at the last minute Miss Corcoran made me talk about the Louisiana Purchase instead. I worked an awful long time on both of them.

GEORGE. Gee, it's funny, Emily. From

my window up there I can just see your head nights when you're doing your homework over in your room.

EMILY. Why, can you?

GEORGE. You certainly do stick to it, Emily. I don't see how you can sit still that long. I guess you like school.

EMILY. Well, I always feel it's something you have to go through.

GEORGE. Yeah.

EMILY. I don't mind it really. It passes the time.

GEORGE. Yeah. . . . Emily, what do you think? We might work out a kinda telegraph from there to there; and once in a while you could give me a kinda hint or two about one of those algebra problems. I don't mean the answers, Emily, of course not . . . just some little hint. . . .

EMILY. Oh, I think *hints* are allowed. So—ah—if you get stuck, George, you whistle to me; and I'll give you some hints.

GEORGE. Emily, you're just naturally bright, I guess.

EMILY. I figure that it's just the way a person's born.

GEORGE. Yeah. But, you see, I want to be a farmer, and my Uncle Luke says whenever I'm ready I can come over and work on his farm, and if I'm any good I can just gradually have it.

EMILY. You mean the house and everything?

[*Enter* MRS. WEBB.]

GEORGE. Yeah. Well, thanks. . . . I better be getting out to the baseball field. Thanks for the talk, Emily. . . . Good afternoon, Mrs. Webb.

MRS. WEBB. Good afternoon, George.

GEORGE. So long, Emily.

EMILY. So long, George.

MRS. WEBB. Emily, come and help me string these beans for the winter. George Gibbs let himself have a real conversation, didn't he? Why, he's growing up. How old would George be?

EMILY. I don't know.

MRS. WEBB. Let's see. He must be almost sixteen.

EMILY. Mamma, I made a speech in class today, and I was very good.

MRS. WEBB. You must recite it to your father at supper. What was it about?

EMILY. The Louisiana Purchase. It was like silk off a spool. I'm going to make speeches all my life. . . . Mamma, are these big enough?

MRS. WEBB. Try and get them a little bigger if you can.

EMILY. Mamma, will you answer me a question, serious?

MRS. WEBB. Seriously dear—not serious.

EMILY. Seriously. Will you?

MRS. WEBB. Of course, I will.

EMILY. Mamma, am I good-looking?

MRS. WEBB. Yes, of course you are. All my children have got good features; I'd be ashamed if they hadn't.

EMILY. Oh, Mamma, that's not what I mean. What I mean is: Am I *pretty?*

MRS. WEBB. I've already told you, yes. Now, that's enough of that. You have a nice, young, pretty face. I never heard of such foolishness.

EMILY. Oh, Mamma, you never tell us the truth about anything.

MRS. WEBB. I *am* telling you the truth.

EMILY. Mamma, were *you* pretty?

MRS. WEBB. Yes, I was, if I do say it. I was the prettiest girl in town next to Mamie Cartwright.

EMILY. But, Mamma, you've got to say *some*thing about me. Am I pretty enough . . . to get anybody . . . to get people interested in me?

MRS. WEBB. Emily, you make me tired. Now stop it. You're pretty enough for all normal purposes. Come along now and bring that bowl with you.

EMILY. But, Mamma, you're no help at all.

STAGE MANAGER. Thank you. Thank you! That'll do. We'll have to interrupt again here. Thank you, Mrs. Webb; thank you, Emily.

[MRS. WEBB *and* EMILY *withdraw.*]

There are some more things we've got to explore about this town. This time we're going to go about it in another way:

we're going to look back on it from the future. I'm not going to tell you what became of these two families we're seeing most of, because the rest of the play will tell you about them. But take some of these others.

Take Joe Crowell, Jr. Joe was a very bright fellow. He graduated with honors and got a scholarship to Boston Tech—M.I.T., that is. But the war broke out, and Joe died in France. All that education for nothing.

Howie Newsome's still delivering milk at Grover's Corners. He's an old man now, has a lot of help; but he still delivers it himself. Says he gets the feel of the town that way. Carries all the accounts in his head; never has to write down a word.

Mr. Morgan's drugstore ain't the same—it's all citified. Mr. Morgan retired and went to live in San Diego, California, where his daughter married a real-estate man, name of Kerby. Mr. Morgan died there in 1935 and was buried in a lot of palm trees. Kinda lost his religion at the end and took up New Thought or something. They read some newfangled poetry over him and cremated him. The New Hampshire in him sort of broke down in that climate, seems like.

The Cartwrights got richer and richer. The house is closed most of the year. They're off eating big dinners in hotels now—in Virginia Hot Springs and Miami Beach. They say the winters are cold here. I see where they've become 'Piscopalians.

The Cartwright interests have just begun building a new bank in Grover's Corners—had to go to Vermont for the marble, sorry to say. And they've asked a friend of mine what they should put in the cornerstone for people to dig up a thousand years from now. Of course, they've put in a copy of the New York *Times* and a copy of Mr. Webb's *Sentinel*. We're kind of interested in this, because some scientific fellas have found a way of painting all that reading matter with a kind of glue—silicate glue—that'll

make it keep a thousand, two thousand, years. We're putting in a Bible . . . and the Constitution of the United States and a copy of William Shakespeare's plays. What do you say, folks? What do you think? Y'know—Babylon once had two million people in it, and all we know about 'em is the names of the kings and some copies of wheat contracts and . . . the sales of slaves. Yes, every night all those families sat down to supper, and the father came home from his work, and the smoke went up the chimney—same as here. And even in Greece and Rome all we know about the real life of the people is what we can piece together out of the joking poems and the comedies they wrote for the theater back then. So I'm going to have a copy of this play put in the cornerstone and the people a thousand years from now'll know a few simple facts about us—more than the Treaty of Versailles [1] and the Lindbergh flight. See what I mean?

Well—you people a thousand years from now—in the provinces north of New York at the beginning of the twentieth century, people et three times a day: soon after sunrise, at noon, and at sunset. Every seventh day, by law and by religion, was a day of rest, and all work came to a stop. The religion at that time was Christianity. I guess you have some other records about Christianity. The domestic setup was marriage: a binding relation between a male and one female that lasted for life. Christianity strictly forbade killing, but you were allowed to kill animals, and you were allowed to kill human beings in war and government punishings. I guess we don't have to tell you about the government and business forms, because that's the kind of thing people seem to hand down first of all. Let me see now if there's anything else. Oh, yes—at death people were buried in the ground just as they are.

So, friends, this is the way we were

---

[1] **Treaty of Versailles:** treaty signed at the end of World War I.

in our growing up and in our marrying and in our doctoring and in our living and in our dying. Now we'll return to our day in Grover's Corners: A lot of time has gone by. It's evening. You can hear choir practice going on in the Congregational Church. All the children are at home doing their schoolwork. The day is running down like a tired clock.

[*A choir partially concealed in the orchestra pit has begun singing "Blest Be the Tie That Binds."* SIMON STIMSON *stands directing them. Two ladders have been pushed onto the stage; they serve as indication of the second story in the Gibbs and Webb houses.* GEORGE *and* EMILY *mount them, and apply themselves to their schoolwork.* DR. GIBBS *has entered and is seated in his kitchen, reading.*]

SIMON STIMSON. Now look here, everybody. Music come into the world to give pleasure. Softer! Softer! Get it out of your heads that music's only good when it's loud. You leave loudness to the Methodists. You couldn't beat 'em, even if you wanted to. Now again. Tenors!

GEORGE. Hssst! Emily!

EMILY. Hello.

GEORGE. Hello.

EMILY. I can't work at all. The moonlight's so *terrible*.

GEORGE. Emily, did you get the third problem?

EMILY. Which?

GEORGE. The *third?*

EMILY. Why, yes, George—that's the easiest of them all.

GEORGE. I don't see it. Emily, can you give me a hint?

EMILY. I'll tell you one thing: the answer's in yards.

GEORGE. In yards! How do you mean?

EMILY. In *square* yards.

GEORGE. Oh . . . in square yards.

EMILY. Yes, George, don't you see?

GEORGE. Yeah.

EMILY. In square yards of *wallpaper*.

GEORGE. Wallpaper—oh, I see. Thanks a lot, Emily.

EMILY. You're welcome. My, isn't the moonlight *terrible?* And choir practice going on. I think if you hold your breath you can hear the train all the way to Contookuck. Hear it?

GEORGE. M-m-m. What do you know!

EMILY. Well, I guess I better go back and try to work.

GEORGE. Good night, Emily. And thanks.

EMILY. Good night, George.

SIMON STIMSON. Before I forget it: How many of you will be able to come in Tuesday afternoon and sing at Fred Hersey's wedding? Show your hands. That'll be fine; that'll be right nice. We'll do the same music we did for Jane Trowbridge's last month. . . . Now we'll do "Art thou weary; art thou languid?" It's a question, ladies and gentlemen; make it talk. Ready.

DR. GIBBS. Oh, George, can you come down a minute?

GEORGE. Yes, Pa. (*He descends the ladder.*)

DR. GIBBS. Make yourself comfortable, George; I'll only keep you a minute. George, how old are you?

GEORGE. I? I'm sixteen, almost seventeen.

DR. GIBBS. What do you want to do after school's over?

GEORGE. Why, you know, Pa, I want to be a farmer on Uncle Luke's farm.

DR. GIBBS. You'll be willing, will you, to get up early and milk and feed the stock . . . and you'll be able to hoe and hay all day?

GEORGE. Sure, I will. What are you . . . what do you mean, Pa?

DR. GIBBS. Well, George, while I was in my office today I heard a funny sound. . . . And what do you think it was? It was your mother chopping wood. There you see your mother—getting up early, cooking meals all day long, washing and ironing; and still she has to go out in the back yard and chop wood. I suppose she just got tired of asking you. She just gave up and decided it was easier to do it herself. And you eat her meals and put on the clothes she keeps nice for you, and you run off and play base-ball—like she's some hired girl we keep around the house but that we don't like very much. Well, I knew all I had to do was call your attention to it. Here's a handkerchief, son. George, I've decided to raise your spending money twenty-five cents a week. Not, of course, for chop-ping wood for your mother, because that's a present you give her, but because you're getting older—and I imagine there are lots of things you must find to do with it.

GEORGE. Thanks, Pa.

DR. GIBBS. Let's see—tomorrow's pay-day. You can count on it. Hmm. Probably Rebecca'll feel she ought to have some more too. Wonder what could have hap-pened to your mother. Choir practice never was as late as this before.

GEORGE. It's only half-past eight, Pa.

DR. GIBBS. I don't know why she's in that old choir. She hasn't any more voice than an old crow.... Traipsin' around the streets at this hour of the night.... Just about time you retired, don't you think?

GEORGE. Yes, Pa.

[GEORGE *mounts to his place on the lad-der. Laughter and good nights can be heard on stage left, and presently* MRS. GIBBS, MRS. SOAMES, *and* MRS. WEBB *come down Main Street. When they ar-rive at the center of the stage, they stop.*]

MRS. SOAMES. Good night, Martha. Good night, Mr. Foster.

MRS. WEBB. I'll tell Mr. Webb; I *know* he'll want to put it in the paper.

MRS. GIBBS. My, it's late!

MRS. SOAMES. Good night, Irma.

MRS. GIBBS. Real nice choir practice, wa'n't it? Myrtle Webb! Look at that moon, will you! Tsk-tsk-tsk. Potato weather, for sure.

MRS. SOAMES. Naturally I didn't want to say a word about it in front of those others, but now we're alone—really, it's the worst scandal that ever was in this town!

MRS. GIBBS. What?

MRS. SOAMES. Simon Stimson!

MRS. GIBBS. Now, Louella!

MRS. SOAMES. But, Julia! To have the organist of a church drink and drink year after year. You know he was drunk to-night.

MRS. GIBBS. Now, Louella. We all know about Mr. Stimson, and we all know about the troubles he's been through, and Dr. Ferguson knows too; and if Dr. Ferguson keeps him on there in his job, the only thing the rest of us can do is just not to notice it.

MRS. SOAMES. Not to notice it! But it's getting worse.

MRS. WEBB. No, it isn't, Louella. It's getting better. I've been in that choir twice as long as you have. It doesn't hap-pen anywhere near so often.... My, I hate to go to bed on a night like this. I better hurry. Those children'll be sitting up till all hours. Good night, Louella. (*She hurries downstage, enters her house, and disappears.*)

MRS. GIBBS. Can you get home safe, Louella?

MRS. SOAMES. It's as bright as day. I can see Mr. Soames scowling at the win-dow now. You'd think we'd been to a dance the way the menfolk carry on.

[*Repeated good nights.* MRS. GIBBS *ar-rives at her home.*]

MRS. GIBBS. Well, we had a real good time.

DR. GIBBS. You're late enough.

MRS. GIBBS. Why, Frank, it ain't any later 'n usual.

DR. GIBBS. And you stopping at the corner to gossip with a lot of hens.

MRS. GIBBS. Now, Frank, don't be grouchy. Come out and smell my helio-trope in the moonlight. (*They stroll out arm in arm along the footlights.*) Isn't that wonderful? What did you do all the time I was away?

DR. GIBBS. Oh, I read—as usual. What were the girls gossiping about tonight?

MRS. GIBBS. Well, believe me, Frank— there is something to gossip about.

DR. GIBBS. Hmm! Simon Stimson far gone, was he?

MRS. GIBBS. Worst I've ever seen him. How'll that end, Frank? Dr. Ferguson can't forgive him forever.

DR. GIBBS. I guess I know more about Simon Stimson's affairs than anybody in this town. Some people ain't made for small-town life. I don't know how that'll end; but there's nothing we can do but just leave it alone. Come, get in.

MRS. GIBBS. No, not yet. . . . Oh, Frank, I'm worried about you.

DR. GIBBS. What are you worried about?

MRS. GIBBS. I think it's my duty to make plans for you to get a real rest and change. And if I get that legacy, well, I'm going to insist on it.

DR. GIBBS. Now, Julia, there's no sense in going over that again.

MRS. GIBBS. Frank, you're just *unreasonable!*

DR. GIBBS. Come on, Julia, it's getting late. First thing you know you'll catch cold. I gave George a piece of my mind tonight. I reckon you'll have your wood chopped for a while anyway. No, no, start getting upstairs.

MRS. GIBBS. Oh, dear. There's always so many things to pick up, seems like. You know, Frank, Mrs. Fairchild always locks her front door every night. All those people up that part of town do.

DR. GIBBS. They're all getting citified, that's the trouble with them. They haven't got nothing fit to burgle and everybody knows it.

[*They disappear.* REBECCA *climbs up the ladder beside* GEORGE.]

GEORGE. Get out, Rebecca. There's only room for one at this window. You're always spoiling everything.

REBECCA. Well, let me just look a minute.

GEORGE. Use your own window.

REBECCA. I did; but there's no moon there. . . . George, do you know what I think, do you? I think maybe the moon's getting nearer and nearer and there'll be a big 'splosion.

GEORGE. Rebecca, you don't know anything. If the moon were getting nearer, the guys that sit up all night with telescopes would see it first and they'd tell about it, and it'd be in all the newspapers.

REBECCA. George, is the moon shining on South America, Canada, and half the whole world?

GEORGE. Well—prob'ly is.

[*The* STAGE MANAGER *strolls on.*]

STAGE MANAGER. Nine-thirty. Most of the lights are out. No, there's Constable Warren trying a few doors on Main Street. And here comes Editor Webb, after putting his newspaper to bed.

MR. WEBB. Good evening, Bill.

CONSTABLE WARREN. Evenin', Mr. Webb.

MR. WEBB. Quite a moon!

CONSTABLE WARREN. Yep.

MR. WEBB. All quiet tonight?

CONSTABLE WARREN. Simon Stimson is rollin' around a little. Just saw his wife movin' out to hunt for him, so I looked the other way—there he is now.

[SIMON STIMSON *comes down Main Street from the left, only a trace of unsteadiness in his walk.*]

MR. WEBB. Good evening, Simon. . . . Town seems to have settled down for the night pretty well. . . .

[SIMON STIMSON *comes up to him and pauses a moment.*]

Good evening. . . . Yes, most of the town's settled down for the night, Simon. . . . I guess we better do the same. Can I walk along a ways with you?

[SIMON STIMSON *continues on his way without a word and disappears at the right.*]

Good night.

CONSTABLE WARREN. I don't know how that's goin' to end, Mr. Webb.

MR. WEBB. Well, he's seen a peck of trouble, one thing after another. . . . Oh, Bill . . . if you see my boy smoking cigarettes, just give him a word, will you? He thinks a lot of you, Bill.

CONSTABLE WARREN. I don't think he smokes no cigarettes, Mr. Webb. Leastways, not more'n two or three a year. He don't belong to that crowd that hangs out down by the gully.

MR. WEBB. Mm.... I hope not. Well, good night, Bill.

CONSTABLE WARREN. Good night, Mr. Webb. *(Exit.)*

MR. WEBB. Who's that up there? Is that you, Myrtle?

EMILY. No, it's me, Papa.

MR. WEBB. Why aren't you in bed?

EMILY. I don't know. I just can't sleep yet, Papa. The moonlight's so *won*-derful. And the smell of Mrs. Gibbs's heliotrope. Can you smell it?

MR. WEBB. Hm.... Yes. Haven't any troubles on your mind, have you, Emily?

EMILY. *Troubles,* Papa? *No.*

MR. WEBB. Well, enjoy yourself, but don't let your mother catch you. Good night, Emily.

EMILY. Good night, Papa.

[MR. WEBB *crosses into the house, whistling "Blest Be the Tie That Binds," and disappears.*]

REBECCA. I never told you about that letter Jane Crofut got from her minister when she was sick. The minister of her church in the town she was in before she came here. He wrote Jane a letter and on the envelope the address was like this. It said: Jane Crofut, The Crofut Farm, Grover's Corners, Sutton County, New Hampshire, United States of America.

GEORGE. What's funny about that?

REBECCA. But listen, it's not finished: The United States of America, Continent of North America, Western Hemisphere, The Earth, The Solar System, The Universe, The Mind of God—that's what it said on the envelope.

GEORGE. What do you know!

REBECCA. And the postman brought it just the same.

GEORGE. What do you know!

STAGE MANAGER. That's the end of the first act, friends. You can go and smoke now, those that smoke.

COMMENTARY

By now you are probably aware of the tension between the commonplace simplicity of the events of *Our Town* and the unusually sophisticated way in which these events are presented on the stage. Certainly this play would seem to be a departure both from the soaring poetry of Shakespeare and from suspenseful, well-constructed plays like *Beyond the Horizon* (page 804).

As far as the events of his play are concerned, Thornton Wilder seems particularly interested in stressing the ordinary over the extraordinary, the typical rather than the usual. He concentrates on two families, the Gibbses and the Webbs, both of whom seem to live routine and conventional lives. We see Doctor Gibbs making his usual rounds and Editor Webb mowing his ever-growing lawn. We see their children getting ready for school, coming home, doing their homework. We see the two mothers at typically domestic chores or going to what seems like a routine choir practice. Even the minor characters in the play are shown in everyday circumstances. Joe Crowell delivers, as always, the morning paper, and his knee, as always, predicts rain. Constable Warren makes his regular rounds. Howie Newsome's horse does what it has always done. The first act of *Our Town*, then, is permeated with a sense of the ever-occurring, predictable, circular patterns of daily life.

True, there are a few hints of potentially unusual events in the play. For instance, Mrs. Gibbs says she may sell an antique and take a trip abroad; and Simon Stimson, the church organist, apparently has been drinking. But when we consider these details, we realize that the playwright introduces them only to emphasize the idea of orderly routine. Mrs. Gibbs, we feel, will forego her trip to Paris and settle for the usual trip to Gettysburg. A prospective change in routine will be defeated by the routine itself. Simon Stimson drinks, we learn, because "some people ain't made for small-town life." His drinking is a protest against commonplace routines, and yet, ironically, his drinking has become a routine itself, a commonplace, expected part of the life of Grover's Corners.

Routine, then, seems to be the word which best describes the events of Act I of *Our Town*. And behind these events there are reminders of other routines. A rooster crows at daybreak; a school bell calls children to school; a whistle calls workers to the factory. The whole act, in fact, is bracketed by two cosmically continual events: the rising of the sun in the morning and the rising of the moon in the evening.

Yet if the events of the play are consistently and constantly commonplace, they are presented to us in a theatrically unusual way. The playwright always attempts to make the ordinary *seem* extraordinary, by throwing a very different sort of light upon it. The staging of the play constantly calls attention to the fact that these events are being presented before an audience. Normally, plays use curtains, scenery, lighting, every effect they can, to draw us into the imaginary world up on the stage. But here, the playwright seems to be doing the very opposite: there is no curtain at the beginning, very little scenery throughout, and the actors use imaginary or crudely representative props. George and Emily converse not from windowsills but from stepladders, and behind them is the dull brick backstage wall. Apparently, in *Our Town,* we are not supposed to lose ourselves in the story, but rather remain removed and detached from it because of the obvious artificiality of its staging. Moreover, the constant presence of the Stage Manager contributes to this effect of detachment. He pulls the strings of the play before our eyes, bringing characters on and off, tampering with time sequences, commenting on what is happening. We are asked to think about what we see and hear, rather than

to respond emotionally to it. The humdrum life of a small New Hampshire town is put under a cool, intellectual light so that this life—as it unfolds during the course of this play—will gain new meaning, new significance.

Thus there is an odd contrast between the events themselves and the attitude we are encouraged to take toward these events. The characters respond with great feeling to what is happening, but we the audience are supposed to remain aloof and thoughtful. Emily finds the moonlight "terrible" and emotes about algebra, but the audience sees the more general issue of two young people falling in love; George apparently cries when he is reprimanded by his father, but we probably don't cry with him, knowing as we do that the scene is really about all boys growing up. The characters respond to specific things; the audience understands the general implications. The characters are involved; the audience is presumably detached.

Perhaps the whole effect can best be summarized in the address on Jane Crofut's letter:

> "Jane Crofut, The Crofut Farm, Grover's Corners, Sutton County, New Hampshire; United States of America, . . . Continent of North America, Western Hemisphere, The Earth, The Solar System, The Universe, The Mind of God . . ."

Now from Jane Crofut's point of view, the address is particularly exciting because she is linked with a vast cosmic concept. To us the audience, however, the address also emphasizes the unimportance of Jane when she is viewed against such a sweeping backdrop. The address, like the play itself, connects both viewpoints: the intense concern of the individual and the cosmic detachment of a deity. And the letter is delivered: "the postman brought it just the same." A wonderful line, suggesting that the routines of life go on no matter what the point of view.

1. How good is Emily at schoolwork? How good a student is George? By what means does the playwright suggest George's and Emily's abilities?

2. How does the playwright hint that George and Emily will fall in love? How does he suggest that Mrs. Gibbs will never go to Paris?

3. After the Stage Manager sets the stage for us and begins to introduce the characters, he tells us that "Doc Gibbs died in 1930. The new hospital's named after him. Mrs. Gibbs died first—long ago in fact" (page 756). Why does he bother to tell us this? How does it affect our attitude toward him and toward the characters themselves?

4. Professor Willard describes Grover's Corners scientifically: Emily and George are called "brachycephalic stock" and the New Hampshire countryside "a shelf of Devonian basalt." Grover's Corners itself is said to lie "on the old Archeozoic granite of the Appalachian range" (page 760). Mr. Webb, in addition, gives us a great many statistics about Grover's Corners. What is the effect of all this information on the audience? How does it contribute to what appears to be the playwright's purpose?

5. About halfway through Act I, the Stage Manager gives a long speech about a time capsule. Reread this speech. This would seem to be another example of the playwright's distortion of the normal rules of stage chronology. Why? What do Babylon, Greece, and some future civilization have to do with Grover's Corners in the early years of the twentieth century?

6. Review the last part of Act I (from page 766). Lots of things are going on, almost simultaneously: Dr. and Mrs. Gibbs chat in the moonlight; George and Rebecca talk about the universe; Mr. Webb talks with Constable Warren; the Stage Manager meets the unhappy Simon Stimson. Is there any common denominator to all these events? Do they add up to any total effect?

7. What seems to set the Stage Manager apart from the other characters? What does the Stage Manager have in common with the other characters?

8. Despite the ordinariness of the events in *Our Town,* does the playwright keep us in suspense? What threads are introduced in Act I which make us anticipate Acts II and III?

ACT II

The tables and chairs of the two kitchens are still on the stage. The ladders have been withdrawn. The STAGE MANAGER *has been at his accustomed place, watching the audience return to its seats.*

STAGE MANAGER. Three years have gone by. Yes, the sun's come up over a thousand times. Summers and winters have cracked the mountains a little bit more, and the rains have brought down some of the dirt. Some babies that weren't even born before have begun talking regular sentences already; and a number of people who thought they were right young and spry have noticed that they can't bound up a flight of stairs like they used to, without their heart fluttering a little. Some older sons are sitting at the head of the table, and some people I know are having their meat cut up for them.

All that can happen in a thousand days. Nature's been pushing and contriving in other ways, too: a number of young people fell in love and got married. Yes, the mountain got bit away a few fractions of an inch, millions of gallons of water went by the mill, and here and there a new home was set up under a roof. Almost everybody in the world gets married. You know what I mean? In our town there aren't hardly any exceptions. Most everybody in the world climbs into their graves married.

The first act was called "The Daily Life." This act is called "Love and Marriage." There's another act coming after this; I reckon you can guess what that's about.

So it's three years later. It's 1904. It's July 7, just after high school commencement. That's the time most of our young people jump up and get married. Soon as they've passed their last examinations in solid geometry and Cicero's [1] orations,

---

[1] **Cicero:** a Roman statesman and orator, 106–43 B.C. His speeches are often studied in advanced Latin classes.

looks like they suddenly feel themselves fit to be married.

It's early morning. Only this time it's been raining. It's been pouring and thundering. Mrs. Gibbs's garden, and Mrs. Webb's here—drenched. All those bean poles and pea vines—drenched. All yesterday over there on Main Street the rain looked like curtains being blown along. Hm . . . it may begin again any minute.

There! You can hear the five-forty-five for Boston. And here comes Howie Newsome delivering the milk. And there's Si Crowell delivering the papers like his brother before him. You remember about his brother—all that education he's going to get and that'll be wasted? And there's Mrs. Gibbs and Mrs. Webb come down to make breakfast, just as though it were an ordinary day. I don't have to point out to the women in my audience that those ladies they see before them, both those ladies cooked three meals a day—one of 'em for twenty years, the other for forty—and no summer vacation. They brought up two children apiece, washed, cleaned the house—and never a nervous breakdown. Never thought themselves hard-used, either.

It's like what one of those Middle West poets said: You've got to love life to have life, and you've got to have life to love life.[1] . . . It's what they call a vicious circle.

[SI CROWELL *has entered, hurling imaginary newspapers into doorways.* HOWIE NEWSOME *has come along Main Street with* BESSIE.]

HOWIE NEWSOME. Git-ap, Bessie.

SI CROWELL. Morning, Howie.

HOWIE NEWSOME. Morning, Si. Anything in the papers I ought to know?

SI CROWELL. Nothing much, except we're losing about the best baseball pitcher Grover's Corners ever had.

HOWIE NEWSOME. Reckon he was. He's been standing off the whole of south New Hampshire singlehanded, looks like.

[1] **You've . . . life:** The lines, an approximate quotation, are from "Lucinda Matlock" in Edgar Lee Masters' *Spoon River Anthology.*

SI CROWELL. He could hit and run bases, too.

HOWIE NEWSOME. Yep. Mighty fine ballplayer. . . . Bessie! I guess I can stop and talk if I've a mind to!

SI CROWELL. I don't see how he could give up a thing like that just to get married. Would you, Howie?

HOWIE NEWSOME. Can't tell, Si. Never had no talent that way.

[CONSTABLE WARREN *enters. They exchange good mornings.*]

You're up early, Bill.

CONSTABLE WARREN. Seein' if there's anything I can do to prevent a flood. River's been risin' all night.

HOWIE NEWSOME. Si Crowell's all worked up here about George Gibbs's retiring from baseball.

CONSTABLE WARREN. Yes, sir; that's the way it goes. Back in eighty-four we had a player, Si—even George Gibbs couldn't touch him. Name of Hank Todd. Went down to Maine and become a parson. Wonderful ballplayer. . . . Howie, how did the weather look to you?

HOWIE NEWSOME. No, 'tain't bad. Think maybe it'll clear up for good.

[CONSTABLE WARREN *and* SI CROWELL *continue on their way.* HOWIE NEWSOME *brings the milk first to* MRS. GIBBS'S *house. She meets him by the trellis.*]

MRS. GIBBS. Good morning, Howie. Do you think it's going to rain again?

HOWIE NEWSOME. Morning, Mrs. Gibbs. It rained so heavy, I think maybe it'll clear up.

MRS. GIBBS. Certainly hope it will.

HOWIE NEWSOME. How much did you want today?

MRS. GIBBS. I guess I'll need three-a-milk and two-a-cream, Howie. I'm going to have a house full of relations.

HOWIE NEWSOME. My wife says to tell you we both hope they'll be very happy, Mrs. Gibbs. Know they *will.*

MRS. GIBBS. Thanks a lot, Howie. Tell

your wife I hope she gits there to the wedding.

HOWIE NEWSOME. Yes, she'll be there; she'll be there if she kin. (*He crosses to* MRS. WEBB'S *house.*) Morning, Mrs. Webb.

MRS. WEBB. Oh, good morning, Mr. Newsome. I told you four quarts of milk, but I hope you can spare me another.

HOWIE NEWSOME. Yes'm . . . and the two of cream.

MRS. WEBB. Will it rain all day, Mr. Newsome?

HOWIE NEWSOME. No'm. Just sayin' to Mrs. Gibbs as how it may lighten up. Mrs. Newsome told me to tell you as how we hope they'll both be very happy, Mrs. Webb. Know they *will*.

MRS. WEBB. Thank you, and thank Mrs. Newsome; and we hope to see you all at the wedding.

HOWIE NEWSOME. Yes, Mrs. Webb. We hope to git there. Couldn't miss that. Chck! Bessie!

[*Exit* HOWIE NEWSOME. DR. GIBBS *descends in his shirt sleeves, and sits down at his breakfast table.*]

DR. GIBBS. Well, Ma, the day has come. You're losin' one of your chicks.

MRS. GIBBS. Frank Gibbs, don't you say another word. I feel like crying every minute. Sit down and drink your coffee.

DR. GIBBS. The groom's up shaving himself. Whistling and singing, like he's glad to leave us. Every now and then he says "I do" to the mirror, but it don't sound convincing to me.

MRS. GIBBS. I declare I don't know how he'll get along. I've arranged his clothes and seen to it he's put warm things on— Frank, they're too young! Emily won't think of such things. He'll catch his death of cold within a week. . . . Here's something I made for you.

DR. GIBBS. Why, Julia Hersey! French toast!

MRS. GIBBS. 'Tain't hard to make, and I had to do something.

DR. GIBBS. I remember my wedding morning, Julia.

MRS. GIBBS. Now, don't start that, Frank Gibbs. I tell you I can't stand it.

DR. GIBBS. I was the scaredest young fella in the State of New Hampshire. I thought I'd made a mistake for sure. And when I saw you comin' down that aisle I thought you were the prettiest girl I'd ever seen, but the only trouble was that I'd never seen you before. There I was in the Congregational Church marryin' a total stranger.

MRS. GIBBS. And how do you think I felt! . . . Did you hear Rebecca stirring about upstairs?

DR. GIBBS. Only morning in the year she hasn't been managing everybody's business. She's shut up in her room. I got the impression that maybe she's crying.

MRS. GIBBS. Good Lord! This has got to stop. . . . Rebecca! Rebecca! Everything's getting cold down here.

[GEORGE *comes rattling down the stairs, very brisk.*]

GEORGE. Good morning, everybody. Only five more hours to live. (*Makes the gesture of cutting his throat*)

MRS. GIBBS. Where are you going?

GEORGE. Just stepping across the grass to see my girl.

MRS. GIBBS. Now, George! You take an umbrella, or I won't let you out of this house.

GEORGE. Aw, Ma. It's just a *step!*

MRS. GIBBS. From tomorrow on you can kill yourself in all weathers; but while you're in my house you live wisely, thank you. There are your overshoes right there in the hall. And here's an umbrella.

GEORGE. Aw, Ma!

MRS. GIBBS. Maybe Mrs. Webb isn't used to callers at seven in the morning. Take a cup-a-coffee first.

GEORGE. Be back in a minute. (*He crosses the stage, leaping over the puddles.*) Good morning, Mother Webb.

MRS. WEBB. Goodness! You frightened me! Now, George, you can come in a minute out of the wet, but you know I can't ask you in.

GEORGE. Why not?

MRS. WEBB. George, you know's well as I do: the groom can't see his bride on his wedding day, not until he sees her in church.

GEORGE. Aw! That's just a superstition.

[*Enter* MR. WEBB.]

MR. WEBB. Good morning, George.

GEORGE. Mr. Webb, you don't believe in that superstition, do you?

MR. WEBB. There's a lot of common sense in some superstitions, George.

MRS. WEBB. Millions have folla'd it, George, and you don't want to be the first to fly in the face of custom.

GEORGE. How is Emily?

MRS. WEBB. She hasn't waked up yet. I haven't heard a sound out of her.

GEORGE. Emily's *asleep!*

MRS. WEBB. No wonder! We were up till all hours, sewing and packing. I'll tell you what I'll do; you set down here a minute with Mr. Webb and drink this cup of coffee, and I'll go upstairs and see she doesn't come down and surprise you. There's some bacon, too; but don't be long about it.

[*Exit* MRS. WEBB. *Embarrassed silence.*]

MR. WEBB. Well, George, how are you?

GEORGE. Oh, fine. I'm fine. (*Pause*) Mr. Webb, what sense could there be in a superstition like that?

MR. WEBB. Well, you see, on her wedding morning a girl's head's apt to be full of . . . clothes and things like that. Don't you think that's probably it?

GEORGE. Ye-e-s. I never thought of that.

MR. WEBB. A girl's apt to be a mite nervous on her wedding day. (*Pause*)

GEORGE. I wish a fellow could get married without all that marching up and down.

MR. WEBB. Well, every man that's ever lived has felt that way about it, George; but it hasn't done much good. It's the women that have built up weddings, my boy. From now on they have it pretty much as they like. . . . All those good women standing shoulder to shoulder making sure that the knot's tied in a mighty public way.

GEORGE. But . . . you *believe* in it, don't you, Mr. Webb?

MR. WEBB. Oh, yes; oh, yes. Don't you misunderstand me, my boy. Marriage is a wonderful thing—wonderful thing. And don't you forget that, George.

GEORGE. No, sir. Mr. Webb, how old were you when you got married?

MR. WEBB. Well, you see, I'd been to college and I'd taken a little time to get settled. But Mrs. Webb—she wasn't much older than what Emily is. Oh, age hasn't much to do with it, George—not compared to other things.

GEORGE. What were you going to say, Mr. Webb?

MR. WEBB. Oh, I don't know—was I going to say something? (*Pause*) George, I was thinking the other night of some advice my father gave me when I got married. Charles, he said, Charles, start out early showing who's boss, he said. Best thing to do is to give an order, even if it don't make sense; just so she'll learn to obey. And he said: If anything about your wife irritates you—her conversation, or anything—just get up and leave the house. That'll make it clear to her, he said. And, ah, yes! he said never, *never* let your wife know how much money you have, never.

GEORGE. Well, Mr. Webb . . . I don't think I could. . . .

MR. WEBB. So I took the opposite of my father's advice and I've been happy ever since. And let that be a lesson to you, George, never to ask advice on personal matters. . . . George, are you going to raise chickens on your farm?

GEORGE. What?

MR. WEBB. Are you going to raise chickens on your farm?

GEORGE. Uncle Luke's never been much interested, but I thought——

MR. WEBB. A book came into my office the other day, George, on the Philo System of raising chickens. I want you to read it. I'm thinking of beginning in a small way in the back yard, and I'm going to put an incubator in the cellar——

[*Enter* MRS. WEBB.]

MRS. WEBB. Charles, are you talking about that old incubator again? I thought you two'd be talking about things worthwhile.

MR. WEBB. Well, Myrtle, if you want to give the boy some good advice, I'll go upstairs and leave you alone with him.

MRS. WEBB. Now, George, I'm sorry, but I've got to send you away so that Emily can come down and get some breakfast. She told me to tell you that she sends you her love, but that she doesn't want to lay eyes on you. So good-by, George.

[GEORGE *crosses the stage to his own home and disappears.*]

MR. WEBB. Myrtle, I guess you don't know about that older superstition.

MRS. WEBB. What do you mean, Charles?

MR. WEBB. Since the cave men: the groom shouldn't be left alone with his father-in-law on the day of the wedding, or near it. Now don't forget that!

STAGE MANAGER. Thank you. Thank you, everybody. Now I have to interrupt again here. You see, we want to know how all this began—this wedding, this plan to spend a lifetime together. I'm awfully interested in how big things like that begin. You know how it is. You're twenty-one or twenty-two, and you make some decisions; then whisssh! you're seventy. You've been a lawyer for fifty years, and that white-haired lady at your side has eaten over fifty thousand meals with you. How do such things begin?

George and Emily are going to show you now the conversation they had when they first knew that . . . that . . . as the saying goes . . . they were meant for one another. But before they do it I want you to try and remember what it was like when you were young, when you were fifteen or sixteen. For some reason it is very hard to do: those days when even the little things in life could be almost too exciting to bear. And particularly the days when you were first in love; when you were like a person sleepwalking, and you didn't quite see the street you were in and didn't quite hear everything that was said to you. You're just a little bit crazy. Will you remember that, please?

Now they'll be coming out of high school at three o'clock. George has just been elected president of the junior class; and, as it's June, that means he'll be president of the senior class all next year. And Emily's just been elected secretary and treasurer. I don't have to tell you how important that is. (*He places a board across the backs of two chairs, parallel to the footlights, and places two high stools behind it. This is the counter of* MR. MORGAN'S *drugstore.*) All ready!

[EMILY, *carrying an armful of imaginary schoolbooks, comes along Main Street from the left.*]

EMILY. I can't, Louise. I've got to go home. Good-by. . . . Oh, Earnestine! Earnestine! Can you come over tonight and do algebra? I did the first and third in study hall. No, they're not hard. But, Earnestine, that Caesar's awful hard. I don't see why we have to do a thing like that. Come over about seven. Tell your mother you *have* to. G'by. . . . G'by, Helen. G'by, Fred.

[GEORGE, *also carrying books, catches up with her.*]

GEORGE. Can I carry your books home for you, Emily?

EMILY (*coldly*). Thank you. (*She gives them to him.*)

GEORGE. Excuse me a minute, Emily. . . . Say, Bob, get everything ready. I'll be there in a quarter of an hour. If I'm a little late, start practice anyway. And give Herb some long high ones. His eye needs a lot of practice. Seeya later.

EMILY. Good-by, Lizzy.

GEORGE. Good-by, Lizzy. . . . I'm awfully glad you were elected, too, Emily.

EMILY. Thank you.

[*They have been standing on Main Street,*

almost against the back wall. GEORGE *is about to take the first steps toward the audience when he stops again.*]

GEORGE. Emily, why are you mad at me?

EMILY. I'm not mad at you. '

GEORGE. You . . . you treat me so funny.

EMILY. Well, I might as well say it right out, George. I don't like the whole change that's come over you in the last year. I'm sorry if that hurts your feelings, but I've just got to tell the truth and shame the devil.

GEORGE. I'm awfully sorry, Emily. Wha-a-what do you mean?

EMILY. Well, up to a year ago I used to like you a lot. And I used to watch you as you did everything . . . because we'd been friends so long . . . and then you began spending all your time at baseball . . . and you never even spoke to anybody any more; not even to your own family you didn't . . . and, George, it's a fact, you've got awful conceited and stuck-up, and all the girls say so. They may not say so to your face, but that's what they say about you behind your back; and it hurts me to hear them say it, but I've got to agree with them a little. I'm sorry if it hurts your feelings . . . but I can't be sorry I said it.

GEORGE. I . . . I'm glad you said it, Emily. I never thought that such a thing was happening to me. I guess it's hard for a fella not to have faults creep into his character.

[*They take a step or two in silence, then stand still in misery.*]

EMILY. I always expect a man to be perfect, and I think he should be.

GEORGE. Oh . . . I don't think it's possible to be perfect, Emily.

EMILY. Well, my father is and, as far as I can see, your father is. There's no reason on earth why you shouldn't be, too.

GEORGE. Well, Emily . . . I feel it's the other way round. That men aren't naturally good, but girls are. Like you and your mother and my mother.

EMILY. Well, you might as well know right now that I'm not perfect. It's not as easy for a girl to be perfect as a man, because we girls are more nervous. Now I'm sorry I said all that about you. I don't know what made me say it.

GEORGE. No, no—I guess if it's the truth you ought to say it. You stick to it, Emily.

EMILY. I don't know if it's the truth or not. And I suddenly feel that it isn't important at all.

GEORGE. Emily, would you like an ice-cream soda, or something, before you go home?

EMILY. Well, thank you. . . . I would.

[*They come into the drugstore and seat themselves on the stools.*]

STAGE MANAGER (*as* MR. MORGAN). Hello, George. Hello, Emily. What'll you have? Why, Emily Webb, what've you been crying about?

GEORGE (*groping for an explanation*). She . . . she just got an awful scare, Mr. Morgan. She almost got run over by that hardware-store wagon. Everybody always says that Tom Huckins drives like a crazy man.

STAGE MANAGER. Here, take a drink of water, Emily. You look all shook up. . . . There! Now, what'll you have?

EMILY. I'll have a strawberry phosphate, thank you, Mr. Morgan.

GEORGE. No, no. You go and have an ice-cream soda with me, Emily. Two strawberry ice-cream sodas, Mr. Morgan.

STAGE MANAGER (*working, the faucets*). Yes, sir. I tell you, you've got to look both ways before you cross Main Street these days. Gets worse every year. There are a hundred and twenty-five horses in Grover's Corners this minute I'm talking to you. State inspector was in here yesterday. And now they're bringing in these auto-mobiles, the best thing to do is to just stay home. Why, I can remember the time when a dog could lie down all day in the middle of Main Street and nothing would come to disturb him. . . . Yes, Miss Ellis; be with you in a minute. . . .

Here are your sodas. Enjoy 'em. (*He goes off.*)

EMILY. They're so expensive.

GEORGE. No, no—don't you think of that. We're celebrating. First, we're celebrating our election. And then do you know what else I'm celebrating?

EMILY. No.

GEORGE. I'm celebrating because I've got a friend who tells me all the things that ought to be told me.

EMILY. George, *please* don't think of that. I don't know why I said it. It's not true. You're——

GEORGE. No, you stick to it, Emily. I'm glad you spoke to me like you did. But you'll see: I'm going to change so quick —you bet I'm going to change. And, Emily, I want to ask you a favor.

EMILY. What?

GEORGE. Emily, if I go away to State Agriculture College next year, will you write me a letter once in a while?

EMILY. I certainly will. I certainly will, George. (*Pause*) It certainly seems like being away three years you'd get out of touch with things.

GEORGE. No, no. I mustn't do that. You see, I'm not only going to be just a farmer. After a while, maybe, I'll run for something to get elected. So your letters'll be very important to me; you know, telling me what's going on here and everything. . . .

EMILY. Just the same, three years is a long time. Maybe letters from Grover's Corners wouldn't be so interesting after a while. Grover's Corners isn't a very important place when you think of all New Hampshire; but I think it's a very nice town.

GEORGE. The day wouldn't come when I wouldn't want to know everything that's happening here. I know *that's* true, Emily.

EMILY. Well, I'll try to make my letters interesting. (*Pause*)

GEORGE. Y'know, Emily, whenever I meet a farmer, I ask him if he thinks it's important to go to agricultural school to be a good farmer.

EMILY. Why, George——

GEORGE. Yeah, and some of them say that it's even a waste of time. You can get all those things, anyway, out of the pamphlets the government sends out. And Uncle Luke's getting old—he's about ready for me to start in taking over his farm tomorrow, if I could.

EMILY. My!

GEORGE. And, like you say, being gone all that time . . . in other places and meeting other people. . . . If anything like that can happen, I don't want to go away. I guess new people aren't any better than old ones. I'll bet they almost never are. Emily, I feel that you're as good a friend as I've got. I don't need to go and meet the people in other towns.

EMILY. But, George, maybe it's very important for you to go and learn all that about cattle judging and soils and those things. And if you're going into politics, maybe you ought to meet people from other parts of the state . . . of course, I don't know.

GEORGE (*after a pause*). Emily, I'm going to make up my mind right now. I won't go. I'll tell Pa about it tonight.

EMILY. Why, George, I don't see why you have to decide right now. It's a whole year away.

GEORGE. Emily, I'm glad you spoke to me about that . . . that fault in my character. And what you said was right; but there was *one* thing wrong in it, and that was when you said that for a year I wasn't noticing people, and . . . you, for instance. Listen, Emily . . . you say you were watching me when I did everything. . . . Why, I was doing the same about you all the time. Why, sure—I always thought about you as one of the chief people I thought about. I always made sure where you were sitting on the bleachers, and who you were with. And we've always had lots of talks . . . and joking, in the halls; and they always meant a lot to me. Of course, they weren't as good as the talk we're having now. Lately I'd been noticing that you'd been acting kind of funny to me; and for three days

I've been trying to walk home with you, but something's always got in the way. Yesterday I was standing over against the wall waiting for you, and you walked home with Miss Corcoran.

EMILY. George! . . . Life's awful funny! How could I have known that? Why, I thought——

GEORGE. Listen, Emily, I'm going to tell you why I'm not going to agricultural school. I think that once you've found a person that you're very fond of . . . I mean a person who's fond of you, too—at least enough to be interested in your character. . . . Well, I think that's just as important as college is, and even more so. That's what I think.

EMILY. I think it's awfully important, too.

GEORGE. Emily.

EMILY. Yes, George.

GEORGE. Emily, if I improve and make a big change . . . would you be . . . I mean, *could* you be . . .

EMILY. I . . . I am now; I always have been. *(Pause)*

GEORGE. So I guess this is an important talk we've been having.

EMILY. Yes.

GEORGE *(taking a deep breath and straightening his back)*. Wait just a minute and I'll take you home. *(He rises and goes to the* STAGE MANAGER, *who appears and comes toward him.)* Mr. Morgan, I'll have to go home and get the money to pay you for this. It'll only take a minute.

STAGE MANAGER. What's that? George Gibbs, do you mean to tell me——

GEORGE. Yes, but I had reasons, Mr. Morgan. Look, here's my gold watch to keep until I come back with the money.

STAGE MANAGER. That's all right. Keep your watch. I'll trust you.

GEORGE. I'll be back in five minutes.

STAGE MANAGER. I'll trust you ten years, George—not a day more. . . . Got all over your shock, Emily?

EMILY. Yes, thank you, Mr. Morgan. It was nothing.

GEORGE *(taking up the books from the counter)*. I'm ready.

[*They walk in grave silence down the stage, turn, and pass through the trellis at the Webb's back door and disappear.*]

STAGE MANAGER. Thank you, Emily. Thank you, George. . . . Now before we go on to the wedding, there are still some more things we ought to know about this —about this marriage. I want to know some more about how the parents took it; but what I want to know most of all is—oh, you know what I mean—what Grover's Corners thought about marriage, anyway. You know's well as I do: people are never able to say right out what they think of money, or death, or fame or marriage. You've got to catch it between the lines; you've got to *over*hear it.

Oh, Doctor! Mrs. Gibbs!

[*They appear at their side of the stage and exchange a glance of understanding with him. The* STAGE MANAGER *lays across two chairs the same plank that served as a drugstore counter, and it has now become* MRS. GIBBS'S *ironing board.* DR. GIBBS *sits down in a rocker and smokes.* MRS. GIBBS *irons a moment in silence, then goes to the foot of the stairs.*]

MRS. GIBBS *(calling)*. Rebecca! It's time you turned out your light and went to sleep. George, you'd better get some sleep, too.

REBECCA'S VOICE. Ma, I haven't finished my English.

MRS. GIBBS. What? Well, I bet you haven't been working, Rebecca. You've been reading that Sears Roebuck catalogue, that's what you've been doing. All right, I'll give you ten more minutes. If you haven't finished by then, you'll just have to fail the course and be a disgrace to your father and me. . . . George, what are you doing?

GEORGE'S VOICE *(hurt)*. I'm doing history.

MRS. GIBBS. Well, you'd better go to bed. You're probably sleeping at the desk as it is. *(She casts an amused eye at her husband and returns to her ironing.)*

DR. GIBBS. I had a long talk with the boy today.

MRS. GIBBS. Did you?

DR. GIBBS. I tell you, Mrs. G., there's nothing so terrifying in the world as a son. The relation of a father to a son is the confounded awkwardest—I always come away feeling like a soggy sponge of hypocrisy.

MRS. GIBBS. Well, a mother and a daughter's no picnic, let me tell you.

DR. GIBBS. George is set on it: he wants to marry Emily soon as school's out and take her right on to the farm. *(Pause)* He says he can sit up nights and learn agriculture from government pamphlets, without going to college for it.

MRS. GIBBS. He always was crazy about farming. Gets that from my people.

DR. GIBBS. At a pinch I guess he could start in farming, but I swear I think he's too young to get married. Julia, he's just a green, half-grown kid. He isn't ready to be a family man.

MRS. GIBBS. No, he ain't. You're right. But he's a good boy and I wouldn't like to think of him being alone out there . . . coming into town Satiddy nights, like any old farm hand, tuckered out from work and looking for excitement. He might get into bad ways. It wouldn't be enough fun for him to come and sit by our stove, and holding hands with Emily for a year mightn't be enough either. He might lose interest in her.

DR. GIBBS. Hm.

MRS. GIBBS. Frank, I been watching her. George is a lucky boy when you think of all the silly girls in the world.

DR. GIBBS. But, Julia, George *married*. That great, gangling, selfish nincompoop.

MRS. GIBBS. Yes, I know. *(She takes up a collar and examines it.)* Frank, what do you do to your collars? Do you gnaw 'em? I never saw such a man for collars.

DR. GIBBS. Julia, when I married you, do you know what one of my terrors was in getting married?

MRS. GIBBS. Pshaw! Go on with you!

DR. GIBBS. I was afraid we weren't going to have material for conversation more'n'd last us a few weeks. I was afraid we'd run out and eat our meals in silence. That's a fact. You and I've been conversing for twenty years now without any noticeable barren spells.

MRS. GIBBS. Well, good weather, bad weather, 'tain't very choice, but I always manage to find something to say. *(Pause)*

DR. GIBBS. What do you think? What do you think, Julia? Shall we tell the boy he can go ahead and get married?

MRS. GIBBS. Seems like it's up to us to decide. Myrtle and Charles Webb are willing. They think it's a good idea to throw the young people into the sea and let 'em sink or swim, as soon as they're ready.

DR. GIBBS. What does that mean? Must we decide right now? This minute?

MRS. GIBBS. There you go putting the responsibility on me!

DR. GIBBS. Here it is, almost April. . . . I'll go up and say a word to him right now before he goes to bed. *(He rises.)* You're sure, Julia? You've nothing more to add?

MRS. GIBBS *(stops ironing a moment).* I don't know what to say. Seems like it's too much to ask, for a big outdoor boy like that to go and get shut up in classrooms for three years. And once he's on the farm, he might just as well have a companion, seeing he's found a fine girl like Emily. . . . People are meant to live two-by-two in this world. . . . Yes, Frank, go up and tell him it's all right.

[DR. GIBBS *crosses and is about to call when* MRS. GIBBS, *her hands on her cheeks, staring into the audience, speaks in sharp alarm.*]

Wait a minute! Wait a minute! *(Then, resuming her ironing)* No—go and tell him.

DR. GIBBS. Why did you stop then, Julia?

MRS. GIBBS. Oh, you know: I thought of all those times we went through in the first years when George and Rebecca were babies—you walking up and down with them at three in the morning, the whooping cough, the time George fell off the porch. You and I were twenty-five years old, and more. It's wonderful how one forgets one's troubles like that.... Yes, Frank, go upstairs and tell him. It's worth it.

DR. GIBBS. Yes, they'll have a lot of troubles, but that's none of our business. Let'm. Everybody has a right to his own troubles. You ought to be present, Julia— important occasion like that. I'll call him.... George! Oh, George!

GEORGE'S VOICE. Yes, Pa.

DR. GIBBS. Can you come down a minute? Your mother and I want to speak to you.

GEORGE. Yeah, sure.

MRS. GIBBS (*putting her arm through her husband's*). Lord, what a fool I am; I'm trembling all over. There's nothing to tremble about.

STAGE MANAGER. Thank you! Thank you! ... Now we're ready to go on with the wedding.

[*While he talks, the actors remove the chairs and tables and trellises from the Gibbs and Webb homes. They arrange the pews for the church in the back of the stage. The congregation will sit facing the back wall. The aisle of the church is in the middle of the scene. A small platform is placed against the back wall; on this the STAGE MANAGER, as minister, can stand.*]

There are a lot of things to be said about a wedding; there are a lot of thoughts that go on during a wedding. We can't get them all into one wedding, naturally, and especially not into a wedding at Grover's Corners, where they're awfully plain and short. In this wedding I play the minister. That gives me the right to say a few more things about it.

For a while now, the play gets pretty serious. Y'see, some churches say that marriage is a sacrament. I don't quite know what that means, but I can guess. Like Mrs. Gibbs said a few minutes ago: People were made to live two-by-two.

This is a good wedding, but people are so put together that even at a good wedding there's a lot of confusion way down deep in people's minds; and we thought that that ought to be in our play, too.

The real hero of this scene isn't on the stage at all, and you know who that is. It's like what one of those European fellas said: Every child born into the world is nature's attempt to make a perfect human being. Well, we've seen nature pushing and contriving for some time now. We all know that nature's interested in quantity; but I think she's interested in quality, too—that's why I'm in the ministry. Maybe she's trying to make another good governor for New Hampshire. And don't forget the other witnesses at this wedding —the ancestors. Millions of them. Most of them set out to live two-by-two, also. Millions of them.

Well, that's all my sermon. 'Twan't very long, anyway.

[*The organ starts playing Handel's "Largo." The congregation streams into the church and sits in silence. MRS. WEBB, on the way to her place, turns back and speaks to the audience.*]

MRS. WEBB. I don't know why on earth I should be crying. I suppose there's nothing to cry about. It came over me at breakfast this morning; there was Emily eating her breakfast as she's done for seventeen years, and now she's going off to eat it in someone else's house. I suppose that's it. And Emily! She suddenly said: I can't eat another mouthful, and she put her head down on the table and *she* cried.

[*The choir starts singing "Love Divine, All Love Excelling." GEORGE, coming through the audience, has reached the stage. He stares at the congregation a moment, then takes a few steps of withdrawal toward the right proscenium pillar.*]

GEORGE (*darkly, to himself*). I wish I were back at school.... I don't want to get married.

[*His mother has left her seat and come toward him. She stops, looking at him anxiously.*]

MRS. GIBBS. George, what's the matter?

GEORGE. Ma, I don't want to grow *old*. Why's everybody pushing me so?

MRS. GIBBS. Why, George . . . you wanted it.

GEORGE. Why do I have to get married at all? Listen, Ma, for the last time I ask you——

MRS. GIBBS. No, no George . . . you're a man now.

GEORGE. Listen, Ma, you never listen to me. All I want to do is to be a fella. Why do——

MRS. GIBBS. George! If anyone should hear you! Now stop. Why, I'm ashamed of you!

GEORGE (*passing his hand over his forehead*). What's the matter? I've been dreaming. Where's Emily?

MRS. GIBBS. Gracious! You gave me such a turn.

GEORGE. Cheer up, Ma. What are you looking so funny for? Cheer up; I'm getting married.

MRS. GIBBS. Let me catch my breath a minute.

GEORGE. Now, Ma, you save Thursday nights. Emily and I are coming over to dinner every Thursday night . . . you'll see. Ma, what are you crying for? Come on, we've got to get ready for this.

[*In the meantime* EMILY, *in white and wearing her wedding veil, has come through the audience and mounted onto the stage. She, too, draws back when she sees the congregation in the church. The choir begins "Blest Be the Tie That Binds."*]

EMILY. I never felt so alone in my whole life. And George over there, looking so . . . I *hate* him, I wish I were dead. Papa! Papa!

MR. WEBB (*leaving his seat in the pews and coming toward her anxiously*). Emily! Emily! Now don't get upset.

EMILY. But Papa, I don't want to get married.

MR. WEBB. Sh-sh—Emily. Everything's all right.

EMILY. Why can't I stay for a while just as I am? Let's go away.

MR. WEBB. No, no, Emily. Now stop and think.

EMILY. Don't you remember that you used to say—all the time you used to say that I was *your* girl. There must be lots of places we can go to. Let's go away. I'll work for you. I could keep house.

MR. WEBB. Sh. . . . You mustn't think of such things. You're just nervous, Emily. Now, now—you're marrying the best young fellow in the world. George is a fine fellow.

EMILY. But, Papa——

MR. WEBB. George! George!

[MRS. GIBBS *returns to her seat.* GEORGE *hears* MR. WEBB *and looks up.* MR. WEBB *beckons to him. They move to the center of the stage.*]

I'm giving away my daughter, George. Do you think you can take care of her?

GEORGE. Mr. Webb, I want to . . . I want to try. Emily, I'm going to do my best. I love you, Emily. I need you.

EMILY. Well, if you love me, help me. All I want is someone to love me.

GEORGE. I will, Emily.

EMILY. If ever I'm sick or in trouble, that's what I mean.

GEORGE. Emily, I'll try. I'll try.

EMILY. And I mean for ever. Do you hear? For ever and ever.

[*They fall into each other's arms. The March from* Lohengrin *is heard.*]

MR. WEBB. Come, they're waiting for us. Now you know it'll be all right. Come, quick.

[GEORGE *slips away and takes his place beside the* STAGE MANAGER–CLERGY-MAN. EMILY *proceeds up the aisle on her father's arm.*]

STAGE MANAGER. Do you, George, take this woman, Emily, to be your wedded wife, to have . . .

[MRS. SOAMES *has been sitting in the last row of the congregation. She now turns to her neighbors and speaks in a shrill voice.*]

MRS. SOAMES. Perfectly lovely wedding! Loveliest wedding I ever saw. Oh, I do love a good wedding, don't you? Doesn't she make a lovely bride?

GEORGE. I do.

STAGE MANAGER. Do you, Emily, take this man, George, to be your wedded husband . . .

MRS. SOAMES. Don't know *when* I've seen such a lovely wedding. But I always cry. Don't know why it is, but I always cry. I just like to see young people happy, don't you? Oh, I think it's lovely.

[*The ring. The kiss. The stage is suddenly arrested into silent tableau.*]

STAGE MANAGER (*his eyes on the distance, says to the audience*). I've married two hundred couples in my day. Do I believe in it? I don't know. M____ marries N____. Millions of them. The cottage, the gocart, the Sunday afternoon drives in the Ford, the first rheumatism, the grandchildren, the second rheumatism, the deathbed, the reading of the will—Once in a thousand times it's interesting. Well, let's have Mendelssohn's "Wedding March"!

[*The organ picks up the march. The bride and groom come down the aisle, radiant but trying to be very dignified.*]

MRS. SOAMES. Aren't they a lovely couple? Oh, I've never been to such a nice wedding. I'm sure they'll be happy. I always say *happiness,* that's the great thing! The important thing is to be happy.

[*The bride and groom reach the steps leading into the audience. A bright light is thrown upon them. They descend into the auditorium and run up the aisle joyously.*]

STAGE MANAGER. That's all the second act. Ten minutes' intermission, folks.

COMMENTARY

Early in Act II, the Stage Manager tells us that all the acts have titles: "The first act was called 'The Daily Life.' This act is called 'Love and Marriage.' " And he assumes that we expect the last act to be entitled "Death." We realize more and more, as we read on in Act II, that Thornton Wilder intends to give us a panoramic picture of the human experience, as exemplified by the events in Grover's Corners, particularly by what happens to George Gibbs and Emily Webb. In his first speech, the Stage Manager tells us what he thinks is behind the whole experience: "Nature's been pushing and contriving," he says, implying that marriage is as natural a process as erosion or gravity. "Most everybody in the world climbs into their graves married," he goes on, and by associating marriage with the grave, he again stresses the natural inevitability of both events.

Hence we can say that in Act II, as in Act I, the Stage Manager maintains his remote, slightly bemused, calmly detached attitude toward the events of the play, and he invites the audience to share his point of view. But the other characters are intensely concerned with their own issues of love and marriage. George says jokingly that he has "only five more hours to live," and later we see him momentarily panic at the whole idea. Emily also becomes frightened, and even their parents, who have been through it all before, become awkward and confused. Marriage, to those who are involved, is obviously an important occurrence, and we, as readers and audience, tend to catch some of the excitement.

Act II intensifies the contrast between the attitudes of involvement and detachment. The characters seem to ask the audience to respond emotionally to all the excitements and fears which go with "this plan to spend a lifetime together"; but the Stage Manager constantly reminds us that a wedding is simply a natural, inevitable event and that we should concentrate on the implications behind it. The clash continues between the specific and the general. For example, notice how the Stage Manager uses time. He shows us the morning of the marriage before we see George and Emily become engaged. Hence as we watch the scenes where they fall in love, we already know the outcome and can concentrate on the undercurrents behind the obvious. We are aware of the slow "contriving" of nature as it "pushes" two people toward a new stage in life. George and Emily occasionally feel this pressure (George once protests "Why's everybody pushing me so?") but we, as audience, see nature behind the entire process. Thus we can sit back and watch with an almost godlike comprehension.

The Stage Manager finally tells us that we should know who "the real hero" of the wedding scene is: "Every child born into the world is nature's attempt to make a perfect human being." Nature's purpose in all her efforts becomes clearer: the eventual perfection of the human race. Behind all the events of Act I and Act II, there is a universal process, even if the characters on the stage are unaware of it. The Stage Manager's remark about the millions of ancestors witnessing the wedding makes sense when we recall that they, too, were part of nature's movement toward a perfect man. The address on Jane Crofut's letter now gains additional meaning. It expresses a continuity between the individual and the Mind of God, which universal forces work to join through events such as marriage and birth.

Yet the process of nature is painful for those who live through it. We observe and respond to the private pain of George and Emily as they halt on the brink of a new stage of life. We respond also to the confusion of their parents. "There's a lot of confusion way down deep in people's minds," we are told, and this confusion seems to be at the heart of the human predicament. Living under the influence of such a powerful impetus toward perfection, yet not fully understanding why the present moment must be left behind, the characters in this play cannot both experience the transitory pleasures of life and comprehend the purpose behind them. Mrs. Soames, gushing about the wedding at the end of Act II, sees only the immediate picture; but the Stage Manager calmly points out that weddings are interesting only "once in a thousand times." We the audience, being human and sentimental and at the same time outside of the play, can embrace both points of view at once, and the result is an exhilarating and moving theatrical experience.

FOR STUDY AND DISCUSSION

1. What was George's father worried about when he got married? What age-old rule does Mr. Webb recite for future fathers—and sons-in-law? How does this advice contribute to the contrast between involvement and detachment? What does Mrs. Soames's behavior at the wedding contribute to this contrast?

2. Reread the Stage Manager's descriptions of nature. Is this an unusual view of nature? Would a modern scientist support it?

3. Reread the scene in the drugstore. How important to you are all the details about the cost of the soda, agricultural college, and writing letters? How important do they eventually become to George and Emily?

4. Reread the Stage Manager's long speech about weddings toward the end of Act II. How does it tie in with his other remarks on nature? The Stage Manager remarks that a wedding is interesting only once in a thousand times. Why then does he show a wedding?

5. Has the unusual use of time in Act II been prepared for in Act I? Explain.

6. In Act II, Mr. Webb feels uneasy with George. Mrs. Gibbs has second thoughts about the wedding. Can it be said that they represent society in general? Why or why not?

7. Consider the characters' attitudes toward past events, particularly toward events which were once of high importance to them. Is there any consistency in all their attitudes? How does this attitude compare with the attitudes of the audience?

[THORNTON WILDER CONTINUED ON PAGE 791]

AMERICAN PAINTING

New Developments at Mid-Century

Although regionalism and social protest were important forces in American art of the 'thirties, a more abstract type of painting was being developed at the same time by artists who had acquired a broader world outlook. Mark Tobey, for example, traveled in France, Greece, and the Near East and studied Oriental brushwork in Japan. In his tempera painting of 1936 titled *Broadway* (PLATE 1), what captures our attention is not so much the subject matter as Tobey's fascinating linear style—a kind of "white writing." Tobey later explained that he had painted *Broadway* from memory while living in England. He felt he could best paint something he loved when he was far away from it.

In contrast to Tobey's vision of Broadway at night, Stuart Davis's *Owh! In San Paō* (PLATE 2) suggests the garish colors of city billboards in broad daylight. Though based on his earlier experiments in the French Cubist style, Davis's picture is typically American in its jumpy, staccato patterns, which are somewhat like the syncopated rhythms of jazz, to which Davis was passionately devoted. Notice how the title sets up a teasing rhyme with the word NOW. This word plays an important part in the design of the picture, and at the same time plays a sort of nonsense game with other words and scribbles around it. Davis here has transformed haphazard fragments of modern city life into a kind of visual music.

During the 1940's, New York became the center of a tremendous ferment in American art. Artists driven from Europe by Nazi persecution brought to this country exciting new ideas which fired the imagination of certain young American painters. One such painter was Jackson Pollock, who gradually developed an abstract style of great expressive power and originality. Setting his large canvases on his studio floor, he applied his pigment by dripping or spattering it from the brush. In this way he could paint with broad, swinging motions of his arm. He even brought into play the action of his entire body, though always with extraordinary control. In his painting called *Number 27, 1950* (PLATE 3), you can see the unique richness of color and texture and the furious interweaving of lines and shapes that Pollock achieved with his unconventional technique.

Pollock was one of several famous American artists who pioneered an important new world movement known as Abstract Expressionism. In this type of art the very act of painting became extremely important, for, instead of working from preliminary sketches, the "action" painter composed his picture as he went along, expressing his subconscious feelings through abstract forms conjured up in the intensity of the moment. Of course the cry has often been that anyone can do this kind of painting, but only skill and inventiveness have ever made an Abstract Expressionist painting really interesting. It is worth noting, for example, that Willem de Kooning, one of the leading Abstract Expressionists, was trained as a realistic painter in his native Holland before he came to this country. His *Easter Monday* (PLATE 4), might seem at first merely a wild free-for-all. By looking at it carefully, however, we can sense the artist's expert craftsmanship. In some areas he applied the paint with a brush, in others with a palette knife, and in still others he rubbed and smeared and scraped it— creating an effect somewhat like that of a billboard with many layers of torn, blistered posters showing through. Every form and color seems to be struggling either to overpower its neighbors or to wrench itself free. Yet, running through this furious activity is a strong zigzag design which gives the picture unity.

In Franz Kline's paintings, a very different sort of struggle goes on. Most of his pictures consist of huge dark "structures" boldly silhouetted against a light background. But since Kline brings these dark forms close to us, so that they almost fill the picture, the leftover pieces of white background suddenly become "forms" themselves—forms which struggle against the dark shapes in front of them. Look, for example, at *The Bridge* (PLATE 5). Here the great masonry towers and swinging cables of Brooklyn Bridge loom up in such a way that they threaten to overwhelm the space around them. Kline applied his few well-chosen colors with sure, rapid movements of his arm, often using large house painters' brushes. By subtly varying the pressure of each stroke, he has made seemingly flat silhouettes appear unusually solid, as if they were truly massive forms in a three-dimensional world.

Several Abstract Expressionists continued to produce fine paintings well into the 1960's, but by this time new movements had developed. Throughout all these changes, however, a few excellent painters have continued to work in the native American tradition of realism inherited from Homer and Eakins. By far the best known is Andrew Wyeth. Wyeth is an extraordinary master of tempera painting, an opaque, fast-drying medium which he applies with very small, delicate strokes of the brush. In *River Cove* (PLATE 6), he rendered the tiniest details of a sandy shore in an almost breathtaking way. Wyeth makes us sense, in an exciting moment of discovery, the infinitely complex world of nature which exists all around us.

PLATE 1. MARK TOBEY (1890–): *Broadway*. 1936. Tempera, 26 x 19$\frac{1}{4}$ inches. (The Metropolitan Museum of Art, New York)

PLATE 2. STUART DAVIS (1894–1964): *Owh! In San Paō*. 1951. Oil on canvas, $52\frac{1}{4}$ x $41\frac{3}{4}$ inches. (Collection of the Whitney Museum of American Art, New York)

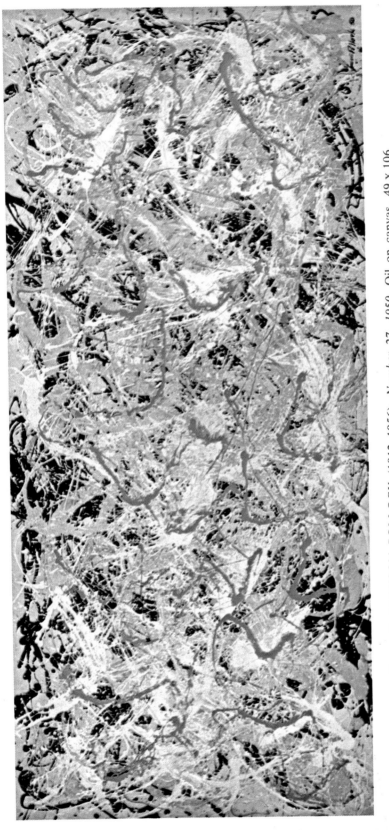

PLATE 3. JACKSON POLLOCK (1912–1956): *Number 27, 1950.* Oil on canvas, 49 x 106 inches. (Collection of the Whitney Museum of American Art, New York)

PLATE 4. WILLEM DE KOONING (1904–   ): *Easter Monday*. 1956. Oil and newspaper transfer on canvas, 96 x 74 inches. (The Metropolitan Museum of Art, New York, Rogers Fund, 1956)

PLATE 5. FRANS KLINE (1910–1962): *The Bridge*. 1955. Oil on canvas, 80 x 52¾ inches. (Munson-Williams-Proctor Institute, Utica, New York)

PLATE 6. ANDREW WYETH (1917–   ): *River Cove*. 1958. Tempera on masonite, 48 x 30 inches. (Private Collection, New York)

[THORNTON WILDER, CONTINUED FROM
PAGE 782]

ACT III

*During the intermission the audience
has seen the actors arranging the stage.
On the right-hand side, a little right of the
center, ten or twelve ordinary chairs have
been placed in three openly spaced rows
facing the audience. These are graves in
the cemetery.*

*Toward the end of the intermission the
actors enter and take their places. The
front row contains, toward the center of
the stage, an empty chair; then* MRS.
GIBBS *and* SIMON STIMSON. *The second
row contains, among others,* MRS. SOAMES.
The third row has WALLY WEBB. *The
dead sit in a quiet without stiffness and in
a patience without listlessness.*

The STAGE MANAGER *takes his accustomed place and waits for the house lights
to go down.*

STAGE MANAGER. This time nine years
have gone by, friends—summer, 1913.
Gradual changes in Grover's Corners.
Horses are getting rarer. Farmers coming
into town in Fords. Chief difference is in
the young people, far as I can see. They
want to go to the moving pictures all the
time. They want to wear clothes like they
see there . . . want to be citified. Everybody locks their house doors now at night.
Ain't seen any burglars in town yet, but
everybody's heard about 'em. But you'd
be surprised, though—on the whole, things
don't change much at Grover's Corners.

Guess you want to know what all these
chairs are here fur. Smarter ones have
guessed it already. I don't know how you
feel about such things, but this certainly
is a beautiful place. It's on a hilltop—a
windy hilltop—lots of sky, lots of clouds,
often lots of sun and moon and stars. You
come up here on a fine afternoon and you
can see range on range of hills—awful
blue they are—up there by Lake Sunapee
and Lake Winnipesaukee . . . and way up,
if you've got a glass, you can see the
White Mountains and Mt. Washington—
where North Conway and Conway is.
And, of course, our favorite mountain,
Mt. Monadnock's right here—and all
around it lie these towns—Jaffrey, 'n East
Jaffrey, 'n Peterborough, 'n Dublin; and
(Then, pointing down in the audience)
there, quite a ways down, is Grover's
Corners.

Yes, beautiful spot up here. Mountain
laurel and li-lacks. I often wonder why
people like to be buried in Woodlawn and
Brooklyn when they might pass the same
time up here in New Hampshire. Over in
that corner *(Pointing to stage left)* are the
old stones—1670, 1680. Strong-minded
people that come a long way to be independent. Summer people walk around
there laughing at the funny words on the
tombstones . . . it don't do any harm. And
genealogists come up from Boston—get
paid by city people for looking up their
ancestors. They want to make sure they're
Daughters of the American Revolution
and of the *Mayflower*. . . . Well, I guess that
don't do any harm, either. Wherever you
come near the human race, there's layers
and layers of nonsense.

Over there are some Civil War veterans
too. Iron flags on their graves. . . . New
Hampshire boys . . . had a notion that the
Union ought to be kept together, though
they'd never seen more than fifty miles of
it themselves. All they knew was the
name, friends—the United States of America. The United States of America. And
they went and died about it.

This here is the new part of the cemetery.
Here's your friend Mrs. Gibbs. 'N let
me see—Here's Mr. Stimson, organist at
the Congregational Church. And over
there's Mrs. Soames, who enjoyed the
wedding so—you remember? Oh, and a
lot of others. And Editor Webb's boy Wallace, whose appendix burst while he was
on a Boy Scout trip to Crawford Notch.
Yes, an awful lot of sorrow has sort of
quieted down up here. People just wild
with grief have brought their relatives up
to this hill. We all know how it is. And

then time . . . and sunny days . . . and rainy days . . . 'n snow . . . tz-tz-tz. We're all glad they're in a beautiful place, and we're coming up here ourselves when our fit's over. This certainly is an important part of Grover's Corners. A lot of thoughts come up here, night and day, but there's no post office.

Now I'm going to tell you some things you know already. You know'm as well as I do, but you don't take'm out and look at'm very often. I don't care what they say with their mouths—everybody knows that *something* is eternal. And it ain't houses, and it ain't names, and it ain't earth, and it ain't even the stars . . . everybody knows in their bones that *something* is eternal, and that something has to do with human beings. All the greatest people ever lived have been telling us that for five thousand years, and yet you'd be surprised how people are always losing hold of it. There's something way down deep that's eternal about every human being. *(Pause)* You know as well as I do that the dead don't stay interested in us living people for very long. Gradually, gradually, they lose hold of the earth . . . and the ambitions they had . . . and the pleasures they had . . . and the things they suffered . . . and the people they loved. They get weaned away from earth. That's the way I put it—weaned away. Yes, they stay here while the earth part of 'em burns away, burns out; and all that time they slowly get indifferent to what's goin' on in Grover's Corners.

They're waitin'. They're waitin' for something that they feel is comin'. Something important and great. Aren't they waitin' for the eternal part in them to come out clear? Some of the things they're going to say maybe'll hurt your feelings—but that's the way it is: mother 'n daughter . . . husband 'n wife . . . enemy 'n enemy . . . money 'n miser—all those terribly important things kind of grow pale around here. And what's left? What's left when memory's gone, and your identity, Mrs. Smith? *(He looks at the audience a minute, then turns to the stage.)*

Well! There are some *living* people. There's Joe Stoddard, our undertaker, supervising a new-made grave. And here comes a Grover's Corners boy that left town to go out West.

[JOE STODDARD *has hovered about in the background.* SAM CRAIG *enters left, wiping his forehead from the exertion. He carries an umbrella and strolls front.*]

SAM CRAIG. Good afternoon, Joe Stoddard.

JOE STODDARD. Good afternoon, good afternoon. Let me see now: Do I know you?

SAM CRAIG. I'm Sam Craig.

JOE STODDARD. Gracious sakes' alive! Of all people! I should'a knowed you'd be back for the funeral. You've been away a long time, Sam.

SAM CRAIG. Yes, I've been away over twelve years. I'm in business out in Buffalo now, Joe. But I was in the East when I got news of my cousin's death, so I thought I'd combine things a little and come and see the old home. You look well.

JOE STODDARD. Yes, yes, can't complain. Very sad, our journey today, Samuel.

SAM CRAIG. Yes.

JOE STODDARD. Yes, yes; I always say I hate to supervise when a young person is taken. I see you brought your umbrella. It's going to rain and make it sadder still, seems like. They'll be here in a few minutes now. I had to come here early today —my son's supervisin' at the home.

SAM CRAIG (*reading stones*). Old Farmer McCarty. I used to do chores for him—after school. He had the lumbago.

JOE STODDARD. Yes, we brought Farmer McCarty here a number of years ago now.

SAM CRAIG (*staring at* MRS. GIBBS'S *knees*). Why, this is my Aunt Julia.... I'd forgotten that she'd ... of course, of course.

JOE STODDARD. Yes, Doc Gibbs lost his wife two, three years ago ... about this time. And today's another pretty bad blow for him, too.

MRS. GIBBS (*to* SIMON STIMSON, *in an even voice*). That's my sister Carrie's boy, Sam—Sam Craig.

SIMON STIMSON. I'm always uncomfortable when *they're* around.

MRS. GIBBS. Simon.

SIMON STIMSON. They and their nonsense and their idiotic glee at being alive.

MRS. GIBBS. Simon, be patient.

SAM CRAIG. Do they choose their own verses much, Joe?

JOE STODDARD. No ... not usual. Mostly the bereaved pick a verse.

SAM CRAIG. Doesn't sound like Aunt Julia. There aren't many of those Hersey sisters, left now. Let me see. Where are —I wanted to look at my father's and mother's ...

JOE STODDARD. Over there with the Craigs.... Avenue F.

SAM CRAIG (*reading* SIMON STIMSON's *epitaph*). He was organist at church, wasn't he? Hm, drank a lot, we used to say.

JOE STODDARD. Nobody was supposed to know about it. He'd seen a peck of trouble. Those musical fellas ain't like the rest of us, I reckon. (*Behind his hand*) Took his own life, y'know?

SAM CRAIG. Oh, did he?

JOE STODDARD. Hung himself in the attic. They tried to hush it up, but of course it got around. His wife's just married Senator Barstow. Many a time I've seen her, eleven o'clock at night, goin' around the streets huntin' for her husband. Think o' that! Now she's married to Senator Barstow over at Manchester. He chose his own epy-taph. You can see it there. It ain't a verse exactly.

SAM CRAIG. Why, it's just some notes of music! What is it?

JOE STODDARD. Oh, I wouldn't know. It was wrote up in the Boston papers at the time.

SAM CRAIG. Joe, what did she die of?

JOE STODDARD. Who?

SAM CRAIG. My cousin.

JOE STODDARD. Oh, didn't you know? Had some trouble bringing a baby into the world. Let's see, today's Friday—'twas almost a week ago now.

SAM CRAIG (*putting up his umbrella*). Did the baby live?

JOE STODDARD (*raising his coat collar*). No. 'Twas her second, though. There's a little boy 'bout four years old.

SAM CRAIG. The grave's going to be over there?

JOE STODDARD. Yes, there ain't much more room over here among the Gibbses, so they're opening up a whole new Gibbs section over by Avenue B. You'll excuse me now. I see they're comin'.

THE DEAD (*not lugubrious, and*

strongly New England in accent). Rain'll do a lot of good. . . . Yes, reckon things were gettin' downright parched. Don't look like it's goin' to last long, tho'. . . . Lemuel, you remember the flood of seventy-nine? Carried away all the bridges but one.

[*From left to right, at the back of the stage, comes a procession. Four men carry a casket, invisible to us. All the rest are under umbrellas. One can vaguely see* DR. GIBBS, GEORGE, *the* WEBBS, *etc. They gather about a grave in the back center of the stage, a little to the left of center.*]

MRS. SOAMES. Who is it, Julia?

MRS. GIBBS *(without raising her eyes).* My daughter-in-law, Emily Webb.

MRS. SOAMES *(a little surprised, but no emotion).* Well, I declare! The road up here must have been awful muddy. What did she die of, Julia?

MRS. GIBBS. In childbirth.

MRS. SOAMES. Childbirth. *(Almost with a laugh)* I'd forgotten all about that! My, wasn't life awful—*(With a sigh)* and wonderful.

SIMON STIMSON *(with a sideways glance).* Wonderful, was it?

MRS. GIBBS. Simon! Now, remember!

MRS. SOAMES. I remember Emily's wedding. Wasn't it a lovely wedding! And I remember her reading the class poem at graduation exercises. Emily was one of the brightest girls ever graduated from high school. I've heard Principal Wilkins say so time after time. I called on them at their new farm just before I died. Perfectly beautiful farm.

A WOMAN FROM AMONG THE DEAD. It's on the same road we lived on.

A MAN AMONG THE DEAD. Yes, just near the Elks's picnic grounds. Remember, Joe? By the lake where we always used to go Fourth of July? Right smart farm.

[*They subside. The group by the grave starts singing "Blest Be the Tie That Binds."*]

A WOMAN AMONG THE DEAD. I always liked that hymn. I was hopin' they'd sing a hymn.

A MAN AMONG THE DEAD. My wife— my second wife—knows all the verses of about every hymn there is. It just beats the Dutch—she can go through them all by heart.

[*Pause. Suddenly* EMILY *appears from among the umbrellas. She is wearing a white dress. Her hair is down her back and tied by a white ribbon like a little girl's. She comes slowly, gazing wonderingly at* THE DEAD, *a little dazed. She stops halfway and smiles faintly.*]

EMILY. Hello.

VOICES AMONG THE DEAD. Hello, Emily. H'lo, M's. Gibbs.

EMILY. Hello, Mother Gibbs.

MRS. GIBBS. Emily.

EMILY. Hello. (*The hymn continues.* EMILY *looks back at the funeral. She says dreamily*) It's raining.

MRS. GIBBS. Yes.... They'll be gone soon, dear. Just rest yourself.

[EMILY *sits down in the empty chair by* MRS. GIBBS.]

EMILY. It seems thousands and thousands of years since I ... How stupid they all look. They don't have to look like that!

MRS. GIBBS. Don't look at them now, dear. They'll be gone soon.

EMILY. Oh, I wish I'd been here a long time. I don't like being new here.... How do you do, Mr. Stimson?

SIMON STIMSON. How do you do, Emily.

[EMILY *continues to look about her with a wan and wondering smile, but for a moment her eyes do not return to the funeral group. As though to shut out from her mind the thought of that group, she starts speaking to* MRS. GIBBS *with a touch of nervousness.*]

EMILY. Mother Gibbs, George and I have made that farm into just the best place you ever saw. We thought of you all the time. We wanted to show you the new barn and a great long ce-ment drinking fountain for the stock. We bought that out of the money you left us.

MRS. GIBBS. I did?

EMILY. Don't you remember, Mother Gibbs—the legacy you left us? Why, it was over three hundred and fifty dollars.

MRS. GIBBS. Yes, yes, Emily.

EMILY. Well, there's a patent device on this drinking fountain so that it never overflows, Mother Gibbs, and it never sinks below a certain mark they have there. It's fine. (*Her voice trails off, and her eyes return to the funeral group.*) It won't be the same to George without me, but it's a lovely farm. (*Suddenly she looks directly at* MRS. GIBBS.) Live people don't understand, do they?

MRS. GIBBS. No, dear—not very much.

EMILY. They're sort of shut up in little boxes, aren't they? I feel as though I knew them last a thousand years ago.... My boy is spending the day at Mrs. Carter's. (*She sees* MR. CARTER *among* THE DEAD.) Oh, Mr. Carter, my little boy is spending the day at your house.

MR. CARTER. Is he?

EMILY. Yes, he loves it there.... Mother Gibbs, we have a Ford, too. Never gives any trouble. I don't drive, though. Mother Gibbs, when does this feeling go away? Of being ... one of *them?* How long does it ...

MRS. GIBBS. Sh! dear. Just wait and be patient.

EMILY (*with a sigh*). I know.... Look, they're finished. They're going.

MRS. GIBBS. Sh....

[*The umbrellas leave the stage.* DR. GIBBS *comes over to his wife's grave and stands before it a moment.* EMILY *looks up at his face.* MRS. GIBBS *does not raise her eyes.*]

EMILY. Look! Father Gibbs is bringing some of my flowers to you. He looks just like George, doesn't he? Oh, Mother Gibbs, I never realized before how troubled and how ... how in the dark live persons are. From morning till night that's all they are—troubled.

[DR. GIBBS *goes off.*]

THE DEAD. Little cooler than it was.... Yes, that rain cooled it off a little. Those northeast winds always do the same thing, don't they? If it isn't a rain, it's a three-day blow.... Reckon it may clear up before night; often does.

[*A patient calm falls on the stage. The* STAGE MANAGER *appears at his proscenium pillar, smoking.* EMILY *sits up abruptly, with an idea.*]

EMILY. But, Mother Gibbs, one can go back; one can go back there again ... into living. I feel it. I know it. Why, just then for a moment I was thinking about ... about the farm ... and for a minute I *was* there, and my baby was on my lap as plain as day.

MRS. GIBBS. Yes, of course you can.

EMILY. I can go back there and live all those days over again ... why not?

MRS. GIBBS. All I can say is, Emily, *don't.*

EMILY (*taking a few steps toward the* STAGE MANAGER). But it's true, isn't it? I can go and live ... back there ... again.

STAGE MANAGER. Yes, some have tried —but they soon come back here.

MRS. GIBBS. Don't do it, Emily.

MRS. SOAMES. Emily, don't. It's not what you think it'd be.

EMILY. But I won't live over a sad day. I'll choose a happy one—I'll choose the day I first knew that I loved George. Why should that be painful?

[*They are silent. Her question turns to the* STAGE MANAGER.]

STAGE MANAGER. You not only live it, but you watch yourself living it.

EMILY. Yes?

STAGE MANAGER. And as you watch it, you see the thing that they—down there— never know. You see the future. You know what's going to happen afterward.

EMILY. But is that—painful? Why?

MRS. GIBBS. That's not the only reason why you shouldn't do it, Emily. When you've been here longer, you'll see that our life here is our hope that soon we'll forget all that, and think only of what's ahead, and be ready for what's ahead.

When you've been here longer, you'll understand.

EMILY (*softly*). But, Mother Gibbs, how can I ever forget that life? It's all I know. It's all I had.

[MRS. GIBBS *does not answer.*]

Mr. Stimson, did you go back?

SIMON STIMSON (*sharply*). No.

EMILY. Did you, Mrs. Soames?

MRS. SOAMES. Oh, Emily. It isn't wise. Really, it isn't. All we can do is just warn you. It won't be what you expect.

EMILY (*slowly*). But it's a thing I must know for myself. I'll choose a happy day, anyway.

MRS. GIBBS. No. At least choose an unimportant day. Choose the least important day in your life. It will be important enough.

EMILY (*to the* STAGE MANAGER). Then it can't be since I was married, or since the baby was born. I can choose a birthday at least, can't I? ... I choose my twelfth birthday.

STAGE MANAGER. All right. February 11, 1899. A Tuesday.... Do you want any special time of day?

EMILY. Oh, I want the whole day.

STAGE MANAGER. We'll begin at dawn. You remember it had been snowing for several days; but it had stopped the night before, and they had begun clearing the roads. The sun's coming up.

EMILY (*with a cry*). There's Main Street.... Why, that's Mr. Morgan's drugstore before he changed it! ... And there's the livery stable. (*She walks toward the back of the stage.*)

STAGE MANAGER. Yes, it's 1899. This is fourteen years ago.

EMILY. Oh, that's the town I knew as a little girl. And, look, there's the old white fence that used to be around our house. Oh, I'd forgotten that! Oh, I love it so! Are *they* inside?

STAGE MANAGER. Yes, your mother'll be coming downstairs in a minute to make breakfast.

EMILY (*softly*). Will she?

STAGE MANAGER. And you remember:

your father had been away for several days; he came back on the early-morning train.

EMILY. No . . .

STAGE MANAGER. He'd been back to his college to make a speech—in western New York, at Clinton.

EMILY. Look! There's Howie Newsome. There's our policeman. But he's *dead; he died.*

[*The* STAGE MANAGER *retires to his corner. The voices of* HOWIE NEWSOME, CONSTABLE WARREN, *and* JOE CROWELL, JR., *are heard at the left of the stage.*]

HOWIE NEWSOME. Whoa, Bessie! Bessie! . . . Morning, Bill.

CONSTABLE WARREN. Morning, Howie.

HOWIE NEWSOME. You're up early.

CONSTABLE WARREN. Been rescuin' a party; darn near froze to death, down by Polish Town thar. Got drunk and lay out in the snowdrifts. Thought he was in bed when I shook'm.

EMILY. Why, there's Joe Crowell.

JOE CROWELL, JR. Good morning, Mr. Warren. Morning, Howie.

[MRS. WEBB *has appeared in her kitchen, but* EMILY *does not see her until she calls.*]

MRS. WEBB. Chil-*dren!* Wally! Emily! . . . Time to get up.

EMILY. Mamma, here I am! Oh, how young Mamma looks! I didn't know Mamma was ever that young. Oh!

MRS. WEBB. You can come and dress by the kitchen fire, if you like; but hurry.

[HOWIE NEWSOME *has entered along Main Street and brings the milk to* MRS. WEBB's *door.*]

Good morning, Mr. Newsome. Whhhh— it's cold.

HOWIE NEWSOME. Ten below by my barn, Mrs. Webb.

MRS. WEBB. Think of it. Keep yourself wrapped up. (*She takes her bottles in, shuddering.*)

EMILY (*with an effort*). Mamma, I can't find my blue hair ribbon anywhere.

MRS. WEBB. Just open your eyes, dear, that's all. I laid it out for you special—on the dresser, there. If it were a snake, it would bite you.

EMILY. Yes, yes. . . . (*She puts her hand on her heart.*)

[MR. WEBB *comes along Main Street, where he meets* CONSTABLE WARREN.]

MR. WEBB. Good morning, Bill.

CONSTABLE WARREN. Good morning, Mr. Webb. You're up early.

MR. WEBB. Yes, just been back to my old college in New York State. Been any trouble here?

CONSTABLE WARREN. Well, I was called up this mornin' to rescue a Polish fella—darn near froze to death he was.

MR. WEBB. We must get it in the paper.

CONSTABLE WARREN. 'Twan't much.

EMILY (*whispers*). Papa.

[MR. WEBB *shakes the snow off his feet and enters his house.*]

MR. WEBB. Good morning, Mother.

MRS. WEBB. How did it go, Charles?

MR. WEBB. Oh, fine, I guess. I told'm a few things.

MRS. WEBB. Did you sit up on the train all night?

MR. WEBB. Yes. Never could sleep on a Pullman anyway.

MRS. WEBB. Charles, seems to me— we're rich enough so that you could sleep in a train once in a while.

MR. WEBB. Everything all right here?

MRS. WEBB. Yes—can't think of anything that's happened, special. Been right cold. Howie Newsome says it's ten below over to his barn.

MR. WEBB. Yes? Well, it's colder than that at Hamilton College. Students' ears are falling off. It ain't Christian. . . . Paper have any mistakes in it?

MRS. WEBB. None that I noticed. Coffee's ready when you want it.

[*He starts upstairs.*]

Charles! Don't forget; it's Emily's birthday. Did you remember to get her something?

MR. WEBB (*patting his pocket*). Yes, I've got something here.

MRS. WEBB. Goodness sakes! I hope she likes what I got for her. I hunted hard enough for it. Chil*dren!* Hurry up! Hurry up!

MR. WEBB. Where's my girl? Where's my birthday girl? (*He goes off left.*)

MRS. WEBB. Don't interrupt her now, Charles. You can see her at breakfast. She's slow enough as it is. Hurry up, children! It's seven o'clock. Now, I don't want to call you again.

EMILY (*softly, more in wonder than in grief*). I can't bear it. They're so young and beautiful. Why did they ever have to get old? Mamma, I'm here. I'm grown up. I love you all, everything. . . . I can't look at everything hard enough. There's the butternut tree. (*She wanders up Main Street.*) There's Mr. Morgan's drugstore. And there's the high school, for ever and ever and ever. And there's the Congregational Church where I got married. Oh, dear. Oh, dear. Oh, dear!

[*The* STAGE MANAGER *beckons partially to her. He points to the house. She says a breathless "yes" and goes to the house.*]

Good morning, Mamma.

MRS. WEBB (*at the foot of the stairs, kissing her in a matter-of-fact way*). Well, now, dear, a very happy birthday to my girl and many happy returns. There are some surprises waiting for you on the kitchen table.

EMILY. Oh, Mamma, you *shouldn't* have. (*She throws an anguished glance at the* STAGE MANAGER.) I can't—I can't.

MRS. WEBB (*facing the audience, over her stove*). But birthday or no birthday, I want you to eat your breakfast good and slow. I want you to grow up and be a good strong girl. (*She goes to the stairs and calls.*) Wally! Wally, wash yourself good. Everything's getting cold down here. (*She returns to the stove with her back to* EMILY.)

[EMILY *opens her parcels.*]

That in the blue paper is from your Aunt Carrie, and I reckon you can guess who brought the post-card album. I found it on the doorstep when I brought in the milk. George Gibbs must have come over in the cold pretty early . . . right nice of him.

EMILY (*to herself*). Oh, George! I'd forgotten that.

MRS. WEBB. Chew that bacon slow. It'll help keep you warm on a cold day.

EMILY (*beginning softly but urgently*). Oh, Mamma, just look at me one minute as though you really saw me. Mamma, fourteen years have gone by. I'm dead. You're a grandmother, Mamma. I married George Gibbs, Mamma. Wally's dead, too. Mamma, his appendix burst on a camping trip to North Conway. We felt just terrible about it—don't you remember? But, just for a moment now we're all together. Mamma, just for a moment we're happy. Let's look at one another.

MRS. WEBB. That in the yellow paper is

something I found in the attic among your grandmother's things. You're old enough to wear it now, and I thought you'd like it.

EMILY. And this is from you. Why, Mamma, it's just lovely and it's just what I wanted. It's beautiful! (*She flings her arms around her mother's neck.*)

[*Her mother goes on with her cooking, but is pleased.*]

MRS. WEBB. Well, I hoped you'd like it. Hunted all over. Your Aunt Norah couldn't find one in Concord, so I had to send all the way to Boston. (*Laughingly*) Wally has something for you, too. He made it at manual-training class, and he's very proud of it. Be sure you make a big fuss about it. Your father has a surprise for you, too; don't know what it is myself. Sh—here he comes.

MR. WEBB (*offstage*). Where's my girl? Where's my birthday girl?

EMILY (*in a loud voice to the STAGE MANAGER*). I can't. I can't go on. Oh! Oh. It goes so fast. We don't have time to look at one another. (*She breaks down, sobbing.*)

[*At a gesture from the STAGE MANAGER, MRS. WEBB disappears.*]

I didn't realize. So all that was going on and we never noticed. Take me back— up the hill—to my grave. But first— wait! One more look. Good-by, good-by, world. Good-by, Grover's Corners . . . Mamma and Papa. Good-by to clocks ticking . . . and Mamma's sunflowers. And food and coffee. And new-ironed dresses and hot baths . . . and sleeping and waking up. Oh, earth, you're too wonderful for anybody to realize you. (*She looks toward the STAGE MANAGER and asks, abruptly, through her tears*) Do any human beings ever realize life while they live it—every, every minute?

STAGE MANAGER. No. (*Pause*) The saints and poets, maybe—they do some.

EMILY. I'm ready to go back. (*She returns to her chair beside MRS. GIBBS.*) Mother Gibbs, I should have listened to you. Now I want to be quiet for a while.

. . . Oh, Mother Gibbs, I saw it all. I saw your garden.

MRS. GIBBS. Did you, dear?

EMILY. That's all human beings are! Just blind people.

MRS. GIBBS. Look, it's clearing up. The stars are coming out.

EMILY. Oh, Mr. Stimson, I should have listened to them.

SIMON STIMSON (*with mounting violence; bitingly*). Yes, now you know. Now you know! That's what it was to be alive. To move about in a cloud of ignorance, to go up and down trampling on the feelings of those . . . of those about you. To spend and waste time as though you had a million years. To be always at the mercy of one self-centered passion or another. Now you know—that's the happy existence you wanted to go back and see. Did you shout to 'em? Did you call to 'em?

EMILY. Yes, I did.

SIMON STIMSON. Now you know them as they are: in ignorance and blindness.

MRS. GIBBS (*spiritedly*). Simon Stimson, that ain't the whole truth, and you know it.

[THE DEAD *have begun to stir.*]

THE DEAD. Lemuel, wind's coming up, seems like. . . . Oh, dear, I keep remembering things tonight. . . . It's right cold for June, ain't it?

MRS. GIBBS. Look what you've done, you and your rebellious spirit stirring us up here. . . . Emily, look at that star. I forget its name.

THE DEAD. I'm getting to know them all, but I don't know their names. My boy, Joel, was a sailor—knew 'em all. He'd set on the porch evenings and tell 'em all by name. Yes, sir, it was wonderful. A star's mighty good company. Yes, yes. Yes, 'tis.

SIMON STIMSON. Here's one of *them* coming.

THE DEAD. That's funny. 'Tain't no time for one of them to be here. Goodness sakes.

EMILY. Mother Gibbs, it's George.

which he slowly draws across the scene. In the distance a clock is heard striking the hour very faintly.]

STAGE MANAGER. Most everybody's asleep in Grover's Corners. There are a few lights on. Shorty Hawkins, down at the depot, has just watched the Albany train go by. And at the livery stable somebody's setting up late and talking. . . . Yes, it's clearing up. There are the stars—doing their old, old crisscross journeys in the sky. Scholars haven't settled the matter yet, but they seem to think there are no living beings up there. They're just chalk . . . or fire. Only this one is straining away, straining away all the time to make something of itself. The strain's so bad that every sixteen hours everybody lies down and gets a rest. (*He winds his watch.*) Hm. . . . Eleven o'clock in Grover's Corners. . . . You get a good rest, too. Good night.

MRS. GIBBS. Sh, dear. You just rest yourself.

EMILY. It's George.

[GEORGE *enters from the left and slowly comes toward them.*]

A MAN FROM AMONG THE DEAD. And my boy, Joel, who knew the stars—he used to say it took millions of years for that speck o' light to git to the earth. Don't seem like a body could believe it, but that's what he used to say—millions of years.

ANOTHER. That's what they say.

[GEORGE *flings himself on* EMILY'S *grave.*]

THE DEAD. Goodness! That ain't no way to behave! He ought to be home.

EMILY. Mother Gibbs?

MRS. GIBBS. Yes, Emily?

EMILY. They don't understand much, do they?

MRS. GIBBS. No, dear, not very much.

[*The* STAGE MANAGER *appears at the right, one hand on a dark curtain,*

COMMENTARY

Act III is about death. We've been slyly warned about it in Act II, so presumably we are somewhat prepared for it. We are aware that death, to the playwright, like the birth which introduces his play or the love and marriage which occupy the center of it, is a natural, inevitable occurrence which happens to every human being. But when we discover that it is Emily who has died, it is not easy for us to maintain a cool, unruffled state of mind. For all the efforts of the Stage Manager, he cannot prevent the audience from sensing the quiet pathos in this last act, particularly when it is contrasted to the hopeful warmheartedness of Act II.

Yet the Stage Manager, or really the playwright, uses a number of devices to mitigate the funereal atmosphere and underscore his optimistic sense of a movement toward perfection. The third act opens with a long speech describing the dead. The graveyard is, we are told, a beautiful spot, above the busy life of the town, with a view of the mountains and the stars. Generations of New Englanders have been buried there. Hence the emphasis is upon geographical and temporal removal from the workaday world. Here too there is a vast emotional distance from life. People may come up here "wild with grief," but the dead have been "weaned away from earth," and so "slowly get indifferent to what's goin' on in Grover's Corners." Furthermore, the dead "sit in a quiet without stiffness and in a patience without listlessness." They speak evenly with no emotion. In other words, they are as emotionally disengaged from life as they are physically "waitin' for the eternal part in them to come out clear."

Death, then, would seem to be merely another rung on the ladder of existence, leading toward perfection and God. Just as, in Act II, George and Emily looked back on their old quarrel as trivial and unimportant compared with the marriage they look forward to, so the dead view all their past lives as insignificant compared with "something that they feel is comin'." The process is as natural as growing up; in fact, the expression "weaned away from earth" suggests that life on earth is merely the childhood of total existence. Life and time, both so important in Grover's Corners, have ceased to be important when they are placed against eternity. The attitude of the dead is detached, very similar really to the attitude that the Stage Manager has maintained all along, and to the attitude that he attempts to instill in the audience.

Yet if death is the process of being removed from all the tense considerations of life, it is bound to be at least as painful for those going through it as birth, or growing up, or marriage has been in the past. And so when Emily arrives on the scene, we observe once again the conflict between two stages of existence as she reminisces about her old life and antici-

pates the new. She can talk about her farm with pride, and yet the funeral seems "stupid" and trivial. Moreover, the manner of her death emphasizes nature's continual drive for perfection. If the real hero of Act II was the baby which her marriage was to create, the baby in a sense is now the villain of Act III, since its mother has died in childbirth. Yet the word *villain* hardly works here. Nature's efforts to create a perfect human being caused Emily's death, just as they caused her birth, her love, and her marriage. As Emily says, "Oh earth, you're too wonderful for anyone to realize you."

FOR STUDY AND DISCUSSION

1. How significant is the cause of Emily's death in terms of the overall theme of the play?

2. Why does Mrs. Gibbs urge Emily to return to life on an insignificant day? What do you think her reaction would be if she returned on an important day?

3. Why does the playwright include the scene between Joe Stoddard, the undertaker, and Sam Craig, the out-of-town visitor? What effect does it have on us to hear first about Emily's death from these two? How do the dead respond to Joe and Sam?

4. What, in general, do the dead talk about? What evidence is there of "the eternal part" in them?

5. Reread the remarks of Simon Stimson and Mrs. Soames in Act III. Compare and contrast them. What in particular seems to be Simon's difficulty all along in the play? Why does he drink? How does his state of mind relate to the theme of the play as a whole? Why is it appropriate that Stimson be an organist?

COMMENTARY
The Play as a Whole

The Stage Manager points out that only a few people, a few poets and saints, can both feel the wonder of life and understand its purpose simultaneously. Saints are said to be more attuned to the working of God in this world, while poets have a heightened ability to respond to particular moments. But otherwise, according to *Our Town,* the human predicament is to know and feel only partially, and to suffer because we can never completely reconcile feeling and understanding. The contrasting attitudes of involvement and detachment, of the living versus the dead, are most effectively dramatized when George throws himself onto Emily's grave, while the dead talk about the stars and light years. The space between the live George and the dead Emily seems to be as wide as that between Jane Crofut and God.

We must not forget our own attitudes as we read *Our Town* and imagine it being performed on a stage that seems curiously empty. The staging of the play, and the efforts of the Stage Manager, tend to remove us from the particular events, even though we are alive and human enough to respond emotionally to them. Is it not true that we can feel George's grief even as we understand Emily's tranquillity? In other words, aren't we, the audience, responding to the play with the same double attitude with which poets and saints respond to actual life? We accomplish, watching the play, what Emily couldn't in her return home. And if, as the Stage Manager says in his last speech, the earth "is straining away all the time to make something of itself," then we must assume that plays are written to contribute to this process of creative growth. We ourselves have been "pushed" and "contrived" by nature's emissary, the Stage Manager, into a keener awareness of life. But, as the Stage Manager reminds us, the strain of living gets so difficult that "every sixteen hours everybody lies down and gets a rest." Grover's Corners is now resting, and we (the audience) feel like resting too.

FOR STUDY AND DISCUSSION:
THE PLAY AS A WHOLE

1. Why is "Grover's Corners" a good name for Our Town? Why is "Blest Be the Tie That Binds" a particularly fitting hymn to be sung in all three acts? In what way does the title *Our Town* have special relevance by the end of Act III?

2. Discuss the staging of *Our Town.* Where is it particularly effective in disengaging or qualifying the sympathies of the audience? What effect do you suppose the playwright intends by having the wedding members enter from the audience? Can you give examples of similar staging—in dramas, motion pictures, or television plays—that does not attempt to give an illusion of real life but that deliberately calls attention to itself?

3. Do you think *Our Town* seems old-fashioned? Do its truths apply to our highly industrialized society? What would the Stage Manager say, for example, about the effect of present-day technology upon the essential events of life?

4. Is *Our Town* sentimental? Do you think it gives too rosy a view of life? Do you think it accounts for the injustices and evils which exist in the world?

FOR COMPOSITION

1. Write a composition in which you agree or disagree with the author's ideas about nature, as these ideas are expressed in the play and brought out in the Commentaries. Use incidents from the play and from your own knowledge and experience to support your point of view.

2. One of the most important features of the play is the author's use of dialogue and staging devices to set up an opposition between involvement and detachment, feeling and comprehension (see pages 769, 781). Write a composition in which you contrast an involved and a detached point of view. You might tell how you felt about a certain event in your life while it was taking place and how you can regard it more objectively now. Or you might show how a person can become more involved or more detached while examining a familiar object—for example, a flower.

3. *Our Town* presents a cross section of life in Grover's Corners. Present a cross section of life in your town, either in the form of an essay describing various people in your town or in the form of a dramatic sketch in which the people speak for themselves. (You might have a stage manager introduce them.) Choose your characters carefully and be sure they are significant figures in the life of your town.

BEYOND THE HORIZON

EUGENE O'NEILL

Eugene O'Neill (1888–1953) was born in New York City, the son of James O'Neill, a famous actor of melodramas. During his youth, Eugene traveled with his father's theatrical company and the stage was an important part of his life. He turned to playwriting, however, only after a troubled youth that included several sea voyages, a marriage and divorce, and a bout with tuberculosis.

During his life, O'Neill was regarded as the foremost American dramatist. His restless experimentation, in plays such as *The Emperor Jones* (1920), *The Great God Brown* (1926), and *Strange Interlude* (1928), gave the American theater a needed shot in the arm. The anguished intensity of his later plays, such as *The Iceman Cometh* (1948) and *Long Day's Journey into Night* (1956), seems to have solidified a reputation that has continued to grow beyond his death. He was a considerable influence in turning the American drama away from contrived and frivolous hack work. Whatever is serious and ambitious on our stage today owes a great deal to the trail he blazed.

Beyond the Horizon, Eugene O'Neill's first important full-length drama, made its author famous. Produced in 1920, it won the Pulitzer prize for that year and prepared the way for the impressive group of dramas which O'Neill was to write until his death in 1953. This play, unlike most of its successors, is written in the realistic tradition; the audience is asked to view the action as if through a fourth wall, and the events unfold in an orderly, chronological manner, allowing for leaps of time to take place between acts. Plenty of painted, representational scenery is required to suggest the concrete influence of the surroundings, and the characters are supposed to speak a recognizably rural dialect.

On the other hand, there are seeds, even in this early play, of the restless experimentation that characterizes O'Neill's subsequent work. The setting—mountains, the fences, the sea beyond—takes on a certain symbolic quality before the play has gone very far, and the alternation between outdoors and indoors conveys a fundamental rhythm. The purposely vague geography suggests that O'Neill does not intend to write simply about a local incident, while his characters, in the harsh directness of their confrontations, also seem to strive for universality.

As you read *Beyond the Horizon,* it might be a good idea to ask yourself whether or not it approaches tragedy (see page 751). Do you feel a sense of struggle against insurmountable odds, for example, and does this struggle seem to add up to anything meaningful at the end of the play? This problem should be discussed in detail after you have read the play, but the issue should be at least in the back of your mind from the start.

Beyond the Horizon

Characters

JAMES MAYO, *a farmer*

KATE MAYO, *his wife*

CAPTAIN DICK SCOTT, *of the bark* Sunda, *her brother*

ANDREW MAYO ⎫
ROBERT MAYO ⎬ *sons of* JAMES MAYO

RUTH ATKINS

MRS. ATKINS, *her widowed mother*

MARY

BEN, *a farm hand*

DOCTOR FAWCETT

ACT I

SCENE 1

A section of country highway. The road runs diagonally from the left, forward, to the right, rear, and can be seen in the distance winding toward the horizon like a pale ribbon between the low, rolling hills with their freshly plowed fields clearly divided from each other, checkerboard fashion, by the lines of stone walls and rough snake fences.

The forward triangle cut off by the road is a section of a field from the dark earth of which myriad bright-green blades of fall-sown rye are sprouting. A straggling line of piled rocks, too low to be called a wall, separates this field from the road.

To the rear of the road is a ditch with a sloping, grassy bank on the far side. From the center of this an old, gnarled apple tree, just budding into leaf, strains its twisted branches heavenward, black against the pallor of distance. A snake fence sidles from left to right along the top of the bank, passing beneath the apple tree.

The hushed twilight of a day in May is just beginning. The horizon hills are still rimmed by a faint line of flame, and the sky above them glows with the crimson flush of the sunset. This fades gradually as the action of the scene progresses.

At the rise of the curtain, ROBERT MAYO *is discovered sitting on the fence. He is a tall, slender young man of twenty-three. There is a touch of the poet about him expressed in his high forehead and wide, dark eyes. His features are delicate and refined, leaning to weakness in the mouth and chin. He is dressed in gray corduroy trousers pushed into high laced boots, and a blue flannel shirt with a bright colored tie. He is reading a book by the fading sunset light. He shuts this, keeping a finger in to mark the place, and turns his head toward the horizon, gazing out over the fields and hills. His lips move as if he were reciting something to himself.*

His brother ANDREW *comes along the road from the right, returning from his work in the fields. He is twenty-seven years old, an opposite type to* ROBERT— *husky, sun-bronzed, handsome in a large-featured, manly fashion—a son of the soil, intelligent in a shrewd way, but with nothing of the intellectual about him. He wears overalls, leather boots, a gray flannel shirt open at the neck, and a soft, mud-stained hat pushed back on his head. He stops to talk to* ROBERT, *leaning on the hoe he carries.*

ANDREW (*seeing* ROBERT *has not noticed his presence—in a loud shout*). Hey there! (ROBERT *turns with a start.*

Beyond the Horizon from *Ah Wilderness! And Two Other Plays* by Eugene O'Neill, copyright 1920, 1947 by Eugene O'Neill. Reprinted by permission of Random House, Inc.

Seeing who it is, he smiles.) Gosh, you do take the prize for daydreaming! And I see you've toted one of the old books along with you. *(He crosses the ditch and sits on the fence near his brother.)* What is it this time—poetry, I'll bet. *(He reaches for the book.)* Let me see.

ROBERT *(handing it to him rather reluctantly).* Look out you don't get it full of dirt.

ANDREW *(glancing at his hands).* That isn't dirt—it's good clean earth. *(He turns over the pages. His eyes read something and he gives an exclamation of disgust.)* Hump! *(With a provoking grin at his brother he reads aloud in a doleful, singsong voice.)* "I have loved wind and light and the bright sea. But holy and most sacred night, not as I love and have loved thee." *(He hands the book back.)* Here! Take it and bury it. I suppose it's that year in college gave you a liking for that kind of stuff. I'm darn glad I stopped at high school, or maybe I'd been crazy too. *(He grins and slaps* ROBERT *on the back affectionately.)* Imagine me reading poetry and plowing at the same time! The team'd run away, I'll bet.

ROBERT *(laughing).* Or picture me plowing.

ANDREW. You should have gone back to college last fall, like I know you wanted to. You're fitted for that sort of thing—just as I ain't.

ROBERT. You know why I didn't go back, Andy. Pa didn't like the idea, even if he didn't say so; and I know he wanted the money to use improving the farm. And besides, I'm not keen on being a student, just because you see me reading books all the time. What I want to do now is keep on moving so that I won't take root in any one place.

ANDREW. Well, the trip you're leaving on tomorrow will keep you moving all right. *(At this mention of the trip they both fall silent. There is a pause. Finally* ANDREW *goes on, awkwardly, attempting to speak casually.)* Uncle says you'll be gone three years.

ROBERT. About that, he figures.

ANDREW *(moodily).* That's a long time.

ROBERT. Not so long when you come to consider it. You know the *Sunda* sails around the Horn for Yokohama first, and that's a long voyage on a sailing ship; and if we go to any of the other places Uncle Dick mentions—India, or Australia, or South Africa, or South America —they'll be long voyages, too.

ANDREW. You can have all those foreign parts for all of me. *(After a pause)* Ma's going to miss you a lot, Rob.

ROBERT. Yes—and I'll miss her.

ANDREW. And Pa ain't feeling none too happy to have you go—though he's been trying not to show it.

ROBERT. I can see how he feels.

ANDREW. And you can bet that I'm not giving any cheers about it. *(He puts one hand on the fence near* ROBERT.)

ROBERT *(putting one hand on top of* ANDREW'S *with a gesture almost of shyness).* I know that, too, Andy.

ANDREW. I'll miss you as much as anybody, I guess. You see, you and I ain't like most brothers—always fighting and separated a lot of the time, while we've always been together—just the two of us. It's different with us. That's why it hits so hard, I guess.

ROBERT *(with feeling).* It's just as hard for me, Andy—believe that! I hate to leave you and the old folks—but—I feel I've got to. There's something calling me—— *(He points to the horizon.)* Oh, I can't just explain it to you, Andy.

ANDREW. No need to, Rob. *(Angry at himself)* You want to go—that's all there is to it; and I wouldn't have you miss this chance for the world.

ROBERT. It's fine of you to feel that way, Andy.

ANDREW. Huh! I'd be a nice son-of-a-gun if I didn't, wouldn't I? When I know how you need this sea trip to make a new man of you—in the body, I mean— and give you your full health back.

ROBERT *(a trifle impatiently).* All of you seem to keep harping on my health.

You were so used to seeing me lying around the house in the old days that you never will get over the notion that I'm a chronic invalid. You don't realize how I've bucked up in the past few years. If I had no other excuse for going on Uncle Dick's ship but just my health, I'd stay right here and start in plowing.

ANDREW. Can't be done. Farming ain't your nature. There's all the difference shown in just the way us two feel about the farm. You—well, you like the home part of it, I expect; but as a place to work and grow things, you hate it. Ain't that right?

ROBERT. Yes, I suppose it is. For you it's different. You're a Mayo through and through. You're wedded to the soil. You're as much a product of it as an ear of corn is, or a tree. Father is the same. This farm is his lifework, and he's happy in knowing that another Mayo, inspired by the same love, will take up the work where he leaves off. I can understand your attitude, and Pa's; and I think it's wonderful and sincere. But I—well, I'm not made that way.

ANDREW. No, you ain't; but when it comes to understanding, I guess I realize that you've got your own angle of looking at things.

ROBERT (*musingly*). I wonder if you do, really.

ANDREW (*confidently*). Sure I do. You've seen a bit of the world, enough to make the farm seem small, and you've got the itch to see it all.

ROBERT. It's more than that, Andy.

ANDREW. Oh, of course. I know you're going to learn navigation, and all about a ship, so's you can be an officer. That's natural, too. There's fair pay in it, I expect, when you consider that you've always got a home and grub thrown in; and if you're set on traveling, you can go anywhere you're a mind to without paying fare.

ROBERT (*with a smile that is half sad*). It's more than that, Andy.

ANDREW. Sure it is. There's always a chance of a good thing coming your way in some of those foreign ports or other. I've heard there are great opportunities for a young fellow with his eyes open in some of those new countries that are just being opened up. *(Jovially)* I'll bet that's what you've been turning over in your mind under all your quietness! *(He slaps his brother on the back with a laugh.)* Well, if you get to be a millionaire all of a sudden, call 'round once in a while and I'll pass the plate to you. We could use a lot of money right here on the farm without hurting it any.

ROBERT *(forced to laugh)*. I've never considered that practical side of it for a minute, Andy.

ANDREW. Well, you ought to.

ROBERT. No, I oughtn't. *(Pointing to the horizon—dreamily)* Supposing I was to tell you that it's just Beauty that's calling me, the beauty of the far off and unknown, the mystery and spell of the East which lures me in the books I've read, the need of the freedom of great wide spaces, the joy of wandering on and on— in quest of the secret which is hidden over there, beyond the horizon? Suppose I told you that was the one and only reason for my going?

ANDREW. I should say you were nutty.

ROBERT *(frowning)*. Don't, Andy. I'm serious.

ANDREW. Then you might as well stay here, because we've got all you're looking for right on this farm. There's wide space enough, Lord knows; and you can have all the sea you want by walking a mile down to the beach; and there's plenty of horizon to look at, and beauty enough for anyone, except in the winter. *(He grins.)* As for the mystery and spell, I haven't met 'em yet, but they're probably lying around somewheres. I'll have you understand this is a first-class farm with all the fixings. *(He laughs.)*

ROBERT *(joining in the laughter in spite of himself)*. It's no use talking to you, you chump!

ANDREW. You'd better not say anything to Uncle Dick about spells and things when you're on the ship. He'll likely chuck you overboard for a Jonah. *(He jumps down from fence.)* I'd better run along. I've got to wash up some as long as Ruth's Ma is coming over for supper.

ROBERT *(pointedly—almost bitterly)*. And Ruth.

ANDREW *(confused—looking everywhere except at* ROBERT—*trying to appear unconcerned)*. Yes, Ruth'll be staying too. Well, I better hustle, I guess, and—— *(He steps over the ditch to the road while he is talking.)*

ROBERT *(who appears to be fighting some strong inward emotion—impulsively)*. Wait a minute, Andy! *(He jumps down from the fence.)* There is something I want to—— *(He stops abruptly, biting his lips, his face coloring.)*

ANDREW *(facing him; half-defiantly)*. Yes?

ROBERT *(confusedly)*. No—never mind —it doesn't matter, it was nothing.

ANDREW *(after a pause, during which he stares fixedly at* ROBERT'S *averted face)*. Maybe I can guess—what you were going to say—but I guess you're right not to talk about it. *(He pulls* ROBERT'S *hand from his side and grips it tensely; the two brothers stand looking into each other's eyes for a minute.)* We can't help those things, Rob. *(He turns away, suddenly releasing* ROBERT'S *hand.)* You'll be coming along shortly, won't you?

ROBERT *(dully)*. Yes.

ANDREW. See you later, then. *(He walks off down the road to the left.* ROBERT *stares after him for a moment; then climbs to the fence rail again and looks out over the hills, an expression of deep grief on his face. After a moment or so,* RUTH *enters hurriedly from the left. She is a healthy, blonde, out-of-door girl of twenty, with a graceful, slender figure. Her face, though inclined to roundness, is undeniably pretty, its large eyes of a deep blue set off strikingly by the sun-bronzed complexion. Her small, regular features are marked by a certain strength—an underlying, stubborn fixity of purpose hidden in the frankly appealing charm of her fresh youthfulness. She wears a simple white dress but no hat.)*

RUTH (*seeing him*). Hello, Rob!

ROBERT (*startled*). Hello, Ruth!

RUTH (*jumps the ditch and perches on the fence beside him*). I was looking for you.

ROBERT (*pointedly*). Andy just left here.

RUTH. I know. I met him on the road a second ago. He told me you were here. (*Tenderly playful*) I wasn't looking for Andy, Smarty, if that's what you mean. I was looking for *you*.

ROBERT. Because I'm going away tomorrow?

RUTH. Because your mother was anxious to have you come home and asked me to look for you. I just wheeled Ma over to your house.

ROBERT (*perfunctorily*). How is your mother?

RUTH (*a shadow coming over her face*). She's about the same. She never seems to get any better or any worse. Oh, Rob, I do wish she'd try to make the best of things that can't be helped.

ROBERT. Has she been nagging at you again?

RUTH (*nods her head, and then breaks forth rebelliously*). She never stops nagging. No matter what I do for her she finds fault. If only Pa was still living—— (*She stops as if ashamed of her outburst.*) I suppose I shouldn't complain this way. (*She sighs.*) Poor Ma, Lord knows it's hard enough for her. I suppose it's natural to be cross when you're not able ever to walk a step. Oh, I'd like to be going away some place—like you!

ROBERT. It's hard to stay—and equally hard to go, sometimes.

RUTH. There! If I'm not the stupid body! I swore I wasn't going to speak about your trip—until after you'd gone; and there I go, first thing!

ROBERT. Why didn't you want to speak of it?

RUTH. Because I didn't want to spoil this last night you're here. Oh, Rob, I'm going to—we're all going to miss you so awfully. Your mother is going around looking as if she'd burst out crying any minute. You ought to know how I feel.

Andy and you and I—why it seems as if we'd always been together.

ROBERT (*with a wry attempt at a smile*). You and Andy will still have each other. It'll be harder for me without anyone.

RUTH. But you'll have new sights and new people to take your mind off; while we'll be here with the old, familiar place to remind us every minute of the day. It's a shame you're going—just at this time, in spring, when everything is getting so nice. (*With a sigh*) I oughtn't to talk that way when I know going's the best thing for you. You're bound to find all sorts of opportunities to get on, your father says.

ROBERT (*heatedly*). I don't give a damn about that! I wouldn't take a voyage across the road for the best opportunity in the world of the kind Pa thinks of. (*He smiles at his own irritation.*) Excuse me, Ruth, for getting worked up over it; but Andy gave me an overdose of the practical considerations.

RUTH (*slowly, puzzled*). Well, then, if it isn't—— (*With sudden intensity*) Oh, Rob, why *do* you want to go?

ROBERT (*turning to her quickly, in surprise—slowly*). Why do you ask that, Ruth?

RUTH (*dropping her eyes before his searching glance*). Because—— (*Lamely*) It seems such a shame.

ROBERT (*insistently*). Why?

RUTH. Oh, because—everything.

ROBERT. I could hardly back out now, even if I wanted to. And I'll be forgotten before you know it.

RUTH (*indignantly*). You won't! I'll never forget—— (*She stops and turns away to hide her confusion.*)

ROBERT (*softly*). Will you promise me that?

RUTH (*evasively*). Of course. It's mean of you to think that any of us would forget so easily.

ROBERT (*disappointedly*). Oh!

RUTH (*with an attempt at lightness*). But you haven't told me your reason for leaving yet?

ROBERT (*moodily*). I doubt if you'll understand. It's difficult to explain, even to myself. Either you feel it, or you don't. I can remember being conscious of it first when I was only a kid—you haven't forgotten what a sickly specimen I was then, in those days, have you?

RUTH (with a shudder). Let's not think about them.

ROBERT. You'll have to, to understand. Well, in those days, when Ma was fixing meals, she used to get me out of the way by pushing my chair to the west window and telling me to look out and be quiet. That wasn't hard. I guess I was always quiet.

RUTH (compassionately). Yes, you always were—and you suffering so much, too!

ROBERT (musingly). So I used to stare out over the fields to the hills, out there—(He points to the horizon) and somehow after a time I'd forget any pain I was in, and start dreaming. I knew the sea was over beyond those hills—the folks had told me—and I used to wonder what the sea was like and try to form a picture of it in my mind. (With a smile) There was all the mystery in the world to me then about that—far-off sea—and there still is! It called to me then just as it does now. (After a slight pause) And other times my eyes would follow this road, winding off into the distance, toward the hills, as if it, too, was searching for the sea. And I'd promise myself that when I grew up and was strong, I'd follow that road, and it and I would find the sea together. (With a smile) You see, my making this trip is only keeping that promise of long ago.

RUTH (charmed by his low, musical voice telling the dreams of his childhood). Yes, I see.

ROBERT. Those were the only happy moments of my life then, dreaming there at the window. I liked to be all alone—those times. I got to know all the different kinds of sunsets by heart. And all those sunsets took place over there—(He points) beyond the horizon. So gradually I came to believe that all the wonders of the world happened on the other side of those hills. There was the home of the good fairies who performed beautiful miracles. I believed in fairies then. (With a smile) Perhaps I still do believe in them. Anyway, in those days they were real enough, and sometimes I could actually hear them calling to me to come out and play with them, dance with them down the road in the dusk in a game of hide-and-seek to find out where the sun was hiding himself. They sang their little songs to me, songs that told of all the wonderful things they had in their home on the other side of the hills; and they promised to show me all of them, if I'd only come, come! But I couldn't come then, and I used to cry sometimes and Ma would think I was in pain. (He breaks off suddenly with a laugh.) That's why I'm going now, I suppose. For I can still hear them calling. But the horizon is as far away and as luring as ever. (He turns to her—softly.) Do you understand now, Ruth?

RUTH (spellbound, in a whisper). Yes.

ROBERT. You feel it then?

RUTH. Yes, yes, I do! (Unconsciously she snuggles close against his side. His arm steals about her as if he were not aware of the action.) Oh, Rob, how could I help feeling it? You tell things so beautifully!

ROBERT (suddenly realizing that his arm is around her, and that her head is resting on his shoulder, gently takes his arm away. RUTH, brought back to herself, is overcome with confusion). So now you know why I'm going. It's for that reason—that and one other.

RUTH. You've another? Then you must tell me that, too.

ROBERT (looking at her searchingly. She drops her eyes before his gaze). I wonder if I ought to! You'll promise not to be angry—whatever it is?

RUTH (softly, her face still averted). Yes, I promise.

ROBERT (simply). I love you. That's the other reason.

RUTH (hiding her face in her hands). Oh, Rob!

ROBERT. I wasn't going to tell you, but

I feel I have to. It can't matter now that I'm going so far away, and for so long—perhaps forever. I've loved you all these years, but the realization never came 'til I agreed to go away with Uncle Dick. Then I thought of leaving you, and the pain of that thought revealed to me in a flash—that I loved you, had loved you as long as I could remember. *(He gently pulls one of* RUTH's *hands away from her face.)* You mustn't mind my telling you this, Ruth. I realize how impossible it all is—and I understand; for the revelation of my own love seemed to open my eyes to the love of others. I saw Andy's love for you—and I knew that you must love him.

RUTH *(breaking out stormily).* I don't! I don't love Andy! I don't! (ROBERT *stares at her in stupid astonishment.* RUTH *weeps hysterically.)* Whatever—put such a fool notion into—into your head? *(She suddenly throws her arms about his neck and hides her head on his shoulder.)* Oh, Rob! Don't go away! Please! You mustn't, now! You can't! I won't let you! It'd break my—my heart!

ROBERT *(the expression of stupid bewilderment giving way to one of overwhelming joy. He presses her close to him—slowly and tenderly).* Do you mean that—that you love me?

RUTH *(sobbing).* Yes, yes—of course I do—what d'you s'pose? *(She lifts up her head and looks into his eyes with a tremulous smile.)* You stupid thing! *(He kisses her.)* I've loved you right along.

ROBERT *(mystified).* But you and Andy were always together!

RUTH. Because you never seemed to want to go anyplace with me. You were always reading an old book, and not paying any attention to me. I was too proud to let you see I cared because I thought the year you had away to college had made you stuckup, and you thought yourself too educated to waste any time on me.

ROBERT *(kissing her).* And I was thinking—— *(With a laugh)* What fools we've both been!

RUTH *(overcome by a sudden fear).* You won't go away on the trip, will you, Rob? You'll tell them you can't go on account of me, won't you? You can't go now! You can't!

ROBERT *(bewildered).* Perhaps—you can come too.

RUTH. Oh, Rob, don't be so foolish. You know I can't. Who'd take care of ma? Don't you see I couldn't go—on her account? *(She clings to him imploringly.)* Please don't go—not now. Tell them you've decided not to. They won't mind. I know your mother and father'll be glad. They'll all be. They don't want you to go so far away from them. Please, Rob! We'll be so happy here together where it's natural and we know things. Please tell me you won't go!

ROBERT *(face to face with a definite,*

final decision, betrays the conflict going on within him). But—Ruth—I—Uncle Dick——

RUTH. He won't mind when he knows it's for your happiness to stay. How could he? *(As* ROBERT *remains silent, she bursts into sobs again.)* Oh, Rob! And you said—you loved me!

ROBERT *(conquered by this appeal—an irrevocable decision in his voice).* I won't go, Ruth. I promise you. There! Don't cry! *(He presses her to him, stroking her hair tenderly. After a pause he speaks with happy hopefulness.)* Perhaps after all Andy was right—righter than he knew—when he said I could find all the things I was seeking for here, at home on the farm. I think love must have been the secret—the secret that called to me from over the world's rim—the secret beyond every horizon; and when I did not come, it came to me. *(He clasps* RUTH *to him fiercely.)* Oh, Ruth, our love is sweeter than any distant dream! *(He kisses her passionately and steps to the ground, lifting* RUTH *in his arms and carrying her to the road where he puts her down.)*

RUTH *(with a happy laugh).* My, but you're strong!

ROBERT. Come! We'll go and tell them at once.

RUTH *(dismayed).* Oh, no, don't, Rob, not 'til after I've gone. There'd be bound to be such a scene with them all together.

ROBERT *(kissing her—gayly).* As you like—little Miss Common Sense!

RUTH. Let's go, then. *(She takes his hand, and they start to go off left.* ROBERT *suddenly stops and turns as though for a last look at the hills and the dying sunset flush.)*

ROBERT *(looking upward and pointing).* See! The first star. *(He bends down and kisses her tenderly.) Our* star!

RUTH *(in a soft murmur).* Yes. Our very own star. *(They stand for a moment looking up at it, their arms around each other. Then* RUTH *takes his hand again and starts to lead him away.)* Come, Rob, let's go. *(His eyes are fixed again on the*

horizon as he half turns to follow her. RUTH *urges.)* We'll be late for supper, Rob.

ROBERT *(shakes his head impatiently, as though he were throwing off some disturbing thought—with a laugh).* All right. We'll run then. Come on! *(They run off laughing as*

[*The Curtain Falls.*]

SCENE 2

The sitting room of the Mayo farmhouse about nine o'clock the same night. On the left, two windows looking out on the fields. Against the wall between the windows, an old-fashioned walnut desk. In the left corner, rear, a sideboard with a mirror. In the rear wall to the right of the sideboard, a window looking out on the road. Next to the window a door leading out into the yard. Farther right, a black horsehair sofa and another door opening on a bedroom. In the corner, a straight-backed chair. In the right wall, near the middle, an open doorway leading to the kitchen. Farther forward a double-heater stove with coal scuttle, etc. In the center of the newly carpeted floor, an oak dining-room table with a red cover. In the center of the table, a large oil reading lamp. Four chairs, three rockers with crocheted tidies on their backs and one straight-backed, are placed about the table. The walls are papered a dark red with a scrolly-figured pattern.

Everything in the room is clean, well kept, and in its exact place, yet there is no suggestion of primness about the whole. Rather the atmosphere is one of the orderly comfort of a simple, hard-earned prosperity, enjoyed and maintained by the family as a unit.

JAMES MAYO, *his wife, her brother,* CAPTAIN DICK SCOTT, *and* ANDREW *are discovered.* MAYO *is his son* ANDREW *over again in body and face—an* ANDREW *sixty-five years old with a short, square, white beard.* MRS. MAYO *is a slight, round-*

faced, rather prim-looking woman of fifty-five who had once been a schoolteacher. The labors of a farmer's wife have bent but not broken her, and she retains a certain refinement of movement and expression foreign to the MAYO part of the family. Whatever of resemblance ROBERT has to his parents may be traced to her. Her brother, the CAPTAIN, is short and stocky, with a weather-beaten, jovial face and a white mustache —a typical old salt, loud of voice and given to gesture. He is fifty-eight years old.

JAMES MAYO sits in front of the table. He wears spectacles, and a farm journal which he has been reading lies in his lap. The CAPTAIN leans forward from a chair in the rear, his hands on the table in front of him. ANDREW is tilted back on the straight-backed chair to the left, his chin sunk forward on his chest, staring at the carpet, preoccupied and frowning.

As the Curtain rises, the CAPTAIN is just finishing the relation of some sea episode. The others are pretending an interest which is belied by the absent-minded expressions on their faces.

THE CAPTAIN (chuckling). And that mission woman, she hails me on the dock as I was acomin' ashore, and she says— with her silly face all screwed up serious as judgment—"Captain," she says, "would you be so kind as to tell me where the sea gulls sleeps at nights?" Blow me if them warn't her exact words! (He slaps the table with the palm of his hands and laughs loudly. The others force smiles.) Ain't that just like a fool woman's question? And I looks at her serious as I could, "Ma'm," says I, "I couldn't rightly answer that question. I ain't never seed a sea gull in his bunk yet. The next time I hears one snorin'," I says, "I'll make a note of where he's turned in, and write you a letter 'bout it." And then she calls me a fool real spiteful and tacks away from me quick. (He laughs again uproariously.) So I got rid of her that way. (The others smile but immediately relapse

into expressions of gloom again.)

MRS. MAYO (absent-mindedly—feeling that she has to say something). But when it comes to that, where do sea gulls sleep, Dick?

SCOTT (slapping the table). Ho! Ho! Listen to her, James. 'Nother one! Well, if that don't beat all.

MAYO (with a twinkle in his eyes). They unhitch their wings, Katey, and spreads 'em out on a wave for a bed.

SCOTT. And then they tells the fish to whistle to 'em when it's time to turn out. Ho! Ho!

MRS. MAYO (with a forced smile). You men folks are too smart to live, aren't you? (She resumes her knitting. MAYO pretends to read his paper; ANDREW stares at the floor.)

SCOTT (looks from one to the other of them with a puzzled air. Finally he is unable to bear the thick silence a minute longer, and blurts out). You folks look as if you was settin' up with a corpse. (With exaggerated concern) There ain't anyone dead, be there?

MAYO (sharply). Don't play the dunce, Dick! You know as well as we do there ain't no great cause to be feelin' chipper.

SCOTT (argumentatively). And there ain't no cause to be wearin' mourning, either, I can make out.

MRS. MAYO (indignantly). How can you talk that way, Dick Scott, when you're taking our Robbie away from us, in the middle of the night, you might say, just to get on that old boat of yours on time! I think you might wait until morning when he's had his breakfast.

SCOTT (appealing to the others hopelessly). Ain't that a woman's way o' seein' things for you? I can't give orders to the tide that it's got to be high just when it suits me to have it. I ain't gettin' no fun out o' missin' sleep and leavin' here at six bells myself. (Protestingly) And the Sunda ain't an old ship—leastways, not very old—and she's good's she ever was.

MRS. MAYO (her lips trembling). I wish Robbie weren't going.

MAYO (looking at her over his glasses—

consolingly). There, Katey!

MRS. MAYO *(rebelliously).* Well, I *do* wish he wasn't!

SCOTT. You shouldn't be taking it so hard, 's far as I kin see. This vige'll make a man of him. I'll see to it he learns how to navigate, 'n' study for a mate's c'tificate right off—and it'll give him a trade for the rest of his life, if he wants to travel.

MRS. MAYO. But I don't want him to travel all his life. You've got to see he comes home when this trip is over. Then he'll be all well, and he'll want to—to marry—(ANDREW *sits forward in his chair with an abrupt movement)*—and settle down right here. *(She stares down at the knitting in her lap—after a pause.)* I never realized how hard it was going to be for me to have Robbie go—or I wouldn't have considered it a minute.

SCOTT. It ain't no good goin' on that way, Kate, now it's all settled.

MRS. MAYO *(on the verge of tears).* It's all right for *you* to talk. You've never had any children. You don't know what it means to be parted from them—and Robbie my youngest, too. (ANDREW *frowns and fidgets in his chair.)*

ANDREW *(suddenly turning to them).* There's one thing none of you seem to take into consideration—that Rob wants to go. He's dead set on it. He's been dreaming over this trip ever since it was first talked about. It wouldn't be fair to him not to have him go. *(A sudden uneasiness seems to strike him.)* At least, not if he still feels the same way about it he did when he was talking to me this evening.

MAYO *(with an air of decision).* Andy's right, Katey. That ends all argyment, you can see that. *(Looking at his big silver watch)* Wonder what's happened to Robert? He's been gone long enough to wheel the widder to home, certain. He can't be out dreamin' at the stars his last night.

MRS. MAYO *(a bit reproachfully).* Why didn't you wheel Mrs. Atkins back tonight, Andy? You usually do when she and Ruth come over.

ANDREW *(avoiding her eyes).* I thought maybe Robert wanted to tonight. He offered to go right away when they were leaving.

MRS. MAYO. He only wanted to be polite.

ANDREW *(gets to his feet).* Well, he'll be right back, I guess. *(He turns to his father.)* Guess I'll go take a look at the black cow, Pa—see if she's ailing any.

MAYO. Yes—better had, son. (ANDREW *goes into the kitchen on the right.)*

SCOTT *(as he goes out—in a low tone).* There's the boy that would make a good, strong seafarin' man—if he'd a mind to.

MAYO *(sharply).* Don't you put no such fool notions in Andy's head, Dick—or you 'n' me's goin' to fall out. *(Then he smiles.)* You couldn't tempt him, no ways. Andy's a Mayo bred in the bone, and he's a born farmer, and a damn good one, too. He'll live and die right here on this farm, like I expect to. *(With proud confidence)* And he'll make this one of the slickest, best-payin' farms in the state, too, afore he gits through!

SCOTT. Seems to me it's a pretty slick place right now.

MAYO *(shaking his head).* It's too small. We need more land to make it amount to much, and we ain't got the capital to buy it. (ANDREW *enters from the kitchen. His hat is on, and he carries a lighted lantern in his hand. He goes to the door in the rear leading out.)*

ANDREW *(opens the door and pauses).* Anything else you can think of to be done, Pa?

MAYO. No, nothin' I know of. (ANDREW *goes out, shutting the door.)*

MRS. MAYO *(after a pause).* What's come over Andy tonight, I wonder? He acts so strange.

MAYO. He does seem sort o' glum and out of sorts. It's 'count o' Robert leavin', I s'pose. *(To SCOTT)* Dick, you wouldn't believe how them boys o' mine sticks together. They ain't like most brothers. They've been thick as thieves all their lives, with nary a quarrel I kin remember.

SCOTT. No need to tell me that. I can see how they take to each other.

MRS. MAYO (*pursuing her train of thought*). Did you notice, James, how queer everyone was at supper? Robert seemed stirred up about something; and Ruth was so flustered and giggly; and Andy sat there dumb, looking as if he'd lost his best friend; and all of them only nibbled at their food.

MAYO. Guess they was all thinkin' about tomorrow, same as us.

MRS. MAYO (*shaking her head*). No. I'm afraid somethin's happened—somethin' else.

MAYO. You mean—'bout Ruth?

MRS. MAYO. Yes.

MAYO (*after a pause—frowning*). I hope her and Andy ain't had a serious fallin'-out. I always sorter hoped they'd hitch up together sooner or later. What d'you say, Dick? Don't you think them two'd pair up well?

SCOTT (*nodding his head approvingly*). A sweet, wholesome couple they'd make.

MAYO. It'd be a good thing for Andy in more ways than one. I ain't what you'd call calculatin' generally, and I b'lieve in lettin' young folks run their affairs to suit themselves; but there's advantages for both o' them in this match you can't overlook in reason. The Atkins farm is right next to ourn. Jined together they'd make a jim-dandy of a place, with plenty o' room to work in. And bein' a widder with only a daughter, and laid up all the time to boot, Mrs. Atkins can't do nothin' with the place as it ought to be done. She needs a man, a first-class farmer, to take hold o' things; and Andy's just the one.

MRS. MAYO (*abruptly*). I don't think Ruth loves Andy.

MAYO. You don't? Well, maybe a woman's eyes is sharper in such things, but—they're always together. And if she don't love him now, she'll likely come around to it in time. (*As* MRS. MAYO *shakes her head*) You seem mighty fixed in your opinion, Katey. How d'you know?

MRS. MAYO. It's just—what I feel.

MAYO (*a light breaking over him*). You don't mean to say—— (MRS. MAYO *nods.* MAYO *chuckles scornfully.*) Shucks! I'm losin' my respect for your eyesight, Katey. Why, Robert ain't got no time for Ruth, 'cept as a friend!

MRS. MAYO (*warningly*). Sss-h-h! (*The door from the yard opens, and* ROBERT *enters. He is smiling happily and humming a song to himself, but as he comes into the room, an undercurrent of nervous uneasiness manifests itself in his bearing.*)

MAYO. So here you be at last! (ROBERT *comes forward and sits on* ANDY'S *chair.* MAYO *smiles slyly at his wife.*) What have you been doin' all this time—countin' the stars to see if they all come out right and proper?

ROBERT. There's only one I'll ever look for any more, Pa.

MAYO (*reproachfully*). You might've even not wasted time lookin' for that one —your last night.

MRS. MAYO (*as if she were speaking to a child*). You ought to have worn your coat a sharp night like this, Robbie.

SCOTT (*disgustedly*). God A'mighty, Kate, you treat Robert as if he was one-year-old!

MRS. MAYO (*notices* ROBERT'S *nervous uneasiness*). You look all worked up over something, Robbie. What is it?

ROBERT (*swallowing hard, looks quickly from one to the other of them—then begins determinedly*). Yes, there *is* something—something I must tell you—all of you. (*As he begins to talk,* ANDREW *enters quietly from the rear, closing the door behind him and setting the lighted lantern on the floor. He remains standing by the door, his arms folded, listening to* ROBERT *with a repressed expression of pain on his face.* ROBERT *is so much taken up with what he is going to say that he does not notice* ANDREW'S *presence.*) Something I discovered only this evening—very beautiful and wonderful—something I did not take into consideration previously because I hadn't dared to hope that such happiness could ever come to me. (*Appealingly*) You must all remember that fact, won't you?

MAYO (*frowning*). Let's get to the point, son.

ROBERT (*with a trace of defiance*). Well, the point is this, Pa: I'm not going—I mean—I can't go tomorrow with Uncle Dick—or at any future time, either.

MRS. MAYO (*with a sharp sigh of joyful relief*). Oh, Robbie, I'm so glad!

MAYO (*astounded*). You ain't serious, be you, Robert? (*Severely*) Seems to me it's a pretty late hour in the day for you to be upsettin' all your plans so sudden!

ROBERT. I asked you to remember that until this evening I didn't know myself. I had never dared to dream——

MAYO (*irritably*). What is this foolishness you're talkin' of?

ROBERT (*flushing*). Ruth told me this evening that—she loved me. It was after I'd confessed I loved her. I told her I hadn't been conscious of my love until after the trip had been arranged, and I realized it would mean—leaving her. That was the truth. I *didn't* know until then. (*As if justifying himself to the others*) I hadn't intended telling her anything but— suddenly—I felt I must. I didn't think it would matter, because I was going away. And I thought she loved—someone else. (*Slowly—his eyes shining*) And then she cried and said it was I she'd loved all the time, but I hadn't seen it.

MRS. MAYO (*rushes over and throws her arms about him*). I knew it! I was just telling your father when you came in— and, oh, Robbie, I'm so happy you're not going!

ROBERT (*kissing her*). I knew you'd be glad, Ma.

MAYO (*bewilderedly*). Well, I'll be damned! You do beat all for gettin' folks' minds all tangled up, Robert. And Ruth too! Whatever got into her of a sudden? Why, I was thinkin'——

MRS. MAYO (*hurriedly—in a tone of warning*). Never mind what you were thinking, James. It wouldn't be any use telling us that now. (*Meaningly*) And what you were hoping for turns out just the same almost, doesn't it?

MAYO (*thoughtfully—beginning to see this side of the argument*). Yes; I suppose you're right, Katey. (*Scratching his* head in puzzlement) But how it ever come about! It do beat anything ever I heard. (*Finally he gets up with a sheepish grin and walks over to* ROBERT.) We're glad you ain't goin', your Ma and I, for we'd have missed you terrible, that's certain and sure; and we're glad you've found happiness. Ruth's a fine girl and'll make a good wife to you.

ROBERT (*much moved*). Thank you, Pa. (*He grips his father's hand in his.*)

ANDREW (*his face tense and drawn, comes forward and holds out his hand, forcing a smile*). I guess it's my turn to offer congratulations, isn't it?

ROBERT (*with a startled cry when his brother appears before him so suddenly*). Andy! (*Confused*) Why—I—I didn't see you. Were you here when——

ANDREW. I heard everything you said; and here's wishing you every happiness, you and Ruth. You both deserve the best there is.

ROBERT (*taking his hand*). Thanks, Andy, it's fine of you to—— (*His voice dies away as he sees the pain in* ANDREW'S *eyes.*)

ANDREW (*giving his brother's hand a final grip*). Good luck to you both! (*He turns away and goes back to the rear where he bends over the lantern, fumbling with it to hide his emotion from the others.*)

MRS. MAYO (*to the* CAPTAIN, *who has been too flabbergasted by* ROBERT'S *decision to say a word*). What's the matter, Dick? Aren't you going to congratulate Robbie?

SCOTT (*embarrassed*). Of course I be! (*He gets to his feet and shakes* ROBERT'S *hand, muttering a vague*) Luck to you, boy. (*He stands beside* ROBERT *as if he wanted to say something more but doesn't know how to go about it.*)

ROBERT. Thanks, Uncle Dick.

SCOTT. So you're not acomin' on the *Sunda* with me? (*His voice indicates disbelief.*)

ROBERT. I can't, Uncle—not now. I wouldn't miss it for anything else in the world under any other circumstances.

(He sighs unconsciously.) But you see I've found—a bigger dream. (Then with joyous high spirits) I want you all to understand one thing—I'm not going to be a loafer on your hands any longer. This means the beginning of a new life for me in every way. I'm going to settle right down and take a real interest in the farm, and do my share. I'll prove to you, Pa, that I'm as good a Mayo as you are—or Andy, when I want to be.

MAYO (kindly but skeptically). That's the right spirit, Robert. Ain't none of us doubts your willin'ness, but you ain't never learned——

ROBERT. Then I'm going to start learning right away, and you'll teach me, won't you?

MAYO (mollifyingly). Of course I will, boy, and be glad to, only you'd best go easy at first.

SCOTT (who has listened to this conversation in mingled consternation and amazement). You don't mean to tell me you're goin' to let him stay, do you, James?

MAYO. Why, things bein' as they be, Robert's free to do as he's a mind to.

MRS. MAYO. Let him! The very idea!

SCOTT (more and more ruffled). Then all I got to say is, you're a soft, weak-willed critter to be permittin' a boy—and women, too—to be layin' your course for you wherever they damn pleases.

MAYO (slyly amused). It's just the same with me as 'twas with you, Dick. You can't order the tides on the seas to suit you, and I ain't pretendin' I can reg'late love for young folks.

SCOTT (scornfully). Love! They ain't old enough to know love when they sight it! Love! I'm ashamed of you, Robert, to go lettin' a little huggin' and kissin' in the dark spile your chances to make a man out o' yourself. It ain't common sense—no siree, it ain't—not by a hell of a sight! (He pounds the table with his fists in exasperation.)

MRS. MAYO (laughing provokingly at her brother). A fine one you are to be talking about love, Dick—an old cranky bachelor like you. Goodness sakes!

SCOTT (exasperated by their joking). I've never been a damn fool like most, if that's what you're steerin' at.

MRS. MAYO (tauntingly). Sour grapes, aren't they, Dick? (She laughs. ROBERT and his father chuckle. SCOTT sputters with annoyance.) Good gracious, Dick, you do act silly, flying into a temper over nothing.

SCOTT (indignantly). Nothin'! You talk as if I wasn't concerned nohow in this here business. Seems to me I've got a right to have my say. Ain't I made all arrangements with the owners and stocked up with some special grub all on Robert's account?

ROBERT. You've been fine, Uncle Dick; and I appreciate it. Truly.

MAYO. 'Course; we all does, Dick.

SCOTT (unplacated). I've been countin' sure on havin' Robert for company on this vige—to sorta talk to and show things to, and teach, kinda, and I got my mind so set on havin' him I'm goin' to be double lonesome this vige. (He pounds on the table, attempting to cover up this confession of weakness.) Darn all this silly lovin' business, anyway. (Irritably) But all this talk ain't tellin' me what I'm to do with that sta'b'd [1] cabin I fixed up. It's all painted white, an' a bran new mattress on the bunk, 'n' new sheets 'n' blankets 'n' things. And Chips built in a bookcase so's Robert could take his books along—with a slidin' bar fixed across't it, mind, so's they couldn't fall out no matter how she rolled. (With excited consternation) What d'you suppose my officers is goin' to think when there's no one comes aboard to occupy that sta'b'd cabin? And the men what did the work on it—what'll they think? (He shakes his finger indignantly.) They're liable as not to suspicion it was a woman I'd planned to ship along, and that she gave me the go-by at the last moment! (He wipes

[1] sta'b'd: starboard.

his perspiring brow in anguish at this thought.) Gawd A'mighty! They're only lookin' to have the laugh on me for something like that. They're liable to b'lieve anything, those fellers is!

MAYO *(with a wink)*. Then there's nothing to it but for you to get right out and hunt up a wife somewheres for that spick 'n' span cabin. She'll have to be a pretty one, too, to match it. *(He looks at his watch with exaggerated concern.)* You ain't got much time to find her, Dick.

SCOTT *(as the others smile—sulkily)*. You kin go to thunder, Jim Mayo!

ANDREW *(comes forward from where he has been standing by the door, rear, brooding. His face is set in a look of grim determination)*. You needn't worry about that spare cabin, Uncle Dick, if you've a mind to take me in Robert's place.

ROBERT *(turning to him quickly)*. Andy! *(He sees at once the fixed resolve in his brother's eyes and realizes immediately the reason for it—in consternation.)* Andy, you mustn't!

ANDREW. You've made your decision, Rob, and now I've made mine. You're out of this, remember.

ROBERT *(hurt by his brother's tone)*. But Andy——

ANDREW. Don't interfere, Rob—that's all I ask. *(Turning to his uncle)* You haven't answered my question, Uncle Dick.

SCOTT *(clearing his throat, with an uneasy side glance at JAMES MAYO who is staring at his elder son as if he thought he had suddenly gone mad)*. O' course, I'd be glad to have you, Andy.

ANDREW. It's settled then. I can pack the little I want to take in a few minutes.

MRS. MAYO. Don't be a fool, Dick. Andy's only joking you.

SCOTT *(disgruntledly)*. It's hard to tell who's jokin' and who's not in this house.

ANDREW *(firmly)*. I'm not joking, Uncle Dick. *(As SCOTT looks at him uncertainly)* You needn't be afraid I'll go back on my word.

ROBERT *(hurt by the insinuation he feels in* ANDREW'S *tone)*. Andy! That isn't fair!

MAYO *(frowning)*. Seems to me this ain't no subject to joke over—not for Andy.

ANDREW *(facing his father)*. I agree with you, Pa, and I tell you again, once and for all, that I've made up my mind to go.

MAYO *(dumbfounded—unable to doubt the determination in* ANDREW'S *voice—helplessly)*. But why, son? Why?

ANDREW *(evasively)*. I've always wanted to go.

ROBERT. Andy!

ANDREW *(half angrily)*. You shut up, Rob! *(Turning to his father again)* I didn't ever mention it because as long as Rob was going I knew it was no use; but now Rob's staying on here, there isn't any reason for me not to go.

MAYO *(breathing hard)*. No reason? Can you stand there and say that to me, Andrew?

MRS. MAYO *(hastily—seeing the gathering storm)*. He doesn't mean a word of it, James.

MAYO *(making a gesture to her to keep silence)*. Let me talk, Katey. *(In a more kindly tone)* What's come over you so sudden, Andy? You know's well as I do that it wouldn't be fair o' you to run off at a moment's notice right now when we're up to our necks in hard work.

ANDREW *(avoiding his eyes)*. Rob'll hold his end up as soon as he learns.

MAYO. Robert was never cut out for a farmer, and you was.

ANDREW. You can easily get a man to do my work.

MAYO *(restraining his anger with an effort)*. It sounds strange to hear you, Andy, that I always thought had good sense, talkin' crazy like that. *(Scornfully)* Get a man to take your place! You ain't been workin' here for no hire, Andy, that you kin give me your notice to quit like you've done. The farm is your'n as well as mine. You've always worked on it with that understanding; and what you're sayin' you intend doin' is just skulkin' out o' your rightful responsibility.

ANDREW (looking at the floor—simply). I'm sorry, Pa. (After a slight pause) It's no use talking any more about it.

MRS. MAYO (in relief). There! I knew Andy'd come to his senses!

ANDREW. Don't get the wrong idea, Ma. I'm not backing out.

MAYO. You mean you're goin' in spite of—everythin'?

ANDREW. Yes. I'm going. I've got to. (He looks at his father defiantly.) I feel I oughtn't to miss this chance to go out into the world and see things, and—I want to go.

MAYO (with bitter scorn). So—you want to go out into the world and see thin's! (His voice raised and quivering with anger) I never thought I'd live to see the day when a son o' mine 'd look me in the face and tell a bare-faced lie! (Bursting out) You're a liar, Andy Mayo, and a mean one to boot!

MRS. MAYO. James!

ROBERT. Pa!

SCOTT. Steady there, Jim!

MAYO (waving their protests aside). He is and he knows it.

ANDREW (his face flushed). I won't argue with you, Pa. You can think as badly of me as you like.

MAYO (shaking his finger at ANDY, in a cold rage). You know I'm speakin' truth—that's why you're afraid to argy! You lie when you say you want to go 'way—and see thin's! You ain't got no likin' in the world to go. I've watched you grow up, and I know your ways, and they're my ways. You're runnin' against your own nature, and you're goin' to be a'mighty sorry for it if you do. 'S if I didn't know your real reason for runnin' away! And runnin' away's the only words to fit it. You're runnin' away 'cause you're put out and riled 'cause your own brother's got Ruth 'stead o' you, and——

ANDREW (his face crimson—tensely). Stop, Pa! I won't stand hearing that—not even from you!

MRS. MAYO (rushing to ANDY and putting her arms about him protectingly).

Don't mind him, Andy dear. He don't mean a word he's saying! (ROBERT stands rigidly, his hands clenched, his face contracted by pain. SCOTT sits dumbfounded and open-mouthed. ANDREW soothes his mother who is on the verge of tears.)

MAYO (in angry triumph). It's the truth, Andy Mayo! And you ought to be bowed in shame to think of it!

ROBERT (protestingly). Pa!

MRS. MAYO (coming from ANDREW to his father; puts her hands on his shoulders as though to try and push him back in the chair from which he has risen). Won't you be still, James? Please won't you?

MAYO (looking at ANDREW over his wife's shoulder—stubbornly). The truth—God's truth!

MRS. MAYO. Sh-h-h! (She tries to put a finger across his lips, but he twists his head away.)

ANDREW (who has regained control over himself). You're wrong, Pa, it isn't truth. (With defiant assertiveness) I don't love Ruth. I never loved her, and the thought of such a thing never entered my head.

MAYO (with an angry snort of disbelief). Hump! You're pilin' lie on lie!

ANDREW (losing his temper—bitterly). I suppose it'd be hard for you to explain anyone's wanting to leave this blessed farm except for some outside reason like that. But I'm sick and tired of it—whether you want to believe me or not—and that's why I'm glad to get a chance to move on.

ROBERT. Andy! Don't! You're only making it worse.

ANDREW (sulkily). I don't care. I've done my share of work here. I've earned my right to quit when I want to. (Suddenly overcome with anger and grief; with rising intensity) I'm sick and tired of the whole damn business. I hate the farm and every inch of ground in it. I'm sick of digging in the dirt and sweating in the sun like a slave without getting a word of thanks for it. (Tears of rage starting to his eyes—hoarsely) I'm through, through for good and all; and if Uncle Dick won't take me on his ship, I'll find another. I'll get away somewhere, somehow.

MRS. MAYO (*in a frightened voice*). Don't you answer him, James. He doesn't know what he's saying. Don't say a word to him 'til he's in his right senses again. Please James, don't——

MAYO (*pushes her away from him; his face is drawn and pale with the violence of his passion. He glares at* ANDREW *as if he hated him*). You dare to—you dare to speak like that to me? You talk like that 'bout this farm—the Mayo farm—where you was born—you—you—— (*He clenches his fist above his head and advances threateningly on* ANDREW.) You whelp!

MRS. MAYO (*with a shriek*). James! (*She covers her face with her hands and sinks weakly into* MAYO'S *chair.* ANDREW *remains standing motionless, his face pale and set.*)

SCOTT (*starting to his feet and stretching his arms across the table toward* MAYO). Easy there, Jim!

ROBERT (*throwing himself between father and brother*). Stop! Are you mad?

MAYO (*grabs* ROBERT'S *arm and pushes him aside—then stands for a moment gasping for breath before* ANDREW. *He points to the door with a shaking finger*). Yes—go!—go!—You're no son o' mine—no son o' mine! You can go to hell if you want to! Don't let me find you here—in the mornin'—or—or—I'll *throw* you out!

ROBERT. Pa! For God's sake! (MRS. MAYO *bursts into noisy sobbing.*)

MAYO (*he gulps convulsively and glares at* ANDREW). You go—tomorrow mornin' —and don't come back—don't dare come back—not while I'm livin'—or I'll—I'll —— (*He shakes over his muttered threat and strides toward the door rear, right.*)

MRS. MAYO (*rising and throwing her arms around him—hysterically*). James! James! Where are you going?

MAYO (*incoherently*). I'm goin'—to bed, Katey. It's late, Katey—it's late. (*He goes out.*)

MRS. MAYO (*following him, pleading hysterically*). James! Take back what you've said to Andy. James! (*She follows him out.* ROBERT *and the* CAPTAIN *stare after them with horrified eyes.* ANDREW *stands rigidly looking straight in front of him, his fists clenched at his sides.*)

SCOTT (*the first to find his voice—with an explosive sigh*). Well, if he ain't the devil himself when he's roused! You oughtn't to have talked to him that way, Andy, 'bout the farm, knowin' how touchy he is about it. (*With another sigh*) Well, you won't mind what he's said in anger. He'll be sorry for it when he's calmed down a bit.

ANDREW (*in a dead voice*). You don't know him. (*Defiantly*) What's said is said and can't be unsaid; and I've chosen.

ROBERT (*with violent protest*). Andy! You can't go! This is all so stupid—and terrible!

ANDREW (*coldly*). I'll talk to you in a minute, Rob. (*Crushed by his brother's attitude* ROBERT *sinks down into a chair, holding his head in his hands.*)

SCOTT (*comes and slaps* ANDREW *on the back*). I'm glad you're shippin' on, Andy. I like your spirit, and the way you spoke up to him. (*Lowering his voice to a cautious whisper*) The sea's the place for a young feller like you that isn't half dead 'n' alive. (*He gives* ANDY *a final approving slap.*) You 'n' me'll get along like twins, see if we don't. I'm goin' aloft to turn in. Don't forget to pack your dunnage. And git some sleep, if you kin. We'll want to sneak out extra early b'fore they're up. It'll do away with more argyments. Robert can drive us down to the town and bring back the team. (*He goes to the door in the rear, left.*) Well, good night.

ANDREW. Good night. (SCOTT *goes out. The two brothers remain silent for a moment. Then* ANDREW *comes over to his brother and puts a hand on his back. He speaks in a low voice, full of feeling.*) Buck up, Rob. It ain't any use crying over spilt milk; and it'll all turn out for the best —let's hope. It couldn't be helped— what's happened.

ROBERT (*wildly*). But it's a lie, Andy, a lie!

ANDREW. Of course it's a lie. You know it and I know it—but that's all ought to know it.

ROBERT. Pa'll never forgive you. Oh, the whole affair is so senseless—and tragic. Why did you think you must go away?

ANDREW. You know better than to ask that. You know why. (*Fiercely*) I can wish you and Ruth all the good luck in the world, and I do, and I mean it; but you can't expect me to stay around here and watch you two together, day after day—and me alone. I couldn't stand it—not after all the plans I'd made to happen on this place thinking—— (*His voice breaks*) thinking she cared for me.

ROBERT (*putting a hand on his brother's arm*). It's horrible! I feel so guilty—to think that I should be the cause of your suffering, after we've been such pals all our lives. If I could have foreseen what'd happen, I swear to you I'd have never said a word to Ruth. I swear I wouldn't have, Andy!

ANDREW. I know you wouldn't; and that would've been worse, for Ruth would've suffered then. (*He pats his brother's shoulder.*) It's best as it is. It had to be, and I've got to stand the gaff, that's all. Pa'll see how I felt—after a time (*As* ROBERT *shakes his head*)—and if he don't—well, it can't be helped.

ROBERT. But think of Ma! Andy, you can't go! You can't!

ANDREW (*fiercely*). I've got to go—to get away! I've got to, I tell you. I'd go crazy here, bein' reminded every second of the day what a fool I'd made of myself. I've got to get away and try and forget, if I can. And I'd hate the farm if I stayed, hate it for bringin' things back. I couldn't take interest in the work any more, work with no purpose in sight. Can't you see what a hell it'd be? You love her too, Rob. Put yourself in my place, and remember I haven't stopped loving her, and couldn't if I was to stay. Would that be fair to you or to her? Put yourself in my place. (*He shakes his brother fiercely by the shoulder.*) What'd you do then? Tell me the truth! You love her. What'd you do?

ROBERT (*chokingly*). I'd—I'd go, Andy! (*He buries his face in his hands with a shuddering sob.*) God!

ANDREW (*seeming to relax suddenly all over his body—in a low, steady voice*). Then you know why I got to go; and there's nothing more to be said.

ROBERT (*in a frenzy of rebellion*). Why did this have to happen to us? It's damnable! (*He looks about him wildly, as if his vengeance were seeking the responsible fate.*)

ANDREW (*soothingly—again putting his hands on his brother's shoulder*). It's no use fussing any more, Rob. It's done. (*Forcing a smile*) I guess Ruth's got a right to have who she likes. She made a good choice—and God bless her for it!

ROBERT. Andy! Oh, I wish I could tell you half I feel of how fine you are!

ANDREW (*interrupting him quickly*). Shut up! Let's go to bed. I've got to be up long before sunup. You, too, if you're going to drive us down.

ROBERT. Yes. Yes.

ANDREW (*turning down the lamp*). And I've got to pack yet. (*He yawns with utter weariness.*) I'm as tired as if I'd been plowing twenty-four hours at a stretch. (*Dully*) I feel—dead. (ROBERT *covers his face again with his hands.* ANDREW *shakes his head as if to get rid of his thoughts and continues with a poor attempt at cheery briskness.*) I'm going to douse the light. Come on. (*He slaps his brother on the back.* ROBERT *does not move.* ANDREW *bends over and blows out the lamp. His voice comes from the darkness.*) Don't sit there mourning, Rob. It'll all come out in the wash. Come on and get some sleep. Everything'll turn out all right in the end. (ROBERT *can be heard stumbling to his feet, and the dark figures of the two brothers can be seen groping their way toward the doorway in the rear as*

[*The Curtain Falls.*]

COMMENTARY

O'Neill's starkly dramatic way of looking at the world should be apparent after reading Act I. He works in harsh contrasts, which are established even in his initial description of the scenery. The promise conveyed by the road and the rolling hills is juxtaposed against the sense of containment and restriction of the stone wall, the ditch, and the fence. The lush fertility suggested by the young green stalks of rye contrasts with the gnarled old apple tree, which "strains its twisted branches heavenward." Even the time of day, sunset, has a feeling of tension, beautiful now but transitory, leading to the bleak night. As the curtain rises on this play, then, we are shown a world of opposition and contrast—openness and containment, aspiration and despair.

When we consider the appearances and behavior of Robert and Andrew Mayo, moreover, we are again dealing with opposites: "a touch of the poet" as against "a son of the soil," the book opposed to the hoe, the flashy, romantic clothes opposed to overalls. What is "dirt" to Robert is "good clean earth" to Andrew, while the poetry which the younger brother admires is simply "stuff" to the elder. For all these contrasts, no one is particularly unhappy at the beginning of the play. Each youth has staked out his respective claim on life, just as the land behind them has been ordered and divided up, and the truce between the two points of view appears to be a genial and healthy one. The world may be a world of tension and contrast, but these youths seem to have realized it, and each has committed himself to his own sphere.

Yet before the first scene has progressed very far, we see these firm boundaries of interest become confused and muddied by the influence of a woman. To Robert, Ruth seems to bring together the world of romantic dreams and the world of tangible reality; her very presence is a concrete personification of all he has longed for. And before they return to the farmhouse, when we hear Robert and Ruth talking about their "very own star," we may wonder whether there isn't something ironic about their referring to something so unattainable in such possessive terms. Ruth's character is still unclear to us at the end of the first scene, but we know Robert well enough to feel that he can never be "wedded to the soil."

The second scene develops the themes introduced in the first scene. The setting itself continues to reflect the basic opposition: a neat, orderly, contained interior contrasts immediately with the expansive openness of the out-of-doors, where Robert likes to read and dream. The contrast is further developed in the characters of the two parents: James Mayo, the vigorous, no-nonsense farmer as opposed to Katey, the mother, with her schoolteacher background and her "certain refinement of movement." Before Robert's supposed departure and again when he decides to stay, the parental differences come out clearly. The vague shadow of Ruth, which broods over this scene, has blotted out the clear-cut, accepted lines of separation which we saw at the beginning of the play. Truthful awareness has turned into a lie for all three men: the father lies in rejecting Andrew; Andrew lies in his turning to a sea voyage; and Robert lies in insisting on his romantic infatuation with Ruth.

Moreover, it seems at this point that women, in their urge to combine and blend and modify the clean contrasts accepted by men, are to some extent the cause of the difficulty. Ruth's role has already been discussed. Mrs. Mayo's maternal, pacifying attempts only make the situation worse. O'Neill suggests that the influence of women befuddles and complicates the clean lines of male commitment. The strong men in the play either reject women, avoid them, or overrule them. Even Ruth's invalid mother has a disturbing, inhibiting influence which prevents Robert and Ruth from at least leaving the farm together.

1. What kind of men are Robert and Andrew Mayo? How does Eugene O'Neill bring out the differences between these two characters at the very beginning of *Beyond the Horizon*? In answering, remember the importance of staging devices as well as dialogue. How, at the beginning of Scene 1, are Robert and Andrew characterized by actions as well as words?

2. Where in Scene 1 is the issue of Ruth first introduced? What happens to the relationship between the two brothers at even the mention of her name?

3. Compare Robert's relationship with his brother to his relationship with Ruth. Which would you say is the deeper relationship? Defend your answers with specific references to the play.

4. In Scene 1 we hear about James Mayo, Captain Scott, and Mrs. Mayo long before we meet them in Scene 2. In what ways and how well does O'Neill prepare us for the kind of characters that James Mayo, Mrs. Mayo, and Captain Scott turn out to be?

5. Locate some of the references to sickness in Act I. How does the idea of sickness relate to what O'Neill seems to be saying about the nature of Robert's dream?

6. What is the poetic difference between the sea and the land: what connotations are normally associated with each? Discuss how O'Neill uses imagery associated with the sea.

7. There are several references to stars in Act I. What is a star generally a symbol of? How is a star used as a symbol in this act of the play?

8. What other images or patterns of imagery run through Act I?

9. How does Captain Scott contribute to what appears to be the general issue of the play? Consider not only how he affects the plot, but also what he seems to stand for.

10. Consider in more detail Captain Scott's remarks about the old mission woman and her question on sea gulls. How is this speech significant in the play? How does it convey the difference between a sea and a land point of view?

11. Thus far, how would you say that *Beyond the Horizon* is developing, according to your ideas of tragedy? (You may wish to review the discussion of tragedy on pages 751 and 854.)

ACT II

SCENE 1

Same as Act I, Scene 2. Sitting room of the farmhouse about half past twelve in the afternoon of a hot, sun-baked day in midsummer, three years later. All the windows are open, but no breeze stirs the soiled white curtains. A patched screen door is in the rear. Through it the yard can be seen, its small stretch of lawn divided by the dirt path leading to the door from the gate in the white picket fence which borders the road.

The room has changed, not so much in its outward appearance as in its general atmosphere. Little significant details give evidence of carelessness, of inefficiency, of an industry gone to seed. The chairs appear shabby from lack of paint; the table cover is spotted and askew; holes show in the curtains; a child's doll, with one arm gone, lies under the table; a hoe stands in a corner; a man's coat is flung on the couch in the rear; the desk is cluttered up with odds and ends; a number of books are piled carelessly on the sideboard. The noon enervation of the sultry, scorching day seems to have penetrated indoors, causing even inanimate objects to wear an aspect of despondent exhaustion.

A place is set at the end of the table, left, for someone's dinner. Through the open door to the kitchen comes the clatter of dishes being washed, interrupted at intervals by a woman's irritated voice and the peevish whining of a child.

At the rise of the curtain MRS. MAYO *and* MRS. ATKINS *are discovered sitting facing each other,* MRS. MAYO *to the rear,* MRS. ATKINS *to the right of the table.* MRS. MAYO'S *face has lost all character, disintegrated, become a weak mask wearing a helpless, doleful expression of being constantly on the verge of comfortless tears. She speaks in an uncertain voice, without assertiveness, as if all power of willing had deserted her.* MRS. ATKINS *is*

in her wheelchair. She is a thin, pale-faced, unintelligent-looking woman of about forty-eight, with hard, bright eyes. A victim of partial paralysis for many years, condemned to be pushed from day to day of her life in a wheelchair, she has developed the selfish, irritable nature of the chronic invalid. Both women are dressed in black. MRS. ATKINS knits nervously as she talks. A ball of unused yarn, with needles stuck through it, lies on the table before MRS. MAYO.

MRS. ATKINS (with a disapproving glance at the place set on the table). Robert's late for his dinner again, as usual. I don't see why Ruth puts up with it, and I've told her so. Many's the time I've said to her "It's about time you put a stop to his nonsense. Does he suppose you're runnin' a hotel—with no one to help with things?" But she don't pay no attention. She's as bad as he is, a'most—thinks she knows better than an old, sick body like me.

MRS. MAYO (dully). Robbie's always late for things. He can't help it, Sarah.

MRS. ATKINS (with a snort). Can't help it! How you do go on, Kate, findin' excuses for him! Anybody can help anything they've a mind to—as long as they've got health and ain't rendered helpless like me—(She adds as a pious afterthought)—through the will of God.

MRS. MAYO. Robbie can't.

MRS. ATKINS. Can't! It do make me mad, Kate Mayo, to see folks that God gave all the use of their limbs to potterin' round and wastin' time doin' everything the wrong way—and me powerless to help and at their mercy, you might say. And it ain't that I haven't pointed the right way to 'em. I've talked to Robert thousands of times and told him how things ought to be done. You know that, Kate Mayo. But d'you s'pose he takes any notice of what I say? Or Ruth, either—my own daughter? No, they think I'm a crazy, cranky old woman, half dead a'ready, and the sooner I'm in the grave and out o' their way the better it'd suit them.

MRS. MAYO. You mustn't talk that way, Sarah. They're not as wicked as that. And you've got years and years before you.

MRS. ATKINS. You're like the rest, Kate. You don't know how near the end I am. Well, at least I can go to my eternal rest with a clear conscience. I've done all a body could do to avert ruin from this house. On their heads be it!

MRS. MAYO (with hopeless indifference). Things might be worse. Robert never had any experience in farming. You can't expect him to learn in a day.

MRS. ATKINS (snappily). He's had three years to learn, and he's gettin' worse 'stead of better. Not on'y your place but mine too is driftin' to rack and ruin, and I can't do nothin' to prevent.

MRS. MAYO (with a spark of assertiveness). You can't say but Robbie works hard, Sarah.

MRS. ATKINS. What good's workin' hard if it don't accomplish anythin', I'd like to know?

MRS. MAYO. Robbie's had bad luck against him.

MRS. ATKINS. Say what you've a mind to, Kate, the proof of the puddin's in the eatin'; and you can't deny that things have been goin' from bad to worse ever since your husband died two years back.

MRS. MAYO (*wiping tears from her eyes with her handkerchief*). It was God's will that he should be taken.

MRS. ATKINS (*triumphantly*). It was God's punishment on James Mayo for the blasphemin' and denyin' of God he done all his sinful life! (MRS. MAYO *begins to weep softly.*) There, Kate, I shouldn't be remindin' you, I know. He's at peace, poor man, and forgiven, let's pray.

MRS. MAYO (*wiping her eyes—simply*). James was a good man.

MRS. ATKINS (*ignoring this remark*). What I was sayin' was that since Robert's been in charge things've been goin' downhill steady. You don't know *how* bad they are. Robert don't let on to you what's happenin'; and you'd never see it yourself if 'twas under your nose. But, thank the Lord, Ruth still comes to me once in a while for advice when she's worried near out of her senses by his goin's-on. Do you know what she told me last night? But I forgot, she said not to tell you—still I think you've got a right to know, and it's my duty not to let such things go on behind your back.

MRS. MAYO (*wearily*). You can tell me if you want to.

MRS. ATKINS (*bending over toward her —in a low voice*). Ruth was almost crazy about it. Robert told her he'd have to mortgage the farm—said he didn't know how he'd pull through 'til harvest without it, and he can't get money any other way. (*She straightens up—indignantly.*) Now what do you think of your Robert?

MRS. MAYO (*resignedly*). If it has to be——

MRS. ATKINS. You don't mean to say you're goin' to sign away your farm. Kate Mayo—after me warnin' you?

MRS. MAYO. I'll do what Robbie says is needful.

MRS. ATKINS (*holding up her hands*). Well, of all the foolishness!—well, it's your farm, not mine, and I've nothin' more to say.

MRS. MAYO. Maybe Robbie'll manage till Andy gets back and sees to things. It can't be long now.

MRS. ATKINS (*with keen interest*). Ruth says Andy ought to turn up any day. When does Robert figger he'll get here?

MRS. MAYO. He says he can't calculate exactly on account o' the *Sunda* being a sailboat. Last letter he got was from England, the day they were sailing for home. That was over a month ago, and Robbie thinks they're overdue now.

MRS. ATKINS. We can give praise to God then that he'll be back in the nick o' time. He ought to be tired of travelin' and anxious to get home and settle down to work again.

MRS. MAYO. Andy *has* been working. He's head officer on Dick's boat, he wrote Robbie. You know that.

MRS. ATKINS. That foolin' on ships is all right for a spell, but he must be right sick of it by this.

MRS. MAYO (*musingly*). I wonder if he's changed much. He used to be so fine-looking and strong. (*With a sigh*) Three years! It seems more like three hundred. (*Her eyes filling—piteously*) Oh, if James could only have lived 'til he came back—and forgiven him!

MRS. ATKINS. He never would have— not James Mayo! Didn't he keep his heart hardened against him till the last in spite of all you and Robert did to soften him?

MRS. MAYO (*with a feeble flash of anger*). Don't you dare say that! (*Brokenly*) Oh, I know deep down in his heart he forgave Andy, though he was too stubborn ever to own up to it. It was that brought on his death—breaking his heart just on account of his stubborn pride. (*She wipes her eyes with her handkerchief and sobs.*)

MRS. ATKINS (*piously*). It was the will of God. (*The whining crying of the child sounds from the kitchen.* MRS. ATKINS *frowns irritably.*) Drat that young one! Seems as if she cries all the time on purpose to set a body's nerves on edge.

MRS. MAYO (*wiping her eyes*). It's the

heat upsets her. Mary doesn't feel any too well these days, poor little child!

MRS. ATKINS. She gets it right from her Pa—bein' sickly all the time. You can't deny Robert was always ailin' as a child. (*She sighs heavily.*) It was a crazy mistake for them two to get married. I argued against it at the time, but Ruth was so spelled with Robert's wild poetry notions she wouldn't listen to sense. Andy was the one would have been the match for her.

MRS. MAYO. I've often thought since it might have been better the other way. But Ruth and Robbie seem happy enough together.

MRS. ATKINS. At any rate it was God's work—and His will be done. (*The two women sit in silence for a moment.* RUTH *enters from the kitchen, carrying in her arms her two-year-old daughter,* MARY, *a pretty but sickly and anemic-looking child with a tear-stained face.* RUTH *has aged appreciably. Her face has lost its youth and freshness. There is a trace in her expression of something hard and spiteful. She sits in the rocker in front of the table and sighs wearily. She wears a gingham dress with a soiled apron tied around her waist.*)

RUTH. Land sakes, if this isn't a scorcher! That kitchen's like a furnace. Phew! (*She pushes the damp hair back from her forehead.*)

MRS. MAYO. Why didn't you call me to help with the dishes?

RUTH (*shortly*). No. The heat in there'd kill you.

MARY (*sees the doll under the table and struggles on her mother's lap*). Dolly, Mama! Dolly!

RUTH (*pulling her back*). It's time for your nap. You can't play with Dolly now.

MARY (*commencing to cry whiningly*). Dolly!

MRS. ATKINS (*irritably*). Can't you keep that child still? Her racket's enough to split a body's ears. Put her down and let her play with the doll if it'll quiet her.

RUTH (*lifting* MARY *to the floor*). There! I hope you'll be satisfied and keep still. (MARY *sits down on the floor before the table and plays with the doll in silence.* RUTH *glances at the place set on the table.*) It's a wonder Rob wouldn't try to get to meals on time once in a while.

MRS. MAYO (*dully*). Something must have gone wrong again.

RUTH (*wearily*). I s'pose so. Something's always going wrong these days, it looks like.

MRS. ATKINS (*snappily*). It wouldn't if you possessed a bit of spunk. The idea of you permittin' him to come in to meals at all hours—and you doin' the work! I never heard of such a thin'. You're too easy goin', that's the trouble.

RUTH. Do stop your nagging at me, Ma! I'm sick of hearing you. I'll do as I please about it; and thank you for not interfering. (*She wipes her moist forehead—wearily.*) Phew! It's too hot to argue. Let's talk of something pleasant. (*Curiously*) Didn't I hear you speaking about Andy a while ago?

MRS. MAYO. We were wondering when he'd get home.

RUTH (*brightening*). Rob says any day now he's liable to drop in and surprise us —him and the Captain. It'll certainly look natural to see him around the farm again.

MRS. ATKINS. Let's hope the farm'll look more natural, too, when he's had a hand at it. The way thin's are now!

RUTH (*irritably*). Will you stop harping on that, Ma? We all know things aren't as they might be. What's the good of your complaining all the time?

MRS. ATKINS. There, Kate Mayo. Ain't that just what I told you? I can't say a word of advice to my own daughter even, she's that stubborn and self-willed.

RUTH (*putting her hands over her ears —in exasperation*). For goodness sakes, Ma!

MRS. MAYO (*dully*). Never mind. Andy'll fix everything when he comes.

RUTH (*hopefully*). Oh, yes, I know he will. He always did know just the right thing ought to be done. (*With weary vexation*) It's a shame for him to come home and have to start in with things in such a topsy-turvy.

MRS. MAYO. Andy'll manage.

RUTH (*sighing*). I s'pose it isn't Rob's fault things go wrong with him.

MRS. ATKINS (*scornfully*). Hump! (*She fans herself nervously.*) Land o' Goshen, but it's bakin' in here! Let's go out in under the trees in back where there's a breath of fresh air. Come, Kate. (MRS. MAYO *gets up obediently and starts to wheel the invalid's chair toward the screen door.*) You better come too, Ruth. It'll do you good. Learn him a lesson and let him get his own dinner. Don't be such a fool.

RUTH (*going and holding the screen door open for them—listlessly*). He wouldn't mind. He doesn't eat much. But I can't go anyway. I've got to put baby to bed.

MRS. ATKINS. Let's go, Kate. I'm boilin' in here. (MRS. MAYO *wheels her out and off left.* RUTH *comes back and sits down in her chair.*)

RUTH (*mechanically*). Come and let me take off your shoes and stockings, Mary, that's a good girl. You've got to take your nap now. (*The child continues to play as if*

she hadn't heard, absorbed in her doll. An eager expression comes over RUTH'S tired face. She glances toward the door furtively—then gets up and goes to the desk. Her movements indicate a guilty fear of discovery. She takes a letter from a pigeonhole and retreats swiftly to her chair with it. She opens the envelope and reads the letter with great interest, a flush of excitement coming to her cheeks. ROBERT walks up the path and opens the screen door quietly and comes into the room. He, too, has aged. His shoulders are stooped as if under too great a burden. His eyes are dull and lifeless, his face burned by the sun and unshaven for days. Streaks of sweat have smudged the layer of dust on his cheeks. His lips, drawn down at the corners, give him a hopeless, resigned expression. The three years have accentuated the weakness of his mouth and chin. He is dressed in overalls, laced boots, and a flannel shirt open at the neck.*)

ROBERT (*throwing his hat over on the sofa—with a great sigh of exhaustion*). Phew! The sun's hot today! (RUTH *is startled. At first she makes an instinctive motion as if to hide the letter in her bosom. She immediately thinks better of this and sits with the letter in her hands, looking at him with defiant eyes. He bends down and kisses her.*)

RUTH (*feeling of her cheek—irritably*). Why don't you shave? You look awful.

ROBERT (*indifferently*). I forgot—and it's too much trouble in this weather.

MARY (*throwing aside her doll, runs to him with a happy cry*). Dada! Dada!

ROBERT (*swinging her up above his head—lovingly*). And how's this little girl of mine this hot day, eh?

MARY (*screeching happily*). Dada! Dada!

RUTH (*in annoyance*). Don't do that to her! You know it's time for her nap and you'll get her all waked up; then I'll be the one that'll have to sit beside her till she falls asleep.

ROBERT (*sitting down in the chair on the*

left of table and cuddling MARY *on his lap).* You needn't bother. I'll put her to bed.

RUTH *(shortly).* You've got to get back to your work, I s'pose.

ROBERT *(with a sigh).* Yes, I was forgetting. *(He glances at the open letter on* RUTH'S *lap.)* Reading Andy's letter again? I should think you'd know it by heart by this time.

RUTH *(coloring as if she'd been accused of something—defiantly).* I've got a right to read it, haven't I? He says it's meant for all of us.

ROBERT *(with a trace of irritation).* Right? Don't be so silly. There's no question of right. I was only saying that you must know all that's in it after so many readings.

RUTH. Well, I don't. *(She puts the letter on the table and gets wearily to her feet.)* I s'pose you'll be wanting your dinner now.

ROBERT *(listlessly).* I don't care. I'm not hungry.

RUTH. And here I been keeping it hot for you!

ROBERT *(irritably).* Oh, all right then. Bring it in and I'll try to eat.

RUTH. I've got to get her to bed first. *(She goes to lift* MARY *off his lap.)* Come, dear. It's after time and you can hardly keep your eyes open now.

MARY *(crying).* No, no! *(Appealing to her father)* Dada! No!

RUTH *(accusingly to* ROBERT*).* There! Now see what you've done! I told you not to——

ROBERT *(shortly).* Let her alone, then. She's all right where she is. She'll fall asleep on my lap in a minute if you'll stop bothering her.

RUTH *(hotly).* She'll not do any such thing! She's got to learn to mind me! *(Shaking her finger at* MARY.*)* You naughty child! Will you come with Mama when she tells you for your own good?

MARY *(clinging to her father).* No, Dada!

RUTH *(losing her temper).* A good spanking's what you need, my young lady —and you'll get one from me if you don't mind better, d'you hear? *(*MARY *starts to whimper frightenedly.)*

ROBERT *(with sudden anger).* Leave her alone! How often have I told you not to threaten her with whipping? I won't have it. *(Soothing the wailing* MARY*)* There! There, little girl! Baby mustn't cry. Dada won't like you if you do. Dada'll hold you and you must promise to go to sleep like a good little girl. Will you when Dada asks you?

MARY *(cuddling up to him).* Yes, Dada.

RUTH *(looking at them, her pale face set and drawn).* A fine one you are to be telling folks how to do things! *(She bites her lips. Husband and wife look into each other's eyes with something akin to hatred in their expressions; then* RUTH *turns away with a shrug of affected indifference.)* All right, take care of her then, if you think it's so easy. *(She walks away into the kitchen.)*

ROBERT *(smoothing* MARY'S *hair—tenderly).* We'll show Mama you're a good little girl, won't we?

MARY *(crooning drowsily).* Dada, Dada.

ROBERT. Let's see: Does your mother take off your shoes and stockings before your nap?

MARY *(nodding with half-shut eyes).* Yes, Dada.

ROBERT *(taking off her shoes and stockings).* We'll show Mama we know how to do those things, won't we? There's one old shoe off—and there's the other old shoe—and here's one old stocking—and there's the other old stocking. There we are, all nice and cool and comfy. *(He bends down and kisses her.)* And now will you promise to go right to sleep if Dada takes you to bed? *(*MARY *nods sleepily.)* That's the good little girl. *(He gathers her up in his arms carefully and carries her into the bedroom. His voice can be heard faintly as he lulls the child to sleep.* RUTH *comes out of the kitchen and gets the plate from the table. She hears the voice from the room and tiptoes to the door to look in.*

Then she starts for the kitchen but stands for a moment thinking, a look of ill-concealed jealousy on her face. At a noise from inside she hurriedly disappears into the kitchen. A moment later ROBERT *re-enters. He comes forward and picks up the shoes and stockings which he shoves carelessly under the table. Then, seeing no one about, he goes to the sideboard and selects a book. Coming back to his chair, he sits down and immediately becomes absorbed in reading.* RUTH *returns from the kitchen, bringing his plate heaped with food and a cup of tea. She sets those before him and sits down in her former place.* ROBERT *continues to read, oblivious to the food on the table.)*

RUTH *(after watching him irritably for a moment).* For heaven's sakes, put down that old book! Don't you see your dinner's getting cold?

ROBERT *(closing his book).* Excuse me, Ruth. I didn't notice. *(He picks up his knife and fork and begins to eat gingerly, without appetite.)*

RUTH. I should think you might have some feeling for me, Rob, and not always be late for meals. If you think it's fun sweltering in that oven of a kitchen to keep things warm for you, you're mistaken.

ROBERT. I'm sorry, Ruth, really I am. Something crops up every day to delay me. I mean to be here on time.

RUTH *(with a sigh).* Mean-tos don't count.

ROBERT *(with a conciliating smile).* Then punish me, Ruth. Let the food get cold and don't bother about me.

RUTH. I'd have to wait just the same to wash up after you.

ROBERT. But I can wash up.

RUTH. A nice mess there'd be then!

ROBERT *(with an attempt at lightness).* The food is lucky to be able to get cold this weather. *(As* RUTH *doesn't answer or smile he opens his book and resumes his reading, forcing himself to take a mouthful of food every now and then.* RUTH *stares at him in annoyance.)*

RUTH. And besides, you've got your own work that's got to be done.

ROBERT *(absent-mindedly, without taking his eyes from the book).* Yes, of couse.

RUTH *(spitefully).* Work you'll never get done by reading books all the time.

ROBERT *(shutting the book with a snap).* Why do you persist in nagging at me for getting pleasure out of reading? Is it because—— *(He checks himself abruptly.)*

RUTH *(coloring).* Because I'm too stupid to understand them, I s'pose you were going to say.

ROBERT *(shamefacedly).* No—no. *(In exasperation)* Why do you goad me into saying things I don't mean? Haven't I got my share of troubles trying to work this cursed farm without your adding to them? You know how hard I've tried to keep things going in spite of bad luck——

RUTH *(scornfully).* Bad luck!

ROBERT. And my own very apparent unfitness for the job, I was going to add; but you can't deny there's been bad luck to it, too. Why don't you take things into consideration? Why can't we pull together? We used to. I know it's hard on you also. Then why can't we help each other instead of hindering?

RUTH *(sullenly).* I do the best I know how.

ROBERT *(gets up and puts his hand on her shoulder).* I know you do. But let's both of us try to do better. We can both improve. Say a word of encouragement once in a while when things go wrong, even if it is my fault. You know the odds I've been up against since Pa died. I'm not a farmer. I've never claimed to be one. But there's nothing else I can do under the circumstances, and I've got to pull things through somehow. With your help, I can do it. With you against me— *(He shrugs his shoulders. There is a pause. Then he bends down and kisses her hair—with an attempt at cheerfulness.)* So you promise that; and I'll promise to be here when the clock strikes—and anything else you tell me to. Is it a bargain?

RUTH *(dully).* I s'pose so. *(They are in-*

terrupted by the sound of a loud knock at the kitchen door.) There's someone at the kitchen door. (She hurries out. A moment later she reappears.) It's Ben.

ROBERT (frowning). What's the trouble now, I wonder? (In a loud voice) Come on in here, Ben. (BEN slouches in from the kitchen. He is a hulking, awkward young fellow with a heavy, stupid face and shifty, cunning eyes. He is dressed in overalls, boots, etc., and wears a broad-brimmed hat of coarse straw pushed back on his head.) Well, Ben, what's the matter?

BEN (drawlingly). The mowin' machine's bust.

ROBERT. Why, that can't be. The man fixed it only last week.

BEN. It's bust just the same.

ROBERT. And can't you fix it?

BEN. No. Don't know what's the matter with the goll-darned thing. 'Twon't work, anyhow.

ROBERT (getting up and going for his hat). Wait a minute and I'll go look it over. There can't be much the matter with it.

BEN (impudently). Don't make no diff'-rence t' me whether there be or not. I'm quittin'.

ROBERT (anxiously). You don't mean you're throwing up your job here?

BEN. That's what! My month's up today and I want what's owin' t' me.

ROBERT. But why are you quitting now, Ben, when you know I've so much work on hand? I'll have a hard time getting another man at such short notice.

BEN. That's for you to figger. I'm quittin'.

ROBERT. But what's your reason? You haven't any complaint to make about the way you've been treated, have you?

BEN. No. 'Tain't that. (Shaking his finger) Look-a-here. I'm sick o' being made fun at, that's what; an' I got a job up to Timms' place; an' I'm quittin' here.

ROBERT. Being made fun of? I don't understand you. Who's making fun of you?

BEN. They all do. When I drive down with the milk in the mornin' they all laughs and jokes at me—that boy up to Harris' and the new feller up to Slocum's, and Bill Evans down to Meade's, and all the rest on 'em.

ROBERT. That's a queer reason for leaving me flat. Won't they laugh at you just the same when you're working for Timms?

BEN. They wouldn't dare to. Timms is the best farm hereabouts. They was laughin' at me for workin' for you, that's what! "How're things up to the Mayo place?" they hollers every mornin'. "What's Robert doin' now—pasturin' the cattle in the cornlot? Is he seasonin' his hay with rain this year, same as last?" they shouts. "Or is he inventin' some 'lectrical milkin' engine to fool them dry cows o' his into givin' hard cider?" (Very much ruffled) That's like they talks; and I ain't goin' to put up with it no longer. Everyone's always knowed me as a first-class hand hereabouts, and I ain't wantin' 'em to get no different notion. So I'm quittin' you. And I wants what's comin' to me.

ROBERT (coldly). Oh, if that's the case, you can go to the devil. You'll get your money tomorrow when I get back from town—not before!

BEN (turning to doorway to kitchen). That suits me. (As he goes out he speaks back over his shoulder.) And see that I do get it, or there'll be trouble. (He disappears and the slamming of the kitchen door is heard.)

ROBERT (as RUTH comes from where she has been standing by the doorway and sits down dejectedly in her old place). The stupid fool! And now what about the haying? That's an example of what I'm up against. No one can say I'm responsible for that.

RUTH. He wouldn't dare act that way with anyone else! (Spitefully, with a glance at ANDREW's letter on the table) It's lucky Andy's coming back.

ROBERT (without resentment). Yes, Andy'll see the right thing to do in a jiffy. (With an affectionate smile) I wonder if the old chump's changed much? He doesn't seem to from his letters, does he? (Shaking his head) But just the same I doubt if he'll want to settle down to a humdrum farm life, after all he's been through.

RUTH (*resentfully*). Andy's not like you. He likes the farm.

ROBERT (*immersed in his own thoughts—enthusiastically*). Gad, the things he's seen and experienced! Think of the places he's been! All the wonderful far places I used to dream about! God, how I envy him! What a trip! (*He springs to his feet and instinctively goes to the window and stares out at the horizon.*)

RUTH (*bitterly*). I s'pose you're sorry now you didn't go?

ROBERT (*too occupied with his own thoughts to hear her—vindictively*). Oh, those cursed hills out there that I used to think promised me so much! How I've grown to hate the sight of them! They're like the walls of a narrow prison yard shutting me in from all the freedom and wonder of life! (*He turns back to the room with a gesture of loathing.*) Sometimes I think if it wasn't for you, Ruth, and—(*His voice softening*)—little Mary, I'd chuck everything up and walk down the road with just one desire in my heart—to put the whole rim of the world between me and those hills and be able to breathe freely once more! (*He sinks down into his chair and smiles with bitter self-scorn.*) There I go dreaming again—my old fool dreams.

RUTH (*in a low, repressed voice—her eyes smoldering*). You're not the only one!

ROBERT (*buried in his own thoughts—bitterly*). And Andy, who's had the chance—what has he got out of it? His letters read like the diary of a—of a farmer! "We're in Singapore now. It's a dirty hole of a place and hotter than hell. Two of the crew are down with fever and we're short-handed on the work. I'll be glad when we sail again, although tacking back and forth in these blistering seas is a rotten job too!" (*Scornfully*) That's about the way he summed up his impressions of the East.

RUTH (*her repressed voice trembling*). You needn't make fun of Andy.

ROBERT. When I think—but what's the use? You know I wasn't making fun of Andy personally, but his attitude toward things is——

RUTH (*her eyes flashing—bursting into uncontrollable rage*). You was too making fun of him! And I ain't going to stand for it! You ought to be ashamed of yourself! (ROBERT *stares at her in amazement. She continues furiously.*) A fine one to talk about anyone else—after the way you've ruined everything with your lazy loafing! —and the stupid way you do things!

ROBERT (*angrily*). Stop that kind of talk, do you hear?

RUTH. You findin' fault—with your own brother who's ten times the man you ever was or ever will be! You're jealous, that's what! Jealous because he's made a man of himself, while you're nothing but a— but a—— (*She stutters incoherently, overcome by rage.*)

ROBERT. Ruth! Ruth! You'll be sorry for talking like that.

RUTH. I won't! I won't never be sorry! I'm only saying what I've been thinking for years.

ROBERT (*aghast*). Ruth! You can't mean that!

RUTH. What do you think—living with a man like you—having to suffer all the time because you've never been man enough to work and do things like other people. But no! You never own up to that. You think you're so much better than other folks, with your college education, where you never learned a thing, and always reading your stupid books instead of working. I s'pose you think I ought to be *proud* to be your wife—a poor, ignorant thing like me! (*Fiercely*) But I'm not. I hate it! I hate the sight of you. Oh, if I'd only known! If I hadn't been such a fool to listen to your cheap, silly poetry talk that you learned out of books! If I could have seen how you were in your true self—like you are now—I'd have killed myself before I'd have married you! I was sorry for it before we'd been together a month. I knew what you were really like—when it was too late.

ROBERT (*his voice raised loudly*). And now—I'm finding out what you're really like—what a—a creature I've been living with. *(With a harsh laugh)* It wasn't that I haven't guessed how mean and small you are—but I've kept on telling myself that I must be wrong—like a fool! —like a damned fool!

RUTH. You were saying you'd go out on the road if it wasn't for me. Well, you can go, and the sooner the better! I don't care! I'll be glad to get rid of you! The farm'll be better off too. There's been a curse on it ever since you took hold. So go! Go and be a tramp like you've always wanted. It's all you're good for. I can get along without you, don't you worry. *(Exulting fiercely)* Andy's coming back, don't forget that! He'll attend to things like they should be. He'll show what a man can do! I don't need you. Andy's coming!

ROBERT *(they are both standing.* ROBERT *grabs her by the shoulders and glares into her eyes).* What do you mean? *(He shakes her violently.)* What are you thinking of? What's in your evil mind, you—you—— *(His voice is a harsh shout.)*

RUTH *(in a defiant scream).* Yes I do mean it! I'd say it if you was to kill me! I do love Andy. I do! I do! I always loved him. *(Exultantly)* And he loves me! He loves me! I know he does. He always did! And you know he did, too! So go! Go if you want to!

ROBERT *(throwing her away from him. She staggers back against the table—thickly).* You—you slut! *(He stands glaring at her as she leans back, supporting herself by the table, gasping for breath. A loud frightened whimper sounds from the awakened child in the bedroom. It continues. The man and woman stand looking at one another in horror, the extent of their terrible quarrel suddenly brought home to them. A pause. The noise of a horse and carriage comes from the road before the house. The two, suddenly struck by the same premonition, listen to it breathlessly, as to a sound heard in a dream. It stops. They hear* ANDY'S *voice from the road shouting a long hail—"Ahoy there!")*

RUTH *(with a strangled cry of joy).* Andy! Andy! *(She rushes and grabs the knob of the screen door, about to fling it open.)*

ROBERT *(in a voice of command that forces obedience).* Stop! *(He goes to the door and gently pushes the trembling* RUTH *away from it. The child's crying rises to a louder pitch.)* I'll meet Andy. You better go in to Mary, Ruth. *(She looks at him defiantly for a moment, but there is something in his eyes that makes her turn and walk slowly into the bedroom.)*

ANDY'S VOICE *(in a louder shout).* Ahoy there, Rob!

ROBERT *(in an answering shout of forced cheeriness).* Hello, Andy! *(He opens the door and walks out as*

[*The Curtain Falls.*]

SCENE 2

The top of a hill on the farm. It is about eleven o'clock the next morning. The day is hot and cloudless. In the distance the sea can be seen.

The top of the hill slopes downward slightly toward the left. A big boulder stands in the center toward the rear. Further right, a large oak tree. The faint trace of a path leading upward to it from the left foreground can be detected through the bleached, sun-scorched grass.

ROBERT *is discovered sitting on the boulder, his chin resting on his hands, staring out toward the horizon seaward. His face is pale and haggard, his expression one of utter despondency.* MARY *is sitting on the grass near him in the shade, playing with her doll, singing happily to herself. Presently she casts a curious glance at her father, and, propping her doll up against the tree, comes over and clambers to his side.*

MARY *(pulling at his hand—solicitously).* Dada sick?

ROBERT *(looking at her with a forced smile).* No, dear. Why?

MARY. Play wif Mary.

ROBERT *(gently).* No, dear, not today. Dada doesn't feel like playing today.

MARY (*protestingly*). Yes, Dada!

ROBERT. No, dear. Dada does feel sick—a little. He's got a bad headache.

MARY. Mary see. (*He bends his head. She pats his hair.*) Bad head.

ROBERT (*kissing her—with a smile*). There! It's better now, dear, thank you. (*She cuddles up close against him. There is a pause during which each of them looks out seaward. Finally* ROBERT *turns to her tenderly.*) Would you like Dada to go away?—far, far away?

MARY (*tearfully*). No! No! No, Dada, no!

ROBERT. Don't you like Uncle Andy—the man that came yesterday—not the old man with the white mustache—the other?

MARY. Mary loves Dada.

ROBERT (*with fierce determination*). He won't go away, baby. He was only joking. He couldn't leave his little Mary. (*He presses the child in his arms.*)

MARY (*with an exclamation of pain*). Oh! Hurt!

ROBERT. I'm sorry, little girl. (*He lifts her down to the grass.*) Go play with Dolly, that's a good girl; and be careful to keep in the shade. (*She reluctantly leaves him and takes up her doll again. A moment later she points down the hill to the left.*)

MARY. Mans, Dada.

ROBERT (*looking that way*). It's your Uncle Andy. (*A moment later* ANDREW *comes up from the left, whistling cheerfully. He has changed but little in appearance, except for the fact that his face has been deeply bronzed by his years in the tropics; but there is a decided change in his manner. The old easy-going good nature seems to have been partly lost in a breezy, businesslike briskness of voice and gesture. There is an authoritative note in his speech as though he were accustomed to give orders and have them obeyed as a matter of course. He is dressed in the simple blue uniform and cap of a merchant ship's officer.*)

ANDREW. Here you are, eh?

ROBERT. Hello, Andy.

ANDREW (*going over to* MARY). And who's this young lady I find you all alone with, eh? Who's this pretty young lady? (*He tickles the laughing, squirming* MARY, *then lifts her up at arm's length over his head.*) Upsy—daisy! (*He sets her down on the ground again.*) And there you are! (*He walks over and sits down on the boulder beside* ROBERT *who moves to one side to make room for him.*) Ruth told me I'd probably find you up topside here; but I'd have guessed it, anyway. (*He digs his brother in the ribs affectionately.*) Still up to your old tricks, you old beggar! I can remember how you used to come up here to mope and dream in the old days.

ROBERT (*with a smile*). I come up here now because it's the coolest place on the farm. I've given up dreaming.

ANDREW (*grinning*). I don't believe it. You can't have changed that much. (*After a pause—with boyish enthusiasm*) Say, it sure brings back old times to be up here with you having a chin all by our lonesomes again. I feel great being back home.

ROBERT. It's great for us to have you back.

ANDREW (*after a pause—meaningly*). I've been looking over the old place with Ruth. Things don't seem to be——

ROBERT (*his face flushing—interrupts his brother shortly*). Never mind the farm! Let's talk about something interesting. This is the first chance I've had to have a word with you alone. Tell me about your trip.

ANDREW. Why, I thought I told you everything in my letters.

ROBERT (*smiling*). Your letters were—sketchy, to say the least.

ANDREW. Oh, I know I'm no author. You needn't be afraid of hurting my feelings. I'd rather go through a typhoon again than write a letter.

ROBERT (*with eager interest*). Then you were through a typhoon?

ANDREW. Yes—in the China sea. Had to run before it under bare poles [1] for two

---

[1] **under bare poles:** with the sails down.

days. I thought we were bound down for Davy Jones, sure. Never dreamed waves could get so big or the wind blow so hard. If it hadn't been for Uncle Dick being such a good skipper we'd have gone to the sharks, all of us. As it was we came out minus a main topmast and had to beat back to Hong Kong for repairs. But I must have written you all this.

ROBERT. You never mentioned it.

ANDREW. Well, there was so much dirty work getting things shipshape again I must have forgotten about it.

ROBERT (*looking at* ANDREW—*marveling*). Forget a typhoon? (*With a trace of scorn*) You're a strange combination, Andy. And is what you've told me all you remember about it?

ANDREW. Oh, I could give you your bellyful of details if I wanted to turn loose on you. It was all-wool-and-a-yard-wide-Hell, I'll tell you. You ought to have been there. I remember thinking about you at the worst of it, and saying to myself: "This'd cure Rob of them ideas of his about the beautiful sea, if he could see it." And it would have too, you bet! (*He nods emphatically.*)

ROBERT (*dryly*). The sea doesn't seem to have impressed you very favorably.

ANDREW. I should say it didn't! I'll never set foot on a ship again if I can help it—except to carry me some place I can't get to by train.

ROBERT. But you studied to become an officer!

ANDREW. Had to do something or I'd gone mad. The days were like years. (*He laughs.*) And as for the East you used to rave about—well, you ought to see it, and *smell* it! One walk down one of their filthy narrow streets with the tropic sun beating on it would sicken you for life with the "wonder and mystery" you used to dream of.

ROBERT (*shrinking from his brother with a glance of aversion*). So all you found in the East was a stench?

ANDREW. *A* stench! Ten thousand of them!

ROBERT. But you did like some of the places, judging from your letters—Sydney, Buenos Aires——

ANDREW. Yes, Sydney's a good town. (*Enthusiastically*) But Buenos Aires—there's the place for you. Argentine's a country where a fellow has a chance to make good. You're right I like it. And I'll tell you, Rob, that's right where I'm going just as soon as I've seen you folks for a while and can get a ship. I can get a berth as second officer, and I'll jump the ship when I get there. I'll need every cent of the wages Uncle's paid me to get a start at something in B. A.

ROBERT (*staring at his brother—slowly*). So you're not going to stay on the farm?

ANDREW. Why sure not! Did you think I was? There wouldn't be any sense. One of us is enough to run this little place.

ROBERT. I suppose it does seem small to you now.

ANDREW (*not noticing the sarcasm in* ROBERT'S *tone*). You've no idea, Rob, what a splendid place Argentine is. I had a letter from a marine insurance chap that I'd made friends with in Hong Kong to his brother, who's in the grain business in Buenos Aires. He took quite a fancy to me, and what's more important, he offered me a job if I'd come back there. I'd have taken it on the spot, only I couldn't leave Uncle Dick in the lurch, and I'd promised you folks to come home. But I'm going back there, you bet, and then you watch me get on! (*He slaps* ROBERT *on the back.*) But don't you think it's a big chance, Rob?

ROBERT. It's fine—for you, Andy.

ANDREW. We call this a farm—but you ought to hear about the farms down there —ten square miles where we've got an acre. It's a new country where big things are opening up—and I want to get in on something big before I die. I'm no fool when it comes to farming, and I know something about grain. I've been reading up a lot on it, too, lately. (*He notices* ROBERT'S *absent-minded expression and laughs.*) Wake up, you old poetry bookworm, you! I know my talking about business makes you want to choke me, doesn't it?

ROBERT (*with an embarrassed smile*). No, Andy, I—I just happened to think of something else. (*Frowning*) There've been lots of times lately that I've wished I had some of your faculty for business.

ANDREW (*soberly*). There's something I want to talk about, Rob—the farm. You don't mind, do you?

ROBERT. No.

ANDREW. I walked over it this morning with Ruth—and she told me about things —— (*Evasively*) I could see the place had run down; but you mustn't blame yourself. When luck's against anyone——

ROBERT. Don't, Andy! It *is* my fault. You know it as well as I do. The best I've ever done was to make ends meet.

ANDREW (*after a pause*). I've got over a thousand saved, and you can have that.

ROBERT (*firmly*). No. You need that for your start in Buenos Aires.

ANDREW. I don't. I can——

ROBERT (*determinedly*). No, Andy! Once and for all, no! I won't hear of it!

ANDREW (*protestingly*). You obstinate old son of a gun!

ROBERT. Oh, everything'll be on a sound footing after harvest. Don't worry about it.

ANDREW (*doubtfully*). Maybe. (*After a pause*) It's too bad Pa couldn't have lived to see things through. (*With feeling*) It cut me up a lot—hearing he was dead. He never—softened up, did he—about me, I mean?

ROBERT. He never understood, that's a kinder way of putting it. He does now.

ANDREW (*after a pause*). You've forgotten all about what—caused me to go, haven't you, Rob? (ROBERT *nods but keeps his face averted.*) I was a slushier damn fool in those days than you were. But it was an act of Providence I did go. It opened my eyes to how I'd been fooling myself. Why, I'd forgotten all about— that—before I'd been at sea six months.

ROBERT (*turns and looks into* ANDREW'S *eyes searchingly*). You're speaking of— Ruth?

ANDREW (*confused*). Yes. I didn't want you to get false notions in your head, or I wouldn't say anything. (*Looking* ROBERT *squarely in the eyes*) I'm telling you the truth when I say I'd forgotten long ago. It don't sound well for me, getting over things so easy, but I guess it never really amounted to more than a kid idea I was letting rule me. I'm certain now I never was in love—I was getting fun out of thinking I was—and being a hero to myself. (*He heaves a great sigh of relief.*) There! Gosh, I'm glad that's off my chest. I've been feeling sort of awkward ever since I've been home, thinking of what you two might think. (*A trace of appeal in his voice*) You've got it all straight now, haven't you, Rob?

ROBERT (*in a low voice*). Yes, Andy.

ANDREW. And I'll tell Ruth, too, if I can get up the nerve. She must feel kind of funny having me round—after what used to be—and not knowing how I feel about it.

ROBERT (*slowly*). Perhaps—for her sake —you'd better not tell her.

ANDREW. For her sake? Oh, you mean she wouldn't want to be reminded of my foolishness? Still, I think it'd be worse if——

ROBERT (*breaking out—in an agonized voice*). Do as you please, Andy; but for God's sake, let's not talk about it! (*There is a pause.* ANDREW *stares at* ROBERT *in hurt stupefaction.* ROBERT *continues after a moment in a voice which he vainly attempts to keep calm.*) Excuse me, Andy. This rotten headache has my nerves shot to pieces.

ANDREW (*mumbling*). It's all right, Rob —long as you're not sore at me.

ROBERT. Where did Uncle Dick disappear to this morning?

ANDREW. He went down to the port to see to things on the *Sunda*. He said he didn't know exactly when he'd be back. I'll have to go down and tend to the ship when he comes. That's why I dressed up in these togs.

MARY (*pointing down the hill to the left*). See! Mama! Mama! (*She struggles to her feet.* RUTH *appears at left. She is dressed in white, shows she has been fixing up. She looks pretty, flushed and full of life.)*

MARY *(running to her mother).* Mama!

RUTH *(kissing her).* Hello, dear! *(She walks toward the rock and addresses* ROBERT *coldly.)* Jake wants to see you about something. He finished working where he was. He's waiting for you at the road.

ROBERT *(getting up—wearily).* I'll go down right away. *(As he looks at* RUTH, *noting her changed appearance, his face darkens with pain.)*

RUTH. And take Mary with you, please. *(To* MARY) Go with Dada, that's a good girl. Grandma has your dinner most ready for you.

ROBERT *(shortly).* Come, Mary!

MARY *(taking his hand and dancing happily beside him).* Dada! Dada! *(They go down the hill to the left.)*

RUTH *(looks after them for a moment, frowning—then turns to* ANDY *with a smile).* I'm going to sit down. Come on, Andy. It'll be like old times. *(She jumps lightly to the top of the rock and sits down.)* It's so fine and cool up here after the house.

ANDREW *(half-sitting on the side of the boulder).* Yes. It's great.

RUTH. I've taken a holiday in honor of your arrival. *(Laughing excitedly)* I feel so free I'd like to have wings and fly over the sea. You're a man. You can't know how awful and stupid it is—cooking and washing dishes all the time.

ANDREW *(making a wry face).* I can guess.

RUTH. Besides, your mother just insisted on getting your first dinner to home, she's that happy at having you back. You'd think I was planning to poison you the flurried way she shooed me out of the kitchen.

ANDREW. That's just like Ma, bless her!

RUTH. She's missed you terrible. We all have. And you can't deny the farm has, after what I showed you and told you when we was looking over the place this morning.

ANDREW *(with a frown).* Things are run down, that's a fact! It's too darn hard on poor old Rob.

RUTH *(scornfully).* It's his own fault. He never takes any interest in things.

ANDREW *(reprovingly).* You can't blame him. He wasn't born for it; but I know he's done his best for your sake and the old folks and the little girl.

RUTH *(indifferently).* Yes, I suppose he has. *(Gayly)* But thank the Lord, all those days are over now. The "hard luck" Rob's always blaming won't last long when you take hold, Andy. All the farm's ever needed was someone with the knack of looking ahead and preparing for what's going to happen.

ANDREW. Yes, Rob hasn't got that. He's frank to own up to that himself. I'm going to try and hire a good man for him— an experienced farmer—to work the place on a salary and percentage. That'll take it off of Rob's hands, and he needn't be worrying himself to death any more. He looks all worn out, Ruth. He ought to be careful.

RUTH *(absent-mindedly).* Yes, I s'pose. *(Her mind is filled with premonitions by the first part of his statement.)* Why do you want to hire a man to oversee things? Seems as if now that you're back it wouldn't be needful.

ANDREW. Oh, of course I'll attend to everything while I'm here. I mean after I'm gone.

RUTH *(as if she couldn't believe her ears).* Gone!

ANDREW. Yes. When I leave for the Argentine again.

RUTH *(aghast).* You're going away to sea!

ANDREW. Not to sea, no; I'm through with the sea for good as a job. I'm going down to Buenos Aires to get in the grain business.

RUTH. But—that's far off—isn't it?

ANDREW *(easily).* Six thousand miles more or less. It's quite a trip. *(With enthusiasm)* I've got a peach of a chance down there, Ruth. Ask Rob if I haven't. I've just been telling him all about it.

RUTH *(a flash of anger coming over her*

face). And didn't he try to stop you from going?

ANDREW *(in surprise).* No, of course not. Why?

RUTH *(slowly and vindictively).* That's just like him—not to.

ANDREW *(resentfully).* Rob's too good a chum to try and stop me when he knows I'm set on a thing. And he could see just as soon's I told him what a good chance it was.

RUTH *(dazedly).* And you're bound on going?

ANDREW. Sure thing. Oh, I don't mean right off. I'll have to wait for a ship sailing there for quite a while, likely. Anyway, I want to stay to home and visit with you folks a spell before I go.

RUTH *(dumbly).* I s'pose. *(With sudden anguish)* Oh, Andy, you can't go! You can't. Why we've all thought—we've all been hoping and praying you was coming home to stay, to settle down on the farm and see to things. You mustn't go! Think of how your Ma'll take on if you go—and how the farm'll be ruined if you leave it to Rob to look after. You can see that.

ANDREW *(frowning).* Rob hasn't done so bad. When I get a man to direct things, the farm'll be safe enough.

RUTH *(insistently).* But your Ma—think of her.

ANDREW. She's used to me being away. She won't object when she knows it's best for her and all of us for me to go. You ask Rob. In a couple of years down there I'll make my pile, see if I don't; and then I'll come back and settle down and turn this farm into the crackiest place in the whole state. In the meantime, I can help you both from down there. *(Earnestly)* I tell you, Ruth, I'm going to make good right from the minute I land, if working hard and a determination to get on can do it; and I *know* they can! *(Excitedly—in a rather boastful tone)* I tell you, I feel ripe for bigger things than settling down here. The trip did that for me, anyway. It showed me the world is a larger proposition than ever I thought it was in the old days. I couldn't be content any more stuck

here like a fly in molasses. It all seems trifling, somehow. You ought to be able to understand what I feel.

RUTH *(dully).* Yes—I s'pose I ought. *(After a pause—a sudden suspicion forming in her mind)* What did Rob tell you—about me?

ANDREW. Tell? About you? Why, nothing.

RUTH *(staring at him intensely).* Are you telling me the truth, Andy Mayo? Didn't he say—I—— *(She stops confusedly.)*

ANDREW *(surprised).* No, he didn't mention you, I can remember. Why? What made you think he did?

RUTH *(wringing her hands).* Oh, I wish I could tell if you're lying or not!

ANDREW *(indignantly).* What're you talking about? I didn't used to lie to you, did I? And what in the name of God is there to lie for?

RUTH *(still unconvinced).* Are you sure —will you swear—it isn't the reason—— *(She lowers her eyes and half turns away from him.)* The same reason that made you go last time that's driving you away again? 'Cause if it is—I was going to say— you mustn't go—on that account. *(Her voice sinks to a tremulous, tender whisper as she finishes.)*

ANDREW *(confused—forces a laugh).* Oh, is *that* what you're driving at? Well, you needn't worry about that no more—— *(Soberly)* I don't blame you, Ruth, feeling embarrassed having me around again, after the way I played the dumb fool about going away last time.

RUTH *(her hope crushed—with a gasp of pain).* Oh, Andy!

ANDREW *(misunderstanding).* I know I oughtn't to talk about such foolishness to you. Still I figure it's better to get it out of my system so's we three can be together same's years ago, and not be worried thinking one of us might have the wrong notion.

RUTH. Andy! Please! Don't!

ANDREW. Let me finish now that I've started. It'll help clear things up. I don't want you to think once a fool always a fool, and be upset all the time I'm here on my fool account. I want you to believe I put all that silly nonsense back of me a long time ago—and now—it seems—well—as if you'd always been my sister, that's what, Ruth.

RUTH (*at the end of her endurance—laughing hysterically*). For God's sake, Andy—won't you please stop talking! (*She again hides her face in her hands, her bowed shoulders trembling.*)

ANDREW (*ruefully*). Seem's if I put my foot in it whenever I open my mouth today. Rob shut me up with almost the same words when I tried speaking to him about it.

RUTH (*fiercely*). You told him—what you've told me?

ANDREW (*astounded*). Why sure! Why not?

RUTH (*shuddering*). Oh, my God!

ANDREW (*alarmed*). Why? Shouldn't I have?

RUTH (*hysterically*). Oh, I don't care what you do! I don't care! Leave me alone! (ANDREW *gets up and walks down the hill to the left, embarrassed, hurt, and greatly puzzled by her behavior.*)

ANDREW (*after a pause—pointing down the hill*). Hello! Here they come back—and the Captain's with them. How'd he come to get back so soon, I wonder? That means I've got to hustle down to the port and get on board. Rob's got the baby with him. (*He comes back to the boulder.* RUTH *keeps her face averted from him.*) Gosh, I never saw a father so tied up in a kid as Rob is! He just watches every move she makes. And I don't blame him. You both got a right to feel proud of her. She's surely a little winner. (*He glances at* RUTH *to see if this very obvious attempt to get back in her good graces is having any effect.*) I can see the likeness to Rob standing out all over her, can't you? But there's no denying she's your young one, either. There's something about her eyes——

RUTH (*piteously*). Oh, Andy, I've a headache! I don't want to talk! Leave me alone, won't you please?

ANDREW (*stands staring at her for a moment—then walks away saying in a hurt tone*). Everybody hereabouts seems to be on edge today. I begin to feel as if I'm not wanted around. (*He stands near the path, left, kicking at the grass with the toe of his shoe. A moment later* CAPTAIN DICK SCOTT *enters, followed by* ROBERT *carrying* MARY. *The* CAPTAIN *seems scarcely to have changed at all from the jovial, booming person he was three years before. He wears a uniform similar to* ANDREW'S. *He is puffing and breathless from his climb and mops wildly at his perspiring countenance.* ROBERT *casts a quick glance at* ANDREW, *noticing the latter's discomfited look, and then turns his eyes on* RUTH *who, at their approach, has moved so her back is toward them, her chin resting on her hands as she stares out seaward.*)

MARY. Mama! Mama! (ROBERT *puts her down and she runs to her mother.* RUTH *turns and grabs her up in her arms with a sudden fierce tenderness, quickly turning away again from the others. During the following scene she keeps* MARY *in her arms.*)

SCOTT (*wheezily*). Phew! I got great news for you, Andy. Let me get my wind first. Phew! Mountin' this damned hill is worser'n goin' aloft to the skys'l yard in a blow. I got to lay to a while. (*He sits down on the grass, mopping his face.*)

ANDREW. I didn't look for you this soon, Uncle.

SCOTT. I didn't figger it, neither; but I run across a bit o' news down to the Seamen's Home made me 'bout ship and set all sail back here to find you.

ANDREW (*eagerly*). What is it, Uncle?

SCOTT. Passin' by the Home I thought I'd drop in an' let 'em know I'd be lackin' a mate next trip count o' your leavin'. Their man in charge o' the shippin' asked after you 'special curious. "Do you think he'd consider a berth as Second on a steamer, Captain?" he asks. I was goin' to say no when I thinks o' you wantin' to get back down south to the Plate agen; so I asks him: "What is she and where's she bound?" "She's the *El Paso,* a brand new tramp," he says, "and she's bound for Buenos Aires."

ANDREW (*his eyes lighting up—excitedly*). Gosh, that is luck! When does she sail?

SCOTT. Tomorrow mornin'. I didn't know if you'd want to ship away again so quick an' I told him so. "Tell him I'll hold the berth open for him until late this afternoon," he says. So there you be, an' you can make your own choice.

ANDREW. I'd like to take it. There may not be another ship for Buenos Aires with a vacancy in months. (*His eyes roving from* ROBERT *to* RUTH *and back again—uncertainly*) Still—damn it all—tomorrow morning *is* soon. I wish she wasn't leaving for a week or so. That'd give me a chance —it seems hard to go right away again when I've just got home. And yet it's a chance in a thousand—— (*Appealing to* ROBERT) What do you think, Rob? What would you do?

ROBERT (*forcing a smile*). He who hesitates, you know. (*Frowning*) It's a piece of good luck thrown in your way—and—I think you owe it to yourself to jump at it. But don't ask me to decide for you.

RUTH (*turning to look at* ANDREW—*in a tone of fierce resentment*). Yes, go, Andy! (*She turns quickly away again. There is a moment of embarrassed silence.*)

ANDREW (*thoughtfully*). Yes, I guess I will. It'll be the best thing for all of us in the end, don't you think so, Rob? (ROBERT *nods but remains silent.*)

SCOTT (*getting to his feet*). Then, that's settled.

ANDREW (*now that he has definitely made a decision his voice rings with hopeful strength and energy*). Yes, I'll take the berth. The sooner I go the sooner I'll be back, that's a certainty; and I won't come back with empty hands next time. You bet I won't!

SCOTT. You ain't got so much time, Andy. To make sure you'd best leave here soon's you kin. I got to get right back aboard. You'd best come with me.

ANDREW. I'll go to the house and repack my bag right away.

ROBERT (*quietly*). You'll both be here for dinner, won't you?

ANDREW (*worriedly*). I don't know. Will there be time? What time is it now, I wonder?

ROBERT (*reproachfully*). Ma's been getting dinner especially for you, Andy.

ANDREW (*flushing—shamefacedly*). Hell! And I was forgetting! Of course I'll stay for dinner if I missed every damned ship in the world. (*He turns to the* CAPTAIN—*briskly.*) Come on, Uncle. Walk down with me to the house and you can tell me more about this berth on the way. I've got to pack before dinner. (*He and the* CAPTAIN *start down to the left.* ANDREW *calls back over his shoulder.*) You're coming soon, aren't you, Rob?

ROBERT. Yes. I'll be right down. (AN-DREW *and the* CAPTAIN *leave.* RUTH *puts* MARY *on the ground and hides her face in her hands. Her shoulders shake as if she were sobbing.* ROBERT *stares at her with a grim, somber expression.* MARY *walks backward toward* ROBERT, *her wondering eyes fixed on her mother.*)

MARY (*her voice vaguely frightened, taking her father's hand*). Dada, Mama's cryin', Dada.

ROBERT (*bending down and stroking her hair—in a voice he endeavors to keep from being harsh*). No, she isn't, little girl. The sun hurts her eyes, that's all. Aren't you beginning to feel hungry, Mary?

MARY (*decidedly*). Yes, Dada.

ROBERT (*meaningly*). It must be your dinner time now.

RUTH (*in a muffled voice*). I'm coming, Mary. (*She wipes her eyes quickly and, without looking at* ROBERT, *comes and takes* MARY'S *hand—in a dead voice.*) Come on and I'll get your dinner for you. (*She walks out left, her eyes fixed on the ground, the skipping* MARY *tugging at her hand.* ROBERT *waits a moment for them to get ahead and then slowly follows as*

[*The Curtain Falls.*]

COMMENTARY

Act II parallels Act I in its scenic alternation between the stifling interior and the expansive out-of-doors. Yet O'Neill does more than simply repeat the contrasts he introduced in Act I. There we saw Robert and Andrew make decisions which we knew were based on what their father called a lie, all because of the intrusive influence of Ruth. Here, in Act II, we begin to see the results of those decisions. The first scene takes a long look at Robert and Ruth; the second scene focuses on Andrew and how his impulsive decision to leave the farm has changed him.

The new disorder and shabbiness of the farmhouse sitting room is apparent at the rise of the curtain. From then on to the conclusion of this first scene, O'Neill piles on detail after detail to give a picture of unhappiness and inefficiency. The hot weather, the cold food, the complaining women, the whining child, the broken machinery, the quitting farm hand, the mortgage—all these signs of an unhappy home are here. Thus when Ruth and Robert finally turn on each other, enraged by their frustration and disappointment, we can understand how they feel. Here, it seems, is where their bright star has settled.

Two points of light, of hope, flicker in this scene: Robert's relationship with his child, Mary, suggests that some good may come out of this bad dream. Furthermore, we know that Andrew is coming home, and we hear him call out greetings at the end of the scene.

Yet by the time Scene 2 is over, the change that time has wrought in Andrew is also clear. If Robert's sea-dream has withered on the land, then Andrew's practical, earthy, active nature has hardened into insensitivity at sea. He has hardly responded to the adventures and sights he has seen; he is in fact giving up the sea for the sake of making a fast peso by selling grain in Argentina.

1. Enumerate all the different means by which O'Neill suggests the nature of Robert's and Ruth's life together.

2. The end of Scene 1, Act II, comes at about the middle of the play and is certainly a point of high climax. Discuss how O'Neill prepares for and accomplishes this climax. In your discussion, make specific references to preceding actions and speeches.

3. How does O'Neill use stagecraft or specifically theatrical devices to prepare us for Ruth's hidden love of Andrew? (For a discussion of staging devices, see page 751.)

4. Does Ruth have a new attitude toward Mary toward the end of the act? If so, why? How does the playwright suggest it?

5. What is Andrew's impression of a typhoon? of Asia? What would Robert's response be? Why did Andrew decide to become a ship's officer? Why is the *way* Andrew plans to make money ironic? How does this detail, in itself, dramatize the change in Andrew?

6. Describe Robert's and Ruth's state of mind at the end of Act II. How do the stage directions suggest this? Do Robert and Ruth have any hope for the future at the end of this act?

7. Discuss the role of Mrs. Atkins as it contributes to the unity of the play. What is her attitude toward suffering and adversity? Do you agree with her and feel she is right in this attitude?

8. Why do you think O'Neill sets the second scene of Act II out-of-doors? What theatrical advantage does this setting have at this time?

9. O'Neill contrives his plot so that Andrew will have to leave the farm much earlier than was expected. Why do you think the playwright bothers to do this? What new insights does this development give us about Andrew and others?

10. How are the images of sickness developed in Act II? How are the images involving books and dreams developed?

11. After Act I, it was suggested that women seem to muddy and complicate the clear thoughts of the men in this play. Does this idea prove true in Act II as well? If so, where and how?

12. O'Neill uses a number of excuses to have his characters enter or leave the stage, so that other characters can be alone or get together. Enumerate some of these excuses. Do they seem natural or contrived?

EUGENE O'NEILL   839

ACT III

SCENE 1

Same as Act II, Scene 1—The sitting room of the farmhouse about six o'clock in the morning of a day toward the end of October, five years later. It is not yet dawn, but as the action progresses the darkness outside the windows gradually fades to gray.

The room, seen by the light of the shadeless oil lamp with a smoky chimney which stands on the table, presents an appearance of decay, of dissolution. The curtains at the windows are torn and dirty and one of them is missing. The closed desk is gray with accumulated dust as if it had not been used in years. Blotches of dampness disfigure the wall paper. Threadbare trails, leading to the kitchen and outer doors, show in the faded carpet. The top of the coverless table is stained with the imprints of hot dishes and spilt food. The rung of one rocker has been clumsily mended with a piece of plain board. A brown coating of rust covers the unblacked stove. A pile of wood is stacked up carelessly against the wall by the stove.

The whole atmosphere of the room, contrasted with that of former years, is one of a habitual poverty too hopelessly resigned to be any longer ashamed or even conscious of itself.

At the rise of the curtain RUTH *is discovered sitting by the stove, with hands outstretched to the warmth as if the air in the room were damp and cold. A heavy shawl is wrapped about her shoulders, half-concealing her dress of deep mourning. She has aged horribly. Her pale, deeply lined face has the stony lack of expression of one to whom nothing more can ever happen, whose capacity for emotion has been exhausted. When she speaks her voice is without timbre, low and monotonous. The negligent disorder of her dress, the slovenly arrangement of her hair, now streaked with gray, her muddied shoes run down at the heel, give full evidence of the apathy in which she lives.*

Her mother is asleep in her wheelchair beside the stove toward the rear, wrapped up in a blanket.

There is a sound from the open bedroom door in the rear as if someone were getting out of bed. RUTH *turns in that direction with a look of dull annoyance. A moment later* ROBERT *appears in the doorway, leaning weakly against it for support. His hair is long and unkempt, his face and body emaciated. There are bright patches of crimson over his cheekbones and his eyes are burning with fever. He is dressed in corduroy pants, a flannel shirt, and wears worn carpet slippers on his bare feet.*

RUTH (*dully*). S-s-s-h-! Ma's asleep.

ROBERT (*speaking with an effort*). I won't wake her. (*He walks weakly to a rocker by the side of the table and sinks down in it exhausted.*)

RUTH (*staring at the stove*). You better come near the fire where it's warm.

ROBERT. No. I'm burning up now.

RUTH. That's the fever. You know the doctor told you not to get up and move round.

ROBERT (*irritably*). That old fossil! He doesn't know anything. Go to bed and stay there—that's his only prescription.

RUTH (*indifferently*). How are you feeling now?

ROBERT (*buoyantly*). Better! Much better than I've felt in ages. Really I'm fine now—only very weak. It's the turning point, I guess. From now on I'll pick up so quick I'll surprise you—and no thanks to that old fool of a country quack, either.

RUTH. He's always tended to us.

ROBERT. Always helped us to die, you mean! He "tended" to Pa and Ma and—(*His voice breaks*)—and to—Mary.

RUTH (*dully*). He did the best he knew, I s'pose. (*After a pause*) Well, Andy's bringing a specialist with him when he comes. That ought to suit you.

ROBERT (*bitterly*). Is that why you're waiting up all night?

RUTH. Yes.

ROBERT. For Andy?

RUTH (*without a trace of feeling*). Somebody had got to. It's only right for someone to meet him after he's been gone five years.

ROBERT (*with bitter mockery*). Five years! It's a long time.

RUTH. Yes.

ROBERT (*meaningly*). To *wait*!

RUTH (*indifferently*). It's past now.

ROBERT. Yes, it's past. (*After a pause*) Have you got his two telegrams with you? (RUTH *nods.*) Let me see them, will you? My head was so full of fever when they came I couldn't make head or tail to them. (*Hastily*) But I'm feeling fine now. Let me read them again. (RUTH *takes them from the bosom of her dress and hands them to him.*)

RUTH. Here. The first one's on top.

ROBERT (*opening it*). New York. "Just landed from steamer. Have important business to wind up here. Will be home as soon as deal is completed." (*He smiles bitterly.*) Business first was always Andy's motto. (*He reads.*) "Hope you are all well. Andy." (*He repeats ironically.*) "Hope you are all well!"

RUTH (*dully*). He couldn't know you'd been took sick till I answered that and told him.

ROBERT (*contritely*). Of course he couldn't. I'm a fool. I'm touchy about nothing lately. Just what did you say in your reply?

RUTH (*inconsequentially*). I had to send it collect.

ROBERT (*irritably*). What did you say was the matter with me?

RUTH. I wrote you had lung trouble.

ROBERT (*flying into a petty temper*). You *are* a fool! How often have I explained to you that it's *pleurisy* is the matter with me. You can't seem to get it in your head that the pleura is outside the lungs, not in them!

RUTH (*callously*). I only wrote what Doctor Smith told me.

ROBERT (*angrily*). He's a damned ignoramus!

RUTH (*dully*). Makes no difference. I had to tell Andy something, didn't I?

ROBERT (*after a pause, opening the other telegram*). He sent this last evening. Let's see. (*He reads.*) "Leave for home on midnight train. Just received your wire. Am bringing specialist to see Rob. Will motor to farm from Port." (*He calculates.*) What time is it now?

RUTH. Round six, must be.

ROBERT. He ought to be here soon. I'm glad he's bringing a doctor who knows something. A specialist will tell you in a second that there's nothing the matter with my lungs.

RUTH (*stolidly*). You've been coughing an awful lot lately.

ROBERT (*irritably*). What nonsense! Haven't you ever had a bad cold yourself? (RUTH *stares at the stove in silence.* ROBERT *fidgets in his chair. There is a pause. Finally* ROBERT'S *eyes are fixed on the sleeping* MRS. ATKINS.) Your mother is lucky to be able to sleep so soundly.

RUTH. Ma's tired. She's been sitting up with me most of the night.

ROBERT (*mockingly*). Is she waiting for Andy, too? (*There is a pause.* ROBERT *sighs.*) I couldn't get to sleep to save my soul. I counted ten million sheep if

I counted one. No use! I gave up trying finally and just laid there in the dark thinking. *(He pauses, then continues in a tone of tender sympathy.)* I was thinking about you, Ruth—of how hard these last years must have been for you. *(Appealingly)* I'm sorry, Ruth.

RUTH *(in a dead voice)*. I don't know. They're past now. They were hard on all of us.

ROBERT. Yes; on all of us but Andy. *(With a flash of sick jealousy)* Andy's made a big success of himself—the kind he wanted. *(Mockingly)* And now he's coming home to let us admire his greatness. *(Frowning—irritably)* What am I talking about? My brain must be sick, too. *(After a pause)* Yes, these years have been terrible for both of us. *(His voice is lowered to a trembling whisper.)* Especially the last eight months since Mary —died. *(He forces back a sob with a convulsive shudder—then breaks out in a passionate agony.)* Our last hope of happiness! I could curse God from the bottom of my soul—if there was a God! *(He is racked by a violent fit of coughing and hurriedly puts his handkerchief to his lips.)*

RUTH *(without looking at him)*. Mary's better off—being dead.

ROBERT *(gloomily)*. We'd all be better off for that matter. *(With a sudden exasperation)* You tell that mother of yours she's got to stop saying that Mary's death was due to a weak constitution inherited from me. *(On the verge of tears of weakness)* It's got to stop, I tell you!

RUTH *(sharply)*. S-h-h! You'll wake her; and then she'll nag at me—not you.

ROBERT *(coughs and lies back in his chair weakly—a pause)*. It's all because your mother's down on me for not begging Andy for help.

RUTH *(resentfully)*. You might have. He's got plenty.

ROBERT. How can *you* of all people think of taking money from *him?*

RUTH *(dully)*. I don't see the harm. He's your own brother.

ROBERT *(shrugging his shoulders)*.

What's the use of talking to you? Well, *I* couldn't. *(Proudly)* And I've managed to keep things going, thank God. You can't deny that without help I've succeeded in—— *(He breaks off with a bitter laugh.)* My God, what am I boasting of? Debts to this one and that, taxes, interest unpaid! I'm a fool! *(He lies back in his chair closing his eyes for a moment, then speaks in a low voice.)* I'll be frank, Ruth. I've been an utter failure, and I've dragged you with me. I couldn't blame you in all justice—for hating me.

RUTH *(without feeling)*. I don't hate you. It's been my fault too, I s'pose.

ROBERT. No. You couldn't help loving —Andy.

RUTH *(dully)*. I don't love anyone.

ROBERT *(waving her remark aside)*. You needn't deny it. It doesn't matter. *(After a pause—with a tender smile)* Do you know, Ruth, what I've been dreaming back there in the dark? *(With a short laugh)* I was planning our future when I get well. *(He looks at her with appealing eyes as if afraid she will sneer at him. Her expression does not change. She stares at the stove. His voice takes on a note of eagerness.)* After all, why shouldn't we have a future? We're young yet. If we can only shake off the curse of this farm! It's the farm that's ruined our lives! And now that Andy's coming back—I'm going to sink my foolish pride, Ruth! I'll borrow the money from him to give us a good start in the city. We'll go where people live instead of stagnating, and start all over again. *(Confidently)* I won't be the failure there that I've been here, Ruth. You won't need to be ashamed of me there. I'll prove to you the reading I've done can be put to some use. *(Vaguely)* I'll write, or something of that sort. I've always wanted to write. *(Pleadingly)* You'll want to do that, won't you, Ruth?

RUTH *(dully)*. There's Ma.

ROBERT. She can come with us.

RUTH. She wouldn't.

ROBERT *(angrily)*. So that's your answer! *(He trembles with violent passion.*

His voice is so strange that RUTH *turns to look at him in alarm.*) You're lying, Ruth! Your mother's just an excuse. You want to stay here. You think that because Andy's coming back that—— (*He chokes and has an attack of coughing.*)

RUTH (*getting up—in a frightened voice*). What's the matter? (*She goes to him.*) I'll go with you, Rob. Stop that coughing for goodness' sake! It's awful bad for you. (*She soothes him in dull tones.*) I'll go with you to the city—soon's you're well again. Honest I will, Rob, I promise! (ROB *lies back and closes his eyes. She stands looking down at him anxiously.*) Do you feel better now?

ROBERT. Yes. (RUTH *goes back to her chair. After a pause he opens his eyes and sits up in his chair. His face is flushed and happy.*) Then you *will* go, Ruth?

RUTH. Yes.

ROBERT (*excitedly*). We'll make a new start, Ruth—just you and I. Life owes us some happiness after what we've been through. (*Vehemently*) It must! Otherwise our suffering would be meaningless—and that is unthinkable.

RUTH (*worried by his excitement*). Yes, yes, of course, Rob, but you mustn't——

ROBERT. Oh, don't be afraid. I feel completely well, really I do—now that I can hope again. Oh, if you knew how glorious it feels to have something to look forward to! Can't you feel the thrill of it, too—the vision of a new life opening up after all the horrible years?

RUTH. Yes, yes, but do be——

ROBERT. Nonsense! I won't be careful. I'm getting back all my strength. (*He gets lightly to his feet.*) See! I feel light as a feather. (*He walks to her chair and bends down to kiss her smilingly.*) One kiss—the first in years, isn't it?—to greet the dawn of a new life together.

RUTH (*submitting to his kiss—worriedly*). Sit down, Rob, for goodness' sake!

ROBERT (*with tender obstinacy—stroking her hair*). I won't sit down. You're silly to worry. (*He rests one hand on the back of her chair.*) Listen. All our suffering has been a test through which we had to pass to prove ourselves worthy of a finer realization. (*Exultingly*) And we did pass through it! It hasn't broken us! And now the dream is to come true! Don't you see?

RUTH (*looking at him with frightened eyes as if she thought he had gone mad*). Yes, Rob, I see; but won't you go back to bed now and rest?

ROBERT. No. I'm going to see the sun rise. It's an augury of good fortune. (*He goes quickly to the window in the rear left, and pushing the curtains aside, stands looking out.* RUTH *springs to her feet and comes quickly to the table, left, where she remains watching* ROBERT *in a tense, expectant attitude. As he peers out his body seems gradually to sag, to grow limp and tired. His voice is mournful as he speaks.*) No sun yet. It isn't time. All I can see is the black rim of the damned hills outlined against a creeping grayness. (*He turns around; letting the curtains fall back, stretching a hand out to the wall to support himself. His false strength of a moment has evaporated, leaving his face drawn and hollow-eyed. He makes a pitiful attempt to smile.*) That's not a very happy augury, is it? But the sun'll come—soon. (*He sways weakly.*)

RUTH (*hurrying to his side and supporting him*). Please go to bed, won't you, Rob? You don't want to be all wore out when the specialist comes, do you?

ROBERT (*quickly*). No. That's right. He mustn't think I'm sicker than I am. And I feel as if I could sleep now—(*Cheerfully*)—a good, sound, restful sleep.

RUTH (*helping him to the bedroom door*). That's what you need most. (*They go inside. A moment later she reappears calling back.*) I'll shut this door so's you'll be quiet. (*She closes the door and goes quickly to her mother and shakes her by the shoulder.*) Ma! Ma! Wake up!

MRS. ATKINS (*coming out of her sleep with a start*). Glory be! What's the matter with you?

RUTH. It was Rob. He's just been talking to me out here. I put him back to bed. (*Now that she is sure her mother is awake* her fear passes and she relapses into *dull indifference. She sits down in her chair and stares at the stove—dully.)* He acted—funny; and his eyes looked so—so wild like.

MRS. ATKINS *(with asperity)*. And is that all you woke me out of a sound sleep for, and scared me near out of my wits?

RUTH. I was afraid. He talked so crazy. I couldn't quiet him. I didn't want to be alone with him that way. Lord knows what he might do.

MRS. ATKINS *(scornfully)*. Humph! A help I'd be to you and me not able to move a step! Why didn't you run and get Jake?

RUTH *(dully)*. Jake isn't here. He quit last night. He hasn't been paid in three months.

MRS. ATKINS *(indignantly)*. I can't blame him. What decent person'd want to work on a place like this? *(With sudden exasperation)* Oh, I wish you'd never married that man!

RUTH *(wearily)*. You oughtn't to talk about him now when he's sick in his bed.

MRS. ATKINS *(working herself into a fit of rage)*. You know very well, Ruth Mayo, if it wasn't for me helpin' you on the sly out of my savin's, you'd both been in the poorhouse—and all 'count of his pigheaded pride in not lettin' Andy know the state thin's were in. A nice thin' for me to have to support him out of what I'd saved for my last days—and me an invalid with no one to look to!

RUTH. Andy'll pay you back, Ma. I can tell him so's Rob'll never know.

MRS. ATKINS *(with a snort)*. What'd Rob think you and him was livin' on, I'd like to know?

RUTH *(dully)*. He didn't think about it, I s'pose. *(After a slight pause)* He said he'd made up his mind to ask Andy for help when he comes. *(As a clock in the kitchen strikes six)* Six o'clock. Andy ought to get here directly.

MRS. ATKINS. D'you think this special doctor'll do Rob any good?

RUTH *(hopelessly)*. I don't know. *(The two women remain silent for a time, staring dejectedly at the stove.)*

MRS. ATKINS *(shivering irritably)*. For goodness' sake put some wood on that fire. I'm most freezin'!

RUTH *(pointing to the door in the rear)*. Don't talk so loud. Let him sleep if he can. *(She gets wearily from the chair and puts a few pieces of wood in the stove.)* This is the last of the wood. I don't know who'll cut more now that Jake's left. *(She sighs and walks to the window in the rear, left, pulls the curtains aside, and looks out.)* It's getting gray out. *(She comes back to the stove.)* Looks like it'd be a nice day. *(She stretches out her hands to warm them.)* Must've been a heavy frost last night. We're paying for the spell of warm weather we've been having. *(The throbbing whine of a motor sounds from the distance outside.)*

MRS. ATKINS *(sharply)*. S-h-h! Listen! Ain't that an auto I hear?

RUTH *(without interest)*. Yes. It's Andy, I s'pose.

MRS. ATKINS *(with nervous irritation)*. Don't sit there like a silly goose. Look at the state of this room! What'll this strange doctor think of us? Look at that lamp chimney all smoke! Gracious sakes, Ruth——

RUTH *(indifferently)*. I've got a lamp all cleaned up in the kitchen.

MRS. ATKINS *(peremptorily)*. Wheel me in there this minute. I don't want him to see me looking a sight. I'll lay down in the room the other side. You don't need me now and I'm dead for sleep. *(RUTH wheels her mother off right. The noise of the motor grows louder and finally ceases as the car stops on the road before the farmhouse.* RUTH *returns from the kitchen with a lighted lamp in her hand which she sets on the table beside the other. The sound of footsteps on the path is heard—then a sharp rap on the door.* RUTH *goes and opens it.* ANDREW *enters, followed by* DOCTOR FAWCETT *carrying a small black bag.* ANDREW *has changed greatly. His face seems to have grown highstrung, hardened by the look of decisiveness which comes from being constantly under a strain where judgments on the spur of the moment are compelled to be accurate. His eyes are keener and more alert. There is even a suggestion of ruthless cunning about them. At present, however, his expression is one of tense anxiety. DOCTOR FAWCETT is a short, dark, middle-aged man with a Vandyke beard. He wears glasses.)*

RUTH. Hello, Andy! I've been waiting——

ANDREW *(kissing her hastily).* I got here as soon as I could. *(He throws off his cap and heavy overcoat on the table, introducing RUTH and the DOCTOR as he does so. He is dressed in an expensive business suit and appears stouter.)* My sister-in-law, Mrs. Mayo—Doctor Fawcett. *(They bow to each other silently. ANDREW casts*

a quick glance about the room.) Where's Rob?

RUTH *(pointing).* In there.

ANDREW. I'll take your coat and hat, Doctor. *(As he helps the DOCTOR with his things)* Is he very bad, Ruth?

RUTH *(dully).* He's been getting weaker.

ANDREW. Damn! This way, Doctor. Bring the lamp, Ruth. *(He goes into the bedroom, followed by the DOCTOR and RUTH carrying the clean lamp. RUTH reappears almost immediately, closing the door behind her, and goes slowly to the outside door, which she opens, and stands in the doorway looking out. The sound of ANDREW'S and ROBERT'S voices comes from the bedroom. A moment later ANDREW reenters, closing the door softly. He comes forward and sinks down in the rocker on the right of table, leaning his head on his hand. His face is drawn in a shocked expression of great grief. He sighs heavily, staring mournfully in front of him. RUTH turns and stands watching him. Then she shuts the door and returns to her chair by the stove, turning it so she can face him.)*

ANDREW *(glancing up quickly—in a harsh voice).* How long has this been going on?

RUTH. You mean—how long has he been sick?

ANDREW *(shortly).* Of course! What else?

RUTH. It was last summer he had a bad spell first, but he's been ailin' ever since Mary died—eight months ago.

ANDREW *(harshly).* Why didn't you let me know—cable me? Do you want him to die, all of you? I'm damned if it doesn't look that way! *(His voice breaking)* Poor old chap! To be sick in this out-of-the-way hole without anyone to attend to him but a country quack! It's a damned shame!

RUTH *(dully).* I wanted to send you word once, but he only got mad when I told him. He was too proud to ask anything, he said.

ANDREW. Proud? To ask *me*? *(He jumps to his feet and paces nervously back and forth.)* I can't understand the way you've acted. Didn't you see how sick he was getting? Couldn't you realize —why, I nearly dropped in my tracks when I saw him! He looks—*(He shudders)*—terrible! *(With fierce scorn)* I suppose you're so used to the idea of his being delicate that you took his sickness as a matter of course. If I'd only known!

RUTH *(without emotion)*. A letter takes so long to get where you were—and we couldn't afford to telegraph. We owed everyone already, and I couldn't ask Ma. She'd been giving me money out of her savings till she hadn't much left. Don't say anything to Rob about it. I never told him. He'd only be mad at me if he knew. But I had to, because—God knows how we'd have got on if I hadn't.

ANDREW. You mean to say—— *(His eyes seem to take in the poverty-stricken appearance of the room for the first time.)* You sent that telegram to me collect. Was it because—— (RUTH *nods silently.* ANDREW *pounds on the table with his fist.)* Good God! And all this time I've been— why I've had everything! *(He sits down in his chair and pulls it close to* RUTH's— *impulsively.)* But—I can't get it through my head. Why? Why? What has happened? How did it ever come about? Tell me!

RUTH *(dully)*. There's nothing much to tell. Things kept getting worse, that's all—and Rob didn't seem to care. He never took any interest since way back when your Ma died. After that he got men to take charge, and they nearly all cheated him—he couldn't tell—and left one after another. Then after Mary died he didn't pay no heed to anything any more—just stayed indoors and took to reading books again. So I had to ask Ma if she wouldn't help us some.

ANDREW *(surprised and horrified)*. Why, damn it, this is frightful! Rob must be mad not to have let me know. Too proud to ask help of *me!* What's the matter with him in God's name? *(A sudden, horrible suspicion entering his mind)*

Ruth! Tell me the truth. His mind hasn't gone back on him, has it?

RUTH *(dully)*. I don't know. Mary's dying broke him up terrible—but he's used to her being gone by this, I s'pose.

ANDREW *(looking at her queerly)*. Do you mean to say *you're* used to it?

RUTH *(in a dead tone)*. There's a time comes—when you don't mind any more— anything.

ANDREW *(looks at her fixedly for a moment—with great pity)*. I'm sorry, Ruth— if I seemed to blame you. I didn't realize —— The sight of Rob lying in bed there, so gone to pieces—it made me furious at everyone. Forgive me, Ruth.

RUTH. There's nothing to forgive. It doesn't matter.

ANDREW *(springing to his feet again and pacing up and down)*. Thank God I came back before it was too late. This doctor will know exactly what to do. That's the first thing to think of. When Rob's on his feet again we can get the farm working on a sound basis once more. I'll see to that—before I leave.

RUTH. You're going away again?

ANDREW. I've got to.

RUTH. You wrote Rob you was coming back to stay this time.

ANDREW. I expected to—until I got to New York. Then I learned certain facts that make it necessary. *(With a short laugh)* To be candid, Ruth, I'm not the rich man you've probably been led to believe by my letters—not now. I was when I wrote them. I made money hand over fist as long as I stuck to legitimate trading; but I wasn't content with that. I wanted it to come easier, so like all the rest of the idiots, I tried speculation. Oh, I won all right! Several times I've been almost a millionaire—on paper—and then come down to earth again with a bump. Finally the strain was too much. I got disgusted with myself and made up my mind to get out and come home and forget it and really live again. *(He gives a harsh laugh.)* And now comes the funny part. The day before the steamer sailed I saw what I thought was a chance to become a millionaire again. *(He snaps his fingers.)* That easy! I plunged. Then, before things broke, I left—I was so confident I couldn't be wrong. But when I landed in New York —I wired you I had business to wind up, didn't I? Well, it was the business that wound me up! *(He smiles grimly, pacing up and down, his hands in his pockets.)*

RUTH *(dully).* You found—you'd lost everything?

ANDREW *(sitting down again).* Practically. *(He takes a cigar from his pocket, bites the end off, and lights it.)* Oh, I don't mean I'm dead broke. I've saved ten thousand from the wreckage, maybe twenty. But that's a poor showing for five years' hard work. That's why I'll have to go back. *(Confidently)* I can make it up in a year or so down there—and I don't need but a shoestring to start with. *(A weary expression comes over his face and he sighs heavily.)* I wish I didn't have to. I'm sick of it all.

RUTH. It's too bad—things seem to go wrong so.

ANDREW *(shaking off his depression— briskly).* They might be much worse. There's enough left to fix the farm OK before I go. I won't leave 'til Rob's on his feet again. In the meantime I'll make things fly around here. *(With satisfaction)* I need a rest, and the kind of rest I need is hard work in the open—just like I used to do in the old days. *(Stopping abruptly and lowering his voice cautiously)* Not a word to Rob about my losing money! Remember that, Ruth! You can see why. If he's grown so touchy, he'd never accept a cent if he thought I was hard up; see?

RUTH. Yes, Andy. *(After a pause, during which* ANDREW *puffs at his cigar abstractedly, his mind evidently busy with plans for the future, the bedroom door is opened and* DOCTOR FAWCETT *enters, carrying a bag. He closes the door quietly behind him and comes forward, a grave expression on his face.* ANDREW *springs out of his chair.)*

ANDREW. Ah, Doctor! *(He pushes a chair between his own and* RUTH'S.*)* Won't you have a chair?

FAWCETT *(glancing at his watch).* I must catch the nine o'clock back to the city. It's imperative. I have only a moment. *(Sitting down and clearing his throat—in a perfunctory, impersonal voice)* The case of your brother, Mr. Mayo, is—— *(He stops and glances at* RUTH *and says meaningly to* ANDREW.*)* Perhaps it would be better if you and I——

RUTH *(with dogged resentment).* I know what you mean, Doctor. *(Dully)* Don't be afraid I can't stand it. I'm used to bearing trouble by this; and I can guess what you've found out. *(She hesitates for a moment—then continues in a monotonous voice.)* Rob's going to die.

ANDREW *(angrily).* Ruth!

FAWCETT *(raising his hand as if to command silence).* I am afraid my diagnosis of your brother's condition forces me to the same conclusion as Mrs. Mayo's.

ANDREW *(groaning).* But, Doctor, surely——

FAWCETT *(calmly).* Your brother hasn't long to live—perhaps a few days, perhaps only a few hours. It's a marvel that he's alive at this moment. My examination revealed that both of his lungs are terribly affected.

ANDREW *(brokenly).* Good God! *(*RUTH *keeps her eyes fixed on her lap in a trance-like stare.)*

FAWCETT. I am sorry I have to tell you this. If there was anything that could be done——

ANDREW. There isn't anything?

FAWCETT *(shaking his head).* Six months ago there might have——

ANDREW *(in anguish).* But if we were to take him to the mountains—or to Arizona—or——

FAWCETT. That might have prolonged his life six months ago. *(*ANDREW *groans.)* But now—— *(He shrugs his shoulders significantly.)*

ANDREW *(appalled by a sudden thought).* Good heavens, you haven't told him this, have you, Doctor?

FAWCETT. No. I lied to him. I said a change of climate—— *(He looks at his* watch again nervously.) I must leave you. (He gets up.)

ANDREW (getting to his feet—insistently). But there must still be some chance——

FAWCETT (as if he were reassuring a child). There is always that last chance—the miracle. (He puts on his hat and coat—bowing to RUTH.) Good-by, Mrs. Mayo.

RUTH (without raising her eyes—dully). Good-by.

ANDREW (mechanically). I'll walk to the car with you, Doctor. (They go out of the door. RUTH sits motionlessly. The motor is heard starting and the noise gradually recedes into the distance. ANDREW reenters and sits down in his chair, holding his head in his hands.) Ruth! (She lifts her eyes to his.) Hadn't we better go in and see him? I'm afraid to! I know he'll read it in my face. (The bedroom door is noiselessly opened and ROBERT appears in the doorway. His cheeks are flushed with fever, and his eyes appear unusually large and brilliant. ANDREW continues with a groan.) It can't be, Ruth. It can't be as hopeless as he said. There's always a fighting chance. We'll take Rob to Arizona. He's got to get well. There must be a chance!

ROBERT (in a gentle tone). Why must there, Andy? (RUTH turns and stares at him with terrified eyes.)

ANDREW (whirling around). Rob! (Scoldingly) What are you doing out of bed? (He gets up and goes to him.) Get right back now and obey the Doc, or you're going to get a licking from me!

ROBERT (ignoring these remarks). Help me over to the chair, please, Andy.

ANDREW. Like hell I will! You're going right back to bed, that's where you're going, and stay there! (He takes hold of ROBERT's arm.)

ROBERT (mockingly). Stay there 'til I die, eh, Andy? (Coldly) Don't behave like a child. I'm sick of lying down. I'll be more rested sitting up. (As ANDREW hesitates—violently) I swear I'll get out of bed every time you put me there. You'll have to sit on my chest, and that wouldn't help my health any. Come on, Andy. Don't play the fool. I want to talk to you, and I'm going to. (With a grim smile) A dying man has some rights, hasn't he?

ANDREW (with a shudder). Don't talk that way, for God's sake! I'll only let you sit down if you'll promise that. Remember. (He helps ROBERT to the chair between his own and RUTH's.) Easy now! There you are! Wait, and I'll get a pillow for you. (He goes into the bedroom. ROBERT looks at RUTH, who shrinks away from him in terror. ROBERT smiles bitterly. ANDREW comes back with the pillow, which he places behind ROBERT's back.) How's that?

ROBERT (with an affectionate smile). Fine! Thank you! (As ANDREW sits down) Listen, Andy. You've asked me not to talk—and I won't after I've made my position clear. (Slowly) In the first place I know I'm dying. (RUTH bows her head and covers her face with her hands. She remains like this all during the scene between the two brothers.)

ANDREW. Rob! That isn't so!

ROBERT (wearily). It is so! Don't lie to me. After Ruth put me to bed before you came, I saw it clearly for the first time. (Bitterly) I'd been making plans for our future—Ruth's and mine—so it came hard at first—the realization. Then when the doctor examined me, I knew—although he tried to lie about it. And then to make sure I listened at the door to what he told you. So don't mock me with fairy tales about Arizona, or any such rot as that. Because I'm dying is no reason you should treat me as an imbecile or a coward. Now that I'm sure what's happening I can say Kismet to it with all my heart. It was only the silly uncertainty that hurt. (There is a pause. ANDREW looks around in impotent anguish, not knowing what to say. ROBERT regards him with an affectionate smile.)

ANDREW (finally blurts out). It isn't foolish. You have got a chance. If you heard all the Doctor said, that ought to prove it to you.

ROBERT. Oh, you mean when he spoke of the miracle? (*Dryly*) I don't believe in miracles—in my case. Besides, I know more than any doctor on earth *could* know—because I *feel* what's coming. (*Dismissing the subject*) But we've agreed not to talk of it. Tell me about yourself, Andy. That's what I'm interested in. Your letters were too brief and far apart to be illuminating.

ANDREW. I meant to write oftener.

ROBERT (*with a faint trace of irony*). I judge from them you've accomplished all you set out to do five years ago?

ANDREW. That isn't much to boast of.

ROBERT (*surprised*). Have you really, honestly reached that conclusion?

ANDREW. Well, it doesn't seem to amount to much now.

ROBERT. But you're rich, aren't you?

ANDREW (*with a quick glance at* RUTH). Yes, I s'pose so.

ROBERT. I'm glad. You can do to the farm all I've undone. But what did you do down there? Tell me. You went in the grain business with that friend of yours?

ANDREW. Yes. After two years I had a share in it. I sold out last year. (*He is answering* ROBERT'S *questions with great reluctance*.)

ROBERT. And then?

ANDREW. I went in on my own.

ROBERT. Still in grain?

ANDREW. Yes.

ROBERT. What's the matter? You look as if I were accusing you of something.

ANDREW. I'm proud enough of the first four years. It's after that I'm not boasting of. I took to speculating.

ROBERT. In wheat?

ANDREW. Yes.

ROBERT. And you made money—gambling?

ANDREW. Yes.

ROBERT (*thoughtfully*). I've been wondering what the great change was in you. (*After a pause*) You—a farmer—to gamble in a wheat pit [1] with scraps of paper.

[1] **wheat pit:** section of an exchange where trading in wheat is done.

There's a spiritual significance in that picture, Andy. (*He smiles bitterly*.) I'm a failure, and Ruth's another—but we can both justly lay some of the blame for our stumbling on God. But you're the deepest-dyed failure of the three, Andy. You've spent eight years running away from yourself. Do you see what I mean? You used to be a creator when you loved the farm. You and life were in harmonious partnership. And now—— (*He stops as if seeking vainly for words*.) My brain is muddled. But part of what I mean is that your gambling with the thing you used to love to create proves how far astray—— So you'll be punished. You'll have to suffer to win back—— (*His voice grows weaker and he sighs wearily*.) It's no use. I can't say it. (*He lies back and closes his eyes, breathing pantingly*.)

ANDREW (*slowly*). I think I know what you're driving at, Rob—and it's true, I guess. (ROBERT *smiles gratefully and stretches out his hand, which* ANDREW *takes in his*.)

ROBERT. I want you to promise me to do one thing, Andy, after——

ANDREW. I'll promise anything, as God is my Judge!

ROBERT. Remember, Andy, Ruth has suffered double her share. (*His voice faltering with weakness*) Only through contact with suffering, Andy, will you—awaken. Listen. You must marry Ruth—afterward.

RUTH (*with a cry*). Rob! (ROBERT *lies back, his eyes closed, gasping heavily for breath*.)

ANDREW (*making signs to her to humor him—gently*). You're tired out, Rob. You better lie down and rest a while, don't you think? We can talk later on.

ROBERT (*with a mocking smile*). Later on! You always were an optimist, Andy! (*He sighs with exhaustion*.) Yes, I'll go and rest a while. (*As* ANDREW *comes to help him*) It must be near sunrise, isn't it?

ANDREW. It's after six.

ROBERT (*as* ANDREW *helps him into the bedroom*). Shut the door, Andy. I want to be alone. (ANDREW *reappears and shuts the door softly. He comes and sits down on his chair again, supporting his head on his hands. His face is drawn with the intensity of his dry-eyed anguish.)*

RUTH *(glancing at him—fearfully).* He's out of his mind now, isn't he?

ANDREW. He may be a little delirious. The fever would do that. *(With impotent rage)* What a shame! And there's nothing we can do but sit and—wait! *(He springs from his chair and walks to the stove.)*

RUTH *(dully).* He was talking—wild—like he used to—only this time it sounded —unnatural, don't you think?

ANDREW. I don't know. The things he said to me had truth in them—even if he did talk them way up in the air, like he always sees things. Still—— *(He glances at* RUTH *keenly.)* Why do you suppose he wanted us to promise we'd—— *(Confusedly)* You know what he said.

RUTH *(dully).* His mind was wandering, I s'pose.

ANDREW *(with conviction).* No—there was something back of it.

RUTH. He wanted to make sure I'd be all right—after he'd gone, I expect.

ANDREW. No, it wasn't that. He knows very well I'd naturally look after you without—anything like that.

RUTH. He might be thinking of—something happened five years back, the time you came home from the trip.

ANDREW. What happened? What do you mean?

RUTH *(dully).* We had a fight.

ANDREW. A fight? What has that to do with me?

RUTH. It was about you—in a way.

ANDREW *(amazed).* About *me?*

RUTH. Yes, mostly. You see I'd found out I'd made a mistake about Rob soon after we were married—when it was too late.

ANDREW. Mistake? *(Slowly)* You mean —you found out you didn't love Rob?

RUTH. Yes.

ANDREW. Good God!

RUTH. And then I thought that when Mary came it'd be different, and I'd love him; but it didn't happen that way. And I couldn't bear with his blundering and book-reading—and I grew to hate him, almost.

ANDREW. Ruth!

RUTH. I couldn't help it. No woman could. It had to be because I loved someone else, I'd found out. *(She sighs wearily.)* It can't do no harm to tell you now— when it's all past and gone—and dead. *You* were the one I really loved—only I didn't come to the knowledge of it 'til too late.

ANDREW *(stunned).* Ruth! Do you know what you're saying?

RUTH. It was true—then. *(With sudden fierceness)* How could I help it? No woman could.

ANDREW. Then—you loved me—that time I came home?

RUTH *(doggedly).* I'd known your real reason for leaving home the first time— everybody knew it—and for three years I'd been thinking——

ANDREW. That I loved you?

RUTH. Yes. Then that day on the hill you laughed about what a fool you'd been for loving me once—and I knew it was all over.

ANDREW. Good God, but I never thought—— *(He stops, shuddering at his remembrance.)* And did Rob——

RUTH. That was what I'd started to tell. We'd had a fight just before you came and I got crazy mad—and I told him all I've told you.

ANDREW *(gaping at her speechlessly for a moment).* You told Rob—you loved me?

RUTH. Yes.

ANDREW *(shrinking away from her in horror).* You—you—you mad fool, you! How could you do such a thing?

RUTH. I couldn't help it. I'd got to the end of bearing things—without talking.

ANDREW. Then Rob must have known every moment I stayed here! And yet he never said or showed—God, how he must have suffered! Didn't you know how much he loved you?

RUTH *(dully).* Yes. I knew he liked me.

ANDREW. Liked you! What kind of a woman are you? Couldn't you have kept silent? Did you have to torture him? No wonder he's dying! And you've lived together for five years with this between you?

RUTH. We've lived in the same house.

ANDREW. Does he still think——

RUTH. I don't know. We've never spoke a word about it since that day. Maybe, from the way he went on, he s'poses I care for you yet.

ANDREW. But you don't. It's outrageous. It's stupid! You don't love me!

RUTH (slowly). I wouldn't know how to feel love, even if I tried, any more.

ANDREW (brutally). And I don't love you, that's sure! (He sinks into his chair, his head between his hands.) It's damnable such a thing should be between Rob and me. Why, I love Rob better'n anybody in the world and always did. There isn't a thing on God's green earth I wouldn't have done to keep trouble away from him. And I have to be the very one— it's damnable! How am I going to face him again? What can I say to him now? (He groans with anguished rage. After a pause) He asked me to promise—what am I going to do?

RUTH. You can promise—so's it'll ease his mind—and not mean anything.

ANDREW. What? Lie to him now—when he's dying? (Determinedly) No! It's you who'll have to do the lying, since it must be done. You've got a chance now to undo some of all the suffering you've brought on Rob. Go in to him! Tell him you never loved me—it was all a mistake. Tell him you only said so because you were mad and didn't know what you were saying! Tell him something, anything, that'll bring him peace!

RUTH (dully). He wouldn't believe me.

ANDREW (furiously). You've got to make him believe you, do you hear? You've got to—now—hurry—you never know when it may be too late. (As she hesitates—imploringly) For God's sake, Ruth! Don't you see you owe it to him? You'll never forgive yourself if you don't.

RUTH (dully). I'll go. (She gets wearily to her feet and walks slowly toward the bedroom.) But it won't do any good. (ANDREW's eyes are fixed on her anxiously. She opens the door and steps inside the room. She remains standing there for a minute. Then she calls in a frightened voice.) Rob! Where are you? (Then she hurries back, trembling with fright.) Andy! Andy! He's gone!

ANDREW (misunderstanding her—his face pale with dread). He's not——

RUTH (interrupting him—hysterically). He's gone! The bed's empty. The window's wide open. He must have crawled out into the yard!

ANDREW (springing to his feet. He rushes into the bedroom and returns immediately with an expression of alarmed amazement on his face). Come! He can't have gone far! (Grabbing his hat he takes RUTH's arm and shoves her toward the door.) Come on! (Opening the door) Let's hope to God—— (The door closes behind them, cutting off his words as

[The Curtain Falls.]

SCENE 2

Same as Act I, Scene 1—A section of country highway. The sky to the east is already alight with bright color and a thin, quivering line of flame is spreading slowly along the horizon rim of the dark hills. The roadside, however, is still steeped in the grayness of the dawn, shadowy and vague. The field in the foreground has a wild uncultivated appearance as if it had been allowed to remain fallow the preceding summer. Parts of the snake fence in the rear have been broken down. The apple tree is leafless and seems dead.

ROBERT staggers weakly in from the left. He stumbles into the ditch and lies there for a moment; then crawls with a great effort to the top of the bank where he can see the sun rise, and collapses weakly. RUTH and ANDREW come hurriedly along the road from the left.

ANDREW (*stopping and looking about him*). There he is! I knew it! I knew we'd find him here.

ROBERT (*trying to raise himself to a sitting position as they hasten to his side—with a wan smile*). I thought I'd given you the slip.

ANDREW (*with kindly bullying*). Well you didn't, you old scoundrel, and we're going to take you right back where you belong—in bed. (*He makes a motion to lift* ROBERT.)

ROBERT. Don't, Andy. Don't, I tell you!

ANDREW. You're in pain?

ROBERT (*simply*). No. I'm dying. (*He falls back weakly.* RUTH *sinks down beside him with a sob and pillows his head on her lap.* ANDREW *stands looking down at him helplessly.* ROBERT *moves his head restlessly on* RUTH'S *lap.*) I couldn't stand it back there in the room. It seemed as if all my life—I'd been cooped in a room. So I thought I'd try to end as I might have —if I'd had the courage—alone—in a ditch by the open road—watching the sun rise.

ANDREW. Rob! Don't talk. You're wasting your strength. Rest a while and then we'll carry you——

ROBERT. Still hoping, Andy? Don't. I know. (*There is a pause during which he breathes heavily, straining his eyes toward the horizon.*) The sun comes so slowly. (*With an ironical smile*) The doctor told me to go to the far-off places—and I'd be cured. He was right. That was always the cure for me. It's too late—for this life— but—— (*He has a fit of coughing which racks his body.*)

ANDREW (*with a hoarse sob*). Rob! (*He clenches his fists in an impotent rage against Fate.*) God! God! (RUTH *sobs brokenly and wipes* ROBERT'S *lips with her handkerchief.*)

ROBERT (*in a voice which is suddenly ringing with the happiness of hope*). You mustn't feel sorry for me. Don't you see I'm happy at last—free—free!—freed from the farm—free to wander on and on— eternally! (*He raises himself on his elbow, his face radiant, and points to the horizon.*) Look! Isn't it beautiful beyond the hills? I can hear the old voices calling me to come—— (*Exultantly*) And this time I'm going! It isn't the end. It's a free beginning—the start of my voyage! I've won to my trip—the right of release—beyond the horizon! Oh, you ought to be glad— glad—for my sake! (*He collapses weakly.*) Andy! (ANDREW *bends down to him.*) Remember Ruth——

ANDREW. I'll take care of her, I swear to you, Rob!

ROBERT. Ruth has suffered—remember,

Andy—only through sacrifice—the secret beyond there—— *(He suddenly raises himself with his last remaining strength and points to the horizon where the edge of the sun's disc is rising from the rim of the hills.)* The sun! *(He remains with his eyes fixed on it for a moment. A rattling noise throbs from his throat. He mumbles.)* Remember! *(And falls back and is still.* RUTH *gives a cry of horror and springs to her feet, shuddering, her hands over her eyes.* ANDREW *bends on one knee beside the body, placing a hand over* ROB-ERT'S *heart, then he kisses his brother reverentially on the forehead and stands up.)*

ANDREW *(facing* RUTH, *the body between them—in a dead voice).* He's dead. *(With a sudden burst of fury)* God damn you, you never told him!

RUTH *(piteously).* He was so happy without my lying to him.

ANDREW *(pointing to the body—trembling with the violence of his rage).* This is your doing, you damn woman, you coward, you murderess!

RUTH *(sobbing).* Don't, Andy! I couldn't help it—and he knew how I'd suffered, too. He told you—to remember.

ANDREW *(stares at her for a moment, his rage ebbing away, an expression of deep pity gradually coming over his face. Then he glances down at his brother and speaks brokenly in a compassionate voice).* Forgive me, Ruth—for his sake—and I'll remember—— *(*RUTH *lets her hands fall from her face and looks at him uncomprehendingly. He lifts his eyes to hers and forces out falteringly)* I—you—we've both made a mess of things! We must try to help each other—and—in time—we'll come to know what's right—— *(Desperately)* And perhaps we—— *(But* RUTH, *if she is aware of his words, gives no sign. She remains silent, gazing at him dully with the sad humility of exhaustion, her mind already sinking back into that spent calm beyond the further troubling of any hope.)*

[*The Curtain Falls.*]

COMMENTARY

O'Neill's view of a relentless destiny continues to pervade the third act of *Beyond the Horizon.* Here again, the unkempt, decayed setting of the farmhouse accurately reflects the wasted, apathetic lives which it now contains. Even the time, dark night, supports the bleakness of tone, just as the rosy glow of sunset contributed to the false romantic flush of Act I.

Moreover, we learn before long that Robert's sickness, hinted at obliquely during the two preceding acts, has now become serious. Decay now pervades his body as well as his soul and his surroundings. The dream is dead, and the dreamer is dying. Ruth, who once responded so strongly to Robert's wanderlust, has become spiritually dead herself. "There's a time come," she says, "when you don't mind any more."

The description of Andrew, when he once more returns, indicates that time has taken its toll of him, too. His old practicality is visibly marred by "a suggestion of ruthless cunning." As he says himself, "I'm sick of it all." Only old Mrs. Atkins, a querulous invalid, still able to sleep and to protest, seems to have survived the blows of fate unchanged.

Early in the first scene of Act III, there is a surge toward hope. Robert feverishly and momentarily talks about a new life for himself and Ruth in the city, but we know by now that this is a false dawn, which O'Neill underscores by the blackness of the night outside the window. Another false promise of redemption is offered by Andrew, when he urges Ruth to lie to Robert so that the latter will at least die in a happy delusion. Yet we know, as does Ruth, that there have been enough lies; we have seen the anguish that lies have caused. Truth, not lies, are what one now must subscribe to; self-awareness, not delusion, is what Robert can still long for. And these, O'Neill shows, can be reached only at the rock bottom of suffering, as Andrew finally realizes at the end of the play.

O'Neill risks breaking the momentum of Act III by shifting scenes, so that Robert can die out-of-doors, seeing the dawn at last appearing on his horizon. His last word is "Remember!" as he asks his wife and brother to see that "only through sacrifice" can you become aware of "the secret beyond there." Andrew berates Ruth for not lying to the dying man but then changes his mind, realizing at last, as she does, that falsehoods are no substitute for the hard, clear insights which come only through suffering.

FOR STUDY AND DISCUSSION

1. Do Robert and Ruth show any new sympathy or understanding toward each other in Act III? If so, where and how? What does Robert learn about himself and the world in Act III that he didn't know in Act II? How about Andrew? Ruth?

2. How does O'Neill suggest, early in Act III, that Robert's illness is more serious than he thinks?

3. How does O'Neill explain Andrew's delay in returning? Why do you think he introduces this delay?

4. Why is tuberculosis, a sickness associated with nineteenth-century poets and operatic heroines, a particularly appropriate disease for Robert to die of?

5. Robert tells Andrew, "Don't mock me with fairy tales about Arizona." Why is the phrase "fairy tales" significant here? Has Robert previously responded to fairy tales or used the phrase? Why is it important that he considers them mockery now?

6. In your opinion, is Mary's death simply bad luck, or were Robert and Ruth in some way responsible for it? Explain.

7. Critics have claimed that the last act of *Beyond the Horizon* is anticlimactic and marred by the break between scenes. It has also been argued that Robert has nothing really to do in this last act except die. Do you agree with these criticisms? Why or why not?

8. What do the hills symbolize in the last scene of the play? What do the apple tree and the fence symbolize?

COMMENTARY
The Play as a Whole

When it was first produced, *Beyond the Horizon* was called a tragedy by many critics. It might now be well to reexamine this term briefly as it applies to this play. While we cannot, in this small space, arrive at any final and comprehensive definition of what a tragedy is, we can certainly suggest some of its characteristics. A tragedy is traditionally a play in which the leading character (or characters) struggles to attain some significant objective and in the end is destroyed in the attempt, partly because he is pitted against forces too great for him to conquer (page 751), and partly because of some flaw in his own character. The struggle and the destruction should not be meaningless, however. The main character, as well as those who surround him, must have learned something through his agony, and those who survive him must normally continue living on a new, more fruitful basis.

It is wise to keep in mind, too, that normally in a tragedy there is no particular focus of blame. The main character may have his flaw, but his defeat should not simply be a question of personality or misjudgment. There must be some sense of fate, of cosmic rules by which the hero plays out his serious and ultimately disastrous game. In Greek tragedy, for example, a hero (or heroine) pits himself vainly but gloriously against the gods, or fate, a contest which we know he cannot win. In Shakespearean tragedy a character upsets or attempts to change God's divinely ordained and ordered universe. Lately, in O'Neill's time and our own, the uncompromising opposition is more difficult to pin down. Some playwrights throw their heroes against society; others against a weakness of character; in some O'Neill plays a malevolent fate works against the character. In all tragedies there is a sense of an unbreakable net tightening on a man in spite of his efforts to break out of it— and even because of these efforts. If there seems to be some simple solution—some circumstance or condition which can be easily remedied—then, generally speaking, the play is not a tragedy at all.

Considering O'Neill's *Beyond the Horizon* as a tragedy, then, we can try to apply the rules we've just raised. Certainly Robert, in his struggle for a more romantic world, is destroyed by this struggle and thereby comes to a more profound understanding of what the real world is all about. Ruth and Andrew also seem to gain wisdom through and because of his death. Yet Robert's dreamy longing is not the sole cause of all the trouble. Everyone, and no one, is to blame for how things work out. O'Neill's characters shake their fists at God, at fate, and at each other, and we do have the sense that an uncompromising destiny broods over the Mayos and their farm.

Whom or what do we blame in *Beyond the Horizon?* If we turn on Ruth for muddying the situation at the beginning, we also sympathize with her at the end, when she says, "I couldn't help it. No woman could." Robert's decision to stay, Andrew's to leave, are both feasible and understandable. The play moves toward its grim ending primarily, it seems, because people are born to lie to themselves and to act on these lies. And the world, to O'Neill, is somehow put together so they can't get away with it. This is a big theme, and O'Neill strives toward universality with all the imagery of land, sea, and sky. Whether or not it is a tragic theme depends on how convincingly it comes across.

FOR STUDY AND DISCUSSION:
THE PLAY AS A WHOLE

1. O'Neill presents his theme through a series of contrasts, such as reading and activity, outdoors and indoors, land and sea. Cite other sets of opposites used in this play and show how they bring out its theme.

2. Some critics have said that Robert is too inactive to be a truly dramatic figure. Do you agree? Is he really inactive or does he merely seem so? Would it be fair to say that he has a more active *mind* than anyone else?

3. The name of Ruth comes from the heroine of "The Book of Ruth." Does Ruth's name seem appropriate for the O'Neill heroine? Why? (If you are not familiar with this short book of the Bible, you may want to read it.)

4. Because O'Neill's father, James O'Neill, was a famous nineteenth-century actor of melodrama, Eugene O'Neill was brought up in a theatrical environment and was used to the flamboyant, histrionic excesses of the theater at that time. Can you see any melodramatic influences in *Beyond the Horizon?* Do any scenes or characters seem to you particularly melodramatic?

5. In what ways might *Beyond the Horizon* be called a study of moral corruption and confusion? How might society be to blame for this corruption and confusion? Support your answer with examples from the text.

FOR COMPOSITION

1. "Character is destiny" is a well-known saying. Write a composition in which you apply this saying to *Beyond the Horizon.* To what extent is the fate of Robert, Ruth, and Andrew dependent on their character? To what extent are forces beyond their control? Can O'Neill be called a realistic dramatist? a naturalistic dramatist?

2. When O'Neill's father saw *Beyond the Horizon,* he is reported to have told his son, "People come to the theater to forget their troubles, not to be reminded of them. What are you trying to do—send them home to commit suicide?" Write a composition in which you discuss what reply O'Neill might have made to his father. Remember that the senior O'Neill was a leading actor in an old melodramatic tradition, while his son was trying to write a new kind of drama.

3. O'Neill once wrote, "To me the tragic alone had that significant beauty which is truth. It is the meaning of life and the hope . . . only through the unattainable does man achieve a hope worth living and dying for—and so attain himself." Apply this quotation to *Beyond the Horizon.* To what extent does the play achieve the "significant beauty" to which O'Neill refers?

The Literature of Modern America

The selections in this final unit take American literature into the present and, in a sense, into the future. Some of the writers represented—such as John Updike, Robert Lowell, Richard Wilbur, and James Baldwin—are among the most important writing today and will almost certainly continue to produce important works. Just as the life around us seems to be more various and confusing than accounts of life in bygone ages, so it is more difficult to identify contemporary literary movements than to comment on past literature. Yet keeping in mind the basic themes of this book—the conflict between ideals and realities and the attempt to create a distinctive national literature—it is easy to see how these basic concerns continue to influence our national literature.

One advantage that the modern American writer enjoys over the writers of the nineteenth century is that he can look back on a tradition (or several traditions) of American writing. He can refer to past American writers and see how they came to terms with the realities of living in this country, just as Robert Lowell has turned to Nathaniel Hawthorne to see how the earlier writer dealt with common problems (pages 677–79). In dealing with present realities, the modern writer can draw on what Van Wyck Brooks has called a "usable past." At the same time, the contemporary writer responds strongly to the continuing conflict between desire and actuality, the American dream and the small and large betrayals of that dream.

THEMES IN CONTEMPORARY AMERICAN LITERATURE

The literature of this unit deals with a world that you know from personal experience. As you discuss the following questions, keep in mind the important events of the recent past and consider how poems, stories, essays, and plays can throw light on these events and on your own world.

1. The British scholar and critic Marcus Cunliffe has remarked, "With the Armistice of 1918, and the peacemaking of 1919, the American prose-writer entered a new period of revolt. In some ways this was a continuation of earlier movements. . . . His principal theme—that of secession from society—was one that had long engaged the American writer." Discuss.

2. How does each of the following selections deal with the theme of "secession from society": Ernest Hemingway's "Big Two-Hearted River," John Steinbeck's "Flight," Shirley Jackson's "The Lottery," Stewart Holbrook's "The Beard of Joseph Palmer," and F. Scott Fitzgerald's "The Crack-Up"? Which selections criticize society, either explicitly or implicitly? What selections in previous units dealt with this theme?

3. Judging from the selections in this book, how do the following writers draw on one or more American traditions, the "usable past" that is the cultural heritage of all Americans: Katherine Anne Porter, Van Wyck Brooks, William Faulkner, Stephen Vincent Benét, E. B. White, Robert Lowell?

TYPES OF LITERATURE

In this unit, unlike previous units, the selections have been arranged according to the type of literature they represent. The following questions will help you to draw together what you have learned about each type.

1. *Short Stories.* Modern fiction writers have been working away from the neatly plotted "well-made" short story. Which stories in the unit depend most on clever plots? Which stories have little or no plot? Do these stories seem to you poorly written or constructed? Why or why not? Which kind of story do you prefer? Defend your choice. Why do you think some modern writers became impatient with the neatly plotted story? What are the limitations of this kind of story in conveying human experience? (See page 520 for a discussion of plot.)

2. *Poetry.* Some modern poets have done a great deal of experimenting with new forms (primarily free verse) and new technical devices. Other poets have sought to revitalize traditional forms. Many poets have moved in both directions. Almost all contemporary poets, whether formalist or experimental, have gained from the efforts of poets such as William Carlos Williams, E. E. Cummings, and Marianne Moore to startle the reader into a new awareness. Find examples of the following devices, which are characteristic of much modern poetry, and point out how each device contributes to the effect of a specific poem: (a) an unusual arrangement of words on a page, (b) startling images and metaphors, (c) the use of words that are not usually considered "poetic," (d) sudden breathtaking leaps from one idea to another, (e) the use of unusual quotations, (f) an attempt to capture the precise look or feel of a thing.

3. *Essays.* Why is the essay called "the open form"? Apply the following sentence from the discussion of the essay (page 683) to three essays in the unit: "No matter how much an essay meanders, always there is some thread running through it, holding it together and giving it unity."

4. *Drama.* In this unit, you have studied one play written in the realistic tradition and one experimental play. What have you discovered from reading each of these plays about the potentialities of the drama as an artistic form? How may a play influence an audience through devices of staging (page 751)? How may a play affect an audience by deliberately disregarding the conventions of the realistic theater?

FOR COMPOSITION: INTERPRETING LITERATURE

Ernest Hemingway once said, "Read anything I write for the pleasure of reading it. Whatever else you find will be the measure of what you brought to the reading." Good writers often deliberately attempt to compress many experiences and perceptions into a single story, poem, essay, or drama. A good reader, like a good critic, approaches a literary work as a complex artistic creation. He brings his entire sensitivity and intelligence to bear on the work so that he can get out of it most of what the writer has put into it.

1. Many of the discussion questions in this book have been designed to help you appreciate particular works as *artistic wholes*—that is, to understand how all the details in a work are arranged in a particular pattern to achieve a particular effect or set of effects. But literature can be appreciated as well for its insights into the world around us. The following questions may help you arrive at these insights:

    a. Does the work reveal anything about the inner individual experience? That is, can any *psychological* insights be derived from a particular selection?

    b. Does the work reveal anything about people's relationships to each other in society or in groups? That is, can any *social* or *historical* criticisms be derived from a particular selection?

    c. Does the work reveal anything about man's relationship to a set of values, to a higher power, or to some ideal beyond himself? That is, can any *philosophical* insights be derived from the work?

    d. Does the work reveal anything about its author as a person or as an artist? That is, can any *biographical* insights be derived from the work?

    e. Does the work reveal anything about writing as an art? That is, can any *esthetic* or *critical* insights be derived from the work?

It is possible to interpret some works of literature on all these levels. But remember that such levels of meaning must exist *in the work itself* and not simply in the reader's own mind. You must be able to cite passages, sentences, and words to support your findings, and you should be able to find more than one example to support your interpretation. If your interpretation is valid and is important in understanding the work of art as a whole, you will almost always be able to find several passages to support it.

2. Write a composition in which you apply at least two of the above guides for interpretation to one of the selections in the unit. Exchange papers with a classmate. Study your classmate's interpretation of a literary work, and write a paragraph explaining why you agree or disagree with him.

ART AND LITERATURE

Art as well as literature may give us insights into or make comments about society. Study the paintings on pages 641–46, 713–18, and 785–90. Then write a composition explaining how a number of these paintings make a social comment. Note, for example, the artists' use of color, composition, and use of details. How are they combined for maximum effect?

Literary Terms and Techniques

Glossary of Literary Terms

Numbers after entries are page references indicating principal discussions of literary terms.

ALLEGORY A tale in verse or prose in which the characters all represent abstract ideas or moral qualities. 253

ALLITERATION The repetition of initial consonant sounds of words as in "*d*ark *d*readful *d*en." 122

ALLUSION A reference to something in literature, mythology, history, and the like, which the author expects the reader to recognize. 53

ANALOGY A comparison between two objects to show the similarities between them. Analogies are often used for illustration (to explain something unfamiliar by comparing it to something familiar) or for argument (to persuade that what holds true for one thing should hold true for the thing to which it is compared).

ANAPEST A poetic foot consisting of two unstressed syllables followed by a stressed syllable. 204

ANTAGONIST A person opposing the PROTAGONIST (see page 751) in a dramatic or narrative work.

APPROXIMATE RHYME Rhyme in which (as opposed to *exact rhyme*) only the final consonant sounds of the words are identical. *Cook-look* is an exact rhyme. *Cook-lack* is an approximate rhyme.

ASSONANCE The repetition of vowel sounds, especially in poetry, as in "h*i*gh fl*i*er." 122

BLANK VERSE Poetic lines of unrhymed iambic pentameter, often used in verse drama and in long meditative poems. 116, 625

CAESURA A break or pause in a line of poetry. 116

CATALOGUE A device used in poetry to suggest largeness and inclusiveness by giving long lists of things. The catalogue was a favorite device of Walt Whitman. 328

CHARACTER A person in a story, novel, play, or narrative poem; one of the basic elements of narrative writing, especially fiction. 548

CLASSICISM A movement or tendency in literature, art, and music which pursues the traditional and the universal and which values clarity, balance, and order. 89

CLIMAX The decisive point of a narrative or dramatic work of art; the point of greatest intensity or interest.

COMEDY A kind of play that seeks to amuse its audience and make it think as well. 751

CONCEIT A kind of METAPHOR (see page 860) which makes a comparison between two startlingly different things. 23, 286

CONFLICT A struggle between two or more opposing forces. Most narrative and dramatic works of art are organized around one or more conflicts. 520

CONNOTATION The emotional and intellectual associations a word may bring up. Connotation is usually opposed to DENOTATION, the literal meaning of a word. 300

CONSONANCE The repetition of consonant sounds, as in "wo*r*ld of me*rr*iment." 122

CONTEXT The situation in which a word occurs: that is, the words surrounding it and the general meaning of the passage. Context clarifies the meaning of the word. 18

COUPLET A pair of rhymed poetic lines.

CRITIC A writer who studies, analyzes, and evaluates literary works of art.

DACTYL A poetic foot consisting of a stressed syllable followed by two unstressed syllables. 204

DENOTATION See CONNOTATION.

DESCRIPTION A form of discourse; the kind of writing that deals with the appearance of a person, object, or place. 29, 78, 150

DIALOGUE Conversation between two or more persons; the conversational element in a play, story, or novel. In plays dialogue, together with staging, is one of the two basic tools of the dramatist. 751

DICTION An author's choice of words, one aspect of his style. (See STYLE).

DRAMATIC MONOLOGUE A poem consisting of a long speech by one character who, through his words, reveals himself and the dramatic situation he is in.

ELEGY A poem mourning the death of an individual. Whitman's "When Lilacs Last in the Dooryard Bloomed" (page 320) is a famous example.

END RHYME Rhyme that occurs at the ends of lines of poetry.

EPIC A long narrative poem, told in an elevated style, that relates the deeds of a hero of national or international importance.

EPITHET A word or phrase used to characterize someone or something, such as *fleet-footed Achilles*.

ESTHETIC DISTANCE. The distance a writer places between the events of his story or novel and the reader. The concept of esthetic distance is closely related to point of view. 474

EXPOSITION A form of discourse; the kind of writing that seeks primarily to present information. 29, 290 Also, in a story, novel, or play, the part that helps the reader or audience to understand the situation.

FARCE A kind of play designed to make the audience laugh through a series of outrageous events.

FIGURATIVE LANGUAGE Language that departs from the strictly literal to achieve special effects. Such language makes use of devices called figures of speech (see FIGURE OF SPEECH).

FIGURE OF SPEECH A device that permits the writer to say one thing and mean another. The most common kinds of figures of speech—SIMILE, METAPHOR, PERSONIFICATION—involve a comparison of unlike things.

FLASHBACK A scene in a story or novel that goes back to an event in the past. 558

FOOT A combination of stressed and, usually, unstressed syllables forming a rhythmic unit, like a measure in music. The most common feet in English prosody are the IAMB, TROCHEE, ANAPEST, and DACTYL. 116, 204

FORM The arrangement of all aspects of a work of art to make a unified whole. The form of a work is frequently opposed to its *content*. Content refers to what the work is about while *form* refers to the way the work is organized and designed.

FORMS OF DISCOURSE A way of classifying writing under four types: EXPOSITION, DESCRIPTION, PERSUASION, and NARRATION (see pages 859, 860, and 861). This approach to writing seeks to determine the special skills and procedures necessary for each kind of writing. 29, 78, 150

FREE VERSE Poetry that follows no regular pattern of rhythm. 317, 393, 628

HONORIFIC AND DEROGATORY WORDS Words which express approval and disapproval and which are usually chosen deliberately to influence a reader's attitudes. 339

IAMB A poetic foot consisting of an unstressed syllable followed by a stressed syllable. 116

IMAGE A word or phrase appealing to one or more of the senses. 220

IMPRESSIONISM The rendering of events or details as they appear to the senses. 504

IN MEDIAS RES A Latin phrase meaning "in the middle of things." The phrase refers to the practice of some writers of plunging into the middle of a story and only later telling what has happened previously. 558

INTERNAL RHYME Rhyme that occurs within a single line of poetry, as in the following line by Poe: "For the moon never *beams* without bringing me *dreams.*" 669

IRONY An attitude or a way of writing that depends on a discrepancy between what is apparent and what is real. Three kinds of irony are (1) *verbal irony,* in which a writer says one thing and means another; (2) *dramatic irony,* in which a reader or audience perceives a character's mistakes or misunderstandings; (3) *irony of situation,* in which there is a discrepancy between purpose and result. 49

LOCAL COLOR In fiction, the use of details associated with a particular region or section of the country. 291–92

MELODRAMA A kind of play designed to thrill the audience through an exciting (although not always logical) series of events.

METAPHOR A figure of speech in which two unlike things are compared but in which no word of comparison (such as *like* or *as)* is used. 286

METER A regular pattern of rhythm in poetry. 204; see also 116

MYTH A traditional story, connected with religious beliefs or practices and seeking to explain and justify them. Also any story that is felt to have a deep, general significance.

NARRATION A form of discourse; the kind of writing that relates an event or series of events. 29

NATURALISM An extreme form of realism. Naturalist writers begin with a view of man's place in the universe and seek to show how man is affected by his heredity and environment. 388, 476, 503

ONOMATOPOEIA The use of a word, especially in poetry, whose sound imitates or suggests its meaning; for example, "buzz." 122

ORNATE STYLE See PLAIN STYLE.

PARABLE A short tale that illustrates a moral lesson. 253

PARADOX A statement that is true in fact, although it seems to contradict itself, such as "wasteful efficiency."

PATHOS The quality or qualities in a work that arouse pity or sorrow.

PENTAMETER A poetic line consisting of five verse feet. 116, 204

PERIODIC SENTENCE A sentence in which an important part of the meaning is withheld until the very end, as opposed to a loose sentence in which the words follow in normal order. 113

PERSONIFICATION A figure of speech in which something nonhuman is given human qualities.

PERSUASION A form of discourse; the kind of writing that offers intellectual or emotional arguments to persuade readers to accept an idea or take a course of action. 29, 78

PLAIN STYLE A style which strives after clarity and simplicity, as opposed to an *ornate style,* which seeks to call attention to its own intricacy. 12, 78

PLOT The sequence of events in a narrative or dramatic work. Plots may be simple or complicated, loosely or tightly constructed, but to satisfy, every plot must appear to be made of incidents that belong together. 520, 558, 566

POETIC INVERSION Words arranged in an unusual or confusing order in a poetic line, usually to force the line into a particular metrical pattern or to have the line end with a particular word for the sake of rhyme.

POINT OF VIEW The position in which a reader is placed in relation to a story or novel. 604

PROSODY The study of rhythm in language and especially in poetry.

PROTAGONIST The main character or hero of a dramatic or narrative work. 751

QUATRAIN A poetic stanza of four lines. 212

REALISM The attempt to present life as it really is, without sentimentalizing or idealizing it. As a movement in literature, realism arose as a protest against romanticism. 385–89, 476, 502–04, 752–53

REVELATION The focal point of many modern short stories. In such a story, all the details are organized to provide a moment of insight into a character or a situation as the climax of the work. 520

RHYME SCHEME The pattern made by the rhymes in a poem. 204

ROMANCE At first used to describe a verse or prose tale, written in medieval times and dealing with the loves and adventures of kings and heroes. Such tales contained a number of unlikely or supernatural happenings. Later, the term *romance* was applied to a long prose tale that was more colorful and imaginative than the novel.

ROMANTICISM A movement or tendency in literature, art, music and philosophy which favors the imagination and emotions over reason and which pursues the original, the strange, and the deeply personal. Now applied to a work of any period showing these tendencies, the term *romanticism* was originally used for developments which began near the end of the eighteenth century and which arose as a rebellion against CLASSICISM (see page 859). This movement showed an increased interest in the past, in the primitive and the exotic, and in unspoiled nature. 89–90, 149–50, 289

SATIRE A piece of writing that holds up to ridicule or contempt the weaknesses and the wrongdoing of individuals, groups, or humanity in general. Satire often seeks to persuade through the force of laughter. 49

SCANSION The analysis of a poem's rhythm by dividing it into metrical feet and marking the stressed and unstressed syllables. 204

SCENE AND SUMMARY Two ways of dealing with time in a story or novel. In a scene, a single event is dramatized at some length. In a summary, a large period of time is briefly passed over. 520

SETTING The place and time of a story, novel, or play. 587

SIMILE A figure of speech in which two unlike things are explicitly compared and in which a word of comparison (such as *like* or *as*) is used to signal the reader. 286

SLICE OF LIFE A term used in connection with realistic and naturalistic writing. It refers to the desire of the realist or naturalist to lift a sample of real life and transfer it, just as it is, to the printed page. 752

SONNET A poem of fourteen lines (usually of iambic pentameter) that may follow one of several patterns. 212, 634

STAGING (or STAGECRAFT). All the devices aside from dialogue which a dramatist uses to communicate with the audience. 751

Exercises in the Text

The page numbers cited in this index indicate the location of the major exercises on the topics listed below.

Index of Fine Art

THE COMPOSITION AND LANGUAGE PROGRAM

Assignments Based on Selections

Unless otherwise designated, all assignments are presented in the anthology under the heading *For Composition*. Numbers in parentheses refer to the numbered items in the text under the heading *For Composition*.

DESCRIPTION

Writing unified description that will create a dominant impression or mood 150
Analysis and Composition (number 3)

Describing an interior in such a way as to suggest something about its inhabitant 501
"The Sculptor's Funeral," Willa Cather (number 1)

Writing description in the Romantic manner (Poe) and in the Realist manner (Crane or Cather) 503
Analysis and Composition (number 1)

Writing an opening paragraph (as though for a short story) in which a particular setting is established 587
"Flight," John Steinbeck

Writing an evocative description of a remembered place 728
"The Dogwood Tree: Boyhood in the 1940's," John Updike

NARRATION

Paraphrasing a poem 123
"The Bells," Edgar Allan Poe

Writing a historical narrative 339
"The Hardihood of LaSalle," Francis Parkman

Rewriting an episode from a different point of view 501
"The Sculptor's Funeral," Willa Cather (number 2)

Writing a realistic narrative 504
Analysis and Composition

EXPOSITION

Comparing the characters of two men 18
FROM *Of Plymouth Plantation*, William Bradford
FROM *History of the Dividing Line*, William Byrd

Comparing the personalities and outlook of two men 42
FROM *His Autobiography*, Benjamin Franklin
FROM "Sinners in the Hands of an Angry God," Jonathan Edwards

Comparing two examples of persuasive writing 57
"Speech in the Virginia Convention," Patrick Henry
FROM *The Crisis, Number 1*, Thomas Paine

Comparing different kinds of persuasive writing 78
Analysis and Composition

Analyzing proverbial sayings 108
"The Devil and Tom Walker" Washington Irving (number 1)

Explaining quotations 179
"The American Scholar," Ralph Waldo Emerson (number 1)

Comparing two poems 233
"To a Waterfowl," William Cullen Bryant
"The Chambered Nautilus," Oliver Wendell Holmes

Comparing the treatment of death in two poems 287
"Thanatopsis," William Cullen Bryant and "Because I Could Not Stop for Death," Emily Dickinson

Analyzing expository prose 290
Analysis and Composition (numbers 1 and 2)

Analyzing persuasive writing 300
"Gettysburg Address," Abraham Lincoln

Comparing Mark Twain with one or two contemporary American humorists 367

Interpreting a novel 475
The Red Badge of Courage, Stephen Crane (number 3)

Glossary

Listed below are words from selections in this book that you will find useful to add to your vocabulary. Proper names and words that are specialized, archaic, or not generally useful are not included in this glossary but have been footnoted, as appropriate, in the text. The pronunciation key is that of the Funk and Wagnalls *Standard College Dictionary* and the definitions are based on those given in the *Standard College Dictionary*.

A

abate (ə·bāt′) To become less in force, intensity, or value.

aberration (ab′ə·rā′shən) **1.** Deviation from a right, customary, prescribed, or natural course or condition. **2.** Partial mental derangement.

abhor (ab·hôr′) To regard with repugnance; detest; loathe. **—ab·hor′rence** *n.*

abject (ab′jekt, ab·jekt′) Humble; cast down.

abominable (ə·bom′in·ə·bəl) **1.** Very bad or disgusting. **2.** Hateful.

abrogate (ab′rə·gāt) To annul by authority, as in law; abolish; repeal. **—ab′ro·ga′tion** *n.*

abstemious (ab·stē′mē·əs) Eating and drinking sparingly; abstinent; temperate. **—ab·ste′mi·ous·ness** *n.*

abstraction (ab·strak′shən) **1.** The process of separating qualities or attributes from the individual objects to which they belong. **2.** A product of this process; a concept: Beauty is an *abstraction*.

accede (ak·sēd′) **1.** To give one's consent or adherence; agree; assent: with *to*. **2.** To come into or enter upon an office or dignity: with *to*.

accouterment (ə·kōō′tər·mənt) *pl.* Equipment; trappings; especially, the equipment of a soldier other than arms and dress.

acquiesce (ak′wē·es′) To consent or concur tacitly; assent; comply; with *in* (formerly with *to*): The candidate *acquiesced* in all his party's plans. **—ac′qui·es′cence** *n.*

acrid (ak′rid) **1.** Of a cutting, burning taste; pungent; bitter. **2.** Of a sharp, satirical nature, speech, etc.; acrimonious.

admonish (ad·mon′ish) To criticize mildly, often with some attention to faults.

advent (ad′vent) The coming or arrival of a person or thing.

adversity (ad·vûr′sə·tē) Great hardship, misfortune, or trouble.

advert (ad·vûrt′) To call attention; refer: with *to*.

affinity (ə·fin′ə·tē) **1.** A natural attraction or inclination: an *affinity* between opposite natures. **2.** Any close relation or agreement; kinship in general; similarity: an *affinity* of colors.

affluence (af′lōō·əns) A profuse or abundant supply, as of riches; wealth; abundance; opulence.

affront (ə·frunt′) **1.** To insult openly; treat with insolence; offend by word or act. **2.** To confront in defiance; accost. **3.** *Archaic* To face toward.

agape (ə·gāp′, ə·gap′) In a gaping state; gaping.

aggregate (ag′rə·gāt) **1.** To bring or gather together, as into a mass, sum, or body; collect; mass. **2.** To amount to; form a total of. **—ag′gre·ga′tion** *n.*

ague (ā′gyōō) **1.** *Pathol.* A periodic malarial fever marked by intermittent chills and sweating. **2.** A chill or paroxysm.

alacrity (ə·lak′rə·tē) Cheerful willingness and promptitude; liveliness.

alienate (āl′yən·āt, ā′lē·ən-) **1.** To make indifferent or unfriendly; estrange: to *alienate* a friend. **2.** *Law* To make over; transfer, as property. **—al′ien·a′tion** *n.*

alluvion (ə·lōō′vē·ən) **1.** Inundation; flood. **2.** *Geol.* A downpour of volcanic cinder mud.

altercation (ôl′tər·kā′shən, al′-) A heated dispute; angry controversy; wrangling.

ambiguous (am·big′yōō·əs) **1.** Capable of being understood in more senses than one; having a double meaning; equivocal. **2.** Obscure; indistinct: *ambiguous* shadows. **—am·bi·gu′i·ty** *n.*

analogy (ə·nal′ə·jē) **1.** Agreement or resemblance in certain aspects, as form or function, between otherwise dissimilar things; similarity without identity. **2.** Any similarity or agreement. **—a·nal′o·gous** *adj.*

annals (an′əlz) *pl.* **1.** A record of events in their chronological order, year by year. **2.** History or records in general. **3.** A periodical publication of discoveries, transactions, etc.

annihilate (ə·nī′ə·lāt) **1.** To destroy utterly. **2.** To annul; abolish; make void. **—an·ni′hi·la′tion** *n.*

anomalous (ə·nom′ə·ləs) Deviating from the common rule; irregular; exceptional; abnormal.

anomaly (ə·nom′ə·lē) Deviation from rule, type, or form; irregularity. **—a·nom′a·lous** *adj.*

apocryphal (ə·pok′rə·fəl) Having little or no authenticity.

apothegm (ap′ə·them) A terse, instructive, practical saying; maxim: also spelled *apophthegm.*

appellation (ap′ə·lā′shən) **1.** A name or title. **2.** The act of calling or naming.

apprehensive (ap′rə·hen′siv) Fearful concerning the future; anxious; uneasy. **—ap′pre·hen′sive·ly** *adv.*

approbation (ap′rə·bā′shən) **1.** The act of approving; approval. **2.** Sanction.

artifice (är′ti·fis) **1.** An ingenious expedient; stratagem; maneuver. **2.** Subtle or deceptive craft; trickery.

ascendant (ə·sen′dənt) **1.** Ascending; rising. **2.** Superior; dominant. Also **as·cen′dent. —as·cen′dan·cy** *n.*

ascertain (as′ər·tān′) To learn with certainty; find out by experiment or investigation. **—as′cer·tain′a·ble** *adj.*

PRONUNCIATION: add, āce, câre, pälm; end, ēven; it, īce; odd, ōpen, ôrder; tŏŏk, pōōl; up, bûrn; ə = a in *above*, e in *sicken*, i in *flexible*, o in *melon*, u in *focus*; yōō = u in *fuse*; oil; pout; check; go; ring; thin; this; zh, vision.

868

athwart (ə·thwôrt′) **1.** From side to side of. **2.** Contrary to; in opposition to.

attenuate (ə·ten′yŏŏ·āt) **1.** To make thin, small, or fine; draw out, as a wire. **2.** To reduce in value, quantity, size, or strength; weaken; impair.

aught (ôt) **1.** Anything; any part or item. **2.** The figure 0; cipher; a naught; nothing: also spelled *ought.*

auroral (ô·rôr′əl, ô·rō′rəl) Pertaining to or like the dawn; dawning; roseate.

auspicious (ôs·pish′əs) **1.** Of good omen; propitious. **2.** Prosperous; fortunate.

austere (ô·stir′) **1.** Severe, grave, or stern, as in aspect or conduct. **2.** Morally strict; abstemious; ascetic.

autocrat (ô′tə·krat) **1.** A supreme ruler of unrestricted power. **2.** An arrogant, dictatorial person. —**au′to·crat′ic** *adj.*

avarice (av′ə·ris) Too much eagerness for riches; greed.

avocation (av′ə·kā′shən) An occupation that is not one's regular work; a hobby.

awry (ə·rī′) **1.** Toward one side; askew. **2.** Out of the right course; amiss; wrong.

B

ballast (bal′əst) **1.** Any heavy substance, as sand, stone, etc., laid in the hold of a vessel or in the car of a balloon to steady it. **2.** That which gives stability to character, morality, etc.

bamboozle (bam·bōō′zəl) To practice trickery or deception.

banal (bā′nəl, bə·nal′, ban′əl) Meaningless from overuse; hackneyed; trivial. —**ba·nal′i·ty** *n.*

bauble (bô′bəl) A worthless, showy trinket.

bayou (bī′ōō) *U.S.* A marshy inlet or outlet of a lake, river, etc.

beatitude (bē·at′ə·tōōd, -tyōōd) Supreme blessedness or felicity.

bedraggle (bi·drag′əl) To make wet, spoiled, or untidy, as by dragging through mire.

beholden (bi·hōl′dən) Indebted; obligated.

beneficent (bə·nef′ə·sənt) **1.** Bringing about or doing good. **2.** Resulting in benefit. —**be·nef′i·cence** *n.*

benevolence (bə·nev′ə·ləns) **1.** Disposition to do good; kindliness; charitableness. **2.** Any act of kindness; a gift of charity. —**be·nev′o·lent** *adj.*

benign (bi·nīn′) **1.** Of a kind disposition; kindly. **2.** Favorable.

berate (bi·rāt′) To scold severely.

bespeak (bi·spēk′) **1.** To ask or arrange for in advance; reserve. **2.** To give evidence of; indicate: His face *bespeaks* good news.

billet (bil′it) **1.** Lodging for troops in private or non-military buildings. **2.** A job; berth. **3.** *Archaic* A brief note.

bittern (bit′ərn) Any of various wading birds related to the heron.

bivouac (biv′ōō·ak, biv′wak) To camp out in a bivouac or temporary encampment.

blasé (blä·zā′, blä′zā) Wearied or bored, as from overindulgence in pleasure.

blatant (blā′tənt) **1.** Offensively loud or noisy; clamorous. **2.** Obvious; obtrusive: *blatant* stupidity.

blithe (blīth, blīth) **1.** Characterized by cheerfulness or mirth; joyous; gay. **2.** Casual or indifferent in manner; airy. —**blithe′ly** *adv.*

bludgeon (bluj′ən) A short club, commonly loaded at one end, used as a weapon. —*v.*

bounden (boun′dən) **1.** Obligatory: our *bounden* duty. **2.** Under obligations; obliged.

brackish (brak′ish) **1.** Somewhat saline; briny. **2.** Distasteful.

brazen (brā′zən) **1.** Made of brass. **2.** Resembling brass in hardness, color, sound, etc. **3.** Impudent; shameless.

bruit (brōōt) To noise abroad; talk about: usually in the passive.

buccaneer (buk′ə·nir′) **1.** A pirate or freebooter. **2.** One of the piratical rovers of the 17th and 18th centuries who preyed along the Spanish coasts of America. —*v.i.*

bullion (bŏŏl′yən) **1.** Gold or silver uncoined or in mass, as in bars, plates, etc. **2.** A heavy, twisted cord fringe, especially one made with fine gold or silver wire.

bulwark (bŏŏl′wərk) **1.** A defensive wall or rampart; fortification. **2.** Any safeguard or defense.

burgeon (bûr′jən) **1.** To flourish; grow. **2.** To bud; sprout.

C

cache (kash) To store away in concealment.

cadaverous (kə·dav′ər·əs) Resembling or characteristic of a corpse; pale; ghastly; gaunt. —**ca·dav′er·ous·ness** *n.*

calumniate (kə·lum′nē·āt) To accuse falsely; defame; slander.

capricious (kə·prish′əs) Characterized by or resulting from caprice; fickle; whimsical. —**ca·pri′cious·ness** *n.*

catamount (kat′ə·mount) **1.** *U.S.* The puma; also, the lynx. **2.** A catamountain.

cataract (kat′ə·rakt) **1.** A waterfall of great size. **2.** *Pathol.* **a** Opacity of the lens of the eye, causing partial or total blindness. **b** The opaque area.

catechize (kat′ə·kīz) **1.** To instruct, especially in the principles of Christianity, by asking a series of set questions and discussing the answers. **2.** To question searchingly and at length. Also **cat′e·chise.**

caulk (kôk) **1.** *Naut.* To make tight, as a boat's seams, by plugging with soft material, such as oakum or hemp fiber. **2.** To hammer or fasten together, as the edges of boiler's plates.

causeway (kôz′wā′) A raised road or way, as over marshy ground.

celerity (sə·ler′ə·tē) Quickness of motion; speed.

celestial (sə·les′chəl) **1.** Of or pertaining to the sky or heavens. **2.** Of heaven; divine.

chaff (chaf, chäf) To poke fun (at).

charger (chär′jər) **1.** One who, or that which, charges. **2.** A horse trained for use in battle; a war horse.

churlish (chûr′lish) **1.** Of or like a churl; rude; boorish; niggardly. **2.** Hard to work or manage; intractable. —**churl′ish·ly** *adv.*

circumambient (sûr′kəm·am′bē·ənt) Encompassing; surrounding.

citadel (sit′ə·dəl, -del) **1.** A fortress commanding a city. **2.** Any fortress or stronghold.

clangor (klang′gər, klang′ər) Repeated clanging; clamor; din. —**clan′gor·ous** *adj.*

cleave (klēv) **1.** To split or sunder, as with an ax or wedge. **2.** To part or divide along natural lines of separation. —**clo′ven** Alternative past participle of CLEAVE: *cloven* hoof. —**cleft** *adj.*

cleft (kleft) See CLEAVE.

coffer (kôf′ər, kof′-) **1.** A chest or box, especially one for valuables; a strongbox; safe. **2.** *pl.* Financial resources; a treasury.

PRONUNCIATION: add, āce, câre, pälm; end, ēven; it, īce; odd, ōpen, ôrder; tŏŏk, pōōl; up, bûrn; ə = a in *above,* e in *sicken,* i in *flexible,* o in *melon,* u in *focus;* yōō = u in *fuse;* oil; pout; check; go; ring; thin; this; zh, vision.

cohere (kō·hir') **1.** To stick or hold firmly together. **2.** To be logically connected; be consistent, as the parts of a speech or story.

collocate (kol'ō·kāt) To place together or in relation; arrange. —**col'lo·ca'tion** *n.*

commingle (kə·ming'gəl) To mix together; mingle.

commiserate (kə·miz'ə·rāt) To feel or express sympathy for; pity. —**com·mis'er·a'tion** *n.*

compatriot (kəm·pā'trē·ət, -pat'rē·ət) A fellow countryman.

complaisance (kəm·plā'zəns, kom'plə·zans) The disposition to defer to the wishes, views, or convenience of others; desire to please; obligingness. —**com·plai'sant** *adj.*

complement (kom'plə·ment) **1.** That which fills up or completes a thing; that which must be added to make up a whole. **2.** One of two parts that mutually complete each other. —*v.t.*

composite (kəm·poz'it) Made up of separate parts or elements; combined or compounded.

compunction (kəm·pungk'shən) An uneasiness of mind arising from wrongdoing; a sense of guilt or remorse.

concerted (kən·sûr'tid) Arranged, agreed upon, or done together; combined.

conciliate (kən·sil'ē·āt) To overcome the hostility or suspicion of; secure the friendship of; win over; placate; appease; propitiate.

concurrent (kən·kûr'ənt) **1.** Occurring together at the same time or place; existing in close association. **2.** United in action or application; cooperating; coordinate. **3.** Having the same authority or jurisdiction.

conduce (kən·dōōs', -dyōōs') To help or tend toward a result; contribute: with *to.*

conformation (kon'fôr·mā'shən) **1.** The manner in which a thing is formed; structure or outline. **2.** The symmetrical arrangement and shaping of parts.

congenital (kən·jen'ə·təl) **1.** Existing prior to or at birth, but not inherited: distinguished from *hereditary*: a *congenital* defect. **2.** Loosely, disposed as if by birth: a *congenital* liar.

conjoin (kən·join') To join together; associate; connect; unite.

conjure (kon'jər) **1.** To summon by incantation or spell, as the devil. **2.** To accomplish or effect by or as by magic.

consecrate (kon'sə·krāt) **1.** To set apart as sacred; dedicate to sacred uses with appointed ceremonies. **2.** To dedicate; devote: He *consecrated* his life to the cause.

consort (kən·sôrt') **1.** To keep company; associate. **2.** *Obs.* To accompany; escort.

consternation (kon'stər·nā'shən) Sudden, paralyzing fear or amazement; panic.

constituent (kən·stich'ōō·ənt) **1.** Serving to form or compose; constituting. **2.** Entitled to elect a representative. —*n.*

constrain (kən·strān') **1.** To compel by physical or moral means; coerce. **2.** To confine, as by bonds. **3.** To restrain: compel to inaction.

convex (kon'veks) Curving outward.

conveyance (kən·vā'əns) **1.** The act of conveying; communication; transportation. **2.** Something used for conveying, as a truck or bus. **3.** *Law* The transfer of title to property; also, the document whereby title is transferred. —**con·vey'anc·er** *n.*

convivial (kən·viv'ē·əl) **1.** Fond of feasting and good fellowship; jovial; sociable. **2.** Of or befitting a feast; festive. —**con·viv'i·al'i·ty** *n.*

copestone (kōp'stōn) **1.** The top stone of a wall or building. **2.** The final or crowning stroke; culmination. Also called *capstone, topstone.*

cornice (kôr'nis) **1.** *Archit.* The horizontal molded projection at the top of a building or of a component part of a building, usually under the eaves. **2.** A frame fastened to a wall or window so as to cover the rods and hooks used for hanging curtains, etc.

corpulent (kôr'pyə·lənt) Having a fleshy body; fat.

corrosive (kə·rō'siv) **1.** Having the power of corroding or eating away. **2.** Having the power to hurt one's feelings, etc.; biting; cutting: *corrosive* wit.

countenance (coun'tə·nəns) **1.** The face or features. **2.** An encouraging look or expression; also, approval; support. **3.** Self-control; composure.

countervail (koun'tər·vāl', koun'tər·vāl) To oppose with equal force or effect; avail against; counteract.

covert (kuv'ərt, kō'vərt) **1.** Concealed; secret. **2.** Covered over; sheltered. —**cov'ert·ly** *adv.*

covetous (kuv'ə·təs) Excessively desirous (of something); avaricious; greedy.

cowl (koul) **1.** A monk's hood; also, a hooded garment. **2.** A hood-shaped top for a chimney, to increase the draft. —*v.t.*

craven (krā'vən) Conspicuously lacking in courage; cowardly.

credence (krēd'ns) **1.** Belief, especially as based upon the evidence or reports of others. **2.** Recommendation or accreditation: letters of *credence.*

crepe (krāp) **1.** A thin fabric of silk, cotton, wool, or synthetic fiber, having a crinkled surface. **2.** Black crepe used as a sign of mourning, as in an armband: in this sense sometimes *crape.*

crone (krōn) **1.** A withered old woman. **2.** *Rare.* A senile man.

cryptic (krip'tik) **1.** Secret or hidden; occult. **2.** Puzzling; mystifying: a *cryptic* remark.

crystalline (kris'tə·lin, -lēn) **1.** Of, pertaining to, or like crystal or crystals. **2.** Transparent; clear; pure.

culminate (kul'min·āt) **1.** To reach the highest point or degree; come to a final result or effect: with *in.* **2.** *Astron.* To reach the meridian, or the point of greatest or least altitude.

cursory (kûr'sər·ē) Rapid and superficial; not thorough; hasty.

D

debacle (dā·bäk'əl, -bak'əl, di-) **1.** A sudden and disastrous breakdown or collapse; ruin; rout. **2.** A violent flood.

declaim (di·klām') **1.** To speak loudly and rhetorically. **2.** To give a formal, set speech or recitation.

declamation (dek'lə·mā'shən) **1.** A prepared speech or recitation. **2.** Bombastic or empty oratory.

decorous (dek'ə·rəs, di·kôr'əs) Decent; proper or dignified.

decorum (di·kôr'əm, -kō'rəm) Conformity to the requirements of good taste or social convention; propriety in behavior, dress, etc.; seemliness.

decrepit (di·krep'it) Enfeebled or worn out by old age or excessive use. —**de·crep'i·tude** *n.*

deferential (def'ə·ren'shəl) Marked by deference; respectful; courteous. —**def'er·en'tial·ly** *adv.*

definitive (di·fin'ə·tiv) **1.** Sharply defining or limiting; precise; explicit. **2.** Bringing to an end; conclusive and unalterable; final.

PRONUNCIATION: add, āce, câre, pälm; end, ēven; it, īce; odd, ōpen, ôrder; tŏŏk, pōōl; up, bûrn; ə = a in *above*, e in *sicken*, i in *flexible*, o in *melon*, u in *focus*; yōō = u in *fuse*; oil; pout; check; go; ring; thin; this; zh, vision.

defunct (di·fungkt′) Dead; deceased; extinct.

degenerate (di·jen′ə·rāt) 1. To become worse, inferior, or more debased. 2. *Biol.* To revert to a lower type; decline; deteriorate. —**di·jen′ər·it** *adj. & n.*

delineate (di·lin′ē·āt) 1. To draw in outline; trace out. 2. To represent by a drawing; depict. 3. To portray verbally; describe.

delusive (di·loo′siv) 1. Tending to delude; misleading; deceptive. 2. Like a delusion; unreal.

delve (delv) 1. To make careful investigation; search for information: to *delve* into a crime. 2. *Archaic & Dial.* To turn over or dig (ground).

demean (di·mēn′) 1. To behave or conduct (oneself) in a particular way. 2. To lower in dignity or reputation; debase; degrade.

demeanor (di·mē′nər) The manner in which one behaves or bears oneself; deportment; mien.

demented (di·men′tid) Out of one's mind; insane.

demure (di·myoor′) Having a sedate or sober demeanor; grave; reserved.

denunciation (di·nun′sē·ā′shən, -shē-) 1. Open disapproval or condemnation of a person or action. 2. Accusation before public authorities; arraignment.

deploy (di·ploi′) 1. To place or position (forces, people, etc.) according to a plan. 2. *Mil.* To spread out (troops, etc.) in battle formation.

deride (di·rīd′) To treat with scornful mirth; ridicule. —**de·ri′sion** *n.* —**de·ri′sive** *adj.*

despondent (di·spon′dənt) Dejected in spirit; disheartened.

dexterous (dek′strəs, -stər·əs) Possessing dexterity; skillful or adroit; artful. Also **dex′trous.**

diadem (dī′ə·dem) A crown or headband worn as a symbol of royalty or honor.

diaphanous (dī·af′ə·nəs) Showing light through its substance; transparent; translucent.

diffuse (di·fyooz′) To pour or send out so as to spread in all directions; circulate; permeate.

dilate (dī·lāt′, di·lāt′) To widen or enlarge; become wider or larger.

dirge (dûrj) 1. A song or melody expressing mourning; a lament. 2. A hymn or choral service at a funeral.

disaffected (dis′ə·fek′tid) Alienated in feeling or loyalty; estranged; unfriendly. —**dis′af·fec′tion** *n.*

disburse (dis·bûrs′) To pay out; expend. —**dis·burse′ment** *n.*

discern (di·sûrn′, di·zûrn′) To perceive, as with sight or mind; recognize; apprehend.

discernible (di·sûr′nə·bəl, -zûr′-) Capable of being discerned; perceptible.

discerning (di·sûr′ning, -zûr′-) Quick to discern; discriminating; penetrating.

disconcert (dis′kən·sûrt′) 1. To disturb the self-possession or composure of; confuse; upset. 2. To throw into confusion; frustrate, as a plan.

discountenance (dis·koun′tə·nəns) 1. To look upon with disfavor; disapprove of. 2. To abash; disconcert.

dishearten (dis·här′tən) To weaken the spirit or courage of; discourage.

disheveled (di·shev′əld) 1. Tousled or rumpled. 2. Untidy; unkempt.

disparate (dis′pər·it) Essentially different; altogether dissimilar; totally distinct in kind.

dispassionate (dis·pash′ən·it) Free from passion or bias; calmly objective; impartial; unbiased.

dissension (di·sen′shən) 1. Difference of opinion, especially arising from dissatisfaction or anger; discord; strife.

2. A heated quarrel or disagreement.

dissipate (dis′ə·pāt) 1. To disperse or drive away; dispel. 2. To spend wastefully; squander. 3. To engage in excessive or dissolute pleasures. —**dis′si·pā′tion** *n.*

dissolution (dis′ə·loo′shən) Breakup; disintegration.

distend (dis·tend′) 1. To expand by or as by pressure from within. 2. To stretch out; swell.

dogged (dôg′id, dog′-) Stubborn; obdurate. —**dog′ged·ly** *adv.*

doleful (dōl′fəl) Melancholy; mournful.

doughty (dou′tē) Valiant; brave.

draggletail (drag′əl·tāl) An untidy person.

dramaturgy (dram′ə·tûr′jē) The art of writing or producing plays, or of acting in them; dramatics.

draught (draft, dräft) 1. A current of air. 2. A quantity of liquid for drinking; a drink: a *draft* of ale. 3. The act of drawing air, smoke, etc., into the lungs; also, the quantity of air, etc., taken in.

droll (drōl) Humorously odd; charmingly amusing; comical; funny. —**droll′er·y** *n.*

dun (dun) Of a grayish brown or reddish brown color.

dunnage (dun′ij) 1. *Naut.* Mats and battens used to protect cargo. 2. Baggage.

duplicity (doo·plis′ə·tē, dyoo-) Tricky deceitfulness; double-dealing.

dyspepsia (dis·pep′shə, -sē·ə) Difficult or painful digestion, usually chronic.

E

efface (i·fās′) 1. To rub out, as written characters; erase; cancel. 2. To obliterate or destroy, as a memory.

effectual (i·fek′choo·əl) Producing or having adequate power to produce an intended effect; efficacious: *effectual* measures.

effervescent (ef′ər·ves′ənt) 1. Giving off bubbles of gas; bubbling up. 2. Vivacious; lively.

efficacy (ef′ə·kə·sē) Power to produce a desired or intended result.

effrontery (i·frun′tər·ē) Shameless or insolent boldness; audacity; impudence.

emaciated (i·mā′shē·ā′tid) Very thin; wasted away.

emolument (i·mol′yə·mənt) Salary or fees connected with one's job or position.

empyrean (em′pə·rē′ən, -pī-) The highest heaven; the abode of God and the angels, anciently conceived as a region of pure fire.

engraft (en·graft′, -gräft) 1. *Bot.* To graft (a cion) to another type of tree or plant for propagation. 2. To set firmly; implant.

enigmatic (en′ig·mat′ik) Puzzling; baffling.

enjoin (in·join′) 1. To order authoritatively and emphatically; direct or command (a person or group) to a course of action, conduct, etc. 2. To forbid or prohibit, especially by judicial order or injunction.

enshroud (in·shroud′) To shroud; conceal.

enthrall (in·thrôl′) To fascinate; hold spellbound.

entrench (in·trench′) 1. To fortify or protect with or as with a trench or trenches. 2. To establish firmly: the idea was *entrenched* in his mind. —**en·trench′ment** *n.*

ephemeral (i·fem′ər·əl) Lasting but a short time; transitory.

epithet (ep′ə·thet) 1. An adjective or other descriptive word or phrase qualifying or used in place of the usual name of a person or thing, as *rosy-fingered* in "the rosy-fingered dawn" or *the Bold* in "Philip the Bold." 2. Loosely, any disparaging name, especially for a person.

PRONUNCIATION: add, āce, câre, pälm; end, ēven; it, īce; odd, ōpen, ôrder; took, pool; up, bûrn; ə = a in *above*, e in *sicken*, i in *flexible*, o in *melon*, u in *focus*; yoo = u in *fuse*; oil; pout; check; go; ring; thin; this; zh, vision.

871

eradicate (i·rad′ə·kāt) **1.** To pull up by the roots; root out. **2.** To destroy utterly; extirpate; erase.

ethereal (i·thir′ē·əl) **1.** Resembling ether or air, as in lightness; airy: an *ethereal* substance. **2.** Delicate or exquisite in line, feature, etc.: an *ethereal* face.

evince (i·vins′) To indicate clearly; demonstrate convincingly; make evident; prove: His loyalty was *evinced* by this heroic act.

evocative (i·vok′ə·tiv) Tending to call up feelings, memories, etc.

execrable (ek′sə·krə·bəl) **1.** Detestable and revolting; abominable: an *execrable* crime. **2.** Appallingly inferior; extremely bad: an *execrable* speller.

execrate (ek′sə·krāt) **1.** To call down evil upon; curse. **2.** To denounce violently. —**ex′e·cra′tion** *n.*

exemplary (ig·zem′plər·ē) Deserving to be imitated; model.

exhort (ig·zôrt′) **1.** To urge by earnest appeal or argument; advise or recommend strongly. **2.** To utter or give exhortation. —**ex·hor·ta′tion** *n.*

exodus (ek′sə·dəs) A going forth, as of a multitude, from a place or country.

expedient (ik·spē′dē·ənt) **1.** Serving to promote a desired end; suitable, advisable, or proper under the circumstances. **2.** Pertaining to or prompted by utility, interest, or advantage rather than by what is right. —*n.*

expletive (eks′plə·tiv) An exclamation, often profane.

expostulate (ik·spos′chōō·lāt) To reason earnestly with a person concerning the impropriety or inadvisability of his actions, etc.; remonstrate: usually with *with*. —**ex·pos′-tu·la′tion** *n.*

expunge (ik·spunj′) **1.** To strike out (something written); delete; erase. **2.** To get rid of as if by erasing; wipe out.

extort (ik·stôrt′) To get (money, a confession, or the like) from a person by threats or force.

extricate (eks′trə·kāt) To free from entanglement, hindrance, or difficulties; disentangle.

exultant (ig·zul′tənt) Jubilant, triumphant; elated.

F

falsetto (fôl·set′ō) The higher, less colorful register of a voice, especially an adult male voice: also called *head voice.*

farthing (fär′thing) **1.** A small, bronze, English coin worth one fourth of a penny, no longer legal tender. **2.** Something of no value; a trifle.

fastidious (fas·tid′ē·əs, fəs-) Hard to please in matters of taste; exceedingly delicate or refined; overnice; squeamish.

feign (fān) To make a false show of; put on a deceptive appearance of; sham; to *feign* madness.

felicity (fə·lis′ə·tē) **1.** Happiness, especially when very great; bliss. **2.** An agreeably pertinent or effective manner or style: *felicity* of expression.

fervid (fûr′vid) Fervent, especially to an extreme degree; most impassioned.

fetish (fet′ish, fē′tish) **1.** An object, as a stone or a tree, superstitiously regarded as being the embodiment or dwelling place of a spirit or as having magical powers that can benefit or injure human beings. **2.** Something which one cultivates or to which one is devoted excessively or irrationally: to make a *fetish* of being punctual.

fetter (fet′ər) **1.** To put fetters upon; shackle; bind. **2.** To prevent the free movement or expression of; hold in check; confine; restrain.

fissure (fish′ər) A narrow opening, cleft, crevice, or furrow. —*v.* To crack, split; cleave.

folkways (fōk′wāz′) *Sociol.* The traditional habits, customs, and behavior of a group, tribe, or nation.

forbear (fôr·bâr′) **1.** To refrain or abstain from (some action): to *forbear* speaking. **2.** *Archaic* To put up with; endure.

forestall (fôr·stôl′, fōr-) To hinder, prevent, or guard against in advance.

forestick (fôr′stik′) The front log in a log fire.

formidable (fôr′mi·də·bəl) **1.** Exciting fear or dread by reason of strength, size, etc. **2.** Extremely difficult: a *formidable* undertaking.

forthwith (fôrth′with′, -with′, fôrth′-) Without delay; immediately.

founder (found′ər) **1.** To sink after filling with water, as a boat or ship. **2.** To fail completely; collapse. **3.** To stumble and become lame, as a horse.

fracas (frā′kəs) A noisy disturbance, fight, or dispute; brawl; row.

freshet (fresh′it) **1.** A sudden rise or overflow of a stream. **2.** A fresh-water stream emptying into the sea.

frigate (frig′it) A medium-sized, square-rigged warship used in the eighteenth and early nineteenth centuries. *Poetic* A light, fast sailboat or rowboat.

furl (fûrl) To roll up (a sail, flag, etc.) and make secure, as to a mast or staff.

furrow (fûr′ō) **1.** To make furrows in. **2.** To make deep wrinkles in. **3.** To plow.

G

gainsay (gān′sā′) **1.** To deny. **2.** To contradict; controvert.

gall (gôl) **1.** To make sore or injure (the skin) by friction; chafe. **2.** To vex or irritate.

garrison (gar′ə·sən) **1.** To place troops in, as a fort or town, for defense. **2.** To station (troops) in a fort, town, etc. **3.** To occupy as a garrison.

gauntlet (gônt′lit, gänt′-) In medieval armor, a glove covered with metal plates to protect the hand.

genealogy (jē′nē·al′ə·jē, jen′ē-, -nē·ol′-) **1.** A record or table showing the descent of an individual or family from a certain ancestor. **2.** The study of pedigrees. —**ge′ne·al′o·gist** *n.*

gesticulate (jes·tik′yə·lāt) **1.** To make emphatic or expressive gestures, as in speaking. **2.** To express by gestures.

ghoul (gōōl) **1.** One who robs graves. **2.** One who takes pleasure in revolting things or practices.

gibber (jib′ər, gib′-) To talk rapidly and incoherently; jabber.

globule (glob′yōōl) A tiny sphere of matter or drop of liquid.

goatee (gō·tē′) A man's beard trimmed short to a pointed end below the chin.

grandiloquent (gran·dil′ə·kwənt) Speaking in or characterized by a pompous or bombastic style.

gratify (grat′ə·fī) **1.** To give pleasure or satisfaction to. **2.** To satisfy, humor, or indulge, as a desire or need. —**grat′i·fi·ca′tion** *n.*

guttural (gut′ər·əl) **1.** Pertaining to the throat. **2.** Having a harsh, or muffled, grating quality, as sounds produced in the throat.

gyrate (jī′rāt) To rotate or revolve, usually around a fixed point or axis.

PRONUNCIATION: add, āce, câre, pälm; end, ēven; it, īce; odd, ōpen, ôrder; tŏŏk, pōōl; up, bûrn; ə = a in *above*. e in *sicken*, i in *flexible*, o in *melon*, u in *focus*; yōō = u in *fuse*; oil; pout; check; go; ring; thin; this; zh, vision,

872

H

hallucination (hə·lōō´sə·nā´shən) **1.** *Psychol.* Any of numerous auditory, visual, or tactile perceptions that have no external cause or stimulus: distinguished from *illusion.* **2.** The seemingly real object of such a perception.

harangue (hə·rang´) A lengthy, loud, and vehement speech; tirade. —*v.t. & v.i.*

harrow (har´ō) A farm implement set with spikes or disks, for leveling plowed ground, breaking clods, etc. —*v.t. & v.i.*

haversack (hav´ər·sak) A bag for carrying rations, etc., on a march or hike.

heinous (hā´nəs) Extremely wicked; atrocious; odious.

hermitage (hûr´mə·tij) **1.** The retreat or dwelling of a hermit. **2.** Any secluded dwelling place.

hirsute (hûr´sōōt, hûr·sōōt´) Covered with hair; hairy.

hoary (hôr´ē, hō´rē) **1.** Ancient; aged; venerable. **2.** Gray or white with age.

hypochondria' (hī´pə·kon´drē·ə, hip´ə-) **1.** A persistent anxiety about one's health, usually associated with one or another part of the body and imagined symptoms of illness. **2.** A morbid melancholy and depression of mind or spirits. —**hy´po·chon´dri·ac** *adj. & n.*

I

ignominious (ig´nə·min´ē·əs) Marked by or involving dishonor or disgrace; shameful. —**ig´no·min´i·ous·ly** *adv.*

ilk (ilk) Breed; sort; class: Smith and others of his *ilk.*

illimitable (i·lim´it·ə·bəl) Incapable of being limited; limitless; boundless.

illustrious (i·lus´trē·əs) **1.** Greatly distinguished; renowned. **2.** Conferring greatness or glory: *illustrious deeds.*

imminent (im´ə·nənt) Likely to happen soon; probable.

immutable (i·myōō´tə·bəl) Not mutable; unchanging; unalterable. —**im·mu´ta·bil´i·ty** *n.*

impalpable (im·pal´pə·bəl) **1.** Not capable of being perceived by the sense of touch. **2.** Not capable of being distinguished by the mind; intangible.

impediment (im·ped´ə·mənt) **1.** That which hinders or obstructs; an obstacle. **2.** A physical handicap, especially a speech defect.

impetus (im´pə·təs) **1.** The force that sets a body in motion; also, the energy with which a body moves or is driven. **2.** Any motivating force; stimulus; incentive.

impious (im´pē·əs) **1.** Lacking in reverence for God; ungodly; blasphemous. **2.** Lacking in due respect, as for one's parents.

implacable (im·plā´kə·bəl, -plak´ə-) That cannot be appeased or pacified; inexorable.

imponderable (im·pon´dər·ə·bəl) Incapable of being estimated, calculated, or valued.

importunate (im·pôr´chə·nit) Urgently or stubbornly persistent in demand; insistent: an *importunate* creditor.

imposture (im·pos´chər) Deception by means of false pretenses; especially, the act of posing under a false name or character.

impound (im·pound´) **1.** To shut up in a pound, as a stray dog. **2.** To seize and place in custody of a court of law. **3.** To collect (water) in a pond, reservoir, etc., as for irrigation.

imprecate (im´prə·kāt) To invoke or call down (some curse or calamity): to *imprecate* evil upon a person. —**im´pre·ca´tion** *n.*

impregnable (im·preg´nə·bəl) **1.** Incapable of being taken by force; proof against attack: an *impregnable* fortress. **2.** Incapable of being overcome; firmly resistant; unyielding: *impregnable* moral strength.

imprimis (im·prī´mis) In the first place; firstly.

impromptu (im·promp´tōō, -tyōō) Made, done, or uttered on the spur of the moment; extempore; offhand.

impunity (im·pyōō´nə·tē) Freedom or exemption from punishment, harm, or unpleasant consequence.

inadvertent (in´əd·vûr´tənt) **1.** Not exercising due care or consideration; negligent. **2.** Resulting from inattention or oversight; unintentional. —**in´ad·ver´tence** *n.*

inauspicious (in´ô·spish´əs) Not auspicious; ill-omened; unfavorable.

incandescent (in´kən·des´ənt) **1.** Luminous or glowing with intense heat. **2.** Shining with intense brilliance.

incantation (in´kan·tā´shən) The uttering or intoning of words or syllables supposed to produce magical results.

incessant (in·ses´ənt) Unceasing; uninterrupted; continuing without letup.

incipient (in·sip´ē·ənt) Coming into existence; just beginning to appear.

incongruous (in·kong´grōō·əs) Inconsistent with what is suitable, reasonable, or proper; not suited to the circumstances; out of place.

inconsequential (in´kon·sə·kwen´shəl, in·kon´-) Having little or no consequence; unimportant; trivial.

incontinently (in·kon´tə·nənt·lē) Immediately; with no delay.

incorrigible (in·kôr´ə·jə·bəl, -kor´-) Incapable of being reformed or chastened; irreclaimable.

incredulous (in·krej´ə·ləs) Not willing or not disposed to believe; skeptical. —**in·cred´u·lous·ly** *adv.*

incubus (in´kyə·bəs) **1.** Anything that tends to oppress or discourage. **2.** A nightmare.

incursion (in·kûr´zhən, -shən) A hostile, often sudden, entrance into a territory; an invasion; raid.

indenture (in·den´chər) **1.** *Law* A deed or contract made between two or more parties. **2.** *Usually pl.* Such a contract between master and apprentice.

indigent (in´də·jənt) **1.** Lacking means of subsistence; needy; poor. **2.** *Archaic* Lacking; deficient: often with *of.* —**in´di·gence** *n.*

indolent (in´də·lənt) Averse to exertion or work; lazy; idle.

indubitable (in·dōō´bə·tə·bəl) Not to be doubted; unquestionable; certain. —**in·du´bi·ta·bly** *adv.*

ineffable (in·ef´ə·bəl) **1.** Too overpowering to be expressed in words; unutterable: *ineffable* joy. **2.** Too lofty or sacred to be uttered: the *ineffable* name of Jehovah.

inert (in·ûrt´) Very slow to move or act, or entirely unable to move.

inexorable (in·ek´sər·ə·bəl) **1.** Not to be moved by entreaty or persuasion; unyielding. **2.** Unalterable; relentless.

infectious (in·fek´shəs) **1.** Liable to produce infection; carrying disease-producing organisms. **2.** Tending to excite similar reactions in others: *infectious* laughter.

influx (in´fluks) **1.** A flowing in, as of a liquid or gas. **2.** A continuous coming, as of people or things.

ingratiate (in·grā´shē·āt) To bring (oneself) deliberately into the favor or confidence of others.

iniquity (in·ik´wə·tē) **1.** Grievous violation of right or justice; wickedness. **2.** A wrongful act; unjust thing or deed; sin.

PRONUNCIATION: add, āce, câre, pälm; end, ēven; it, īce; odd, ōpen, ôrder; tŏŏk, pōōl; up, bûrn; ə = a in *above,* e in *sicken,* i in *flexible,* o in *melon,* u in *focus;* yōō = u in *fuse;* oil; pout; check; go; ring; thin; this; zh, vision.

innate (i·nāt′, in′āt) Inborn; natural.

inordinate (in·ôr′də·nit) Exceeding proper limits; immoderate; excessive: *inordinate* pride.

inscrutable (in·skrōō′tə·bəl) That cannot be searched into or understood; incomprehensible.

insidious (in·sid′ē·əs) 1. Subtly cunning or deceitful; treacherous; wily. 2. Progressing imperceptibly but harmfully: *insidious* disease. —in·sid′i·ous·ly *adv.*

insolent (in′sə·lənt) Deliberately rude; insulting.

insular (in′sə·lər, -syə-) 1. Of, like, or pertaining to an island. 2. Narrow or limited in customs, opinions, etc.; provincial.

intermittent (in′tər·mit′ənt) Ceasing from time to time; coming at intervals.

intrepid (in·trep′id) Fearless; undaunted.

inviolable (in·vī′ə·lə·bəl) 1. Not to be profaned, defiled, etc.; sacrosanct. 2. Not to be violated or broken: an *inviolable* law.

inviolate (in·vī′ə·lit) 1. Not violated; not profaned or broken; intact. 2. Inviolable.

invulnerable (in·vul′nər·ə·bəl) 1. Not capable of being wounded or physically injured. 2. Not to be overcome or damaged by attack; unconquerable. —in·vul′ner·a·bil′i·ty *n.*

iridescent (ir′ə·des′ənt) Displaying the colors of the rainbow in shifting hues and patterns, as soap bubbles, mother-of-pearl, etc.

irreclaimable (ir′i·klā′mə·bəl) Incapable of being reclaimed.

irredeemable (ir′i·dē′mə·bəl) 1. Incapable of being recovered, bought back, or paid off. 2. Not to be converted into coin: said of some types of paper money.

irreparable (i·rep′ər·ə·bəl) Incapable of being repaired, rectified, remedied, or made good.

irreproachable (ir′i·prō′chə·bəl) Not meriting reproach; blameless.

irreversible (ir′i·vûr′sə·bəl) 1. Incapable of being turned in the opposite direction. 2. Incapable of being annulled, repealed, or undone.

J

jaded (jā′did) 1. Worn-out; exhausted. 2. Dulled, as from overindulgence; sated.

jaundice (jôn′dis, jän′-) 1. A diseased condition of the liver due to the presence of bile pigments in the blood and characterized by yellowness of the skin and eyeballs. 2. A state of mind, feeling, perception, etc., that distorts the judgment. —*v.t.*

juxtapose (juks′tə·pōz′) To place close together; put side by side.

K

kindred (kin′drid) 1. Belonging to the same family; related by blood; akin. 2. Having a like nature or character; similar; cognate; related. —*n.*

kismet (kiz′met, kis′-) Appointed lot; fate.

knoll (nōl) A small round hill; a mound.

L

laconic (lə·kon′ik) Brief and concise in expression; pithy.

laggard (lag′ərd) One who lags; loiterer; straggler.

lateral (lat′ər·əl) Pertaining to the side or sides; situated at, occurring, or coming from the side.

lethargy (leth′ər·jē) A state of sluggish inaction, indifference, or dullness; apathy. —le·thar′gic *adj.*

limbo (lim′bō) 1. *Theol.* A region on the edge of hell for the souls of the righteous who died before the coming of Christ and for those of infants who die before baptism. 2. A place or condition for the relegation of unwanted or forgotten persons, things, etc.

loath (lōth) Strongly disinclined; reluctant; unwilling: often followed by *to*.

lucid (lōō′sid) 1. Easily understood; rational; clear: a *lucid* explanation. 2. Shining; bright.

ludicrous (lōō′də·krəs) Exciting laughter or ridicule; ridiculous; absurd.

lugubrious (lōō·gōō′brē·əs, -gyōō′-) Very sad, or mournful, especially in a ludicrous manner.

luminous (lōō′mə·nəs) 1. Full of light; glowing. 2. Easily understood; clear: a *luminous* comment. —lu′mi·nous·ness *n.*

lurid (lōōr′id, lyōōr-) 1. Shocking, vivid, or sensational. 2. Pale and sickly in color. 3. Sending out or lighted up with a yellowish red glare or glow especially in smoke or darkness.

M

malediction (mal′ə·dik′shən) 1. The pronouncing of a curse against someone: opposed to *benediction*. 2. Slander; calumny.

malign (mə·līn′) Having an evil disposition toward others; ill-disposed; malevolent.

manifold (man′ə·fōld) Having many and varied forms, types, instances, etc.; multiple: *manifold* sorrows.

marshal (mär′shəl) 1. To arrange or dispose in order, as facts. 2. To array or draw up, as troops for battle.

melee (mā′lā, mā·lā′) A confused, general hand-to-hand fight; affray.

mendicant (men′də·kənt) 1. Begging; depending on alms for a living. 2. Pertaining to or characteristic of a beggar.

mercenary (mûr′sə·ner′ē) 1. Influenced by a desire for gain or reward; greedy. 2. Serving for pay: now said only of soldiers hired by a foreign state. —*n.*

meridian (mə·rid′ē·ən) 1. *Astron.* An imaginary great circle of the celestial sphere passing through its poles and the zenith of an observer at any point. 2. The highest or culminating point of anything; zenith: the *meridian* of life.

metamorphose (met′ə·môr′fōz) To change the form of; transmute.

mettlesome (met′l·səm) Full of spirit; courageous; valiant.

millennium (mi·len′ē·əm) 1. A period of a thousand years. 2. The thousand years during which Christ is to rule the world, according to the New Testament. *Rev.* xx 1–5. 3. Any period of happiness, prosperity, etc.

missive (mis′iv) Sent or designed to be sent. —*n.*

mitigate (mit′ə·gāt) To make milder or less severe.

mizzenmast (miz′ən·məst′, -mast′, -mäst′) *Naut.* 1. In a ship with three masts, the mast nearest the stern. 2. In a ship having more than three masts, the third mast from the forward end of the ship.

mode (mōd) 1. Manner or form of being, doing, etc.; way; method: a *mode* of political thought. 2. Prevailing or current style or fashion, as in dress.

molder (mōl′dər) 1. To decay gradually and turn to dust; crumble. 2. To atrophy from lack of use.

PRONUNCIATION: add, āce, câre, pälm; end, ēven; it, īce; odd, ōpen, ôrder; tŏŏk, pōōl; up, bûrn; ə = a in *above*, e in *sicken*, i in *flexible*, o in *melon*, u in *focus*; yōō = u in *fuse*; oil; pout; check; go; ring; thin; this; zh, vision.

874

monitory (mon′ə·tôr′ē, -tō′rē) Conveying a warning or monition; admonitory: a *monitory* look.

morass (mə·ras′, mô-, mō-) **1.** A tract of low-lying, soft wet ground; marsh; bog. **2.** Anything that impedes, perplexes, or traps, as a difficult situation.

myriad (mir′ē·əd) Composed of a very large indefinite number; innumerable. —*n.*

N

nebulous (neb′yə·ləs) **1.** Vague or confused; unclear; hazy: a *nebulous* idea. **2.** Cloudlike; misty.

nil (nil) Nothing.

nimbus (nim′bəs) **1.** A luminous emanation or atmosphere believed to envelop a deity or holy person; glory; also, the representation of this in art. **2.** Any atmosphere or aura, as of fame, etc., about a person or thing.

nostrum (nos′trəm) **1.** A medicine of one's own invention or preparation; also, a quack medicine. **2.** A favorite remedy or plan.

noxious (nok′shəs) Causing or tending to cause injury to health or morals; hurtful.

nullify (nul′ə·fī) **1.** To make useless or ineffective; bring to naught; undo. **2.** To deprive of legal force or effect; annul.

nullity (nul′ə·tē) **1.** The state of being null. **2.** That which is null.

O

obeisance (ō·bā′səns, ō·bē′-) Courtesy, reverence, or homage; also, an act or gesture expressing this: chiefly in phrases **to do (make, or pay) obeisance.**

obliterate (ə·blit′ə·rāt) **1.** To destroy utterly; leave no trace of. **2.** To blot or wipe out; erase, as writing.

oblivion (ə·bliv′ē·ən) **1.** The state or fact of being completely forgotten. **2.** Heedlessness; disregard.

obsequious (ob·sē′kwē·əs) Excessively obedient or submissive; sycophantic; servile.

obsess (əb·ses′) To occupy or trouble the mind of to an excessive degree; preoccupy; harass; haunt. —**ob·ses′-sion** *n.*

obstreperous (əb·strep′ər·əs) Unruly, noisy, or boisterous, especially in resistance to control, advice, etc. —**ob-strep′er·ous·ness** *n.*

obtrude (əb·trōōd′) To thrust or force (oneself, an opinion, etc.) upon another without request or warrant. —**ob-tru′sive** *adj.*

ocher (ō′kər) **1.** A naturally occurring hydrated iron oxide mixed with various earthy materials and varying from light yellow to deep orange or red, largely used as a pigment. **2.** A dark yellow color derived from or resembling ocher. Also *Brit.* **o′chre.**

odious (ō′dē·əs) Arousing hate or disgust; detestable.

omniscience (om·nish′əns) **1.** Infinite knowledge. **2.** *Usually cap.* God.

opprobrium (ə·prō′brē·əm) **1.** The state of being scornfully reproached; ignominy. **2.** A cause of disgrace or reproach.

ostentation (os′tən·tā′shən) The act of displaying vainly or pretentiously, as in order to excite admiration, awe, etc. —**os′ten·ta′tious** *adj.*

P

pall (pôl) **1.** A covering, usually of black cloth, thrown over a coffin or over a tomb. **2.** A gloomy or oppressive atmosphere, effect, etc. —**pall** *v.t.*

pall (pôl) **1.** To become insipid or uninteresting. **2.** To have a dulling or displeasing effect: followed by *on.*

pallid (pal′id) Of a pale or wan appearance; weak or lacking in color. —**pal′lid·ly** *adv.*

palpable (pal′pə·bəl) **1.** Capable of being touched or felt. **2.** Readily perceived; obvious.

palpitate (pal′pə·tāt) **1.** To quiver; tremble. **2.** To beat more rapidly than normal; flutter: said especially of the heart.

palsy (pôl′zē) **1.** Paralysis. **2.** Any impairment or loss of ability to control movement.

panorama (pan′ə·ram′ə, -rä′mə) A complete view in every direction; also, a complete or comprehensive view of a subject or of passing events. —**pan′o·ram′ic** *adj.*

pantaloon (pan′tə·lōōn′) *pl.* Formerly, a tight-fitting garment for the hips and legs; trousers.

paradox (par′ə·doks) **1.** A statement seemingly absurd or contradictory, yet in fact true. **2.** A statement essentially self-contradictory, false, or absurd. —**par′a·dox′i·cal** *adj.*

paramount (par′ə·mount) Superior to all others; chief in importance.

paroxysm (par′ək·siz′əm) A sudden and violent outburst, as of emotion or action: a *paroxysm* of tears.

parsimony (pär′sə·mō′nē) Undue sparingness in the expenditure of money; niggardliness; stinginess.

partiality (pär′shē·al′ə·tē) *pl.* **1.** The state of being partial. **2.** Unfairness; bias. **3.** A particular fondness; predilection.

pathos (pā′thos) The quality in speech, music, or expression which arouses a feeling of sympathetic sadness or pity.

patrimony (pat′rə·mō′nē) An inheritance from a father or an ancestor; also, anything inherited.

pecuniary (pi·kyōō′nē·er′ē) Consisting of or relating to money.

pendant (pen′dənt) Anything that hangs from something else, either for ornament or for use.

pensive (pen′siv) **1.** Engaged in or addicted to serious, quiet reflection, often with a touch of sadness. **2.** Expressive of, suggesting, or causing a sad or melancholy thoughtfulness.

perambulate (pə·ram′byə·lāt) **1.** To walk through or over. **2.** To walk around or around so as to inspect, etc.

peremptory (pə·remp′tər·ē, per′əmp·tôr′ē, -tō′rē) **1.** Not admitting of debate or appeal; decisive; absolute. **2.** Intolerant of opposition; dictatorial.

perfidy (pûr′fə·dē) The act of violating faith, trust, or allegiance; treachery.

perfunctory (pər·fungk′tər·ē) Done or performed mechanically and merely for the sake of getting through; careless; superficial; cursory.

periphery (pə·rif′ər·ē) **1.** The outer part, surface, or boundary of something. **2.** A surrounding region, area, or country.

pernicious (pər·nish′əs) Having the power of destroying or injuring; tending to kill or hurt; very injurious; deadly.

perturb (pər·tûrb′) **1.** To disquiet or disturb greatly; alarm; agitate. **2.** To throw into disorder; cause confusion in. —**per′tur·ba′tion** *n.*

pervade (pər·vād′) To spread through every part of; be diffused throughout; permeate.

pestilence (pes′tə·ləns) **1.** Any widespread, often fatal, infectious or contagious disease, as cholera or the bubonic plague. **2.** A noxious or malign doctrine, influence, etc. —**pes′ti·len′tial** *adj.*

PRONUNCIATION: add, āce, câre, pälm; end, ēven; it, īce; odd, ōpen, ôrder; tŏŏk, pōōl; up, bûrn; ə = a in *above*, e in *sicken*, i in *flexible*, o in *melon*, u in *focus*; yōō = u in *fuse*; oil; pout; check; go; ring; thin; ḫis, zh, vision.

petulant (pech′ŏŏ·lənt) **1.** Displaying or characterized by capricious fretfulness; peevish. **2.** *Obs.* Saucily rude; insolent; pert. —**pet′u·lant·ly** *adv.*

phantasmagoria (fan·taz′mə·gôr′ē·ə, -gō′rē·ə) A changing, incoherent series of apparitions or phantasms, as in a dream. —**phan·tas′ma·gor′ic** *adj.*

phosphorescence (fos′fə·res′əns) The property of continuing to shine in the dark after exposure to light, shown by many mineral substances: distinguished from *fluorescence.*

pinion (pin′yən) **1.** The wing of a bird. **2.** A feather; quill.

pique (pēk) A feeling of irritation or resentment. —*v.t.*

plash (plash) A slight splash. —**plash′y** *adj.*

platitude (plat′ə·tōōd, -tyōōd) A flat, dull, or commonplace statement; an obvious truism.

pleurisy (plŏŏr′ə·sē) *Pathol.* Inflammation of the pleura, commonly attended with fever, pain in the chest, difficult breathing, exudation, etc.

plight (plīt) **1.** To pledge (one's word, faith, etc.). **2.** To promise, as in marriage; betroth.

ply (plī) **1.** To use in working, fighting, etc.; wield; employ. **2.** To work at; be engaged in. **3.** To supply with or offer repeatedly.

polarity (pō·lar′ə·tē, -lâr′-) **1.** The quality or condition of having poles. **2.** The quality or condition of being attracted to one pole and repelled from the other. **3.** The possession or demonstration of two opposite or contrary qualities or tendencies.

polestar (pōl′stär) **1.** Polaris. **2.** That which governs, guides, or directs; a controlling principle.

pommel (pum′əl, pom′-) **1.** To beat with or as with the fists or the pommel of a sword. **2.** A knob at the front and on the top of a saddle.

ponder (pon′dər) **1.** To weigh in the mind; consider carefully. **2.** To meditate; reflect.

portent (pôr′tent, pōr′-) An indication or sign of what is to happen, especially of something momentous or calamitous.

posterity (pos·ter′ə·tē) All of a person's descendants.

potation (pō·tā′shən) The act of drinking; also a drink, especially of an alcoholic beverage.

potter (pot′ər) To putter.

poultice (pōl′tis) A moist, mealy mass of flour, mustard, etc., applied hot to a sore or inflamed part of the body.

powwow (pou′wou′) *U.S.* **1.** *Informal* Any meeting or conference. **2.** A conference with or of American Indians.

prate (prāt) To talk idly and at length; chatter.

prattle (prat′l) **1.** To talk foolishly or like a child; prate. **2.** To utter in a foolish or childish way.

precarious (pri·kâr′ē·əs) **1.** Subject to continued risk; uncertain. **2.** Subject or exposed to danger; hazardous.

precept (prē′sept) **1.** A rule prescribing a particular kind of conduct or action. **2.** A proverbial standard or guide to morals; a maxim.

preceptor (pri·sep′tər) **1.** A teacher; instructor. **2.** The principal of a school.

precipitous (pri·sip′ə·təs) **1.** Consisting of or like a precipice; very steep. **2.** Precipitate; hasty.

predestine (prē·des′tin) To destine or decree beforehand; foreordain; predestinate.

prenatal (prē·nāt′l) Prior to birth: *prenatal* care.

prerogative (pri·rog′ə·tiv) **1.** An exclusive and unquestionable right belonging to a person or body of persons; especially, a hereditary or official right: the royal *prerogative.* **2.** Any characteristic privilege peculiar to a person

or class: It is a woman's *prerogative* to change her mind.

presentiment (pri·zen′tə·mənt) A prophetic sense of something to come; a foreboding.

preternatural (prē′tər·nach′ər·əl) **1.** Diverging from or exceeding the common order of nature, but not outside the natural order: distinguished from *supernatural.* **2.** Outside the natural order; supernatural.

prevalent (prev′ə·lənt) **1.** Of wide extent or frequent occurrence; common. **2.** Predominant; superior.

pristine (pris′tēn, -tin) **1.** Of or pertaining to the earliest state or time; primitive. **2.** Extremely pure; untouched; unspoiled.

profuse (prə·fyōōs′, prō-) **1.** Giving or given forth lavishly; liberal; extravagant; prodigal. **2.** Copious; overflowing; abundant: *profuse* vegetation.

progenitor (prō·jen′ə·tər) A forefather or parent.

projectile (prə·jek′təl, *esp. Brit.* -tīl) **1.** A body projected or thrown forth by force. **2.** *Mil.* A missile for discharge from a gun or cannon.

prolix (prō′liks, prō·liks′) **1.** Unduly long and verbose, as an address. **2.** Indulging in long and wordy discourse; tedious: a *prolix* orator. —**pro·lix′i·ty** *n.*

propitiate (prō·pish′ē·āt) To cause to be favorably disposed; appease; conciliate. —**pro·pi′ti·a·to·ry** *adj.*

propriety (prə·prī′ə·tē) **1.** The character or quality of being proper; especially, accordance with recognized usage, custom, or principles. **2.** *Obs.* An exclusive right of possession; also, a possession or property owned.

provender (prov′ən·dər) **1.** Food for cattle; especially, dry food. **2.** Provisions generally.

prudent (prōōd′ənt) Wise; sensible; showing good judgment.

pugilist (pyōō′jə·list) One who fights with his fists; especially, a prize fighter. —**pu′gi·lis′tic** *adj.*

punctilious (pungk·til′ē·əs) Very careful or exact in the observance of forms of etiquette, etc.

purl (pûrl) **1.** To whirl; turn. **2.** To flow with a bubbling sound; ripple. **3.** To move in eddies.

pursy (pûr′sē) **1.** Short of breath, often because of fatness. **2.** Fat; corpulent.

pusillanimous (pyōō′sə·lan′ə·məs) Lacking strength of mind, courage, or spirit; cowardly.

Q

quaff (kwaf, kwof, kwôf) To drink, especially copiously or with relish. —*n.*

quagmire (kwag′mīr′, kwog′-) **1.** Marshy ground that gives way under the foot; bog. **2.** A difficult situation.

querulous (kwer′ə·ləs, -yə·ləs) Disposed to complain or be fretful; captious.

quiescent (kwi·es′ənt) **1.** Being in a state of repose or inaction; quiet; still. **2.** Resting free from anxiety, emotion, or agitation.

quoit (kwoit, *esp. Brit.* koit) **1.** A disk of iron or other material with a round hole in the center to be thrown in a game at a short stake, either encircling it or coming as close to it as possible. **2.** *pl.* The game so played.

R

rail (rāl) **1.** To use scornful, insolent, or abusive language; scold: with *at* or *against.* **2.** To drive or force by railing.

rapacious (rə·pā′shəs) **1.** Given to plunder or rapine. **2.** Grasping; greedy.

rebuke (ri·byōōk′) To scold sharply; reprimand.

PRONUNCIATION: add, āce, câre, pälm; end, ēven; it, īce; odd, ōpen, ôrder; tŏŏk, pōōl; up, bûrn; ə = a in *above* e in *sicken*, i in *flexible*, o in *melon*, u in *focus*; yōō = u in *fuse*; oil; pout; check; go; ring; thin; this; zh, vision

876

reciprocal (ri·sip'rə·kəl) **1.** Done or given by each of two to the other; mutual. **2.** Mutually interchangeable.

recluse (ri·klōōs'; *for n., also* rek'lōōs) **1.** One who lives in retirement or seclusion. **2.** A religious devotee who lives voluntarily shut up in a cell and practices exceptional austerities. —*adj.*

recondite (rek'ən·dīt, ri·kon'dīt) **1.** Remote from ordinary or easy perception; abstruse; secret. **2.** Hidden; not readily observed.

reconnoiter (rē'kə·noi'tər, rek'ə-) To examine the country and note anything of interest.

rectitude (rek'tə·tōōd, -tyōōd) **1.** Uprightness in principles and conduct. **2.** Correctness, as of judgment.

recumbent (ri·kum'bənt) Wholly or partly lying down; reclining.

redoubtable (ri·dou'tə·bəl) **1.** Inspiring fear; formidable. **2.** Deserving respect or deference.

redress (ri·dres'; *for n., also* rē'dres) To set right, as a wrong, by compensation or by punishment of the wrongdoer; make reparation for.

rejuvenescence (ri·jōō'və·nes'əns) A renewal of youth. —**re·ju've·nes'cent** *adj.*

remonstrate (ri·mon'strāt) To urge strong reasons against any course or action; protest; object.

remunerative (ri·myōō'nə·rā'tiv, -nər·ə·tiv) **1.** Profitable; lucrative. **2.** Serving to pay or remunerate: *remunerative justice.*

reprobate (rep'rə·bāt) To disapprove of heartily; condemn.

reproof (ri·prōōf') **1.** Faultfinding; rebuke. **2.** Words of blame.

requiem (rek'wē·əm, rē'kwē-) Music written for parts of a Mass for the dead.

requite (ri·kwīt') **1.** To make equivalent return for, as kindness, service, or injury; make up for. **2.** To make return to; compensate or repay in kind.

retrograde (ret'rə·grād) **1.** To move or appear to move backward; recede. **2.** To grow worse; degenerate.

retrospective (ret'rə·spek'tiv) **1.** Looking back on the past. **2.** Applying retroactively, as legislation. —**ret'ro·spec'tive·ly** *adv.*

reverberate (ri·vûr'bə·rāt) **1.** To resound or re-echo. **2.** To rebound or recoil. —**re·ver'ber·a'tion** *n.*

rheum (rōōm) *Pathol.* **1.** A thin, watery catarrhal discharge from the nose and eyes. **2.** A cold; catarrh.

rigmarole (rig'mə·rōl) A succession of confused or nonsensical statements; incoherent talk or writing; nonsense.

ruche (rōōsh) A quilted or ruffled strip of fine fabric, worn about the neck or wrists of a woman's costume: also spelled *rouche*. —**ruch'ing** *n.*

ruminate (rōō'mə·nāt) **1.** To chew (food previously swallowed and regurgitated) over again; chew (the cud). **2.** To meditate or reflect (upon); ponder.

S

sagacious (sə·gā'shəs) Characterized by discernment, shrewdness, and wisdom.

sallow (sal'ō) Having or being an unhealthy, yellowish color.

salutary (sal'yə·ter'ē) Calculated to bring about a sound condition by correcting evil or promoting good; beneficial.

sanguinary (sang'gwə·ner'ē) **1.** Attended with bloodshed. **2.** Bloodthirsty.

sanguine (sang'gwin) **1.** Of buoyant disposition; hopeful; confident; cheerful. **2.** Ruddy; robust.

sarcophagus (sär·kof'ə·gəs) **1.** A stone coffin or tomb. **2.** A large ornamental coffin of marble or stone placed in a crypt or exposed to view.

satiety (sə·tī'ə·tē) The state of being satiated; repletion; surfeit.

savant (sə·vänt', sav'ənt; *Fr.* sà·vän') A man of exceptional learning.

scruple (skrōō'pəl) To hold back from (an action) because of doubts of its rightness.

scrutinize (skrōō'tə·nīz) To examine very carefully; look at closely.

secular (sek'yə·lər) **1.** Of or pertaining to this world or the present life; temporal; worldly: distinguished from *spiritual*. **2.** Not under the control of the church; civil; not ecclesiastical.

semblance (sem'bləns) **1.** A mere show without reality; pretense. **2.** Outward appearance; look; aspect. **3.** A likeness or resemblance.

sensibility (sen'sə·bil'ə·tē) **1.** The capability of sensation; power to perceive or feel. **2.** *Often pl.* Susceptibility or sensitiveness to outside influences or mental impressions; also, abnormal sensitiveness.

sepulcher (sep'əl·kər) A burial place, especially one found or made in a rock or solidly built of stone; tomb; vault. —*v.t.*

seraph (ser'əf) *pl.* **ser·aphs** or **ser·a·phim** (ser'ə·fim) **1.** A celestial being having three pairs of wings. *Isaiah* vi 2. **2.** *pl. Theol.* The highest of the nine orders of angels.

sere (sir) **1.** To wither; dry up. **2.** To burn the surface of; scorch. —*adj.*

servitor (sûr'və·tər) One who waits upon and serves another; an attendant; servant.

shoal (shōl) **1.** A shallow place in any body of water; a sandbank or bar. **2.** An assemblage or multitude; a school of fish.

shroud (shroud) **1.** A dress or garment for the dead; winding sheet. **2.** Something that envelops or conceals like a garment: the *shroud* of night.

sinuous (sin'yōō·əs) **1.** Characterized by bends, curves, or folds; winding; undulating. **2.** Devious; erring.

skirmish (skûr'mish) To fight in a preliminary or desultory way. —**skir'mish·er** *n.*

slough (slou) **1.** A place of deep mud or mire; bog. **2.** A state of moral depravity or despair.

smirch (smûrch) To soil; dishonor.

smite (smīt) To strike; hit hard. —**smiting** *adj.* Very intense; overwhelming.

sojourn (sō'jûrn, sō·jûrn') To stay or dwell temporarily; abide for a time. —*n.*

solicitude (sə·lis'ə·tōōd, -tyōōd) The state of being solicitous; anxiety or concern.

somnolence (som'nə·ləns) Oppressive drowsiness or inclination to sleep.

sonorous (sə·nôr'əs, -nō'rəs, son'ər·əs) **1.** Productive or capable of sound vibrations; sounding. **2.** Loud and full-sounding; resonant. —**so·no'rous·ly** *adv.*

sovereign (sov'rən, suv'-) Free, independent, and in no way limited by external authority or influence: a *sovereign* state.

spasmodic (spaz·mod'ik) **1.** Of the nature of a spasm; convulsive. **2.** Violent, or impulsive and transitory.

spawn (spôn) **1.** *Zool.* The eggs of fishes, amphibians, mollusks, etc., especially in masses. **2.** Outcome or results; product; yield.

specter (spek'tər) **1.** A ghost or apparition. **2.** Anything of a fearful or horrible nature. —**spec'tral** *adj.*

PRONUNCIATION: add, āce, câre, pälm; end, ēven; it, īce; odd, ōpen, ôrder; tōōk, pōōl; up, bûrn; ə = a in *above*, e in *sicken*, i in *flexible*, o in *melon*, u in *focus*; yōō = u in *fuse*; oil; pout; check; go; ring; thin; this; zh, vision.

877

speculate (spek´yə·lāt) **1.** To form conjectures regarding anything without experimentation; theorize, conjecture. **2.** To make an investment involving a risk, but with hope of gain. —**spec´u·la·tive** *adj.*

sporadic (spô·rad´ik, spō-) **1.** Occurring here and there; occasional. **2.** Separate; isolated.

stanchion (stan´shən) An upright bar forming a principal support.

starboard (stär´bərd) The right-hand side of a vessel as one faces the front or bow.

stolid (stol´id) Having or showing little feeling or perception; impassive; dull.

stupefy (stoo´pə·fī, styoo´-) **1.** To dull the senses or faculties of; stun. **2.** To amaze; astound.

sublime (sə·blīm´) Grand; supreme.

subsist (səb·sist´) **1.** To have existence or reality; continue to exist. **2.** To maintain one's existence; manage to live, often with *on* or *by:* to *subsist* on vegetables. —**sub·sis´tence** *n.*

succinct (sək·singkt´) Consisting of or characterized by brief and meaningful language; terse; concise.

succor (suk´ər) **1.** Help or relief rendered in danger, difficulty, or distress. **2.** One who or that which affords relief. —*v.t.*

succulent (suk´yə·lənt) **1.** Full of juice; juicy. **2.** Rich or vigorous; a *succulent* theme. —**suc´cu·lence** *n.*

suffuse (sə·fyooz´) To overspread, as with a vapor, fluid, or color. —**suf·fu´sion** *n.*

sulfureous (sul·fyoor´ē·əs) Of or like sulfur: also spelled *sulphureous.*

sumptuous (sump´choo·əs) **1.** Involving or showing lavish expenditure. **2.** Luxurious.

superfluous (soo·pûr´floo·əs) **1.** Exceeding what is needed; excessively abundant; surplus. **2.** Unnecessary; uncalled for; irrelevant: a *superfluous* question. —**su´per·flu´ity** *n.*

supernal (soo·pûr´nəl) **1.** Heavenly; celestial. **2.** Placed or located above; lofty; overhead; towering.

supernumerary (soo´pər·noo´mə·rer´ē, nyoo´-) **1.** Being beyond a fixed or standard number. **2.** Beyond a customary or necessary number; superfluous. —*n.*

supersede (soo´pər·sēd´) To take the place of, as by reason of superior worth, right, or appropriateness; replace; supplant.

supine (soo·pīn´) **1.** Lying on the back, or with the face turned upward. **2.** Having no interest or care; inactive; indolent; listless. **3.** Having an inclined position; sloping, as a hill.

supplication (sup´lə·kā´shən) An earnest plea, prayer, or entreaty.

supposition (sup´ə·zish´ən) **1.** The act of supposing; conjecture. **2.** That which is supposed or conjectured; hypothesis. —**sup·pos´i´tious** *adj.*

surcease (sûr·sēs´, sûr´sēs) Absolute cessation; end. —*v.t. & v.i.*

susceptible (sə·sep´tə·bəl) Yielding readily; capable of being influenced, acted on, or determined; open; liable: usually with *of* or *to.*

swathe (swāth) **1.** To bind or wrap, as in bandages. **2.** To envelop; surround.

T

tableau (tab´lō, ta·blō´) Any picture or picturesque representation; especially, a striking scene presented dramatically.

tangent (tan´jənt) **1.** A line that touches a curve at a particular point but does not cross it there. **2.** Angle; slant.

temporal (tem´pər·əl) **1.** Pertaining to affairs of the present life; earthly. **2.** Temporary; transitory. **3.** Pertaining to civil law or authority; lay; secular.

tenet (ten´it, tē´nit) An opinion, principle, dogma, etc., that a person or organization believes or maintains as true.

tenuity (ten·yoo´ə·tē, ti·noo´-) Thinness; weakness; delicacy.

termagant (tûr´mə·gənt) A scolding or abusive woman; shrew. —*adj.*

terrestrial (tə·res´trē·əl) **1.** Of, pertaining to, or consisting of earth or land. **2.** Worldly; mundane.

tether (teth´ər) To fasten or confine with a tether or rope. —**tethered** *adj.* Tied up with a rope.

timbre (tim´bər, tam´-; *Fr.* tan´br´) The attribute of a sound resulting from the number and relative strength of its partial tones, and distinguishing one vowel from another, the tone of one musical instrument from another, etc.; quality; tone.

tincture (tingk´chər) **1.** A solution, usually in alcohol, of some substance used in medicine; *tincture* of iodine. **2.** A slight additional flavor, quality, etc.

tintinnabulation (tin´ti·nab´yə·lā´shən) The pealing, tinkling, or ringing of bells.

traipse (trāps) To walk about in an idle or aimless manner: also spelled *trapes.*

transfigure (trans·fig´yər) **1.** To change the outward form or appearance of. **2.** To make glorious; idealize.

transfix (trans·fiks´) **1.** To pierce through; impale. **2.** To fix in place by impaling. **3.** To make motionless, as with horror, awe, etc.

transmute (trans·myoot´, tranz-) To change in nature, form, quality, etc.; transform.

travesty (trav´is·tē) **1.** A grotesque imitation; burlesque. **2.** In literature, a burlesque treatment of a lofty subject. —*v.t.*

trellis (trel´is) **1.** A crossbarred structure or panel of wood, metal, or other material, used as a screen or a support for vines, etc. **2.** A summer-house, archway, etc., made from or consisting of such a structure.

tremulous (trem´yə·ləs) **1.** Characterized or affected by trembling: *tremulous* speech. **2.** Showing timidity or fear; timorous.

trepidation (trep´ə·dā´shən) **1.** A state of agitation or alarm; perturbation. **2.** An involuntary trembling.

trestle (tres´əl) **1.** A beam or bar supported by four divergent legs, for bearing platforms, etc. **2.** An open braced framework for supporting a railway bridge, etc.

triptych (trip´tik) **1.** A triple tablet; especially, a Greek or Roman hinged triple writing tablet. **2.** A triple picture or carving on three hinged panels, often depicting a religious subject.

turgid (tûr´jid) **1.** Unnaturally distended, as by contained air or liquid; swollen. **2.** Inflated; bombastic, as language, literary style, etc.

U

ubiquity (yoo·bik´wə·tē) The state of being in an indefinite number of places at once; omnipresence.

undulate (un´dyə·lāt, -də-) **1.** To cause to move like a wave or in waves. **2.** To give a wavy appearance to. —**un´du·la´tion** *n.*

---

unscrupulous (un·skrōō′pyə·ləs) Not scrupulous; having no scruples or morals; unprincipled.

unversed (un·vûrst′) See VERSED.

unwonted (un·wun′tid, -wōn′-) Not according to habit or custom; unusual.

usurer (yōō′zhər·ər) One who practices usury; one who lends money, especially at an exorbitant or illegal rate.

usurp (yōō·zûrp′, -sûrp′) 1. To seize and hold (the office, rights, or powers of another) without right or legal authority; take possession of by force. 2. To take arrogantly, as if by right. **—u′sur·pa′tion** *n.*

V

vacuous (vak′yōō·əs) 1. Having no contents; containing no matter; empty. 2. Lacking intelligence; blank.

vagary (və·gâr′ē, vā′gər·ē) A wild fancy; extravagant notion.

vainglory (vān·glôr′ē, -glō′rē) Excessive or groundless vanity; also, vain pomp; boastfulness.

variegated (vâr′ē·ə·gā′tid) 1. Having diverse color, varied in color, as with streaks or blotches. 2. Having or exhibiting different forms, styles, or varieties.

venerable (ven′ər·ə·bəl) 1. Meriting or commanding veneration; worthy of reverence; now usually implying age. 2. Exciting reverential feelings because of sacred or historic associations.

veracious (və·rā′shəs) 1. Habitually disposed to speak the truth; truthful. 2. Conforming to or expressing truth; true; accurate.

versed (vûrst) Thoroughly acquainted; adept; proficient: with *in.*

vestment (vest′mənt) 1. An article of dress; especially, a garment or robe of state or office. 2. *Eccl.* One of the ritual garments of the clergy; especially, a garment worn at the Eucharist; a chasuble.

viand (vī′ənd) 1. An article of food, especially meat. 2. *pl.* Victuals; provisions; food; especially, choice food.

vicissitudes (vi·sis′ə·tōōds, -tyōōdz) *pl.* Irregular changes or variations, as of fortune: the *vicissitudes* of life.

victual (vit′l) 1. *pl.* Food for human beings, as prepared for eating: also, *Informal, vittles.* 2. *Obs.* Provisions of any kind.

vindicate (vin′də·kāt) To clear of accusation, censure, suspicion, etc. **—vin′di·ca′tion** *n.*

vintner (vint′nər) A wine merchant.

vista (vis′tə) 1. A view or prospect, as along an avenue; an outlook. 2. A mental view embracing a series of events.

vitiate (vish′ē·āt) 1. To impair the use or value of; spoil. 2. To debase or corrupt. 3. To render legally ineffective.

viva (vē′vä) Live! Long live!: a shout of applause; an acclamation or salute.

vivacious (vi·vā′shəs, vī-) Full of life and spirits; lively; active.

vociferate (vō·sif′ə·rāt) To cry out with a loud voice; exclaim noisily; shout; bawl. **—vo·cif′er·a′tion** *n.*

vociferous (vō·sif′ər·əs) Making or characterized by a loud outcry; clamorous; noisy.

votive (vō′tiv) Dedicated by a vow; performed in fulfillment of a vow.

vouchsafe (vouch′sāf′) 1. To grant, as with condescension; permit; deign. 2. *Obs.* To assure or guarantee.

W

waive (wāv) 1. To give up or relinquish a claim to. 2. To refrain from insisting upon or taking advantage of; forgo.

wan (won) 1. Pale, as from sickness or anxiety; pallid. 2. *Obs.* Having a gloomy aspect; dismal; dark; said of scenes or landscapes.

wend (wend) 1. To direct or proceed on (one's course or way). 2. To travel; proceed; go.

whelp (hwelp) To give birth (to): said of dogs, lions, etc.

whirligig (hwûr′lə·gig) 1. Any toy or small device that revolves rapidly on an axis. 2. Anything that seems to perform quick revolutions or moves in a cycle: the *whirligig* of time.

wicker (wik′ər) Made of twigs, osiers, etc.

woof (wōōf) The weft of a woven fabric; the threads carried back and forth across the fixed threads of the warp in a loom.

Y

yeoman (yō′mən) 1. A petty officer in the U.S. Navy or Coast Guard who performs clerical duties. 2. *Brit.* One who cultivates his own farm. 3. Formerly, a freeholder next below the gentry who owned a small landed estate or farm.

Z

zenith (zē′nith) 1. The point of the celestial sphere that is exactly overhead, and opposite to the nadir. 2. The highest or culminating point; peak: the *zenith* of one's career: opposed to *nadir.*

PRONUNCIATION: add, āce, câre, pälm; end, ēven; it, īce; odd, ōpen, ôrder; tŏŏk, pōōl; up, bûrn; ə = a in *above*, e in *sicken*, i in *flexible*, o in *melon*, u in *focus*; yōō = u in *fuse*; oil; pout; check; go; ring; thin; this; zh, vision.

General Index

Names of authors represented in the text appear in small capitals; numbers in italics refer to the pages on which author biographies appear. Titles of selections presented in the text are shown in italics. Other references are shown in regular type.

PICTURE ACKNOWLEDGMENTS

Page 2, Culver Pictures, Inc.; 3, New York Public Library; 9, Historical Picture Service, Chicago; 11, Erik S. Monberg; 13, Bettmann Archive; 15, The American Museum of Natural History; 16, The American Museum of Natural History; 20, Collection of The American Numismatic Society; 24, courtesy of Yale University; 30, Bettmann Archive; 31, Historical Pictures Service, Chicago; 40, Sy Seidman; 43, New York Public Library, Stokes Collection; 44, Library of Congress; 45, Massachusetts Historical Society; 46, New York Public Library, Manuscript Division; 47, Library of Congress; 50, Bettmann Archive; 51, Colonial Williamsburg, Inc.; 54, Bettmann Archive; 57, Erik S. Monberg; 58, Boston Athenaeum; 63, Stokes Collection, New York Public Library; 65, New York Historical Society; 67, courtesy of Yale University; 75, New York Public Library; 88, New York Public Library; 92, Bettmann Archive; 93, Bettmann Archive; 97, Library of Congress; 99, Bettmann Archive; 109, Historical Pictures Service, Chicago; 111, New York Historical Society; 117, Bettmann Archive; 156, Frank Rollins; 157, courtesy of Yale University; 165, Bettmann Archive; 175, Stanley Rice; 183, Bettmann Archive; 197, Library of Congress; 203, Metropolitan Museum of Art; 205, Brown Brothers; 213, Brown Brothers; 221, Brown Brothers; 225, Sandak, Incorporated, New York City; 228, The Metropolitan Museum of Art; 235, Essex Institute Collection; 254, Brown Brothers; 282, Fogg Art Museum; 292, Library of Congress, Brady Collection; 295 a, Granger Collection; 295 b, Bettmann Archive; 296, Bettmann Archive; 297, Bettmann Archive; 298, Culver Pictures, Inc.; 301, Bettmann Archive; 304, Brown Brothers; 307, Bettmann Archive; 310, Bettmann Archive; 332, Bettmann Archive; 340, Bettmann Archive; 349, Bettmann Archive; 363, Joseph Klima, Jr.; 386, Erik S. Monberg; 388, Harpers Weekly, March 1880, from The Picture Collection, New York Public Library; 389, Granger Collection; 391, Bettmann Archive; 465, John Webb, F.R.P.S., Brompton Studios; 466, Harbrace; 469, Henry B. Beville; 480, The Macmillan Company; 487, Pix, Inc.; 491, Brown Brothers; 507, Wide World; 509, Brown Brothers; 511, Culver Pictures, Inc.; 521, Brown Brothers; 536, Robert Capa, Magnum; 550, Wide World; 559, Paul Porter, Harcourt, Brace & World, Inc.; 569, Henry B. Beville; 570, Henry B. Beville; 574, Sherwin Greenberg; 575, Hans Nemuth; 588, courtesy Museum of Fine Arts, Boston; 599, Harcourt, Brace & World, Inc.; 605, courtesy Viking Press, Eric Hartmann; 613, Burt Glinn, Magnum; 626, Edward Steichen; 630, Brown Brothers; 635, Harcourt, Brace & World, Inc.; 646, Harbrace; 647, Alfred Knopf; 652, Eve Arnold, Magnum; 655, George Platt-Lynes; 658, James R. Deaver; 661, Houghton-Mifflin Company; 664, New York Public Library; 666, Random House; 670, Burt Glinn, Magnum; 673, Harper & Brothers; 676, Harcourt, Brace & World, Inc.; 680, Harcourt, Brace & World, Inc.; 684, Harper & Brothers; 689, Tony Rollo, *Newsweek;* 695, Philippe Halsman; 696, "Home" from *The Thurber Carnival,* Harper & Row, Publishers, copyright, © 1945 by James Thurber. Originally printed in *The New Yorker.* Reprinted by permission of Helen Thurber. 699, Wide World; 706, Brown Brothers; 716, Blomstrann; 719, Fred Kaplan from Black Star; 729, E. P. Dutton & Co., Inc.; 738, Steve Shapiro, from Black Star; 742, Wide World; 743, Harper & Row; 746, Harvard College Library, Theater Collection; 747, Harvard College Library, Theater Collection; 748, Harvard College Library, Theater Collection; 785, The Museum of Modern Art.

ART CREDITS

JOHN GRETZER. 721, 724, 726, 727, 728.

MANNY HALLER. 22, 35, 52, 61, 73, 95, 112, 232, 267, 279, 318, 488, 490, 494, 513, 515, 517, 698, 700, 702, 703, 704, 705, 756, 792, 794, 798, 800, 806, 810, 823, 826, 840, 845, 852.

KEN LONGTEMPS. 101, 106, 107, 126, 134, 138, 238, 239, 240, 241, 242, 249, 330, 398, 406, 417, 425, 436, 461, 692, 693, 708, 731, 735, 736, 737.

ALLAN MARDON. 180, 186, 215, 216, 219, 220, 334, 686, 687, 688.

JAMES AND RUTH MCCREA. 284, 285, 485, 525, 526, 531, 637, 650, 653, 654, 671, 678, 682.

MARIE NONAST. 342, 343, 344, 347, 590, 596, 600, 601, 602.

SIMEON SHIMIN. 542, 543, 545, 546, 547.

EARL THOLLANDER. 142, 147, 371, 372, 373, 374, 375, 377, 378, 379, 579, 581, 584.

E 6
F 7
G 8
H 9
I 0
J 1